Fodor's 99

France

The complete guide, thoroughly up-to-date

Packed with details that will make your trip

The must-see sights, off and on the beaten path

What to see, what to skip

Mix-and-match vacation itineraries

City strolls, countryside adventures

Smart lodging and dining options

Essential local do's and taboos

Transportation tips, distances and directions

Key contacts, savvy travel tips

When to go, what to pack

Clear, accurate, easy-to-use maps

Books to read, videos to watch, background essays

Fodor's Travel Publications, Inc.
New York • Toronto • London • Sydney • Auckland
www.fodors.com

Fodor's France '99

EDITOR: Natasha Lesser

Editorial Contributors: David Brown, Nancy Coons, Nigel Fisher, Simon Hewitt, Rebecca Hirschfield, Suzanne Rowan Kelleher, Christina Knight, Alexander Lobrano, Jennifer Paull, Ian Phillips, Helayne Schiff, M. T. Schwartzman (Gold Guide editor), George Semler, Nancy Van Itallie

Editorial Production: Tom Holton

Maps: David Lindroth, *cartographer*; Mapping Specialists Ltd., *cartographers*; Robert Blake, *map editor*

Design: Fabrizio La Rocca, *creative director*; Guido Caroti, *associate art director*; Jolie Novak, *photo editor*

Production/Manufacturing: Mike Costa

Cover Photograph: Suzanne and Nick Geary/Tony Stone Images

Design: Between the Covers

Copyright

Special Sales

CONTENTS

Maps

ON THE ROAD WITH FODOR'S

WHEN I PLAN A VACATION, the first thing I do is cast around among my friends and colleagues to find someone who's just been where I'm going. That's because there's no substitute for a recommendation from a good friend who knows your tastes, your budget, and your circumstances, someone who's just been there. Unfortunately, such friends are few and far between. So it's nice to know that there's *Fodor's France*.

In the first place, this book won't stay home when you hit the road. It will accompany you every step of the way, steering you away from wrong turns and wrong choices and never expecting a thing in return. It includes a wonderful, full-color map from Rand McNally, the world's largest commercial mapmaker. Most important of all, it's written and assiduously updated by the kind of people you *would* hit up for travel tips if you knew them. They're as choosy as your pickiest friend, except they've probably seen a lot more of France. In these pages, they don't send you chasing down every town and sight in France, but have instead selected the best ones, the ones that are worthy of your time and money. To make it easy for you to put it all together in the time you have, they've created short, medium, and long itineraries and, in cities, neighborhood walks that you can mix and match in a snap. Just tear out the map at the perforation, and join us on the road in France.

About Our Writers

Our success in achieving our goals—and in helping to make your trip the best of all possible vacations—is a credit to the hard work of our extraordinary writers and editors.

Nancy Coons, who has been based in Europe since 1987, has covered much of northeastern France (and many neighboring countries) for Fodor's. This year she adds the Riviera to her list. She works from her 300-year-old farmhouse in Lorraine. She has written on European culture and food for *The Wall Street Journal*, *European Travel & Life, Opera News,* and *National Geographic Traveler*.

Nigel Fisher, the peripatetic writer and knowledgeable publisher of "Voyager International," a newsletter on world travel, updated much of this book. His particular interests are in telling his readers about art, about divine places to stay, and about the most delicious food. Everywhere he goes, he talks to people and makes friends, so he always knows which chefs are striving for the stars and which are resting on their laurels.

Simon Hewitt, who first wrote much of this book, headed to Paris straight from studying French and Art History at Oxford. It was a return to base: His grandmother was French, as are his wife and daughter. He recently moved to Versailles to gain a different perspective on life in and around the French capital. When not contemplating the Sacré-Coeur's aesthetic fallout or the Sun King's bigger-than-life Baroque home, his thoughts often turn to cricket—he is captain of the French national team.

Rebecca Hirschfield, a native New Yorker now living in Paris, has done work for the *International Herald Tribune, Boulevard* magazine, and *Time Out Paris*. Her passion is learning about the medieval beginnings of modern France and exploring *La France Profonde* (that is, everything outside of Paris). This time, she helps us find out all there is to know about the North and Champagne.

Nicola Keegan was born in Ireland and raised in Iowa. But after spending a year at the Sorbonne, she knew France was going to be her home forever. Nine years later she is still there—and married to a Frenchman. An expert at finding her way around France, she provides smart travel tips in the Gold Guide to make your trip easier.

Suzanne Rowan Kelleher traded bagels for croissants when she moved from New York to Paris in 1993. A wayfarer by nature, Suzanne is a travel writer who contributes to *Esquire* and *Travel Holiday*. She has good news about shopping and lodging in Paris: France's recession has forced the city to become more value-oriented.

Editor **Natasha Lesser** has lived in Washington, D.C., California, Iowa, Kenya, and France, and traveled to many other places. After exploring every boulevard and back rue in Paris, many a mile of coast in Normandy, a number of Roman amphitheaters in Provence, and the heights of the French Alps, she has stayed long enough at her desk in New York to pass her knowledge on to you.

Alexander Lobrano has lived in Paris for 11 years, after eating his way through Boston, New York, and London. He writes a weekly dining column for *Paris Time Out* and has reported on French food for many publications, including *Food & Wine* and *Travel & Leisure*. The best meal he has had recently in Paris? At Les Élysées.

Ian Phillips, who reports on what's going on at night and in the arts scene in Paris, originally moved from Britain to the French capital by mistake. He had applied for a job in the Mediterranean, following his dream of sailing yachts, but ended up taking Bateaux Mouches down the Seine instead. He swiftly found his way around the city, and finally found his footing as a freelance journalist, writing on culture and fashion for publications in Paris, London, and New York.

George Semler lives over the border in Spain, but he has skied, hiked, fly-fished, and explored both sides of the Pyrénées for the last quarter of a century. He can say that he's acquainted with each trout in the Pyrénées, of Spanish *and* French persuasion, as well as every wild mushroom and Romanesque chapel. Corsica is his second love and his mountain in the sea.

We'd especially like to thank the staff at the French Government Tourist Office in New York for fact-finding assistance.

Connections

We're pleased that the American Society of Travel Agents continues to endorse Fodor's as its guidebook of choice. ASTA is the world's largest and most influential travel trade association, operating in more than 170 countries, with 27,000 members pledged to adhere to a strict code of ethics reflecting the Society's motto, "Integrity in Travel." ASTA shares Fodor's devotion to providing smart, honest travel information

and advice to travelers, and we've long recommended that our readers—even those who have guidebooks and traveling friends—consult ASTA member agents for the experience and professionalism they bring to your vacation planning.

On Fodor's Web site (www.fodors.com), check out the new Resource Center, an online companion to the Gold Guide chapter of this book, complete with useful hot links to related sites. In our forums, you can also get lively advice from other travelers and more great tips from Fodor's experts worldwide.

How to Use This Book

Organization

Up front is the **Gold Guide,** an easy-to-use section arranged alphabetically by topic. Under each listing you'll find tips and information that will help you accomplish what you need to in France. You'll also find addresses and telephone numbers of organizations and companies that offer destination-related services and detailed information and publications.

The first chapter in the guide, **Destination: France** helps get you in the mood for your trip. New and Noteworthy cues you in on trends and happenings, What's Where gets you oriented, Pleasures and Pastimes describes the activities and sights that make France unique, Great Itineraries lays out a selection of complete trips, Fodor's Choice showcases our top picks, and Festivals and Seasonal Events alerts you to special events to seek out.

Chapters in *France* are arranged regionally, beginning with the capital, Paris, and the region around it, Ile-de-France, then spiraling clockwise around the country from west to east. Each city chapter begins with Exploring information, which is divided into neighborhood sections; each recommends a walking or driving tour and lists sights in alphabetical order. Each regional chapter is divided by geographical area; within each area, towns are covered in logical geographical order, and attractive stretches of road and minor points of interest between them are indicated by the designation *En Route*. And within town sections, all restaurants and lodgings are grouped.

To help you decide what to visit in the time you have, all chapters begin with our recommended itineraries. The A to Z section that ends all chapters covers getting there and getting around. It also provides helpful contacts and resources.

At the end of the book you'll find **Portraits,** wonderful essays about food, wine, and architecture in France, followed by suggestions for pretrip research, from recommended reading to movies on tape that use France as a backdrop.

Icons and Symbols

★   Our special recommendations
✕   Restaurant
🏠   Lodging establishment
✕🏠   Lodging establishment whose restaurant warrants a special trip
☻   Good for kids (rubber duck)
☞   Sends you to another section of the guide for more information
✉   Address
☎   Telephone number
🕙   Opening and closing times
💶   Admission prices (those we give apply to adults; substantially reduced fees are almost always available for children, students, and senior citizens)

Numbers in white and black circles (e.g., ③ and ❸) that appear on the maps, in the margins, and within the tours correspond to one another.

Dining and Lodging

The restaurants and lodgings we list are the cream of the crop in each price range. Price charts appear in the Pleasures and Pastimes section that follows each chapter introduction.

Hotel Facilities

We always list the facilities that are available—but we don't specify whether you'll be charged extra to use them: When pricing accommodations, always ask what's included. In addition, assume that all rooms have private bathrooms unless otherwise noted (and then be sure to ask for a private bathroom, if you want one). Note that private bathrooms may have either a bathtub or a shower (which is not noted), and not necessarily both; if you prefer one or the other, be sure to ask when making the reservation. In addition, when you book a room, be sure to mention if you have a disability or are traveling with children, if you prefer a certain type of bed, or if you have specific dietary needs or other concerns.

Restaurant Reservations and Dress Codes

Reservations are always a good idea; we mention them only when they're essential or are not accepted. Book as far ahead as you can, and reconfirm as soon as you arrive. Unless otherwise noted, the restaurants listed are open daily for lunch and dinner. We mention dress only when men are required to wear a jacket or a jacket and tie. Look for an overview of local dining-out habits in the Gold Guide and in the Pleasures and Pastimes section that follows each chapter introduction.

Credit Cards

The following abbreviations are used: **AE,** American Express; **DC,** Diners Club; **MC,** MasterCard; and **V,** Visa.

Don't Forget to Write

You can use this book in the confidence that all prices and opening times are based on information supplied to us at press time; Fodor's cannot accept responsibility for any errors. Time inevitably brings changes, so always confirm information when it matters—especially if you're making a detour to visit a specific place.

Were the restaurants we recommended as described? Did our hotel picks exceed your expectations? Did you find a museum we recommended a waste of time? Keeping a travel guide fresh and up-to-date is a big job, and we welcome your feedback, positive *and* negative. If you have complaints, we'll look into them and revise our entries when the facts warrant it. If you've discovered a special place that we haven't included, we'll pass the information along to our correspondents and have them check it out. So send us your thoughts via e-mail at editors@fodors.com (specifying the name of the book on the subject line) or on paper in care of the France editor at Fodor's, 201 East 50th Street, New York, New York 10022. In the meantime, have a wonderful trip!

Karen Cure

Karen Cure
Editorial Director

ENGLAND

La Manche
(English Channel)

Boulogne

Cherbourg

Dieppe

Ami

Le Havre

Rouen

Caen

NORMANDY

Chartres

Roscoff

Brest

St-Malo

Morlaix

St-Brieuc

BRITTANY

Rennes

Le Mans

Quimper

Vannes

Angers

Blois

Lorient

Nantes

PAYS-DE-LOIRE

Loire

Tours

VAL DE LOTRE

ATLANTIC
OCEAN

Les Sables
d'Olonne

Poitiers

Montlu

Niort

La Rochelle

POITOU-CHARENTES

Saintes

Limoges

Royan

Angoulême

LIMOUSIN

Périgueux

Brive-la-Gaillarde

Bay of Biscay

Bordeaux

Garonne

Dordogne

Cahors

Langon

AQUITAINE

Montauban

Bayonne

Albi

Biarritz

Pau

MIDI-PYRÉNÉES

Toulouse

LAN-ROU

Tarbes

Carcassonne

SPAIN

ANDORRA

Calais
BELGIUM
NORTH
Lille
Arras
PICARDY
niens
Cambrai
St. Quentin
Beauvais
CHAMPAGNE
ARDENNES
Reims
ILE-DE-
FRANCE
Metz
ALSACE
LORRAINE
Paris
Châlons-en-
Champagne
Nancy
Sens
Strasbourg
GERMANY
Troyes
Colmar
Orléans
Mulhouse
Auxerre
Belfort
Bourges
Dijon
Besançon
Nevers
Beaune
SWITZERLAND
BURGUNDY
FRANCHE-
COMTÉ
luçon
Mâcon
Bourg-en-
Bresse
Clermont-
Ferrand
Lyon
Rhône
ALPES
ITALY
AUVERGNE
Chambéry
Le Puy
Aurillac
RHÔNE
VALLEY
Grenoble
Rodez
Montélimar
Gap
Millau
PROVENCE
Sisteron
Nîmes
Avignon
RIVIERA
NGUEDOC
USSILLON
Montpellier
Aix-en-Provence
Nice
MONACO
Monte Carlo
Cannes
Narbonne
Marseille
Perpignan
Toulon
Mediterranean Sea
Corsica
0   50 mi
0   75 km

Corsica
Calvi
Bastia
Corte
Ajaccio
N198
Bonifacio

LUXEMBOURG

Europe

SMART TRAVEL TIPS A TO Z

Basic Information on Traveling in France, Savvy Tips to Make Your Trip a Breeze, and Companies and Organizations to Contact

AIR TRAVEL

BOOKING YOUR FLIGHT

Price is just one factor to consider when booking a flight: frequency of service and even a carrier's safety record are often just as important. Major airlines offer the greatest number of departures. Smaller airlines—including regional and no-frills airlines—usually have a limited number of flights daily. On the other hand, so-called low-cost airlines usually are cheaper, and their fares impose fewer restrictions, such as advance-purchase requirements. Safety-wise, low-cost carriers as a group have a good history—about equal to that of major carriers.

When you book, **look for nonstop flights** and **remember that "direct" flights stop at least once.** Try to **avoid connecting flights,** which require a change of plane.

Ask your airline if it offers electronic ticketing, which eliminates all paperwork. You go directly to the gate and give the agent your confirmation number.

CARRIERS

➤ MAJOR AIRLINES: **Air France** (☎ 800/237–2747 in the U.S., 08–02–80–28–02 in France) to Charles de Gaulle. **American Airlines** (☎ 800/433–7300 in the U.S., 01–69–32–73–07 in France) to Charles de Gaulle, Orly. **Continental** (☎ 800/231–0856 in the U.S., 01–42–99–09–09 in France) to Charles de Gaulle. **Delta** (☎ 800/241–4141 in the U.S., 01–47–68–92–92 in France) to Charles de Gaulle. **Northwest** (☎ 800/225–2525 in the U.S., 01–42–66–90–00 in France) to Charles de Gaulle. **TWA** (☎ 800/892–4141 in the U.S., 01–49–19–20–00 in France) to Charles de Gaulle. **United** (☎ 800/538–2929 in the U.S., 08–01–72–72–72 in

France) to Charles de Gaulle. **US Airways** (☎ 800/428–4322 in the U.S., 01–49–10–29–00 in France) to Charles de Gaulle.

➤ FROM THE U.K.: **Air France** (☎ 0181/742–6600 in the U.K., 08–02–80–28–02 in France). **British Airways** (☎ 0345/222–111 in the U.K., 08–02–80–29–02 in France). **Air U.K.** (☎ 0345/666–777 in the U.K., 01–44–56–18–08 in France). **British Midland** (☎ 0181/754–7321 or 0345/554–554 in the U.K., 01–48–62–55–65 in France). **Easyjet** (☎ 0990/292–929 in the U.K., 04–93–21–48–33 in France) runs scheduled services to Nice from Luton.

➤ SMALLER LOCAL AIRLINES: **Air Inter-Europe** (☎ 800/237–2747 in the U.S., 01–45–46–90–00 in France), a subsidiary of Air France, flies all over the country. **Air Liberté** (☎ 08–03–80–58–05) flies from Paris to the Riviera and the southwest region of France.

CHARTERS

Charters usually have the lowest fares but are the least dependable. Departures are infrequent and seldom on time, flights can be delayed for up to 48 hours or can be canceled for any reason up to 10 days before you're scheduled to leave. Itineraries and prices can change after you've booked.

In the U.S., the Department of Transportation's Aviation Consumer Protection Division has jurisdiction over charters and provides a certain degree of protection. The DOT requires that money paid to charter operators be held in escrow, so if you can't pay with a credit card, **always make your check payable to a charter carrier's escrow account.** The name of the bank should be in the charter contract. If you have any problems with a charter operator, contact the DOT (☞ Airline Complaints, *below*). If you buy a charter package that includes both air and land arrangements, remember that the escrow requirement applies only to the air component.

➤ CHARTER CARRIER: **Tower Air** (☎ 800/34–TOWER).

CONSOLIDATORS

Consolidators buy tickets for scheduled international flights at reduced rates from the airlines, then sell them at prices that beat the best fare available directly from the airlines, usually without restrictions. Sometimes you can even get your money back if you need to return the ticket. Carefully read the fine print detailing penalties for changes and cancellations, and **confirm your consolidator reservation with the airline.**

➤ CONSOLIDATORS: **Cheap Tickets** (☎ 800/377–1000). **DER Travel Services** (☎ 800/717–4247). **Up & Away Travel** (☎ 212/889–2345). **Discount Travel Network** (☎ 800/576–1600). **Unitravel** (☎ 800/325–2222). **World Travel Network** (☎ 800/409–6753).

COURIERS

When you fly as a courier, you trade your checked-luggage space for a ticket deeply subsidized by a courier service. It's all perfectly legitimate, but there are restrictions: You can usually book your flight only a week or two in advance, your length of stay may be set for a certain number of days, and you probably won't be able to book a companion on the same flight.

➤ COURIER COMPANIES: **Air Courier Association** (✉ 15000 W. 6th Ave., Suite 203, Golden, CO 80401, ☎ 800/282–1202, www.aircourier.org).

International Association of Air Travel Couriers (✉ 220 South Dixie Highway #3, P.O. Box 1349, Lake Worth, FL, 33460, ☎ 561/582–8320, FAX 561/582–1581. www.courier.org).

Now Voyager Travel (✉ 74 Varick St., Suite 307, New York, NY 10013 ☎ 212/431–1616, FAX 212/219–1753 or 212/334–5243, www.nowvoyagertravel.com).

CUTTING COSTS

The least-expensive airfares to France are priced for round-trip travel and usually must be purchased in advance. It's smart to **call a number of airlines, and when you are quoted a good price, book it on the spot**—the same fare may not be available the next day. Airlines generally allow you to change your return date for a fee. However, most low-fare tickets are nonrefundable. To get the lowest airfare, **check different routings.** Compare prices of flights to and from different airports if your destination or home city has more than one gateway. Also price off-peak flights.

Travel agents, especially those who specialize in finding the lowest fares (☞ Discounts & Deals, *below*), can be especially helpful when booking a plane ticket. When you're quoted a price, **ask your agent if the price is likely to get any lower.**

DISCOUNT PASSES

You can **save on air travel** within Europe if you plan on traveling to and from Paris aboard Air France. As part of their Euro Flyer program, you then can buy between three and nine flight coupons, valid on these airlines' flights to more than 100 European cities. At $120 each (April–September) and $99 each (October–April 1), these coupons are a good deal, and the fine print still allows you plenty of freedom.

CHECK IN & BOARDING

The first to get bumped are passengers who checked in late and those flying on discounted tickets, so **get to the gate and check in as early as possible,** especially during peak periods.

Although the trend on international flights is to drop reconfirmation requirements, many airlines still ask you to reconfirm each leg of your international itinerary. Failure to do so may result in your reservation being canceled.

To enter France, you need to **carry your passport.** You will be asked to show it when you check in. For more information, *see* Passports & Visas, *below.*

THE GOLD GUIDE / SMART TRAVEL TIPS

ENJOYING THE FLIGHT

For more legroom, **request an emergency-aisle seat.** Don't sit in the row in front of the emergency aisle or in front of a bulkhead, where seats may not recline.

If you don't like airline food, **ask for special meals when booking.** These can be vegetarian, low-cholesterol, or kosher, for example.

When flying internationally, try to maintain a normal routine, to help fight jet-lag. At night, **get some sleep. By day, eat light meals, drink water (not alcohol), and move around the cabin** to stretch your legs.

Many carriers have prohibited smoking on all of their international flights; others allow smoking only on certain routes or certain departures, so **contact your carrier regarding its smoking policy.**

FLYING TIMES

Flying time to Paris is 7½ hours from New York, 9 hours from Chicago, and 11 hours from Los Angeles. Flying time between Paris and Nice is approximately 1 hour.

HOW TO COMPLAIN

If your baggage goes astray or your flight goes awry, complain right away. Most carriers require that you **file a claim immediately.**

➤ AIRLINE COMPLAINTS: U.S. Department of Transportation **Aviation Consumer Protection Division** (✉ C-75, Room 4107, Washington, DC 20590, ☎ 202/366–2220). **Federal Aviation Administration Consumer Hotline** (☎ 800/322–7873).

AIRPORTS

The major gateways to France are Orly and Charles de Gaulle (also known as Roissy), outside of Paris. It doesn't really matter which one you fly into; both are easily accessible to Paris, though Roissy is the only one with a TGV station. Many major airlines also have (less-frequent) flights to Lyon, Nice, Marseille, Bordeaux, and Toulouse, or you can catch a connecting flight in Paris to other destinations in France.

➤ AIRPORT INFORMATION: **Charles de Gaulle/Roissy** (✉ 26 km (16 mi) northeast of Paris, ☎ 01–48–62–12–12).**Orly** (✉ 16 km (10 mi) south of Paris, ☎ 01–49–75–15–15).

DUTY-FREE SHOPPING

Duty-free cosmetics and perfumes are generally a good buy, but you are better off purchasing wine, chocolates, mustard, coffee, and other food items in shops throughout the country.

BARGE TRAVEL

Canal and river trips are popular in France, particularly along the picturesque waterways in Brittany, Burgundy, and the Midi. For further information, contact a travel agent; ask for a "Tourisme Fluvial" brochure in any French tourist office; or get in touch with one of the companies that organizes barge trips. Also *see* Theme Trips *in* Tour Operators, *below.*

➤ BARGE COMPANIES: **Bourgogne Voies Navigables** (✉ 1 quai de la République, 89000 Auxerre, ☎ 03–86–72–92–10). **Connoisseur Cruisers** (✉ Halye Nautique, Ile Sauzay, 70100 Gray, ☎ 03–84–64–95–20).

BIKE TRAVEL

The French are great bicycling enthusiasts—witness the Tour de France—and there are many good bicycling routes in France. For 44 francs a day (55 francs for a 10-speed touring bike) **you can rent a bike from one of 30 train stations;** you need to show your passport and leave a deposit of 1,000 francs or a Visa or MasterCard. Mountain bikes (known as VTT or Vélo Touts Terrains) can be rented from many shops, as well as from some train stations. Bikes may be taken as accompanied luggage from any station in France; some trains in rural areas don't even charge for this. Tourist offices supply details on the more than 200 local shops that rent bikes, or you can get the SNCF brochure "Guide du Train et du Vélo" from any station.

Several good routes are described in detail in the chapters that follow, or contact the Fédération Française de Cyclotourisme for information. The yellow Michelin maps (1:200,000 scale) are fine for roads, but for off-road bicycling you may want to get one of the Institut Géographique National's detailed, large-scale maps. Try their blue series (1:25,000) or orange series (1:50,000). For more bicycling trips, *see* Theme Trips *in* Tour Operators, *below.*

➤ BICYCLING INFORMATION: **Fédération Française de Cyclotourisme** (✉ 8 rue Jean-Marie-Jégo, 75013 Paris, ☎ 01–44–16–88–88). **Institut Géographique National** (✉ IGN, 107 rue La Boétie, 75008 Paris, ☎ 01–42–56–06–68).

BIKES IN FLIGHT

Most airlines will accommodate bikes as luggage, provided they are dismantled and put into a box. Call to see if your airline sells bike boxes (about $5; bike bags are at least $100) although you can often pick them up free at bike shops. International travelers can sometimes substitute a bike for a piece of checked luggage for free; otherwise, it will cost about $100.

BOAT & FERRY TRAVEL

A number of ferry and hovercraft routes link the United Kingdom and France, as well as mainland France and Corsica (☞ Chapter 14 for more information). Driving distances from the French ports to Paris are as follows: from Calais, 290 km (180 mi); from Boulogne, 243 km (151 mi); from Dieppe, 193 km (120 mi); from Dunkerque, 257 km (160 mi). The fastest routes to Paris from each port are via the N43, A26, and A1 from Calais and the Channel Tunnel; via the N1 from Boulogne; via the N15 from Le Havre; via the D915 and N1 from Dieppe; and via the A25 and A1 from Dunkerque.

➤ DOVER–CALAIS: **Hoverspeed** (✉ International Hoverport, Marine Parade, Dover CT17 9TG, ☎ 01304/865000; 03–21–46–14–14 in Calais) operates up to 15 crossings a day by Hovercraft and catamaran. The crossings take 35 minutes (Hovercraft) or 55 minutes (catamaran). **P&O European Ferries** (✉ Channel House, Channel View Rd., Dover, Kent CT17 9TJ, ☎ 01304/863000; 03–21–46–10–20 in Calais) has up to 25 sailings a day; the crossing

takes about 75 minutes. **Sealink** (✉ Charter House, Park St., Ashford, Kent TN24 8EX, ☎ 01233/646801; 03–21–46–78–30 in Calais) operates up to 25 sailings a day; the crossing takes about 90 minutes.

➤ FOLKESTONE–BOULOGNE: **Hoverspeed** (☎ 03–21–30–27–26 in Boulogne or Dover–Calais, ☞ *above*) is the sole operator on this route, with 10 35-minute crossings a day.

➤ NEWHAVEN–DIEPPE: **Sealink** (☞ Dover–Calais, *above*) has as many as four sailings a day, and the crossing takes four hours.

➤ PORTSMOUTH–LE HAVRE: **P&O European Ferries** (☎ 02–35–19–78–50 in Le Havre or Dover–Calais, ☞ *above*) has up to three sailings a day, and the crossing takes 5½ hours by day, 7½ by night.

➤ RAMSGATE–DUNKERQUE: **Sally Line** (✉ Argyle Centre, York St., Ramsgate, Kent CT11 9DS, ☎ 01843/595522; 03–28–26–70–70 in Dunkerque) has up to six 2½-hour crossings a day.

BUS TRAVEL

France's excellent train service means that long-distance buses are rare; **regional buses are found mainly where train service is spotty.** Excursions and bus tours are organized by the SNCF and other tourist organizations. Ask for a brochure at any major travel agent or contact France-Tourisme. Bus tours from the U.K. generally depart from London, for Paris, the Atlantic Coast, Chamonix and the Alps, Grenoble, Lyon, and the Riviera.

➤ TO THE U.K. AND OTHER EUROPEAN COUNTRIES: **Eurolines** (✉ 28 av. Général-de-Gaulle, Bagnolet, ☎ 01–49–72–51–51 in France, 0171/730–3499 in the U.K.) runs bus trips (via Hovercraft or ferry) from Paris to London and many other European cites.

➤ WITHIN FRANCE: **Paris Vision** (✉ 1 rue d'Auber, 75009 Paris, ☎ 01–47–42–27–40). **SNCF** (✉ 88 rue St-Lazare, 75009 Paris, ☎ 08–36–35–35–39 in English).

BUSINESS HOURS

BANKS

Generally, **banks are open weekdays, from 9:30 to 4:30.** Most take a one-hour, or even a 90-minute, lunch break, except for those in Paris.

MUSEUMS

Usual opening times are from 9:30 to 5 or 6, but some are only open Sunday afternoons. Many close for lunch (noon–2). Most are closed one day a week (generally Monday or Tuesday) and on national holidays: **check museum hours before you go.**

SHOPS

Large stores in big towns are open from 9 or 9:30 until 7 or 8. Smaller shops often open earlier (8 AM) and close later (8 PM) but take a lengthy lunch break (1–4), particularly in the south of France. Corner groceries frequently stay open until around 10 PM. Some Paris stores are beginning to stay open on Sundays.

CAMERAS & COMPUTERS

EQUIPMENT PRECAUTIONS

Always **keep your film, tape, or computer disks out of the sun.** Carry an extra supply of batteries, and **be prepared to turn on your camera, camcorder, or laptop** to prove to security personnel that the device is real. Always **ask for hand inspection of film,** which becomes clouded after successive exposure to airport X-ray machines, and **keep videotapes and computer disks away from metal detectors.**

ONLINE ON THE ROAD

If you use a major internet provider, getting online in Paris shouldn't be difficult. Call your internet provider to get the local access number in Paris. Some hotels even have in-room modem lines. You may, however, need an adapter for your computer (☞ *above*).

➤ ACCESS NUMBERS IN PARIS: **AOL** (☎ 01–40–64–16–70). **Compu-serve** (☎ 01–41–02–03–04).

➤ INTERNET CAFÉS: **Internet Café** (✉ 27 rue Lacepède, 5ᵉ, Paris, ☎ 01–43–36–70–46, métro Place Monge). **Internet Cyberia Café** (✉ 23 rue du Renard, 4ᵉ Paris, ☎ 01–44–54–53–49, métro Hôtel-de-Ville).

➤ PHOTO HELP: **Kodak Information Center** (☎ 800/242–2424). *Kodak Guide to Shooting Great Travel Pictures,* available in bookstores or from Fodor's Travel Publications (☎ 800/533–6478; $16.50 plus $4 shipping).

CAR RENTAL

Though renting a car in France is expensive—about twice as much as in the United States—as is gas (5.80 francs to 6.80 francs per liter), it may pay off if you are traveling with two or more people. In addition, renting a car gives you a kind of freedom that the train does not. Rates in Paris begin at about $70 a day and $200 per week for an economy car with air conditioning, a manual transmission, and unlimited mileage. The price doesn't usually take into account the 20.6% VAT tax or, if you pick it up from the airport, the airport tax. You won't need a car in the capital, so **wait to pick up your rental until the day you leave Paris.**

➤ MAJOR AGENCIES: **Alamo** (☎ 800/522–9696, 0800/272–2000 in the U.K.). **Avis** (☎ 800/331–1084, 800/879–2847 in Canada, 008/225–533 in Australia). **Budget** (☎ 800/527–0700, 0800/181181 in the U.K.). **Dollar** (☎ 800/800–4000; 0990/565656 in the U.K., where it is known as Eurodollar). **Hertz** (☎ 800/654–3001, 800/263–0600 in Canada, 0345/555888 in the U.K., 03/9222–2523 in Australia, 03/358–6777 in New Zealand). **National InterRent** (☎ 800/227–3876; 0345/222525 in the U.K., where it is known as Europcar InterRent).

➤ LOCAL AGENCIES: **ACAR** (✉ 99 bd. Auguste-Blanqui, 75013 Paris, ☎ 01–45–88–28–38). **Locabest** (✉ 104 bd. Magenta, 75010 Paris, ☎ 01–44–72–08–05). **Rent-A-Car** (✉ 79 rue de Bercy, 75012 Paris, ☎ 01–43–45–98–99).

CUTTING COSTS

To get the best deal, **shop around,** either through a travel agent or on your own, and make arrangements before you go to France.

Also **ask your travel agent about a company's customer-service record.** How has the company responded to late plane arrivals and vehicle mishaps? Are there often lines at the rental counter? If you're traveling during a holiday period, does a confirmed reservation guarantee you a car?

Be sure to **look into wholesalers,** companies that do not own fleets but rent in bulk from those that do and often offer better rates than traditional car-rental operations. Prices are best during off-peak periods. Rentals booked through wholesalers must be paid for before you leave the United States.

If you are planning on being in France for at least 17 days, **look into leasing a car;** rates include all taxes, insurance, and unlimited mileage.

In addition, **look into car rental and train travel packages,** these may end up saving you some money and time (☞ Train Travel, *below*).

➤ LONG-TERM LEASING: **Renault Eurodrive** (☎ 800/221–1052 east; ☎ 800/477–7716 west; and ☎ 800/777–7131 FL and Puerto Rico).

➤ RENTAL WHOLESALERS: **Auto Europe** (☎ 207/842–2000 or 800/223–5555, FAX 800–235–6321). **Europe by Car** (☎ 212/581–3040 or 800/223–1516, FAX 212/246–1458). **DER Travel Services** (✉ 9501 W. Devon Ave., Rosemont, IL 60018, ☎ 800/782–2424, FAX 800/282–7474 for information or 800/860–9944 for brochures). **Kemwel Holiday Autos** (☎ 914/835–5555 or 800/678–0678, FAX 914/835–5126).

INSURANCE

When driving a rented car you are generally responsible for any damage to or loss of the vehicle. Before you rent, **see what coverage you already have** under the terms of your personal auto-insurance policy and credit cards, and ask what coverage you may be able to get when you rent the car. Collision policies that car-rental companies sell for European rentals typically do not cover stolen vehicles.

REQUIREMENTS

In France your own driver's license is acceptable. You don't need an International Driver's Permit, unless you are planning on a long-term stay; you can get one from the American or Canadian automobile association, and, in the United Kingdom, from the Automobile Association or Royal Automobile Club.

SURCHARGES

Before you pick up a car in one city and leave it in another, **ask about drop-off charges or one-way service fees,** which can be substantial. Note, too, that some rental agencies charge extra if you return the car before the time specified in your contract. To avoid a hefty refueling fee, **fill the tank just before you turn in the car,** but be aware that gas stations near the rental outlet may overcharge.

CAR TRAVEL

AUTO CLUBS

➤ IN AUSTRALIA: **Australian Automobile Association** (☎ 06/247–7311).

➤ IN CANADA: **Canadian Automobile Association** (CAA, ☎ 613/247–0117).

➤ IN NEW ZEALAND: **New Zealand Automobile Association** (☎ 09/377–4660).

➤ IN THE U.K.: **Automobile Association** (AA, ☎ 0990/500–600), **Royal Automobile Club** (RAC, ☎ 0990/722–722 for membership, 0345/121–345 for insurance).

➤ IN THE U.S.: **American Automobile Association** (☎ 800/564–6222).

EMERGENCY SERVICES

If your car breaks down on an expressway, **go to a roadside emergency telephone** and call the breakdown service. If you have a breakdown anywhere else, find the nearest garage or contact the police (dial 17).

GASOLINE

Gas is expensive, especially on expressways and in rural areas. When possible, **buy gas before you get on the expressway** and keep an eye on pump prices as you go. These vary enormously; anything from 5.80 to 6.80 francs per liter. The cheapest gas can be found at *hypermarchés* (very large supermarkets). It is possible to go for many miles in the country without passing a gas station—**don't let your tank get too low in rural areas.**

PARKING

Parking is a nightmare in Paris and often difficult in other large towns. Meters and ticket machines (pay and display) are common: Make sure you **have a supply of 1-, 2-, 5-, and 10-franc coins.** Parking is free during August in most of Paris, but **be sure to always check the signs before you park, as rules vary.** In smaller towns, parking may be permitted on one side of the street only—alternating every two weeks—so pay attention to signs.

ROADS

France's roads are classified into five types, numbered and prefixed *A, N, D, C,* or *V.* For the fastest roads between two points, **look for roads marked A for *autoroutes.*** A *péage* (toll) must be paid on most express-ways: The rate varies but can be steep.

The *N* (Route Nationale) roads—which are sometimes divided high-ways—and *D* (Route Départementale) roads are usually also wide and fast. Don't be daunted by smaller (*C* and *V*) roads, either.

There are excellent links between Paris and most French cities, but poor ones between the provinces (the principal exceptions being A26 from Calais to Reims, A62 between Bordeaux and Toulouse, and A9/A8 the length of the Mediterranean coast).

It is often difficult to avoid Paris when crossing France—just **try to steer clear of the rush hours** (7–9:30 AM and 4:30–7:30 PM). To leave Paris by car, figure out which of the *portes* (gates) correspond to the direction you are going. Major highways connect to Paris at these points and directions are indicated by major cities. For instance, heading north, look for Porte de la Chapelle (direction Lille and Charles de Gaulle Airport); east, for Porte de Bagnolet (direction Metz and Nancy); south, for Porte d'Orléans (diretion Lyon and Bordeaux); and west, for Porte d'Auteuil (direction Rouen and Chartres) or Porte de St-Cloud.

ROAD MAPS

If you plan to drive through France, **get a yellow Michelin map** for each region you'll be visiting. The maps are available from most bookshops and newsagents.

RULES OF THE ROAD

In France, **you may use your own driver's license,** but you must be able to prove you have third-party insur-ance. Drive on the right and **yield to drivers coming from streets to the right.** However, this rule does not necessarily apply at roundabouts, where you should watch out for just about everyone. You must **wear your seat belt,** and children under 12 may not travel in the front seat. Speed limits are 130 kph (80 mph) on expressways, 110 kph (70 mph) on divided highways, 90 kph (55 mph) on other roads, 50 kph (30 mph) in towns. French drivers break these limits and police dish out hefty on-the-spot fines with equal abandon.

U.K. TO FRANCE BY CAR

☞ Boat & Ferry Travel, *above.*

CHILDREN & TRAVEL

CHILDREN IN FRANCE

Be sure to plan ahead and **involve your youngsters** as you outline your trip. When packing, include things to keep them busy en route. On sightsee-ing days try to schedule activities of special interest to your children. If you are renting a car don't forget to **arrange for a car seat** when you reserve.

Many restaurants serve children's portions and have high chairs, and larger hotels will provide cribs free to guests with young children. (This is often not the case in pensions and smaller hotels.) A supplement may be requested for children over three.

Supermarkets carry several major brands of diapers (*couches à jeter*) and baby food, and pharmacies provide the essentials.

There are plenty of diversions for the young (noted by a duck icon through-out this book), and **almost all muse-ums and movie theaters offer discounted rates** to children.

Playgrounds can be found off of many highways. Most rest stop bathrooms have changing tables.

Getting around **Paris and other major cities with a stroller can be a challenge.** Not all métro stations have escalators. Buses are a better bet in off-peak hours since they are often not as crowded as the métro. Many museums require you to check strollers at the entrance.

➤ LOCAL INFORMATION: Contact the **CIDJ** (✉ Centre d'Information et de Documentation pour la Jeunesse, 101 quai Branly, 75015 Paris, ☎ 01–44–49–12–00) for information about activities and events for youngsters in Paris. *Pariscope* and *L'Officiel* are two weekly publications that have sections in English about entertainment for children in Paris.

FLYING

If your children are two or older, **ask about children's airfares.** As a general rule, infants under two not occupying a seat fly at greatly reduced fares or even for free.

Experts agree that it's a good idea to use safety seats aloft for children weighing less than 40 pounds. Airlines, however, can set their own policies: U.S. carriers allow FAA-approved models but usually require that you buy a ticket, even if your child would otherwise ride free, since the seats must be strapped into regular seats. Airline rules vary, so it's important to **check your airline's policy about using safety seats during takeoff and landing.** Safety seats cannot obstruct the movement of other passengers in the row, so get an appropriate seat assignment as early as possible.

When making your reservation, **request children's meals or a freestanding bassinet** if you need them; the latter are available only to those seated at the bulkhead.

GROUP TRAVEL

When planning to take your kids on a tour, look for companies that specialize in family travel.

➤ FAMILY-FRIENDLY TOUR OPERATORS: **Grandtravel** (✉ 6900 Wisconsin Ave., Suite 706, Chevy Chase, MD 20815, ☎ 301/986–0790 or 800/247–7651) for people traveling with grandchildren ages 7–17. **Families Welcome!** (✉ 92 N. Main St., Ashland, OR 97520, ☎ 541/482–6121 or 800/326–0724, FAX 541/482–0660). **A Touch of France** (✉ 660 King Rd., Fords, NJ 08863, ☎ 800/738–5240).

LODGING

Most hotels in France allow children under a certain age to stay in their parents' room at no extra charge, but others charge them as extra adults; be sure to **ask about the cutoff age for children's discounts.**

Some hotel chains offer discounts for families and programs for children. Club Med is particularly family friendly: it has a "Baby Club" (from age four months) at its resort in Chamonix, and "Mini Clubs" (for ages four to six or eight, depending on the resort), and "Kids Clubs" (for ages eight and up during school holidays) at all its resort villages in France except in Val d'Isère. Some clubs are only French-speaking, so check first.

Another option: **consider a short-term apartment or house rental or home exchange.** *See* Lodging, *below,* for information about organizations.

➤ FAMILY-FRIENDLY LODGING: **Club Med** (✉ 40 W. 57th St., New York, NY 10019, ☎ 800/258–2633). **Novotel** (☎ 800/221–4542). **Sofitel hotels** (☎ 800/221–4542).

TRAIN TRAVEL

The SNCF allows children under 4 to travel free (provided they don't occupy a seat) and children 4 to 11 to travel at half fare. The Carte Kiwi (285 francs) allows children under 16 and as many as four accompanying adults to make four journeys at half fare.

Changing compartments for infants are available on all TGVs, although not on all local trains. For more information, *see* Train Travel, *below.*

CONSUMER PROTECTION

Whenever possible, **pay with a major credit card** so you can cancel payment or get reimbursed if there's a problem, provided that you can provide documentation. This is the best way to pay, whether you're buying travel arrangements before your trip or shopping at your destination.

If you're doing business with a particular company for the first time, **contact your local Better Business Bureau and the attorney general's offices** in your state and the company's home state, as well. Have any complaints been filed?

Finally, if you're buying a package or tour, always **consider travel insurance** that includes default coverage (☞ Insurance, *below*).

➤ LOCAL BBBs: **Council of Better Business Bureaus** (✉ 4200 Wilson Blvd., Suite 800, Arlington, VA 22203, ☎ 703/276–0100, 🖷 703/525–8277).

CUSTOMS & DUTIES

When shopping, **keep receipts** for all of your purchases. Upon reentering your country of origin, **be ready to show customs officials what you've bought.** If you feel a duty is incorrect, appeal the assessment. If you object to the way your clearance was handled, get the inspector's badge number. In either case, first ask to see a supervisor, then write to the appropriate authorities, beginning with the port director at your point of entry.

IN FRANCE

There are two levels of duty-free allowance for travelers entering France: one for goods obtained (tax paid) within another European Union (EU) country and the other for goods obtained anywhere outside the EU or for goods purchased in a duty-free shop within the EU.

In the first category, you may import duty-free: 300 cigarettes or 150 cigarillos or 75 cigars or 400 grams of tobacco; 5 liters of table wine and (1) 1½ liters of alcohol over 22% volume (most spirits), (2) 3 liters of alcohol under 22% by volume (fortified or sparkling wine), or (3) 3 more liters of table wine; 90 milliliters of perfume; 375 milliliters of toilet water; and other goods to the value of 2,400 francs (620 francs for those under 15).

In the second category, you may import duty-free: 200 cigarettes or 100 cigarillos or 50 cigars or 250 grams of tobacco (these allowances are doubled if you live outside Europe); 2 liters of wine and (1) 1 liter of alcohol over 22% volume (most spirits), (2) two liters of alcohol under 22% volume (fortified or sparkling wine), or (3) 2 more liters of table wine; 60 milliliters of perfume; 250 milliliters of toilet water; and other goods to the value of 300 francs (150 francs for those under 15).

IN AUSTRALIA

Australia residents who are 18 or older may bring back $A400 worth of souvenirs and gifts (including jewelry), 250 cigarettes or 250 grams of tobacco, and 1,125 ml of alcohol (including wine, beer, and spirits). Residents under 18 may bring back $A200 worth of goods.

➤ INFORMATION: **Australian Customs Service** (Regional Director, ✉ Box 8, Sydney, NSW 2001, ☎ 02/9213–2000, 🖷 02/9213–4000).

IN CANADA

Canadian residents who have been out of Canada for at least 7 days may bring in C$500 worth of goods duty-free. If you've been away less than 7 days but more than 48 hours, the duty-free allowance drops to C$200; if your trip lasts 24–48 hours, the allowance is C$50. You may not pool allowances with family members. Goods claimed under the C$500 exemption may follow you by mail; those claimed under the lesser exemptions must accompany you. Alcohol and tobacco products may be included in the 7-day and 48-hour exemptions but not in the 24-hour exemption. If you meet the age requirements of the province or territory through which you reenter Canada, you may bring in, duty-free, 1.14 liters (40 imperial ounces) of wine or liquor *or* 24 12-ounce cans or bottles of beer or ale. If you are 16 or older you may bring in, duty-free, 200 cigarettes and 50 cigars.

You may send an unlimited number of gifts worth up to C$60 each duty-free to Canada. Label the package UNSOLICITED GIFT—VALUE UNDER $60. Alcohol and tobacco are excluded.

➤ INFORMATION: **Revenue Canada**
(✉ 2265 St. Laurent Blvd. S, Ottawa,
Ontario K1G 4K3, ☎ 613/993–
0534, 800/461–9999 in Canada).

IN NEW ZEALAND

Homeward-bound residents with
goods to declare must present themselves for inspection. If you're 17 or
older, you may bring back $700
worth of souvenirs and gifts. Your
duty-free allowance also includes 4.5
liters of wine or beer; one 1,125-ml
bottle of spirits; and either 200
cigarettes, 250 grams of tobacco, 50
cigars, or a combo of all three up to
250 grams.

➤ INFORMATION: **New Zealand Customs** (✉ Custom House, ✉ 50 Anzac
Ave., Box 29, Auckland, New Zealand,
☎ 09/359–6655, ☎ 09/309–2978).

IN THE U.K.

If you are a U.K. resident and your
journey was wholly within the European Union (EU), you won't have to
pass through customs when you
return to the United Kingdom. If you
plan to bring back large quantities of
alcohol or tobacco, check EU limits
beforehand.

➤ INFORMATION: **HM Customs and
Excise** (✉ Dorset House, ✉ Stamford
St., London SE1 9NG, ☎ 0171/202–
4227).

IN THE U.S.

U.S. residents may bring home $400
worth of foreign goods duty-free if
they've been out of the country for at
least 48 hours (and if they haven't
used the $400 allowance or any part
of it in the past 30 days).

U.S. residents 21 and older may bring
back 1 liter of alcohol duty-free. In
addition, regardless of your age, you
are allowed 200 cigarettes and 100
non-Cuban cigars. Antiques, which
the U.S. Customs Service defines as
objects more than 100 years old,
enter duty-free, as do original works
of art.

You may also send packages home
duty-free: up to $200 worth of goods
for personal use, with a limit of one
parcel per addressee per day (and no
alcohol or tobacco products or perfume worth more than $5); label the
package PERSONAL USE, and attach a
list of its contents and their retail
value. Do not label the package
UNSOLICITED GIFT, or your duty-free
exemption will drop to $100. Mailed
items do not affect your duty-free
allowance on your return.

➤ INFORMATION: **U.S. Customs Service**
(Inquiries, ✉ Box 7407, Washington,
DC 20044, ☎ 202/927–6724; com-
plaints, Office of Regulations and
Rulings, ✉ 1301 Constitution Ave.
NW, Washington, DC 20229; registra-
tion of equipment, Resource Manage-
ment, ✉ 1301 Constitution Ave. NW,
Washington DC 20229, ☎ 202/927–
0540).

DINING

France is two-big-meals-a-day country, with good restaurants around
every corner. If you prefer to eat
lighter, you can **try a brasserie or a
café for rapid, straightforward fare.**
French breakfasts are relatively simple: good coffee, fruit juice if you
request it, bread, butter, and croissants. Although many hotels serve
breakfast, it make sense to **eat breakfast in local cafés:** It is less expensive
and often more enjoyable. Tap water
is safe, though not always appetizing
(least of all in Paris). There is no need
to wear a tie and jacket at most
restaurants (unless specified), even
fancy ones. For more on what to wear
in France, *see* Packing for France,
below.

MEALTIMES

Breakfast is usually served from
7:30–10 AM; lunch from noon–1:30;
and dinner from 8–10 PM.

DISABILITIES & ACCESSIBILITY

ACCESS IN FRANCE

Though the French government is
doing much to ensure that public
facilities provide for visitors with
disabilities, it still has a long way to
go. Only some monuments, hotels,
and museums—especially those
constructed within the past decade—
are equipped with ramps, elevators,
and special toilet facilities. Lists of
regional hotels include a symbol to
indicate which hotels have rooms that
are accessible to people using
wheelchairs.

The SNCF has special cars on some trains that have been reserved exclusively for people using wheelchairs and can arrange for those passengers to be escorted on and off trains and assisted in making connections (the latter service must, however, be requested in advance).

Unfortunately, there are very few métro stations in Paris that are wheelchair accessible and only some RER stations.

➤ LOCAL RESOURCES: **Association des Paralysés de France** (✉ 17 bd. Auguste-Blanqui, 75013 Paris, ☎ 01–40–78–69–00) for a list of Paris hotels. **Comité Nationale Français de Liaison pour la Réadaptation des Handicapés** (✉ 236-B rue de Tolbiac, 75013 Paris, ☎ 01–53–80–66–66).

MAKING RESERVATIONS

When discussing accessibility with an operator or reservations agent, be sure to **discuss your needs before booking.** Are there any stairs, inside *or* out? Are there grab bars next to the toilet *and* in the shower/tub? How wide is the doorway to the room? To the bathroom? For the most extensive facilities meeting the latest legal specifications, **opt for newer accommodations,** which are more likely to have been designed with access in mind. Older buildings or ships may have more limited facilities.

TRAVEL AGENCIES & TOUR OPERATORS

As a whole, the travel industry has become more aware of the needs of travelers with disabilities. In the U.S., the Americans with Disabilities Act requires that travel firms serve the needs of all travelers. Note, though, that some agencies and operators specialize in making travel arrangements for individuals and groups with disabilities.

➤ TRAVELERS WITH MOBILITY PROBLEMS: **Access Adventures** (✉ 206 Chestnut Ridge Rd., Rochester, NY 14624, ☎ 716/889–9096), run by a former physical-rehabilitation counselor. **Accessible Journeys** (✉ 35 W. Sellers Ave., Ridley Park, PA 19078, ☎ 610/521–0339 or 800/846–4537, FAX 610/521–6959), for escorted tours exclusively for travelers with mobility

impairments. **CareVacations** (✉ 5019 49th Ave., Suite 102, Leduc, Alberta T9E 6T5, ☎ 403/986–6404, 800/648–1116 in Canada) has group tours and is especially helpful with cruise vacations. **Flying Wheels Travel** (✉ 143 W. Bridge St., Box 382, Owatonna, MN 55060, ☎ 507/451–5005 or 800/535–6790, FAX 507/451–1685), a travel agency specializing in customized tours and itineraries worldwide. **Hinsdale Travel Service** (✉ 201 E. Ogden Ave., Suite 100, Hinsdale, IL 60521, ☎ 630/325–1335), a travel agency that benefits from the advice of wheelchair traveler Janice Perkins.

DISCOUNTS & DEALS

Be a smart shopper and **compare all your options** before making any choice. A plane ticket bought with a promotional coupon may not be cheaper than the least expensive fare from a discount ticket agency. For high-price travel purchases, such as packages or tours, keep in mind that what you get is just as important as what you save. Just because something is cheap doesn't mean it's a bargain.

CLUBS & COUPONS

Many companies sell discounts in the form of travel clubs and coupon books, but these cost money. You must use participating advertisers to get a deal, and only after you recoup the initial membership cost or book price do you begin to save. If you plan to use the club or coupons frequently, you may save considerably. Before signing up, find out what discounts you get for free.

➤ DISCOUNT CLUBS: **Entertainment Travel Editions** (✉ 2125 Butterfield Rd., Troy, MI 48084, ☎ 800/445–4137; $20–$51, depending on destination). **Great American Traveler** (✉ Box 27965, Salt Lake City, UT 84127, ☎ 801/974–3033 or 800/548–2812; $49.95 per year). **Moment's Notice Discount Travel Club** (✉ 7301 New Utrecht Ave., Brooklyn, NY 11204, ☎ 718/234–6295; $25 per year, single or family). **Privilege Card International** (✉ 237 E. Front St., Youngstown, OH 44503, ☎ 330/746–5211 or 800/236–9732;

$74.95 per year). **Sears's Mature Outlook** (✉ Box 9390, Des Moines, IA 50306, ☎ 800/336–6330; $19.95 per year). **Travelers Advantage** (✉ CUC Travel Service, ✉ 3033 S. Parker Rd., Suite 1000, Aurora, CO 80014, ☎ 800/548–1116 or 800/648–4037; $59.95 per year, single or family). **Worldwide Discount Travel Club** (✉ 1674 Meridian Ave., Miami Beach, FL 33139, ☎ 305/534–2082; $50 per year family, $40 single).

CREDIT-CARD BENEFITS

When you use your credit card to make travel purchases you may get free travel-accident insurance, collision-damage insurance, and medical or legal assistance, depending on the card and the bank that issued it. American Express, MasterCard, and Visa provide one or more of these services, so **get a copy of your credit card's travel-benefits policy.** If you are a member of an auto club, **ask hotel and car-rental reservations agents about auto-club discounts.** Some clubs offer additional discounts on tours, cruises, and admission to attractions.

DISCOUNT RESERVATIONS

To save money, **look into discount-reservations services** with toll-free numbers, which use their buying power to get a better price on hotels, airline tickets, even car rentals. When booking a room, always **call the hotel's local toll-free number** (if one is available) rather than the central reservations number—you'll often get a better price. Always ask about special packages or corporate rates.

When shopping for the best deal on hotels and car rentals, **look for guaranteed exchange rates,** which protect you against a falling dollar. With your rate locked in, you won't pay more, even if the price goes up in the local currency.

➤ AIRLINE TICKETS: ☎ 800/FLY–4–LESS.

➤ HOTEL ROOMS: **Hotels Plus** (☎ 800/235–0909). **Hotel Reservations Network** (☎ 800/964–6835). **International Marketing & Travel Concepts** (☎ 800/790–4682). **Steigenberger Reservation Service** (☎ 800/223–5652). **Travel Interlink** (☎ 800/888–5898).

PACKAGE DEALS

Packages and guided tours can save you money, but don't confuse the two. When you buy a package, your travel remains independent, just as though you had planned and booked the trip yourself. Fly/drive packages, which combine airfare and car rental, are often a good deal. In cities, ask the local visitor's bureau about hotel packages. These often include tickets to major museum exhibits and other special events. With a **a rail/drive pass, you may get substantial savings** on train tickets and car rentals. All Eurail- and Europass holders get a discount on Eurostar fares through the Channel Tunnel.

ELECTRICITY

To use your U.S.-purchased electric-powered equipment, **bring a converter and adapter.** The electrical current in France is 220 volts, 50 cycles alternating current (AC); wall outlets take continental-type plugs, with two round prongs.

If your appliances are dual-voltage, you'll need only an adapter. Don't use 110-volt outlets, marked FOR SHAVERS ONLY, for high-wattage appliances such as blow-dryers. Most laptops operate equally well on 110 and 220 volts and so require only an adapter.

EMBASSIES

If you need assistance in an emergency, you can go to your country's embassy. Proof of identity and citizenship are generally required to enter. If your passport has been stolen, get a police report then contact your embassy for assistance.

➤ EMBASSY ADDRESSES: **Australia** (✉ 4 rue Jean-Rey, Paris, 15ᵉ, ☎ 01–40–59–33–00, métro Bir Hakeim, ⊙ weekdays 9:15–12:15) **Canada** (✉ 35 av. Montaigne, Paris, 8ᵉ, ☎ 01–44–43–29–00, métro Franklin-D.-Roosevelt, ⊙ weekdays 8:30–11). **New Zealand** (✉ 7 ter rue Léonardo da Vinci, Paris, 16ᵉ, métro Victor Hugo ☎ 01–45–00–24–11, ⊙ weekdays 9–1). **United Kingdom** (✉ 35 rue du Faubourg-St-Honoré, Paris, 8ᵉ, ☎ 01–44–51–31–00, ⊙ métro Madeleine), ⊙ weekdays 9:30–12:30 and 2:30–5. **United States** (✉ 2 rue St-Florentin, Paris, 1ᵉʳ, ☎ 01–43–12–22–22 in

English or ☎ 01–43–12–23–47
in emergencies, métro Concorde),
⊙ weekdays 9–3.

EMERGENCIES

In France, call the fire department or
the police in emergencies. *See* also
Health, *below,* and Emergencies *in* A
to Z sections *in* individual chapters
for information on regional hospitals.

➤ EMERGENCIES: **Ambulance** (☎ 15).
Fire Department (☎ 18). **Police** (☎ 17).

GAY & LESBIAN TRAVEL

The largest gay and lesbian communities, which are in Paris, are low-key
and reserved in public, although
active and easily accessible to visitors.
Discos and nightclubs are numerous
and popular; it takes a serious
couche-tard (night owl) to keep up
with the hip scene (☞ Arts and
Nightlife *in* Chapter 2). A number of
informative newspapers and magazines that cover the Parisian gay/les-
bian scene are available at stores and
kiosks in the city: *Gai Guide, Gai Pied
Hebdo, Lesbia,* and *Paris Exit.*

➤ GAY & LESBIAN ORGANIZATIONS IN
PARIS: **Agora** (✉ 33 bd. Picpus, 12ᵉ,
☎ 01–43–42–19–02) provides
information on events, meetings, and
rallies. **Association des Médecins Gais**
(☎ 01–48–05–81–71) offers advice
and information over the phone.
Centre Gai et Lesbien (✉ 3 rue Keller,
11ᵉ, ☎ 01–43–57–21–47) offers a
wide range of information on events.

➤ GAY- AND LESBIAN-FRIENDLY TRAVEL
AGENCIES: **Corniche Travel** (✉ 8721
Sunset Blvd., Suite 200, West Hollywood, CA 90069, ☎ 310/854–6000
or 800/429–8747, FAX 310/659–
7441). **Islanders Kennedy Travel**
(✉ 183 W. 10th St., New York, NY
10014, ☎ 212/242–3222 or 800/
988–1181, FAX 212/929–8530). **Now
Voyager** (✉ 4406 18th St., San Francisco, CA 94114, ☎ 415/626–1169
or 800/255–6951, FAX 415/626–
8626). **Yellowbrick Road** (✉ 1500 W.
Balmoral Ave., Chicago, IL 60640,
☎ 773/561–1800 or 800/642–2488,
FAX 773/561–4497). **Skylink Travel
and Tour** (✉ 3577 Moorland Ave.,
Santa Rosa, CA 95407, ☎ 707/585–
8355 or 800/225–5759, FAX 707/
584–5637), serving lesbian travelers.

HEALTH

Note that outside of Paris it's very
difficult to find English-speaking
doctors.

DOCTORS & HOSPITALS

For information on doctors and
hospitals throughout France, *see* A to
Z sections *in* individual chapters.

MEDICAL PLANS

No one plans to get sick while traveling, but it happens, so **consider signing up with a medical-assistance
company.** Members get doctor referrals, emergency evacuation or repatri-
ation, 24-hour telephone hot lines for
medical consultation, cash for emergencies, and other personal and legal
assistance. Coverage varies by plan, so
review the benefits of each carefully.

➤ MEDICAL-ASSISTANCE COMPANIES:
International SOS Assistance (✉ 8
Neshaminy Interplex, Suite 207,
Trevose, PA 19053, ☎ 215/245–
4707 or 800/523–6586, FAX 215/
244–9617; ✉ 12 Chemin Riant-
bosson, 1217 Meyrin 1, Geneva,
Switzerland, ☎ 4122/785–6464,
FAX 4122/785–6424; ✉ 10 Anson
Rd., 14-07/08 International Plaza,
Singapore, 079903, ☎ 65/226–3936,
FAX 65/226–3937).

HIKING

France has many good places to hike
and an extensive network of mapped-
out Grands Randonnées (GRs or
Long Trails) that range from easy to
challenging. For details on hiking in
France and guides to GRs in specific
areas, contact the Club Alpin Français
or the Fédération Française de la
Randonnée Pédestre, which also
publishes good topographical maps.
The IGN maps sold in many bookshops are also invaluable (☞ Bicycling, *above*).

➤ HIKING ORGANIZATIONS: **Club
Alpin Français** (✉ 24 av. Laumière,
75019 Paris, ☎ 01–53–72–87–00).
**Fédération Française de la Randonnée
Pédestre** (✉ 64 rue de Gergovie,
75014 Paris, ☎ 01–45–45–31–02).

HOLIDAYS

With 11 national *jours feriés* (holidays) and 5 weeks of paid vacation,

the French have their share of repose. In May, there is a holiday nearly every week, so be prepared for stores, banks, and museums to shut their doors for days at a time. Be sure to **call museums, restaurants, and hotels in advance to make sure they will be open.**

The following dates are for 1999: January 1 (New Year's Day); April 5 (Easter Monday); May 1 (Labor Day); May 8 (VE Day); May 13 (Ascension); May 23 (Pentecost Monday); July 14 (Bastille Day); August 15 (Assumption); November 1 (All Saints); November 11 (Armistice); December 25 (Christmas).

INSURANCE

Travel insurance is the best way to **protect yourself against financial loss.** The most useful plan is a comprehensive policy that includes coverage for trip cancellation and interruption, default, trip delay, and medical expenses (with a waiver for preexisting conditions).

Without insurance, you will lose all or most of your money if you cancel your trip, regardless of the reason. Default insurance covers you if your tour operator, airline, or cruise line goes out of business. Trip-delay covers unforeseen expenses that you may incur due to bad weather or mechanical delays. It's important to compare the fine print regarding trip-delay coverage when comparing policies.

For overseas travel, one of the most important components of travel insurance is its medical coverage. Supplemental health insurance will pick up the cost of your medical bills should you get sick or injured while traveling. U.S. residents should note that Medicare generally does not cover health-care costs outside the United States, nor do many privately issued policies. Residents of the United Kingdom can buy an annual travel-insurance policy valid for most vacations taken during the year in which the coverage is purchased. If you are pregnant or have a pre-existing condition, make sure you're covered. British citizens should buy extra medical coverage when travel-ing overseas, according to the Association of British Insurers. Australian travelers should buy travel insurance, including extra medical coverage, whenever they go abroad, according to the Insurance Council of Australia.

Always **buy travel insurance directly from the insurance company;** if you buy it from a cruise line, airline, or tour operator that goes out of business you probably will not be covered for the agency or operator's default, a major risk. Before you make any purchase, **review your existing health and home-owner's policies** to find out whether they cover expenses incurred while traveling.

➤ TRAVEL INSURERS: In the U.S., **Access America** (✉ 6600 W. Broad St., Richmond, VA 23230, ☎ 804/285–3300 or 800/284–8300). **Travel Guard International** (✉ 1145 Clark St., Stevens Point, WI 54481, ☎ 715/345–0505 or 800/826–1300). In Canada, **Mutual of Omaha** (✉ Travel Division, ✉ 500 University Ave., Toronto, Ontario M5G 1V8, ☎ 416/598–4083, 800/268–8825 in Canada).

➤ INSURANCE INFORMATION: In the U.K., **Association of British Insurers** (✉ 51 Gresham St., London EC2V 7HQ, ☎ 0171/600–3333). In Australia, the **Insurance Council of Australia** (☎ 613/9614–1077, FAX 613/9614–7924).

LANGUAGE

Although many French people, especially in major tourist areas, speak some English, it's important to remember that you are going to France and that people speak French. However, generally at least one person in most hotels can explain things to you in English (unless you are in a very rural area). Be patient, and speak English slowly.

The French may appear prickly at first to English-speaking visitors. But it usually helps if you **make an effort to speak a little French.** So even if your own French is terrible, try to master a few words. A simple, friendly "bonjour" (hello) will do, as will asking if the person you are greeting speaks English ("Parlez-vous anglais?"). *See* the French Vocabulary and Menu Guide at the back of the book, for more suggestions.

LANGUAGES FOR TRAVELERS

A phrase book and language tape set can help get you started.

➤ PHRASE BOOKS AND LANGUAGE-TAPE SETS: *Fodor's French for Travelers* ($7; 800/533–6478 to order).

LODGING

APARTMENT & HOUSE RENTALS

If you want a home base that's roomy enough for a family or group and comes with cooking facilities, **consider a furnished rental.** Renting an apartment or a *gîte rural*—a furnished house in the country—for a week or month can save families and small groups money. You can even rent a more luxurious property.

➤ GÎTE RENTALS: **Fédération Nationale des Gîtes de France** (⊠ 59 rue St-Lazare, 75009 Paris, ☎ 01–49–70–75–75, FAX 01–42–81–28–53) lists gîtes ruraux for rent; indicate the region that interests you or order their annual nationwide guide (115 francs). **French Government Tourist Office** (☞ Visitor Information, *below*) is another source for information about gîtes.

➤ RENTAL AGENTS: **Chez Vous** (⊠ 1001 Bridgeway, Suite 245, Sausalito, CA 94965, ☎ 415/331–2535, FAX 415/331–5296). **Drawbridge to Europe** (⊠ 5456 Adams Rd., Talent, OR 97540, ☎ 541/512–8927 or 888/268–1148, FAX 541/512–0978). **Europa-Let/Tropical Inn-Let** (⊠ 92 N. Main St., Ashland, OR 97520, ☎ 541/482–5806 or 800/462–4486, FAX 541/482–0660). **French Experience** (⊠ 370 Lexington Ave., New York, NY 10017, ☎ 212/986–1115, FAX 212/986–3808). **Hometours International** (⊠ Box 11503, Knoxville, TN 37939, ☎ 423/690–8484 or 800/367–4668). **Interhome** (⊠ 124 Little Falls Rd., Fairfield, NJ 07004, ☎ 973/882–6864 or 800/882–6864, FAX 973/808–1742) **Orion** (⊠ 140 E. 56th St., New York, NY 10022, ☎ 800/755–8266, FAX 212/688–9467). **Property Rentals International** (⊠ 1008 Mansfield Crossing Rd., Richmond, VA 23236, ☎ 804/378–6054 or 800/220–3332, FAX 804/379–2073). **Rental Directories International** (⊠ 2044 Rittenhouse Sq., Philadelphia, PA 19103, ☎ 215/985–4001, FAX 215/985–0323). **Rent-a-Home International** (⊠ 7200 34th Ave. NW, Seattle, WA 98117, ☎ 206/789–9377 or 800/488–7368, FAX 206/789–9379). **Vacation Home Rentals Worldwide** (⊠ 235 Kensington Ave., Norwood, NJ 07648, ☎ 201/767–9393 or 800/633–3284, FAX 201/767–5510). **Villas and Apartments Abroad** (⊠ 420 Madison Ave., Suite 1003, New York, NY 10017, ☎ 212/759–1025 or 800/433–3020, FAX 212/755–8316). **Villas International** (⊠ 950 Northgate Dr., Suite 206, San Rafael, CA 94903, ☎ 415/499–9490 or 800/221–2260, FAX 415/499–9491). **Hideaways International** (⊠ 767 Islington St., Portsmouth, NH 03801, ☎ 603/430–4433 or 800/843–4433, FAX 603/430–4444; membership $99) is a club for travelers who arrange rentals among themselves.

B&BS

B&Bs, known in France as *chambres d'hôte or gîtes,* are becoming increasingly popular, especially in rural areas, as well as in Paris. Check local tourist offices for details; contact Gîtes de France, the national organization that lists bed-and-breakfasts all over the country, from rustic to more luxurious ones; or get in touch with private reservation agencies. Often table d'hôte dinners (meals cooked by and eaten with the owners) can be arranged for an extra, fairly nominal fee. Note that in bed-and-breakfasts, unlike hotels, it is more likely that the owners will only speak French. Staying in one may, however, give you more of an opportunity to meet French people.

➤ RESERVATION SERVICES: **Maison des Gîtes de France** (⊠ 59 rue St-Lazare, 75439 Cedex 09 Paris, ☎ 01–49–70–75–75). **Paris Bed & Breakfast** (☎ 800/872–2632).

CAMPING

French campsites have a good reputation for organization and amenities but are crowded in July and August. Many campsites welcome reservations, and in summer, it makes sense to book in advance.

➤ CAMPSITE GUIDE: **Fédération Française de Camping et de Caravaning** (✉ 78 rue de Rivoli, 75004 Paris, ☎ 01–42–72–84–08) publishes a guide to France's campsites; they'll send it to you for 100 francs, plus shipping.

HOME EXCHANGES

If you would like to exchange your home for someone else's, **join a home-exchange organization,** which will send you its updated listings of available exchanges for a year and will include your own listing in at least one of them. It's up to you to make specific arrangements. You might also look in the weekly journal *France-USA Contacts* (also known as *FUSAC*), which lists people interested in apartment exchanges.

➤ EXCHANGE CLUBS: **HomeLink International** (✉ Box 650, Key West, FL 33041, ☎ 305/294–7766 or 800/638–3841, 𝔽𝔸𝕏 305/294–1148; $83 per year).

➤ EXCHANGE LISTINGS: **FUSAC** (✉ 3 rue Larochelle, Paris 75014, ☎ 01–45–38–56–57; ✉ Box 115, Cooper Station, New York, NY, 10276, ☎ 212/929–2929).

HOSTELS

No matter what your age, you can **save on lodging costs by staying at hostels** (though some do have age restrictions.) In some 5,000 locations in more than 70 countries around the world, Hostelling International (HI), the umbrella group for a number of national youth hostel associations, offers single-sex, dorm-style beds and, at many hostels, "couples" rooms and family accommodations. Membership in any HI national hostel association, open to travelers of all ages, allows you to stay in HI-affiliated hostels at member rates (one-year membership is about $25 for adults; hostels run about $10–$25 per night). Members also have priority if the hostel is full; they're eligible for discounts around the world, even on rail and bus travel in some countries.

➤ HOSTEL ORGANIZATIONS: **Hostelling International—American Youth Hostels** (✉ 733 15th St. NW, Suite 840, Washington, DC 20005, ☎ 202/783–6161, 𝔽𝔸𝕏 202/783–6171).

Hostelling International—Canada (✉ 400-205 Catherine St., Ottawa, Ontario K2P 1C3, ☎ 613/237–7884, 𝔽𝔸𝕏 613/237–7868). **Youth Hostel Association of England and Wales** (✉ Trevelyan House, ✉ 8 St. Stephen's Hill, St. Albans, Hertfordshire AL1 2DY, ☎ 01727/855215 or 01727/845047, 𝔽𝔸𝕏 01727/844126); membership in the U.S. $25, in Canada C$26.75, in the U.K. £9.30).

HOTELS

Hotels are officially classified from one-star to four-star-deluxe. Prices must, by law, be posted at the hotel entrance and should include taxes and service. Rates are always by room, not per person.

You should always **check what bathroom facilities the price includes,** if any. Because replumbing drains is often prohibitive, if not impossible, old hotels may have added bathrooms—often with *douches* (showers), not *baignoires* (tubs)—to the guest rooms, but not toilets. If you want a private bathroom, state your preference for shower or tub—the latter always costs more. Unless otherwise noted, lodging listings in this book include a private bathroom with a shower and tub.

When making your reservation, **ask for a *grand lit* if you want a double bed.** The quality of accommodations, particularly in older properties and even in luxury hotels, can vary greatly from room to room; **if you don't like the room you're given, ask to see another.**

Breakfast is not always included in the price, but you are sometimes expected to have it and are occasionally charged for it regardless. Make sure to inform the hotel if you are not going to be breakfasting there; you may want to find the nearest café anyway. In smaller rural hotels you may be expected to have your evening meal at the hotel, too.

France has—but is not dominated by—big hotel chains: Examples in the upper price bracket are Frantel, Novotel, Sofitel, and even Marriott, Hilton, and Hyatt. The Best Western, Campanile, Climat de France, Ibis, and Timhotel chains are more moderate.

Typically, **chains offer a consistently acceptable standard of modern features** (modern bathrooms, TV, etc.), but tend to lack atmosphere, with some exceptions. Logis de France hotels are small and inexpensive and can be relied on for comfort, character, and regional cuisine. Look for its distinctive yellow and green sign. The Logis de France paperback guide is widely available in bookshops (100 frs) or from Logis de France.

Relais & Châteaux and Small Luxury Hotels of the World are two prestigious international groups with numerous converted châteaux and manor houses among its members. Booklets listing members are available.

Negotiating rates has become acceptable in Paris and the provinces, especially if you are planning on staying for a week or longer or are coming off season. Although you may not be able to reduce the price, you might get an upgrade to a newly redecorated, larger, or deluxe room. Tourist offices in major train stations can reserve hotels for you, and so can tourist offices in most towns.

It's always a good idea to **make hotel reservations in Paris and other major tourist destinations as far in advance as possible,** especially in late spring, summer, or fall. If you arrive in Paris without a reservation, the Tourist offices in major train stations may be able to reserve a hotel for you.

➤ HOTEL DIRECTORIES: **Best Western** (☎ 800/528–1234 in the U.S.). **Logis de France** (✉ 83 av. d'Italie, 75013 Paris, ☎ 01–45–84–70–00, FAX 01–44–24–08–74), 95 frs. **France-Accueil** (✉ 163 av. d'Italie, 75013 Paris, ☎ 01–45–83–04–22, FAX 01–45–86–49–82). **Relais & Châteaux** (✉ 15 rue Galvani, 75017 Paris, ☎ 01–45–72–96–50, FAX 01–45–72–96–69; ✉ 11 E. 44th St., Suite 707, New York, NY 10017, ☎ 212/856–0115 or 800/860–4930, FAX 212/856–0193). **Small Luxury Hotels of the World** (✉ 1716 Banks St., Houston, TX 77098, ☎ 713/522–9512 or 800/525–4800 in the U.S., FAX 713/524–7412; ✉ James House, Bridge St., Leatherhead, Surrey, KT22 7EP, U.K., ☎ 44/01372–361873, FAX 44/01372–361874).

MAIL

POSTAL RATES

Letters and postcards to the United States and Canada cost 4.40 francs (about 80¢) for 20 grams. Letters and postcards to the United Kingdom cost 3 francs (about 33p) for up to 20 grams. Letters and postcards within France cost 3 francs. Stamps can be bought in post offices (La Poste) and cafés sporting a red TABAC sign outside.

RECEIVING MAIL

If you're uncertain where you'll be staying, **have mail sent to the local post office,** addressed as "poste restante," or to American Express, but remember that during peak seasons, American Express may refuse to accept mail.

MONEY

COSTS

The following prices are for Paris; other cities and areas are often cheaper. Note that it is less expensive to eat or drink standing at a café or bar counter than it is to sit at a table. Two prices are listed, *au comptoir* (at the counter) and *à salle* (at a table). Coffee in a bar: 6–7 francs (standing), 10–30 francs (seated); beer in a bar: 10 francs (standing), 15–40 francs (seated); Coca-Cola: 6–10 francs a can; ham sandwich: 15–25 francs; one-mile taxi ride: 35 francs; movie-theater seat: 50 francs (15%–33% cheaper on Monday and Wednesday); foreign newspaper: 10–15 francs.

CREDIT & DEBIT CARDS & ATMS

Many restaurants and stores take both credit and debit cards, though there is often a 100-franc minimum.

ATMs are fairly common in Paris and other major cities and are one of the easiest ways to get francs; don't, however, count on finding ATMs in smaller towns and rural areas. Banks usually offer excellent, wholesale exchange rates through ATMs.

To get cash at ATMs in France, **your PIN must be four digits long.** You may have more luck with ATMs if you are using a credit card or a debit card that is also a Visa or MasterCard, rather than just your bank card. Note, too, that you may be charged by your bank for using ATMs overseas; inquire at your bank about charges.

Before you go, it's a good idea to **get a list of ATM locations that you can use** in France from your bank.

➤ ATM LOCATIONS: **Cirrus** (☎ 800/424–7787). **Plus** (☎ 800/843–7587) for locations in the U.S. and Canada, or visit your local bank.

➤ REPORTING LOST CARDS: **American Express** (☎ 910/668-5309) call collect. **Diner's Club** (☎ 303/799–1504) call collect. **Mastercard** (☎ 0800/90–1387). **Visa** (☎ 0800/90–1179).

CURRENCY

The units of currency in France are the franc (fr) and the centime. Bills are in denominations of 500, 200, 100, 50, and 20 francs. Coins are 20, 10, 5, 2, and 1 francs and 50, 20, 10, and 5 centimes. At press time (1998), the exchange rate was about 6 francs to the U.S. dollar, 4.09 to the Canadian dollar, 10.07 to the pound sterling, 3.66 to the Australian dollar, 3.12 to the New Zealand dollar, and 8.45 to the Irish punt.

EXCHANGING MONEY

There are a variety of ways to exchange money, though you have greater options in major cities than in rural areas. In general, the **Banque de France has the best rates** of all the banks. In general, however, banks don't always offer great exchange rates.

Another option is to compare rates between booths and banks and **look for exchange booths that clearly state "no commission."** If you are exchanging a large amount of money, you may be able to get a better deal; it's worth asking. Exchange booths in airports, train stations, hotels, and stores generally offer the worst rates, though you may find their hours more convenient.

Although fees charged for ATM transactions may be higher abroad than at home (you may want to check on this before leaving), **ATM exchange rates are often excellent,** because they are based on wholesale rates offered only by major banks. ATMs are also convenient (you get francs right out of the machine), and are found in Paris and other large cities, and in major airports and train stations (☞ Credit & Debit Cards, *above* for information on finding out ATM locations in France).

Using a debit card (with a Visa or MasterCard symbol on it) makes it easier to find ATMs that you can use. If you are concerned that you may not be able to use your bank or debit card at the airport or train station when you first arrive, or you want to avoid lines at airport or train station exchange booths, **consider getting a bit of local currency before you leave home.**

➤ EXCHANGE SERVICES: **Chase *Currency To Go*** (☎ 800/935–9935; 935–9935 in NY, NJ, and CT). **International Currency Express** (☎ 888/842–0880 on the East Coast, 888/278–6628 on the West Coast). **Thomas Cook Currency Services** (☎ 800/287–7362 for telephone orders and retail locations).

TRAVELER'S CHECKS

Do you need traveler's checks? It depends on where you're headed.

If you're going to rural areas and small towns, go with cash; traveler's checks are best used in cities or popular tourist areas.

Although you can usually get cash from ATMs, it makes sense to **bring some money in traveler's checks, just in case.**

If you get traveler's checks in dollars or your country's currency, you can easily exchange these at banks or exchange bureaus, though you must bring along your passport. Lost or stolen checks can usually be replaced within 24 hours. To ensure a speedy refund, buy your own traveler's checks—don't let someone else pay for them: Irregularities like this can cause delays. The person who bought the checks should make the call to request a refund.

THE GOLD GUIDE / SMART TRAVEL TIPS

OUTDOOR ACTIVITIES & SPORTS

France has no shortage of sports facilities. Many seaside resorts are well equipped for water sports, such as windsurfing and waterskiing, and there are public swimming pools in every French town.

In winter, the Alps and the somewhat less pricey Pyrénées and Vosges mountains have excellent skiing facilities—both for *ski alpin* (downhill) and *ski de fond* (cross-country).

Bicycling (☞ Bicycling, *above*) and hiking (☞ Hiking, *above*) are popular and, like *équitation* (horseback riding), possible in many rural areas.

The many rivers of France offer excellent fishing (check locally for authorization rights) and canoeing.

Tennis is phenomenally popular in France, and courts are everywhere: Try to find a typical *terre battue* (clay court) if you can. Golf and squash have caught on; you may be able to find a course or a court not too far away.

The French are not so keen on jogging, but you'll have no difficulty locating a suitable local park or avenue. *See* individual chapters for specific outdoor activities and sports listings.

PACKING

LUGGAGE

How many carry-on bags you can bring with you is up to the airline. Most allow two, but the limit is often reduced to one on certain flights. Gate agents will take excess baggage—including bags they deem oversize—from you as you board and add it to checked luggage. To avoid this situation, make sure that everything you carry aboard will fit under your seat.

On international flights, baggage allowances may be determined not by piece but by weight—generally 88 pounds (40 kilograms) in first class, 66 pounds (30 kilograms) in business class, and 44 pounds (20 kilograms) in economy.

Airline liability for baggage is limited to $1,250 per person on flights within the United States. On international flights it amounts to $9.07 per pound or $20 per kilogram for checked baggage (roughly $640 per 70-pound bag) and $400 per passenger for unchecked baggage. You can buy additional coverage at check-in for about $10 per $1,000 of coverage, but it excludes a rather extensive list of items, shown on your airline ticket.

Before departure, **itemize your bags' contents** and their worth, and label the bags with your name, address, and phone number. (If you use your home address, cover it so that potential thieves can't see it readily.) Inside each bag, **pack a copy of your itinerary.** At check-in, **make sure that each bag is correctly tagged** with the destination airport's three-letter code. If your bags arrive damaged or fail to arrive at all, file a written report with the airline before leaving the airport.

PACKING LIST

Although you'll usually have no trouble finding a baggage cart at the airport, luggage restrictions on international flights are tight and baggage carts at railroad stations are not always available; **pack light.**

Over the years, **casual dress has become more acceptable,** although Paris is still the world's fashion capital and people dress accordingly (and they bring this fashion sense to other major French cities and resorts).

Jeans are very common, though they, too, are worn very stylishly, with a nice button-down shirt, polo, or t-shirt without writing. Shorts are now a popular item for the younger crowd in most cities. More and more people are wearing sneakers, although you may still stand out as a tourist with them on, especially if you wear them when you go out at night.

There is no need to wear a tie and jacket at most restaurants (unless specified), even fancy ones, though you should still try to look nice.

For beach resorts, take a cover-up, as wearing bathing suits on the street is frowned upon. Most casinos and nightclubs along the Riviera require jackets and ties.

Most of France is hot in the summer, cool in the winter. Since it rains all year round, **bring a raincoat and umbrella.** You'll need a sweater or warm jacket for the Mediterranean in winter.

If you are staying in budget hotels, **take along soap; many hotels either do not provide it or give you a very limited number.**

In your carry-on luggage **bring an extra pair of eyeglasses or contact lenses** and **enough of any medication** you take to last the entire trip. You may also want your doctor to write a spare prescription using the drug's generic name, since brand names may vary from country to country. **Never put prescription drugs or valuables in luggage to be checked.** To avoid customs delays, carry medications in their original packaging.

And don't forget to copy down and carry addresses of offices that handle refunds of lost traveler's checks.

PASSPORTS & VISAS

When traveling in France, you must **carry a passport.** It's a good idea to **make two photocopies of the data page** (one for someone at home and another for you, carried separately from your passport). If you lose your passport, promptly call the nearest embassy or consulate and the local police.

ENTERING FRANCE

All Australian, Canadian, New Zealand, U.K, and U.S. citizens, even infants, need only a valid passport to enter France for stays of up to 90 days.

PASSPORT OFFICES

➤ CONTACTS: **Australian Passport Office** (☎ 13/1232). **Canadian Passport Office** (☎ 819/994–3500 or 800/567–6868).**New Zealand Passport Office** (☎ 04/494–0700 for information on how to apply, 0800/727–776 for information on applications already submitted). **United Kingdom Passport Office, London** (☎ 0990/21010), for fees and documentation requirements and to request an emergency passport. **United States National Passport Information Center** (☎ 900/225–5674; calls are charged at 35¢ per minute for automated service, $1.05 per minute for operator service).

PUBLIC TRANSPORTATION

For information about public transportation in France *see* A to Z sections *in* individual chapters.

SAFETY

Beware of petty theft—purse snatching, pickpocketing, and pilfering from automobiles—throughout France, particularly in Paris and along the Riviera. Use common sense: Avoid pulling out a lot of money in public; wear a handbag with long straps that you can sling across your body, bandolier-style, with a zippered compartment for your money and passport; and don't leave your luggage showing in the car in major cities.

SENIOR-CITIZEN TRAVEL

Older travelers (60+) can take advantage of many discounts, such as reduced admissions of 20%–50% to museums and movie theaters. For rail travel in France, the Carte Vermeil entitles travelers 60 years or older to discounts (☞ *Train Travel, below*).

To qualify for age-related discounts, **mention your senior-citizen status up front** when booking hotel reservations (not when checking out) and before you're seated in restaurants (not when paying the bill). Note that discounts may be limited to certain menus, days, or hours. When renting a car, **ask about promotional car-rental discounts,** which can be cheaper than senior-citizen rates.

➤ ADVENTURES: **Overseas Adventure Travel** (✉ Grand Circle Corporation, ✉ 625 Mt. Auburn St., Cambridge, MA 02138, ☎ 617/876–0533 or 800/221–0814, FAX 617/876–0455).

➤ EDUCATIONAL PROGRAMS: **Elderhostel** (✉ 75 Federal St., 3rd floor, Boston, MA 02110, ☎ 617/426–8056). **Interhostel** (✉ University of New Hampshire, ✉ 6 Garrison Ave., Durham, NH 03824, ☎ 603/862–1147 or 800/733–9753, FAX 603/862–1113).

SHOPPING

In France, people don't usually bargain in shops where **prices are clearly marked,** but at outdoor and flea markets, and in antiques stores, bargaining is an accepted way of life. If

SMART TRAVEL TIPS / THE GOLD GUIDE

you're thinking of buying several items, you've nothing to lose by cheerfully suggesting to the proprietor, *"Vous me faites un prix?"* ("How about a discount?").

A number of shops offer VAT tax refunds to foriegn shoppers (☞ Taxes, *below*).

CLOTHING SIZES

To figure out the French equivalent of U.S. clothing and shoe sizes, **do the following, simple calculations.**

To change U.S. men's suit sizes to French suit sizes, add 10 to the U.S. suit size. To change French suit sizes to U.S. suit sizes, subtract 10 from the French suit size. For example, a U.S. size 42 is a French size 52.

To change U.S. men's collar sizes to French collar sizes, multiply the U.S. collar size by 2 and add 8. To change French collar sizes to U.S. collar sizes, subtract 8 from the French collar size and divide by 2. For example, a U.S. size 15 is a French size 38. A U.S. size 15½ is a French size 39.

French men's shoe sizes vary in their relation to U.S. shoe sizes. A U.S. men's size 6½ is a French size 39; a size 7 is a 39; an 8 is a 40; a 9 is a 41; a 10 is a 42; a 10½ is a 43; and an 11 is a 45.

To change U.S. dress/coat/blouse sizes to French sizes, add 28 to the U.S. size. To change French dress/coat/blouse sizes to U.S. sizes, subtract 28 from the French size. For example, a U.S. women's size 8 is a French size 36.

To change U.S. women's shoe sizes to French shoe sizes, add 30 to the U.S. shoe size. To change French shoe sizes to U.S. shoe sizes, subtract 30 from the French shoe size. For example, a U.S. size 7 is a French size 37.

STUDENT TRAVEL

There are student bargains almost everywhere, on train and plane fares, and for movie and museum tickets.

STUDYING ABROAD

Studying in France is the perfect way to shake up your perception of the world, make international friends, and improve your language skills. You may choose to study through a U.S.-sponsored program, usually through an American university, or to enroll in a program sponsored by a French organization. Do your homework: programs vary greatly in expense, academic quality, exposure to language, amount of contact with locals, and living conditions. Working through your local university is the easiest way to find out about study-abroad programs in France. Most universities have staff members who distribute information on programs at European universities, and they might be able to put you in touch with program participants.

➤ RESOURCES: **American Institute for Foreign Study** (⊠ 102 Greenwich Ave., Greenwich, CT 06830, ☎ 203/869–9090 or ☎ 800/727–2437, FAX 203/863–6180). **American Council of International Studies** (ACIS; ⊠ 19 Bay State Rd., Boston, MA 02215, ☎ 617/236–2051 or ☎ 800/888–2247). **Council on International Educational Exchange** (CIEE; ⊠ 205 E. 42nd St., 14th floor, New York, NY 10017, ☎ 212/822–2600 or ☎ 888/268–6245, FAX 212/822–2699). **Institute of International Education** (IIE; ⊠ 809 U.N. Plaza, New York, NY 10017, ☎ 212/984–5413). **World Learning** (⊠ Kipling Rd., Box 676, Brattleboro, VT 05302, ☎ 802/257–7751 or ☎ 800/336–1616, FAX 802/258–3248).

TRAVEL AGENCIES

To save money, **look into deals available through student-oriented travel agencies.** To qualify you'll need a bona fide student I.D. card. Members of international student groups are also eligible.

➤ STUDENT I.D.s & SERVICES: **Council on International Educational Exchange** (⊠ *above*), for mail orders only, in the United States. **Travel Cuts** (⊠ 187 College St., Toronto, Ontario M5T 1P7, ☎ 416/979–2406 or 800/667–2887) in Canada.

➤ STUDENT TOURS: **Contiki Holidays** (⊠ 300 Plaza Alicante, Suite 900, Garden Grove, CA 92840, ☎ 714/740–0808 or 800/266–8454, FAX 714/740–2034). **AESU Travel** (⊠ 2 Hamill Rd., Suite 248, Baltimore, MD 21210-1807, ☎ 410/323–4416 or 800/638–7640, FAX 410/323–4498).

TAXES

All taxes must be included in posted prices in France. The initials TTC (*toutes taxes comprises*—taxes included) sometimes appear on price lists but, strictly speaking, are superfluous. By law, **restaurant and hotel prices must include 20.6% taxes and a service charge.** If they show up as extra charges on your bill, complain.

VALUE-ADDED TAX (V.A.T.)

A number of shops offer VAT refunds to foreign shoppers. You are entitled to an Export Discount of 20.6%, depending on the item purchased, but it is often applicable only if your purchases in the same store reach a minimum of 2,800 francs (for U.K. and EU residents) or 1,200 francs (other residents, including U.S. and Canadian residents). Remember to **ask for the refund, as some stores—especially larger ones—offer the service only upon request.**

TELEPHONES

COUNTRY CODES

The country code for France is 33 and the country code for Monaco is 337. All phone numbers in France have ten digits. The first two digits are a prefix determined by zone: Paris and Ile de France, 01; the northwest, 02; the northeast, 03; the southeast, 04; and the southwest, 05. Numbers beginning with 08 are either toll-free or toll calls (with an additional charge on top of making the call).

CALLING FRANCE

When dialing a French number from abroad, drop the inital 0 from the two-digit prefix. To call France from the United States, for instance, dial 011 (for all international calls), then dial 33 (the country code), and the number in France, minus the inital 0. To call France from the United Kingdom, dial 00–33, then dial the number in France minus any initial 0.

CALLING HOME

To call out of France, dial 00 and wait for the tone, then dial the country code (1 for the United States and Canada, 44 for the United Kingdom) and the area code (minus any intial 0) and number. Expect to be overcharged if you call from your hotel.

AT&T, MCI, and Sprint international access codes make calling the United States relatively convenient, but you may find the local access number blocked in many hotel rooms. First ask the hotel operator to connect you. If the hotel operator balks, ask for an international operator, or dial the international operator yourself. One way to improve your odds of getting connected to your long-distance carrier is to travel with more than one company's calling card (a hotel may block Sprint, for example, but not MCI). If all else fails, call from a pay phone in the hotel lobby.

➤ ACCESS CODES: **AT&T Direct** (☎ 08–00–99–00–11; 800/874–4000 for information). **MCI Call USA** (☎ 08–00–99–00–19; 800/444–4444 for information). **Sprint Express** (☎ 08–00–99–00–87; 800/793–1153⁻ for information).

LONG-DISTANCE CALLS

To call any region in France from another region, dial the full 10-digit number (including the two-digit prefix).

LOCAL CALLS

To make calls in the same city or town, or in the same region, dial the full 10-digit number.

OPERATORS & INFORMATION

To find a number **in France, dial 12 for information.** For international inquiries, dial 00–33 plus the country code.

Another source of information is the Minitel, an online network similar to the Internet. You can find one—they look like a small computer terminal—in most post offices. Available free is an online phone book covering the entire country. To find information, hit the *appel* (call) key, then, when prompted, type the name you are looking for and hit *envoi* (return). It is also useful for tracking down services: choose *activité* (activity), tap in *piscine* (swimming pool), then Chartres, for example, and it will give you a list of all the pools in Chartres. Go to other lines or pages by hitting the *suite* (next) key. Newer models will connect automatically when you hit the book-icon key. To disconnect, hit *fin* (end).

PUBLIC PHONES

Telephone booths **can almost always be found at post offices, métro stations, on the street, and often in cafés.** A local call costs 74 centimes for every three minutes; half-price rates apply weekdays between 9:30 PM and 8 AM, from 1:30 PM Saturday, and all day Sunday.

Most **French pay phones are operated by *télécartes* (phone cards),** which you can buy from post offices, métro stations, and some tabacs (tobacco shops) for a cost of 40.6 francs for 50 units and 97.5 francs for 120. Coin operated pay phones are scarce these days, existing only in cafés (who can set their own rates) and post offices. Phone cards are accepted everywhere else, even the métro. You can also use your own Visa card, which is accepted in all phone booths and works like a télécarte but is more expensive.

TIPPING

The French have a clear idea of when they should be tipped. Bills in bars and restaurants include a service charge, but **it is customary to round out your bill with some small change** unless you're dissatisfied. The amount of this varies: anywhere from 50 centimes if you've merely bought a beer, to 10 francs after a meal. Tip taxi drivers and hairdressers about 10%. Give ushers in theaters and movie theaters 1 or 2 francs. In some theaters and hotels, coat check attendants may expect nothing (if there is a sign saying POURBOIRE INTERDIT—tips forbidden); otherwise give them 2–5 francs. Washroom attendants usually get 2 francs, though the sum is often posted.

If you stay in a hotel for more than two or three days, it is customary to leave something for the chambermaid—about 10 francs per day. In expensive hotels you may well call on the services of a baggage porter (bell boy) and hotel porter and possibly the telephone receptionist. All expect a tip: Plan on about 10 francs per item for the baggage porter, but the other

tips will depend on how much you've used their services—common sense must guide you here. In hotels that provide room service, give 5 francs to the waiter (this does not apply to breakfast served in your room). If the chambermaid does some pressing or laundering for you, give her 5 francs on top of the charge made.

Gas-station attendants get nothing for gas or oil, and 5 or 10 francs for checking tires. Train and airport porters get a fixed 6–10 francs per bag, but you're better off getting your own baggage cart if you can (a 10-franc coin—refundable—is necessary in train stations only). Museum guides should get 5–10 francs after a guided tour, and it is standard practice to tip tour guides (and bus drivers) 10 francs or more after an excursion, depending on its length.

TOUR OPERATORS

Buying a prepackaged tour or independent vacation can make your trip to France less expensive and more hassle-free. Because everything is prearranged, you'll spend less time planning.

Operators that handle several hundred thousand travelers per year can use their purchasing power to give you a good price. Their high volume may also indicate financial stability. But some small companies provide more personalized service; because they tend to specialize, they may also be more knowledgeable about a given area.

BOOKING WITH AN AGENT

Travel agents are excellent resources. In fact, large operators accept bookings made only through travel agents. But it's a good idea to **collect brochures from several agencies,** because some agents' suggestions may be influenced by relationships with tour and package firms that reward them for volume sales. If you have a special interest, **find an agent with expertise in that area;** ASTA (☞ Travel Agencies, *below*) has a database of specialists worldwide.

Make sure your travel agent knows the accommodations and other services. Ask about the hotel's location, room size, beds, and whether it has a pool, room service, or programs for children, if you care about these. Has your agent been there in person or sent others you can contact?

Do some homework on your own, too: Local tourism boards can provide information about lesser-known and small-niche operators, some of which may sell only direct.

BUYER BEWARE

Each year consumers are stranded or lose their money when tour operators—even very large ones with excellent reputations—go out of business. So **check out the operator.** Find out how long the company has been in business, and ask several travel agents about its reputation. If the package or tour you are considering is priced lower than in your wildest dreams, **be skeptical.** Try to **book with a company that has a consumer-protection program.** If the operator has such a program, you'll find information about it in the company's brochure. If the operator you are considering does not offer some kind of consumer protection, then ask for references from satisfied customers.

In the U.S., members of the National Tour Association and United States Tour Operators Association are required to set aside funds to cover your payments and travel arrangements in case the company defaults. It's also a good idea to choose a company that participates in the American Society of Travel Agent's Tour Operator Program (TOP). This gives you a forum if there are any disputes between you and your tour operator; ASTA will act as mediator.

➤ TOUR-OPERATOR RECOMMENDATIONS: **American Society of Travel Agents** (☞ Travel Agencies, *below*). **National Tour Association** (⊠ NTA, ⊠ 546 E. Main St., Lexington, KY 40508, ☎ 606/226–4444 or 800/755–8687). **United States Tour Operators Association** (⊠ USTOA, ⊠ 342 Madison Ave., Suite 1522, New York, NY 10173, ☎ 212/599–6599 or 800/468–7862, FAX 212/599–6744).

COSTS

The more your package or tour includes, the better you can predict the ultimate cost of your vacation. Make sure you know exactly what is covered, and **beware of hidden costs.** Are taxes, tips, and service charges included? Transfers and baggage handling? Entertainment and excursions? These can add up.

Prices for packages and tours are usually quoted per person, based on two sharing a room. If traveling solo, you may be required to pay the full double-occupancy rate. Some operators eliminate this surcharge if you agree to be matched with a roommate of the same sex, even if one is not found by departure time.

GROUP TOURS

Among companies that sell tours to France, the following are nationally known, have a proven reputation, and offer plenty of options. The classifications used below represent different price categories, and you'll probably encounter these terms when talking to a travel agent or tour operator. The key difference is usually in accommodations, which run from budget to better, and better-yet to best.

➤ SUPER-DELUXE: **Abercrombie & Kent** (⊠ 1520 Kensington Rd., Oak Brook, IL 60521-2141, ☎ 630/954–2944 or 800/323–7308, FAX 630/954–3324). **Travcoa** (⊠ Box 2630, 2350 S.E. Bristol St., Newport Beach, CA 92660, ☎ 714/476–2800 or 800/992–2003, FAX 714/476–2538).

➤ DELUXE: **Globus** (⊠ 5301 S. Federal Circle, Littleton, CO 80123-2980, ☎ 303/797–2800 or 800/221–0090, FAX 303/347–2080). **Maupintour** (⊠ 1515 St. Andrews Dr., Lawrence, KS 66047, ☎ 913/843–1211 or 800/255–4266, FAX 913/843–8351). **Tauck Tours** (⊠ Box 5027, 276 Post Rd. W, Westport, CT 06881-5027, ☎ 203/226–6911 or 800/468–2825, FAX 203/221–6866).

➤ FIRST-CLASS: **Brendan Tours** (⊠ 15137 Califa St., Van Nuys, CA 91411, ☎ 818/785–9696 or 800/421–8446, FAX 818/902–9876). **Caravan Tours** (⊠ 401 N. Michigan Ave., Chicago, IL 60611, ☎ 312/

321–9800 or 800/227–2826, FAX 312/ 321–9845). **Collette Tours** (✉ 162 Middle St., Pawtucket, RI 02860, ☎ 401/728–3805 or 800/340–5158, FAX 401/728–4745). **DER Tours** (✉ 9501 W. Devon St., Rosemont, IL 60018, ☎ 800/937–1235, FAX 847/692–4141 or 800/282–7474, 800/860–9944 for brochures). **Insight International Tours** (✉ 745 Atlantic Ave., #720, Boston, MA 02111, ☎ 617/482– 2000 or 800/582–8380, FAX 617/482– 2884 or 800/622–5015). **Trafalgar Tours** (✉ 11 E. 26th St., New York, NY 10010, ☎ 212/689–8977 or 800/ 854–0103, FAX 800/457–6644).

➤ BUDGET: **Cosmos** (☞ Globus, *above*). **Trafalgar** (☞ *above*).

PACKAGES

Like group tours, independent vacation packages are available from major tour operators and airlines. The companies listed below offer vacation packages in a broad price range.

➤ AIR/HOTEL: **Continental Vacations** (☎ 800/634–5555). **Delta Vacations** (☎ 800/872–7786). **DER Tours** (☞ First-Class, *above*). **4th Dimension Tours** (✉ 7101 S.W. 99th Ave., #105, Miami, FL 33173, ☎ 305/279–0014 or 800/644–0438, FAX 305/273– 9777). **TWA Getaway Vacations** (☎ 800/438–2929). **US Airways Vacations** (☎ 800/455–0123).

➤ FLY/DRIVE: **Delta Vacations** (☎ 800/872–7786). **Budget WorldClass Drive** (☎ 800/527–0700; 0800/ 181181 in the U.K.) for self-drive itineraries.

➤ FROM THE U.K.: **British Airways Holidays** (✉ Astral Towers, Betts Way, London Rd., Crawley, West Sussex RH10 2XA, ☎ 01293/722– 727, FAX 01293/722–624). **Cresta Holidays** (✉ Tabley Ct., Victoria St., Altrincham, Cheshire WA14 1EZ, ☎ 0161/927–7000) for hotel and apartment holidays. **Invitation to France** (✉ 4 Alice Ct., 116 Putney Bridge Rd, London SW15 2NQ, ☎ 0181/ 871–3300) for chateaux and country-house hotels. **Thomas Cook** (✉ 45 Berkeley St., London W1A 1EB, ☎ 0171/499–4000) offers fly-drive holidays that may include Disneyland Paris.

THEME TRIPS

➤ TRAVEL AGENCIES: **Maison de la France** (☞ Visitor Information, *below*) publishes many brochures on theme trips in France including "In the Footsteps of the Painters of Light in Provence" and "France for the Jewish Traveler." **Travel Contacts** (✉ Box 173, Camberley, GU15 1YE, England, ☎ 01276/67–7217, FAX 01276/6–3477) represents over 150 tour operators in Europe.

➤ ADVENTURE: **Adventure Center** (✉ 1311 63rd St., #200, Emeryville, CA 94608, ☎ 510/654–1879 or 800/ 227–8747, FAX 510/654–4200). **Mountain Travel-Sobek** (✉ 6420 Fairmount Ave., El Cerrito, CA 94530, ☎ 510/527–8100 or 800/ 227–2384, FAX 510/525–7710). **Safaricentre** (✉ 3201 N. Sepulveda Blvd., Manhattan Beach, CA 90266, ☎ 310/546–4411 or 800/223–6046, FAX 310/546–3188).

➤ ART AND ARCHITECTURE: **Endless Beginnings Tours** (✉ 9285 Dowdy Dr., San Diego, CA 92126, ☎ 619/ 566–4166 or 800/822–7855, FAX 619/544–9655). **Esplanade Tours** (✉ 581 Boylston St., Boston, MA 02116, ☎ 617/266–7465 or 800/426–5492, FAX 617/262–9829).

➤ BALLOONING: **Bonaventura Balloon Company** (✉ 133 Wall Rd., Napa, CA 94558, ☎ 707/944–2822 or 800/ 359–6272, FAX 707/944–2220). **Buddy Bombard European Balloon Adventures** (✉ 333 Pershing Way, West Palm Beach, FL 33401, ☎ 561/ 837–6610 or 800/862–8537, FAX 561/837–6623).

➤ BARGE/RIVER CRUISES: **Abercrombie & Kent** (☞ Group Tours, *above*). **Alden Yacht Charters** (✉ 1909 Alden Landing, Portsmouth, RI 02871, ☎ 401/683–1782 or 800/662–2628, FAX 401/683–3668). **Etoile de Champagne** (✉ 88 Broad St., Boston, MA 02110, ☎ 800/280–1492, FAX 617/ 426–4689). **European Waterways** (✉ 140 E. 56th St., Suite 4C, New York, NY 10022, ☎ 212/688–9489 or 800/ 217–4447, FAX 212/688–3778 or 800/296–4554). **Fenwick & Lang** (✉ 1940 116th Ave. NE, Bellevue, WA 98004, ☎ 425/455–4445 or 800/ 927–3876, FAX 425/455–2111). **French Country Waterways** (✉ Box

2195, Duxbury, MA 02331, ☎ 781/ 934–2454 or 800/222–1236, FAX 781/934–9048). **KD River Cruises of Europe** (⊠ 2500 Westchester Ave., Purchase, NY 10577, ☎ 914/696– 3600 or 800/346–6525, FAX 914/ 696–0833). **Kemwel's Premier Selections** (⊠ 106 Calvert St., Harrison, NY 10528, ☎ 914/835–5555 or 800/ 234–4000, FAX 914/835–5449). **Le Boat** (⊠ 10 S. Franklin Turnpike, #204B, Ramsey, NJ 07446, ☎ 201/ 236–2333 or 800/922–0291).

➤ BICYCLING: **Backroads** (⊠ 801 Cedar St., Berkeley, CA 94710-1800, ☎ 510/527–1555 or 800/462–2848, FAX 510-527–1444). **Bridges Tours** (⊠ 2855 Capital Dr., Eugene, OR 97403, ☎ 541/484–1196 or 800/461–6760, FAX 541/687–9085). **Butterfield & Robinson** (⊠ 70 Bond St., Toronto, Ontario, Canada M5B 1X3, ☎ 416/ 864–1354 or 800/678–1147, FAX 416/864–0541). **Chateaux Bike Tours** (⊠ Box 5706, Denver, CO 80217, ☎ 303/393–6910 or 800/ 678–2453, FAX 303/393–6801). **Classic Adventures** (⊠ Box 153, Hamlin, NY 14464–0153, ☎ 716/ 964–8488 or 800/777–8090, FAX 716/964–7297). **Euro-Bike Tours** (⊠ Box 990, De Kalb, IL 60115, ☎ 815/758–8851 or 800/321–6060). **Europeds** (⊠ 761 Lighthouse Ave., Monterey, CA 93940, ☎ 800/321– 9552, FAX 408/655–4501). **Himalayan Travel** (⊠ 110 Prospect St., Stamford, CT 06901, ☎ 203/359–3711 or 800/225–2380, FAX 203/359–3669). **Imagine Tours** (⊠ Box 123, Davis, CA 95617, ☎ 530/758–8782 or 888/592–8687, FAX 530/758–8778). **Progressive Travels** (⊠ 224 W. Galer Ave., Suite C, Seattle, WA 98119, ☎ 206/285–1987 or 800/245–2229, FAX 206/285–1988). **Rocky Mountain Worldwide Cycle Tours** (⊠ 333 Baker St., Nelson, BC0, Canada V1L 4H6, ☎ 250/354–1241 or 800/661– 2453, FAX 250/354–2058). **Uniquely Europe** (⊠ 1940 116th Ave. NE, Bellevue, WA 98004, ☎ 425/455– 4445 or 800/927–3876, FAX 425/ 455–2111). **Vermont Bicycle Touring** (⊠ Box 711, Bristol, VT, 05443- 0711, ☎ 802/453–4811 or 800/245– 3868, FAX 802/453–4806).

➤ CUSTOMIZED PACKAGES: **Abercrombie & Kent** (☞ Group Tours, *above*).

Alekx Travel (⊠ 519A S. Andrews Ave., Fort Lauderdale, FL 33301, ☎ 954/462–6767, FAX 954/462–8691). **Five Star Touring** (⊠ 60 E. 42nd St., #612, New York, NY 10165, ☎ 212/ 818–9140 or 800/792–7827, FAX 212/818–9142). **The French Experience** (⊠ 370 Lexington Ave., Suite 812, New York, NY 10017, ☎ 212/ 986–1115).

➤ FOOD AND WINE: **Le Cordon Bleu** (⊠ 404 Airport Executive Pk., Nanuet, NY 10954, ☎ 800/457– 2433). **Cuisine International** (⊠ Box 25228, Dallas, TX 75225, ☎ 214/ 373–1161, FAX 214/373–1162). **European Culinary Adventures** (⊠ 5 Ledgewood Way, Suite 6, Peabody, MA 01960, ☎ 508/535–5738 or 800/852–2625). **France In Your Glass** (⊠ 814 35th Ave., Seattle, WA 98122, ☎ 206/325–4324 or 800/ 578–0903, FAX 206/325–1727). **Ritz-Escoffier** (☎ 800/966–5758), in Paris's Ritz hotel.

➤ GOLF: **Golf International** (⊠ 275 Madison Ave., New York, NY 10016, ☎ 212/986–9176 or 800/833–1389, FAX 212/986–3720). **ITC Golf Tours** (⊠ 4134 Atlantic Ave., #205, Long Beach, CA 90807, ☎ 310/595–6905 or 800/257–4981).

➤ HOMES AND GARDENS: **Coopersmith's England** (⊠ Box 900, Inverness, CA 94937, ☎ 415/669–1914, FAX 415/669–1942).

➤ HORSEBACK RIDING: **Cross Country International Equestrian Vacations** (⊠ Box 1170, Millbrook, NY 12545, ☎ 800/828–8768, FAX 914/677– 6077). **Equitour FITS Equestrian** (⊠ Box 807, Dubois, WY 82513, ☎ 307/455–3363 or 800/545–0019, FAX 307/455–2354).

➤ HORTICULTURE: **Expo Garden Tours** (⊠ 70 Great Oak, Redding, CT 06896, ☎ 203/938–0410 or 800/448–2685, FAX 203/938–0427).

➤ LEARNING: **Fresh Pond Travel Vacations** (⊠ 186 Alewife Brook Parkway, Cambridge, MA 02138, ☎ 617/661–9200 or 800/645–0001, FAX 617/661–3354). **IST Cultural Tours** (⊠ 225 W. 34th St., New York, NY 10122-0913, ☎ 212/563–1202 or 800/833–2111, FAX 212/594–6953). **Naturequest** (⊠ 934 Acapulco St.,

Laguna Beach, CA 92651, ☎ 714/
499–9561 or 800/369–3033, FAX
714/499–0812). **Smithsonian Study
Tours and Seminars** (☞ Art and
Architecture, *above*).

➤ MOTORCYCLE: **Beach's Motorcycle
Adventures** (✉ 2763 W. River Pkwy.,
Grand Island, NY 14072-2053, ☎
716/773–4960, FAX 716/773–5227).

➤ MUSIC: **Dailey-Thorp Travel** (✉
330 W. 58th St., #610, New York, NY
10019-1817, ☎ 212/307–1555 or
800/998–4677, FAX 212/974–1420).

➤ NATURAL HISTORY: **Questers** (✉
381 Park Ave. S, New York, NY
10016, ☎ 212/251–0444 or 800/
468–8668, FAX 212/251–0890).

➤ SPAS: **Great Spas of the World** (✉
55 John St., New York, NY 10038,
☎ 212/267–5500 or 800/772–8463,
FAX 212/571–0510). **Spa-Finders** (✉
91 5th Ave., #301, New York, NY
10003-3039, ☎ 212/924–6800 or
800/255–7727). **Spa Trek Travel**
(✉ 475 Park Ave. S, New York, NY
10016, ☎ 212/779–3480 or 800/
272–3480, FAX 212/779–3471).

➤ TENNIS: **Championship Tennis
Tours** (✉ 8040 E. Morgan Trail #12,
Scottsdale, AZ 85258, ☎ 602/443–
9499 or 800/468–3664, FAX 602/
443–9982). **Steve Furgal's International Tennis Tours** (✉ 11828 Ran-
cho Bernardo Rd., #123-305, San
Diego, CA 92128, ☎ 619/675–3555
or 800/258–3664).

➤ WALKING: **Abercrombie & Kent**
(☞ Group Tours, *above*). **Above
the Clouds Trekking** (✉ Box 398,
Worcester, MA 01602-0398, ☎ 508/
799–4499 or 800/233–4499, FAX 508/
797–4779). **Backroads** (☞ Bicycling,
above). **Butterfield & Robinson**
(☞ Bicycling, *above*). **Classic Adventures** (☞ Bicycling, *above*). **Country
Walkers** (✉ Box 180, Waterbury, VT
05676-0180, ☎ 802/244–1387 or
800/464–9255, FAX 802/244–5661).
Euro-Bike Tours (☞ Bicycling, *above*).
Europeds (☞ Bicycling, *above*).
Mountain Travel-Sobek (✉ 6420
Fairmount Ave., El Cerrito, CA
94530, ☎ 510/527–8100 or 800/
227–2384, FAX 510/525–7710).
Progressive Travels (☞ Bicycling,
above). **Uniquely Europe** (☞ Bicy-

cling, *above*). **Wilderness Travel** (✉
1102 Ninth St., Berkeley, CA 94710,
☎ 510/558–2488 or 800/368–2794).

➤ YACHT CHARTERS: **Club Voyages**
(✉ 43 Hooper Ave., Atlantic High-
lands, NJ, 07716, ☎ 732/291–8228
or 888/842–2122). **Huntley Yacht
Vacations** (✉ 210 Preston Rd.,
Wernersville, PA 19565, ☎ 610/
678–2628 or 800/322–9224, FAX
610/670–1767). **Lynn Jachney Charters** (✉ Box 302, Marblehead, MA
01945, ☎ 617/639–0787 or 800/
223–2050, FAX 617/639–0216). **The
Moorings** (✉ 19345 U.S. Hwy. 19 N,
4th floor, Clearwater, FL 34624-
3193, ☎ 813/530–5424 or 800/535–
7289, FAX 813/530–9474). **Ocean
Voyages** (✉ 1709 Bridgeway, Sausalito, CA 94965, ☎ 415/332–4681 or
800/299–4444, FAX 415/332–7460).

TRAIN TRAVEL

The SNCF is recognized as Europe's
best national rail service: It's fast,
punctual, comfortable, and comprehensive. There are various options:
local trains, overnight trains with
sleeping accomodations, and the
high-speed TGV, the *Trains à Grande
Vitesse* (Very Fast Trains).

The TGVs average 255 kph/160 mph
on the Lyon/southeast line, and 300
kph/190 mph on the Lille and Bor-
deaux/southwest lines, and are the best
and the fastest domestic trains. They
operate between Paris and Lille/Calais,
Paris and Brussels, Paris and Amsterdam, Paris and Lyon/Switzerland/the
Riviera, and Angers/Nantes, and
Tours/Poitiers/Bordeaux. As with other
main-line trains, a small supplement
may be assessed at peak hours.

You must **always make a seat reservation for the TGV**—easily obtained at
the ticket window or from an automatic machine. Seat reservations are
reassuring but seldom necessary on
other main-line French trains, except
at certain busy holiday times.

If you know what station you'll
depart from, you can get a free schedule there (while supplies last), or you
can access the new multilingual
computerized schedule information
network at any Paris station and
many provincial ones. You can also

make reservations and buy your ticket while at the computer.

If you are traveling from Paris (or any other terminus), **get to the station half an hour before departure** to ensure that you'll have a good seat. The majority of intercity trains in France consist of open-plan cars and are known as *Corail* trains. They are clean and extremely comfortable, even in second class. Trains on regional branch lines are currently being spruced up but lag behind in style and quality. The food in French trains can be good, but it's poor value for the money.

Before boarding, you must **punch your ticket (but not Eurailpass) in one of the orange machines** at the entrance to the platforms, or else the ticket collector will fine you 100 francs on the spot.

It is possible to get from one end of France to the other without traveling overnight. Otherwise you have the choice between high-priced *wagons-lits* (sleeping cars) and affordable *couchettes* (bunks, six to a compartment in second class, four to a compartment in first, with sheets and pillow provided, priced at around 90 francs). Special summer night trains from Paris to Spain and the Riviera, geared to young people, are equipped with disco and bar.

➤ INFORMATION: SNCF (✉ 88 rue St-Lazare, 75009 Paris, ☎ 08–36–35–35–35); note that a per minute charge is assessed.

➤ WEB SITES: **Eurail/Eurostar** (http://www.eurail.com/). SNCF (http://www.sncf.fr/indexe.htm).

DISCOUNT PASSES

If you plan to travel outside of Paris by train, **consider purchasing a France Rail Pass,** which allows three days of unlimited train travel in a one-month period. Prices begin at $130 each for two adults traveling together in second class and $165 second class for a solo traveler. First-class rates are $156 each for two adults and $195 for a solo traveler. Additional days may be added for $30 a day in either class. Other options include the France Rail 'n Drive Pass (combining rail and rental car), France Rail 'n Fly Pass (rail travel and one air travel journey within France), and the France Fly Rail 'n Drive Pass (a rail, air, and rental car program all in one).

France is one of 17 countries in which you can **use EurailPasses,** which provide unlimited first-class rail travel, in all of the participating countries, for the duration of the pass. If you plan to rack up the miles, get a standard pass. These are available for 15 days ($522), 21 days ($678), one month ($838), two months ($1,148), and three months ($1,468). If your plans call for only limited train travel, **look into a Europass,** which costs less money than a EurailPass. Unlike EurailPasses, however, you get a limited number of travel days, in a limited number of countries, during a specified time period. For example, a two-month Europass ($316) allows between 5 and 15 days of rail travel, but costs $200 less than the least expensive Eurail-Pass. Keep in mind, however, that the Europass is good only in France, Germany, Italy, Spain, and Switzerland, and the number of countries you can visit is further limited by the type of pass you buy.

In addition to standard EurailPasses, **ask about special rail-pass plans.** Among these are the Eurail Youthpass (for those under age 26), the Eurail Saverpass (which gives a discount for two or more people traveling together), a Eurail Flexipass (which allows a certain number of travel days within a set period), the Euraildrive Pass and the Europass Drive (train and rental car).

Whichever of the above you choose, remember that you must **purchase your pass at home before leaving for Europe.**

Don't assume that your rail pass guarantee you a seat on the train you wish to ride. You need to **book seats ahead even if you are using a rail pass;** seat reservations are required on high-speed trains, and are a good idea on trains that may be crowded-particularly in summer on popular routes. You will also need a reservation for sleeping accommodations.

THE GOLD GUIDE / SMART TRAVEL TIPS

➤ TICKET AGENTS: Eurail- and Euro-passes are available through travel agents and a few authorized organizations. **CIT Tours Corp.** (✉ 15 West 44th St., 10th Floor, New York, NY 10036, ☎ 800/248–7245 for rail or 800/248–8687for tours and hotels). **DER Travel Services** (✉ 9501 W. Devon Ave., Rosemont, IL 60018, ☎ 800/782–2424). **Rail Europe**(✉ 226–230 Westchester Ave., White Plains, NY 10604, ☎ 800/438–7245, FAX 800/432–1329; ✉ 2087 Dundas E., Suite 105, Mississauga, Ontario L4X 1M2, ☎ 905/602–4195),

FRENCH RAIL PASSES

SNCF offers a number of discount rail passes available only for purchase in France. When traveling together, **two people (who don't have to be a couple) can save money with the Prix Découverte à Deux.** You'll get a 25% discount during "périodes bleus" (blue periods; weekdays and not on or near any holidays). Note that you have to be with the person you said you would be traveling with.

You can **get a reduced fare if you are a senior citizen (over 60)** with the Carte Vermeil. There are two options: The first, the Carte Vermeil Quatre Temps, costs 143F and gives you a reduction on 4 trips: 50% off in the blue periods and 20% off during the more crowded "périodes blanches" (white periods; weekends or on or around holidays). The second, the Carte Vermeil Plein Temps, is 279F and allows you, for one year, an unlimited number of 30% reductions on trips within France and a 30% discount on trips outside of France.

With the Carte Kiwi, **children under 16 can get 50% off** four trips for 285 francs, or for a full year of travel for 444 francs.

If you purchase an individual ticket from SNCF in France and you're under 26, you will automatically get a 25% reduction (a valid ID, such as an ISIC card or your passport, is necessary). If you're going to be using the train quite a bit during your stay in France and **if you're under 26, consider buying the Carte 12–25** (270F), which offers unlimited 50% reductions for one year (provided that there's space available at that price,

otherwise you'll just get the standard 25% discount).

If you don't benefit from any of these reductions and **if you plan on traveling at least 1,000 km (620 mi) roundtrip (including several stops), look into purchasing a Billet Séjour.** This ticket gives you a 25% reduction if you stay over a Sunday and if you travel only during blue periods. It may be a major organizational feat, but you can save a lot of cash this way.

FROM THE U.K.

Short of flying, the "Chunnel" is the fastest way to cross the English Channel: 3 hours from London's central Waterloo Station to Paris's central Gare du Nord, 35 minutes from Folkestone to Calais, and 60 minutes from motorway to motorway. Round-trip tickets range from 3,400 francs for first class to 690 francs for second class.

British Rail also has four daily departures from London's Victoria Station, all linking with the Dover-Calais/Boulogne ferry services through to Paris. There is also an overnight service on the Newhaven-Dieppe ferry. Journey time is about eight hours. Credit-card bookings are accepted by phone or in person at a British Rail Travel Centre.

➤ CAR TRANSPORT: **Le Shuttle** (☎ 0990/353535 in the U.K.).

➤ PASSENGER SERVICE: In France, **Eurostar** (☎ 08–36–35–35–39). In the U.K., **Eurostar** (☎ 0345/881881), **InterCity Europe** (✉ Victoria Station, London, ☎ 0171/834–2345, 0171/828–0892 for credit-card bookings). In the U.S., **BritRail Travel** (☎ 800/677–8585), **Rail Europe** (☎ 800/942–4866).

➤ SCHEDULE INFORMATION: **British Rail** (☎ 0171/834–2345).

➤ TRAIN-FERRY LINK: **British Rail International** (☎ 0171/834–2345) and **Sealink** (☎ 01–44–94–40–40) provide train-ferry travel between the U.K. and France.

TRAVEL AGENCIES

A good travel agent puts your needs first. Look for an agency that has been in business at least five years, emphasizes customer service, and has someone on staff who specializes in your destination. In addition, **make sure the agency belongs to a professional trade organization,** such as ASTA in the United States. If your travel agency is also acting as your tour operator, *see* Buyer Beware *in* Tour Operators, *above*).

➤ LOCAL AGENT REFERRALS: **American Society of Travel Agents** (ASTA, ☎ 800/965–2782 24-hr hot line, ℻ 703/684–8319). **Association of Canadian Travel Agents** (⊠ Suite 201, 1729 Bank St., Ottawa, Ontario K1V 7Z5, ☎ 613/521–0474, ℻ 613/521–0805). **Association of British Travel Agents** (⊠ 55–57 Newman St., London W1P 4AH, ☎ 0171/637–2444, ℻ 0171/637–0713). **Australian Federation of Travel Agents** (☎ 02/9264–3299). **Travel Agents' Association of New Zealand** (☎ 04/499–0104).

➤ LOCAL AGENCIES: The following locations are in Paris, but most of these agencies have offices all over France. **Access Voyages** (⊠ 6 rue Pierre Lescot, 1ᵉ, métro Châtelet–Les Halles, ☎ 01–44–76–84–50). **Nouvelles Frontiéres** (⊠ 5 ave. de l'Opéra, 1ᵉʳ, métro Pyramides, ☎ 08–03–33–33–33). **Soltours** (⊠ 48 rue de Rivoli, 4ᵉ, métro Hôtel-de-Ville, ☎ 01–42–71–24–34).

VISITOR INFORMATION

TOURIST INFORMATION

➤ FRENCH GOVERNMENT TOURIST OFFICE: **France On-Call** (☎ 202/659–7779; Mon.–Fri. 9–9. **Chicago** (⊠ 676 N. Michigan Ave., Chicago, IL 60611, ☎ 312/751–7800). **Los Angeles** (⊠ 9454 Wilshire Blvd., Suite 715, Beverly Hills, CA 90212, ☎ 310/271–6665, ℻ 310/276–2835).**New York City** (⊠ 444 Madison Ave., 16th floor, New York, NY 10022, ☎ 212/838–7800). **Canada** (⊠ 1981 Ave. McGill College, Suite 490, Montréal, Québec H3A 2W9, ☎ 514/288–4264, ℻ 514/845–4868. **U.K.** ⊠ 178 Piccadilly, London W1V OAL, ☎ 171/629–2869, ℻ 0171/493–6594.

➤ LOCAL TOURIST OFFICES: *See* the A to Z sections *in* individual chapters for local tourist office telephone numbers and addresses.

WORLD WIDE WEB

Do check out the World Wide Web when you're planning. You'll find everything from up-to-date weather forecasts to virtual tours of famous cities. The **Fodor's Web site, www.fodors.com, is a great place to start** your on-line travels. For more information specifically on France, visit the following.

➤ RECOMMENDED WEB SITES: **Bordeaux Tourist Office** (http://www.bordeaux-tourisme.com/). **Eurail/Eurostar** (http://www.eurail.com/). **French Youth Hostel Federation** (http://ww.fuaj.org). **Maison de la France/French Government Tourist Office** (http://www.francetourism.com and http://www.maison-de-la-france.com:8000/). **Monaco Tourist Office** (http://www.monaco.mc/usa/). **Provence Tourist Office** (http://www.visitprovence.com). **Riviera Tourist Office** (http://www.crt-riviera.fr/). **SNCF** (http://www.sncf.fr/indexe.htm). **Strasbourg Tourism Office** (http://www.strasbourg.com/).

VOLUNTEER & EDUCATIONAL TRAVEL

A variety of volunteer programs are available. CIEE (☞ Students, *above*) is a key player, running its own roster of projects and publishing a directory that lists other sponsor organizations, *Volunteer! The Comprehensive Guide to Voluntary Service in the U.S. and Abroad*. Service Civil International (SCI), International Voluntary Service (IVS), and Volunteers for Peace (VFP) run two- and three-week short workcamps; VFP also publishes the *International Workcamp Directory*. WorldTeach programs, run by Harvard University, require that you commit a year to teaching on subjects ranging from English and science to carpentry, forestry, or sports.

➤ ORGANIZATIONS: **SCI/IVS** (⊠ 5474 Walnut Level Rd., Crozet, VA 22932, ☎ 804/823–1826). **VFP** (⊠ 43 Tiffany Rd., Belmont, VT 05730, ☎ 802/259–2759, ℻ 802/259–2922). **WorldTeach** (⊠ 14 Story St., Cambridge, MA 02138, ☎ 617/495–5527, ☎ 800/483–2240, ℻ 617/495–1599).

THE GOLD GUIDE / SMART TRAVEL TIPS

WHEN TO GO

June and September are the best months to be in France, as both are free of the midsummer crowds. June offers the advantage of long daylight hours, while cheaper prices and frequently warm weather (often lasting well into October) make September attractive. Try to avoid the second half of July and all of August, when almost all of France goes on vacation. Huge crowds jam the roads and beaches, and prices are jacked up in resorts. Don't travel on or around July 14 and August 1, 15, and 31. July and August in southern France can be stifling. Paris can be stuffy and uncomfortable in August, especially with the problems that have arisen recently with the record highs in pollution. However, the city is pleasantly deserted. Many restaurants, theaters, and small shops close, but enough stay open these days to make a low-key, unhurried visit a pleasure.

The ski season in the Alps and Pyrénées lasts from Christmas to Easter; if you can, avoid February, when school holidays mean crowds. Anytime between March and November will offer you a good chance to soak up the sun on the Riviera. If Paris and the Loire are among your priorities, remember that the weather is unappealing before Easter. If you're dreaming of Paris in the springtime, May is your best bet, not rainy April. But the capital remains a joy during mid-winter, with plenty of things to see and do.

CLIMATE

What follows are average daily maximum and minimum temperatures for Paris and Nice.

PARIS

Month	°F	°C	Month	°F	°C	Month	°F	°C
Jan.	43F	6C	May	68F	20C	Sept.	70F	21C
	34	1		49	10		53	12
Feb.	45F	7C	June	73F	23C	Oct.	60F	16C
	34	1		55	13		46	8
Mar.	54F	12C	July	76F	25C	Nov.	50F	10C
	39	4		58	15		40	5
Apr.	60F	16C	Aug.	75F	24C	Dec.	44F	7C
	43	6		58	15		36	2

NICE

Month	°F	°C	Month	°F	°C	Month	°F	°C
Jan.	55F	13C	May	68F	20C	Sept.	77F	25C
	39	4		55	13		61	16
Feb.	55F	13C	June	75F	24C	Oct.	70F	21C
	41	5		61	16		54	12
Mar.	59F	15C	July	81F	27C	Nov.	63F	17C
	45	7		64	18		46	8
Apr.	64F	18C	Aug.	81F	27C	Dec.	55F	13C
	46	8		64	18		41	5

➤ FORECASTS: **Weather Channel Connection** (☎ 900/932–8437), 95¢ per minute from a Touch-Tone phone.

1 Destination: France

THE BEST OF ALL POSSIBLE WORLDS

FRANCE IS NEITHER TOO HOT nor too cold, neither too wet nor too dry, neither too flat nor too crammed with inconvenient mountains. At any rate, that is what the French say. They think that countries should be hexagonal in shape and about 600 miles across. Spain is too square, Norway is frayed at the edges, l'Angleterre (which is what they usually call Great Britain) is awkwardly surrounded by cold water, Switzerland is landlocked and too small, and the United States is too large (you cross three time zones and then get the same depressing dinner). After God created France, He belatedly realized that He had gone too far: It was too near perfection. "How can I restore the balance?" He asked Himself. Then He saw what to do—He created the French. That is a French story. The French enjoy grumbling about themselves or, rather, about other French people, but in the same breath they admit that there is only one civilized way for people to live, and that is the French way, *la civilisation française*.

My wife and I have lived in France for many years, and we have come to the conclusion that there is something to be said for this view. Our fellow villagers are kind, patient, and friendly, behaving with natural dignity and good manners, like most of the other French people we meet (except Parisians in the rush hour). Visitors to France, particularly Anglo-Saxon visitors, whether they stay a week or a year, will have a better time if they "go native" as far as they find it practicable—and when and where they don't, they should be philosophically aware of the drawbacks of trying to behave as in dear old Birmingham, Alabama, or the U.K. (I am using the word "Anglo-Saxon" as the French use it. To them, Louis Armstrong, Robert Burns, James Joyce, and Frank Sinatra are representative Anglo-Saxons; Beowulf and King Alfred have nothing to do with it.)

Let's look at the French timetable. Most of the French are up early, gulping a café au lait and getting to work by 8. By 10, Parisian executives are fuming because their London contacts haven't yet answered the phone (it's only 9 in England). There is no coffee break.

At noon, they are hungry. Work stops for two hours or longer. Museums and small shops close. *Le déjeuner* (called *le dîner* in the country) is a sacred rite. Fast-food outlets have multiplied, but the norm is a proper meal, taking an hour and a half; a surprising number manage to get home for it. However, the increasing number of women at work means that 6 lunches out of 10 are eaten at restaurants or canteens—substantial, freshly cooked affairs, eaten with serious critical attention. The French grew rich in the '60s: Back in 1920, they each ate nearly three pounds of bread a day—now it is just under a pound, with a corresponding increase in the consumption of meat, fish, and cheese. Less wine is drunk, but more of it is of higher quality.

There is a typical restaurant in our nearest market town (pop. 6,000). It has only one menu: copious hors d'oeuvres, a fish dish or a light meat dish, a more serious meat dish, vegetables in season, a good cheese board, fruit or ice cream. It's always full by 12:30. A couple from San Francisco who stayed in a rented cottage in our village were hardly ever able to use it. They used to get up at 9 and have an Anglo-Saxon sort of breakfast, and so they were hopelessly out of phase with the commercial travelers (up at 6) who form the restaurant's main clientele. You can't start your lunch there at 1:30 or 2, and there are no doggy bags in France. We are in the Midi, where an early start and a siesta are convenient (many of the shops don't reopen until 3:30). However, the couple happily developed the picnic habit: France is God's own country for picnicking, if only you get to the *charcuterie* and the *boulangerie* and the *pâtisserie* well before they close at noon.

Back to work for another four-hour stretch. No tea or coffee break. Are the French mighty toilers? Yes and no. I have conducted oral language examinations in France and in England. The French expect me to keep on examining nonstop from 8 to 12:30 and again from 2 to 6:30. The merciful (lazy?) English think six hours of attentive interviewing per day, with breaks mid-morning and mid-afternoon, are all the human mind can stand. French schoolchildren have a much longer day than do Anglo-Saxon ones and have more to learn.

On the other hand, wage earners and schoolchildren have many leisure days. In the '80s, the average industrial worker put in 1,872 hours of work per year in the United States, 1,750 in Great Britain, but only 1,650 in France. Five weeks' paid vacation is the official minimum, and there are many public holidays. The French have become addicts of leisure in the past two decades. One family in 10 has a second house in the country, where they go on weekends and vacations, causing astounding traffic jams as they flee the cities.

If he finishes his day's work at 6 or 6:30, will our average Frenchman call in at his favorite café for a chat and an aperitif on his way home? Probably not, nowadays. In the past, the café was used as a sort of extra living room for meeting friends or professional contacts, or even for writing novels if you were Jean-Paul Sartre or Simone de Beauvoir. But today an average of two hours and 50 minutes is spent watching television at home, which reduces the time available for social life.

This is sad. The number of cafés has diminished. Fortunately, there are still a lot left, and how convenient they are for the visitor! On the terrace of a French café, you can bask in the sun or enjoy the shade of a multicolor parasol, sipping a cool beer and keeping an eye on life's passing show. A small black coffee entitles you to spend an hour or two—no hurry.

While we are on the subject: It seems odd to the Anglo-Saxon that in France beer is generally considered a nonalcoholic drink. (Nurses serve it after you give blood.) When you tell the French that some people at home succeed in getting nastily drunk on it, they say, "But they must drink several glasses!" Indeed. A Frenchman will spend half an hour sipping a quarter of a liter. One sees few drunks in France, except in the north, and then very rarely.

I mentioned the apéritif hour to talk not only about cafés but about friendliness. Some people—notably Americans—complain that the French are inhospitable and standoffish. The fact is that they are great respecters of privacy. If the Englishman's home is his castle, the Frenchman's apartment or house is his lair. People simply do not pop into one another's lairs, drinking casual cups of coffee and borrowing half a pound of sugar. They need a neutral place in which to socialize. Britons come somewhere between typical French people and the American middle class. According to Paul Fussell (*Caste Marks*, 1983): "Among the [American] middles there's a convention that erecting a fence or even a tall hedge is an affront."

IT'S DIFFERENT in France. People in the Midi, where we live, just love to talk, and even to listen. But our village neighbors are timid about entering our house. If they want to ask us something, they will wait until we meet, or stay on the doorstep, or phone (from 50 yards away). They penetrate our house, and we penetrate theirs, when specifically invited. That is how they behave among themselves, too. It's not because we are foreigners.

So when do we talk? There are benches everywhere, in the sun and in the shade. The villagers—and we—sit there for hours, chatting. The locals really are interested in you, your habits and tastes, the number and ages of your children, your work, where you come from, and so forth, and are longing to impart a discreet selection of their own personal details. Of course you *may* be invited home. There are no rules about this sort of thing. And if there were, the French would take pleasure in breaking them.

When talking with the French, there are conventions that should be observed if you don't want to be thought a barbarian by people who are unaware of Anglo-Saxon attitudes. You must say *"Bonjour"* followed by *Monsieur, Madame, Mademoiselle, Messieurs, Mesdames,* or *Messieurs-dames* much more often than you would think necessary (on entering a small shop, for instance) and *"Au revoir, Monsieur"* (etc.). Hands are shaken frequently (by colleagues at work, morning and evening, and by the most casual acquaintances). *Bon appétit* can replace *au revoir* shortly before mealtimes. On going through a door, a certain amount of *après-vous*-ing is normal, with *pardon* if you go through first, turning your back. Getting on first-name terms is a sign of much greater intimacy than in England or the United States. Rush-hour Parisian life is more brutal, of course, and, as elsewhere in the world, the driving seat of a car exerts a malign influence. In England or the States, a headlight flash sometimes means "After you"; in France, it means either "After me" or "I am a criminal and I expect you are, too, so watch it, chum, the cops are round the corner."

BACK HOME FROM the café, *le dîner* (called *le souper* in the country) is served around 8, for rich and poor. It's a lighter meal than at midday, with soup replacing hors d'oeuvres. The movies, after a sharp fall as television established itself in every home, have resisted well. Except in Paris, films are dubbed into French, a practice deplored by intellectuals.

Almost all employed people now have a two-day weekend, usually Saturday and Sunday, but Sunday and Monday for many shop workers. Schoolchildren have Wednesday free, but may attend Saturday morning, instead. In recent years, the French have revolutionized their leisure habits: Jogging, swimming, soccer, gymnastics, tennis, and vigorous bicycling (for fun, not transport) are practiced, mainly on weekends, by large numbers of all social classes.

Sunday is a day for enjoying oneself. Though 85% of the population declare themselves Catholics, only 15% of those go to church every week. There is a fairly strong anti-church sentiment among many, even among those who say they are Catholics, but the traditional warfare between priest and primary-school teacher— the one reactionary and the other attached to Republican ideals—is a thing of the past. Divorce, the pill, and legal abortion are widely accepted, even by practicing Catholics.

The great Sunday ritual takes place at noon or soon after. Four out of 10 will visit friends or relations. Sixty percent of families do more cooking on Sundays than on other days. This is also a big day for restaurants that feature a special Sunday menu. Half the French end their Sunday lunch with a fresh fruit tart or some sort of gâteau, which is why the pastry shops are open in the morning and why you see Frenchmen carefully carrying flat cardboard boxes. Then a quarter of the population takes a little siesta.

An essay such as this has to contain rash generalizations. Is there an average French person? Obviously not. There are the rich and the poor, for example. The poor, in France, like champagne, oysters, and foie gras, but they get them less often than do the rich. The same is true of other aspects of life. The gulf between one class and another is not one of tastes and aspirations; rich and poor are in broad agreement on what constitutes a pleasant life. The poor are simply further away from it than are the rich.

Changing France . . . I was there in 1947, and I said to myself: "How wonderful! But it can't last." On the whole it has. The surge of prosperity in the '60s brought improvements to French life, with some drawbacks (traffic in Paris, for example), but basic traditions die hard. The young ape foreign fashions, with a fast-food/motorcycle/mid-Atlantic pop noise/comicstrip culture, but they grow out of it. Official morality has changed. Contraception used to be forbidden; Paris was famed for its elegant brothels, but women had to go to London for diaphragms and to Switzerland for abortions. All that has gone. In 1988, the rise of AIDS caused a quickly smothered quarrel among bishops about the sinfulness of condoms, which are readily available. *Le topless* is seen on most beaches, and total nakedness on some. But the family remains a powerful, cohesive unit.

What do they think of us? Corresponding to the Anglo-Saxon stereotype that depicts all Frenchmen wearing berets and pointed beards, waving their arms wildly and being saucy with the girls, the French picture Americans as rich, generous, overweight, and likely in world politics or personal relationships to behave like wellmeaning bulls in china shops and the English as either tall, silent, inhibited, masochistic, and scrupulously honest or as drunken, sadistic, soccer-watching vandals. Of course nobody really believes any of this, but if you are going to attach a national label to yourself, you might as well be aware of the cliché lurking at the back of the mind.

"Happy as God in France" say the Germans, exaggerating a bit. Anglo-Saxons come in two sorts: Those who love France and those who don't. It's a matter of taste and character. The former find it easy to slip into the French way of life for a week or a month or permanently. The latter are better off in Paris or on the Riviera. But really, the French are canny operators when it comes to enjoying *la douceur de vivre,* the sweetness of life. If you follow their example while in France, you can't go far wrong. (One way to go wrong would be to quote almost any paragraph from this essay to them; at any rate, it will start a vigorously French argument.)

—John P. Harris

Born in England, John P. Harris has lived in a small village in the south of France since 1975. He has written numerous articles for both French and British newspapers and magazines, including the London *Times,* and is the author of a guidebook to France.

NEW AND NOTEWORTHY

Not content with its status as the world's largest museum, the **Louvre** continues to expand: 11 new rooms of Persian and Arab antiquities opened in October 1997, followed in December by an extralarge exhibit space devoted to Greek, Roman, Egyptian, Etruscan, and Coptic art.

The **Centre Pompidou** closed in October 1997 for a $120 million renovation program and will not reopen till the last day of the century—December 31, 1999. In the meantime, you can visit the **Atelier Brancusi** in front of the center—the reconstituted studios of avant-garde sculptor Constantin Brancusi.

The **Bibliothèque Nationale François-Mitterrand,** the new national library building in Paris (which replaced the old national library, the Bibliothèque Nationale Richelieu, on rue Richelieu), has proved a popular addition to the southeast section of the city. The Tolbiac district around the new library was due to be united to cen-

tral Paris by the express **Météor** métro line by late 1998.

Paris is gearing up for **L'An 2000** (The Year 2000) with a host of special events planned to celebrate the millennium. A digital clock on the Eiffel Tower is counting down the days to the end of the century and, more frenetically, the Genitron on place de la Bastille is ticking down the seconds.

In **Versailles,** the Musée des Carrosses, with its parade of historic royal carriages, is now open weekends in the Grandes Écuries. A permanent exhibit charting France's parliamentary history was set up in late 1997 in the south wing of the palace, enabling you to visit the plush but hitherto inaccessible debate-chamber (still occasionally used to vote constitutional amendments). Out in the park, an ambitious tree-replacement scheme was launched in early 1998 to recapture Le Nôtre's original perspectives (the trees had grown too big and old).

After nearly a decade, the reopening of Bayonne's **Musée Basque,** which is dedicated to exhibits on Basque ethnography, is a big event. The exact date of reopening (the end of 1998 or 1999) is as yet undetermined; in the meantime, exhibits are being held at the Château Neuf.

France's **highways** continue to expand: the A26 from Paris, ultimately destined to reach the Channel, is in operation as far as Abbeville; the new A14 tollway opened between La Défense and Orgeval, easing traffic to the west of Paris; and a stretch of the E50 expressway between Angers and Saumur was completed and is soon to be extended as far as Tours.

On the political front, France continues to prepare for the **euro,** the single European currency. Although notes and coins are not expected to be introduced until 2001, many banks and shops are already posting prices in euros as well as francs.

WHAT'S WHERE

Paris

The Eiffel Tower gives you an overview; the Louvre, a good look at the art of the past (with a peek, too, at architecture's present and future). Say a prayer at Notre-Dame, buy a dress you'll love forever, and eat an unforgettable meal anywhere at all. Open your eyes—there's something beautiful or amusing at every step; dawdle around the Latin Quarter, climb up to Montmartre for a peek at Sacré-Coeur, spend a morning at the *marché aux puces* (flea market), and sail down the Seine on the Bateaux Mouches.

Ile-de-France

The green surround of Paris, lushly forested and islanded by meandering rivers, is studded with noble châteaux and their spectacular gardens. Versailles and Fontainebleau, Thoiry, Chantilly, and Maintenon are only a few. From sublime Chartres to Monet's Giverny, then to Disneyland Paris, you can traverse the centuries, all within an hour or so of Paris.

The Loire Valley

Sometimes owned by England, and fought over for centuries, this stretch of the Loire southwest of Paris resounds today with the noise of contented tourists, music festivals, and son-et-lumière spectacles at the extraordinary châteaux. Amboise, Blois, Chenonceau, and Chambord number among the many. Joan of Arc captured Orléans, and here you can learn her history; at Angers, 210 km (130 mi) downriver, you can visit the fortress and the cathedral and get to know the wines of Anjou at the Maison du Vin.

Brittany

Nationalistic Brittany, the northwest arm of France, is full of the sound of the sea. It also has massive castles, vast beaches, and prehistoric standing stones. You'll be charmed, as well, by Rennes (medieval, Renaissance, *and* classical buildings), walled St-Malo, Quimper with its pottery, Dinan's old town, and tranquil Nantes. Come to Finistère (land's end) in August for the classic sailboat rally in the Bay of Douarnenez, and then visit Ste-Anne-la-Palud during the *pardon*, where you'll see traditional Breton lace *coiffes*.

Normandy

With miles of sandy beaches along the English Channel, Normandy also has folksy seaside towns like Dieppe, Fécamp, Honfleur, and plush resort towns like Trouville, Deauville, and Cabourg. Continue west to reach fabulous Mont-St-Michel,

the medieval abbey and village on a rock offshore that's an island at high tide. Inland, you must see Rouen's cathedral and its museums, visit charming Pont-Audemer on a market day, the lace museum in Alençon, and stay a while in Bayeux for the legendary tapestry and the harmonious cathedral. And don't forget Camembert and other marvelous cheeses—or your post-dinner calvados.

The North and Champagne

Lille is one of France's liveliest cities—a vibrant return to reality after the moving World War I battlefields and cemeteries near Albert and Arras—and just an hour from Paris by TGV. The new Channel Tunnel, like the traditional ferries, arrives at Calais; head down the Channel coast's uninterrupted stretch of sandy beaches to the elegant resort of Le Touquet. Inland, admire the palace of Compiègne, the mighty castles of Pierrefonds and Sedan, and the awesome cathedrals of Beauvais, Amiens, Noyon, Laon, and Reims—also center of the champagne industry, where bottles snooze in cavernous, chalky cellars. Away to the northeast lie the game-filled forests of the Ardennes.

Alsace-Lorraine and Franche-Comté

In Alsace, France's Germanic eastern corner, the beautiful Route du Vin winds through vineyards and villages among the Vosges foothills, and medieval half-timber houses lend a storybook air. Strasbourg rivals Paris in culture (it's home to the European Parliament), history, and architecture, not to mention haute cuisine (with local foie gras). Nancy, in Lorraine, is home to Baccarat and St-Louis crystal and adds Art Nouveau to its decorative mix. In the Jura, you can visit pretty little towns and buy wooden toys, clocks, and pipes, and even ski.

Burgundy

Drive southeast from Paris to the land of medieval dukes more powerful than kings, noble vineyards, Gothic cathedrals, and fabulous food. Stop first in Troyes (Champagne) to wander the pedestrian streets, see the old churches, timber houses, and museums. Circle the Morvan Forest, stopping in Autun, once a Roman town, and picturesque Vézelay with its basilica, and push on to Dijon, where the Palais des Ducs now houses the wonderful Musée des

Beaux-Arts. Be sure to taste the wines at the Marché aux Vins in Beaune, and maybe buy some as you head south, visiting Cluny's Abbey on your way to Mâcon's wine fair in May.

Lyon and the Alps

You can zip down from Paris on the TGV in a couple of hours and plant yourself in wonderful Lyon while you take in the rest of the region, from the wine villages of Beaujolais to the lakes and marshes of the Dombes and the medieval hilltop village of Pérouges. Then, venture down the Rhône to Vienne for Roman ruins and Renaissance facades and to the river town of Serrières. Pass through Grenoble with its fine museum en route to the Alps. Aix-les-Bains has ruined Roman baths and modern ones, and Annecy has lively Tuesday and Friday markets. Picturesque Talloires and chic Chamonix, with its cable car up the Aiguille du Midi, are two more enticing spots.

The Massif Central and Auvergne

This unspoiled region, now more easily accessible by autoroute, has volcanoes and ravines, thermal springs, and the dramatic Gorges du Tarn. Visit the exquisite cathedral in the market town of Bourges, elegant Vichy, the museums and cathedral in Clermont-Ferrand, the Parc des Volcans (but not in summer), and wonderful medieval towns and villages like Salers, high-perched Rocamadour, St-Cirq-Lapopie, Figeac, and Ste-Foy.

Provence

Hot, fragrant Provence is full of well-preserved Roman ruins; dozens of produce, flower, and fish markets; and a plethora of outdoor activities to do and see (even bullfighting). Go to Nîmes (in Languedoc) to see the Pont du Gard aqueduct, the amphitheater, the museums, and the beautiful Maison Carrée temple. You'll pass through the marshy Camargue en route to Arles, with its Roman arena and theater. Visit Daudet's Moulin in charming Fontvieille, inspect the tiny medieval streets and ancient houses in Les Baux, and stop in Avignon to see the Papal Palace and the famous bridge. Orange has a Roman theater and triumphal arch, and elegant Aix-en-Provence has museums, fountains, and the beautiful Cours Mirabeau boulevard.

The Riviera

Invisible celebrities, pebbly beaches, backed-up traffic, hordes of sunburned bathers—why do people come? Because the medieval hilltop villages (St-Paul-de-Vence, Mougins, Gassin, Vence, Peillon, even touristy Èze), the fields of fragrant flowers that supply the Grasse perfume factories, the wonderful museums, and the lovely, limpid light are still as magnetic as ever. Stylish boutiques, great art, splendid food, exciting nightlife, and spectacular views of crystal bays and cliff-side villas don't hurt either. Nor do the lively, cobbled streets of Nice's old town; the pretty, pastel colors of St-Tropez; or the splendor of Monte Carlo's casino.

Corsica

This island in the Mediterranean, about 160 km (100 mi) southeast of Monaco, is wonderful in spring and fall and crowded in July and August. You'll need a week to circle it. Visit Bastia's old town; explore the mountains along the Scala di Santa Regina; see Corte's citadel; laze on a beach; hear folk songs in Pigna; tour Napoléon's birthplace, Ajaccio; visit fortified Bonifacio; and splurge at the Grand Hôtel de Cala Rossa in the walled town of Porto-Vecchio.

Toulouse, the Midi-Pyrénées, and Roussillon

Sports and nature lovers flock to southwest France, where lively Toulouse, a university town of rosy pink brick, is the cultural star. As appealing are fortified Cordes and its medieval houses, Albi and its wonderful Toulouse-Lautrec Museum, Moissac and its fine cloister, Mirepoix and its wooden arcades, and medieval Carcassone. Near Tarascon is the Grotte de Niaux, with its marvelous prehistoric paintings, and ski trails descending from snowy peaks. Relaxing spa towns and wonderful views enliven the Pyrénées' twisting roads on the way from Roussillon to Ceret and Perpignan. And when you see picturesque Collioure's stunning Mediterranean setting you'll know why artists such as Matisse and Derain were so inspired.

Pays Basque, Béarn, and the Hautes Pyrénées

Basque country, south from Bayonne to Biarritz and the border with Spain, along the coast and in the Pyrénées, is a world of its own. Come here to discover the ancient and mysterious Basque culture, and dine on the incomparable cuisine. The landscape, too, is stunning, ranging from colorful seaports to rolling hills to the peaks of the Pyrénées. To the east is Béarn and its capital, the elegant city of Pau. The Hautes Pyrénées, the most central and the highest part of the range, hold, among other treasures, two of the region's most famous natural phenomena, the Cirque de Gavarnie and the Brèche de Roland.

Poitou-Charentes, Périgord, and Northern Aquitaine

Whatever you want is what you get in this varied region of southwest France. Castles and châteaux recall medieval battles; Romanesque abbeys and cathedrals echo with history. You may be drawn by the perky resorts of Arcachon and Royan, the vast beaches, marshy "Green Venice" in the north, or the vineyards of Cognac and Bordeaux. Come in May to the elegant city of Bordeaux, the regional capital, for the music festival, or any time to sip splendid wines while you indulge in oysters, truffles, foie gras, and caviar.

PLEASURES AND PASTIMES

Art

It is through the eyes of France's artists that many first get to know the country. No wonder people from across the globe come to find Gauguin's bobbing boats at Pont-Aven, Monet's bridge at Giverny, and the gaslit Moulin Rouge of Toulouse-Lautrec—not framed in gilt and hung in a museum but alive in all their three-dimensional glory. In Arles you can stand on the spot where van Gogh painted and compare his perspective to a placard with his finished work; in Paris you can climb into the garret-atelier where Delacroix created his epic canvases, or wander the redolent streets of Montmartre, once haunted by Renoir, Utrillo, and Modigliani. And, of course, the museums and châteaux hang heavy with masterworks, many of them bringing a telling local insight into French history, culture, and joie de vivre.

Cathedrals

Their extraordinary permanence, their everlasting relevance even in a secular world, and their transcending beauty make the Gothic and Romanesque cathedrals of France a lightning rod if you are in search of the essence of French culture. The product of a peculiarly Gallic mix of mysticism, exquisite taste, and high technology, France's cathedrals provide a thorough grounding in the history of architecture (some say there was nothing new in the art of building between France's Gothic arch and Frank Lloyd Wright's cantilevered slab). Each cathedral imparts its own monumental experience—knee-weakening grandeur, a mighty resonance that touches a chord of awe, and humility in the unbeliever. Even cynics will find satisfaction in the cathedrals' social history—the anonymity of the architects, the solidarity of the artisans, and the astonishing bravery of experiments in suspended stone.

Châteaux

From the humblest feudal ruin to the most delicate Renaissance spires to the grandest of Sun King spreads, the castles, manor houses, and châteaux of France evoke the history of Europe as no museum can. Standing on castellated ramparts overlooking undulating valleys, it is easy to slip into the role of a feudal lord scrambling to protect his patchwork of holdings from the centralized stronghold of kings and dukes. The lovely landscape takes on a strategic air and you find yourself role-playing thus, whether swanning aristocratically over Japanese bridges in the château park or curling a revolutionary lip at the splendid excesses of Versailles. These are, after all, the castles that inspired Sleeping Beauty, Beauty and the Beast, and Snow White, and their fairy-tale magic—rich with history and Disney-free—still holds true.

Cities

Besides being home to the most sophisticated city in the world, France has more to offer than just Paris. Other French cities possess the best of Paris without the staggering crowds, noise, pollution, and traffic. Lille, Lyon, Dijon, Bordeaux, Rennes, Marseille, and Strasbourg all have strong regional identities (and cuisines), as well as historic *vieilles villes* (old towns), sidewalk cafés, vast farmers' markets, and fine old parks. As for the arts, France's ministry of culture ensures that even the country's farthest outreaches have top-notch orchestras, stellar operas, and excellent museums.

Dining

Few countries match France's reputation for good food or offer as many fine restaurants. Eating in France can be a memorable experience, from the simplest picnic lunch of baguette, Camembert, and local *jambon* (ham) *sur l'herbe* (on the grass) to the most magnificent haute cuisine in formal splendor. Don't feel guilty if you spend as much of your day in restaurants as in museums and cathedrals: Dining is at the heart and soul of French culture. Give yourself over to the leisurely meal; two hours for a three-course menu is par, and you may, after relaxing into the routine, feel pressed at less than three.

L'Esprit Sportif

Though the physically inclined would consider walking across Scotland or bicycling across Holland, they often misconstrue France as a sedentary site where one plods from museum to château to restaurant. But it's possible to have a more active approach: Imagine pedaling past barges on the Saône River or along slender poplars on a *route départmentale* (provincial road); hiking through the dramatic gorges in the Massif Central or over Alpine meadows in the Savoie; or sailing the historic ports of Honfleur or Cap d'Antibes. Experiencing this side of France will take you off the beaten path and into the countryside (and away from those rest stops on the autoroute). As you bike along French country roads or along the extensive network of *Grands Randonnées* (Lengthy Trails) crisscrossing the country, you will have time to tune into the landscape—to study crumbling garden walls, smell the honeysuckle, and chat with a farmer in his *potager* (vegetable garden). Moreover, picnics are more sublime after a day of strenuous activity, and you can gorge without guilt on three-hour dinners when you reach your auberge.

The French Coast

Along the miles of French coast you will find broad-brimmed hats, parasols, and opaque sunglasses—their modesty and discretion charmingly contradictory in view of—and we mean full view of—the frankly bare flesh that bobbles up and down the miles of seashore. And not just the famous *seins nus* (topless women), but the bellies of gastronome *pépés* (grandfathers) as well, swinging low over briefs too brief to mention. Naked children crouch over sand châteaux, their unselfconsciousness a reflection of their elders' own. For the French the summer beach holiday is a sacred ritual, a counterbalance to the winter ski trip—a given, deserved and observed without thought of ozone holes, pollution, or disintegrating beachfront rentals.

To avoid the July–August stampede, go in June or September. Ironic as it may be, France's most famous coastline possesses the country's worst beaches: sand along the Riviera is in shorter supply than pebbles. By far the finest French beaches are those facing north (toward the Channel) and west (toward the Atlantic). Many are so vast that you can spread out even at the most popular resorts (like Biarritz, Royan, Dinard, or Le Touquet). Brittany's beaches are the most picturesque, though the water can be chilly, even in summer.

Shopping

Hunting for treasures in France can be a joy, as well as a frustration, as this proud isolationist country increasingly gives itself over to malls and chain stores. Not to worry: Paris is still the firm fashion capital, but more and more small towns are selling generic goods. You may be surprised to find that the same silk scarf you plan to purchase in France costs less in the mall at home, although it may be more fun to buy. For distinctly French souvenirs, it pays to look to the past: flea markets and *brocantes* (second-hand shops) sell Art Deco brooches, tiny eaux-de-vie glasses, and evocative old copies of *Paris Match*. And there's always the chance of finding a stray bit of Quimper faience. Another good bet is purchasing regional specialties, though your exports must be legal—madeleines, say, or nougat—as those savory sausages and glass jars of foie gras may be confiscated by customs.

Wine

From the chipped carafe of a coarse *vin de pays* on a local café table to the Gevrey-Chambertin decanted with surgical concentration by a linen-swathed sommelier to the perfect glass sampled at family-tended vineyard in Burgundy, wine is indispensable to the French experience. Intricately interlaced with the progress of a well-planned menu (the magical combination of certain foods with the right wines is referred to as a *bon mariage,* or a good marriage), wine can dominate your memory of a fine meal.

FODOR'S CHOICE

Châteaux

☆ **Chenonceau, Loire Valley.** The most romantic of them all, with arched galleries spanning the Cher, this palace owes its gardens to Catherine de' Medici.

☆ **Citadelle, Corte.** From its spectacular site high over the junction of three rivers, the fortress protects the earlier "Eagle's Nest" château and contains the Musée de la Corse.

☆ **Hautefort, Périgord.** Part medieval, part Renaissance, vast Hautefort raises an eclectic skyline above its gardens and is full of 17th-century furnishings.

☆ **Pierrefonds, Champagne.** This huge château, begun in the 12th century, was restored in the 1860s by the fairy-tale imagination of Viollet-le-Duc and the money of Napoléon III.

☆ **Vaux-le-Vicomte, Ile-de-France.** Louis XIV was so jealous of Nicolas Fouquet's new château that he jailed him on the spot and started work on Versailles to show who was boss. The sumptuous gardens and interior remain unchanged.

☆ **Versailles, Ile-de-France.** The world's grandest palace has it all: paintings, murals, gold-leafed furniture, the Hall of Mirrors, a landscaped park, a phony village, a giant canal, artful fountains, and shady glades.

☆ **Vitré, Brittany.** This triangular fortress, with fat, round towers, has stood guard at the gateway to Brittany since the 11th century.

Churches and Abbeys

☆ **Abbaye de St-Michel de Cuxa, Prades.** With its 10th-century pre-Romanesque arches and its elegant crypt, this abbey is one of the gems of the eastern Pyrénées.

☆ **Basilique, Vézelay.** This great pilgrim church, part-Romanesque, part-Gothic, gazes serenely over the rolling hills of Burgundy. Marvel at the miniature figures on the carved capitals in the nave.

☆ **Cathédrale, Chartres.** Take your binoculars to survey the world's finest collection of medieval stained-glass windows. The mighty, asymmetric spires dominate the flat grainlands for miles around.

☆ **Cathédrale Notre-Dame, Laon.** The hilltop setting—known as the Crowned Mountain—is the most spectacular of any French cathedral, bristling with elegant, openwork towers.

☆ **Cathédrale Notre-Dame, Amiens.** The colossal cathedral was built in 44 years during the 13th century; note the rose window and humorous carved misericords.

☆ **Cathédrale St-Étienne, Bourges.** Look for the towers of the cathedral as you approach on N151; inside, note its stained glass and the slender columns rising to an extraordinary height.

☆ **Église St-Joseph, Le Havre.** Concrete construction at its most spartan yet spectacular is represented in Auguste Perret's 1950s tour de force: part silo, part movie theater, part rocket.

☆ **Mont-St-Michel, Normandy.** From its silhouette against the horizon to the abbey and gardens at the peak of the rock, you'll never forget this awe-inspiring sight.

☆ **Notre-Dame de l'Espérance, Mézières.** All the windows of this elegant 15th-century church are filled with modern stained glass—the mix is sensational.

☆ **Notre-Dame-du-Haut, Ronchamp.** Some say that this free-form chapel is Le Corbusier's masterpiece—utterly individual, yet imbued with peace and calm.

Dining

☆ **L'Ami Fritz, Obernai.** The owner-chef serves succulent local specialties and his own wine at this rustic yet chic spot. *$$*

☆ **L'Assiette Gourmande, Honfleur.** The harbor-front setting on the coast of Normandy gives a hint that seafood is a strong point, but all Gérard Bonnefoy's food is to die for—including the delectable desserts. *$$–$$$*

⋆ **Bouchon d'Objectif, Cannes.** Popular and unpretentious, this tiny bistro serves inexpensive Provençal cuisine prepared with a sophisticated twist. $

⋆ **Boyer, Reims.** Chef Gérard Boyer's innovative cuisine and his extensive wine list draw sophisticated diners (and lodgers) to this opulent restaurant in a 19th-century château. $$$$

⋆ **Chez Yvonne, Strasbourg.** This chic yet cozy *weinstub* (inn) serves classic Alsatian fare and local wines to hip locals and heads of state. $

⋆ **Le Coq Gadby, Rennes.** Sample superb seafood dishes and traditional Breton specialities at this restaurant in a 19th-century mansion. $$–$$$

⋆ **La Corde, Toulouse.** It's worth finding this doyen of Toulouse restaurants, hidden in a small 15th-century tower in the courtyard of a 16th-century mansion. $$–$$$

⋆ **Euskalduna, Bayonne.** The traditional and rustic setting perfectly matches the authentic Basque *cuisine de terroir* (country cooking). $$

⋆ **Le Ferme Campo di Monte, Murato.** The Julliards prepare some of Corsica's best fare at their lovely 350-year-old farmhouse. $$

⋆ **Les Feuillants, Céret.** The cuisine at this restaurant, one of the best in the area, is yet another manifestation of the town's superb artistic endowment. $$$

⋆ **Les Magnolias, Plaisance.** Superb, sophisticated regional cooking is created by chef Francis Roussel and served in a wonderfully medieval ambience. $$

⋆ **Les Muses, Lyon.** Sit behind enormous statues of the muses on the roof of the opera house while lunching or dining on Philippe Chavent's inspired dishes. $$

⋆ **Philippe Detourbe, Paris.** Spectacular contemporary French cuisine is served at this unexpectedly glamourous restaurant. $$

⋆ **Pierre Gagnaire, Paris.** Legendary chef Pierre Gagnaire brings together at least three or four different tastes and textures in his sensational dishes. $$$$

⋆ **Pigeons Blancs, Cognac.** Chef Jacques Tachet's cooking would be worth a detour even if the handful of rooms weren't

charming and reasonable. His three-course carte du jour is a find. $$

⋆ **La Terrasse at Juana, Juan-les-Pins.** Chef Christian Morisset is on his way to becoming one of France's top chefs, with his delicious and exquisitely presented seafood dishes. $$$$

⋆ **Le Violon d'Ingres, Paris.** Chef Christian Constant, formerly of the Hôtel Crillon, has a hit on his hands with this very stylish spot serving excellent contemporary bistro fare. $$–$$$

Lodging

⋆ **Caron de Beaumarchais, Paris.** The theme of this intimate hotel in the heart of the Marais is the work of Caron de Beaumarchais, who wrote *The Marriage of Figaro* in 1778. Rooms reflect the taste of 18th-century French nobility. $$

⋆ **Castan, Besançon.** This exquisitely restored 18th-century manor house is just below the Citadelle in the heart of the old town; its rooms are lined with Franche-Comté bibelots and reproduction fabrics. $$$

⋆ **Castel-Clara, Belle-Ile.** Ask for a room with a view of the sea at this modern hotel perched on a cliff on the lovely island of Belle-Ile. $$–$$$

⋆ **Château de Courcelles, Soissons.** East of Soissons, along the Vesle River on the Champagne border, is this luxurious and refined château run by easygoing Frédéric Nouhaud. $$$

⋆ **Colombe d'Or, St-Paul-de-Vence.** Once a hangout for the likes of Klee, Picasso, and Utrillo, whose works are on the walls, this country inn now draws the rich and famous, for a meal or a stay. $$$

⋆ **La Cour des Loges, Lyon.** This stylish hotel, carved out of four Renaissance buildings, is an all-round delight. Relax in the tapas bar and swim in the heated pool. $$$$

⋆ **L'Hostellerie du Vieux Cordes, Cordes.** This old house around a wisteria-draped courtyard is an enchanting place to stay and eat in the opulent crimson dining rooms. $$

⋆ **Hôtels St-Albert et Montaigne, Sarlat-la-Canéda.** These comfortable hotels in the Périgord on the delightful town square share a good regional restaurant and the services of the pleasant Garrigou family. $–$$

★ **La Maison des Consuls, Mirepoix.** This extraordinary hotel is on the arcaded, medieval central square. $$$

★ **Le Maquis, Porticcio.** The evocatively named Maquis, by the sea, ranks as one of Corsica's finest *hôtels de charme*. $$$–$$$$

★ **Palais, Biarritz.** The spacious rooms, vast lawns, and the elegant mirrored dining room overlooking the sea recall the grandeur of the days when Empress Eugénie stayed here. $$$$

★ **Relais St-Germain, Paris.** Every room at this outstanding hotel in the heart of St-Germain-des-Prés has its own, unique treasures. $$$

★ **Les Templiers, Collioure.** No visit is complete without a stay at this warm and welcoming hotel filled with more than 2,500 original works of art. $$

★ **Le Tourville, Paris.** Both upscale and cozy, this hotel has crisp, virgin-white damask upholstery, a smattering of antique bureaus, original artwork, and fabulous old mirrors. $$–$$$

★ **La Treille Muscate, Cliousclat.** In this charming village halfway between Lyon and Avignon is this gem of a hotel with individually styled rooms and a delightful, inexpensive restaurant serving regional cuisine. $$

★ **33 rue Thiers, La Rochelle.** Amiable American owner Maybelle Iribe runs this small town-house inn with enthusiasm; rooms are delightfully unique; dinners are splendid. $$

★ **Le Vieux Logis, Les Eyzies-de-Tayac.** A stay at this old stone house, which has a pool and a garden, in the Dordogne is unforgettable; so are the chef's five-course meals. $$$–$$$$

Museums

★ **Fondation Maeght, St-Paul-de-Vence.** A small gem of a museum of modern art, it blends its stunning holdings with stylish presentation.

★ **Historial de la Grande Guerre, Péronne.** A spacious, imaginative display of maps, artifacts, newsreels, guns, and nightmarish lithographs rams home the horror of World War I.

★ **Louvre, Paris.** No matter how many times you've visited, be sure to come again; I. M. Pei's pyramid and newly opened exhibit rooms are stunning.

★ **Musée d'Art Modern, Céret.** This modern art museum has one of the best collections of French and Catalan artists ever assembled outside a major metropolis.

★ **Musée des Arts Décoratifs, Lyon.** You can see the well-displayed furniture, silverware, ceramics, and objects of early Lyonnaise life in a satisfying couple of hours.

★ **Musée des Beaux-Arts, Lille.** This fine-arts museum in Lille is one of the largest French museums outside of Paris.

★ **Musée Condé, Chantilly.** The château houses a remarkable collection of illuminated manuscripts, tapestries, furniture, paintings, Fouquet miniatures, and stained glass.

★ **Musée Fesch, Ajaccio.** Wonderful Italian Old Masters make up the museum's collection.

★ **Musée Ingres, Montauban.** Drawings and paintings by the great French classicist and works from his own collection are housed in this museum in the former Bishop's Palace.

★ **Musée Matisse, Le Cateau.** The Palais Fénelon is now home to paintings, sculpture, and drawings by the town's native son.

★ **Musée de l'Oeuvre Notre-Dame, Strasbourg.** This museum is much more than just a collection of weathered statues rescued from the cathedral; an effort has been made to create a churchlike atmosphere.

★ **Palais de la Berbie, Albi.** The world's greatest collection of works by Henri de Toulouse-Lautrec are housed in this former fortress with gardens designed by André Le Nôtre.

GREAT ITINERARIES

So, you want to taste France, gaze at its beauty, and inhale its special joie de vivre—all in a one-week to 10-day trip. Let's assume at least that you've seen Paris, and you're ready to venture into the countryside. Here are some itineraries to help you plan your trip. Or create your own route using the suggested itineraries in each chapter.

France for First-Timers

If this is your first time in France, this itinerary will give you a feel for the country's tremendous variety—its Continental heart in the north and its Mediterranean soul in the south. This is the route Parisians used to follow, slowly, surely, heading south to the Mediterranean, feasting and sightseeing along the way.

DURATION➤ 7–10 Days.

THE MAIN ROUTE➤ **Two nights: Vézelay, Saulieu,** or **Beaune.** Visit the medieval basilica and Beaune's Hôtel-Dieu. En route note the virgin forests and the hills and small family-tended vineyards of Burgundy, easing your passage with the memorable *dégustation* (tasting) available free at many of them. Dine in Lyon.

Two to three nights: Avignon and **Provence.** Visit the Roman ruins, medieval towns, and the fields of aromatic lavender and of the towering sunflowers that van Gogh painted.

Two to three nights: Cannes and the **Côte d'Azur.** Take a swim in the Mediterranean at one of the trendy (even topless) French beaches. Walk through Èze or another medieval hilltop village. Depending on your inclination, say a prayer at the Matisse Chapel near Vence, or lose your remaining francs at Monte Carlo's Belle Époque casino.

GETTING AROUND➤ It's best to rent a car in Paris for this itinerary. If you travel by train, the TGV speeds through Burgundy and Lyon to the coast, stopping in major cities along the way. You'll have to arrange transport into the countryside or rent a bicycle at the train station.

INFORMATION➤ *See* Chapters 9, 10, 12, and 13.

France for the Family

Suave and sophisticated may be what comes to mind when thinking of France, but there's another side to this varied country: a love for children that extends to even the youngest.

DURATION➤ 6–8 Days.

THE MAIN ROUTE➤ **One or two nights: Étretat and Fécamp.** Take a walk on Étretat's cliffs and explore Fécamp's fishing port.

Two nights: Deauville. Visit the casino and the beach. Make an excursion to the charming fishing town of Honfleur.

One night: Bayeux. Visit the medieval tapestries and the D-day beaches.

Three nights: Brittany. Start at Mont-St-Michel and make your way west. Sample the crepes and enjoy the views.

GETTING AROUND➤ Normandy is only a few hours from Paris, although it takes up to five hours to reach its western end. Traveling around Normandy and Brittany is almost impossible without a car.

Trains leave from Gare St-Lazare for Deauville and other Normandy destinations; trains to Brittany leave from Gare Montparnasse.

INFORMATION➤ *See* Chapters 5 and 6.

France for Wine Lovers

French vineyards can be just as spectacular as the wines they produce. This itinerary concentrates on the eastern corridor of France from Champagne to Châteauneuf-du-Pape, if only because there is more concentrated variety here than in the Loire Valley or the Cognac and Bordeaux regions.

DURATION➤ 8 Days.

THE MAIN ROUTE➤ **One night: Épernay.** Drive to Reims and visit one of the city-based producers. Take the pretty Route du Vin wine road south along the Montagne de Reims, and pay homage to Dom Pérignon, the monk who created champagne, at Hautvillers.

One night: Auxerre. Head south through southern Champagne, via historic Troyes, to Les Riceys, where vertiginous slopes yield France's priciest rosé. Continue southwest to Auxerre via the equally mountainous vineyards of Chablis.

Two nights: Beaune. Visit the pretty wine villages just south of Auxerre. Take the expressway to Dijon to join the short, scenic Route du Vin, lined with some of the world's most famous wine-producing villages, to Beaune. Visit the Marché aux

Vins in Beaune for an extensive sampling. The next day make an excursion to the Jura, visiting Arbois and clifftop Château-Chalon.

One night: Villefranche-sur-Saône. Head south along the west bank of the Saône through the Beaujolais Wine Road.

One night: Valence. Bypass Lyon and drive through (or rather beneath) the increasingly steep vineyards of Côte Rotie and St-Joseph. Cross the Rhône at Tain-l'Hermitage near Tournon to admire the famous Hermitage vineyards. Pause at Cornas just before you reach Valence.

One night: Orange. Tour the rocky, sunbaked vineyards of Châteauneuf-du-Pape, just south of Orange, and explore the villages to the east, beneath the towering slopes of Mont Ventoux.

GETTING AROUND➤ Reims is just 90 minutes east of Paris by car. Visiting vineyards and wine villages is impossible without a car (preferably one with a biggish trunk). But go easy on the *dégustations* (tastings).

INFORMATION➤ *See* Chapters 7, 9, 10, and 12.

Outdoor France

France has far more to offer than just museums, palaces, cathedrals, and restaurants. You can enjoy nature at its most varied, with everything from verdant marshlands and sandy beaches to endless pine forests, deep gorges, and towering mountains—all within a few hours' drive.

DURATION➤ 14 Days.

THE MAIN ROUTE➤ **One night: Coulon.** In this sleepy, waterside village, you will encounter the Marais Poitevin, nicknamed Green Venice for its tree-lined canals. Explore the banks by bike, rowboat, or foot—or hire a punt, a boat maneuvered with a long wooden pole by a garrulous local guide.

Two nights: La Rochelle. Stroll around the pretty port of La Rochelle, and then take a boat trip to any of the neighboring islands—Ile de Ré, Ile de'Aix, or Ile d'Oléron—where you can rent bikes and explore old fortresses. Make an early start south after your second night; walk the ramparts at historic Brouage. Continue via the long sandy beach of the Côte Sauvage—ideal for swimming or sunbathing—to

Royan. From here take the *bac* (ferry) across the Gironde estuary. Head south to Lac d'Hourtin, which has excellent canoeing and waterskiing facilities.

One night: Arcachon. You can ride, dive, and play golf at this busy Belle Époque resort town. Or take a boat across the lagoon to inspect the nearby oyster beds.

One night: Biarritz. Stop en route at the Dune du Pilat, Europe's highest sand dune. Then meander through the pines of the flat Landes forest, stopping for a picnic or a game of boules if the fancy takes you. Ritzy Biarritz has cliffs, magnificent beaches, and the coast's best surfing.

One night: Ste-Engrâce. Head east into the foothills of the Pyrénées. The area around Ste-Engrâce is great hiking country, particularly the Gorges de Kakouetta.

Two nights: Lourdes. Drive east to Lourdes. Spend the afternoon at the spa town of Cauterets, and then take the chairlift at Pont d'Espagne for a view of the bright blue Lac de Gaube and beyond. The next day, head south along spectacular D921 to Gavarnie to see its famous cirque. Rent a horse or donkey to explore the mountains.

One night: Foix. Head east, via St-Gaudens and St-Girons, to the peaceful town of Foix. The rivers here are excellent for fishing. You might also enjoy a boat trip down the Rivière Souterraine de Labouiche, a mysterious underground river.

One night: Plaisance. Wander through the Limoux vineyards, famous for their sparkling wine. Have lunch in Carcassonne, followed by a walk around the spectacular town walls. Continue north over the scenic Montagne Noire and spend the night at the hotel-restaurant in Plaisance.

Two nights: Ispagnac. Drive up through Millau and spend the next two days exploring the Gorges du Tarn and the Gorges de la Jonte. Both are good places to hike, mountain bike, raft, or canoe.

One night: Clermont-Ferrand or La Grande-Motte. From Ispagnac, you have two choices. Either head north, farther into the Massif Central, taking in spectacular Le Puy-en-Velay on your way to the extinct volcanoes (you can survey them from a hot-air balloon at the Puy-du-Dôme) ringing Clermont-Ferrand. Or plunge south toward the bustling city of Montpellier and the nearby Mediterranean resort town of La Grand Motte.

GETTING AROUND➤ Although La Rochelle, Royan, Archachon, Biarritz, Lourdes, and Clermont-Ferrand are all reachable by train, this entire itinerary can only be done by car. Coulon, in the Marais Poitevin, and the first stop on this itinerary, is a four-hour drive from Paris (take A10 as far as Niort).

INFORMATION➤ *See* Chapters 11, 12, 13, 15, 16, and 17.

Palatial France

The French Revolution ended the old regime, but many of the buildings remain—palaces of local seigneurs and châteaux reserved for the king.

DURATION➤ 5–7 Days.

THE MAIN ROUTE➤ **One to two nights: Versailles** and the **Vallée de Chevreuse.** Visit the châteaux and **Chartres Cathedral.**

Three nights: Tours. Visit Blois, Chambord, Cheverny, and Chenonceau in the Loire Valley.

One night: Fontainebleau and **Vaux-le-Vicomte.**

GETTING AROUND➤ Versailles is only a 30-minute drive from downtown Paris (avoid rush hours). The Loire Valley is two hours from the capital via A10, or you can take the more leisurely N10 via Chartres to Tours.

The TGV gets to Tours in little more than an hour, and buses run from the train stations to many of the châteaux. You can also rent bicycles at the train stations to get to the châteaux; the valley is flat and easy to navigate. But by far the easiest way to follow this itinerary is by car.

INFORMATION➤ *See* Chapters 3 and 4.

FESTIVALS AND SEASONAL EVENTS

France is a festival all year round, with special events taking place throughout the country. For full museum, theater, and concert information, be sure to check the listings in *Pariscope* (which includes reviews in English of the week's main events and new restaurants), *Officiel des Spectacles*, or *Figaroscope*, on arrival in Paris. The *International Herald Tribune* also lists special events in its weekend edition, but not in great detail. The most complete listing of festivals comes in a small pamphlet published by the **Maison de la France** (☞ Visitor Information *in* the Gold Guide).

Annual highlights include the Nice Carnival in February, the Cannes Film Festival and the French Open Tennis Championships in May, the Fête de la Musique throughout France in June, the Tour de France bike race and Bastille Day in July, and Paris's Autumn Festival in September.

➤ DEC.: On the 24th, a Christmas celebration known as the **Shepherd's Festival**, featuring midnight Mass and picturesque "living crèches," is held in Les Baux, Provence. From the end of November through the New Year, Strasbourg mounts its famous **Christmas Market**, with echoes of German gemütlichkeit.

Christmas in Paris spells celebrations, especially for children, from late December to early January. A giant crèche is set up on the square in front of the Hôtel de Ville (City Hall), and there are automated window displays in the *grands magasins* (department stores) on boulevard Haussmann. Street illuminations are hung in towns throughout the country. Big events are planned throughout France for New Year's Eve of **L'An 2000** (The Year 2000), especially in Paris and around the Eiffel Tower.

➤ JAN.: The **International Circus Festival**, featuring top acts from around the world, and the **Monte Carlo Motor Rally**, one of the motoring world's most venerable races, are held in Monaco. Wine-producing villages throughout France celebrate **St. Vincent's Day** with festivities on January 22 in honor of their patron saint. The **Tournament St-Vincent**, a colorful Burgundy wine festival, takes place on the third weekend in a different wine village each year. Buy a cup for about 30 francs and then drink as much as you like—or just frolic in the decorated streets. Angoulême hosts the world's biggest and most popular comic-book festival, the **Fête de la Bande Dessinée**.

➤ FEB.: The **Carnival de Nice** provides an exotic blend of parades and revelry during the weeks leading up to Lent. Other cities and villages also have their own smaller versions. **The Carnival de Dunkerque** on the weekend before Shrove Tuesday is the most rambunctious street carnival in northern France. The lively four-day **Carnival de Granville** in Normandy also takes place on the weekend before Shrove Tuesday.

➤ MAR.: The **Salon de Mars**, an art and antiques fair, and the **Salon du Livre**, France's biggest book festival, take place in Paris. The largest international exhibit of flowers and plants from all over the world, **Fleurissimo**, will take place in Dijon this year.

➤ APR.: The **Monte Carlo Open Tennis Championships** get under way at the ultraswank Monte Carlo Country Club. The **son-et-lumière show** at Beaune's Hôtel-Dieu every night from April to mid-November is brilliantly done. The **Foire de Paris** is a giant fair with products, including food, wine, and cheese, and agricultural displays from all over France; it's held at the Porte de Versailles in Paris at the end of the month.

➤ MAY: The **Cannes Film Festival** sees two weeks of star-studded events. Classical concert festivals get under way throughout the country. At the end of the month, the **French Open Tennis Championships** are held at Roland Garros Stadium in Paris. Rouen celebrates the national heroine, Joan of Arc, with the **Fête Jeanne d'Arc.** Until September, the **Grandes Eaux** (Louis XIV's splendid fountains) come alive in the park of Versailles on Sunday afternoons.

SUMMER

➤ JUNE: From now until September you will find **son-et-lumière** (sound-and-light) shows—historical pageants featuring special lighting effects—at many French châteaux, especially in the Loire Valley. Throughout France, there is dancing in the streets during the musical festival, the **Fête de la Musique,** on June 21. Strasbourg's **Fête de la Musique** features concerts in the Cathédrale Notre-Dame and various halls. This is a popular time for horse races: The **Prix du Président de la République** is run at the Hippodrome de Vincennes, the **Grand Steeplechase de Paris** is at the Auteuil Racecourse, and the **Grand Prix de Paris,** for equine three-year-olds, is at Longchamp Racecourse.

The **24 Heures du Mans,** the famous 24-hour car race, is held in Le Mans. The **Paris Air Show,** which takes place in odd-numbered years only, is a display of old and new planes and an update on worldwide technological developments in the aeronautical industry, at Le Bourget Airport near Paris. On the last weekend in June, the **Fête du Cinéma** allows you to take in as many movies

as you can for the price of a single ticket.

➤ JULY: The **summer arts festival season** gets into full swing, particularly in Provence. Avignon offers a month of top-notch theater, Aix-en-Provence specializes in opera, Carpentras in religious music, Nice holds a big Jazz Festival, and Arles mounts a big photography festival. Northern France's spectacular **Fête de Gayant** (festival of the *giant,* in local patois) is held in Douai on the first Sunday after July 5. From July 9 to 18, the **Armada du Siècle,** an amazing regala of antique wood boats, takes place in Rouen. Most important, the **Tour de France,** the world's most famous bicycle race, dominates national attention for three weeks before crossing the finish line on the Champs-Élysées on the last Sunday of the month.

On **Bastille Day** (July 14) all of France commemorates the Storming of the Bastille in 1789—the start of the French Revolution. Look out for fireworks, free concerts, and street festivities beginning the evening of the 13th, including the Bal des Pompiers (Firemen's Ball) organized by local firemen.

➤ AUG.: If you want to see something you're likely never to see again, on August 11 there will be a total **eclipse** of the sun and the best view is in France. Between 10:20 and 10:30 AM, the area between Strasbourg and Le Havre will be in total blackness, something astronomers have not seen for more than one hundred years. On **Assump-**

tion (August 15) many towns, notably Chartres and Lisieux, hold religious festivals and processions dedicated to the Virgin Mary. On the first Sunday following August 15, the **Festival de la Force Basque** in St-Palais brings together participants from eight villages to compete in contests of strength. The most famous annual religious festival in Brittany is the *pardon* in Ste-Anne-la-Palud, near Quimper, on the last Sunday of August.

AUTUMN

➤ SEPT.: The **vendanges,** grape harvests, begin and festivals are held in the country's wine regions. South of Lille, the **Fête d'Ail** in Arleux is a celebration of garlic. The **Grande Braderie** turns Lille into one giant street fair on the month's first weekend. Every two even years (next in 2000), on the first weekend in September, medieval France is re-created at Dinan's **Fête des Remparts.** The **Fête de Musique de Besançon et Franche-Comté** consists of a series of chamber music concerts in and around Besançon during the month. The **Fête d'Automne,** a major arts and film festival, opens in Paris and continues until December. The **Rencontres Polyphoniques** in Calvi is an excellent chance to hear authentic Corsican music. The world's most stylish antiques fair, the **Paris Biennale,** is held in the capital (even years only). The **Journée du**

Patrimoine, on the Sunday nearest to September 21, opens the doors of many official and private buildings usually closed to the public. The **Biarritz Film Festival,** held in late September, features films from Latin America.

➤ OCT.: The **Prix de l'Arc de Triomphe,** horseracing's most prestigious flat race, is held at Longchamp Racecourse in Paris on the first Sunday of the month. A giant contemporary art exhibition called **FIAC** takes place in Paris early in the month. The **Paris**

Auto Show (even-numbered years only) features the latest developments in the international automobile industry. The weeklong **Paris Indoor Open** attracts the world's top tennis players at the end of the month.

➤ NOV.: **Les Trois Glorieuses,** Burgundy's biggest wine festival, features the year's most important wine auction and related merriment in several Burgundy locations. The **Festiventu** in Calvi (Corsica) is a celebration of wind-related

activities ranging from Windsurfers to woodwinds. Nationwide **Armistice Day** ceremonies on November 11 commemorate veterans of World Wars I and II; in Paris, there's a military parade down the Champs-Élysées. On the third Thursday in November, France—especially Paris—celebrates the arrival of the **Beaujolais Nouveau.** The **Salon des Caves Particulières,** a giant wine fair for independent producers, is held in Paris at the end of the month.

2 Paris

Bearing the marks of 2,000 years of history and a rich cultural heritage, Paris overwhelms, astonishes, and surprises. From the heights of the Arc de Triomphe, the city swaggers with the knowledge that it is at the pinnacle of architectural beauty, artistic development, and culinary delight. On its intimate, winding streets, the city invites unhurried exploration.

IF THERE'S A PROBLEM WITH A TRIP TO PARIS, it is the embarrassment of riches that faces you. A city of vast, noble perspectives and winding, hidden streets, Paris remains a combination of the pompous and the intimate. Whether you've come looking for sheer physical beauty, cultural and artistic diversions, world-famous dining and shopping, history, or simply local color, you will find it here in abundance.

Pleasures and Pastimes

Cafés

People-watching, some would say, is what Paris is all about; and there's no better place to indulge in this pursuit than the terrace of a sidewalk café. Favored locales include place St-Michel, boulevard du Montparnasse, and place St-Germain-des-Prés, on the Left Bank; and place de l'Opéra, the Champs-Élysées, and Les Halles, on the Right Bank. But you may enjoy seeking out your own (less expensive) local haunts.

Churches

Paris is rich in churches of two architectural styles: the 15th- to 16th-century overlap of Flamboyant Gothic and Renaissance (at St-Gervais, St-Étienne du Mont, St-Eustache, and St-Séverin) and 17th-century Baroque with domes and two-tiered facades (at Les Invalides, Val de Grâce, and St-Paul–St-Louis). But the city's most enduring religious symbols are medieval (Notre-Dame Cathedral and Ste-Chapelle) and 19th-century (Sacré-Coeur and La Madeleine).

Dining

Whether your dream meal is savoring truffle-studded foie gras on Limoges china or breaking the crust of a steaming cassoulet in a thick crockery bowl, you can find it in Paris. The city remains one of the world's great food capitals, despite some rumblings about sliding standards and increasingly bland fare. For most, the prospect of eating here is exciting; for you, it may be the main reason for a trip.

Museums

Paris has a plethora of museums. Alongside the four superstars—the Louvre, the Musée d'Orsay, the Centre Pompidou (unfortunately, temporarily closed for renovations until 2000), and the Cité des Sciences at la Villette—are such underestimated delights as the Musée National du Moyen Age (medieval works of art) and single-artist museums dedicated to the works of Picasso, Rodin, Dalí, and Maillol.

Shopping

Window-shopping is one of Paris's great spectator sports. Tastefully displayed wares—luscious cream-filled éclairs, lacy lingerie, rare artwork, gleaming copper pots—entice the eye and awaken the imagination. Happily, shopping opportunities in Paris are endless and geared to every taste. You can price emerald earrings at Cartier, spend an afternoon browsing through bookstalls along the Seine, buy silk-lined gloves at Dior, tour the high-gloss department stores, or bargain over prices in the sprawling flea markets on the outskirts of town.

EXPLORING PARIS

Revised and updated by Simon Hewitt

For visitors, Paris is a practical city: It is relatively small as capitals go, with many of its major sites and museums within walking distance of one another. The city is divided into 20 *arrondissements* (districts). The last two digits of the zip code (e.g., 75002) will tell you the arrondissement (the 2e, or 2nd). The city's principal tourist axis is less than 6½ km (4 mi) long, running parallel to the north bank of the Seine between the Arc de Triomphe and the Bastille. In fact, the best method of getting to know Paris is on foot, although public transportation—particularly the métro system—is excellent. Buy a *Plan de Paris* booklet: a city map-guide with a street-name index that also shows métro stations. Note that all métro stations have a detailed neighborhood map just inside the entrance (☞ Getting Around *in* Paris A to Z, *below*, for a map of the Paris métro).

Paris owes both its development and much of its visual appeal to the Seine River, which weaves through it. Each bank of the Seine has its own personality; the *Rive Droite* (Right Bank), with its spacious boulevards and formal buildings, generally has a more genteel feel than the carefree *Rive Gauche* (Left Bank) to the south. The historical and geographical heart of the city is Notre-Dame Cathedral on the Ile de la Cité, the larger of the Seine's two islands (the other is the Ile St-Louis).

Our coverage of Paris is divided into nine neighborhood walks. There are several "musts" that you may not want to miss: the Eiffel Tower, the Champs-Élysées, the Louvre, and Notre-Dame. A few monuments and museums close for lunch, between noon and 2, and many are closed on either Monday or Tuesday. Check before you set off. Admission prices listed are for adults, but often there are special rates for students, children, and senior citizens. Keep in mind that cafés in Paris are open all day long; they are a great boon if you are weary and in need of a coffee, a beer, or a sandwich; *boulangeries* (bakeries) are also good for snacks or sandwiches on the run.

Numbers in the text correspond to numbers in the margin and on the Paris and Montmartre maps.

Great Itineraries

A visit to Paris will never be quite as simple as a quick look at a few landmarks. Each *quartier* (neighborhood) has its own treasures, and you should be ready to explore—a very pleasant prospect in this elegant city. Outlined here are the main areas to concentrate on depending on the length of your stay. Bear in mind that the amount of time spent visiting monuments—and museums in particular—is not something you can, or would want to, predict with any certainty. Also, to see the city's large museums, let alone its smaller ones, you probably need at least a week in Paris.

IF YOU HAVE 3 DAYS

On your first day, get your bearings—and an overview of the city's attractive waterfront—by taking a trip along the Seine on a Bateau Mouche (from place de l'Alma) or a Vedette (from the square du Vert-Galant). Visit Notre-Dame Cathedral and, if you enjoy medieval architecture, the nearby Ste-Chapelle on Ile de la Cité; then cross the Seine to the Left Bank and explore the Latin Quarter, using the Panthéon dome as a landmark. End your day in the Luxembourg Gardens, close by. Spend your second day exploring the noble vista between the Arc de Triomphe and the Louvre: Start at the Arc (that way it's all downhill) and work along the Champs-Élysées, across place de la Concorde and the Tuileries Gardens (with the Orangerie and Jeu de Paume museums) to the Louvre. Divide your third day between the Eiffel Tower, the Musée d'Orsay, and Montmartre.

IF YOU HAVE 6 DAYS

Follow the three-day itinerary; then spend one day exploring the Marais and Ile St-Louis, and another combining a visit to the Left Bank's St-Germain and the nearby Invalides. For good shopping and a look at Haussmann's 19th-century Paris, walk down the Right Bank's rue

Paris with Arrondissements

ST-OUEN

CLICHY

PORTE DE
CLICHY

PORTE DE
ST-OUEN

COURBEVOIE

LEVALLOIS-
PERRET

PORTE
D'ASNIÈRES

bd. Berthier

bd. Bessières

av. de Clichy

av. de St-Ouen

LA
DÉFENSE

PORTE
CHAMPERRET

BATIGNOLLES

17e

Cimetière c
Montmartre

pt. de Neuilly

av. Charles de Gaulle

NEUILLY-SUR-
SEINE

PORTE DES
TERNES

av. de Wagram

av. de Villiers

bd. des Batignolles

R. d'Amsterdam

P

bd.

PORTE
MAILLOT

TERNES

bd. de Courcelles

Parc
Monceau

Gare
St-Lazare

OP

av. de la Grande
Armée

Bois de
Boulogne

PORTE
DAUPHINE

av. Foch

Arc de
Triomphe

av. de Friedland

bd. Haussmann

av. Kléber

av. des Champs

av. Marceau

av. George V

av. F. D. Roosevelt

8e

La Madeleine

Opéra

Opéra

bd. Lannes

av. Victor Hugo

CHAILLOT

Petite
Palais

pl.
Vendôme

r. Faubour

PORTE DE
LA MUETTE

pl. du
Trocadéro

av. du Pres. Wilson

-Elysées

Grand Palais

pl. de la
Concorde

r. de Rivoli

Jardin des
Tuileries

16e

Palais
de Chaillot

quai d'Orsay

Musée
d'Orsay

PASSY

Tour
Eiffel

av. de la Bourdonnais

7e

ST-GERMA

bd. Suchet

bd. Périphérique

av. du Pres. Kennedy

av. de Suffren

bd. de Grenelle

Hôtel des
Invalides

av. de
Breteuil

r. de Sèvres

bd. Raspail

6e

Pe
Lu

Le

AUTEUIL

PORTE
D'AUTEUIL

École
Militaire

av. Emile Zola

GRENELLE

r. Lecourbe

r. de Vaugirard

bd. du Montparnass

bd.
Exelmans

PORTE DE
ST-CLOUD

r. de la Convention

15e

av. F. Faure

Gare
Montparnasse

MONTPARNA

PORTE
DE SÈVRES

bd. Victor

r. de Vaugirard

r. d'Alésia

av. du Maine

av. du Gl. Leclerc

bd. Galliéni

r. Ernest Renan

PORTE DE
VERSAILLES

bd. Lefebvre

14e

bd. Brune

bd. Ma
J

av. Victor Cresson

VANVES

PORTE DE
CHATILLON

Unive

ISSY-LES-
MOULINEAUX

PORTE DE
CHATILLON

MONTROUGE

PORTE
D'ORLEANS

Faubourg St-Honoré and join the Grand Boulevards by the Madeleine church; continue past the Opéra toward place de la République.

You can attack the city's "other" museums—the Picasso and Rodin—after following the six-day itinerary. Check out Montparnasse and some of the attractions on the edge of the city, all reachable by métro: Père Lachaise Cemetery and the Parc de la Villette; the Bois de Boulogne to the west, plus the futuristic area of La Défense; or the Bois de Vincennes to the east. You may also wish to take a day trip to Versailles or other points of interest in the region (☞ Chapter 3).

From the Arc de Triomphe to the Louvre

The Arc de Triomphe stands foursquare at the top of the city's most famous avenue: the Champs-Élysées. Site of most French national celebrations, the Champs-Élysées is the last leg of the Tour de France bicycle race on the third or fourth Sunday in July and the site of vast ceremonies on Bastille Day (July 14) and Armistice Day (November 11). Explore both its commercial upper half and its verdant lower section, sloping down gracefully to place de la Concorde, with its Egyptian obelisk. Beyond lie the Tuileries Gardens and the gleaming glass pyramid of the world's largest museum, the Louvre. Local charm is not a feature of this exclusive sector of western Paris; it's beautiful, grand—and a little impersonal. The French moan that it's losing its character, and, as you notice the number of fast-food joints along the Champs-Élysées, you'll know what they mean—though renovation has gone some way to restoring the street's legendary elegance.

A Good Walk

The colossal, 164-ft **Arc de Triomphe** ① sits on place Charles-de-Gaulle, known to Parisians as "L'Étoile," or "The Star," a reference to the streets that fan out from it. This is Europe's most chaotic traffic circle: Short of a death-defying dash, your only way of getting to the Arc de Triomphe in the middle is to take an underground passage from the far side of avenue des Champs-Élysées. The view from the top of the Arc de Triomphe illustrates the star effect of the 12 radiating avenues and enables you to admire the vista down the **Champs-Élysées** toward place de la Concorde and the distant Louvre. West of the Champs-Élysées, and visible from the Arc de Triomphe, are the beautiful **Bois de Boulogne** ② and the towering office buildings and ultramodern arch of **La Défense** ③.

Walk down the Champs-Élysées and stop by the **Office de Tourisme de la Ville de Paris** at No. 127 (☞ Visitor Information *in* Paris A to Z, *below*). Continue to the Rond-Point and turn right onto the spacious avenue Franklin-D.-Roosevelt. Some 200 yards down is the glass-roofed **Grand Palais** ④, which forms an attractive duo with the Petit Palais on the other side of avenue Winston-Churchill.

The leafy lower reaches of the Champs-Élysées, with well-tended gardens off to the left, lead to the broad, airy **place de la Concorde** ⑤. Across place de la Concorde, facing the Champs-Élysées, two smallish buildings stand sentinel to the Jardin des Tuileries. Nearest the rue de Rivoli is the **Musée du Jeu de Paume** ⑥, and nearer the Seine is the **Musée de l'Orangerie** ⑦.

Stroll through the royally landscaped **Jardin des Tuileries** ⑧ and survey the surrounding cityscape. Manicured lawns and eccentric diagonal hedges lead on toward the Arc du Carrousel, a small relation of the distant Arc de Triomphe. Cross the paved esplanade, past Louis

XIV on his rearing bronze steed, to I. M. Pei's famous glass pyramid entry to the **Louvre** ⑨.

TIMING

You can probably cover this walk in a couple of hours, but if you wish to ascend the Eiffel Tower, take a trip along the Seine, or visit any of the plethora of museums along the way, you'd be best off allowing most of the day.

Sights to See

★ ❶ **Arc de Triomphe.** This colossal, 164-foot arch was planned by Napoléon but not finished until 1836, 20 years after Napoléon's rule. It is decorated with some magnificent sculpture by François Rude, such as the *Departure of the Volunteers*, better known as *La Marseillaise*, situated to the right of the arch when viewed from the Champs-Élysées. There is a small museum halfway up the arch devoted to its history. France's Unknown Soldier is buried beneath the archway; the flame is rekindled every evening at 6:30. ⊠ *pl. Charles-de-Gaulle,* ☎ *01–43–80–31–31.* ⚏ *35 frs.* ☉ *Daily 9:30 AM–11 PM; winter, daily 10–10. Métro, RER: Étoile.*

❷ **Bois de Boulogne** (Boulogne Woods). Class and style have been associated with this 2,200-acre park—known to Parisians as "Le Bois"—ever since it was landscaped into an upper-class playground by Baron Haussmann in the 1850s. That onetime glamour is emphasized by Haussmann's approach road from the Arc de Triomphe: avenue Foch, Paris's widest boulevard (120 yards across). The park is crisscrossed by broad, leafy roads, home to rowers, joggers, strollers, riders, *pétanque* (a game also known as *boules,* similar to boccie) players, picnickers, and lovers. The manifold attractions of Le Bois include cafés, restaurants, lakes, waterfalls, gardens, and museums. Rowboats can be rented at the **Lac Inférieur** and **Lac Supérieur.** The Fête à Neu-Neu, a giant carnival, takes place every September and October around the two lakes. Meetings at **Longchamp** and **Auteuil** racetracks are high on the social calendar, as is the French Open tennis tournament at the beautiful **Roland Garros** stadium in late May. Buses traverse the Bois de Boulogne during the day (service 244 from Porte Maillot), but Le Bois becomes a distinctly adult playground after dark, when prostitutes of various genders come prowling for clients. ⊠ *Main entrance at bottom of av. Foch. Métro: Porte Maillot, Porte Dauphine, or Porte d'Auteuil; Bus 244.*

Champs-Élysées. The 2-km (1-mi) Champs-Élysées was originally laid out in the 1660s by the landscape gardener Le Nôtre as a garden sweeping away from the Tuileries. Explore both its commercial upper half and its verdant lower section. *Métro: George-V, Franklin-D.-Roosevelt.*

❸ **La Défense.** French planners, with their usual desire to rationalize, ordained that modern high-rise development be banished to the outskirts at La Défense, just west of Paris. The soaring skyscrapers are mainly taken up by offices, with no expense spared in the pursuit of visual ingenuity. The highlight is the giant **Grande Arche de La Défense,** aligned with avenue de la Grande-Armée, the Arc de Triomphe, the Champs-Élysées, and the Louvre. Tubular glass elevators whisk you to the top. ⊠ *Parvis de La Défense,* ☎ *01–49–07–27–57.* ⚏ *Arch 40 frs.* ☉ *Arch daily 10–7. Métro: Grande Arche de La Défense; RER: La Défense.*

❹ **Grand Palais** (Grand Palace). With its curved glass roof, the Grand Palais is unmistakable when approached from either the Seine or the Champs-Élysées and forms an attractive duo with the **Petit Palais** on the other side of avenue Winston-Churchill. Both were built for the World's Fair of 1900, and, as with the Eiffel Tower, there was never any intention

Paris

that they would be permanent additions to the city. Unfortunately, the Grand Palais was closed for renovation in 1994 and is unlikely to re-open before 2000. But the Petit Palais contains a permanent collection of French painting and furniture, with splendid canvases by Courbet and Bouguereau. ⊠ *av. Winston-Churchill,* ☎ *01–42–65–12–73.* ⌷ *27 frs.* ⊙ *Tues.–Sun. 10–5:30. Métro: Champs-Élysées–Clemenceau.*

🖐 ❽ **Jardin des Tuileries** (Tuileries Garden). The recently renovated Tuileries Garden is typically French: formal and neatly patterned, with statues, rows of trees, and gravel paths. This is a delightful place to stroll and survey the surrounding cityscape. *Métro: Tuileries.*

❾ **Louvre.** Though it is now a coherent, unified structure, the Louvre—the world's largest museum—is the product of centuries. Originally built by Philippe-Auguste in the 13th century as a fortress, it was not until the reign of pleasure-loving François I, 300 years later, that today's Louvre gradually began to take shape. Through the years, Henri IV (1589–1610), Louis XIII (1610–43), Louis XIV (1643–1715), Napoléon (1804–14), and Napoléon III (1852–70) all contributed to its construction. The recent history of the Louvre centers on I. M. Pei's glass Pyramid, unveiled in March of 1989.

The number one attraction for most visitors is Leonardo da Vinci's enigmatic **Mona Lisa** (*La Joconde* to the French); be forewarned that you will find it encased in glass and surrounded by a mob of tourists. The collections are divided into seven sections: Asian antiquities; Egyptian antiquities; Greek and Roman antiquities; sculpture; paintings, prints, and drawings; furniture; and objets d'art. Don't try to see it all at once; try, instead, to make repeat visits—the admission is nearly half price on Sundays and after 3 PM on other days. (Unless you plan on going to a number of museums every day, the one-, three-, and five-day tourist museum passes probably aren't worth your money since you could easily spend a whole day at the Louvre alone.) Some other highlights of the paintings are *Shepherds in Arcadia,* by Nicolas Poussin (1594–1665); *The Oath of the Horatii,* by Jacques-Louis David (1748–1825); *The Raft of the Medusa,* by Théodore Géricault (1791–1824); and *La Grande Odalisque,* by Jean-Auguste-Dominique Ingres (1780–1867). The French crown jewels (in the objets d'art section of the Richelieu Wing) include the mind-boggling 186-carat Regent diamond. The *Winged Victory of Samothrace* seems poised for flight at the top of the stairs, and another much-loved piece of sculpture is Michelangelo's pair of *Slaves,* intended for the tomb of Pope Julius II. These can be admired in the Denon Wing, where a new medieval and Renaissance sculpture section is housed partly in the former imperial stables. In 1997 new rooms for Persian, Arab, Greek, and Egyptian art were opened. ⊠ *Palais du Louvre,* ☎ *01–40–20–51–51.* ⌷ *45 frs; 26 frs after 3 PM and on Sun.; free 1st Sun. of the month.* ⊙ *Thurs.–Sun. 9–6, Mon. and Wed. 9 AM–9:45 PM. Some sections open limited days. Métro: Palais-Royal.*

❻ **Musée du Jeu de Paume.** At the entrance to the Tuileries Gardens, this museum is an ultramodern, white-walled showcase for excellent temporary exhibits of bold contemporary art. ⊠ *pl. de la Concorde,* ☎ *01–42–60–69–69.* ⌷ *35 frs.* ⊙ *Tues. noon–9:30, Wed.–Fri. noon–7, weekends 10–7. Métro: Concorde.*

❼ **Musée de l'Orangerie.** Several of Claude Monet's *Water Lily* series head the choice array of early 20th-century paintings in this museum in the Tuileries Gardens. ⊠ *pl. de la Concorde,* ☎ *01–42–97–48–16.* ⌷ *30 frs.* ⊙ *Wed.–Mon. 9:45–5:15. Métro: Concorde.*

⑤ Place de la Concorde. This majestic square at the foot of the Champs-Élysées was laid out in the 1770s, but there was nothing in the way of peace or concord about its early years. Between 1793 and 1795 more than a thousand victims, including Louis XVI and Marie-Antoinette, were slashed into oblivion at the guillotine. The **Obelisk,** a present from the viceroy of Egypt, was erected in 1833. *Métro: Concorde.*

From the Eiffel Tower to Pont de l'Alma

The Eiffel Tower lords it over southwest Paris, and wherever you are on this walk, you can see it looming overhead. Water is the second theme: fountains playing beneath place du Trocadéro; tours along the Seine on a Bateau Mouche; and an underground prowl through the city's sewers, if you can stand it. Museums are the third: The area around Trocadéro is full of them. And style is the fourth—not just because the buildings here are overwhelmingly elegant, but also because, with the Champs-Élysées a brief walk to the north, the top names in world fashion are all congregated around avenue Montaigne.

A Good Walk

The verdant expanse of the Champ de Mars, once used as a parade ground by the École Militaire (still in use as a military academy and therefore not open to the public), then as site of the World Exhibitions, provides a thrilling approach to the iron symbol of Paris, the **Tour Eiffel** ⑩. As you get nearer, the Eiffel Tower's colossal bulk (it's far bigger and sturdier than pictures suggest) becomes increasingly more evident. (If you want to skip this walk through the parade grounds to the Eiffel Tower, just take the métro directly there.)

Across the Seine from the Eiffel Tower, above stylish gardens and fountains on the heights of place du Trocadéro, is the Art Deco **Palais de Chaillot** ⑪, a cultural center containing a number of museums: an anthropology museum, a museum of French architecture, and a museum of cinema history (the latter two were damaged by fire in 1997 and their date of reopening was uncertain at press time). The area around place du Trocadéro is a feast for museum lovers. The **Musée Guimet** ⑫, at place d'Iéna, contains three floors of Indo-Chinese and Far Eastern art and is slated to reopen in 1999 after extensive renovation. Farther down the avenue du Président-Wilson is the **Musée d'Art Moderne de la Ville de Paris** ⑬, which has temporary exhibits as well as a permanent collection of modern art.

Continue down to bustling place de l'Alma, where a giant golden torch appears to be saluting the memory of Diana, Princess of Wales, who died in a car crash in the tunnel below in August 1997. Down the sloping side-road to the left of the Pont de l'Alma (Alma Bridge) is the embarkation point of the **Bateaux Mouches** ⑭ and their tours of Paris by water. Stylish avenue Montaigne, home to many of the leading Paris fashion houses (☞ Shopping, *below*), runs up from place de l'Alma toward the Champs-Élysées.

TIMING

You can probably cover this walk in a couple of hours, but if you wish to ascend the Eiffel Tower, take a trip along the Seine, or visit any of the plethora of museums along the way, you'd be best off allowing most of the day.

Sights to See

⑭ **Bateaux Mouches.** These popular motorboats set off on their hour-long tours of Paris waters regularly (every half hour in summer) from place de l'Alma. ⊠ *pl. de l'Alma,* ☎ *01–40–76–99–99.* ✐ *40 frs. Métro: Alma-Marceau.*

⑬ **Musée d'Art Moderne de la Ville de Paris** (City Museum of Modern Art). Both temporary exhibits and a permanent collection of top-quality 20th-century art can be found at this museum. It takes over, chronologically speaking, where the Musée d'Orsay (☞ *below*) leaves off: Among the earliest works are Fauve paintings by Vlaminck and Derain, followed by Picasso's early experiments in Cubism. Other highlights include works by Braque, Rouault, Gleizes, Da Silva, Gromaire, and Modigliani. ⊠ *11 av. du Président-Wilson,* ☎ *01–53–67–40–00.* ☎ *27 frs.* ⊘ *Tues.–Sun. 10–5:30, Wed. 10–8:30. Métro: Iéna.*

⑫ **Musée Guimet.** This Belle Époque museum was founded by Lyonnais industrialist Émile Guimet, who traveled around the world in the late 19th century amassing Indo-Chinese and Far Eastern objets d'art, plus a large collection of Cambodian art. Most of the museum was closed for restoration until 1999, with just the **Heidelbach-Guimet gallery** around the corner (⊠ 19 av. d'Iéna), featuring Buddhist art from China and Japan, staying open in the interim. ⊠ *6 pl. d'Iéna,* ☎ *01–45–05–00–98.* ☎ *16 frs.* ⊘ *Wed.–Mon. 9:45–6. Métro: Iéna.*

⑪ **Palais de Chaillot** (Chaillot Palace). This honey-color, Art Deco culture center facing the Seine, perched atop tumbling gardens with sculpture and fountains, was built in the 1930s and houses four museums: the **Musée de l'Homme** (Museum of Man), with an array of prehistoric artifacts; the **Musée de la Marine** (Maritime Museum), with its salty collection of model ships, marine paintings, and naval paraphernalia; the **Musée des Monuments Français** (Museum of French Monuments); and the **Musée du Cinéma Henri-Langlois** (Cinema Museum). The latter two were badly damaged by fire in 1997 and their date of reopening was uncertain at press time. ⊠ *pl. du Trocadéro. Métro: Trocadéro. Museum of Man:* ☎ *01–44–05–72–72;* ☎ *30 frs;* ⊘ *Wed.–Mon. 9:45–5. Maritime Museum:* ☎ *01–53–65–69–69;* ☎ *38 frs;* ⊘ *Wed.–Mon. 10–6. Museum of French Monuments:* ☎ *01–44–05–39–10. Cinema Museum:* ☎ *01–45–53–74–39.*

★ ☉ ⑩ **Tour Eiffel** (Eiffel Tower). Known to the French as La Tour Eiffel (pronounced *F.L.*), Paris's most famous landmark was built by Gustave Eiffel for the World Exhibition of 1889, the centennial of the French Revolution, and was still in good shape to celebrate its own 100th birthday. Such was Eiffel's engineering wizardry that even in the strongest winds his tower never sways more than 4½ inches. If you're full of energy, stride up the stairs as far as the third deck. If you want to go to the top, you'll have to take the elevator. ⊠ *quai Branly,* ☎ *01–44–11–23–23.* ☎ *By elevator: 2nd floor, 20 frs; 3rd floor, 42 frs; 4th floor, 57 frs. By foot: 2nd and 3rd floors only, 14 frs.* ⊘ *July–Aug., daily 9 AM–midnight; Sept.–June, daily 9 AM–11 PM. Métro: Bir-Hakeim; RER: Champ-de-Mars.*

The Faubourg St-Honoré

The Faubourg St-Honoré, north of the Champs-Élysées and the Tuileries, is synonymous with style—as you will see as you progress from the President's Palace, past a wealth of art galleries, to the monumental Madeleine church and on to stately place Vendôme, home to the Ritz and the world's top jewelers. Leading names in modern fashion are found farther east on place des Victoires, close to what was, for centuries, the gastronomic heart of Paris: Les Halles (pronounced *lay ahl*), once the city's main market.

Les Halles was closed in 1969 and replaced by a park and a modern shopping mall, the Forum des Halles. The surrounding streets underwent a transformation and are now filled with shops, cafés, and restaurants. The brash modernity of the Forum stands in contrast to the august church of St-Eustache nearby. Similarly, the incongruous black-and-white columns in the classical courtyard of Richelieu's neighboring Palais-Royal present a further case of daring modernity—or architectural vandalism, depending on your point of view.

A Good Walk

Start in front of the most important home in France: the **Palais de l'Élysée** ⑮, or Presidential Palace. Crash barriers and stern policemen keep visitors at bay; in fact, there's more to see in the plethora of art galleries and luxury fashion boutiques that line rue du Faubourg–St-Honoré as you head east. Pass the British Embassy and turn left onto rue Boissy-d'Anglas; then cut right through an archway into Cité Berryer, a restored courtyard with several trendy boutiques. It leads to rue Royale, a classy street lined with jewelry stores. Looming to the left is the **Église de la Madeleine** ⑯, a sturdy neoclassical edifice.

Cross boulevard de la Madeleine and take rue Duphot down to rue St-Honoré, where you'll pass Notre-Dame de l'Assomption, noted for its huge dome and solemn interior. Continue to rue de Castiglione and then head left to **place Vendôme** ⑰, one of the world's most opulent squares. Return to rue St-Honoré and follow it to the mighty church of **St-Roch** ⑱.

Take the next right onto rue des Pyramides and cross place des Pyramides, with its gilded statue of Joan of Arc on horseback, to the northernmost wing of the Louvre. Stay on arcaded rue de Rivoli to place du Palais-Royal. On the corner of rue de Richelieu and rue de Rivoli is the **Comédie Française** ⑲, the time-honored setting for performances of classical French drama. To the right of the theater is the unobtrusive entrance to the **Palais-Royal** ⑳; its courtyard is a surprising oasis in the heart of the city. Exit the Palais-Royal courtyard onto rue des Petits-Champs, which heads east to the circular **place des Victoires** ㉑: That's Louis XIV riding the plunging steed in the center of the square. Head south down rue Croix-des-Petits-Champs, past the nondescript Banque de France on your right, and take the second street on the left to the circular **Bourse du Commerce** ㉒, or Commercial Exchange. Alongside it is the 100-ft-high fluted Colonne de Ruggieri.

You don't need to scale Ruggieri's column to spot the bulky outline of the church of **St-Eustache** ㉓, a curious architectural hybrid of Gothic and classical. The vast site next to St-Eustache is now occupied by a garden, the Jardin des Halles, and the modern **Forum des Halles** ㉔ shopping mall. Rue Berger leads from allée de St-Jean-de-Perse to the square des Innocents, with its handsome Renaissance fountain. Head south along rue St-Denis from the far end of square des Innocents to place du Châtelet, with its theaters, fountain, and the Tour St-Jacques, the tower looming up to your left. Turn right along the Seine to reach **St-Germain l'Auxerrois** ㉕, opposite the Louvre, once the French royal family's parish church.

TIMING

With brief visits to churches and monuments, this walk should take three to four hours. On a nice day you may want to linger in the gardens of the Palais-Royal and on a cold day you may want to indulge in an unbelievably thick hot chocolate at the Angélina tearoom.

Sights to See

㉒ **Bourse du Commerce** (Commercial Exchange). The circular, shallow-domed, 18th-century Commercial Exchange near Les Halles began life as a corn exchange; Victor Hugo waggishly likened it to a jockey's cap without the peak. ⊠ *rue de Viarmes. Métro or RER: Les Halles.*

⑲ Comédie Française. This theater is the setting for performances of classical French drama, with tragedies by Racine and Corneille and comedies by Molière regularly on the bill. The building itself dates from 1790, but the Comédie Française company was created by that most theatrical of French monarchs, Louis XIV, back in 1680. ⊠ *pl. André-Malraux,* ☏ *01–44–58–15–15. Métro: Palais-Royal.*

⑯ Église de la Madeleine. With its rows of uncompromising columns, this sturdy neoclassical edifice—designed in 1814 but not consecrated until 1842—looks more like a Greek temple than a Christian church. In fact, La Madeleine, as it is known, was nearly selected as Paris's first train station (the site of the Gare St-Lazare, just up the road, was chosen instead). Inside, the walls are richly and harmoniously decorated; gold glints through the murk. The portico's majestic Corinthian colonnade supports a gigantic pediment with a frieze of the Last Judgment. ⊠ *pl. de la Madeleine.* ☉ *Mon.–Sat. 7:30–7, Sun. 8–7. Métro: Madeleine.*

㉔ Forum des Halles. Les Halles, the iron-and-glass halls of the central Paris food market, were closed in 1969 and replaced in the late '70s by the Forum des Halles, a mundane shopping mall. Unfortunately, much of its plastic, concrete, glass, and mock-marble exterior is already showing signs of wear and tear. ⊠ *Main entrance on rue Pierre-Lescot. Métro: Les Halles; RER: Châtelet–Les Halles.*

NEED A BREAK? | Founded in 1903, **Angélina** (⊠ 226 rue de Rivoli, ☏ 01–42–60–82–00) is an elegant *salon de thé* (tearoom), famous for its hot chocolate so thick you'll need a fork to eat it (irresistible even in the summer).

⑮ Palais de l'Élysée (Élysée Palace). This "palace," known as L'Élysée, where the French president lives, works, and receives official visitors, was originally constructed as a private mansion in 1718 and has housed presidents only since 1873. Although you can catch a glimpse of the palace forecourt and facade through the Faubourg St-Honoré gateway, it is difficult to get much idea of the building's size, or of the extensive gardens that stretch back to the Champs-Élysées. ⊠ *55 rue du Faubourg St-Honoré.* ☉ *Not open to the public. Métro: Miromesnil.*

⑳ Palais-Royal (Royal Palace). The buildings of this former palace—royal only in that all-powerful Cardinal Richelieu (1585–1642) magnanimously bequeathed them to Louis XIII—date from the 1630s. Today, the Palais-Royal is home to the French Ministry of Culture, and its buildings are not open to the public. You can, however, visit the colonnaded courtyard with black-and-white striped half-columns and revolving silver spheres that slither around in two fountains—the controversial work of architect Daniel Buren—and the more classical gardens beyond. ⊠ *pl. du Palais-Royal. Métro: Palais-Royal.*

⑰ Place Vendôme. Mansart's rhythmic, perfectly proportioned example of 17th-century urban architecture shines in all its golden-stone splendor. The square is a fitting showcase for the deluxe Ritz Hotel and the cluster of jewelry display windows found here. Napoléon had the square's central column made from the melted bronze of 1,200 cannons captured at the battle of Austerlitz in 1805. That's Napoléon standing vigilantly at the top. *Métro: Opéra.*

㉑ Place des Victoires. This circular square, now home to many of the city's top fashion boutiques, was laid out in 1685 by Jules-Hardouin Mansart in honor of the military victories (*victoires*) of Louis XIV. The Sun King gallops along on a bronze horse in the middle. *Métro: Sentier.*

㉓ St-Eustache. Since the demolition of the 19th-century market halls at the beginning of the '70s, St-Eustache has reemerged as a dominant element on the central Paris skyline. A huge church, it was built as the market people's Right Bank reply to Notre-Dame, though St-Eustache dates from a couple of hundred years later. The church is a curious architectural hybrid: With the exception of the feeble west front, added between 1754 and 1788, construction lasted from 1532 to 1637, spanning the decline of the Gothic style and the emergence of the Renaissance. ☒ *2 rue du Jour,* ☎ *01–46–27–89–21 for concert information.* ☺ *Daily 8–7. Métro: Les Halles; RER: Châtelet–Les Halles.*

㉕ St-Germain l'Auxerrois. Until 1789, St-Germain was used by the French royal family as their parish church, in the days when the adjacent Louvre was a palace rather than a museum. The facade reveals the influence of 15th-century Flamboyant Gothic style, whereas the fluted columns around the choir, the area surrounding the altar, demonstrate the triumph of classicism. ☒ *pl. du Louvre. Métro: Louvre-Rivoli.*

⑱ St-Roch. Designed by Lemercier in 1653 but completed only in the 1730s, this huge church is almost as long as Notre-Dame (138 yards) thanks to Hardouin-Mansart's domed Lady Chapel at the far end. ☒ *rue St-Honoré. Métro: Tuileries.*

The Grand Boulevards

The focal point of this walk is the uninterrupted avenue that runs in almost a straight line from St-Augustin, the city's grandest Second Empire church, to place de la République, whose very name symbolizes the ultimate downfall of the imperial regime. The avenue's name changes six times along the way, which is why Parisians refer to it as the *Grands Boulevards* in *plural*. The makeup of the neighborhoods along the Grand Boulevards changes steadily as you head east from the posh 8ᵉ arrondissement toward working-class east Paris. The *grands magasins* (department stores) at the start of the walk epitomize upscale Paris shopping. They stand on boulevard Haussmann, named in honor of the regional prefect who oversaw the reconstruction of the city in the 1850s and 1860s (☞ A Survey of French Architecture *in* Chapter 18). The opulent Opéra Garnier, just past the *grands magasins,* is the architectural showpiece of the period (often termed the Second Empire and corresponding to the rule of Napoléon III).

A Good Walk

Step through gold-topped iron gates to enter the **Parc Monceau** ㉖, in the tony 8ᵉ arrondissement. At the middle of the park, head left to avenue Velasquez past the **Musée Cernuschi** ㉗—home to Chinese art from Neolithic pottery to contemporary paintings—to boulevard Malesherbes. Turn right on boulevard Malesherbes and right again on rue de Monceau to reach the **Musée Nissim de Camondo** ㉘, whose aristocratic interior reflects the upbeat tone of this haughty part of Paris.

Turn left down rue de Téhéran, left along avenue de Messine, and left again on rue de Laborde to get to the innovative iron-and-stone church of **St-Augustin** ㉙. Cross the square in front and turn left along boulevard Haussmann to square Louis XVI. Some 300 yards farther down boulevard Haussmann, you'll find the *grands magasins*: Paris's most renowned department stores. First come the cupolas of Au Printemps, then Galeries Lafayette. Opposite looms the massive bulk of the **Opéra Garnier** ㉚.

Boulevard des Capucines, lined with cinemas and restaurants, heads left from in front of the Opera, becoming boulevard des Italiens before colliding with boulevard Haussmann. A left here down rue Drouot will take you to the **Hôtel Drouot** ㉛, Paris's central auction house. Rue Rossini leads from "Drouot" to rue de la Grange-Batelière. Halfway along on the right is the Passage Jouffroy, one of the many covered galleries that honeycomb the center of Paris. Head down to boulevard Montmartre and cross to passage des Panoramas, leading to rue St-Marc. Turn right, then left down rue Vivienne, to find the foresquare, colonnaded **Bourse** ㉜, the Paris Stock Exchange.

Head east along rue Réaumur, once the heart of the French newspaper industry—stationery shops still abound—and cross rue Montmartre. Take the second left up rue de Cléry, a narrow street that is the exclusive domain of fabric wholesalers. Continue up rue de Cléry as far as rue des Degrés—not a street at all, but a 14-step stairway—then look for the crooked church tower of **Notre-Dame de Bonne-Nouvelle** ㉝, hemmed in by rickety housing. The porticoed entrance is around the corner on rue de la Lune, which leads back to the Grand Boulevards, by now going under the name of boulevard de Bonne-Nouvelle.

The Porte St-Denis, a triumphal arch, looms up ahead and, a little farther on, the smaller but similar Porte St-Martin. From here take rue St-Martin south to the **Conservatoire National des Techniques** ㉞, an industrial museum housed partly in the former church of St-Martin. Current restoration may not end before 1999, so console yourself with a glimpse of the solemn domed forecourt and repair to the leafy square opposite, or to the high, narrow, late-Gothic church of **St-Nicolas des Champs** ㉟ across rue Réaumur. Head left on rue de Turbigo, past the cloister ruins and Renaissance gateway that embellish the far side of St-Nicolas. Some 400 yards along on the right is the Baroque church of **Ste-Élisabeth** ㊱; shortly after, you reach **place de la République** ㊲. It's a short métro ride from here to the city's most famous cemetery, the **Cimetière du Père Lachaise** ㊳, or to the **Parc de la Villette** ㊴, with its postmodern science and music museums.

TIMING

The distance between Parc Monceau and place de la République is almost 6 km (4 mi), which will probably take you four hours to walk, including coffee breaks and window-shopping. Allot a few additional hours, if not a whole morning or afternoon, to visit the Père Lachaise Cemetery or the Parc de la Villette. Or return to these on another day.

Sights to See

㉜ **Bourse** (Stock Exchange). The Paris Stock Exchange, a serene, colonnaded 19th-century building, is a far cry from Wall Street. Take your passport if you want to tour it. ⊠ *rue Vivienne.* ▨ *30 frs.* ⊙ *Guided tours only (in French), weekdays every ½ hr 1:15–3:45. Métro: Bourse.*

㊳ **Cimetière du Père Lachaise** (Father Lachaise Cemetery). Cemeteries may not be your idea of the ultimate attraction, but this is the largest and most interesting in Paris. It forms a veritable necropolis with cobbled avenues and tombs competing in pomposity and originality. Leading incumbents include Jim Morrison, Frédéric Chopin, Marcel Proust, Edith Piaf, and Gertrude Stein. Get a map at the entrance and track them down. ⊠ *Entrances on rue des Rondeaux, bd. de Ménilmontant, rue de la Réunion.* ⊙ *Apr.–Sept., daily 8–6, Oct.–Mar., daily 8–5. Métro: Gambetta, Philippe-Auguste, Père Lachaise.*

㉞ **Conservatoire National des Techniques** (National Technical Museum). The former church and priory of St-Martin des Champs, built between the 11th and 13th centuries, is now part of this industrial museum with a varied collection of models (locomotives, vehicles, and agricultural machinery), astronomical instruments, and displays on printing, photography, and television. A major renovation may keep the museum shut until an unspecified date in 1999. ⊠ *292 rue St-Martin,* ☎ *01–40–27–23–31. Métro: Arts et Métiers.*

③ Hôtel Drouot. Paris's central auction house has everything from stamps and toy soldiers to Renoirs and 18th-century commodes. The 16 salesrooms make for fascinating browsing, and there's no obligation to bid. ⊠ *9 rue Drouot,* ☏ *01–48–00–20–00.* ☉ *Viewings Mon.–Sat. 11–noon and 2–6, with auctions starting at 2. Closed mid-July–mid-Sept. Métro: Richelieu-Drouot.*

㉗ Musée Cernuschi. The collection includes Chinese art from Neolithic pottery (3rd century BC) to funeral statuary, painted 8th-century silks, and contemporary paintings, as well as ancient Persian bronze objects. ⊠ *7 av. Velasquez,* ☏ *01–45–63–50–75.* ▦ *17 frs.* ☉ *Tues.–Sun. 10–5:40. Métro: Monceau.*

㉘ Musée Nissim de Camondo. The elegant decadence of the last days of the regal Ancien Régime is fully reflected in the lavish interior of this aristocratic Parisian mansion, built in the style of Louis XVI. ⊠ *63 rue de Monceau,* ☏ *01–53–89–06–40.* ▦ *27 frs.* ☉ *Wed.–Sun. 10–noon and 2–5. Métro: Monceau.*

㉝ Notre-Dame de Bonne-Nouvelle. This wide, soberly neoclassical church, built 1823–29, is tucked away off the Grand Boulevards. ⊠ *rue de la Lune. Métro: Bonne-Nouvelle.*

㉚ Opéra Garnier. The original Paris Opera, begun in 1862 by Charles Garnier at the behest of Napoléon III, was not completed until 1875, five years after the emperor's abdication. It is said that it typifies Second Empire architecture, which is to say that it is a pompous hodgepodge of styles. After paying the entry fee, you can stroll around at leisure. The monumental foyer and staircase are impressive and the stage is the largest in the world. Marc Chagall painted the ceiling in 1964. The **Musée de l'Opéra**, containing a few paintings and theatrical mementos, is unremarkable. ⊠ *pl. de l'Opéra,* ☏ *01–40–01–22–63.* ▦ *30 frs.* ☉ *Daily 10–4:30; closed occasionally for rehearsals; call 01–47–42–57–50 to check. Métro: Opéra.*

NEED A BREAK?	There are few grander cafés in Paris than the Belle Époque **Café de la Paix** (⊠ 5 pl. de l'Opéra, ☏ 01–40–07–30–10), once described as "the center of the civilized world."

☝ ㉖ Parc Monceau. The most picturesque gardens on the Right Bank were laid out as a private park in 1778 and retain some of the fanciful elements then in vogue, including mock ruins and a phony pyramid. ⊠ *Entrances on bd. de Courcelles, av. Velasquez, av. Ruysdaël, av. van Dyck. Métro: Monceau.*

★ ☝ ㉟ Parc de la Villette. Until the 1970s this 130-acre site, in an unfashionable corner of northeast Paris, was home to a cattle market and *abattoir* (slaughterhouse). The site was transformed into an ambitiously landscaped, futuristic park known as La Villette. It has sweeping lawns, a children's playground, canopied walkways, a cinema, two museums, brightly painted pavilions, and a state-of-the-art concert hall, the **Cité de la Musique** (☞ Nightlife and the Arts, *below*). This giant postmodern musical academy also houses the outstanding **Musée de la Musique** (Music Museum). The former slaughterhouse—the **Grande Halle**—is a magnificent structure whose transformation into an arts center provides an intelligent link with the site's historic past. At the **Géode** cinema, which looks like a huge silver golf ball, films are shown on an enormous, 180-degree-curved screen. The **Cité des Sciences et de l'Industrie**, a science museum, contains dozens of try-it-yourself exhibits that make you feel more participant than onlooker (though most displays are in French only). ⊠ *Cité de la Musique: 221 av. Jean-Jaurès,*

☎ *01–44–84–46–21. Musée de la Musique: ⌨ 35 frs; ◷ Tues.–Sun. noon–6. Cité des Sciences et de l'Industrie: ⊠ 30 av. Corentin-Cariou, ☎ 08–36–68–29–30; ⌨ 50 frs, 35 frs Sat.; ◷ Tues.–Sun. 10–noon and 2–6. Métro: Porte de la Villette, Porte de Pantin.*

㊲ **Place de la République.** This large, oblong square, laid out by Haussmann from 1856 to 1865, is dominated by a matronly, Stalin-size statue symbolizing *The Republic* (1883). *Métro: République.*

㉙ **St-Augustin.** This domed church was dexterously constructed in the 1860s within the confines of an awkward, V-shape site. It represented a breakthrough in ecclesiastical engineering, insofar as the use of metal pillars and girders obviated the need for exterior buttressing. ⊠ *pl. St-Augustin. Métro: St-Augustin.*

㊱ **Ste-Élisabeth.** This studied essay in Baroque (1628–46) has brightly restored wall paintings and a wide, semicircular apse around the choir. ⊠ *rue du Temple. Métro: Temple.*

㉟ **St-Nicolas des Champs.** The rounded-arch, fluted Doric capitals in the chancel of this church date from 1560 to 1587, a full century later than the pointed-arch nave (1420–80). ⊠ *rue St-Martin. Métro: Arts-et-Métiers.*

The Marais and the Bastille

The Marais is one of the city's most historic and sought-after residential districts. Renovation is the keynote; well into the '70s, this was one of the city's poorest areas. Regeneration was sparked by the building of the architecturally whimsical Pompidou Center. The gracious architecture of the 17th and early 18th centuries, however, sets the tone for the rest of the Marais. Today, most of the Marais's spectacular *hôtels particuliers*—loosely, "mansions," onetime residences of aristocratic families—have been restored; many are now museums. There are trendy boutiques and cafés among the kosher shops in the formerly run-down streets of the Jewish neighborhood around rue des Rosiers.

The history of the Marais—the word, incidentally, means marsh or swamp—goes back to when Charles V, king of France in the 14th century, moved his court here from the Ile de la Cité. However, it wasn't until Henri IV laid out place Royale, today place des Vosges, in the early 17th century, that the Marais became *the* place to live. After the French Revolution, the Marais rapidly became one of the most dissolute areas in Paris and was spared the attentions of Baron Haussmann, the man who rebuilt so much of Paris in the mid-19th century.

On the eastern edge of the Marais is place de la Bastille, site of the infamous prison stormed on July 14, 1789, an event that came to symbolize the beginning of the French Revolution. Largely in commemoration of the bicentennial of the Revolution, the Bastille area was renovated and became one of the trendiest sections of Paris. Galleries, shops, theaters, cafés, restaurants, and bars now fill formerly decrepit buildings and alleys.

A Good Walk

Make **place de la Bastille** ㊵, which is easily accessible by métro, your starting point. Today the square is dominated by the Colonne de Juillet, the curving glass facade of the modern **Opéra de la Bastille,** and the Genitron digital clock at the start of boulevard Richard-Lenoir, ticking off the seconds to the year 2000.

Walk down rue St-Antoine to the **Hôtel de Sully** ㊶, home to the Caisse Nationale des Monuments Historiques (National Treasury of Historic

Monuments) at No. 62. Cross the road and pause at the mighty Baroque church of **St-Paul–St-Louis** ⑫. Take the left-hand side door out of the church into narrow passage St-Paul; then turn right onto rue St-Paul, past the grid of courtyards that make up the Village St-Paul antiques-shops complex. Wind your way through the small streets to the quai de l'Hôtel-de-Ville.

Turn right on quai de l'Hôtel-de-Ville; *bouquinistes* (booksellers) line the Seine to your left. Pause by the Pont Louis-Philippe to admire the dome of the Panthéon floating above the skyline; then take the next right up picturesque rue des Barres to **St-Gervais–St-Protais** ⑬. Beyond the church stands the **Hôtel de Ville** ⑭, the city hall. From the Hôtel de Ville, cross rue de Rivoli and go up rue du Temple. On your right, you'll pass one of the city's most popular department stores, the Bazar de l'Hôtel de Ville, or "BHV," as it is known (☞ Shopping, *below*). Take rue de la Verrerie, the first street on your left.

Cross rue du Renard and take the second right past the ornate 16th-century church of St-Merri. Rue St-Martin, full of stores, restaurants, and galleries, leads to the **Centre Pompidou** ⑮, sadly closed for renovation until the end of the century. The adjacent square Igor-Stravinsky merits a stop for its unusual fountain, however, and you can visit the **Atelier Brancusi** in front of the Center—the reconstituted studio of sculptor Constantin Brancusi.

Turn left around the back of the Pompidou Center, take rue Rambuteau, then take the first left onto rue du Temple. Note the Hôtel de St-Aignan at No. 71 and the Hôtel de Montmor at No. 79, both splendid Renaissance mansions. Take a right onto rue des Haudriettes; just off to the left at the next corner is the **Musée de la Chasse et de la Nature** ⑯, the Museum of Hunting and Nature, housed in one of the Marais's most stately mansions. Head right on rue des Archives, crossing rue des Haudriettes, and admire the medieval gateway with two fairy-tale towers, now part of the **Archives Nationales** ⑰, the archives museum entered from rue des Francs-Bourgeois (Street of the Free Citizens) around to the left.

Continue past the Crédit Municipal (the city's grandiose pawnbroking concern), the Dômarais restaurant (housed in a circular 18th-century chamber originally used for auctions), and the church of Notre-Dame des Blancs-Manteaux. A corner turret signals rue Vieille-du-Temple: Turn left past the palatial Hôtel de Rohan (now part of the Archives Nationales), then right onto rue de la Perle to the **Musée Bricard** ⑱, occupying a mansion as impressive as the assembly of locks and keys within. From here it is a step down rue de Thorigny (opposite) to the palatial 17th-century Hôtel Salé, now the **Musée Picasso** ⑲.

Backtrack along rue de Thorigny and turn left onto rue du Parc-Royal. Halfway down rue Elzévir is the **Musée Cognacq-Jay** ⑳, a must for fans of 18th-century furniture, porcelain, and paintings. Back on rue des Francs-Bourgeois is the **Musée Carnavalet** ㉑, the Paris history museum, in perhaps the swankiest edifice in the Marais. A short walk along rue des Francs-Bourgeois takes you to large, pink-brick **place des Vosges** ㉒, lined with covered arcades.

TIMING

This walk will comfortably take a morning or an afternoon. If you choose to spend an hour or two in any of the museums along the way, allow a full day. Be prepared to wait in line at the Picasso Museum. Note that some of the museums don't open until the afternoon and that most shops in the Bastille and the Marais don't open until the late morning.

Sights to See

47 **Archives Nationales** (National Archives). If you're a serious history buff, you will be fascinated by the thousands of intricate historical documents, dating from the Merovingian period to the 20th century, at the National Archives. ⊠ *60 rue des Francs-Bourgeois,* ☎ *01–40–27–62–18.* ▣ *15 frs.* ⊙ *Wed.–Mon. 1:45–5:45. Métro: Rambuteau.*

Atelier Brancusi (Brancusi Studio). Romanian-born sculptor Constantin Brancusi settled in Paris in 1898 at age 22. This light, airy museum in front of the Pompidou Center contains four glass-fronted rooms that reconstitute Brancusi's studio, crammed with smooth, stylized works from all periods of his career. ⊠ *11 rue St-Paul,* ☎ *01–44–78–12–33.* ▣ *20 frs.* ⊙ *Wed.–Mon. noon–10. Métro: Rambuteau.*

45 **Centre Pompidou.** The futuristic, funnel-top Pompidou Center—known to Parisians as Beaubourg, after the surrounding district—was built in the mid-1970s and named in honor of former French president Georges Pompidou (1911–74). The Center was soon attracting more than 8 million visitors a year—five times more than intended. Hardly surprising, then, that it was soon showing signs of fatigue: The much-vaunted, gaudily painted service pipes snaking up the exterior needed continual repainting, while the plastic tubing enclosing the exterior escalators was cracked and grimy. In 1996 the government stepped in and took drastic action: shutting the Center until December 1999 and embarking on top-to-bottom renovation. It's still worth passing by to admire the **Atelier Brancusi** (☞ *above*) and the temporary, giant white wigwam lined with computers flashing out data on the Center's manifold (albeit dormant) activities. ⊠ *pl. Georges-Pompidou,* ☎ *01–44–78–12–33. Métro: Rambuteau.*

41 **Hôtel de Sully.** This late-Renaissance mansion, begun in 1624, has a stately garden and a majestic courtyard with statues, richly carved pediments, and dormer windows. It is the headquarters of the **Caisse Nationale des Monuments Historiques** (National Treasury of Historic Monuments), responsible for administering France's historic monuments. Guided visits to Paris sites and buildings begin here, though all are conducted in French. ⊠ *62 rue St-Antoine,* ☎ *01–44–61–20–00. Métro: St-Paul.*

44 **Hôtel de Ville** (City Hall). During the Commune of 1871, the Hôtel de Ville was burned to the ground. Today's exuberant building, based closely on the 16th-century Renaissance original, went up between 1874 and 1884. You can't inspect the lavish interior, but head round left to the traffic-free square, with its fountains and forest of street lamps, to admire the exuberant facade. ⊠ *pl. de l'Hôtel-de-Ville. Métro: Hôtel-de-Ville.*

☜ **48** **Musée Bricard.** This museum—also called the Musée de la Serrure (Lock Museum)—is housed in a sober Baroque mansion designed in 1685 by the architect of Les Invalides, Libéral Bruand, for himself. If you've got a taste for fine craftsmanship, you will appreciate the intricacy and ingenuity of many of the locks displayed here. ⊠ *1 rue de la Perle,* ☎ *01–42–77–79–62.* ▣ *30 frs.* ⊙ *Weekdays 2–5. Métro: St-Paul.*

51 **Musée Carnavalet.** Two adjacent mansions in the heart of the Marais house the Carnavalet Museum, or the Paris History Museum, with material dating from the city's origins to the present. The museum is full of maps and plans, furniture, and busts and portraits of Parisian worthies down the ages. ⊠ *23 rue de Sévigné,* ☎ *01–42–72–21–13.* ▣ *27 frs.* ⊙ *Tues.–Sun. 10–5:30. Métro: St-Paul.*

NEED A
BREAK? **Marais Plus** (☒ 20 rue des Francs-Bourgeois, ☎ 01–48–87–01–40), on
the corner of rue Elzévir and rue des Francs-Bourgeois, is a delightful,
artsy gift shop with a cozy *salon de thé* at the rear.

㊻ Musée de la Chasse et de la Nature (Museum of Hunting and Nature).
This museum is housed in the Hôtel de Guénégaud, designed around
1650 by François Mansart. There is a series of immense 17th- and 18th-
century still lifes (notably by Desportes and Oudry) of dead animals
and a wide variety of swords, guns, muskets, and taxidermy. ☒ *60 rue
des Archives,* ☎ *01–42–72–86–43.* ☜ *25 frs.* ☉ *Wed.–Mon. 10–
12:30 and 1:30–5:30. Métro: Rambuteau.*

㊿ Musée Cognacq-Jay. This museum, devoted to the arts of the 18th century, contains outstanding furniture, porcelain, and paintings (notably
by Watteau, Boucher, and Tiepolo). ☒ *8 rue Elzévir,* ☎ *01–40–27–
07–21.* ☜ *17 frs.* ☉ *Tues.–Sun. 10–5:30. Métro: St-Paul.*

㊾ Musée Picasso. Housed in the 17th-century Hôtel Salé, this museum contains the paintings, sculptures, drawings, prints, ceramics, and assorted
works of art given to the government by Picasso's heirs after the painter's
death in 1973 in lieu of death duties. There are works from every period of Picasso's life, as well as pieces by Cézanne, Miró, Renoir, Braque,
Degas, and Matisse. ☒ *5 rue de Thorigny,* ☎ *01–42–71–25–21.* ☜
30 frs, Sun. 20 frs. ☉ *Thurs.–Mon. 9:30–6. Métro: St-Sébastien.*

Opéra de la Bastille. The state-of-the-art Bastille Opera was erected
on the south side of place de la Bastille. Designed by Argentine-born
Carlos Ott, it opened on July 14, 1989, in commemoration of the bicentennial of the French Revolution. The steep-climbing auditorium
seats more than 3,000 and has earned more plaudits than the curving
glass facade. ☒ *pl. de la Bastille,* ☎ *01–44–73–13–00. Métro: Bastille.*

㊵ Place de la Bastille. Nothing remains of the infamous Bastille prison
destroyed at the beginning of the French Revolution. Until 1988, there
was little more to see here than a huge traffic circle and the **Colonne
de Juillet** (July Column), commemorating the overthrow of Charles X
in July 1830. As part of the countrywide celebrations for July 1989,
the bicentennial of the French Revolution, the Opéra de la Bastille was
erected, inspiring substantial redevelopment on the surrounding streets,
especially along rue de Lappe and rue de la Roquette. What was formerly a humdrum neighborhood rapidly gained streamlined art galleries, funky jazz clubs, and tapas bars. *Métro: Bastille.*

㊾ Place des Vosges. Laid out by Henri IV at the start of the 17th century
and originally known as place Royale, this square is the oldest and one
of the prettiest in Paris. The two larger buildings on either side were
originally the king's and queen's pavilions. The statue in the center is
of Louis XIII. At No. 6 is the **Maison de Victor Hugo** (Victor Hugo
House), where the workaholic French author, famed for *Les Misérables*
and *The Hunchback of Notre-Dame*, lived between 1832 and 1848.
☒ *Maison de Victor Hugo: 6 pl. des Vosges,* ☎ *01–42–72–10–16.*
☜ *27 frs.* ☉ *Tues.–Sun. 10–5:45. Métro: St-Paul, Chemin-Vert.*

㊸ St-Gervais–St-Protais. This imposing church near the Hôtel de Ville is
named after two Roman soldiers martyred by the emperor Nero in the
1st century AD. The church, a riot of Flamboyant style, went up between 1494 and 1598, making it one of the last Gothic constructions
in the country. The facade, constructed between 1616 and 1621, is an
early example of French architects' use of classical decoration on the
capitals (topmost sections) of the columns. ☒ *pl. St-Gervais,* ☎ *01–
47–26–78–38 for concert information.* ☉ *Tues.–Sun. 6:30 AM–8
PM. Métro: Hôtel-de-Ville.*

St-Paul–St-Louis. The leading Baroque church in the Marais was begun in 1627 by the Jesuits and partly modeled on their Gesu church in Rome. Look for Delacroix's dramatic *Christ in the Mount of Olives* high up in the transept. ⊠ *rue St-Antoine. Métro: St-Paul.*

The Islands and the Latin Quarter

Of the two islands in the Seine—the Ile St-Louis and the Ile de la Cité—it is the Ile de la Cité that forms the historic heart of Paris. It was here that the earliest inhabitants of Paris, the Gaulish tribe of the Parisii, settled in about 250 BC. They called their little home Lutetia, meaning "settlement surrounded by water." Whereas the Ile St-Louis is today largely residential, the Ile de la Cité remains deeply historic. It has been inhabited for more than 2,000 years and is the site of one of the most beautiful churches in France—the great, brooding cathedral of Notre-Dame. Most of the island's other medieval buildings fell victim to town planner Baron Haussmann's ambitious rebuilding program of the 1860s. Among the rare survivors are the jewel-like Ste-Chapelle, a vision of shimmering stained glass, and La Conciergerie, the former city prison.

South of Ile de la Cité on the Left Bank of the Seine is the bohemian Quartier Latin, with its warren of steep sloping streets, populated largely by Sorbonne students and academics. The name Latin Quarter comes from the university tradition of studying and speaking in Latin, a tradition that disappeared during the Revolution. The university began as a theological school in the Middle Ages and later became the headquarters of the University of Paris; in 1968 the student revolution here had an explosive effect on French politics, resulting in major reforms in the education system.

A grim modern skyscraper at the Jussieu campus, the science division of the University of Paris, reiterates the area's yen for learning yet fails to outgun the mighty dome of the Panthéon in its challenge for skyline supremacy. Most of the district's appeal is less emphatic: Roman ruins, tumbling street markets, the two oldest trees in Paris, and chance glimpses of Notre-Dame all await your discovery.

A Good Walk

The oldest bridge in Paris, confusingly called the **Pont Neuf** ⑤, or New Bridge, is built across the western tip of Ile de la Cité. Find your way to the middle of the bridge and the square du Vert-Galant below, with its proud equestrian statue of Henri IV. On the quay side of the square, vedette motorboats start their tours along the Seine.

Opposite the square, on the other side of the bridge, is place Dauphine, completed the same year as the Pont Neuf (although much altered since). Cross place Dauphine and head left along quai de l'Horloge, named for the oldest clock (*horloge*) in Paris—marking time since 1370 from high up **La Conciergerie,** the prison where Marie-Antoinette was kept during the French Revolution. Then turn left onto boulevard du Palais to reach the imposing **Palais de Justice** ⑤, the law courts. The real interest here is the medieval **Ste-Chapelle,** tucked away to the left of the main courtyard. Take rue de Lutèce opposite the Palais de Justice, pause at the extensive flower market 150 yards down on the left, then turn right on rue de la Cité to come face to face with the serene, golden facade of **Notre-Dame** ⑤. This is the geographic and historic heart of Paris, and its dark, solemn interior feels suitably reverential.

Cross the Seine on the Pont St-Louis, at the island's eastern tip, to the **Ile St-Louis** ⑤, the smaller of the city's two islands. Just across the bridge is the **Mémorial de la Déportation** ⑤, a starkly moving modern crypt dedicated to the French people who died in Nazi concentration camps.

Rue St-Louis-en-l'Ile runs the length of the island, bisecting it in two. Walk down this street and admire the strange, pierced spire of St-Louis-en-l'Ile, and then stop off for an ice cream at Berthillon at No. 31.

Cross back to the Ile de la Cité and take the Pont au Double across the Seine to square René-Viviani. Behind the square lies the church of **St-Julien-le-Pauvre** ㊳, built at the same time as Notre-Dame, and the tiny, elegant streets of the Maubert district. Turn left out of the church and cross rue St-Jacques to the elegantly proportioned church of **St-Séverin** ㊴. The surrounding streets are pedestrian-only. Take rue St-Séverin, a right on rue Xavier-Privas, and a left on rue de la Huchette to reach place St-Michel. Gabriel Davioud's grandiose 1860 fountain, depicting St. Michael slaying the dragon, is a popular meeting spot at the nerve center of the Left Bank.

Turn left up boulevard St-Michel and cross boulevard St-Germain. To your left, behind some forbidding railings, lurks a garden with ruins that date from Roman times. These belong to the **Musée National du Moyen-Age** ㊿, the National Museum of the Middle Ages. The entrance is down rue Sommerard, the next street on the left. Cross place Paul-Painlevé in front of the museum up toward **La Sorbonne** ㊱ university, fronted by a small plaza where the Left Bank's student population congregates after classes. Continue uphill until you are confronted, up rue Soufflot on your left, by the menacing domed bulk of the **Panthéon** ㊲. On the far left corner of place du Panthéon stands **St-Étienne-du-Mont** ㊳, a church whose facade is a mishmash of architectural styles. Explore the top of quaint rue de la Montagne-Ste-Geneviève, and then turn right onto rue Descartes to reach place de la Contrescarpe. This square looks almost provincial during the day as Parisians flock to the daily market on rue Mouffetard.

Pass the old church of St-Médard at the foot of rue Mouffetard; then head left for 250 yards along rue Censier and turn left again into rue Georges-Desplas to find the beautiful white **Mosquée** ㊽, complete with minaret. On the far side of the mosque extends the **Jardin des Plantes** ㊾, spacious botanical gardens; the first building you'll come to is the **Grande Galerie de l'Évolution,** a museum with a startling collection of stuffed animals, many extinct or endangered. The museums of entomology, paleontology, and mineralogy line one side of the garden; an old-fashioned zoo the other. Farther upriver, via quai d'Austerlitz and quai de la Gare, is the new **Bibliothèque François-Mitterrand** ㊻, the French national library, with its four huge, shiny glass towers.

If you forgo the distant pleasure of the new library, take the northwest exit from the Jardin des Plantes up rue Lacépède, then rue de Navarre to the **Arènes de Lutèce** ㊼, the remains of a Roman amphitheater. Rue des Arènes and rue Limé lead to place Jussieu and its hideous 1960s concrete campus; there's greater refinement around the corner down rue des Fossés-St-Bernard at the glass-facaded **Institut du Monde Arabe** ㊽, a center devoted to Arab culture. End your walk here with a cup of mint tea in the rooftop café that overlooks Paris.

TIMING

This walk can be fitted into a morning or afternoon or serve as the basis for a leisurely day's exploring—given that several sites, notably Notre-Dame and the Musée de Cluny—deserve a lengthy visit. If you're with children, try to do this tour on a Thursday, when the enchanting Grande Galerie d'Évolution stays open till 10 PM. You can easily make a brief excursion to the Bibliothèque François-Mitterrand.

Sights to See

㊼ **Arènes de Lutèce** (Lutèce Arena). This Roman arena was only discovered in 1869 and has since been excavated and landscaped to reveal parts of the original amphitheater. Designed as a theater and circus, the arena was almost totally destroyed by the barbarians in AD 280, although you can still see part of the stage and tiered seating. ✉ *Entrances on rue Monge and rue de Navarre.* ☉ *Daily 8–sunset. Métro: Monge.*

66 **Bibliothèque François-Mitterrand** (François Mitterrand Library). The last of former president Mitterrand's *grands travaux* (great building projects) opened in early 1997. The new library subsumes the majority of the collections in the old Bibliothèque Nationale and, with some 11 million volumes between its walls, surpasses the Library of Congress as the largest library in the world. Architect Dominique Perrault's controversial design features four soaring 24-story towers. A stunning interior courtyard—sunk beneath ground level, with its thicket of mighty evergreens invisible as you approach—provides breathing space. You can visit part of the library for free or pay 20 francs to consult the books. ✉ *11 quai François-Mauriac,* ☎ *01–53–79–53–79.* ☉ *Tues.–Sat. 10–7, Sun. noon–6. Métro: Quai de la Gare.*

La Conciergerie. This turreted medieval building by the Seine was originally part of the royal palace on Ile de la Cité. Most people know it, however, as a prison, whence Danton, Robespierre, and Marie-Antoinette were bundled off to the guillotine. You can visit Marie-Antoinette's cell, the guardroom, and the monumental Salle des Gens d'Armes (Hall of the Men-at-Arms). ✉ *1 quai de l'Horloge,* ☎ *01–53–73–78–50.* ✉ *32 frs.* ☉ *Daily 9:30–6:30; winter, daily 10–5. Métro: Cité.*

☙ **Grande Galerie de l'Évolution** (Great Hall of Evolution). This vast, handsome glass-and-iron structure in the Jardin des Plantes was built, like the Eiffel Tower, in 1889 but abandoned in the 1960s. It reopened amid popular acclaim in 1994 and now contains one of the world's finest collections of taxidermy, including a section devoted to extinct and endangered species. ✉ *36 rue Geoffroy-St-Hilaire,* ☎ *01–40–79–39– 39.* ✉ *40 frs.* ☉ *Wed.–Mon. 10–6, Thurs. 10–10. Métro: Monge.*

56 **Ile St-Louis.** The smaller of the two Paris islands displays striking architectural unity, which stems from the efforts of a group of early 17th-century property speculators led by Christophe Marie. Leading Baroque architect Louis Le Vau (1612–70) was commissioned to erect a series of imposing town houses. *Métro: Pont-Marie.*

NEED A   Cafés all over sell the haute couture of ice cream, but **Berthillon** (✉ 31
BREAK?   rue St-Louis-en-l'Ile, ☎ 01–43–54–31–61) itself is the place to come.
             More than 30 flavors are served; expect to wait in line. The shop is
             open Wednesday–Sunday.

68 **Institut du Monde Arabe** (Arab World Institute). Jean Nouvel's striking 1988 glass-and-steel edifice adroitly fuses Arabic and European styles. Note the 240 shutterlike apertures that open and close to regulate light exposure. Inside, the Institute tries to do for Arab culture what the Pompidou Center does for modern art, with the help of a sound-and-image center; a vast library and documentation center; and an art museum. The top-floor café provides a good view of Paris. ✉ *1 rue des Fossés-St-Bernard,* ☎ *01–40–51–38–38.* ✉ *40 frs.* ☉ *Tues.–Sun. 10–6. Métro: Cardinal-Lemoine.*

☙ **65** **Jardin des Plantes** (Botanical Garden). This enormous swath of greenery contains the botanical garden, the Grande Galerie de l'Évolution (☞ *above*), and three natural history museums: the **Musée Entomologique**, devoted to insects; the **Musée Paléontologique**, to fossils and prehistoric animals; and the **Musée Minéralogique**, to rocks and minerals. There is also an alpine garden, an aquarium, a maze, a number of hothouses, and a small, old-fashioned zoo. ⊠ *Entrances on rue Geoffroy-St-Hilaire and rue Buffon.* 🎟 *Zoo 30 frs; Mineralogy Museum 30 frs; Paleontology Museum 20 frs; Entomology Museum 15 frs.* ☉ *Garden daily 7:30–sunset; zoo daily 9–6; museums Wed.–Mon. 10–5. Métro: Monge.*

⑤⑦ Mémorial de la Déportation (Deportation Memorial). On the eastern tip of the Ile de la Cité, in what was once the city morgue, lies a starkly moving modern crypt, dedicated to those French men, women, and children who died in Nazi concentration camps. 🎟 *Free.* ☉ *Daily 9–6; winter, daily 9–dusk. Métro: Maubert-Mutualité.*

⑥④ Mosquée (Mosque). The city mosque was built from 1922 to 1925, complete with arcades and minaret, and decorated in the style of Moorish Spain. The sunken garden and tiled patios are open to the public (the prayer rooms are not) and so are the *hammams,* or Turkish baths. Venture in and sip a restorative cup of sweet mint tea at the café. ⊠ *2 pl. du Puits-de-l'Ermite,* ☎ *01–45–35–97–33.* 🎟 *15 frs for guided tour, 65 frs for Turkish baths.* ☉ *Baths daily 11 AM–8 PM; Fri. and Sun. men only; Mon., Wed., Thurs., and Sat. women only. Guided tours of mosque Sat.–Thurs. 10–noon and 2–6. Métro: Monge.*

⑥⓪ Musée National du Moyen-Age (National Museum of the Middle Ages). This museum is housed in the 15th-century Hôtel de Cluny. The mansion has an intricately vaulted chapel and a cloistered courtyard with mullioned windows that originally belonged to monks of the Cluny Abbey in Burgundy, hence the museum's former name, the Musée de Cluny. A stunning array of tapestries heads its vast exhibition of medieval decorative arts. Alongside the mansion are the city's Roman baths and the *Boatmen's Pillar,* Paris's oldest sculpture. ⊠ *6 pl. Paul-Painlevé,* ☎ *01–53–73–78–00.* 🎟 *30 frs, Sun. 20 frs.* ☉ *Wed.– Mon. 9:45–5:45. Métro: Cluny–La Sorbonne.*

★ **⑤⑤ Notre-Dame.** Looming above the large, pedestrian place du Parvis is Notre-Dame Cathedral, the most enduring symbol of Paris. Begun in 1163, it was not completed until 1345. The facade seems perfectly proportioned until you notice that the north (left) tower is wider than the south tower. The south tower houses the great bell of Notre-Dame, as tolled by Quasimodo, Victor Hugo's fictional hunchback. The cathedral interior, with its vast proportions, soaring nave, and soft, multicolor light filtering through the stained-glass windows, inspires awe, despite the inevitable throngs of tourists. Visit early in the morning, when the cathedral is at its lightest and least crowded. Window space is limited and filled with shimmering stained glass; the circular rose windows in the transept are particularly delicate. The 387-step climb up the towers is worth the effort for a perfect view of the famous gargoyles and the heart of Paris. ⊠ *pl. du Parvis.* 🎟 *Towers 32 frs.* ☉ *Cathedral 8 AM–7 PM; tower daily (summer) 9:30–12:15 and 2–6, daily (winter) 10–5. Métro: Cité.*

⑥② Panthéon. Originally commissioned as a church by Louis XV, as a mark of gratitude for his recovery from a grave illness in 1744, the Panthéon is now a monument to France's most glorious historical figures, including Voltaire, Zola, Rousseau, and dozens of French statesmen, military heroes, and other thinkers. Germain Soufflot's building was not begun until 1764, or completed until 1790, whereupon during the French Revolution, its windows were blocked and it was transformed into the national shrine it is today. ⊠ *pl. du Panthéon,* ☎ *01–44– 32–18–00.* 🎟 *32 frs.* ☉ *Daily 10–5:30. Métro: Cardinal-Lemoine; RER: Luxembourg.*

54 **Palais de Justice** (Law Courts). In about 1860, the city law courts were built by Baron Haussmann in his characteristically weighty neoclassical style. You can wander around the buildings, watch the bustle of the lawyers, or attend a court hearing. But the real interest here is the medieval part of the complex, spared by Haussmann: La Conciergerie and Ste-Chapelle (☞ *above* and *below*, respectively). ⊠ *bd. du Palais. Métro: Cité.*

53 **Pont Neuf** (New Bridge). Crossing the Ile de la Cité, just behind square du Vert-Galant, is the oldest bridge in Paris, confusingly called the New Bridge, or Pont Neuf. It was completed in 1607 and was the first bridge in the city to be built without houses lining either side. *Métro: Pont-Neuf.*

★ **Ste-Chapelle** (Holy Chapel). This chapel was built by Louis IX (1226–70), later canonized St. Louis, in the 1240s, to house what he believed to be Christ's Crown of Thorns, purchased from Emperor Baldwin of Constantinople. The building's lead-covered wood spire, rebuilt in 1854, rises 246 ft. The somewhat garish lower chapel is less impressive than the upper one, whose walls consist of little else but dazzling 13th-century stained glass. ⊠ *In the Palais de Justice,* ☎ *01–43–54–30–09 for concert information.* ☜ *32 frs.* ☉ *Apr.–Sept., daily 9:30–6:30; Oct.–Mar., daily 10–5. Métro: Cité.*

63 **St-Étienne-du-Mont.** The ornate facade of this mainly 16th-century church combines Gothic, Baroque, and Renaissance elements. Inside, the curly, carved rood screen (1525–35), separating nave and chancel, is the only one of its kind in Paris. ⊠ *pl. de l'Abbé-Basset. Métro: Cardinal-Lemoine.*

58 **St-Julien-le-Pauvre.** This tiny church was built at the same time as Notre-Dame (1165–1220). The church belongs to a Greek Orthodox order today, but was originally named for St. Julien, bishop of Le Mans, who was nicknamed Le Pauvre (The Poor) after he gave all his money away. ⊠ *rue St-Julien-le-Pauvre. Métro: St-Michel.*

59 **St-Séverin.** This unusually wide, Flamboyant Gothic church dominates a Left Bank neighborhood filled with squares and pedestrian streets. Note the splendidly deviant spiraling column in the forest of pillars behind the altar. ⊠ *rue des Prêtres St-Séverin.* ☉ *Weekdays 11–5:30, Sat. 11–10. Métro: St-Michel.*

61 **La Sorbonne.** Named after Robert de Sorbon, a medieval canon who founded a theological college here in 1253, this is one of the oldest universities in Europe. The church and university buildings were restored by Cardinal Richelieu in the 17th century, and the maze of amphitheaters, lecture rooms, and laboratories, and the surrounding courtyards and narrow streets, retains a hallowed air. You can visit the main courtyard on rue de la Sorbonne and peek into the main lecture hall, a major meeting point during the tumultuous student upheavals of 1968. The square is dominated by the noble university church with cupola and Corinthian columns. Inside is the white marble tomb of that ultimate crafty cleric, Cardinal Richelieu himself. ⊠ *rue de la Sorbonne. Métro: Cluny–La Sorbonne.*

From Orsay to St-Germain

This walk covers the Left Bank, from the Musée d'Orsay in the stately 7ᵉ arrondissement to the lively and colorful area around St-Germain-des-Prés in the 6ᵉ. The Musée d'Orsay, in a daringly converted Belle Époque rail station on the Seine, houses one of the world's most spectacular arrays of Impressionist paintings. Farther along the river, the

18th-century Palais Bourbon, home to the National Assembly, sets the tone for the 7ᵉ arrondissement. Luxurious ministries and embassies—including the Hôtel Matignon, residence of the French prime minister—line the surrounding streets, their majestic scale in total keeping with the Hôtel des Invalides, whose gold-leafed dome climbs heavenward above the regal tomb of Napoléon. The splendid Rodin Museum is only a short walk away.

To the east, away from the splendor of the 7ᵉ, the boulevard St-Michel slices the Left Bank in two: on one side, the Latin Quarter (☞ The Islands and the Latin Quarter, *above*); on the other, the Faubourg St-Germain, named for St-Germain-des-Prés, the oldest church in Paris. The venerable church tower has long acted as a beacon for intellectuals, most famously during the 1950s when Albert Camus, Jean-Paul Sartre, and Simone de Beauvoir ate and drank existentialism in the neighborhood cafés. Today most of the philosophizing is done by tourists, yet a wealth of bookshops, art stores, and antiques galleries ensure that "St-Germain," as the area is commonly known, retains its highbrow appeal. In the southern part of this district is the city's most famous and colorful park, the Jardin du Luxembourg.

A Good Walk

Start at the **Musée d'Orsay** ㉖, famed for its collection of art from 1848–1914. A good meeting point is the pedestrian square outside the museum, where huge bronze statues of an elephant and a rhinoceros disprove the idea that the French take their art *too* seriously. Head west along rue de Lille to the **Palais Bourbon** ㉘, home of the Assemblée Nationale (French Parliament).

Rue de l'Université leads from the Assemblée to the grassy Esplanade des Invalides and an encounter with the **Hôtel des Invalides** ㉙, founded by Louis XIV to house wounded (or "invalid") veterans. The most impressive dome in Paris towers over the church at the Invalides—the Église du Dôme. From the church, double back along boulevard des Invalides and take rue de Varenne to the Hôtel Biron, better known as the **Musée Rodin** ㉚, where you can see a fine collection of Auguste Rodin's emotionally charged statues. The quiet, distinguished 18th-century streets between the Rodin Museum and the Parliament are filled with embassies and ministries.

Continue on to rue du Bac, turn left, then take a right onto rue de Grenelle, to the **Musée Maillol** ㉛, dedicated to the work of sculptor Aristide Maillol. Continue on rue de Grenelle past Edme Bouchardon's Fontaine des Quatre Saisons (Four Seasons Fountain) to the carrefour de la Croix-Rouge, with its mighty bronze Centaur by the contemporary sculptor César. Take rue du Vieux-Colombier to place St-Sulpice, a spacious square ringed with cafés. Looming over the square is the enormous church of **St-Sulpice** ㉞.

Exit the church, head back across the square, and turn right on rue Bonaparte to reach **St-Germain-des-Prés** ㉟, Paris's oldest church. Across the cobbled place St-Germain-des-Prés is the café Les Deux Magots, one of the principal haunts of the intelligentsia after World War II. Two doors down boulevard St-Germain is the Café de Flore, another popular spot with the likes of Jean-Paul Sartre and Simone de Beauvoir. Follow rue de l'Abbaye, alongside the far side of the church, to rue de Furstemberg. The street opens out into a quiet square where you'll find Eugène Delacroix's studio, the **Atelier Delacroix** ㊱. Take a left on rue Jacob and turn right down rue Bonaparte to the **École Nationale des Beaux-Arts** ㊲, whose students can often be seen painting and sketching on the nearby quays and bridges.

Continue down to the Seine and turn right along the quai, past the **Institut de France** ⑦. With its distinctive dome, curved facade, and commanding position overlooking the Pont des Arts—a footbridge affording delightful views of the Louvre and Ile de la Cité—the institute is one of the city's most impressive waterside sights. Continue along quai de Conti past the **Hôtel des Monnaies,** the former national mint. Head up rue Dauphine. It's linked 150 yards up by the open-air passage Dauphine to rue Mazarine, which leads left to the carrefour de Buci, where you can find one of the best morning food markets in Paris. Rue de l'Ancienne-Comédie, so named because it was the first home of the legendary Comédie Française, leads up to busy place de l'Odéon. Cross boulevard St-Germain, and climb rue de l'Odéon to the colonnaded Théâtre de l'Odéon (☞ Nightlife and the Arts, *below*). Behind the theater lies the spacious **Jardin du Luxembourg** ⑦, one of the most stylish parks in the city.

TIMING

This walk could take four hours to a couple of days, depending on how long you spend in the plethora of museums along the way. Aim for an early start—that way you can hit the Musée d'Orsay early, when crowds are smaller, then get to the rue de Buci street market in full swing, in the late afternoon (the stalls are generally closed for lunch until 3 PM). Note that the Hôtel des Invalides is open daily, but Orsay is closed Monday. You might consider returning to one or more museums on another day or night—Orsay is open late on Thursday evening.

Sights to See

❼ **Atelier Delacroix** (Delacroix's Studio). The studio of artist Eugène Delacroix (1798–1863) contains only a small collection of his sketches and drawings. But if you want to pay homage to France's foremost Romantic painter, you'll want to visit this museum. ☒ *6 rue Furstemberg,* ☏ *01–43–54–04–87.* 🎟 *15 frs, Sun. 10 frs.* ☉ *Wed.–Mon. 9:45–5:15. Métro: St-Germain-des-Prés.*

❼ **École Nationale des Beaux-Arts** (National Fine Arts College). Occupying three large mansions near the Seine, this school—today the breeding ground for painters, sculptors, and architects—was once the site of a convent, founded in 1608. Only the church and cloister remained by the time the Beaux Arts school was established in 1816. Wander into the courtyard and galleries of the school to see the casts and copies of the statues stored here for safekeeping during the Revolution. ☒ *14 rue Bonaparte.* ☉ *Daily 1–7. Métro: St-Germain-des-Prés.*

NEED A
BREAK?
The popular **La Palette** café (☒ 43 rue de Seine, ☏ 01–43–26–68–15), on the corner of rue de Seine and rue Callot, has long been a favorite haunt of Beaux-Arts students.

❼ **Hôtel des Invalides.** "Les Invalides," as it is widely known, is an outstanding monumental Baroque ensemble, designed by Libéral Bruand in the 1670s at the behest of Louis XIV to house wounded, or "invalid," soldiers. Although no more than a handful of old-timers live at the Invalides today, the military link remains in the form of the **Musée de l'Armée,** a military museum. The **Musée des Plans-Reliefs,** also housed here, contains a fascinating collection of old scale models of French towns. The 17th-century **Église St-Louis des Invalides** is the Invalides's
★ original church. More impressive is Jules Hardouin-Mansart's **Église du Dôme,** built onto the end of the church of St-Louis but blocked off from it in 1793. The remains of Napoléon are here. ☒ *51 bis bd. de la Tour-Maubourg,* ☏ *01–44–42–37–67.* 🎟 *37 frs.* ☉ *Apr.–Sept., daily 10–6; Oct.–Mar., daily 10–5. Métro: Latour-Maubourg.*

Hôtel des Monnaies (Mint). Louis XVI transferred the Royal Mint to this imposing mansion in the late 18th century. Although the mint was moved again, to Pessac, near Bordeaux, in 1973, weights and measures, medals, and limited-edition coins are still made here. The **Musée de la Monnaie** (Coin Museum) has an extensive collection of coins, documents, engravings, and paintings. On Tuesday and Friday at 2 PM you can catch the coin metal craftsmen. ⊠ *11 quai de Conti,* ☎ *01–40–46–55–35.* 🎫 *20 frs.* 🕙 *Tues.–Fri. 11–5:30, weekends noon–5:30. Métro: Pont-Neuf.*

78 Institut de France (French Institute). This is one of France's most revered cultural institutions, and its curved, dome-topped facade is one of the Left Bank's most impressive waterside sights. It was built as a college in 1661; at the beginning of the 19th century, Napóleon had it transferred here from the Louvre. The Académie Française, the oldest of the five academies that compose the Institute, was created by Cardinal Richelieu in 1635. Its first major task (still unfinished) was to edit the definitive French dictionary; it is also charged with safeguarding the purity of the French language. ⊠ *pl. de l'Institut.* 🕙 *Closed to the general public. Métro: Pont-Neuf.*

79 Jardin du Luxembourg (Luxembourg Garden). One of the prettiest of Paris's few large parks, the Luxembourg Garden has fountains, ponds, trim hedges, precisely planted rows of trees, and gravel walks typical of the French fondness for formal landscaping. The 17th-century **Palais de Luxembourg** (Luxembourg Palace), overlooking the gardens, houses the French Senate; it is not open to the public. It was built, like the surrounding garden, for Marie de' Medici, widow of Henri IV. It was not completed until 1627, and Marie lived there for just five years before being expelled from France by Cardinal Richelieu in 1632. *Métro: Odéon; RER: Luxembourg.*

73 Musée Maillol. Plaster casts and bronzes by Art Deco sculptor Aristide Maillol (1861–1944), whose sleek, stylized nudes adorn the Tuileries, can be admired at this handsome town house lovingly restored by his former muse Dina Vierny. ⊠ *61 rue de Grenelle,* ☎ *01–42–22–59–58.* 🎫 *40 frs.* 🕙 *Wed.–Mon. 11–6. Métro: Rue du Bac.*

69 Musée d'Orsay. In a stylishly converted train station, the Orsay Museum—devoted to the arts (mainly French) spanning the period 1848–1914—is one of the city's most popular. The main artistic attraction is the Impressionists: Renoir, Sisley, Pissarro, and Monet are all well represented. The post-Impressionists—Cézanne, van Gogh, Gauguin, and Toulouse-Lautrec—are on the top floor. On the first floor, you'll find the work of Manet and the delicate nuances of Degas. If you prefer more academic paintings, look for Puvis de Chavannes's larger-than-life classical canvases. And if you're excited by more modern developments, look for the early 20th-century Fauves (meaning wild beasts, the name given them by an outraged critic in 1905)—particularly Matisse, Derain, and Vlaminck. Thought-provoking sculptures lurk at every turn. ⊠ *1 rue de Bellechasse,* ☎ *01–40–49–48–14.* 🎫 *39 frs, Sun. 27 frs.* 🕙 *Tues.–Sat. 10–6 (Thurs till 9:30), Sun. 9–6. Métro: Solférino; RER: Musée d'Orsay.*

NEED A BREAK? Find respite from the overwhelming collection of art in the **Musée d'Orsay Café** behind one of the giant station clocks, close to the Impressionist galleries on the top floor.

72 Musée Rodin. The 18th-century Hôtel Biron makes a gracious setting for the sculpture of Auguste Rodin (1840–1917). You'll doubtless recognize the seated *Le Penseur* (*The Thinker*), with his elbow resting on his knee, and the passionate *Le Baiser* (*The Kiss*). From the second-floor rooms, which contain some fine paintings by Rodin's friend Eugène Carrière (1849–1906), and some fine sculptures by Rodin's mistress, Camille Claudel (1864–1943), you can see the large garden behind the house. Don't skip the garden: It is exceptional both for its rosebushes (more than 2,000 of them) and for its sculpture. ⊠ *77 rue de Varenne,* ☎ *01–44–18–61–10.* ✉ *28 frs, Sun. 18 frs.* ☉ *Easter–Oct., Tues.–Sun. 10–6; Nov.–Easter, Tues.–Sun. 10–5. Métro: Varenne.*

⑦ Palais Bourbon. The most prominent feature of the home of the Assemblée Nationale (French Parliament) is its colonnaded facade, commissioned by Napoléon. ⊠ *pl. du Palais-Bourbon.* ☉ *During temporary exhibits only. Métro: Assemblée Nationale.*

⑦ St-Germain-des-Prés. Paris's oldest church was first built to shelter a relic of the true cross, brought back from Spain in AD 542. The chancel was enlarged and the church then consecrated by Pope Alexander III in 1163; the tall, sturdy tower—a Left Bank landmark—dates from this period. The church stages superb organ concerts and recitals. ⊠ *pl. St-Germain.* ☉ *Weekdays 8–7:30, weekends 8–9. Métro: St-Germain-des-Prés.*

⑦ St-Sulpice. Dubbed the "Cathedral of the Left Bank," this enormous 17th-century church has entertained some unlikely christenings, including the Marquis de Sade's and Charles Baudelaire's. The 18th-century facade was never finished, and its unequal towers add a playful touch to an otherwise sober design. ⊠ *pl. St-Sulpice. Métro: St-Sulpice.*

Montparnasse

A mile south of the Seine is the district of Montparnasse, named after Mount Parnassus, the Greek mountain associated with the worship of Apollo and the Muses. Montparnasse's cultural heyday came in the first four decades of the 20th century, when it replaced Montmartre as *the* place for painters and poets to live, and prompted the launch of a string of artsy brasseries along the district's main thoroughfare, the broad boulevard du Montparnasse. The boulevard may lack poetic charm these days, but nightlife stays the pace, as bars, clubs, restaurants, and cinemas crackle with energy beneath Europe's second tallest high-rise: the 59-story Tour Montparnasse. Although the tower itself is a typically bland product of the early 1970s, of note only for the view from the top, several more adventurous buildings have risen in its wake: Ricardo Bofil's semicircular Amphithéâtre housing complex, the glass-cubed Cartier center for contemporary art, and the Montparnasse train station with its giant glass facade and designer garden above the tracks. If you have a deeper feel for history, you may prefer the sumptuous Baroque church of Val-de-Grâce or the quiet earth of Montparnasse Cemetery. After ignoring Hitler's orders to blow up the city, it was in Montparnasse that Governor von Choltitz signed the German surrender in August 1944.

A Good Walk

Walk or take the métro to the Vavin station (only three short stops from St-Sulpice; ☞ From Orsay to St-Germain, *above*), beneath Rodin's 10-ft statue of Balzac, at the corner of boulevards Raspail and Montparnasse. Four cafés, famous since Montparnasse's interwar heyday, are all within a stone's throw on boulevard du Montparnasse: the Café du Dôme at No. 108, La Coupole at No. 102, La Rotonde at No. 105, and La Sélect at No. 99. Head west along boulevard du Montparnasse to **place du 18-Juin-1940.** Towering above it is the **Tour Montparnasse** ⑧. Behind the skyscraper is the huge, gleaming glass facade of the Gare Montparnasse. Take boulevard Edgar-Quinet to the side of the tower and turn right onto rue de la Gaîté.

Cross avenue du Maine and follow rue Vercingétorix to **place de Catalogne** ⑧, dominated by the monumental curves of the postmodern Amphithéâtre housing complex. Explore its arcades and circular forecourts, and compare its impersonal grandeur with the cozy charm of Notre-Dame du Travail, behind. As you reemerge from the Amphithéâtre, Pont des Cinq-Martyres leads left over the rail tracks of Montparnasse station. The tracks are hidden beneath a regimented modern park, the **Jardin Atlantique** ⑧. Rue Jean-Zay leads from place de Catalogne to the corner of the high-walled **Cimetière de Montparnasse** ⑧. Enter the cemetery down rue Froidevaux if you wish to pay homage to local and foreign worthies. Rue Froidevaux continues to place Denfert-Rochereau, where you can admire the huge bronze *Lion of Belfort* by Frédéric-Auguste Bartholdi.

Walk up boulevard Raspail, past the eye-catching glass cubicle that houses the **Fondation Cartier** ⑧. Take the third right onto rue Campagne-Première, a handsome street once inhabited by Picasso, Miró, Kandinsky, and Modigliani. Turn right at the bottom of the street onto boulevard du Montparnasse. At avenue de l'Observatoire stands perhaps the most famous bastion of Left Bank café culture, the Closerie des Lilas. Up avenue de l'Observatoire is the Observatoire de Paris, Louis XIV's astronomical observatory. In the other direction, the tree-lined avenue sweeps past the Fontaine de l'Observatoire. To the right of the fountain, down rue du Val-de-Grâce, is the imposing Baroque dome of the **Val de Grâce** ⑧ church. Straight ahead is the Jardin du Luxembourg (☞ From Orsay to St-Germain, *above*).

TIMING

The walk around Montparnasse is just under 5 km (3 mi) long and will comfortably take a morning or an afternoon if you choose to check out one of the historic cafés and the cemetery along the way.

Sights to See

⑧ **Cimetière de Montparnasse** (Montparnasse Cemetery). This cemetery is not picturesque, but it contains many of the quarter's most illustrious residents: Charles Baudelaire, Auguste Bartholdi, Jean-Paul Sartre, Man Ray, Samuel Beckett, Jean Seberg, and Serge Gainsbourg. ⊠ *Entrances at rue Froidevaux, bd. Edgar-Quinet. Métro: Raspail, Gaîté.*

⑧ **Fondation Cartier** (Cartier Foundation). Architect Jean Nouvel's eye-catching giant glass cubicle is a suitable setting for the temporary, thought-provoking shows of contemporary art organized here by jewelry giant Cartier. ⊠ *261 bd. Raspail,* ☎ *01–42–18–56–50.* 💶 *30 frs.* ☉ *Tues.–Sun. noon–8. Métro: Raspail.*

⑧ **Jardin Atlantique** (Atlantic Garden). This small park, which opened in 1994, was planted on a concourse constructed over the first 100 yards of the tracks leading to the Gare Montparnasse. It features an assortment of trees and plants from countries on the Atlantic Ocean. ⊠ *Pont des Cinq-Martyrs-du-Lycée-Buffon. Métro: Gaîté.*

⑧ **Place de Catalogne.** This square is dominated by Ricardo Boffil's monumental **Amphithéâtre** housing complex, with its chunky reinvention of classical detail, and the turn-of-the-century church of **Notre-Dame du Travail**, which made a powerful statement when it was built. Its riveted iron-and-steel framework was meant to symbolize the work ethos enshrouded in the church's name. *Métro: Gaîté.*

Place du 18-Juin-1940. This square beneath the Tour Montparnasse is named for the date of the radio speech Charles de Gaulle broadcast from London, urging the French to resist the Germans after the Nazi invasion of May 1940. And it was here that German military governor Dietrich von Choltitz surrendered to the Allies in August 1944, ignoring Hitler's orders to destroy the city as he withdrew. A plaque on the wall commemorates the event. *Métro: Montparnasse-Bienvenue.*

⑳ Tour Montparnasse (Montparnasse Tower). As Europe's second tallest skyscraper, completed in 1973, this 685-ft tower offers a stupendous view of Paris from its open-air roof terrace. Fifty-two of the 59 stories are taken up by offices, and a vast commercial complex, including a Galeries Lafayette department store, spreads over the first floor. Banal by day, the tower becomes Montparnasse's neon-lit beacon at night. ✉ *33 av. du Maine.* 🎫 *42 frs.* ☉ *Apr.–Sept., daily 9:30 AM–11:30 PM; Oct.–Mar., Sun.–Thurs. 9:30 AM–10:30 PM, Fri.–Sat. 9:30 AM–11 PM. Métro: Montparnasse-Bienvenue.*

㉟ Val de Grâce. This imposing 17th-century Left Bank church, extensively restored in the early 1990s, was commissioned by Anne of Austria and designed by François Mansart. Its powerfully rhythmic two-story facade rivals the Dôme Church at the Invalides as the city's most striking example of Italianate Baroque. ✉ *1 pl. Alphonse-Laveran. RER: Port-Royal.*

Montmartre

On a dramatic rise above the city is Montmartre, site of the Sacré-Coeur Basilica and home to a once-thriving artistic community. Although the fabled nightlife of old Montmartre has fizzled down to some glitzy nightclubs and porn shows, Montmartre still exudes history and Gallic charm.

Windmills once dotted Montmartre (often referred to by Parisians as *La Butte,* meaning "mound"). They were set up here not just because the hill was a good place to catch the wind—at more than 300 ft, it's the highest point in the city—but because Montmartre was covered with wheat fields and quarries right up to the end of the 19th century. Today, only 2 of the original 20 windmills remain.

Visiting Montmartre means negotiating a lot of steep streets and flights of steps. The crown atop this urban peak, the Sacré-Coeur Basilica, is something of an architectural oddity. It has been called everything from grotesque to sublime; its silhouette, viewed from afar at dusk or sunrise, looks more like a mosque than a cathedral.

A Good Walk

Begin at **place Blanche** ㊏; just off of it is the **Moulin Rouge** ㊐, the windmill turned dance hall, immortalized by Toulouse-Lautrec. Walk up rue Lepic, to the right of the Moulin Rouge, and wind your way up to the **Moulin de la Galette** ㊑, atop its leafy hillock opposite rue Tholozé, once a path over the hill. Turn right down rue Tholozé, past Studio 28, the first cinema built expressly for experimental films. Continue down rue Tholozé to rue des Abbesses, and turn left toward the triangular **place des Abbesses** ㊒. Follow rue Ravignan as it climbs north, via place Émile-Goudeau, an enchanting little cobbled square, to the **Bateau-Lavoir** ㊓, or Boat Wash House, at its northern edge. Painters Picasso and Braque had studios in the original building; this drab concrete edifice was built in its place. Continue up the hill via rue de la Mire to place Jean-Baptiste Clément, where Amedeo Modigliani had a studio.

The upper reaches of rue Lepic lead to rue Norvins, formerly rue des Moulins (Windmill Street). At the end of the street, to the left, is stylish avenue Junot. Continue right past the bars and tourist shops until you reach famous **place du Tertre** ⑨. Around the corner on rue Poulbot, the **Espace Dalí** ⑨ houses works by Salvador Dalí, who once had a studio in the area. Return to place du Tertre. Looming menacingly behind is the scaly white dome of the Basilique du **Sacré-Coeur** ⑨. The cavernous interior is worth visiting for its golden mosaics; climb to the top of the dome for the view of Paris. Walk back toward place du Tertre. Turn right onto rue du Mont-Cenis and left onto rue Cortot, site of the **Musée du Vieux Montmartre** ⑨, which, like the Bateau-Lavoir, once sheltered an illustrious group of painters, writers, and assorted cabaret artists. Another famous Montmartre landmark is at No. 22: the bar-cabaret **Lapin Agile** ⑨. Opposite the Lapin Agile is the tiny Cimetière St-Vincent, where painter Maurice Utrillo is buried.

TIMING

Reserve four to five hours for this walk: Many of the streets are steep and slow. Include half an hour each at Sacré-Coeur and the museums (the Dalí museum is open daily, but the Montmartre museum is closed Monday). From Easter through September, Montmartre is besieged by tourists. Two hints to avoid the worst of the rush: Come on a gray day, when Montmartre's sullen-tone facades suffer less than most others in the city; or during the afternoon, and return to place du Tertre (maybe via the funicular) by the early evening, once the tourist buses have departed.

Sights to See

⑨ **Bateau-Lavoir** (Boat Wash House). Montmartre poet Max Jacob coined the name, meaning Boat Wash House, for the original building on this site (which burned down in 1970), saying it resembled a boat and that the warren of artists' studios within was perpetually paint-splattered and in need of a good hosing down. It was here that Pablo Picasso and Georges Braque made their first bold stabs at the concept of Cubism. The new building also contains art studios, but is the epitome of poured concrete drabness. ⊠ *13 pl. Émile-Goudeau. Métro: Abbesses.*

⑨ **Espace Dalí** (Dalí Center). Some of Salvador Dalí's less familiar works are among the 25 sculptures and 300 prints housed in this museum with an atmosphere that is meant to approximate the surreal experience. ⊠ *11 rue Poulbot,* ☎ *01–42–64–40–10.* ☞ *35 frs.* ☉ *Daily 10–6; summer, daily 10–8. Métro: Abbesses.*

⑨ **Lapin Agile.** This bar-cabaret, originally one of the raunchiest haunts in Montmartre, got its curious name—the Nimble Rabbit—when the owner, André Gill, hung up a sign of a laughing rabbit jumping out of a saucepan clutching a bottle of wine. Locals christened it the Lapin à Gill, meaning Gill's Rabbit. When, in 1886, it was sold to cabaret singer Jules Jouy, he called it the Lapin Agile, which has the same pronunciation in French as Lapin à Gill. In 1903 the premises were bought by the most celebrated cabaret entrepreneur of them all, Aristide Bruand, portrayed by Toulouse-Lautrec in a series of famous posters. ⊠ *22 rue des Saules,* ☎ *01–46–06–85–87. Métro: Lamarck-Caulaincourt.*

⑧ **Moulin de la Galette** (Biscuit Windmill). This is one of two remaining windmills in Montmartre. It was once the focal point of an open-air cabaret (made famous in a painting by Renoir), and rumor has it that the miller, Debray, was strung up on its sails and spun to death after striving vainly to defend it against invading Cossacks in 1814. Unfortunately, it is privately owned and can only be admired from the street below. ⊠ *rue Tholozé. Métro: Abbesses.*

⑧ **Moulin Rouge** (Red Windmill). This world-famous cabaret was built in 1885 as a windmill, then transformed into a dance hall in 1900. Those wild, early days were immortalized by Toulouse-Lautrec in his posters

Montmartre

and paintings. It still trades shamelessly on the notion of Paris as a city of sin: If you fancy a Vegas-style night out, this is the place to go. ⊠ *82 bd. de Clichy,* ☎ *01–53–09–82–82. Métro: Blanche.*

94 **Musée du Vieux Montmartre** (Old Montmartre Museum). In its turn-of-the-century heyday, Montmartre's historical museum was home to an illustrious group of painters, writers, and assorted cabaret artists. Foremost among them were Renoir and Maurice Utrillo. The museum also provides a view of the tiny **vineyard**—the only one in Paris—on neighboring rue des Saules. A symbolic 125 gallons of wine are still produced every year. ⊠ *12 rue Cortot,* ☎ *01–46–06–61–11.* ⊡ *25 frs.* ☉ *Tues.–Sun. 11–6. Métro: Lamarck-Caulaincourt.*

89 **Place des Abbesses.** This triangular square is typical of the picturesque, slightly countrified style that has made Montmartre famous. The entrance to the Abbesses métro station, a curving, sensuous mass of delicate iron, is one of the two original Art Nouveau entrance canopies left in Paris. *Métro: Abbesses.*

86 **Place Blanche** (White Square). The name White 6quare comes from the clouds of chalky dust that used to be churned up by the carts that carried wheat and crushed flour from the nearby windmills, including the Moulin Rouge. *Métro: Blanche.*

91 **Place du Tertre.** This tumbling square (*tertre* means hillock) regains its village atmosphere only in the winter, when the branches of the plane-trees sketch traceries against the sky. At any other time of year you'll be confronted by crowds of tourists and a swarm of third-rate artists clamoring to do your portrait. (If one produces an unsolicited portrait, you are not obligated to buy it.) **La Mère Catherine,** on one corner of the square, was a favorite bistro with the Russian Cossacks who occupied Paris in 1814. *Métro: Abbesses.*

NEED A BREAK? **Patachou** (⊠ 9 pl. du Tertre, ☎ 01–42–51–06–06), serving exquisite, if expensive, cakes and teas, sounds the one classy note on place du Tertre.

93 **Sacré-Coeur.** The Sacred Heart Basilica was erected as a sort of national guilt offering in expiation for the blood shed during the Commune and Franco-Prussian War in 1870–71 and was largely financed by French Catholics fearful of an anticlerical backlash under the new republican regime. The basilica was not consecrated until 1919. Stylistically, the Sacré-Coeur borrows elements from Romanesque and Byzantine models. The gloomy, cavernous interior is worth visiting for its golden mosaics; climb to the top of the dome for the view of Paris. ⊠ *pl. du Parvis-du-Sacré-Coeur.* ⊠ *Free. Métro: Anvers.*

DINING

Revised and updated by Alexander Lobrano

This listing includes restaurants of a variety of styles and price levels, from formal dining rooms serving haute cuisine to fashionable bistros serving classical and contemporary cooking. Generally, Paris restaurants are open from noon to about 2 and from 7:30 or 8 to 10 or 10:30. It's best to make reservations, particularly in summer, although the reviews only state when reservations are absolutely essential. If you want no-smoking seating, make this clear; the mandatory no-smoking area is sometimes limited to a very few tables. Brasseries have longer hours and often serve all day and late into the evening; some are open 24 hours. Assume a restaurant is open every day unless otherwise indicated. Surprisingly, many prestigious restaurants close on Saturday as well as Sunday. July and August are the most common months for annual closings, although Paris in August is no longer the wasteland it used to be.

Most restaurants have two basic types of menu: à la carte and *prix-fixe* (fixed-price, or *un menu*), which is usually the best value, though choices are limited. Most menus begin with a first course, followed by fish and poultry, then meat; it's rare today that anyone orders something from all three. However, outside of brasseries, wine bars, and other simple places, it's inappropriate to order just one dish, as you'll understand when you see the waiter's expression. The popular *menu dégustation* (tasting menu), with many small courses, allows for a wide sampling of the chef's offerings. In general, consider the season and the daily specials when ordering (for help, *see* the Menu Guide at the end of this book).

Although prices include tax and tip, pocket change left on the table in simple places, or an additional 5% in better restaurants, is appreciated. Places where a jacket and tie are de rigueur are noted. Otherwise, use common sense—jeans and T-shirts are not suitable in Paris restaurants, nor are shorts or running clothes, except in the most casual bistros or cafés.

CATEGORY	COST*
$$$$	over 550 frs
$$$	300 frs–550 frs
$$	175 frs–300 frs
$	under 175 frs

*per person for a three-course meal, including 20.6% tax and service but not drinks

1er Arrondissement (Louvre/Les Halles)

FRENCH

$$ ✕ **Restaurant du Palais-Royal.** Tucked away in the northern corner of the magnificent Palais-Royal garden, this pleasant bistro has good food and a charming terrace. A salad of baby scallops and pleurotus mushrooms in a balsamic vinaigrette are among the interesting contemporary dishes. ⊠ *Jardin du Palais-Royal, 110 Galerie Valois,* ☎ *01–40–20–00–27. AE, MC, V. Closed Sun. No lunch Sat. Métro: Palais-Royal.*

$–$$ ✕ **Aux Crus de Bourgogne.** This delightfully old-fashioned bistro, with its bright lights and red-checked tablecloths, attracts a happy, lively crowd. It opened in 1932 and quickly became popular by serving two luxury items—foie gras and cold lobster with homemade mayonnaise—at surprisingly low prices, a tradition that happily continues. ⊠ *3 rue Bachaumont,* ☎ *01–42–33–48–24. V. Closed weekends and Aug. Métro: Sentier.*

2e Arrondissement (Le Bourse)

FRENCH

$$ ✕ **Chez Georges.** The traditional bistro cooking is good—herring, sole, kidneys, steak, and *frites* (fries)—but the atmosphere is better. A wood-paneled entry leads you to an elegant and unpretentious dining room where one long, white-clothed stretch of table lines the mirrored walls. ⊠ *1 rue du Mail,* ☎ *01–42–60–07–11. AE, DC, MC, V. Closed Sun. and Aug. Métro: Sentier.*

VIETNAMESE

$ ✕ **Le Moi.** At this simple but good Vietnamese restaurant, next door to Harry's New York Bar (☞ Nightlife, *below*), sample *nems* (deep-fried mini–spring rolls), steamed dumplings, or poultry, beef, or seafood salads enlivened with fresh Asian herbs like lemongrass and lemon basil. Service is prompt and friendly. ⊠ *5 rue Daunou,* ☎ *01–47–03–92–05. MC, V. Closed Sun. No lunch Sat. Métro: Opéra.*

3ᵉ Arrondissement (Beaubourg/Marais)

FRENCH

$ ✕ **Au Bascou.** Gregarious proprietor Jean-Guy Lousteau enthusiastically shares his knowledge of the wines of southwest France at this fashionable little bistro. The sturdy, savory cuisine of the Basque country stars on the menu; the country ham and cod with broccoli puree are particularly flavorful. ✉ *38 rue Réaumur,* ☎ *01–42–72–69–25. MC, V. Closed weekends. Métro: Arts et Métiers.*

NORTH AFRICAN

$ ✕ **Chez Omar.** Come here for couscous, the signature North African dish, with grilled lamb, *merguez* (spicy, red) sausage, or chicken; portions are generous. The restaurant, in a former turn-of-the-century bistro, is popular with a fashionable crowd. Proprietor Omar Guerida is famously friendly and speaks English. ✉ *47 rue de Bretagne,* ☎ *01–42–72–36–26. MC, V. No lunch Sun. Métro: Filles du Calvaire.*

4ᵉ Arrondissement (Marais/Ile St-Louis)

FRENCH

$$ ✕ **Le Vieux Bistro.** Overlook the touristy location next to Notre-Dame and the corny name, "The Old Bistro." This place really *is* generations old, and its menu is full of bistro classics, such as beef fillet with marrow, and tart Tatin. The decor is nondescript, but the frequently fancy crowd doesn't seem to notice. ✉ *14 rue du Cloître-Notre-Dame,* ☎ *01–43–54–18–95. MC, V. Métro: Hôtel de Ville.*

$ ✕ **Baracane.** The owner of this small, simple place oversees the menu of robust specialties of his native southwest France, including rabbit confit, veal tongue, and pear poached in wine and cassis. The prix-fixe menus make it one of the best values in the Marais. ✉ *38 rue des Tournelles,* ☎ *01–42–71–43–33. MC, V. Closed Sun. No lunch Sat. Métro: Bastille.*

VEGETARIAN

$ ✕ **La Truffe.** In this attractive open-space restaurant with a mezzanine, you can find organic, vegetarian food that is prepared without fat or steaming—special cooking equipment is used so that the grains, mushrooms, and vegetables conserve their taste and vitamins. Smoking is not allowed. ✉ *31 rue Vieille-du-Temple,* ☎ *01–42–71–08–39. MC, V. Métro: St-Paul.*

5ᵉ Arrondissement (Latin Quarter)

FRENCH

$$ ✕ **Campagne et Provence.** On the quai across from Notre-Dame, this very pleasant little restaurant has a rustic Provençal look and a menu to match that includes grilled John Dory with preserved fennel, and peppers stuffed with cod and eggplant. ✉ *25 quai de la Tournelle,* ☎ *01–43–54–05–17. MC, V. Closed Sun. No lunch Sat. or Mon. Métro: Maubert-Mutualité.*

$ ✕ **Chantairelle.** Not only is delicious south-central Auvergne cuisine served, but so is a full regional experience, hence the decor: recycled barn timbers and essential oils diffusing local scents. The food is hearty and the portions of stuffed cabbage and *potée,* a casserole of pork and vegetables in broth, copious. ✉ *17 rue Laplace,* ☎ *01–46–33–18–59. MC, V. Closed Sun. No lunch Sat. Métro: Maubert-Mutualité.*

6ᵉ Arrondissement (St-Germain)

FRENCH

$$ ✕ **L'Épi Dupin.** Half-timber walls, sisal carpeting, and crisp white table linens are the backdrop for this bistro. The menu of delicious and reasonably priced French classics is revised regularly and might include mixed green salad garnished with foie gras and fillet of lamb with rata-

Paris Dining

Alain Ducasse, **3**
Au Bascou, **20**
Au Bon Accueil, **37**
Au Trou Gascon, **25**
Aux Crus de
Bourgogne, **16**
Baracane, **26**
Brasserie Flo, **19**
Campagne et
Provence, **28**
Chantairelle, **30**

Chardenoux, **23**
Chartier, **13**
Chez Georges, **15**
Chez Maître Paul, **33**
Chez Michel, **17**
Chez Omar, **21**
Contre-Allée, **32**
La Dinée, **36**
L'Épi Dupin, **34**
Les Élysées, **4**
Guy Savoy, **7**
Ledoyen, **10**

Le Moi, **11**
Le Moulin à Vins, **12**
Le Petit Rétro, **1**
Le Relais du Parc, **2**
Philippe
Detourbe, **35**
Pierre Gagnaire, **8**
Prunier, **5**
Le Repaire de
Cartouche, **22**
Le Restaurant d'Eric
Frechon, **18**

Restaurant du
Palais-Royal, **14**
Le Square
Trousseau, **24**
Taillevent, **9**
Le Terroir, **31**
Le Timgad, **6**
La Truffe, **27**
Le Vieux Bistro, **29**
Le Violon
d'Ingres, **38**

touille. ✉ *11 rue Dupin,* ☎ *01–42–22–64–56. Reservations essential. MC, V. Closed Sun. Métro: Sèvres-Babylone.*

$ ✕ **Chez Maître Paul.** A few steps from the Odéon, this is a great place to discover the little-known cooking of the Jura and Franche-Comté. Though sturdy, this cuisine appeals to modern palates, too. ✉ *12 rue Monsieur-le-Prince,* ☎ *01–43–54–74–59. AE, DC, MC, V. Metro: Odéon.*

7e Arrondissement (Invalides/École Militaire)

FRENCH

$$–$$$ ✕ **Le Violon d'Ingres.** A diverse crowd comes to sample the regularly
★   revised menu of chef Christian Constant, formerly of the Hôtel Crillon (☞ *Lodging, below*). Sample dishes include cream of pumpkin soup with sheep's cheese, and guinea hen on a bed of diced turnips. It's the perfect place for a dinner out on the town. ✉ *135 rue St-Dominique,* ☎ *01–45–44–15–05. Reservations essential. AE, DC, MC, V. Closed weekends. Métro: École-Militaire.*

$–$$ ✕ **Au Bon Accueil.** If you want to see what well-heeled Parisians like to eat these days, book a table at this popular bistro as soon as you get to town. The excellent, reasonably priced *cuisine du marché* (daily menu based on what's in the markets) has made it a hit. ✉ *14 rue de Montessuy,* ☎ *01–47–05–46–11. Reservations essential. MC, V. Closed Sun. Métro, RER: Pont de l'Alma.*

8e Arrondissement (Champs-Élysées)

FRENCH

$$$$ ✕ **Les Élysées.** Chef Alain Solivères is a passionate cook whose repu-
★   tation continues to grow. Not only is his food—which changes seasonally and draws inspiration from southern France, Basque Country, Bordeaux, and Languedoc—exquisite, but service is also impeccable and the intimate dining room beautiful. ✉ *In the Hôtel Vernet, 25 rue Vernet,* ☎ *01–47–23–43–10. AE, DC, MC, V. Reservations essential. Closed weekends. Métro: George-V.*

$$$$ ✕ **Ledoyen.** Chef Ghislaine Arabian has set gastronomic fashion by concentrating on northern French cuisine and creating specialties with beer sauces, such as *coquilles St-Jacques à la bière* (scallops in beer). The elegant restaurant has gilded ceilings and walls, plush chairs, and tables with candelabra. ✉ *1 av. du Tuit, on the carré des Champs-Élysées,* ☎ *01–47–42–23–23. Reservations essential. AE, DC, MC, V. Closed weekends. Métro: Place de la Concorde or Champs-Élysées–Clemenceau.*

$$$$ ✕ **Pierre Gagnaire.** In a single dish, legendary chef Pierre Gagnaire sen-
★   sationally brings together unexpected tastes and textures. Two intriguing dishes from a recent menu—it changes seasonally—included duck foie gras wrapped in bacon, and sea bass in herbs with tiny clams. Don't miss the *Grand Dessert,* a five-course extravaganza. The only drawbacks: the amateurish service and the puzzlingly brief wine list. ✉ *6 rue de Balzac,* ☎ *01–44–35–18–25. Reservations essential. AE, DC, MC, V. Closed Sun. Métro: Charles-de-Gaulle–Étoile.*

$$$$ ✕ **Taillevent.** Many say this is the best restaurant in Paris—and dining in the paneled rooms of this mid-19th-century mansion is certainly a sublime experience. Service is exceptional, the wine list remarkable, and the classical French cuisine usually perfect. ✉ *15 rue Lamennais,* ☎ *01–45–63–39–94. Reservations 3–4 wks in advance essential. Jacket and tie. AE, MC, V. Closed weekends and Aug. Métro: Charles-de-Gaulle–Étoile.*

9e Arrondissement (Opéra)

FRENCH

$ ✕ **Chartier.** People come to this cavernous turn-of-the-century restaurant more for the bonhomie than the food, which is often rather ordinary. You may find yourself sharing a table as you study the long, old-fashioned menu of such favorites as steak tartare and roast chicken with fries. ⊠ *7 rue du Faubourg-Montmartre,* ☎ *01–47–70–86–29. Reservations not accepted. No credit cards. Métro: Rue Montmartre.*

10ᵉ Arrondissement (République/Gare du Nord)
FRENCH

$$ ✕ **Brasserie Flo.** This place is hard to find down its passageway near Gare de l'Est, but it's worth the effort. The rich wood and stained glass is typically Alsatian, service is enthusiastic, and brasserie standards such as shellfish and *choucroute* (sauerkraut and sausage) are savory. It's open until 1:30 AM, with a special night-owl menu from 11 PM. ⊠ *7 cour des Petites Écuries,* ☎ *01–47–70–13–59. AE, DC, MC, V. Métro: Château d'Eau.*

$–$$ ✕ **Chez Michel.** Chef Thierry Breton pulls a stylish crowd—despite the drab decor and neighborhood—with his wonderful cuisine du marché and dishes from his native Brittany. Typical of Breton's kitchen are the lasagna stuffed with chèvre, and the artichokes and tuna steak with pureed peas. ⊠ *10 rue Belzunce,* ☎ *01–44–53–06–20. Reservations essential. MC, V. Closed Sun.–Mon. No lunch Sat. Métro: Gare du Nord.*

11ᵉ Arrondissement (Bastille/République)
FRENCH

$$ ✕ **Chardenoux.** A bit off the beaten path but well worth the effort, this cozy neighborhood bistro with etched-glass windows and a long zinc bar attracts a cross-section of savvy Parisians. The traditional cooking is first-rate: delicious salads, game dishes, and savory desserts, with a nicely chosen wine list. ⊠ *1 rue Jules-Valles,* ☎ *01–43–71–49–52. AE, V. Closed weekends and Aug. Métro: Charonne.*

$$ ✕ **Le Repaire de Cartouche.** Near the Cirque d'Hiver, in the Bastille,
★ this split-level, '50s-style bistro with dark wood decor is the latest good-value bistro sensation in Paris. Young chef Rodolphe Paquin is a creative and impeccably trained cook who does a stylish take on earthy French regional dishes. The wine list is excellent, with bargains like a Pernand-Vergelesses (red Burgundy) for $20. ⊠ *99 rue Amelot,* ☎ *01–47–00–25–86. AE, MC, V. Reservations essential. Closed Sun. No dinner Mon. Métro: Filles du Calvaire.*

12ᵉ Arrondissement (Bastille/Gare de Lyon)
FRENCH

$$$ ✕ **Au Trou Gascon.** At this successful Belle Époque establishment off place Daumesnil, owner Alain Dutournier serves his version of the cuisine of Gascony—a region of outstanding ham, foie gras, lamb, and poultry—and his now classic white-chocolate mousse. ⊠ *40 rue Taine,* ☎ *01–43–44–34–26. AE, DC, MC, V. Closed weekends, Christmas wk, and Aug. Métro: Daumesnil.*

$$ ✕ **Le Square Trousseau.** Since fashion designer Jean-Paul Gaultier moved his headquarters nearby, this charming turn-of-the-century bistro has become very chic. You might see a supermodel or two while dining on the homemade foie gras and tender baby chicken with mustard and bread-crumb crust. The house wine is a good value, especially the fruity red Morgon. ⊠ *1 rue Antoine Vollon,* ☎ *01–43–44–06–00. MC, V. Métro: Ledru-Rollin.*

13ᵉ Arrondissement (Les Gobelins)
FRENCH

$ ✕ **Le Terroir.** A jolly crowd of regulars makes this little bistro festive. The solidly classical menu, based on first-rate ingredients from all over France, includes salads with chicken livers or fresh marinated anchovies, calves' liver or monkfish with saffron, and pears marinated in wine. ✉ *11 bd. Arago,* ☎ *01–47–07–36–99. Closed Sun. No lunch Sat. Métro: Les Gobelins.*

14ᵉ Arrondissement (Montparnasse)

FRENCH

$$ ✕ **Contre-Allée.** Students and professors crowd this large restaurant, simply decorated with bullfighting posters. The menu has original selections such as squid salad with mussels and roast cod with Parmesan; homemade fresh pasta accompanies many dishes. A sidewalk terrace enlivens shady avenue Denfert-Rochereau in summer. The restaurant serves until 11:30 PM. ✉ *83 av. Denfert-Rochereau,* ☎ *01–43–54–99–86. AE, DC, MC, V. No lunch Sat. Métro: Denfert-Rochereau.*

15ᵉ Arrondissement (Motte-Picquet/Balard)

FRENCH

$$ ✕ **La Dinée.** Chef Christophe Chabanel's restaurant in this rather remote location at the edge of the 15ᵉ arrondissement is filled noon and night by a crowd of stylish regulars. Signature dishes are fillet of sole with baby shrimp, and chicken medallions with peppers in a corn vinaigrette. The dining room, with blue print fabrics and wooden tub chairs, is simple; service is professional. ✉ *85 rue Leblanc,* ☎ *01–45–54–20–49. V. Closed weekends. Métro: Balard.*

$$ ✕ **Philippe Detourbe.** Amidst black lacquer, mirrors, and Burgundy vel-
★ vet upholstery, sample Detourbe's spectacular contemporary French cooking. The menu changes with every meal and may include smoked salmon filled with cabbage *rémoulade* (creamy dressing) or cod steak with white beans and caramelized endives; desserts are fantastic. The wine list is brief but well chosen; service is friendly and efficient. ✉ *8 rue Nicolas Charlet,* ☎ *01–42–19–08–59. Reservations essential. MC, V. Closed Sun. No lunch Sat. Métro: Pasteur.*

16ᵉ Arrondissement (Arc de Triomphe/ Bois de Boulogne)

FRENCH

$$$$ ✕ **Alain Ducasse.** Since he took over from Joël Robuchon, Ducasse has surprised everyone by serving resolutely classical French dishes. Ducasse is a marvelous cook, but his creativity is lost on traditional dishes. Other dishes, though, like the duckling roasted with fig leaves, show his brilliant subtlety. One way or another you can get a solidly luxurious meal here. Be forewarned that service is snippy and that it's staggeringly expensive; the 480-franc lunch menu is your best bet. ✉ *59 av. Raymond-Poincaré,* ☎ *01–47–27–12–27. Reservations several months in advance essential. AE, DC, MC, V. Closed weekends. Métro: Victor Hugo.*

$$–$$$ ✕ **Prunier.** Founded in 1925, this seafood restaurant is one of the best—and the prettiest—in Paris. The famous Art Deco mosaics glitter and the white marble counters shine with impeccably fresh shellfish. The kitchen not only excels at classic French fish dishes but has added some interesting options, like a *Saintongeaise* plate—raw oysters with grilled sausages—eaten in Bordeaux. ✉ *16 av. Victor-Hugo,* ☎ *01–44–17–35–85. Reservations essential in upstairs dining room. Jacket and tie. AE, DC, MC, V. Closed Sun.–Mon. Métro: Charles-de-Gaulle–Étoile.*

$$ ✕ **Le Relais du Parc.** This bistro-annex is the place to try a lighter version of Alain Ducasse's cooking for less. Two delicious starters—the lobster salad, and the baby potatoes with black truffles in a creamy oxtail-stock sauce—make good meals, followed by cheese or dessert. Main courses are also excellent, but the desserts could be better and wine is overpriced. ✉ *55 av. Raymond-Poincaré,* ☎ *01–44–05–66–10. Reservations essential. AE, DC, MC, V. Métro: Victor Hugo.*

$ ✕ **Le Petit Rétro.** Two types of clientele—men in expensive suits at noon and well-dressed couples in the evening—frequent this little bistro with Art Nouveau tiles and bentwood furniture. You can't go wrong with the daily special written on the chalkboard. Come when you want a good solid meal, like the perfect *pavé de boeuf* (thick steak). ⊠ *5 rue Mesnil,* ☎ *01–44–05–06–05. MC, V. Closed Sun. No lunch Mon. Métro: Victor Hugo.*

17ᵉ Arrondissement (Monceau/Clichy)
FRENCH

$$$$ ✕ **Guy Savoy.** Top chef Guy Savoy's other five bistros have not distracted him too much from his handsome luxury restaurant near the Arc de Triomphe. The oysters in aspic and grilled pigeon reveal the magnitude of his talent, and the mille-feuille is a contemporary classic. ⊠ *18 rue Troyon,* ☎ *01–43–80–40–61. Reservations essential. AE, MC, V. Closed Sun. No lunch Sat. Métro: Charles-de-Gaulle–Étoile.*

NORTH AFRICAN

$$ ✕ **Le Timgad.** For a stylish evening out and a night off from French food, try this elegant North African restaurant. Start with a savory *brick* (crispy parchment pastry filled with meat, eggs, or seafood), followed by tasty couscous or succulent *tagine* (meat or poultry that's slowly braised inside a domed pottery casserole). ⊠ *21 rue de Brunel,* ☎ *01–45–74–23–70. MC, V. Métro: Argentine.*

18ᵉ Arrondissement (Montmartre)
FRENCH

$ ✕ **Le Moulin à Vins.** The atmosphere at this popular wine bar–bistro is sepia-toned—both it and the surrounding neighborhood evoke old Paris. It's perfect for lunch while touring Montmartre. In the evening it's livelier, when devoted regulars come for the daily short list of hot dishes. ⊠ *6 rue Burq,* ☎ *01–45–52–81–27. MC, V. Closed Mon. Métro: Abbesses.*

19ᵉ Arrondissement (Buttes Chaumont/La Villette)
FRENCH

$$ ✕ **Le Restaurant d'Eric Frechon.** This simply decorated little place is a
★ sterling example of a price-conscious, market-menu bistro. Chef Frechon worked with Christian Constant at the Hôtel Crillon (☞ Lodging, *below*), which means his cooking is more adventurous and elegant than most other bistro fare. ⊠ *10 rue du Général-Brunet,* ☎ *01–40–40–03–30. V. Closed weekends Métro: Danube.*

Cafés and Salons de Thé

Cafés are found at every bend in Paris; following is just a small selection of cafés and *salons de thé* (tea shops—London isn't the only city that has them) to whet your appetite. **Au Père Tranquille** (⊠ 16 rue Pierre Lescot, 1ᵉʳ, ☎ 01–45–08–00–34, métro Les Halles) is one of the best places in Paris for people-watching. **Café Marly** (⊠ Cour Napoléon du Louvre, 93 rue de Rivoli, 1ᵉʳ, ☎ 01–49–26–06–60, métro Palais-Royal), overlooking the main courtyard of the Louvre, is perfect for an afternoon break or a nightcap. **La Crémaillère** (⊠ 15 pl. du Tertre, 18ᵉ, ☎ 01–46–06–58–59, métro Anvers), a veritable monument to fin-de-siècle art in Monmartre, is decorated with Alphonse Mucha frescoes. **Mariage Frères** (⊠ 30 rue du Bourg-Tibourg, 4ᵉ, ☎ 01–42–72–28–11, métro Hôtel-de-Ville) is an outstanding tea shop serving 500 kinds of tea, along with delicious tarts. **Salon de Thé du Palais Royal** (⊠ Jardins du Palais Royal, 110 Galérie de Valois, 1ᵉʳ, ☎ 01–40–20–00–27, métro Palais-Royal) serves tea on a terrace overlooking the gardens of the Palais Royal. **Le Vieux Colombier** (⊠ 65 rue

de Rennes, 7ᵉ, ☎ 01–45–48–53–81, métro St-Sulpice) is just around
the corner from St-Sulpice and the Vieux Colombier theater.

Wine Bars

Wine bars are a good place to sample a glass (or bottle) of French wine
and have an excellent, simple hot meal or just a plate of cheese or charcuterie. Hours can vary widely, so it's best to check ahead; many close
around 10 PM. **Aux Bons Crus** (✉ 7 rue des Petits-Champs, 1ᵉʳ, ☎ 01–
42–60–06–45, métro Bourse) is a cramped, narrow venue with an au-
thentically Parisian feel. **Le Baron Rouge** (✉ 1 rue Théophile-Roussel,
12ᵉ, ☎ 01–43–43–14–32, métro Ledru-Rollin) is a noisy and convivial haunt, where wine spills from the barrel. **Jacques Mélac** (✉ 42
rue Léon-Frot, 11ᵉ, ☎ 01–43–70–59–27, métro Charonne) is named
after the jolly owner who bottles several of his own wines—try the chewy
red Lirac.

LODGING

Revised and
updated by
Suzanne
Rowan Kelleher

The Paris Tourist Office's annual lodging guide lists some 1,500 member hotels in the city's 20 arrondissements. The true count, though, is
closer to 2,200—some 85,000 rooms in all. Despite the huge choice
of hotels, you should always reserve well in advance.

The criteria when selecting the hotels reviewed below were quality, location, and character. Fewer hotels in outlying arrondissements (the
10ᵉ to the 20ᵉ) are listed because they are farther from the major sites.
Generally, there are more Right Bank hotels offering luxury—or at any
rate, formality—than there are on the Left Bank, where hotels are often
smaller and richer in old-fashioned personality.

As part of a general upgrade of the city's hotels in recent years, scores
of lackluster, cheap Paris lodgings have been replaced by good-value
establishments in the lower to middle price range. Although air-conditioning has become de rigueur in middle- to higher-priced hotels, it
is generally not a prerequisite for comfort (Paris's hot weather season
doesn't usually last long). Hotel rooms in Paris's oldest quarters are
generally much smaller than their American counterparts. Reviews indicate the number of rooms with full bathroom facilities, which may
mean *baignoire* (bathtub) or *douche* (shower); any exceptions are
noted. If you want one or the other, you should specify when you make
reservations. Assume that suites have full bathrooms with tubs. It's rare
to find moderately priced places that offer shared toilets or bathrooms
down the hall, but make sure you know what you are getting when
you book a budget hotel.

Almost all Paris hotels charge extra for breakfast, with prices ranging
from 30 francs to more than 200 francs per person in luxury establishments. For anything more than the standard Continental breakfast
of café au lait (coffee with hot milk) and croissants, the price will be
higher. You're often better off finding the nearest café. A nominal
séjour (lodging) tax of 7 francs per person, per night is charged to pay
for promotion of tourism in Paris.

CATEGORY	COST*
$$$$	over 1,750 frs
$$$	1,000 frs–1,750 frs
$$	600 frs–1,000 frs
$	under 600 frs

All prices are for a standard double room, including 20.6% tax and service.

1er Arrondissement (Louvre/Les Halles)

$$$$
★ **Costes.** Jean-Louis and Gilbert Costes's sumptuous hotel is the darling of the fashion and media set. Conjuring up the palaces of Napoléon III, rooms are swathed in rich garnet and bronze tones and contain a luxurious mélange of patterned fabrics, heavy swags, and enough brocade and fringe to blanket the Champs-Élysées. The bathrooms are truly marvelous affairs. ⊠ *239 rue St-Honoré, 75001,* ☎ *01–42–44–50–50,* FAX *01–42–44–50–01. 85 rooms. Restaurant, bar, air-conditioning, in-room modem lines, in-room safes, no-smoking rooms, room service, indoor pool, sauna, exercise room, laundry service. AE, DC, MC, V. Métro: Tuileries.*

$$$$ **Meurice.** The Meurice, owned by the Italian CIGA chain, is one of the finest hotels in the city. The Louis XVI–style first-floor salons are luxurious and the bedrooms, adorned with Persian carpets, opulent. Book well in advance to land a room or a suite overlooking the Tuileries Gardens. The hotel's restaurant is fabled. ⊠ *228 rue de Rivoli, 75001,* ☎ *01–44–58–10–10,* FAX *01–44–58–10–15. 180 rooms, 28 suites. Restaurant, bar, air-conditioning, no-smoking rooms, room service, laundry service, business services. AE, DC, MC, V. Métro: Tuileries, Concorde.*

$$$$ **Ritz.** The Ritz is the crowning gem of the sparkling place Vendôme. Festooned with gilt and ormolu, dripping with crystal chandeliers, and swathed in heavy silk and tapestries, this hotel, which opened in 1896, is the epitome of fin-de-siècle Paris. Yet it's surprisingly intimate. Don't miss the famous Hemingway Bar (which the writer claimed to have "liberated" in 1944). ⊠ *15 pl. Vendôme, 75001,* ☎ *01–43–16–30–30,* FAX *01–43–16–36–68. 142 rooms, 45 suites. 3 restaurants, 2 bars, air-conditioning, in-room safes, room service, indoor pool, beauty salon, health club, shops, laundry service, meeting rooms, parking (fee). AE, DC, MC, V. Métro: Opéra.*

$$ **Britannique.** Open since 1870, the Britannique blends courteous English service with old-fashioned French elegance. It has retained its handsome winding staircase and has well-appointed, soundproof rooms in chic, warm tones. ⊠ *20 av. Victoria, 75001,* ☎ *01–42–33–74–59,* FAX *01–42–33–82–65. 40 rooms. Bar, in-room safes. AE, DC, MC, V. Métro: Châtelet.*

$
★ **Louvre Forum.** This hotel is a find: Smack in the center of town, it has clean, comfortable, well-equipped rooms (minibars, satellite TV) at extremely reasonable prices, and a friendly feel. ⊠ *25 rue du Bouloi, 75001,* ☎ *01–42–36–54–19,* FAX *01–42–33–66–31. 27 rooms. Bar, minibars. AE, DC, MC, V. Métro: Louvre.*

2e Arrondissement (Le Bourse)

$$ **Hôtel de Noailles.** With a nod to the work of postmodern designers like Putnam and Starck, this new-wave inn (part of the Tulip Inn group) is a star among Paris's new crop of well-priced, style-driven boutique hotels. Though not to everyone's taste, rooms are imaginatively decorated with funky furnishings and contemporary details. A young, cosmopolitan clientele has made this one their own. ⊠ *9 rue de Michodière, 75002,* ☎ *01–47–42–92–90,* FAX *01–49–24–92–71. 53 rooms. Bar, air-conditioning, laundry service. AE, DC, MC, V. Métro: Opéra.*

3e Arrondissement (Beaubourg/Marais)

$$$$ **Pavillon de la Reine.** On lovely place des Vosges, this magnificent mansion reconstructed from original plans is filled with Louis XIII–style fireplaces and antiques. Ask for a duplex with French windows overlooking the first of two flower-filled courtyards behind the historic Queen's Pavilion. ⊠ *28 pl. des Vosges, 75003,* ☎ *01–40–29–19–19, 800/447–7462 in the U.S.,* FAX *01–40–29–19–20. 30 rooms, 25*

64

L'Astor, **5**	Grand Hôtel Inter-Continental, **13**	Lancaster, **4**	Relais Christine, **33**
Atelier Montparnasse, **30**	Grandes Écoles, **25**	Latour Maubourg, **7**	Relais St-Germain, **32**
Bretonnerie, **17**	Hôtel de l'Abbaye, **31**	Louvre Forum, **15**	Ritz, **12**
Britannique, **16**	Hôtel d'Aubusson, **34**	Meurice, **11**	Saint James Paris, **2**
Caron de Beaumarchais, **18**	Hôtel Crillon, **6**	Montalembert, **35**	Le Tourville, **8**
Castex, **21**	Hôtel de Noailles, **14**	Montparnasse, **26**	
Costes, **10**	Hôtel du 7e Art, **22**	Le Pavillon Bastille, **20**	
Deux-Iles, **23**	Hyatt Regency Paris–Madeleine, **9**	Pavillon de la Reine, **19**	
Étoile-Péreire, **3**	Istria, **28**	Queen's Hotel, **1**	
Familia, **24**	Jardin du Luxembourg, **27**	Raspail-Montparnasse, **29**	

suites. Bar, breakfast room, air-conditioning, room service, laundry service, free parking. AE, DC, MC, V. Métro: Bastille, St-Paul.

4e Arrondissement (Marais/Ile St-Louis)

$$ **Bretonnerie.** This small hotel is in a 17th-century *hôtel particulier* (town house) on a tiny street in the Marais, a few minutes' walk from the Pompidou Center. Rooms are done in Louis XIII style, complete with upholstered walls; they vary considerably in size from spacious to cramped. ⌧ *22 rue Ste-Croix-de-la-Bretonnerie, 75004,* ☎ *01–48– 87–77–63,* FAX *01–42–77–26–78. 27 rooms, 3 suites. In-room safes. MC, V. Métro: Hôtel de Ville.*

$$ **Caron de Beaumarchais.** The theme of this intimate jewel is the work
★ of Caron de Beaumarchais, who wrote *The Marriage of Figaro* in 1778. Rooms faithfully reflect the taste of 18th-century French nobility. Fresh flowers and fluffy bathrobes are a bonus for the price. The second- and fifth-floor rooms with balconies are the largest; those on the sixth floor have beguiling views across Right Bank rooftops. ⌧ *12 rue Vieille-du-Temple, 75004,* ☎ *01–42–72–34–12,* FAX *01–42–72– 34–63. 19 rooms. Air-conditioning, in-room safes, laundry service. AE, DC, MC, V. Métro: Hôtel de Ville.*

$$ **Deux-Iles.** This converted 17th-century mansion on the Ile St-Louis has long won plaudits for charm and comfort. Flowers and plants are scattered around the stunning main hall. The delightfully old-fashioned rooms, blessed with exposed beams, are small but airy. Ask for one overlooking the little garden courtyard. In winter, a roaring fire warms the lounge. ⌧ *59 rue St-Louis-en-l'Ile, 75004,* ☎ *01–43–26–13–35,* FAX *01–43–29–60–25. 17 rooms. Air-conditioning, in-room safes, baby-sitting. AE, MC, V. Métro: Pont-Marie.*

$–$$ **Hôtel du 7e Art.** The theme of this hip Marais hotel ("Seventh Art" is what the French call filmmaking) is Hollywood from the '40s to the '60s. Rooms are small and spartan but clean, quiet, and equipped with cable TV. There's no elevator, but there is a pleasant bar. The clientele is young, trendy, and primarily American. ⌧ *20 rue St-Paul, 75004,* ☎ *01–44–54–85–00,* FAX *01–42–77–69–10. 23 rooms. Bar, in-room safes. AE, DC, MC, V. Métro: St-Paul.*

$ **Castex.** This Marais hotel in a Revolution-era building is a bargain-hunter's dream. Rooms are low on frills but squeaky clean and up-to-date, the owners are extremely friendly, and the prices are rock-bottom, which ensures that the hotel is often booked months ahead. There's no elevator, and the only TV is in the ground-floor salon. ⌧ *5 rue Castex, 75004,* ☎ *01–42–72–31–52,* FAX *01–42–72–57–91. 27 rooms, 23 with shower. MC, V. Métro: Bastille.*

5e Arrondissement (Latin Quarter)

$$$ **Jardin du Luxembourg.** Blessed with a charming staff and a stylish look, this hotel is one of the most sought-after in the Latin Quarter. Rooms are a bit small (common for this neighborhood) but intelligently furnished for optimal space, and warmly decorated in ocher, rust, and indigo *à la provençale.* Ask for one with a balcony overlooking the street; the best, No. 25, has a peekaboo view of the Eiffel Tower. ⌧ *5 impasse Royer-Collard, 75005,* ☎ *01–40–46–08–88,* FAX *01–40–46– 02–28. 27 rooms. Air-conditioning, in-room safes, no-smoking rooms, sauna. AE, DC, MC, V. Métro: Luxembourg.*

$ **Familia.** The hospitable Gaucheron family, the owners, bend over
★ backward for you. About half the rooms feature romantic sepia frescoes of celebrated Paris scenes; others are appointed with exquisite Louis XV–style furnishings or have nice mahogany pieces. Book a month ahead for one with a walk-out balcony on the second or fifth floor. ⌧ *11 rue des Écoles, 75005,* ☎ *01–43–54–55–27,* FAX *01–43–29–61– 77. 30 rooms. AE, MC, V. Métro: Cardinal Lemoine.*

$ ⊞ **Grandes Écoles.** This delightfully intimate place looks and feels like a country cottage dropped smack in the middle of the Latin Quarter. It is off the street and occupies three buildings on a beautiful leafy garden. Parquet floors, Louis-Philippe furnishings, lace bedspreads, and the absence of TV all add to the rustic ambience. ✉ *75 rue du Cardinal Lemoine, 75005,* ☎ *01–43–26–79–23,* FAX *01–43–25–28–15. 51 rooms. No-smoking rooms. MC, V. Métro: Cardinal Lemoine.*

6ᵉ Arrondissement (St-Germain/Montparnasse)

$$$$ ⊞ **Relais Christine.** On a quiet street between the Seine and boulevard St-Germain, this luxurious and popular hotel, occupying 16th-century abbey cloisters, oozes romantic ambience. Rooms are spacious (particularly the duplexes on the upper floors) and well appointed in old Parisian style; the best have exposed beams and overlook the garden. ✉ *3 rue Christine, 75006,* ☎ *01–40–51–60–80, 800/447–7462 in the U.S.,* FAX *01–40–51–60–81. 35 rooms, 16 suites. Bar, air-conditioning, no-smoking rooms, room service, baby-sitting, laundry service, meeting rooms, free parking. AE, DC, MC, V. Métro: Odéon.*

$$$$ ⊞ **Relais St-Germain.** The interior-designer owners of this outstand-
★   ing hotel have exquisite taste and a superb respect for tradition and detail. Moreover, the rooms are at least twice the size of those in other hotels in the area for the same price. Much of the furniture was selected with a knowledgeable eye from the city's *brocantes* (secondhand dealers), and every room has its own, unique treasures. Breakfast is included. ✉ *9 carrefour de l'Odéon, 75006,* ☎ *01–43–29–12–05,* FAX *01–46–33–45–30. 21 rooms, 1 suite. AE, DC, MC, V. Métro: Odéon.*

$$$ ⊞ **Hôtel de L'Abbaye.** This delightful hotel near St-Sulpice was transformed from an erstwhile convent. The blend of stylishly rustic antiques and earthy apricot and ocher tones makes for a calm, cozy atmosphere. The first-floor rooms open onto the garden; most of those on the upper floors have oak beams and sitting alcoves. The four duplexes with private terraces are more expensive. Breakfast is included. ✉ *10 rue Cassette, 75006,* ☎ *01–45–44–38–11,* FAX *01–45–48–07–86. 42 rooms, 4 suites. Bar, air-conditioning, no-smoking rooms, room service, baby-sitting, laundry service. AE, MC, V. Métro: St-Sulpice.*

$$–$$$ ⊞ **Hôtel d'Aubusson.** This good-value hotel keeps prices in check
★   while offering original Aubusson tapestries, Versailles-style parquet floors, chiseled stone fireplace, and restored antiques. Even the smallest rooms are good-size by Paris standards, and all are decked out in rich burgundies, greens, or blues. The 10 best rooms have canopied beds and ceiling beams. ✉ *33 rue Dauphine, 75006,* ☎ *01–43–29–43–43,* FAX *01–43–29–12–62. 49 rooms. Bar, air-conditioning, in-room safes, baby-sitting, laundry service. AE, MC, V. Métro: Odéon.*

$$ ⊞ **Atelier Montparnasse.** This Art Deco–inspired gem of a hotel was designed with style and comfort in mind. Rooms are tastefully decorated and spacious, and all the bathrooms feature mosaic reproductions of famous French paintings. One of the rooms sleeps three. The hotel is within walking distance of the Luxembourg Gardens and St-Germain-des-Prés. ✉ *49 rue Vavin, 75006,* ☎ *01–46–33–60–00,* FAX *01–40–51–04–21. 17 rooms. Bar, room service, baby-sitting, laundry service. AE, DC, MC, V. Métro: Vavin.*

7ᵉ Arrondissement (Invalides/École Militaire)

$$$$ ⊞ **Montalembert.** This place is one of Paris's most originally voguish boutique hotels. Whether appointed with traditional or contemporary furnishings, rooms are all about simple lines and chic luxury. Ask about special packages if you're staying for more than three nights. ✉ *3 rue de Montalembert, 75007,* ☎ *01–45–49–68–68, 800/628–8929 in the U.S.,* FAX *01–45–49–69–49. 50 rooms, 6 suites. Restau-*

rant, bar, air-conditioning, in-room modem lines, in-room safes, room service, in-room VCRs, baby-sitting, meeting rooms. AE, DC, MC, V. Métro: Rue du Bac.

$$–$$$ ⊞ **Le Tourville.** Here is a rare find: an intimate, upscale hotel at affordable
★ prices. Each room has crisp, virgin-white damask upholstery set against pastel or ocher walls; a smattering of antiques; original artwork; and fabulous old mirrors. The staff couldn't be more helpful. ⊠ *16 av. de Tourville, 75007, ☎ 01–47–05–62–62, 800/528–3549 in the U.S., FAX 01–47–05–43–90. 27 rooms, 3 junior suites. Bar, air-conditioning, no-smoking rooms, laundry service. AE, DC, MC, V. Métro: École Militaire.*

$$ ⊞ **Latour Maubourg.** In the bourgeois heart of the smart seventh, a stone's throw from Invalides, this hotel with a friendly staff has been inked into many a traveler's journal. Decor is homey and unpretentious, and with just 10 rooms, the accent is on intimacy and personalized service. ⊠ *150 rue de Grenelle, 75007, ☎ 01–47–05–16–16, FAX 01–47–05–16–14. 9 rooms, 1 suite. In-room safes. MC, V. Métro: Latour Maubourg.*

8ᵉ Arrondissement (Champs-Élysées)

$$$$ ⊞ **L'Astor.** Following a top-to-bottom makeover by the Westin-Demeure group, L'Astor has been reborn as a bastion of highly stylized, civilized chic. The Art Deco lobby is decked out in boldly patterned armchairs, huge mirrors, and ceiling frescoes. Guest rooms are testimonials to the sober Regency style, with weighty marble fireplaces and mahogany furnishings. Several suites have walk-out balconies. The hotel's restaurant is supervised by the celebrated chef Joël Robuchon. ⊠ *11 rue d'Astorg, 75008, ☎ 01–53–05–05–05, 800/937–8461 in the U.S., FAX 01–53–05–05–30. 134 rooms, 5 suites. Restaurant, bar, air-conditioning, in-room modem lines, in-room safes, no-smoking rooms, room service, health club, laundry service. AE, DC, MC, V. Métro: Miromesnil, St-Augustin.*

$$$$ ⊞ **Hôtel Crillon.** One of Paris's most famous "palace" hotels, the Crillon comprises two 18th-century town houses on place de la Concorde. Marie-Antoinette took singing lessons here. Rooms are lavishly done with Rococo and Directoire antiques, crystal and gilt wall sconces, and gold fittings. The sheer quantity of marble downstairs—especially in Les Ambassadeurs restaurant—is staggering. ⊠ *10 pl. de la Concorde, 75008, ☎ 01–44–71–15–00, 800/888–4747 in the U.S., FAX 01–44–71–15–02. 118 rooms, 45 suites. 2 restaurants, 2 bars, tea shop, air-conditioning, in-room safes, no-smoking rooms, room service, exercise room, baby-sitting, laundry service, meeting rooms. AE, DC, MC, V. Métro: Concorde.*

$$$$ ⊞ **Hyatt Regency Paris–Madeleine.** This stunning Haussmannesque building near the Opéra Garnier feels more like a boutique hotel than an international business chain, thanks to stylized details like cherry paneling and mismatched bedside tables. Book a room on the seventh or eighth floor facing boulevard Malesherbes for a view of the Eiffel Tower. ⊠ *24 bd. Malesherbes, 75008, ☎ 01–55–27–12–34, 800/223–1234 in the U.S., FAX 01–55–27–12–10. 81 rooms, 5 suites. Restaurant, bar, air-conditioning, in-room modem lines, in-room safes, no-smoking floors, room service, sauna, exercise room, laundry service, meeting rooms. AE, DC, MC, V. Métro: St-Augustin.*

$$$$ ⊞ **Lancaster.** The Lancaster—one of Paris's most venerable institutions,
★ now owned by the Savoy group—has been meticulously transformed into one of the city's most modish, luxury hotels. The clubby decor seamlessly blends the traditional with the contemporary to evoke an overall feeling of timeless elegance. Many of the suites pay homage to the hotel's colorful regulars, from Sir Alec Guinness to Marlene Diet-

rich. ✉ *7 rue de Berri, 75008,* ☎ *01–40–76–40–76, 800/637–2869 in the U.S.,* FAX *01–40–76–40–00. 60 rooms,10 suites. Restaurant, bar, air-conditioning, in-room modem lines, in-room safes, room service, in-room VCRs, sauna, exercise room, baby-sitting, laundry service, meeting rooms. AE, DC, MC, V. Métro: George-V.*

9ᵉ Arrondissement (Opéra)

$$$$ 🏨 **Grand Hôtel Inter-Continental.** Open since 1862, Paris's biggest luxury hotel has a facade that seems as long as the Louvre. The grand salon's Art Deco dome and the restaurant's painted ceilings are registered landmarks. The Art Deco rooms are spacious and light (ask for one on the top floors). Its famed Café de la Paix is one of the city's great people-watching spots. ✉ *2 rue Scribe, 75009,* ☎ *01–40–07– 32–32, 800/327–0200 in the U.S.,* FAX *01–42–66–12–51. 475 rooms, 39 suites. 3 restaurants, 2 bars, air-conditioning, in-room modem lines, in-room safes, no-smoking rooms, room service, in-room VCRs, sauna, health club, laundry service, business services, meeting rooms. AE, DC, MC, V. Métro: Opéra.*

12ᵉ Arrondissement (Bastille/Gare de Lyon)

$$–$$$ 🏨 **Le Pavillon Bastille.** Here's a smart address (across from the Opéra Bastille) if you appreciate getting perks for less. The transformation of this 19th-century *hôtel particulier* into a mod, colorful, high-design hotel garnered architectural awards and a fiercely loyal, hip clientele. ✉ *65 rue de Lyon, 75012,* ☎ *01–43–43–65–65, 800/233–2552 in the U.S.,* FAX *01–43–43–96–52. 24 rooms, 1 suite. Bar, air-conditioning, in-room safes, minibars, room service. AE, DC, MC, V. Métro: Bastille.*

14ᵉ Arrondissement (Montparnasse)

$$ 🏨 **Raspail-Montparnasse.** Rooms in this hotel are named after the artists who made Montparnasse the art capital of the world in the '20s and '30s. All are decorated in pastels and contemporary blonde-wood furniture. Most are at the low end of this price category; five have spectacular panoramic views of Montparnasse and the Eiffel Tower. ✉ *203 bd. Raspail, 75014,* ☎ *01–43–20–62–86,* FAX *01–43–20–50–79. 38 rooms. Bar, air-conditioning, in-room safes, meeting rooms. AE, DC, MC, V. Métro: Vavin.*

$–$$ 🏨 **Istria.** This small, delightful, family-run hotel on a quiet side street was once a Montparnasse artists' hangout. It has a flower-filled courtyard and simple, clean, comfortable rooms with light wood furniture and soft pastel-tone Japanese wallpaper. ✉ *29 rue Campagne-Première, 75014,* ☎ *01–43–20–91–82,* FAX *01–43–22–48–45. 26 rooms. In-room safes, meeting rooms. AE, DC, MC, V. Métro: Raspail.*

$ 🏨 **Parc Montsouris.** This modest hotel in a 1930s villa is on a quiet residential street next to the lovely Parc Montsouris. Attractive oak pieces and high-quality French fabrics embellish the small but clean rooms; satellite TV is another plus. Those with shower are very inexpensive; suites sleep four. ✉ *4 rue du Parc-Montsouris, 75014,* ☎ *01–45–89– 09–72,* FAX *01–45–80–92–72. 28 rooms, 7 suites. Air-conditioning, no-smoking rooms, laundry service. AE, MC, V. Métro: Montparnasse-Bienvenue.*

16ᵉ Arrondissement (Arc de Triomphe/ Bois de Boulogne)

$$$$ 🏨 **Saint James Paris.** Called the "only château-hôtel in Paris," this gracious, late-19th-century neoclassical mansion is surrounded by a lush private park. The lavish Art Deco interior was created by designer Andrée Putman. Ten rooms on the third floor open onto a winter garden. The restaurant is reserved for guests; in warm weather, meals are served in the garden. The poshest option is booking one of the two duplex gatehouses. ✉ *43 av. Bugeaud, 75016,* ☎ *01–44–05–81–81, 800/447–*

7462 in the U.S., ℻ 01–44–05–81–82. 24 rooms, 24 suites. Restaurant, bar, air-conditioning, in-room modem lines, in-room safes, no-smoking rooms, room service, sauna, health club, baby-sitting, laundry service, meeting rooms, free parking. AE, DC, MC, V. Métro: Porte Dauphine.

$ 🏨 **Queen's Hotel.** One of only a handful of hotels in the tony residential district near the Bois de Boulogne, Queen's is a small, comfortable hotel with a high standard of service. Each room focuses on a different 20th-century French artist. The rooms with baths have Jacuzzis. ✉ 4 rue Bastien-Lepage, 75016, ☎ 01–42–88–89–85, ℻ 01–40–50–67–52. 20 rooms. Air-conditioning, in-room safes, no-smoking rooms. AE, DC, MC, V. Métro: Michel-Ange–Auteuil.

17ᵉ Arrondissement (Monceau/Clichy)

$$ 🏨 **Étoile-Péreire.** Behind a quiet, leafy courtyard in this chic residential district is this unique, intimate hotel, consisting of two parts: a fin-de-siècle building on the street and a 1920s annex overlooking an interior courtyard. Rooms and duplexes are done in deep shades of rose or blue with crisp, white damask upholstery; only suites have air-conditioning. ✉ 146 bd. Péreire, 75017, ☎ 01–42–67–60–00, ℻ 01–42–67–02–90. 21 rooms, 5 duplex suites. Bar, in-room safes, no-smoking rooms, laundry service. AE, DC, MC, V. Métro: Péreire.

NIGHTLIFE AND THE ARTS

The Arts

The weekly magazines *Pariscope* (which has an English section), *L'Officiel des Spectacles,* and *Figaroscope* (a supplement to *Le Figaro* newspaper) are published every Wednesday and give detailed entertainment listings. Activities are also listed in **"Saison de Paris,"** a booklet available at the Paris Tourist Office (☞ Visitor Information *in* Paris A to Z, *below*). The Paris Tourist Office's **24-hour hot line** in English (☎ 01–49–52–53–56) is another source of information about events.

The best place to buy tickets is at the venue itself; try to purchase in advance, as many of the more popular performances sell out. Also try your hotel or a travel agency, such as **Paris-Vision** (✉ 1 rue Auber, 9ᵉ, ☎ 01–40–06–01–00, métro Opéra). Tickets for most concerts can be bought at **FNAC** (especially ✉ 1–5 rue Pierre Lescot, Forum des Halles, 3rd level down, 1ᵉʳ, ☎ 01–49–87–50–50, métro Châtelet–Les Halles). **Virgin Megastore** (✉ 52 av. des Champs-Élysées, 8ᵉ, ☎ 01–44–68–44–08, métro Franklin-D.-Roosevelt) sells theater and concert tickets. Half-price tickets for many same-day theater performances are available at the **Kiosques Théâtre** at the Madeleine (✉ across from 15 pl. de la Madeleine, métro Madeleine) and outside the Gare Montparnasse (✉ pl. Raoul Dautry, 15ᵉ, métro Montparnasse-Bienvenüe), open Tuesday–Sunday 12:30–7:30; expect a line.

Classical Music

A varied program of classical and world music concerts is held at the **Cité de la Musique** (✉ 221 av. Jean-Jaurès, 19ᵉ, ☎ 01–44–84–44–84, métro Porte de Pantin). The **Salle Pleyel** (✉ 252 rue du Faubourg-St-Honoré, 8ᵉ, ☎ 01–45–61–53–00, métro Ternes) is Paris's principal home of classical music. The **Théâtre des Champs-Élysées** (✉ 15 av. Montaigne, 8ᵉ, ☎ 01–49–52–50–50, métro Alma-Marceau), an Art Deco temple, hosts concerts and ballet.

Paris has a never-ending stream of inexpensive lunchtime and evening concerts in churches, some scheduled as part of the **Festival d'Art Sacré** (☎ 01–44–70–64–10 for information) between mid-November and

Christmas. **Churches** with classical concerts (often free) include (☞ Exploring, *above*, for addresses): Notre-Dame, Ste-Chapelle, St-Eustache, St-Germain-des-Prés, St-Louis-en-l'Ile, St-Roch, and St-Germain l'Auxerrois.

Dance

The **Opéra Garnier** (⊠ pl. de l'Opéra, 9ᵉ, ☎ 01–40–01–17–89, métro Opéra) is home to the well-reputed Paris Ballet. **Théâtre de la Bastille** (⊠ 76 rue de la Roquette, 11ᵉ, ☎ 01–43–57–42–14, métro Bastille) is an example of the innovative dance activity in the Bastille area. The **Théâtre de la Ville** (⊠ 2 pl. du Châtelet, 4ᵉ, métro Châtelet; ⊠ 31 rue des Abbesses, 18ᵉ, métro Abbesses; ☎ 01–42–74–22–77 for both) is the place for contemporary dance.

Film

Parisians are far more addicted to the cinema as an art form than even Londoners or New Yorkers. A number of theaters, especially in principal tourist areas such as the Champs-Élysées, St-Germain-des-Prés, Les Halles, and the boulevard des Italiens near the Opéra, show first-run films in English. Check the weekly guides for a movie of your choice. Look for the initials "v.o.," which mean *version originale,* i.e., not dubbed. Cinema admission runs from 37 to 51 francs; there are slightly reduced rates on Mondays and, in some cinemas, for morning shows. Most theaters will post two show times: The first is the *séance,* when commercials, previews, and sometimes short films start, and the second is the feature presentation, which usually starts 10–20 minutes later.

Paris has numerous small cinemas showing classic and independent films, especially in the Latin Quarter. Screenings are often organized around retrospectives (check "Festivals" in weekly guides). The **Cinémathèque Française** (⊠ 42 bd. de Bonne-Nouvelle, ☎ 01–47–04–24–24, métro Bonne-Nouvelle) shows classic French and international films Wednesday–Saturday. Big-screen fanatics should try the **Grand Rex** (⊠ 1 bd. Poissonnière, 2ᵉ, ☎ 01–42–36–83–93, métro Bonne Nouvelle). The **Max Linder Panorama** (⊠ 24 bd. Poissonnière, 9ᵉ, ☎ 01–48–24–88–88, métro Rue Montmartre) often shows classics on its big screen. **UGC Ciné Cité Les Halles** (⊠ pl. de la Rotonde, Forum des Halles, 3rd level down, 1ᵉʳ, ☎ 08–36–68–68–58, métro Les Halles) has first-fun films on its big screens.

Opera

Getting tickets to the opera can be difficult on short notice, so it is a good idea to plan ahead. For the schedule, send away for the Paris Tourist Office's *"Saison de Paris"* booklet (☞ Visitor Information *in* Paris A to Z, *below*); then contact the **Opéra de la Bastille** (⊠ 120 rue de Lyon, Paris 75012) well in advance. Buying from a scalper is not recommended, as people have been known to sell counterfeit tickets.

The **Opéra de la Bastille** (⊠ pl. de la Bastille, 12ᵉ, ☎ 01–44–73–13–00, métro Bastille) has taken over the role as Paris's main opera house from the Opéra Garnier (☞ Dance, *above*); tickets range from 45 to 635 francs. The **Opéra Comique** (⊠ 5 rue Favart, 2ᵉ, ☎ 01–42–96–12–20, métro Richelieu-Drouot) is a lofty old hall where you'll hear often excellent comic operas. Better known as the Théâtre du Châtelet, the **Théâtre Musical de Paris** (⊠ pl. du Châtelet, 1ᵉʳ, ☎ 01–40–28–28–40, métro Châtelet) has built up a strong reputation for opera and offers productions for a wider audience, at more reasonable prices.

Theater

A number of theaters line the Grand Boulevards between Opéra and République, but there is no Paris equivalent to Broadway or the West End. Shows are mostly in French. **Bouffes du Nord** (⊠ 37 bis bd. de la Chapelle, 10ᵉ, ☎ 01–46–07–34–50, métro La Chapelle) is home to English director Peter Brook. The **Comédie-Française** (⊠ pl. André-Malraux, 1ᵉʳ, ☎ 01–44–58–15–15, métro Palais-Royal) is a distinguished venue that stages classical drama. The **Théâtre de la Huchette** (⊠ 23 rue de la Huchette, 5ᵉ, ☎ 01–43–26–38–99, métro St-Michel), a tiny Left Bank theater, has been staging Ionesco's "The Bald Primadonna" every night since 1950. **Théâtre de l'Odéon** (⊠ pl. de l'Odéon, 6ᵉ, ☎ 01–44–41–36–36, métro Odéon) has made pan-European theater its primary focus.

Nightlife

So you've immersed yourself in culture all day and you want a night out on the town. The hottest spots are near Menilmontant, the Bastille, and the Marais. The Left Bank is definitely a lot less happening. The Champs-Élysées is making a comeback, though the clientele remains predominantly foreign. Take note: The last métro runs between 12:30 and 1 AM (you can take a cab, but they are sometimes hard to find).

Bars and Clubs

Buddha Bar (⊠ 8 rue Boissy d'Anglas, 8ᵉ, ☎ 01–53–05–90–00, métro Concorde) has a spacious mezzanine bar that overlooks the dining room. **Café Charbon** (⊠ 109 rue Oberkampf, 11ᵉ, ☎ 01–43–57–55–13, métro St-Maur, Parmentier) is a beautifully restored 19th-century café, whose trend-setting clientele chats to jazz in the background. **China Club** (⊠ 50 rue de Charenton, 12ᵉ, ☎ 01–43–43–82–02, métro Ledru-Rollin) has three floors of bars and a restaurant with lacquered furnishings and a colonial Orient theme. **Le Closerie des Lilas** (⊠ 171 bd. de Montparnasse, 6ᵉ, ☎ 01–43–54–21–68, RER Port Royal) has served more than one generation of poets and intellectuals, as the brass plaques around the bar attest; the piano plays until 1 AM. **Harry's New York Bar** (⊠ 5 rue Daunou, 2ᵉ, ☎ 01–42–61–71–14, métro Opéra), a cozy, wood-paneled hangout popular with expatriates, is haunted by the ghosts of Ernest Hemingway and F. Scott Fitzgerald.

It helps to be famous—or look like a model—to get into **Les Bains** (⊠ 7 rue du Bourg-l'Abbé, 3ᵉ, ☎ 01–48–87–01–80, métro Étienne-Marcel), a forever-trendy club (closed Monday). **Le Balajo** (⊠ 9 rue de Lappe, 11ᵉ, ☎ 01–47–00–07–87, métro Bastille) is an old Java ballroom that specializes in salsa and techno; entry is free for women on Thursday. **Le Cabaret** (⊠ 68 rue de Charonne, 8ᵉ, ☎ 01–42–89–44–14, métro Franklin-D.-Roosevelt) used to be just that; now there are still cabaret acts, as well as dancing to soul and funk.

GAY AND LESBIAN BARS AND CLUBS

Gay and lesbian bars and clubs are mostly concentrated in the Marais and include some of the most happening addresses in the city. **Amnésia Café**'s (⊠ 42 rue Vieille-du-Temple, 4ᵉ, ☎ 01–42–72–16–94, métro Rambuteau), with its underlit bar and Art Deco ceiling paintings, attract a young, yuppie, gay and lesbian crowd. Mostly men go to **L'Open Café** (⊠ 17 rue des Archives, 4ᵉ, ☎ 01–42–72–26–18, métro Hôtel-de-Ville), which has sunny decor and a convivial ambience. **Le Pulp!** (⊠ 25 bd. Poissonnière, 2ᵉ, ☎ 01–40–26–01–93, métro Pyramides) is just about the only lesbian nightclub in Paris; it's open Wednesday–Saturday. **Queen** (⊠ 102 av. des Champs-Élysées, 8ᵉ, ☎ 01–42–89–31–32, métro George-V) is one of the hottest nightspots in Paris: Although it's predominantly gay, everyone else lines up to get in, too.

Cabaret

Paris's cabarets are household names—more so abroad than in France, it would seem, judging by the hefty percentage of foreigners present at most shows. You can dine at many of them; prices range from 200 francs (simple admission plus one drink) to more than 800 francs (dinner plus show).

Crazy Horse (⊠ 12 av. George-V, 8ᵉ, ☎ 01–47–23–32–32, métro Alma-Marceau) is one of the best-known cabarets, with pretty dancers and raunchy routines. **Lido** (⊠ 116 bis av. des Champs-Élysées, 8ᵉ, ☎ 01–40–76–56–10, métro George-V) stars the famous Bluebell Girls; the owners claim that no show in Las Vegas can rival it for special effects. That old favorite at the foot of Montmartre, **Moulin Rouge** (⊠ pl. Blanche, 18ᵉ, ☎ 01–46–06–00–19, métro Blanche), mingles the Doriss Girls, the cancan, and a horse in an extravagant spectacle. **Paradis Latin** (⊠ 28 rue du Cardinal Lemoine, 5ᵉ, ☎ 01–43–25–28–28, métro Cardinal Lemoine) is perhaps the liveliest, busiest, and trendiest cabaret on the Left Bank.

Jazz Clubs

Paris is one of the great jazz cities of the world, and the French take jazz seriously. For nightly schedules, consult the specialty magazine *Jazz Hot* or *Jazz Magazine*. Nothing gets going till 10 or 11 PM; entry prices vary widely from about 40 francs to more than 100 francs. At the Méridien Hotel near Porte Maillot, the **Lionel Hampton Jazz Club** (⊠ 81 bd. Gouvion-St-Cyr, 17ᵉ, ☎ 01–40–68–30–42, métro Porte Maillot) hosts a roster of international jazz players. **New Morning** (⊠ 7 rue des Petites-Écuries, 10ᵉ, ☎ 01–45–23–51–41, métro Château-d'Eau) is a premier spot for serious fans of avant-garde jazz, as well as folk and world music. The greatest names in French and international jazz have been playing at **Le Petit Journal** (⊠ 71 bd. St-Michel, 5ᵉ, ☎ 01–43–26–28–59, RER Luxembourg) for decades; Sunday is devoted to the blues. **Le Petit Opportun** (⊠ 15 rue des Lavandières-Ste-Opportune, 1ᵉʳ, ☎ 01–42–36–01–36, métro Châtelet), in a converted bistro, sometimes features top-flight American soloists with French backup.

Rock, Pop, and World Music Venues

Upcoming concerts are posted on boards in FNAC and Virgin Megastores. **Le Bataclan** (⊠ 50 bd. Voltaire, 11ᵉ, ☎ 01–47–00–30–12, métro Oberkampf) is an intimate venue for live rock, rap, and reggae. **Élysée Montmartre** (⊠ 72 bd. Rochechouart, 18ᵉ, ☎ 01–44–92–45–45, métro Anvers) is one of the prime venues for emerging French and international rock groups. **Palais Omnisports de Paris-Bercy** (⊠ rue de Bercy, 12ᵉ, ☎ 01–44–68–44–68, métro Bercy) is the best place to catch big French and international stars. **Zenith** (⊠ Parc de la Villette, 19ᵉ, ☎ 01–42–08–60–00, métro Porte-de-Pantin) stages large rock shows.

OUTDOOR ACTIVITIES AND SPORTS

Participant Sports

Bicycling

Paris has been making valiant efforts to become more biker-friendly. More than 100 km (63 mi) of **bicycle lanes** now cross the city, notably along rue de Rivoli and boulevard St-Germain. Certain roads are banned to cars altogether on Sundays (including the banks of the Seine between the Tuileries and the Eiffel Tower, from 9 AM to 6 PM, and the roads alongside the Canal St-Martin, from 2 PM to 6 PM). With their wide, leafy avenues, the **Bois de Boulogne** (☞ Exploring, *above*) and the **Bois de Vincennes** (métro Porte Dorée, Château de Vincennes) are good places for biking. Bikes can be rented from **Pariscyclo** (⊠ Rond Point de Jardin d'Acclimatation, ☎ 01–47–47–76–50, métro Les Sablons), in the Bois de Boulogne. **Paris à Vélo, C'est Sympa** (⊠ 37 bd. Bourdon, 4ᵉ, ☎ 01–48–87–60–01, métro Bastille) also rents bikes.

Health Clubs and Swimming Pools

A number of hotels, gyms, and clubs in the city offer one-day or short-term memberships. **Aquaboulevard de Paris** (⊠ 4 rue Louis-Armand, 15ᵉ, ☎ 01–40–60–10–00, métro Balard) has a gym, Turkish baths, and the city's best swimming pool, complete with giant slide and wave machine (150 francs per day). **Club Quartier Latin** (⊠ 19 rue de Pontoise, 5ᵉ, ☎ 01–43–54–82–45, métro Maubert Mutualité) has a nice 30-meter skylighted pool, a climbing wall, squash courts, and exercise equipment (70 francs per day and 75 francs an hour for squash). **Espace Vit-Halles** (⊠ 48 rue Rambuteau, 3ᵉ, ☎ 01–42–77–21–71, métro Les Halles) has a broad range of aerobics classes (100 francs a class), exercise machines, sauna, and steam bath. The **Piscine des Halles** (⊠ pl. de la Rotonde, Forum des Halles, 1ᵉʳ, ☎ 01–42–36–98–44) is a beautiful 50-meter pool. Admission is 25 francs; call for hours.

Jogging

The best inner-city running is in the **Champ de Mars,** next to the Eiffel Tower, measuring 2 km (1½ mi) around the perimeter. Shorter and more crowded routes are found in the **Jardin du Luxembourg,** with a 1½-km (about 1-mi) loop just inside the park's fence. The path in the **Jardin des Tuileries** also measures about 1½ km (1 mi). The **Parc Monceau** has a loop of 1 km (½ mi). The **Bois de Boulogne** (☞ Exploring, *above*) has miles of trails through woods and around lakes. The equally bucolic **Bois de Vincennes** has a 15-km (9-mi) circuit or a 1½-km (¾-mi) loop around the Château de Vincennes itself.

Spectator Sports

Information on upcoming events can be found in the weekly guide **Pariscope**, on posters around the city, or by calling the ticket agencies of FNAC (☎ 01–49–87–50–50) or the **Virgin Megastore** (☎ 01–44–68–44–08).

A wide range of sporting events, including indoor athletics, ice-skating, horse shows, gymnastics, and stock-car racing, take place at the **Palais Omnisports de Paris-Bercy** (⊠ 8 bd. de Bercy, 12ᵉ, ☎ 01–44–68–44–68, métro Bercy). **Parc des Princes** (⊠ 24 rue du Cdt. Guilbaud, 16ᵉ, ☎ 01–42–88–02–76, métro Porte de St-Cloud) is where the city's soccer team, Paris St-Germain, plays its home matches. **Roland-Garros** (⊠ 2 av. Gordon Bennett, 16ᵉ, ☎ 01–47–43–48–00, métro Porte d'Auteuil) is the venue for the French Open tennis tournament in May. **Stade de France** (⊠ St-Denis, ☎ 01–55–93–00–00, RER La Plaine–Stade de France) was built for the World Cup in 1998 and is now home to the French national soccer and rugby teams.

SHOPPING

Revised and updated by Suzanne Rowan Kelleher

The shopping opportunities in Paris are endless and geared to every taste. Perfume and designer clothing are perhaps the most coveted Parisian souvenirs. However, even on haute couture's home turf, bargains are surprisingly elusive. It's good to be aware of the slings and arrows of international exchange rates and to know prices at home before you arrive. Even stores that accept currency other than francs will generally give you a lower rate of exchange than banks or exchange offices. You're better off using credit cards. Even the corner newsstand or flea market salesperson is likely to honor plastic for purchases over 100 francs. Visa is the most common and preferred card, followed closely by MasterCard. American Express, Diners Club, and Access are accepted in the larger international stores.

When hunting for bargains, watch for the word *soldes* (sales). The two main sale seasons are January and July. For nice gifts, try the shops in Paris's museums, especially the shops in the Louvre, the Musée Carnavalet, the Opéra Garnier, and the Musée des Arts Décoratifs. If you're from outside the European Union, aged 15 and over, and stay in France and/or the EU for less than six months, you can benefit from Value Added Tax (VAT) reimbursements, known in France as TVA or *détaxe*. To qualify, non-EU residents must spend at least 2,000 francs in a single store. Refunds vary from 13% to 20.6% and are mailed to you by check or credited to your charge card.

Shopping by Neighborhood

Avenue Montaigne
This elegant boulevard is a showcase of international haute-couture houses. American **Calvin Klein** and Italian moguls **Prada** and **Dolce & Gabbana** have joined **Chanel, Dior, Nina Ricci, Jil Sander, Guy Laroche, Jean-Louis Scherrer, Emanuel Ungaro, Céline, Valentino, MaxMara, Genny, Krizia, Escada, Thierry Mugler,** and **Hanae Mori.** Here you'll also find accessories by **S. T. Dupont, Loewe, Salvatore Ferragamo,** and **Louis Vuitton. Yves Saint Laurent** and **Givenchy** are nearby, on avenues Marceau and George-V, respectively, and **Versace** is on rue François I.

Bastille
Scores of trendy boutiques are clustered between art galleries, furniture stores, and bars in this gentrified neighborhood. **Jean-Paul Gaultier** has his flagship boutique on rue Faubourg St-Antoine, and hot lounge-look designer **Christophe Lemaire** is installed on the rue St-Sabin.

Champs-Élysées
Cafés and movie theaters keep the once-chic Champs-Élysées active 24 hours a day, but the invasion of exchange banks, car showrooms, and fast-food chains has lowered the tone. Four glitzy 20th-century arcade malls—**Galerie du Lido, Le Rond-Point, Le Claridge,** and **Élysées 26**—capture most of the retail action.

Left Bank
After decades of clustering on the Right Bank's venerable shopping avenues, the high-fashion houses are now storming the Rive Gauche. Ever since **Louis Vuitton, Giorgio Armani, Thierry Mugler, Christian Dior Men,** and **Romeo Gigli** set up Left Bank shops in 1996, anyone who's anyone has rushed to followed suit. (**Sonia Rykiel** and **Yves Saint Laurent** arrived fashionably early in the 1970s.) This immensely walkable district between rue de Grenelle and rue de Rennes is also known for its top-quality shoe shops (**Maud Frizon, Charles Jourdan, Stéphane Kélian,** and **Harel**).

Les Halles
Most of the narrow pedestrian streets on the former site of Paris's wholesale food market are lined with fast-food joints, sex shops, jeans outlets, and garish souvenir stands, but rue du Jour—featuring **MaxMara, Agnès B.,** and **Junior Gaultier** boutiques—is an attractive exception. Rue Tiquetonne is a vintage clothing mecca, and the fabulously quirky **Comme des Garçons** has shops for both sexes on rue Étienne-Marcel. In the middle of the action is the **Forum des Halles,** a multilevel underground shopping mall, which, though it has its share of teens and chain stores, also has started attracting higher-quality merchants and a clutch of promising designers.

Louvre–Palais Royal

The elegant and eclectic shops clustered in the 18th-century arcades of the Palais-Royal sell antiques, toy soldiers, Shiseido cosmetics, dramatic art jewelry from Siki, and even vintage designer dresses. The glossy marble **Carrousel du Louvre** mall, beneath the Louvre, is lit by an immense inverted glass pyramid. Shops, including **Virgin Megastore,** the **Body Shop,** and **Esprit,** along with a lively international food court, are open on Sunday—still a rare convenience in Paris.

Le Marais

Between the pre-Revolution mansions and tiny kosher food stores that characterize this area are scores of trendy gift shops and clothing stores. Avant-garde designers **Azzedine Alaïa, Lolita Lempicka, Issey Miyake,** and **Romeo Gigli** have boutiques within a few blocks of the stately place des Vosges and the Picasso and Carnavalet museums. Nearly all Marais shops are open on Sunday.

Montparnasse

The bohemian mecca for artists and writers in the '20s and '30s, Montparnasse is better known for bars and restaurants than shops. The commercial center near the train station has a **Galeries Lafayette** outlet, but it's too charmless to attract many tourists. **Rue d'Alésia** on the southern fringe of Montparnasse is known for discount clothing shops.

Opéra to La Madeleine

Three major department stores—**Au Printemps, Galeries Lafayette,** and the British **Marks & Spencer** (☞ Department Stores, *below*)—define boulevard Haussmann, behind Paris's ornate 19th-century Opéra Garnier. Place de la Madeleine is home to two luxurious food stores, **Fauchon** and **Hédiard.** Steps away, on boulevard de la Madeleine, is a classy 75-shop mall, **Les Trois Quartiers. Lalique** and **Baccarat Crystal** also have opulent showrooms near the Église de la Madeleine.

Passy–Victor Hugo

The bourgeois and conservative 16ᵉ arrondissement attracts predictably classic and upscale retailers, most of whom are centered on rue de Passy and place Victor Hugo. A handful of secondhand shops in this wealthy area offer exceptionally good deals. **Réciproque,** on rue de la Pompe, is one of the biggest and best swap shops in Paris.

Place Vendôme and Rue de la Paix

The magnificent 17th-century place Vendôme, home of the Ritz Hotel, and rue de la Paix, leading north from Vendôme, have attracted the world's most elegant jewelers: **Cartier, Boucheron, Buccellati, Van Cleef and Arpels, Répossi, Mellerio, Mauboussin,** and **Mikimoto.**

Place des Victoires

This graceful, circular plaza near the Palais-Royal is the playground of cutting-edge fashion icons such as **Kenzo, Victoire,** and **Thierry Mugler.** Avant-garde boutiques like **Chantal Thomass, Jean-Charles de Castelbajac, Absinthe,** and **En Attendant les Barbares** have fanned into the side streets; **Jean-Paul Gaultier**'s flagship shop is in the nearby Galerie Vivienne arcade. One of the hottest new emporiums to pop up in the neighborhood, **Le Shop,** at 3 rue d'Argout, rents retail space to hip, up-and-coming designers.

Rue du Faubourg–St-Honoré

This chic shopping and residential street is exemplified by the presence of the Élysée Palace and the official residences of the American and British ambassadors. The Paris branch of **Sotheby's** and renowned antiques galleries such as **Didier Aaron** add artistic flavor. Boutiques include **Hermès, Lanvin, Karl Lagerfeld, Reveillon Furs, Louis Feraud,** and **Christian Lacroix.**

Department Stores

Paris's top department stores offer both convenience and style. Most are open Monday through Saturday from about 9:30 AM to 7 PM, and some are open until 10 PM one weekday evening. All six major stores listed below have multilingual guides, international welcome desks, détaxe offices, and restaurants.

Au Bon Marché (⊠ 22 rue de Sèvres, 7ᵉ, ☎ 01–44–39–80–00, métro Sèvres-Babylone), founded in 1852, is an excellent hunting ground for housewares, men's clothes, and gifts.

Au Printemps (⊠ 64 bd. Haussmann, 9ᵉ, ☎ 01–42–82–50–00, métro Havre-Caumartin, Opéra, or Auber) has three floors of women's fashion. Free fashion shows are held on Tuesday (all year) and Friday (March–October) at 10 AM on the seventh floor. The three-store complex also includes La Maison, for housewares and furniture, and Brummel, a six-floor emporium of menswear.

Bazar de l'Hôtel de Ville (⊠ 52–64 rue de Rivoli, 4ᵉ, ☎ 01–42–74–90–00, métro Hôtel de Ville), better known as BHV, has minimal fashion offerings, but is noteworthy for its enormous basement hardware store, quality household goods, and office supplies.

Galeries Lafayette (⊠ 40 bd. Haussmann, 9ᵉ, ☎ 01–42–82–34–56, métro Chaussée d'Antin, Opéra, or Havre-Caumartin; ⊠ Centre Commercial Montparnasse, 15ᵉ, ☎ 01–45–38–52–87, métro Montparnasse-Bienvenue) carries nearly 80,000 fashion labels under its roof. Free fashion shows are held every Wednesday at 11 AM (☎ 01–48–74–02–30 for reservations). Along with the world's largest perfumery, the main store has a huge emporium dedicated to the art of living *à la française* (like the French).

Marks & Spencer (⊠ 35 bd. Haussmann, 9ᵉ, ☎ 01–47–42–42–91, métro Havre-Caumartin, Auber, or Opéra; ⊠ 88 rue de Rivoli, 4ᵉ, ☎ 01–44–61–08–00, métro Hôtel de Ville) is a British chain chiefly noted for its moderately priced basics (underwear, socks, sleep- and sportswear), and its excellent English grocery.

La Samaritaine (⊠ 19 rue de la Monnaie, 1ᵉʳ, ☎ 01–40–41–20–20, métro Pont-Neuf or Châtelet), a sprawling five-story complex, carries everything from designer fashions to cuckoo clocks but is especially known for kitchen supplies, housewares, and furniture. Its most famous asset is the Toupary café in Building 2 with its marvelous views.

Budget

Monoprix and **Prisunic** are French dime stores—with scores of branches throughout the city—that stock inexpensive everyday items like makeup, toothpaste, groceries, toys, and paper—a little of everything. Both chains carry inexpensive children's clothes of surprisingly good quality.

Shopping Arcades and Markets

Paris's 19th-century commercial arcades, called *passages*, are the forerunners of the modern mall. Glass roofs, decorative pillars, and mosaic floors give the passages character. The major arcades are on the Right Bank in central Paris. The **Galerie Vivienne** (⊠ 4 rue des Petits-Champs, 2ᵉ, métro Bourse) is home to a range of interesting shops, an excellent tearoom, and a quality wine shop. The **Passage Jouffroy** (⊠

12 bd. Montmartre, 2ᵉ, métro Montmartre) is full of shops selling toys, postcards, antique canes, and perfumes. The **Passage des Panoramas** (⊠ 11 bd. Montmartre, 2ᵉ, métro Montmartre), built in 1800, is the oldest of them all. The **Passage des Pavillons** (⊠ 6 rue de Beaujolais, 1ᵉʳ, métro Palais-Royal), near the Palais-Royal gardens, is an elegant gallery with shops selling gourmet foods and antiquarian books.

Flea Markets

The **Marché aux Puces** on Paris's northern boundary (métro Porte de Clignancourt), which takes place Saturday through Monday, is a century-old labyrinth of alleyways packed with antiques dealers' booths and junk stalls spreading for more than a square mile. Early birds pick up the most worthwhile loot. But be warned—if there's one place in Paris where you need to know how to bargain, this is it!

Food Markets

The lively atmosphere that reigns in most of Paris's open-air food markets makes them a sight worth seeing even if you don't want or need to buy anything. Every neighborhood has one, although many are open only a few days each week. Sunday morning, till 1 PM, is usually a good time to go; Monday the markets are likely to be closed. Many of the better-known markets are in areas you'd visit for sightseeing: **rue de Buci** (⊠ 6ᵉ, métro Odéon), open daily, near St-Germain-des-Prés; **rue Mouffetard** (⊠ 5ᵉ, métro Monge), best on weekends, near the Jardin des Plantes; **rue Montorgueuil** (⊠ 1ᵉʳ, métro Châtelet–Les Halles), open daily; and **rue Lepic** in Montmartre (⊠ 18ᵉ, métro Blanche or Abbesses), best on weekends.

Specialty Stores

Art and Antiques

Art galleries and antiques shops are scattered throughout the city; often galleries focusing on the same period are clustered in one neighborhood. Many contemporary galleries, for instance, have grown up around the Pompidou Center, the Picasso Museum, and the Bastille Opera. Many of these galleries are hidden away in courtyards, the only sign of their presence a small plaque on the front of the buildings; take these as invitations to push through the double doors. Galleries around St-Germain aren't as avant-garde, though some could certainly fit on either side of the river. The **carré Rive Gauche** (métro St-Germain-des-Prés, Rue du Bac), an area that shelters dozens of art and antiques galleries on its narrow lanes, is a good place to start. Works by old masters and established modern artists dominate the galleries around **rue du Faubourg St-Honoré** and **avenue Matignon.** To plot your course, get the free map published by the Association des Galeries; it's available at many galleries.

Louvre des Antiquaires (⊠ 2 pl. du Palais-Royal, 1ᵉʳ, métro Palais-Royal) is an elegant multifloor complex where 250 of Paris's leading dealers showcase their rarest objects and is open Tuesday to Sunday; it's closed Sunday in July and August.

Bookstores (English-Language)

The scenic open-air bookstalls along the Seine sell secondhand books (mostly in French), prints, and souvenirs. Numerous French-language bookshops—specializing in a wide range of topics, including art, film, literature, and philosophy—are found in the scholarly Latin Quarter and the publishing district, St-Germain-des-Prés. For English-language books, try the following. **Brentano's** (⊠ 37 av. de l'Opéra, 2ᵉ, ☎ 01–42–61–52–50, métro Opéra) is stocked with everything from classics to children's titles. **Shakespeare & Co.** (⊠ 37 rue de la Bûcherie,

5ᵉ, ☎ 01–43–26–96–50, métro St-Michel) specializes in expatriate literature. **W. H. Smith** (✉ 248 rue de Rivoli, 1ᵉʳ, ☎ 01–42–60–37–97, métro Concorde) carries an excellent range of books.

Clothing

CHILDREN'S

Dipaki (✉ 18 rue Vignon, 8ᵉ, ☎ 01–01–42–66–24–74, métro Madeleine) is a mecca for affordably priced infants' and kids' clothing in bold, primary colors. **Du Pareil Au Même** (✉ 15 and 23 rue des Mathurins, 8ᵉ, ☎ 01–42–66–93–80, métro Havre-Caumartin; ✉ 7 rue St-Placide, 6ᵉ, ☎ 01–40–49–00–33, métro St-Placide) is a moderately priced chain selling well-made, adorable basics in soft, brightly colored jersey and cotton.

MEN'S

Charvet (✉ 28 pl. Vendôme, 1ᵉʳ, ☎ 01–42–60–30–70, métro Opéra) is the Parisian equivalent of a Savile Row tailor. **Façonnable** (✉ 9 rue du Faubourg St-Honoré, 8ᵉ, ☎ 01–47–42–72–60, métro Concorde) sells fashionable town and weekend clothes for young urbanites. **Kenzo** (✉ 3 pl. des Victoires, 2ᵉ, ☎ 01–40–39–72–03, métro Bourse; ✉ 17 bd. Raspail, 7ᵉ, ☎ 01–42–22–09–38, métro Rue du Bac) brings exuberant color and fantasy to his menswear collections. **Lanvin** (✉ 15 rue du Faubourg St-Honoré, 8ᵉ, ☎ 01–44–71–33–33, métro Madeleine) has elegant tailoring and sophisticated sportswear; the branch for women is at No. 22.

WOMEN'S

Christophe Lemaire (✉ 4 rue Chérubini, 2ᵉ, ☎ 01–47–03–39–00, métro Quatre Septembre) trained with Lacroix, St-Laurent, and Michel Klein and is now the name to watch in the new generation of French designers. **L'Éclaireur** (✉ 3 rue des Rosiers, 4ᵉ, ☎ 01–48–87–10–22, métro St-Paul) has an uncanny gift for spotting tomorrow's fashion stars. **Et Vous** (✉ 25 rue Royale, 8ᵉ, ☎ 01–47–42–31–00, métro Madeleine) is where hip Parisiennes find their stylish, contemporary womenswear. **Forum des Jeunes Créateurs** (✉ Forum des Halles, 1st level down, 1ᵉʳ, ☎ no phone, métro Châtelet) sells the creations of 50 rising-star designers at wholesale prices.

Joseph (✉ 14 av. Montaigne, 8ᵉ, ☎ 01–47–20–39–55, métro Alma Marceau) has his own collection, as well as clothing by designers such as Azzedine Alaïa and Galliano. **Tara Jarmon** (✉ 18 rue du Four, 6ᵉ, ☎ 01–46–33–26–60, métro St-Sulpice) is a Canadian designer who has garnered plaudits from Paris's trendwatchers. **Victoire** (✉ 12 pl. des Victoires, 2ᵉ, ☎ 01–42–61–09–02, métro Bourse or Palais-Royal; menswear at ✉ 10–12 rue du Col. Driant, 1ᵉʳ, ☎ 01–42–97–44–87, métro Palais-Royal) is a discreet boutique with a knack for identifying new fashions. **Y's** (✉ 59 rue St-Pères, 6ᵉ, ☎ 01–45–48–22–56, métro St-Germain-des-Prés) stocks the simpler, less expensive second line of Japanese wonderboy Yohji Yamamoto (for men, too).

Food and Wine

À la Mère de Famille (✉ 35 rue du Faubourg-Montmartre, 9ᵉ, ☎ 01–47–70–83–69, métro Cadet) is well versed in French regional specialties and old-fashioned bonbons, sugar candy, and more. **Le Cave Augé** (✉ 116 bd. Haussmann, 8ᵉ, ☎ 01–45–22–16–97, métro St-Augustin) has been one of the best wine shops in Paris since 1850. **La Maison du Chocolat** (✉ 52 rue François 1ᵉʳ, 8ᵉ, ☎ 01–47–23–38–25, métro Franklin-D.-Roosevelt; ✉ 8 bd. de la Madeleine, 9ᵉ, ☎ 01–47–42–86–52, métro Madeleine; ✉ 225 rue du Faubourg-St-Honoré, 8ᵉ, ☎ 01–42–27–39–44, métro Ternes) is heaven for cocoa purists. Take home chocolates, or go to the tearoom on rue du Faubourg-St-Honoré.

Housewares

Colette (⊠ 213 rue St-Honoré, 1ᵉʳ, ☎ 01–55–35–33–90, métro Tuileries) is an enormous minimalist space showcasing all that's trendy in home design, art, and fashion accessories. **Geneviève Lethu** (⊠ 28 rue St-Antoine, 4ᵉ, ☎ 01–42–74–21–25, métro St-Paul) sells tea services, potpourri mixtures, and table linens for your real or imagined country house. **La Tuile à Loup** (⊠ 35 rue Daubenton, 5ᵉ, ☎ 01–47–07–28–90, métro Censier-Daubenton) is jam-packed with traditional pottery, faience, basketry, and gift items from every region of France. **La Vaissellerie** (⊠ 85 rue de Rennes, 6ᵉ, ☎ 01–42–22–61–49, métro Rennes; ⊠ 92 rue St-Antoine, 4ᵉ, ☎ 01–42–72–76–66, métro St-Paul; ⊠ 332 rue St-Honoré, 1ᵉʳ, ☎ 01–42–60–64–50, métro Tuileries) is chockablock with the sort of ingenious kitchen accoutrements that the French do so well, priced below what you would pay for such creativity back home.

PARIS A TO Z

Arriving and Departing

By Bus

Long-distance bus journeys within France are uncommon, which may be why Paris has no central bus depot. But if you are arriving or departing by bus, the leading Paris-based bus company is **Eurolines** (⊠ 28 av. du Général-de-Gaulle, Bagnolet, ☎ 01–49–72–51–51) in the near eastern suburbs.

By Car

In a country as highly centralized as France, it is no surprise that expressways converge on the capital from every direction: A1 from the north (225 km/140 mi to Lille); A13 from Normandy (225 km/140 mi to Caen); A4 from the east (499 km/310 mi to Strasbourg); A10 from the southwest (579 km/360 mi to Bordeaux); and A7 from the Alps and Riviera (466 km/290 mi to Lyon). Each connects with the *périphérique*, the beltway, whose exits into the city are named, not numbered.

By Plane

Paris is served by two international airports: **Charles de Gaulle,** also known as Roissy, 26 km (16 mi) northeast; and **Orly,** 16 km (10 mi) south. Major carriers, among them TWA, American Airlines, and Air France, fly daily from the United States, while Air France, British Airways, British Midland, and Air U.K. offer regular flights from London. *See* Air Travel *in* the Gold Guide for details.

BETWEEN THE AIRPORT AND DOWNTOWN

From Charles de Gaulle, you can take the **RER-B,** the suburban commuter train, beneath Terminal 2. Trains to central Paris (Les Halles, St-Michel, Luxembourg) leave every 15 minutes; the fare is 46 francs, and the journey time is 30 minutes. Note: You have to carry your luggage up and down from the platform, and trains can be crowded during rush hour. **Buses** operated by Air France (you need not have flown with the airline) run every 15 minutes between Roissy and western Paris (Porte Maillot and the Arc de Triomphe). The fare is 55 francs, and the journey time is about 40 minutes, though rush-hour traffic may make it longer. Additionally, the **Roissybus,** operated by RATP, runs directly between Roissy and rue Scribe by the Opéra every 15 minutes and costs 40 francs. **Taxis** are readily available; the fare will be around 200–250 francs, depending on traffic. For the same price as a taxi for two or more people, **Paris Airports Service** can meet you on arrival in a private car and drive you to your destination; reservations must be made two to three days in advance; MasterCard and

Visa are accepted; call ☎ 33–1/49–62–78–78 or fax FAX 33–1/49–62–78–79.

From Orly airport, the cheapest way to get to Paris is on the **RER-C** line; there's a free shuttle bus from the terminal building to the train station, and trains leave every 15 minutes. The fare is 30 francs, and the train journey takes about 40 minutes. The **Orlyval** service is a shuttle train that runs direct from each Orly terminal to Antony **RER-B** station every seven minutes; a one-way ticket for the entire trip into Paris is 54 francs. **Buses** operated by Air France (you need not have flown with the airline) run every 12 minutes between Orly airport and the Air France air terminal at Les Invalides on the Left Bank; the fare is 40 francs, and the trip can take from 30 minutes to an hour. RATP also runs the **Orlybus** between Denfert-Rochereau métro station and Orly every 15 minutes for 30 francs. A 25-minute **taxi** ride costs 130–180 francs. With reservations, **Paris Airports Service** (☞ *above*) can pick you up at Orly and drive you directly to your destination.

By Train

Paris has five international train stations: **Gare du Nord** (northern France, northern Europe, and England via Calais or the Channel Tunnel); **Gare St-Lazare** (Normandy and England via Dieppe); **Gare de l'Est** (Strasbourg, Luxembourg, Basel, and Central Europe); **Gare de Lyon** (Lyon, Marseille, the Riviera, Geneva, Italy); and **Gare d'Austerlitz** (Loire Valley, southwest France, Spain). The **Gare Montparnasse** is used by the TGV-*Atlantique* bound for Nantes or Bordeaux. For information contact the **RATP** (✉ 44 quai de la Rapée, ☎ 08–36–68–77–14).

Getting Around

To help you find your way around, buy a *Plan de Paris par Arrondissement*, a city guide available at most kiosks, with separate maps of each district, including the whereabouts of métro stations and an index of street names. Maps of the métro/RER network are available free from any métro station and many hotels. They are also posted on every platform, as are maps of the bus network. Bus routes are also marked at bus stops and on buses. The extensive public transportation system is the best way to get around.

By Bicycle

Despite the recent introduction of bike lanes, bicycling in central Paris is not that safe; definitely wear a helmet. Bicycles can be rented at various locations throughout the city (☞ Outdoor Activities and Sports, *above*).

By Bus

Paris buses are marked with the route number and destination in front, and major stopping places along the sides. Most routes operate from 6 AM to 8:30 PM; some continue until midnight. Ten *Noctambus*, or night buses, operate hourly (1 AM to 6 AM) between Châtelet and various nearby suburbs. The brown bus shelters, topped by red-and-yellow circular signs, contain timetables and route maps. You can use your métro ticket on the buses; if you have individual tickets (as opposed to weekly or monthly tickets), state your destination and be prepared to punch one or more tickets in the red-and-gray machines onboard.

By Car

Don't use a car in Paris unless you have to. Parking is difficult—and expensive—and traffic, except late at night, is awful.

By Métro

The métro is by far the quickest and most efficient way of getting around. Trains run from 5:30 AM until 1:15 AM (be careful—this means

Paris Métro

that the famous "last métro" can pass your station anytime after 12:30). Stations are signaled either by a large yellow "M" within a circle or by their distinctive curly, green Art Nouveau railings and archway entrances bearing the full title (Métropolitain). You must know the name of the last station on the line you take, as this appears on all signs. A connection (you can make as many as you like on one ticket) is called a *correspondance*. At junction stations, illuminated orange signs bearing the name of the line terminal appear over the correct corridors for correspondance. Illuminated blue signs marked *sortie* indicate the station exit. In general, the métro is safe, although try to avoid lines 2 and 13 if you're alone late at night. Access to métro platforms is through an automatic ticket barrier. Slide your ticket in and pick it up as it pops up. Keep your ticket during your journey; you will need it to leave the RER system and in case you run into any green-clad inspectors when you are leaving the métro—they can be very nasty and will impose a big fine on the spot if you do not have a ticket.

All métro tickets and passes are valid for RER and bus travel as well; tickets cost 8 francs each, but it makes more sense to buy a *carnet* (10 tickets) for 48 francs. If you're staying for a week or more, the best deals are the weekly *coupon jaune* (yellow ticket) or monthly *carte orange* (orange card), sold according to zone. Zones 1 and 2 cover the entire métro network; tickets cost 72 francs a week or 243 francs a month. If you plan to take suburban trains to visit places in the Ile-de-France, consider a four-zoner (Versailles, St-Germain-en-Laye; 126 francs a week) or six-zoner (Rambouillet, Fontainebleau; 170 francs a week). Weekly and monthly passes are available from rail and major métro stations; the monthly pass requires a passport-size photograph.

Alternatively, there are two-, three-, and five-day unlimited-travel tickets (*Paris Visite*). Unlike the coupon jaune, good from Monday morning to Sunday evening, the unlimited ticket is valid starting any day of the week and gives you discounts on a limited number of museums and tourist attractions. The prices are, respectively, 80, 110, and 170 francs for Paris only; 170, 230, and 300 francs for the suburbs. The equivalent one-day ticket is called *Formule 1* and costs 40 francs (Paris) or 100 francs (with suburbs).

By RER
RER trains travel between Paris and the suburbs. When they go through Paris they act as a sort of supersonic métro—they connect with the métro network at several points—and can be great time-savers. Access to RER platforms is through the same type of automatic ticket barrier (if you've started your journey on the métro you can use the same ticket), but you'll need to have the same ticket handy to put through another barrier when you leave the system.

By Taxi
Paris taxis may not have the charm of their London counterparts—there is no standard vehicle or color—but they're cheaper. Daytime rates (7 AM to 7:30 PM) are around 2.80 francs per kilometer, and nighttime rates are around 4.50 francs. There is a basic charge of 13 francs for all rides and a 6-franc charge per piece of luggage. Rates are about 40% higher in the suburbs than in the city. You are best off asking your hotel or restaurant to call for a taxi; cruising cabs are difficult to spot, especially late at night. Note that taxis seldom take more than three people at a time.

Contacts and Resources

Baby-Sitters

Baby-sitting services can provide English-speaking baby-sitters with just a few hours' notice. The hourly rate is approximately $7 (three-hour minimum) plus an agency fee of $10. **Ababa** (⊠ 8 av. du Maine, 15e, ☎ 01–45–49–46–46). **Baby Sitting Service** (⊠ 18 rue Tronchet, 8e, ☎ 01–46–37–51–24). **Bébé Cool** (⊠ 4 rue Faustin-Hélie, 16e, ☎ 01–45–04–27–14).

Car Rentals

Cars can be rented at both airports, as well as at locations in the city. **Avis** (⊠ 60 rue de Ponthieu, 8e, métro St-Phillipe du Roule, ☎ 01–45–62–82–50). **Citer** (⊠ 113 bd. de Magenta, 10e, métro Gare du Nord, ☎ 01–53–20–04–75). **Europcar** (⊠ 202 rue de Rivoli, 1er, métro St-Paul, Concorde, ☎ 01–40–15–96–98). **Hertz** (⊠ 193 rue de Bercy, 12e, métro Gare de Lyon, ☎ 01–43–44–06–00).

Embassies

Canada (⊠ 35 av. Montaigne, 8e, métro Franklin-D.-Roosevelt, ☎ 01–44–43–29–00). **U.K.** (⊠ 35 rue du Faubourg-St-Honoré, 8e, métro Concorde, ☎ 01–44–51–31–00). **U.S.** (⊠ 2 av. Gabriel, 8e, métro Concorde, ☎ 01–43–12–22–22).

Emergencies

Ambulance (☎ 15 or 01–45–67–50–50). **Dentist** (☎ 01–43–37–51–00). **Doctor** (☎ 01–43–37–77–77). **Police** (☎ 17).

A 24-hour emergency service is available at **American Hospital** (⊠ 63 bd. Victor-Hugo, Neuilly, ☎ 01–47–45–71–00). **Hertford British Hospital** (⊠ 3 rue Barbès, Levallois-Perret, ☎ 01–47–58–13–12) also has all-night emergency service.

LATE-NIGHT PHARMACIES

The **Pharmacie Dérhy** (⊠ 84 av. des Champs-Élysées, 8e, ☎ 01–45–62–02–41, métro Georges-V) is open 24 hours a day, 365 days a year. The **Pharmacie Européenne de la Place Clichy** (⊠ 6 pl. Clichy, 9e, ☎ 01–48–74–65–18, métro Place de Clichy) is open 24 hours, seven days a week.

Guided Tours

Hour-long boat trips on the Seine can be fun if you're in Paris for the first time; the cost is around 50 francs. Some boats serve lunch and dinner (for an additional cost); make reservations in advance. **Bateaux Mouches** (⊠ Pont de l'Alma, 8e, ☎ 01–42–25–96–10, métro Alma-Marceau) boats depart daily every 15 minutes, 10–noon, 2–7, and 8:30–10:30. **Bateaux Parisiens** (⊠ Pont d'Iéna, 7e, ☎ 01–44–11–33–44, métro Trocadéro) depart every half hour in summer and every hour in winter, starting at 10 AM; the last boat departs at 9 PM (11 PM in summer). **Canauxrama** (☎ 01–42–39–15–00) organizes half- and full-day barge tours along the canals of east Paris; boats depart from: ⊠ 13 quai de la Loire, 19e, métro Jaurès, or from the ⊠ Bassin de l'Arsenal, 12e, opposite 50 bd. de la Bastille, métro Bastille. **Vedettes du Pont-Neuf** (⊠ Depart from the square du Vert Galant, 1er, ☎ 01–46–33–98–38, métro Pont Neuf) depart every half hour 10–noon, 1:30–6:30, and 9–10:30 from March to October.

Cityrama (⊠ 4 pl. des Pyramides, 1er, ☎ 01–44–55–61–00, métro Tuileries) and **Paris Vision** (⊠ 214 rue de Rivoli, 1er, métro Tuileries☎ 01–42–60–31–25) both organize a number of different tours, from two hours on a double-decker bus with live or tape-recorded commentary (English is available) to day trips to sights in the Paris region.

For a more intimate—albeit expensive—tour of the city, Cityrama also runs several minibus excursions per day; the bus can take eight people and can pick up or drop off at hotels; the cost is 210 francs for a two-hour tour, 350 francs for three hours.

For sightseeing at your own pace, take **Paris Bus,** a red double-decker with nine pick-up and drop-off points around Paris. Tours start from Trocadéro at 10:20 AM and every 50 minutes until 5. Tickets are good for two days and cost 120 francs.

Paris Major Limousine (✉ 6 pl. de la Madeleine, 8ᵉ, ☎ 01–42–45–34–14) arranges private tours of Paris in luxury cars or minibuses (holding up to seven passengers) with English-speaking drivers. The price starts at 1,400 francs but varies with time (a minimum of three hours) and number of passengers. Reservations are essential.

There are plenty of guided **walking tours** of specific areas of Paris, often concentrating on a historical or architectural topic. Guides are enthusiastic but not always English-speaking. Charges range from 40 to 60 francs, and tours last about two hours. Details are published in the weekly magazines *Pariscope* and *L'Officiel des Spectacles* under "Conférences." Walking tours are sometimes organized by the **Caisse Nationale des Monuments Historiques,** Bureau des Visites (✉ Hôtel de Sully, 62 rue St-Antoine, 4ᵉ, métro Bastille or St-Paul, ☎ 01–44–61–20–00).

Travel Agencies
Air France (✉ 119 av. des Champs-Élysées, 8ᵉ, ☎ 01–44–08–24–24, métro Charles-de-Gaulle–Étoile). **American Express** (✉ 11 rue Scribe, 9ᵉ, ☎ 01–47–77–70–00, métro Chaussée d'Antin). **Wagon-Lits** (✉ 32 rue du Quatre-Septembre, 2ᵉ, ☎ 01–42–66–15–80, métro Opéra or Quatre Septembre).

Visitor Information
The **Office du Tourisme de la Ville de Paris** (✉ Paris Tourist Office, 127 av. des Champs-Élysées, 75008, métro Charles-de-Gaulle–Étoile, ☎ 01–49–52–53–54, 01–49–52–53–56 for recorded information in English) is open daily 9 AM–8 PM. It has branches at all main-line train stations except Gare St-Lazare.

3 Ile-de-France

Versailles, Chartres,
Fontainebleau

The soft light and lush rolling hills of
the region around Paris inspired
painters and kings. Van Gogh took up
residence here, as did Louis XIV, who
built one of Europe's most fantastic
châteaux at Versailles. Here, too,
Gothic architecture reached a pinnacle
in the soaring towers of Chartres.

PARIS MAY BE SMALL AS CAPITAL CITIES GO, with just over 2 million inhabitants, but Ile-de-France, the region around Paris, contains more than 10 million people—one-sixth of France's entire population. That type of statistic conjures up visions of a gray, never-ending suburban sprawl. Nothing could be further from the truth.

Although not actually an *île* (island), Ile-de-France is figuratively isolated from the rest of France by three rivers—the Seine, the Oise, and the Marne—that weave meandering circles around its periphery. The verdant landscape, within easy reach of the capital, was a strong temptation early on; the region was a favorite retreat of medieval kings and clerics. Castles and palaces went up in the towns of Vincennes, St-Germain-en-Laye, and Provins; abbeys and cathedrals sprang skyward in Chartres, Senlis, and Royaumont.

Ile-de-France never lost favor with the powerful, partly because its many forests—large chunks of which still stand—harbored sufficient game to ensure a regular kill even for bloated, pampered monarchs. First Fontainebleau, in manageable Renaissance proportions, then Versailles, in minion-crushing, bicep-flexing Baroque excess, reflected the royal desire to transform hunting lodges into palatial residences. Vaux-le-Vicomte, Dampierre, Rambouillet, Maisons-Laffitte, and Chantilly exude almost comparable grandeur.

More recently, another kind of magic kingdom was built in this region: Disneyland Paris. Although it did not meet with instant success when it first opened, it finally found its feet. On the whole, however, the architectural impact of the 20th century has been discreet in Ile-de-France. You may find it disorienting that so many rural backwaters exist within 30 minutes' drive of the capital. The Gallic mania for rational planning—with new developments assigned to restricted areas—has limited the impact of suburban sprawl. Students of modern architecture are served food for thought in such so-called "new towns" as Cergy-Pontoise and St-Quentin-en-Yvelines, and sociologists won't lack material in the concrete ghettos of the "red belt" north of Paris (so called because its working-class population traditionally votes communist).

Pleasures and Pastimes

Artists' Residences

Claude Monet's house and garden at Giverny, with its famous lily pond, is a moving visual link to Impressionist painting. In Auvers-sur-Oise, Vincent van Gogh had a final burst of creativity before committing suicide. André Derain lived in Chambourcy; Camille Pissarro at Pontoise; Alfred Sisley at Moret-sur-Loing. Rousseau, Millet, and Corot paved the way for Impressionism with their penchant for outdoor landscape painting at Barbizon.

Châteaux

The majestic château of Versailles, perhaps the most famous palace in the world, is not to be missed. Nor are its splendid neighbors—Fontainebleau, Vaux-le-Vicomte, St-Germain-en-Laye, and Chantilly. And there are another dozen châteaux almost as grand—led by Dampierre, Rambouillet, Maintenon, Maisons-Laffitte, and Thoiry.

Dining

Ile-de-France's smart restaurants can be just as pricey as their Parisian counterparts. But in smaller towns, and for those prepared to venture off the beaten tourist path, nourishing, well-priced meals are not hard to find. The style of cuisine mirrors that of Paris. "Local delicacies" cited by earnest textbooks—lamb stew, *pâté de Pantin* (pastry filled with meat or fish), or pig's trotters—tend to be obsolete. Instead, look for sumptuous game and asparagus in season in the south of the region, and the soft, creamy cheese of Meaux and Coulommiers to the east. Reservations are a must at all restaurants in summer.

CATEGORY	COST*
$$$$	over 400 frs
$$$	250 frs–400 frs
$$	125 frs–250 frs
$	under 125 frs

per person for a three-course meal, including tax (20.6%) and tip but not wine

Forests

Vast tracts of forest around Paris still resist the onset of urbanization. The forests of St-Germain, Rambouillet, Chantilly, and Fontainebleau are the largest and most famous; they are ideal for taking long walks or bike rides.

Lodging

In summer, hotel rooms are at a premium and reservations are essential; almost all accommodations in the swankier towns—Versailles, Rambouillet, and Fontainebleau—are on the costly side. Take nothing for granted. Picturesque Senlis, for instance, does not have a single hotel in its historic downtown area.

CATEGORY	COST*
$$$$	over 800 frs
$$$	550 frs–800 frs
$$	300 frs–550 frs
$	under 300 frs

All prices are for a standard double room for two, including tax (20.6%) and service charge.

Exploring Ile-de-France

The region can be covered in a series of loops: west from Paris to Versailles, Chartres, and Giverny; north and east along the Oise Valley via Chantilly to Disneyland; and southeast from Evry to Fontainebleau and Provins.

Numbers in the text correspond to numbers in the margin and on the Ile-de-France, Versailles, and Fontainebleau maps.

Great Itineraries

You could spend weeks visiting the dozens of châteaux and historic towns in the region. But if you don't have that much time, try one of the following shorter itineraries. Spend two to eight days exploring the area or take day trips from Paris—most sites are within easy reach of the capital by car or train.

IF YOU HAVE 2 DAYS

Head west from Paris to nearby **St-Germain-en-Laye** ② and visit either the château or the Prieuré museum. Try to reach 🚉 **Versailles** ③–⑮ for lunch, and then visit the château and the park. The next morning spend more time in Versailles or leave early and visit **Rambouillet** ⑰ or **Maintenon** ⑱ on your way to 🚉 **Chartres** ⑲; spend half a day exploring the cathedral and the old town.

Take the expressway north from Paris to **Senlis** ㉛, visit the old town and cathedral, then head to 🏰 **Chantilly** ㉚ for the afternoon. The next morning follow the Oise Valley, stopping briefly in **Auvers-sur-Oise** ㉘, en route to 🏰 **Versailles** ③–⑮. Spend the morning of your third day in Versailles or **Rambouillet** ⑰; try to be in 🏰 **Chartres** ⑲ by early afternoon. Spend the night there and drive to 🏰 **Fontainebleau** ㊳–㊻ the following morning, perhaps visiting **Barbizon** ㊲ on your way.

Spend your first day in **Senlis** ㉛ and 🏰 **Chantilly** ㉚. On the second day, head down the Oise Valley, via **Auvers-sur-Oise** ㉘ to 🏰 **St-Germain-en-Laye** ②. Head northwest through the Seine Valley to **Giverny** ㉓ on the third day; spend the night near 🏰 **Vernon** ㉒. The following day, take the expressway to 🏰 **Versailles** ③–⑮. On the fifth day, go southwest to 🏰 **Chartres** ⑲, with a stop in **Rambouillet** ⑰ or **Maintenon** ⑱ if time allows. On day six head to **Barbizon** ㊲ and 🏰 **Fontainebleau** ㊳–㊻; make it your base for two nights. On day seven make sure to visit **Vaux-le-Vicomte** ㊱ and perhaps **Moret-sur-Loing** ㊼; finish up on day eight at either **Disneyland Paris** ㉞ or **Provins** ㊽.

When to Tour Ile-de-France

With its extensive forests, Ile-de-France is especially beautiful in the fall, particularly October. June and July are good months, too, whereas August can be sultry and crowded. On Saturday nights in summer you can see son-et-lumière shows in Moret-sur-Loing and make candlelit visits to Vaux-le-Vicomte. Be aware when making your travel plans that some places are closed one or two days a week: The châteaux of Versailles and Auvers are closed on Monday; the Prieuré museum in St-Germain is closed both Monday and Tuesday; and the châteaux of Chantilly and Fontainebleau are closed Tuesday. Disneyland Paris gets really crowded on summer weekends. So does Giverny (Monet's garden), which is at its best May–June and, like Vaux-le-Vicomte, is closed November–March.

WEST TO VERSAILLES, CHARTRES, AND GIVERNY

Not only is majestic Versailles one of the most unforgettable sights in Ile-de-France, but it is also within easy reach of Paris, less than 30 minutes by either train (☞ Arriving and Departing *in* Ile-de-France A to Z, *below*) or car (A13 expressway from Porte d'Auteuil). With neighboring St-Germain-en-Laye, it's also the starting point for a visit to western Ile-de-France, anchored by Chartres to the south and Monet's home at Giverny to the north.

Rueil-Malmaison

❶   *8 km (5 mi) west of Paris on N13 via La Défense.*

Rueil-Malmaison is a slightly dreary western suburb of Paris, but the memory of the legendary pair Napoléon and Joséphine still haunts its ★ château. Built in 1622, **La Malmaison** was bought by the future Empress Joséphine in 1799 as a love nest for Napoléon and herself (they had married three years earlier). After the childless Joséphine was divorced by the heir-hungry emperor in 1809, she retired to La Malmaison and died here on May 29, 1814. The château has 24 rooms furnished with exquisite tables, chairs, and sofas of the Napoleonic period; of special note are the library, game room, and dining room. The walls are adorned with works by artists of the day, such as Jacques-Louis

David, Pierre-Paul Prud'hon, and Baron Gérard. Take time to admire the clothes and hats that belonged to Napoléon and Joséphine, particularly the empress's gowns. Their carriage can be seen in one of the garden pavilions, and another pavilion contains a unique collection of snuffboxes donated by Prince George of Greece. The gardens themselves are delightful, especially the regimented rows of spring tulips. ⊠ *15 av. du Château,* ☎ *01–41–29–05–55.* 🎫 *30 frs (including Bois Préau;* ☞ *below).* ⊘ *Wed.–Mon. 9:30–12:30 and 1:30–5:45.*

The **Bois Préau,** a smaller mansion dating from the 17th century, is close to La Malmaison (and included in the same admission ticket). It was acquired by Joséphine in 1810, after her divorce, but was subsequently reconstructed in the 1850s. Today its 10 rooms, complete with furniture and objects from the Empire period, are devoted mainly to souvenirs of Napoléon's exile on the island of St. Helena. ⊠ *av. de l'Impératrice,* ☎ *01–47–08–37–67.* 🎫 *16 frs.* ⊘ *Thurs.–Sun. 12:30–6:30.*

Festivals

Ile-de-France was once a wine-producing center—though there's little evidence these days—and one of the few places where the tradition lingers is in the hilly neighboring suburb of Suresnes, where a **Fête des Vendanges** (Grape Harvest Festival) is staged after the harvest on the first weekend of October.

St-Germain-en-Laye

❷ *8 km (5 mi) west of Rueil-Malmaison on N13, 16 km (10 mi) west of Paris.*

The elegant town of St-Germain-en-Laye, perched on a hill above the Seine and encircled by forest, has lost little of its original cachet, despite the invasion of wealthy, former Parisians who commute to work on the RER. If you're fond of the swashbuckling novels of Alexandre Dumas, then you'll enjoy the **Château de Monte-Cristo** (Monte Cristo Castle) at Port-Marly on the southern fringe of St-Germain (signposted to your left as you arrive from Rueil-Malmaison). Purists may find that its fanciful exterior, where pilasters, cupolas, and stone carvings compete for attention, has crossed the line from opulence to tastelessness, but—as in the novels, *The Count of Monte Cristo* and *The Three Musketeers*—swagger, not subtlety, is what counts. Dumas built the château after his books' surging popularity made him rich in the 1840s. Construction costs and lavish partying meant he went broke just as quickly, and he skedaddled to a Belgian exile in 1849. The château contains pictures, Dumas mementos, and the luxurious Moorish Chamber, with spellbinding, interlacing plasterwork executed by Arab craftsmen (lent by the Bey of Tunis) and recently restored by a donation from Moroccan king Hassan II. There's also a miniature version of the Château d'If in Marseille—scene of the Count of Monte Cristo's most heroic exploits—in a miniature lake in the château park. ⊠ *av. du Président-Kennedy,* ☎ *01–30–61–61–35.* 🎫 *30 frs.* ⊘ *Apr.–Oct., Tues.–Sun. 10–6; Nov.–Mar, Sun. 2–5.*

Next to the St-Germain RER train station is the stone-and-brick **Château de St-Germain,** with its dry moat and intimidating circular towers; it dates from the 16th and 17th centuries. A royal palace has existed here since the early 12th century, when Louis VI—known as Le Gros (The Fat)—exploited St-Germain's defensive potential in his bid to pacify Ile-de-France. A hundred years later, Louis IX (St. Louis) added the elegant **Ste-Chapelle,** the château's oldest remaining section. The figures on the tympanum (the inset triangular area over the main door) are believed to be the first known representations of French roy-

Ile-de-France

alty, portraying Louis with his mother, Blanche de Castille, and other members of his family.

Charles V (1364–80) built a powerful defensive keep in the mid-14th century, but from the 1540s, François I and his successors transformed St-Germain into a palace of more domestic, and less warlike, vocation. Louis XIV was born here, and it was here that his father, Louis XIII, died. Until 1682—when the court moved to Versailles—it remained the country's foremost royal residence outside Paris. Since 1867 the château has housed the impressive **Musée des Antiquités Nationales** (Museum of Ancient History), holding a trove of artifacts, figurines, brooches, and weapons from the Stone Age to the 8th century. ✉ *pl. Charles-de-Gaulle,* ☏ *01–34–51–53–65.* ✉ *25 frs, 17 frs on Sun.* ☉ *Wed.– Mon. 9–5:15.*

★ The quaint **Musée du Prieuré** (Priory Museum) is devoted to the work of the artist Maurice Denis (1870–1943) and his fellow Symbolists and Nabis—painters opposed to the naturalism of their 19th-century Impressionist contemporaries. Denis found the calm of the former Jesuit priory, set above tiered gardens, ideally suited to his spiritual themes, which he expressed in stained glass, ceramics, and frescoes, as well as oils. ✉ *2 bis rue Maurice-Denis,* ☏ *01–39–73–77–87.* ✉ *25 frs.* ☉ *Wed.–Fri. 10–5:30, weekends 10–6:30.*

In the village of Chambourcy, 3 km (2 mi) northwest of St-Germain-en-Laye via N13, you'll find the stately **Maison André-Derain** (André Derain House). This 17th-century building is where the versatile Derain (1880–1954), best known for his pioneering, hotly colored Fauve paintings, lived from 1935 until his death. You can admire his well-preserved studio and a smattering of his works and watch a 12-minute film about his career. ✉ *64 Grande Rue,* ☏ *01–30–74–70–04.* ✉ *20 frs.* ☉ *Weekends 2–4:30.*

OFF THE   **MÉDAN** – Émile Zola moved to the village of Médan, 11 km (7 mi)
BEATEN PATH northwest of St-Germain-en-Laye, in 1877 after the runaway success of his novel *L'Assommoir*. Until the 1980s, Zola's house, overlooking the Seine and the Paris–Le Havre rail line he smokily evokes in *La Bête Humaine*, was used as an orphanage. You can now visit the spacious rooms (including the study where Zola wrote many of his novels) furnished in the surprisingly ostentatious, bourgeois taste of one of France's most rebellious writers, renowned for his defense of the working classes. ✉ *26 rue Pasteur,* ☏ *01–39–75–35–65.* ✉ *30 frs.* ☉ *Weekends 2–6.*

Dining and Lodging

$$ ✕ **La Feuillantine.** Friendly service and an imaginative, good-value prix-fixe menu have made this restaurant a success. Gizzard salad, salmon with endive, and herbed chicken fricassee with morels are among the specialties. ✉ *10 rue des Louviers,* ☏ *01–34–51–04–24. MC, V.*

$$$–$$$$ ▣ **La Forestière.** Opened in 1928, this is St-Germain's most stylish hotel
★ and a member of the deluxe Relais & Châteaux chain. Its forest setting, its 18th-century-style furniture, and its fine restaurant, the Cazaudehore, contribute to a sense of well-being. The restaurant is closed to nonguests on Monday (except holidays). ✉ *1 av. du Président-Kennedy, 78100,* ☏ *01–39–10–38–38,* 𝔽𝔸𝕏 *01–39–73–73–88. 25 rooms, 5 suites. Restaurant. MC, V.*

Nightlife and the Arts

The **Fête des Loges** (Loges Festival) is a giant fair and carnival held in the Forest of St-Germain from July to mid-August.

Versailles

14 km (9 mi) south of St-Germain-en-Laye via N186, 16 km (10 mi) west of Paris.

Paris in the 17th century was a rowdy, rabble-ridden city; Louis XIV hated it. He lost no time in casting his cantankerous royal eye over Ile-de-France in search of a new power base. Marshy, inhospitable Versailles became the place of his dreams. Down came his father's modest royal hunting lodge and up went a new château. The town itself—capital of France from 1682 to 1789 and again from 1871 to 1879—is easily underestimated, despite its broad, leafy boulevards and majestic buildings. Most people are usually exhausted from exploring the palace and park to spend time visiting the town—but it's worth taking a little time to wander around.

★ ❸ The **Château de Versailles** seems monstrous, but it wasn't big enough for the army of 20,000 noblemen, servants, and sycophants who moved in with Louis XIV. A new city had to be constructed from scratch to accommodate them. Town planners dreamt up vast mansions and avenues broader than the Champs-Élysées, all in Baroque.

It is hardly surprising that Louis XIV's successors felt out of sync with their architectural inheritance. Louis XV transformed the royal apartments into places to live in rather than pose. The hapless Louis XVI cowered in the Petit Trianon in the leafy depths of Versailles's gardens, out of the mighty château's shadow. His queen, Marie-Antoinette, lost her head well before her trip to the guillotine in 1793, pretending to be a peasant shepherdess amid the ersatz rusticity of her oh-so-cute Potemkin hamlet.

You enter the château—built by architects Louis Le Vau and Jules Hardouin-Mansart between 1662 and 1690—through the gilt iron gates from the huge place d'Armes. On the first floor of the château, dead center as you pass the Sun King's statue and across the sprawling cobbled forecourt, is Louis XIV's bedchamber. The two wings were occupied by the royal children and princes of the blood, while courtiers made do in the attics.

One of the palace's trademark sights is the sparkling **Galerie des Glaces** (Hall of Mirrors). It was here, after France's capitulation, that Otto von Bismarck proclaimed the unified German Empire in 1871; and here that the Treaty of Versailles, asserting Germany's responsibility for World War I, was signed in 1919. The **Grands Appartements** (Big Apartments, or State Rooms) that flank the Hall of Mirrors retain much of their original Baroque decoration: gilt stucco, painted ceilings, and marble sculpture. Perhaps the most extravagant is the **Salon d'Apollon** (Apollo Room), the former throne room, dedicated to the sun god Apollo, Louis XIV's mythical hero. Equally interesting are the **Petits Appartements** (Small, or Private, Apartments), where the royal family and friends lived in (relative) privacy.

In the north wing of the château you'll find the solemn white-and-gold **chapelle** (chapel), completed in 1710; the intimate **Opéra Royal** (Opera House), the first oval hall in France, built by J. A. Gabriel for Louis XV in 1770; and, connecting the two, the 17th-century **Galeries,** with exhibits retracing the château's history. The south wing contains the majestically proportioned **Galerie des Batailles** (Gallery of Battles), lined with gigantic canvases extolling French military glory. In 1997 the former state rooms and sumptuous debate-chamber of the **Aile du Midi** (South Wing) were opened to the public, with infrared headphones (English commentary available) explaining Versailles's parliamentary his-

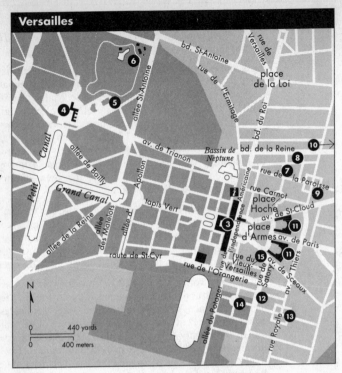

tory. ☎ 01–30–84–76–18. ☞ *Château 45 frs, parliament exhibition 25 frs extra.* ☉ *Tues.–Sun. 9–6:30, 9–5:30 in winter (Galerie des Glaces 9:45–5; Opéra Royal 9:45–3:30). Tours of Opéra Royal and Petits Appartements every 15 mins.*

★ After the awesome feast of interior decor, the **Parc de Versailles** (Versailles Park) is an ideal place to catch your breath. The gardens were designed by André Le Nôtre, whose work here represents classical French landscaping at its most formal and sophisticated. The 250-acre grounds include woods, lawns, flower beds, statues, artificial lakes, and fountains galore. An extensive tree-replacement scheme—necessary once a century—was launched at the start of 1998 to recapture the full impact of Le Nôtres's artful vistas. The distances are vast—the Trianons themselves are more than a mile from the château—so you might like to rent a bike from the Grille de la Reine on boulevard de la Reine (near the Trianon Palace hotel). The park is at its golden-leafed best in the fall but is also enticing in summer—especially on Sundays when the fountains are in full flow. They become a spectacle of rare grandeur during the Fêtes de Nuit, light-and-fireworks shows in July and September. ☎ 01–39–50–36–22 *for details of the Fêtes de Nuit.* ☞ *25 frs Sun., May–Sept., free other times.* ☉ *Grounds daily 7 AM–8 PM or dusk.*

❹ The **Grand Trianon,** built by Hardouin-Mansart in 1687, is a pink-marble pleasure palace occasionally used to entertain visiting heads of state. Most of the time it's open for you to admire its lavish interior and early 19th-century furniture. ☎ 01–30–84–75–43. ☞ *25 frs.* ☉ *Oct.–Apr., Tues.–Sun. 10–12:30 and 2–5:30; May–Sept., Tues.–Sun. 10–6:30.*

❺ The comparatively dainty **Petit Trianon** was built by J. A. Gabriel in 1768. It's a mansion, not a palace—modest by Versailles standards, albeit sumptuously furnished and stuffed with mementos of Marie-Antoinette. Look for her initials wrought into the iron railings of the main staircase. ⌨ *15 frs.* ☉ *Oct.–Apr., Tues.–Fri. 10–noon and 2–5:30; May–Sept., Tues.–Sun. 10–6:30.*

❻ Beyond the Petit Trianon and across the Petit Lac—which looks more like a wriggly stream—is the queen's **Hameau** (Hamlet), where Marie-Antoinette lived out her romanticized dreams of peasant life. With its water mill, genuine small lake (Grand Lac), and pigeon loft, this make-believe village is outrageously pretty.

Make sure to leave a little time for the majestic **town of Versailles**, which is worth a visit in its own right. Leave the château park by the Bassin de Neptune and turn right onto rue des Réservoirs, past the classical Théâtre Montansier, and pause at the Office de Tourisme before making a left on rue Carnot. Up ahead you can make out Louis XIV's equestrian statue in the château courtyard; in the other direction is the church spire of neighboring Le Chesnay. Rue Carnot leads past the stately Écuries de la Reine, once the queen's stables, now a law court, to octagonal place Hoche. Down rue Hoche to the left is the sturdy Baroque
❼ church of **Notre-Dame**, built from 1684 to 1686 by Jules Hardouin-Mansart as the parish church for Louis XIV's brand-new town. Around the back of Notre-Dame, on boulevard de la Reine (note the regimented lines of trees), is the elegant Hôtel de Neyret, now used by the Banque
❽ de France, and the **Musée Lambinet**, a sumptuous mansion from 1751, furnished with paintings, weapons, fans, and porcelain. ✉ *54 bd. de la Reine,* ☏ *01–39–50–30–32.* ⌨ *25 frs.* ☉ *Tues.–Sun. 2–6.*

Take a right onto rue Le Nôtre, then left and right again into passage de la Geôle, a cobbled alley lined with quaint antiques shops that
❾ climbs up to **place du Marché-Notre-Dame**, whose open-air market on Tuesday, Friday, and Sunday is famed throughout the region; there are also four 19th-century timber-roofed halls with fish, meat, and spice stalls. Cross the square and head up rue de la Paroisse to avenue de
❿ St-Cloud. Around to the left is the **Lycée Hoche**, whose domed, colonnaded chapel was once part of a convent built for Louis XV's queen Marie Leszczynska in 1767.

Cross avenue de St-Cloud and head along rue Montbauron to **avenue de Paris**. At 120 yards across, it's wider than the Champs-Élysées; its buildings are just as grand and more historic. Note the mighty doorway at the **Hôtel de Police** on your left and then, at No. 21, the pretty **Hôtel du Barry**. Cross the avenue and return toward the château, past the **Hôtel des Menus-Plaisirs**, where the States General held their first session in May 1789. Just opposite, behind an imposing grille, is the elaborate 19th-century **Prêfecture** (the local government building), confronting the even bigger—but uglier—stone-and-brick **Hôtel de Ville** (City Hall). Avenue de Paris leads down to place d'Armes, a vast sloping plaza usually filled with tourist buses. Facing the château are
⓫ the Trojan-size royal stables. One wing of the **Grandes Écuries** (Large Stables), to the left, houses a distinguished parade of royal and imperial carriages in what is known as the **Musée des Carrosses** (Carriage Museum). ✉ *1 av. de Paris,* ☏ *01–30–21–54–82.* ⌨ *20 frs.* ☉ *Weekends 2–6.*

Cross avenue de Sceaux, pass the imposing chancellery on the corner, and take rue de Satory—a cute pedestrian shopping-street—to the
⓬ domed **Cathédrale St-Louis**, with its powerful two-towered facade, built from 1743 to 1754 and endowed with a fine organ and paintings. Turn left down narrow rue du Marché to reach the ramshackle
⓭ but photogenic **Carrés St-Louis**, a prototype 18th-century housing es-
⓮ tate. Rue d'Anjou leads down to the **Potager du Roi**, the lovingly restored royal fruit and vegetable garden. ✉ *Entrance at 40 rue Hardy,*

☎ *01–39–24–62–62.* ✉ *40 frs.* ☉ *Guided tours Apr.–Oct., Wed.–Sun. at 2:30; June–Sept., Wed.–Fri. at 2:30, weekends at 2:30 and 4:30.*

From the garden, return to rue de Satory and take rue du Vieux-Versailles, just as old—in parts decrepit—and full of character as its name suggests. The **Salle du Jeu de Paume,** the indoor sports hall (built in 1686) where the Third Estate swore to transform absolutist France into a constitutional monarchy on June 20, 1789, is off to the right. ✉ *1 rue du Jeu-de-Paume.* ☉ *June–Sept., Wed. 2–5.*

Rue de l'Indépendance-Américaine leads from the top of rue du Vieux-Versailles up to the château, where Louis XIV, quite uncoincidentally, is clearly visible on his prancing steed at the top of the hill. Admire the sculpted porticoes and gilded Sun King emblems on the row of monumental 17th- and 18th-century state buildings.

Dining and Lodging

$$$$ ✕ **Les Trois Marches.** The restaurant at the Trianon Palace hotel (☞ ★ *below*) is recognized as one of the best in Ile-de-France. It's hard to wait for your meal after perusing Gérard Vié's menu, which may include lobster bisque, salmon with fennel, and turbot *galette* (cake). When it's nice out, you can eat on the huge terrace. ✉ *1 bd. de la Reine,* ☎ *01–39–50–13–21. Reservations essential. Jacket and tie. AE, DC, MC, V. Closed Sun.–Mon. and Aug.*

$$–$$$ ✕ **Brasserie La Fontaine.** If you have neither the time nor the budget to do justice to Gérard Vié's cuisine at Les Trois Marches (☞ *above*), head for his "annex" across the garden. Designed as a true brasserie, with crimson velvet seats and aproned waiters, the restaurant is exceptional when it comes to the zesty simmered snails, pollack roasted with carrots, and chocolate fritters. ✉ *1 bd. de la Reine,* ☎ *01–30–84–38–47. AE, DC, MC, V.*

$$ ✕ **Quai No. 1.** Fish and seafood rule supreme amid the sails, barometers, and model ships of this quaintly decked-out restaurant. Home-smoked salmon and sauerkraut with fish are specialties. Eating à la carte isn't too expensive, and there are good-value prix-fixe menus. ✉ *1 av. de St-Cloud,* ☎ *01–39–50–42–26. MC, V. Closed Mon. No dinner Sun.*

$$$$ 🏨 **Sofitel.** Nestled behind the giant triumphal arch dating from the Sun King's era, this luxury hotel is closer to the old town and the château than the Trianon Palace (☞ *below*). It's also a bit cheaper. Rooms are spacious and decor subdued to the point of blandness. Prix-fixe menus in the Manèges restaurant start at around 160 francs. ✉ *2 bis av. de Paris, 78000,* ☎ *01–39–07–46–46,* FAX *01–39–07–46–49. 146 rooms, 6 suites. Restaurant, bar, business services. AE, DC, MC, V.*

$$$$ 🏨 **Trianon Palace.** This deluxe hotel, a turn-of-the-century creation of ★ imposing size, is in a huge garden close to the château park. Its once-faded charm was given a thorough overhaul by its new Japanese owners, and the results are spectacular: The health club alone is worth the price of admission. ✉ *1 bd. de la Reine, 78000,* ☎ *01–30–84–38–00,* FAX *01–39–49–00–77. 97 rooms, 32 suites. Restaurant, pool, health club, business services. AE, DC, MC, V.*

$$$ 🏨 **Le Versailles.** This unpretentious 1950s hotel, renovated in the early 1990s, is close to the château and recommended if you plan to explore the town on foot. Rooms are comfortable but lack character. ✉ *7 rue Ste-Anne, 78000,* ☎ *01–39–50–64–65,* FAX *01–39–02–37–85. 50 rooms. AE, DC, MC, V.*

$$ 🏨 **Home St-Louis.** This small hotel is a good, cheap, quiet bet—close to the cathedral and not too far from the château. ✉ *28 rue St-Louis, 78000,* ☎ *01–39–50–23–55,* FAX *01–39–21–62–45. 27 rooms. MC, V.*

Nightlife and the Arts

A **music festival,** with concerts and operas in the town and château, runs May–June; call the tourist office (☎ 01–30–97–81–03) for details.

Shopping

Aux Colonnes (⊠ 14 rue Hoche) is a highly rated *confiserie* (candy shop) with an astounding array of chocolates and candies; it's closed Monday. **Les Délices du Palais** (⊠ 4 rue Maréchal-Foch) has everything for the makings of an impromptu picnic (cold cuts, cheese, salads); it's closed Monday. **Eugène Le Gall** (⊠ 15 rue Ducis) has a huge choice of cheeses—including one of France's widest selection of goat cheeses; it's closed Sunday afternoon and Monday. **Passage de la Geôle** (⊠ 10 rue Rameau), open Friday–Sunday 9–7, is the site of a good antiques market.

En Route   From Versailles, take D91 south for 14 km (9 mi) to the ruined **Abbaye de Port-Royal-des-Champs,** where France's greatest playwright, Jean Racine, studied in the 1650s. From the Abbaye de Port-Royal-des-Champs, turn left on D46 through the glades and folds of the Chevreuse Valley, then right on D906. Watch for a left turn 5 km (3 mi) farther on, leading to the steep-roofed **Château de Breteuil,** which has been owned by the same family since the 17th century. Interior highlights range from Swedish porcelain to Gobelin tapestries and a richly inlaid Teschen table, encrusted with pearls and precious stones—an 18th-century present from Austrian empress Maria Theresa. The vast wooded park has picnic areas and playgrounds. Life-size wax figures—including English king Edward VII and novelist Marcel Proust (a onetime guest)—lurk in many of the rooms. ☎ 01–30–52–05–02. ☞ *Château and grounds 52 frs, grounds only 34 frs.* ☉ *Château Mon.–Sat. 2:30–6, Sun. 11–6; grounds daily 10–6.*

Dampierre

16   *5 km (3 mi) northwest of Breteuil via D906 and D149, 21 km (13 mi) southwest of Versailles via D91.*

The unspoiled village of Dampierre is home to one of the most charming family seats in Ile-de-France. The stone-and-brick **Château de Dampierre,** surrounded by a moat and set well back from the road, was rebuilt in the 1670s by Hardouin-Mansart for the Duc de Luynes. Much of the interior has kept its 17th-century decoration—portraits, wood paneling, furniture, and works of art. But the main staircase, with its trompe l'oeil murals, and the richly gilded **Salle des Fêtes** (Ballroom) date from the last century. This second-floor chamber contains a huge wall painting by the celebrated artist Jean-Auguste Ingres (1780–1867): a mythical evocation of the Age d'Or (Golden Age). The large park was planned by Versailles designer Le Nôtre. ☎ 01–30–52–53–24. ☞ *52 frs, grounds only 34 frs.* ☉ *Apr.–Oct., Mon.–Sat. 2–6, Sun. 11–noon and 2–6.*

Rambouillet

17   *16 km (10 mi) southwest of Dampierre via D91 and D906, 32 km (20 mi) southwest of Versailles, 42 km (26 mi) southwest of Paris.*

Haughty Rambouillet, once favored by kings and dukes, is now home to affluent gentry and, occasionally, the French president. The **Château,** surrounded by a magnificent 30,000-acre forest (reason enough for hikers and bikers to plan an excursion this way), is a favored retreat for guests of state; but usually the château and its grounds are open to the public. Most of the château dates from the early 18th century, but the brawny **Tour François I** (François I Tower), named for the king who died here in 1547, was part of the 14th-century fortified castle that first stood on this site. Highlights include the wood-paneled apartments, especially the **Boudoir de la Comtesse** (Countess's Dressing Room); the marble-walled **Salle de Marbre** (Marble Room), dating from the Renaissance; and the **Salle de Bains de Napoléon** (Napoléon's Bathroom), adorned with Pompeii-style frescoes. The lakeside facade of the château is a sight of unsuspected serenity and, as more flowers spill from its balconies, cheerful informality. ☎ 01–34–94–28–00. 🎫 27 frs. ☉ Daily 10–11:30 and 2–5:30.

An extensive **park** stretches behind the château; it includes a lake with small islands. The **Laiterie de la Reine** (Queen's Dairy) was built as a dairy for Marie-Antoinette, and has a small temple, grotto, and the shell-lined Chaumière des Coquillages (Shell Pavilion). The **Bergerie Nationale** (National Sheepfold) is the site of a more serious agricultural venture: The merino sheep reared here, prized for the quality and yield of their wool, are descendants of beasts imported from Spain by Louis XVI in 1786. ☉ Laiterie Wed.–Mon. 10–11:30 and 2–4:30 (until 4 Nov.–Easter); Bergerie Fri.–Sun. 2–5 (Oct.–June, Sun. only, 2–5) . 🎫 Laiterie 15 frs, Bergerie 21 frs.

☾ Some 4,000 models and more than 1,300 ft of track make the **Musée Rambolitrain,** France's leading model-train museum. There are historic steam engines, old-time stations, and a realistic points and signaling system. ✉ 4 pl. Jeanne-d'Arc, ☎ 01–34–83–15–93. 🎫 20 frs. ☉ Wed.–Sun. 10–noon and 2–5:30.

Dining

$ ✕ **Poste.** You can bank on traditional, unpretentious cooking at this former coaching inn right in the center of town. Service is good, as is the selection of prix-fixe menus. Game is a specialty in season. ✉ 101 rue du Général-de-Gaulle, ☎ 01–34–83–03–01. AE, MC, V.

Maintenon

⑱ 23 km (14 mi) southwest of Rambouillet via D906, 65 km (41 mi) southwest of Paris.

Vestiges of Louis XIV, both atmospheric and architectural, make Maintenon an intriguing stopover on the road to Chartres. The **Château de Maintenon** once belonged to Louis XIV's second wife, Françoise Scarron—better known as Madame de Maintenon—whom he married morganatically in 1684. (As social inferiors, neither she nor her children could claim a royal title.) She had acquired the château as a young widow 10 years earlier, and her private apartments form the hub of the interior visit. A round brick tower (16th century) and square 12th-century keep give the ensemble a muscular dignity at odds with the picturesque back garden, with its lawns, canal, and prim hedges. ✉ pl. Aristide Briand, ☎ 02–37–23–00–09. 🎫 33 frs. ☉ Apr.–Oct., Wed.–Mon. 2–6; Nov.–Mar., weekends 2–5; closed mid-Dec.–end of Jan.

Looming at the back of the château garden and extending through the village from the train station to highway D6 are the unlikely ivy-covered arches of a ruined **Aqueduc** (Aqueduct), one of the Sun King's most outrageous projects. The original scheme aimed to provide the ornamental lakes in the gardens of Versailles (some 50 km/31 mi away) with water from the River Eure. In 1684, 30,000 men were signed up to construct a three-tiered, 5-km (3-mi) aqueduct as part of the project. Many died in the process, and construction was called off in 1689.

Dining and Lodging

$$$–$$$$ ✕🏨 **Château d'Esclimont.** The 16th-century château is well worth seeking out if you wish to eat and sleep like royalty. On luxurious

grounds, with lawns, a lake, and a heliport, this member of the Relais & Châteaux group is a regular spot for Parisian power brokers. Rooms are luxuriously furnished in reproduction 18th-century French pieces. The cuisine is sophisticated and varied: Quail, lamb, lobster, and game in season top the menu. Dinner reservations are essential and a jacket and tie are required. ⊠ *2 rue Château-d'Esclimont, 28700 St-Symphorien-le-Château (19 km/12 mi southeast of Maintenon: take D116 to village of Gaillardon, keep an eye out for church, then turn left),* ☎ *02–37–31–15–15,* FAX *02–37–31–57–91. 48 rooms. Restaurant, pool, 2 tennis courts, fishing, helipad. MC, V.*

Chartres

⑲ *19 km (12 mi) southwest of Maintenon via D906, 88 km (55 mi) southwest of Paris.*

Although Chartres is chiefly visited for its magnificent Gothic cathedral with world-famous stained-glass windows, the whole town—with its old houses and picturesque streets—is worth leisurely exploration. Ancient streets tumble down from the cathedral to the River Eure; there is a lovely view of the rooftops beneath the cathedral from rue du Pont-St-Hilaire. Each year on August 15, pilgrims and tourists flock here for the **Procession du Voeu de Louis XIII,** a religious procession through the streets, commemorating the French monarchy's vow to serve the Virgin Mary.

★ Worship on the site of the **Cathédrale Notre-Dame,** also known as Chartres Cathedral, goes back to before the Gallo-Roman period; the crypt contains a well that was the focus of Druid ceremonies. In the late 9th century, Charles II (known as the Bald) presented Chartres with what was believed to be the tunic of the Virgin Mary, a precious relic that attracted hordes of pilgrims. The current cathedral, the sixth church on the spot, dates mainly from the 12th and 13th centuries and was erected after the previous, 11th-century building burned down in 1194. A well-chronicled outburst of religious fervor followed the discovery that the Virgin Mary's relic had miraculously survived unsinged. Reconstruction went ahead at a breathtaking pace. Just 25 years were needed for Chartres Cathedral to rise again, and it has remained substantially unchanged ever since.

The lower half of the facade is a survivor of the earlier Romanesque church: This can be seen most clearly in the use of round arches rather than the pointed Gothic type. The **Portail Royal** (Royal Portal) is richly sculpted with scenes from the Life of Christ, and the flanking towers are also Romanesque. The taller of the two spires (380 ft versus 350 ft) was built at the start of the 16th century, after its predecessor was destroyed by fire; its fanciful Flamboyant intricacy contrasts sharply with the stumpy solemnity of its Romanesque counterpart. The **rose window** above the main portal dates from the 13th century, and the three windows below it contain some of the finest examples of 12th-century stained glass in France.

The interior is somber, and your eyes will need time to adjust. The reward: the gemlike richness of the stained glass, with the famous deep "Chartres blue" predominating. The oldest window is arguably the most beautiful: **Notre-Dame de la Belle Verrière** (Our Lady of the Beautiful Window) in the south choir. The cathedral's windows are being gradually cleaned—a lengthy, painstaking process—and the contrast with those still covered in the grime of centuries is staggering. It is well worth taking a pair of binoculars to pick out the details. If you wish to know more about stained-glass techniques and the motifs used, visit the small exhibit in the gallery opposite the north porch. For even more detail, try to arrange a tour (in English) with local institution Malcolm Miller, who has a formidable knowledge of the cathedral's windows. (He leads tours twice a day, Monday through Saturday; the cost is 30 francs. You can reach him at the telephone number below.) The vast black-and-white labyrinth on the floor of the nave is one of the few to have survived from the Middle Ages. The faithful were expected to travel along its entire length (some 300 yards) on their knees. Guided tours of the **Crypte** start from the Maison de la Crypte opposite the south porch. You can also see a 4th-century Gallo-Roman wall and some 12th-century wall paintings. ⊠ *16 cloître Notre-Dame,* ☎ *02–37–21–56– 33.* ✒ *10 frs.* ☼ *Church 8–6. Guided tours of crypt Easter–Oct., daily at 11, 2:15, 3:30, 4:30, 5:15; Nov.–Easter, daily at 11 and 4.*

The **Musée des Beaux-Arts** (Fine Arts Museum) is in a handsome 18th-century building just behind the cathedral that used to serve as the bishop's palace. Its varied collection includes Renaissance enamels, a portrait of Erasmus by Holbein, tapestries, armor, and some fine, mainly French, paintings of the 17th, 18th, and 19th centuries. There is also a room devoted to the forceful 20th-century land- and snowscapes of Maurice de Vlaminck, who lived in the region. ⊠ *29 cloître Notre-Dame,* ☎ *02–37–36–41–39.* ✒ *10 frs (20 frs for special exhibitions).* ☼ *Apr.–Oct., Wed.–Mon. 10–6; Nov.–Mar., Wed.–Mon. 10–noon and 2–5.*

The Gothic church of **St-Pierre** (⊠ rue St-Pierre) near the River Eure has magnificent medieval windows from a period (circa 1300) not represented at the cathedral. The oldest stained glass here, portraying Old Testament worthies, is to the right of the choir and dates from the late 13th century. Exquisite 17th-century stained glass can be admired at the church of **St-Aignan** (⊠ rue des Grenets) around the corner from St-Pierre.

Dining and Lodging

$$$ ✕ **La Vieille Maison.** Occupying a pretty 14th-century building just 100 yards from the cathedral, this restaurant is a fine choice for either lunch or dinner. The setting—on a flower-decked patio—is charming. The menu changes regularly but invariably includes regional specialties, such as asparagus, rich duck pâté, and superb homemade foie gras. Prices, though justified, can be steep, but the 160-franc lunch menu is a good bet. ⊠ *5 rue au Lait,* ☎ *02–37–34–10–67. Jacket and tie. AE, MC, V. Closed Mon. No dinner Sun.*

$$ ✕ **Buisson Ardent.** In an attractive, old, oak-beam building almost within
★   sight of the cathedral's south portal, this popular restaurant has inexpensive prix-fixe menus (especially on weekdays) and a choice of imaginative à la carte dishes made with delicious sauces. Try the chicken ravioli with leeks or the rolled beef with spinach. Service is gratifyingly attentive. ⊠ *10 rue au Lait,* ☎ *02–37–34–04–66. AE, DC, MC, V. No dinner Sun.*

$$$ ▥ **Grand Monarque.** The most popular rooms in this 18th-century coaching inn, part of the Best Western chain, are in a separate turn-of-the-century building overlooking a garden. The most atmospheric are tucked away in the attic. There's also a fine restaurant with a varied choice of prix-fixe menus for 150, 210, and 275 francs. ⊠ *22 pl. des Épars, 28000,* ☎ *02–37–21–00–72,* ℻ *02–37–36–34–18. 54 rooms, 52 with bath. Restaurant. AE, DC, MC, V.*

Shopping
Vitrail (stained glass) being the key to Chartres's fame, you may want to visit the **Galerie du Vitrail** (⊠ 17 rue Cloître-Notre-Dame, ☎ 02–

37–36–10–03), which specializes in the noble art. Pieces range from small plaques to entire windows, and there are books on the subject in English and French.

Dreux

⑳   *35 km (22 mi) north of Chartres via N154, 74 km (46 mi) west of Paris.*

Dreux, center of an independent county during the Middle Ages, enjoyed an upsurge in prosperity after being united to the French crown in 1556. This was shortly after completion of the beefy belfry on the main square. The early 19th century conferred lasting glory on the town in the form of the burial chapel of the royal House of Orléans.

★ In 1816, the Orléans family, France's ruling house from 1830 to 1848, began the construction of a circular chapel-mausoleum on the hill behind the town center. The **Chapelle Royale St-Louis** is built in sugary but not unappealing neo-Gothic style: superficial ornament rather than structure recalls the medieval style. The magnificently decorated interior can be visited only with a French-speaking guide, but an English written text is provided. And no linguistic explanations are needed to prompt wonder at either the Sèvres-manufactured "stained glass"—thin layers of glass coated with painted enamel (an extremely rare, fragile, and vivid technique)—or the funereal statuary. Some of the **tombs**—an imploring hand reaching through a window to a loved one or an infant wrapped in a cloak of transparent gauze—may evoke morbid sentimentality, but their technical skill and compositional drama belie this mawkishness. ⊠ *2 square d'Aumale,* ☎ *02–37–46–07–06.* 🎫 *32 frs.* ◐ *Apr.–Nov., Wed.–Mon. 9–11:30 and 2:30–6.*

The church of **St-Pierre,** across the road from the belfry, is an interesting jumble of styles with pretty stained glass and a 17th-century organ loft. It presents a curious silhouette, with its unfinished classical towers cut off midway. ⊠ *pl. Métezeau,* ☎ *02–37–42–06–89.*

Lodging

$$ 🏨 **Le Beffroi.** This modest country hotel is on the historic square that links the church to the belfry. Ask for a room with a view. ⊠ *12 pl. Métezeau, 28100,* ☎ *02–37–50–02–03,* 𝐅𝐀𝐗 *02–37–42–07–69. 16 rooms. AE, DC, MC, V.*

OFF THE BEATEN PATH   **VERNEUIL-SUR-AVRE** – This old market town, 33 km (21 mi) west of Dreux via N12, retains a number of half-timber houses. But it's mainly of interest for its soaring, richly sculpted belfry, built around 1500. The tower, one of the most eye-catching in France, is visible for miles around.

Anet

㉑   *16 km (10 mi) north of Dreux via D928, 73 km (46 mi) west of Paris.*

Only picturesque ruins remain of the **Château d'Anet,** begun in 1548 for Henri II's mistress Diane de Poitiers. Her bedchamber can be visited in the Left Wing, the finest surviving section, with its 17th-century **Escalier d'Honneur** (Staircase of Honor) and tapestries in the **Salle des Gardes** (Guard Room), depicting the adventures of the huntress Diana. The chapel has a 16th-century dome, one of the earliest in France. As you enter the grounds, look up at the tympanum over the gate to admire the cast of Benvenuto Cellini's *Nymph with a Stag* (the original is now in the Louvre). ☎ *02–37–41–90–07.* 🎫 *36 frs.* ◐ *Apr.–Oct., Mon.–Sat. 2:30–6:30, Sun. 10–11:30 and 2:30–6:30.*

Vernon

㉒   *36 km (22 mi) north of Anet via Pacy-sur-Eure, 76 km (48 mi) north-west of Paris.*

The old town of Vernon, on the Seine, has a medieval church often painted by Impressionist artist Claude Monet, and several fine medieval timber-frame houses (the best, on rue Carnot, houses the tourist office). The church of **Notre-Dame,** across from the tourist office, has an arresting rose-window facade that, like the high nave, dates from the 15th century. Rounded Romanesque arches in the choir, however, attest to the building's 12th-century origins. The church is a fine sight when viewed from behind: Monet liked to paint it from across the Seine.

A few minor Monet canvases, along with other late-19th-century paintings, can be admired in the **Musée Poulain** (the town museum). This rambling old mansion is seldom crowded, and the helpful curators are happy to explain local history if you are intrigued by the town's English-sounding name. ⊠ *12 rue du Pont,* ☎ *02–32–21–28–09.* ⊡ *15 frs.* ☉ *Tues.–Fri. 11–1 and 2–6, weekends 2–6.*

Dining and Lodging

$$$ ✕▥ **Château de Brécourt.** This 17th-century stone-and-brick château,
★ outside of Vernon, has high-pitched roofs, an imposing forecourt, and extensive grounds. Guest room decor follows exuberant turn-of-the-century lines. Even if you're not spending a night here, dine on the inventive food in the august restaurant, Le Grand Siècle. Dishes such as lobster mousse and veal with truffles make it a popular spot—and it's even easy to get to from Giverny, which is just across the Seine from Vernon. As such châteaux-hotels go, a stay here is a relatively good value. ⊠ *Douains 27120 (10 km/6 mi south of Vernon on D181),* ☎ *02–32–52–40–50,* ℻ *02–32–52–69–65. 24, 5 suites. Restaurant, pool, tennis court. AE, DC, MC, V.*

Giverny

㉓   *5 km (3 mi) southeast of Vernon via D5 across the Seine, 72 km (45 mi) northwest of Paris.*

The small village of Giverny, just beyond the official limits of Ile-de-France, has become a place of pilgrimage for art lovers. It was here that Claude Monet lived for 43 years, until his death in 1926 at the age of 86.

★   With its pretty pink walls and green shutters, the **Maison and Jardin de Claude Monet** (Claude Monet House and Garden), has been lovingly restored, just like the spectacular garden with its famous lily pond. Monet was brought up in Normandy and, like many of the Impressionists, was sold on the soft light of the Seine Valley. After several years at Argenteuil, just north of Paris, he moved downriver to Giverny in 1883 along with his two sons, his mistress Alice Hoschedé (whom he later married), and her six children. By 1890, a prospering Monet was able to buy the house outright. The house has a warm family feeling that may come as a welcome break after visiting stately French châteaux. Rooms have been restored to Monet's original designs: the kitchen with its blue tiles, the buttercup-yellow dining room, and Monet's bedroom on the second floor. Reproductions of his works, and some of the Japanese prints he avidly collected, crowd the walls.

Three years after buying his house, Monet purchased another plot of land across the lane to continue his gardening experiments, even diverting the River Epte to make a pond. The resulting garden, with flowers spilling out across the paths, is as cheerful and natural as the house. The famous Japanese bridge and water-lily pond, flanked by a mighty willow and rhododendrons, are across the lane that runs to the side of the house and can be reached through a tunnel. Images of the bridge and the water lilies during various seasons appear in much of Monet's later work. Looking across the pond, it is easy to conjure up the grizzle-bearded painter dabbing at his canvases—capturing changes in light and a breakdown in form that were to have a major influence on 20th-century art. ⊠ *84 rue Claude-Monet,* ☎ *02–32–51–28–21.* ☒ *35 frs for gardens and home, gardens only 25 frs.* ⊙ *Tues.–Sun. 10–noon and 2–6.*

The spacious, airy **Musée Américain** (American Museum), endowed by Chicago art patrons Daniel and Judith Terra, displays works by American Impressionists who were influenced by—and often studied with—Claude Monet. ⊠ *99 rue Claude-Monet,* ☎ *02–32–51–94–65.* ☒ *35 frs.* ⊙ *Apr.–Oct., Tues.–Sun. 10–6.*

Dining

$$–$$$ ✕ **Moulin de Fourges.** Local connoisseurs find this little mill irresistible. Nestled in verdant countryside by the River Epte, just minutes from the American Impressionist museum, its setting alone is enough to make you ravenous. ⊠ *Rue du Moulin, Fourges,* ☎ *02–32–52–12–12. Reservations essential. AE, DC, MC, V. Closed Mon. and Jan.–mid-Feb. No dinner Sun.*

$$ ✕ **Les Jardins de Giverny.** This commendable restaurant, with an old-fashioned dining room that overlooks a rose garden, is close to Monet's house. Enjoy the 130-franc lunch menu or choose from a repertoire of inventive dishes such as foie gras spiked with applejack or scallops with wild mushrooms. ⊠ *1 rue Milieu,* ☎ *02–32–21–60–80. AE, V. Closed Mon. and Feb. Dinner Sat. only.*

En Route The road south of Giverny has difficulty matching the bends of the meandering Seine. Follow signs to Mantes and you'll next encounter the river at the village of **La Roche-Guyon,** dominated by chalky cliffs and a classical château. A few miles farther upriver is the tumbling village of **Vétheuil,** with its 12th-century church. The road (now D147) abandons the riverbank until it reaches **Mantes-la-Jolie,** whose vast 12th-century **Notre-Dame** church has a twin-towered facade strikingly similar to that of Notre-Dame in Paris. The small, circular windows that ring the east end of the church are an unusual local characteristic, as you may have spotted at Vétheuil.

Thoiry

㉔ *40 km (25 mi) southeast of Giverny (cross the Seine at Bonnières, then take N13), 17 km (11 mi) southeast of Mantes-la-Jolie via Arnouville, 43 km (27 mi) west of Paris.*

Thoiry is most famous for its 16th-century château with beautiful gardens, wild animal reserve, and gastronomy museum. The village makes an excellent day trip from Paris if you are traveling with children.

Built by Philibert de l'Orme in 1564, the **Château de Thoiry** has a handsome Renaissance facade set off by gardens landscaped in the disciplined French fashion by Le Nôtre, in this case with unexpected justification: The château is positioned directly in line with the sun as it sets in the west at the winter solstice (December 21) and as it rises in the east at the summer solstice (June 21). Heightening the effect, the central part of the château appears to be a transparent arch of light, owing to its huge glass doors and windows.

Owners Vicomte Paul de La Panouse and his American wife, Annabelle, have restored the château and park, opening both to the public. The distinguished history of the La Panouse family—a Comte César even fought in the American Revolution—is retraced in the **Musée des Archives** (Archives Museum), where papal bulls and Napoleonic letters mingle with missives from Thomas Jefferson and Benjamin Franklin. The neighboring pantries house a **Musée de la Gastronomie** (Gastronomy Museum), whose tempting display of *pièces montées*—virtuoso banquet showpieces—re-creates the designs of famed 19th-century chef Antoine Carême. Early recipe books, engravings, and old copper pots are also displayed.

Other highlights of the château interior include the grand staircase, the **Escalier d'Honneur,** with its 18th-century Gobelin tapestries; the **Salon Vert** and **Salon Blanc** (Green and White Salons), with their antique painted harpsichord and portraits; and the **Salon de la Tapisserie** (Tapestry Salon), with its monumental Don Quixote tapestry bearing the rather gruesome arms (three severed raven's heads) of former owner Machault d'Arnouville. An authentic, homey, faintly faded charm pervades these rooms, especially when fires crackle in their enormous hearths on damp afternoons.

The viscountess is a keen gardener and enjoys experimenting in the less formal **Jardin Anglais** (English Garden), where cricket is played on weekend afternoons during summer, and in her late-flowering **Jardin d'Automne** (Autumn Garden). You're allowed to wander at leisure, although it's best not to stray too far from the official footpath through the **Parc Zoologique** (an animal reserve). Note that the parts of the reserve that contain the wilder beasts—deer, zebra, camels, hippos, bears, elephants, and lions—can be visited only by car. The reserve hit the headlines when the first-ever ligrons—a cross between a lion and a tiger—were born here a few years ago. These beasts (bigger than either a lion or a tiger) are now in their second generation and can be seen from the safety of a raised footbridge in the **Parc des Tigres** (Tiger Park). Nearby is a children's play area with a burrow to wriggle through and a huge netted cobweb to bounce around in. ☎ *01–34–87–52–25.* ✉ *Château 30 frs; Château, park, and game reserve 100 frs.* ☉ *Summer, weekdays 10–6, weekends 10–6:30; winter, daily 10–5.*

Dining and Lodging

$ ✕ **Commerce.** This bar on Thoiry's main street has an attractive upstairs dining room where locals come for hearty weekday lunches. Start with the extensive buffet—pâté, salami, and carrot salad are favorites—followed by a sturdy main course such as steak and chips or beef Wellington. ✉ *rue de la Porte-St-Martin,* ☎ *01–34–87–40–18. No credit cards. Closed Sat. No dinner.*

$ ✕▥ **Étoile.** This dowdy hotel-restaurant, just 300 yards from the château along the main street, is more convenient than appealing. Rooms need redecorating, but the fine restaurant serves a good *menu touristique* (special tourist menu, which doesn't always mean you should go running the other way) of robust French dishes. ✉ *38 rue de la Porte-St-Martin, 78770,* ☎ *01–34–87–40–21,* ℻ *01–34–87–49–57. 12 rooms. Restaurant. AE, DC, MC, V. Closed Mon.*

Montfort-L'Amaury

㉕ *13 km (8 mi) south of Thoiry via D76, 42 km (26 mi) west of Paris.*

Montfort-L'Amaury, with its twisting, narrow streets clustered around an old church, is one of the prettiest towns in Ile-de-France. The bulky Renaissance tower of the church of **St-Pierre** dominates the town square. Note the gargoyles around the far end and, inside, the splendid Renaissance stained glass.

Composer Maurice Ravel lived in Montfort from 1921 until his death in 1937; he composed his famous *Bolero* in 1928 in his "Japanese" garden. His tiny house, now the **Musée Ravel** (Ravel Museum), has been reconstituted with many of his souvenirs and furnishings (including his piano). ⊠ *Le Belvédère, rue Maurice-Ravel,* ☎ *01–34–86–00–89.* 🎟 *21 frs.* ☉ *Mon.–Thurs. 2–5, weekends 10–noon and 2–5.*

Shortly after moving into his attractive, thatched house 5 km (3 mi) east of Montfort-L'Amaury, politician Jean Monnet, often known as the Father of Europe, is said to have conceived the idea of a European Community in 1950. He lived here until his death in 1979 and was accorded the supreme state accolade of burial in the Paris Panthéon. The **Maison Jean-Monnet** (Jean Monnet House), where Monnet once hobnobbed with world leaders, is now owned by the European Parliament and displays information on the present European Union, Monnet mementos, and a film on his life and ideas—all in 11 different languages, in time-honored Eurocrat tradition. ⊠ *Houjarray (take D13 east from Montfort and turn right at the entry to Bazoches-sur-Guyonne),* ☎ *01–34–86–12–43.* 🎟 *Free.* ☉ *Wed.–Sun. 2–6.*

Lodging

$–$$ 🏨 **Voyageurs.** This small, homey hotel at the bottom of Montfort's
★ cobbled main street, with wood-beam bedrooms, a well-priced restaurant (menus from 75 to 135 francs), and a cheerful bar with incongruous but appealing '50s decor, is a handy base for exploring Thoiry, Dreux, or Rambouillet. ⊠ *49 rue de Paris, 78490,* ☎ *01–34–86–00–14,* FAX *01–34–86–14–56. 7 rooms.Restaurant, bar. MC, V. Closed mid- to late Aug.*

THE OISE VALLEY AND EAST TO DISNEYLAND PARIS

This area covers a broad arc beginning north of Paris at Maisons-Laffitte, heading east through the Oise Valley to Chantilly, and continuing southeast through Meaux. Besides being the old stomping grounds for several world-famous artists, the area is now the domain of Disneyland Paris.

Maisons-Laffitte

㉖ *7 km (4 mi) northeast of St-Germain-en-Laye via D157, 16 km (10 mi) northwest of Paris via N308.*

The riverside suburb of Maisons-Laffitte has an unusually high proportion of elegant villas, many of which were built with profits from the town's famous racecourse and training stables. It is also home to one of France's finest 17th-century properties. The early Baroque
★ **Château de Maisons,** constructed by architect François Mansart from 1642 to 1651, is one of the least-known châteaux in Ile-de-France. This was not always the case: Sun King Louis XIV came to the housewarming party, and Louis XV, Louis XVI, the 18th-century writer Voltaire, and Napoléon all stayed here. The interior clearly met their exacting standards, thanks to the well-proportioned entrance vestibule with its rich sculpture; the winding **Escalier d'Honneur,** a majestic staircase adorned with paintings and statues; and the royal apartments, above, with their parquet floors and elegant wall paneling. ☎ *01–39–62–01–49.* 🎟 *32 frs.* ☉ *Daily 10–noon and 1:30–5.*

En Route   Take D308 west into the Forêt de St-Germain, and then turn right after
4 km (2½ mi) on N184 to **Conflans-Ste-Honorine,** the capital of France's
inland waterway network. Barges arrive from as far afield as the ports
of Le Havre and Dunkerque, on the north coast, and are often moored
up to six-abreast along the mile-long quayside, near the *conflans* (confluence) of the Rivers Seine and Oise.

Pontoise

㉗ *8 km (5 mi) north of Conflans-Ste-Honorine via N184/N14, 29 km
(19 mi) northwest of Paris via A15.*

A pleasant old town on the banks of the Oise, Pontoise is famous for its
link with the Impressionists. The small **Musée Pissarro,** high up in the
old town, pays tribute to one of Pontoise's most illustrious past residents:
Impressionist painter Camille Pissarro (1830–1903). The collection of
prints and drawings is of interest mainly to specialists, but the view across
the valley from the museum gardens will appeal to all. ⊠ *17 rue du
Château,* ☎ *01–30–32–06–75.* 🎟 *Free.* ☉ *Wed.–Sun. 2–6.*

The **Musée Tavet-Delacour,** housed in a turreted mansion in the center of Pontoise, stages good exhibitions and has a permanent collection that includes landscapes by various local painters and a top floor
devoted to contemporary art, with intriguing abstract geometric compositions by Otto Freundlich. ⊠ *4 rue Lemercier,* ☎ *01–30–38–02–
40.* 🎟 *20 frs.* ☉ *Wed.–Mon. 10–12:30 and 1:30–6.*

Auvers-sur-Oise

㉘ *7 km (4 mi) east of Pontoise via D4, 33 km (21 mi) northwest of Paris
via N328.*

The tranquil Oise River valley, which runs northeast from Pontoise,
retains much of the charm that attracted Pissarro, Paul Cézanne,
Camille Corot, Charles-François Daubigny, and Berthe Morisot to
Auvers-sur-Oise in the second half of the 19th century. But it is the
shadow of Vincent van Gogh that haunts every nook and cranny of
this pretty riverside village.

Van Gogh moved here from Arles in 1890 to be with his brother,
Theo. Little has changed since the summer of 1890, during the last 10
weeks of van Gogh's life, when he painted no fewer than 70 pictures
and then shot himself behind the village château. He is buried next to
his brother in a simple, ivy-covered grave in the village cemetery. The
whole village is peppered with plaques marking the spots that inspired
his art. The plaques bear reproductions of his paintings, enabling you
to compare his final works with the scenes as they are today. After years
of indifference and neglect, his last abode has been turned into a shrine.
You can also visit the medieval village church, subject of one of van
Gogh's most famous paintings, *L'Église d'Auvers,* and admire Osip Zad-
kine's powerful modern statue of van Gogh in the village park.

The Auberge Ravoux, the inn where van Gogh stayed, is now the **Maison de van Gogh** (Van Gogh House). A dingy staircase leads up to the
tiny, spartan, wood-floor attic where van Gogh stored some of modern art's most famous pictures under his bed. A short film retraces van
Gogh's time at Auvers, and there is a well-stocked souvenir shop. Stop
for a drink or for lunch at the ground-floor restaurant. ⊠ *8 rue de la
Sansonne,* ☎ *01–30–36–60–60.* 🎟 *30 frs.* ☉ *Tues.–Sun. 10–6.*

★ ♺   The elegant 17th-century village château, set above split-level gardens, is home to the **Voyage au Temps des Impressionnistes** (Journey
Through the Impressionist Era). You'll receive a set of infrared head-

phones (English available), with commentary that guides you past various tableaux illustrating life in the Impressionist era. Although there are no Impressionist originals—500 reproductions pop up on screens interspersed between the tableaux—some say this is one of France's most imaginative, enjoyable, and innovative museums. Some of the special effects—talking mirrors, computerized cabaret dancing girls, and a simulated train ride past Impressionist landscapes—are worthy of Disney at its best. ⊠ *rue de Léry,* ☎ *01–34–48–48–48.* ▧ *55 frs.* ☉ *May–Oct., daily 10–8; Nov.–Apr., Tues.–Sun. 10–6:30.*

The landscapist Charles-François Daubigny, a precursor of the Impressionists, lived in Auvers from 1861 until his death in 1878. You can visit his studio, the **Atelier Daubigny,** and admire the remarkable array of mural and roof paintings by Daubigny and fellow artists Camille Corot and Honoré Daumier. ⊠ *61 rue Daubigny,* ☎ *01–34–48–03–03.* ▧ *25 frs.* ☉ *Tues.–Sun. 2–6:30.*

You may also want to visit the modest **Musée Daubigny** to admire the drawings, lithographs, and occasional oils by local 19th-century artists, some of which were collected by Daubigny himself. The museum is opposite the Maison de van Gogh, above the tourist office. ⊠ *Manoir des Colombières, rue de la Sansonne,* ☎ *01–30–36–80–20.* ▧ *20 frs.* ☉ *May–Oct., Wed.–Sun. 2:30–6:30; Nov.–Apr., Wed.–Sun. 2–5:30.*

The small **Musée de l'Absinthe** (Absinthe Museum), near the château, contains publicity posters and other Belle Époque artifacts evoking the history of absinthe—a forerunner of today's anise-based aperitifs like Ricard and Pernod. Look out for the special spoons used to add sugar to absinthe. Before it was banned in 1915 because of its negative effects on the nervous system, absinthe was France's national drink. A famous painting by Edgar Degas shows two absinthe drinkers; van Gogh, too, probably downed a few glasses at the Auberge Ravoux (☞ *below*). ⊠ *44 rue Callé,* ☎ *01–30–36–83–26.* ▧ *25 frs.* ☉ *Oct.–May, weekends 11–6; June–Sept., Wed.–Sun. 11–6.*

Dining

$$ ✕ **Auberge Ravoux.** For total van Gogh immersion, have lunch in the
★ same restaurant he patronized more than a hundred years ago. The 150-franc, three-course menu changes regularly, but it's the setting that makes eating here special, with glasswork, lace curtains, and wall decor carefully modeled on the original designs. ⊠ *52 rue Général-de-Gaulle,* ☎ *01–30–36–60–63. Reservations essential. AE, DC, MC, V.*

L'Isle-Adam

㉙ *6 km (4 mi) northeast of Auvers-sur-Oise via D4, 35 km (22 mi) north of Paris via N1.*

Residentially exclusive L'Isle-Adam is one of the most picturesque towns in Ile-de-France. Paris lies just 40 km (25 mi) south, but it could be 100 miles and as many years away. There is a sandy beach along one stretch of the River Oise (via rue de Beaumont); a curious pagodalike folly, the Pavillon Chinois de Cassan; and an unassuming local museum. The **Musée Louis-Senlecq,** on the main street, often stages painting exhibitions and contains numerous attractive works by local landscapists. ⊠ *46 Grande Rue,* ☎ *01–34–69–45–44.* ▧ *15 frs.* ☉ *Thurs.–Mon. 3–6.*

Dining and Lodging

$$–$$$ ✕▨ **Le Cabouillet.** The riverside Cabouillet aptly reflects the quiet charm of L'Isle-Adam, thanks to its pretty views over the Oise. You can savor these from each of its eight rooms or from the chic restau-

rant, where the cooking can be inspired (go for the crawfish in Sauternes sauce, if it's on the menu). The restaurant is closed Wednesday. ⊠ *5 quai de l'Oise, 95290,* ☎ *01–34–69–00–90,* FAX *01–34–69–33–88. 8 rooms. Restaurant. AE, DC, MC, V. Closed Dec. 25–early Feb.*

En Route   From L'Isle-Adam, D922 leads to the small hilltop town of **Beaumont-sur-Oise**—worth a quick peek for its attractive 12th- to 13th-century church of **St-Laurent,** transformed into a cathedral by Émile Zola as the setting for his romantic novel *Le Rêve (The Dream).* Some 6 km (4 mi) farther east (via D922 and D909) is the medieval **Abbaye de Royaumont,** founded by Louis IX in 1228. You can visit the only part of the abbey church still standing (the south transept), along with the ivy-clad cloisters, the refectory, and the vaulted kitchens. The monks' dormitories, chapter house, and library are now part of an international cultural center and seldom open to the public; a music festival (☎ 01–30–35–30–16 for details) is held here in August and September. ☒ *22 frs.* ☉ *Easter–Oct., Wed.–Mon. 10–12:30 and 2–6; Nov.–Easter, weekends 10–12:30 and 2–5.*

Chantilly

③⓪   *10 km (6 mi) northeast of Royaumont via D909, 23 km (14 mi) east of L'Isle-Adam via D4, 37 km (23 mi) north of Paris via N16.*

Romantic Chantilly has a host of attractions: a faux Renaissance château, an eye-popping art collection, splendid Baroque stables, a classy racecourse, and a 16,000-acre forest. Yet it attracts far fewer sightseeing hordes than either Versailles or Fontainebleau.

Although its lavish exterior may be 19th-century Renaissance pastiche, the **Château de Chantilly,** sitting snugly behind an artificial lake, houses
★   the outstanding **Musée Condé,** with illuminated medieval manuscripts, tapestries, furniture, and paintings. The most famous room, the **Santuario** (Sanctuary), contains two celebrated works by Italian painter Raphael (1483–1520)—the *Three Ages of Woman* and the *Orleans Virgin*—plus an exquisite ensemble of 15th-century miniatures by the most illustrious French painter of his time, Jean Fouquet (1420–81). Farther on, in the *Cabinet des Livres* (Book Room), is the Book of Hours of the Duc de Berry, one of the finest medieval manuscripts. Other highlights of this unusual museum are the **Galerie de Psyché** (Psyche Gallery), with 16th-century stained glass and portrait drawings by Flemish artist Jean Clouet II; the **chapelle** (chapel), with sculptures by Jean Goujon and Jacques Sarrazin; and the extensive collection of paintings by 19th-century French artists, headed by Jean-Auguste Ingres. The large **park** behind the château is based on that familiar combination of formal (neatly planned parterres and a mighty straight-banked canal) and romantic eccentricity (the waterfall and the make-believe village that inspired Marie-Antoinette's version at Versailles). ☎ *03–44–57–08–00.* ☒ *39 frs, park only 17 frs.* ☉ *Mar.–Oct., Wed.–Mon. 10–6; Nov.–Feb., 10:30–12:45 and 2–5.*

★ ☾   The majestic 18th-century **Grandes Écuries** are the grandest stables in France and still in use as the **Musée Vivant du Cheval** (Living Museum of the Horse), with a glittering array of carriages and 40 horses and ponies performing dressage exercises. The stables, by the racecourse opposite the château, were designed by Jean Aubert to accommodate 240 horses and 500 hounds in straw-lined comfort, ready for stag and boar hunts in the forests nearby. ⊠ *7 rue du Connétable,* ☎ *03–44–57–40–40.* ☒ *50 frs.* ☉ *Wed.–Mon. 10:30–5:30.*

OFF THE BEATEN PATH

ÉCOUEN – This small town, 21 km (13 mi) south of Chantilly along N16, is renowned for its **Musée de la Renaissance** (Renaissance Museum), housed in a turreted château, with a strong collection of 16th- and 17th-century tapestries and furniture from France, Italy, and Holland. ☎ 01–34–38–38–50. ✎ 25 frs, 17 frs Sun.. ☉ Wed.–Mon. 9:45–12:30 and 2–5:15.

Dining and Lodging

$$ ✕ **La Ferme de Condé.** Opposite the racecourse, in a building that originally served as an Anglican chapel, is one of the classiest restaurants in Chantilly. Elegant dishes including duck with honey and spices and lobster terrine. A reasonably priced menu makes it a suitable lunch spot. There is a good wine list. ✉ 42 av. du Maréchal-Joffre, ☎ 03–44–57–32–31. Reservations essential. AE, MC, V. Closed Tues.

$ ✕ **Capitainerie.** Since the château is a fair walk from the town's main street, it makes sense to have a quick lunch on the spot. This self-service restaurant is in the château's medieval basement, adorned with old kitchen utensils. The buffet is available nonstop from 10:30 through 6:30; you'll find salads, cheeses, and desserts, along with a few hot dishes. ✉ In the Château de Chantilly, ☎ 03–44–57–15–89. Reservations not accepted. No credit cards. Closed Tues.

$$ ▥ **Calèche.** Although it's small and underwhelming, and your reception may be somewhat lacking in warmth, this hotel-restaurant on the avenue leading from the train station to the château is cheap and acceptable for a night's stopover. ✉ 3 av. du Maréchal-Joffre, 60500, ☎ 03–44–57–02–55. 15 rooms. MC, V.

$$ ▥ **Campanile.** This functional, modern motel is in quiet, relaxing Les Huit Curés, just outside Chantilly, on the edge of the forest (which compensates for the lack of interior atmosphere). There's a grillroom for straightforward, if unexciting, meals. You can dine outside on the terrace in summer. ✉ rte. de Creil (on N16 toward Creil), 60500, ☎ 03–44–57–39–24, ℻ 03–44–58–10–05. 47 rooms. Grill. MC, V.

Outdoor Activities and Sports

Chantilly's fabled racecourse comes into its own each June with two of Europe's most prestigious events: the **Prix du Jockey-Club** (Jockey Club Prize) on the first Sunday of the month, and the **Prix de Diane** (Diana Prize) the Sunday after.

Senlis

③ 10 km (6 mi) east of Chantilly via D924, 45 km (28 mi) north of Paris via A1.

Senlis is an exceptionally well-preserved medieval town with crooked, mazelike streets dominated by the svelte, soaring spire of its Gothic cathedral. Two museums—one on hunting and the other centering on fine art and archaeology—are also worth a visit.

The **Cathédrale Notre-Dame,** one of France's oldest and narrowest cathedrals, dates from the second half of the 12th century. The superb ★ spire—arguably the most elegant in France—was added around 1240 and has recently been cleaned and restored. ✉ pl. de Parvis.

The **Musée de la Vénerie** (Hunting Museum), across from the cathedral on the grounds of the ruined royal castle, is one of France's few full-fledged hunting museums. Displayed are artifacts, prints, and paintings, including excellent works by 18th-century animal portraitist, Jean-Baptiste Oudry. ✉ Château Royal, ☎ 03–44–53–00–80. ✎ 14 frs. ☉ Mid-Jan.–mid-Dec., Wed. 2–6, Thurs.–Mon. 10–noon and 2–6.

The town's **Musée d'Art et Archéologie** (Museum of Art and Archaeology), built atop an ancient Gallo-Roman residence, displays some excellent finds, from Gallo-Roman votive objects, unearthed in the neighboring Halatte Forest, to the building's own excavated foundations (found in the basement). Upstairs, the museum presents paintings by—among others—Thomas Couture, Manet's teacher, who lived in Senlis. ⊠ *Palais Épiscopal, pl. du Parvis-Notre-Dame,* ☏ *03–44–53–00–80.* ☑ *14 frs.* ⊙ *Thurs.–Mon. 9–noon and 1:30–5:30.*

OFF THE BEATEN PATH **PARC ASTÉRIX –** Great for kids of all ages, this Gallic theme park, 10 km (6 mi) south of Senlis via A1, takes its cue from a French comic-book figure whose adventures are set during the Roman invasion of France 2,000 years ago. Highlights include a mock Gallo-Roman village, a dolphin lake, and a giant roller coaster. ☏ *08–36–68–30–10.* ☑ *160 frs.* ⊙ *Apr.–early Sept., daily 10–6, except certain Fri. and Mon.; early Sept.–mid-Oct., Wed. and weekends 10–6.*

Dining and Lodging

$$ ✗ **Le Bourgeois Gentilhomme.** This cozy, two-floor restaurant in old Senlis serves some interesting dishes: fricassee of burbot with mushrooms and marjoram-scented rabbit with tiny vegetable ravioli, to name just two. ⊠ *3 pl. de la Halle,* ☏ *03–44–53–13–22. V. Closed Mon. and 3 wks in Aug. No dinner Sun.*

$ 🏨 **Hostellerie Porte-Bellon.** This is the closest you'll get to spending a night in the historic center of Senlis. A modest yet efficient hotel, the Porte-Bellon is just a five-minute walk from the cathedral and close to the bus station. ⊠ *51 rue Bellon, 60300,* ☏ *03–44–53–03–05,* ꜰᴀx *03–44–53–29–94. 20 rooms, 14 with bath. Restaurant. MC, V. Closed mid-Dec.–mid-Jan.*

Ermenonville

❸❷ *13 km (8 mi) southeast of Senlis via N330, 43 km (27 mi) northeast of Paris.*

A ruined abbey and children's amusement park, both nearby, add to the appeal of the village of Ermenonville, best known as the final haunt of the 18th-century French philosopher Jean-Jacques Rousseau.

The Cistercian **Abbaye de Chaalis,** just off the N330 as you arrive from Senlis, has photogenic 13th-century ruins, a landscaped park that has been restored to its 18th-century appearance, and a château with an eclectic collection of Egyptian antiquities and medieval paintings, together with three rooms displaying manuscripts and other mementos of Jean-Jacques Rousseau. ⊠ *Just off N330.* ☑ *Abbey and park 30 frs, park only 12 frs.* ⊙ *Abbey Mar.–Oct., Mon. and Wed.–Fri. 2–6:30, weekends 10:30–12:30 and 2–6:30. Park Wed.–Mon. 9–7.*

⊙ The **Mer de Sable** (Sea of Sand) playground, opposite the abbey of Chaalis, is a cheerful place for children, with its miniature train, giant slide, small zoo, and curious natural "desert" of sand. ⊠ *Parc d'Attractions Jean-Richard,* ☏ *03–44–54–00–96.* ☑ *70 frs.* ⊙ *Apr.–May and Sept., weekdays 11–6:30, weekends 11–7; June, weekdays 10–6, weekends 11–7; July–Aug., daily 10:30–6:30, Sun. 10:30–7; closed Oct.–Mar.*

The elegant **Parc Jean-Jacques Rousseau,** in the center of Ermenonville, is famous as the initial resting place of the influential writer, who spent the last three months of his life in Ermenonville in 1778 and was buried on the Ile des Peupliers in the middle of the lake. Rousseau's ideas about natural equality made him a hero of the French Revolution, and in 1794 his body was removed to the Panthéon in Paris. A few years later, Napoléon came to Ermenonville to pay homage to Rousseau, saying: "It would have been better for the peace of France if this man had never existed; he paved the way for the French Revolution." When it was pointed out that he could hardly complain about the turn of Revolutionary events, Napoléon is said to have replied: "Time will tell whether it would have been better for peace on earth if Rousseau and I had never lived."

Lodging

$–$$ ✕🏠 **Auberge de la Croix d'Or.** For lunch or an overnight stop in tiny
★ Ermenonville, the Croix d'Or is the place. Its small rooms and homey restaurant have the welcoming feel of a village inn. The attractive park where Jean-Jacques Rousseau was buried is nearby. The restaurant is closed Monday and Sunday dinner, in winter. ⊠ *2 rue du Prince-Radziwill, 60950,* ☎ *03–44–54–00–04,* 𝔽𝔸𝕏 *03–44–54–05–44. 11 rooms. MC, V. Closed mid-Dec.–1st wk of Feb.*

Meaux

③③ *24 km (15 mi) southeast of Ermenonville via N330, 40 km (25 mi) east of Paris via N3.*

A sturdy cathedral and well-preserved bishop's palace embellish Meaux, a dignified old market-town on the banks of the Marne. An excellent variety of the creamy Brie cheese is produced locally.

Above the Marne River, the **Cathédrale St-Étienne** took more than 300 years to complete and stylistically is a bit of a hodgepodge. The stonework in the soaring interior becomes increasingly decorative as you approach the west end, culminating in a notable Flamboyant Gothic rose window. The exterior is somewhat eroded and looks sadly battered—or pleasingly authentic, according to taste. A son-et-lumière with medieval costumes is staged outside the cathedral most weekends in June and July. ⊠ *rue St-Étienne.* ☎ *01–60–23–40–00 for details about the son-et-lumière.* ☉ *Daily 8–noon and 2–6.*

The former bishop's palace next to the cathedral, overlooking a trimly patterned garden with remains of the town wall, now houses the **Musée Bossuet.** The museum combines French old masters with a quirky collection of medals commemorating the Paris Commune and Franco-Prussian War, and documents and mementos detailing the life of former bishop Jacques Bossuet, a noted 17th-century theologian. ⊠ *Ancien Palais Épiscopal,* ☎ *01–64–34–84–45.* 🎫 *15 frs, free Wed.* ☉ *Wed.–Mon. 10–noon and 2–6.*

Disneyland Paris

🎡 ③④ *20 km (13 mi) southwest of Meaux via A140 and A4, 38 km (24 mi) east of Paris via A4.*

Disneyland Paris (originally called Euro Disney) is not what most people travel to France to experience. But if you have a child in tow, the promise of a day there may get you through an afternoon at Versailles or Fontainebleau. If you're a dyed-in-the-wool Disney fan, you'll want to make a beeline for the park to see how it has been molded to appeal to the tastes of Europeans. (Disney's "Imagineers" call it their most lovingly detailed park.) And if you've never experienced this particular form of Disney showmanship, you may want to put in an appearance, if only to see what the fuss is all about.

Although great fanfare greeted the opening of Euro Disney, the resort has had its share of troubles: image problems, reports of technical glitches, feuds with neighbors objecting to noisy fireworks, and—worst of all—low attendance levels. But the change of name, lowering of admission prices, and the sale of alcohol in theme-park restaurants have helped reverse the slide.

The theme park is made up of five "lands": Main Street U.S.A., Frontierland, Adventureland, Fantasyland, and Discoveryland. The central theme of each land is relentlessly echoed in every detail, from attractions to restaurant menus to souvenirs. The park is circled by a railroad, which stops three times along the perimeter.

Main Street U.S.A. goes under the railroad and past shops and restaurants toward the main plaza; the Disney Parades are held here every afternoon and—during holiday periods—every evening.

Top attractions at **Frontierland** are the chilling Phantom Manor, haunted by holographic spooks, and the thrilling runaway mine train of Big Thunder Mountain, a roller coaster that plunges wildly through floods and avalanches in a setting meant to evoke Utah's Monument Valley.

Whiffs of Arabia, Africa, and the West Indies give **Adventureland** its exotic cachet; the spicy meals and snacks served here rank among the best food in the park. Don't miss the Pirates of the Caribbean, an exciting mise-en-scène populated by eerily human, computer-driven figures, or one of Disney's newest attractions, Indiana Jones and the Temple of Doom, a breathtaking ride that relives some of this luckless hero's most exciting moments.

Fantasyland charms the youngest park goers with familiar cartoon characters from such classic Disney films as *Snow White, Pinocchio, Dumbo,* and *Peter Pan.* The focal point of Fantasyland, and indeed Disneyland Paris, is Le Château de la Belle au Bois Dormant (Sleeping Beauty's Castle), a 140-ft, bubble-gum-pink structure topped with 16 blue- and gold-tipped turrets. Its design was allegedly inspired by illustrations from a medieval Book of Hours. The castle's dungeon conceals a scaly, green, 2-ton dragon who rumbles in his sleep and occasionally rouses to roar—an impressive feat of engineering, producing an answering chorus of shrieks from younger children.

Discoveryland is a futuristic setting for high-tech Disney entertainment. Robots on roller skates welcome you on your way to Star Tours, a pitching, plunging, sense-confounding ride based on the *Star Wars* films. In Le Visionarium, a simulated space journey is presented by 9-Eye, a staggeringly realistic robot. Space Mountain pretends to catapult riders through the Milky Way. ☎ 01–60–30–60–30. 🖾 *Apr.–Sept. and Christmas period 200 frs (380 frs for 2-day Passport, 515 frs for 3-day Passport); Oct.–Mar., except Christmas period, 160 frs (305 frs for 2-day Passport, 415 frs for 3-day Passport); includes admission to all individual attractions within the park but not meals. AE, DC, MC, V.* ☺ *Mid-June–mid-Sept., daily 9 AM–10 PM; mid-Sept.–mid-June, Sun.–Fri. 10–6, Sat. 9–8; Dec. 23–Jan. 6, daily 9–8.*

Dining and Lodging

$–$$ ✕ **Disneyland Restaurants.** Disneyland Paris is peppered with places to eat, ranging from snack bars and fast-food joints to five full-service restaurants—all with a distinguishing theme. In addition, Disney Village (☞ *below*) and Disney hotels have restaurants that are open to the public. But since these are outside the park, it is not recommended that you waste time traveling to them for lunch. Disneyland Paris has relaxed its no-alcohol policy and now serves wine and beer in the park's sit-down restaurants, as well as in the hotels and restaurants outside the park. Eateries serve nonstop as long as the park is open. ☎ *01–*

60–45–65–40. *Sit-down restaurants: AE, DC, MC, V; counter-service restaurants: no credit cards.*

$$–$$$$ 🏨 **Disneyland Hotels.** The resort has 5,000 rooms in six hotels, all a short distance from the park, ranging from the luxurious Disneyland Hotel to the not-so-rustic Camp Davy Crockett. Free transportation to the park is available at every hotel. Several packages that include Disneyland lodging, entertainment, and admission are available through travel agents in Europe. ⊠ *Centre de Réservations, B.P. 100, 77777 Marne-la-Vallée cedex 4,* ☎ *01–60–30–60–30, 407/934–7639 in the U.S.,* ℻ *01–49–30–71–00. All hotels have at least 1 restaurant, bar, café, indoor pool, sauna, exercise facilities, and free parking. AE, DC, MC, V.*

Nightlife and the Arts

Nocturnal entertainment outside the park centers in **Disney Village,** a vast pleasure mall designed by American architect Frank Gehry. Featured are American-style restaurants (crab shack, diner, deli, steak house), including **Billybob's Country Western Saloon** (☎ 01–60–45–70–79) and **Hurricane's** disco with giant video screen (☎ 01–60–45–70–70). Also in Disney Village is **Buffalo Bill's Wild West Show** (☎ 01–60–45–71–00 for reservations), a two-hour dinner extravaganza with a menu of sausages, spareribs, and chili; performances by a talented troupe of stunt riders, bronco busters, tribal dancers, and musicians; plus some 50 horses, a dozen buffalo, a bull, and an Annie Oakley–style sharpshooter, with a golden-maned "Buffalo Bill" as emcee. A re-creation of a show that dazzled Parisians a hundred years ago, it's corny but great fun if you can manage the appropriate suspension of disbelief. There are two shows nightly, at 6:30 and 9:30; the cost is 295 francs (it's closed in January).

Outdoor Activities and Sports

A 27-hole **golf course** (☎ 01–60–45–68–04) is open to the public at Disneyland; rental clubs are available, and some special golf packages are available through travel agents.

En Route There are three châteaux just west of Disneyland that merit a stop if you have time. The lavishly furnished **Château de Ferrières** (just off the expressway, 8 km/5 mi west of Disneyland) was built by the Rothschilds in the 19th century; it's open afternoons only, Wednesday–Sunday in summer, Sundays only in winter. The 17th-century **Château de Guermantes** (5 km/3 mi north of Ferrières on D35) has Italianate decor and is open weekends from March through November. The 18th-century **Château de Champs-sur-Marne** (8 km/5 mi west of Guermantes) has gardens with an assortment of ingeniously trimmed hedges; it's open daily except Tuesday.

SOUTHEAST TO FONTAINEBLEAU AND PROVINS

Fontainebleau forms the hub of this heavily wooded southeast region of Ile-de-France. But don't bypass Vaux-le-Vicomte, a masterpiece of 17th-century architecture and garden design; the pretty painters' villages of Barbizon and Moret-sur-Loing; or hilltop Provins, with its well-preserved medieval walls.

Evry

㉟ *24 km (15 mi) south of Paris via N7.*

One of five "new towns" constructed in the Paris region since the 1960s to house the overspill from the capital, Evry has made a determined bid to escape faceless concrete anonymity by building Europe's newest and weirdest cathedral. The **Cathédrale d'Evry,** completed in 1995, is a circular, redbrick building shaped like a drum with the top sliced off, and a ring of trees planted on the roof symbolizing Christ's crown of thorns. The sober interior makes discreet use of different woods and marbles and incorporates high-tech sound and lighting controls that may not surprise Americans but that, by traditionalist European standards, are revolutionary. ✉ *cours Monseigneur-Roméro,* ☎ *01–64– 97–85–21.*

Vaux-le-Vicomte

★ ❸ *24 km (15 mi) southeast of Evry via N446 to Melun, 5 km (3 mi) northeast of Melun via N36 and D215.*

Wonderful proportions and exquisite gardens characterize the stunning **Château de Vaux-le-Vicomte,** built between 1656 and 1661 for finance minister Nicolas Fouquet. The construction of this château was monstrous even for those days: Entire villages were razed, 18,000 workmen called in, and architect Louis Le Vau, painter Charles Le Brun, and landscape architect André Le Nôtre were hired to prove that Fouquet's refined tastes matched his business acumen. The housewarming party was so lavish that star guest Louis XIV, tetchy at the best of times, threw a jealous fit. He hurled Fouquet in the slammer and promptly began building Versailles to prove just who was boss.

The high-roofed château, partially surrounded by a moat, is set well back from the road behind iron railings topped with sculpted heads. A cobbled avenue stretches up to the entrance and stone steps lead to the entrance hall, which, given the noble scale of the exterior, seems small. There is no grand staircase, either—the stairs are tucked away in the left wing and lead to the private apartments—rooms designed on an intimate scale for daily living. Charles Le Brun's captivating decoration includes the ceiling of the **Chambre du Roi** (Royal Bedchamber), depicting *Time Bearing Truth Heavenward*, framed by stucco work by sculptors François Girardon and Legendre. Along the frieze you can make out small squirrels, the Fouquet family's emblem—even now squirrels are known as *fouquets* in local dialect. But Le Brun's masterwork is the ceiling in the **Salon des Muses** (Hall of Muses), a brilliant allegorical composition painted in glowing, sensuous colors that surpasses his work at Versailles.

On the ground floor, the impressive **Grand Salon** (Great Hall), with its unusual oval form and 16 caryatid pillars symbolizing the months and seasons, possesses harmony and style despite its unfinished state. In fact, the lack of decoration only points up Le Vau's architectural genius.

In the basement, whose cool, dim rooms were used to store food and wine and house the château's staff, you'll find rotating exhibits about the château's past. Life-size wax figures illustrate the château's history. The **cuisine** (kitchen), a cheerful sight with its gleaming copperware and old menus, is also down here.

Unlike Fontainebleau, Vaux-le-Vicomte is still privately owned, and as such, it doesn't have a perfectly restored interior. But there is no mistaking the grandeur of Le Nôtre's **gardens,** which have been carefully restored; these are at their best when the fountains are turned on (the second and fourth Saturdays of each month, at 3 and 6 PM). Also visit the **Musée des Équipages** (Carriage Museum) in the stables and inspect a host of carriages and coaches in wonderful condition. ☎ *01–64–14– 41–90.* ✉ *Château and grounds 56 frs, grounds only 30 frs, candle-*

light visits 75 frs. ☉ *Apr.–Oct., daily 10–6; Mar. and early–mid-Nov., daily 11–1 and 2–5. Candlelight visits May–Oct., Sat. 8:30 PM–11 PM.*

Dining

$ ✕ **L'Écureuil.** An imposing barn to the right of the château entrance has been transformed into this self-service cafeteria where you can enjoy fine steaks (insist yours is cooked enough), coffee, or a snack beneath the ancient rafters of a wood-beam roof. The restaurant is open daily for lunch and tea, and for dinner during candlelight visits. ✉ *Château de Vaux-le-Vicomte. Reservations not accepted. MC, V.*

Barbizon

37 *17 km (11 mi) southwest of Vaux-le-Vicomte via Melun and D64, 50 km (31 mi) southeast of Paris.*

On the western edge of the 62,000-acre Fontainebleau forest, the painters' village of Barbizon retains its atmosphere despite the intrusion of art galleries, souvenir shops, and weekending Parisians. The group of landscape painters known as the Barbizon School—Camille Corot, Jean-François Millet, Narcisse Diaz de la Peña, and Théodore Rousseau, among others—lived here from the 1830s on, paving the way for the Impressionists by their willingness to accept nature on its own terms, rather than use it as an idealized base for carefully structured compositions. In the forest, sealed to one of the famous sandstone rocks, is a bronze medallion by sculptor Henri Chapu, which pays homage to Millet and Rousseau.

Corot and company would often repair to the **Auberge du Père Ganne** after painting; the inn still stands and is now the **Musée de l'École de Barbizon** (Barbizon School Museum). The museum contains documents of the village as it was in the 19th century as well as a few original works—in addition, the Barbizon artists painted on every available surface, and even now you can see some originals on the walls and in the buffet. ✉ *92 Grande-Rue,* ☎ *01–60–66–22–27.* 🎟 *25 frs (joint admission with Maison-Atelier Théodore Rousseau; ☞ below)* . ☉ *Wed.–Mon. 10–12:30 and 2–5.*

You can also soak up the artsy mood at the **Atelier Jean-François Millet** (Jean-François Millet's Studio). Though there are no actual Millet works, this studio is where the artist painted some of his most renowned pieces, including *The Gleaners.* ✉ *27 Grande-Rue,* ☎ *01–60–66–21–55.* 🎟 *Free.* ☉ *Wed.–Mon. 9:30–12:30 and 2–5:30.*

The **Maison-Atelier Théodore Rousseau** was painter Théodore Rousseau's house-cum-studio—in a converted barn. Temporary exhibitions are now staged here. ✉ *55 Grande-Rue,* ☎ *01–60-66–22–38.* 🎟 *25 frs (joint ticket with the Barbizon School Museum; ☞ above).* ☉ *Mon. and Wed.—Fri. 10–12:30 and 2–5, weekends 10–5.*

Dining and Lodging

$–$$ ✕ **Le Relais.** Large portions of delicious French country specialties are served at this spacious restaurant with a big open fire and paintings and hunting trophies adorning the walls. The choice of prix-fixe menus is good and you can eat on a large terrace, in the shade of lime and chestnut trees. ✉ *2 av. Général-de-Gaulle,* ☎ *01–60–66–40–28. Reservations essential on weekends. MC, V. Closed Wed. No dinner Tues.*

$$ ✕🖼 **Auberge des Alouettes.** This delightful, family-run 19th-century
★ inn is on 2 acres of grounds (which the better rooms overlook). The interior has been redecorated in '30s style, but many rooms still have their original oak beams. The popular restaurant (reservations are essential), with its large open terrace, serves light cuisine and barbecued

beef in summer. The restaurant is closed Sunday night in winter. ⊠ *4 rue Antoine-Barye, 77630,* ☎ *01–60–66–41–98,* 🖷 *01–60–66–20–69. 22 rooms. Restaurant, tennis court. AE, DC, MC, V.*

Fontainebleau

8 km (5 mi) southeast of Barbizon via N7, 64 km (40 mi) southeast of Paris via A6/N7.

★ Like Chambord in the Loire Valley or Compiègne to the north, Fontainebleau was a favorite spot for royal hunting parties before it hosted one of France's grandest residences. Begun under the flamboyant Renaissance prince François I, the French contemporary of England's Henry VIII, the **Château de Fontainebleau** was embellished by Italian artists Il Rosso (a pupil of Michelangelo; 1494–1540) and Francesco Primaticcio (1504–70). In fact, they did much more: By introducing the pagan allegories and elegant lines of Mannerism to France, they revolutionized French decorative art. Their extraordinary frescoes and stuccowork can be admired in the **Galerie François I** and the glorious **Salle de Bal** (☞ *below*), completed under Henri II, François I's successor. The decorative interlaced initials found throughout the château are also an addition of Henri II; while you might expect to see the royal "H" woven with a "C" (for Catherine de' Medici, his wife), instead you'll find a "D"—indicating his mistress, Diane de Poitiers.

Even Sun King Louis XIV turned his architectural attentions to Fontainebleau, commissioning Hardouin-Mansart to design new pavilions and André Le Nôtre to replant the **Jardins** (Gardens). Despite the allure of his main project, Versailles, he and his court returned faithfully each autumn for the hunting season. However, it was Napoléon who made a Versailles, as it were, out of Fontainebleau, by spending lavishly to restore it to its former glory. He held Pope Pius VII prisoner here in 1812 and signed the second church-state concordat here in 1813. The formal, flowery **Parterre** (Flower Garden) faces the leafy **Jardin Anglais** (English Garden) across the **Étang des Carpes** (Carp Pond), where ancient carp are alleged to swim. Allied soldiers drained the pond in 1915 and ate the fish, and, in the event they missed some, Hitler's hordes did likewise in 1940.

38 The domed **Porte du Baptistère** (Baptism Gateway) is named for the baptism of the Dauphin—the heir to the throne, later to become Louis XIII—which took place under the arch of the gateway in 1606. The **39** gateway fronts the **Cour Ovale** (Oval Courtyard), shaped like a flat-**40** tened egg. Opposite the courtyard is the **Cour Henri IV** (Henry IV Courtyard), a large, severe square built at the same time as the place des Vosges in Paris (1609). Around the corner is the informal **Jardin 41** **de Diane** (Diana's Garden), with peacocks and a statue of the hunting goddess surrounded by mournful hounds. The palace's most majestic **42** courtyard, the **Cour du Cheval-Blanc** (White Horse Courtyard), contains the famous horseshoe staircase built by Jean du Cerceau in the early 17th century; it can be reached from the garden. Here Napoléon bade farewell to his Old Guard in 1814 before his brief exile on the Mediterranean island of Elba—hence the courtyard's other name, the Cour des Adieux (Courtyard of Farewells).

43 The **Musée Napoléon** (Napoléon Museum) contains a lock of his hair, his Légion d'Honneur medal, his imperial uniform, the hat he wore on his return from Elba in 1815, and a bed in which he once slept. There **44** is also a **Salle du Trône** (Throne Room)—Napoléon spurned the throne room at Versailles, a palace he disliked, and established his imperial

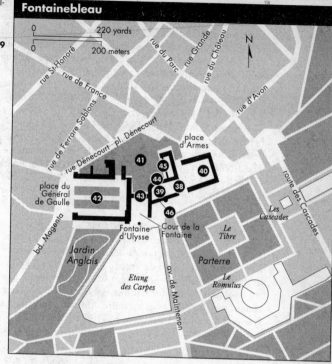

seat here in the former **Chambre du Roi** (King's Bedchamber), a room
with a suitably majestic decor—and the **Boudoir de la Reine** (Queen's
Boudoir), known as the Room of the Six Maries.

45 The sweeping **Galerie de Diane,** built during the reign of Henri IV (1589–
1610), was converted to a library in the 1860s. Other salons have 17th-
century tapestries, marble reliefs by Jacquet de Grenoble, and paintings
and frescoes by Primaticcio, Niccolò dell'Abbate, and other members
of the Fontainebleau School.

46 The jewel of the interior is the ceremonial ballroom—the **Salle de
Bal**—nearly 100 ft long, with wood paneling, 16th-century frescoes and
gilding, and, reputedly, the first coffered ceiling in France, its intricate
pattern echoed by the splendid 19th-century parquet floor. ☎ 01–60–
71–50–70. 🎫 Château 35 frs, gardens free. ☉ Château Wed.–Mon.
9:30–5; gardens daily 9–dusk.

Dining and Lodging

$–$$ ✕ **La Route du Beaujolais.** The food is cheap and the atmosphere
cheerful at this jolly eatery near the château, where Lyonnais-style cold
cuts and bottles of Beaujolais are the mainstays. For something a little more upscale, try the beef fillet with Brie or the braised veal kidney. Prix-fixe meals are priced at 88 and 130 francs. ✉ 3 rue Montebello,
☎ 01–64–22–27–98. AE, DC, MC, V.

$$$$ ✕🏨 **Aigle-Noir.** This may be Fontainebleau's costliest hotel, but you
★ can't go wrong if you request one of the rooms overlooking either the
garden or the château. They have late-18th- or early 19th-century reproduction furniture, evoking a Napoleonic mood. The restaurant, Le
Beauharnais, serves subtle, imaginative cuisine—duck with marjoram
is a good choice. There's a tranquil garden for alfresco dining in summer. Reservations are essential and jacket and tie are required. ✉ 27
pl. Napoléon-Bonaparte, 77300, ☎ 01–64–22–32–65, FAX 01–64–

22–17–33. 56 rooms. Restaurant, pool, sauna, exercise room, convention center. AE, DC, MC, V.

$$$　🏨 **Napoléon.** Opposite the château, this is surely one of the best local properties. Pastel-color rooms have modern furniture and marble baths and look out onto terraces or the indoor garden. The restaurant, La Table des Maréchaux, serves satisfying, deftly prepared classics, and the 130-franc menu is an excellent deal. ⊠ *9 rue Grande, 77300,* ☎ *01–60–74–60–00,* FAX *01–60–74–60–61. 57 rooms. Restaurant. AE, DC, MC, V. Closed end of Dec.*

$$　🏨 **Londres.** Established in 1850, the Londres is a tranquil, family-style hotel with Louis XV decor. Balconies overlook the château and the Cour des Adieux, where Napoléon bade his troops an emotional farewell. The austere 19th-century facade is a registered landmark. ⊠ *1 pl. du Général-de-Gaulle, 77300,* ☎ *01–64–22–20–21,* FAX *01–60–72–39–16. 22 rooms. Restaurant, bar. AE, DC, MC, V. Closed mid-Dec.–early Jan.*

Outdoor Activities and Sports

The forest of Fontainebleau is laced with hiking trails; for more information, ask for the *Guide des Sentiers* at the tourist office (☞ Visitor Information *in* Ile-de-France A to Z, *below*). Bikes can be rented at the Fontainebleau-Avon train station. The forest is also famed for its fascinating rock formations, where many a novice alpinist first caught the climbing bug; for more information contact the **Club Alpin Français** (⊠ 24 av. Laumière, 75019 Paris, ☎ 01–53–38–88–61).

Moret-sur-Loing

47 *10 km (6 mi) southeast of Fontainebleau via N6, 74 km (46 mi) southeast of Paris.*

Close to the confluence of the Rivers Seine and Yonne is the endearing village of Moret-sur-Loing, immortalized by Impressionist painter Alfred Sisley, who lived here for 20 years at 19 rue Montmartre (not open to the public), around the corner from the church. A narrow bridge, one of the oldest in France, leads across the River Loing and provides a view of the village walls, rooftops, and church tower. Those with a sweet tooth, take note: Moret is also renowned for its barley sugar. A good time to visit the town is on a Saturday evening in summer (mid-June through early September), when 500 locals stage son-et-lumière pageants illustrating the town's history.

Truculent World War I leader Georges Clemenceau (1841–1929), known as the Tiger, is the subject of a cozy museum at **La Grange-Batelière,** the thatched house he used to live in. His taste for Asian art and his friendship with Impressionist Claude Monet are evoked here. ⊠ *Access via rue du Peintre-Sisley,* ☎ *01–60–70–51–21.* 🎟 *Guided tours only 35 frs.* ⊘ *Easter–mid-Nov., weekends 3–6.*

En Route　From Moret, head north to neighboring St-Mammès, at the confluence of the Loing and Seine rivers, and then head east along D39 to **Montereau-Fault-Yonne**—where the Seine meets the great river of northern Burgundy, the Yonne. Montereau was a renowned pottery center until the 1950s, as you will learn at the small **Musée de la Faïence** (Faience Museum; ⊠ 2 pl. René-Cassin, ☎ 01–64–32–95–64). From Montereau continue along D403, through **Donnemarie,** with its huge belfry, and past hilltop **St-Loup-de-Naud,** with its richly sculpted church portal, to Provins.

Provins

★ **48** *48 km (30 mi) northeast of Moret-sur-Loing, 48 km (30 mi) east of Melun, 80 km (50 mi) southeast of Paris via N19.*

On the hilltop site of a Roman camp, Provins developed into the third most important commercial center in France (after Paris and Rouen) during the Middle Ages. Under the influence of the counts of Champagne, it acquired international renown as a rose-growing center.

★ Climb up to the **Tour de César**, a circular 12th-century keep on a sturdy mound, to admire the panoramic view of the town and its **Remparts**, some of the best-preserved medieval town walls in France. ⊠ *7 rue du Palais,* ☎ *01–64–01–40–19.* ☎ *22 frs.* ☉ *June–Sept., daily 10–5; Oct.–May, weekends 2–5.*

Note the incongruous 17th-century classical dome on the 12th-century Gothic church of **St-Quiriace**, beneath the Tour de César. The **Jardin des Brébans** (Brébans' Garden), close to the church, is a pleasant place for a walk. From the garden, rue du Palais leads to place du Châtel, a sloping square with restaurants at the far end.

The 13th-century **Grange aux Dîmes** (Tithe Barn), on rue de Jouy, just off the square, houses a good collection of medieval stone sculptures in its vaulted ground floor. ☎ *22 frs.* ☉ *Weekends 2–6.*

In a bid to liven up its image, Provins stages **Soirées Médiévales** (Medieval Evenings) in summer, with pageants and costumes; call the tourist office (☎ 01–64–60–26–26) for details. There is also a **Fête des Moissons** (Harvest Festival) on the last Sunday of August.

Lodging

$$–$$$ 🏠 **Vieux Remparts.** Old wood beams inside the attractive old building and a cheerful, leafy courtyard make for a cheerful atmosphere. Rooms are small but have good light and modern furnishings. ⊠ *3 rue Couverte, 77160,* ☎ *01–64–08–94–00,* FAX *01–60–67–77–22. 25 rooms. Restaurant. AE, DC, MC, V.*

ILE-DE-FRANCE A TO Z

Arriving and Departing

By Car

Expressway A13, from the Porte d'Auteuil, links Paris to Versailles. You can get to Chartres on A10 from Porte d'Orléans. For Fontainebleau, take A6 from Porte d'Orléans, or, for a more attractive route through the Forest of Sénart and the northern part of the Forest of Fontainebleau, take N6 from Porte de Charenton via Melun. The A4 expressway runs from Paris to Disneyland.

By Plane

Major airports in the Ile-de-France area are **Charles de Gaulle** (☎ 01–48–62–22–80), known as Roissy, 25 km (16 mi) northwest of Paris, and **Orly** (☎ 01–49–75–15–15), 16 km (10 mi) south. Shuttle buses link Disneyland to the airports at Roissy, 56 km (35 mi) away, and Orly, 50 km (31 mi) distant; buses take 45 minutes and run every 45 minutes from Roissy, every 60 minutes from Orly (less frequently in low season), and cost 75 francs.

By Train

Many of the sights mentioned can be reached by train from Paris. Both regional and mainline (Le Mans–bound) trains leave the **Gare Montparnasse** for Chartres; the former also stop at Versailles, Rambouillet, and Maintenon. Gare Montparnasse is also the terminal for trains to Dreux (Granville line) and for the suburban trains that stop at Montfort-l'Amaury, the nearest station to Thoiry.

Some mainline trains from **Gare St-Lazare** stop at Mantes-la-Jolie and Vernon on their way to Rouen and Le Havre. Suburban trains leave the **Gare du Nord** for L'Isle-Adam. Chantilly is on the main northbound line from Gare du Nord (Senlis can be reached by bus from Chantilly) and Provins on a suburban line from **Gare de l'Est.** Fontainebleau— or, rather, neighboring Avon, 2 km (1½ mi) away (there is frequent bus service)—is 45 minutes from **Gare de Lyon.**

St-Germain-en-Laye is a terminal of the **RER-A** (commuter train) that tunnels through Paris (main stations at Étoile, Auber, and Les Halles). The RER-A also accesses Maisons-Laffitte and, at the other end, the new suburban station for Disneyland Paris (called Marne-la-Vallée– Chessy), within 100 yards of the entrance to both the theme park and Disney Village. Journey time is around 40 minutes and trains operate every 10–30 minutes, depending on the time of day. The handiest of Versailles's three train stations is the one reached by the **RER-C** line (main stations at Austerlitz, St-Michel, Invalides, and Champ-de-Mars). Evry can be reached on **RER-D.**

A mainline **TGV** (*Trains à Grande Vitesse*) station links Disneyland to Lille, Lyon, Brussels, and London (via Lille and the Channel Tunnel).

Getting Around

Although a comprehensive rail network ensures that most towns in Ile-de-France can make comfortable day trips from Paris, the only way to crisscross the region without returning to the capital is by car. There is no shortage of expressways or fast highways, but be prepared for delays close to Paris and during the morning and evening rush hours.

Contacts and Resources

Car Rentals
Cars can be rented from agencies in Paris (☞ Contacts and Resources *in* Chapter 2).

Emergencies
Ambulance (☎ 15). **Regional hospitals:** Chartres (✉ 34 rue du Dr-Maunoury, ☎ 02–37–30–30–30); Melun (✉ 2 rue Fréteau-de-Pény, ☎ 01–64–71–60–06); and **Versailles** (✉ 177 rue de Versailles, in neighboring Le Chesnay, ☎ 01–39–63–91–33). Hospitals closer to Paris: The **American Hospital** in Neuilly (✉ 63 bd. Victor-Hugo, ☎ 01–47–45–71–00); and the **British Hospital** in Levallois-Perret (✉ 3 rue Barbès, ☎ 01–47–58–13–12).

Guided Tours
Alliance Autos (✉ 10 bis rue Jeanne-d'Arc, St-Mandé, near the Bois de Vincennes, ☎ 01–43–28–20–20) has bilingual guides who will take you on a private tour around the Paris area in luxury cars or a minibus for a minimum of four hours for about 500 francs an hour (call to check details and prices).

Guided excursions to Giverny are organized by **American Express** (✉ 11 rue Scribe, Paris, 9ᵉ, ☎ 01–47–77–77–37) from April through October. **Cityrama** (✉ 147 rue St-Honoré, Paris, 1ᵉʳ, ☎ 01–44–55–61–00) and **Paris Vision** (✉ 214 rue de Rivoli, Paris, 1ᵉʳ, ☎ 01–42–86–95–36) run half-day guided trips three times a week (195–450 francs) to Chartres, Fontainebleau, and Barbizon (with additional departures scheduled in summer) and daily trips to Versailles.

Visitor Information

For written inquiries only, contact the **Comité Régional de Tourisme d'Ile-de-France** (⊠ 26 av. de l'Opéra, 75001 Paris, ☎ 01–42–60–28–62). Information on Disneyland is available from the **Disneyland Paris Reservations Office** (⊠ B.P. 100, 77777 Marne-la-Vallée cedex 4, ☎ 01–60–30–60–30, 407/824–4321 in the U.S.).

Local tourist offices: **Barbizon** (⊠ 55 Grande Rue, ☎ 01–60–66–41–87). **Chartres** (⊠ pl. de la Cathédrale, ☎ 02–37–21–50–00). **Fontainebleau** (⊠ 4 rue Royale, ☎ 01–60–74–99–99). **Rambouillet** (⊠ 8 pl. de la Libération, ☎ 01–34–83–21–21). **Versailles** (⊠ 7 rue des Réservoirs, ☎ 01–39–50–36–22).

4 The Loire Valley

Château Country

Sometimes owned by England, and fought over for centuries, this stretch of the Loire Valley is renowned for its extraordinary châteaux. Ranging from majestic Chambord and Saumur to the palatial Cheverny and Azay-le-Rideau to scenic Chenonceau and Ussé, these châteaux have become almost synonymous with France. At Orléans, too, you can see the country's history: It was here that Joan of Arc had her most rousing successes against the English.

Revised and updated by Simon Hewitt

THE LOIRE IS THE LONGEST RIVER IN FRANCE, originating deep in the heart of the Massif Central and winding its way north and then west for more than 960 km (600 mi) before reaching the Atlantic beyond Nantes. Halfway along, just outside the city of Orléans, the river makes a wide, westward bend, gliding languidly through low, rich country known as the Val de Loire—the Loire Valley. In this temperate "garden" region—a 225-km (140-mi) stretch between Orléans and Angers—scores of châteaux rise from the rocky banks of the Loire and its tributaries: the rivers Cher, Indre, Vienne, and Loir (with no *e*).

For centuries the Loire River was the area's principal means of transportation and an important barrier against invading armies. Towns arose at strategic bridgeheads, and fortresses—the earliest châteaux—appeared on the slopes of towering hills. The Loire Valley was hotly disputed by France and England during the Middle Ages; it belonged to England (under the Anjou Plantagenet family) between 1154 and 1216 and again during the Hundred Years' War (1337–1453). It was the example of Joan of Arc, the Maid of Orléans (scene of her most stirring victories), that crystallized French efforts to expel the English.

The Loire Valley's golden age came under François I (1515–47), flamboyant contemporary of Henry VIII. His salamander emblem can be seen in many châteaux, including Chambord, the mightiest one. He hired Renaissance craftsmen from Italy and hobnobbed with the aging Leonardo da Vinci, his guest at Amboise. Although the nation's power base shifted to Paris around 1600, aristocrats continued to erect luxurious palaces along the Loire until the end of the 18th century. Since that time, many châteaux—too expensive now for even the wealthiest to maintain—have fallen to the care of the state and are now preserved as cultural and historic monuments.

Pleasures and Pastimes

Châteaux

"Loire" and "château" are almost synonymous; even the word, "château"—part fortress, part palace, part mansion—has no English equivalent. More than 20 are described in this chapter, from grandiose Chambord and Saumur to the more intimate Cheverny and Azay-le-Rideau to the incredibly scenic Chenonceau and Ussé. There are genuine castles to admire, too—either preserved in intimidating glory, such as Langeais, Loches, and Angers, or gloriously ruined, like Chinon.

Dining

The Loire region, known as the Garden of France, produces a cornucopia—from beef, poultry, game, and fish to butter, cream, wine, fruit, and vegetables (especially asparagus and mushrooms). It sends its early crops to the best Parisian tables yet keeps more than enough for local use. Loire wines can be extremely good—and varied. Among the best are Savennières and Cheverny (dry white); Coteau du Layon and Montlouis (sweet white); Cabernet d'Anjou (rosé); Bourgueil, Chinon, and Saumur-Champigny (red); and Vouvray (white—dry, sweet, or sparkling).

CATEGORY	COST*
$$$$	over 500 frs
$$$	250 frs–500 frs
$$	125 frs–250 frs
$	under 125 frs

*per person for a three-course meal, including tax (20.6%) and tip but not wine

Lodging

Even before the age of the train, the Loire Valley drew visitors from far and wide. Hundreds of hotels of all kinds have sprung up to accommodate today's travelers. At the higher end of the price scale is the Relais & Châteaux group; some of their best hotels are converted châteaux. At the lower end are the Logis de France hotels: small, traditional inns in towns and villages throughout the region that usually offer terrific value for the money. The Loire Valley is one of the country's most popular vacation destinations, so be sure to make reservations well in advance.

CATEGORY	COST*
$$$$	over 800 frs
$$$	550 frs–800 frs
$$	300 frs–550 frs
$	under 300 frs

All prices are for a standard double room for two, including tax (20.6%) and service charge.

Outdoor Activities

Besides the châteaux, the Loire Valley offers a great variety of outdoor activities, from bicycling to picnicking to walking through rolling hills and along riverbanks. The short distances between châteaux and other attractions make for pleasant bicycling even if you don't want to spend all day pedaling. Bicycles can be rented from many train stations.

Son-et-Lumière

In summer, concerts, music festivals, fairs, and the celebrated son-et-lumière (sound-and-light) extravaganzas held on the grounds of many châteaux abound. Dramatic spectacles that take place after dark, son-et-lumière shows can take the form of historical pageants—with huge casts of people in period costume and caparisoned horses, all floodlit and backed by music and commentary, sometimes in English. They also consist of shows with spoken commentary and dialogue but no visible figures, as at Chenonceau. The most magnificent, with more than 100 performers, takes place at Le Lude.

Exploring the Loire Valley

Pick up the Loire River halfway along its voyage from central France to the Atlantic Ocean. Châteaux and vineyards will accompany you throughout your 340-km (210-mi) westbound course from the hilltop wine town of Sancerre to the bustling city of Angers. Lively towns punctuate the route at almost equal distances—Orléans, Blois, Tours, and Saumur—and are useful bases if you're relying on public transportation. Although you may be rushing around to see as many famous châteaux as possible, try to make time to walk through the poppy-covered hills, picnic along the riverbanks, and sample the local wines. If you want an escape from the usual tourist track, explore the lakes and forests of Sologne or wend your way back along the gentle, confusingly named Loir Valley.

Great Itineraries

You need a fortnight to cover the Loire Valley region in its entirety. But even if you don't have that long, you can still see many of the Loire's finest châteaux in three days by concentrating on the area between Blois and Amboise. Five days will give you time to explore these châteaux as well as visit Tours and Angers, two of the region's major cities. In 10 days you can follow the Loire from Orléans to Angers.

Numbers in the text correspond to numbers in the margin and on the Loire Valley, Orléans, and Tours maps.

IF YOU HAVE 3 DAYS

Begin in **Blois** ⑮ and move inland through the forest to spend the night at 🏰 **Chambord** ⑬. The next day take in nearby **Cheverny** ⑭ and return to the river at 🏰 **Chaumont-sur-Loire** ⑯. Two attractions await just downstream at **Amboise** ⑰: the château and the Clos-Lucé mansion devoted to Leonardo da Vinci. Afterward, take in the Château de Chenonceau (no *x*) in the town of **Chenonceaux** ⑱, for a fitting climax for a visit to this area.

IF YOU HAVE 6 DAYS

Start by following the three-day itinerary through **Blois** ⑮, 🏰 **Chambord** ⑬, **Cheverny** ⑭, 🏰 **Chaumont-sur-Loire** ⑯, and **Amboise** ⑰, spending your third night in either 🏰 **Chenonceaux** ⑱ or the region's major city, 🏰 **Tours** ⑳–㉔. On day four head west to the attractive châteaux of **Azay-le-Rideau** ㉗, **Ussé** ㉚, and 🏰 **Chinon** ㉛. The next day continue downstream to the venerable abbey at **Fontevraud** ㉞ and spend the fifth night in 🏰 **Saumur** ㉟. End up in **Angers** ㊲, a lively city with a dramatic castle and good museums and shops.

IF YOU HAVE 10 DAYS

Stop in **Orléans** ⑦–⑩ on your way west along the Loire, if you are coming from Paris. From there, head to 🏰 **Blois** ⑮ for the night. Over the next two days, explore **Cheverny** ⑭, 🏰 **Chambord** ⑬, **Chaumont-sur-Loire** ⑯, **Amboise** ⑰, and 🏰 **Chenonceaux** ⑱. On day four, detour south to the mighty citadel of **Loches** ⑲, before an overnight stop in 🏰 **Tours** ⑳–㉔. Take in the reconstituted gardens at **Villandry** ㉕ en route to see the Renaissance pleasure palace at 🏰 **Azay-le-Rideau** ㉗. The following day head to the château of **Ussé** ㉚ and the castle at 🏰 **Chinon** ㉛. From Chinon, a short excursion south brings you to the chapel in **Champigny-sur-Veude** ㉜ and the unchanged 17th-century town of **Richelieu** ㉝. Continue west on day eight from Chinon to **Fontevraud** ㉞ and 🏰 **Saumur** ㉟. Spend the next night in 🏰 **Angers** ㊲, with a detour to the imposing Château de Serrant if you have time. Finish with a leisurely drive east through the other Loir Valley, from **Le Lude** ㊴ to the historic town of **Vendôme** ㊵.

When to Tour the Loire Valley

The Loire is at its best in May and June, when it still looks like a river; come midsummer, the water level drops, marooning unsightly sandbanks. The valley can be sultry, stuffy, and crowded in July and August, although most of the son-et-lumière shows take place at this time. October is a good off-season option, when all is mist and mellow fruitfulness along the Loire and the mysterious pools of the Sologne, and the trees are turning russet and gold. The fall is also the best time to sample regional specialties such as wild mushrooms and game. On Sundays, try to avoid the main cities, Orléans, Tours, and Angers—most shops are closed.

THE LOIRE VALLEY

Although Orléans is considered the gateway to the Loire—especially if you're coming from Paris—you may want to start exploring this area farther east. Take in the hilltop wine town of Sancerre, the hunting and ceramics center of Gien, and the ancient abbey of St-Benoît. A string of fine châteaux dominates the valley west of Orléans—Blois, Chaumont, and Amboise lead the way—but the area's most stunning monuments lie inland: romantic Chenonceau, with its arches half-straddling the River Cher, and colossal Chambord, its forest of chimneys and turrets visible above the treetops. Tours, the largest and most central of the cities in the Loire Valley, leads to Ussé and Azay-le-Rideau and the

The Loire Valley

more muscular castles of Chinon and Saumur. At Angers you can drive northeast to explore the winding, intimate Loir Valley all the way to Châteaudun, just south of Chartres and the Ile-de-France; or continue along the Loire as far as Nantes, the gateway to Brittany.

Sancerre

❶ *200 km (125 mi) south of Paris via A6 and N7, 120 km (75 mi) southeast of Orléans.*

The hilltop town of Sancerre is a maze of old cobbled streets offering dramatic views of the mountainous vineyards that produce its flinty white wine. Forget about the Loire's reputation for soft pastures and gentle hills: The vineyards of Sancerre (like the town itself) stand on rugged, towering mounds and are among the most scenic in France. The steep, climbing country roads west of town provide panoramic views. Head for **Chavignol,** just over 3 km (2 mi) away, a wine village with a number of producers who offer sales and tastings. Chavignol is also home to a delicious small round goat cheese, Crottin de Chavignol, that comes soft or hard, depending on the time of year. This famous goat cheese, and other local cheeses, is celebrated in Sancerre every April during the **Fête du Crottin.**

En Route   Head north from Sancerre on D955 and D951 along the west bank of the Loire for 36 km (22 mi) to Châtillon. Stay on D951 and pause to admire the **Pont-Canal de Briare,** a splendid, lamp-lined aqueduct built by Gustave Eiffel in 1890 (the year after his tower) to transport the Canal Latéral de la Loire (Loire Side Canal) across the river. You can walk along the top to admire the view, then have a drink outside the café at the far end of the aqueduct, or saunter into the village of Briare to admire the colorful riverboats moored along the pretty quay. A few miles farther along the west bank of the Loire is the 12th-century castle of **St-Brisson,** whose collection of 13th-century mangonels (giant catapults) is activated by local strongmen every Sunday in summer. The biggest catapult, known as a *couillard,* sends rocks that weigh 45 pounds spinning as high as the castle roof before crashing 150 yards away. From Brisson, continue on to Gien.

Gien

❷ *6 km (4 mi) northwest of St-Brisson; 51 km (32 mi) northwest of Sancerre via D955 and D951; 67 km (42 mi) southeast of Orléans.*

Ceramics and hunting are the twin historical attractions of the pleasant riverside town of Gien. Its redbrick château, completed in 1484, ★ houses the unexpectedly fine **Musée International de la Chasse** (International Hunting Museum). Exhibits trace the various types of hunt—shooting, trapping, fox hunting with hounds—and the display of firearms ranges from harquebuses to rifles. A 13-ft horn (the usual length before a hunting horn is coiled up into its familiar circle) sounds an offbeat note from the ceiling of one room; vast 18th-century hunting pictures by François Desportes and Jean-Baptiste Oudry, dogs and boar to the fore, line the stately hall with its superb beamed roof. ✉ *pl. du Château,* ☎ *02–38–67–69–69.* ✇ *35 frs.* ☉ *Apr.–Oct., daily 9:30–6:30; Nov.–Mar., daily 9–noon and 2–5.*

At the **Musée de la Faïencerie** (Earthenware Factory Museum), in an old paste store, admire local Gien earthenware (both old and new), with its distinctive deep blue glaze and golden decoration. Call ahead to arrange a tour of the factory; there's also a shop. ✉ *78 pl. de la Victoire,* ☎ *02–38–67–00–05.* ✇ *20 frs.* ☉ *Apr.–Sept., daily 9–11:45 and 2–5:45; Oct.–Mar., daily 2–6.*

Dining and Lodging

$$ ✕🏨 **Rivage.** Jolly *patron* Christian Gaillard, unmistakable behind his huge Gallic moustache, presides over the finest hotel in Gien. Rooms are large and airy, breakfasts are copious, and the piano bar, with its terrace overlooking Loire, is the ideal place to relax before or after a dinner. Fish and herbs are likely to figure in your meal at the restaurant, unless you opt for the snails or veal kidneys with fresh pasta. Menus start at around 150 francs, and there is an extensive wine cellar. ✉ *1 quai de Nice, 45500,* ☎ *02–38–37–79–00,* FAX *02–38–38–10–21. 16 rooms, 9 with shower, 7 with bath. Restaurant. AE, DC, MC, V.*

Sully-sur-Loire

❸ *24 km (15 mi) northwest of Gien via D951, 48 km (30 mi) southeast of Orléans.*

An imposing castle with a park, moat, and spectacular medieval roof makes Sully-sur-Loire worth visiting. The **Château de Sully** dates from the first half of the 14th century. It has a sturdy keep with the finest chestnut roof anywhere along the Loire—a vast structure in the form of an upturned boat, constructed in 1400. The chestnut has the useful property of repelling insects; no sensible spider would spin a web in it. ☎ *02–38–36–36–86.* 🎫 *25 frs.* ⊙ *June–Aug., daily 10–6; Sept.–May, daily 10–noon and 2–5.*

St-Benoît-sur-Loire

❹ *8 km (5 mi) northwest of Sully-sur-Loire via D60, 40 km (30 mi) southeast of Orléans.*

The highlight of St-Benoît-sur-Loire is its ancient abbey, often called the greatest Romanesque church in France. Village signposts refer to it as "La Basilique."

St-Benoît (St. Benedict) was the founder of the Benedictine monastic order. In AD 650, a group of monks chose this safe and fertile spot for their new monastery, then returned to Monte Cassino, Italy, to retrieve the bones of St. Benedict with which to bless the site. Despite demands from priests at Monte Cassino for the return of the bones, some of the relics remain here, in the 11th-century **Abbaye St-Benoît.** Following the Hundred Years' War in the 14th and 15th centuries, the monastery fell into a decline, and the Wars of Religion (1562–98) wrought further damage. During the French Revolution, the monks dispersed and all the buildings were destroyed, except the abbey church itself, which became the parish church.

Monastic life here began anew in 1944, when the monks rebuilt their monastery and regained the church for their own use. The pillars of the tower porch are noted for their intricately carved capitals, and the choir floor is an amazing patchwork of many-color marble. Gregorian chants can be heard daily, at mass or vespers, and Sunday services attract worshipers and music lovers from all around. You are welcome to explore the church crypt. ☎ *02–38–35–72–43.* ⊙ *Mass and vespers Sun. 11 AM and 6:15 PM, Mon.–Sat. noon and 6:15 PM. Guided English-language tours of the monastic buildings can be arranged; inquire at the monastery shop.*

Germigny-des-Prés

❺ *6 km (4 mi) northwest of St-Benoît-sur-Loire via D60, 34 km (21 mi) southeast of Orléans.*

The village of Germigny-des-Prés is famous for its church, one of the oldest in France. Around AD 800, Theodulf, an abbot of St-Benoît, built the tiny **Église de Germigny-les-Prés**—a Byzantine arrangement of round arches on square pillars, with indirect light filtering from smaller arches above the central square. The church was carefully restored to its original condition during the last century. Though Theodulf himself brought most of the original mosaics from Italy, only one—covered by plaster and not discovered until 1848—survives. Made of 130,000 cubes of colored glass, it shows the Ark of the Covenant transported by angels with golden halos. The Latin inscription asks us not to forget Theodulf in our prayers. ☉ *Daily 9–noon and 2–5.*

Châteauneuf-sur-Loire

6 *5 km (3 mi) northwest of Germigny-des-Prés.*

The village of Châteauneuf-sur-Loire has a delightful public park with giant tulip trees, magnolias, weeping willows, and rhododendrons and is especially beautiful in late May and early June. Little streams on their way to the Loire snake their way across the parkland, past benches, shady copses, and scenic picnic spots.

In the town hall is the small **Musée de la Marine** (Maritime Museum), chronicling the history of navigation on the Loire. ⊠ *1 pl. Aristide-Briand,* ☎ *02–38–58–41–18.* ⊡ *12 frs.* ☉ *July–Aug., Wed.–Mon. 10–noon and 2–6; June, Mon. and Wed.–Fri. 2–6; Jan.–Mar., Sun. 2–5:30.*

Orléans

125 km (78 mi) south of Paris; 112 km (70 mi) northeast of Tours.

As a natural bridgehead over the Loire, Orléans has long been the focus of hostile confrontations and invasions. In 52 BC Julius Caesar slaughtered its inhabitants and burned it to the ground. Five centuries later, Attila and the Huns did much the same. Next came the Normans; then the Valois kings turned it into a secondary capital. The story of the Hundred Years' War, Joan of Arc, and the Siege of Orléans is widely known. During the Wars of Religion (1562–98), much of the cathedral was destroyed. A century ago, ham-fisted town planners razed many of the city's fine old buildings. Both German and Allied bombs helped finish the job during World War II. Today, however, Orléans is a thriving commercial city; sensitive urban renewal has done much to bring it back to life, especially the medieval streets between the Loire and the cathedral.

7 The **Cathédrale Ste-Croix** is a riot of pinnacles and gargoyles, both Gothic and pseudo-Gothic, embellished with 18th-century wedding-cake towers. After most of the cathedral was destroyed in the 16th century during the Wars of Religion, Henry IV and his successors rebuilt it. Novelist Marcel Proust (1871–1922) called it France's ugliest church, but most people find it impressive. Inside are vast quantities of stained glass and 18th-century wood carving, plus the modern **Chapelle de Jeanne d'Arc** (Joan of Arc Chapel), with plaques in memory of the British and American war dead. ⊠ *pl. Ste-Croix.* ☉ *Daily 9–noon and 2–6.*

8 The modern **Musée des Beaux-Arts** (Fine Arts Museum) is across from the cathedral. Take the elevator to the top of the five-story building; then make your way down to see works by such artists as Tintoretto, Velázquez, Watteau, Boucher, Rodin, and Gauguin. The museum's richest collection is its 17th-century French paintings. ⊠ *1 rue Ferdinand-Rabier,* ☎ *02–38–53–39–22.* ⊡ *20 frs.* ☉ *Wed.–Mon. 11–6.*

132

Cathédrale
Ste-Croix, **7**
Maison de
Jeanne d'Arc, **10**
Musée des
Beaux-Arts, **8**
Musée
Historique, **9**

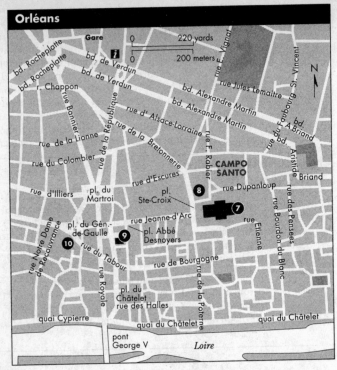

Orléans

9 The **Musée Historique** (Orléans's History Museum) is housed in the **Hôtel Cabu**, a Renaissance mansion restored after World War II. It contains both "fine" and "popular" works of art connected with the town's past, including a remarkable collection of pagan bronzes of animals and dancers. These bronzes were hidden from zealous Christian missionaries in the 4th century and discovered in a sandpit near St-Benoît in 1861. ⊠ *pl. de l'Abbé-Desnoyers*, ☎ *02–38–79–25–60.* ⊡ *13 frs.* ☉ *July–Aug., Tues.–Sun. 10–6; Sept.–June, Wed. and weekends 2–6.*

During the 10-day Siege of Orléans in 1429, 17-year-old Joan of Arc **10** stayed on the site of the **Maison de Jeanne d'Arc** (Joan of Arc's House). This faithful reconstruction of the house she knew contains exhibits about her life and costumes and weapons of her time. Several dioramas modeled by Lucien Harmey recount the main episodes in her life, from the audience at Chinon to the coronation at Reims; her seizure at Compiègne; and the stake at Rouen. ⊠ *3 pl. du Général-de-Gaulle,* ☎ *02–38–52–99–89.* ⊡ *13 frs.* ☉ *May–Oct., Tues.–Sun. 10–noon and 2–6; Nov.–Apr., Tues.–Sun. 2–6.*

Dining and Lodging

$$ ✕ **Au Rétro.** Although this bustling restaurant, decorated with old movie posters, stays open late (orders are taken until 10:30 PM), service is unflappable. House specialties include ravioli with scallops, bream with smoked ham, and baked apple desserts. ⊠ *34 rue Notre-Dame-de-Recouvrance,* ☎ *02–38–53–49–17. AE, DC, MC, V. Closed Sun.*

$$ ✕▦ **Rivage.** This small, white-walled hotel south of Orléans is a pleasant base for exploring the city. Each of the compact rooms has a little balcony with a view of the tree-lined river; the bathrooms are tiny. There is no elevator. The dining room opens onto a terrace facing the Loire. The menu changes with the season—if you're lucky, chef François

Tassain's memorable crayfish, lamb marinated in paprika, and glazed green apple soufflé with apple marmalade will be on the menu. ⊠ *635 rue de la Reine-Blanche, 45160 Olivet (5 km/3 mi south of Orléans), ☎ 02–38–66–02–93, FAX 02–38–56–31–11. 17 rooms, 11 with shower, 6 with bath. Restaurant, tennis court. AE, DC, MC, V. Closed late Dec.–mid-Jan.*

Nightlife and the Arts

The two-day **Fête de Jeanne d'Arc** (Joan of Arc Festival), on May 7 and 8, celebrates the heroic Maid of Orléans with a military parade and religious procession.

Meung-sur-Loire

⓫ *16 km (10 mi) southwest of Orléans via N152.*

Intimate Meung-sur-Loire is not as commercial as Amboise or Azay-le-Rideau. The town's most famous citizen was Jehan de Meung, born in 1260 and author of the best-selling *Roman de la Rose* (Geoffrey Chaucer produced a well-known English translation). Give yourself time to wander down rue Jehan-de-Meung, the street that leads off the main square away from the château, to see the half-timber houses.

The **Château de Meung** is part 12th-century fortress, part 18th-century residence. From the 12th century to the French Revolution, it served mainly as the official residence of the bishops of Orléans, although, in 1429, Lord Salisbury used it as his headquarters during the Siege of Orléans. (When he was killed in the fray, Lord Talbot took over but could not prevent Joan of Arc from capturing the château.) It was sold after the French Revolution, and had stood empty and derelict for years before private restoration began in the early 1970s. It has since been furnished with a diverse collection of items that range from 12th-century antiques to medieval crossbows, World War II submachine guns, and military helmets from the Middle Ages to 1945. The most unusual part of the château is underground: a network of tunnels, dungeons, and storehouses, with a chapel and torture chamber. ⊠ *16 pl. du Martroi, ☎ 02–38–44–36–47. ⊡ 35 frs. ☉ Apr.–Oct., daily 9:30–5; Nov.–Mar., daily 10:30–noon and 2:30–4:30; guided visits only.*

Dining and Lodging

$–$$ ✕🏠 **St-Jacques.** This inn, on Meung's busy main road, is just a five-★ minute walk from the château and the river. At the family-run restaurant (closed Monday), excellent fresh food is served without fuss at deliciously low prices. The prix-fixe menus might include oysters, fillet of duck in a raspberry vinaigrette, lamb or fish, cheese, and dessert. The clean, simple rooms either have a shower or, for 20 francs more, a full bath. ⊠ *60 rue du Général-de-Gaulle, 45130, ☎ 02–38–44–30–39, FAX 02–38–45–17–02. 12 rooms. Restaurant. AE, MC, V. Closed last 2 wks in Jan.*

Beaugency

⓬ *7 km (4 mi) southwest of Meung.*

A clutch of historic towers and buildings around a 14th-century bridge over the Loire gives Beaugency its charm. The buildings include the massive 11th-century **Donjon** (Keep), the Romanesque church of **Notre-Dame**, and the **Tour du Diable** (Devil's Tower) overlooking the river. The **Château Dunois** contains a regional museum with traditional costumes and peasant furniture. ⊠ *2 pl. Dunois, ☎ 02–38–44–55–23. ⊡ 22 frs. ☉ Apr.–Oct., Wed.–Mon. 10–noon and 2–5.*

Chambord

★ ⑬ *24 km (15 mi) southwest of Beaugency via D925, D951, and D112;*
19 km (12 mi) east of Blois; 45 km (28 mi) southwest of Orléans; 175
km (109 mi) southwest of Paris.

The largest of the Loire châteaux, the **Château de Chambord** is in the
middle of a royal game forest with a cluster of buildings—barely a village—across the road. Chambord is the kind of place William Ran-
dolph Hearst might have built if he'd had more money. Variously
dubbed "megalomaniac" and "an enormous film-set extravaganza,"
this is one of the most extraordinary structures in Europe.

A few facts about the château set the tone: The facade is 420 ft long,
there are 440 rooms and 365 chimneys, and a wall 32 km (20 mi) long
encloses the 13,000-acre forest (you can wander through 3,000 acres
of it; the rest is reserved for wild boar and other game). Under François
I, building began in 1519, a job that took 12 years and required 1,800
workers. His original grandiose idea was to divert the Loire to form
a moat, but someone (perhaps his adviser, Leonardo da Vinci) persuaded
him to make do with the River Cosson. François I used the château
only for short stays; yet when he came, 12,000 horses were required
to transport his luggage, servants, and entourage! Later kings also used
Chambord as an occasional retreat, and Louis XIV, the Sun King, had
Molière perform here. In the 18th century, Louis XV gave the château
to Maréchal de Saxe as a reward for his victory over the English and
Dutch at Fontenoy (southern Belgium) in 1745. When not besporting
himself with wine, women, and song, the marshal stood on the roof
to oversee the exercises of his own regiment of 1,000 cavalry. Now,
after long neglect—all the original furnishings vanished during the French
Revolution—Chambord belongs to the state.

You can wander freely through the vast rooms, filled with a variety of
exhibits (including a hunting museum opened in 1997)—not all concerned with Chambord, but interesting nonetheless. The enormous, dou-
ble-helix staircase looks like a single staircase, but an entire regiment
could march up one spiral while a second came down the other, and
they would never meet. Also be sure to visit the roof terrace, whose forest of towers, turrets, cupolas, gables, and chimneys was described by
19th-century novelist Henry James as "more like the spires of a city than
the salient points of a single building." The château is sumptuously illuminated at night, and a short **son-et-lumière** show in French, English,
and German, successively, is held on many evenings from mid-May to
mid-October; admission is 50 francs. ☎ *02–54–50–40–28.* 🖾 *40 frs.*
🕙 *Apr.–Aug., daily 9:30–6:30; Sept.–Mar., daily 9:30–5:15.*

Dining and Lodging

$$ ✕🏨 **Grand St-Michel.** Enjoy simple and comfortable quarters in this
revamped country house at the edge of the woods, across from the
château. A few of the rooms have spectacular views, the restaurant serves
hearty local fare (including game in the fall), and there's a pleasant café-
terrace—just the place for contemplation while sipping a drink. 🖂 *103*
pl. St-Michel, 41250, ☎ *02–54–20–31–31,* 🅵🅰🆇 *02–54–20–36–40.*
39 rooms, 31 with bath. Restaurant, tennis court. MC, V. Closed mid-
Nov.–late Dec.

$$ 🏨 **Château de Colliers.** Rooms at this 18th-century manor are simply
★ furnished. Bathrooms are country-house style—the tub has a handheld
showerhead. The Empire Room not only contains marvelous antiques,
but it also has a private rooftop terrace with views of the Loire. Dine
on a wholesome table d'hôte dinner (make arrangements in advance)
in the dining room, where there are murals on the walls and ceilings.

Afternoon tea or an aperitif on the terrace overlooking the Loire is an ideal way to end the day. ✉ *41500 Muides-sur-Loire (6 km/4 mi north of Chambord)*, ☎ *02–54–87–50–75,* FAX *02–54–87–03–64. 5 rooms. Pool, tennis court. MC, V. Closed Dec.–mid-Mar.*

Outdoor Activities and Sports

Rent a horse from the former stables of the **Maréchal de Saxe** (✉ on grounds of Château de Chambord, ☎ 02–54–20–31–01) and ride through the vast national park that surrounds the château. From March through October you can hire a boat to explore the château moat and the **Grand Canal** linking it to the River Cosson (☎ 02–54–56–00–43 for details).

Cheverny

⑭ *17 km (11 mi) south of Chambord via D112 and D102, 13 km (8 mi) southeast of Blois via D765.*

Cheverny has become synonymous with its restrained, classical château, although the village is officially named Cour-Cheverny.

One of the last in the area to be built, the **Château de Cheverny** was finished in 1634. Its white, elegantly proportioned, classical facade greets you across manicured lawns. The interior—with its painted and gilded rooms, splendid furniture, and rich tapestries depicting the *Labors of Hercules*—is one of the grandest in the Loire region. In the gallery there's a bronze of George Washington alongside a document that bears his signature.

Unfortunately, the gardens are off-limits, as is the orangery, where the *Mona Lisa* and other masterpieces were hidden during World War II. But you are free to contemplate the antlers of 2,000 stags in the Trophy Room. Hunting, called "venery" in the leaflets, continues vigorously here, with red coats, bugles, and all. In the château's kennels, hordes of hungry hounds lounge about, dreaming of their next kill. Feeding times—*la soupe aux chiens*—are posted on a notice board, and you are welcome to watch the dogs wolf down their dinner. You can visit the château grounds by either boat or electric buggy, or get a bird's-eye view from 500 ft up in a hot-air balloon; purchase tickets on the spot. ☎ 02–54–79–96–29. ⊟ 32 frs. ⊙ Mar.–Sept., daily 9–6:30; Oct.–Feb., daily 9:30–noon and 2:15–5.

OFF THE BEATEN PATH **SOLOGNE –** This flat, wooded region, famed for its game, mushrooms, asparagus, and hidden lakes, occupies a vast area of partly drained marshland south of the Loire, between Cour-Cheverny in the west and Gien in the east. With rare exceptions, such as the market town of Romorantin-Lanthenay or the Royal Scottish Stuarts' onetime stronghold of Aubigny-sur-Nère (their 16th-century château is now the town hall), nature—and silence—holds peaceful sway.

Dining

$$$ ✗ **Relais de Bracieux.** Chef Bernard Robin produces fine nouvelle cuisine in his gleaming kitchens, but connoisseurs savor his simpler dishes: carp, game in season, and salmon with beef marrow. The attentive staff brings delicious tidbits to keep you busy between courses. ✉ *1 av. de Chambord, Bracieux (9 km/6 mi northeast of Cour-Cheverny on the road to Chambord)*, ☎ 02–54–46–41–22. *Reservations essential. Jacket and tie. AE, MC, V. Closed Wed. (except July–Aug.). No dinner Tues.*

Blois

★ ⓵⑤   *13 km (8 mi) northwest of Cour-Cheverny via D765, 54 km (34 mi) southwest of Orléans, 58 km (36 mi) northeast of Tours.*

Perched on a steep hillside that overlooks the Loire, bustling Blois is a convenient base for exploring the eastern Loire and is well served by train and expressway. There is a signposted route for a walking tour of the **Vieille Ville** (Old Town)—maps are available from the tourist office. The best view of the town, with its château and numerous church spires rising sharply above the river, is from the Pont Gabriel bridge, on the other side of the Loire.

The massive **Château de Blois** spans several architectural periods and is among the valley's finest. Your ticket entitles you to a guided tour—in English when there are enough visitors who can't understand French—but you are more than welcome to roam around without a guide if you visit between mid-March and August. Before you enter, stand in the courtyard to admire four centuries of architecture. On one side stand the 13th-century hall and tower, the latter offering a stunning view of the town and countryside. The Renaissance begins to flower in the Louis XII wing (built between 1498 and 1503), through which you enter, and comes to full bloom in the François I wing (1515–24). The masterpiece here is the openwork spiral staircase, painstakingly restored. The fourth side consists of the classical Gaston d'Orléans wing (1635–38).

At the bottom of the spiral staircase is a *diaporama*, an audiovisual display that traces the château's history. Upstairs is a series of enormous rooms with tremendous fireplaces, decorated with the gilded porcupine, emblem of Louis XII; the ermine of Anne of Brittany; and, of course, François I's salamander, breathing fire and surrounded by flickering flames. Many rooms have intricate ceilings and carved, gilded paneling; there is even a sad little picture of Mary, Queen of Scots. In the great council room, the Duc de Guise was murdered on the orders of Henri III in 1588. In the **Musée des Beaux-Arts** (Fine Arts Museum), in the Louis XII wing, you'll find royal portraits, including Rubens's puffy portrayal of Maria de' Medici as France Personified. Most evenings from April through September, **son-et-lumière** shows in French and English are staged. Call the château or the tourist office (☞ The Loire Valley A to Z, *below*) for details; admission is 50 francs. ☎ 02–54–74–16–06. 🖼 35 frs. ☉ Apr.–Aug., daily 9–6; Sept.–Mar., daily 9–12:30 and 2–5:30.

Dining and Lodging

$$$ ✕ **Péniche.** This innovative restaurant is actually a luxurious barge moored on the bank of the Loire. Chef Germain Bosque serves beautifully presented fresh seafood dishes (notably lobsters and oysters). ⊠ *promenade du Mail, quai St-Jean,* ☎ 02–54–74–37–23. AE, DC, MC, V.

$$ ✕ **Rendez-Vous des Pêcheurs.** This modest restaurant near the Loire
★   has simple decor but offers excellent value for its creative cooking. Chef Eric Reithler studied under Guy Savoy in Paris and has brought inventiveness to his fish and seafood specialties. ⊠ *27 rue du Foix,* ☎ 02–54–74–67–48. MC, V. Closed Sun. and Aug. No dinner Mon.

$$ ✕🏠 **Médicis.** Rooms at this smart little hotel about 1 km (½ mi) from the château are comfortable, air-conditioned, and soundproof. All share a joyous color scheme but are individually furnished. If you wish to splurge, the suite has a whirlpool. The restaurant alone makes a stay here worthwhile. Chef-owner Christian Garanger turns his innovative classical dishes into a presentation—*coquilles St-Jacques* (scallops) with a pear fondue and thin slices of roast hare with black-currant sauce. (The restaurant is closed dinner Sunday off-season.) The staff

is cheerful. ✉ *2 allée François-Ier, 41000,* ☎ *02–54–43–94–04,* FAX *02–54–42–04–05. 12 rooms, 1 suite. Restaurant, air-conditioning. AE, DC, MC, V. Closed Jan.*

\$\$ 🏨 **Anne de Bretagne.** Although this simple pension—on a small square across from the cathedral—is nothing to rave about, the rooms, up rather steep stairs, are clean and neat, with bright bedspreads and curtains. There's space to keep your car on the street, which is a plus, and a small bar next door, a congenial spot for a nightcap. ✉ *31 av. du Dr- Jean-Laigret, 41000,* ☎ *02–54–78–05–38,* FAX *02–54–74–37–79. 30 rooms, 24 with bath. AE, DC, MC, V. Closed mid-Feb.–mid-Mar.*

Chaumont-sur-Loire

⑯ *21 km (13 mi) southwest of Blois via D751.*

Chaumont is best known for its sturdy castle with famous stables and magnificent panorama of the Loire. Built between 1465 and 1510, the **Château de Chaumont** was given to Henri II's mistress, Diane de Poitiers, by his wife, Catherine de' Medici, to get her out of the Château de Chenonceau. Benjamin Franklin was a regular visitor here. The interior has been extensively restored but retains less cachet than the majestic stables, where purebreds dined like royalty. ☎ *02–54–51–26–26.* 🎫 *32 frs.* ⊙ *Apr.–Sept., daily 9:30–6:30; Oct.–Mar., daily 10–5.*

Dining and Lodging

\$\$\$ ✕🏨 **Domaine des Hauts-de-Loire.** Across the river from Chaumont is
★ this exquisite hotel in an 18th-century, turreted, vine-covered hunting lodge on 180 acres. Rooms in the main house are furnished with antiques, which creates an aristocratic air; those in the adjacent carriage houses have a mix of old and modern furnishings that harmonize with the exposed brick walls and gabled ceilings. Service is relaxed and unpretentious; the restaurant (closed Monday and Tuesday lunch off-season) is first-class, and in 1993 chef Rémy Giraud was justifiably awarded his second Michelin star. ✉ *rte. de Mesland, 41150 Onzain (on the other side of the river from Chaumont),* ☎ *02–54–20–72–57,* FAX *02–54–20–77–32. 28 rooms, 7 suites. Restaurant, pool, tennis court, fishing, helipad. AE, DC, MC, V. Closed Dec.–Feb.*

Amboise

★ ⑰ *17 km (11 mi) southwest of Chaumont-sur-Loire via D751, 26 km (16 mi) east of Tours.*

Memories of Leonardo da Vinci, a historic château that overlooks the Loire, bustling markets, narrow medieval streets, and plenty of hotels and restaurants make Amboise a superb base.

The **Château d'Amboise** stands on a flattened hill that was originally a Stone Age settlement, fortified in the Iron Age by a ditch and a rampart. An early bridge gave the stronghold strategic importance. In AD 503, Clovis, king of the Franks, met with Alaric, king of the Visigoths, at Amboise. But the 15th and 16th centuries were Amboise's golden age, when the château, enlarged and embellished, became a royal palace. Charles VII stayed here, as did the unfortunate Charles VIII, best remembered for banging his head on a low doorway (you will be shown it) and dying as a result. François I, whose long nose appears in so many château paintings, based his court here. In 1560 his son, François II, settled here with his wife, Mary Stuart (otherwise known as Mary, Queen of Scots), and his mother, Catherine de' Medici. The castle was also the setting for the Amboise Conspiracy, an ill-fated Protestant plot organized against François II; you are shown where the corpses of 1,200 conspirators dangled from the castle walls. Decline and demolition occurred before and after the Revolution; today only about a third of the original building remains.

The château's interior is partly furnished, though not with the original objects; these vanished when the building was converted into a barracks and then a button factory. The great round tower has a spiral ramp rather than a staircase; designed for horsemen, it is wide enough to accommodate a small car. You are free to explore the grounds at your own pace, including the little chapel of St-Hubert with its carvings of the Virgin and Child, Charles VIII, and Anne of Brittany. Son-et-lumière pageants take place at the château daily in July and August. ☎ 02–47–57–00–98. ▣ 37 frs; son-et-lumière 30 frs–90 frs. ☉ Oct.–Mar., daily 9–noon and 2–5; Apr.–June and Sept., daily 9–noon and 2–6:30; July–Aug., daily 9–6:30.

☾ The **Clos Lucé,** a few hundred yards up rue Victor-Hugo from the château, is a handsome Renaissance manor where Leonardo da Vinci spent the last four years of his life and died in 1519. The basement contains working models built by IBM engineers (using the detailed sketches in his notebooks) of some of Leonardo's extraordinary inventions. Mechanisms on display include three-speed gearboxes, a military tank, a clockwork car, and even a flying machine complete with designs for parachutes. Leonardo was several centuries ahead of his time. ⌧ 2 rue du Clos-Lucé, ☎ 02–47–57–62–88. ▣ 38 frs. ☉ Sept.–Oct. and Apr.–June, daily 9–6; Nov.–Mar., daily 10–5; July–Aug., daily 9–7.

Dining and Lodging

$$$ ✕ **Manoir St-Thomas.** Between the château and the Clos Lucé, this restaurant occupies a fine Renaissance building with an adjacent garden. Chef François Le Coz serves elegant, traditional food, including ravioli aux huîtres (with oysters and caviar), and suprême de pintade farci (stuffed guinea-fowl breast). The list of Touraine wines is enticing. ⌧ 1 mail St-Thomas, ☎ 02–47–57–22–52. Jacket and tie. AE, DC, MC, V. Closed Mon.

$$–$$$ ✕▥ **Château de Pray.** This former 13th-century fortress transformed during the Renaissance into a pleasant manor is surrounded by a 25-acre park and a lovely garden. The inside has a cozy, hunting-lodge ambience; the elegantly appointed guest rooms have carved wooden furniture and modern conveniences. One drawback is the hotel's lack of comfortable public spaces. The restaurant has improved greatly under chef Bruno Delagneau, and you can enjoy a roaring fire and fine views of the river. ⌧ rte. de Chargé, 37530 Chargé (1½ km/1 mi east of Amboise via D751, on the south bank of the Loire), ☎ 02–47–57–23–67, ⅻ 02–47–57–32–50. 17 rooms, 2 suites. Restaurant, pool. AE, DC, MC, V. Closed Jan.

$ ✕▥ **Le Blason.** Behind the château and a five-minute walk from the center of town, this delightful, small hotel is enlivened by its enthusiastic
★   owners. The old building has rooms of different shapes and sizes: No. 229, for example, has exposed beams and a cathedral ceiling; No. 109 is comfortably spacious and has a good view of the square. In the restaurant, superior, reasonably priced fare is served. The menu changes seasonally, but may include roast lamb with garlic and salmon carpaccio with mustard dressing. ⌧ 11 pl. Richelieu, 37400, ☎ 02–47–23–22–41, ⅻ 02–47–57–56–18. 29 rooms. Restaurant. AE, DC, MC, V.

$$$ ✕▥ **Choiseul.** Classical elegance and a superb restaurant characterize this Relais & Châteaux hotel on the bank of the Loire, just below the château. The grounds are small but neat. Be sure to visit the caverns, where temporary art exhibits are often held. Though rooms are modern, they retain an old and distinctive feel. The highly rated young chef, Pascal Bouvier, cooks up such specialties as lobster in pastry and beef

with truffles. Prix-fixe menus start at 190 francs at lunch and 280 francs at dinner. ✉ *36 quai Charles-Guinot, 37400,* ☎ *02–47–30–45–45,* FAX *02–47–30–46–10. 32 rooms. Restaurant, pool. AE, DC, MC, V. Closed Dec.–Jan.*

En Route Just 3 km (2 mi) south of Amboise on the road to the town of Chenonceaux, pause at the **Pagode de Chanteloup,** an extraordinary 140-ft, seven-story Chinese-style pagoda built for the Duc de Choiseul in 1778.

Chenonceaux

⓳ *12 km (8 mi) south of Amboise via D81 and D40; 32 km (20 mi) east of Tours.*

★ The small village of Chenonceaux, on the River Cher, is best known as the site of the **Château de Chenonceau** (without the *x*). From historical figures like Diane de Poitiers, Catherine de' Medici, and Mary, Queen of Scots, to a host of modern travel writers, many have called it the "most romantic" of all the Loire châteaux. Its site, straddling the river, is one of the prettiest and most unusual in France. You could happily spend half a day wandering through the château and grounds. During the peak summer season the château is open—unlike many others—all day. The only drawback is its popularity: If you want to avoid a roomful of English schoolchildren, take a stroll in the grounds and come back when they stop for lunch.

More pleasure palace than fortress, the château was built in 1520 by Thomas Bohier, a wealthy tax collector. When he went bankrupt, it passed to François I. Later, Henri II gave it to his mistress, Diane de Poitiers. After his death, Henri's not-so-understanding widow, Catherine de' Medici, expelled Diane to nearby Chaumont and took back the château. It is to Catherine that we owe the lovely gardens and the handsome, three-story extension whose arches span the River Cher.

Before you go inside, pick up an English leaflet at the gate. Then walk around to the right of the main building to see the harmonious, delicate architecture beyond the formal garden, with the river gliding under the arches. The romantically inclined may want to rent a rowboat and spend an hour drifting. Inside the château are splendid ceilings, colossal fireplaces, authentic furnishings, and paintings by Rubens, del Sarto, and Correggio. As you tour the rooms, be sure to pay your respects to former owner Mme. Dupin, tellingly captured in Nattier's charming portrait: Thanks to the great affection she inspired among her proletarian neighbors, the château and its treasures survived the Revolution intact. The château's history is illustrated with wax figures in the **Musée des Cires,** housed in one of the château's outbuildings. Every night from mid-June to mid-September, excellent **son-et-lumière** shows are performed in the illuminated château gardens. ☎ *02–47–23–90–07.* 🎫 *Château 45 frs, wax museum 10 frs, son-et-lumière 40 frs.* ☉ *Mid-Feb.–mid-Nov., daily 9–5, 6, or 7, depending on the season; mid-Nov.–mid-Feb., daily 9–4:30.*

OFF THE BEATEN PATH **VALENÇAY –** Although 49 km (31 mi) southeast of Chenonceaux, Valençay may entice you and your family with its lusciously furnished château, collection of vintage cars, son-et-lumière shows, and eccentric outdoor appeal: The grounds include statues, manicured hedges, peacocks, llamas, and intrepid kangaroos. ☎ *02–54–00–15–69.* 🎫 *42 frs.* ☉ *Mid-Mar.–mid-Nov., daily 9–noon and 2–dusk or 8; mid-Nov.–mid-Mar., weekends 2–5.*

Dining and Lodging

$$–$$$ ✕▥ **Bon Laboureur.** In 1882 this place won Henry James's praise as
★ a simple, rustic inn. Since then, through four generations of the Jeudi
family, it has become an elegantly modern hotel. Rooms in the old house
are comfortably traditional; those in the former stables are larger and
more contemporary; the biggest and most elegant are in the manor house
across the street. For honeymooners there is a small separate house. A
large garden, with fountains and streams, supplies vegetables and
herbs for the kitchen. The food is commendable—try the excellent turbot with hollandaise or the braised rabbit with dried fruits. Make your
dinner reservations early for a table in the original dining room rather
than in the annex. ✉ *6 rue du Dr-Bretonneau, 37150,* ☎ *02–47–23–
90–02,* ℻ *02–47–23–82–01. 36 rooms. Restaurant, pool, bicycles.
AE, DC, MC, V. Closed mid-Nov.–mid-Dec.*

Loches

⑲   *27 km (17 mi) south of Chenonceaux via D40, D80, and D31; 49 km
(31 mi) west of Valençay; 39 km (24 mi) southeast of Tours.*

On a rocky spur just beside the River Indre is small, picturesque, medieval Loches. The town is dominated by its **Citadelle.** Unlike Chinon's,
which is a ruined shell, much of Loches's defensive walls are well preserved and function as part of the town. At one end is the castle,
whose terrace provides a fine view of the roofs and river below and
the towers and swallows' nests above; on the other end is the keep.

Inside the **Logis Royaux** (château), on the north end of the citadel, look
for the vicious, two-man crossbow that could pierce an oak door at
200 yards. There are some interesting pictures, too, including a copy
of the well-known portrait that shows an extremely disgruntled Charles
VII and one of his mistresses, Agnès Sorel, poised as a virtuous Virgin
Mary (though semi-topless). Her alabaster image decorates her tomb,
guarded by angels and lambs. Agnès died in 1450 at age 28, probably
poisoned by Charles's son, the future Louis XI. The little chapel was
built by Charles VIII for his queen, Anne of Brittany, and is lavishly
decorated with sculpted ermine tails, the lady's emblem. In the **donjon** (keep), on the south side of the citadel, one 11th-century tower,
half-ruined and roofless, is open for exploration; the others require guided
supervision. These towers contain dungeons and will delight anyone
who revels in prison cells and torture chambers. The citadel church of
St-Ours has a striking roof formed of octagonal pyramids, which dates
from the 12th century; a doorway sculpted with owls, monkeys, and
mythical beasts; and a baptismal font converted from a Roman altar.
✉ *pl. Charles-VII,* ☎ *02–47–59–01–32.* 🎟 *30 frs.* ☉ *Jan.–mid-Mar.
and Sept.–Nov., Thurs.–Tues. 9–noon and 2–5; mid-Mar.–June,
daily 9–noon and 2–6; July–Aug., daily 9–6.*

Tours

*39 km (24 mi) northwest of Loches via N143; 112 km (70 mi) south-
west of Orléans; 240 km (150 mi) southwest of Paris.*

Little remains of Tours's château—one of France's finest cathedrals more
than compensates—but the city makes an ideal center from which to
tour the Loire Valley's attractions by public transportation. Trains from
Tours run along the river in both directions, and regular bus services
radiate from here; in addition, the city is the starting point for a variety of organized bus excursions (many with English-speaking guides).
The formerly small town has mushroomed into a city of a quarter of a
million inhabitants, with an ugly modern sprawl of factories, high-rise

blocks, and overhead expressway junctions cluttering up the outskirts. But the timber-framed houses in **Vieux Tours** (Old Tours), the attractive medieval center around place Plumereau, have been tastefully restored after extensive damage during World War II. Tours is easy to get around by public buses. If you have a car, you may prefer to base yourself in any of a dozen smaller towns within a half-hour drive.

★ ⑳ The **Cathédrale St-Gatien,** built between 1239 and 1484, reveals a mixture of architectural styles. The richly sculpted stonework of its majestic, soaring, two-tower facade betrays the Renaissance influence among local château-trained craftsmen. The stained glass dates from the 13th century (if you have binoculars, bring them). Also take a look at the little tomb with kneeling angels built in memory of Charles VIII and Anne of Brittany's two children. ⊠ *rue Lavoisier.* ☉ *Daily 8–noon and 2–6.*

🐾 ㉑ Alongside the château ruins you will find the **Historial de la Touraine** (Regional History Museum)—a group of more than 150 waxwork models that represent historic figures like St. Martin and Joan of Arc, whose deeds helped shape this region for more than 15 centuries. There's also a small aquarium (open daily 2–6) next door. ⊠ *quai d'Orléans,* ☎ *02–47–61–02–95.* ☒ *Wax museum 35 frs, aquarium 30 frs.* ☉ *Mid-Mar.–June and Sept.–Oct., daily 9–noon and 2–6; Nov.–mid-Mar., daily 2–5:30; July–Aug., daily 9–6:30.*

㉒ The **Musée des Beaux-Arts** (Fine Arts Museum), in what was once the archbishop's palace, has an eclectic selection of treasures: works by Rubens, Rembrandt, Boucher, Degas, Calder—even Fritz the Elephant, stuffed in 1902. ⊠ *18 pl. François-Sicard,* ☎ *02–47–05–68–73.* ☒ *30 frs.* ☉ *Wed.–Mon. 9–12:45 and 2–6.*

㉓ Two museums, the **Musée du Vin** (Wine Museum) and the **Musée du Compagnonnage** (Guild Museum), are in and around the cloisters of the 13th-century church of St-Julien, near the Loire. *Compagnonnage* is a sort of apprenticeship–cum–trade-union system, and here you see the masterpieces of the candidates for guild membership: virtuoso craftwork, some of it eccentric (an Eiffel Tower made of slate, for instance, or a varnished noodle château). These stand as evidence of the devotion to craftsmanship that is still an important feature of French life. You are free to visit both the guild and wine museums at your own pace. ⊠ *8 rue Nationale,* ☎ *02–47–61–07–93.* ☒ *Musée du Compagnonnage 25 frs, Musée du Vin 15 frs.* ☉ *Wed.–Mon. 9–noon and 2–6.*

🐾 ㉔ The **Musée du Gemmail,** in the imposing 19th-century Hôtel Raimbault, contains an unusual collection of three-dimensional, colored-glass window panels. Depicting patterns, figures, and even portraits, the panels are both beautiful and intriguing, since most of the gemlike fragments of glass come from broken bottles. Incidentally, Jean Cocteau coined the word *gemmail* by combining *gemme* (gem) with *émail* (enamel). ⊠ *7 rue du Mûrier,* ☎ *02–47–61–01–19.* ☒ *30 frs.* ☉ *Mar.–mid-Oct., Tues.–Sun. 10–noon and 2:30–6; mid-Oct.–Feb., weekends 10–noon and 2–6:15.*

Dining and Lodging

$$ ✕ **Les Tuffeaux.** This restaurant, between the cathedral and the Loire, retains its place as one of Tours's best—without breaking your budget. Chef Gildas Marsollier wins customers with delicious fennel-perfumed salmon, oysters in an egg sauce seasoned with Roquefort, and remarkable desserts. Gentle lighting and a wood-beamed, stone-walled decor provide a soothing background. ⊠ *19 rue Lavoisier,* ☎ *02–47–47–19–89. MC, V. Closed Sun. No lunch Mon.*

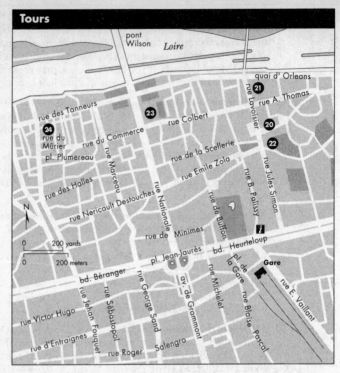

$$$$ ✗⌂ **Château d'Artigny.** The ambience of this Relais & Châteaux hotel—built by the Coty perfume tycoon in 1912 as a vast, pseudo–Louis XV house—recalls a perfume ad: Gilt, marble, and plush abound, creating a perfect backdrop for the frequent celebrity guests. The spacious rooms have 18th-century-style French furnishings. The nouvelle restaurant is excellent but expensive. You can jog away the calories in the 60-acre park. ⊠ *rte. d'Azay-le-Rideau, 37250 Montbazon (13 km/8 mi south of Tours, west of Montbazon on D17),* ☎ *02–47–34–30–30,* ℻ *02–47–65–92–79. 55 rooms. Restaurant, pool, tennis court. AE, DC, MC, V. Closed Dec.–early Jan.*

$$$$ ✗⌂ **Jean Bardet.** Bardet, one of France's top 20 chefs, serves an eight-
★ course *menu dégustation* (tasting menu) for 620 francs and an à la carte menu that includes oysters poached in Muscadet on a puree of watercress, and grilled lobster. Reservations are essential, and the restaurant is closed Monday. One downside: Both the food and the service can be erratic—not to be expected when the tab for two is close to 1,000 francs. The suites and rooms, though luxurious, are on the exorbitant side. For real style, you can hire Bardet's Rolls-Royce Silver Shadow II to take you on a tour of the Loire. ⊠ *57 rue Groison, 37100,* ☎ *02–47–41–41–11,* ℻ *02–47–51–68–72. 15 rooms, 6 suites. Restaurant. AE, DC, MC, V.*

$$$ ✗⌂ **Domaine de la Tortinière.** Subtle elegance exudes from this little
★ 19th-century château south of Tours. Rooms in the main building convey quiet, rustic luxury; those in the modern annex are less desirable. Some negatives in the old house: the morning gurgle of the water pipes and the sound of doors opening and closing along the corridor. But the beds are so comfy it's a pleasure to wake up in them. Room 15, small but pleasant (680 frs), is quieter. Dinner is a delightful occasion, even if the fare does not quite live up to its reputation. The pi-

geon in a rich wine sauce, and the lobster bisque with a pastry top, though, are excellent. ⊠ *10 rte. de Ballan, 37250 Veigné (about 12 km/7 mi south of Tours in Veigné),* ☎ *02–47–34–35–00,* FAX *02–47–65–25–70. 21 rooms. Restaurant, pool, tennis court. AE, MC, V. Closed mid-Dec.–Mar.*

$$$ ⊞ **Univers.** The Univers is the best hotel in Tours. Murals in the salon
★ depict some of the famous people who have stayed here: Winston Churchill, Sarah Bernhardt, Maurice Chevalier, Rudyard Kipling, and the Duke of Windsor. Wood panels and soft colors add traditional warmth to the rooms, of which only 10 face the street; the others look onto a flower garden. ⊠ *5 bd. Heurteloup, 37000,* ☎ *02–47–05–37–12,* FAX *02–47–61–51–80. 80 rooms, 8 suites. Restaurant, bar, meeting room. AE, DC, MC, V.*

Villandry

㉕ *16 km (10 mi) west of Tours via D7.*

Villandry is renowned for its extravagant, terraced gardens—the finest in the Loire Valley—reconstituted according to original plans. In 1906 Spanish doctor Joachim Carvalla and his wife, American heiress Ann Coleman, bought the **Château de Villandry** and began a long process of restoration. Both the château and the gardens are from the 16th century, but over the years they had fallen into disrepair. The château has a remarkable gilded ceiling—imported from Toledo, Spain—and a collection of fine Spanish paintings.

★ The **gardens** are unquestionably the main attraction, replanted according to their original, rigorous, geometric design, with zigzagging hedges around flower beds, vegetable plots, and gravel walks. The result is an aristocratic 16th-century *jardin à la française* (French-style garden). Below an avenue of 1,500 precisely pruned lime trees lies an ornamental lake filled with swans: Not a ripple is out of place. The aromatic and medicinal garden, its plots neatly labeled in three languages, is especially appealing. The quietest time to visit is usually during the two-hour French lunch break. ☎ *02–47–50–02–09.* ⊠ *Château and gardens 45 frs, gardens only 32 frs.* ☉ *June–Sept., daily 9–6, gardens 9–8; Oct.–May, daily 9:30–12:30 and 2–5:30, gardens 9–dusk. Château closed Jan. (gardens remain open).*

Dining and Lodging

$$ ✕⊞ **Cheval Rouge.** The restaurant in this fine, old-fashioned hotel is popular with locals. They come to eat the surprisingly good classical food—considering its touristy location next to the château—and drink good wine. Best bets are the terrine of foie gras, the calf sweetbreads, and the wood-fired-grill fare. Rooms are modern and tidy. ⊠ *9 rue de la Mairie, 37510 Villandry,* ☎ *02–47–50–02–07,* FAX *02–47–50–08–77. 20 rooms. Restaurant. MC, V. Closed Mon. and Feb.*

Langeais

㉖ *8 km (5 mi) west of Villandry.*

Across the Loire from Villandry is the small, old town of Langeais, with a Renaissance church-tower and some 16th-century houses, crushed beneath its massive castle. The **Château de Langeais,** built in the 1460s and never altered, contains a superb collection of fireplaces, tapestries, chests, and beds. Outside, tidy gardens nestle behind sturdy walls and battlements. ☎ *02–47–96–72–60.* ⊠ *40 frs.* ☉ *Easter–Oct., Tues.–Sun. 9–6:30; Nov.–Easter, daily 9–noon and 2–5.*

Azay-le-Rideau

㉗ *10 km (6 mi) southeast of Langeais via D57, 24 km (15 mi) southwest of Tours.*

Nestled in a sylvan setting on the banks of the River Indre, the pleasant village of Azay-le-Rideau is famed for its white-walled Renaissance
★ pleasure palace. The 16th-century **Château d'Azay-le-Rideau** was never a serious fortress. It certainly offered no protection to its builder, royal financier Gilles Berthelot, when a financial scandal forced him to flee France shortly after the château's completion in 1529. For centuries, the château passed from one private owner to another and was finally bought by the state in 1905. Though the interior contains an interesting blend of furniture and artwork, you may wish to spend most of your time exploring the enchanting private park, complete with a moatlike lake. Delightful **son-et-lumière** shows are held on the château grounds on summer evenings. ☎ *02–47–45–42–04.* 🎫 *Château 32 frs, son-et-lumière 50 frs.* ⊘ *Apr.–Sept., daily 9:30–6; Oct.–Mar., daily 9:30–noon and 2–5.*

Dining and Lodging

$$ ✕🏨 **Grand Monarque.** Just yards from the château, this old hotel has a captive audience, which shows in its offhand service. However, rooms, which vary in size and style, have character; most are simply decorated with an antique or two, and many have exposed beams. The restaurant serves good, traditional food and an extensive selection of Loire wines (it's closed Monday lunch and Thursday in winter). The 99-franc lunch menu is a particularly good value. Weekend stays must include dinner. ✉ *3 pl. de la République, 37190,* ☎ *02–47–45–40–08,* FAX *02–47–45–46–25. 25 rooms, 22 with bath. Restaurant. AE, DC, MC, V. Closed mid-Dec.–end of Jan.*

Outdoor Activities and Sports

Rent bikes from **Leprovost** (✉ *13 rue Carnot,* ☎ *02–47–45–40–94*) and ride along the River Indre.

Saché

㉘ *7 km (4 mi) east of Azay-le-Rideau via D17.*

Saché is best known for its associations with the novelist Honoré de Balzac (1799–1850), who lived and wrote in its **Château.** If you've never read Balzac and don't understand spoken French, you may find little of interest here; but if you have, and do, you'll return to the novels with fresh enthusiasm and understanding. The present château, built between the 16th and 18th centuries, is more of a comfortable country house than a fortress. Balzac came here—to stay with his friends, the Margonnes—during the 1830s, both to write and to escape his creditors. The château houses the substantial **Musée Balzac** (Balzac Museum), where exhibits range from photographs to original manuscripts to the coffeepot Balzac used to help keep him writing up to 16 hours a day. ☎ *02–47–26–86–50.* 🎫 *24 frs.* ⊘ *Feb.–mid-Mar. and Oct.–Nov. Thurs.–Tues. 9:30–11:45 and 2:15–4:30; mid-Mar.–Sept., daily 9–noon and 2–6.*

Villaines-les-Rochers

㉙ *6 km (4 mi) southeast of Azay-le-Rideau via D57.*

Osier (wicker) products have been made for centuries in Villaines. In 1849, when the craft was threatened with extinction, the parish priest persuaded 65 small groups of basket weavers to form France's first agricultural workers' cooperative. These days craftspeople settle here from all over France—and abroad—attracted by the troglodyte cliff dwellings and back-to-nature lifestyle: The willow reeds are cultivated in nearby fields and dried in the sun each May, before being transformed into sofas, cat baskets, or babies' rattles (all available at the village shop). A small exhibition in the **Coopératif de la Vannerie** (Wickerwork Cooperative) tells the cooperative's story; you can also buy wicker items here. ⊠ *1 rue de la Cheneillère,* ☎ *02–47–45–43–03.* ⌑ *Free.* ☉ *Sat. 10–noon and 2–7, Sun. 2–7.*

Ussé

★ ㉚ *14 km (9 mi) west of Azay-le-Rideau via D17 and D7, 36 km (23 mi) southwest of Tours.*

As you approach the **Château d'Ussé** (actually in the village of Rigny-Ussé), between the Forest of Chinon and the Loire, an astonishing array of delicate towers and turrets greets you. Literature describes this château as the original Sleeping Beauty castle—the inspiration for Charles Perrault's beloved 17th-century tale. Though parts of the castle are from the 1400s, most of it was completed two centuries later. It is a flamboyant mix of Gothic and Renaissance styles—stylish and romantic, built for fun, not for fighting. Its history supports this playful image: It suffered no bloodbaths—no political conquests or conflicts. And a tablet in the chapel indicates that even the French Revolution passed it by.

After admiring the château's luxurious furnishings and 19th-century French fashion exhibit, climb the spiral stairway to the tower to view the River Indre through the battlements. Here you also find a waxwork effigy of Sleeping Beauty herself. Before you leave, visit the 16th-century chapel in the garden; its door is decorated with pleasingly sinister skull-and-crossbones carvings. ☎ *02–47–95–54–05.* ⌑ *60 frs.* ☉ *Mid-Feb.–mid-Nov., daily 9–noon and 2–6.*

Dining

$$ ✕ **Atlantide.** This restaurant is worth seeking out. The small dining room,
★ dressed in white tablecloths, potted plants, and a Grecian statue, has a classic simplicity that allows you to focus on the food. The 105-franc, fixed-price three-course menu may include chicken *à la chinoise* (Chinese-style) with a thick mushroom wine sauce, a delicate goat cheese salad, and dessert. ⊠ *17 rue Nationale, Avoine (8 km/5 mi southwest of Ussé),* ☎ *02–47–58–81–85. MC, V.*

Chinon

★ ㉛ *13 km (8 mi) southwest of Rigny-Ussé via D7 and D16, 44 km (28 mi) southwest of Tours.*

The town of Chinon—birthplace of author François Rabelais (1494–1553)—is dominated by the towering ruins of its medieval castle perched high above the River Vienne. Though the main tourist office is in the town below, in summer a special annex operates from the castle grounds. The town is a warren of narrow, cobbled streets (some are pedestrian only), lined with half-timber medieval houses. Since both the village and the château are on steep, cobbled slopes, it's a good idea to wear comfortable walking shoes.

The vast **Château de Chinon,** a veritable fortress with walls 400 yards long, is from the time of Henry II of England, who died here in 1189 and was buried at Fontevraud. Two centuries later, the castle witnessed an important historic moment: Joan of Arc's recognition of the disguised dauphin, later Charles VII. In the early 17th century, the castle was partially dismantled by Cardinal Richelieu (1585–1642), who used many of its stones to build a new palace 21 km (13 mi) to the south, in Richelieu.

At Chinon, everything is open to the elements, except the **Logis Royal** (Royal Chambers). Here there is a small museum containing a model of the castle when it was intact, various old tapestries, and precious stones. For a fine view of the region, climb the **Tour Coudray** (Coudray Tower), where in 1307 leading members of the crusading Knights Templar were imprisoned before being taken to Paris, tried, and burned at the stake. The **Tour de l'Horloge** (Clock Tower), whose bell has sounded the hours since 1399, contains the **Musée Jeanne d'Arc** (Joan of Arc Museum). There are sensational views from the ramparts over Chinon and the Vienne Valley. ☎ 02–47–93–13–45. 🖼 Château 27 frs. ⊙ Mid-Mar.–June and Sept., daily 9–6; July and Aug., daily 9–7; Oct., daily 9–5; Nov.–mid-Mar., daily 9–noon and 2–5.

The **Musée du Vin** (Wine Museum), in a vaulted cellar beneath one of Chinon's fine medieval streets, has a fascinating presentation about vine growing and wine and barrel making. English commentary is available, and the admission charge entitles you to a sample of the local product. ✉ 12 rue Voltaire, ☎ 02–47–93–25–63. 🖼 22 frs. ⊙ Apr.–Oct., Fri.–Wed. 10–noon and 2–6.

Dining and Lodging

$$ ✕ **Au Plaisir Gourmand.** Gourmets from all over come to celebrate,
★ and lucky tourists will get a table only if they make reservations (the dining room in this charming old house seats only 30). Chef Jérôme Rigollet uses fresh, local produce inventively. For a real treat, try the Vienne River trout and one of the exceptional local wines. ✉ 2 rue Parmentier, ☎ 02–47–93–20–48. Reservations essential. Jacket and tie. AE, MC, V. Closed Mon. and mid-Jan.–mid-Feb. No dinner Sun.

$ ✕ **Jeanne de France.** Local families and swarms of young people patronize this lively little pizzeria in the town's main square. It's a far cry from an American pizza joint, though: Here you can also order jugs of local wine, steaks, and french fries. ✉ 12 pl. du Général-de-Gaulle, ☎ 02–47–93–20–12. AE, MC, V. Closed Wed. and Jan.

$$$ ✕🏨 **Château de Marçay.** An efficient staff serves the fashionable guests
★ at this ultrasophisticated château-hotel outside of Chinon. Rooms in the "pavilion," 50 yards from the main hotel, are pleasantly furnished but have little charm; the more expensive ones in the château have more to offer. Beams and gables add a cozy warmth to the spacious rooms, decorated with antiques. Chef Pascal Bodin serves excellent carpaccio de canard (thin slices of marinated cold duck), tournedos of salmon in a Chinon wine sauce, and an extensive cheese board (sample the Ste-Marie chèvre). The wine list is one of the most extensive in France. ✉ 37500 Marçay (6 km/4 mi south of Chinon), ☎ 02–47–93–03–47, FAX 02–47–93–45–33. 35 rooms. Restaurant, pool, tennis court. AE, DC, MC, V. Closed Feb.–mid-Mar.

$$ ✕🏨 **Gargantua.** This small, quiet hotel in the center of the medieval city was a bailiff's palace in the 15th century. It has an array of rooms in various sizes and styles; simple good taste prevails throughout. Rooms 7 and 9, with views of the château, are good choices. In the old dining room, delicious local specialties are served, such as fillet of barbue (a white fish) with a marmalade, thyme, and citron sauce. On Friday and Saturday evenings waitresses dress up in medieval costume; in summer you can dine outside and admire Chinon Castle. ✉ 73 rue Voltaire, 37500, ☎ 02–47–93–04–71. 8 rooms, 4 with bath. AE, DC, MC, V. Closed Wed. and Feb.

$$ ⌧ **Hôtel de France.** Just off Chinon's main square is one of the oldest buildings in town. Built in the 16th century, it was home to many notables until the Revolution, when it became known as the Hôtel de France. Rooms are all comfortable, but ask for one of the more recently refurbished ones with a view of the castle. On the ground floor, the restaurant doubles as a bar, a congenial place to regroup your energies before your next adventure. ⌧ *47 pl. du Général-de-Gaulle, 37500,* ☎ *02–47–93–33–91,* 𝔽𝔸𝕏 *02–47–98–37–03. 30 rooms. Restaurant. AE, DC, MC, V. Closed Dec.–Jan.*

Nightlife and the Arts

Chinon stages a **Marché Médiéval** (Medieval Market) during the first weekend of August. The streets are decked with flags and bunting, craftsmen ply their wares, ancient recipes are resurrected, and locals dress up in medieval costumes, with minstrels, jesters, and troubadours on the prowl.

Champigny-sur-Veude

32 *15 km (9 mi) south of Chinon via D749.*

Some of the best Renaissance stained glass in the world is in the village of Champigny-sur-Veude. In the dainty, white-stone **Sainte-Chapelle,** the 16th-century windows relate scenes from the Passion, Crucifixion, and the life of the 13th-century French king St. Louis; note the vividness and harmony of the colors, especially the purplish blues. The church was originally part of a château built between 1508 and 1543, but it was razed a century later by order of jealous neighbor Cardinal Richelieu. ☎ *02–47–95–73–48.* ⌧ *20 frs.* ☉ *Apr.–Sept., daily 9–noon and 2–6.*

Richelieu

33 *6 km (4 mi) south of Champigny-sur-Veude.*

The eerie town of Richelieu was founded by Cardinal Richelieu in 1631, along with a megalomaniac château intended to be one of the most lavish in Christendom. The town remains a rare example of rigid, symmetrical, and unspoiled classical town planning, with 28 identical mansions lining the main street. Its bombastic scale and state of preservation are unique; the severe, straight streets have not changed for 350 years, give or take the odd traffic sign. All that's left of the cardinal's vainglorious country retreat, however, are a few outbuildings and parkland.

Fontevraud

34 *20 km (12 mi) northwest of Chinon via D751, 15 km (9 mi) southeast of Saumur.*

The small village of Fontevraud is famous for its large, medieval abbey, of central importance in the history of both England and France. Founded in 1099, the **Abbaye Royale de Fontevraud** had separate churches and living quarters for nuns, monks, lepers, "repentant" female sinners, and the sick. Between 1115 and the French Revolution in 1789, 39 different abbesses—among them a granddaughter of William the Conqueror—directed operations.

The great 12th-century **Église Abbatiale** (Abbey Church), one of the most eclectic architectural structures in France, contains the tombs of Henry II of England; his wife, Eleanor of Aquitaine; and their son, Richard Coeur de Lion—Richard the Lionhearted. Though their bones were scattered during the Revolution, their effigies remain. Napoléon turned the abbey church into a prison, and so it remained until 1963, when historical restoration work—still under way—began. The **Salle Capitulaire** (Chapter House), adjacent to the church, with its collection of 16th-century religious wall paintings (prominent abbesses served as models), is unmistakably Renaissance; the paving stones bear the salamander emblem of François I. Next to the long refectory is the unusual, octagonal **cuisine** (kitchen), topped by 20 scaly-looking stone chimneys led by the **Tour d'Evrault**. ⊠ *pl. des Plantagenêts,* ☎ *02–41–51–71–41.* ⊡ *32 frs.* ☉ *May–mid-Sept., daily 9–noon and 2–6:30; mid-Sept.–Apr., daily 9:30–noon and 2–5.*

Saumur

★ ㉟ *15 km (9 mi) northwest of Fontevraud via D947, 65 km (41 mi) west of Tours, 46 km (29 mi) southeast of Angers.*

The ancient town of Saumur, dominated by its mighty, turreted château, which perches high above town and river, is an excellent base for exploring the western Loire Valley. It's also known for its riding school and flourishing mushroom industry, which produces 100,000 tons per year. The same cool tunnels in which the mushrooms grow also provide an ideal storage place for the local *mousseux* (sparkling wines).

If you arrive in the evening, the sight of the floodlit, elegant, white, 14th-century **Château de Saumur** will take your breath away. Looks familiar? Probably because you've seen it in countless reproductions from the famous *Très Riches Heures* (*Book of Hours*), painted for the Duc de Berri in 1416 (now in the Musée Condé at Chantilly). Inside it's bright and cheerful, with a fairy-tale gateway and plentiful potted flowers. There are two museums here: the **Musée des Arts Décoratifs** (Decorative Arts Museum), with its fine collection of medieval objets d'art and 18th- and 19th-century porcelain, and the **Musée du Cheval** (Horse Museum). Both are included in the guided tour. Afterward, climb the **Tour de Guet** (Watchtower) for an impressive view. ⊠ *esplanade du Château,* ☎ *02–41–40–24–40.* ⊡ *37 frs.* ☉ *July–Sept., daily 9–6:30; Oct. and May–June, daily 9–11:30 and 2–6; Nov.–Apr., Wed.–Mon. 9:30–noon and 2–5:30.*

Ⓒ In the old powder house at the château is the **Musée de la Figurine-Jouet** (Toy Figurine Museum), with more than 2,000 toy figurines on display. ☎ *02–41–67–39–23.* ⊡ *12 frs.* ☉ *June and Sept., Wed.–Mon. 2–6; July–Aug., Wed.–Mon. 10–6.*

The **Musée du Champignon** (Mushroom Museum) on the outskirts of Saumur offers an intriguing subterranean tour through fossil-filled caverns where edible fungi are grown. ⊠ *rte. de Gennes, St-Hilaire-St-Florent,* ☎ *02–41–50–31–55.* ⊡ *38 frs.* ☉ *Mid-Feb.–mid-Sept., daily 10–7.*

Dining and Lodging

$$ ✕ **Les Ménestrels.** Chef Lucien Von cooks very acceptable fare in a restored, white-stone, 18th-century mansion up against the castle cliff. Specialties include pheasant casserole, fried mushrooms, perch with spring-onion fondue, and beef in a local red-wine sauce. ⊠ *11 rue Raspail,* ☎ *02–41–67–71–10.* AE, DC, MC, V. *No dinner Sun. (except July–Aug.).*

$$$$ ✕⊡ **Prieuré.** This gracious manor west of Saumur is from medieval times but has been tastefully modernized. Rooms are large; the nicest are in the main building. Room 5 overlooks the Loire. Though the garden chalets are luxurious and neatly appointed, they are short on character. In the spacious dining room with a view of the river, crystal and silver clink discreetly. Behind the scenes, chef Jean-Noël Lumineau pro-

duces well-executed classics. ⊠ *49350 Chênehutte-les-Tuffeaux (8 km/5 mi west of Saumur on D751 toward Angers),* ☎ *02–41–67–90–14,* FAX *02–41–67–92–24. 33 rooms. Restaurant, pool, tennis court. AE, MC, V. Closed Jan.–early Mar.*

$$–$$$ 🔟 **Loire.** This member of the Best Western chain wins no prizes for charm or friendly service, but it is clean, spacious, and functional. It's also inconveniently located across the river from the main part of town, though this makes parking easier and makes for a stunning view of the château from the restaurant. ⊠ *rue de Vieux-Pont, 49400,* ☎ *02–41–67–22–42, 800/528–1234 for U.S. reservations, 0181/541–0033 for U.K. reservations;* FAX *02–41–67–88–80. 45 rooms. Restaurant. AE, DC, MC, V.*

$$ 🔟 **Anne d'Anjou.** Close to the center of town, this hotel facing the river has a view of the château (floodlit at night) above. Inside the 18th-century building is an astounding staircase, which circles up to the top floor, where there is an impressive mural. Most rooms are simply decorated with old or contemporary furniture and are reasonably priced. Owners Yves and Anne-Marie Touzé will point you to their best, Room 102 (650 frs), with its wood-panel paintings and Empire furnishings. ⊠ *32 quai Mayaud, 49400,* ☎ *02–41–67–30–30,* FAX *02–41–67–51–00. 50 rooms. Restaurant. AE, DC, MC, V.*

Outdoor Activities and Sports

If you want to ride through the rolling hills or take a weeklong equestrian tour of the Loire Valley, head to the **Centre Équestre St-Hilaire–St-Florent** (⊠ Petit Souper, St-Hilaire, ☎ 02–41–50–29–90), 3 km (2 mi) northwest of Saumur.

Shopping

Loire wine is not a practical buy—except for instant consumption—but if wine-tasting tours of vineyards inspire you, enterprising wine makers will arrange shipment to the United States. For sparkling wine, try **Ackerman** (⊠ 19 rue Léopold-Palustre, St-Hilaire, ☎ 02–41–53–30–20). Just southeast of Saumur in Dampierre-sur-Loire, stop in at the **Château de Chaintres** (⊠ 54 rue de la Croix-de-Chaintre, ☎ 02–41–52–90–54), where affable Krishna Lester, an English eccentric, produces the region's finest still red and enjoys talking visitors through the production process. **Veuve Amiot** (⊠ 21 rue Jean-Ackerman, St-Hilaire, ☎ 02–41–83–14–14) is another place for sparkling wine.

Montreuil-Bellay

㊱ *18 km (11 mi) south of Saumur via N147.*

Montreuil-Bellay is a small riverside town with many 18th- and 19th-century houses, lovely public gardens, and a leafy square next to its castle. The grandiose exterior—majestic towers and pointed roofs—of the 15th-century **Château de Montreuil-Bellay** is as fascinating as its interior. Inside is a fine collection of furniture and tapestries, a fully equipped medieval kitchen, and a chapel adorned with frescoes of angelic musicians. For a memorable view, take a stroll in the gardens; graceful white turrets tower high above the trees and rosebushes, and down below, the little River Thouet winds its lazy way to the Loire. ⊠ *pl. des Ormeaux,* ☎ *02–41–52–33–06.* 🎫 *45 frs.* ☉ *Apr.–Nov., Wed.–Mon. 10–noon and 2–5:30.*

En Route   From Montreuil-Bellay, take D761 northwest to Doué-la-Fontaine, 12 km (8 mi) away. The town is home to a zoo, the **Parc Zoologique des Minières** (⊠ rte. de Cholet, ☎ 02–41–59–18–58) where deer, emu, and monkeys roam happily, surrounded by golden limestone quarries. It's open daily May–September 9–7, and October–April 9–12:30

and 2–6; admission is 60 francs. From the zoo, return to D761 to continue to Angers, pausing along the way to admire the towering **Château de Brissac.**

Angers

㊲ *51 km (28 mi) northwest of Montreuil-Bellay via D761, 10 km (69 mi) west of Tours, 88 km (55 mi) east of Nantes.*

The bustling city of Angers, on the banks of the River Maine just north of the Loire, is famous for its towering castle filled with extraordinary tapestries. But there's also a fine Gothic cathedral, a selection of art galleries, and a network of pleasant, traffic-free shopping streets. The town's principal sights lie within a compact square formed by the three main boulevards and the River Maine.

The massive **Château d'Angers,** built by St. Louis (1228–38), glowers over the town from behind turreted moats, now laid out as gardens and overrun with flowers and deer. As you explore the grounds, note the startling contrast between the thick, defensive walls, defended by a drawbridge and 17 massive round towers, and the formal garden, with its delicate, white tufa-stone chapel, erected in the 16th century. For a sweeping view of the city and surrounding countryside, climb one of the castle towers. A well-integrated modern gallery on the castle grounds contains the great **Tenture de l'Apocalypse** (Apocalypse Tapestry), woven in Paris in the 1380s and restored to almost pristine glory in 1996. Measuring 16 ft high and 120 yards long, it shows a series of 70 horrifying and humorous scenes from the Book of Revelation. In one, mountains of fire fall from heaven while boats capsize and men struggle in the water. Another has the beast with seven heads. ✉ *pl. du Président-Kennedy,* ☎ *02–41–87–43–47.* 🎫 *35 frs.* ☉ *July–Aug., daily 10–7; Sept.–June, daily 10–5.*

★

The **Cathédrale St-Maurice** is a 12th- and 13th-century Gothic cathedral noted for its curious Romanesque facade and original stained-glass windows; bring binoculars to appreciate both fully. ✉ *pl. Freppel.*

The **Musée des Beaux-Arts** (Fine Arts Museum), just south of the cathedral in a house that once sheltered Cesare Borgia and Mary, Queen of Scots, has an impressive collection of old masters from the 17th and 18th centuries, including paintings by Raphael, Watteau, Fragonard, and Boucher. ✉ *10 rue du Musée,* ☎ *02–41–88–64–65.* 🎫 *10 frs.* ☉ *Tues.–Sun. 10–noon and 2–6.*

The **Musée David d'Angers,** in a refurbished, glass-roofed medieval church, has a collection of dramatic sculptures by Jean-Pierre David (1788–1859), the city's favorite son. ✉ *33 rue Toussaint,* ☎ *02–41–87–21–03.* 🎫 *10 frs.* ☉ *Tues.–Sun. 10–noon and 2–6.*

To learn about the heartwarming liqueur made in Angers since 1849, head to the **Distillerie Cointreau** on the east of the city. The guided visit of the distillery starts with an introductory film; moves through the bottling plant and alembic room, with its gleaming copper pot stills; and ends with a tasting. ✉ *rue de la Croix-Blanche, St-Barthélémy d'Anjou,* ☎ *02–41–31–50–50.* 🎫 *20 frs.* ☉ *Tours June–Sept., weekdays every hr at 10, 11, and 2–5, weekends at 3 and 4:30; tours Oct.–May, Mon.–Sat. at 3, Sun. at 3 and 4:30.*

OFF THE
BEATEN PATH

CHÂTEAU DE SERRANT – This sumptuous château 17 km (11 mi) southwest of Angers on N23, flanked by stately lawns and a moat, dates from 1546, with additions from the 17th and 18th centuries. The lush, paneled interior is hung with tapestries; the magnificent library is lined with 10,000 books. ☎ 02–41–39–13–01. 🖾 45 frs. ☉ Apr.–Oct., Wed.–Mon. 9–11:30 and 2–6.

Dining and Lodging

$$–$$$ ✕ **La Salamandre.** Carefully prepared classical cuisine is served in this restaurant in the Anjou Hotel (☞ *below*). Lamb, duck with cranberries, and calamari with crab sauce are just a few of the dishes served amid the Renaissance-style decor and stained-glass windows. Opt for one of the reasonably priced prix-fixe menus. ⊠ *1 bd. du Maréchal-Foch,* ☎ *02–41–88–99–55. AE, DC, MC, V. Closed Sun.*

$$ ✕ **Toussaint.** Chef Michel Bignon serves nouvelle versions of traditional
★ local dishes, plus fine wines and tasty desserts. Local river fish with beurre blanc is a particular specialty. There are two dining rooms: The ground floor is less formal; upstairs, the neoclassical room has a better view of the castle. Reserve your table accordingly. ⊠ *7 pl. du Président-Kennedy,* ☎ *02–41–87–46–20. Reservations essential. Jacket required. AE, MC, V. Closed Mon. No dinner Sun.*

$ ✕ **La Boucherie.** If you have an appetite for steak and good value, this place is for you. There are various menus with different cuts of beef, but for 55 francs you can get a sirloin, a small salad, crusty bread, and a ¼-liter carafe of wine. Service is friendly, cheerful, and swift. If there is a wait for a table, don't despair: The action is fast. Tables are close together, and lively conversation adds to the robust atmosphere. ⊠ *27 bd. du Maréchal-Foch,* ☎ *02–41–25–39–25. Reservations not accepted. MC, V.*

$ ✕ **La Treille.** For traditional, simple fare at affordable prices, try this small, two-story mom-and-pop restaurant, off place Ste-Croix and across from Maison d'Adam, Angers's finest timber house. The prix-fixe menu may start with a *salade au chèvre chaud* (warm goat cheese salad), followed by confit of duck and an apple tart. The upstairs dining room draws a lively crowd; downstairs is quieter. ⊠ *12 rue Montault,* ☎ *02–41–88–45–51. MC, V. Closed Sun.*

$$$ 🏨 **Bleu Marine.** You won't find individuality in this standardized chain hotel, but you won't find problems either. Rooms are bright and modern and furnished with a copious amount of Formica. There's a spacious lobby and a good classical restaurant on the ground floor that looks out at Angers's main boulevard. The breakfast buffet is large and good. ⊠ *18 bd. du Maréchal-Foch, 49100,* ☎ *02–41–87–37–20, 800/ 888–4747 in the U.S.,* FAX *02–41–87–49–54. 75 rooms. Restaurant, health club. AE, DC, MC, V.*

$$ 🏨 **Anjou.** In business since 1850, the Anjou, now part of the Best Western chain, is decorated in a vaguely 18th-century style, including stained-glass windows in the lobby. The spacious rooms have high ceilings, double doors, and modern bathrooms with terry-cloth bathrobes. ⊠ *1 bd. du Maréchal-Foch, 49000,* ☎ *02–41–88–24–82, 800/528– 1324 in the U.S.,* FAX *02–41–87–22–21. 53 rooms. Restaurant. AE, DC, MC, V.*

Nightlife and the Arts

For four weeks beginning in mid-June, the **Fête d'Anjou** (Anjou Festival) enlivens the area around Angers with music, theater, and dance. Call the tourist office (☞ The Loire Valley A to Z, *below*) for details.

Outdoor Activities and Sports

Go canoeing, sailing, fishing, and windsurfing at the **Centre Nautique du Lac de Maine** (Maine Lake Nautical Center; ⊠ 75 av. du Lac-de-Maine, ☎ 02–41–22–32–20), 5 km (3 mi) southwest of the city.

Le Plessis-Bourré

㊳ *20 km (12 mi) north of Angers via D107, off D508 south of Écuillé.*

The reason to visit Le Plessis-Bourré is to see its Renaissance castle. The **Château du Plessis-Bourré,** built between 1468 and 1473 by Jean Bourré (one of Louis XI's top-ranking civil servants), looks like a traditional grim fortress: The bridge across its moat is nearly 50 yards long. Once you step into the central courtyard, however, the gentler mood of the Renaissance takes over.

What makes this place special is the painted wooden ceiling in the **Salle des Gardes** (Guards' Room). Jean Bourré's hobby was alchemy—an ancient branch of chemistry with more than a touch of the occult—and the ceiling's 24 hexagonal panels are covered with scenes illustrating the craft. Some have overtones of the grotesque dream world of late-medieval Dutch painter Hieronymus Bosch, while others illustrate folktales or proverbs. A few must have been painted just for fun: A topless lady steers a land yacht with wooden wheels (thought to be an allegory of spirit and matter); people urinate ceremoniously (ammonia was extracted from urine); an emaciated wolf takes a bite out of a startled lady (according to folk legend, the wolf's diet consisted of faithful wives, apparently in short supply); and Thurberesque dogs gambol in between. You may want to ignore the guide's lecture on furniture and spend your time gazing upward. ☎ *02–41–32–06–01.* 🎫 *45 frs.* ⊙ *Apr.–Aug., Thurs.–Tues. 10–noon and 2–6; Sept.–Nov. and Feb.–Mar., Thurs.–Tues. 2–5.*

Le Lude

㊴ *62 km (39 mi) east of Le Plessis-Bourré via D74, D766, and D305; 47 km (29 mi) northeast of Saumur; 44 km (28 mi) south of Le Mans.*

One of France's most spectacular son-et-lumière shows takes place in Le Lude in the Loir Valley. The **Château du Lude** has three wings. The north, or Louis XII, wing is the earliest, dating from the early 16th century; it houses a ballroom and a spacious, 19th-century library. The François I wing, which faces the park, combines round fortress towers with dainty Renaissance detail and contains Flemish and Gobelin tapestries and a chimneypiece with the king's carved salamander emblem. The 18th-century Louis XVI wing overlooking the river displays severe, classical symmetry. Interior highlights (guided tours only) include the oval saloon, ornate bedroom, and murals by followers of Raphael. On Friday and Saturday evenings from mid-June to mid-September, more than 130 costumed performers, assisted by fountains

★ and fireworks, take part in Le Lude's **son-et-lumière** pageant chronicling the history of the château and the region from the Hundred Years' War onward. ⊠ *pl. François-de-Nicolay,* ☎ *02–43–94–40–54.* 🎫 *32 frs, park only 21 frs, son-et-lumière 90 frs.* ⊙ *Château Apr.–Sept., daily 2–6; park daily 10–noon.*

OFF THE
BEATEN PATH
LE MANS – Best known for its 24-hour automobile race in the second half of June, Le Mans (44 km/28 mi north of Le Lude via D307) is a bustling city with Gallo-Roman ramparts, a well-preserved old quarter, and a magnificent cathedral—part Gothic, part Romanesque—perched precariously on a hilltop overlooking the River Sarthe.

En Route   As you head east from Le Lude on D305, the gentle **Loir Valley** serves up troglodyte dwellings; the sedate little towns of Château-du-Loir and La Chartre-sur-le-Loir (home to a fine dry white wine, Jasnières); hilltop Trôo with its feudal burial mound; and Montoire, scene of Hitler's meeting with Pétain in 1940.

Vendôme

40 *80 km (50 mi) east of Le Lude via D305 and D917, 32 km (20 mi) northwest of Blois, 70 km (44 mi) west of Orléans.*

The enchanting town of Vendôme may not be on your itinerary, but its picturesque appeal—the Loir River splits here into numerous arms, creating a canal-like effect—amply merits a visit. Take time to stroll through the narrow streets, and climb up to the gardens of the ruined castle for knockout views of the town center.

★ The Flamboyant Gothic abbey church of **La Trinité,** dominated by a solemn, 12th-century, 262-ft bell tower that served as a model for the elder spire at Chartres, has a dramatic west front with lacy, petal-like stonework by Jean de Beauce. The earliest part of the interior dates from the 11th century. Note the amusingly carved choir stalls and fine stained glass. The adjacent cloisters lead to the chapter house, whose wall paintings depict the life of Christ. ⊠ *rue de l'Abbaye.*

Dining and Lodging

$$ ✕▥ **Vendôme.** This traditional hotel, a few minutes' walk from the town center, has pleasant rooms in pastel colors, although they are a bit on the small side. The restaurant, La Cloche Rouge, exudes hushed provincial formality, as local gentry concentrate reverentially on their crayfish mousse or *lapin à la solognote* (rabbit cooked in wine with onions and mushrooms). The wine list is strong on local Loire *and* Loir wines. ⊠ *15 rue Faubourg Chartrain, 41100,* ☏ *02–54–77–02–88,* ℻ *02–54–73–90–71. 35 rooms, 21 with shower, 14 with bath. Restaurant. MC, V. Closed late Dec.–early Jan.*

Châteaudun

41 *45 km (28 mi) northeast of Vendôme via N10, 44 km (28 mi) south of Chartres, 29 km (18 mi) southeast of Illiers-Combray.*

The small town of Châteaudun, perched on the only hill for miles around, grew up as the market center for grain produced from the flat farmlands of the Beauce. Although the town took a battering from the Prussians in 1870, a well-indicated pedestrian circuit enables you to admire the 16th- and 17th-century houses that line the tumbling streets between the colossal castle and the 12th-century church of La Madeleine.

The **Château de Châteaudun** stands resplendent on a steep promontory 200 ft above the Loir. The courtyard presents a stylistic clash between cheerful, 16th-century buildings and the circular 12th-century **Grosse Tour** (Great Tower), with its pointed roof like a witch's hat—one of France's bulkiest and best-preserved keeps, with walls more than 12 ft thick. Originally, the ground floor was used solely to store food, and to reinforce its defensive impregnability, the only way in was through a hole in the ceiling; the entrance to the tower itself was halfway up, through a door in a gallery above the chapel. The **Sainte-Chapelle** (Holy Chapel) has a noted collection of 15th-century statues. The other château buildings, with their wonky brick flooring, host a smattering of tapestries and architectural exhibitions. There are also some vaulted medieval kitchens and two fine stone staircases: one Gothic, the other Renaissance. ⊠ *pl. Jehan-du-Dunois,* ☏ *02–37–94–02–90.* ◻ *32 frs.* ☉ *Mid-Mar.–Sept., daily 8–11:45 and 2–6; Oct.–mid-Mar., daily 10–12:30 and 2–5. Guided tours (in English in summer) at 10:30 and 3.*

En Route   From Châteaudun, a fast straight road (N10) heads a half hour north to Chartres. If you're a fan of author Marcel Proust, you may want to make a pilgrimage northwest to **Illiers-Combray,** to visit the house where he spent his summers as a boy, painstakingly evoked in *Swann's Way* and *The Guermantes' Way* in his tome *À la Recherche du Temps Perdu* (*In Search of Lost Time*).

THE LOIRE VALLEY A TO Z

Arriving and Departing

By Car

The Loire Valley is an easy drive from Paris. A10 runs from Paris to Orléans—a distance of 130 km (80 mi)—and on to Tours, with exits at Meung, Blois, and Amboise. After Tours, A10 veers south, toward Poitiers and Bordeaux. A11 links Paris to Angers via Le Mans. Slower but more scenic routes run from the Channel ports down through Normandy into the Loire region.

By Plane

The closest international airports are Paris's Charles-de-Gaulle and Orly (☞ Air Travel *in* the Gold Guide).

By Train

Tours and Angers are both served by the superfast TGV (*Trains à Grande Vitesse*) from Paris (Gare Montparnasse), and three TGV daily reach Vendôme in 40 minutes. Express trains run every two hours from Paris (Gare d'Austerlitz) to Orléans (usually you must change at Les Aubrais) and Blois. Note that trains for Gien leave from Paris's Gare de Lyon (direction Nevers) and that the nearest station to Sancerre is across the Loire at Tracy.

Getting Around

By Bus

Local bus services are extensive and reliable and are a link between train stations and scenic areas off the river. Inquire at tourist offices for information about routes and timetables.

By Car

By far the easiest way to visit the Loire châteaux is by car; N152 hugs the riverbank and offers excellent sightseeing possibilities. You can arrange to rent a car in all the large towns in the region, or at train stations in Orléans, Blois, Tours, or Angers, or in Paris.

By Train

The Loire region's local train network is good but not great: although it's possible to reach many of the châteaux by train, it's not that easy if you have limited time (having a car makes getting around much easier). The main line follows the Loire from Orléans to Blois, Tours, Langeais, Saumur, and Angers, with trains every two hours. There are branch lines from Tours, with less frequent trains, to Loches, Azay-le-Rideau and Chinon, and Vendôme and Châteaudun. Ask the SNCF for the brochure *"Les Chateaux de la Loire en Train"* for more detailed information.

Contacts and Resources

Car Rental

Avis (⊠ 6 rue Jean-Moulin, Blois, ☎ 02–54–74–48–15; ⊠ 13 rue Sansonnières, Orléans, ☎ 02–38–62–27–04; ⊠ Gare SNCF, Tours, ☎ 02–47–20–53–27). **Hertz** (⊠ chaussée St-Victor [on N7], Blois, ☎ 02–54–74–03–03; ⊠ 57 rue Marcel-Tribut, Tours, ☎ 02–47–20–40–24). **Europcar** (⊠ 81 rue André-Dessaux, Fleury-les-Aubrais, near Orléans, ☎ 02–33–73–00–40; ⊠ 76 rue Bernard-Palissy, Tours, ☎ 02–47–64–47–76).

Emergencies

Ambulance (☎ 15). **Regional hospitals:** Angers (⊠ 4 rue Larrey, ☎ 02–41–35–36–37); **Orléans** (⊠ 14 av. de l' Hôpital, ☎ 02–38–51–44–44); **Tours** (⊠ 2 bd. Tonnellé, ☎ 02–47–47–47–47).

Guided Tours

Bus tours of the main châteaux leave daily in summer from Tours, Blois, Angers, Orléans, and Saumur: Ask at the relevant tourist office for latest times and prices. Most châteaux insist that you follow one of their own tours, but try to get a booklet in English before joining, as most are in French. The tourist offices in Tours and Angers also arrange city and regional excursions with **personal guides.** A **walking tour** of Tours sets out from the tourist office every morning at 10 AM from mid-April through October for 40 francs. English-speaking guides show you around the historic city of Blois during a walk that starts from the château at 4; the cost is about 30 francs.

Travel Agencies

American Express (⊠ pl. Albert-Ier, Orléans, ☎ 02–38–53–63–52). **Wagons-Lits** (⊠ 9 rue Marceau, Tours, ☎ 02–47–20–40–54).

Visitor Information

The Loire region has two area tourist offices, for written inquiries only. For Chinon and points east, contact the **Comité Régional du Tourisme Centre-Val de Loire** (⊠ 10 rue Étienne-Dolet, 45000 Orléans). For Fontevraud and points west, contact the **Comité Régional du Tourisme des Pays-de-Loire** (⊠ 2 rue de la Loire, 44200 Nantes).

Others are as follows: **Amboise** (⊠ quai Général-de-Gaulle, ☎ 02–47–57–01–37). **Angers** (⊠ 1 pl. du Président-Kennedy, ☎ 02–41–23–51–11). **Blois** (⊠ 3 av. du Dr-Jean-Laigret, ☎ 02–54–74–06–49). **Orléans** (⊠ pl. Albert-Ier, ☎ 02–38–24–05–05). **Saumur** (⊠ pl. de la Bilange, ☎ 02–41–40–20–60). **Tours** (⊠ 78 rue Bernard-Palissy, ☎ 02–47–70–37–37).

5 Brittany

St-Malo and the Channel Coast, Nantes and the Atlantic Shore

Thanks to its proximity to Great Britain, its folklore, and its spectacular coastline, Brittany is a favorite destination among English-speaking vacationers. It also has massive castles, prehistoric standing stones, and picturesque medieval towns. The French love the area, too, but don't worry about hordes of tourists— Brittany's vast beaches aren't easily crowded and there are enough châteaux to go around.

EVEN THE FRENCH FEEL THEY ARE IN A FOREIGN land
when they visit Brittany (Bretagne in French), the
bulbous portion of western France jutting far out
into the Atlantic. Cut off from mainstream France, the Bretons are an
independent lot who have closer cultural affinities with the Celts across
the Channel than with their fellow countrymen. Both Brittany and Cornwall claim Merlin, King Arthur, and the Druids as cult figures; huge
Stonehenge-like menhirs and dolmens (prehistoric standing stones) litter the Breton countryside and islands.

Revised and
updated by
Simon Hewitt

Brittany became part of France in 1532, but regional folklore is still
very much alive. An annual village *pardon* (religious festival) will give
you a good idea of Breton traditions: Banners and saintly statues are
borne in colorful parades, accompanied by hymns, and the whole
event is rounded off by food of all kinds. The most famous pardon is
held on the last Sunday of August at Sainte-Anne-la-Palud, near Quimper. The surrounding Finistère (from *Finis Terrae,* or Land's End) *département* (province), Brittany's westernmost, is renowned for the
costumes worn on such occasions—notably the lace bonnets, or *coiffes*,
which can tower 15 inches above the wearer's head.

Although Brittany's towns took a mighty hammering during the Nazi
retreat in 1944, most have been restored, except for the large concrete-
cluttered naval base at Brest. Rennes, the only Breton city with more
than 200,000 inhabitants, retains its traditional charm, as do the towns
of Dinan, Quimper, St-Malo, and Vannes. Many ancient man-made delights are still found in the region's villages, and castles and cathedrals
dot the landscape. Geographically, Brittany remains the land of *Armor*
(the sea) and *Argoat* (the forest).

Pleasures and Pastimes

Beaches

Wherever you go in Brittany, the coast is close by: In winter, the frenzied, cliff-bashing Atlantic pounds the shore; in summer, the sprawling beaches and bustling harbors are filled with frolicking bathers and
boaters. Dozens of islands, many inhabited and within easy reach of
the mainland, dot the coastal waters. The best sandy beaches and a
multitude of water sports are found at Dinard, Perros-Guirec, Trégastel-
Plage, Douarnenez, Carnac, La Trinité-sur-Mer, and La Baule.

Dining

Not surprisingly, Breton cuisine is dominated by seafood—often lobster, grilled or prepared in a cream sauce. Popular meats include smoked
ham and lamb, frequently served with green kidney beans. Fried eel is
a traditional dish in Nantes. Brittany is particularly famous for its crepes,
served with both sweet and savory fillings. Accompanied by a glass of
local cider, they are an ideal light, inexpensive meal.

CATEGORY	COST*
$$$$	over 400 frs
$$$	250 frs–400 frs
$$	125 frs–250 frs
$	under 125 frs

*per person for a three-course meal, including tax (20.6%) and tip but not
wine

Lodging

Brittany has plenty of small, charming, family-run hotels with friendly
and personal service, as well as a growing number of luxury hotels and

châteaux. Dinard, on the English Channel, and La Baule, on the Atlantic, are the area's two most expensive resorts. In summer, there are large crowds, so make reservations far in advance and reconfirm.

CATEGORY	COST*
$$$$	over 800 frs
$$$	600 frs–800 frs
$$	300 frs–600 frs
$	under 300 frs

All prices are for a standard double room for two, including tax (20.6%) and service charge.

Exploring Brittany

Brittany can be divided into two basic areas: the northeast, stretching from Rennes to St-Malo and along the Channel coast, with mighty medieval castles surveying the land and quaint resort towns by the sea; and the Atlantic coast between Brest and Nantes, where frenzied surf crashes against the cliffs, alternating with sprawling beaches and bustling harbors.

Great Itineraries

If you only have a short amount of time—three days, for instance—concentrate on northeast Brittany. With five days you can explore this area in greater depth, including the capital city of Rennes. In 10 days, you can cover the entire region, if you don't spend too much time in any one place. A car is necessary for getting to the small medieval towns and deserted coastline.

Numbers in the text correspond to numbers in the margin and on the Brittany and Nantes maps.

IF YOU HAVE 3 DAYS

Make either the fortified port of ⛱ **St-Malo** ⑨ or the medieval town of ⛱ **Dinan** ⑤ your base for exploring northeast Brittany. Be sure to visit seaside **Dinard** ⑩, ancient **Dol-de-Bretagne** ⑦, Chateaubriand's boyhood home at **Combourg** ⑥, or the 16th-century castle at **La Bourbansais,** all within a 30-km (20-mi) radius. In addition, the magnificent rock island of **Mont-St-Michel** (☞ Chapter 6) is only 50 km (30 mi) away in Normandy.

IF YOU HAVE 5 DAYS

Follow the three-day itinerary, and then on the fourth day, stop at the castle at **Montmuran** ④ on your way to ⛱ **Rennes** ③, the region's capital. Visit the formidable castle in **Vitré** ② and the medieval military town of **Fougères** ① on day five.

IF YOU HAVE 10 DAYS

Make ⛱ **Rennes** ③ your base for exploring the castles, châteaux, and fortresses at **Vitré** ②, **Fougères** ①, and **Montmuran** ④, making an excursion to the Château de Caradeuc, if you have time. On day three, stop at **La Bourbansais, Combourg** ⑥, or **Dol-de-Bretagne** ⑦ on your way to ⛱ **Dinan** ⑤ or ⛱ **St-Malo** ⑨ for the night. Head west the following day on a scenic tour of the coast and spend the night in ⛱ **Trébeurden** ⑫, on the tip of the Corniche Bretonne. Start early the next day for **Morlaix** ⑬, with its quaint streets. Continue west and briefly visit the market town of **St-Pol-de-Léon** ⑭, the fortified château of **Kerjean,** or the splendid basilica at **Le Folgoët.** Eat lunch in **Brest** ⑮, a huge, modern port town. By late afternoon plan on being in **Locronan,** where sails used to be made for French fleets. Try to reach picturesque ⛱ **Douarnenez** ⑯ by evening. On the sixth day, head to **Audierne** ⑰ and on to the rugged Pointe du Raz; then double back to **Quimper** ⑱, with its lovely river bank and cathedral. Stop briefly to see the offshore stronghold at **Concarneau** ⑲, and aim to reach ☒ **Pont-Aven** ⑳ by the end of the day; then dine on oysters in nearby **Riec-sur-Belon.** Drive down the Atlantic seaboard, on day seven, to the beaches of **Quiberon** ㉒ and catch the ferry to the pretty island of ☒ **Belle-Ile** ㉓. On day eight, return to the mainland and meander along the coast through the beach resorts of **Carnac** ㉔ and **La Trinité-sur-Mer,** stopping in the medieval town of **Vannes** ㉖ and exploring the marshy parkland of **La Grande Brière.** Spend the night in seaside ☒ **La Baule** ㉗. The following day head to tranquil, prosperous ☒ **Nantes** ㉘–㉞.

When to Tour Brittany

The tourist season is short in Brittany. Long, damp winters keep visitors away, and many hotels are closed until Easter. Brittany is particularly crowded in July and August, when most French people are on vacation, so choose crowd-free June, September, or early October, when autumnal colors and crisp evenings make for a particularly invigorating visit. Late summer, however, is the most festive time in Brittany: The two biggest pardons take place on July 26 (Sainte-Anne d'Auray) and the last Sunday in August (Sainte-Anne-la-Palud); the Celtic Festival de Cornouaille takes place at Quimper in late July.

NORTHEAST BRITTANY AND THE CHANNEL COAST

Northeast Brittany extends from the city of Rennes to the coast. The rolling farmland around Rennes is strewn with mighty castles in Vitré, Fougères, and Dinan—remnants of Brittany's ceaseless efforts to repel invaders during the Middle Ages and a testimony to the wealth derived from pirate and merchant ships. The beautiful Côte d'Émeraude (Emerald Coast) stretches west from Cancale to St-Brieuc, and the dramatic Côte de Granit Rose (Pink Granite Coast) extends from Paimpol to Trébeurden and the Corniche Bretonne. Follow the coastal routes D786 and D34, winding, narrow roads that total less than 100 km (60 mi) but can take five hours to drive; all along there are spectacular views.

Fougères

❶ *320 km (200 mi) west of Paris via A11, A81, and D30; 47 km (29 mi) southeast of Mont-St-Michel; 48 km (30 mi) northeast of Rennes.*

For many centuries, Fougères, a traditional cobbling and cider-making center, was a frontier town, valiantly attempting to guard Brittany against attack. One of the reasons for its conspicuous lack of success is the site of its castle: Instead of sitting high up on the hill, it spreads out down in the valley, though the sinuous River Nançon does make an admirable moat. A number of medieval houses line rue de la Pinterie, which leads directly from the castle up to the undistinguished heart of town.

The 13-tower **Château de Fougères,** one of the largest in Europe, covers more than 5 acres. Although largely in ruins, it is an excellent example of the military architecture of the Middle Ages, impressive both inside and out. The thick walls—20 ft across in places—were intended to resist 15th-century artillery fire, but the castle proved vulnerable to surprise attacks and sieges. A visit inside the castle walls reveals three lines of fortification, with the keep at their heart. There are memorable views over Fougères from the **Tour Mélusine** (tower) and, in the **Tour Raoul,** a small shoe museum. The second and third stories of the **Tour de Coigny** were transformed into a chapel during the 16th century. ☒

English Channel (La Manche)

Corniche Bretonne
Perros-Guirec

Ile de Batz
Roscoff
St-Pol-de-Léon 14
Trébeurden 12
Lannion

Kerjean
Le Folgoët
D10
D788
D30
Morlaix 13
D786
N12-E50
Guingamp
D767

Ile d'Ouessant
Ile Molène
N12
Brest 15
D789
N165
Daoulas
D764
Carhaix-Plouguer
D787
N164

Aulne
Port Launay

Baie de Douarnenez
Ste-Anne-la-Palud
Locronan
Treboul
Douarnenez 16
Steir
Odet
D769

Ile de Sein
17 **Audierne**
D765
Quimper 18
D784
Pointe du Raz

Concarneau 19
D783
N165
Pont-Aven
20
Riec-Sur-Belon
N165
N24

Iles de Glénan
Lorient 21
Hennebo
Port-Louis
D781

Ile de Groix
Carnac
24
La
22
Quiberon

ATLANTIC OCEAN

Sauzon
Belle-Ile 23

N

0   20 miles
0   30 km

pl. Symon, ☎ *02–99–99–79–59.* 🎫 *22 frs.* 🕑 *Feb.–Mar. and Oct.–Dec., daily 10–noon and 2–5; Apr.–mid-June, daily 9:30–noon and 2–6; mid-June–Sept., daily 9–7.*

The oldest streets are alongside the castle, clustered around the elegant slate spire of **St-Sulpice,** a Flamboyant Gothic church with several fine altarpieces. ✉ *rue Le Bouteiller.*

In the 1790s Fougères was a center of Royalist resistance to the French Revolution. Much of the action in 19th-century writer Honoré de Balzac's bloodcurdling novel *Les Chouans* takes place hereabouts. The novel's heroine, Marie de Verneuil, had rooms close to the church of **St-Léonard,** which overlooks the Nançon Valley. To get there from the cathedral, follow the river south. Both the footpath leading to the building and the church, with its ornate facade and 17th-century tower, have changed little; the garden through which the path leads is known today as the **Jardin Public** (Public Garden). ✉ *rue de la Porte-St-Léonard.*

Another man who was inspired by the scenery of Fougères was locally born Emmanuel de La Villéon (1858–1944), a little-known Impressionist painter. More than 100 paintings, pastels, watercolors, and drawings—revealing a serene, underestimated talent—are on display at the **Musée La Villéon.** It is in one of the oldest surviving houses (dating from the 16th century) in Fougères. The artist's work ranges from compassionate studies of toiling peasants to pretty landscapes where soft shades of green melt into hazy blue horizons. To reach it from the Jardin Public, head left past St-Léonard and cross the square into the adjacent rue Nationale. ✉ *51 rue Nationale.* 🎫 *10 frs.* 🕑 *Easter–mid-June, weekends 11–12:30 and 2:30–5; mid-June–mid-Sept., weekdays 10:30–12:30 and 2:30–5:30, weekends 11–12:30 and 2:30–5.*

Dining and Lodging

$$ ✕🏨 **Les Voyageurs.** The refined cuisine—local foie gras and sweetbreads in Madeira sauce—has made this hotel-restaurant a favorite. Save room for the dessert cart loaded with homemade pastries. The restaurant is closed the last two weeks in August and weekend nights, September to June. Some of the rooms have been pleasantly redecorated in light colors and chintzes: Ask for one of these. ✉ *10 pl. Gambetta, 35300,* ☎ *02–99–99–08–20,* 🆕 *02–99–99–99–04. 37 rooms, 17 with bath, 20 with shower. Restaurant. Closed mid-Dec.–early Jan.*

Vitré

② *30 km (19 mi) south of Fougères via D798 and D178, 36 km (22 mi) east of Rennes.*

Built high above the Vilaine Valley, Vitré (pronounced vee-*tray*) is one of the age-old gateways to Brittany: There's still a feel of the Middle Ages about its formidable castle, tightly packed and half-timbered houses, remaining ramparts, and dark, narrow alleys. The castle stands at the west end of town, facing narrow, cobbled streets, as picturesque as any in Brittany—rue Poterie, rue d'Embas, and rue Beaudrairie, originally the home of tanners (the name comes from *baudoyers,* leather workers).

★   Rebuilt in the 14th and 15th centuries to protect Brittany from invasion, the 11th-century **Château de Vitré**—shaped in an imposing triangle with fat, round towers—proved to be one of the province's most successful fortresses: During the Hundred Years' War (1337–1453), the English repeatedly failed to take it, even though they occupied the rest of the town. It is a splendid sight, especially from the vantage point of rue de Fougères across the river valley below. Time, not foreigners, came closest to ravaging the castle, which was heavily, though tastefully, restored during the past century. The **Hôtel de Ville** (Town Hall), however, is an unfortunate 1913 addition to the castle courtyard. You can visit the wing to the left of the entrance, beginning with the **Tour St-Laurent** and its museum containing 15th- and 16th-century sculptures, Aubusson tapestries, and engravings. Continue along the walls via the **Tour de l'Argenterie** (Silver Tower)—which contains a macabre collection of stuffed frogs and reptiles preserved in glass jars—to the **Tour de l'Oratoire**. (Oratory Tower). ☎ 02–99–96–76–51. ☎ 21 frs. ☉ Apr.–June, Wed.–Mon. 10–noon and 2–5:30; July–Sept., daily 10–12:30 and 2–6:15; Oct.–Mar., Mon. 2–5:30, Wed.–Fri. 10–noon and 2–5:30 .

Fragments of the town's medieval ramparts include the 15th-century **Tour de la Bridolle** (⌧ pl. de la République), five blocks up from the castle. The **Notre-Dame** church (⌧ pl. Notre-Dame), with its fine, pinnacled south front, was built in the 15th and 16th centuries.

Dining and Lodging

$$ ✗▥ **Le Petit Billot.** Carved wood paneling and faded pastels give this hotel a delightful, French provincial atmosphere. The staff is friendly and the restaurant serves good food: Try the vegetable terrine with a chopped tomato sauce or the fresh grilled mackerel. ⌧ 5 pl. du Général-de-Gaulle, 35500, ☎ 02–99–75–02–10, ℻ 02–99–74–72–96. 22 rooms, 5 with bath. Restaurant. Closed last wk of Dec.

Rennes

❸ 36 km (22 mi) west of Vitré via D857/N157, 348 km (216 mi) west of Paris, 107 km (66 mi) north of Nantes.

Rennes (pronounced ren) is the traditional capital of Brittany. It has a different flavor from other towns in the region, mainly because of a terrible fire in 1720, which lasted a week and destroyed half the city. The remaining cobbled streets and half-timber, 15th-century houses form an interesting contrast to the classical feel of the cathedral and Jacques Gabriel's disciplined granite buildings, broad avenues, and spacious squares. Many of the 15th- and 16th-century houses in the streets surrounding the cathedral have been converted into shops, boutiques, restaurants, and crêperies (crepe houses).

A late-18th-century building in classical style that took 57 years to construct, the **Cathédrale St-Pierre** looms above rue de la Monnaie at the west end of the old town, bordered by the River Rance. Stop in to admire its richly decorated interior and outstanding 16th-century Flemish altarpiece. ⌧ pl. St-Pierre. ☉ Mon.–Sat. 8:30–noon and 2–5, Sun. 8:30–noon.

The **Palais de Justice** (Law Courts), the palatial original home of the Breton Parliament and now the Rennes law courts, was designed in 1618 by Salomon de Brosse, architect of the Luxembourg Palace in Paris. It was the most important building in Rennes to escape the 1720 fire, but in February 1994, following a massive demonstration by Breton fishermen demanding state subsidies, a disastrous fire broke out at the Parliament building that left it just a charred shell. Much of the art work—though damaged—was saved by firefighters, who arrived at the scene after the building was already engulfed in flames. It was a case of the fire bell that cried "fire" once too often; a faulty bell, which went off regularly for no reason, had led the man on duty to ignore the ringing. As for the cause of the fire itself, rumors abound, and the building is not likely to be restored until 2002. In the meantime, the art treasures are hidden away for safekeeping. ⌧ rue Nationale.

The **Musée des Beaux-Arts** (Fine Arts Museum), south of the Palais de Justice and left across the quai Émile-Zola, contains one of the country's best collections of paintings outside Paris, featuring works by Georges de La Tour, Jean-Baptiste Chardin, Camille Corot, Paul Gauguin, and Maurice Utrillo, to name a few. ⊠ *20 quai Émile-Zola,* ☎ *02–99–28–55–84.* 🎫 *20 frs.* ⊙ *Wed.–Mon. 10–noon and 2–6.*

Take a stroll through the lovely **Jardin du Thabor,** east of the Palais des Musées and a five-minute walk via rue Victor-Hugo. It's a large, formal French garden with regimented rows of trees, shrubs, and flowers. There is a notable view of the church of **Notre-Dame-en-St-Melaine** from the garden. ⊠ *rue de Paris.*

Dining and Lodging

$ ╳ **Piccadilly Tavern.** Around the corner from the Palais de Justice and next to the municipal theater is this oddly named tavern. Its huge, sunny terrace is the perfect place to people-watch while enjoying a half dozen fresh oysters and an aperitif. ⊠ *15 Galerie du Théâtre,* ☎ *02–99–78–17–17. MC, V.*

$$–$$$ ╳🏨 **Le Coq Gadby.** A 19th-century mansion with huge fireplaces and
★ antiques sets the stage for this cozy hotel-restaurant. Rooms have a homey feel and four-poster beds with floral covers; some have fireplaces. French presidents have come here to dine on traditional Breton specialties—*biscuit de langoustines aux olives noires* (puff pastry filled with langoustines and black olives) and *frigousse aux trois volailles* (poultry stew). It's a popular place, so reserve ahead; there's no dinner Sunday. ⊠ *156 rue d'Antrain, 35300,* ☎ *02–99–38–05–55,* 𝖥𝖠𝖷 *02–99–38–53–40. 11 rooms. Restaurant. MC, V.*

$$$ 🏨 **Garden Hôtel.** This delightful hotel has an age-old wooden gallery overlooking the sunny inner courtyard where breakfast is served. Rooms are small but nicely decorated with bright colors and antiques. ⊠ *3 rue Duhamel, 35000,* ☎ *02–99–65–45–06,* 𝖥𝖠𝖷 *02–99–65–02–62. 24 rooms, 8 with bath, 16 with shower. AE, DC, MC, V.*

$$ 🏨 **Central.** This stately 19th-century hotel is in a quiet, narrow backstreet close to the cathedral. Rooms look out over the street or the courtyard, but the best part about this place is its central location. ⊠ *6 rue Lanjuinais, 35000,* ☎ *02–99–79–12–36,* 𝖥𝖠𝖷 *02–99–79–65–76. 43 rooms. AE, DC, MC, V.*

Nightlife and the Arts

Dance the night away at **L'Espace** (⊠ 45 bd. de la Tour d'Auvergne, ☎ 02–99–30–21–95). Relax with a drink at **Pym's** (⊠ 27 pl. du Colombier, ☎ 02–99–67–30–00).

Brittany's principal theater is the **Opéra de Rennes** (⊠ pl. de la Mairie, ☎ 02–99–28–55–87). All kinds of performances are staged at the **Théâtre National de Bretagne** (⊠ 1 rue St-Hélier, ☎ 02–99–31–55–33). The famous, annual international rock-and-roll festival, **Les Transmusicales** (☎ 02–99–31–12–10 for information), takes place the second week of December in bars around town and at the Théâtre National de Bretagne. The first week of July is **Les Tombées de la Nuit** (Nightfall) festival, featuring ballet, music, and theater performances staged in old historic streets and churches (☎ 02–99–30–38–01 for information).

Shopping

A lively **street market** is held on place des Lices on Saturday morning.

Montmuran

❹ *24 km (15 mi) northwest of Rennes via N137/D221.*

The **Château de Montmuran** was once home to one of France's finest knights, Bertrand du Guesclin (1320–80). Commemorated in countless squares and hostelries across the province, du Guesclin sprang to prominence at the age of 17, when he entered a jousting tournament in disguise and successfully unseated several hoarier knights. He went on to become one of France's greatest warriors, leading the onslaught against the English during the Hundred Years' War. An alley of oak and beech trees leads up to the main 17th-century building of du Guesclin's château, which is surrounded by a moat and flanked by four towers, two built in the 12th century, two in the 14th. You can visit the towers and a small museum devoted to the castle's history. The château also has two pleasant guest rooms, which are open from May to October. Call to reserve. ⊠ *35630 Les Iffs (right next to Montmuran),* ☎ *02–99–45–88–88.* ▨ *20 frs.* ☉ *Easter–Oct., daily 2–7; Nov.–Easter, weekends 2–5.*

OFF THE **CHÂTEAU DE CARADEUC** – Ambitiously dubbed the Versailles of Brittany,
BEATEN PATH this château, 8 km (5 mi) west of Montmuran just beyond Bécherel, is privately owned and not open to the public. But you can explore the surrounding park—Brittany's largest—and admire its statues, flower beds, and leafy alleys. ⊠ *rte. de Chateaubriand,* ☎ *02–99–66–77–76.* ▨ *15 frs.* ☉ *Apr.–Oct., daily 10–6; Nov.–Mar., weekends 2–6.*

Dinan

★ ❺ *29 km (18 mi) northwest of Montmuran via D27 and D68, 24 km (15 mi) south of Dinard.*

Dinan, too, has close links with warrior-hero Bertrand du Guesclin (☞ Montmuran, *above*), who won a famous victory here in 1359 and promptly married a local girl, Tiphaine Raguenel. When he died in the siege of Auvergne (central France) in 1380, his body was dispatched home to Dinan. Owing to the great man's popularity, only his heart completed the journey (it rests in the basilica); the rest of him was confiscated by devoted followers along the way.

On **place des Merciers, rue de l'Apport,** and **rue de la Poissonnerie,** note the splendid triangular-gable wooden houses. These cobbled streets are so pretty you may think you've stumbled onto a movie set. **Rue du Jerzual,** which leads down to Dinan's harbor, is also a beautifully preserved medieval street, divided halfway down by the town walls and the massive **Porte du Jerzual** gateway and lined with boutiques and crafts shops in 15th- and 16th-century houses. A few restaurants brighten the area around the harbor and boats sail up the Rance River in summer, but the abandoned warehouses mostly bear witness to the town's vanished commercial activity. Above the harbor, near Porte St-Malo, is the leafy **promenade des Grands Fossés,** the best-preserved section of the town walls, which leads to the castle. The **tourist office** (⊠ rue de l'Horloge, ☎ 02–96–39–75–40) is housed in a 16th-century building in the old town.

For a superb view of the town, climb to the top of the medieval **Tour de l'Horloge** (Clock Tower). ⊠ *rue de l'Horloge.* ▨ *10 frs.* ☉ *July–Sept., daily 10:45–1:15 and 3–6.*

Breton warrior-hero du Guesclin's heart lies in the north transept of
★ the **Basilique St-Sauveur,** off rue de l'Horloge, one block north of the tourist office. The church's style ranges from the Romanesque south

front to the Flamboyant Gothic facade and Renaissance side chapels. The old trees in the **Jardin Anglais** (English Garden) behind the church provide a nice frame. More spectacular views can be found at the bottom of the garden, which looks down the plummeting Rance Valley to the river 250 ft below. ⊠ *pl. St-Sauveur.*

The **Château,** at the end of the promenade des Petits Fossés, has a two-story tower, the **Tour du Coëtquen,** and a 100-ft, 14th-century **donjon** (keep), containing a museum with varied displays of medieval effigies and statues, Breton furniture, and local lace coiffes. ⊠ *Porte de Guichet,* ☎ 02–96–39–45–20. 🎫 25 frs. ☉ *Mar.–May and mid-Sept.–mid-Nov., daily 10–11:30 and 2–5:30; June–mid-Sept., daily 10–5:30; mid-Nov.–Feb., Thurs.–Tues. 1:30–5.*

Dining and Lodging

$$ ✕ **La Poudrière.** Under the vaulted ceilings of this restaurant, which is in the cellar of the D'Avaugour hotel (☞ *below*), hearty fare—from *cuisse canard en confit* (duck thigh in its fat) to lobster in a rich wine sauce—is served. ⊠ *1 pl. du Champ-Clos,* ☎ 02–96–39–79–84. *AE, DC, MC, V.*

$ ✕ **Relais des Corsaires.** On the banks of the Rance is this spot that was named, after the pirates, it is said, who raided Dinan. The mid-range prix-fixe menu provides an ample four-course meal. The welcoming proprietors, Jacques and Barbel Pauwels, also have a more informal grill, Au Petit Corsair, in the 15th-century building next door. ⊠ *7 rue du Quai,* ☎ 02–96–39–40–17. *AE, DC, MC, V. Closed Jan.–Feb.*

$$ 🏨 **Arvor.** The cobbled streets of the old town are visible from this comfortably converted 18th-century convent across from the tourist office. It's run by the convivial Brigitte Urvoy, and is a good value without frills. ⊠ *5 rue Auguste-Pavie, 22100,* ☎ 02–96–39–21–22, FAX 02–96–39–83–09. *23 rooms. AE, MC, V.*

$$ 🏨 **D'Avaugour.** This hotel, opposite the castle tower, has a sunny
★ flower garden where breakfast and afternoon tea are served. Most rooms are cozy and look out onto either the garden or the castle. Start the day with the full buffet breakfast. Mme. Quinton is fluent in English and enjoys helping plan day trips. ⊠ *1 pl. du Champ-Clos, 22100,* ☎ 02–96–39–07–49, FAX 02–96–85–43–04. *27 rooms. Restaurant, breakfast room. AE, DC, MC, V.*

Nightlife and the Arts

Every two years (next in 2000), on the first weekend in September, medieval France is re-created with a market, parade, jousting tournament, and street music for **La Fête des Remparts** (Ramparts Festival), one of the largest medieval festivals in Europe.

Shopping

The cobbled, sloping **rue de Jerzual** is lined with medieval houses containing shops selling crafts by local wood-carvers, jewelers, leather workers, glass specialists, and silk painters.

En Route Halfway between Dinan and Combourg is the castle of **La Bourban-sais,** built in the 1580s. Most of the interior furnishings date from the 18th century, including the fine collection of porcelain and tapestries. Its extensive gardens contain a small zoo and a pack of hunting hounds. ☎ 02–99–69–40–07. 🎫 *Castle 45 frs, park 45 frs, castle and park 60 frs.* ☉ *Castle Apr.–Oct., daily 2–6; Nov.–Mar., Sun. 3:30–5; park daily 2–6.*

Combourg

❻ *24 km (15 mi) southeast of Dinan via D794, 39 km (24 mi) north of Rennes.*

The pretty, lakeside village of Combourg is dominated by the boyhood home of Romantic writer Viscount Chateaubriand (1768–1848), the thick-walled, four-tower **Château de Combourg.** The castle dates mainly from the 14th and 15th centuries. You can visit the Chateaubriand archives and the writer's austere bedroom in the **Tour du Chat** (Cat's Tower). The grounds—ponds, woods, and cattle-strewn meadowland—are suitably mournful and can seem positively desolate under leaden skies. ☎ 02–99–73–22–95. ⌑ *25 frs, park only 8 frs. ☉ Apr.– June and Sept., Wed.–Mon. 9–noon and 2–5; July–Aug., daily 9–5; Oct., Wed.–Mon. 2–4.*

Dol-de-Bretagne

❼ *17 km (11 mi) north of Combourg via D795, 56 km (35 mi) north of Rennes.*

The ancient town of Dol-de-Bretagne, which still has its original ramparts, looks out over the Marais de Dol, a marshy plain stretching across to Mont-St-Michel, 21 km (13 mi) northeast. For extensive views of the Marais as well as Mont-Dol, a 200-ft windmill-topped mound 3 km (2 mi) north and the legendary scene of combat between St. Michael and the devil, walk along the **Promenade des Douves,** on the northern part of the original ramparts. Also explore Dol's picturesque main street, **Grand-Rue des Stuarts,** lined with medieval houses; the oldest, the **Maison des Palets,** at No. 17, has a chunky row of Romanesque arches.

The **Cathédrale St-Samson** is a damp, soaring, fortresslike bulk of granite dating mainly from the 12th to the 14th centuries. This mighty building shows just how influential the bishopric of Dol was in days gone by. The richly sculpted Great Porch, carved wooden choir stalls, and stained glass in the chancel deserve close scrutiny. ⌑ *pl. de la Cathédrale.*

During a short, cheerfully guided tour of the small **Musée Historique d'Art Populaire** (Museum of Popular Art) opposite the cathedral, you can see costumes, weapons, and models retracing life in Dol since prehistoric times. The pride of the museum is its assembly of colored wooden religious statues. ✉ *2 pl. de la Trésorerie,* ☎ *02–99–48–09–38.* ⌑ *20 frs. ☉ Easter–Oct., Wed.–Mon. 9:30–noon and 2–5:30.*

On the third Sunday of September, traditional farming tools and methods are on display during **La Fête du Blé Noir** (Black Wheat Festival) at the Musée de la Paysannerie (Peasantry Museum; ✉ Baguer Morvan, 4 km/2 mi north of Dol-de-Bretagne, ☎ 02–99–48–04–04).

Dining and Lodging

$$ ✕▣ **La Bresche Arthur.** With its crisp outlines, white walls, and glassed-in terrace, this hotel doesn't look as historic as it sounds. But it is cozy, and rooms are inexpensive if functional. Character, smartness, and indulgence are reserved for the restaurant, where chef-owner Philippe Martel serves classically inspired roast pigeon with black currant and ginger, and ravioli stuffed with *petits gris* (small snails). ✉ *36 bd. Deminiac, 35120,* ☎ *02–99–48–01–44,* FAX *02–99–48–16–32. 24 rooms. Restaurant. AE, DC, MC, V. Closed Feb.*

$$ ✕▣ **Domaine des Ormes.** The former country retreat of the bishops of Dol, just south of town, serves as the backdrop for this tasteful leisure complex. It has a campsite, rental chalets, a golf course, artificial lakes, an outdoor pool, an archery concourse, a cricket ground, and a modern hotel with spacious rooms and a bilingual staff. Decor throughout is bland, but the restaurant's menu is inventive, with a fine array of meats, shellfish, and pâtés for 95 francs and up. The salads at the golf club are a good lunchtime bet. ✉ *35120 Épiniac (7 km/4 mi south*

of Dol-de-Bretagne), ☎ 02–99–73–43–33, FAX 02–99–73–40–84.
*32 rooms. Restaurant, bars, pool, 19-hole golf course, 2 tennis courts,
archery. AE, DC, MC, V.*

Cancale

8 *22 km (14 mi) northwest of Dol via D155 and D76.*

If you enjoy eating oysters, be sure to get to Cancale, a picturesque
fishing village renowned for its *bancs d'huîtres* (oyster beds). You can
sample the little brutes at countless stalls or restaurants along the
quay. At the **Musée de l'Huître** (Oyster Museum), you can learn all about
how oysters are farmed. ⊠ *Les Parcs St-Kerber, plage de l'Aurore,* ☎
02–99–89–69–99. ☉ *Guided 1-hr tours mid-June–mid-Sept., daily
11 and 3–5; mid-Feb.–mid-June and Oct., daily 3 PM.*

Dining and Lodging

\$\$\$\$ ✕🏨 **Bricourt.** Mont-St-Michel is visible from the large stone house where
chef Olivier Roellinger grew up and now runs one of the region's best
restaurants. Murals, stone fireplaces, and antique tiles create an imposing yet cozy atmosphere. Local seafood dishes seasoned with exotic spices are the specialty. Don't skip dessert. The restaurant is closed
Tuesday and Wednesday in winter. If you wish to stay the night, there
are attractive rooms in the main building and the annex. ⊠ *62 rue Ri-
mains, 35260,* ☎ *02–99–89–64–76,* FAX *02–99–89–88–47. 19
rooms. Restaurant. AE, DC, MC, V.*

\$\$\$\$ ✕🏨 **Richeux.** One of three hotels in Cancale owned by the Roellingers
of the Bricourt (☞ *above*), it occupies an imposing turn-of-the-century
waterfront mansion built on the ruins of the du Guesclin family's
11th-century château. Request one of the tower rooms, which have stunning views of Mont-St-Michel Bay. Le Coquillage, a small restaurant,
closed from mid-November to mid-December, serves local oysters. ⊠
Le Point du Jour, St-Méloir des Ondes, 35350, ☎ *02–99–89–25–
25,* FAX *02–99–89–18–49. 11 rooms. Restaurant. AE, DC, MC, V.*

St-Malo

★ **9** *23 km (14 mi) west of Cancale via coastal D201, 69 km (43 mi) north
of Rennes.*

Facing Dinard across the Rance Estuary lies the ancient walled town
of St-Malo. The stone ramparts of this onetime pirate base have withstood the Atlantic since the 12th century. They were considerably enlarged and modified in the 18th century and now extend for more than
1½ km (1 mi) around the old town—known as *intra-muros* (within the
walls)—from the castle in St-Malo's northeast corner. The views are
stupendous, especially at high tide.

The town itself has proved less resistant: A weeklong fire in 1944, kin-
dled by retreating Nazis, wiped out nearly all the old buildings. Restoration work was more painstaking than brilliant, but the narrow streets
and granite houses of the old town were satisfactorily re-created, enabling St-Malo to regain its role as a busy fishing port, seaside resort,
and tourist destination. Millions of tourists invade this quaint town,
so if you want to avoid crowds, don't come here in summer.

At the edge of the ramparts is the **Château,** whose great keep and watchtowers command an impressive view of the harbor and coastline. It
houses the **Musée d'Histoire de la Ville** (Town History Museum), devoted to local history, and the **Galerie Quic-en-Grogne,** a museum in
a tower, where various episodes and celebrities from St-Malo's past are
recalled by way of waxworks. ⊠ *Hôtel de Ville,* ☎ *02–99–40–71–*

57 for museums, 02–99–40–80–26 for château. ⌸ Museums 25 frs, château 20 frs. ☉ Museums Easter–Sept., Wed.–Mon. 10–noon and 2–6. Château Easter–June and Sept.–Oct., daily 9:30–11:15 and 2–5:15; July–Aug., daily 9:30–11:45 and 2–5:45.

Five hundred yards offshore is the **Ile du Grand Bé,** a small island housing the somber military tomb of Viscount Chateaubriand, who was born in St-Malo. The islet can be reached by a causeway at low tide.

The **Fort National,** also offshore and only accessible by causeway at low tide, is a massive fortress with a dungeon constructed in 1689 by that military-engineering genius Sébastien de Vauban. ☎ 02–99–46–91–25. ⌸ 10 frs. ☉ Easter–Oct.; call ahead. Times of ½-hr guided tours depend on the tides.

You can pay homage to Jacques Cartier, who set sail from St-Malo in 1535 to discover the St. Lawrence River and found Québec, at his tomb in the church of **St-Vincent** (⌷ At the top of Grande-Rue). His statue looks out over the town ramparts, four blocks away, along with that of swashbuckling corsair Robert Surcouf, hero of many daring 18th-century raids on the British navy (he's the one pointing an accusing finger over the waves at England).

Dining and Lodging

$–$$ ✕ **Le Chalut.** Locals and tourists come to this simple, casual, friendly restaurant for fish. You can inspect the night's fare on ice in front and in a large tank in the dining room. Decor is plain—the emphasis is on the food. ⌷ 8 rue de la Corne-du-Cerf, ☎ 02–99–56–71–58. Reservations not accepted. MC, V. Closed Jan. and 2 wks in Oct. No dinner Sun. off-season.

$ ✕ **Café de la Bourse.** Prawns and oysters are downed by the shovelful in this bustling brasserie in the old town. The decor, replete with wooden seats, ships' wheels, and posters of grizzled old sea dogs, is hardly artistic. But the large, L-shape dining room makes amends with friendly service and a seafood platter for two that includes at least three tanklike crabs plus an army of cockles, snails, and periwinkles. ⌷ 1 rue de Dinan, ☎ 02–99–56–47–17. MC, V. Closed Wed. off-season.

$$–$$$ 🏨 **Atlantis.** The view of the sea is magnificent from the hotel's terrace and rooms. The largest and most luxurious rooms are pricey, but others are quite reasonable. The bar, overlooking the water, and the salon de thé (tea shop) also add to the hotel's charm. ⌷ 49 chaussée du Sillon, 35400, ☎ 02–99–56–09–26, FAX 02–99–56–41–65. 53 rooms. Bar, tea shop. AE, V. Closed Jan.

$$ 🏨 **Elizabeth.** In a town house built into the ramparts of the city wall,
★ the Elizabeth, near the Porte St-Louis, is a little gem of sophistication in touristy St-Malo. Rooms are generally small but tastefully furnished; rates vary with size. ⌷ 2 rue des Cordiers, 35400, ☎ 02–99–56–24–98, FAX 02–99–56–39–24. 17 rooms. AE, DC, MC, V.

$$ 🏨 **Jean-Bart.** This clean, quiet hotel next to the ramparts is done in cool blues. Beds are comfortable and bathrooms modern, but the rooms, some with sea views, are somewhat small. ⌷ 12 rue de Chartres, 35400, ☎ 02–99–40–33–88, FAX 02–99–40–33–88. 17 rooms. MC, V. Closed mid-Nov.–mid-Feb.

Nightlife and the Arts

Bar de L'Univers (⌷ pl. Chateaubriand) is a nice spot to sip a drink in a pirate's lair setting. **La Belle Époque** (⌷ 11 rue de Dinan) is a popular hangout for all ages till the wee hours. **L'Escalier** (⌷ La Buzardière, rue de la Tour-du-Bonheur) is the place for dancing the night away.

In summer, performances are held at the **Théâtre Chateaubriand** (⌷ 6 rue Groult-de-St-Georges, ☎ 02–99–40–98–05). On July 14 (Bastille

Day) the **Fête du Clos Poulet** (Clos Poulet Festival), a neighborhood event with traditional dancing, takes place. August brings a religious music festival, the **Festival de la Musique Sacrée.**

Outdoor Activities and Sports

The **Club Hippique** at St-Coulomb (☎ 02–99–81–65–03) is the source for horses. Sailboats can be rented from **Naviloc** (⊠ quai des Bas-Sablons, ☎ 02–99–82–12–72). The harbor and area outside the breakwater are popular sailing spots.

Shopping

A lively **outdoor market** takes place in the streets of old St-Malo every Tuesday and Friday.

Dinard

⑩ *13 km (8 mi) west of St-Malo via D168, 71 km (44 mi) north of Rennes.*

Dinard is the most elegant resort town on this stretch of the Brittany coast. Its picture-book setting on the Rance Estuary opposite the walled city of St-Malo lured the English aristocracy here in droves after it was discovered in the 1850s by an American named Coppinger. What started out as a small fishing port soon became a seaside mecca of lavish turn-of-the-century villas, grand hotels, and a bustling casino. A number of modern establishments punctuate the landscape, but the town still retains something of an Edwardian tone. To make the most of Dinard's beauty, head down to the Pointe de la Vicomte, at the town's southern tip, where the cliffs give panoramic views across the Baie du Prieuré and Rance Estuary, or stroll along the promenade.

The **Promenade Clair de Lune** hugs the seacoast on its way toward the English Channel and passes in front of the small jetty used by boats crossing to St-Malo. It really hits its stride as it rounds the **Pointe du Moulinet** and heads toward the sandy **Plage du Prieuré,** named after a priory that once stood here. River meets sea in a foaming mass of rock-pounding surf: Be careful as you walk along the slippery path to the calm shelter of the **Plage de l'Écluse,** an inviting sandy beach, bordered by a casino and numerous stylish hotels. The coastal path picks up on the west side of Plage de l'Écluse, ringing the Pointe de la Malouine and the Pointe des Étêtés before arriving at the **Plage de St-Enogat.**

☾ At the **Musée de la Mer** (Marine Museum and Aquarium), almost every known species of Breton bird and sea creature is on display in two rooms and 24 pools. Another room is devoted to the polar expeditions of explorer Jean Charcot, one of the first men to chart the Antarctic. ⊠ *17 av. George-V,* ☎ *02–99–46–13–90.* ☜ *15 frs.* ☉ *Ascension Day–mid-Sept., daily 10:30–12:30 and 3:30–7:30.*

Dining

$$ ✕ **La Présidence.** Imaginatively prepared fish and seafood are the credo of this green-fronted restaurant near the casino: Fillet of John Dory cooked in sherry and scallops with lentils in curry sauce are just two choice examples from the menu. The eye-easy, salmon-pink decor makes for a relaxing evening. ⊠ *29 bd. du Président-Wilson,* ☎ *02–99–46–44–27. MC, V. Closed Mon. No dinner Sun.*

Nightlife

As befitting a fashionable resort, Dinard has a **casino** (⊠ 4 bd. du Président-Wilson, ☎ 02–99–16–30–30).

Outdoor Activities and Sports

Go horseback riding at the **Centre Équestre de la Côte d'Émeraude** (⊠ Le Val Porée, ☎ 02–99–46–23–57). For windsurfing, wander over

to the **Wishbone Club** (⊠ Digue de l'Écluse, ☎ 02–99–88–15–20).
Rent boats from the **Yacht Club** (⊠ promenade Clair de Lune, ☎ 02–99–46–14–32).

En Route   Follow the coast west from Dinard to **Cap Fréhel**, 40 km (25 mi) away, where dramatic pink cliffs rise vertically from the sea. The colors are best in the evening, but at any time of day the sight is formidable. Pick your way through the seagulls and cormorants, and if you're not afraid of heights, walk down past the small restaurant for a vertiginous glimpse of the rocks below. Then climb up to the lighthouse, whose beam winks at ships more than 96 km (60 mi) away. If you've got time, check out the **Fort de Latte** nearby, a 17th-century fort linked to the mainland by a drawbridge. Then head west, past fine beaches at Pléhérel and Sables-d'Or, to pick up D786 and skirt around the Bay of St-Brieuc.

Paimpol

⓫   *92 km (57 mi) west of Cap Fréhel via D786, 45 km (28 mi) northwest of St-Brieuc.*

Paimpol is one of the best fishing ports in the area and a good base for exploring this part of the coast. The town is a maze of narrow streets lined with local shops, a number of restaurants, and the inevitable souvenir shops. The harbor is its main focal point: Fishermen used to unload their catch from far-off seas; today, most of the fish is caught in the Channel. From the sharp cliffs you can see the coast's famous pink granite rocks.

The **Fête des Terres-Neuvas** is a celebration of the traditional return from Newfoundland of the Breton fishing fleets on the third Sunday in July. For centuries, but no longer, Breton fishermen sailed to Newfoundland each spring to harvest cod—a long and perilous journey.

Dining and Lodging

\$\$–\$\$\$ ✕🛏 **Le Repaire de Kerroch.** This delightful hotel overlooking the harbor has spacious rooms, with artfully used odd angles. A favorite, Les Sept Isles, faces the street and has a view of boats. Chef-owner Jean Claude Broc prepares delicious seafood dishes—skate with zesty beurre blanc and sea trout—as well as *lapereau confit* (young rabbit confit). Be sure to have breakfast if just for the homemade confitures of bananas and green tomatoes. The restaurant is closed on Tuesday and Wednesday, except in July and August. ⊠ *29 quai Morand,* ☎ *02–96–20–50–13,* 𝖥𝖠𝖷 *02–96–22–07–46. 12 rooms. Restaurant. MC, V. Closed early Jan.–mid-Feb.*

Trébeurden

⓬   *42 km (26 mi) west of Paimpol via D786/D65, 9 km (6 mi) northwest of Lannion.*

A small, pleasant fishing village that is now a summer resort town, Trébeurden makes a good base for exploring the pink granite cliffs of the Corniche Bretonne, starting with the rocky point at nearby Le Castel. Take a look at the profile of the dramatic rocks off the coast near Trégastel and Perros-Guirec and use your imagination to see Tête de Mort (Death's Head), La Tortoise, Le Sentinel, and Le Chapeau de Wellington (Wellington's Hat). The scene changes with the sunlight and the sweep and retreat of the tide, which strands fishing boats among islands that were, only hours before, hidden beneath the sea.

Dining and Lodging

$$$–$$$$ ✕🏨 **Manoir de Lan Kerellec.** The beauty of the Breton coastline is embraced by this Relais & Châteaux hotel. Choose from a range of comfortable accommodations. The restaurant, whose circular dining room has a delightful model of the *St-Yves* ship suspended from its ceiling, mostly serves seafood, but the roast lamb is also good; it's closed Monday and Tuesday off-season. ⊠ *11 allée Centrale, 22560,* ☎ *02–96–15–47–47,* FAX *02–96–23–66–88. 16 rooms, 5 suites. Restaurant, tennis court. AE, DC, MC, V. Closed mid-Nov.–mid-Mar.*

Morlaix

🔞   *45 km (28 mi) southwest of Trébeurden via D65 and D786, 60 km (37 mi) east of Brest.*

The town-spanning, 19th-century stone railroad viaduct—300 yards long and 200 ft high—in Morlaix (pronounced mor-*lay*) is an unforgettable sight. The old town is an attractive mix of half-timber houses and shops that deserve unhurried exploration. At its commercial heart is the pedestrian **Grand'Rue,** lined with quaint 15th-century houses. In the adjacent rue du Mur, the three-story, 16th-century **Maison de la Reine Anne** (Queen Anne House) is adorned with statuettes of saints.

Known as the **Musée des Jacobins** because it is housed in a former Jacobin church (note the early 15th-century rose window at one end), the town museum—just off rue d'Aiguillon, parallel to Grand'Rue—has an eclectic collection ranging from religious statues to archaeological finds and modern paintings. ⊠ *pl. des Jacobins,* ☎ *02–98–88–68–88.* 🎫 *25 frs.* ☉ *Apr.–Oct., daily 10–12:30 and 2–6:30; Nov.–Mar., Wed.–Mon. 10–noon and 2–5.*

Every year, 3 million tons of cigars are rolled in the **Manufacture de Cigares** (Cigar Factory). Tours can be arranged year-round with advance notice. ⊠ *41 quai de Léon,* ☎ *02–98–88–15–32.*

At the **Brasserie des Deux Rivières** (Two Rivers Brewery), the beer is brewed according to traditional Breton methods; you can even quaff one on the spot. ⊠ *1 pl. de la Madeleine,* ☎ *02–98–63–41–92.* 🎫 *Free.* ☉ *July–Aug., tours Mon.–Wed. 10:30, 2, and 3:30.*

Dining and Lodging

$–$$ ✕🏨 **Europe.** Though rooms—as in many other old French hotels—are dreary, this place is convenient. The welcoming, many-mirrored restaurant, however, has a low-cost prix-fixe menu that might include lobster (try the fricassee of Breton lobster with chervil and garlic confit), warm oysters, and smoked salmon. ⊠ *1 rue d'Aiguillon, 29600,* ☎ *02–98–62–11–99,* FAX *02–98–88–83–38. 60 rooms, 41 with bath. Restaurant. AE, DC, MC, V.*

St-Pol-de-Léon

🔞   *18 km (11 mi) northwest of Morlaix via D58.*

St-Pol-de-Léon is a lively market town famous for its cauliflowers, artichokes, and three spires: Two belong to the cathedral, the highest to the chapel.

The pleasingly proportioned **Ancienne Cathédrale** was built between the 13th and 16th centuries and has finely carved 16th-century choir stalls that warrant a trip inside. ⊠ *rue Général-Leclerc.*

The **Chapelle Notre-Dame du Kreisker,** once used for meetings by the town council, has a magnificent 250-ft, 15th-century granite spire, flanked at each corner by tiny spires known as *fillettes* ("girls"): the prototype for countless bell towers in Brittany. From the top there is a resounding view across the Bay of Morlaix toward the English Channel. ✉ *rue du Général-Leclerc,* ☎ *02–98–69–01–15.* 🎫 *Tower 5 frs.* 🕑 *Mid-June–mid-Sept., daily 10–noon and 2–5.*

OFF THE
BEATEN PATH

KERJEAN – With its vast park, ditch, and 40-ft-thick defensive walls, the 15th-century Château de Kerjean, 19 km (12 mi) southwest of St-Pol-de-Léon, looks like a fortress until you see its domestically large windows, tall chimney stacks, and high-pitched roofs. The chapel, kitchens, and main apartments, full of regional furniture, can be visited. Note the old well in the main courtyard. ☎ 02-98-69-93-69. 🎫 25 frs. 🕑 July-Aug., daily 10–7; June and Sept., Wed.-Mon. 10-6; Oct., Dec., and Apr.-May, Wed.-Mon. 2-5; Nov. and Feb.-Mar., Wed. and Sun. 2-5.

BRITTANY'S ATLANTIC COAST

Brittany's Atlantic coast runs southeast from the down-to-earth port of Brest to the tony city of Nantes at the mouth of the Loire River. The wild, rugged creeks around the little-visited northwestern tip of Finistère (Land's End) gradually give way to sandy beaches south of Concarneau. Inland, the bent trees and craggy rocks look like they've been bewitched by Merlin in a bad mood.

Brest

⑮ *75 km (47 mi) southwest of Morlaix, 244 km (151 mi) west of Rennes.*

Brest's enormous, sheltered bay is strategically positioned close to the Atlantic and the English Channel. You need not spend much time here: World War II left the city in ruins. Postwar reconstruction, resulting in long, straight streets of reinforced concrete, has given latter-day Brest the unenviable reputation of being one of France's least inviting cities. Its waterfront, however, is worth visiting for the few old buildings, castle, and museums, as well as for dramatic views across the bay toward the Plougastel Peninsula. The **Pont de Recouvrance,** which crosses the Penfeld River, is Europe's longest lift bridge, at 95 yards.

Begin your visit at one of the town's oldest monuments, the **Tour Tanguy,** next to the bridge. This bulky, round 14th-century tower, once used as a lookout post, contains a museum of local history with scale models of the Brest of yore. 🎫 *Free.* 🕑 *Oct.–May, Wed.–Sun. 2–6; June–Sept., daily 10–noon and 2–7.*

Brest's medieval **Château,** across the bridge from the Tour Tanguy, is home to the **Musée de la Marine** (Naval Museum), containing boat models, sculpture, pictures, and naval instruments. A section is devoted to the castle's 700-year history. The dungeons can also be visited. ☎ *02-98-22-12-39.* 🎫 *29 frs.* 🕑 *Wed.–Mon. 9:15–noon and 2–6.*

French, Flemish, and Italian paintings, spanning the period from the 17th to the 20th century, make up the collection at the **Musée Municipal** (Town Museum). ✉ *rue Traverse.* 🎫 *Free.* 🕑 *Mon. and Wed.–Sat. 10–11:45 and 2–6:45, Sun. 2–6:45.*

Maritime technology, fauna, and flora are the themes of the exhibits at the futuristic **Océanopolis** center. But the biggest attraction is the aquarium—the largest in Europe. ✉ *rue Alain-Colas,* ☎ *02–98–34–40–40.* 🎫 *50 frs.* 🕑 *July–Sept., daily 9:30–6; Oct.–June, Mon. 2–5, Tues.–Fri. 9:30–5, weekends 9–6.*

The **Festival des Trois Mers** (Three Seas Festival), in July and August, is famous for its sacred and choral music performances.

OFF THE   **LE FOLGOËT –** Pilgrims come from afar to Le Folgoët, 24 km (15 mi)
BEATEN PATH northeast of Brest, to attend the pardon in early September, and drink
             from the Salaün fountain behind the splendid church, whose water
             comes from a spring beneath the altar. The church, known as the
             Basilique, has a sturdy north tower that serves as a beacon for miles
             around and, inside, a rare, intricately carved granite rood screen, sepa-
             rating the choir and nave.

Dining

$ ✕⊞ **Maison de l'Océan.** This giant, split-level brasserie by the water-
front mirrors the city of Brest: all earnest bustle with no frills. It serves
the freshest seafood at top value—three prix-fixe menus are under 100
francs, and the 149-franc menu includes a seafood platter. In finest French
tradition, the service remains hectically unflappable. ⊠ *2 quai de la
Douane,* ☏ *02–98–80–44–84. MC, V.*

Outdoor Activities and Sports

Rent sailboats from **Centre Nautique Municipal** (Port de Plaisance, ☏
02–98–34–64–64).

En Route   Stop in **Daoulas,** 19 km (12 mi) southeast of Brest, to admire its 12th-
century, still-functioning Romanesque abbey, with cloisters and herbal
garden. Then head south on N165 and D7 to the old weaving town
of **Locronan,** 46 km (29 mi) away, and visit the 15th-century **Église St-
Ronan** and the adjacent **Chapelle du Penity,** dominating the magnificently preserved ensemble of houses and main square.

Douarnenez

⑯   *10 km (6 mi) west of Locronan via D7, 86 km (54 mi) south of Brest.*

Douarnenez is a quaint old fishing town of quayside paths and zigzag-
ging narrow streets. Boats come in from the Atlantic to unload their
catches of mackerel, sardines, and tuna. Just over the Port-Rhu Estuary is Tréboul, a seaside resort town favored by French families.

Ꮯ   One of the three town harbors is home to the unique **Port-Musée** (Port
Museum). Along the wharves, you can visit the workshops of wooden-
boat wrights, sail makers, and other old-time craftspeople, then go
aboard the historic trawlers, lobster boats, Thames barges, and a former lightship anchored alongside. You can also sail on an antique
fishing boat on the second weekend of May. ⊠ *quai de Port-Rhu,*
☏ *02–98–92–65–20.* ⊡ *40 frs June–Sept., 30 frs Oct.–May.* ☉
*June–Sept., daily 10–7; Oct.–Dec. and May, Tues.–Sun. 10–12:30
and 2–6.*

A few miles north of Douarnenez is the seaside village of Sainte-Anne-
la-Palud, whose **pardon** on the last Sunday in August is one of the finest
and most authentic age-old religious festivals in Brittany.

Dining and Lodging

$$$–$$$$ ✕⊞ **Hôtel de la Plage.** This former private house sits nestled in a cove
on a quiet strip of sandy beach around the bay at Sainte-Anne-la-
Palud—a remote setting perfect for long, restorative walks. Some of the
comfortably furnished rooms face the sea. The hotel, however, has less
of a feeling of Brittany than you might want. The food in the restau-
rant is consistently good, especially the seafood dishes, but not very in-
novative; reservations are essential and a jacket is required. ⊠
Sainte-Anne-la-Palud 29127 (11 km/7 mi north of Douarnenez), ☏ *02–*

98–92–50–12, FAX 02–98–92–56–54. *26 rooms. Restaurant, tennis court, beach. AE, DC, MC, V. Closed mid-Oct.–early Apr.*

$$ ✕🏠 **Hôtel Ty' Mad.** Artists and writers like Picasso and Breton native
★ Max Jacob frequented this small hotel, in a quiet residential area, in the 1920s. Rooms are not big, but the sea views are great. The delicious dishes, including skate pâté with mint sauce and monkfish flambéed with tarragon are served in the glass-enclosed restaurant. ⊠ *3 rue St-Jean, 29100,* ☎ *02–98–74–00–53,* FAX *02–98–74–15–16. 23 rooms. Restaurant. MC, V. Closed Nov.–Easter.*

$–$$ ✕🏠 **Manoir de Moëllien.** This lovely 15th-century manor house, filled with precious antiques, is famous for its local seafood dishes. Sample the *terrine de poisson chaud* (seafood terrine) or the *duo de truites de mer* (poached sea trout). Rooms have terraces overlooking the garden, which makes for a peaceful, country atmosphere. ⊠ *29550 Plonevez-Porzay (12 km/7 mi northeast of Douarnenez),* ☎ *02–98–92–50–40,* FAX *02–98–92–55–21. 10 rooms. Restaurant. AE, DC, MC, V. Closed Jan.–Mar.*

Outdoor Activities and Sports

Sailboats can be rented from **Les Voiles d'Iroise** (52 rue Ernest-Renan, ☎ 02–98–92–76–25), on the bay.

Audierne

⑰ *22 km (14 mi) southwest of Douarnenez via D765.*

In summer, the small working port of Audierne, where the fishermen come daily bearing the day's catch of langoustines, is a busy pleasure-boat center that is never overcrowded. Most of the visitors are locals, which makes for a nontouristy, welcoming atmosphere.

West of Audierne is the **Cap Sizun** peninsula, whose dramatic, jagged coastline culminates with the 300-ft drop at the Pointe du Raz, the westernmost tip of France.

Dining and Lodging

$$$ ✕🏠 **Le Goyen.** In the early morning you can watch the activity in the
★ bustling fishing port from the balcony of your very pretty room (or ultramodern suite) in this modern hotel. In the evening, aperitifs are served while you wait for chef Adolphe Bosser's superb Breton cuisine. Watch the port as you dine on baked turbot with a beef stock sauce, Breton lobster, or aromatic *ris de veau* (veal sweetbread). The restaurant is closed Monday off-season. ⊠ *pl. Jean-Simon, 29770,* ☎ *02–98–70–08–88,* FAX *02–98–70–18–77. 126 rooms, 3 suites. AE, MC, V. Closed mid-Nov.–mid-Dec.*

Quimper

⑱ *35 km (22 mi) east of Audierne via D784, 72 km (45 mi) south of Brest.*

Lively, commercial Quimper is the ancient capital of the Cornouaille province, founded, it is said, by King Gradlon 1,500 years ago. Quimper (pronounced cam-*pair*) owes its strange name to its site at the confluence (*kemper* in Breton) of the Odet and Steir rivers. Stroll along the banks of the Odet and through the old town, with its cathedral. Then walk along the lively shopping street, rue Kéréon, and down medieval rue du Guéodet (note the house with caryatids), rue St-Mathieu, and rue du Sallé.

The **Cathédrale St-Corentin** is a masterpiece of Gothic architecture and the second-largest cathedral in Brittany (after Dol-de-Bretagne's). Legendary King Gradlon is represented on horseback just below the base of the spires, harmonious mid-19th-century additions to the medieval ensemble. The 15th-century stained glass is luminous. Behind the cathedral is the stately **Jardin de l'Évêché** (Bishop's Garden). ✉ *pl. St-Corentin.*

Works by major masters, such as Rubens, Corot, and Picasso, mingle with pretty landscapes from the local Gauguin-inspired Pont-Aven school in the **Musée des Beaux-Arts** (Fine Arts Museum), next to the cathedral. ✉ *40 pl. St-Corentin,* ☎ *02–98–95–45–20.* ✆ *25 frs.* ☉ *July–Aug., daily 9–7; Sept.–June, Wed.–Mon. 10–noon and 2–6.*

Local furniture, ceramics, and folklore top the bill in the **Musée Départemental** (Breton Regional Museum) on rue du Roi-Gradlon, adjacent to place St-Corentin. ✉ *1 rue du Roi-Gradlon,* ☎ *02–98–95–21–60.* ✆ *20 frs.* ☉ *June–Sept., daily 9–6; Oct.–May, Tues.–Sun. 9–noon and 2–5.*

In the mid-18th century, Quimper sprang to nationwide attention as a ceramic manufacturing center when it began producing second-rate imitations of faience, the Rouen ceramics with blue Asian motifs. Today's more colorful designs, based on floral arrangements and marine fauna, are still often hand-painted. Guided tours are available at the **Musée de la Faïence** (Faience Museum). ✉ *14 rue Jean-Baptiste-Bousquet,* ☎ *02–98–90–12–72.* ✆ *26 frs.* ☉ *Mid-Apr.–Oct., Mon.–Sat. 10–6.*

Dining

$$ ✕ **Ambroisie.** With its yellow walls, huge paintings by Francis Bacon, and different settings at every table, this place looks modern. But the food remains resolutely old-style Breton, such as rolled whole-wheat crepes with smoked salmon and crab crepes. ✉ *49 rue Élie-Féron,* ☎ *02–98–95–00–02. Reservations essential. AE, MC, V. Closed 1 wk in June and Oct.*

Nightlife and the Arts

The Celtic **Festival de Cornouaille** (☎ 02–98–55–53–33 for information) is held in Quimper in late July.

Shopping

Keep an eye out for such typical Breton products as woven and embroidered cloth, woolen goods, brass and wooden goods, puppets, dolls, and locally designed jewelry. When it comes to distinctive Breton folk costumes, Quimper is the best place to look. The streets around the cathedral, especially **rue du Parc,** are full of shops selling the woolen goods (notably thick marine sweaters). Faience and a wide selection of hand-painted pottery can be purchased at the **Faïencerie d'Art Breton** (✉ 16 bis rue du Parc, ☎ 02–98–95–34–13).

Concarneau

🄌 *21 km (13 mi) south of Quimper via D783, 93 km (58 mi) southeast of Brest.*

Concarneau is the third-largest fishing port in France. A busy industrial town, it has a grain of charm and an abundance of tacky souvenir shops. But it's worth visiting to see its fort in the middle of the harbor. Entered by a quaint drawbridge, the **Ville Close,** the fortified islet in the harbor, was, from early medieval times, regarded as impregnable. The fortifications were further strengthened by the English under John de Montfort during the War of Succession (1341–64). Three hundred years later, Sébastien de Vauban remodeled the ramparts into what you see today: 1 km long (½ mi long) with splendid views across the two harbors on either side. During the second half of August enjoy the Fête des Filets Bleus (Blue Net Festival) in the Ville Close, a weeklong folk celebration in which Bretons in costume swirl and dance to the wail of bagpipes. ✉ *Ramparts 5 frs.* ☉ *Easter–Sept., daily 10–7:30; Oct.–Easter, daily 10–noon and 2–5.*

The **Musée de la Pêche** (Fishing Museum), close to the island gateway, has aquariums and exhibits on fishing techniques from around the world. ✉ *3 rue Vauban,* ☎ *02–98–97–10–20.* ✉ *30 frs.* ☉ *July–Aug., daily 9:30–7:30; Sept.–June, Tues.–Sun. 10–noon and 2–6.*

Dining

$$–$$$ ✕ **Le Galion.** Nestled in a stone house in the fortified old town, this restaurant, with traditional nautical decor, has a modern, trendy menu. The langoustine fricassee and the *St-Pierre à la rhubarbe* (fish with rhubarb sauce) are excellent. ✉ *15 rue Guénolé,* ☎ *02–98–97–30–16. MC, V. Closed Mon. Oct.–Easter. No dinner Sun.*

Pont-Aven

⑳ *14 km (9 mi) east of Concarneau via D783, 91 km (56 mi) northwest of Vannes.*

Pont-Aven is a former artists' colony where Paul Gauguin lived before he headed off to the South Seas. While you're here, visit the museum dedicated to the school, cool off (in summer) with a boat trip down the estuary from Pont-Aven, or take a walk in the hills among the pastures to the Tremalo chapel, where there is a crucifix attributed to Gauguin. A permanent photography exhibition documenting the Pont Aven School and works by its participants are found at the **Musée Municipal** (Town Museum). ✉ *pl. de l'Hôtel-de-Ville,* ☎ *02–98–06–14–43.* ✉ *25 frs July–Aug., 20 frs Feb.–June and Sept.–Dec.* ☉ *July–Aug., daily 9:30–7:30; Feb.–June and Sept.–Dec., Tues.–Sun. 10–noon and 2–6.*

Dining and Lodging

$$$ ✕ **La Taupinière.** On the road from Concarneau, in the outskirts of Pont-Aven, is this roadside inn with an attractive garden. The food isn't cheap, but chef Guy Guilloux's fish, crab, crayfish, and Breton ham (grilled over the large, open fire) are worth it. And his wine cellar is renowned. ✉ *Croissant St-André,* ☎ *02–98–06–03–12. Reservations essential. Jacket required. AE, DC, MC, V. Closed Tues. and mid-Sept.–mid-Oct. No dinner Mon.*

$$$ ✕⊡ **Moulin de Rosmadec.** The Sébilleaus' old mill sits in the middle of the rushing, rocky Aven River. You can hear the sound of water gently spilling over the stones beneath your window. In the rustic-looking restaurant, one of the best in France, have lobster or langoustine ravioli, and opt for the prix-fixe menus. Reservations are essential and a jacket is required; the restaurant is closed dinner Sunday and Wednesday, mid-September to mid-June. ✉ *pl. Paul-Gauguin, 29930,* ☎ *02–98–06–00–22,* 🄵🄰🄾 *02–98–06–18–00. 4 rooms. Restaurant. MC, V. Closed mid-Nov.–late Nov. and Feb.*

$$ ✕⊡ **Roz-Aven.** Built into a rock face on the banks of the River Aven, this efficiently run hotel has simple, clean rooms. The owner, Yann Souffez, speaks excellent English. He describes the furnishings as Louis XVI, but, at best, they appear petit bourgeois. The restaurant has a limited selection of fine prix-fixe menus and wines, priced 20% less than some fancier restaurants. ✉ *11 quai Théodore-Botrel, 29930,* ☎ *02–98–06–13–06,* 🄵🄰🄾 *02–98–06–03–89. 24 rooms. Restaurant. MC, V.*

Lorient

㉑   *36 km (22 mi) southeast of Pont-Aven via D24.*

France's most exotically named town—founded by Colbert in 1666 as a base for the spice-seeking vessels of France's East India Company (Compagnie des Indes), bound for the Orient—was smashed into semi-oblivion during World War II. A handful of Art Deco mansions survived, and you may like to visit the brazen concrete church of Notre-Dame-de-Victoire for its modern frescoes and stained glass.

Fish and submarines have fueled Lorient's resurrection: This is France's leading Atlantic submarine base, and the fishing port is second only to that of Boulogne. Both types of vessel rub shoulders along the mile-long quayside, and the choice at the fish market (Halles de Merville) is unsurpassed. The town itself is at its liveliest during the Interceltic Festival in August (☞ *below*). From Lorient you can visit the beach 5 km (3 mi) south at **Larmor-Plage,** or take a ferry to the rocky **Ile de Groix** or across the bay to **Port-Louis,** a harbor renowned for tuna fishing and its 17th-century fort and ramparts.

Dining and Lodging

$$$$ ✕▦ **Château de Locquénolé.** The château's squat, imposing architecture is countered by the peaceful setting of lawns and woods, through which the River Blavet flows. Design takes a turn for the better inside, with 19th-century furnishings and tapestries. The spacious rooms are similarly decorated; ask for one with a view of the river. Or you may prefer to stay in the rustic, cozy rooms in the renovated stables, 3 km (2 mi) away. Marc Angelle, one of France's top chefs, cooks with a keen creativity in the restaurant, which is closed Monday. ✉ *rte. de Port-Louis, 56700 Kervignac (13 km/8 mi east of Lorient via D170),* ☎ *02–97–76–29–04,* 𝔽𝔸𝕏 *02–97–76–39–47. 31 rooms, 4 suites. Restaurant, pool, sauna. AE, DC, MC, V. Closed Jan.–mid-Feb.*

Nightlife and the Arts

The **Festival Interceltique** (☎ 02–97–21–24–29) in the first half of August is a jamboree of Celtic culture—music, drama, poetry, dance—when fellow Celts pour into Lorient from all over northwest Europe (Cornwall, Wales, Ireland, and Galicia) to celebrate with their Breton brethren.

Quiberon

㉒   *40 km (25 mi) southeast of Lorient via D781 and D768.*

Quiberon is a spa town with pearl-like beaches on the eastern side of the 16-km-long (10-mi-long) Presqu'île de Quiberon (the "almost island" or Quiberon Peninsula), a stretch of rough coastal cliffs and beaches joined to the mainland by a hairbreadth of sand. Its dramatic western coast is dubbed the Côte Sauvage (Wild Coast), a mix of crevices, coves, and rocky grottoes lashed by the sea. A word to the wise: The coast is extremely dangerous and swimming is prohibited. Quiberon's best beach is the Grande Plage (Great Beach), on the protected side of the peninsula. Boats for nearby Belle-Ile leave from the harbor of Port-Maria.

Nightlife

Quiberon's **casino** (✉ 2 bd. René-Cassin, ☎ 02–97–50–23–57) has the standard games of chance, as well as shows in summer.

Outdoor Activities and Sports

An 18-km (11-mi) footpath follows the Côte Sauvage, as does the boulevard de la Côte Sauvage, which is perfect for cycling. Bicycles can be rented from **Cyclomar** (✉ 47 pl. Hoche, ☎ 02–97–50–26–00).

Shopping

In a country where gourmandism is virtually a cultural pursuit, **Henri Le Roux** (⊠ 18 rue du Port-Maria, ☎ 02–97–50–06–83) has taken the art of chocolatiering to dizzying heights. Check out his delicious displays at his shop near Quiberon Harbor.

Belle-Ile

㉓ *45 mins by boat from Quiberon.*

At 18 km (11 mi) long, Belle-Ile is the largest of Brittany's islands. It also lives up to its name: It's beautiful and much less commercialized than Quiberon. Because of the cost and inconvenience of reserving car berths on the ferry, cross over as a pedestrian and rent a car—or, better still, a bicycle—on the island.

The ferry lands at **Le Palais,** where there is a Vauban **citadelle.** From Le Palais, head to **Sauzon,** the prettiest fishing harbor, where you can see across to the Quiberon Peninsula and the Gulf of Morbihan to Belle Époque actress Sarah Bernhardt's summer home. Continue on to the **Grotte de l'Apothicairerie,** which derives its name from the local cormorants' nests, said to resemble apothecary bottles. At Port Goulphar is the **Grand Phare** (Great Lighthouse). Built in 1835, it rises 275 ft above sea level and has one of the most powerful lights in Europe, visible from 120 km (75 mi) across the Atlantic. If the keeper is available, you may be able to climb to the top.

Dining and Lodging

$$–$$$ ✕▥ **Castel-Clara.** This modern hotel is perched on a cliff overlooking
★ the surf and the narrow Anse de Goulphar bay. Ask for a room with a view. In the bright, airy restaurant, chef Christophe specializes in seafood, literally caught just offshore. The St-Pierre fish baked in sea salt, and the grilled sea bream are simple but delicious. ⊠ *Port-Goulphar, 56360 Bangor,* ☎ *02–97–31–84–21,* ℻ *02–97–31–51–69. 32 rooms, 10 suites. Restaurant, indoor pool, spa, tennis court. MC, V. Closed mid-Nov.–mid-Feb.*

Carnac

★ ㉔ *16 km (10 mi) northeast of Quiberon via D768/D781, 32 km (20 mi) southeast of Lorient.*

At the north end of Quiberon Bay, Carnac is famed for its fabulous beaches but is especially known for its ancient stone monuments. Dating from the Neolithic to early Bronze ages (3500–1800 BC), the origin of Carnac's **megalithic monuments** remains as obscure as those of their English contemporary, Stonehenge, although religious beliefs and astrology were doubtless an influence. The 2,395 menhirs that make up the three **Alignements du Ménec**—Kermario, Kerlescan, and Ménec—are positioned with astounding astronomical accuracy in semicircles and parallel lines over about 1 km (½ mi). There are also smaller-scale dolmen ensembles and three tumuli (mounds or barrows), including the 130-yard-long, 38-ft-high **Tumulus de St-Michel,** topped by a small chapel with views of the rock-strewn countryside. ▨ *10 frs.* ⊙ *Easter–Oct.; guided tours of tumulus daily Apr.–Sept. 10, 11, 2, 3:30*

Nightlife and the Arts

A cosmopolitan crowd goes dancing at **Les Chandelles** (⊠ 24 av. des Druides).

Outdoor Activities and Sports

Horseback riding can be arranged through the **Centre Équestre des Menhirs** (☎ 02–97–55–73–45). Windsurfing equipment can be rented from **De Petigny** (⊠ 90 rue du Pô, ☎ 02–97–52–02–41).

Auray

㉕ *14 km (12 mi) north of Carnac via D119/D768, 38 km (24 mi) southeast of Lorient.*

The ancient town of Auray grew up along the banks of the Loch River, best admired from the promenade du Loch overlooking the quayside. Cross the river to explore the old, cobbled streets of the St-Goustan district. Across the old bridge at the harbor is the **Goélette St-Sauveur,** an old sailing ship tied alongside the quay. In its hold is a sailing museum with many unusual nautical artifacts. ☎ 02–97–40–37–05. ☉ *July–Aug., daily 10–noon; Sept.–June by appointment.*

Dining

$$–$$$ ✕ **Closerie de Kerdrain.** Chef Fernand Corfmat presides over the kitchen in this large Breton house draped in wisteria, where he inventively blends traditional and contemporary cuisine. The vegetable and langoustine tart, and the ravioli stuffed with seafood in lobster sauce are unusual but delicious versions of local recipes. ⊠ *20 rue Louis-Billet,* ☎ *02–97–56–61–27. AE, DC, MC, V. Closed Mon. mid-Nov.–Mar., last 2 wks of Nov., and 1st 2 wks of Mar. No dinner Sun.*

Nightlife and the Arts

In July, the biggest **pardon** in Brittany is held at the sanctuary of Sainte-Anne d'Auray (☎ 02–97–57–69–16 for information).

Outdoor Activities and Sports

Take a cruise down the Auray River on the **Navix-Vedettes du Golfe** (☎ 02–97–56–59–47) and you'll discover the lovely, 16th-century Château du Plessis-Kaer, and the tiny, tidal fishing port of Bono tucked between the steep banks and the oysters beds of the Pô estuary.

Vannes

㉖ *16 km (10 mi) east of Auray via N165, 108 km (67 mi) southwest of Rennes.*

Scene of the declaration of unity between France and Brittany in 1532, Vannes is one of the few towns in Brittany to have been spared damage during World War II, so its authentic regional charm remains intact. This also means that the town is packed with tourists in summer. If this doesn't stop you, be sure to walk along the promenade de la Garenne and the ramparts, visit the medieval wash houses and cathedral, browse in the small boutiques and antiques shops in the pedestrian streets around the picturesque place Henri IV, and check out the Cohue, formerly a medieval market hall, now a temporary exhibition center. Boat trips of the scenic Golfe du Morbihan depart from the port.

Inside the **Cathédrale St-Pierre** is a 1537 Renaissance chapel, a Flamboyant Gothic transept portal, and a treasury. ⊠ *pl. de la Cathédrale.* 🎫 *5 frs.* ☉ *Treasury mid-June–mid-Sept., Mon.–Sat. 2–6.*

The **Musée d'Archéologie** (Archaeology Museum) houses a collection of ancient tools and artifacts dating from the Paleolithic to the Middle Ages. ⊠ *2 rue Noé,* ☎ *02–97–42–59–80.* ☉ *Mon.–Sat. 9:30–noon and 2–6.*

OFF THE
BEATEN PATH

FORTERESSE DE LARGOËT – The imposing ruins of this fortress, 16 km (10 mi) northeast of Vannes, is in a wooded park near the village of Elven, just off the N166. Its 170-ft, 14th-century octagonal keep is the highest in France; its walls are up to 30 ft thick. Alongside is a faithfully restored 15th-century tower. Henry Tudor was held prisoner here before his return to England and the triumphant 1485 military campaign that led to his crowning as Henry VII. Don't miss the magnificent evening son-et-lumière shows from mid-June to mid-September. ☎ 02-97-53-35-96. ✆ 15 frs. ⊙ Apr.–Sept., daily 8–6; Oct. and Mar., weekends 10–noon and 2–5.

JOSSELIN – The quaint medieval town of Josselin, on the Oust River, 38 km (24 mi) north of Vannes via D126, is known for its two-faced castle. On the side facing the river, it looks like a defensive stronghold with three stout turreted towers linked by austere, near-windowless walls. The landward facade, however, is a riot of intricate pinnacles, gables, and stone ornament, surrounded by gardens. You can visit the library, wood-panel dining room, portrait gallery, and Grand Salon, with its ornate fireplace (only the ground floor is open to the public). The former stables house some 500 old dolls, many dressed in traditional costume and dating from the 18th century (22 frs extra). ⊠ pl. de la Congrégation, ☎ 02-97-22-22-50. ✆ 22 frs. ⊙ July–Aug., daily 10–noon and 2–6; June and Sept., daily 2–6; Apr.–May, Wed. and Sun. 2–6.

Dining and Lodging

$$–$$$ ✕ **Régis Mahé.** Step off the train and right into this popular spot, a haven of refinement where seafood reigns supreme. The chef's delicate poached snapper and grilled sea bass garnished with vegetables are so fresh you can still smell the sea. The prix-fixe menus are your best bet. ⊠ 24 pl. de la Gare, ☎ 02-97-42-61-41. AE, V. Closed Mon., late Nov., and late Feb. No dinner Sun.

$$$$ ✕▦ **Domaine de Rochevilaine.** At sunset on summer evenings, the view of the sea is magnificent. Wealthy Parisians come to this resort in summer to relax; businesspeople come for seminars in winter. Rooms are arranged on two sides of a courtyard, surrounded by terraced gardens; all have modern furnishings but vary in size; not all face the ocean. Chef Patrice Caillaut's cuisine is excitingly creative, but the prices are somewhat inflated. ⊠ 16 rue du Phare, 56190 Billiers (28 km/18 mi southeast of Vannes, at the tip of the Pointe de Pen-Lan), ☎ 02-97-41-61-61, FAX 02-97-41-44-85. 36 rooms, 2 suites. Restaurant, pool, meeting rooms. AE, DC, MC, V. Closed Feb.–mid-Mar.

$$ ✕▦ **Image Ste-Anne.** A varied foreign clientele stays in this hotel in an old, rustic building. The comfortable rooms and welcoming staff make the price of a night here seem more than acceptable. Mussels, sole in cider, and duck are featured in the restaurant, which has a very reasonable prix-fixe menu; it's closed dinner Sunday, November–March. ⊠ 8 pl. de la Libération, 56000, ☎ 02-97-63-27-36, FAX 02-97-40-97-02. 35 rooms. Restaurant. MC, V.

En Route   From Josselin, head southeast to the cozy, ivy-clad medieval castle at **Rochefort-en-Terre,** restored by the American artists Alfred and Trafford Klots. Then stop off at **Redon,** once a busy commercial port at the junction of the River Vilaine and the Nantes–Brest canal. The quays are lined with stylish 17th- to 19th-century mansions, with large windows and wrought-iron balconies; wood-frame medieval houses front the main street, dominated by the slender spire and magnificent Romanesque tower of the church of St-Sauveur.

La Grande Brière

Missillac is 22 km (14 mi) south of Redon and 53 km (33 mi) south-east of Vannes.

Missillac is the gateway to the low-lying Grande Brière regional park. Made up of reed marshes and crisscrossed by long, narrow canals, the park is a bird-watcher's delight. In Missillac, be sure to take a look at the **Château de la Bretesche**, rebuilt in the 16th century with ornate ramparts and a water-filled moat.

The best way to explore La Grande Brière is to take a boat trip organized by the **Maison du Parc Naturel Régional de Brière** (⊠ 177 rte. de Fédrun, ☎ 02–40–92–68–68), 16 km (10 mi) south of Missillac in St-Joachim. You should also visit the small village of **St-Lyphard** to the west, and climb up the church tower for a panoramic view. Five kilometers (3 miles) south of St-Lyphard on D51 is the curious **Dolmen de Kerbourg**, a table-shape megalith. Continue on to **Guérande**, an appealing 15th-century town with towers and moat, surrounded by salt flats.

La Baule

㉗ *6 km (4 mi) south of Guérande via D92, 72 km (45 mi) southeast of Vannes.*

One of the most fashionable—and pricey—resorts in France, La Baule has a 5-km (3-mi) seafront promenade lined with hotels. Like Le Touquet and Dinard, it is a 19th-century creation, founded in 1879 to make the most of the excellent sandy beaches that extend around the broad, sheltered bay between Pornichet and Le Pouliguen. A pine forest, planted in 1840, keeps the shifting local sand dunes firmly at bay.

Dining and Lodging

$$$ ✕ **La Marcanderie.** This warm, yellow-walled restaurant run by cheerful owner Jean-Luc Giraud is widely considered the best in town. Potato and scampi tart, lobster salad, monkfish in cider, and scallops in endive top the menu, which starts at 190 francs. ⊠ *5 av. d'Agen,* ☎ *02–40–24–03–12. Reservations essential. Jacket and tie. AE, MC, V. Closed Mon. No dinner Sun.*

$$ ✕ **Ferme du Grand Clos.** At this lively restaurant in an old farm house, wafer-thin crepes are served with every imaginable filling, from sweet to savory—mussels, fish, chicken, or chocolate—take your pick. Come early for a table; it's a popular place. ⊠ *52 av. du Maréchal-de-Lattre-de-Tassigny,* ☎ *02–40–60–03–30. MC, V. Closed Wed. Sept.–June.*

$$ 🏨 **Concorde.** This establishment numbers among the least expensive good hotels in pricey La Baule. It's calm, comfortable, modernized, and a short block from the beach (ask for a room with a sea view). ⊠ *1 bis av. de la Concorde, 44500,* ☎ *02–40–60–23–09,* FAX *02–40–42–72–14. 47 rooms. Closed Oct.–Easter.*

$$ 🏨 **Hôtel de la Plage.** One of the few hotels on the beach in St-Marc-sur-Mer, this comfortable place was the setting for Jacques Tati's classic comedy movie, *Les Vacances de Monsieur Hulot.* It has been updated since, and *hélas*, the swinging door to the dining room is no longer there. But the view of the sea and the sound of the surf remain. ⊠ *37 rue du Commandant-Charcot, 44600 St-Marc-sur-Mer (10 km/6 mi south of La Baule),* ☎ *02–40–91–99–01,* FAX *02–40–91–92–00. 33 rooms. Restaurant. MC, V. Closed early–late Jan.*

Nightlife

Occasionally you see high stakes on the tables at La Baule's **casino** (⊠ 6 av. Pierre-Loti, ☎ 02–40–11–48–28).

Nantes

72 km (45 mi) east of La Baule via N171/N165, 108 km (67 mi) south of Rennes, 114 km (71 mi) southeast of Vannes.

The tranquil, prosperous city of Nantes seems to pursue its existence without too much concern for what's going on elsewhere in France. Cobbled streets surround its castle and cathedral in the town's medieval sector. Across the broad boulevard, **cours des 50-Otages**, is the 19th-century city. Although Nantes is officially part of the Pays de la Loire, its historic ties with Brittany are embodied in its imposing castle.

28 Built by the dukes of Brittany, who had no doubt that Nantes belonged in their domain, the **Château des Ducs de Bretagne** is a massive, well-preserved 15th-century fortress with a neatly grassed moat. François II, the duke responsible for building most of it, led a hedonistic existence here, surrounded by ministers, chamberlains, and an army of servants. Numerous monarchs later stayed in the castle, where, in 1598, Henry IV signed the famous Edict of Nantes advocating religious tolerance.

The **Harnachement** (saddlery)—a separate building inside the castle walls—is home to the **Musée des Salorges** (Naval Museum), devoted principally to the history of seafaring; a separate section outlines the triangular trade that involved transportation of Africans to America to be sold as slaves. As you cross the courtyard to the Grand Gouvernement wing, home to the **Musée d'Art Breton Régional** (Regional Folk Art Museum), look for the old well, where the ducal coat of arms is entwined in a magnificent wrought-iron decoration. The **Musée d'Art Populaire** (Folk Art Museum) features an array of armor, furniture, 19th-century Breton costumes, and reconstituted interiors illustrating the former life of the Vendée region to the south. ⊠ *rue du Château,* ☎ *02–40–41–56–56.* ☑ *10 frs, free Sun.* ☉ *Castle and museums July–Aug., daily 10–noon and 2–6; Sept.–June, Wed.–Mon. 10–noon and 2–6.*

29 The **Cathédrale St-Pierre,** 200 yards north of the castle, is one of France's last Gothic cathedrals, begun in 1434, well after most other medieval cathedrals had been completed. The facade is ponderous and austere, in contrast to the light, wide, elegant interior, whose vaults rise higher (120 ft) than those of Notre-Dame in Paris. In the transept, notice Michel Colombe's early 16th-century tomb of François II and his wife, Marguerite de Foix, one of France's finest examples of funerary sculpture. ⊠ *pl. St-Pierre,* ☎ *02–51–88–95–47.* ☑ *20 frs.* ☉ *Crypt Mon.–Sat. 10–12:30 and 2–6, Sun. 2–6:30.*

30 A fine collection of paintings from the Renaissance, including works by Jacopo Tintoretto, Georges de La Tour, Jean-Auguste Ingres, and Gustave Courbet can be found at the **Musée des Beaux-Arts** behind the Cathédrale St-Pierre, past the 15th-century Porte St-Pierre. ⊠ *10 rue Georges-Clemenceau,* ☎ *02–40–41–65–65.* ☑ *20 frs, free Sun.* ☉ *Mon. and Wed.–Thurs. 10–6, Fri. 10–9, weekends 11–6.*

31 Erected in 1843, the **Passage Pommeraye** (⊠ rue Crébillon) is an el-**32** egant shopping gallery in the 19th-century part of town. The **Grand Théâtre** (⊠ pl. Graslin), down the block from the Passage Pommeraye, was built in 1783.

33 The 15th-century **Manoir de la Touche** (⊠ rue Voltaire) was once home **34** to the bishops of Nantes. The mock Romanesque **Musée Dobrée**, offsetting the medieval silhouette of the Manoir de la Touche across the way, was built by arts connoisseur Thomas Dobrée during the past century. Among the treasures within are miniatures, tapestries, medieval

Nantes

manuscripts, and enamels; one room is devoted to the Revolutionary War in Vendée. ⊠ *rue Voltaire,* ☎ *02–40–71–03–50.* ☞ *20 frs, free Sun.* ☉ *Tues.–Sun. 10–noon and 1:30–5:30.*

Dining and Lodging

$$$ ╳ **Villa Mon Rêve.** This cozy little restaurant is in delightful parkland. Chef Gérard Ryngel concocts elegantly inventive regional fare (the duck or rabbit in muscadet are good choices) and you can sample one of the 45 varieties of muscadet, the local wine. ⊠ *506 rte. des Bords de Loire, Basse-Goulaine (8 km/5 mi east of Nantes),* ☎ *02–40–03–55–50. AE, DC, MC, V. Closed last wk of Oct.*

$$ ╳ **L'Embellie.** Chef Claude Scheiber's cooking at this small, modern
★   bistro is serious and traditional and makes the most of herbs to bring out the natural flavors in the seafood and game dishes. The lunchtime menu is a particularly good value. ⊠ *14 rue Armand-Brossard,* ☎ *02–40–48–20–02. AE, MC, V. Closed Sun. and 2nd wk in Aug. No lunch Sat.*

$ ╳ **La Cigale.** Miniature palm trees, gleaming woodwork, colorful enamel tiles, and painted ceilings have led to the official recognition of La Cigale as a *monument historique.* You can savor its Belle Époque ambience without spending a fortune—the prix-fixe lunch menus are a good value. But the banks of fresh oysters and well-stacked dessert cart may tempt you to order à la carte. ⊠ *4 pl. Graslin,* ☎ *02–51–84–94–94. Reservations essential. MC, V.*

$$$ ▦ **Hôtel La Pérouse.** Bare parquet floors, plain off-white walls, simple high-tech lighting, and minimal contemporary furnishings make rooms feel spacious. Bathrooms are equally modern. The amiable staff speaks fluent English. A pedestrian zone full of boutiques and restaurants is right outside the door, and place Royale is less than 10 minutes away. ⊠ *3 allée Dusquesne, 44000,* ☎ *02–40–89–75–00,* FAX *02–40–89–76–00. 47 rooms. AE, MC, V.*

Nightlife and the Arts

For live jazz, go to the informal **Pub Univers** (⊠ 16 rue Jean-Jacques Rousseau). Or head to the piano bar, **Le Tie Break** (⊠ 1 rue des Petites-Écuries), a popular drinking hole.

The **Théâtre Graslin** (⊠ rue Scribe, ☎ 02–40–69–77–18) is Nantes's principal theater; performance listings are available at the tourist office (⊠ 1 rue Molière, ☎ 02–40–41–90–60).

Shopping

The commercial quarter of Nantes stretches from place Royale to place Graslin. For antiques, try **Cibot** (⊠ 7 rue Voltaire). Since 1803 the Devineau family has been selling wax fruit and vegetables at **Devineau** (⊠ 6 pl. Ste-Croix); for 75 francs, you can take home a basket of purple grapes or a cauliflower, as well as handmade candles and wildflower honey. Don't miss chocolate specialists **Gautier-Debotté** (⊠ 9 rue de la Fosse) or their Muscadets Nantais grapes dipped in brandy and covered with chocolate.

BRITTANY A TO Z

Arriving and Departing

By Car

Rennes, the gateway to Brittany, is 312 km (195 mi) west of Paris. It can be reached in about four hours via Le Mans and A81 and A11 (A11 continues southwest from Le Mans to Nantes).

By Train

There are numerous daily high-speed TGVs (*Trains à Grande Vitesse*) between Paris (Gare Montparnasse) and both Nantes and Rennes, making this region easily accessible. The trip to either city takes about 2¼ hours. There is also regular train service up the west coast to Nantes from La Rochelle and Bordeaux.

Getting Around

By Car

Rennes, a strategic base for penetrating Brittany, is linked by good roads to Morlaix and Brest (E50), Quimper (N24/N165), and Vannes (N24/N166).

By Plane

There are domestic airports at Rennes, Brest, Nantes, Quimper, and Lorient. **Air France** (☞ Air Travel *in* the Gold Guide).

By Train

Most towns in this region are accessible by train, though you may need a car to get to some of the more out-of-the-way places. Some trains from Paris stop at Vitré before forking at Rennes on their way to either Brest (via Morlaix) or Quimper (via Vannes). Change at Rennes for Dol-de-Bretagne and St-Malo; at Dol-de-Bretagne for Dinan and Dinard (bus link); at Morlaix for Roscoff; at Rosporden, 19 km (12 mi) south of Quimper, for Concarneau (bus link); and at Auray for Quiberon.

Contacts and Resources

Bicycling

Bikes can be rented at most major train stations.

Car Rental

Avis (☎ 01–46–10–60–60 national reservations number in Paris; ⊠ pl. Rhin-et-Danube, La Baule, ☎ 02–40–60–36–28; ⊠ 20 bis rue de

Siam, Brest, ☎ 02–98–44–63–02; ⊠ aéroport, Dinard, ☎ 02–99–46–25–20; ⊠ 27 bd. de Stalingrad, Nantes, ☎ 02–40–89–25–50; ⊠ 8 av. de la Gare, Quimper, ☎ 02–98–90–31–34).

Guided Tours

Information about organized tours of Brittany is available from the very helpful **Maison de la Bretagne** (⊠ 203 bd. St-Germain, 75007 Paris, ☎ 01–53–63–11–50, FAX 01–53–63–11–57). The following regional offices can also provide information about guided tours of Brittany: in **Brest** (⊠ 8 av. Georges-Clemenceau, ☎ 02–98–44–24–96) and **Quimper** (⊠ 11 rue Théodore-le-Hac, ☎ 02–98–76–20–70).

France Tourisme (⊠ 3 rue d'Alger, 75001 Paris, ☎ 01–44–50–44–20) organizes three-day tours of Normandy and Brittany from April through October.

Travel Agencies

Wagons-Lits (⊠ 22 rue du Calvaire, Nantes, ☎ 02–40–08–29–18; ⊠ 2 rue Jules-Simon, Rennes, ☎ 02–99–79–45–96).

Visitor Information

The principal regional tourist offices follow. **Brest** (⊠ 8 av. Georges-Clemenceau, ☎ 02–98–44–24–96). **Nantes** (⊠ pl. du Commerce, ☎ 02–40–20–60–60). **Rennes** (⊠ Pont de Nemours, ☎ 02–99–79–01–98).

The following smaller towns also have tourist offices: **Carnac** (⊠ 74 av. des Druides, ☎ 02–97–52–13–52). **Concarneau** (⊠ quai d'Aiguillon, ☎ 02–98–97–01–44). **Dinan** (⊠ 6 rue de l'Horloge, ☎ 02–96–39–75–40). **Dinard** (⊠ 2 bd. Féart, ☎ 02–99–46–94–12). **Dol-de-Bretagne** (⊠ 3 Grand Rue, ☎ 02–99–48–15–37). **Douarnenez** (⊠ 1 rue du Dr-Mével, ☎ 02–98–92–13–35). **La Baule** (⊠ 8 pl. de la Victoire, ☎ 02–40–24–34–44). **Lorient** (⊠ Maison de la Mer, quai de Rohan, ☎ 02–97–21–07–84). **Morlaix** (⊠ pl. des Otages, ☎ 02–98–62–14–94). **Quiberon** (⊠ 14 rue de Verdun, ☎ 02–97–50–07–84). **Quimper** (⊠ 7 rue Déesse, ☎ 02–98–53–04–05). **St-Malo** (⊠ esplanade St-Vincent, ☎ 02–99–56–64–48). **Vannes** (⊠ 1 rue Thiers, ☎ 02–97–47–24–34). **Vitré** (⊠ pl. St-Yves, ☎ 02–99–75–04–46).

6 Normandy

Rouen to Mont-St-Michel

On the miles of sandy or pebbly beaches along the English Channel are bustling towns such as Dieppe, Étretat, Honfleur, and Deauville. To the west is Mont-St-Michel, the famous medieval abbey crowning a rock offshore. Inland, Rouen's cathedral and museums, Pont-Audemer's colorful market, and the legendary Bayeux Tapestry beckon, as do calvados and marvelous cheeses.

Revised and
updated by
Simon Hewitt

NORMANDY (OR NORMANDIE, as the French spell
it), the coastal region northwest of Paris, probably has more associations for English speakers
than any other part of France: William the Conqueror, Joan of Arc,
and D day are household names in English, just as they are in French.

The area is popular with British vacationers not only because it's right
across the Channel but also because of its countryside: wild, granite cliffs
in the west; long, sandy beaches along the coast; wooded valleys in the
south; and lush green meadows and apple orchards in the center.

Historic buildings—castles, churches, and monuments—pepper the
Norman countryside. Following the 1066 invasion of England by the
Norman duke William (the Conqueror), Normandy oscillated between
English and French control for several centuries. In Rouen, in 1431,
Joan of Arc was burned at the stake, marking a turning point in the
Hundred Years' War between the French and the English. The coastline east of the Cotentin Peninsula is lined with the World War II D-
day beaches, where the colossal Allied amphibious landings took place
in June 1944. But perhaps Normandy's most celebrated sight is the abbey
of Mont-St-Michel, erected on a 264-ft mound of granite cut off from
the mainland at high tide; this architectural marvel is the country's most
visited spot outside Paris.

Pleasures and Pastimes

Bicycling
The Cotentin Peninsula, jutting out into the English Channel, is suited
for easy cycling, particularly the west coast, which doesn't get much
traffic. The rolling hills of La Suisse Normande, south of Caen, are dotted with little villages and picnic spots connected by country roads that
make the area ideal for touring by bike.

The Coast
Normandy has 605 km (375 mi) of coastline bordering the English Channel. There are four major ports—Le Havre, Rouen, Dieppe, and Cherbourg, plus coastal towns with seafaring pasts, like Honfleur, and
former fishing villages like Fécamp. Sandwiched between are beaches
and fashionable resort towns—Deauville, Cabourg, and Étretat—where
you might find yourself reclining in a deck chair. Though the waters
are chilly, you might be tempted to take a dip on a hot, sunny day.

Dining
The Normans are notoriously big eaters: On festive occasions, in the
old days, they wouldn't bat an eye at tucking away 24 courses. Between
the warm-up and the main course there was a *trou Normand* (Norman hole), a break often lasting several hours, during which lots of
calvados (apple brandy) was downed to make room for more food.
And Norman food isn't light. Many dishes are cooked with rich cream
sauces and apple flavoring—hence *à la normande* (with cream sauce
or apples). Rich local milk makes excellent cheese: Pont-l'Évêque
(known since the 13th century) is made in the Pays d'Auge with milk
that is still warm and creamy; Livarot (also produced for centuries) uses
milk that has stood for a while—don't be put off by its pungent smell.
The excellent Pavé d'Auge is a firm, square-shape cheese with a strong
flavor. Best known of them all is creamy Camembert, a relative newcomer invented by a farmer's wife in the late 18th century. Although
Normandy is not a wine-growing area, it produces excellent hard cider
(the best comes from the Vallée d'Auge) and calvados.

Local specialties differ from place to place. Rouen is famous for its *canard à la rouennaise* (duck in blood sauce); Caen, for its *tripes à la mode de Caen* (tripe cooked with carrots in a seasoned cider stock); Mont-St-Michel for *omelettes Mère Poulard* (a secret recipe first made by a local hotel manager in the late 19th century). From the Vallée d'Auge there's *sole dieppoise* (sole poached in a sauce with cream and mussels) and *pré-salé* (lamb from the salt marshes). If you like *boudin noir* (blood sausage), this is the region; for seafood lovers, the coast provides oysters, lobster, and shrimp. In summer, be sure to make reservations at restaurants to assure you can indulge in all these Norman treats.

CATEGORY	COST*
$$$$	over 400 frs
$$$	250 frs–400 frs
$$	125 frs–250 frs
$	under 125 frs

*per person for a three-course meal, including tax (20.6%) and tip but not wine

Hiking

Gentle rolling countryside makes Normandy ideal for rambling or serious hiking. There are 10 long-distance, signposted itineraries and countless well-indicated footpaths for shorter walks in La Suisse Normande and the Cotentin Peninsula; hostels are found in many of the villages along the trails.

Lodging

Accommodations to suit every taste can be found in Normandy. The beach resort season is very short—July and August only—but weekends are busy most of the year, especially during school holidays. In June and September, lodging is usually available on short notice, and good discounts are given off-season, particularly for stays of more than one night.

CATEGORY	COST*
$$$$	over 800 frs
$$$	600 frs–800 frs
$$	300 frs–600 frs
$	under 300 frs

*All prices are for a standard double room for two, including tax (20.6%) and service charge.

Exploring Normandy

You won't want to miss medieval Rouen, seaside Deauville, or magnificent Mont-St-Michel. But if you get away from these popular spots, you can lose yourself along the cliff-lined coast and the green spaces inland, where the closest thing to a crowd is a farmer with his herd of brown-and-white cows. From Rouen northeast to the coast—the area known as Upper Normandy—medieval castles and abbeys stand guard above the rolling countryside, while resort and fishing towns line the white cliffs of the Côte d'Alabâtre. Popular seaside resorts and the D-day landing sites occupy the sandy beaches along the Côte Fleurie; apple orchards and dairy farms dot the countryside in the area known as Lower Normandy. The Cotentin Peninsula to the west juts out into the English Channel. Central Normandy encompasses the peacefully rural, hilly region of La Suisse Normande, along the scenic Orne River.

Numbers in the text correspond to numbers in the margin and on the Normandy and Rouen maps.

Great Itineraries

Without spending too much time in any one place, you can see most of Normandy in about nine days, from the best-known spots along the coast to the smaller, rural towns inland. Five days gives you time to meander through the countryside and down the coast. In three days you can just get a feel for the region.

IF YOU HAVE 3 DAYS

Head straight to ⊡ **Rouen** ④–⑬ and spend a day and a half in the region's cultural capital; then go to ⊡ **Honfleur** ⑰, the fishing port that caught the Impressionists' eye.

IF YOU HAVE 5 DAYS

Follow the Seine as it snakes through the gentle rolling countryside, on your way from Paris to Rouen. Stop at the formidable fortress at **Les Andelys** ③ before going to ⊡ **Rouen** ④–⑬ for a night and a day. On the third day continue along the Seine Valley on the Route des Abbayes to the abbeys at **Jumièges** ⑭ and **St-Wandrille** ⑮. Cross the Pont de Normandie and spend the night in ⊡ **Honfleur** ⑰. The next day travel along the Côte Fleurie to the fashionable resort towns of **Deauville, Trouville** ㉕, and **Cabourg** ㉗. By early afternoon try to reach **Caen** ㉘, site of some of World War II's fiercest fighting and home to William the Conqueror's fortress. Spend the night in ⊡ **Bayeux** ㉚, famous for its medieval tapestry. On the fifth day explore the D-day landing beaches, **Arromanches** ㉙ and Omaha Beach; then head southwest to **Coutances** ㉛, with its elegant cathedral, and **Granville** ㉜, an old harbor town. Reach the majestic abbey on a rock, ⊡ **Mont-St-Michel** ㉝, before sundown.

IF YOU HAVE 9 DAYS

Follow the Seine en route from Paris to ⊡ **Rouen** ④–⑬, visiting **Les Andelys** ③ and **Lyons-la-Forêt** ② along the way. On the third day wind along the Route des Abbayes to the abbeys of **Jumièges** ⑭ and **St-Wandrille** ⑮. Drive north to the port of **Dieppe** ㉑ and stop briefly before heading down the Côte d'Albâtre to the fishing town of **Fécamp** ⑳ and the popular beach town of **Étretat** ⑲. Return south, cross the Pont de Normandie and spend the night in ⊡ **Honfleur** ⑰. The next day travel along the Côte Fleurie to the seaside resorts, **Deauville** and **Trouville** ㉕, and **Cabourg** ㉗. Get to **Caen** ㉘ by mid-afternoon for a visit to the "men's" and "ladies'" abbeys. Stay in medieval ⊡ **Bayeux** ㉚ overnight. Set aside a day for historic **Arromanches** ㉙ and Omaha Beach. On day seven ramble south through La Suisse Normande's rocky expanse of hills, passing through Thury-Harcourt and **Clécy** ㉞, on the Orne River. Stop for a picnic lunch at the Roche d'Oëtre, a rock with a spectacular view of the countryside. By late afternoon try to be in the spa town of ⊡ **Bagnoles-de-l'Orne** ㊲. Then, on day nine, hurry west via Domfront to dramatic ⊡ **Mont-St-Michel** ㉝.

When to Tour Normandy

July and August—when French families vacation—are the busiest months, but also the most activity-filled: Concerts are held every evening at Mont-St-Michel, and the region's most important horse races take place in Deauville in the second half of August. June 6, the anniversary of the Allied invasion, is the most popular time to visit the D-day beaches. If you're trying to avoid crowds, your best bet is late spring and early autumn, when it is still fairly temperate. Some of the biggest events of the region take place during these seasons: in Rouen, at the end of May, Joan of Arc is celebrated at a festival in her name; in Deauville, the first week of September, the American Film Festival takes place. If you're hearty, winter offers the pleasures of Normandy without the crowds (most places remain open throughout the year, except January).

UPPER NORMANDY

Upper Normandy is delineated by the Seine, which winds northwest out of Paris through the rolling hills around Rouen, the region's cultural and commercial capital, on its way to meet the English Channel. Between Rouen and Le Havre, the Seine winds its way along the Route des Abbayes, past ancient abbeys and small towns, amid some lovely scenery. The impressive chalky cliffs and pebbly beaches of the Côte d'Albâtre stretch from Le Havre to the fishing town of Dieppe. In the 19th century, the bathing resorts along the coast attracted writers and artists like Maupassant, Monet, and Braque, who were inspired by the dramatic scenery.

Gisors

❶ *64 km (40 mi) northwest of Paris via A15 and D915, 35 km (24 mi) northeast of Vernon.*

Gisors, a peaceful market town evoked by Impressionist painter Camille Pissarro (who lived just to the north at Eragny-sur-Epte), has several half-timbered houses along the sloping rue de Vienne and a fine hilltop castle standing sentinel at the confines of Normandy. The town church, lovingly restored after damage in World War II, is a charming jumble of styles; the elaborate, two-towered 16th-century facade and florid vaulting in the side chapels clash with the sober choir consecrated in 1249. The royal fleur-de-lys emblem keeps cropping up unexpectedly—carved on a spiral-patterned pillar, in a modern stained-glass window, or woven into the stone balustrade above the side-chapels outside.

The **Château Fort** was begun in 1097 by the English king William Rufus, son of the Conqueror. The castle has two parts. One is the drumlike ring of curtain walls with a dozen towers, surrounded by a big ditch and enclosing a park filled with flowers and evergreens. The park is open daily without charge and offers a fine view of the church above the roofs of the old town. The other is the 70-ft artificial mound in the middle, the foresquare keep, with a staircase leading to the top—and down to the dungeon. ⊠ *pl. Blanmont,* ☎ *02–32–55–59–36.* ⊡ *25 frs.* ⊙ *Apr.–Sept., Wed.–Mon. 10–noon and 2–6; Oct.–Nov. and Feb.– Mar., weekends 10–noon and 2–5.*

In the pretty village of Boury-en-Vexin 8 km (5 mi) southwest of Gisors, the steep-roofed **Château de Boury,** built in 1685 by Jules Hardouin-Mansart, displays the same monumental dignity as the architect's work at Versailles. The two-tiered facade, with arched ground-flower windows and Ionic pilasters above, surveys a trim lawn with cone-shape topiary bushes. The château has remained in the same family since it was built, and has a homey, lived-in feel to complement its grand furniture, portraits, and crystal chandeliers. ⊠ *Boury-en-Vexin,* ☎ *02–32–55–15–10.* ⊡ *25 frs.* ⊙ *July–Aug., Wed.–Mon. 2:30– 6:30; mid-Apr.–June and Sept.–mid-Oct., weekends 2:30–6:30.*

En Route From Gisors, follow D17 north along the winding Levrière Valley river to Bézu-la-Forêt; then take D14 to **Fleury-la-Forêt,** pausing to admire the village green and, farther on, the imposing flint and redbrick 17th-century château.

Lyons-la-Forêt

❷ *34 km (21 mi) northwest of Gisors, 36 km (23 mi) east of Rouen.*

Few villages in France are as pretty as Lyons-la-Forêt, built in a verdant clearing surrounded by a noble beech forest. Lyons has entire streets

Normandy

0 ——————— 20 miles
0 ——————— 30 km

N

TO ROSSLARE
TO POOLE
TO PORTSMOUTH
TO CA' DE LA HAGUE

TO PORTSMA
TO ROSSLARE
TO CORK
TO PORTSMOUTH

Cherbourg

N13

Cotentin Peninsula

Valognes

Carteret

Portbail

Utah Beach

Ste-Mere L'Eglise

St-Laurent-sur-Mer

Vierville-sur-Mer

Omaha Beach

Port-en-Bessin-Huppain

Arromanches

Côte Fleuri

Courseulles

La Haye-du-Puits

D2

D903

Colleville-sur-Mer

D514

D516

29

D514

Cabourg

27

2

Isigny-sur-Mer

Bayeux

N13

Bénouville

30

D513

La Haye-du-Puits

D900

D971

D572

Balleroy

Caen

28

Troarn

St-Lô

D972

D173

N174

N175

D212

Orne

Laize-la-Ville

N158

Coutances

31

D571

D669

Thury-Harcourt

D562

Percy

D577

Clécy

34

Pont d'Ouilly

Falaise

Granville

32

D973

Villedieu-les-Poêles

N175

Conde-Sur-Noireau

Vire

Roche d' Oëtre

Rabodanges

D909

Avranches

Flers

Putanges-Pont-Ecrepin

D909

Mont-St-Michel

33

N175

Domfront

Bagnoles-de-l'Orne

37

D916

Dol-de-Bretagne

D795

D155

Antrain

D998

D177

N176

D23

Pré-en-Pail

Combourg

Fougères

N12

Mayenne

D35

English Channel
(La Manche)

TO NEWHAVEN

Le Tréport
Eu

Côte d' Albâtre

Dieppe **21**

St-Valéry-en-Caux

Veules-les-Roses

Varengeville-sur-Mer

D68

D925

N28

Neufchatel-en-Bray

Fécamp **20**

D79

D925

Cany-Barville

Étretat **19**

D926

N27

N29

D915/N15

Forges-les-Eaux

Cleres

D6

N28

Caudebec-en-Caux

Villequier

St-Wandrille

Duclair

Rouen
4 — **13**

N31

Lyons-la-Forêt **2**

Gisors **1**

Le Havre **18**

A29

D81

D81

A131

Jumièges

D082

15

14

St-Martin de Boscherville

Bonsecour

N15

N14

Les Andelys **3**

Honfleur **17**

Pont-Audemer **16**

A13

Seine

Seine

Louviers

auville–ouville **25**

D579

lgate sur-Mer

Manerbe

ron-uge

Pont l'Evêque

D810

Le Bec-Hellouin **23**

Brionne

Lisieux **24**

N13

Bernay

Risle

D139

Touques

N138

Conches-en-Ouche

Evreux 22

N13

D316

A13

Eure

Bonnieres-sur-Siene

N183

D313

moutiers

Risle

D840

Houdan

gentan

L'Aigle

N26

Verneuil-sur-Avre

Dreux

Eure

Orne

Château d'O

Sées **35**

N138

N12

Chateauneuf-en-Thymerais

D928

N154

Mortagne

Alençon **36**

Eure

Chartres

Nogent-le-Rotrou

full of rickety, half-timbered houses and a venerable market hall built of robust medieval oaks on its main square. In fact, the square is more of a tumbling triangle—all bustle in summer but, come winter when most of the hotels and restaurants are shut, as forlorn as the leafless beech trees all around. Lyons is built on two levels, and if you arrive from Gisors, take care not to miss the lower road—a black-and-white quilt of medieval frontages, leading to the village church and its life-size wooden statues.

The scenic ruins of the Cistercian **Abbaye de Mortemer** lie by a small lake in the heart of the forest 5 km (3 mi) south of Lyons. The 100-yard-long church was built at the start of the 13th century but destroyed during the Revolution. Some of the abbey buildings survive, including the large 15th-century pigeon loft that was also used as a prison. A small museum evokes aspects of monastic life. ⊠ *rue de Mortemer, Lisors,* ☎ *02–32–49–54–37.* 🎫 *25 frs.* ☉ *Easter–Oct., daily 2–6:30; Nov.–Easter, Sun. 2–6.*

Dining and Lodging

$$–$$$ ✕📷 **Licorne.** This venerable inn at the top of the village square has comfortably restored rooms with rustic wooden furniture. The colorful garden at the back of the hotel is a fine place for a pre-dinner drink before repairing to the dining room, where a fire crackles in the hearth on cooler evenings. For a main course, try grilled salmon or guinea fowl cooked with peaches. ⊠ *pl. du Marché, 27480,* ☎ *02–32–49–62–02,* 𝖥𝖠𝖷 *02–32–49–80–09. 21 rooms, 15 with bath or shower. Restaurant. AE, DC, MC, V. Closed Dec.–Mar.*

Les Andelys

❸   *20 km (13 mi) southwest of Lyons-la-Forêt, 88 km (55 mi) northwest of Paris, 40 km (25 mi) southeast of Rouen.*

In one of the most picturesque loops of the Seine, the small town of Les Andelys, birthplace of France's leading classical painter, Nicolas Poussin, is set against magnificent chalky cliffs. The **Château Gaillard,** a formidable fortress built by England's King Richard the Lionhearted in 1196, overlooks Les Andelys from the cliff tops, with spectacular views in both directions. Despite its solid defenses, the castle fell to the French in 1204. It suffered considerable damage during the assault, and sections were eventually torn down at the end of the 16th century; only one of its five main towers remains intact, but the location and the ruins bring alive a history long forgotten. ⊠ *rue Richard-Coeur-de-Lion,* ☎ *02–32–54–41–93.* 🎫 *15 frs.* ☉ *Thurs.–Mon. 10–noon and 2–5, Wed. 2–5.*

Dining and Lodging

$$$ ✕📷 **Hostellerie St-Pierre.** This hotel, west of Les Andelys on the road to Rouen, is the perfect place to stay in the Seine Valley. Room 27 has the best view of the river and French windows that open onto a terrace. Its size, like that of most others, is modest; all have comfortingly traditional decor. At dinner, sample the *rable de lapin farci* (saddle of rabbit) stuffed with mushrooms in a cider sauce, or the *boudin de poisson* (fish mousse) in beurre blanc. Desserts are generally good, though the *assiette tout chocolat* (all-chocolate plate) is less luscious than expected. ⊠ *6 chemin de la Digue, 27430 St-Pierre-du-Vauvray (11 km/7 mi west of Les Andelys),* ☎ *02–32–59–93–29,* 𝖥𝖠𝖷 *02–32–59–41–93. 14 rooms. Restaurant. MC, V. Closed mid-Nov.–mid-Mar.*

En Route   From Les Andelys, stay on the right bank of the Seine for 24 km (15 mi) to Amfreville; then turn right up steep D508 to what is known as the **Côte des Deux Amants** (Lovers' Mount) for a spectacular view of the Seine Valley and its chalky cliffs. Follow the road to Pont-St-Pierre and then head northwest on D138 toward Rouen, pausing in the suburb of **Bonsecours** to check out the **Basilique Notre-Dame**, a fine neo-Gothic church built in 1840 on a hilltop overlooking the Seine.

Rouen

★ *30 km (19 mi) north of Louviers, 40 km (25 mi) northwest of Les Andelys, 86 km (53 mi) east of Le Havre, 132 km (82 mi) northwest of Paris.*

Rouen has a surprising wealth of medieval buildings, despite the fact that a large part of the city was destroyed during World War II and subsequently rebuilt. But even before its massive reconstruction, Rouen had expanded with the development of industries spawned by its increasingly busy port, now the fifth largest in France. Cobblestone streets lined with ancient Norman buildings—like rue d'Amiette, a pedestrians-only street harboring restaurants and small shops—fan out from place St-Maclou, an attractive square surrounded by picturesque half-timber houses. In its more distant past, Rouen gained celebrity when Joan of Arc was burned at the stake here in 1431.

Rouen is known as the City of a Hundred Spires because many of its important edifices are churches. Lording over them all is the magnif-
❹ icent **Cathédrale Notre-Dame.** If you are familiar with the works of Impressionist Claude Monet, you will immediately recognize the cathedral's immense west facade, rendered in an increasingly hazy fashion in his series *Cathédrales de Rouen*. The original 12th-century construction was replaced after a terrible fire in 1200; only the left-hand spire, the **Tour St-Romain** (St. Romanus Tower), survived the flames. The imposing 250-ft steeple on the right, known as the **Tour de Beurre** (Butter Tower), was added in the 15th and 16th centuries and completed in the 17th, when a group of wealthy citizens donated large sums of money for the privilege of eating butter during Lent. Interior highlights include the 13th-century choir, with its pointed arcades; vibrant stained glass depicting the crucified Christ (restored after heavy damage during World War II); and massive stone columns topped by some intriguing carved faces. The first flight of the famous **Escalier de la Librairie** (Booksellers' Stairway), attributed to Guillaume Pontifs (also responsible for most of the 15th-century work seen in the cathedral), rises from a tiny balcony just to the left of the transept. ⊠ *pl. de la Cathédrale,* ☎ *02–35–71–00–48.* ☉ *Mon.–Sat. 8–7, Sun. 8–6.*

❺ The late-Gothic church of **St-Maclou,** across rue de la République behind Cathédrale Notre-Dame, bears testimony to the wild excesses of Flamboyant architecture; take time to examine the central and left-hand portals on the main facade, covered with little bronze lion heads and pagan engravings. Inside, note the 16th-century organ, with its Renaissance wood carving, and the fine marble columns. ⊠ *pl. St-Maclou,* ☎ *02–35–71–71–72.* ☉ *Mon.–Sat. 10–noon and 2:30–6, Sun. 3–5:30.*

❻ A former ossuary (a charnel house used for the bodies of plague victims), the **Aître St-Maclou,** east of place St-Maclou, is one of the last reminders of the plague that devastated Europe during the Middle Ages; these days, it holds Rouen's School of Art and Architecture. French composer Camille Saint-Saëns (1835–1921) is said to have been inspired by the ossuary when he was working on his *Danse Macabre*. The building's massive double frieze is carved with some graphic skulls, bones, and grave diggers' tools. ⊠ *184 rue Martainville.*

❼ A fine example of late Gothic architecture is the **Abbaye St-Ouen** on the square at the end of rue de la République. The stained-glass windows, dating from the 14th to the 16th centuries, are the most spec-

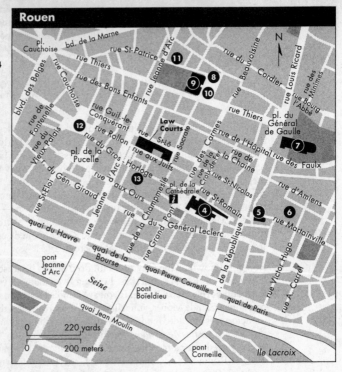

tacular features of the otherwise spare abbey. The church's 19th-century pipe organs have few equals in France. ✉ *pl. du Général-de-Gaulle.* ⊙ *Mid-Mar.–Oct., Wed.–Mon. 8–noon and 2–6; Nov.–mid-Dec. and mid-Jan.–mid-Mar., Wed. and weekends 10–12:30 and 2–6.*

8 A painted wooden ceiling and fine medieval stained glass, especially the *Tree of Jesse* dating from 1506, distinguish the church of **St-Godard.** ✉ *pl. St-Godard,* ☎ *02–35–71–47–12.*

9 One of Rouen's cultural mainstays is the **Musée des Beaux-Arts** (Fine Arts Museum). It contains a good collection of French paintings from the 17th and 19th centuries, including works by Claude Monet, Alfred Sisley, Auguste Renoir, Eugène Delacroix, and Théodore Chassériau. An entire room is devoted to Rouen-born Théodore Géricault. ✉ *square Verdrel, off rue Thiers,* ☎ *02–35–71–28–40.* 🎫 *25 frs.* ⊙ *Wed.–Mon. 10–6.*

10 The **Musée Le Secq des Tournelles** (Wrought Ironwork Museum), behind the Musée des Beaux-Arts, claims to possess the world's finest collection of wrought iron, with exhibits spanning the 3rd through the 19th century. Displays include a range of items used in daily life, accessories, and professional instruments used by surgeons, barbers, carpenters, clock makers, and gardeners. ✉ *square Verdrel,* ☎ *02–35–07–31–74.* 🎫 *15 frs.* ⊙ *Wed.–Mon. 10–1 and 2–6.*

11 A superb array of local faience is in the **Musée de la Céramique** (Ceramics Museum) near the Musée des Beaux-Arts. ✉ *rue Faucon,* ☎ *02–35–07–31–74.* 🎫 *15 frs.* ⊙ *Wed.–Mon. 10–1 and 2–6.*

12 Dedicated to Joan of Arc, the modern **Église Jeanne d'Arc** (Joan of Arc Church), a few blocks from rue Thiers, just off rue Jeanne-d'Arc, was built on the spot where she was burned to death in 1431. Not all is new, however: The church incorporates some remarkable 16th-century stained-glass windows taken from the former Église St-Vincent, destroyed in 1944. ⊠ *pl. du Vieux-Marché.* ⊗ *Daily 10–12:15 and 2–6, except Fri. and Sun. mornings.*

⑬ The name of the pedestrian rue du Gros-Horloge, Rouen's most popular street, comes from the **Gros-Horloge** itself, a giant Renaissance clock. In 1527 the Rouennais had a splendid arch built especially for it, and today its golden face looks out over the street. You can see the clock's inner workings from a 15th-century belfry. Though the street is crammed with boutiques and fast-food joints, a few old houses, dating from the 16th century, remain. Wander through the surrounding old town, a warren of tiny streets lined with more than 700 half-timber houses, many artfully transformed into fashionable shops. ⊠ *rue du Gros-Horloge.* 🎟 *Clock 10 frs.* ⊗ *Wed.–Mon. 10–1 and 2–6.*

OFF THE BEATEN PATH

PARC ZOOLOGIQUE DE CLÈRES – This wildlife park on the grounds of a stately Renaissance château in the tiny village of Clères, 22 km (14 mi) north of Rouen via N15 and D155, is home to more than 750 species of birds, plus a motley assortment of free-roaming antelope, deer, kangaroos, and gibbons. ⊠ *32 av. du Parc, close to D155,* ☎ *02–35–33–23–08.* 🎟 *30 frs.* ⊗ *June–Aug., daily 9–6; Mar.–May and Sept.–Nov., daily 9–noon and 1:30–5.*

Dining and Lodging

$$$ ✕ **Auberge de la Butte.** Chef Pierre Hervé is renowned for his subtle
★ fish and seafood dishes, including poached oysters wrapped in spinach leaves and fricasseed fillet of sole. The magnificent Norman dining room has exposed beams and half-timber walls adorned with paintings and shining copper pots. This former 18th-century post house, in the suburb of Bonsecours, is well worth seeking out (you'll need a car). ⊠ *69 rte. de Paris, Bonsecours (about 3 km/2 mi east of the city center),* ☎ *02–35–80–43–11. Jacket and tie. AE, DC, MC, V. Closed Sun.–Mon., late Dec.–early Jan., and Aug.*

$$$ ✕ **La Couronne.** In a 15th-century Norman building, this restaurant is crammed with leather-upholstered chairs and a scattering of sculpture. The traditional Norman cuisine—crayfish salad with foie gras and caviar, duck with orange sauce—makes few modern concessions. ⊠ *31 pl. du Vieux-Marché,* ☎ *02–35–71–66–66. Jacket and tie. AE, DC, MC, V.*

$$ ✕ **La Toque d'Or.** This large, bustling bistro next to the market and the Église Jeanne d'Arc has a helpful staff and a huge menu. Excellent specialties include oysters, mussels, and delicious tripe. ⊠ *11 pl. du Vieux-Marché,* ☎ *02–35–71–46–29. AE, DC, V.*

$$ ✕🏨 **Dieppe.** Dating from the late 19th century, the Dieppe remains up-to-date thanks to the strong management of four generations of the same family. Staff members are helpful and speak English. The compact rooms are furnished in cheerful, modern style. Street noise can be a problem, though, despite double-glazed windows. The restaurant, Les Quatre Saisons, has a well-earned reputation and serves English-style roasts, as well as traditional Norman dishes. ⊠ *pl. Bernard-Tissot, 76000,* ☎ *02–35–71–96–00, 800/528–1324 for U.S. reservations,* 𝔽𝔸𝕏 *02–35–89–65–21. 42 rooms. Restaurant, breakfast room. AE, DC, MC, V.*

$$ 🏨 **Mercure Rouen-Centre.** In the jumble of streets near the cathedral— a navigational challenge if you arrive by car—this modern chain hotel has small, comfortable rooms, in breezy pastels. The location makes this hotel ideal for touring the old streets of the city center. Service, too, is efficient. ⊠ *7 rue de la Croix-de-Fer, 76000,* ☎ *02–35–52–69–52,* 𝔽𝔸𝕏 *02–35–89–41–46. 125 rooms. Bar. AE, DC, MC, V.*

$–$$ 🏨 **Cathédrale.** This hotel is in a medieval building on a narrow pedestrian street behind the cathedral. (You can sleep soundly, though: The cathedral bells do not boom out the hour at night.) Rooms are petite but neat and comfortable. Breakfast is served in the beamed dining room. ⊠ *12 rue St-Romain, 76000,* ☎ *02–35–71–57–95,* F̄AX̄ *02–35–70–15–54. 25 rooms. Breakfast room, parking (fee). MC, V.*

Nightlife and the Arts

The **Fête Jeanne d'Arc** (Joan of Arc Festival) takes place on the Sunday nearest to May 30, with parades, street plays, concerts, and exhibitions. Evening **concerts** and organ recitals are held at St-Maclou in August and at St-Ouen throughout the year; get details from the Rouen Tourist Office (☞ Contacts and Resources *in* Normandy A to Z, *below*). Operas are staged at the **Théâtre des Arts** (⊠ 111 rue du Gal-Leclerc, ☎ 02–35–71–41–36).

Jumièges

⑭   *24 km (15 mi) west of Rouen: Head west on D982 through St-Martin de Boscherville, and then turn off left on D143 to get to the Abbaye de Jumièges.*

★   Imposing ruins are all that is left of the once-mighty Benedictine **Abbaye de Jumièges,** founded in 654 by St-Philbert, plundered by Vikings in 841, then rebuilt by William Longswood, Duke of Normandy, around 940, though not consecrated until 1067. The French Revolution forced the evacuation of the remaining 16 monks, whereupon the abbey was auctioned off to a timber merchant, who promptly demolished part of the building to sell the stones. What remains is impressive enough. ⊠ *24 rue Guillaume-le-Conquérant,* ☎ *02–35–37–24–02.* 🎫 *32 frs.* ☉ *Apr.–Sept., daily 9–7; Oct.–Mar., daily 9:30–12:30 and 2–5:30.*

St-Wandrille

⑮   *14 km (9 mi) north of the Abbaye de Jumièes via D982, 37 km (23 mi) northwest of Rouen.*

The Benedictine **Abbaye de St-Wandrille** is still active today. Founded in the 7th century, the abbey was sacked by the Normans and rebuilt in the 10th century—although what you see today is an ensemble of styles from the 11th century through the early 18th (mainly the latter). You can hear the monks sing their Gregorian chants at morning mass if you arrive early (9:25 AM weekdays and 10 AM Sunday and holidays). Be sure to visit the abbey shop down the hill. Everything it sells— from floor polish to spiritual aids—is monk-made. ☎ *02–35–96–23–11.* 🎫 *25 frs.* ☉ *Guided tour weekdays at 3:30, Sun. at 11:30.*

Pont-Audemer

⑯   *32 km (20 mi) southwest of St-Wandrille, 50 km (31 mi) west of Rouen.*

Pont-Audemer, on the banks of the River Risle in the heart of calvados country, luckily escaped destruction by warfare and bulldozers. Today, many of its buildings are still as they were in the 16th century when the town made its mark as an important trading center. After taking in the colorful market square, be sure to stroll along impasse St-Ouen and impasse de l'Épée, narrow streets lined with timber-framed medieval houses. Don't miss the church of **St-Ouen** with its pleasing modern stained-glass windows that blend with richly sculpted medieval stonework. ⊠ *rue de la République,* ☎ *02–32–41–12–88.*

Dining and Lodging

$$$ ✕⊞ **Belle-Isle sur Risle.** It's hard not to feel like a guest of this private
★ manor—an impression somehow heightened by a few rough edges. The
newer, more modern rooms have wall-to-wall carpeting and depart-
ment-store furniture, but the older ones have wood floors with rugs
and assorted traditional furniture. Rooms on the first floor have bal-
conies. In the restaurant, chef Laurent Matuit turns out tasty foie gras
blinis, *coquilles St-Jacques* (scallops) with a coulis (thick sauce) of
mushrooms, and light pastry tarts with honeyed apples and sorbet. ⊠
112 rte. de Rouen, 27500, ☎ *02–32–56–96–22,* FAX *02–32–42–88–
96. 15 rooms, 4 suites. Restaurant, pool, sauna, tennis court. MC, V.*

$$–$$$ ✕⊞ **Auberge du Vieux Puits.** Gustave Flaubert, an early admirer of
this hotel in a trellised and beamed cottage, gave it a few lines in his
notorious novel *Madame Bovary.* The quiet rooms, furnished with heavy
wooden pieces and pretty curtains, overlook the courtyard. The restau-
rant serves first-rate, rich, innovative Norman cuisine—trout in cham-
pagne sauce, duckling stew with sour cherries, local cheeses, and fresh
fruit tarts. (It is closed Monday and Tuesday dinner off-season.) Since
this place is first and foremost a restaurant, you are expected to eat
dinner here when you stay. ⊠ *6 rue Notre-Dame-du-Pré, 27500,* ☎
02–32–41–01–48, FAX *02–32–42–37–28. 11 rooms, 7 with bath, 4
with shower. Restaurant. MC, V. Closed mid-Dec.–late Jan.*

$$$ ⊞ **Petit Coq aux Champs.** Rooms at this small luxury hotel in a Nor-
man-style, thatch-roof farmhouse are not large, but they have balconies.
No. 39 has two especially comfortable beds, a porthole window, and
a good-size bathroom. Though the food isn't particularly exciting, the
beamed dining room is cozy and full of antiques. (Meals are not
mandatory.) The owner speaks excellent English. ⊠ *La Pommeraie,
27500 Campigny (take D810 and D29 from Pont-Audemer),* ☎ *02–
32–41–04–19,* FAX *02–32–56–06–25. 12 rooms. Restaurant, pool.
AE, DC, MC, V. Closed Jan.*

Honfleur

★ ⑰ *24 km (15 mi) northwest of Pont-Audemer via N175 and D80, 80 km
(50 mi) west of Rouen.*

The colorful port of Honfleur on the Seine estuary has become increasingly crowded since the Pont de Normandie suspension bridge—
providing a direct link with Le Havre and Upper Normandy—opened
in 1995. The town, full of half-timber houses and cobbled streets, was
once an important departure point for maritime expeditions, including the first voyages to Canada in the 15th and 16th centuries. The
17th-century harbor is fronted on one side by two-story stone houses
with low, sloping roofs and on the other by tall, narrow houses whose
wooden facades are topped by slate roofs.

Soak up the seafaring atmosphere by strolling around the old harbor
and paying a visit to the wooden church of **Ste-Catherine,** which dominates the harbor's northern corner. It was built by townspeople to show
their gratitude for the departure of the English at the end of the Hundred Years' War (1453). ⊠ *rue des Logettes,* ☎ *02–31–89–11–83.*

Dining and Lodging

$$$ ✕ **Absinthe.** A 17th-century dining room, with stone walls and beamed
ceilings, is the magnificent setting for Antoine Ceffrey's masterly
seafood and fish creations, such as *barbet* (freshwater cod) prepared
with ginger. On sunny days you'll probably want to eat on the sunny
terrace. ⊠ *10 quai de la Quarantaine,* ☎ *02–31–89–39–00. Jacket
and tie. AE, DC, MC, V. Closed 2nd ½ Nov. No dinner Mon.*

$$-$$$ ✕ **L'Assiette Gourmande.** This is one of Honfleur's unsung top restau-
★   rants. On the seasonal menu, you might find chef Gérard Bonnefoy's
superb *coquilles St-Jacques* (scallops) grilled with sautéed asparagus
in a raspberry vinaigrette and orange sauce; huge, succulent *noix de
St-Jacques* (scallops with hazelnut risotto); or roast lamb from the salt
marshes. ⊠ *2 quai des Passagers,* ☎ *02–31–89–24–88.* .

$$ ✕ **Ancrage.** Massive seafood platters top the bill at this delightful old
restaurant occupying a two-story 17th-century building overlooking
the harbor. The cuisine is authentically Norman—simple but good. If
you want a change, try the succulent calf sweetbreads. ⊠ *16 rue Mont-
pensier,* ☎ *02–31–89–00–70. Reservations essential. MC, V. Closed
Wed. and Jan. No dinner Tues.*

$$ ✕ **La Terrasse de l'Assiette.** This restaurant near the church has an excellent prix-fixe menu. The oysters, marinated salmon and haddock,
and grilled tuna with tart lemon sauce are uniformly satisfying. The
wine list is limited but well priced. ⊠ *8 pl. Ste-Catherine,* ☎ *02–31–
89–31–33. AE, MC, V. Closed Dec. No dinner Tues. or Sun.*

$$$$ 🏨 **Ferme St-Siméon.** It is claimed that this 19th-century manor house
was the birthplace of Impressionism and that its park inspired Claude
Monet and Alfred Sisley. Rooms are decorated in a style that attempts
to be opulent: pastel colors and floral wallpaper, antiques and period
decor. Those in the converted stables are quieter but have less character.
Be aware, however, that the high prices have more to do with the hotel's
reputation than with what it offers. The sophisticated restaurant specializes
in fish; the cheese board does justice to the region. ⊠ *rue Adolphe-Marais,
on D513 to Trouville, 14600,* ☎ *02–31–89–23–61,* 🖷 *02–31–89–
48–48. 22 rooms, 16 suites. Restaurant, pool, tennis court. MC, V.*

$$ 🏨 **Cheval Blanc.** Alain Petit, the owner of this friendly inn by the har-
★   bor, is a humorous and helpful Frenchman who speaks English excel-
lently. Rooms have fine views of the port; No. 34 is larger, better
furnished, and twice as expensive as the rest, with a couch, queen-size
bed, gabled ceilings, and Jacuzzi. ⊠ *2 quai des Passagers, 14600,* ☎
02–31–81–65–00, 🖷 *02–31–89–52–80. 33 rooms, 14 with bath.
Breakfast room. MC, V. Closed Jan.*

$$ 🏨 **Hostellerie Lechat.** This typical 18th-century Norman building is in
a pretty square just behind the harbor. The well-maintained, spacious
rooms are filled with French provincial prints—ask for one with a view
of Ste-Catherine. Hearty, Norman cuisine is served in the rustic, beamed
restaurant (closed in January). ⊠ *13 pl. Ste-Catherine, 14600,* ☎ *02–
31–89–23–85,* 🖷 *02–31–14–49–49. 23 rooms, 1 suite. Restaurant,
bar. AE, DC, MC, V.*

Nightlife and the Arts

The two-day **Fête des Marins** (Marine Festival), including a fishermen's
pilgrimage that started in 1861, is held on Pentecost Sunday and Monday. On the Sunday, all the boats in the harbor are decked out in flags
and paper roses, and a priest bestows his blessing at high tide. The next
day, model boats and local children head a musical procession.

En Route   Three kilometers (2 miles) east of Honfleur is the turnoff to the elegant **Pont de Normandie,** a suspension bridge (toll 32 francs) across
the Seine. This is the world's largest cable-stayed bridge, supported by
two concrete pylons taller than the Eiffel Tower, and is designed to resist winds of 160 mph. To reach Le Havre, continue west for 16 km
(10 mi) on A131.

Le Havre

⑱   *23 km (14 mi) northwest of Honfleur via the Pont de Normandie, 88
km (55 mi) west of Rouen, 200 km (125 mi) northwest of Paris.*

Le Havre, France's second-largest port (after Marseille), was bombarded no fewer than 146 times during World War II. You may find the rebuilt city, with its uncompromising recourse to reinforced concrete and open spaces, bleak and uninviting; or you may admire its rational planning and audacious modern architecture. The hilly suburb of **Ste-Adresse** just west is resplendent with Belle Époque villas and an old fortress and is also worth a visit for its beach and fine views of the sea and port.

The **Musée André-Malraux,** the city art museum, is an innovative 1960s building surrounded by a moat. From the outside, this metal-and-glass structure looks in need of repair; inside, however, its spacious, airy design lets daylight flood in. Two local artists are showcased here—Raoul Dufy (1877–1953), with a remarkable collection of his brightly colored oils, watercolors, and sketches on the ground floor; and, upstairs, Eugène Boudin (1824–98), a forerunner of Impressionism, whose compelling beach scenes and landscapes tellingly evoke the Normandy coast and skyline. ⊠ *23 bd. Clemenceau,* ☎ *02–35–42–33–97.* 🎟 *Free.* ☉ *Wed.–Mon. 10–noon and 2–6.*

★ Perhaps the outstanding postwar building in Le Havre, and one of the most impressive 20th-century churches in France, is the **Église St-Joseph,** built to the plans of Auguste Perret from 1951 to 1957. The church's 350-ft tower powers into the sky like a fat rocket. The inside is thrilling. No frills here: The 270-ft octagonal lantern towers over the crossing, filled almost to the top with abstract stained glass that hurls colored light over the bare concrete walls. ⊠ *bd. François-I,* ☎ *02–35–42–20–03.*

Dining and Lodging

$$$ ✕ **Odyssée.** This restaurant is gaining a reputation as the finest place in town for fish, and with the port and fish-market both within netting distance, fresh produce is guaranteed. There are no frills about the light, airy decor. Visual appeal is on your plate, in the pinks and greens of the smoked salmon and avocado sauce that accompany the chef's homemade fish terrine. Other inventive dishes include fried sole with lemon sabayon, and grilled turbot with poppy seeds in cream sauce. ⊠ *41 rue du Général-Faidherbe,* ☎ *02–35–21–32–42. MC, V. Closed Mon. No dinner Sun., no lunch Sat.*

$$ 🏨 **Bordeaux.** The location of this hotel, just one block from the central square, is its main plus—as are its welcoming owners. The light, airy rooms have modern furniture; many have views of the port. As at all other hotels in Le Havre, prices are high for room size. The small bathrooms have hand-held showers in the tubs. ⊠ *147 rue Louis-Brindeau, 76600,* ☎ *02–35–22–69–44,* ℻ *02–35–42–09–27. 31 rooms. Parking (fee). MC, V.*

Étretat

★ ⑲ *28 km (17 mi) north of Le Havre via D940, 88 km (55 mi) northwest of Rouen.*

Although the promenade running the length of the town's pebble beach has been marred by a proliferation of seedy cafés and french-fry stands, this town is justly famous for the magnificent tall rock formations that extend out into the sea. The **Falaises d'Étretat** are white cliffs that are as famous in France as Dover's are in England. At low tide, it is possible to walk through the huge archways formed by the rocks to neighboring beaches. The biggest arch is at the **Falaise d'Aval,** to the south. For a breathtaking view of the whole bay, take the path up to the Falaise d'Aval, from which you can hike for miles across the

Manneporte hills . . . or play a round of golf on one of Europe's windiest, and most scenic, courses. Farther south is the appropriately named **Aiguille** (Needle), a 300-ft spire of rock jutting into the air just off the coast. To the north towers the **Falaise d'Amont.**

Dining and Lodging

$$ ✕ **Roches Blanches.** The exterior of this family-owned restaurant off the beach is a concrete post–World War II eyesore. But take a table by the window with a view of the cliffs, order Georges Trézeux's superb fresh seafood (try the mussels), and you'll be glad you came. ⊠ *rue Abbé-Cochet,* ☎ *02–35–27–07–34. Reservations essential Sun. lunch. MC, V. Closed Tues.–Thurs. (Wed. only July–early Sept.), Jan., and Oct.*

$$–$$$ ✕▥ **Donjon.** This endearing little château has lovely bay views from
★ a park overlooking town. Rooms, individually furnished with flair, are huge, comfortable, and quiet. Prix-fixe menus and reliable French cuisine—scallops and a seafood platter with lobster—are served in the cozy restaurant. ⊠ *chemin de St-Clair, 76790,* ☎ *02–35–27–08–23,* FAX *02–35–29–92–24. 10 rooms, 7 with bath. Restaurant, pool. AE, DC, MC, V.*

Outdoor Activities and Sports

Don't miss the chance to play on the breathtaking course at the **Golf d'Étretat** (⊠ rte. du Havre, ☎ 02–35–27–04–89), 6,580 yards long (par 72) across the cliff tops of the Falaise d'Aval; it's closed Tuesday.

Fécamp

⓴ *17 km (11 mi) northeast of Étretat via D940, 42 km (26 mi) northeast of Le Havre.*

An ancient fishing port on the Côte d'Alabâtre, Fécamp no longer has a commercial fishing fleet, but you can still see lots of boats in the private marina. Before Mont-St-Michel stole the limelight, the town was Normandy's primary place of pilgrimage. The magnificent abbeychurch, the **Église de La Trinité,** bears witness to Fécamp's religious past. The Benedictine abbey was founded by the Duke of Normandy in the 11th century and became the home of the monastic order of the Précieux Sang et de la Trinité (referring to Christ's blood, which supposedly arrived here in the 7th century). ⊠ *rue Leroux.*

Fécamp is also the home of the liqueur Benedictine. The **Palais de la Bénédictine** (Benedictine Palace), seven blocks from La Trinité and across from the tourist office, is housed in a building dating from 1892. A florid mixture of neo-Gothic and Renaissance styles, it's one of Normandy's most popular attractions. You can drop in for a sample—at 12 francs a shot—or browse through the shop selling Benedictine products and souvenirs. ⊠ *110 rue Alexandre-le-Grand,* ☎ *02–35–10–26–10.* ▱ *27 frs (including tasting).* ☉ *Daily 10–noon and 2–5.*

Dining and Lodging

$ ✕ **L'Escalier.** This delightfully simple little restaurant overlooking the harbor serves traditional Norman cuisine. The prix-fixe menus, beginning at 60 francs, consist mainly of fish and seafood dishes. ⊠ *101 quai Bérigny,* ☎ *02–35–28–26–79. Reservations essential in summer. DC, MC, V. Closed Mon. and 2 wks in Nov.*

$$$ ✕▥ **Les Hêtres.** One of the most highly rated chefs in Normandy, Bertrand Warin, runs this restaurant in Ingouville, east of Fécamp. In the elegant dining room, half-timber walls and Louis XIII chairs contrast with sleek, modern furnishings. Large windows look out onto the garden. The restaurant is closed Sunday dinner and Monday; reservations are essential and a jacket and tie are required. There are also four pretty

rooms for diners (only) who want to stay the night; they have old wooden furniture and engravings. The largest has a terrace looking onto the garden. ⊠ *rue des Fleurs, Ingouville, 76460 (28 km/17 mi east of Fécamp),* ☎ *02–35–57–09–30,* ℻ *02–35–57–09–31. 4 rooms. Restaurant. MC, V. Closed 1st ½ of Jan., last 2 wks in Aug.*

$$ ✕🔟 **Auberge de la Rouge.** In a little hamlet just south of Fécamp is
★ this small inn. Rooms are simply decorated and moderately priced and have modern amenities (TVs). The menu features a mix of classic and modern dishes, including local specialties; the lobster is good, but the *coquilles St-Jacques* (scallops) with herbs and the wild pressed duck are the true temptations. The restaurant is closed Sunday dinner and Monday. Meals are not mandatory if you stay overnight. ⊠ *1 rue du Bois-de-Boclion, St-Léonard, 76400 (1 km/½ mi south of Fécamp),* ☎ *02–35–28–07–59,* ℻ *02–35–28–70–55. 8 rooms. Restaurant, minibars. AE, DC, MC, V.*

En Route From Fécamp, take the scenic coastal road (D79), via the quaint harbor of St-Valery-en-Caux. Before you reach Dieppe, look for the tiny hilltop church in **Varengeville-sur-Mer**; the 20th-century painter Georges Braque (1882–1963)—who, with Picasso, is credited with inventing Cubism—is buried in its graveyard. Nearby, visit the **Parc Floral des Moustiers** (Moustiers Flower Garden) to admire the colorful collection of rare flowers and giant 100-year-old rhododendrons. ⊠ *La Haie des Moustiers,* ☎ *02–35–85–10–02.* ▦ *40 frs.* ☉ *Apr.–Oct., daily 10– noon and 2–6.*

Dieppe

🔞 *11 km (7 mi) east of Varengeville-sur-Mer via D75, 64 km (40 mi) northeast of Fécamp, 64 km (40 mi) north of Rouen.*

Bustling Dieppe is part fishing and commercial port and part Norman seaside town, though its era in the fashionable spotlight is past and its hotels have seen better days. It is now mostly a transit stop for the ferries that run from Dieppe three times a day across the Channel to Newhaven, near Brighton. The seafront promenade, boulevard du Maréchal-Foch, separates an immense lawn from an unspoiled pebble beach where, in 1942, many Canadian soldiers were killed during the so-called Jubilee Raid. The town castle surveys the scene from the cliff top.

The 15th-century **Château,** overlooking the Channel at the western end of the bay, contains a museum, well known for its collection of ivories. In the 17th century, Dieppe imported vast quantities of elephant tusks from Africa and Asia, and as many as 350 craftsmen settled here to work the ivory; their efforts can be seen in the form of ship models, nautical accessories, religious artifacts, and day-to-day objects. The museum also has a room devoted to sketches by Georges Braque. ⊠ *square du Canada,* ☎ *02–35–84–19–76.* ▦ *13 frs.* ☉ *Wed.–Mon. 10–noon and 2–5 (until 6 Sun.).*

Dining and Lodging

$$ ✕🔟 **Windsor.** Of the hotels facing the sea, the Windsor is the best kept, with modern rooms, functional furniture, and reasonably sized bathrooms. Request a room with a sea view. The restaurant on the second floor is popular for its panoramic view of the Channel. ⊠ *18 bd. de Verdun, 76200,* ☎ *02–35–84–15–23,* ℻ *02–35–84–74–52. 48 rooms. Restaurant. AE, DC, MC, V.*

Nightlife and the Arts

At night, the **casino** at the Grand Hotel (⊠ 3 bd. de Verdun, ☎ 02–35–82–33–60) comes alive with shows and gambling. If you love jazz, come for the **Festival Européen de Jazz Traditionnel** (European Traditional Jazz Festival), held in mid-June at Luneray, 8 km (5 mi) southwest of Dieppe. For information, contact the Dieppe tourist office (☞ Normandy A to Z, *below*).

Outdoor Activities and Sports

Bicycles can be rented from Dieppe's train station for 44–55 francs a day; the flat terrain around the city is great for biking. For information on routes, check with the tourist office (☞ Contacts and Resources, *in* Normandy A to Z, *below*).

LOWER NORMANDY

Lower Normandy encompasses the sandy Côte Fleurie (Flower Coast), stretching from the resorts of Trouville and Deauville to the D-day landing site of Omaha Beach. Lush green meadows and apple orchards cover the countryside from west of the market town of Lisieux—the heart of calvados country. Some of the fiercest fighting after the World War II D-day landings took place around Caen and Bayeux, as many monuments and memorials testify. To the south, in the prosperous Pays d'Auge, dairy farms produce the region's famous cheeses. Rising to the west is the fabled Mont-St-Michel.

Évreux

㉒ *102 km (63 mi) northwest of Paris via A13 and N13, 50 km (31 mi) south of Rouen via N15 and N154.*

From the 5th century on, Évreux, capital of the Eure *département* (province), was ravaged and burnt by a succession of armies—first the Vandals, then the Normans, the English, and various French kings. World War II played its part as well. But the town has been restored and is now embellished by gardens and calm overgrown footpaths.

Évreux's principal historic site is the **Cathédrale Notre-Dame,** in the heart of town just off rue Corbeau. Unfortunately, it was an easy victim of the many fires and raids that took place over the centuries; all that's left of the original 12th-century construction are the nave arcades. The lower parts of the chancel date from 1260, the chapels from the 14th century. Yet it's an outstanding example of Flamboyant Gothic inside and out. Don't miss the choir triforium and transept, the 14th-century stained-glass windows in the apse, or the entrance to the fourth chapel. ⊠ *pl. Notre-Dame,* ☎ *02–32–33–06–57.*

Le Bec-Hellouin

㉓ *46 km (29 mi) northwest of Évreux via N13 and D130, 39 km (24 mi) southwest of Rouen.*

Le Bec-Hellouin is centered on its abbey. Dating from 1034 when the knight Herluin exchanged his charger for a donkey and took up the simple life, the **Abbaye du Bec-Hellouin** was demolished during the French Revolution and the monks driven out. Only the 15th-century **Tour St-Nicolas,** part of the south transept, and the bases of some of the 11th-century pillars remain, together with a 13th-century Gothic door and some statues from the 14th and 15th centuries. ⊠ *Abbaye du Bec-Hellouin,* ☎ *02–32–43–72–60.* ☜ *25 frs.* ☉ *Guided tours only June–Sept., Wed.–Mon. at 10, 11, 3, 4, and 5; Sun. at 12:15, 3:30, 4, and 6; Oct.–May, Wed.–Mon. at 11 and 3:15; Sun. at noon, 3, and 4.*

Dining and Lodging

$$ ✕🏠 **Auberge de l'Abbaye.** You can find fantastic, traditional Norman cooking (including an exceptional apple tart) at this rustic inn with a classic *colombage* facade (exposed timber in stucco walls). The restaurant is closed Monday dinner and Tuesday off-season. Inside, beamed ceilings and stone walls are hung with ornamental copper pans. The delightfully old-fashioned, small bedrooms are reserved for diners only (though you don't have to stay to eat). ✉ *pl. Guillaume-le-Conquérant, 27800,* ☎ *02–32–44–86–02,* FAX *02–32–46–32–23. 8 rooms. Restaurant. MC, V. Closed Jan.–Feb.*

Lisieux

24 *47 km (29 mi) west of Le Bec-Hellouin via D130, N138, and N13; 82 km (51 mi) southwest of Rouen.*

Lisieux is the main market town of the prosperous Pays d'Auge, an agricultural region famous for cheeses named after such towns as Camembert, Pont l'Évêque, and Livarot. It is also a land of apple orchards, used for the finest calvados. Although Lisieux emerged relatively unscathed from World War II, it has few historic monuments beyond the 12th- and 13th-century **Cathédrale St-Pierre.** (The tower to the left of the imposing facade is later than it looks—it's a rare example of 17th century neo-Gothic reconstruction.) ✉ *pl. François-Mitterrand,* ☎ *02–31–62–09–82.*

The town's fame stems from St. Theresa (1873–97), who came to Lisieux as a child, joined a convent at 15, and spent the last 10 years of her life as a Carmelite nun. Theresa was canonized in 1925, and in 1954 the **Basilique Ste-Thérèse**—one of the world's largest 20th-century churches, with a huge dome and an interior of colored marble—was built in her honor. From the cathedral, walk up avenue Victor-Hugo and branch left onto avenue Jean-XXIII. A **son-et-lumière** show, running through 2,000 years of history, is presented at the basilica every evening (bar Sunday) at 9:45 from June to September. The **Procession de la Vierge** (Virgin's Procession) is held on August 15. The **Procession de la Fête Ste-Thérèse** (St. Theresa Festival Procession) takes place on the last Sunday in September. ✉ *av. Jean-XXIII,* ☎ *02–31–78–52–62.* 🎞 *Son-et-lumière 35 frs.*

En Route If you're a connoisseur of apple brandy, or just want to try some, definitely explore the **Pays d'Auge** between Lisieux and Beuvron-sur-Auge, 27 km (17 mi) to the west. This is the heart of calvados country: You don't need a fixed itinerary; just follow your nose and the minor roads, keeping an eye out for local farmers selling calvados. From Beuvron, nearby A13 speeds to Deauville, 40 km (25 mi) away, in about half an hour.

Deauville–Trouville

25 *29 km (17 mi) north of Lisieux via D579 and N177, 92 km (57 mi) west of Rouen.*

The twin seaside resorts of Deauville and Trouville are separated by the estuary of the River Touques and joined by a bridge. The two towns have distinctly different atmospheres, but it's easy (and common) to shuttle between them.

Deauville is a chic watering hole for the French bourgeoisie and would-be fashionable personalities from farther afield, attracted by its racecourse, casino, marina and regattas, palaces and gardens, and, of course, its sandy beach. The **Promenade des Planches**—the boardwalk extending along the seafront and lined with deck chairs, bars, and striped cabanas—is the place for celebrity spotting. With high-price hotels, designer boutiques, and one of the smartest, gilt-edge casinos in Europe, Deauville's fashionable image attracts the wealthy throughout the year.

Although Trouville is now considered an overflow town for its more prestigious neighbor, it became one of France's first seaside resorts when Parisians began flocking here in the mid-19th century. In contrast to Deauville, Trouville is more of a family resort with few pretensions. If you'd like to see a typical French holiday spot rather than look for glamour, stay in Trouville. It, too, has a casino and boardwalk, a bustling fishing port, and a native population that makes it a livelier place out of season than Deauville.

Dining and Lodging

$$$$ ✕⌂ **Normandy.** The fashionable and monied from Paris have been attracted to this hotel, with its traditional Norman facade and underground passage to the casino, since it opened in 1912. A luxurious sense of well-being pervades the chandeliers and columns of the public areas. Request a room with a sea view. Breakfast (96 francs) is served around the indoor pool. The gourmet restaurant, La Potinière, and the large dining room both serve mouthwatering variations of Norman cuisine. ⌂ 38 rue Jean-Mermoz, 14800 Deauville, ☎ 02–31–98–66–22, 800/223–5652 for U.S. reservations, ℻ 02–31–98–66–23. 271 rooms. 2 restaurants, indoor pool, sauna. AE, DC, MC, V.

$$$$ ⌂ **Royal.** This gigantic five-star hotel, overlooking the sea and close to the casino, is more than a little self-important. Many of the rooms are decorated in traditional, warm colors, with dark wood cabinetry; ask for one facing the sea. Of the two restaurants, L'Étrier has the stronger emphasis on haute cuisine. ⌂ bd. Eugène-Cornuché, 14800 Deauville, ☎ 02–31–98–66–33, 800/223–5652 for U.S. reservations, ℻ 02–31–98–66–34. 281 rooms. 2 restaurants, pool, sauna. AE, DC, MC, V. Closed mid-Nov.–early Mar.

$$–$$$ ⌂ **Beach Hotel.** Although it lacks character, this hotel, one of the newer ones in town, is handy because of its location behind the casino. Print fabrics add color to the pristine white rooms; most rooms overlook the sea or the harbor. Public rooms are designed for the flow of guests who often arrive on package tours, so expect efficiency rather than personal service. ⌂ quai Albert-I, 14360 Trouville, ☎ 02–31–98–12–00, ℻ 02–31–87–30–29. 110 rooms. Restaurant, pool, meeting rooms. AE, DC, MC, V.

$$ ⌂ **Continental.** One of Deauville's oldest buildings is now this provincial hotel, four blocks from the sea and within easy walking distance of the town center and downtown Trouville. Rooms are small but simple, pristine, and reasonably priced for Deauville. ⌂ 1 rue Désiré-Le-Hoc, 14800 Deauville, ☎ 02–31–88–21–06, ℻ 02–31–98–93–67. 42 rooms. AE, DC, MC, V. Closed mid-Nov.–mid-Mar.

$–$$ ⌂ **Carmen.** This straightforward, unpretentious little hotel is around the corner from the casino and a block from the sea. Rooms range from plain and inexpensive to comfortable and moderate. The owners, the Bude family, are on hand to give advice. ⌂ 24 rue Carnot, 14360 Trouville, ☎ 02–31–88–35–43, ℻ 02–31–88–08–03. 18 rooms. Restaurant. AE, DC, MC, V. Closed Jan.–mid-Feb. and 10 days in Oct.

Nightlife and the Arts

One of the biggest cultural events on the Norman calendar is the **American Film Festival,** held in Deauville during the first week of September. Formal attire is required at Deauville's smart **casino** (⌂ 2 rue Edmond-Blanc, ☎ 02–31–14–31–14). Trouville's **casino** is slightly less highbrow than Deauville's (✉ pl. du Maréchal-Foch, ☎ 02–31–87–75–00). Night owls enjoy the smoky ambience of the **Mélody** (✉ 13 rue Albert-Fracasse, Deauville); it's open until 5 AM. **Y Club** (✉ 14 bis rue Désiré-le-Hoc, Deauville) is the place for dancing.

Outdoor Activities and Sports

At the **Club Nautique de Deauville** (✉ quai de la Marine, ☎ 02–31–88–38–19), hiring the smallest boat (16 ft) costs just 100 francs, while a day on an 80-ft yacht will set you back about 500 francs per person. Small and large sailing boats may also be rented from the **Club Nautique de Trouville** (✉ Digue des Roches Noires, ☎ 02–31–88–13–59). Deauville becomes Europe's horse capital in August, when breeders jet in from around the world for its yearling auctions and the races at its two attractive **Hippodromes** (racetracks).

Houlgate

㉖ *14 km (9 mi) southwest of Deauville via D513, 27 km (17 mi) northeast of Caen.*

Cheerful Houlgate, bursting with wood-beamed, striped-brick Belle Époque villas and thatched-roof houses, is a personable alternative to its pricier neighbors Deauville and Cabourg. The setting is prettier, too, with the steep **Falaise des Vaches Noires** (Black Cow Cliff) providing a rocky backdrop to the town's enormous sandy beach.

Dining and Lodging

$–$$ ✕🏠 **1900.** Don't be misled by the tacky glass veranda: A wonderful dining room lurks behind, with Art Nouveau lamps and a fine, carved bar almost as old as the regiment of varied-size calvados bottles that parade across the top. Claire is the good-humored *patronne*; her husband, Alain, is a deft cook with a penchant for fish and seafood. Service from the young trainees, impeccable in their black-and-white aprons, is discreet and helpful. You can stay the night here, too: Rooms in the modernized annex, 100 yards down the street, are preferable to the slightly dowdy ones in the main building. ✉ *17 rue des Bains, 14510,* ☎ *02–31–28–77–77,* FAX *02–31–28–08–07. 21 rooms, 14 with bath or shower. Restaurant. MC, V.*

En Route As you drive west along the seafront toward Cabourg, pause to visit the center of historic **Dives-sur-Mer,** with its oak-beamed medieval market hall, rickety square, and chunky Gothic church.

Cabourg

㉗ *4 km (2 mi) west of Houlgate via D513, 25 km (16 mi) northeast of Caen.*

Cabourg still takes itself seriously and retains a certain frowsy 19th-century elegance. Its streets fan out from a central hub near the seafront where the casino and the Grand Hôtel are situated. Marcel Proust, the early 20th-century novelist, often vacationed here. One of the volumes in his epic *À la Recherche du Temps Perdu* (*Rembrance of Things Past*) paints an evocative picture of life in the resort, named Balbec in the novel; Cabourg responded by naming its magnificent seafront promenade after him.

Lodging

$$$$ 🏠 **Pullman Grand Hôtel.** This luxurious white-stucco hotel, on the seafront in the heart of town, is connected to the casino and has a lively piano bar in summer. Many rooms have balconies overlooking the sea; Proust used to stay in Room 147. In the restaurant, Le Balbec, you can dine on traditional French cuisine of a high standard but no great sophistication. ✉ *promenade Marcel-Proust, 14390,* ☎ *02–31–91–01–79,* FAX *02–31–24–03–20. 70 rooms. Restaurant, bar. AE, DC, MC, V.*

Caen

②⑧   *24 km (15 mi) southwest of Cabourg, 120 km (75 mi) west of Rouen, 150 km (94 mi) north of Le Mans.*

With its abbeys and castle, Caen, a busy commercial city and the capital of Lower Normandy, is very different from the coastal resorts. William of Normandy ruled from Caen in the 11th century before he conquered England. Nine hundred years later, the two-month Battle of Caen in 1944 devastated the town. Much of the city burned in a fire that raged for 11 days, and the downtown area was almost entirely—yet tastefully—rebuilt after the war.

A good place to begin exploring Caen is the **Hôtel d'Escoville,** a stately mansion in the city center, built by a wealthy merchant Nicolas Le Valois d'Escoville in the 1530s. The building was badly damaged during the war but has since been restored; the austere facade conceals an elaborate inner courtyard, reflecting the Italian influence on early Renaissance Norman architecture. The city **tourist office** is housed here and has excellent resources. ✉ *pl. St-Pierre,* ☎ *02–31–27–14–14.*

Across the square is the late-Gothic church of **St-Pierre,** a riot of ornamental stonework. Looming on a mound ahead of the church is the **Château**—the ruins of William the Conqueror's fortress, built in 1060 and sensitively restored after the war. The castle gardens are a perfect spot for strolling, and the ramparts afford good views of the city. The citadel also contains two museums (☞ *below*) and the medieval Chapelle St-Georges.

The **Musée des Beaux-Arts,** within the castle's walls, built an airy new wing in 1994. It's a heavyweight among France's provincial fine-arts museums; its old master collection includes works by Poussin, Rembrandt, Titian, Tintoretto, van der Weyden, and Paolo Veronese. ✉ *Entrance by the castle gateway,* ☎ *02–31–85–28–63.* 🎫 *25 frs (free Wed.).* ☉ *Wed.–Mon. 10–6.*

The **Musée de Normandie** (Normandy Museum), also within the castle precincts, is dedicated to regional arts, such as ceramics and sculpture, plus some local archaeological finds. ✉ *Entrance by the castle gateway,* ☎ *02–31–86–06–24.* 🎫 *10 frs (free Wed.).* ☉ *Wed.–Mon. 9:30–12:30 and 2–6.*

★   Caen's finest church, of cathedral proportions, is part of the **Abbaye aux Hommes** (Men's Abbey), a monastery built by William the Conqueror. The abbey was begun in Romanesque style in 1066 and added to in the 18th century. Note the magnificent yet spare facade of the abbey church of **St-Étienne,** whose spareness is enhanced by two 11th-century towers topped by octagonal spires. Inside, what had been William the Conqueror's tomb was destroyed by 16th-century Huguenots during the Wars of Religion. However, the choir still stands; it was the first to be built in Norman Gothic style, and many subsequent choirs were modeled after it. ✉ *pl. Louis-Guillouard,* ☎ *02–31–30–41–00.* 🎫 *Guided tours 10 frs.* ☉ *Tours daily at 9:30, 11, 2:30, 4.*

The **Abbaye aux Dames** (Ladies' Abbey) was founded by William the Conqueror's wife, Matilda, in 1062. Once a hospital, the abbey—rebuilt in the 18th century—was restored in the 1980s by the Regional Council, who promptly requisitioned it for office space; however, its elegant arcaded courtyard and ground-floor reception rooms can be admired during a (free) guided tour. You can also visit the squat **Église de la Trinité**, a fine example of 11th-century Romanesque architecture, though its original spires were replaced by bulky balustrades in the early 18th century. The 11th-century crypt once held Matilda's tomb, destroyed during the French Revolution. Note the intricate carvings on columns and arches in the chapel. ⊠ *pl. de la Reine-Mathilde,* ☎ *02–31–06–98–98.* ⊠ *Free.* ☉ *Guided tours daily at 2:30 and 4.*

A good introduction to the Normandy landings of 1944 is available at the stark modern **Mémorial.** At this museum, videos, photos, arms, paintings, and prints detail the Battle of Normandy and the French Liberation within a historical context, from the 1930s to the 1960s. Multimedia screens also depict D day and the Battle of Normandy. ⊠ *esplanade Dwight-D.-Eisenhower,* ☎ *02–31–06–06–44.* ⊠ *69 frs.* ☉ *Jan.–June and Sept.–Dec., daily 9–6; July–Aug., daily 9–9.*

Dining and Lodging

$$$ ✕ **Bourride.** On one of Caen's oldest streets, near the castle, this restau-
★ rant is one of the region's best. Chef Michel Bruneau's specialties include baked *St-Pierre* (whitefish) with green mango and baby pigeon in a salted bean crust. The small dining room is typically Norman—stone walls, beamed ceilings, and a large fireplace. ⊠ *15 rue de Vaugueux,* ☎ *02–31–93–50–76. Reservations essential. Jacket and tie. AE, DC, MC, V. Closed Mon., most of Jan., and 2nd ½ of Aug. No dinner Sun.*

$$$ ✕ **La Pommeraie.** Chef-owner José Aparicio's celebrated restaurant is found in a 17th-century former priory in the small village of Bénouville outside of Caen. The excellent fish and seafood come off without a hitch. Aperitifs and coffee are served in the garden. If you eat here, you can stay overnight in the 11 expensive rooms (800 francs) in the adjoining hotel, Le Manoir d'Hastings. ⊠ *18 av. de la Côte-de-Nacre, 14970 Bénouville (10 km/6 mi northeast of Caen),* ☎ *02–31–44–62–43. Reservations essential. Jacket and tie. AE, DC, MC, V. Closed Mon. and mid-Nov.–mid-Apr. No dinner Sun.*

$$–$$$ ▦ **Relais des Gourmets.** The hotel's comfortable, pastel-color modern rooms are reasonably large, though they vary in size; those with showers cost less (450 francs) than the ones with full baths (580 francs). As icing on the cake, the restaurant is terrific; you can dine in the garden in summer. ⊠ *15 rue de la Geôle, 14000,* ☎ *02–31–86–06–01,* 𝖥𝖠𝖷 *02–31–39–06–00, 0181/541–0033 for U.K. reservations, 800/528–1234 for U.S. reservations. 32 rooms. Restaurant. AE, DC, MC, V.*

$$ ▦ **Dauphin.** Although it's downtown, Le Dauphin is peaceful and quiet. The building is a former priory dating from the 12th century, but the smallish rooms are modern. Those overlooking the street are soundproof; the ones in back look out on the serene garden courtyard. Service is friendly and efficient, both in the hotel and in the excellent, though rather expensive, restaurant (closed Saturday). ⊠ *29 rue Gémare, 14000,* ☎ *02–31–86–22–26,* 𝖥𝖠𝖷 *02–31–86–35–14. 21 rooms. Restaurant. AE, DC, MC, V.*

Shopping

A **marché aux puces** (flea market) takes place on Friday morning on place St-Saveur and on Sunday morning on place Courtonne. In June, collectors and dealers flock to Caen's bric-a-brac and **antiques fair.**

En Route Take D514 north from Caen and turn right at Bénouville to see the famous **Pegasus Bridge** across the Canal de Caen. Early on June 6, 1944, the British 6th Airborne Division landed by glider and captured the bridge (named for the division's emblem, showing Bellerophon astride his winged horse, Pegasus). This proved the first symbolic step toward the liberation of France from Nazi occupation. The original drawbridge—

erected in 1935 but replaced by a replica for safety reasons in 1993—was moved 200 yards away in 1997. Continue north past the port of Ouistreham, and then follow the coast west along Sword Beach, Juno Beach, and Gold Beach, through unassuming resort towns like Langrune and Courseulles, whose slender church spires patrol the vast, flat horizon.

Arromanches

㉙ *31 km (19 mi) northwest of Caen, 10 km (6 mi) northeast of Bayeux.*

Little remains to mark the furious fighting waged hereabouts after D day. In the bay off of Arromanches, however, some elements of the floating harbor are still visible. Contemplate those seemingly insignificant hunks of concrete protruding from the water, and try to imagine the extraordinary technical feat involved in towing two floating harbors across the Channel from England. (The other, moored at Omaha Beach, was destroyed on June 19, 1944, by a violent storm.)

The **Musée du Débarquement** on the seafront, has models, mock-ups, and photographs depicting Operation Overlord—the code name for the Invasion of Normandy. Five beachheads (dubbed Utah, Omaha, Gold, Juno, and Sword) were established along the coast to either side of Arromanches. Preparations started in mid-1943, and British shipyards worked furiously through the following winter and spring building two artificial harbors (called mulberries), boats, and landing equipment. The British troops that landed on Sword, Juno, and Gold on June 6, 1944, quickly pushed inland and joined with parachute regiments that had been dropped behind the German lines. U.S. forces met with far tougher opposition on Omaha and Utah beaches, however, and it took them six days to secure their positions and meet the other Allied forces. From there, they pushed south and west, cutting off the Cotentin Peninsula on June 18 and taking Cherbourg on June 26. Meanwhile, British forces were encountering fierce resistance at Caen and did not take it until July 9; St-Lô was not liberated until July 19. ✉ *pl. du 6-Juin,* ☎ *02–31–22–34–31.* 🎫 *32 frs.* ☉ *May–Sept., daily 9–7; Oct.–Dec. and Feb.–Apr., daily 9:30–4:30.*

Bayeux

㉚ *10 km (6 mi) southwest of Arromanches via D516, 28 km (17 mi) northwest of Caen.*

Bayeux, the first town to be liberated during the Battle of Normandy, is steeped in history—home to a Norman-Gothic cathedral, a museum dedicated to the Battle of Normandy, and the world's most celebrated piece of needlework: the Bayeux Tapestry. Bayeux's medieval atmosphere makes it a popular base, especially among British travelers, from which to make day trips to other towns in Normandy; the tourist office (☞ Contacts and Resources *in* Normandy A to Z, *below*) can help you plan sightseeing trips in the area.

★ Really a 225-ft-long embroidered scroll stitched in 1067, the Bayeux Tapestry, known in French as the **Tapisserie de la Reine Mathilde** (Queen Matilde's Tapestry), depicts, in 58 separate scenes, the epic story of William of Normandy's conquest of England in 1066. The tapestry was probably commissioned from Saxon embroiderers by the count of Kent—who was also the bishop of Bayeux—to be displayed in his newly built cathedral, the Cathédrale Notre-Dame (☞ *below*). Despite its age, the tapestry is in remarkably good condition; the extremely detailed, often homey scenes provide an unequaled record of the clothes, weapons, ships, and lifestyles of the day. It's showcased in the **Musée** de la Tapisserie (Tapestry Museum), in an 18th-century building; for 5 francs, you can hire headphones and listen to an English commentary on the tapestry, scene by scene. ⊠ *Centre Guillaume le Conquérant, 13 bis rue de Nesmond,* ☎ *02–31–51–25–50.* ▣ *38 frs (joint ticket with Musée Baron-Gérard; ☞ below) .* ☉ *May–mid-Sept., daily 9–6:30; mid-Sept.–Apr., daily 9:30–12:30 and 2–6.*

The **Musée Baron-Gérard** contains a fine collection of Bayeux porcelain and lace, ceramics from Rouen, a marvelous collection of apothecary jars from the 17th and 18th centuries, and 16th- to 19th-century furniture and paintings. From the Tapestry Museum (☞ *above*) head up rue de Nesmond to rue Larchet, turning left into lovely place des Tribuneaux. ⊠ *1 rue la Chaîne, pl. des Tribuneaux,* ☎ *02–31–92–14–21.* ▣ *38 frs (joint ticket with Tapestry Museum; ☞ above).* ☉ *June–mid-Sept., daily 9–7; mid-Sept.–May, 10–12:30 and 2–6; closed 2 wks in Jan.*

Bayeux's mightiest edifice, the **Cathédrale Notre-Dame** is a harmonious mixture of Norman and Gothic architecture. Note the portal on the south side of the transept that depicts the assassination of English Archbishop Thomas à Becket in Canterbury Cathedral in 1170, following his opposition to King Henry II's attempts to control the church. ⊠ *rue de Bienvenu,* ☎ *02–31–92–01–85.*

At the **Musée de la Bataille de Normandie** (Battle of Normandy Museum) detailed exhibits trace the story of the Battle of Normandy from June 7 to August 22, 1944. The ultramodern museum, sunk partly beneath the level of its surrounding lawns, contains an impressive array of war paraphernalia, including uniforms, weapons, equipment, 150 waxworks, and a film depicting scenes and tactics of the invasion. ⊠ *bd. Général-Fabian-Ware,* ☎ *02–31–92–93–41.* ▣ *30 frs.* ☉ *May–mid-Sept., daily 9–6:30; mid-Sept.–Apr., daily 10–noon and 2–6.*

Dining and Lodging

$ ✕ **Amaryllis.** You get to choose from a number of dishes from this small restaurant's prix-fixe menu. But the three-course dinner, with six selections per course, may include a half dozen oysters, fillet of sole with a cider-based sauce, and pastries for dessert. ⊠ *32 rue St-Patrice,* ☎ *02–31–22–47–94. AE, DC, MC, V. Closed Mon. and mid-Dec.–mid-Jan.*

$$$$ ✕▣ **Château d'Audrieu.** The Hollywood version of a palatial château
★ is fulfilled at this family-owned property. An avenue leads to an imposing, elegant 18th-century facade that sets the tone for what lies within—Old World opulence, with wall sconces, overstuffed chairs, and antiques. Rooms 50 and 51 have gabled ceilings with exposed-wood beams. The restaurant has an extensive wine list, and chef Alain Cornet keeps to a classical repertoire of dishes. The restaurant is closed Monday. ⊠ *14250 Audrieu (15 km/9 mi southeast of Bayeux off N13),* ☎ *02–31–80–21–52,* ℻ *02–31–80–24–73. 30 rooms. Restaurant, bar, pool, helipad. MC, V. Closed Dec.–Feb.*

$$$–$$$$ ✕▣ **Chenevière.** This hotel is in a 19th-century grand manor in parkland between Bayeux and the coast. Rooms have modern furnishings, with plain draperies on the floor-to-ceiling windows and flowered bedspreads. The restaurant lives up to its surroundings; Claude Esprabens's roasted scampi with sesame seeds and fresh chanterelles is delicious, as is the warm sliced duck liver with raspberry sauce. Try one of the not-too-sweet desserts, like the goat cheese in puff pastry or the apple stuffed with Camembert. ⊠ *Les Escures, 14520 Commes (9 km/5½ mi north of Bayeux via D6),* ☎ *02–31–51–25–25,* ℻ *02–31–51–25–20. 19 rooms. Restaurant. AE, DC, MC, V.*

$$–$$$ ✕▣ **Grand Hôtel du Luxembourg.** The Luxembourg, a Best Western affiliate, has small but adequate rooms; all but two face the courtyard

garden. Off-season rates are only slightly higher than at the town's two-star hotels, which makes this place a good choice in winter. It's also got one of the town's best restaurants, Les Quatre Saisons. The menu is seasonal; depending on the time of year, you might have a salmon *galette* (buckwheat pancake) or chicken roasted with cider. ⊠ *25 rue des Bouchers, 14400,* ☎ *02–31–92–00–04, 800/528–1234 for U.S. reservations,* 🖷 *02–31–92–54–26. 19 rooms, 3 suites. Restaurant, bar, dance club. AE, DC, MC, V.*

$$ ✕☎ **Lion d'Or.** The Lion d'Or is a handsome '30s creation in the center of town. Palm trees arch over the garden courtyard, and flowers cascade from balcony window boxes. The comfortable rooms are decorated with pretty fabrics. In the chic, apricot-color restaurant, *andouille chaude Bovary*—perhaps Madame's own recipe for hot sausage—is served. ⊠ *71 rue St-Jean, 14400,* ☎ *02–31–92–06–90,* 🖷 *02–31–22–15–64. 25 rooms. Restaurant. AE, DC, MC, V. Closed late Dec.–mid-Jan.*

$$ ☎ **Manoir du Carel.** Archives suggest that the Manoir du Carel, an ideal
★ spot halfway between Bayeux and the Normandy beaches, was constructed as a fortified manor by an Englishman during the Hundred Years' War. Certainly the narrow slits serving as windows on the tower suggest a defensive stance. Current owner Jacques Aumond offers comfortable rooms with modern furnishings. The cottage on the grounds has a kitchen plus a fireplace that masks a brick oven where, prior to the revolution, villagers had their bread baked. The lounges have turn-of-the-century furniture and are perfect places for a glass of wine before going out to dinner. ⊠ *14400 Maisons (5 km/3 mi northwest of Bayeux),* ☎ *02–31–22–37–00,* 🖷 *02–31–21–57–00. 3 rooms, 1 cottage. Breakfast room.*

Outdoor Activities and Sports

Bicycles can be rented from **Family Home** (⊠ 39 rue Général-de-Dais, ☎ 02–31–92–15–22) for around 50 francs a day. Ask the tourist office for trail information (☞ Contacts and Resources *in* Normandy A to Z, *below*).

The **Rassemblement International de Ballons** (International Balloon Festival) (☎ 02–31–21–62–19 for information) takes place in mid-June at the 17th-century château of Balleroy, 16 km (10 mi) southwest of Bayeux. Hot-air balloons fill the Normandy skies as a fair with dancing, acrobatics, and horse-drawn carriages takes place on the château grounds.

Shopping

Handmade lace is a specialty of Bayeux. Although it's expensive, it's exceptional, particularly at the **Conservatoire de la Dentelle** (⊠ Hôtel du Doyen, rue Leforestier, ☎ 02–31–92–73–80), open daily 9–noon and 2–5.

The D-Day Landing Beaches

Along with the nearby villages of St-Laurent-sur-Mer and Vierville-sur-Mer, **Omaha Beach,** 20 km (12 mi) west of Arromanches, saw some of the heaviest fighting during the D-day invasions. Nearly 10,000 soldiers spearheading the Allied invasion lost their lives here. Most of the 4,659 American casualties on D day occurred here, and many of the fallen are buried at the moving **Cimetière du St-Laurent** (St-Laurent Cemetery) above the beach. Stroll around the beach and grassy tops of the dunes in St-Laurent-sur-Mer and you'll see sad remnants of the war—ruined bunkers, rows of trenches, the remains of barbed-wire defenses, and the **Monument du Débarquement** (Monument to the Normandy Landings). In **Vierville-sur-Mer,** the Monument to the Members of the U.S. National Guard who fought in both world wars stands just back from the beach.

From Vierville it is a 45-minute drive around the coast to **Utah Beach,** 48 km (30 mi) away. Unless you are an assiduous student of World War II—or keen to drive up to Cherbourg at the top of the Cotentin Peninsula, where ferries cross the Channel to England—head southwest from Omaha Beach to **Isigny-sur-Mer** (known for its small, tasty oysters); pass through Carentan, with its mighty octagonal church spire; and continue via D971 to Coutances.

Coutances

③ *66 km (41 mi) southwest of Omaha Beach, 64 km (40 mi) southwest of Bayeux via D572 and D972, 76 km (47 mi) south of Cherbourg.*

★ If you're interested in cathedral architecture, you'll want to stop off in Coutances. Many consider the largely 13th-century **Cathédrale Notre-Dame,** with its famous octagonal lantern rising 135 ft above the nave, to be the most harmonious Gothic building in Normandy. On the outside, especially the facade, note the obsessive use of turrets, spires, slender shafts, and ultranarrow pointed arches squeezed senseless in their architectural pursuit of vertical takeoff.

Lodging

$ ⊡ **Moulin Girard.** If you have a hankering for English hospitality, cheerful conversation, and inexpensive accommodations, Roger and Jasmine Albon's inn is the place to head. The main house has three very small rooms, and the Norman-style cottage has a two-bedroom suite—for 350 francs, including breakfast, it's ideal for a family or two couples. This is a great base for exploring the area. ⊠ *50410 Le Chefresne (26 km/16 mi southeast of Coutances; from Villedieu-les-Poêles, take a right on D98 as you enter Percy in the direction of Tessy-sur-Vire, and then right on D452 for Le Chefresne),* ☎ FAX *02–33–61–62–06. 3 rooms, 1 suite. No credit cards.*

Granville

③ *30 km (19 mi) south of Coutances via D971, 107 km (67 mi) southwest of Caen.*

Proud locals like to call Granville the "Monaco of the North." It's perched on a rocky outcrop and has a sea-water therapy center, and . . . the similarities end there. Free of casinos and sequins, Granville instead has a down-to-earth feel. Granite houses cluster around the church in the old town, while the harbor below is full of working boats. There are fine views of the English Channel from the ramparts; catamarans spurt over to Jersey daily in summer. Drive a few miles down the coast to find sandy beaches and a view of distant Mont-St-Michel.

Nightlife and the Arts

The rambunctious **Carnaval de Granville** involves four days of parades and festivities, culminating each year on Shrove Tuesday. The **Grand Pardon des Corporations de la Mer,** a *pardon,* or religious festival, this one devoted to the sea, is celebrated on the last Sunday of July with a military parade, regatta, and platefuls of shellfish.

Outdoor Activities and Sports

Granville is a center for aquatic sports; inquire about sailboat jaunts at the **Centre Régional de Nautisme de Granville** (⊠ bd. des Amiraux, ☎ 02–33–91–22–60). **Lepesqueux Voile** (⊠ 3 rue Clément-Desmaisons, ☎ 02–33–50–18–97) rents boats and yachts.

Shopping

It is said that every kitchen worth its salt in France buys its pans from **Villedieu-les-Poêles,** 28 km (18 mi) east of Granville. The town is famous for its copperware and shops line the main street, rue Carnot, but you can find smaller outlets, with better buys, on the parallel rue du Dr-Harvard. Note that Tuesday is market day, so parking becomes a bit of a problem.

Mont-St-Michel

★ ③ *44 km (27 mi) south of Granville via D973, N175, and D43; 123 km (77 mi) southwest of Caen; 67 km (42 mi) north of Rennes.*

The dramatic silhouette of Mont-St-Michel against the horizon may well be your most lasting image of Normandy. The abbey's fascination stems not only from its rocky perch a few hundred yards off the coast (it's cut off from the mainland at high tide) but from its legendary origins and the sheer exploit of its construction. The abbey stands at the top of a 264-ft mound of rock; the granite used to build it was transported from the Isles of Chausey (just beyond Mont-St-Michel Bay) and Brittany and laboriously hauled up to the site.

Before you visit this awe-inspiring monument, be warned that the sea that separates the rock from the mainland is extremely dangerous: It's subject to tidal movements that produce a difference of up to 45 ft between low and high tides, and because of the extremely flat bay bed, the water rushes in at an incredible speed. Also, there are patches of quicksand, so walk carefully!

The abbey's construction took more than 500 years, from 1017 to 1521. Legend has it that the Archangel Michael appeared to Aubert, bishop of Avranches, inspiring him to build an oratory on what was then called Mont Tombe. The original church was completed in 1144, but new buildings were added in the 13th century to accommodate the monks, as well as the hordes of pilgrims who flocked here even during the Hundred Years' War, when the region was in English hands. The Romanesque choir was rebuilt in an ornate Gothic style during the 15th and 16th centuries. The abbey's monastic vocation was undermined during the 17th century, when the monks began to flout the strict rules and discipline of their order, drifting into a state of decadence that culminated in the monks' dispersal and the abbey's conversion into a prison, well before the French Revolution. In 1874 the former abbey was handed over to a governmental agency responsible for the preservation of historic monuments; only within the past 20 years have monks been able to live and work here once more.

A causeway—to be replaced eventually by a bridge, thus allowing the bay waters to circulate freely—links Mont-St-Michel to the mainland. Leave your car in the parking lot (10 francs) along the causeway, outside the main gateway. If you are staying the night on Mont-St-Michel, take what you need in a small suitcase; you cannot gain access to your hotel by car.

The island village, with its steep, narrow streets, is best visited out of season, from September to May. The hordes of tourists and souvenir sellers can be stifling in summer. From the ramparts in general and the North Tower in particular there are dramatic views of the bay. Give yourself at least a couple of hours here. However, with the mount's inflated prices you may want to stay elsewhere.

The climb to the abbey is hard going, but it's worth it. Head first for the **Grand Degré,** the steep, narrow staircase on the north side. Once past the ramparts, you come to the pink-and-gray granite towers of the **Châtelet** and then to the **Salle des Gardes** (Guards' Room), the central point of the abbey. Guided tours start from the **Saut Gautier** terrace (named after a prisoner who jumped to his death from it): You must join one of these groups if you want to see the beautifully wrought **Escalier de Dentelle** (Lace Staircase) inside the church. In July and August, evening concerts are held in the abbey during the **Heures Musicales** (Musical Hours). ☎ 02–33–60–14–14. ⊠ 40 frs. ☉ May–Sept., daily 9:30–11:30 and 1:30–6; Oct.–Apr., Wed.–Mon. 9:30–4:30.

Dining and Lodging

$$$$ ✕⊞ **Mère Poulard.** The hotel of the most celebrated restaurant on the mount consists of adjoining houses with small, simple, clean rooms, up three steep flights of narrow stairs. The restaurant's reputation derives partly from Mère Poulard's famous secret omelet recipe and partly from its location, overlooking the bay. The owners trade on a captive market—prices are exorbitant and the menu doesn't accurately reflect what you will pay. Room prices start low but ratchet upward the bigger they get. Also, you are usually requested to book two meals with the room. Reservations are essential for the restaurant. ⊠ Grande Rue, 50116, ☎ 02–33–60–14–01, ⅢX 02–33–48–52–31. 26 rooms. Restaurant, piano bar. AE, DC, MC, V.

$$–$$$ ⊞ **Terrasses Poulard.** Hordes of tourists come to this ensemble of buildings clustered around a small garden in the middle of the mount. Rooms at this hotel are some of the best—with rustic-style furnishings—and the most spacious on the mount; many have views of the bay. ⊠ Grand Rue, opposite the parish church, 50116, ☎ 02–33–60–14–09, ⅢX 02–33–60–37–31. 29 rooms. Restaurant, billiards, library. AE, DC, MC, V.

$$ ⊞ **Roche Turin.** This small, ivy-clad manor house on 4 acres of park-
★ land is a delightful alternative to the high price of staying on Mont-St-Michel. Rooms are pleasantly old-fashioned, but the bathrooms are modern. The owners, M. and Mme. Barraux, run a comfortable dining room with an open fireplace: the *pré-salé* (salt-marsh lamb) is superb. In summer, aperitifs are served in the garden, where there's a view of Mont-St-Michel. The restaurant is closed Monday. ⊠ 34 rte. de la Roche-Turin, 50220 Courtils (9 km/5 mi from Mont-St-Michel), ☎ 02–33–70–96–55, ⅢX 02–33–48–35–20. 11 rooms, 1 suite. Restaurant. MC, V. Closed mid-Nov.–mid-Mar.

LA SUISSE NORMANDE

La Suisse Normande (Swiss Normandy), a rocky expanse of hills and gullies south of Caen, has an abundance of natural beauty with few man-made sights. Striking as the scenery is, however, you need to exert your powers of imagination to spot much resemblance to the Swiss Alps. The small town of Thury-Harcourt is considered the gateway to La Suisse Normande; it's famous for the beautiful gardens of its ruined castle. Routes D212 and D562 are particularly scenic roads through this region.

Clécy

34 *44 km (28 mi) south of Caen.*

La Suisse Normande's main tourist center is on the Orne River at Clécy. Take the steep roads up to the cliff tops overlooking the river, where there are lovely views of the woods on the other bank.

Dining

$ ✕ **La Potinière.** Stop for a drink or a snack at this great, open-air, river-bank café. Crepes with either sweet or savory fillings are the biggest temptations. ⊠ *La Cambronnerie,* ☎ *02–31–69–76–75. Closed Oct.–Apr.*

En Route   From Clécy, take D562 south for just over 3 km (2 mi), and turn left at Le Fresne onto D1, which winds its way through the valley of the Noireau to another riverside resort town, **Pont d'Ouilly** (home to a fa-mous pardon on the first Sunday after August 15). Head south along the Orne on D167, veer right at Pont-des-Vers onto D43, and turn left
★   at Rouvrou to reach the **Roche d'Oëtre,** a rock with spectacular views of the craggy hills that give the region its name. Follow the Orne Val-ley on D301 to the dramatic **Gorges de St-Aubert** (St. Aubert Gorge); park and follow the signs on foot if you want to admire the gorge up close. Continue on D301 to Rabodanges, and then go south on D121 to get to the **Barrage de Rabodanges** (Rabodanges Dam), which dams the Orne and forms a small lake. The dam is best admired from the Pont Ste-Croix, 1½ km (1 mi) farther on. Cross the lake on the Pont Ste-Croix and continue to the tumbling little town of **Putanges-Pont-Écrepin,** with its distinctive, pointed church tower. From Putanges, the Orne winds east through **Argentan,** heavily damaged during the last days of the Battle of Normandy, and on toward Sées.

Sées

❸❺   *22 km (14 mi) southeast of Argentan, 130 km (81 mi) southeast of Clecy.*

The small town of Sées exudes faded charm, with old houses, churches, a stately town hall, majestic bishop's palace and former abbey, and a quaint circular market hall, all paying tribute to its onetime importance as the religious center of southern Normandy.

The **Cathédrale St-Latrium** rises from the sleepy heart of Sées, its 200-ft spires visible for miles around. Apart from the tower, the main ex-ternal feature is the huge porch, reinforced by extra buttressing when it started leaning on the sloping ground in the 16th century. The ele-gant interior has an airy east end, with the huge windows of the choir, and the rose window in the transepts, filled with exquisite 13th-cen-tury stained glass. ⊠ *pl. du Général-de-Gaulle.*

The turrets and improbably steep slate roofs of the **Château d'O** rise above rich meadowland near Mortrée, 7 km (4 mi) northwest of Sées. The three-winged château, surrounded by a moat patroled by regal swans, has checkerboard brick and stone walls and an interior refur-bished in the 18th century; look out for the sculpted ermine emblem of the O family, distinguished both as royal courtiers and for possess-ing the shortest family name in France. ☎ *02–33–35–34–69.* ▨ *35 frs.* ☉ *Mar.–Nov., Wed.–Mon. 2–5.*

Alençon

❸❻   *22 km (14 mi) south of Sées via N138, 49 km (31 mi) north of Le Mans.*

Historic Alençon, an attractive town with many old buildings and an impressive church, is south of the Écouves Forest on the eastern edge of the Normandie-Maine nature park. It has been a lace-making cen-ter since 1665. By the end of the 17th century, *point d'Alençon* (nee-dle-point lace) was de rigueur on women's and men's clothing and in interior decor in all fashionable circles.

The **Musée des Beaux-Arts et de la Dentelle** (Museum of Fine Arts and Lace) contains a sophisticated collection of lace from Italy, Flanders, and France, along with paintings from the French school that span the 17th to the 20th century. ⊠ *rue du Capitaine-Charles-Aveline*, ☎ *02–33–32–40–07.* ⊟ *18 frs.* ☉ *Tues.–Sun. 10–noon and 2–6.*

Shopping
Handmade lace is a rarity and prices are high, though this kind of labor-intensive, superior-quality creation never comes cheap: The **Musée de la Dentelle** (⊠ 31 rue du Pont-Neuf, ☎ 02–33–26–27–26) has an excellent selection.

Bagnoles-de-l'Orne

③⑦ *48 km (30 mi) northwest of Alençon via N12 and N176, 80 km (50 mi) south of Caen.*

Bagnoles-de-l'Orne, the region's most beautiful spa town, overlooks a forest-fringed lake formed by the Yée River. Forty-five hotels and a casino are only part of what draws people here: From April through October some 20,000 people come to cure their blood-related ailments by soaking in the chemical-laden waters; the town is nicknamed the Capital of Veins.

An attractive road heads west from Bagnoles to the spectacular hilltop town of Domfront and on toward Mont-St-Michel.

Dining and Lodging
$$ ✕☎ **Manoir de Lys.** This warm, inviting Norman country house presides over a beautifully landscaped park on the forest's edge. Room size varies—some have French windows that open onto the gardens; others, in the newer wing, are slightly larger and have exposed beams. Chef Franck Quinton has won accolades for creations like lobster tournedos and ravioli with frogs' legs. He also leads weeklong cooking classes several times a year. The restaurant is closed Sunday night and Monday (November–Easter). ⊠ *Rte. de Juvigny, 61140 Croix Gauthier (1½ km/1 mi from the casino),* ☎ *02–33–37–80–69,* ⨳ *02–33–30–05–80. 20 rooms. Restaurant, tennis court. AE, MC, V. Closed Jan.–mid-Feb.*

Nightlife and the Arts
Among France's best, Bagnoles's **casino** (⊠ 6 av. Robert-Cousin, ☎ 02–33–37–84–00) has the usual games, plus a cabaret.

NORMANDY A TO Z

Arriving and Departing

By Boat
A number of ferry companies sail between the United Kingdom and ports in Normandy. **Brittany Ferries** (☎ 01705/82–7701 in U.K., 08–03–82–82–82 in France) travels between Caen (Ouistreham) and Portsmouth, and Poole and Cherbourg. **P&O European Ferries** (☎ 0130/21–0004 in Portsmouth, 02–35–19–78–78 in Le Havre) travels between Le Havre and Portsmouth, and Cherbourg and Portsmouth. **Stena** (☎ 01273/51–6699 in Newhaven, 02–35–06–39–03 in Dieppe) travels between Dieppe and Newhaven, and Cherbourg and Southampton.

By Car
From Paris, A13 slices its way to Rouen in 1½ hours (toll 35 francs) before continuing to Caen (2½ hours) with a fork to Le Havre (A131). N13 continues from Caen to Cherbourg via Bayeux in another two hours.

By Plane

Paris's Charles de Gaulle (Roissy) and Orly airports are the closest international links with the region. **Air Inter** (☞ Air Travel *in* the Gold Guide) flies to Caen (☎ 02–31–26–58–00 for airport information), but tickets are expensive. From the United Kingdom, there are regular flights to Caen and Deauville (☎ 02–31–64–81–81 for airport information) from London, and to Cherbourg (☎ 02–33–88–57–60 for airport information) from Southampton and the Channel Islands (☞ Air Travel *in* the Gold Guide).

By Train

From Paris (Gare St-Lazare), separate train lines head to Upper Normandy (Rouen and Le Havre or Dieppe) and Lower Normandy (Caen, Bayeux, and Cherbourg, via Évreux and Lisieux). If you're thinking about taking the train from Paris to Mont-St-Michel, forget it: Connections are so complicated it will take you all day.

Getting Around

By Car

The 1995 opening of the Pont de Normandie, between Le Havre and Honfleur, has effectively united Upper and Lower Normandy and made driving between the two regions a lot easier. A13/N13, linking Rouen to Caen, Bayeux, and Cherbourg, is the backbone of Normandy. If you have extra time, taking Normandy's scenic minor roads can be very rewarding.

By Train

Unless you are content to stick to the major towns (Rouen, Le Havre, Dieppe, Caen, Bayeux), visiting Normandy by train may prove frustrating. You can reach several smaller towns (Fécamp, Deauville, Cabourg), and even Mont-St-Michel (sort of—it's a 15-minute taxi ride from Pontorson), on snail-paced branch lines, but the intricacies of what is arguably Europe's most complicated regional timetable will probably have driven you nuts by the time you get there.

Contacts and Resources

Bike Rental

You can rent bicycles from several major train stations for about 45 francs per day.

Car Rental

Avis (⊠ 44 pl. de la Gare, Caen, ☎ 02–31–84–73–80; ⊠ 24 rue Malouet, Rouen, ☎ 02–35–72–77–50). **Europcar** (⊠ 8 rue du Dr-Piasecki, Le Havre, ☎ 02–35–25–21–95).

Emergencies

Ambulance (☎ 15). **Regional hospitals:** Caen (⊠ av. de la Côte-de-Nacre, ☎ 02–31–06–31–06); Le Havre (⊠ 29 av. Pierre-Mendès-France, Montivilliers, ☎ 02–32–73–32–32); Rouen (⊠ 1 rue Germont, ☎ 02–32–88–89–90).

Guided Tours

Périer Voyages (⊠ 130 rue Martainville, 76000 Rouen, ☎ 02–35–07–93–46) arranges personalized driving tours with an English-speaking driver. **Viking Voyages** (⊠ 16 rue du Général-Giraud, 14000 Caen, ☎ 02–31–27–12–34) specializes in two-day packages by car, with overnight stays in private châteaux, as well as bike trips around the region and a "Normandy Antiques" tour by car.

Cityrama (⊠ 147 rue St-Honoré, 75001 Paris, ☎ 01–44–55–61–00) organizes one-day bus excursions from Paris to Mont-St-Michel on Saturdays with meals included; the cost is 975 francs. There is also a two-day package that includes the châteaux of the Loire. **Paris-Vision** (⊠ 214 rue de Rivoli, 75001 Paris, ☎ 01–42–60–31–25) also runs one-day bus excursions from Paris to Mont-St-Michel on Saturdays, as well as two-day trips to the Loire.

Outdoor Activities and Sports

For information on trails and hiking courses, contact the **Comité Départemental de la Randonnée Pédestre de Seine-Maritime** (⊠ B.P. 666, 76008 Rouen, ☎ no phone). For information regarding stables, get in touch with the **Ligne de Normandie de Sports Équestres** (⊠ 10 pl. de Demi-Lune, 14039 Caen, ☎ 02–31–84–61–87).

Travel Agencies

American Express (⊠ 1–3 pl. Jacques-Le-Lieur, Rouen, ☎ 02–32–08–19–20; ⊠ 57 quai George-V, Le Havre, ☎ 02–32–74–75–76).
Havas (⊠ 25 Grande-Rue, Alençon, ☎ 02–33–82–59–00; ⊠ 80 rue St-Jean, Caen, ☎ 02–31–27–10–50; ⊠ 63 rue St-Jacques, Dieppe, ☎ 02–35–82–46–98).

Visitor Information

Each of Normandy's five *départements* has its own central tourist office. **Alençon** (⊠ 88 rue St-Blaise, ☎ 02–33–28–88–71) for the Orne. **Caen** (⊠ pl. du Canada, ☎ 02–31–27–90–30) for Calvados. **Évreux** (⊠ bd. Georges-Chauvin, ☎ 02–32–31–51–51) for the Eure. **Rouen** (⊠ 6 rue de la Couronne, Bihorel-les-Rouen, ☎ 02–35–59–26–26) for the Seine-Maritime. **St-Lô** (⊠ rte. de Villedieu, ☎ 02–33–05–98–70) for La Manche.

Other major Norman towns with tourist offices include the following: **Bayeux** (⊠ 3 rue St-Jean, ☎ 02–31–51–28–28). **Dieppe** (⊠ Pont Jehan-Ango, ☎ 02–35–84–11–77). **Fécamp** (⊠ 113 rue Alexandre-le-Grand, ☎ 02–35–28–51–01). **Le Havre** (⊠ 1 pl. de l'Hôtel-de-Ville, ☎ 02–32–74–04–04). **Honfleur** (⊠ 9 rue de la Ville, ☎ 02–31–89–23–30).

7 The North, Southern Picardy, and Champagne

Lille, Reims, and the Ardennes

Just an hour from Paris on the TGV and right across the English Channel, the North and Southern Picardy harbor many treasures: uninterrupted stretches of sandy beach, moving World War I battlefields, mighty castles, beefy belfries, and awesome cathedrals. Lille, one of France's liveliest cities, is here, as is Reims, the capital of bubbly. To the northeast lies the thick forest of the Ardennes.

TOO FEW PEOPLE VISIT NORTHERN FRANCE. Most French vacationers flock south each year in search of a suntan. The millions of tourists who buzz through the Channel ports of Calais and Dunkerque make a beeline to Paris. But the Channel Tunnel, perhaps the most ambitious engineering project of the late 20th century, is beginning to change this, making it easier and less expensive for the British to flit across for day and weekend trips.

Revised and updated by Rebecca Hirschfield

The north of France is an industrial region, but don't look for slag heaps and smokestacks everywhere; heavy industry is highly centralized. This is a green and pleasant land where wooded, restful landscapes predominate. It also has a shared history with Dutch-speaking territories. Lille, France's northern metropolis, is the capital of what is known as French Flanders, which stretches northwest from the city to the coastal areas around Dunkirk and Gravelines. This was one of several regions heavily disputed by France and Spain during the 16th century when Spain controlled the Low Countries. What is now the French side of the border with Belgium was deemed French (more or less) under the 1713 Treaty of Utrecht.

West and north of Lille extends the Côte d'Opale, the Atlantic and Channel coastline so named for the color of its sea and sky. To the southeast, the grapes of Champagne flourish on the steep slopes of the Marne Valley and the Montagne de Reims, really more of a mighty hill than a mountain. Reims is the only city in Champagne, and one of France's richest tourist venues. The kings of France were crowned in its cathedral until 1825, and every age since the Roman period has left an architectural mark. The thriving champagne business has conferred wealth and, sometimes, an arrogant reserve on the region's inhabitants. The down-to-earth folk of the North reserve a warmer welcome.

Pleasures and Pastimes

Beaches
The northern French coast, from Dunkerque to Berck-sur-Mer, is one long, sandy beach, known as the Côte d'Opale. It is sometimes short of sun, but not of space or beach sports like *char à voile* (sand sailing), involving windsurfing boards on wheels that race along the sands at up to 112 kph (70 mph). The climate is bracing, often windy, but there are wonderful scenic spots along the cliffs south of Calais at Cap Gris Nez and Cap Blanc Nez. Le Touquet is one of France's fanciest coastal resort towns; Le Crotoy, Wimereux, and Hardelot are more family-oriented.

Champagne
The world's most famous sparkling wine comes from France's northernmost vineyards along the towering Marne Valley between Épernay and Château-Thierry, and on the slopes of the Montagne de Reims, between Épernay and Reims. Champagne firms, in these two towns and in Ay, welcome you into their chalky, mazelike cellars. You can also visit the tomb of Dom Perignon, the inventor of champagne, in Hautvillers. Just follow the Route du Vin south of Reims.

Churches and Cathedrals
Northern France contains many of France's most remarkable Gothic cathedrals: Amiens, the largest; Beauvais, the highest; Noyon, the earliest; Abbeville, the last; Reims, the most royal; and Laon, with the most towers (and the most spectacular hilltop setting). The region's smaller churches are also admirable—the intricate stonework of Rue and

L'Épine; the ruined drama of Mont St-Eloi; the modern stained glass of Mézières; and the Baroque brickwork of Asfeld.

Dining

The cuisine of northern France is robust and hearty. In French Flanders, beer is often used as a base for sauces. French fries and mussels are featured on most menus; vans selling fries and hot dogs are a common sight; and large quantities of mussels and fish, notably herring, are consumed. Smoked ham and, in season, boar and venison are specialties of the Ardennes. Be sure to sample creamy cheeses in the southernmost part of the region: the soft, square *Maroilles*, with its orange rind; and the spicy, pyramid-shape *boulette d'Avesnes*. To satisfy your sweet tooth, try the macaroons and *bêtises de Cambrai* (minty lollipops) in French Flanders. Ham, pigs' feet, gingerbread, and champagne-based mustard are specialties of the Reims area, as is ratafia, a sweet aperitif made from grape juice and brandy. To the north, a glass of *genièvre* (gin flavored with juniper berries, which is sometimes added to black coffee to make a *bistouille*) is the classic conclusion to a good meal.

CATEGORY	COST*
$$$$	over 400 frs
$$$	250 frs–400 frs
$$	125 frs–250 frs
$	under 125 frs

*per person for a three-course meal, including tax (20.6%) and tip but not wine

Lodging

Northern France is overladen with old hotels, often rambling and simple, seldom pretentious; there are also luxurious châteaux-cum–fine restaurants. Good value married with top quality is hard to come by, except in major cities (Amiens, Lille, and Reims) or at Le Touquet, whose Westminster Hotel numbers among the country's best.

CATEGORY	COST*
$$$$	over 800 frs
$$$	550 frs–800 frs
$$	300 frs–550 frs
$	under 300 frs

*All prices are for a standard double room for two, including tax (20.6%) and service charge.

War Memorials

Northern France was in the frontline of battle during the world wars and suffered heavily. The city of Reims was shelled incessantly during World War I, and such names as the Somme and Vimy Ridge evoke the bloody, deadlocked battles that raged from 1914 to 1918. Cemeteries and war memorials may not be the most cheerful items on your itinerary, but they do have a melancholy, thought-provoking beauty.

Exploring The North, Southern Picardy, and Champagne

The area known as the North (Nord, in French) stretches from the River Somme up to Calais and the Channel Tunnel, including the vibrant city of Lille and French Flanders to the northeast. Champagne encompasses Reims and the extreme northeast of Paris, including the Ardennes by the Belgian border. In between is southern Picardy, traversed by the Aisne and Oise rivers.

Great Itineraries

With about a week and a half you can cover most of the region, beginning on the coast in Calais and ending in L'Épine. Five days will give you time to explore inland, from Lille to Châlons-en-Champagne. With only three days, concentrate on the most scenic attractions in Picardy and Champagne.

IF YOU HAVE 3 DAYS

Numbers in the text correspond to numbers in the margin and on the North; Southern Picardy, Champagne, and the Ardennes; Lille; and Reims maps.

Start in **Compiègne** ㉚ at its elegant palace, and then head to **Pierrefonds** ㉛ to see its mighty castle. By dinnertime, be in the hilltop cathedral town of ⊞ **Laon** ㊱. After visiting Laon the next morning, drive to ⊞ **Reims** ㊹–㊾ for the afternoon, the night, and maybe part of the third morning. Make the champagne vineyards to the south—on the Montagne de Reims, along the **Route du Vin,** and in the steeply terraced Marne Valley west of **Épernay** ㉝—your next destination.

IF YOU HAVE 5 DAYS

Begin with a day in the vibrant city of ⊞ **Lille** ③–⑭. The next morning take in stately **Arras** ① and the moving war cemeteries nearby, en route to ⊞ **Compiègne** ㉚. Devote day three to **Pierrefonds** ㉛ and ⊞ **Laon** ㊱ and day four to ⊞ **Reims** ㊹–㊾. Spend your last day touring the Montagne de Reims and the **Route du Vin,** and then head east from **Épernay** ㉝ to the historic town of **Châlons-en-Champagne** �554.

IF YOU HAVE 9 DAYS

Start in **Calais** ⑲ and venture along the Channel cliffs to **Boulogne-sur-Mer** ⑳. If want to go to the beach, head down the coast to **Le Touquet** ㉑ and rejoin the itinerary at Amiens. If you prefer history and culture, head inland from Boulogne to ⊞ **Lille** ③–⑭ for the night and following morning. That afternoon go south to ⊞ **Arras** ①. On day four, cross the **Somme battlefields** via **Albert** ㉖, ending the day in the cathedral city of ⊞ **Amiens** ㉕. The next day visit **Beauvais** ㉙, home to another cathedral and a fine tapestry museum; then go east to ⊞ **Compiègne** ㉚. Spend day six in **Pierrefonds** ㉛ and ⊞ **Laon** ㊱. Day seven head northeast into the Ardennes to explore historic **Charleville-Mézières** ㊵; stay overnight in ⊞ **Sedan** ㊶, home to Europe's largest castle. The following morning go to ⊞ **Reims** ㊹–㊾. On day nine, head to the champagne vineyards south of Reims en route to **Châlons-en-Champagne** �554 and the fine hotel-restaurant by the basilica in ⊞ **L'Épine** �555.

When to Tour the North and Champagne

Compared to many other regions of France, the North remains relatively uncrowded in July and August, and the huge Channel beaches have room for everyone. The liveliest time in Lille is the first weekend in September during its three-day street fair, La Grande Braderie. Other local fairs include the Dunkerque Carnival in February and the Giants' Carnival in Douai in July. Make sure to visit Reims and Champagne between May and October; the region's ubiquitous vineyards are a dismal, leafless sight the rest of the year. The wooded Ardennes are attractive in fall, when local game highlights menus.

BETWEEN THE CHANNEL AND THE SOMME

Starting from Arras—easily accessible by expressway and TGV from Paris—this region extends counterclockwise to Lille, passing northwest through French Flanders to the Channel Coast and down to St-Valery-sur-Somme, then east through the Somme Valley, taking in Amiens, Albert, and many World War I battlefields. Around the city of Arras you can also see many memorials to World War I. Along the coast, you can

The North

Southern Picardy, Champagne, and the Ardennes

find mile upon mile of empty, sandy beaches. Unfortunately, Calais and Dunkerque, your first ports of call coming from England, are among the country's ugliest towns. But the old sections of neighboring Boulogne-sur-Mer are far more appealing, as are the narrow streets of ancient Montreuil and the posh avenues of fashionable Le Touquet.

Arras

❶ *178 km (105 mi) north of Paris via A1, 113 km (70 mi) southeast of Calais via A26.*

At first glance you might not guess that Arras, the capital of the historic Artois region between Flanders and Picardy, was badly mauled during World War I. But its historic core, with two of the finest squares in the country, has been skillfully restored to its 17th- and 18th-century grandeur, when Arras was an important trading and cloth-making center.

★ **Grand'Place,** among Europe's biggest, is one of two main squares in Arras: a grand, harmonious showcase of 17th- and 18th-century Flemish civil architecture. The 155 gabled facades recall those in Belgium and Holland and are a reminder of the unifying influence of the Spanish colonizers of the "Low Lands" during the 17th century. The smaller, arcaded **place des Héros,** separated by a short block from the Grand'-Place, is dominated by the richly worked—and much restored—Hôtel de Ville (Town Hall), capped by a 240-ft belfry.

The **Musée des Beaux-Arts** (Fine Arts Museum), in an imposing 18th-century former abbey, houses a rich collection of porcelain and paintings, as well as the 13th-century gilded wooden *Anges de Saudémont* from Arras's cathedral. ⊠ *20 rue Paul-Doumer,* ☎ *03–21–71–26–43.* ⌸ *15 frs.* ☯ *Apr.–mid-Oct., Wed.–Mon. 10–noon and 2–6; mid-Oct.–Mar., Wed.–Mon. 10–noon and 2–5:30.*

The 19th-century **Cathédrale St-Vaast,** behind the Fine Arts Museum, is a white-stone classical building, every bit as vast as its name (pronounced *va*) almost suggests. It replaced the previous Gothic church that was destroyed in 1799; though it was half-razed during World War I, restoration was so skillfully done you'd never know. ⊠ *rue des Teinturiers.*

Dining and Lodging

$$$ ✕ **La Faisanderie.** In a former stable, this splendid restaurant serves memorable variations on international fare: *pied de veau* (calf's foot), pike baked with frogs' legs, and cod with local Arleux garlic. A loyal clientele supports its longstanding gastronomic reputation. ⊠ *45 Grand'Place,* ☎ *03–21–48–20–76. Reservations essential. Jacket and tie. AE, DC, MC, V. Closed Mon. No dinner Sun.*

$ ✕ **La Rapière.** This lively alternative to its posh neighbor, La Faisanderie, dishes up distinctly local cuisine, including andouillettes and *poule à la bière* (hen in beer), as well as specialties like *flan aux maroilles* (flan made with regional cheese) and *foie gras maison* (house foie gras), all in a casual setting. ⊠ *44 Grand'Place,* ☎ *03–21–55–09–92. AE, MC, V. No dinner Sun.*

$$ 🏩 **Univers.** Once an 18th-century monastery, this stylish hotel has a ★ pretty garden and a charming restaurant. Its central location and courtyard and garden views make it a favorite stop. The interior has been modernized but retains rustic provincial furniture. ⊠ *5 pl. de la Croix-Rouge, 62000,* ☎ *03–21–71–34–01,* FAX *03–21–71–41–42. 38 rooms. Restaurant. AE, MC, V.*

Outdoor Activities and Sports

Crazy as it may seem in this least mountainous of regions, the small mining town of **Noeux-les-Mines,** 24 km (15 mi) north of Arras, has made a name for itself recently as France's leading ski center between the Alps and the Channel. Imaginative local councillors have transformed one of the giant *terrils* (slag heaps) into an artificial ski run. ⊠ *Loisi-nord, rue Léon-Blum,* ☎ *03–21–26–84–84.*

The Artois Battlefields

North of Arras are several of the superbly cared-for war cemeteries that count among the most moving sights in northern France, recalling the murderous stalemate that raged locally for much of World War I.

Legend has it that the once-vast abbey of **Mont St-Eloi,** 8 km (5 mi) north-west of Arras via D341—razed during the French Revolution—is connected to Arras by an enormous underground tunnel. Its ghostly towers, peering mournfully over the tiny village and surrounding countryside, are visible for miles around. They were one story higher before World War I, when their lookout potential invited constant bombardment.

With its gentle slopes, trees, and manicured lawns, **La Targette,** 4 km (2½ mi) east of Mont St-Eloi via D49, is one of the most serene and beautiful of all French war cemeteries. Take the main road, D937, to get to the small **Musée de la Guerre 1914–18** (World War I Museum), opposite a stark war memorial in the form of a giant torch. It has a dusty collection of posters, documents, costumes, and weapons.

★ The road opposite the World War I Museum leads to **Neuville-St-Vaast,** where its Art Deco church is a stately example of 1920s reconstruction. From Neuville, take D55 to **Vimy Ridge,** now a park commemorating a Canadian victory during World War I. With its woods and lush grass, this has become a popular picnic spot—yet the preserved trenches and savagely undulating terrain are harsh reminders of the combat waged here in 1917. The simple, soaring, white-stone **Canadian War Memorial,** a cleft rectangular tower adorned with female figures in tearful lament, is highly effective. Its base is inscribed with thousands of names of the fallen.

From Vimy, return to Neuville and take D937 north, past the beautiful circular cemetery of the **Cabaret Rouge.** Just north of Souchez is **Notre-Dame de Lorette,** a colossal cemetery standing on a windswept hill 500 ft above the plain. There is a mock-Byzantine church and a huge tower, which serves as an ossuary for 6,000 bodies; you can also visit the small war museum. From the top there are extensive views of the surrounding countryside. Return to Souchez, follow signs to Liévin, take A21 around **Lens**—whose giant soccer stadium hosted games in the 1998 World Cup—then follow A21 to Douai.

Douai

❷ *24 km (15 mi) northeast of Arras via N50, 21 km (13 mi) east of Lens, 35 km (22 mi) south of Lille.*

The industrial town of Douai still has several imposing mansions recalling its 18th-century importance as a commercial capital of the French province of Flanders. But Douai is most noteworthy as the home of northern France's most famous **Beffroi** (Belfry), whose turrets and pinnacles are immortalized in a painting by Camille Corot, now in the Louvre. The sturdy tower, completed in 1410, rises 210 ft from the ground and is topped by a huge weather vane in the form of a Flanders Lion. The peal of bells—62 of them!—sounds the quarter hours with a variety of tunes. Climb the 193 steps to the top for a view of the town and the Scarpe River. ⊠ *rue de la Mairie,* ☎ *03–27–87–*

26–63. ☉ *Sept.–June, Mon.–Sat. at 2, 3, 4, and 5, Sun. at 10, 11, 3, 4 and 5; July–Aug., daily at 10, 11, 2, 3, 4 and 5.*

Few herbs are more readily associated with France than *ail* (garlic), and France's unofficial Garlic Capital is **Arleux,** 11 km (7 mi) south of Douai, where a Fête d'Ail (Garlic Festival) is held the first weekend of September. Smoked garlic cloves are the local specialty. Just south of Arleux, the ponds and small lakes known as the **Étangs de la Sensée** provide a scenic backdrop for strolls and picnics.

The abandoned mine at Lewarde, 7 km (4 mi) east of Douai, has been skillfully converted into the **Centre Historique Minier,** a museum charting the history of the local coal industry. You can admire beefy machinery, stroll around an interesting photographic exhibit, and take a mine car ride through reconstructed coal galleries. Wear sturdy shoes and allow two hours for the visit. ☎ *03–27–95–82–82.* ✆ *52 frs (60 frs. Nov.–Feb.).* ☉ *Nov.–Feb., Mon.–Sat. noon–4, Sun. 10–4; Mar.–Oct., daily 10–4.*

Nightlife and the Arts

Giants and processions go together in northern France, most famously during the **Fêtes de Gayant** (Festival of the Giant, in local patois), which has been held in Douai on the first Sunday after July 5 ever since Flanders and France signed a peace treaty in 1530. A family of five giants, more than 25 ft tall, are borne through the streets by dozens of invisible porters, pursued by a float with an outsize Wheel of Fortune. At 11 o'clock the city bells ring out and hundreds of pigeons are released from the town hall.

En Route   To get a feel for the area between Lewarde and Valenciennes—chosen by Émile Zola as the setting for his epic mining novel *Germinal*—take D13 then D47 northeast from Lewarde to Marchiennes. Continue on D35 to **St-Amand-les-Eaux** to admire its 270-ft, 17th-century Baroque abbey tower, topped by a cupola, then head northwest to Lille.

Lille

220 km (137 mi) north of Paris, 100 km (63 mi) southeast of Calais, 56 km (35 mi) northeast of Arras, 100 km (62 mi) west of Brussels.

For a big city supposedly reeling from the problems of its main industry, textiles, Lille—the name comes from *l'isle* ("the island") in the Deûle River, where the city began—is remarkably dynamic and attractive. After experiencing Flemish, Austrian, and Spanish rule, Lille passed into French hands for good in 1668. Since the arrival of the TGV in 1994, it is again a European crossroads, a quick trip by train from Paris, London, and Brussels.

❸ The shiny glass towers of the new **Euralille** complex, the high-tech commercial center that is Lille's answer to La Défense near Paris, greet travelers arriving at the new TGV station, **Lille-Europe.** Hotels and shops dominate the complex, which you may find interesting if you like modern architecture. Avenue Le Corbusier links Euralille to the original rail station, still used for non-TGV services and now renamed Lille-Flandres. The station building, originally the Gare du Nord in Paris, was moved brick by brick to Lille in 1866.

❹ The sumptuous church of **St-Maurice,** just off place de la Gare, is a large, five-aisle structure built between the 14th and 19th centuries. ✉ *rue de Paris.*

❺ The majestic **Porte de Paris,** overlooked by the 340-ft brick tower of the Hôtel de Ville, is a cross between a mansion and a triumphal arch.

It was built by Simon Vollant in the 1680s in honor of Louis XIV and was originally part of the city walls. ⊠ *rue de Paris.*

★ ⑥ The **Musée des Beaux-Arts** is the country's largest fine arts museum outside of Paris. It houses a noteworthy collection of Dutch and Flemish paintings (Anthony Van Dyck, Peter Paul Rubens, Flemish Primitives, and Dutch landscapists) as well as some charmingly understated still lifes by Chardin, works by the Impressionists, and dramatic canvases by El Greco, Tintoretto, Paolo Veronese, and Goya (including two of his most famous—*Les Jeunes* and the ghastly *Les Vieilles*). A ceramics section displays some fine examples of Lille faience (earthenware). ⊠ *pl. de la République,* ☎ *03–20–06–78–17.* ⊡ *30 frs.* ☼ *Wed.–Thurs. and Sat.–Mon. noon–6, Fri. noon–8.*

⑦ The late-15th-century **Palais Rihour** (Rihour Palace), built for Philippe le Bon, duke of Burgundy, is famed for its octagonal turret and staircase with intricate, swirling-pattern brickwork. The city **tourist office** is housed in the vaulted, former guardroom on the ground floor. ⊠ *pl. Rihour.*

⑧ Lille's most famous square, Grand'Place, is next door to place Rihour and is now officially called **place du Général-de-Gaulle.** The *Déesse* (Goddess) atop her giant column, clutching a linstock (used to fire a cannon), has dominated the square since 1845; she commemorates Lille's heroic resistance to an Austrian siege in 1792. Other landmarks include the handsome, gabled 1936 facade of *La Voix du Nord* (the main regional newspaper), topped by three gilded statues symbolizing the three historic regions of Flanders, Artois, and Hainaut; and the Furet du Nord, which immodestly claims to be the world's largest bookshop.

⑨ The elegant **Vieille Bourse** (Old Commercial Exchange), on one side of Grand'Place, was built in 1653 by Julien Destrées as a commercial exchange to rival those of the Low Countries. Note the bronze busts, sculpted medallions, and ornate stonework of its arcaded quadrangle.

🔟 **Le Vieux Lille** (Old Lille) dates mainly from the 17th and 18th centuries; its richly sculpted facades, often combining stone facings with pale pink brickwork, have been tastefully restored. Rue de la Grande-Chaussée, quaintly named rue des Chats-Bossus (Street of the Hunchbacked Cats), and rue de la Monnaie wind north from the Vieille Bourse through the heart of the old town. Perhaps the most ornate building, on place Louise-de-Bettignies, is the **Maison de Gilles Le Boë,** built in 1636 for a rich grocer.

⓫ The **Hospice Comtesse** (Countess Hospital), founded in 1237 by Jeanne de Constantinople, countess of Flanders, as a hospital, was rebuilt in the 15th century after a fire destroyed most of the original building. Local artifacts from the 17th and 18th centuries form the backbone of the museum now housed here, but its star attraction is the **Salle des Malades** (Sick Ward), featuring a majestic wooden ceiling. ⊠ *32 rue de la Monnaie,* ☎ *03–20–49–50–90.* ☑ *15 frs (5 frs Sat. afternoon and Wed.).* ☉ *Wed.–Mon. 10–12:30 and 2–6.*

⓬ The unfinished cathedral **Notre-Dame de la Treille** stands on the spot of a medieval church dismantled during the Revolution. The present building was begun—in a suitably neo-Gothic style—in 1854. Building was halted from 1869 to 1893, and by World War I only the choir was finished. The roof vaults were only finished in 1973, and the west front, with its dismal expanses of gray concrete, was until recently despairingly incomplete. But grandiose plans for the cathedral's new face are finally taking form: At press time, a translucent marble facade, held up by steel cables, was in the process of being constructed. ⊠ *rue des Trois-Mollettes.*

President and general Charles de Gaulle (1890–1970) was born in Lille.

⓭ His birthplace, the **Maison Natale du Général de Gaulle,** is now a museum. ⊠ *9 rue Princesse,* ☎ *03–20–31–96–03.* ☑ *15 frs.* ☉ *Wed.–Sun. 10–noon and 2–5.*

⓮ Lille's gigantic **Citadelle** patrols the northwest of the city from the enchanting Bois de Boulogne gardens, whose leafy walkways alongside photogenic streams attract hordes of strollers, cyclists, and joggers. The colossal walls of the citadel are immaculately preserved, no doubt because the site is still inhabited by the French military (you can only visit the interior on Sunday afternoons). It was constructed rapidly between 1667 and 1670; of course that genius of military engineering Sébastien de Vauban got the commission. Some 60 million bricks were baked in record time—Louis XIV's prime northern outpost needed urgent defending—and the result is a fortified town in its own right. ☎ *03–20–21–94–21 for tourist office to arrange tours.* ☑ *40 frs.* ☉ *Guided tours only Sun. 3–5 PM.*

Dining and Lodging

$$$ ✗ **L'Huîtrière.** Behind a magnificent Art Deco fish shop is this elegant seafood restaurant serving fresh, local seafood, simply prepared in regional (Flemish) style—turbot hollandaise, *waterzooie* (a mild, creamy fish stew), and oysters from La Manche (the English Channel). The clientele is chic, well heeled; the decor luxurious; and prices justifiably high. ⊠ *3 rue des Chats-Bossus,* ☎ *03–20–55–43–41. Jacket and tie. AE, DC, MC, V. Closed end July–Aug. No dinner Sun.*

$$ ✗ **Le Lion Bossu.** Old bricks and beams distinguish the 17th-century interior of this restaurant in the heart of Old Lille. This cozy, old-fashioned spot serves simple, homey regional food. ⊠ *1 rue St-Jacques,* ☎ *03–20–06–06–88. AE, V. Closed Sun. No lunch Mon.*

$ ✕ Les Brasseurs. This dark, wood-paneled brasserie beside Lille-Flandres station brews its own beer. There are four types—blond (lager), amber, dark (stout), and white (wheat beer)—and *La Palette du Barman* lets you sample all four for 24 francs. *Carbonnade flamande* (Flemish-style beef cooked in a sweet and sour sauce) and *flammekueches* (crispy pancakes topped with bacon and onions) are served as accompaniment. ⊠ *22 pl. de la Gare,* ☎ *03–20–06–46–25. AE, V.*

$$ ⛫ Bellevue. The former Hôtel de Bourbon, home to Mozart in the year 1765, is now an elegant, central hotel favored by British travelers. Large, comfortable Art Deco rooms and impeccably modern bathrooms are complemented by the sort of deferential service you can no longer take for granted. There is also a leather-lined bar. ⊠ *5 rue Jean-Roisin, 59800,* ☎ *03–20–57–45–64,* ꜰᴀx *03–20–40–07–93. 80 rooms. Bar. AE, DC, MC, V.*

Nightlife and the Arts

Lille is at its liveliest during the first weekend of September, when the **Grande Braderie** summons folk from miles around to what is theoretically a giant street market but has now become a 36-hour party, awash in oceans of beer and swimming with mussels.

Jazz clubs, piano bars, nightclubs, and all kinds of performances are listed in *Lille by Night,* available at the Lille tourist office. One of Lille's most prominent theaters is **Le Métaphore** (⊠ Grand'Place, ☎ 03–20–14–24–24). The **Opéra de Lille** (⊠ pl. du Théâtre, ☎ 03–20–14–48–61) is one of France's few opera houses; the season runs October–June. The **Orchestre National de Lille** (⊠ 30 pl. Mendès-France, ☎ 03–20–12–82–40) is a well-respected symphony orchestra.

Cassel

⑮ *45 km (28 mi) northwest of Lille via A25 and D948 from Steenvoorde (Exit 13).*

At Cassel, the North's ubiquitous image as Le Plat Pays (The Flat Land) is given a nasty jolt by a 580-ft mound towering over the plain like a land-bound Mont-St-Michel. Sailors use it as a landmark from the English Channel—27 km (17 mi) away. **Mont-Cassel** is the highest of a series of outcrops known as the Monts de Flandre, although the 520-ft Mont des Réollets (to the east) runs a close second. There's a wooden windmill at the top. The views from the surrounding gardens extend over higgledy-piggledy roofs to a patchwork quilt of wheat fields. The sloping town square, more than 200 yards long, lurches around nearby in search of a ruler. A lively Carnival provides a couple of candidates on Easter Monday: giants Reuze-Papa and Reuze-Maman.

St-Omer

⑯ *23 km (14 mi) southwest of Cassel via D933, 64 km (40 mi) northwest of Lille.*

St-Omer is not the archetypal northern industrial town. With its yellow-brick buildings it looks different from its neighbors, and an air of 18th-century prosperity hovers about the place.

The **Basilique Notre-Dame,** surrounded by narrow streets at the top end of the main town square, is a large, homely cathedral-size church, whose relatively low ceiling and broad windows with geometric tracery bear testimony to the local influence of the English Perpendicular style during the 15th century. ⊠ *rue Henri-Dupuis.*

The town museum is in the **Hôtel Sandelin,** a 1776 mansion containing period furnishings and paintings and, above all, an exceptional collection of porcelain and faience, with more than 700 pieces of delft-ware. ⊠ *14 rue Carnot,* ☎ *03–21–38–00–94.* ☜ *17 frs.* ☉ *Wed. and weekends 10–noon and 2–6, Thurs.–Fri. 10–noon and 2–5.*

Vestiges of World War I pepper the north of France, but none of them are as grisly as the Nazi specter lurking in the forest near Watten, 13 km (8 mi) north of St-Omer. Claimed to be the biggest ever built, the **Blockhaus d'Eperlecques,** a bunker of monstrous size and intent, is 80 ft high with concrete walls 20 ft thick. It was erected in 1943 by 35,000 slave laborers as the secret base for the assembly and launch of the V2 rocket-bomb, whose destination would have been London. The structure is so secret, in fact, that you can't even see it from the entrance 100 yards away. Yet it was not secret enough to escape Allied reconnaissance: RAF bombers destroyed the bunker and saved London from being blown to smithereens. Strategic loudspeakers fire out French commentary as you walk around—but the site's message is essentially unspeakable, even if tourist leaflets like to claim that this is where the Space Race began (the V2's creator, Wernher von Braun, defected to the West and helped pioneer the U.S. space program). ⊠ *Off D205 west of Watten,* ☎ *03–21–88–44–22.* ☜ *35 frs.* ☉ *Mar.–Nov. and July–Aug., daily 10–7; call for other times.*

Aspiring rocket scientists appreciate **La Coupole,** a center devoted to World War II and the postwar Space Race, 5 km (3 mi) south of St-Omer. Hitler had this concrete dome erected by Russian and Polish prisoners to house a subterranean V2 rocket storage site. ⊠ *Off A26 south of St-Omer,* ☎ *03–21–93–07–07.* ☜ *55 frs.* ☉ *Apr.–Oct., daily 9–7; Nov.–Mar., daily 10–6.*

Dining and Lodging

$$$ ✕☷ **Moulin de Mombreux.** Huge cogs and waterwheels, skillfully integrated into the decor, reflect the 18th-century watermill origins of the Moulin, west of St-Omer in Lumbres. Chef Jean-Marc Gaudry cooks up tasty cuisine—poached oysters in fennel, lamb in foie gras sauce, and raspberry soufflé. Silver candlesticks and original wood beams lend the dining room atmosphere. The discreet, if unoriginal, charm of pastel painted rooms is augmented by a spacious breakfast room with large windows and wicker chairs. ⊠ *rte. de Bayenghem, 62380 Lumbres (9 km/6 mi from St-Omer),* ☎ *03–21–39–62–44,* ℻ *03–21–93–61–34. 30 rooms. Restaurant, breakfast room. AE, DC, MC, V. Closed mid-Dec.–early Jan.*

$$ ✕☷ **Le Château de Cocove.** This classical, sprawling 18th-century château, west of St-Omer, has a fine restaurant with views over its 28-acre park. Regional specialties include *volailles de Licques* (turkey raised, as it has been for centuries, in neighboring Licques) and *raviolles de Maroilles au jus de truffes* (cheese dumplings in truffle sauce). Rooms are comfortable, if not as elegant as the exterior. A sauna, practice golf range, and horseback riding are other pluses. ⊠ *Off A26 (take Exit 2 to Ardres-Licques) 62890 Recques-sur-Hem (15 km/9 mi west of St-Omer),* ☎ *03–21–82–68–29,* ℻ *03–21–82–72–59. 22 rooms. Restaurant, sauna, 8-hole golf course, horseback riding. AE, MC, V.*

En Route   If you have gone to the Eperlecques Blockhaus (☞ *above*), return to Watten, cross the Aa River, and turn right up to the top of **Mont Watten,** where you will find a ruined abbey, an old windmill, and a sweeping panorama of the surrounding forest and countryside. There is another impressive view 8 km (5 mi) farther along the hilltop road D226, at **Merckeghem:** You can sometimes see to Dunkerque and the sea, 24 km (15 mi) away. Continuing north via D928, you come to the attractive walled town of **Bergues,** partly surrounded by a moat and canals and home to a **beer festival** at the end of May and the Christmastime Fête St-Nicolas on the first Sunday of December.

Dunkerque

⑰ *9 km (6 mi) north of Bergues via D916, 37 km (23 mi) north of St-Omer, 73 km (46 mi) northwest of Lille.*

For English-speakers, "Dunkirk" conjures up the evacuation of May 28, 1940, known as operation "Dynamo." Almost 350,000 British and French soldiers escaped the Nazi advance, ferried to safety across the Channel by an impromptu fleet consisting in large part of small private boats. Dunkerque was three-quarters destroyed in World War II but remains the third largest port in France. One of the historic buildings left is the 14th-century **Leughenaer** (⌧ rue de Leughenaer), one of 28 towers that once circled the town. Also remaining is the 16th-century church of **St-Eloi** (⌧ rue Clemenceau), and the 190-ft **Beffroi**, opposite, built in 1440 as the church belltower, with 48 bells that chime every quarter hour.

Nightlife and the Arts

Dunkerque is renowned for its rambunctious three-day **Carnival** starting the weekend before Shrove Tuesday, when locals throng the streets in fancy dress and the mayor flings herrings at the crowd from the town-hall balcony. The rest of the year you can fling your francs into the one-armed bandits at the **casino** (⌧ pl. du Casino, ☎ 03–28–59–18–23) in neighboring Malo-les-Bains.

Gravelines

⑱ *17 km (11 mi) west of Dunkerque via N1.*

The fortified town of Gravelines is noteworthy for its solid walls and star-shape ramparts, surrounded by a moat fed from the Aa River. These were first constructed by Holy Roman Emperor and Spanish king Charles Quint to protect this border town of the Spanish-controlled Low Countries from France. Louis XIV, however, regained Gravelines by the 1659 Treaty of the Pyrénées and engaged Vauban to beef up the town's defenses, which were completed in the early 1700s.

Calais

⑲ *44 km (28 mi) southwest of Dunkerque, 40 km (25 mi) northwest of St-Omer.*

On account of the devastation of two world wars, few vestiges remain of the old, once-pretty port of Calais, which owed its wealth to the lace industry. Today, money is made from the day-trippers come across the Channel by ferry to shop for tax-free wine and beer. You probably won't want to stay in Calais long, but there are a few sights to see before dashing off.

You don't need to be a sculpture fanatic to appreciate Auguste Rodin's powerful bronze **Monument des Bourgeois de Calais,** which dominates the Parc St-Pierre by the town hall (whose sturdy brick tower is visible for miles around). The bourgeois in question were townspeople who, in 1347, when Calais fell to English king Edward III after resisting siege for 11 months, offered their lives in exchange for his sparing the town. Edward's queen, Philippa, intervened on their behalf, and the courageous men were saved. Calais, on the other hand, remained in English hands until 1558 and was the last English toehold in France. The much-restored 13th-century **Tour du Guet** (Watchtower), the bourgeois's meeting place, is also the last vestige of medieval Calais.

The **Musée des Beaux-Arts et de la Dentelle** (Fine Arts and Lace Museum) contains some fine 19th- and 20th-century paintings, Rodin bronzes, local historical displays, and exhibits documenting the Calais lace industry. ⊠ *25 rue Richelieu,* ☎ *03–21–46–48–40.* ⊡ *15 frs (free Wed.).* ⊙ *Weekdays 10–noon and 2–5:30, Sat. 10–noon and 2–6:30, Sun. 2–6:30.*

The much-restored **Notre-Dame** church, where Général de Gaulle married a native *Calaisienne* in 1921, was built by the English in the 14th century of local yellow brick. Admire the simple, vertical elegance of the windows and the ornate fan vaulting. ⊠ *rue Notre-Dame.*

Napoléon dreamed of it and the Victorians even started digging it, but it was only in May 1994 that the **Channel Tunnel** (Tunnel sous la Manche) was finally inaugurated by Queen Elizabeth II and late president François Mitterrand. Eurostar rail service between Paris and London began in the fall of 1994. Le Shuttle's special double-decker trains for cars run continually and there is no need to book ahead. If you're arriving from England by car, disembark at **Coquelles,** 5 km (3 mi) from Calais. If you're a Eurostar passenger and wish to visit Calais and its surroundings disembark at **Fréthun,** 1 km (½ mi) from Coquelles. England- and Brussels-bound passengers can also get on the Eurostar at the **Lille-Europe** station in the Euralille complex. Reservations can be made at the stations themselves or by phone. ☎ *08–36–35–35–35 for Eurostar; 03–21–00–61–00 for Le Shuttle.*

Dining

$–$$ ✕ **La Pléiade.** This cozy restaurant with a nautical ambience specializes in seafood. ⊠ *32 rue Jean Quehen,* ☎ *03–21–34–03–70. AE, DC, MC, V. Closed Mon. No lunch Sat.*

En Route   Southwest of Calais, on the D940 coast road, are two points, Cap Blanc-Nez and **Cap Gris-Nez.** Stop at the latter for a bracing stroll along the cliff tops beneath a lighthouse and the ominous outlines of a World War II concrete bunker. On a clear day you may be able to spot the white cliffs of Dover across the Channel. D940 continues south, winding past **Ambleteuse,** with its small fort built by Vauban in the 1680s. Farther south along D940, just before Boulogne-sur-Mer, is **Wimereux,** a cheerful Belle Époque resort town.

Boulogne-sur-Mer

⓴   *42 km (26 mi) southwest of Calais via D940, 88 km (55 mi) west of Lille.*

Boulogne-sur-Mer, famous for its kippers (smoked herring), is France's largest fishing port. The rebuilt concrete streets around the port are ugly and unpleasant, but the old town on the hill is a different world—pretty, well kept, and full of character. Perhaps this is why Napoléon chose Boulogne as his base in 1803 while making his fruitless plans to cross the Channel.

The **Colonne de la Grande Armée,** a 160-ft marble column begun in 1804 to commemorate Napoléon's invasion of England, is north of the town just off the road to Calais. The idea was shelved in 1805, and the column was only finished 30 years later under Louis-Philippe. The 263 steps take you to the top and a wide-reaching panoramic view; if the weather is clear, and you're blessed with Napoleonic vision, you may be able to make out the distant cliffs of Dover. ⊠ *Off A6, the road to Calais,* ☎ *03–21–80–43–69.* ⊡ *20 frs.* ⊙ *Apr.–Sept., Thurs.–Mon. 9–noon and 2–6; Oct.–Mar., Thurs.–Mon. 9–noon and 2–5.*

The four main streets of the **Ville Haute** (Upper Town) intersect at **place Bouillon.** Here you will find the 18th-century rose brick **Hôtel de Ville** and the 12th- to 13th-century belfry, as well as the **Hôtel Desandrouins,** where Napoléon spent many long nights pondering how to invade Britain. Dominating them all is the formidable **Basilique Notre-Dame,** its distinctive elongated dome visible from far out at sea. Reconstructed on top of the 12th-century ruins of an abbey church destroyed during the Revolution, its crypt contains painted pillars. Surrounding the basilica and the town are cobbled streets and tower-flanked ramparts, begun in the 13th century and offering excellent views.

The pièce de résistance of Boulogne's city ramparts is its polygonal *château-fort,* the best-preserved of its kind in northern France. Today it's known as the **Château-Musée.** Built for the counts of Boulogne, the fort dates in part from the 13th-century and houses a fine collection of Egyptian artifacts donated by the celebrated Louvre Egyptologist Auguste Mariette, who was born in Boulogne in 1821. The museum's collection of Greek vases is considered second only to that of the Louvre. ✉ *rue de Bernet,* ☎ *03–21–10–02–20.* 🎫 *20 frs.* ☾ *Mon.–Sat. 10–12:30 and 2–7, Sun. 10–12:30 and 2:30–5:30.*

☾ **Nausicaà,** the Centre National de la Mer (National Marine Center), claims to be Europe's largest marine complex, with a battery of aquariums containing no fewer than 4,000 fish. There are also films and exhibitions, as well as a library, large bookshop, and restaurant. ✉ *bd. Ste-Beuve,* ☎ *03–21–30–99–99.* 🎫 *53 frs.* ☾ *Oct.–May, weekdays 10–6, weekends 10–7; June–mid-Sept., daily 10–8.*

Dining and Lodging

$$ ✕ **La Matelote.** The name of this restaurant, across the way from Nausicaà, means "The Sailor's Wife." Here you can enjoy seafood specialities ★ such as *darnes de turbot rôties au thym* (roast fillet of turbot with thyme) in the bright yellow interior. ✉ *80 bd. Ste-Beuve,* ☎ *03–21–30–17–97. AE, DC, V. Closed late Dec.–mid-Jan.*

$$ 🏨 **Cléry.** Extensive lawns and an avenue of trees lead to this stylish hotel in an 18th-century château in the tiny village of Hesdin-l'Abbé. Enter to find an old wooden staircase with wrought-iron banisters. Rooms vary in price and decor; those in the former stables were converted into light, spacious, and modern spaces. It was at this château that Napoléon decided to abandon his plans to invade England. As you bask in the peace and quiet of the beautiful grounds, you'll understand why. ✉ *62360 Hesdin-l'Abbé (8 km/5 mi inland from Boulogne, along N1),* ☎ *03–21–83–19–83,* ℻ *03–21–87–52–59. 19 rooms. Breakfast room, tennis court. AE, DC, MC, V.*

$$ 🏨 **Métropole.** This small hotel is handy for ferry passengers but, like most of the Ville Basse (Lower Town), no great architectural shakes. Although no exciting views are to be had from the rather faceless '50s building, the small garden is pleasant for breakfast in summer and rooms are adequately furnished and individually decorated. ✉ *51 rue Thiers, 62200,* ☎ *03–21–31–54–30,* ℻ *03–21–30–45–72. 25 rooms. AE, DC, MC, V. Closed late Dec.–early Jan.*

Outdoor Activities and Sports

The coast is a popular spot for speed sailing and sand sailing, particularly at Le Touquet, Hardelot, Dunkerque, Bray-Dunes, and Berck-sur-Mer (it costs about 80 francs per hour). For details, contact the **Drakkars** club (✉ Base Nautique Sud, 62152 Hardelot-Plage, ☎ 03–21–83–27–93), 14 km (9 mi) south of Boulogne.

Le Touquet

★ ㉑ *28 km (17 mi) south of Boulogne via D940, 95 km (59 mi) west of Arras.*

At the mouth of the Canche estuary, Le Touquet is an elegant Victorian seaside resort town that grew up like a sprawling sand castle. First transformed into a sandy pine forest by Alphonse Daloz in the mid-19th century, the site was developed by Yorkshire businessman John White to attract English vacationers. On the Paris end, the newspaper *Le Figaro* baptized the site "Paris-Plage" and launched a huge advertising campaign to lure well-to-do Parisians. A cosmopolitan atmosphere remains, and many French people, attracted by the airy, elegant avenues and invigorating climate, have moved here for good. On one side is a fine sandy beach; on the other, the flourishing pine forest. A casino, golf courses, and a racetrack cater to fashionable leisure activities.

Dining and Lodging

$$$ ✕ **Flavio.** Fish is the star at this elegant spot near the casino. Chef Guy Delmotte specializes in lobster and charges whale-size prices for the lobster menu. The other two prix-fixe menus will please most (wine is included in the 230-franc, weekday carte du jour). Cut glass and Oriental carpets add a note of dated glamour. ⊠ *1 av. du Verger,* ☎ *03–21–05–10–22. Reservations essential. Jacket and tie. AE, DC, MC, V. Closed Mon. (except July–Aug.) and Jan.*

$$$ 🏨 **Westminster.** The Westminster's mammoth redbrick facade looks
★ as if it were built just a few years ago; in fact, it dates from the 1930s and, like the rest of the hotel, has been extensively restored. The enormous double rooms are a good value and the bridal suite is the last word in thick-carpeted extravagance. The hotel's brasserie is modestly priced (lunch and dinner); the Pavillon restaurant serves inventive French cuisine. ⊠ *av. du Verger, 62520,* ☎ *03–21–05–48–48,* 🆂 *03–21–05–45–45. 115 rooms. Restaurant, bar, brasserie, indoor pool, hot tub, sauna, squash. AE, DC, MC, V. Closed mid-Jan.–early Mar.*

Outdoor Activities and Sports

Aqualud, a water park on the beachfront, has numerous water-sports facilities, half outdoors, half in, including a giant slide, a large pool with wave machine, and a sauna. ⊠ *bd. de la Mer,* ☎ *03–21–05–90–96.* 🆂 *55 frs for 3 hrs, 61 frs for 4 hrs, 67 frs for 5 hrs, 72 frs all day.* ☉ *Sept.–June, daily 10–6; July–Aug., daily 10–7 (call for schedule changes).*

Montreuil-sur-Mer

㉒ *18 km (11 mi) east of Le Touquet, 80 km (50 mi) west of Arras.*

Despite its seaside-sounding name, Montreuil-sur-Mer is 18 km (11 mi) inland. It was once a port, but the River Canche silted up and left it high and dry. The ancient town has majestic walls and ramparts, as well as a faded, nostalgic charm to which various authors, notably Victor Hugo, have succumbed; an episode of *Les Misérables* is set here.

Wherever citadels and city walls loom on the French horizon, it's a fair bet that Vauban had a hand in their construction. Montreuil is no exception. First Errard de Bar-le-Duc and then Vauban supplemented the existing 16th-century towers of the **Citadelle** with an imposing wall, whose grassy banks and mossy flagstones can be explored at leisure. There are extensive views on all sides. ⊠ *rue Carnot,* ☎ *03–21–06–10–83.* 🆂 *10 frs.* ☉ *Wed.–Mon. 9–11:30 and 2–5:30; closed Oct.*

OFF THE
BEATEN PATH

AZINCOURT – The Battle of Agincourt (Azincourt in French), one of the proudest dates in English history, took place 35 km (22 mi) east of Montreuil in October 1415 when, in boggy conditions, Henry V's well-grouped, lightly clad longbowmen defeated Charles VI's more numerous, but heavily armored, French troops. There's an orientation map and a clearly marked trail.

Dining and Lodging

$$$–$$$$
★

X⛫ **Château de Montreuil.** At this manor house facing the citadel, rooms are furnished with 18th- and 19th-century antiques. No. 208 has a large sitting area and a view of the garden. The less expensive rooms, in the converted stables, are also pleasantly furnished but smaller. Owner Lindsay Germain is English. Her husband Christian is an excellent chef: His forte is bringing out the natural flavor in such dishes as lightly sautéed scallops served with *pompadour* (a variety of potato) and lamb chops with a wine sauce glaze. The restaurant is closed Thursday lunch and Monday. ⊠ *4 chaussée des Capucins, 62170,* ☎ *03–21–81–53–04,* FAX *03–21–81–36–43. 14 rooms. Restaurant. MC, V. Closed mid-Dec.–Feb.*

En Route
Driving from Montreuil-sur-Mer to St-Valery-sur-Somme, you pass the small town of **Rue,** 28 km (17 mi) south. It is known for its extravagantly sculpted **Chapelle du St-Esprit,** with lacelike stonework and stellar-patterned vaulting. Some 6 km (4 mi) south of Rue is the cheerful, unpretentious resort town of **Le Crotoy** on the northern edge of the **Baie de Somme** (Bay of the Somme), where sheep graze peacefully on the salt marshes. Skirt around the bay on D940 to St-Valery-sur-Somme.

St-Valery-sur-Somme

➁ *37 km (23 mi) south of Montreuil-sur-Mer via D940, 65 km (41 mi) northwest of Amiens.*

St-Valery-sur-Somme is a pretty fishing (squid and shellfish are specialties) and resort town with a shady seaside promenade, medieval fortifications, and the remains of St-Valery himself. The flint-and-sandstone-checkerboard **Chapelle des Marins** (Mariners' Chapel), an 18th-century chapel at the far end of the town's bay-side promenade (where there are views of the Somme estuary), houses the tomb of St-Valery.

☉ The **Chemin de Fer de la Baie de Somme** (Somme Bay Steam Railway) chugs around the marshy Somme Bay between St-Valery and Le Crotoy (the trip takes an hour). In 1994 the railway acquired the *130T* locomotive used during construction of the Panama Canal, owned by Detroit's Ford Museum until 1977. ⊠ *Departs from the Crotoy and St-Valery-sur-Somme train stations,* ☎ *03–22–26–96–96.* ▣ *50–56 frs.* ☉ *Departures at 3:30 and return trips 5:30: Apr.–June and Sept., Wed. and weekends; July–Aug., Tues.–Sun.; Oct. 1st 3 Sun.*

☉ The **Maison de l'Oiseau** (Bird House), just west of St-Valery on D204 (direction Cayeux-sur-Mer), has a collection of 400 stuffed birds and a video presentation of their local habitats. ⊠ *carrefour du Hourdel,* ☎ *03–22–26–93–93.* ▣ *34 frs.* ☉ *Mid-Feb.–June and Sept.–mid-Nov., daily 10–6; July–Aug., daily 10–7.*

OFF THE
BEATEN PATH

EU and LE TRÉPORT – The neighboring towns of Eu and Le Tréport are 24 km (15 mi) southwest of St-Valery, just over the regional boundary in Normandy. Eu, slightly inland, has a stately church and a brick château where King Louis-Philippe once entertained Queen Victoria. Le Tréport has a lively harbor and cliff-top promenade.

Abbeville

㉔ *20 km (12 mi) southeast of St-Valery-sur-Somme via D40, 43 km (27 mi) northwest of Amiens.*

The historic town of Abbeville was heavily reconstructed after being reduced to rubble in 1940. Its most admirable building is its Gothic church. Begun in 1488, **St-Vulfran** was the last cathedral-size church to be constructed in the Gothic style. It was here that, according to 19th-century art historian John Ruskin, Gothic "lay down and died." After decades of restoration, the riotous tracery and ornament of its much-mauled facade have been revived. The tall, elegant nave retains fine medieval stained glass. Work is still in progress on the 17th-century choir. ⊠ *rue St-Vulfran.*

Another magnificent church, **St-Riquier** is 9 km (6 mi) northeast of Abbeville via D925 in the village of the same name. Its nave is more than 100 yards long and the majestic Flamboyant Gothic facade is dominated by a weighty, richly sculpted tower.

OFF THE
BEATEN PATH   **CRÉCY-EN-PONTHIEU –** This small town, 19 km (12 mi) north of Abbeville, was the scene of a famous English victory during the Hundred Years' War in 1346, when 20,000 Frenchmen perished at the hands of Edward III. North of the town, on D111, is a hillock known as the Moulin Édouard-III, said to be the site of a windmill where Edward surveyed the battlefield. Just southeast of Crécy on D56 is the Croix de Bohême, a cross marking the spot where France's hapless ally John the Blind, King of Bohemia, stumbled into oblivion.

Amiens

㉕ *43 km (27 mi) southeast of Abbeville via N1, 64 km (40 mi) southwest of Arras.*

Although much of the city counts as a catastrophic example of post–World War I and II reconstruction, Amiens's Gothic cathedral survived unscathed. The waterfront quarter of St-Leu, around the cathedral, is a lively spot to explore: It has colorful, restored houses and eclectic shops.

★   By far the largest church in France, the **Cathédrale Notre-Dame** could fit Paris's Notre-Dame inside twice. It may lack the stained glass of Chartres or the sculpture of Reims, but for architectural harmony, engineering proficiency, and sheer size, it has no peer. The soaring, asymmetrical facade of the cathedral has a notable Flamboyant Gothic rose window and dominates the surrounding nondescript brick streets. Inside, the overwhelming sensation of space is enhanced by the absence of pews in the nave, a return to medieval tradition. There is no stylistic disunity to mar the perspective: Construction took place between 1220 and 1264, a remarkably short period in cathedral-building terms. One of the highlights of a visit here is hidden from the eye, at least until you lift up some of the 110 choir stalls and admire the humorous, skillful misericord (seat) carvings executed between 1508 and 1518. ⊠ *pl. St-Michel,* ☎ *03–22–92–77–29, 03–22–91–83–83 for son-et-lumière information.* 🎫 *60 frs.*

The **Hôtel de Berny,** around the corner from the cathedral, is an elegant brick mansion built in 1633, filled with 18th-century furniture and tapestries, and objets d'art. ⊠ *36 rue Victor-Hugo,* ☎ *03–22–91–36–44.* 🎫 *10 frs.* ☉ *Oct.–mid-Apr., Sun. 10–12:30 and 2–6; mid-Apr.–Sept., Thurs.–Sun. 1–6.*

Jules Verne (1828–1905) lived in Amiens for some 35 years, and his former home has become the **Centre de Documentation Jules Verne** (⊠ 2 rue Charles-Dubois, ☎ 03–22–45–37–84). It contains some 15,000 documents about Verne's life as well as original furniture and a reconstruction of the writing studio where he created his science fiction classics. If you're a true Verne fan, you might want to visit his dramatically sculpted tomb in the **Cimetière de la Madeleine** (⊠ 2 rue de la Poudrière).

The **Hortillonnages,** on the east side of town, are commercial watergardens—more than 700 acres—where vegetables have been grown since Roman times. They're best visited by boat. ⊠ *Boats leave from 54 bd. de Beauvillé,* ☎ *03–22–92–12–18.* ⊡ *28 frs.* ☉ *Apr.–Oct., daily 2–6.*

Dining and Lodging

$$ ✕ **Joséphine.** This unpretentious, good-value restaurant in central Amiens is a reliable choice. Solid fare, decent wines, and rustic decor (a bit on the stodgy side, like the sauces) pull in many foreign customers, notably Brits. ⊠ *20 rue Sire-Firmin-Leroux,* ☎ *03–22–91–47–38. AE, MC, V. Closed Mon. and 3rd wk in Aug. No dinner Sun.*

$$ ✕ **Les Marissons.** In the prettiest and oldest section of Amiens, near the cathedral, this restaurant serves creative takes on regional ingredients. Few of the burbot swimming in the Somme could ever have dreamed they would end up being cooked with apricots, for example; rabbit is accompanied by mint and goat cheese, and black currants add tang to the local pigeon. To avoid pricey dining à la carte, order from one of the three prix-fixe menus. ⊠ *68 rue des Marissons,* ☎ *03–22–92–96–66. Jacket and tie. AE, DC, MC, V. Closed Sun. No lunch Sat.*

$–$$ ⊡ **La Paix.** This hotel in an old quarter of Amiens was reconstructed after World War II. Convenience, private parking, and a view of a nearby church from some of the rooms offset a certain lack of personality, though the breakfast room tries valiantly to suggest an 18th-century Louis XV salon. Foreign guests are common and English is spoken. ⊠ *8 rue de la République, 80000,* ☎ *03–22–91–39–21,* ⒻⒶⓍ *03–22–92–02–65. 26 rooms, 11 with bath. Breakfast room, free parking. AE, MC, V.*

Nightlife and the Arts

The **Théâtre d'Animation Picard** (⊠ 24 rue St-Leu, ☎ 03–22–92–42–06) presents a rare glimpse of the traditional Picardy marionettes, wooden puppets in bright costumes known locally as Chès Cabotans d'Amiens. Shows are performed on weekends in French (daily in August), with plot synopses in English; admission is 50 francs.

Albert

㉖ *28 km (17 mi) northeast of Amiens via D929, 41 km (25 mi) south of Arras.*

Like nearby Amiens, the dour brick town of Albert stands in the *département* (province) of the Somme—a name forever etched into history as site of one of the bloodiest battles of World War I. On July 1, 1916, whole regiments of Allied soldiers went "over the top" only to be mowed down by a hail of German machine-gun fire. When the front stabilized in late November, the Allies had advanced just 8 km (5 mi). Even now, 80 years later, shells and grenades still rise to the surface of the fields hereabouts; 90 tons of these dormant time bombs are collected and destroyed every year.

The **Musée des Abris** (Trenches Museum) uses photographs, costumes, guns, and sandbags to evoke the soldiers' life in the trenches. The museum is almost entirely underground (wear a sweater) and, by the time you come up for air, you've tunneled your way through to a tranquil park 100 yards from where you started. ⊠ *rue Anicet-Godin,* ☎ *03–22–75–16–17.* 🖾 *20 frs.* ⊘ *Jan.–mid-Dec., 9:30–noon and 2–6 (no midday closure in July and Aug.).*

Looming above the museum is the neo-Byzantine, brick **Basilique Notre-Dame-de-Brébières,** an ostentatious country cousin of churches like Fourvière in Lyon and Sacré-Coeur in Paris. Its wealth derives from an 11th-century statue of the Virgin Mary, still venerated by pilgrims. The stone sculpture was discovered "miraculously," the story goes, by a shepherd whose obstinate sheep (*brébis*) wouldn't budge from the spot where the statue was buried. But it is another miraculous statue of the Virgin—the one on top of the 220-ft tower—that captivates most visitors. When the basilica was nearly reduced to rubble in 1916, this mighty gold Virgin, holding aloft the infant Jesus, was left dangling from the tower at right angles, as if held in place by a magic thread. Postcards showing this astonishing scene look like primitive examples of trick photography; in fact, they capture one of the most poignant, symbolic images of World War I. ⊠ *pl. d'Armes,* ☎ *03–22–75–09–54.*

Dining

$$ ✕ **L'Escale.** This vine-covered restaurant in the tiny village of Cappy, southeast of Albert, is worth seeking out: With its antiques and needlework tablecloths and menu illustrated with poems and old photos, it has the feel of a country cottage. The seasonal, regional dishes (smoked eel, duck, and black pudding) are accompanied by subtle, refined sauces. ⊠ *22 chaussée Léon-Blum, Cappy (10 km/6 mi southeast of Albert),* ☎ *03–22–76–02–03. MC, V. No dinner Sun.–Wed.*

The Somme Battlefields

The Battle of the Somme raged from July through November 1916 and left a million dead. During those five futile months, the Allies, including Irish, Canadian, and South African soldiers, progressed about 8 km (5 mi) along the hills above the Ancre River north of Albert.

From Albert, take D929 (direction Bapaume) and stop after 2 km (1 mi) at **La Boisselle** to inspect the awesome **Lochnagar Crater** caused by German shellfire. Follow D20 west from La Boisselle, then D50 north, to reach the **Beaumont-Hamel Parc Mémorial,** where a bronze caribou—emblem of the Newfoundland regiments that fought here—peers mournfully over trenches and undulating, shell-shocked terrain. Backtrack down the hill from the Newfoundland memorial, cross the Ancre River, and head up the hill on the other side. On the left is the **Tour Ulster** (Ulster Tower) commemorating troops from Belfast. A few hundred yards past the Ulster Tower is the village of Thiepval; follow signs to the bombastic brick **British War Memorial,** a disjointed triumphal arch that looks as if it were made of giant Lego blocks. Take D73 to

★ Bazentin, then turn left to Longueval, site of the **Delville Wood Memorial:** A long lawn framed by a stately avenue of oaks leads to an airy, white-stone pentagon, modeled on the Castle of Good Hope in Cape Town. Here giant photographs and etched-glass panels evoke the memories of South Africans who fought in the war.

Péronne

㉗ *15 km (10 mi) southeast of Longueval via D20 and N17, 27 km (17 mi) southeast of Albert, 50 km (31 mi) east of Amiens.*

The small, brick town of Péronne was almost entirely razed in 1916.
★ It is now home to a fine World War I museum, the **Historial de la Grande Guerre.** Tastefully integrated within a ruined brick castle, this spacious

modern museum has a thought-provoking variety of exhibits, from TV monitors playing old newsreel to soldiers' uniforms strung out on the floor surrounded by machine guns and a dim roomful of nightmarish war lithographs by Otto Dix. There is a good shop, with books in English, and a café with views of a leafy-banked lake. Walk around to the end and you'll find the Somme River, strewn with islands, languidly colliding with its tributary, the Cologne. ⊠ *pl. du Château,* ☎ *03– 22–83–14–18.* ⌨ *39 frs.* ☉ *May–Sept., daily 10–6; Oct.–mid-Dec. and mid-Jan.–Apr., Tues.–Sun. 10–5:30.*

Le Cateau

㉘ *50 km (31 mi) northeast of Péronne via D6 and D932.*

★ Artist Henri Matisse (1869–1954) was born in Le Cateau. The **Musée Matisse** (Matisse Museum), housed in the **Palais Fénelon** (former home to the archbishops of Cambrai), contains a number of early oil paintings and sculptures, plus a superb collection of 50 drawings selected by Matisse himself. Two large collages have recently been donated by his family. Call ahead for a guided visit. ⊠ *Palais Fénelon,* ☎ *03–27– 84–13–15.* ⌨ *16 frs.* ☉ *Mon. and Wed.–Sat. 10–12:30 and 2–6, Sun. 10–12:30 and 2:30–6. Free guided tour Sun. at 3 PM.*

Dining and Lodging

$$$ ✕🏨 **Château de Ligny.** Dominating the sleepy village of Ligny, west of Le Cateau, is this château. Despite its modern surroundings and fenced-in park, its grassed-in moat and crenellated gateway make it romantic. The 12th-century tower and 15th- to 18th-century wings are furnished in a busy mix of chintz, lace, and green leather chairs. But the dining room, with its stained-glass windows and a carved-wood fireplace, is magnificent. Rooms, though cozy, are disappointingly small; some bathrooms, however, are surprisingly roomy. The best deal is the Blue Room, overlooking the courtyard and its circular fountain. In the restaurant, it's better to order à la carte—try the delicious artichoke and foie gras salad, if available. ⊠ *2 rue Pierre Curie, 59191, Ligny-en-Cambresis (14 km/9 mi northeast of Le Cateau via N47 and D15),* ☎ *03– 27–85–25–84,* 🖷 *03–27–85–79–79. 11 rooms in chateau, 2 suites in separate building on property. Restaurant. AE, MC, V.*

SOUTHERN PICARDY, CHAMPAGNE, AND THE ARDENNES

As you head east from Beauvais to Laon, the plains of Picardy gradually give way to rolling, wooded hills, then, closer to the Belgian border, to the rugged Ardennes forests. Farther south, the cheerful villages and vine-covered slopes of Champagne, around Reims, provide a scenic circuit if you love the world's bubbliest wine. Châlons-en-Champagne, the administrative capital of Champagne country, is easily accessible from Paris, the Channel, and Lorraine (☞ Chapter 8).

Beauvais

㉙ *60 km (18 mi) south of Amiens via A16; 95 km (59 mi) southwest of Péronne via N17, D930, and N1; 76 km (48 mi) north of Paris.*

Beauvais and its neighbor Amiens have been rivals since the 13th century, when they locked horns over who could build the bigger cathedral. Beauvais lost—gloriously.

A work-in-progress preserved for all time, soaring above the characterless modern blocks of the town center, is the tallest cathedral in France:

★ the **Cathédrale St-Pierre.** You may have an attack of vertigo just gazing up at its vaults, 153 ft off the ground. Tallest, yes; biggest, no. Paid for by the riches of Beauvais's wool industry, the choir collapsed in 1284, shortly after completion, and was only rebuilt with the aid of extra pillars. This engineering fiasco proved so costly that the transept was not attempted until the 16th century. It was worth the wait: The transept is an outstanding example of Flamboyant Gothic, its exterior bristling with pinnacles and flying buttresses. It is also still standing—which is more than can be said for the megalomaniac 450-ft spire erected at the same time. This lasted precisely four years and, when it came crashing down, the transept was damaged, all remaining funds were hurled at an emergency consolidation program, and Beauvais's dream of having the largest church in Christendom disappeared. Now the cathedral is starting to lean and cracks have appeared in the choir vaults because of changing water levels in the soil. No such problems bedevil the **Basse Oeuvre** (Lower Edifice; closed to the public), which juts out impertinently where the nave should have been. It has been there for a thousand years.

Fittingly donated to the cathedral by the canon Étienne Musique, the oldest surviving **Chiming Clock** in the world, a 1302 model with a 15th-century painted wooden face and most of its original clockwork, is built into the wall of the cathedral. Perhaps Auguste Verité drew his inspiration from this humbler timepiece when he made a gift of the gilded, temple-like **Astrological Clock** to his hometown in 1868. Animated religious figurines surrounded by all sorts of gears and dials emerge for their short program at erratic times, although there is a schedule for commentated visits. ☉ *May–Oct., daily 9–12:15 and 2–6:15; Nov.–Apr., daily 9–12:15 and 2–5:30.*

From 1664 to 1939, Beauvais was one of France's leading tapestry centers; it reached its zenith in the mid-18th century. The modern **Galerie Nationale de la Tapisserie** (National Museum of Tapestry), next to the cathedral, has examples from all periods. ⊠ *1 rue St-Pierre,* ☎ *03–44–05–14–28.* ☏ *25 frs.* ☉ *Apr.–Sept., Tues.–Sun. 9:30–11:30 and 2–6; Oct.–Mar., Tues.–Sun. 10–11:30 and 2:30–4:30.*

One of the few remaining testaments to Beauvais's glorious past, the beautiful old Bishop's Palace is now the **Musée Départemental de l'Oise** (Oise Museum). Unfortunately, the museum's pièce de résistance, Thomas Couture's epic canvas of the French Revolution, is currently inaccesible due to renovations that will last until the end of 1999; it can be imagined, however, through a series of original sketches. Don't miss the 14th-century frescoes of instrument-playing sirens on a section of the palace's vaults and the 1st-century brass *Guerrier Gaulois* (Gallic Warrior), as well as the eclectic local ceramic collection. ⊠ *1 rue du Musée,* ☎ *03–44–11–43–83.* ☏ *16 frs.* ☉ *Wed.–Mon. 10–noon and 2–6.*

Compiègne

 60 km (38 mi) east of Beauvais via N31, 82 km (51 mi) northeast of Paris.

Compiègne, a bustling town of some 40,000 people, is at the northern limit of the **Forêt de Compiègne,** on the edge of the misty plains of Picardy: prime hunting country, a sure sign that there's a former royal hunting lodge in the vicinity. The one here enjoyed its heyday in the mid-19th century under Napoléon III. But the town's place in history looks farther back: Joan of Arc was captured in battle and held prisoner here, and the 15th-century Hôtel de Ville possesses an exceptional

Flamboyant Gothic facade. Its place also goes farther forward: The World War I armistice was signed in Compiègne Forest on November 11, 1918.

★ The **Palais de Compiègne** was a humbler château in the 18th century. But it was restored and transformed into a pseudo-royal residence by Napoléon I. It was here that his nephew Napoléon III hosted his famous *séries*—exclusive grand parties and hunting excursions, including visits to Pierrefonds (☞ *below*), under construction at the time. This "Club Med" of its day reflects both Napoléons' taste: Don't miss his study, lined with rare Cuban mahogany and linked to his second wife Marie-Louise's apartments by a door hidden behind fake book-bindings. Most impressive are the bedrooms, spangled with stars and draped in scarlet and gauze. Much of the original furnishings and decorations adorn the rooms. Behind the palace is a gently rising, 4-km (2½-mi) park, inspired by the one at Schönbrunn in Vienna, where Marie-Louise grew up. Also here is the **Musée du Second Empire**, a collection of Napoléon III–era decorative arts, including works by the caricaturist par excellence Honoré Daumier and the painter Thomas Couture. ⊠ *pl. du Général- de-Gaulle,* ☎ *03–44–38–47–00.* ⌲ *23 frs.* ⊙ *Apr.–Sept., Wed.–Mon. 9:15–6; Oct.–Mar., Wed.–Mon. 9:15–3:45 (tours of Empress Marie-Louise's apartments and the Musée du Second Empire by appointment only).*

An amazing collection of 85,000 miniature soldiers fashioned out of lead, cardboard, and other materials depicting military uniforms through the ages is found in the **Musée de la Figurine** (Figurine Museum). ⊠ *28 pl. de l'Hôtel-de-Ville.* ☎ *03–44–40–72–55.* ⌲ *12 frs.* ⊙ *Mar.–Oct., Tues.–Sat. 9–noon and 2–6, Sun. 2–6; Nov.–Feb., Tues.–Sat. 9–noon and 2–5, Sun. 2–5.*

Some 7 km (4 mi) east of Compiègne via N31, near Rethondes, is the **Wagon de l'Armistice** (Armistice Rail Car), a replica of the one where the World War I armistice was signed in 1918. In 1940 the Nazis turned the tables and made the French sign their own surrender in the same place—accompanied by Hitler's famous jig for joy—then tugged the car off to Berlin, where it was later destroyed. The car is part of a small museum in a leafy clearing. ⊠ *Near Rethondes off N31,* ☎ *03–44–40–09–27.* ⌲ *10 frs.* ⊙ *Apr.–Oct., Wed.–Mon. 9–noon and 2–6:30; Nov.–Mar., Wed.–Mon. 9–noon and 2–5:30.*

Dining and Lodging

$$ ✕⊡ **Hôtel de France.** A former 17th-century posting inn, the hotel is central, cheap, and the epitome of French provincial—rooms have creaky, uneven floors, and the prim *patronne,* Mme. Robert, appears from nowhere as you cross the threshold with officious alacrity. The labyrinth of rooms, with their matching fruit-and-flower wallpaper and bedspreads, ranges from nooks and crannies to family sleepers. The intriguing name of the restaurant, La Rôtisserie du Chat Qui Tourne (The Cat That Turns the Spit), recalls a legendary street performance involving a cat roasting a chicken. With its brass lights and plush curtains and waiters in black tie it tries valiantly to be upper-crust. The scallops in pastry soufflé and the langoustines in cream are especially good. ⊠ *17 rue Eugène-Floquet, 60200,* ☎ *03–44–40–02–74,* ℻ *03–44–40–48–37. 20 rooms. Bar, restaurant. MC, V.*

Pierrefonds

★ ㉛ *14 km (9 mi) southeast of Compiègne via D973, 77 km (48 mi) northeast of Paris.*

Dominating the attractive lakeside village of Pierrefonds is its huge ersatz medieval castle. Built on a mound in the 15th century, the **Château**

de Pierrefonds was comprehensively restored and re-created in the 1860s to imagined former glory at the behest of upstart emperor Napoléon III. Architect Viollet-le-Duc left a crenellated fortress with a fairy-tale silhouette, although, like the fortified town of Carcassonne, which he also restored, Pierrefonds is more a construct of what Viollet-le-Duc thought it should have looked like than what it really was. A visit takes in the chapel, barracks, and the majestic keep holding the lord's bedchamber and reception hall, which is bordered by a spiral staircase whose lower and upper sections reveal clearly what is ancient and modern in this former fortress. Never furnished because the Paris Commune of 1870 deposed its developer, the Château de Pierrefonds became a depot for all sorts of government-owned collections: Don't miss the plaster casts of tomb sculptures from all over France in the cellars, and the newly opened **Collection Monduit**—industrially produced, larger-than-life lead decorations made by the 19th-century firm that brought the Statue of Liberty to life. ☎ 03–44–42–72–72. ☞ 32 frs. ☼ Mar.– Apr. and Sept.–Oct., Mon.–Sat. 10–noon and 2–6, Sun. 10–6; May– Aug., Mon.–Sun. 10–6; Nov.–Feb., Mon.–Sat. 10–noon and 2–5, Sun. 10–5:30. (Last admission ¾ hr before closing.)

Dining and Lodging

$$ ✕🏨 **Relais Brunehaut.** Just down the valley from Pierrefonds, in the hamlet of Chelles, is this quaint hotel-restaurant. It's made up of a tiny ensemble of stucco buildings, bordered by several acres of pleasant park and a small, duck-populated river. There's a view of the abbey church next door. An old wooden watermill in the dining room and the good, simple seasonal fare makes eating here a pleasure. ⊠ 3 rue de l'Église, 60350 Chelles (3 km/2 mi from Pierrefonds), ☎ 03–44–42–85–05, 🆚 03–44–42–83–30. 7 rooms. Restaurant. MC, V.

Morienval

③ 6 km (4 mi) south of Pierrefonds via D335.

The village of Morienval is best known for its elegant but relatively modest 11th-century Romanesque church, one of the key buildings in architectural history. Legend has it that the translation of the relics of St. Annobert to the **Église Notre-Dame** in 1122 necessitated a new ambulatory (so everyone could get a look at the saintly remains). But it is now thought that Morienval's masons hit on the innovative idea of using stone vaults supported on "ribs" springing diagonally from column to column in order to extend the church beyond its raised mound and support two additional towers. Few dispute, however, that this architectural breakthrough, the structural basis of the Gothic style (along with pointed arches), occurred at Morienval in the 1120s. This trend was soon picked up at the great basilica of St-Denis near Paris and swept through northern France during the years that followed. Much of the original church remains, notably the east tower and the columns in the nave, whose carved capitals feature spirals, masks, and animals.

Soissons

③ 31 km (19 mi) east of Pierrefonds via D335 and N31, 96 km (60 mi) northeast of Paris via N2, 56 km (35 mi) west of Reims.

Although much damaged in World War I, Soissons commands attention for its two huge churches: one intact, one in ruins.

The Gothic **Cathédrale Notre-Dame** was appreciated by Rodin, who declared famously that "there are no hours in this cathedral, but rather eternity." The interior, with its pure lines and restrained ornament, creates a more harmonious impression than the asymmetrical, one-towered facade. The most remarkable feature, however, is the rounded, two-story transept, a feature more frequently found in the German Rhineland than in France. Rubens's freshly restored *Adoration of the Shepherds* hangs on the other side of the transept. ⊠ *pl. Fernand-Marquigny.*

The twin-spired facade and airy refectory, constructed from the 13th to the 15th century, are all that is left of the abbey church of **St-Jean-des-Vignes,** which was largely destroyed just after the Revolution. Its stones were used to restore the cathedral and neighboring homes. But St-Jean-des-Vignes remains the most impressive sight in Soissons, its hollow rose window peering out over the town like the eye of some giant Cyclops. ⊠ *cours St-Jean-des-Vignes.* ☉ *Mon.–Sat. 9–noon and 2–6, Sun. 10–noon and 2–6.*

OFF THE
BEATEN PATH

D1 leads southeast from Soissons to the 14th-century **Donjon de Septmonts,** a keep that is the last vestige of the Bishop of Soissons's summer residence. The reason for its many levels of towers and turrets remains a mystery, but they definitely make the château look like the classic image of a castle.

Dining and Lodging

$$$ ✕🏨 **Château de Courcelles.** East of Soissons, along the Vesle River on
★ the Champagne border, is this luxurious and refined château run by easygoing and chatty Frédéric Nouhaud. Its pure, classical Louis XIV facade—through which Racine, Rousseau, and others have passed—harmonizes oddly well with the sweeping brass and pewter main staircase attributed to Jean Cocteau and the red teapot-patterned wallpaper on the upper floors. Rooms vary in size and grandeur; the former outbuildings have been converted into large family-size suites. Wind down in the cozy, antechamber-like bar next to a roaring fire while anticipating excellent fare, including seasonal game, prepared by chef Pascal Mottet and served up in the stately dining room. A formal garden and pool are the gateway to 40 acres of parkland and a tree-shaded canal. ⊠ *Château de Courcelles, 02220 Courcelles-sur-Vesle (20 km/12 mi east of Soissons via N31),* ☎ *03-23-74-13-53,* ℻ *03-23-74-06-41. 13 rooms, 5 suites. Restaurant, bar, pool, sauna, tennis court, horseback riding. AE, MC, V.*

Blérancourt

㉞ *23 km (14 mi) northwest of Soissons via D6.*

Blérancourt is home to the **Musée National de la Coopération Franco-Américain** (Museum of French-American Cooperation). Two pavilions and monumental archways are all that remain of the original 17th-century château, demolished during the French Revolution. American Anne Morgan founded the museum in 1924. Pictures, sculptures, and documents chart Franco-American relations, with emphasis on the American Revolution and the two world wars. The grounds include gardens and an arboretum. ⊠ *Off D939,* ☎ *03-23-39-60-16.* 🖾 *16 frs.* ☉ *Wed.–Mon. 10–12:30 and 2–5:30.*

Noyon

㉟ *14 km (9 mi) northwest of Blérancourt, 37 km (23 mi) northwest of Soissons, 24 km (15 mi) northeast of Compiègne.*

Noyon is a frequently overlooked cathedral town that owed its medieval importance to the cult of 7th-century St. Eloi, patron of blacksmiths and a former town bishop. Its second famous son, the Protestant theologian John Calvin, was born here in 1509. The old streets around the cathedral are at their liveliest during the Saturday morning market.

Constructed between 1140 and 1290, the **Cathédrale St-Eloi** was one of the earliest attempts at what was to become the Gothic cathedral. This is evident in the four-story nave; the intermittent use of rounded as well as pointed arches; and the thin, pointed lancet (as opposed to rose) windows in the austere facade. Pause for a wry smile at the "piazza" in front of the cathedral, with its elegant town houses arranged in a semicircle in bashful imitation of St. Peter's in Rome; then head down the cobbled lane to the left of the facade to admire the timber-fronted, 16th-century library behind the cathedral.

Dining and Lodging

$$ 🏨 **St-Eloi.** Between the train station and the cathedral, this hotel charms with its faded elegance. The redbrick and timber Victorian exterior, marble-lined reception area, and airy, pastel dining room are staunchly French bourgeois. The spacious rooms have high ceilings; several have views of the interior courtyard. Avoid, however, the chain-hotel–like annex. Affordable prix-fixe menus are available in the restaurant, which is closed Sunday dinner and the end of July to mid-August. ⊠ *81 bd. Carnot, 60400,* ☎ *03–44–44–01–49,* ℻ *03–44–09–20–90. 18 rooms. Bar, restaurant. AE, MC, V.*

Laon

★ 🌑 *53 km (33 mi) east of Noyon, 47 km (29 mi) northwest of Reims, 47 km (29 mi) southeast of St-Quentin.*

On a splendid hilltop site reached by a winding road, Laon is called the "crowned mountain"—a reference to the forest of towers sprouting from its ancient cathedral. The cathedral and enchanting old town are a must, but strangely, the French ignore Laon as a tourist venue. The medieval ramparts, virtually undisturbed by passing traffic, provide a ready-made itinerary for a tour of old Laon. Panoramic views, sturdy gateways, and intriguing glimpses of the cathedral lurk around every bend. There's even a funicular, the panoramic **POMA,** which makes frequent trips up and down the hillside (except on Sundays during the winter).

★ The **Cathédrale Notre-Dame,** constructed between 1150 and 1230, is a superb example of early Gothic. The light interior gives the impression of order and immense length, and the first flourishing of Gothic architecture is reflected in the harmony of the four-tiered nave: From the bottom up, observe the wide arcades, the double windows of the *tribune,* the squat windows of the *triforium,* and, finally, the *fenêtres hautes* (upper windows). Unfortunately, the upper galleries that extend around the building, so typical of early Gothic, can no longer be visited, for safety reasons. The majestic towers, however, are still deemed secure; guided visits leave from the tourist office, which is housed in a 12th-century hospital on the cathedral square. The filigreed elegance of these five remaining towers is audacious and rare, more along the lines of Romanesque architectural planning than of Gothic. Note the sense of movement imparted by Laon's majestic west front; compare it with the more placid, two-dimensional feel of its contemporary Notre-Dame in Paris. Look, too, for the stone oxen protruding from the towers—there are 16 in all, a tribute to the stalwart 12th-century beasts who carted up blocks of stone from quarries far below. Medieval stained-glass windows not to be missed include the *rosace* with the eight liberal arts in the left transept and those at the end of the nave. ⊠ *pl.*

du Parvis. ⊡ *Tower 35 frs.* ⊙ *Tower visits July–Aug., daily 3 PM; Easter–Oct., weekends 3 PM.*

The **Chapelle des Templiers** is a small, well-preserved, octagonal 12th-century chapel on the grounds of the **Musée de Laon.** Chock-full of medieval curiosities, the chapel contains fragments of the cathedral's gable and some of its original sculptures, and a tiny Lamb of God decorates the cupola. But the star of the collection is the tomb effigy of Guillaume de Harcigny, doctor to the insane king Charles VI, whose death from natural causes in 1393 did not prevent his memorializers from chiseling a skeletal portrait that recalls the Black Death. It is one of the most famous—and chilling—effigies of its style. ⊠ *32 rue Georges-Ermant.* ⊡ *Museum 16 frs.* ⊙ *Apr.–Sept., Wed.–Mon. 10–noon and 2–6; Oct.–Mar., Wed.–Mon. 10–noon and 2–5.*

Dining and Lodging

$$ ✕⊡ **Bannière de France.** In business since 1685, this old-fashioned, uneven-floored hostelry is just five minutes from the cathedral. Mme. Lefèvre, the patronne, speaks fluent German and English. Rooms are cozy and quaint. The restaurant's venerable dining room features sturdy cuisine (trout, guinea fowl, lemon sole à la Normande) and good-value, prix-fixe menus. ⊠ *11 rue Franklin-Roosevelt, 02000,* ☎ FAX *03–23–23–21–44. 18 rooms, 14 with bath or shower. Restaurant. AE, DC, MC, V. Closed late Dec.–early Jan.*

En Route   The **Forêt de St-Gobain** lies just west of Laon via D7 and is dotted with pastoral treasures enveloped in silence. D7 also takes you to the **Abbaye de St-Nicolas aux Bois,** 17 km (10 mi) west of Laon, and the 14th-century fortified priory and barn built as its annex, **Le Tortoir.** Both are privately owned but can be viewed from the road. Continue along D7 to the town of **St-Gobain,** 20 km (12 mi) from Laon. It was once famous for its royal glassworks.

Coucy

③⑦   *11 km (7 mi) south of St-Gobain via D13; 30 km (19 mi) southwest of Laon.*

★   Accessible from the small town of Coucy, which grew up below it, **Coucy-le-Château** is a majestic hilltop fortress whose 13th- and 14th-century *seigneurs* (lords), the Enguerrands de Coucy, rivaled the king of France. (American historian Barbara Tuchman's history of the 14th-century, *A Distant Mirror,* is fascinating background reading.) The story (and tangibility) of Coucy's demise is more compelling than that told by most war memorials: Its *donjon* (keep), once the largest in Europe, was hollowed out in punishment by Mazarin, who also halved many of its 28 towers. The final coup, however, was the dynamiting of the château by the Germans during their 1917 retreat—the great donjon is now nothing more than a pile of rubble. Some vaulted *caves* (cellars) are still intact, giving a sense of the ensemble's former vastness. ☎ *03–23–52–71–28.* ⊡ *25 frs.* ⊙ *Apr.–Sept., daily 9–noon and 2–6; Oct.–Mar., Wed.–Mon. 10–noon and 1:30–4.*

En Route   From Coucy, drive southeast through Pinon, turning left onto N2 and right along D18, to arrive at the hilltop road separating the Aisne and Ailette valleys. Known as the **Chemin des Dames,** the road was named after the daughters of King Louis XV, who came often from Versailles to visit a countess friend. This route was the scene of a disastrous French offensive in April 1917 that led to futile slaughter and mutiny. Pass through **Cerny-en-Laonnois:** Here, the **Caverne du Dragon,** a former quarry, was used as an arsenal and living quarters by both the Germans and the Allies during World War I. Now it is both a museum detailing WWI history and a testament to the soldiers' suffering: The cavern is filled with rock-carvings executed by the cavern's hapless wartime inhabitants. At the **Plateau de Californie** (near Craonne), which was named at the turn-of-the-century in honor of its natural beauty, there is a panoramic view of a WWI battlefield.

Vervins

38 *36 km (22 mi) northeast of Laon via N2, 48 km (30 mi) east of St-Quentin.*

Vervins embodies the idea of a picture-postcard French village. Snugly tucked in behind crumbling ramparts, the town's steep, purplish slate roofs are set off against slender redbrick chimneys. Explore its tumbling cobbled streets and inspect its church of **Notre-Dame,** with its 13th-century choir, wall paintings (notably Jouvenet's vast 1699 *Le Repas Chez Simon*), and 16th-century tower propped up by bulky corner buttressing.

Vervins is the gateway to **Thiérache,** known as the Pays des Églises Fortifiées (Land of Fortified Churches) for the famous redbrick churches that were fortified in the 16th century when the Low Countries' ruler Charles Quint of Spain and French king François I were fighting for supremacy. There are about 60 of these proud, fortresslike places of worship, each with its own peculiarities. A list and a map can be acquired from the Vervins **tourist office** (⊠ pl. du Général de Gaulle, ☎ 03–23–98–11–98), open Monday–Saturday 10–noon and 2–6. Among the most noteworthy are **Jeantes,** whose postwar religious frescoes by Charles Eyck are reminiscent of Marc Chagall's work; and **Burelles,** whose construction reflects Thiérache's tempestuous history. In the 16th century, defensive towers were added to its 13th-century nave, and menaced locals could seek refuge in the right-hand tower (to which you have free access). The second "emergency" level of the tower retains its original chestnut roof beams. Have a glance at **Beaurain,** off of D960, which is impressive for its massive hilltop site but is not open to visitors—and then continue on D960 to the **Château-Fort de Guise.**

Dining and Lodging

$$$ ✕🏠 **Tour du Roy.** This eclectic pink and blue hotel, in a converted medieval manor built of stone from the town's ramparts, is run by garrulous Claude Desvignes. While he rattles amusingly away, his wife, Annie, holds sway in the kitchen. An excellent cook, she creates classical dishes with an emphasis on seasonal produce, including *sanglier* (wild boar) in a cream and peppercorn sauce. Rooms display the character of the owners, a blend of French traditional and charming kitsch: The best suite, in the donjon, has a claw-footed tub and a musical toilet, and a fairy-tale bedroom upstairs. Its haughty title, the *Chambre du Sire de Coucy* (Lord of Coucy's Bedroom), describes a valiant—if a tad cotton-candied—attempt at grandeur. ⊠ *45 rue du Général-Leclerc, 02140,* ☎ *03–23–98–00–11,* ℻ *03–23–98–00–72. 13 rooms, 5 suites. Restaurant. AE, DC, MC, V.*

Guise

39 *17 km (10 mi) northwest of Vervins via D960.*

On a gloomy day, creeping up the dark, ominous covered passageway that leads to the **Château-Fort de Guise** gives you the impression that you are indeed entering the guarded domain of François I's close allies, the Ducs de Guise. This influential line of dukes produced the throne-coveting Henri I, *Le Balafré* (Scarface), who plotted the St.

Bartholomew's Day massacre of August 1572, the great slaughter of Paris's Protestant notables. The imposing remains of the fortress were fortified in the style of Italian Rennaissance military architecture to defend the northeastern route from Paris against Spanish monarch Charles Quint's ambitions. Heavy French bombardment in 1917 chased the Germans out of the town of Guise but also destroyed much of the complex. The fortress is currently being slowly restored by volunteer members of the Club du Vieux Manoir preservation movement, and a fascinating "visit in the rough" of about 1½ hours is best done with Welsh guide Rosalind Guillemin (if she's around). Tours take in the 11th- to 13th-century donjon, one of the best preserved in Picardy, and the artifact-filled subterranean passageways. ☎ 03–23–61–11–76. ⌨ 30 frs. ☉ Daily 10–noon and 2–6; closed late Dec.–early Jan.

Charleville-Mézières

⓵ 69 km (43 mi) southeast of Vervins, 80 km (50 mi) northeast of Reims.

Charleville-Mézières, in the Ardennes, was originally two towns separated by a branch of the capricious River Meuse. Mézières, an administrative and military center, has a more regimented feel than folksy Charleville, where a warren of narrow pedestrian streets encircles a large, shambling square. The two towns were officially united in 1966.

With its pink brick, arcades, and steep slate roofs, Charleville's **place Ducale,** designed around 1610 by Clément Métezeau, recalls place des Vosges in Paris, designed by his elder brother Louis. Place Ducale has no trees or railings to mask the view; its original symmetry, however, has been zapped by rooftop accretions and a 19th-century church and town hall. The square is at its liveliest during the market on Tuesday, Thursday, and Saturday mornings.

The **Vieux Moulin** (Old Mill), a majestic 1626 watermill straddling a branch of the Meuse, hosts temporary art exhibits and a museum devoted to Charleville's most famous son: precocious "punk" poet Arthur Rimbaud. Pictures, souvenirs, and photographs chart his turbulent career, revealing that he fled Charleville at age 17, after writing his masterpiece, *"Le Bateau Ivre"* ("The Drunken Boat"). He died in 1891 in Marseille at age 37 but is buried in Charleville's town cemetery. ✉ *quai Arthur-Rimbaud,* ☎ *03–24–32–44–65.* ⌨ *20 frs.* ☉ *Tues.–Sun. 10–noon and 2–6.*

The subtle lighting and spacious, imaginative layout at the **Musée de l'Ardennes** (Ardennes Museum) lend its displays of guns, coins, keys, pottery, and archaeological findings an almost abstract aesthetic appeal. There are also local paintings and a re-created, rustic regional interior. ✉ *31 pl. Ducale,* ☎ *03–24–32–44–60.* ⌨ *25 frs.* ☉ *Tues.–Sun. 10–noon and 2–6.*

☝ **Le Grand Marionnettiste** (The Giant Puppeteer), tucked away between the Musée de l'Ardennes (☞ *above*) and place Winston Churchill, was commissioned in 1991 by Charleville's International Puppet Institute. It is a surreal spectacle: a huge turquoise frame, topped by a clock and a gold mask peeping out of the roof, with a pair of giant gold legs in the alleyway beneath. Every hour from 10 AM to 9 PM, the red stage curtains slide open to reveal gold hands pulling the strings of a plethora of puppets enacting the local legend of the *Quatre Fils Aymon* (*Aymon's Four Sons*), after which the rock formations north of town (☞ *below*) are named. On Saturday at 9:15 PM, all 12 tableaus appear in sequence.

★ In the 16th-century basilica of **Notre-Dame de l'Espérance,** in Mézières, Charles IX married Elizabeth of Austria in 1570. It has a foursquare

Renaissance tower topped by a fancy 19th-century spire, but the real attraction lies inside. "The church of Mézières is reputed for its stained glass," wrote Victor Hugo in 1838. Alas, the windows he admired have long since been blasted into oblivion during repeated invasions, but today you can admire the most ambitious modern stained glass anywhere in France: an entire church of abstract, geometric designs by René Dürrbach. The overall effect is a breathtaking collision of old and new, one of the most homogeneous displays of stained glass outside Chartres. A guidebook to its biblical symbolism is available from the presbytery. ⊠ *av. de St-Julien.*

Due north of Charleville-Mézières are the four spiky quartzite summits of the **Rocher des Quatre Fils Aymon** (Rock of Aymon's Four Sons), a steep rock formation rising above Château-Regnault.

Dining

$$ ✕ **La Côte à l'Os.** Fish is the specialty here: Sea bass, marinated salmon, and braised pike often figure on the menu. The long, cheerful dining room, decked out with fresh flowers, is popular with locals for its 79-franc, prix-fixe menu. Service is welcoming but low-key. ⊠ *11 cours Aristide-Briand,* ☎ *03–24–59–20–16. AE, MC, V.*

Sedan

④ *21 km (13 mi) southeast of Charleville-Mézières via A203.*

The fame of Sedan far outweighs its modest size. To English speakers its name has become associated with cars and chairs—accidentally, say sedentary etymologists. In France, Sedan is forever written into the national psyche because here, in 1870, Napoléon III's Second Empire came crashing down as the Prussian army smashed through, taking Napoléon and 83,000 soldiers prisoner, then steaming on toward Paris. Émile Zola captured the mayhem in his epic novel *Le Débâcle.*

★ The grim, massive **Château Fort** that dominates Sedan may not be the most impregnable in Europe, but it claims to be the largest. The colossal front, illuminated at night, dominates the town like a Wall of Jericho; the daunting courtyard is hemmed in by bleak walls seven stories high and up to 24 ft thick. The castle was used as a prison during World War II, and you can see why.

Founded in 1424 by the Lords of Sedan, the castle was basically a town in its own right and could house 4,000 soldiers. Its sturdy walls withstood sieges in 1495 and 1521, when Charles V was forced to seek a truce despite attacking with more than 30,000 men. Elizabeth of Austria stayed here in 1570 before her marriage to Charles IX in Mézières, as did Henri II and Catherine de' Medici, and Henri IV and Maria de' Medici. Sedan became part of France only in 1642; Louis XIV stayed here during the siege of Stenay. Documents relating the castle's history can be examined in the **museum** in the south wing, along with archaeological finds. The castle visit is called the **Historium** and involves tableaux depicting the château's history and a self-guided tour with wireless headsets and multilingual commentary. Try to visit at nightfall on Friday or Saturday in summer for a guided tour by torchlight. ☎ *03–24–27–73–75.* 🎫 *45 frs.* ☼ *Mid-Mar.–June and early to mid-Sept., daily 10–6; July–Aug., daily 10–8; mid-Sept.–mid-Mar., Tues.–Sun. 1:30–5:30.*

In the **Vieille Ville** (Old Town), between the castle and the Meuse, several streets are pedestrians-only, especially around place d'Armes. The square is dominated by the church of **St-Charles,** with its pepper-pot towers. The triangular **place de la Halle** leads into **rue du Ménil,** lined with 17th- and 18th-century houses. **Place Turenne,** by the river, is spoiled by the five skyscrapers that glower down from the hill behind, although from here you can glimpse remnants of the awesome walls and catch a rooftop view of higgledy-piggledy chimneys gushing smoke in a satisfyingly Dickensian manner.

Dining and Lodging

$ ✕▥ **Europe.** Convenience is the main reason to stay at this modern hotel by the train station, on the outskirts of town. Rooms are clean, comfortable, and soundproof, if a little characterless. The spacious bar is a fine place to have an aperitif before dining on boar or venison (in season) at the hotel restaurant. ✉ *2 pl. de la Gare, 08200,* ☎ *03–24–27–18–71,* ℻ *03–24–29–32–00. 26 rooms. Restaurant, bar. MC, V.*

OFF THE **DOUZY –** The small aerodrome in Douzy, 8 km (5 mi) south of Sedan
BEATEN PATH via N43, is home to the Musée des Débuts de l'Aviation (Museum of the Origins of Aviation), devoted, in particular, to the pioneering exploits of Roger Sommer (1877–1965), who edged past Wilbur Wright's previous best to set a flight record of 2 hours, 27 minutes at Châlons-en-Champagne on August 7, 1909. ☎ *03–24–29–33–40.* ▱ *13 frs.* ⊙ *June–Aug., Tues.–Sun. 10–noon and 2–6; May and Sept., Tues.–Sun. 2–6; Apr. and Oct., weekends 2–6.*

Mouzon

④ *9 km (6 mi) south of Douzy via D964, 17 km (11 mi) southeast of Sedan.*

The small village of Mouzon, on the Meuse River, is dwarfed beneath the twin towers of its 13th-century abbey church. With fat, round columns and a second-story gallery, the imposing edifice of the **Église Notre-Dame,** 215 ft long and 70 ft high, is a stylistic successor to the cathedrals of Laon and Notre-Dame in Paris.

The **Musée du Feutre** (Felt Museum) outlines the 8,000-year history of felt, from its immemorial manufacture in Turkey, Afghanistan, and Mongolia to its latter-day use in games, decorations, cars, and pens. ✉ *rue Jean-Claude Stoltz,* ☎ *03–24–26–10–63.* ▱ *20 frs.* ⊙ *May–Sept., daily 2–6; Apr. and Oct., weekends 2–6.*

Asfeld

④ *84 km (52 mi) southwest of Mouzon via D19, D30, and D926; 28 km (17 mi) north of Reims.*

The tiny village of Asfeld is home to one of France's most surprising churches. The **Église St-Didier,** designed by Father François Romain for the Count d'Avaux in 1683, is a whimsical essay in Roman Baroque, with curves, cupolas, a rotunda, colonnades, oval side chapels, and hardly a straight line in sight. The ground plan is said to be based on a viola, and the individual bricks are not rectangular but concave or convex. The church would look great in a tony sector of Rome; in this tiny village it hovers between the sublime and the ridiculous. ☎ *03–24–72–95–46.* ⊙ *Daily noon–7.*

Reims

27 km (17 mi) south of Asfeld via D926, D37, and D274; 144 km (90 mi) east of Paris.

Although most of its historic buildings were flattened in World War I and replaced by drab, modern architecture, those that do remain are of royal magnitude. Reims sparkles with some of the biggest names in champagne production. The maze of champagne cellars makes the city a must, as do the splendid cathedral and the fine arts museum. Several champagne producers organize visits to their cellars, combining video presentations with guided tours of their cavernous, chalk-hewn underground warehouses. For a complete list, contact the **Reims Tourist Office** (⊠ 2 rue Guillaume-de-Machault, ☎ 03–26–77–45–25), next to the cathedral.

★ ㊹ The tour of the **Taittinger** cellars is the most spectacular of the champagne producer visits. It includes a champagne *dégustation* (tasting) after the tour. ⊠ *9 pl. St-Niçaise,* ☎ *03–26–85–45–35.* ▣ *20 frs.* ☉ *Weekdays 9:30–noon and 2–4:30, weekends 9–11 and 2–5; closed weekends Dec.–Feb.*

㊺ **Mumm** is another one of the few champagne houses to give out free samples after the tour. ⊠ *34 rue du Champ-de-Mars,* ☎ *03–26–49–59–70.* ▣ *20 frs.* ☉ *Mar.–Oct., daily 9–11 and 2–5; Nov.–Feb., weekdays 9–11 and 2–5, weekends 2–5.*

★ ㊻ The **Cathédrale Notre-Dame** was the age-old setting for the coronations of the French kings. Clovis, king of the Franks in the 6th century, was baptized in an early structure on this site; Joan of Arc led her recalcitrant dauphin here to be crowned King Charles VII; Charles X's coronation, in 1825, was the last. The high, solemn nave is at its best in summer when the light shows up the plain lower walls. The east-end windows have stained glass by Marc Chagall. Admire the vista toward the west end, with an interplay of narrow pointed arches.

The glory of Reims's cathedral is its facade: It's so skillfully proportioned that initially you have little idea of its monumental size. Above the north (left) door hovers the *Laughing Angel,* a delightful statue whose famous smile threatens to melt into an acid-rain scowl. Pollution has succeeded war as the ravager of the building's fabric. Restoration is an ongoing process. With the exception of the 15th-century towers, most of the original building went up in the 100 years after 1211. A stroll around the outside reinforces the impression of harmony, discipline, and decorative richness. The east end presents an idyllic sight across well-tended lawns. Spectacular **son-et-lumière** shows are performed both inside (50 francs) and outside (free) the cathedral on Friday and Saturday evenings from July to mid-September. ⊠ *pl. du Cardinal-Luçon.* ☉ *Daily 7:30–7:30.*

㊽ The **Palais du Tau** (the former Archbishop's Palace), alongside the cathedral, houses an impressive display of tapestries and coronation robes, as well as several statues rescued from the cathedral facade before they fell off. The second-floor views of Notre-Dame are terrific. ⊠ *2 pl. du Cardinal Luçon,* ☎ *03–26–47–81–79.* ▣ *32 frs.* ☉ *July–Aug., daily 9:30–6:30; mid-Mar.–June and Sept.–mid-Nov., daily 9:30–12:30 and 2–6; mid-Nov.–mid-Mar., weekdays 10–noon and 2–5, weekends 10–noon and 2–6.*

㊾ The **Musée des Beaux-Arts,** two blocks southwest of the cathedral, has an outstanding collection of paintings: no fewer than 27 Corots, and Jacques-Louis David's celebrated portrait of the Revolutionary polemicist Jean-Paul Marat stabbed in his bath by Charlotte Corday. ⊠ *8 rue Chanzy,* ☎ *03–26–47–28–44.* ▣ *10 frs, or 15 frs for joint ticket with the Salle de Reddition (☞ below).* ☉ *Wed.–Mon. 10–noon and 2–6.*

㊿ The 11th-century **Basilique St-Rémi,** down rue Chanzy and rue Gambetta, honors the 5th-century saint who gave his name to the city. St-Rémi is nearly as long as the cathedral, and its interior seems to stretch

Reims

into the endless distance, an impression created by its relative murk and lowness. The airy, four-story Gothic choir contains some fine original 12th-century stained glass. Like its sister cathedral, the basilica puts on summer **son-et-lumière** shows inside every Saturday evening at 9:30 PM from late June to early October. They are preceded by a tour of the building and are free. ⊠ *53 rue St-Rémi,* ☎ *03–26–85–31–20.* ☉ *Sun.–Wed. 8–6 or 7, Thurs. and Sat. 8–9.*

50 The Gallo-Roman **Cryptoportique,** an underground gallery and crypt, now a semisubterranean passageway, was constructed around AD 200 under the forum of what was Reim's predecessor, the Roman town of Durocortorum. ⊠ *pl. du Forum,* ☎ *03–26–85–23–36.* ☉ *Mid-June–mid-Sept., Tues.–Sun. 2–6.*

51 The **Porte Mars,** an unlikely but impressive 3rd-century Roman arch adorned by faded bas-reliefs depicting Jupiter, Romulus, and Remus, looms up across from the train station. ⊠ *rue de Mars.*

52 The **Salle de Reddition** (Surrender Room), near the train station, also known as the Salle du 8 mai 1945, is a well-preserved, map-covered room used by General Eisenhower as Allied headquarters at the end of World War II. It was here that General Alfred Jodl signed the German surrender at 2:41 AM on May 7, 1945. Fighting officially ceased at midnight the next day. ⊠ *12 rue Franklin-Roosevelt,* ☎ *03–26–47–84–19.* ▨ *10 frs.* ☉ *Apr.–mid-Nov., Wed.–Mon. 10–noon and 2–6.*

Dining and Lodging

$$ ✕ **Vigneron.** This little brasserie in a 17th-century mansion is cozy and cheerful, with two tiny dining rooms displaying a jumble of champagne-related paraphernalia. The food is delightful as well: relatively cheap, distinctly hearty, and prepared with finesse. Try the pigs' feet or andouillettes slathered with delicious mustard made with champagne. ⊠

pl. Paul-Jamot, ☎ *03–26–79–86–86. MC, V. Closed Sun., late Dec.– early Jan., and most of Aug. No lunch Sat.*

$$$$ ✕🏠 **Boyer.** Gérard Boyer, one of the country's most highly rated chefs,
★ impresses with creations from wild mushrooms in cream to scallops with endive confit. The extensive wine list pays homage to Reims's champagne heritage. The restaurant is closed Monday all day and Tuesday lunch; make reservations and wear a jacket and tie. The building is magnificent, too: a late 19th-century château surrounded by an extensive park. The decor is opulent, typified by ornate chandeliers, towering ceilings, and gilt mirrors. The 19 luxurious suites have wonderful views. ✉ *Les Crayères, 64 bd. Henri-Vasnier, 51100,* ☎ *03–26–82– 80–80,* 🖷 *03–26–82–65–52. 19 rooms. Restaurant. AE, DC, MC, V. Closed late Dec.–mid-Jan.*

$$$ ✕🏠 **La Paix.** A modern, eight-story hotel, 10 minutes' walk from the cathedral, La Paix has stylish rooms with 18th- and 19th-century reproductions, a pretty garden, and a rather incongruous chapel. Its brasserie-style restaurant serves good, though not inexpensive, cuisine (mainly grilled meats and seafood). ✉ *9 rue Buirette, 51100,* ☎ *03– 26–40–04–08,* 🖷 *03–26–47–75–04. 106 rooms. Restaurant, bar, pool. AE, DC, MC, V.*

$$–$$$ ✕🏠 **Cheval Blanc.** This hotel, owned for five generations by the hospitable Robert family, is in the small village of Sept-Saulx, southeast of Reims. Rooms are across the road in a parklike setting—with swings for kids and a tennis court—on the small River Vesle. Some rooms are quite small, but opening the French doors onto the garden helps. The newer suites are larger and have modern furnishings. Restaurant specialties include St-Pierre fish, seasoned with Chinese pepper, and pigeon with dried raisins. ✉ *rue du Moulin, 51400 Sept-Saulx (20 km/12 mi south of Reims, just off D8),* ☎ *03–26–03–90–27,* 🖷 *03–26– 03–97–09. 25 rooms. Restaurant, tennis court, fishing, playground. AE, DC, MC, V. Closed late Jan.–mid-Feb.*

$$ ✕🏠 **Gambetta.** Primarily foreigners stay at this modest, comfortable
★ hotel near the cathedral. The smallish rooms, with modern furnishings and pastel-color walls, have all the creature comforts. The restaurant, Le Vonelly, serves regional specialties like guinea fowl with cabbage in a champagne vinegar–based sauce, and *Bavarois au Marc de Champagne* (a mousse pastry flavored with Marc de Champagne, a regional distillation). It's closed Sunday dinner and all day Monday. ✉ *9 rue Gambetta, 51100,* ☎ *03–26–47–41–64,* 🖷 *03–26–47–22–43. 14 rooms. Restaurant. AE, MC, V.*

Route du Vin

9 km (6 mi) south of Reims via N51 and D26.

The grapes of Champagne flourish on the steep slopes of the Marne Valley and the Montagne de Reims—more of a forest-topped plateau than a mountain—south of Reims. As you begin to climb the Montagne de Reims, spin off left onto D26: This is the Route du Vin—the Wine Road—so named because it winds around the vine-entangled eastern slopes of the Montagne. Drive along it to pass through such pretty wine villages as **Chigny-les-Roses, Rilly-la-Montagne, Mailly-Champagne,** Verzy, and the aptly named **Bouzy,** where a fashionable but overpriced red wine is produced. **Ay,** along the north bank of the Marne River, was once capital of the champagne vineyards; Henry VIII was a keen tippler of its wines.

To understand how the still wine of King Harry's time became sparkling champagne, continue west to **Hautvillers.** Here the monk Dom Pérignon (1638–1715) —whom, as legend has it, was gifted with exceptional taste buds and sense of smell by blindness—invented champagne as we know it by using corks for stoppers and blending wines from different vineyards. Dom Pérignon's simple tomb slab, in a damp, dreary Benedictine abbey church (now owned by Moët et Chandon), is a forlorn memorial to the hero of one of the world's most lucrative drink industries. Champagne vineyards extend west from Hautvillers all the way to **Château-Thierry,** 50 km (31 mi) away, as well as along D1, which provides many a scenic overview as it hugs the steeply sloped Marne Valley. Look out for signs that read DÉGUSTATION (tasting).

Épernay

⑤ *6 km (4 mi) south of Hautvillers, 26 km (16 mi) south of Reims.*

Unlike Reims with its numerous treasures, the town of Épernay, on the south bank of the Marne, appears to live only for champagne. Unfortunately, no relation exists between the fabulous wealth of Épernay's illustrious wine houses and the drab, dreary appearance of the town as a whole. Most of the champagne firms are spaced out along the long, straight avenue de Champagne, and although their names may provoke sighs of wonder, their facades are either functional or overdressy. The attractions are underground, in the cellars.

Of the various champagne houses open to the public, **Mercier** offers the best deal; its sculpted, labyrinthine caves contain one of the world's largest wooden barrels (with a capacity of more than 215,000 bottles). A tour of the cellars takes 45 minutes in the speed and comfort of a small train. A generous glass of champagne is your post-visit reward. ⊠ *75 av. de Champagne,* ☎ *03–26–51–22–22.* 🎫 *25 frs weekdays, 30 frs weekends.* ☉ *Mon.–Sat. 9:30–11:30 and 2–4:30, Sun. 9:30–11:30 and 2–5:30; closed Dec. 25–Jan. 1.*

Dining and Lodging

$$$ ✕🏨 **La Briqueterie.** Épernay is short on good hotels, so it's worth driving south to Vinay to find this commodious, luxurious, and comfortable hotel in a former manor on large grounds. The spacious rooms are modern; ask for one overlooking the garden. The chef has his mind on the Mediterranean: hence the lobster and prawns in citrus sauce. For more regional fare, try the Champagne snails with herbed butter and, for dessert, the *crêpe soufflée au Marc de Champagne* (a crepe filled with pastry cream and flavored with brandy). ⊠ *4 rte. de Sézanne, 51530 Vinay (6 km/4 mi south of Épernay),* ☎ *03–26–59–99–99,* 🖷 *03–26–59–92–10. 40 rooms, 2 suites. Restaurant, indoor pool, sauna, exercise room. AE, MC, V. Closed late Dec.*

Nightlife and the Arts

The leading wine festival in the Champagne region is the **Fête St-Vincent** (named for the patron saint of vine growers), held on January 22 or the following Saturday in Ambonnay, 24 km (15 mi) east of Épernay.

Châlons-en-Champagne

⑤ *34 km (21 mi) east of Épernay via N3, 44 km (28 mi) southeast of Reims.*

Strangely enough, the official administrative center of the champagne industry is not Reims or Épernay but Châlons-en-Champagne. Yet this large town is of principal interest to fans of medieval architecture on account of its vast cathedral and smaller church.

The 13th-century **Cathédrale St-Étienne** is a harmonious structure with large nave windows and tidy flying buttresses; the exterior effect is marred only by the bulky 17th-century Baroque west front. ⊠ *rue de la Marne.*

★ With its twin spires, Romanesque nave, and early Gothic choir and vaults, the church of **Notre-Dame-en-Vaux** bears eloquent testimony to Châlons's medieval importance. The small **museum** beside the excavated cloister contains outstanding medieval statuary. ⊠ *rue Nicolas-Durand,* ☎ *03–26–64–03–87.* 🎫 *25 frs.* ☉ *Apr.–Sept., Wed.–Mon. 10–noon and 2–6; Oct.–Mar., Wed.–Fri. 10–noon and 2–5, weekends 10–noon and 2–6.*

Dining and Lodging

$$–$$$ ✕🏨 **Angleterre.** Rooms at this stylish spot in central Châlons have elaborate decor and marble bathrooms; those in the back are quietest. The restaurant, in particular, stands apart: Chef Jacky Michel's creations include *sandre* (a perchlike fish) cooked in champagne and seasoned roast duck, as well as the seasonal dessert *tout-pommes,* featuring five variations on the humble apple. Breakfast is a superb buffet. ⊠ *19 pl. Monseigneur-Tissier, 51000,* ☎ *03–26–68–21–51,* 🆉🆇 *03–26–70–51–67. 18 rooms. Restaurant. AE, DC, MC, V. Closed mid-July–early Aug. and late Dec.–early Jan.*

L'Épine

55 *7 km (4 mi) east of Châlons-en-Champagne via N3.*

The tiny village of L'Épine is dominated by its church. The twin-towered Flamboyant Gothic **Basilique de Notre-Dame de l'Épine** has a magnificent facade of intricate patterns, spires, and an interior that exudes elegance and restraint.

Dining and Lodging

$$$ ✕🏨 **Aux Armes de Champagne.** The highlight of this cozy former coaching inn opposite the basilica is the restaurant, with its renowned champagne list and imaginative, often spectacular cuisine by chef Gilles Blandin. Among his specialties are artichokes with local goat cheese, and red mullet prepared with juice from roast veal. Ask for a table by the window, with a view of the church. (It's closed Sunday dinner and Monday.) Rooms are furnished with solid, traditional reproductions; wall hangings; and thick carpets. No. 21, with wood beams, is especially nice. ⊠ *31 av. du Luxembourg, 51460,* ☎ *03–26–69–30–30,* 🆉🆇 *03–26–69–30–26. 37 rooms. Restaurant, tennis court. AE, DC, MC, V. Closed Jan.–mid-Feb. and Nov.–Mar.*

THE NORTH, SOUTHERN PICARDY, AND CHAMPAGNE A TO Z

Arriving and Departing

By Car

Highway A1 from Paris passes close to Compiègne (N32 heads off to Noyon) and Arras (where A26 branches off to Calais) before reaching Lille. Journey time is about 100 minutes to Arras and 2½ hours to Lille. If you're arriving by car via the Channel Tunnel, disembark at Coquelles, near Calais, and join A26 heading to Arras (75 minutes) and Reims (2½ hours).

By Ferry

A few ferry and hovercraft companies travel between the northern region of France and the United Kingdom. Companies traveling between Calais and Dover include **Hoverspeed, P&O European Ferries, Seafrance,** and **Stena Line**. The sole operator of the route between Boulogne and Folkestone is **Hoverspeed**. For more information, *see* Ferry & Hovercraft Travel *in* the Gold Guide.

By Plane
If you are coming from the United States or most other destinations, count on arriving at Paris's Charles-de-Gaulle airport, handily placed on northbound A1 and the TGV line to Lille. If coming from London, consider the occasional direct flights from Heathrow to Lille-Lesquin and from Gatwick to Beauvais.

By Train
TGV (*Trains à Grande Vitesse*) speed from Paris (Gare du Nord) to Lille (256 km/160 mi) in just one hour. A separate TGV service links Paris (Gare du Nord) to Arras (50 minutes) and Dunkerque (2 hours). The Paris–Calais train chugs unhurriedly around the coast, taking nearly three hours to cover 300 km (186 mi) via Amiens. There is also frequent daily service from Paris (Gare du Nord) to Compiègne and Noyon, as well as to Laon (taking up to two leisurely hours to cover 140 km/87 mi). Regular trains cover the 175 km (109 mi) from Paris (Gare de l'Est) to Reims in 1½ hours, continuing to Charleville and Sedan. TGV, via the Channel Tunnel, link London to Lille in two hours; some stop at Calais.

Getting Around

By Car
A26 heads inland from Calais and St-Omer to Arras (where it intersects with A1), Laon, and Reims, which is directly linked to Paris by A4. N1 follows the railroad around the coast from Belgium and Dunkerque through Calais, Boulogne, Montreuil-sur-Mer, Amiens, and Beauvais to Paris. A new expressway, route A16, is under construction: It will follow the coast from Dunkerque to Abbeville before heading inland to Paris via Amiens and Beauvais. The Amiens-Abbeville section is now open, and, at press time, the Abbeville-Boulogne stretch was slated for completion.

By Train
It's easy to get around this region by train. Most sites can be reached by regular train service, except for the war cemeteries and the château in Pierrefonds. From Calais, the main line (Grande Ligne) follows the coast. The Lille–Calais regional line (T.E.R.) stops at St-Omer. From Calais, it follows the coast to Boulogne, Montreuil, Étaples (bus link to Le Touquet 6½ km/4 mi away), Abbeville, and Amiens, where a change is needed to reach Beauvais or Reims (via Laon). Trains leave Reims for Épernay, Châlons, and Charleville/Sedan.

Contacts and Resources

Car Rentals
Be aware that the Avis offices at the Calais car ferry and Hoverport terminals may not always be staffed. Look for instructions on how to use the red phones provided in these offices to reach the central office in the town of Calais, which will handle your rental.

Avis (✉ 36 pl. d'Armes, Calais, ☎ 03–21–34–66–50; ✉ Calais car ferry terminal, ☎ 03–21–96–47–65; ✉ Calais Hoverport, ☎ 03–21–96–66–52; ✉ cour de la Gare, Reims, ☎ 03–26–47–10–08). **Europcar** (✉ 32 pl. de la Gare, Lille, ☎ 03–20–06–18–80). **Hertz** (✉ 5 bd. d'Alsace-Lorraine, Amiens, ☎ 03–22–91–26–24; ✉ 10 bd. Daunou, Boulogne, ☎ 03–21–31–53–14).

Emergencies
Ambulance (☎ 15). **Hospitals:** Amiens (✉ 1 pl. Victor-Pauchet, ☎ 03–22–66–80–00); **Charleville-Mézières** (✉ 28 rue Aubilly, ☎ 03–24–56–70–70); **Compiègne** (✉ 8 av. Henri-Adnot, ☎ 03–44–23–60–00);

Lille (⊠ bd. de Belfort, ☎ 03–20–87–48–48); Reims (⊠ American Hospital, 47 rue Cognacq-Jay, ☎ 03–26–78–78–78).

Guided Tours

The **Lille Tourist Office** (⊠ pl. Rihour, ☎ 03–20–21–94–21) is a mine of information about companies that give bus tours of northern France. **Loisirs-Accueil Nord** (⊠ 6 rue Gauthier de Châtillon, Lille, ☎ 03–20–57–59–59) organizes bus trips to Boulogne and Flanders and can arrange fishing, walking, and beer-tasting tours. The **Service des Visites Guidées** in Boulogne's Château-Musée (⊠ rue Bernet, Boulogne-sur-Mer, ☎ 03–21–80–56–78) arranges trips to Boulogne's old town and port for groups of up to 30 people; the cost for two hours is 400 francs whether you are two or more.

Travel Agencies

Wagons-Lits (⊠ 1 rue Paul-Bert, Calais, ☎ 03–21–34–79–25; ⊠ 9 rue Faidherbe, Lille, ☎ 03–20–55–05–76).

Visitor Information

The principal regional tourist offices in Amiens, Lille, and Reims are good sources of information about the region. Other, smaller towns also have their own tourist offices: **Abbeville** (⊠ 1 pl. de l'Amiral-Courbet, ☎ 03–22–24–27–92). **Amiens** (⊠ 6 bis rue Dusevel, ☎ 03–22–71–60–50). **Arras** (⊠ pl. des Héros, ☎ 03–21–51–26–95). **Beauvais** (⊠ 1 rue Beauregard, ☎ 03–44–45–08–18). **Boulogne** (⊠ Forum Jean-Noël, quai de la Poste, ☎ 03–21–31–68–38). **Calais** (⊠ 12 bd. Clemenceau, ☎ 03–21–96–62–40). **Charleville-Mézières** (⊠ 22 pl. Ducale, ☎ 03–24–56–06–08). **Compiègne** (⊠ pl. de l'Hôtel-de-Ville, ☎ 03–44–40–01–00). **Laon** (⊠ pl. du Parvis, ☎ 03–23–20–28–62). **Le Touquet** (⊠ Palais de l'Europe, pl. de l'Hermitage, ☎ 03–21–06–72–00). **Lille** (⊠ pl. Rihour, ☎ 03–20–21–94–21). **Montreuil-sur-Mer** (⊠ 21 rue Carnot, ☎ 03–21–06–04–27). **Noyon** (⊠ pl. de l'Hôtel-de-Ville, ☎ 03–44–44–21–88). **Pierrefonds** (⊠ pl. de l'Hôtel-de-Ville, ☎ 03–44–42–81–44). **Reims** (⊠ 2 rue Guillaume-de-Machault, ☎ 03–26–77–45–25). **St-Omer** (⊠ Hôtel de Ville, pl. Foch, ☎ 03–21–98–08–51). **Sedan** (⊠ pl. du Château, ☎ 03–24–27–73–73).

8 Alsace-Lorraine and Franche-Comté

Nancy, Strasbourg, and the Jura

In Alsace-Lorraine you can wind along the Route du Vin through vineyards and villages among the Vosges foothills; see medieval, half-timber houses with a storybook air; visit churches that tell Joan of Arc's heroic story; and explore Strasbourg, which rivals Paris in culture, history, architecture, and haute cuisine. Then head southeast to the Franche-Comté, where you can find pretty gray-stone towns and go hiking in the Jura Mountains.

ALSACE AND LORRAINE ARE OFTEN linked, but the two regions have always had strong individual cultures, cuisines, and architectural styles. Only their recent past ties them together: In 1871, after France's defeat in the Franco-Prussian War, Alsace and the Moselle district of Lorraine, sutured together by Bismarck, were ceded to Germany as part of the spoils of war. The region was systematically (but unsuccessfully) Teutonized, and two generations grew up culturally torn—until 1919, when, after World War I, France reclaimed the territory.

Revised and updated by Nancy Coons

But no matter how forcefully the French tout its Frenchness, Alsace's German roots go deeper than the late 19th century, as one look at its storybook medieval architecture will prove. In fact, this strip of flatland and vine-covered hills squeezed between the Rhine and the Vosges mountains was called Prima Germania by the Romans and belonged to the fiercely German Holy Roman Empire for more than 700 years. A heavy German influence is still evident. Regional dialect is widespread; conversations between locals are incomprehensible even to most Frenchmen; town names look German; and the main daily paper, *Les Dernières Nouvelles d'Alsace*, is published in both languages. It seems ironic that France's famous national anthem, "La Marseillaise" (composed by Rouget de Lisle) was first sung in Strasbourg—as the battle song of the Rhine Army—in 1792.

Lorraine, west of the Vosges, creased by the serene Moselle Valley, evolved as decidedly less German than its neighbor. It served French and Burgundian lords as well as the Holy Roman Empire, coming into its own under the powerful dukes of Lorraine in the Middle Ages and the Renaissance.

In the Franche-Comté region to the south, the Jura Mountains form a natural border more than 160 km (100 mi) long between France and Switzerland and provide a winter-sports alternative to the Alps. Birthplace of Louis Pasteur and Victor Hugo and home to the celebrated aperitif Pernod, the Jura offers rugged gorges, forests, and vineyards dotted with pretty gray-stone towns.

Pleasures and Pastimes

Dining

Alsace cooking tends to be heavy: *choucroute* (sauerkraut served with ham and sausages) and *baeckoffe* (a hearty meat and potato casserole). But there is sophistication, too: foie gras accompanied by a *vendanges tardives* (late-harvested) glass of Gewürztraminer; and trout and chicken cooked in Riesling, the classic wine of Alsace. Snails and seasonal game are other favorites, as are Muenster cheese, salty *bretzel* loaves, and briochelike *kouglof* bread. Carp fried in bread crumbs is a specialty of southern Alsace. Lorraine, renowned for quiches, is also famous for its madeleines, *dragées* (almond candies), macaroons, and the lovely little *mirabelle,* a small yellow plum filled with heady, perfumed juice. Lorraine shares the Alsatian love of pastry and fruit tarts, served as often at 4 o'clock with coffee as for dessert after dinner. Restaurant prices tend to be lower in Lorraine than in Alsace, but only in German-influenced Alsace will you find *winstubs* (pronounced vin-stüb; cozy paneled inns serving wine and snacks or meals). Mountain-smoked hams and sausages and freshwater fish are menu mainstays in the Jura. Hard, flavorsome Comté and Beaufort are the choice local Gruyère-style cheeses, along with blue-striped Morbier, satiny Vacherin (often served melted in its vat), and Cancaillotte, its flavor milder than its reek. Fondue is a popular winter dish.

CATEGORY	COST*
$$$$	over 400 frs
$$$	250 frs–400 frs
$$	125 frs–250 frs
$	under 125 frs

*per person for a three-course meal, including tax (20.6%) and tip but not wine

Lodging

Accommodations are easier to find in Lorraine and the Jura than in Alsace, where advance reservations are essential in summer. Alsace is rich in *gîtes*—rented country houses or bed-and-breakfasts. Throughout Alsace, hotels are well scrubbed, with tile bathrooms, good mattresses, and geraniums spilling from every window sill. Lorraine tends to lack the Teutonic comforts of Alsace, subscribing to the more Latin laissez-faire school of innkeeping (concave mattresses, dusty bolsters, creaky floors).

CATEGORY	COST*
$$$$	over 800 frs
$$$	500 frs–800 frs
$$	250 frs–500 frs
$	under 250 frs

*All prices are for a standard double room for two, including tax (20.6%) and service charge.

Outdoor Activities and Sports

The region is ideal for a variety of outdoor activities: bicycling along the rivers of Lorraine, horseback riding through the forests, fishing in the angler's paradise of Franche-Comté, or hiking in the Vosges and Jura mountains.

Wine and Brew

Some of France's finest white wines are produced in Alsace—Riesling, Gewürztraminer, Pinot Gris, and Muscat, as well as light-red Pinot Noir. Alsace is also a major brewing area—cafés throughout France usually serve Kronenbourg and Kanterbräu blond beers, as well as the strong gold Fischer, brewed in Strasbourg. Lorraine is renowned for its fruit-based eaux-de-vie, made from cherries (kirsch) or plums (mirabelle and quetsche). In the Jura, look out for sweet *vin de Paille* (straw wine), made from late-harvest, sugar-heavy grapes dried on straw, and for sharp, dry *vin jaune* (yellow wine) made from savagnin grapes.

Exploring Alsace-Lorraine and Franche-Comté

Begin exploring this region to the west—nearest Paris—where the battlegrounds of Verdun provide a poignant introduction to Lorraine. Linger in the artistic city of Nancy and then spear east to Strasbourg (146 km/91 mi east), a city of such historic and cultural importance that it is well worth exploring in depth. From here, tour the rest of Alsace, following the photogenic Route du Vin (Wine Road) to Mulhouse. Finally, head south to Besançon and the spectacular scenery of Franche-Comté and the Jura.

Great Itineraries

You can cover most of the Alsace-Lorraine and Franche-Comté in about nine days. With five days, you can see the northern part of Lorraine, from Verdun to Nancy, and most of Alsace. Three days will give you just enough time to explore Alsace, including the cosmopolitan city of Strasbourg.

Lorraine

Alsace

TO METZ

N

TO NANCY

0 — 15 km
0 — 10 miles

Bitche

Hèming

Saverne **42**

Marmoutier **43**

Strasbourg **29** — **41**

Marlenheim

Rosheim

Boersch

Ottrott

Obernai **44**

Mont-Ste-Odile **45**

Barr **46**

Andlau **47**

Itterswiller

Dambach-la-Ville

Lubine

Provenchères

St-Dié

Châtenois

48

Sélestat **49**

Haut-Koenigsbourg **50**

Ribeauvillé **51**

Riquewihr **52**

Col du Bonhomme

Kaysersberg

Colmar **53**

Munster

Turckheim

Route des Crêtes

Route des Crêtes

Guebwiller

Ungersheim

Murbach **55** **54**

Bussang

Cernay

Thann

Mulhouse **56**

Ronchamp

Belfort

GERMANY

Rhine

Basel

Montbéliard

Pont-de-Roide

SWITZERLAND

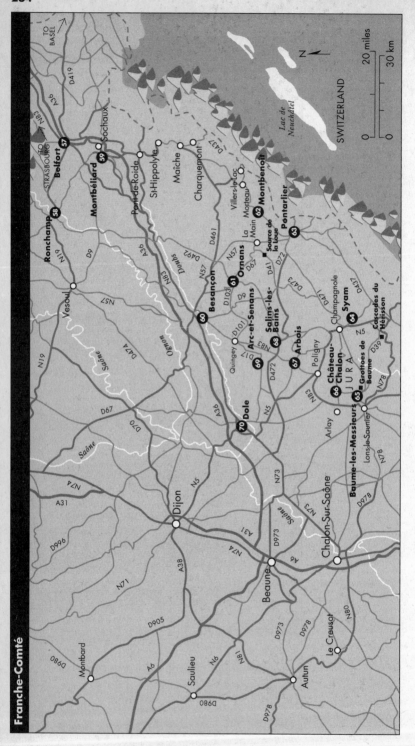

Franche-Comté

Numbers in the text correspond to numbers in the margin and on the Lorraine, Alsace, Franche-Comté, Nancy, and Strasbourg maps.

IF YOU HAVE 3 DAYS

Explore Alsace, beginning with a day and night in the delightful city of ⊞ **Strasbourg** ㉙–㊶. The next day start out early, cruising south along the Route du Vin to pretty **Obernai** ㊹; the charming villages of **Barr** ㊻, **Andlau** ㊼, and **Dambach-la-Ville** ㊽; and the dramatic castle in **Haut-Koenigsbourg** ㊿. Spend the night in impeccably medieval ⊞ **Riquewihr** ㊾. On day three visit **Ribeauvillé** ㊿ and one of the museum towns in **Colmar** ㊾ and **Mulhouse** ㊾.

IF YOU HAVE 6 DAYS

Coming from Paris, start at Lorraine's moving battlefields of **Verdun** ⑲; then head east to the cathedral city of ⊞ **Metz** ㉑. On day two, concentrate on ⊞ **Nancy** ①–⑱. Another option is to go to Nancy first and take day trips from there. Spend your third evening in ⊞ **Strasbourg** ㉙–㊶ and your fourth in or around ⊞ **Obernai** ㊹, visiting **Barr** ㊻ and environs en route. Take in bustling **Sélestat** ㊾, with its fine churches, on day five, along with **Haut-Koenigsbourg** ㊿ and **Ribeauvillé** ㊿, ending up in ⊞ **Riquewihr** ㊾. On day six head to **Colmar** ㊾ or **Mulhouse** ㊾.

IF YOU HAVE 9 DAYS

Begin in **Verdun** ⑲ and ⊞ **Metz** ㉑; then head south through Lorraine to the crumbling cathedral town of **Toul** ㉔ and Joan of Arc's birthplace at ⊞ **Domrémy-la-Pucelle** ㉖. Spend day three in ⊞ **Nancy** ①–⑱. On day four make ⊞ **Strasbourg** ㉙–㊶ your goal. The next day, follow the Route du Vin to **Obernai** ㊹, **Mont-Ste-Odile** ㊺, and ⊞ **Barr** ㊻. Continue south to **Sélestat** ㊾, **Haut-Koenigsbourg** ㊿, **Ribeauvillé** ㊿, and ⊞ **Riquewihr** ㊾. On day seven head to one of the following cities: ⊞ **Colmar** ㊾, to see its splendid Unterlinden Museum; **Mulhouse** ㊾, if you're interested in visiting museums of industry and technology; or ⊞ **Belfort** ㊼ for its monuments. Spend the night in Colmar or Belfort, or head that night to ⊞ **Besançon** ㊿. Explore this historic Franche-Comté town on the morning of day eight; then head to scenic riverside **Ornans** ㊶ and the waterfall at the Source de la Loue, before wheeling west to the wine town of ⊞ **Arbois** ㊸. Use Arbois as a base to explore the grandiose Jura scenery at the Reculée des Planches, the Cirque du Fer-à-Cheval, **Baume-les-Messieurs** ㊺, and the hilltop village of **Château-Châlon** ㊻. If time allows, end your tour at the "ideal village" of **Arc-et-Senans** ㊹.

When to Tour Alsace-Lorraine and Franche-Comté

June and September are warmest and sunniest. Many regional towns and villages, especially the wine villages of Alsace, stage summer festivals; note the spectacular pagan-inspired burning of the three pine trees at Thann (late June), the Flower Carnival at Sélestat (mid-August), and the wine fair at Colmar (first half of August). Some of the region's top sights, however—notably Haut-Koenigsbourg—can be besieged by tourists in July and August, so go early in the morning. Although Lorraine is a lusterless place in winter, the Vosges and Jura mountains make tentative attempts to challenge the Alps as skiing venues—plentiful snow cannot always be guaranteed—while Strasbourg pays tribute to Germanic tradition with a Christmas Fair.

NANCY

For architectural variety, few French cities match Nancy, which is in the heart of Lorraine (146 km/91 mi east of Paris). Medieval ornament, 18th-century grandeur, and Belle Époque fluidity rub shoulders in a town center that mingles commercial bustle with stately elegance. Its majesty derives from a long history as home to the powerful dukes of Lorraine, whose double-barred crosses figure prominently on statues and buildings. Never having fallen under the rule of the Holy Roman Empire or, more recently, the Germans, this Lorraine city retains an eminently Gallic charm.

The Historic Center

Concentrated northeast of the train station, this neighborhood—rich in architectural treasures as well as museums—includes the classical place Stanislas and the shuttered, medieval Vieille Ville (Old Town).

A Good Walk

Begin your walk at the symbolic heart of Nancy, **place Stanislas** ①. On the western corner is the **Musée des Beaux-Arts** ②, the fine arts museum. Cross place Stanislas diagonally and head south down rue Maurice Barrès to the Baroque **Cathédrale** ③. On leaving, turn left down rue St-Georges and right up rue des Dominicains, stopping to admire the elegant stonework on No. 57, the Maison des Adams, named for the sculptors who lived in (and decorated) the edifice in the 18th century.

Recross place Stanislas and go through the monumental Arc de Triomphe, entering into peaceful **place de la Carrière** ④. At the colonnaded Palais du Gouvernement, former home of the governors of Lorraine, turn right into the vast, formal city park known as **La Pépinière** ⑤. From the park's entrance at the foot of place de la Carrière, head straight under the arches and into the Vieille Ville. Dominating the square is the basilica of **St-Epvre** ⑥, clearly constructed to make up for the lack of a Gothic cathedral in Nancy.

Head immediately right up the picturesque Grande-Rue, with its antiques shops, bookstores, and artisanal bakeries behind brightly painted facades. On your right is the **Palais Ducal** ⑦. Here is the main branch of the Musée Historique Lorraine, a marvelous complex that includes the neighboring **Couvent des Cordeliers** ⑧, with its small, Gothic church and folk arts museum. At the end of Grande-Rue is the **Porte de la Craffe** ⑨, the last of Nancy's medieval fortifications.

TIMING
Depending on how much time you spend in the museums, this walk could take an hour or a whole day. Note that all the museums are closed on Tuesday.

Sights to See

❸ **Cathédrale.** This vast, frigid edifice was built in the 1740s in a ponderous Baroque style that has none of the ease and grace of the 18th-century place Stanislas. Its most notable interior feature is a murky 19th-century fresco in the dome. The **Trésor** (Treasury) contains minute 10th-century splendors in carved ivory and gold. ✉ *pl. Stanislas.*

★ ❽ **Couvent des Cordeliers** (Convent of the Franciscans, who were known as Cordeliers until the revolution). Housed in this church complex just up the street from the Palais Ducal is the quirky, appealing **Musée des Arts et Traditions Populaires** (Museum of Folk Arts and Traditions). It re-creates how local people lived in pre-industrial times, in a series of evocative rural interiors. Craftsmen's tools, colorful crockery, stark stone fireplaces, and dark waxed-oak furniture trim the tableau-like settings. The dukes of Lorraine are buried in the crypt of the adjoining **Église des Cordeliers,** a Flamboyant Gothic church; the *gisant* (reclining statue) of Philippa de Gueldra, second wife of René II, is a moving example of Renaissance portraiture, executed in limestone in flowing detail. The octagonal Ducal Chapel was begun in 1607 in the classical style, modeled on the Medici Chapel in Florence. ⊠ *66 Grande-Rue*, ☎ *03–83–32–18–74.* ⊡ *20 frs.* ☉ *May–Sept., Wed.–Mon. 10–6; Oct.–Apr., Wed.–Mon. 10–noon and 2–5, Sun. 10–noon and 2–6.*

★ ❷ **Musée des Beaux-Arts** (Fine Arts Museum). Housed in this splendid building, which now spills over into an impressive new wing, are art treasures of merit equal to the noble white Héré facade. You'll find 19th- and 20th-century paintings by Monet, Manet, Utrillo, and Modigliani; a hefty *Transfiguration* by Rubens; a Caravaggio *Annunciation* and a wealth of old masters from the Italian, Dutch, Flemish, and French schools; and impressive glassworks by Nancy-native Antonin and succeeding generations of his family. ⊠ *pl. Stanislas,* ☎ *03–83–85–30–72.* ⊡ *20 frs.* ☉ *Mon. 2–6, Wed.–Sun. 10:30–6.*

❼ **Palais Ducal** (Ducal Palace). This palace was built in the 13th century and completely restored at the end of the 15th century and again after a fire at the end of the 19th century. The main entrance to the palace, and the **Musée Historique Lorrain** (Lorraine History Museum), which it now houses, is 80 yards down the street from the spectacularly flamboyant Renaissance portal. A spiral stone staircase leads up to the palace's most impressive room, the **Galerie des Cerfs** (Stags Gallery). Exhibits here (including pictures, armor, and books) recapture the Renaissance mood of the 16th and 17th centuries—one of elegance and merrymaking, though not devoid of stern morality: An elaborate series of huge tapestries, *La Condemnation du Banquet* (Condemnation of the Banquet), expounds on the evils of drink and gluttony. Exhibits feature Stanislas and his court, including "his" oft-portrayed dwarf; *Nancy in the Revolution*; and works of Lorraine native sons, including a collection of Jacques Callot engravings and a handful of Georges de La Tours.

✉ *64 Grande-Rue,* ☎ *03–83–32–18–74.* 🎫 *20 frs.* 🕐 *May–Sept., Wed.–Mon. 10–6; Oct.–Apr., Wed.–Mon. 10–noon and 2–5.*

❺ **La Pépinière.** This lovely, landscaped city park contains labeled ancient trees, a rose garden, playgrounds, a carousel, and a small zoo. ✉ *Entrance off pl. de la Carrière.*

❹ **Place de la Carrière.** Lined with pollards and handsome 18th-century mansions (another successful collaboration between Stanislas and Héré), this elegant rectangle leads from place Stanislas to the colonnaded facade of the **Palais du Gouvernement** (Government Palace), former home of the governors of Lorraine.

★ ❶ **Place Stanislas.** The severe, gleaming-white classical facades of this imposing square are given a touch of rococo jollity by fancifully wrought gilt-iron railings. The square is named for Stanislas Leszczynski, twice dethroned as King of Poland but offered the throne of Lorraine by Louis XV (his son-in-law) in 1736. Stanislas left a legacy of spectacular buildings, undertaken between 1751 and 1760 by architect Emmanuel Héré and ironwork genius Jean Lamour. The sculpture of Stanislas that dominates the square went up in the 1830s when the square was named after him. Framing the exit is the **Arc de Triomphe** (Triumphal Arch), erected in the 1750s to honor Louis XV. The facade features the gods of war and the gods of peace; Louis's portrait is here.

❾ **Porte de la Craffe.** The only remains of Nancy's medieval fortifications looms at one end of the Grande-Rue. Built in the 14th and 15th centuries, this arch served as a prison through the Revolution. The thistle and cross are symbols of Lorraine.

❻ **St-Epvre.** A 275-ft spire towers over this splendid neo-Gothic church rebuilt in the 1860s. Most of the 2,800 square yards of stained glass were created by the Geyling workshop in Vienna; the chandeliers were made in Liège, Belgium; many carvings are the work of Margraff of Munich; the heaviest of the eight bells was cast in Budapest; and the organ, though manufactured by Merklin of Paris, was inaugurated in 1869 by Austrian composer Anton Bruckner. ✉ *pl. de la Carrière.*

Art Nouveau Nancy

Nancy was a principal source of the revolution in decorative arts that produced Art Nouveau and *Jugendstil* (the German version of Art Nouveau). Inspired and coordinated by the glass master Émile Gallé, the local movement, formalized in 1901 as L'École de Nancy, nurtured the floral *pâte de verre* (literally, glass dough) works of Antonin Daum and Gallé; the Tiffanesque stained-glass windows of Jacques Gruber; the fluid furniture of Louis Majorelle; and the sinuous architecture of Lucien Weissenburger, Émile André, and Eugène Vallin. Thanks to these artists, Nancy's downtown architecture flows and flowers above the sidewalks like a living garden.

A Good Walk

The **Musée de l'École de Nancy** ⑩ is the best place to immerse yourself in the fanciful style that crept into interiors and exteriors throughout Nancy. To get to the museum from the busy shopping street rue St-Jean (just up rue des Dominicains from place Stanislas), take Bus 5 or 25 uphill; get off at place Pain-Levée. From the museum, turn left down rue du Sergent Blandan and walk about four blocks to **No. 1 rue Louis-Majorelle** ⑪. Cut east to place de la Commanderie and head up **avenue Foch** ⑫ to admire the colorful structures at No. 71, No. 69, and No. 41. Hike over the viaduct Kennedy and the *gare* (train station), turn left past the department store Printemps, and follow rue Mazagran to the **Brasserie l'Excelsior** ⑬. Turn right toward **No. 40 rue Henri-Poincaré** ⑭. Turn right and walk past **No. 9 rue Chanzy** ⑮ (now the Banque Nationale de Paris). Head left to find **No. 2 rue Bénit** ⑯ with its ornate metal structure. Head south to rue St-Jean; at the corner of **rue Raugraff** ⑰ are two bay windows, remnants of stores that were once here. Continue down rue St-Jean and turn right to find **Nos. 42–44 rue St-Dizier** ⑱. Many more Art Nouveau addresses are scattered throughout the city; you can get a detailed map at the tourist office.

TIMING

Allow a full morning to linger in the Musée de l'École de Nancy and then, over an hour and a half or so, wander back circuitously toward the Vieille Ville, stopping to admire Art Nouveau masterworks along the way.

Sights to See

⑫ **Avenue Foch.** This busy boulevard lined with solid mansions was built for Nancy's affluent 19th-century middle class. At No. 69, the occasional pinnacle suggests Gothic influence on a house built in 1902 by Émile André, who designed the neighboring No. 71 two years later. No. 41, built by Paul Charbonnier in 1905, bears ironwork by Majorelle.

⑬ **Brasserie l'Excelsior.** This bustling brasserie has a severely rhythmic facade that is invitingly illuminated at night. The popular restaurant continues to evoke the turn of the century. ✉ *5 rue Mazagran.*

★ ⑩ **Musée de l'École de Nancy** (The School of Nancy Museum). The only museum in France devoted to Art Nouveau is housed in an airy, turn-of-the-century garden–town house. It was built by Eugène Corbin, an early patron of the School of Nancy. There isn't a straight line in the house; pianos ooze, bedsteads undulate; the wood itself, hard and burnished as it is, seems to have melted and re-formed. ✉ *36 rue du Sergent-Blandon,* ☎ *03–83–40–14–86.* ✉ *20 frs, 30 frs for joint ticket with Musée des Beaux-Arts (☞ above).* ☉ *Mon. 2–6, Wed.–Sun. 10:30–6.*

⑪ **No. 1 rue Louis-Majorelle.** This villa was built in 1902 by Paris architect Henri Sauvage for Majorelle himself. Sinuous metal supports seem to sneak up on the unsuspecting balcony like swaying cobras, and there are two grand windows by Gruber: one lighting the staircase (visible from the street), and the other the dining room on the south side of the villa (peek around from the garden side).

⑯ **No. 2 rue Bénit.** This elaborately worked metal exoskeleton, the first in Nancy (1901), is as functional as it is beautiful. The fluid decoration reminds you of the building's past as a seed supply store. Windows were worked by Gruber; the builders were Henry-Barthélemy Gutton (architect) and Henri Gutton (engineer); Victor Schertzer conceived the metal frame.

⑮ **No. 9 rue Chanzy.** Designed by architect Émile André, this lovely structure—now a bank—can be visited during business hours to view the cabinetry of Majorelle, decor of Paul Charbonnier, and stained-glass windows of Gruber.

⑭ **No. 40 rue Henri-Poincaré.** The Lorraine thistle and brasserie hops weave through this undulating exterior, designed by architects Émile Toussaint and Louis Marchal. Victor Schertzer conceived this metal structure in 1908, after the success of No. 2 rue Bénit. Gruber's windows are enhanced by the curving metalwork of Majorelle.

⑱ **Nos. 42–44 rue St-Dizier.** Eugène Vallin and Georges Biet left their mark on this graceful 1903 bank structure; it's open weekdays 8:30–5:30.

⑰ Rue Raugraff. Once there were two stores here, built in 1901. The bay windows are the last vestiges of the work of Charles Vallin, Émile André, and Eugène Vallin. ⊠ *At the corner of rue St-Jean.*

Dining and Lodging

$$$ ✕ **Capucin Gourmand.** Art Nouveau decor and faultless service set the
★ tone at one of Nancy's finest restaurants. Chef Gérard Veissière's menu includes such regional specialties as foie gras, game in casserole, and classic quiche Lorraine. Desserts are superb, the Toul wines admirable. ⊠ *31 rue Gambetta,* ☎ *03–83–35–26–98. Reservations essential. Jacket and tie. V. Closed Sun.–Mon. and Aug.*

$$ ✕ **Comptoir du Petit Gastrolâtre.** Under the direction of chef Patrick Tanesy, this pleasant, low-key bistro serves sophisticated regional cooking. Recommended dishes include baeckoffe with foie gras, pike roasted with garlic, a delectable fricassee of snails, and gingerbread. ⊠ *1 pl. Vaudemont,* ☎ *03–83–35–51–94. MC, V. Closed Sun.–Mon.*

$ ✕ **Au P'tit Cuny.** From the Musée des Arts et Traditions Populaires,
★ cross the street to sink your teeth into authentic Lorraine cuisine in the form of choucroute, *tête de veau* (veal head), or tangy veal *tourte* (pie). The beams and collected farm tools comfort the neighborhood's *intellos* (intellectuals) and *bohèmes* (bohemians). ⊠ *97–99 Grande-Rue,* ☎ *03–83–32–85–94. MC, V. Closed Sun.–Mon.*

$$$ 🏨 **Grand Hôtel de la Reine.** This hotel is every bit as swanky as place
★ Stanislas on which it stands; the magnificent 18th-century building is officially classified as a historic monument. Rooms are decorated in a suitably grand Louis XV style; the most luxurious look out onto the square. The costly restaurant, Le Stanislas, serves classic-nouvelle cuisine; the prix-fixe weekday lunch menus are the best value. ⊠ *2 pl. Stanislas, 54000,* ☎ *03–83–35–03–01,* FAX *03–83–32–86–04. 48 rooms. Restaurant, bar. AE, DC, MC, V.*

$ 🏨 **Carnot.** This somewhat generic downtown hotel, with 1950s-style comforts and mostly tiny rooms, is handy to cours Léopold parking and backs up on the old town. Corner rooms are sizable, back rooms quiet. ⊠ *4 cours Léopold, 54000,* ☎ *03–83–36–59–58,* FAX *03–83–37–00–19. 28 rooms. Breakfast room. MC, V.*

$ 🏨 **De Guise.** Deep in the shuttered old town, this hotel is in a formerly noble mansion with a magnificent stone-floor entry. Unfortunately, the dramatic sweeping stairs wind up to a standard, creaky renovation job. Breakfast on the once-grand main floor and an excellent location make this a good choice for bargain-hunting romantics. ⊠ *18 rue de Guise, 54000,* ☎ *03–83–32–24–68,* FAX *03–83–35–75–63. 42 rooms. MC, V. Closed 2 wks in Dec. and Aug.*

Nightlife and the Arts

Nancy's **Orchestre Symphonique et Lyrique** (⊠ 1 rue Ste-Catherine, ☎ 03–83–85–30–65) is a highly rated classical orchestra.

The **Majéstic** (⊠ 22 rue St-Dizier, ☎ 03–83–32–83–42) has a bar, dance floor, and occasional live music. **Métro** (⊠ 1 rue du Général-Hoche, ☎ 03–83–40–25–13) is a popular dance club. **La Place** (⊠ 9 pl. Stanislas, ☎ 03–83–35–24–14) attracts a young upscale crowd that comes to dance.

Shopping

Daum (⊠ 17 rue des Cristalleries, ☎ 03–83–30–80–20) sells deluxe crystal and examples of the city's traditional Art Nouveau pâte de verre. **Librairie Lorraine** (⊠ 93 Grande-Rue, ☎ 03–83–36–79–52), across from the Musée des Arts et Traditions, is an excellent bookstore devoted entirely to Lorraine history and culture.

LORRAINE

Although the present-day decline of the steel and coal industries and the miseries of its small farmers have left parts of Lorraine tarnished and neglected—some might say unspoiled—its rolling countryside is dotted with orchards and crumbling stucco villages, abbeys, fortresses, and historic towns. It is the home of Baccarat and St-Louis crystal and was once a great faience center; it is also the birthplace of Joan of Arc, Gregorian chant, and Art Nouveau. Majestic Nancy (☞ *above*) is at its heart. Throughout Lorraine you'll find the statue of the region's patron saint, St. Nicholas—old Saint Nick himself—with three children in a *saloir,* or saltbox. Every December 6, Lorraine schoolchildren reenact the legend: A greedy butcher slaughtered and salted down three children as hams, but when St. Nicholas dropped by his place for a meal, he discovered the deed and brought them back to life.

Verdun

⑲ *66 km (41 mi) west of Metz, 93 km (58 mi) northwest of Nancy, 262 km (164 mi) east of Paris.*

A key strategic site along the Meuse Valley, Verdun is famous, above all, for the 18-month battle between the French and the Germans in World War I. It left more than 700,000 dead and nine villages wiped off the map. Both sides fought with suicidal fury, yet no significant ground was gained or lost. To this day, the scenes of battle are scarred by bomb craters, stunted vegetation, and thousands of unexploded mines and shells, rendering the area permanently uninhabitable.

Verdun's leading World War I memorial is at **Douaumont,** 10 km (6 mi) north. The bizarre, evocative structure—a little like a cross, a lot like a bomb—rears up over an endless sea of graves, its ground-level windows revealing undignified heaps of human bones harvested from the killing fields. Climb to the top of the tower (6 francs) for a view of the cemetery. In the basement a film dwells on the agony of the futile butchery. ☎ 03–29–84–54–81. ☞ *Film 15 frs.* ⊙ *Mar.–Apr. and Oct., daily 9–noon and 2–5:30; Nov., daily 9–noon and 2–5; May–June, daily 9–6; July–Aug., daily 9–6:30; Sept., daily 9–noon and 2–6.*

The square, modern **Mémorial de Verdun** (Verdun Memorial), in the town of Fleury-devant-Douaumont, is a World War I museum with emotionally charged texts and video commentary, as well as uniforms, weapons, and the artwork of soldiers (Art Nouveau vases hammered from artillery shells). ☎ 03–29–84–35–34. ☞ *20 frs.* ⊙ *Mid-Apr.–Dec., daily 9–6; Feb.–mid-Apr., daily 9–noon and 2–5:30.*

OFF THE BEATEN PATH

MONTMÉDY – When Louis XVI was arrested at Varennes in 1791, he was fleeing by coach toward the refuge of Montmédy, 48 km (30 mi) north of Verdun. The mighty hilltop citadel was redesigned and reinforced by the great military architect Vauban. His signature star-shape fortifications thrust out over the valley, and drivers still enter the tiny upper village over a drawbridge. Once inside, there's not much to see but a sleepy, undeveloped town, but the spectacular approach is worth the trip.

Dining and Lodging

$$$ ✕ 🏨 **Coq Hardi.** This large, steep-roofed, half-timber hotel, built in 1827 on the banks of the Meuse, is furnished in solid regional style. A familylike welcome pervades here and in the large restaurant, where traditional cuisine dominates without stuffiness: foie gras on quail eggs, suckling pig larded with truffles, and strawberry tart Tatin (upside-down, caramelized tart). ⊠ *8 av. de la Victoire, 55100,* ☎ *03–29–86–36–36,* 🆀 *03–29–86–09–21. 35 rooms. Restaurant. AE, DC, MC, V.*

Avioth

❷⓿ *56 km (35 mi) north of Verdun, 149 km (92 mi) northwest of Nancy, 8 km (5 mi) north of Montmédy.*

The tiny village of Avioth is most famous for its sumptuous **Basilique d'Avioth** (Avioth Basilica). A mysterious statue of the Virgin was discovered by shepherds on a nearby hillside in the 11th century. After the statue was found, a number of miraculous cures took place, and the faithful poured in for the next 300 years. This explains the basilica's surprising richness of workmanship, evolving and being embellished from the dawn to the peak of the elaborate Flamboyant Gothic style (from the late 13th to the early 15th century). The interior contains a 14th-century altar and medieval frescoes on the choir vaults. The *recevresse,* a free-standing Flamboyant tower in front of the main entrance, once held the miraculous statue and received the offerings of pilgrims.

Metz

★ **❷⓵** *66 km (41 mi) east of Verdun, 53 km (33 mi) north of Nancy, 160 km (100 mi) northwest of Strasbourg.*

Despite its industrial background, Metz, the capital of the Moselle region, is officially classed as one of France's greenest cities: Parks, gardens, and leafy squares abound. At its heart you'll find one of the finest Gothic cathedrals in France.

At 137 ft from floor to roof, the **Cathédrale St-Étienne** is one of France's highest; and, thanks to nearly 1½ acres of window space, one of the lightest. The narrow 13th- to 14th-century nave channels the eye toward the dramatically raised 16th-century choir, whose walls have given way to huge sheets of richly colored, gemlike glass by masters old and modern, including artist Marc Chagall (1887–1985). The oldest windows—on the right rear wall of the transepts, over the modern organ—date from the 12th century and, in their dark, mosaiclike simplicity, are a stark contrast to the ethereal new stained glass. A pair of symmetrical 290-ft towers flank the nave, marking the division between the two churches merged to form the cathedral. The tower, with a fussy 15th-century pinnacle, houses **Dame Mutte,** an enormous bell cast in 1605 and tolled on momentous occasions. The **Grand Portal** beneath the large rose window was reconstructed by the Germans at the turn of the century; the statues of the prophets include, on the right, *Daniel,* sculpted to resemble Kaiser Wilhelm II (his unmistakable upturned mustachio was shaved off in 1940). ⊠ *pl. des Armes.*

The **Musée d'Art et d'Histoire** (Museum of Art and History), in a 17th-century former convent, has a wide-ranging collection of French and German paintings from the 18th century on; military arms and uniforms; and religious works of art stored in the **Grenier de Chèvremont,** a granary built in 1457. Best by far are the stelae, statuary, jewelry, arms, clothing, and plumbing evoking the city's Gallo-Roman and Merovingian past. Not to be missed include the ethereal reconstruction of the ancient chapel of St-Pierre-aux-Nonnains (☞ *below*). Unfortunately, the museum's Escherlike labyrinth of stairways excludes wheelchairs, strollers, and poor navigators. ⊠ *2 rue du Haut-Poirier,* ☎ *03–87–75–10–18.* ⊡ *20 frs.* ⊘ *Daily 10–noon and 2–5.*

The small, heavily restored church of **St-Pierre-aux-Nonnains** has round stones and rows of red bricks that are thought to date from the 4th century, predating Attila the Hun's sacking of Metz; thus, Metz claims the oldest church in France. The best of the rare Merovingian ornaments salvaged from the 6th-century version of the chapel are displayed in a full reproduction in the Museum of Art and History (☞ *above*), demonstrating as chronologies never can how early Christian times mixed the culture and tastes of Celts, Romans, and Gauls. ⊠ *rue Poncelet.*

Ⓒ **Walibi Schtroumpf,** a theme park north of Metz, has 30 attractions featuring the cuddly blue dwarfs known in English as Smurfs. A sizable roller coaster and water rides need no translation. ⊠ *Voie Romaine, Maizières-les-Metz (just off A31, 10 km/6 mi north of Metz),* ☎ *03–87–51–73–90.* ⊡ *105 frs.* ⊘ *Mid-Apr.–May 1, daily 10–6; May and Sept., Wed. and weekends 10–6; June, daily 10–6; July–Aug., daily 10–7.*

Dining and Lodging

$$$ ✕ **La Dinanderie.** Chef Claude Piergiorgi serves inventive cuisine—scallops with delicate bacon threads, lamb crisped in honey and thyme, sugar-frosted oranges—with dependable flair. The intimate restaurant, attractively refurbished in pastels, lies across the Moselle, a 10-minute hike from the cathedral. ⊠ *2 rue de Paris,* ☎ *03–87–30–14–40. AE, MC, V. Closed Sun.–Mon.*

$$ ✕ **À la Ville de Lyon.** Just below the cathedral in a venerable vaulted setting, this charming eatery serves solid cuisine that is beginning to venture beyond the standards. Dishes range from tournedos Rossini to roast monkfish with lemon grass. Rely on the encyclopedic knowledge of the young sommelier to choose from the fabulous wine list (30,000 bottles in stock). ⊠ *7 rue des Piques,* ☎ *03–87–36–07–01. AE, DC, MC, V. Closed Mon. and most of Aug. No dinner Sun.*

$$ ✕ **La Baraka.** Below the cathedral is this classic French-Moroccan couscous spot with a lively, unstuffy ambience. It offers a fiery but digestible break from French cooking. If you burned out on couscous in Paris, venture toward *méchoui* (lamb shish kebab) or *tajine,* a meat stew simmered in terra-cotta. ⊠ *24 pl. de Chambre,* ☎ *03–87–36–33–92. MC, V. Closed Wed.*

$ ✕ **La Dauphiné.** Stop at this unpretentious barrel-vaulted tearoom to have *tourte Lorraine* (meat pie), the plat du jour with delicious gratin potatoes, and a generous slice of fruit tart. Locals claim permanent lunch stations, but there's room upstairs, too. ⊠ *8 rue du Chanoine-Collin,* ☎ *03–87–36–03–04. MC, V. Closed Tues.*

$ ✕ **Le Grand Café.** Catercorner from the cathedral entrance, this former pinball dive has metamorphosed into a chic Belle Époque brasserie with tables spilling onto place d'Armes. Lorraine specialties include *cochon de lait* (suckling pig), local lamb and rabbit, and succulent lard-roasted potatoes. ⊠ *14 pl. d'Armes,* ☎ *03–87–75–35–09. MC, V.*

$$–$$$ ▦ **Royal Bleu Marine.** This fully modernized hotel, taken over and buffed
★ up by the Campanile chain, occupies a sumptuous Belle Époque building not far from the train station. Rooms come in a choice of styles (old-fashioned luxury versus simpler modernity). All are soundproof.

⊠ *23 av. Foch, 57011,* ☎ *03–87–66–81–11,* FAX *03–87–56–13–16.
76 rooms. Restaurant, bar, sauna, exercise room. AE, DC, MC, V.*

Pont-à-Mousson

㉒ *27 km (17 mi) south of Metz on N57, 27 km (17 mi) northwest of Nancy.*

The name Pont-à-Mousson may ring a bell if you've strolled a few French streets: It adorns most of the manhole covers in France, all made in the town's foundries along the Moselle river. The town's ornate 15th-century church of **St-Martin** has a host of gravity-defying sculptures and gargoyles. The Baroque **Abbaye des Prémontrés,** begun in 1608, displays sharp contrast between its serene, classical exterior and its flamboyant interior. East of the town, a steep climb leads to the summit of the **Butte de Mousson,** a feudal stronghold where a ruined chapel and fortification walls frame spectacular views over the Moselle Valley.

St-Nicolas-de-Port

㉓ *20 km (12 mi) southeast of Nancy.*

The small industrial town of St-Nicolas-de-Port is saved from mediocrity by its colossal basilica. Legend has it that a finger of St. Nicholas was brought to the town during the 11th-century Crusades. Holding such a priceless relic, the **Basilique de St-Nicolas-de-Port** (1495–1555) was rapidly besieged by pilgrims (including Joan of Arc, who came to ask St. Nicolas's blessings on her famous journey to Orléans). The simplified column capitals and elaborate rib vaulting are shining examples of Flamboyant Gothic enjoying a final fling before the gathering impetus of the Renaissance, as are the 280-ft onion-dome towers, almost symmetrical but, as was the Gothic wont, not quite. Inside, the slender, freestanding 90-ft pillars in the transept are the highest in France.

Toul

㉔ *23 km (14 mi) west of Nancy.*

The old town of Toul, nestled behind mossy, star-shape ramparts, has been a bishopric since AD 365, and merited visits from the Frankish king Clovis to study the Christian faith; from Charlemagne in passing; and from a young, premilitary Joan of Arc, who was sued in the Toul court for breach of promise when she threw over a beau for the voice of God. In 1700, under Louis XIV, the military engineer Vauban built the thrusting ramparts around the town.

The ramshackle streets of central Toul haven't changed much for centuries—not since the embroidered, twin-tower facade, a Flamboyant Gothic masterpiece, was woven onto the **Cathédrale St-Étienne** in the second half of the 15th century. The cathedral's interior, begun in 1204, is long (321 ft), airy (105 ft high), and more restrained than its exuberant facade. On one side of the cathedral are the 14th-century **cloisters,** and on the other a pleasant **garden** behind the **Hôtel de Ville** (Town Hall), built in 1740 as the Bishop's Palace. ☉ *Summer, daily 9–6; winter, daily 9–dark.*

The **Musée Municipal** (Town Museum), housed in a former medieval hospital, has a well- *Salle des Malades* (Patients' Ward) dating from the 13th century. Archaeological finds, ceramics, tapestries, and medieval sculpture are on display. ⊠ *25 rue Gouvion-St-Cyr,* ☎ *03–83–64–13–38.* 🎫 *17 frs.* ☉ *Apr.–Oct., Wed.–Mon. 10–noon and 2–6; Nov.–Mar., Wed.–Mon. 2–6.*

The choir of the attractive church of **St-Gengoult** has beautifully 13th-century stained-glass windows. Unfortunately, because of repeated vandalism, it is closed to the public, although attending Sunday Mass (10:30 AM) will reward the devout. The adjoining Flamboyant Gothic cloisters, later than those of the cathedral but equally picturesque, are also inaccessible to weekday visitors. ⊠ *pl. du Marché.*

Dining

$$$ ✕ **Le Dauphin.** The large, flower-laden dining room was once a G.I. canteen, and the setting (in an industrial area 5 km/3 mi from town) has little of the ambience of historic Toul. Yet Christophe Vohmann entices with cooking of great finesse, tapping local farms and forests, as well as the seafood market, to make such dishes as langoustines with radish and ginger, and soufflé of dried mirabelles. Prices à la carte run quickly out of hand. ⊠ *rte. de Villey-St-Étienne,* ☎ *03–83–43–13–46. Reservations essential. Jacket and tie. AE, MC, V. Closed Mon. No dinner Sun.*

Vaucouleurs

㉕ *24 km (15 mi) southwest of Toul on D960.*

Below the medieval walls and ruins of Robert de Baudricourt's ancient château in the modest market town of Vaucouleurs, you can see the Porte de France, through which Joan of Arc led her armed soldiers to Orléans. The barefoot Maid spent a year within these walls, first wheedling an audience with Baudricourt, then, having convinced him of her mission, learning to ride and swordfight.

Dining and Lodging

$ ✕🏠 **De la Poste.** On the main street, this simple place has quiet rooms over a pleasant, intimate restaurant. The good regional menu is served noon and night, except Sunday night and Monday. A friendly family cooks, serves the meals, and checks you in. ⊠ *12 av. André Maginot, 55140,* ☎ *03–29–89–40–01,* FAX *03–29–89–40–93. 9 rooms. Restaurant. MC, V. Closed end Dec.–Jan.*

Domrémy-la-Pucelle

㉖ *40 km (25 mi) southwest of Toul, 19 km (12 mi) south of Vaucouleurs.*

Joan of Arc was born in a stone hut in Domrémy-la-Pucelle. You can see it, as well as the church where she was baptized, the figure of Ste-Marguerite she prayed before, and the hillside where she tended sheep and first heard voices telling her to take up arms and save France from the English.

The humble stone-and-stucco **Maison Natale Jeanne d'Arc** (Joan of Arc Birthplace)—an irregular, slope-roofed former cowshed—has been with some reverence, and an attached museum retells her story. After she heard the voices, Joan walked 19 km (12 mi) to Vaucouleurs (☞ *above*). Dressed and mounted like a man, she led her forces to lift the siege of Orléans, defeated the English, and escorted the unseated Charles VII to Reims, to be crowned king of France. Military missions after Orléans failed—including an attempt to retake Paris—and she was captured at Compiègne. The English turned her over to the Church, which sent her to be tried by the Inquisition for witchcraft and heresy. She was convicted, excommunicated, and burned at the stake in Rouen (☞ Chapter 6). ⊠ *2 rue de la Basilique,* ☎ *03–29–06–95–86.* 🎫 6 *frs.* ☉ *Apr.–Sept., daily 9–12:30 and 2–7; Oct.–Mar., Wed.–Mon. 9:30–noon and 2–5.*

The ornate, late-19th-century **Basilique du Bois-Chenu** (Aged-Forest Basilica), a pleasant walk up a country road from Joan of Arc's birthplace, has enormous painted panels telling her story in glowing Pre-Raphaelite tones. Here you can see Joan's budding role as symbol of French nationalist pride, passionately illustrated in the shadow of Prussian defeat.

Lodging

$ 🏨 **Jeanne d'Arc.** Stay next door to Joan of Arc's childhood church and wake to the bells that summoned her voices. Accommodations are considerably less evocative, in jazzy '60s tile and paneling, but bathrooms are spotless and breakfasts (in-room only) generous. ⊠ *1 rue Principale, 88630,* ☎ *03–29–06–96–06. 12 rooms. No credit cards. Closed mid-Nov.–Mar.*

Grand

㉗ *15 km (9 mi) northwest of Domrémy-la-Pucelle: From Domrémy, follow signs down country roads west toward Grand.*

In the tiny, enigmatic architectural treasure of Grand, a spring developed into a center for the worship of the Gallo-Roman sun god Apollo-Grannus. It was important enough to draw the Roman emperors Caracalla and Constantine. At the entry to the village, the remains of a large **amphitheater** that once seated 20,000 are being reconstructed as an outdoor theatre; displays illustrate its history. In a tiny museum in the upper village there is a marvelously expressive floor **mosaic** with realistic animal details. Surrounding the mosaic are scraps of exotic stone and relics transported from across two continents, bearing witness to this isolated village's opulent past. ☎ *03–29–06–63–43.* 🎫 *Amphitheater and mosaic 20 frs.* ⊙ *Apr.–Sept., daily 9–noon and 2–7; Oct.–Mar., daily 10–noon and 2–5.*

Épinal

㉘ *84 km (53 mi) southeast of Domrémy, 69 km (43 mi) south of Nancy, 97 km (61 mi) north of Belfort.*

A printing center since 1735, Épinal, on the Moselle River at the feet of the Vosges, is famous throughout France for boldly colored prints, popular illustrations, and hand-colored stencils. **L'Imagerie Pellerin,** the artisanal workshop, has a slide show tracing the history of local printing. ⊠ *42 bis quai de Dogneville,* ☎ *03–29–34–21–87.* 🎫 *Free; guided tour with slide show 25 frs.* ⊙ *Tours at 10, 11, 3, and 4:30 for 45 mins. Gallery-salesroom open between tours Mon.–Sat. 8:30–noon and 2–6:30, Sun. 2–6:30.*

On an island in the Moselle in the center of Épinal, the spectacular **Musée Départemental d'Art Ancien et Contemporain** (Museum of Ancient and Contemporary Art) is in a renovated 17th-century hospital, whose classical traces are still visible under a dramatic barrel-vaulted skylight. It contains France's fourth largest collection of contemporary art, as well as Gallo-Roman artifacts; rural tools and local faience; and old masters, including some fine drawings and watercolors by Fragonard and Boucher. ⊠ *1 pl. Lagarde,* ☎ *03–29–82–20–33.* 🎫 *30 frs.* ⊙ *Apr.–Sept., Wed.–Mon. 10–noon and 2–6; Oct.–Mar., Wed.–Mon. 10–noon and 2–5.*

Épinal's small but bustling old town is anchored by the lovely old **Basilique St-Maurice,** a low gray-stone basilica blending Romanesque and Gothic styles. Its deep 15th-century entry porch prepares you for passing into dark and holy space—a detail of Gothic architecture not to be re-explored until Frank Lloyd Wright. ✉ *pl. St-Goëry,* ☎ *03–29–82–58–36.*

STRASBOURG

Although centered in the heart of Alsace (490 km/304 mi east of Paris) and drawing appealingly on Alsatian gemütlichkeit (friendliness), the city of Strasbourg is a cosmopolitan French cultural center and, in many ways, the unofficial "capital" of Europe. Against an irresistible backdrop of old half-timber houses, waterways, and the colossal single spire of the red sandstone cathedral, Strasbourg is an incongruously sophisticated mix of museums, elite schools (including the notorious hothouse for blooming politicos, the École Nationale d'Administration, or National Administration School), international think tanks, and the European Parliament.

The Romans knew Strasbourg as Argentoratum before it came to be known as Strateburgum, or City of (Cross) Roads. After centuries as part of the Germanic Holy Roman Empire, the city was united with France in 1681, but retained independence regarding legislation, education, and religion under the honorific title Free Royal City. Since World War II, Strasbourg has become a symbolic city, embodying Franco-German reconciliation and the wider idea of a united Europe. The city center is effectively an island within two arms of the River Ill; most major sites are found here, but the northern districts also contain some fine buildings erected over the last 100 years, culminating in the Palais de l'Europe.

The Historic Heart

This central area, from the cathedral to picturesque Petite France, concentrates on the best of old Strasbourg, with its twisting backstreets, flower-lined courts, tempting shops, and inviting winstubs.

A Good Walk

Begin at place Gutenberg and head up rue Mercière, lined with souvenir shops. To see a bit of Strasbourg's appealing combination of cozy winstubs, medieval alleys, and chic shops, turn left up rue des Tailleurs, and head right up rue des Hallebardes. Duck left up "rue pittoresque" (really rue des Orfevres); then circle right down rue Chaudron and again down rue du Sanglier. Head back right down rue des Hallebardes and cut into place de la Cathédrale, passing the landmark Maison Kammerzell (☞ Dining and Lodging, *below*).

Emerging from this close-packed warren of dark-timber buildings and narrow streets, you'll confront the magnificent **Cathédrale Notre-Dame** ㉙. Continue across the square to the **Musée de l'Oeuvre Notre-Dame** ㉚, with its collection of statuary. Leaving the museum, turn right and approach the vast neighboring palace, the **Palais Rohan** ㉛. Once the headquarters of the powerful prince-bishops, the Rohans, it now houses the art and archaeology museums.

Once out of the château's entry court, double back left and turn left again, following rue des Rohans to the river. From here you can take a boat tour (☞ Outdoor Activities, *below*) of the old town. Veer away from the water and cross place du Marché aux Cochons du Lait (Suckling Pig Market Square) and place de la Grande Boucherie (Grand Slaughterhouse Square) to reach the **Musée Historique** ㉜, with its collection of paintings, weapons, and furniture from Strasbourg (closed at press time for renovations). Across the street is the modern glass entrance to the **Ancienne Douane** ㉝, the former customs house, now a vast venue

278

Ancienne Douane, **33**
Barrage Vauban, **37**
Cathédrale
Notre-Dame, **29**
Musée Alsacien, **34**
Musée d'Art
Moderne, **38**

Musée Historique, **32**
Musée de l'Oeuvre
Notre-Dame, **30**
Orangerie, **41**
Palais de l'Europe, **40**
Palais Rohan, **31**
Petite France, **35**

Place de la
République, **39**
Ponts Couverts, **36**

Personal training for Europe

Takes the work out of your travel

Europe by train is a sophisticated workout for your senses, that lets your body sit back and relax. Go the distance from city center to city center, leaving airport hassles and traffic behind. And meet like-minded people in the comfortable, convivial atmosphere that makes European train travel an experience like no other.

Rail Europe offers a wide range of rail options, from the legendary Eurailpass to individual country passes to flexible Rail 'n Drive alternatives, even packages that include hotel and air. No matter what your travel plans, the train makes the trip.

Call your travel agent or Rail Europe today.

You've read the book. Now book the trip.

For all the best deals on flights, hotels, rental cars, and vacation packages, book them online at www.previewtravel.com. Then click on our Destination Guides featuring content from Fodor's and more. You'll find hotels, restaurants, attractions, and things to do around the globe. There are even interactive maps, videos, and weather forecasts. You'll have everything you need to make your vacation exactly what you want it to be. All it takes is a trip online.

Travel on Your Terms™
www.previewtravel.com
aol keyword: previewtravel

preview travel℠

for temporary exhibitions. Over the Ill, cross Pont du Corbeau to cour du Corbeau, a ramshackle 16th-century courtyard whose hostelry once welcomed kings and emperors. Back to the left, fronting the quai, is the **Musée Alsacien** ㉞, where you can get a glimpse of how Alsatian families used to live.

If time and energy allow, strike out toward the picturesque quarter of **Petite France** ㉟. Cross Pont St-Nicolas and follow the riverside promenade west. At Pont St-Martin, take rue des Dentelles to rue du Bain aux Plantes. Explore the alleys, courts, cafés, and shop windows at will as you work your way west. Eventually you will reach the three monumental **Ponts Couverts** ㊱. Just beyond the bridges lies the grass-roof dam, the **Barrage Vauban** ㊲. Climb to the top; from here you'll see a gleaming glass-framed building, the new **Musée d'Art Moderne** ㊳.

TIMING

Allow at least a full day to see Strasbourg—perhaps visiting the old town and cathedral in the morning, ending at 12:30 with the mechanical clock, and then lunch on a nearby backstreet. The afternoon might allow two museum stops or time to wander through Petite France. Two days would allow more museum time; a third day would allow you to take in the monumental sights at place de la République and the Palais de l'Europe (☞ *below*).

Sights to See

㉝ **Ancienne Douane** (Old Customs House). The airport-hangar scale and flexible walls lend themselves to enormous expositions of old master paintings as well as archaeology and history at this gallery in a former customs house on the Ill River. ⊠ *1 rue de Vieux-Marché-aux-Poissons,* ☎ *03–88–52–50–04.* ⊡ *30 frs.* ☉ *Daily 11–6:30, Thurs. 11–10.*

㉛ **Barrage Vauban** (Vauban Dam). Just beyond the Ponts Couverts is the grass-roof Vauban Dam, built by its namesake in 1682. Climb to the top for a stunning view across the roofs of old Strasbourg. ⊠ *Ponts Couverts.* ⊡ *Free.* ☉ *Mid-Oct.–mid-Mar., daily 9–7; mid-Mar.–mid-Oct., daily 9–8.*

★ ㉙ **Cathédrale Notre-Dame.** Rosy, ornately carved Vosges sandstone masonry covers the facade of this most novel and Germanic of French cathedrals, a triumph of Gothic art completed in 1284. Not content with the outlines of the walls themselves, medieval builders encased them in a lacy exoskeleton of slender shafts of stone. The off-center **spire**, finished in 1439, looks absurdly fragile as it tapers skyward some 466 ft; you can nonetheless climb its 330 steps to the top to take in sweeping views of the city, the Vosges mountains, and the Black Forest.

The interior presents a stark contrast to the facade: It is older (mostly finished by 1275), and the nave's broad windows emphasize the horizontal rather than the vertical. Note Hans Hammer's ornately sculpted pulpit (1484–86) and the richly painted 14th- to 15th-century organ loft that rises from pillar to ceiling. The left side of the nave is flanked with richly colored Gothic windows honoring the early leaders of the Holy Roman Empire—Otto I and II, and Heinrich I and II. The **choir** is not ablaze with stained glass but framed by chunky masonry. The fact that the choir is raised above the level of the rest of the church reinforces an aura of murky mystical sanctity. The elaborate 16th-century **Chapelle St-Laurent**, to the left of the choir, merits a visit; turn to the right to admire the **Pilier des Anges** (Angels' Pillar), an intricate column dating from 1230.

☾ The Renaissance machinery of the 16th-century **Horloge Astronomique** (Astronomical Clock) whirs into action daily at 12:30 PM (but the line starts at the south door at 11:45 AM): Macabre clockwork figures enact the story of Christ's Passion. Every evening from April through the end of September, the cathedral is the sight of a son-et-lumière show in French or German (but virtuoso lighting effects translate into any language). ⊠ *pl. de la Cathédrale.* ⌚ *Clock 5 frs; son-et-lumière 34 frs; spire 20 frs.* ☉ *Performances at 8:15 PM in German and 9:15 PM in French.*

㉞ Musée Alsacien (Alsatian Museum). In this labyrinthine half-timber home, with layers of carved balconies sagging over a cobbled inner courtyard, local interiors have been faithfully reconstituted. The diverse activities of blacksmiths, clog makers, saddlers, and makers of artificial flowers are explained with the help of old-time artisans' tools and equipment. ⊠ *23–25 quai St-Nicolas,* ☎ *03–88–52–50–00.* ⌚ *20 frs.* ☉ *Mon. and Wed.–Sat. 10–noon and 1:30–6, Sun. 10–5.*

㊳ Musée d'Art Moderne et Contemporain (Modern and Contemporary Art Museum). Opened in the fall of 1998, this brand-new museum features high-quality temporary expositions of new, esoteric, and unsung contemporary art. Its permanent collection ranges from the Impressionists to postwar abstract painters. Native son Jean Arp, the Dadaist, is prominently featured, as are the drawings, aquarelles, and paintings of Gustave Doré, also from Alsace. ⊠ *1 pl. Hans-Jean Arp,* ☎ *03–88–52–50–00.* ☉ *Tues.–Sat. 11–6, Sun. 11–5.*

㉜ Musée Historique (Local History Museum). This museum, in a 1588, step-gabled slaughterhouse, was temporarily closed for extensive renovations at press time. Hopefully, it will reopen before spring 2000. It contains a collection of maps, armor, arms, bells, uniforms, traditional dress, printing paraphernalia, and two huge relief models of Strasbourg. ⊠ *2 rue du Vieux-Marché-aux-Poissons,* ☎ *03–88–52–00–00.*

★ **㉚ Musée de l'Oeuvre Notre-Dame** (Museum of Works from Notre-Dame). There is more to this museum than the usual assembly of dilapidated statues rescued from the local cathedral before they fell off. A conscious effort has been made to create a church atmosphere and to provide an appropriate setting for the works of art. Secular exhibits include a wealth of Flemish and Upper Rhine paintings, stained glass, gold objects, and massive, heavily carved bourgeois furniture. ⊠ *3 pl. du Château,* ☎ *03–88–52–50–00.* ⌚ *20 frs.* ☉ *Tues.–Sat. 10–noon and 1:30–6, Sun. 10–5.*

㉛ Palais Rohan (Rohan Palace). The exterior of Robert de Cotte's neoclassical building (1732–42) is starkly austere. But the glamour is inside, in Robert le Lorrain's magnificent ground-floor rooms, led by the great **Salon d'Assemblée** (Assembly Room) and the book- and tapestry-lined **Bibliothèque des Cardinaux** (Cardinals' Library). The library leads to a series of less august rooms that house the **Musée des Arts Décoratifs** (Decorative Arts Museum) and its elaborate display of ceramics. Works by Hannong, a porcelain manufacturer active in Strasbourg from 1721 to 1782, are comprehensively represented; dinner services by other local kilns reveal the influence of Chinese porcelain. The **Musée des Beaux-Arts** (Fine-Arts Museum), also in the château, features masterworks of European paintings from Giotto and Memling to El Greco, Rubens, and Goya. Downstairs, the **Musée Archéologique** (Archaeology Museum) displays regional archaeological finds. ⊠ *2 pl. du Château,* ☎ *03–88–52–50–00.* ⌚ *40 frs all museums; per museum, 20 frs.* ☉ *Mon. and Wed.–Sat. 10–noon and 1:30–6, Sun. 10–5.*

㉟ Petite France. With its gingerbread half-timber houses that seem to lean precariously over the canals of the Ill, its novel shops, and inviting little restaurants, this is the most charming and magical neighborhood in Strasbourg. Wander up and down the tiny streets that connect rue du Bain aux Plantes and rue des Dentelles to Grand' Rue, and stroll the waterfront promenade.

③⑥ **Ponts Couverts** (Covered Bridges). These three bridges, distinguished by their three stone towers, were once covered with wooden shelters. Part of the 14th-century ramparts that framed old Strasbourg, they span the Ill as it branches into four fingerlike canals.

Beyond the Ill

If you've seen the center and have time to strike out in new directions, head across the Ill to view two architectural landmarks unrelated to Strasbourg's famous medieval past: place de la République and the European Union's Palais de l'Europe.

A Good Walk
North of the cathedral, walk up rue des Hallebardes and turn left on rue du Dôme. Take a right onto place Broglie and continue up this main thoroughfare across the river to the striking circle of red sandstone buildings on **place de la République** ㉟. Back at the river, head for a bus stop on avenue de la Marseillaise and take Bus 23 to the **Palais de l'Europe** ㊵ for a guided tour (by appointment, arranged in advance). From here, plunge into the greenery of the **Orangerie** ㊶. Either indulge in a three-hour lunch at the stellar Buerehiesel (☞ Dining and Lodging, *below*) or picnic on a bench.

TIMING
Basing your schedule on your tour appointment at the Palais de l'Europe, allow about a half day for this walk; if need be, you can while away the wait in the Orangerie.

Sights to See
㊶ **Orangerie.** Like a private backyard to the Eurocrats in the Palais de l'Europe, this delightful park is laden with flowers and punctuated by noble copper beeches. It contains a lake and, close by, a small reserve of rare birds, including flamingos and noisy local storks. ✉ *av. de l'Europe.*

㊵ **Palais de l'Europe.** Designed by Paris architect Henri Bernard in 1977, this Continental landmark is headquarters to the Council of Europe, founded in 1949 and independent of the European Union. It also houses (until its new building is completed) the European Parliament, which participates in legislation of the European Union. A guided tour introduces you to the intricacies of their workings and may allow you to eavesdrop on a session. Arrange your tour by telephone in advance; appointments are fixed according to language demands and usually take place in the afternoon. Note: You must provide a *pièce d'identité* (ID) before entering. ✉ *av. de l'Europe,* ☎ *03–88–41–20–29 for information, 03–88–17–20–07 for appointments.* ☝ *Free.* ☉ *Guided tours by appointment weekdays.*

㊴ **Place de la République.** The spacious layout and ponderous architecture of this monumental *cirque* (circle) have nothing in common with the old town, except the local red sandstone. A different hand was at work here—that of occupying Germans, who erected the former Ministry (1902); the Academy of Music (1882–92); and the Palais du Rhin (1883–88). The handsome neo-Gothic church of **St-Paul** and the pseudo-Renaissance **Palais de l'Université** (University Palace), constructed between 1875 and 1885, also bear the German stamp. Heavy, turn-of-the-century houses, some betraying the whimsical curves of the Art Nouveau style, frame **allée de la Robertsau**, a tree-lined boulevard that would not look out of place in Berlin.

Dining and Lodging

$$$$ ✕ **Buerehiesel.** This lovely Alsatian farmhouse, reconstructed in the
★   Orangerie, warrants a pilgrimage if you are willing to pay for the
finest cooking in Alsace and some of the best in France. Antoine West-
ermann stands in the upper echelon of chefs while remaining true to
the ingredients and specialties of his native Alsace: roast eel with coriander, guinea hen with morels, and fresh foie gras. European *par-
lementaires* come on foot; others might come on their knees. ⊠ *4 Parc
de l'Orangerie,* ☎ *03–88–45–56–65. Reservations essential. AE,
DC, MC, V. Closed Tues.–Wed.*

$$$$ ✕ **Crocodile.** Chef Émile Jung is celebrated throughout the region for
his Alsatian dishes prepared with an urbane finesse: truffle turnover,
warmed goose liver with rhubarb, and bitter-chocolate cherry cake. The
restaurant's opulent decor makes a sophisticated backdrop for a sensual meal. It's more central than the Buerehiesel and nearly as revered.
⊠ *10 rue de l'Outre,* ☎ *03–88–32–13–02. Reservations essential.
Jacket and tie. AE, DC, MC, V. Closed Sun., Mon.*

$$ ✕ **Chez Yvonne.** Behind red-checked curtains, you'll find artists,
★   tourists, lovers, and heads of state sitting elbow-to-elbow in this clas-
sic winstub. They come to savor steaming platters of duck confit on
juniper-peppered choucroute or *tête de veau* (veal head) in white wine.
Warm Alsatian fabrics dress tables and lamps, the china is regional,
the photos historic, and the ambience all chic—and no kitsch. ⊠ *10
rue du Sanglier,* ☎ *03–88–32–84–15. AE, DC, MC, V. Closed Sun.
No lunch Mon.*

$$ ✕ **Maison Kammerzell.** This restaurant glories in its richly carved,
half-timber, 15th-century building—probably the most familiar house
in Strasbourg. Fight your way through the tourist hordes on the terrace and ground floor to one of the atmospheric rooms above, with
their gleaming wooden furniture and stained-glass windows. Foie gras
and choucroute are best bets, though you may want to try the chef's
pet discovery, choucroute with freshwater fish. Portions are large, but
service can be slipshod: Eat here to gain access to history and atmosphere. ⊠ *16 pl. de la Cathédrale,* ☎ *03–88–32–42–14. AE, DC,
MC, V.*

$ ✕ **Au Tire-Bouchon.** Near the cathedral on a small backstreet, this
★   comfortable winstub, whose name means "Corkscrew," serves classic
choucroute and grilled *quenelles de foie* (liver dumplings), plus lighter
options: *salade de Gruyère* (nutty cheese and onion bits in a rich vinaigrette)—and local wines by the carafe. ⊠ *5 rue des Tailleurs-de-Pierre,*
☎ *03–88–32–47–86. MC, V. Closed Sun.*

$$$$ 🏨 **Régent-Contades.** This sleek, modern hotel is in a revamped mansion in a residential, turn-of-the-century district close to the River Ill
(ask for a room with a view of St-Paul's). First-class amenities add to
the appeal of the spacious rooms. ⊠ *8 av. de la Liberté, 67000,* ☎ *03–
88–15–05–05,* 𝔽𝔸𝕏 *03–88–15–05–15. 44 rooms. Bar, sauna. AE, DC,
MC, V.*

$$$$ 🏨 **Régent-Petite France.** Opposite the Ponts Couverts and surrounded
by rushing canals is the newest and smartest of the city's hotels. The
outside of the building (originally an ice factory) is almost unchanged—
but the inside is jazzily modern, with a spacious marble vestibule and
sculptural room furnishings. Some rooms overlook the river; all vary
considerably in size (and price). ⊠ *5 rue des Moulins, 67000 (aim for
Pont St-Thomas, opposite St-Thomas church, then head west on quai
Finkwiller, before bearing right onto rue des Moulins),* ☎ *03–88–76–
43–43,* 𝔽𝔸𝕏 *03–88–76–43–76. 72 rooms. Restaurant, piano bar. AE,
DC, MC, V.*

$$ 🏨 **Rohan.** Just a block from the cathedral on one of the picturesque pedestrian (read: tourist) streets, this gracious old-city hotel has a welcoming atmosphere and modern though fussily decorated rooms. Despite your placement at the heart of old-town action, quarters are surprisingly quiet. ✉ *17–19 rue Maroquin, 67000,* ☎ *03–88–32–85–11,* FAX *03–88–75–65–37. 36 rooms. MC, V.*

$ 🏨 **Gutenberg.** A 200-year-old mansion is the setting of this hotel, just off place Gutenberg. Several rooms, as well as the reception and breakfast area, have been modernized with a sleek, scrubbed decor, though enough antique oak details remain to remind you of the building's history. Ask for one of the top-floor rooms, as they are the most up-to-date. ✉ *31 rue des Serruriers, 67000,* ☎ *03–88–32–17–15,* FAX *03–88–75–76–67. 50 rooms. Breakfast room. MC, V. Closed 1st wk in Jan.*

Nightlife and the Arts

The annual **Festival de Musique** (Music Festival) is held from June to early July at the modern Palais des Congrès and at the cathedral; contact the Amis de la Musique (✉ 1 av. de la Marseillaise, ☎ 03–88–39–64–10) for more information. The **Opéra du Rhin** (✉ 19 pl. Broglie, ☎ 03–88–75–48–23) has a sizable repertoire. Classical concerts are staged by the **Orchestre Philharmonique** (✉ Palais des Congrès, ☎ 03–88–15–09–09).

Le Bambou (✉ 366 rte. de la Wantzeneau, ☎ 03–88–41–87–17) is a disco for the young and *branché* (hip). **Le Feeling** (✉ 19 rue du Marais-Vert, ☎ 03–88–22–05–58) is a popular bar and disco.

Outdoor Activities

The **Port Autonome de Strasbourg** (☎ 03–88–84–13–13) organizes 75-minute boat tours daily, every half hour from 9:30 to 9, April–October, along the River Ill, leaving from behind the Palais Rohan; the cost is 38 francs.

Shopping

· The lively city center is full of specialized shops and boutiques, including chocolate shops and delicatessens selling local foie gras. Watch for warm paisley linens and rustic homespun fabrics, Alsatian pottery, and local wines. Rue des Hallebardes, next to the cathedral; rue des Grandes Arcades, with its shopping mall; and place Kléber form the city's commercial heart.

ALSACE

The Rhine River forms the eastern boundary of both Alsace and France. But the best of Alsace is not found along the Rhine's industrial waterfront. Instead it's nestled in the Ill Valley at the base of the Vosges, southwest of cosmopolitan Strasbourg (☞ *above*). Northwest is Saverne, and the beginning of the Route du Vin, the great Alsace Wine Road, which winds its way south through the Vosges foothills, fruitful vineyards, and medieval villages that would serve well on a film set for William Tell. Signs for the road help you keep your bearings on the twisty way south, and you'll find limitless opportunity to stop at wineries and sample the local wares. At the industrial town of Mulhouse, you leave behind the charms of Alsace and head into the historic wilds of Franche-Comté.

Saverne

42 *37 km (23 mi) northwest of Strasbourg.*

Saverne, gateway to the northern Vosges, has a stately castle and an exuberant rose garden. Built out of red sandstone, the 18th-century **Château** is renowned for its majestic north facade, lined by fluted pilasters and a Corinthian colonnade. Housed in the right wing is a museum devoted to archaeology, religious statuary, and local history. ☎ *03–88–91–06–28.* ⊠ *Château 15 frs.* ☉ *Mar.–mid-June, Wed.–Mon. 2–5; mid-June–mid-Sept., Wed.–Mon. 10–noon and 2–6; mid-Sept.–Nov., Wed.–Mon. 2–5; Dec.–Feb., Sun. 2–5.*

Don't miss the **Roseraie** (Rose Garden), on the western side of town (off N4). It has some 8,000 roses of 550 varieties. ⊠ *Off N4.* ⊠ *7 frs.* ☉ *Sunrise–sunset.*

Marmoutier

43 *6 km (4 mi) south of Saverne, 41 km (25 mi) northwest of Strasbourg.*

Marmoutier is worth a stop to see its handsome Romanesque **Église Abbatiale** (Abbey Church). The facade, dating from the 11th and 12th centuries, is pure Lombard Romanesque, built from local Vosges sandstone. Inside, you'll find a handsome 1710 organ, built by Silbermann (organ maker to J. S. Bach).

Obernai

44 *35 km (22 mi) south of Saverne, 27 km (17 mi) southwest of Strasbourg.*

Obernai is a thriving, colorful Renaissance market town with a medieval belfry, a Renaissance well, and a late-19th-century church. Place du Marché, in the heart of town, is dominated by the stout, square 13th-century **Kapelturm Beffroi** (Chapel Tower Belfry), topped by a pointed steeple flanked at each corner by frilly openwork turrets added in 1597. An elaborate Renaissance well near the belfry, the **Puits à Six-Seaux** (Well of Six Buckets), was constructed in 1579; its name recalls the six buckets suspended from its metal chains. The twin spires of the parish church of **St-Pierre–St-Paul** compete with the belfry for skyline preeminence. They date, like the rest of the church, from the 1860s, although the 1504 Holy Sepulchre altarpiece in the north transept is a survivor from the previous church, along with some 15th-century stained glass.

Dining and Lodging

$$ ✕☑ **L'Ami Fritz.** In the hilltop village of Ottrott, west of Obernai, this
★ welcoming inn combines chic, warmth, and a rustic atmosphere. The chef's specialties include succulent *presskopf* (head cheese), tender onion tarts, and seasonal game; don't miss the fruity red wine, an Ottrott exclusive. In winter, head for the stone-and-beam *caveau* (cellar), with roaring fireplace; in summer, dine in the garden. The weekday lunch menu is a great deal (the restaurant is closed Wednesday). Now pretty, impeccable rooms are available in the historic house as well as in the all-modern residence 300 yards away. ⊠ *8 rue des Châteaux, 67530 Ottrott (about 3 km/2 mi from Obernai),* ☎ *03–88–95–80–81,* ℻ *03–88–95–84–85. 39 rooms. Restaurant. AE, DC, MC, V.*

$$ ✕☑ **La Cloche.** This sturdy, half-timbered, 14th-century classic on the market square serves simple local specialties. Leaded glass, dark oak, and Hansi-like murals set the tone. Blackboard specials draw locals on market days. Rooms are basic but well equipped and country-

pretty. ✉ *90 rue Général Gouraud, 67210,* ☎ *03–88–95–52–89,* ⨳
03–88–95–07–63. 12 rooms. Restaurant. AE, DC, MC, V.

Shopping

Dietrich (✉ 58 and 74 rue du Général-Gouraud, ☎ 03–88–95–57–
58), on the town market square, has a varied selection of beautifully
crafted household goods.

Mont-Ste-Odile

★ ④⑤ *12 km (8 mi) southwest of Obernai, 42 km (26 mi) southwest of Strasbourg.*

Mont-Ste-Odile, a 2,500-ft mound, has been an important religious
and military site for 3,000 years. An eerie 9½-km-long (6-mi-long) **mur
païen** (pagan wall), up to 12 ft high and, in parts, several feet thick,
rings the summit; its mysterious origins and purpose still baffle ar-
chaeologists. The Romans established a settlement here, and at the start
of the 8th century, Odile, daughter of Duke Etichon of Obernai,
founded a convent on the same spot after recovering her sight while
being baptized (she had been born blind). Odile—the patron saint of
Alsace—died here in AD 720; her sarcophagus rests in the 12th-cen-
tury **Chapelle Ste-Odile.** The spare Romanesque **Chapelle de la Croix**
adjoins the St. Odile chapel. Both churches stand within the confines
of the relatively modern **convent,** now a work-a-day hostelry for modern pilgrims on group retreats.

Barr

④⑥ *11 km (7 mi) southeast of Mont Ste-Odile, 8 km (5 mi) south of Obernai, 33 km (20 mi) southwest of Strasbourg.*

Barr is a thriving semi-industrial town surrounded by vines, with some
charming narrow streets (notably rue des Cigognes, rue Neuve, and
the tiny rue de l'Essieu), a cheerful Hôtel de Ville, and a decorative arts
museum, the Folie Marco. Most buildings date from after a catastrophic fire of 1678; the only medieval survivor is the Romanesque
tower of St-Martin, the Protestant church.

Admire original furniture, local porcelain, earthenware, and pewter at
the **Musée de la Folie Marco,** housed in a steep-tiled mansion built by
local magistrate Félix Marco in 1763. One section of the museum explains the traditional process of *schlittage*: Sleds, bearing bundles of
freshly sawed tree trunks, once slid down forest slopes along a "cor-
duroy road" made of logs. ✉ *30 rue du Dr-Sultzer,* ☎ *03–88–08–
94–72.* ⊡ *20 frs.* ☉ *May–Sept., Wed.–Mon. 10–noon and 2–6;
Oct., weekends 10–noon and 2–6.*

Dining and Lodging

$$ ✕⊡ **Gilg.** Looking over the tiny medieval village of Mittelbergheim,
outside Barr, is this historic inn. The specialty is a pleasant mix of clas-
sic and regional cuisine (fish presskopf, frogs' legs in Riesling) and wines
from neighboring vineyards. It's all served in a timbered and vaulted
winstub (closed Tuesday dinner and Wednesday). Rooms are more at-
mospheric than comfortable, and the 17th-century stone spiral stair-
case leading upstairs is best suited to limber romantics. ✉ *1 rue
Rotland, 67140 Mittelbergheim,* ☎ *03–88–08–91–37,* ⨳ *03–88–
08–45–17. 10 rooms. Restaurant. AE, DC, MC, V. Closed last 3 wks
of Jan. and late June–early July.*

Andlau

47 *3 km (2 mi) southwest of Barr, 37 km (23 mi) southwest of Strasbourg.*

Andlau has long been known for its magnificent abbey. Built in the 12th century, the **Abbaye d'Andlau** has the richest ensemble of Romanesque sculpture in Alsace. Sculpted vines wind their way around the doorway as a reminder of wine's time-honored importance to the local economy. A statue of a female bear, the abbey mascot—bears used to roam local forests and were bred at the abbey until the 16th century—can be seen in the north transept. Legend has it that Queen Richarde, spurned by her husband Charles the Fat, founded the abbey in AD 887 when an angel enjoined her to construct a church on a site to be shown to her by a female bear.

Dambach-la-Ville

48 *5 km (3 mi) southwest of Andlau, 42 km (26 mi) southwest of Strasbourg. From Andlau, take D253 to the junction with D603; keep right; about 1 km (½ mi) later, turn right, then left through Itterswiller before turning right toward Dambach-la-Ville.*

Dambach-la-Ville is a fortified medieval town protected by ramparts and three powerful 13th-century gateways. Dambach is particularly rich in half-timber, high-roof houses from the 17th and 18th centuries, clustered mainly around **place du Marché** (Market Square). Also on the square is the 16th-century **Hôtel de Ville.**

En Route   Just south of Dambach is the imposing **Château d'Ortenburg** on the hilltop to your right, constructed in 1000 by Wernher d'Ortenburg and restored in 1258 by Rodolphe de Habsbourg, a reigning Hapsburg.

Sélestat

49 *9 km (5 mi) southeast of Dambach, 19 km (12 mi) south of Barr, 47 km (29 mi) southwest of Strasbourg.*

Sélestat, midway between Strasbourg and Colmar, is a lively, historic town with a Romanesque church and a library of medieval manuscripts. The church of **St-Foy** dates from between 1155 and 1190; its Romanesque facade remains largely intact (the spires were added in the 19th century), as does the 140-ft octagonal tower over the crossing. Sadly, the interior was mangled during the centuries, chiefly by the Jesuits; their most inspired legacy is the Baroque pulpit of 1733 illustrating the life of St. Francis Xavier. Note the Romanesque bas-relief next to the baptistery, originally the lid of a sarcophagus. ⊠ *pl. du Marché-Vert.*

Among the precious manuscripts on display at the **Bibliothèque Humaniste** (Humanist Library), a major library founded in 1452 and installed in the former Halle aux Blés, are a 7th-century lectionary and a 12th-century Book of Miracles. ⊠ *1 rue de la Bibliothèque,* ☎ *03–88–92–03–24.* ⊡ *20 frs.* ☉ *Weekdays 9–noon and 2–6, Sat. 9–noon; July–Aug., also weekends 2–5.*

Nightlife and the Arts

The colorful **Corso Fleuri** (Flower Carnival) takes place on the second Sunday in August, when the town decks itself—and the floats in its vivid parade—with a magnificent display of dahlias.

Haut-Koenigsbourg

50 *12 km (8 mi) west of Sélestat, 59 km (36½ mi) southwest of Strasbourg.*

★ ☽ One of the most popular spots in Alsace is the romantic, crag-top castle of Haut-Koenigsbourg, originally built as a fortress in the 12th century. The ruins of the **Château du Haut-Koenigsbourg** were presented by the town of Sélestat (or Schelestadt; the German name was used then) to German emperor Wilhelm II in 1901. The château looked just as a kaiser thought it should, and he restored it with some diligence and no lack of imagination—squaring the main tower's original circle, for instance. The site, panorama, drawbridge, and amply furnished imperial chambers may lack authenticity, but they are undeniably dramatic. ☎ *03–88–92–11–46.* 🎟 *Château 36 frs.* ☉ *June–Sept., daily 9–6; Apr.–May, daily 9–noon and 1–6; Oct. and Mar., daily 9–noon and 1–5; Nov.–Feb., daily 9–noon and 1–4.*

Ribeauvillé

🖲 *14 km (9 mi) southwest of Sélestat, 63 km (39 mi) southwest of Strasbourg.*

The beautifully , half-timber town of Ribeauvillé, surrounded by rolling vineyards and three imposing châteaux, produces some of the best Riesling in Alsace. Its narrow main street, crowded with winstubs, pottery shops, bakeries, and wine sellers, is bisected by the 13th-century **Tour des Bouchers,** a clock-belfry completed (gargoyles and all) in the 15th century. Storks' nests crown several towers in the village. The Trimbach family has made Riesling and superb Gewürztraminer here since 1626.

Dining and Lodging

$ ✕ **Caveau de l'Ami Fritz.** Tucked into a low-vaulted hall, with glowing fireplace, paisley linens, and polished wood, this simple, casual spot serves good, hot food all day. Full meals include choucroute and game, but there are also soups, salads, mouthwatering onion tarts, and *tarte flambée* (a delicate bacon-and-crème-fraîche pizza). ⊠ *1 pl. Ancien Hôpital,* ☎ *03–89–73–68–11. MC, V.*

$$ 🏨 **De la Tour.** In the center of Ribeauvillé and across from the Tour des Bouchers, this hotel, with an ornate Renaissance fountain outside its front door, is a good choice for experiencing the atmospheric town by night. Rooms and amenities are modern; those on the top floor have exposed timbers and wonderful views of ramshackle roof-tops. ⊠ *1 rue de la Mairie, 68150,* ☎ *03–89–73–72–73,* 🖷 *03–89–73–38–74. 35 rooms. Breakfast room, hot tub, sauna. MC, V.*

Shopping

Find rich paisley Alsatian tablecloths at the factory outlet for **Beauvillé** (⊠ 19 rte. de Ste-Marie-aux-Mines, ☎ 03–89–73–32–17).

Riquewihr

★ 🖲 *5 km (3 mi) south of Ribeauvillé, 68 km (42 mi) south of Strasbourg.*

Riquewihr is a living museum to the quaint architecture and storybook atmosphere of old Alsace. Its steep main street, ramparts, and winding back alleys have scarcely changed since the 16th century and could easily serve as a film set. Merchants cater to the sizable influx of tourists with a plethora of kitschy souvenir shops; bypass them to peep into courtyards with massive wine presses, study the woodwork and ornately decorated houses, stand in the narrow old courtyard that was once the Jewish quarter, or climb up a narrow wooden stair to the ramparts. You would also do well to settle into a winstub to sample some of Riquewihr's famous wines.

Dining and Lodging

$$ ✕🏨 **Sarment d'Or.** This cozy little hotel stands apart for its irreproachable modern comforts tactfully dovetailed with stone, dark timbers, and thick walls. The restaurant downstairs offers firelit romance and delicious cuisine—pastry-wrapped pâté, presskopf, and breast of duck in Pinot Noir. It has a reasonable daily menu, despite ambitious à la carte prices, and it's closed Sunday dinner and Monday. ⊠ *4 rue du Cerf, 68340,* ☎ *03–89–47–92–85,* 🗚 *03–89–47–99–23. 9 rooms. Restaurant. MC, V. Closed Jan.*

Colmar

🟢 *16 km (10 mi) southeast of Riquewihr, 71 km (44 mi) southwest of Strasbourg.*

Much of Colmar's architecture is modern, on account of the destruction of World Wars I and II. But the heart of this proud merchant town is still a web of well- pedestrian streets that fan out from the beefy-towered church of **St-Martin.** These lead toward the 15th-century customs house, the **Ancienne Douane.** The **Maison aux Arcades** (Arcades House), up the street, was built in 1609 in high Renaissance style and features a series of arched porches (arcades) anchored by two octagonal towers. Calm canals wind through **La Petite Venise** (Little Venice), an area of bright Alsatian houses with colorful shutters and window boxes south of the center of town. Colmar is also home to the finest art museum in Alsace and was once home to Bartholdi, designer of the Statue of Liberty.

★ The **Musée d'Unterlinden** was once a medieval convent and is now a museum. The star attraction is the *Retable d'Issenheim* (Issenheim Altarpiece; 1512–16) by Matthias Grünewald, majestically displayed in the convent's Gothic chapel. Originally painted for the Antoine convent at Issenheim, 32 km (20 mi) south of Colmar, the altarpiece was believed to have miraculous healing powers over ergotism, a widespread disease in the Middle Ages. The enormous work's raw emotional drama and fantasy move sharply away from the stilted restraint of earlier paintings toward the humanistic realism of the Renaissance. Modern art, stone sculpture, ancient wine presses and barrels, and local crafts cluster around the enchanting 13th-century cloister. ⊠ *1 rue Unterlinden,* ☎ *03–89–20–15–50.* 🗓 *30 frs.* ☉ *Apr.–Oct., daily 9–6; Nov.–Mar., Wed.–Mon. 9–noon and 2–5.*

The **Église des Dominicains** (Dominican Church), southeast of the museum off rue Unterlinden, houses the Flemish-influenced *Madonna of the Rosebush* (1473) by Martin Schongauer (1445–91). This work, stolen from St-Martin's in 1972 and later recovered and hung here, has almost certainly been reduced in size from its original state but retains enormous impact. The grace and intensity of the Virgin match that of the Christ child; yet her slender fingers dent the child's soft flesh (and his fingers entwine her curls) with immediate intimacy. Schongauer's text for her crown: *"Me carpes genito tuo o santissima virgo"* ("Choose me also for your child, o holiest Virgin"). ⊠ *pl. des Dominicains,* ☎ *03–89–24–46–57.* 🗓 *8 frs.* ☉ *Mid-Mar.–Dec., daily 10–6.*

The **Maison Pfister** (Pfister House), built in 1537, is the most striking of Colmar's many old dwellings. Note its decorative frescoes and medallions, carved balcony, and ground-floor arcades. ⊠ *11 rue Mercière.*

The **Musée Bartholdi** (Bartholdi Museum) is the former home of Frédéric-Auguste Bartholdi (1834–1904), the local sculptor who designed the Statue of Liberty. Temporary exhibits of contemporary artists claim the ground floor; the artist's apartments and furniture are upstairs; and on the top floor, the creation of Lady Liberty is explored.

⊠ *30 rue des Marchands,* ☎ *03–89–41–90–60.* ⊠ *20 frs.* ☉ *Apr.–Dec., Wed.–Mon. 10–noon and 2–6.*

Dining and Lodging

$$$ ✕ **À l'Échevin.** This restaurant in Le Maréchal hotel (☞ *below*) is atmospheric, if pricey. Meals, served in the garden along the canal, might include freshwater fish choucroute, frogs' legs soup with truffle juice, and farm-raised pigeon. ⊠ *5 pl. des Six-Montagnes-Noires,* ☎ *03–89–41–60–32. MC, V.*

$$ ✕ **Caveau Hansi.** Named for the Rockwell-like illustrator whose beclogged folk children adorn most of the souvenirs of Alsace, this hyper-traditional beamed tavern in the old town serves excellent down-home classics such as choucroute and pot-au-feu, prepared and served with a sophisticated touch despite the waitresses' dirndls. ⊠ *23 rue des Marchands,* ☎ *03–89–41–37–84. MC, V. Closed Thurs. and Jan. No dinner Wed.*

$ ✕ **Au Koïfhus.** Not to be confused with the shabby little Koïfhus on rue des Marchands, this popular landmark serves huge portions of regional standards, plus a variety of changing specialties: roast quail and foie gras on full-dinner salads, game stews with spaetzle (dumplings), and fresh-water fish. Choose between the big, open dining room, glowing with wood and warm fabric, and a shaded table on the broad, lovely square. ⊠ *2 pl. de l'Ancienne-Douane,* ☎ *03–89–23–04–90. DC, MC, V. Closed Thurs. and Jan.*

$$$ 🏠 **Le Maréchal.** A maze of corridors connects the three Renaissance
★ town houses that make up this hotel near the Lauch River. Some of the rooms are small, decorated predominantly in light, cheerful colors; some are endearingly rustic, with beams and curvy walls and floors; those in back have good river views. ⊠ *5 pl. des Six-Montagnes-Noires, 68000,* ☎ *03–89–41–60–32,* 🖷 *03–89–23–73–61. 30 rooms. Restaurant. MC, V.*

$$ 🏠 **Colbert.** The convenient location, halfway between the train station and the ancient town center, is a plus. Rooms are well equipped and air-conditioned, though decor is somewhat overbright. Ask for a quieter room along rue des Taillandiers. ⊠ *2 rue des Trois-Épis, 68000,* ☎ *03–89–41–31–05,* 🖷 *03–89–23–66–75. 50 rooms. Bar, air-conditioning. AE, MC, V.*

$$ 🏠 **Rapp.** In the old town, just off the Champ de Mars, this solid, modern hotel has business-class comforts, a professional and welcoming staff, German-scale breakfast, and an extensive indoor-pool complex, including sauna, steam bath, and workout equipment. ⊠ *1–5 rue Weinemer, 68000,* ☎ *03–89–41–62–10,* 🖷 *03–89–24–13–58. 42 rooms. Restaurant, breakfast room, winstub, indoor pool, sauna, steam room, exercise room. AE, DC, MC, V.*

The Arts

During the first half of August, Colmar celebrates with its annual **Foire Régionale des Vins d'Alsace,** an Alsatian wine fair in the Parc d'Exposition. Events include folk music and theater performances, and, above all, the tasting and selling of wine.

Guebwiller

🅸 *26 km (16 mi) southwest of Colmar, 25 km (16 mi) north of Mulhouse, 94 km (58 mi) south of Strasbourg.*

Despite its admirable churches, fine old buildings, and pleasantly authentic feeling, Guebwiller is often overlooked.

The **Église St-Léger** (1180–1280) is one of the most harmonious Romanesque churches in Alsace, though its original choir was replaced by the current Gothic one in 1336. The bare, solemn interior is of less interest than the three-tower exterior. The towers match—almost: The one on the left has small turrets at the base of its steeple, whereas the one on the right is ringed by triangular gables. The octagonal tower over the crossing looms above them both, topped by a seldom-visited stork's nest. The surrounding square is home to a lively weekly market. ⊠ *pl. St-Léger.*

The **Église Dominicaine** (Dominican Church) has an unmistakable silhouette thanks to the thin, lacy lantern that sticks out of its roof like an effeminate chimney. Its large, 14th-century nave is adorned with frescoes and contains a fine rood screen. ⊠ *rue de l'Hôpital.*

Guebwiller's third and largest church, **Notre-Dame,** possesses a Baroque grandeur that would not be out of keeping in Paris—a reflection of the wealth of the Benedictine abbey at nearby Murbach, whose worldly friars, fed up with country life, opted for the bright lights of Guebwiller in the mid-18th century. The monks—who needed a noble pedigree of four generations to take the cloth—outmaneuvered church authorities by pretending to take temporary exile in Guebwiller while "modernizing" Murbach Abbey, thus circumnavigating the papal permission required before abbeys could move. As a token gesture, the crafty clerics smashed the nave of Murbach Abbey but failed to replace it and refused to budge from their "temporary" home. Instead, they commissioned Louis Beuque to design this new church in Guebwiller (1762–85). The interior is majestic but not overbearing. The gold-and-marble high altar fits in better, perhaps, than does the trick 3-D-effect stucco Assumption (1783), an example of Baroque craftsmanship at its most outlandish. ⊠ *rue de la République.*

The **Musée du Florival** occupies one of the 18th-century canon's houses alongside Notre-Dame. It has a fine collection of ceramics designed by Théodore Deck (1823–91), a native of Guebwiller and director of the renowned Sèvres porcelain factory near Paris. It also contains archaeological treasures, artifacts from everyday life, and religious sculpture. ⊠ *1 rue du 4-Février,* ☎ *03–89–74–22–89.* ☞ *15 frs.* ⊘ *Mon. and Wed.–Fri. 2–6, weekends 10–noon and 2–6.*

OFF THE
BEATEN PATH

ÉCOMUSÉE DE HAUTE-ALSACE – Great for kids, this open-air museum near Ungersheim, southeast of Guebwiller (via D430), is really a small village created from scratch in 1980, including 65 historic peasant houses and buildings typical of the region. An entire sawmill demonstrates its conversion from waterwheel to dynamo; an apiary swarms with honeybees; apples are pressed and cider tasted; and pigs are slopped. Storks are nurtured here in a reserve and perch on chimneys everywhere. The village is crisscrossed by donkey carts and wagons, and behind every door lie entertaining demonstrations of the old ways. An off-season visit is a study in local architecture; in high season the place comes alive. Small restaurants, snack bars, a playground, and a few amusement rides are scattered about for breaks. Inexpensive lodging is available on-site. ☎ *03–89–74–44–74.* ☞ *69 frs.* ⊘ *July–Aug., daily 9–7; June and Sept., daily 9–6; Apr.–May and Oct., daily 10–5; Nov.–Mar., daily 11–5.*

Murbach

⑤ *5 km (3 mi) west of Guebwiller, 23 km (14 mi) northwest of Mulhouse.*

In the tiny village of Murbach, a vast rump of a church towers above the hillside. Only the east end remains of the church of **St-Léger,** once part of the most powerful abbey in Alsace. Roofs and towers create a geometric interplay of squares and triangles, lent rhythm and variety by those round-arched windows and arcades so loved by Romanesque architects. Note the tympanum above the door to the south transept: Its elongated lions, seen in profile, resemble stone images found more commonly in the Middle East.

Mulhouse

56 *23 km (14 mi) southeast of Guebwiller, 35 km (22 mi) south of Colmar.*

A pleasant, if unremarkable, industrial town, Mulhouse rates a visit for its superb car and train museums, as well as for its art museum.

Some 500 vintage and modern cars, dating from the steam-powered Jacquot of 1878 and spanning 100 different makes, are housed at the **Musée National de l'Automobile** (National Car Museum). ✉ *192 av. de Colmar,* ☎ *03–89–33–23–23.* 🎟 *57 frs.* ⊙ *Wed.–Mon. 10–6.*

A reconstructed Stephenson locomotive of 1846 sets the wheels rolling at the **Musée Français du Chemin de Fer** (National Train Museum). Rolling stock is spread over 12 tracks, including a vast array of steam trains and the BB 9004 electric train. ✉ *2 rue Alfred-de-Glehn,* ☎ *03–89–42–25–67.* 🎟 *44 frs.* ⊙ *Apr.–Sept., daily 9–6; Oct. and Mar., daily 9–5.*

Dutch and Flemish masters of the 17th to 18th centuries—including Brueghel, Teniers, and Ruisdael—top the bill at the **Musée des Beaux-Arts** (Fine Arts Museum), complemented by French painters such as Boudin, Courbet, and Bouguereau. ✉ *4 pl. Guillaume-Tell,* ☎ *03–89–45–43–19.* 🎟 *20 frs.* ⊙ *Oct.–May, Wed.–Mon. 10–noon and 2–5; June–Sept., Wed.–Mon. 10–noon and 2–6.*

FRANCHE-COMTÉ

This area extends from Belfort to Besançon, then clockwise through the Jura—which has great expanses of quiet, untouched land with rivers, waterfalls, and cirques, and a challenging range of mountains where you can climb, ski, and enjoy the solitude—to Dole. From here it is an easy trip to Burgundy (☞ Chapter 9) and the Rhône Valley (☞ Chapter 10).

Belfort

57 *40 km (25 mi) southwest of Mulhouse, 146 km (90½ mi) southwest of Strasbourg.*

A beefy citadel and colossal stone lion bear witness to the distinguished military history of the stubborn warrior-town of Belfort. In the heart of town is a 36-ft-high **Lion,** sculpted in red sandstone by Frédéric-Auguste Bartholdi, best known as the sculptor of the Statue of Liberty in New York. The lion was commissioned to celebrate Belfort's heroic resistance during the Franco-Prussian War (1870–71) when the town of Belfort, under the leadership of General Denfert-Rochereau, withstood a 103-day siege and surrendered only after the rest of France had capitulated. The Prussian leader Otto von Bismarck was so impressed by Belfort's plucky resistance that he granted Belfort independent status. Although Alsace was returned to France in 1918, Belfort maintained its special status—meaning that the *Territoire de Belfort* (Belfort Territory) remains by far the smallest *département* (province) in France. ✉ *pl. des Bourgeois.* 🎟 *Climbing up to see Lion 3 frs.*

Belfort's Lion sits proudly at the foot of Vauban's impregnable hilltop château, now home to the **Musée d'Art et d'Histoire** (Museum of Art and History), containing Vauban's 1687 scale model of the town, plus a detailed section on military history. There's also a collection of paintings and sculpture from the 16th through 19th centuries. From the ramparts you can look out over the old town, toward the Vosges Mountains to the north and the Jura to the south. ☎ 03–84–54–25–52. ⊠ *Château free, museum 11 frs (free Wed.).* ☉ *May–Sept., daily 10–7; Oct.–Apr., Wed.–Mon. 10–noon and 2–5.*

Dining and Lodging

$$ ✕ **Pot-au-Feu.** This rustic bistro, tucked in a 16th-century *cave* (cellar) at the foot of the citadel, serves good regional specialties and features—of course—a savory, long-simmered pot-au-feu. Two of the prix-fixe lunch menus include wine. ⊠ *27 bis Grande-Rue,* ☎ *03–84–28–57–84. AE, MC, V. Closed 2 wks in Aug. No lunch Sat. or Mon., no dinner Sun.*

$$ ✕▥ **Château Servin.** Off the city streets in an intimate garden, this hotel was built in 1885 and maintains that era's stuffy grandeur. Dark polished woodwork, heavy floral carpets, fringe, gilt, and lace close you in, whether in the velour-beswagged rooms or the stately restaurant. Chef Dominique Mathy creates classic menus, including sole soufflé in lobster sauce, fresh foie gras with poppy seeds, and hot cherry soufflé. The restaurant (in the $$$ category) is closed Sunday dinner and Friday. ⊠ *9 rue du Général-Négrier, 90000,* ☎ *03–84–21–41–85,* ℻ *03–84–57–05–57. 10 rooms. Restaurant. AE, DC, MC, V.*

Ronchamp

58 *21 km (13 mi) west of Belfort via N19.*

The little town of Ronchamp, in the windswept *département* of Haute-Saône, was once renowned for having France's deepest coal mine shaft (3,300 ft). The mine's huge chimney still towers above the valley, but Ronchamp is now the site of one of Europe's most famous postwar

★ buildings. The hilltop chapel of **Notre-Dame-du-Haut** was designed by Swiss-born French architect Le Corbusier in 1951 to replace a church destroyed during World War II. The chapel's curved, sloping white walls; small, irregularly placed windows; and unadorned, slug-shape gray concrete roof are unique. Many consider it to be Le Corbusier's masterpiece. ☎ *03–84–20–65–13.* ⊠ *10 frs.* ☉ *Mid-Mar.–Oct., daily 9–7; Nov.–mid-Mar., daily 9–4.*

Dining and Lodging

$$ ✕▥ **Pomme d'Or.** At the foot of the road that leads up to the chapel, this jazzed-up roadhouse has all the comforts—full tile baths, bright-decked rooms, a neo-Grecian restaurant with fountain, and a terrace café. Top-floor rooms are less up-to-date but cheaper. ⊠ *34 rue Le Corbusier, 70250,* ☎ *03–84–20–62–12,* ℻ *03–84–63–59–45. 34 rooms. Restaurant, café. AE, DC, MC, V.*

Montbéliard

59 *16 km (10 mi) south of Belfort.*

Montbéliard is an industrial town that is home to the giant Peugeot automobile company and a stately castle. Only the two round towers of the **Château** remain from the heyday of the princes of Würtemberg who once ruled this Renaissance principality; its more classical 18th-century portions contain a museum devoted to insects, geological and archaeological finds, and local clocks and musical boxes. ⊠ *rue du Château,* ☎ *03–81–99–22–61.* ⊠ *Free.* ☉ *May–June, Wed.–Mon.*

2–6:30; July–Aug., daily 10:30–6:30; Sept., daily 10–noon and 1:30–
6:30; Oct.–Apr., Wed.–Mon. 2–6.

Across the rail line in the neighboring suburb of Sochaux, Peugeot's
production methods and colorful history can be explored at the **Musée
de l'Aventure Peugeot** (Peugeot Adventure Museum). You can also tour
the factory (children are not allowed). ✉ *carrefour de l'Europe,* ☎ *03–
81–94–48–21; 03–81–33–47–80 to arrange factory tours.* 🎫 *Museum 30 frs, factory tour free.* ☉ *Museum daily 10–6; factory tours
8:30 AM weekdays (English-speaking guides are available).*

Besançon

60 *80 km (50 mi) southwest of Montbéliard, 238 km (147 mi) southwest
of Strasbourg.*

The former capital of the Franche-Comté, Besançon is a graceful old,
gray-stone city nestled in a vast bend of the River Doubs. Its defensive
potential was quickly realized by Vauban, whose imposing citadel remains the town's architectural focal point. The town has long been a
clock-making center and, more recently, was the birthplace of the
rayon industry. Famous offspring include Auguste and Louis Lumière,
the inventors of a motion-picture camera, and the poet Victor Hugo,
born while his father was garrisoned here in 1802. Hugo is no local
hero, though, having dismissed Besançon as an "old Spanish town,"
a reference to the lip service the town's inhabitants paid to the Aus-
tro-Spanish Habsburgs during medieval times.

☝ A 75-minute **boat trip** along the River Doubs provides a good introduction to Besançon. Boats leave from Pont de la République and take
in a lock and the 400-yard tunnel under the citadel. ☎ *03–81–68–
13–25.* 🎫 *43 frs.* ☉ *July–early Sept., weekdays 10:30, 2:30, 4:30, weekends also at 6:15; May–June, weekends 2:30 and 4:30.*

Wander around the quayside to the **Musée des Beaux-Arts et d'Archéologie** (Museum of Fine Arts and Archaeology) to see its collection of
tapestries, ceramics, and paintings by Bonnard, Renoir, and Courbet.
There's also a section devoted to clocks and watches through the ages.
✉ *1 pl. de la Révolution,* ☎ *03–81–82–39–89.* 🎫 *21 frs.* ☉ *Wed.–
Mon. 9:30–noon and 2–6.*

Grande-Rue, Besançon's oldest street, leads from the river toward the
citadel, past fountains, wrought-iron railings, and stately 16th- to
18th-century mansions, the most stunning of which is the Renaissance
Palais Granvelle (1540). Hugo was born at No. 140, the Lumière
brothers just opposite.

☝ The **Horloge Astronomique,** at the foot of the citadel, is a stupendous
19th-century astronomical clock with 62 dials and an array of automatons that spurt into action just before the hours are sounded. ✉
2 rue du Chapitre, ☎ *03–81–81–12–76.* 🎫 *15 frs.* ☉ *Tours hourly
Wed.–Mon. 9:45–11:45 and 2:45–5:45; closed Wed. Oct.–Mar.*

The **Citadelle** is perched on a rocky spur 350 ft above the town. From
its triple ring of ramparts, now laid out as promenades and peppered
with Vauban's original watchtowers, you can see the city and the
countryside. The buildings contain a series of museums devoted to natural history, regional folklore, agricultural tools, and the French Resistance during World War II. There also are shops and restaurants.
☎ *03–81–65–07–44.* 🎫 *Joint ticket with citadel and museums 50
frs.* ☉ *Late Mar.–Sept., daily 9–7; Oct.–Mar., daily 10–5.*

Dining and Lodging

$$$ ✕ **Mungo Park.** This former warehouse on the banks of the River Doubs is now a bright, glassed-in restaurant. Locals and Parisians pile in to appreciate the inspired works of Jocelyne Choquart and Benoît Rotschi, who bring local ingredients into this century—Jura snails in horseradish cream, pigeon in a sauce flavored with the local aperitif Macvin, and a sweet, hot dessert soup of walnuts, vin jaune, and nutmeg. ⊠ *11 rue Jean-Petit,* ☎ *03–81–81–28–01. Reservations essential. MC, V. Closed Sun., 1 wk in Feb., and 2 wks in Aug. No lunch Sat.*

$$ ✕ **Poker d'As.** Carved-wood tables and cowbells counterbalanced by
★ swagged tulle and porcelain capture the ethnic-chic of this landmark restaurant's cuisine. Earning kudos for his *cuisine du terroir* (regional cooking), chef Raymond Ferreux animates his upscale experiments with splashes of local color: Jura *morteau* (sausage) sautéed with artichokes and cèpes, and pressed partridge with wild mushrooms. ⊠ *14 square St-Amour,* ☎ *03–81–81–42–49. AE, DC, MC, V. Closed Mon. and late July–early Aug. No dinner Sun.*

$ ✕ **Bistrot du Jura.** In an intimate, downscale setting of checkered tiles and bentwood, sample home-cooked regional specialties such as herring with steamed potatoes, and andouillette in Jura wine—a fine selection of which is served by the glass. The owner keeps proud standards but irregular hours; call in advance. ⊠ *35 rue Charles-Nodier,* ☎ *03–81–82–03–48. V.*

$ ✕ **Quignon Comtois.** The dreadful setting—in a former shop cozied up with mail-order decor—is more than offset by earthy and delicious Franche-Comté cooking, served to loyal crowds of young locals. Try the simple fried carp, rich ham gratin with mushrooms, and Swiss-style *roëstis* (hash browns). Jura house wines are sold by the carafe. ⊠ *10 rue G. Courbet,* ☎ *03–81–83–36–13. MC, V.*

$$$ ▦ **Castan.** Just below the citadel, in a courtyard behind a tangle of an-
★ cient trees and crumbling Roman pillars, is this noble 17th- and 18th-century mansion that has become a chic *relais* (inn). Rooms are atmospheric and exquisitely decorated. Regency moldings, period fabrics, luxurious baths, and a private collection of regional bibelots set the tone. ⊠ *6 square Castan, 25000,* ☎ *03–81–65–02–00,* ℻ *03–81–83–01–02. 8 rooms. Breakfast room, free parking. MC, V.*

$$ ▦ **Paris.** There are few decent hotels in the heart of Besançon. This one, though it is on main shopping streets, is a good bet. It's well run, unpretentious, and brightened by a tree-lined garden courtyard. ⊠ *33 rue des Granges, 25000,* ☎ *03–81–81–36–56,* ℻ *03–81–61–94–90. 55 rooms, 54 with bath or shower. Breakfast room. AE, DC, MC, V.*

$ ▦ **Granvelle.** Convenient to the citadel and set back from old-town streets, this modest, straightforward lodging has freshly decorated rooms, including some bargains without bathrooms. ⊠ *13 rue du Général-Lecourbe, 25000,* ☎ *03–81–81–33–92,* ℻ *03–81–81–31–77. 30 rooms, 27 with bath. Breakfast room. DC, MC, V.*

The Arts

A **jazz festival** (☎ 03–80–83–39–09) takes place in July. An **international music festival** (☎ 03–81–80–73–26) is held in September.

Outdoor Activities and Sports

Rent canoes and kayaks from **Sport Nautique** (⊠ 2 av. Chardonnet, ☎ 03–81–80–56–01) for 140–200 francs per day.

Ornans

⑥ *26 km (16 mi) south of Besançon.*

There are two reasons to visit the pretty village of Ornans: to enjoy the view of the steep-roof old houses that line the River Loue and to see the birthplace of Gustave Courbet (1819–77), the pioneering French Realist painter who influenced Édouard Manet. Gustave Courbet was an assertive, full-bearded radical who spent his last years in Swiss exile after toppling Napoléon's column on place Vendôme during the Paris Commune in 1871. The **Musée de la Maison Natale de Courbet** (Courbet's Birthplace Museum)—a rambling 18th-century mansion—hardly goes with his tempestuous image and provides a sedate setting for souvenirs, documents, drawings, sculptures, and paintings. Courbet is best known for his *Burial at Ornans* (now in the Musée d'Orsay in Paris; ☞ Chapter 2), with its procession of somber peasants. ⊠ *pl. Robert-Fernier,* ☎ *03–81–62–23–30.* ⊠ *20 frs; temporary exhibits 40 frs.* ☉ *Apr.–June and Sept.–Oct., daily 10–noon and 2–6; Nov.–Mar., Wed.–Mon. 10–noon and 2–6.*

OFF THE BEATEN PATH	**SOURCE DE LA LOUE –** From Ornans, take D67 down the steeply banked Loue Valley, through the picturesque villages of Vuillafans (with its 16th-century bridge and restored water mill), Lods, and Mouthier-Haute-Pierre, and turn right at La Main onto D41. Turn right again in Ouhans, and follow signs to the spectacular Source de la Loue, where the Loue River gushes from a cliff face, cascading past ruined water mills. To get to the source from the parking lot, take the stony path (for about 20 minutes). The trip from Ornans to the source is about 20 km (12 mi).

Montbenoît

62 *40 km (25 mi) southeast of Ornans.*

The tiny village of Montbenoît is dominated by its **Ancienne Abbaye,** which dates from the 11th century. The vast cloisters, conservative for their flamboyant times, were added in the 15th century. Take time to study the superbly carved wooden **choir stalls** (1525–27), which give a Renaissance interpretation of biblical tales. Samson, for instance, wears natty hose and a lace ruff collar as Delilah takes to his flowing locks with a pair of oversize scissors. ☎ *03–81–38–10–32.* ⊠ *15 frs.* ☉ *Mon.–Sat. 9–noon and 2–6, Sun. 2–6. Guided tours with kitchen and refectory July–Aug. by request.*

Dining and Lodging

$$ ╳▥ **France.** Swiss gourmets flock across the border, just two minutes away, to Villers-le-Lac, to savor chef Hugues Droz's lobster with morels and escargots in absinthe. Hugues's family runs the hotel and will happily book you a two-hour boat trip (40 francs) along the Gorges du Doubs. Breakfasts are large, but the rooms are somewhat noisy. The restaurant is closed Sunday evening and Monday. ⊠ *8 pl. Maxime-Cupillard, 25130 Villers-le-Lac (24 km/15 mi northeast of Montbenoît),* ☎ *03–81–68–00–06,* 〚FAX〛 *03–81–68–09–22. 14 rooms. Restaurant. AE, DC, MC, V. Closed late Jan.*

Pontarlier

63 *14 km (9 mi) southwest of Montbenoît.*

Pontarlier, with its old streets, churches, and gateways, was once home to absinthe—a notorious anise-based aperitif, the forerunner of Ricard and Pernod. It was banned in 1915 for inducing alcoholism and even madness. The **Musée Municipal** has a section on the history of the *fée verte* (green fairy), as absinthe was called. Porcelain and local paintings are also on display. ⊠ *2 pl. d'Arçon,* ☎ *03–81–46–73–68.* ⊠ *10 frs.* ☉ *Weekdays 10–noon and 2–6, Sat. 2–6, Sun. 3–7.*

OFF THE
BEATEN PATH

CHÂTEAU DE JOUX – Just south of Pontarlier via N57, this fortress perched on a steep hill glowers across the Jura landscape toward the Swiss border. Founded in the 11th century, it retains its round medieval towers, drawbridges, and 17th-century ramparts. The dungeon holds a sturdy collection of old guns and weapons (guided tours only; allow one hour). ☎ 03–81–69–47–95. 🎟 30 frs. ⏱ July–Aug., daily 9–6; Mar.– June and Sept., daily 10–11:30 and 2–4:30; Oct.–Mar., daily tours at 10, 11:15, 2, and 3:30.

Syam

64 *48 km (30 mi) southwest of Pontarlier: Take D72 and D471 to Champagnole, then N5 south (toward Geneva) before bearing left on D127.*

Syam, nestled in the lush Ain Valley, forged into the limelight in the second decade of the 19th century as an ironworks center. The **Forges de Syam** (Syam Ironworks) was built in 1813; iron was hauled in by train, then dragged down to the riverside by oxen. Simple lodging was built on-site, now occupied by the nearly 50 people who still work here, making nails, locks, tools, and machinery. "Hot-rolling" and "hard-drawing" techniques are explained at the museum (with video presentation). ☎ 03–84–51–61–00. 🎟 12 frs. ⏱ July–Aug., Wed.–Mon. 10–6; May–June and Sept., weekends 10–6.

The founder of the forge, Alphonse Jobez, was clearly flushed with pride when he had himself built the **Château de Syam,** a sturdy, square, yellow-fronted neo-Palladian villa. Finished in 1818, this grandiose self-homage has outsized Ionic pilasters at each corner and, inside, a theatrical, colonnaded rotunda ringed with balconies and Pompeiian grotesques. Guided tours take you through restored rooms. ☎ 03–84–51–61–25. 🎟 20 frs. ⏱ July–Sept., Fri.–Mon. 2–6.

OFF THE
BEATEN PATH

CASCADES DU HÉRISSON – To get to the Hérisson waterfalls from Syam, take N5 south; turn right on D75 to Ilay; take D39 west (direction Doucier); then double back on narrow, winding D326. It dead-ends at the parking lot, from which it's a 10-minute, uphill walk to L'Éventail, the first waterfall, with its 210-ft drop. If you come after heavy rains, the noise is deafening, and the path is slippery. It's exhilarating but drenching, so dress accordingly. In summer you can usually progress beyond L'Éventail, along a rugged path past five more cascades, all the way to Le Saut Girard, 3 km (2 mi) away (allow three hours for the round-trip).

Baume-les-Messieurs

65 *33 km (21 mi) west of Syam.*

A rambling little stone village in a breathtaking setting of cliffs and forests, Baume-les-Messieurs has a venerable medieval abbey and an underground network of caves. Its Romanesque stonework resonant with history, the 12th-century **Abbaye** has time-worn courtyards and a tenderly painted 16th-century Flemish altarpiece donated by the Belgian town of Ghent. ☎ 03–81–84–27–98. 🎟 Free. ⏱ Daily 9–8.

The **Grottes de Baume,** 2 km (1 mi) outside of town, consists of 650 yards of skillfully lit galleries 400 ft underground, containing a river, a lake, and weird-shape stalactites and stalagmites (the temperature is chilly, so take a sweater). The largest cave is more than 200 ft high, and classical music blasts out to heighten the dramatic effect. The ceilings are clustered with hundreds of tiny, mink-brown bats. ✉ *Chalet* *de Guide, ☎ 03–84–44–61–58. 🎫 25 frs. ⊙ Apr.–Sept., daily 9:30–noon and 2–6.*

Five kilometers (3 miles) outside of Baume-les-Messieurs (south on D4 then west on D71) is the **Belvedère des Roches de Baume** (Baume Rocks Overlook). The plummeting view of the ring of chalky cliffs hemming the village is spectacular; watch for signs. You can also hike the rim of the cirque, following the Grand Randonée (the name of the trail).

Dining and Lodging

$$ ✕🏨 **Parenthèse.** Though its odd geometry and vivid color schemes deny its origins as a sturdy, rustic mansion, this ultramodern retreat in the tiny stone village of Chillé (southwest of Baume) pampers you with a pool and whirlpool baths. The ambitious, mid-priced restaurant features regional specialties with sophisticated twists: breast of Bresse chicken with morels and vin jaune, and saddle of rabbit in Macvin (the local aperitif). The restaurant is closed Sunday dinner and Monday. ⊠ *111 Grande-Rue, 39570 Chillé (20 km/12 mi southwest of Baume, via D157 and Lons),* ☎ *03–84–47–55–44,* 🅵🅰🆇 *03–84–24–92–13. 31 rooms. Restaurant, grill, pool. MC, V.*

$ ✕🏨 **Chambre d'Hôte/Étape Gourmande.** This bed-and-breakfast and
★ restaurant is in the abbey. Come here to sample the simple yet chic specialties of the ex-Parisian owner-hosts, such as toast spread with duck paté and slivers of smoked duck breast, and *tartiflette* (potato and bacon gratin with Vacherin cheese). You'll dine under the groin-vaulted stonework, along the weathered refractory table or on the terrace overlooking the grounds. And if you're lucky, you can even climb up the spiral stone stair to vast beamed rooms furnished casually with mismatched collectibles, woodstoves, and minirefrigerators. Views defy description. A deli downstairs sells local picnic products and wine. ⊠ *Abbaye de Baume-les-Messieurs, 39210,* ☎ *03–84–44–64–47. 3 rooms. Restaurant, breakfast room, deli. MC, V.*

Château-Chalon

★ ⑥⑥ *13 km (8 mi) north of Baume-les-Messieurs.*

The medieval village of Château-Chalon, perched on a rocky promontory high above vertiginous local vineyards, is renowned for its legendary vin jaune, said to keep for 200 years without losing its vigor. A charming place to sample the wine's nutty, sherrylike flavor is opposite the 10th-century church of **St-Pierre,** on the tiny square where the **Fruitière Vinicole** runs generous tastings from an old cellar. Walk off any aftereffects with a stroll through the narrow, twisting streets. Though there's very little to "do" here, you could easily lose yourself for a day in its atmosphere: The restored stonework, restrained shop fronts, and archaic street signs help to keep out the 20th century.

OFF THE **CHÂTEAU D'ARLAY** – This 18th-century château, 8 km (5 mi) west of
BEATEN PATH Château-Chalon, contains sumptuously carved regional furniture dating from the same period. The outstanding wine produced here can be sampled (and purchased) in the château's cellar, open Monday–Saturday 8–noon and 2–6. Combine your visit with a walk around the magnificent park, with its grotto, medieval ruins, and alley of ancient *tilleuls* (basswood trees), and a stop at the Volerie des Rapaces, where (at 4 and 5 PM) trained eagles and other birds of prey perform wide-winged acrobatics overhead. ⊠ *rue Haute-du-Bourg,* ☎ *03–84–85–04–22.* 🎫 *Château and volerie: 45 frs.* ⊙ *July–Aug., Mon.–Sun. 2–6. Volerie also open Apr.–Oct., Wed. and weekends 2–6.*

Arbois

⑥⑦ *24 km (15 mi) north of Château-Chalon.*

The pretty wine market town of Arbois is worth a stop for its fine restaurant, Jean-Paul Jeûnet (☞ Dining and Lodging, *below*). It also has a museum dedicated to the vine and to Louis Pasteur (1822–95), the famous bacteriologist and father of pasteurization, who grew up in Arbois.

The **Maison de Pasteur,** Louis Pasteur's family home, is fully furnished in authentic style, containing many of his possessions. ⊠ *83 rue de Courcelles,* ☎ *03–84–66–11–72.* ⊡ *30 frs.* ☉ *Guided tours hourly mid-May–mid-Sept., daily 9:45–11:45 and 2:15–5:15; mid-Sept.–mid-Nov., last two weeks in Dec., and mid-Feb.–mid-May, Fri.–Wed. at 10, 11, 2, 3, and 4.*

The Arbois vineyard is one of the finest in eastern France; to learn more about it, visit the **Musée de la Vigne et du Vin** (Vineyard and Wine Museum) and peruse its collection of tools and documents. ⊠ *Château Pécauld,* ☎ *03–84–66–26–14.* ⊡ *17 frs.* ☉ *Sept.–June, Wed.–Mon. 10–noon and 2–6; July–Aug., Wed.–Mon. 10–6.*

A short excursion south along D469 will take you into the magnificent **Reculée des Planches,** a dramatic rocky valley created by glacial erosion and peppered with caves and waterfalls. ⊡ *Caves 30 frs.* ☉ *Mar.–mid-Nov., daily 10–noon and 2–5; July–Aug., daily 9:30–6; Oct.–mid-Nov., daily 10–noon and 2:30–4:30.*

Continue along D469 from the Reculée des Planches to the beautiful, rocky **Cirque du Fer à Cheval** (Horseshoe Cirque), with its panoramic view of U-shape cliffs (10 minutes' walk from parking.) Watch for signs.

Dining and Lodging

$ ✕ **La Finette.** In a kitschy log-cabin setting, you can find hot, hearty local cooking at all hours: tripe in a casserole, sausage with lentils, and fondue. ⊠ *22 av. Pasteur,* ☎ *03–84–66–06–78. MC, V.*

$$$ ✕🏠 **Jean-Paul Jeûnet.** This ancient stone convent, its massive beams
★ enhanced with subtle lighting and contemporary art, is one of the most recognized eateries in the Jura. Chef Jeûnet's devotion to local flora and fauna has evolved into a bold, earthy, flavorful cuisine: crayfish sausage, prawns with heather flowers, and even sheeps' milk sorbet. The chef's father, once an award-winning sommelier, has established a worthy cellar. The restaurant is closed Tuesday, and Wednesday lunch. Rooms have pleasant modern decor and pretty pine furniture. ⊠ *9 rue de l'Hôtel-de-Ville, 39600,* ☎ *03–84–66–05–67,* 🇫🇦🇽 *03–84–66–24–20. 17 rooms. Restaurant. DC, MC, V. Closed Dec.–Jan.*

$$ 🏠 **Hôtel des Messageries.** This dignified, vine-covered inn on Arbois's main street has moderate rooms with flossy Baroque decor and a warm public ambience enhanced by grand spaces full of old wood and stone. ⊠ *2 rue des Courcelles, 39600,* ☎ *03–84–66–15–45,* 🇫🇦🇽 *03–84–37–41–09. 26 rooms. Breakfast room. MC, V. Closed Dec.–Jan.*

Outdoor Activities and Sports

Contact **Le Petit Cheval Blanc** (⊠ 39800 Fay-en-Montagne, ☎ 03–84–85–32–07) for details on renting horses, whether for an afternoon promenade or for an eight-day, farm-to-farm self-guided circuit (Apr.–Oct.).

Salins-les-Bains

⑥⑧ *14 km (9 mi) northwest of Arbois.*

If you want to learn about the salt industry in the area, head to Salins-les-Bains. **Les Salines** (The Saltworks), tucked away in the steep valley of the River Furieuse, functioned until 1962. Local salty water was pumped to the surface and then evaporated; it was a sticky, sweaty process that you can fully appreciate in the humid "heating room." ✉ *pl. des Salines,* ☎ *03–84–73–01–34.* 🎫 *23 frs.* ⏱ *Easter–mid-Sept. guided tours daily at 9, 10, 11, 2:30, 3:30, 4:30 and 5:30; mid-Sept.–Nov. and Feb.–Easter guided tours daily at 10:30, 2:30, and 4.*

Arc-et-Senans

★ ⑥⑨ *18 km (11 mi) north of Arbois.*

For a glimpse of the palatial pretensions of the erstwhile salt industry, explore Arc-et-Senans. The **Saline Royale** (Royal Saltworks), built 1774–79 by Claude-Nicolas Ledoux, is an extraordinary example of neoclassical industrial architecture. With their Palladian porticoes, rustication, and towering columns, the buildings—arranged in a gracious semicircle around sweeping lawns—display a grandeur worthy of the Romans. Originally they were intended to form part of a rationally planned, circular *ville idéale* (ideal town). ☎ *03–81–54–45–45.* 🎫 *35 frs.* ⏱ *July–Aug., daily 9–7; Apr.–June and Sept.–Oct., daily 9–noon and 2–6; Nov.–Mar., daily 10–noon and 2–5.*

Dole

⑦⓪ *28 km (18 mi) northwest of Arc-et-Senans, 48 km (30 mi) southeast of Dijon, 48 km (30 mi) southwest of Besançon.*

The sturdy old hilltop town of Dole, where Louis Pasteur was born in 1822, climbs above the River Doubs, a cohesive mass of graystone planes. Visible above the rooftops for miles around is the muscular 250-ft tower of the 16th-century **Église Notre-Dame.** The warren of dank alleyways beneath the church invites exploration. Pasteur's birthplace, the **Maison Natale de Pasteur,** is now a museum, restored to its 1744 look, with original beams and waxed plank floors. It contains documents and mementos, plus the restored tanner's workshop of Pasteur's father who, like most of his neighbors, was a leather worker. ✉ *43 rue Pasteur,* ☎ *03–84–72–20–61.* 🎫 *20 frs.* ⏱ *July–Aug., Wed.–Mon. 10–6; Apr.–June and Sept.–Oct., Wed.–Mon. 10–noon and 2–6.*

Dining

$$ ✕ **Les Templiers.** With its vaulted stone ceiling and pointed Gothic
★ archways, this restaurant in a 16th-century building has an archetypal Old World feel enhanced by tapestry-upholstered high-back chairs and stained-glass windows. Chef Joël Césari's cuisine is a shade more nouvelle: Try the turbot with licorice sauce, the Bresse pigeon with caramelized radish, and the lemon shortbread. ✉ *35 Grande-Rue,* ☎ *03–84–82–78–78. AE, DC, MC, V. Closed Mon., and Nov.–Mar. No dinner Sun.*

ALSACE-LORRAINE AND FRANCHE-COMTÉ A TO Z

Arriving and Departing

By Car
The A4 toll expressway heads east from Paris to Strasbourg, via Verdun, Metz, and Saverne. It is met by A26, descending from the English Channel, at Reims. A31 links Metz to Nancy, continuing south to Burgundy and Lyon. The quickest route from Paris to Besançon and the Jura is on A6 (to Beaune) and then A36; A5 from Paris to Besançon is swift and direct.

By Plane

Most international flights to Alsace land at Mulhouse-Basel airport on the Franco-Swiss border. There are also tiny airports at Strasbourg, Metz-Nancy, Dole, and Mirecourt (Vittel/Épinal) for charter or private plane landings.

By Train

Mainline trains leave Paris (Gare de l'Est) every couple of hours for the four-hour, 504-km (315-mi) journey to Strasbourg. Some stop at Toul and all stop at Nancy, where there are connections for Épinal and Gérardmer. Trains run three times daily from Paris to Verdun and more often to Metz (around three hours to each). Mainline trains stop at Mulhouse (four to five hours) en route to Basel. Three high-speed TGV (*Trains à Grande Vitesse*) leave Paris (Gare de Lyon) daily for Besançon (2½ to 3 hours).

Getting Around

By Car

N83/A35 connects Strasbourg, Colmar, and Mulhouse. A36 continues to Belfort and Besançon. A4, linking Paris to Strasbourg, passes through Lorraine via Metz, linking Lorraine and Alsace. Picturesque secondary roads lead from Nancy and Toul through Joan of Arc country and onto Épinal. Several scenic roads climb switchbacks over forested mountain passes through the Vosges, connecting Lorraine to Alsace and Alsace to Belfort. And Alsace's Route du Vin, winding from Marlenheim in the north all the way south to Guebwiller, is the ultimate touring experience.

By Train

Several local trains a day run between Strasbourg and Mulhouse, stopping at Sélestat and Colmar. Several continue to Belfort and Besançon. Local trains link Besançon to Lons-le-Saunier, occasionally stopping at Arbois. Other towns, such as Dole, Arbois, Montbenoit, and Pontarlier, are accessible, with planning, by train. But you'll need a car to visit smaller villages and the region's spectacular natural sights.

Contacts and Resources

Bed-and-Breakfast Information

Contact the **Service Tourisme** (⊠ Chambre d'Agriculture, B.P. 417, 39016 Lons-le-Saunier) for its brochure on "Gîtes de France" in the Jura. The list includes both bed-and-breakfasts and houses for rent.

Car Rentals

Avis (⊠ 7 pl. Flore, Besançon, ☎ 03–81–80–91–08; ⊠ pl. de la Gare, Strasbourg, ☎ 03–88–32–30–44). **Europcar** (⊠ 18 rue de Serre, Nancy, ☎ 03–83–37–57–24). **Hertz** (⊠ 7 pl. Thiers, Nancy, ☎ 03–83–32–13–14; ⊠ place Flore, Besançon, ☎ 03–81–47–43–23).

Guided Tours

Aéroclub d'Alsace (☎ 03–88–34–00–98) arranges plane rides over Strasbourg and the Vosges from the Aérodrome du Polygone. Balloon trips are organized by **Air Adventures** of Arc-et-Senans (☎ 03–81–57–45–51). **Tecnavia** (☎ 03–83–29–80–60) gives 15-minute helicopter tours of Nancy.

Outdoor Activities and Sports

A guide to bicycling in the Lorraine is available from the **Comité Départemental de Cyclotourisme** (⊠ 33 rue de la République, 54950 Laronxe). For information on biking in the Jura contact the **Comité Ré-**

gional de Cyclotourisme VTT de Franche-Comté (⊠ 12 rue Charles-Dornier, 25000 Besançon, ☎ 03–81–52–17–13).

A brochure on fishing is available by writing to **A.D.E.D.** (⊠ ave. de la Gare d'Eau, 25031 Besançon). For information on horseback riding in the area, contact the **Délégation Départementale de Tourisme Équestre** (⊠ 4 rue des Violettes, 67201 Eckbolsheim, ☎ 03–88–77–39–64).

The **Comité Régional de Tourisme** (⊠ 9 rue de Pontarlier, 25000 Besançon) provides full details on hiking in Franche-Comté. The **Fédération Jurassienne de Randonnée Pédestre** (⊠ Hôtel du Département, B.P. 652, 39021 Lons-le-Saunier) publishes a brochure on trails in the Jura. For a list of signposted trails in the Vosges foothills, contact the **Sélestat Tourist Office** (☞ *below*).

Travel Agencies
Havas Voyages (⊠ 23 rue de la Haute-Montée, Strasbourg, ☎ 03–88–32–99–77). **Wagons-Lits** (⊠ 30 pl. Kléber, Strasbourg, ☎ 03–88–32–16–34; ⊠ 2 rue Raymond-Poincaré, Nancy, ☎ 03–83–35–06–97).

Visitor Information
The principal regional tourist offices are in the following towns: **Besançon** (⊠ 2 pl. de la 1ᵉ-Armée Française, ☎ 03–81–80–92–55). **Nancy** (⊠ 14 pl. Stanislas, ☎ 03–83–35–22–41). **Strasbourg** (⊠ 9 rue du Dôme, ☎ 03–88–21–01–02; ⊠ 17 pl. de la Cathédrale, ☎ 03–88–52–28–28). In **Strasbourg,** there is also a city tourist office (⊠ pl. de la Gare, ☎ 03–88–32–51–49).

Other tourist offices: **Belfort** (⊠ 2 bis bd. Clemenceau , ☎ 03–84–55–90–99). **Colmar** (⊠ 4 rue Unterlinden, ☎ 03–89–20–68–92). **Guebwiller** (⊠ 73 rue de la République, ☎ 03–89–76–10–63). **Lons-le-Saunier** (⊠ 1 rue Louis-Pasteur, ☎ 03–84–24–65–01). **Metz** (⊠ pl. d'Armes, ☎ 03–87–55–53–76). **Mulhouse** (⊠ 9 av. du Maréchal-Foch, ☎ 03–89–45–68–31). **Obernai** (⊠ 59 rue du Général-Gouraud, ☎ 03–88–95–64–13). **Saverne** (⊠ Château des Rohan, ☎ 03–88–91–80–47). **Sélestat** (⊠ 10 bd. Leclerc, ☎ 03–88–58–87–20). **Toul** (⊠ Parvis de la Cathédrale, ☎ 03–83–64–11–69). **Verdun** (⊠ pl. de la Nation, ☎ 03–29–86–14–18).

9 Burgundy

Beaune, Dijon, and Chablis Country

First and foremost are Burgundy's vineyards, producing complex and diverse wines, from the crisp white of Chablis to the rich reds of Côte de Nuits and Côte de Beaune. And then there is its history: the Roman ruins at Autun and the abbeys at Cluny and Vézelay, whose power still reverberates through the region in bare, ruined choirs and echoing cloisters. In the midst of all this is the wonderfully varied Parc du Morvan, full of hikers and bicyclists, bird-watchers and botanists.

Revised and
updated by
Nigel Fisher

FOR A REGION WHOSE POWERFUL MEDIEVAL dukes ruled over large tracts of Western Europe and whose glamorous image is closely allied to its expensive and treasured wine, Burgundy (Bourgogne in French)—just southeast of Paris—can seem a surprisingly rustic backwater. Here "life in the fast lane" refers exclusively to the Paris-bound A6 expressway.

In the Middle Ages, Sens, Auxerre, and Troyes, in neighboring Champagne (but included here), came under the sway of the Paris-based Capetian kings, who erected mighty Gothic cathedrals in those towns. Burgundy's leading religious monuments, however, are the older, Romanesque basilica at Vézelay, once one of Christianity's most important centers of pilgrimage and today a tiny village hidden in the folds of rolling, verdant hills; and the ruined Abbey of Cluny, once a religious center as important as Vézelay.

Chablis is renowned for its excellent bone-dry white wine, although better value for the money can be found at St-Bris-le-Vineux and Irancy, south of Auxerre. The great red wine lands of Burgundy are farther east. Dijon, the province's only city, retains something of the opulence it acquired under the rich, powerful dukes of Burgundy who ruled in the late Middle Ages, but its latter-day reputation is essentially gastronomic.

Pleasures and Pastimes

Abbeys
From the sober beauty of splendid and well-preserved Fontenay and Pontigny to the romantic ruins of Cluny that is a ghost of its former glory, the abbeys of Burgundy are an evocative part of its history.

Dining
Dijon ranks with Lyon as one of the unofficial gastronomic capitals of France. Wealthy Parisian gourmets think nothing of driving three hours to sample the cuisine of Beaune's Jean Crotet or Vézelay's Marc Meneau. Game, freshwater trout, garlicky *jambon persillé* (ham flavored with parsley), goat cheese, coq au vin, snails, mustard, and mushrooms number among the region's specialties. Meat is often served in rich, wine-based sauces.

CATEGORY	COST*
$$$$	over 400 frs
$$$	250 frs–400 frs
$$	125 frs–250 frs
$	under 125 frs

*per person for a three-course meal, including tax (20.6%) and tip but not wine

Hiking and Horseback Riding
The Parc Naturel Régional du Morvan, with its rocky escarpments, hidden valleys, rushing streams, thick forests, and wooded hills, is marvelous for hiking and horseback riding especially in spring and fall.

Lodging
Burgundy is seldom deluged by tourists, so finding accommodations is not hard. But it is still wise to make advance reservations, especially in the wine country (from Dijon to Beaune). If you intend to visit Beaune for the Trois Glorieuses wine festival in November, make your hotel reservation several months in advance. Note that nearly all country hotels have restaurants, and you are usually expected to eat at them. Some

towns have a large number of inexpensive hotels. In Dijon, you can find them around place Émile Zola; in Beaune, look around place Madeleine; in Auxerre, they're tucked away in the streets down from Cathédrale St-Étienne; in Tournus and Avallon, check out their old towns.

CATEGORY	COST*
$$$$	over 800 frs
$$$	550 frs–800 frs
$$	300 frs–550 frs
$	under 300 frs

All prices are for a standard double room for two, including tax (20.6%) and service charge.

Wine

The famous vineyards south of Dijon—the Côte de Nuits and Côte de Beaune—are among the world's most distinguished and picturesque. Don't expect to unearth many bargains here, but a good place for sampling is the Marché aux Vins in Beaune, an old town clustered around the patterned-tile roofs of its medieval Hôtel-Dieu (hospital). However, most vineyards welcome visitors and will invite you to sample their wines in the hope that you will purchase a case. Less expensive Burgundies can be found between Chalon and Mâcon.

Exploring Burgundy

The best way to enter Burgundy is southeast from Paris—by car. First explore the northwest part of the region, from Sens to Autun, with a rewarding detour to the town of Troyes, in Champagne, and the Loire, in the west, around the Parc du Morvan. Go next to Burgundy's wine country, which begins at Dijon and stretches south down the Saône Valley through charming Beaune to Mâcon.

Great Itineraries

You could easily spend two weeks in Burgundy—visiting the sights, tasting the wine, and filling up on the rich food. If, however, you only have three days, you can see two of Burgundy's most interesting cities—Dijon and Beaune. With five days you can explore the northeast part of the region, from Sens to Beaune. Eight days will give you time to get to the Parc du Morvan and the Côte d'Or—home to Burgundy's finest vineyards.

Numbers in the text correspond to numbers in the margin and on the Burgundy, Troyes, and Dijon maps.

IF YOU HAVE 3 DAYS

Start with Burgundy's two most interesting cities—first, the age-old capital of Burgundy, ⚅ **Dijon** ㉝–㊶, then, medieval ⚅ **Beaune** ㊹. Between the two towns, visit the famous Burgundy vineyards around **Clos de Vougeot** ㊷.

IF YOU HAVE 5 DAYS

Make your first stop out of Paris the small town of **Sens** ①, with its vast cathedral and its 13th-century Palais Synodal. Then head for the serene abbey in **Pontigny** ⑮ and the Ancien Hôpital in **Tonnerre** ⑱. End the day tasting the famous white wine in ⚅ **Chablis** ⑰, and spend the night there. Begin day two with a visit to **Auxerre** ⑯ and its cathedral before going on to ancient **Clamecy** ㉙ and the world-famous basilica at **Vézelay** ㉚. Stay overnight in dramatic ⚅ **Avallon** ㉛, with its medieval St-Lazarus church. By day three, get to ⚅ **Dijon** ㉝–㊶ and stay two nights. On day five, take a short run down the wine-producing Côte d'Or to ⚅ **Beaune** ㊹.

Burgundy

Piney

Lusigny

Bar-sur-Aube

N
0 — 20 miles
0 — 30 km

1 Sens

TO PARIS

Joigny

St-Florentin

Charny

Pontigny
15 — Tonnerre
18 — 19 — Tanlay

Châtillon-sur-Seine

Auxerre
16 — 17 — Chablis
20 — Ancy-le-Franc

Pimelles

Toucy

Leugny

Irancy

Montbard

21 — Abbaye de Fontenay

Clamecy
29 — Vézelay — 30 — 31 — Avallon

Semur-en-Auxois

Dijon
33 — 41

Tannay

Saulieu
22 — Châteauneuf-en-Auxois
23 — Clos de Vougeot
42 — Nuits-St-Georges
43

La Charité-sur-Loire
28

32 — Parc Naturel Régional du Morvan

Arnay-le-Duc

Beaune

TO BOURGES

Château-Chinon
26 — Château de Sully
24

44 — Meursault

Nevers
27

Autun
25

Nolay

Chagny

Decize

Montceau-les-Mines

Chalon-sur-Saône

45

Moulins

Bourbon-Lancy

Tournus
46 — Brancion

Cluny
47

Paray-le-Monial

Solutré

Mâcon
48

Lapalisse

Vichy

Roanne

Riom

Thiers

Lyon

Make ⊞ **Troyes** ②–⑭, with its medieval pedestrian streets, your first stop. On day two head south to see **Tonnerre** ⑱, the Renaissance châteaux of **Tanlay** ⑲ and **Ancy-le-Franc** ⑳, and the Cistercian **Abbaye de Fontenay** ㉑. End the day in ⊞ **Dijon** ㉝–㊶. Give yourself two days and nights in Dijon and then go to ⊞ **Beaune** ㊸ for another night. While you're in the vicinity, drive south down the Saône River to medieval **Tournus** ㊻ and the abbey of St-Philibert, as well as the ruined abbey of ⊞ **Cluny** ㊼. The next day, drive north to see the cathedral and Roman remains in **Autun** ㉕, the **Château de Sully** ㉔, the hilltop town of ⊞ **Châteauneuf-en-Auxois** ㉓, and the basilica in **Saulieu** ㉒; end up in ⊞ **Avallon** ㉛. Spend day six driving through the **Parc Naturel Régional du Morvan** ㉜ and visiting the village of **Château-Chinon** ㉖, the imposing cathedral in **Nevers** ㉗, and the abbey-church in **La Charité-sur-Loire** ㉘, before returning to Avallon. Spend the next two days and nights around ⊞ **Auxerre** ⑯, ⊞ **Chablis** ⑰, or ⊞ **Sens** ①. These make good bases for exploring unspoiled **Clamecy** ㉙, the vineyards around Chablis, the abbey in **Pontigny** ⑮, and the basilica in **Vézelay** ㉚.

When to Tour Burgundy

May in Burgundy is especially nice, as are September and October, when the sun is still warm on the shimmering golden trees, and grapes are ready for harvest, scenting the air with anticipation. Many festivals also take place around this time.

NORTHWEST BURGUNDY

From Paris, drive southeast into Burgundy on autoroute A6 (or, alternately, on A5 direct to Troyes, first sneaking into Champagne), before making a clockwise loop around the Parc du Morvan, visiting the small cities and ancient abbeys in the area. The towns and villages are largely preserved, with few industrial suburbs, and the surprisingly rural landscape seems to have remained the same for centuries.

Sens

❶ *112 km (70 mi) southeast of Paris on N6.*

It makes sense for Sens to be your first stop in Burgundy, since it is only 80 minutes by car from Paris on N6, a fast road that hugs the pretty Yonne Valley south of Fontainebleau. Sens was for centuries the ecclesiastical center of France and is still dominated by its **Cathédrale St-Étienne.** You can see the cathedral's 240-ft south tower from far away; the highway forges straight past it. The pompous 19th-century buildings that line this road can give you a false impression if you're in a hurry: The streets leading off it near the cathedral (notably rue Abelard and rue Jean-Cousin) are full of half-timber medieval houses, and within their midst sits the 13th-century church of **St-Pierre-le-Rond,** with its unusual wooden roof and 16th-century stained glass. On Monday, the cathedral square is crowded with stalls, while the colorful covered market throbs with people buying meat and produce. A smaller market is held on Friday mornings.

Begun around 1140, the cathedral used to have two towers; one was topped in 1532 by an elegant, though somewhat incongruous, Renaissance campanile that contains two monster bells, and the other was destroyed in the 19th century. The gallery, with statues of former archbishops of Sens, is a 19th-century addition, but the statue of St. Stephen, between the doors of the central portal, is thought to date from the late 12th century. The vast, harmonious interior is justly renowned for its stained-glass windows. The oldest (circa 1200) are in the north choir;

those in the south transept were manufactured in 1500 at nearby Troyes and include a much-admired *Tree of Jesse*. The cathedral treasury (access near the sacristy to the south of the choir) is one of the richest in France, comparable to that of Conques. It contains a collection of miters, ivories, shrouds of St. Sivard and St. Loup, and gold plates, together with the richly woven gold-and-silver robes of the archbishops of Sens and Thomas à Becket. Becket fled to Sens from England to escape the wrath of Henry II before returning to his cathedral in Canterbury where, in 1170, he was murdered. Stained-glass windows in the north of the chancel retrace his story. ⊠ *pl. de la République,* ☎ *03–86–64–15–27.* ⌨ *Admission to treasury included in ticket to Palais Synodal (☞ below).*

The 13th-century **Palais Synodal** (Synodal Palace), alongside Sens's cathedral, provides an encounter with Burgundy's multicolor tile roofs: From its courtyard, there is a fine view of the cathedral's Flamboyant Gothic south transept, constructed by master stonemason Martin Chambiges at the start of the 16th century. (Rose windows were his specialty, as you can appreciate here.) The Palais Synodal houses a museum with archaeological finds from the Gallo-Roman period, including monumental blocks from public edifices, statues, mosaics, and tapestries, but its six grand windows and the vaulted Synodal Hall are the outstanding features. ☎ *03–86–64–46–27.* ⌨ *22 frs.* ☉ *June–Sept., daily 10–noon and 2–6; Oct.–May, Wed. and weekends 10–noon and 2–6, Mon. and Thurs.–Fri. 2–6.*

Dining and Lodging

$$–$$$ ✕▥ **Paris & Poste.** Owned for the last several decades by the Godard ★ family, the modernized Paris & Poste, which began life as a post house in the 1700s, is a convenient and pleasant stopping point. Rooms are clean, bright, and airy. No. 42, facing the inner courtyard, is especially nice. Sumptuous breakfasts confirm the sense of well-being—further reinforced by a robust evening meal of roast duck or grilled salmon, served in the comfortable, traditional restaurant. ⊠ *97 rue de la République, 89100,* ☎ *03–86–65–17–43,* ℻ *03–86–64–48–45. 25 rooms. Restaurant. AE, DC, MC, V.*

$ ✕▥ **Croix Blanche.** A five-minute walk from the cathedral will take you to this calm, straightforward hotel. Its two-room restaurant (plus veranda) provides three good-value menus, headed by turbot in crayfish sauce, salmon with sorrel, and beef with Roquefort sauce. ⊠ *9 rue Victor-Guichard, 89100,* ☎ *03–86–64–00–02,* ℻ *03–86–65–29–19. 25 rooms. Restaurant. MC, V.*

$$$ ▥ **Château de Prunoy.** Though it's a little out of the way, you may want to venture southwest to this vast château built by one of Louis XVI's finance ministers. It can seem a little haphazard, but if you don't expect prompt service or mind Labradors running around, you'll enjoy it. The comfortable rooms have idiosyncratic flair: One has a pair of carved, 7-ft-tall gilded wings guarding an 18th-century ivory-and-pearl-inlaid jewelry stand; another is designed as a Japanese tea house. Dinner is not especially grand, but there are few options nearby. ⊠ *89120 Charny (40 km/25 mi southwest of Sens, 40 km/25 mi northwest of Auxerre on N6 to D943 to D18),* ☎ *03–86–63–66–91,* ℻ *03–86–63–77–79. 19 rooms. Restaurant, pool, exercise room, meeting rooms. AE, DC, MC, V.*

Troyes

★ *64 km (40 mi) northeast of Sens, 179 km (111 mi) east of Paris.*

The inhabitants of Troyes would be insulted if you mistook them for Burgundians. Troyes is the capital of southern Champagne; as if to prove the point, its historic town center is shaped like a champagne cork, the rounded top enclosed by a loop of the Seine. Few, if any, French town centers contain so much to see and do. A web of enchanting pedestrian streets with timber-frame houses, magnificent churches, and fine museums and a wide choice of restaurants make it appealing. The center of Troyes is divided by quai Dampierre, a broad, busy boulevard. On one side is the quiet cathedral quarter, on the other the more upbeat, commercial part. Consider buying a Museum Passport ticket from the **tourist office** (✉ 16 bd. Carnot, ☎ 03–25–82–62–70); it admits you to the four major museums for 60 francs—a 50% savings.

❷ Although Troyes is on the Seine, it is the capital of the Aube *département* (province), run from the elegant **Préfecture** (government building) that looks out across both the artificial lake, known as the Bassin de la Préfecture, and place de la Libération from behind its gleaming gilt-iron railings.

❸ The best view from place de la Libération is undoubtedly that of the **Cathédrale St-Pierre–St-Paul**, whose 200-ft tower peeps through the trees above the statue and old lamps of the central flower garden. (At press time the tower was undergoing restoration.) Note the incomplete one-tower facade; the small Renaissance campaniles on top of the tower; and the artistry of Martin Chambiges, who worked on Troyes's facade (with its characteristic large rose window) around the same time as he did the transept of Sens. At night, the floodlit features are thrown into dramatic relief. The cathedral's vast five-aisle interior, refreshingly light thanks to large windows and the near-whiteness of the local stone, dates mainly from the 13th century. Like Sens, it has renowned stained glass—fine examples of primitive 13th-century glass in the choir and richly colored 16th-century glass in the nave and facade rose window. The arcaded triforium above the pillars of the choir was one of the first in France to be glazed rather than filled with stone. Son-et-lumière shows are held in the cathedral at varying hours in summer; contact the tourist office (☞ *above*) for details. ⊠ *pl. St-Pierre.* 🎦 *Free.* ☉ *July–mid-Sept., daily 9–1 and 2–7; mid-Sept.–June, daily 10–noon and 2–6.*

④ Just south of Troyes's cathedral is the **Musée d'Art Moderne** (Modern Art Museum), housed in the 16th- to 17th-century former Bishop's Palace. Its magnificent interior, with huge fireplaces, ceilings with carved wood beams, and a Renaissance staircase, plays host to the Levy Collection of modern art—drawings, sculpture, and nearly 400 paintings. ⊠ *Palais Épiscopal, pl. St-Pierre,* ☏ *03–25–80–57–30.* 🎟 *32 frs.* ☉ *Wed.–Mon. 11–6.*

Facing the cathedral square, the buildings of the former Abbaye St-Loup
⑤ now house the **Musée des Beaux-Arts et d'Archéologie** (Fine Arts and Archaeology Museum), often referred to as the Musée St-Loup. There are exhibits devoted to natural history, with impressive collections of birds and meteorites; local archaeological finds, especially gold-mounted 5th-century jewelry and a Gallo-Roman bronze statue of Apollo; medieval statuary and gargoyles; and paintings from the 15th to the 19th century, including works by Rubens, Anthony Van Dyck, Antoine Watteau, François Boucher, and Jacques-Louis David. ⊠ *1 rue Chrétien-de-Troyes,* ☏ *03–25–42–33–33, ext. 35–92.* 🎟 *32 frs.* ☉ *Wed.–Mon. 10–noon and 2–6.*

Where the rue de la Cité, packed with restaurants, joins quai Dampierre, it passes in front of the superb wrought-iron gates of the 18th-century
⑥ **Hôtel-Dieu** (hospital), topped with the blue-and-gold fleurs-de-lis emblems of the French monarchy. Around the corner is the entrance to the **pharmacie,** the former medical laboratory, the only part of the Hôtel-Dieu open to visitors. ⊠ *quai des Comtes-de-Champagne,* ☏ *03–25–42–33–33, ext. 35–92.* 🎟 *20 frs.* ☉ *Wed.–Mon. 10–noon and 2–6.*

⑦ Southwest of quai Dampierre, on rue Clemenceau, is the **Basilique St-Urbain,** built between 1262 and 1286 by Pope Urban IV, who was born in Troyes. St-Urbain is one of the most remarkable churches in France, a perfect culmination of Gothic's quest to replace stone walls with stained glass. Huge windows, containing much of their original glass, ring the church, while the exterior bristles with the thrust-bearing flying buttresses that made this daring structure possible. ⊠ *pl. Vernier.* 🎦 *Free.* ☉ *July–mid-Sept., daily 10:30–5; mid-Sept.–June, daily 10–noon and 2–6.*

Place du Maréchal-Foch, the main square of central Troyes, is flanked
⑧ by cafés, shops, and the delightful early 17th-century facade of the **Hôtel de Ville** (Town Hall). In summer, the square is filled from morning to night.

⑨ The clock tower of the church of **St-Jean** is an unmistakable landmark. England's warrior king, Henry V, married Catherine of France in 1420 here. The church's tall 16th-century choir contrasts with the low earlier nave. ⊠ *pl. du Marché au Pain.* 🎦 *Free.* ☉ *July–mid-Sept., daily 10:30–5; mid-Sept.–June, daily 10–noon and 2–6.*

⑩ The church of **Ste-Madeleine,** the oldest in Troyes, is best known for its elaborate triple-arched stone rood screen separating the nave and the choir. Only six other such screens still remain in France—most were dismantled during the French Revolution—and this one was carved with panache by Jean Gailde between 1508 and 1517. ⊠ *rue de la Madeleine.* 🎦 *Free.* ☉ *July–mid-Sept., daily 10:30–5; mid-Sept.–June, daily 10–noon and 2–6.*

⓫ The private museum known as **Maison de l'Outil** (Tool House), in the 16th-century Hôtel de Mauroy, contains a collection of paintings, models, and tools relevant to such traditional wood-related trades as carpentry, clog making, and barrel making. ⊠ *7 rue de la Trinité*, ☎ *03–25–73–28–26.* ➾ *30 frs.* ☉ *Daily 9–noon and 2–6.*

⓬ The 16th-century church of **St-Pantaléon,** which primarily serves the local Polish community, is close to the Maison de l'Outil, via Bordet. A number of fine stone statues, surmounted by canopies, cluster around its pillars. The tall, narrow walls are topped not by stone vaults but by a wooden roof, unusual for such a late church. ⊠ *rue de Turenne.* ➾ *Free.* ☉ *July–mid-Sept., daily 10:30–5; mid-Sept.–June, daily 10–noon and 2–6.*

⓭ The Renaissance **Hôtel de Vauluisant** houses two museums: the **Musée Historique** (History Museum) and the **Musée de la Bonneterie** (Bonnet-Making Museum). The former traces the development of Troyes and southern Champagne, with a section devoted to religious art, and the latter outlines the history and manufacturing process of the town's traditional bonnet-making industry. ⊠ *4 rue Vauluisant*, ☎ *03–25–42–33–33, ext. 35–92.* ➾ *Joint ticket for both museums 30 frs.* ☉ *Wed.–Mon. 10–noon and 2–6.*

⓮ **St-Nicolas** (⊠ *blvd. Victor-Hugo*) is another of Troyes's many churches. You may not be tempted by its grimy exterior, but undaunted souls will be rewarded by the chance to scale a wide stone staircase up to an exuberantly decorated chapel and an unexpected view over the nave.

Dining and Lodging

The pleasure of Troyes is its old town, Vieux Troyes. This is where you want your hotel to be or at least within walking distance. If you want to dine informally, it is also the area to find a restaurant. There are many on rue Champeraux: A popular one is **Grill St-Jean** (⊠ *19 rue Champeraux*, ☎ *03–25–73–57–26*) with menus starting at 85 francs. Rue St-Jean also has lots of low-key bars and bistros frequented by a youthful crowd.

$$$ ✕ **Valentino.** The restaurant is in an old, half-timber building on a pedestrian street next to the Hôtel de Ville, but its flowery interior makes a bold effort to mimic Art Deco chic. Tables are set outside in summer. Oysters are served as a complement to the menu's fish specialties—grilled crayfish with poppy seeds, and Brittany lobster in a casserole flavored with ginger. ⊠ *11 cour de la Rencontre*, ☎ *03–25–73–14–14. Jacket and tie. AE, DC, MC, V. Closed Mon. and mid-Aug.–early Sept. No dinner Sun.*

$$$ ☵ **Relais St-Jean.** This calm, stylish hotel, in the pedestrian zone near St-Jean, has fully equipped, good-size rooms. Service is personal—the staff knows guests by name. The hotel has no restaurant, but next door is the friendly Valentino (⊠ *8 rue St-Jean*, ☎ *03–25–73–14–14*), with dining in its courtyard. ⊠ *49 rue Paillot-de-Montabert, 10000*, ☎ *03–25–73–89–90*, ℻ *03–25–73–88–60. 22 rooms. Bar, air-conditioning. AE, DC, MC, V. Closed mid-Dec.–early Jan.*

$$ ☵ **Royal.** This renovated 19th-century hotel benefits by being less than a five-minute walk from Vieux Troyes and from the train and bus station (with windows open, you can hear the passing TGV—close them and it's quiet). Rooms are standard for a refurbished hotel: smallish, with either a double or single beds, a desk, and a couple of chairs. There's no lounge area, but the bar serves well in the evening. ⊠ *22 bd. Carnot, 10000 Troyes*, ☎ *03–25–73–19–99*, ℻ *03–25–73–47–85. 37 rooms. Bar, restaurant. AE, DC, MC, V.*

BONUS MILES MAKE GREAT SOUVENIRS.

Earn Miles With Your MCI Card.

Take the MCI Card along on this trip and start earning miles for the next one. You'll earn frequent flyer miles on all your calls and save with the low rates you've come to expect from MCI. Before you know it, you'll be on your way to some other international destination.

Sign up for MCI by calling 1-800-FLY-FREE

Earn Frequent Flyer Miles.

Is this a great time, or what? :-)

Easy To Call Home.

1. To use your MCI Card, just dial the WorldPhone access number of the country you're calling from.
2. Dial or give the operator your MCI Card number.
3. Dial or give the number you're calling.

# Austria (CC) ♦	022-903-012
# Belarus (CC)	
From Brest, Vitebsk, Grodno, Minsk	8-800-103
From Gomel and Mogilev regions	8-10-800-103
# Belgium (CC) ♦	0800-10012
# Bulgaria	00800-0001
# Croatia (CC) ★	0800-22-0112
# Czech Republic (CC) ♦	00-42-000112
# Denmark (CC) ♦	8001-0022
# Finland (CC) ♦	08001-102-80
# France (CC) ♦	0-800-99-0019
# Germany (CC)	0800-888-8000
# Greece (CC) ♦	00-800-1211
# Hungary (CC) ♦	00▼800-01411
# Iceland (CC) ♦	800-9002
# Ireland (CC)	1-800-55-1001
# Italy (CC) ♦	172-1022
# Kazakhstan (CC)	8-800-131-4321
# Liechtenstein (CC) ♦	0800-89-0222
# Luxembourg	0800-0112
# Monaco (CC) ♦	800-90-019
# Netherlands (CC) ♦	0800-022-9122
# Norway (CC) ♦	800-19912
# Poland (CC) ÷	00-800-111-21-22
# Portugal (CC) ÷	05-017-1234
Romania (CC) ÷	01-800-1800
# Russia (CC) ÷ ♦	
To call using ROSTELCOM ■	747-3322
For a Russian-speaking operator	747-3320
To call using SOVINTEL ■	960-2222
# San Marino (CC) ♦	172-1022
# Slovak Republic (CC)	00-421-00112
# Slovenia	080-8808
# Spain (CC)	900-99-0014
# Sweden (CC) ♦	020-795-922
# Switzerland (CC) ♦	0800-89-0222
# Turkey (CC) ♦	00-8001-1177
# Ukraine (CC) ÷	8▼10-013
# United Kingdom (CC)	
To call using BT ■	0800-89-0222
To call using C&W ■	0500-89-0222
# Vatican City (CC)	172-1022

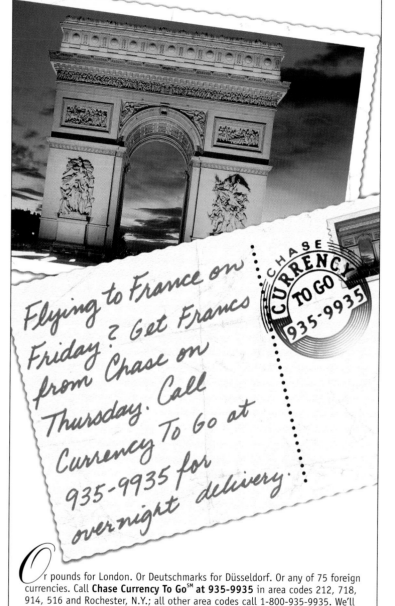

$ 🏨 **Les Comptes de Champagne.** In a 12th-century house in Vieux Troyes, this small hotel offers a step back in time if you're traveling on a near-empty wallet. Rooms are basic, with enough space for a bed and a table; a few have a shower and toilet, whereas the rest share. The whole hotel is a little dark since the light has a hard time finding its way into the narrow streets of Vieux Troyes, but it's all part of the medieval quaintness. ⊠ *56 rue de la Monnaie, 10000,* ☎ *03–25–73–11–70,* FAX *03–25–73–06–02. 28 rooms, 23 with bath. MC, V.*

Shopping

If there is an ideal place for a shopping spree, it's Troyes. Many clothing manufacturers are just outside town, so prices in stores are often 50% cheaper than elsewhere in France. Rue des Bas-Trévois, rue Bégand, and rue Cartalon are good places to look.

Pontigny

⑮ *60 km (37 mi) south of Troyes, 56 km (35 mi) southeast of Sens.*

Pontigny can easily be mistaken for another drowsy, dusty village, but its once-proud abbey is as large as many cathedrals; in the 12th and 13th centuries, it sheltered three archbishops of Canterbury, including St. Thomas à Becket. The **Abbaye de Pontigny** was founded in 1114, but the current church was begun in 1150. The monks belonged to the Cistercian order, which, frowning on the opulence of the rival House of Cluny, fostered buildings of intense sobriety. Small, even-spaced windows render the abbey's silhouette monotonous, but inside, they serenely illuminate the tall, pale shafts of stone. The single tower, that of the facade, scrambles almost apologetically to roof level. The only ornament is provided by the late-17th-century wooden choir stalls, carved with garlands and angels. ☎ *03–86–47–54–99.* 🎟 *Free, 20 frs for a guided tour.* ☉ *Daily 9–7, except during services.*

Auxerre

⑯ *21 km (13 mi) southwest of Pontigny, 58 km (36 mi) southeast of Sens.*

Auxerre is a small, peaceful town perched on a steep hill overlooking the River Yonne. The town's dominant feature is the **Cathédrale St-Étienne,** rising majestically from the squat houses around it. The 13th-century choir, the oldest part of the edifice, contains its original stained glass, dominated by dazzling reds and blues. Beneath the choir, the frescoed 11th-century Romanesque crypt keeps company with the treasury, which features medieval enamels, manuscripts, and miniatures. A 75-minute son-et-lumière show focusing on Roman Gaul is presented every evening from June to September. ⊠ *pl. St-Étienne,* ☎ *03–86–52–31–68.* 🎟 *Crypt and treasury 8 frs each; 25-fr Passport Ticket allows entry to crypt and treasury plus St-Germain (☞ below).* ☉ *Easter–Nov., Mon.–Sat. 9–noon and 2–6, Sun. 2–6.*

Fanning out from Auxerre's main square, **place des Cordeliers** (just up from the cathedral), are a number of venerable streets lined with 16th-century houses worth exploring. North of place des Cordeliers is the town's most interesting church, the former **Abbaye de St-Germain,** which stands parallel to the cathedral some 300 yards away. The church's earliest section above ground is the 11th-century Romanesque bell tower, but the extensive underground crypt dates from the 9th century and contains its original frescoes. ⊠ *pl. St-Germain,* ☎ *03–86–51–09–74.* 🎟 *20 frs.* ☉ *Guided tours of the crypt Wed.–Mon. 9–11:30 and 2–5:30.*

Dining and Lodging

$$ ✕ **La Chamaille.** This restaurant, behind the church in the small village of Chevannes, south of Auxerre, is remarkably low key for its culinary aspirations, especially in contrast to the much more formal, Michelin-starred Barnabet in central Auxerre. The mood is set by the babbling brook running through the garden and the exposed brick walls in the dining room. For starters, the chef makes a marvelous oysters in wine sauce. Follow this with the rabbit in a rich brown sauce, in a pastry. You'll be hard pressed to find room for the apple flan, but you must—it's delectable. Prices are reasonable, especially the four-course menu, which includes a half bottle of regional wine, for 210 francs. ✉ *4 rte. de Boiloup, Chevannes (10 km/6 mi south of Auxerre),* ☎ *03–86–41–24–80. MC, V. Closed Mon., Tues.*

$$ ✕ **Jardin Gourmand.** As its name implies, this restaurant features a pretty garden where you can eat in summer. The interior of this former manor house, accented by light-color oak, is equally congenial. The cuisine is innovative but simple—ravioli and foie gras, and duck with black currants. Service is discreet and the ambience elegant. ✉ *56 bd. Vauban,* ☎ *03–86–51–53–52. MC, V. Closed Mon. No lunch Tues.*

$$$ 🛏 **La Borde.** The Duclos, in their inn, a former granary of a manorial
★   estate southwest of Auxerre, offer four delightful, large rooms. You'll find exposed timbers, walls painted golden hues, and Indian rugs scattered on clay-tile floors. Furniture is kept to a minimum, except for a few antiques. Table d'hôte dinners (for just under 200 francs) are served in the huge kitchen and may include homemade terrine, roast leg of pork, cheese, and local Burgundy wine. Conversation is usually in English (the owners speak it fluently), since most guests come from the States. Advance reservations are essential. ✉ *89130 Leugny (20 km/12 mi southwest of Auxerre on D50 east of Toucy),* ☎ *03–86–47–64–28,* 🖷 *03–86–47–60–28. 4 rooms. No credit cards.*

$$ 🛏 **Le Maxime.** This slightly old-fashioned, family-run hotel on the banks of the Yonne, a five-minute walk from the old town, is appealing if you like a personal touch. Rooms are smallish but quite adequate and neat. Though you may hear a little street noise during the day, ask for a room with a river view. The bar, Le Cave de Bourgogne, with its exposed beams and copper pots, is a comfortable place for a drink. Closed garage parking is conveniently adjacent to the hotel. ✉ *2 quai de la Marine, 89000,* ☎ *03–86–52–14–19,* 🖷 *03–86–52–21–70. 25 rooms. Bar, parking. AE, DC, MC, V. Closed late Dec.–late Jan.*

$–$$ 🛏 **Normandie.** The grand-looking, vine-covered Normandie is in the center of Auxerre, a short walk from the cathedral. Rooms are unpretentious and clean and have such pleasantries as hair dryers in the bathroom. The garden is a nice place to relax. ✉ *41 bd. Vauban, 89000,* ☎ *03–86–52–57–80,* 🖷 *03–86–51–54–33. 48 rooms. Bar, sauna, exercise room. AE, DC, MC, V.*

Chablis

17   *16 km (10 mi) east of Auxerre, 74 km (45 mi) south of Troyes, 183 km (114 mi) southeast of Paris.*

The pretty little village of Chablis, famous for its white wine, nestles on the banks of the River Serein ("serene") and is protected by the massive, round, turreted towers of the Porte Noël gateway. Although "Chablis" in America has become a generic name for cheap white wine, not so in France: It's a fine, slightly oak-tasting wine of tremendous character, with the Premier Cru and Grand Cru wines standing head-to-head with the best French whites. Prices in the local shops tend to be inflated, so your best bet is to buy directly from a vineyard; keep in mind that most are closed Sunday.

Dining and Lodging

$$–$$$ ✕🏠 **Hostellerie des Clos.** The moderately priced, simple yet comfort-
★ able rooms at this inn have floral curtains and wicker tables with
chairs. Most of all, come here for the food; it's the best in the region.
Chef Michel Vignaud cooks superb cuisine: *sandre* (whitefish) served
with a chicken-based sauce, casserole of hare, and *huîtres d'Isgny*
(small oysters) in a dill and Chablis sauce. Desserts are equally splendid. ⊠ *rue Jules-Rathier, 89800,* ☎ *03–86–42–10–63,* 𝔉𝔸𝔛 *03–86–
42–17–11. 26 rooms. Restaurant. AE, DC, MC, V.*

$ 🏠 **Domaine de Montpierreux.** This private manor on a truffle farm south
of Chablis has five immaculate rooms on its top floor. All are delightfully decorated in paisley fabrics and at least one piece of provincial
antique furniture. The friendly owners help to make this a very comfortable base for exploring the area. Breakfast is served. ⊠ *89290 Venoy
(6 km/4 mi south of Chablis, 10 km/6 mi north of Auxerre on D965),*
☎ *03–86–40–20–91,* 𝔉𝔸𝔛 *03–86–40–28–00. 5 rooms. No credit cards.*

Tonnerre

⓲ *16 km (10 mi) northeast of Chablis, 60 km (37 mi) south of Troyes.*

The small town of Tonnerre was mostly rebuilt after a devastating fire
in 1556. Survey the 16th-century reconstruction and the Armançon Valley from the terrace of **St-Pierre** church. The chief attraction, the high-
roofed **Ancien Hôpital,** or Hôtel-Dieu (hospital), was built in 1293 and
has survived the passing centuries—flames and all—largely intact. The
main room, the **Grande Salle,** is 280 ft long and retains its oak ceiling;
it was conceived as the hospital ward and after 1650 served as the parish
church. The original hospital church leads off from the Grande Salle;
in the adjoining **Chapelle du Revestière,** a dramatic 15th-century stone
group represents the *Burial of Christ.* Look for good finds at the **Salon
des Antiquaires** (Antiques Fair), held here on All Saints weekend (second weekend in November). ⊠ *rue du Prieuré,* ☎ *03–86–54–33–
00.* 🎫 *26 frs.* ☉ *June–Sept., Wed.–Mon. 10–noon and 1–6; Apr.–May
and Oct., weekends 1–6.*

Tanlay

⓳ *10 km (6 mi) east of Tonnerre, 45 km (28 mi) northeast of Auxerre.*

Tanlay is best known for its castle, the **Château de Tanlay.** Built around
1550, it is an example of the classical influence of the Renaissance. The
vestibule, framed by wrought-iron railings, leads to a wood-paneled
salon and dining room filled with period furniture. A graceful staircase climbs to the second floor with a frescoed gallery and ornate fireplaces. A small room in the tower above was used as a secret meeting
place by Huguenot Protestants during the 1562–98 Wars of Religion;
note the cupola with its fresco of scantily clad 16th-century religious
personalities. ☎ *03–86–75–70–61.* 🎫 *Guided tours 40 frs, grounds
only 15 frs.* ☉ *Apr.–Nov. 11, Wed.–Mon. 9:30–11:30 and 2:15–5:15.*

Lodging

$ 🏠 **Chez Bateau.** The lovely little farming village of Cuzy-le-Chatel,
on a hillside close to Tanlay, is home to this inn in a walled garden.
The large rooms are decorated with family furnishings and the beds
sag a little. Nonetheless, the rooms are good value for the money, especially the one at the end of the hall, whose exposed timbers and cross
beams form a sort of loft. ⊠ *89740 Cruzy-le-Chatel (12 km/7 mi from
Tanlay),* ☎ *03–86–75–22–78. 4 rooms, 2 with bath. No credit cards.*

Ancy-le-Franc

⑳ *11 km (7 mi) southeast of Tanlay, 55 km (34 mi) northeast of Auxerre and north of Avallon.*

Ancy-le-Franc is famous for its Renaissance château. Built from Sebastiano Serlio's designs with interior decor by Primaticcio, both of whom worked at the court of François I (1515–47), the **Château d'Ancy-le-Franc** has an Italian flavor. The plain, majestic exterior contrasts with the sumptuous rooms and apartments, many—particularly the magnificent Chambre des Arts (Art Gallery)—with carved or painted walls and ceilings and their original furniture. Such grandeur won the approval of Sun King Louis XIV, no less, who once stayed in the Salon Bleu (Blue Room). Adjoining the château is a small **Musée Automobile** (Automobile Museum). ✉ *pl. Clermont-Tonnerre,* ☎ *03–86–75–14–63.* 🎫 *Château and museum 42 frs, museum only 20 frs.* ☉ *Late Mar.–mid-Nov. 10–5 10–5 or (until 6. May–Sept.). Guided château tours at 10, 11, 2, 3, 4, 5, and (May–Sept.) 6.*

Abbaye de Fontenay

★ ㉑ *50 km (31 mi) southeast of Tonnerre, 72 km (45 mi) east of Auxerre.*

Just east of Montbard is the Cistercian Abbaye de Fontenay, founded by St. Bernard in 1118. The same Cistercian criteria applied to Fontenay as to Pontigny (☞ *above*): no-frills architecture and an isolated site. By the end of the 12th century, the buildings were finished, and the abbey's community grew to some 300 monks. It prospered until the 16th century, when religious wars and administrative mayhem hastened its decline. Dissolved during the French Revolution, the abbey was used as a paper factory until 1906. Fortunately, the historic buildings emerged unscathed.

The abbey is surrounded by extensive gardens dotted with the fountains that gave it its name. The church's solemn interior is lit by windows in the facade and by a double row of three narrow windows, representing the Trinity, in the choir. A staircase in the south transept leads to the wood-roofed dormitory (spare a thought for the bleary-eyed monks, obliged to stagger down for services in the dead of night). The chapter house, flanked by a majestic arcade, and the scriptorium, where monks worked on their manuscripts, lead off from the adjoining cloisters. ✉ *Montbard,* ☎ *03–80–92–15–00.* 🎫 *50 frs.* ☉ *Daily 9–noon and 2–6; guided tours only on the hr mid-Mar.–mid-Nov. (every ½ hr July–Aug.).*

Saulieu

㉒ *49 km (30 mi) south of Fontenay, 62 km (37 mi) northwest of Beaune, 77 km (49 mi) west of Dijon.*

Saulieu's reputation belies its size: It is renowned for good food (Rabelais, that roly-poly 16th-century man of letters, extolled its gargantuan hospitality) and Christmas trees (a million are packed off from the area each year).

The town's **Basilique de St-Andoche** is almost as old as that of Vézelay, though less imposing and much restored.

The **Musée François Pompon,** adjoining the basilica, is a museum devoted, in part, to the work of animal-bronze sculptor Pompon (1855–1933), whose smooth, stylized creations seem contemporary but predate World War II. The museum also contains Gallo-Roman funeral stones, sacred art, and a room devoted to local gastronomic lore. ✉ *rue Sal-*

lier, ☎ *03–80–64–19–51.* 🎫 *22 frs.* ⊙ *Apr.–Sept., Wed.–Mon. 10–12:30 and 2–6 (until 5:30, Oct.–Mar.).*

Dining and Lodging

$$
★ ✕⚏ **Chez Camille.** Small, quiet, and friendly sum up this hotel in a 16th-century house with an exterior that looks so ordinary you might easily pass it by. Rooms have period furniture and original wooden beams. Ask for No. 22 or No. 23, the most dramatic, with a beamed ceiling that looks like spokes in a wheel. Traditional Burgundian fare—duck and boar are specialties—makes up the menu in the glass-roofed restaurant. ⊠ *1 pl. Édouard-Herriot, 21230 Arnay-le-Duc (on N6 between Saulieu and Beaune),* ☎ *03–80–90–01–38,* ℻ *03–80–90–04–64. 12 rooms. Restaurant. AE, DC, MC, V.*

Châteauneuf-en-Auxois

㉓ *48 km (30 mi) east of Saulieu, 35 km (22 mi) northwest of Beaune.*

The tiny hilltop town of Châteauneuf-en-Auxois catches your eye from A6. Turn off at the marked exit and take any one of the three narrow, winding roads up and you'll suddenly feel you've entered the Middle Ages. The town's modest 15th-century church was the salvation for perhaps as many as 500 souls when the village was at its zenith. In the last few years tourists have discovered the charm of this village, so try to avoid it on weekends.

The 12th-century **Château** (with some later modifications) still commands the same breadth of view over rolling farmland as far as the eye can see. ☎ *03–80–49–21–89.* 🎫 *21 frs.* ⊙ *Apr.–Sept., tours daily at 9:30, 10:30, 11:30, 2, 3, 4, and 5. Oct.–Mar., Thurs.–Mon. at 10, 11, 2, and 3.*

Clustered behind the château are houses for ordinary folk, at least a score of them notable for their 14th- and 15th-century charm, where today just 63 people live. One of them, **M. Simon** (☎ *03–80–49–21–59*), is so proud of his village that he gladly takes small groups on tours of the sights.

Dining and Lodging

$$$$ ✕⚏ **Château la Chassagne.** Feel like a king or a queen for a night at this former country estate where you can even arrive by private plane or helicopter and be picked up in a Rolls-Royce. Rooms are high ceilinged and spacious—their best attribute; for although the modern wrought-iron and cane furnishings are obviously expensive, they are of disputable taste. The extensive grounds include a golf driving range, tennis courts, and a swimming pool. The restaurant, managed separately, is quite formal. Nouvelle cuisine is served, but the chef seems to focus more on artistic presentation than creative tastes; still it's enjoyable. ⊠ *21410 Pont de Pany (12 km/7 mi from Châteauneuf-en-Auxois off A38, shortly after the junction with A8),* ☎ *03–80–40–47–50,* ℻ *03–80–23–66–28. 33 rooms. Restaurant, pool, driving range, 2 tennis courts, helipad, private airstrip. AE, DC, MC, V.*

$$ ✕⚏ **Hostellerie du Château.** This hotel is in an ancient timbered building in the shadow of the castle. The restaurant serves classical Bourgogne fare—roasted *époisses* (local cow's milk cheese) on a salad bed with walnuts, noisettes of lamb with thyme, and coq au vin. Rooms vary considerably—from small to much more commodious. The best have a view of the castle. ⊠ *Châteauneuf-en-Auxois, 21320 Pouilly,* ☎ *03–80–49–22–00,* ℻ *03–80–49–21–27. 17 rooms. Restaurant. Closed Nov.–mid-Mar.*

Château de Sully

㉔ *37 km (28 mi) south of Châteauneuf-en-Auxois, 33 km (20 mi) south-east of Saulieu.*

The turreted Renaissance Château de Sully stands in a stately park, surrounded by a moat. A monumental staircase leads to the north front and a broad terrace. Marshal MacMahon, president of France from 1873 to 1879, was born here in 1808. ☎ 03–85–82–10–27. ✉ *Guided tours 35 frs, grounds 15 frs.* ☉ *Château 45-min guided tours June–Sept. (call for times). Grounds daily 10–noon and 2–6.*

Autun

㉕ *9 km (6 mi) southwest of Sully, 41 km (25 mi) south of Saulieu, 49 km (30 mi) west of Beaune.*

Autun has been an important town since Roman times, as you can detect from the well-preserved archways, Porte St-André and Porte d'Arroux, and the Théâtre Romain, once the largest arena in Gaul. Julius Caesar even referred to Autun as the "sister and rival of Rome itself." Another famous warrior, Napoléon, studied here in 1779 at the military academy (now the Lycée Bonaparte).

★ Autun's principal monument is the **Cathédrale St-Lazarus,** built from 1120 to 1146 to house the relics of St. Lazarus; the main tower, spire, and upper reaches of the chancel were added in the late 15th century. The influx of medieval pilgrims accounts for the building's size (35 yards wide and nearly 80 yards long). Lazarus's tomb was dismantled in 1766 by canons who were believers in the rationalist credo of the Enlightenment. They also did their best to transform the Romanesque-Gothic cathedral into a classical temple at the same time, adding pilasters and classical ornaments willy-nilly. Fortunately, some of the best Romanesque stonework, including the inspired nave capitals and the tympanum above the main door—a gracefully elongated *Last Judgment* sculpted by Gislebertus in the 1130s—emerged unscathed. Jean-Auguste Ingres's painting depicting the *Martyrdom of St. Symphorien* has been relegated to a dingy chapel in the north aisle of the nave. The cathedral provides a stunning setting for **Musique en Morvan,** a classical music festival in July. ✉ *pl. St-Louis.*

The **Musée Rolin,** across from the cathedral, contains several fine paintings from the Middle Ages and good examples of Burgundian sculpture, including a Gislebertus masterpiece, the *Temptation of Eve,* which originally topped one of the side doors of the cathedral. ✉ *pl. St-Louis,* ☎ 03–85–52–09–76. ✉ *18 frs.* ☉ *Nov.–Mar., Mon. and Wed.–Sat. 10–noon and 2–6, Sun. 10–noon and 2–5; Apr.–Sept., Wed.–Mon. 9:30–noon and 1:30–6; Oct., Mon. and Wed.–Sat. 10–noon and 2–5, Sun. 10–noon and 2:30–5.*

The **Amphithéâtre Roman** at the edge of town on the road to Chalon-sur-Saône is a historic spot for lunch. Pick up the makings in town and eat your picnic on the stepped seats where as many as 15,000 Gallo-Roman spectators sat two millennia ago. In August, a Gallo-Roman performance—the only one of its kind—is performed by 1,600 local residents in period costume in the amphitheater. If you're in a classical mood, don't miss the **Temple of Janus,** in a field at the other edge of town as you leave for Château-Chinon. Keep your eyes peeled to the right for the turnoff.

Dining and Lodging

$ ✕ **Chalet Bleu.** Solid, traditional French cuisine is served in a setting that resembles a converted conservatory. Foie gras and beef with shallots are trustworthy choices, but chef Philippe Bouché is creative with Bourgogne recipes, so be adventuresome. ⌧ *3 rue Jeannin,* ☎ *03–85–86–27–30. AE, DC, MC, V. Closed Tues. No dinner Mon.*

$$ 🏨 **St-Louis.** This comfortable hotel, on a quiet street away from the traffic noise, dates from the 17th century; legend has it that Napoléon once slept here. His room is now a suite with a bed in each of the two alcoves. Renovated in 1997, the hotel now has lots of well-designed wrought-iron furnishings, including beds and lighting fixtures, imported from Mexico. Even the new manager hails from North America. The pleasant patio-garden is a delight for breakfast or an evening libation, and the restaurant, La Rotonde, is one of Autun's best. ⌧ *6 rue de l'Arbalète, 71400,* ☎ *03–85–52–01–01,* FAX *03–85–86–32–54. 52 rooms. Restaurant. AE, DC, MC, V.*

Château-Chinon

㉖ *37 km (23 mi) west of Autun, 58 km (36 mi) south of Avallon.*

Late president François Mitterrand was the former mayor of the small town of Château-Chinon, the capital of the Morvan. One of his legacies is the brash, colorful, and controversial **Niki de St-Phalle Fontaine,** in front of the Hôtel de Ville. The **Musée du Septennat** (Septannate Museum) contains an astonishing variety of gifts Mitterrand received while president. ⌧ *6 rue du Château,* ☎ *03–86–85–19–23.* 🎫 *25 frs.* ⊘ *May–Oct., daily 10–6; Nov.–Apr., weekends 10–6.*

☾ The **Musée du Costume** (Costume Museum) has exhibits on the traditions of the Morvan. ⌧ *16–18 rue St-Christophe,* ☎ *03–86–85–18–55.* 🎫 *25 frs.* ⊘ *Nov.–May, weekends 10–6; June and Sept.–Oct., daily 10–6; July–Aug., daily 10–7.*

Nevers

㉗ *64 km (40 mi) west of Château-Chinon, 119 km (74 mi) south of Auxerre, 239 km (149 mi) southeast of Paris.*

Burgundy's western outpost, Nevers, on the banks of the Loire, has been producing earthenware since the late 16th century. Promoted initially by Italian craftsmen, the industry suffered during the French Revolution, but three traditional manufacturers remain. An extensive selection of Nevers earthenware, retracing its stylistic development, can be admired at the **Musée Municipal** (Town Museum). ⌧ *promenade des Remparts,* ☎ *03–86–68–45–62.* 🎫 *10 frs.* ⊘ *May–Sept., Wed.–Mon. 10–5:15; Oct.–Apr., Wed.–Mon. 10–11:45 and 2–5:15.*

Part of Nevers's medieval walls extend behind the Town Museum, culminating in the intimidating gateway known as the **Porte du Croux** (built in 1393), which, thanks to its turrets and huge, sloping roof, resembles a small castle.

The **Cathédrale** (⌧ rue du Cloître-St-Cyr), with its 170-ft square tower and two apses, is an enormous building, constructed during several periods of the Middle Ages. The **Palais Ducal,** beyond the cathedral, has a sumptuous, large-windowed Renaissance facade but, unfortunately, is closed to the public.

Across a park that can be entered from the central place Carnot, a few hundred yards north of the Palais Ducal, is the **Couvent St-Gildard,** the convent where St. Bernadette of Lourdes (1844–79) spent the last 13 years of her life. A small museum contains mementos and outlines her life story (she claimed to have seen the Virgin several times in 1858 and was canonized in 1933). ⌧ *rue St-Gildard,* ☎ *03–86–36–91–45.* 🎫 *Free.* ⊘ *Daily 10–5.*

Dining

$–$$ ✕ **Cours St-Étienne.** Not only is the food delicious, exquisitely presented, and of excellent value, but the ambience is also serene. Enjoy lunch on the terrace overlooking the courtyard of St-Étienne or in one of the cozy dining rooms. The 82-franc lunch menu may start with smoked trout with peaches or a terrine of mushrooms; then move on to chicken *ballotine* (rolled and stuffed with chives); and end with dessert or cheese. The more expensive 100- and 120-franc menus have wider selections. ✉ *33 rue St-Étienne,* ☎ *03–86–36–74–57. Reservations essential. Closed Aug. and 1st 2 wks of Jan. No dinner Sun., no lunch Mon. MC, V.*

The Arts

Musique en Nivernais, a classical music festival, takes place in September and October.

La Charité-sur-Loire

㉘ *24 km (15 mi) northwest of Nevers, 91 km (57 mi) south of Auxerre.*

La Charité-sur-Loire is best known for its medieval church. Unlike those of Pontigny and Fontenay, the abbey church of **Ste-Croix-Notre-Dame** was dependent on Cluny; when it was consecrated by Pope Pascal II in 1107, it was the country's second largest church. Fire and neglect have taken their toll on the massive original edifice, and these days the church is cut in two, with the single-tower facade separated from the imposing choir and transept by pretty place Ste-Croix (where the nave used to be). A fine view of the church's exterior can be seen from square des Bénédictins, just off Grande-Rue.

Clamecy

㉙ *51 km (32 mi) northeast of La Charité-sur-Loire, 44 km (27 mi) south of Auxerre.*

Slow-moving Clamecy is not on many tourist itineraries, but its tumbling alleyways and untouched, ancient houses epitomize *La France Profonde.* The multishape roofs, dominated by the majestic square tower of the church of **St-Martin,** are best viewed from the banks of the Yonne River. The river played a crucial role in Clamecy's development; trees from the nearby Morvan Forest were chopped down and floated to Paris in huge convoys. The history of this form of transport (*flottage*), which lasted until 1923, is detailed in the Musée Municipal (Town Museum), also known as the **Musée d'Art et d'Histoire Romain Rolland** (Romain Rolland Museum of Art and History) for native son Rolland, Nobel laureate for literature in 1915. Faience and paintings from the 17th– 19th centuries are also on display. ✉ *av. de la République,* ☎ *03–86– 27–17–99.* 🎟 *15 frs.* ☼ *Nov.–Easter, Mon. and Wed.–Sat. 10–noon and 3–6; Easter–Oct., Wed.–Mon. 10–noon and 2–6.*

In homage to the logs that were once floated downriver, *bûchette* (a log-shape, sugared-almond candy) has long been a favorite of Clamecyçois. Sample it at **Avignon** (✉ *22 rue de la Monnaie,* near steps leading to St-Martin), a pastry shop and tearoom.

Dining and Lodging

$–$$ ✕🏠 **Hostellerie de la Poste.** This family-run hotel, in an old coaching stop in the heart of Clamecy, has a welcoming feel. The old-fashioned rooms are small and worn but tidy and clean. It's a popular place for lunching locals, who all seem to be greeted warmly by madame at the desk. Regional fare is served; menus start at 100 francs. ✉ *9 pl. Émile Zola, 58500,* ☎ *03–86–27–01–55,* 🅵🅰🆇 *03–86–27–05–99. 16 rooms. Bar, restaurant, meeting rooms. MC, V.*

Vézelay

30 *24 km (15 mi) east of Clamecy, 51 km (32 mi) south of Auxerre, 13 km (8 mi) southwest of Avallon.*

The somewhat isolated, picturesque town of Vézelay is on a peak, with one main street, rue St-Étienne, climbing steeply to its summit and its medieval basilica. In summer, you'll have to leave your car at the bottom and walk up. Off-season, you can drive up and look for a spot to park in the square.

★ In the 11th and 12th centuries, the celebrated **Basilique Ste-Madeleine** was one of the focal points of Christendom. Pilgrims poured in to gasp at the relics of St. Mary Magdalene before setting off on the great trek to the shrine of St. James at Santiago de Compostela in northwest Spain. By the mid-13th century, the authenticity of St. Mary's relics was in doubt; others had been discovered in Provence. The basilica's decline continued until the French Revolution, when the basilica and adjoining monastery buildings were sold by the state. Only the basilica escaped demolition and was falling into ruin when ace restorer Viollet-le-Duc rode to the rescue in 1840 (he also restored the cathedrals of Laon and Amiens and Paris's Notre-Dame).

Today the basilica, under the patrimony of UNESCO, has recaptured its onetime glory and is considered to be France's most prestigious Romanesque showcase. Note the wonderful decoration in the nave, whose column capitals, imaginatively designed and superbly carved, represent miniature medieval men in all manner of situations. The basilica's exterior is best seen from the leafy terrace to the right of the facade. Opposite, a vast, verdant panorama encompasses lush valleys and rolling hills and hedgerows. In the forefront is the Flamboyant Gothic spire of St-Père-sous-Vézelay, a tiny village 3 km (2 mi) away that is the site of Marc Meneau's famed restaurant (☞ Dining and Lodging, *below*). ☒ *pl. de la Basilique,* ☎ *03–86–33–27–73.* ◻ *Free, but a donation of 15 frs is appreciated.* ◷ *8–8, except during offices Mon.– Sat. 12:15–1:15 and 5:15–7:15, and Sun. 10:30–12:30.*

Just 10 km (6 mi) out of Vézelay in the small town of Bazoches-du-Morvan is the **Château de Bazoches,** the former home of Maréchal de Vauban. Built in the 12th century in the form of a trapezium with four towers and a keep, the building was bought by Vauban in 1675 with the money Louis XIV awarded him for devising the parallel trenches successfully used in the siege of Maastricht. Vauban transformed the building into a fortress and created many of his military engineering designs here. These, and furnishings of his day, are on display. ☒ *Bazoches-du-Morvan,* ☎ *03–86–22–10–22.* ◻ *Free.* ◷ *Late Mar.– early Nov., 9:30–noon and 2:15–6.*

Dining and Lodging

$$$$ ✕▦ **L'Espérance.** Chef Marc Meneau is not the most modest of men— his monogram appears everywhere—but he is renowned for his subtle, original cuisine: delicate lobster soup and scallops in lemon marmalade, for instance. The setting—by a stream and a large, statue-filled garden with Vézelay in the background—is delightful. The restaurant is closed Tuesday and lunch Wednesday; reservations are essential and a jacket required. Rooms are in different buildings and vary in price and style.☒ *89450 Vézelay,* ☎ *03–86–33–39–10,* 𝖥𝖠𝖷 *03–86–33– 26–15. 40 rooms. Restaurant. AE, DC, MC, V. Closed Feb.*

$$$ ▦ **Résidence Hôtel Le Pontot.** With Vezelay's limited lodging, you would do well to book ahead, especially in this historic fortified house with sumptuous little rooms and a lovely garden. Another advantage is the hotel's location in the center of the village halfway up the hill.

⊠ *pl. du Pontot, 89450,* ☎ *03–86–33–24–40,* FAX *no fax. 10 rooms. DC, MC, V. Closed Nov.–Apr.*

$$ 🏨 **Hôtel de la Poste et du Lion d'Or.** On a small square in the lower part of town is the old-fashioned, rambling Lion d'Or. A terrace out front welcomes you; the good-size rooms are decorated with traditional chintzes. The comfortable restaurant is a popular spot with locals who come for the regional fare, such as roast partridge in black currant sauce, and rabbit casserole. ⊠ *pl. du Champ de Foire, 89450,* ☎ *03–86–33–21–23,* FAX *03–86–32–30–92. 39 rooms. Bar, restaurant. AE, MC, V. Closed mid-Nov.–mid-Mar.*

Avallon

③① *13 km (8 mi) east of Vézelay, 97 km (60 mi) northeast of Nevers, 60 km (37 mi) southeast of Auxerre.*

Avallon is spectacularly situated on a promontory jutting over the Vallée du Cousin. The town's old streets and ramparts are pleasant places for strolling, before or after viewing the works of medieval stone carvers whose imaginations ran riot on the portals of the venerable church of **St-Lazarus.** The real delight of Avallon, though, is its medieval market town ambience. It also has enough cafés, bars, and shops to make it interesting, yet it's small enough that you can quickly become familiar with it and turn it into your base for exploring the rest of the region.

Dining and Lodging

$$ ✕🏨 **Moulin des Ruats.** Once an old flour mill, the Moulin des Ruats became a family hotel in 1924 and is now a comfortable country inn run by M. Rossi. Rooms have pretty country-French decor; some have balconies overlooking the Cousin River. Ask for one that has been recently renovated; for example, Room 11, with its exposed beams and an alcove that separates the bed from the settee and table. The restaurant, fronting the river, serves traditional Bourgogne fare with a strong Provençal accent. The best option is the 230-franc menu (try the distinctive foie gras salad), but be warned that too much comes on each plate both in quantity and flavor and that dishes can be uneven. You're better off choosing simple rather than complex dishes. ⊠ *Vallée du Cousin, 89200 (4 km/2 mi southwest of Avallon),* ☎ *03–86–34–07–14,* FAX *03–86–31–65–47. 26 rooms. Restaurant. AE, DC, MC, V. Closed Nov.–Feb.*

$–$$ ✕🏨 **Les Capucins.** On a peaceful square 10 minutes from the town cen-
★ ter, this intimate hotel has rooms in a range of prices. It's better known for its restaurant, however, which features four prix-fixe menus dominated by regional cooking—duck, trout in flaky pastry, and the very local *oeufs en meurette* (eggs poached in broth and red wine). There's a pleasing garden for breakfast and aperitifs and small cozy rooms for a postprandial drink. ⊠ *6 av. Paul-Doumer (also known as av. de la Gare), 89200,* ☎ *03–86–34–06–52,* FAX *03–86–34–58–47. 8 rooms, 7 with bath. Restaurant. AE, MC, V. Closed mid-Nov.–mid-Jan.*

Parc Naturel Régional du Morvan

③② *Take D944 out of Avallon and then turn left on D10 to Quarré-les-Tombes.*

The vast Parc du Morvan encompasses a 3,500-square-km (1,290-square-mi) chunk of Burgundy. A network of roads and *Grandes Randonnées* (GRs, or big trails) winds around the park's lush forests, photogenic lakes, wooded hills, idyllic farms, and tiny villages. Hiking in the Morvan is not strenuous, but it is enchanting: Every turn down a trail provides a new country scene. Numerous itineraries through the park are mapped and marked (maps for specific trails are available from local tourist offices). About fifty 5- to 15-km (3- to 9-mi) routes are good for day hikes; another 10 or so trails of around 110 km (68 mi) each are good for much longer walks. **Quarré-les-Tombes,** one of the best little villages peppering the park, is so named because of the empty prehistoric stone tombs discovered eerily arrayed in a ring around its church. Eight kilometers (5 miles) south of Quarré-les-Tombes is **Rocher de la Pérouse,** a mighty outcrop worth scrambling up for a view of the park and the Cure Valley.

Some 25 *gîtes d'étapes* (simple bed-and-breakfasts, also known as *chambres d'hôte*) en route provide for overnight stays (to make reservations, call ☎ 03–86–78–74–93). If you are going on horseback, there are 21 gîtes with facilities for you and your horse to stay overnight. You can get horses from several stables: **La Ferme des Ruats** (⊠ Off of N6, between St-Émilion and Bussières, ☎ 03–86–33–16–57); **Le Triangle** (⊠ In Usy, ☎ 03–86–33–32–78); and **La Vieille Diligence** (⊠ Rive Droite, Lac des Settons, 58230 Montsauche, ☎ 03–86–84–55–22). For a pamphlet, *"Le Morvan à Cheval,"* that lists stables and gîtes for overnight accommodations, contact the **Parc Natural Régional du Morvan** (⊠ Maison du Parc, 58230 St-Brisson, ☎ 03–86–78–79–00, FAX 03–86–78–74–22).

WINE COUNTRY

East of the Parc du Morvan the low hills and woodland gradually open up, and vineyards, clothing the contour of the land in orderly beauty, even in winter, appear on all sides. The vineyards' steeply banked hills stand in contrast to the region's characteristic gentle slopes. Burgundy's most famous vineyards run south from Dijon through Beaune to Mâcon along what has become known as the Côte d'Or.

Dijon

314 km (195 mi) southeast of Paris, 119 km (74 mi) east of Avallon.

Dijon, linked to Paris by expressway (A6/A38) and high-speed TGV (*Trains à Grande Vitesse*), is the age-old capital of Burgundy. Throughout the Middle Ages, Burgundy was a duchy that led a separate existence from the rest of France, culminating in the rule of the four "Grand Dukes of the West" between 1364 and 1477. A number of monuments date from this period, including the Palais des Ducs (Ducal Palace), now largely converted into an art museum.

Dijon's fame and fortune outlasted its dukes, and the city continued to flourish under French rule from the 17th century on. It has remained the major city of Burgundy—the only one, in fact, with more than 100,000 inhabitants. Its site, on the major European north–south trade route and within striking distance of the Swiss and German borders, has helped maintain its economic importance. It's also a cultural center—a few of its 10 museums are mentioned below. And many of its gastronomic specialties are known worldwide: snails, mustard, and cassis (a black-currant liqueur often mixed with white wine—preferably Burgundy Aligoté—to make *kir,* the popular aperitif).

★ ㉝ The **Palais des Ducs** is Dijon's leading testimony to bygone splendor. The elegant, classical exterior of the former palace can best be admired from place de la Libération and cour d'Honneur. These days, it's home to one of France's major art museums, the **Musée des Beaux-Arts** (Fine Arts Museum), where the tombs of two of the aforementioned dukes—Philip the Bold and John the Fearless—are the center of a rich

322

Dijon

Cathédrale
St-Bénigne, **37**
Chartreuse de
Champmol, **41**

Musée
Archéologique, **38**
Musée d'Art Sacré, **39**

Musée d'Histoire
Naturelle/Jardin de
l'Arquebuse, **40**
Musée Magnin, **36**

Notre-Dame, **34**
Palais des Ducs/
Musée des Beaux-
Arts, **33**

St-Michel, **35**

collection of medieval objects and Renaissance furniture. Among the paintings are works by Italian old masters and French 19th-century artists, such as Théodore Géricault and Gustave Courbet, and their Realist and Impressionist successors, notably Édouard Manet and Claude Monet. The **kitchens** (circa 1435), with their six huge fireplaces, and the 14th-century **chapter house** catch the eye, as does the 15th-century **Salle des Gardes** (Guards' Room), with its richly carved and colored tombs and late-14th-century altarpieces. ✉ *pl. de la Ste-Chapelle,* ☎ *03–80–74–52–70.* 🎫 *15 frs.* ⊘ *Wed.–Mon. 10–6.*

❸❹ Notre-Dame, one of the city's oldest churches, stands out with its elegant towers, delicate nave stonework, 13th-century stained glass, and soaring chancel. ✉ *rue de la Préfecture.*

❸❺ The church of **St-Michel,** to the east of the palace, takes you forward 300 years from Notre-Dame with its chunky Renaissance facade. ✉ *pl. St-Michel.*

❸❻ The **Musée Magnin,** in a 17th-century mansion, showcases original furnishings and a variety of paintings from the 16th to the 19th century. ✉ *4 rue des Bons-Enfants,* ☎ *03–80–67–11–10.* 🎫 *15 frs.* ⊘ *June–Sept., Tues.–Sun. 10–6; Oct.–May, Tues.–Sun. 10–noon and 2–6.*

❸❼ The **Cathédrale St-Bénigne** is comparatively austere; its chief glory is the 10th-century crypt—a forest of pillars surmounted by a rotunda. ✉ *pl. St-Bénigne.*

❸❽ The **Musée Archéologique** (Archaeological Museum), housed in the former abbey buildings of St-Bénigne, traces the history of the region through archaeological discoveries. ✉ *5 rue du Dr-Maret,* ☎ *03–80–30–88–54.* 🎫 *11 frs.* ⊘ *June–Sept., Wed.–Mon. 9:30–6; Oct.–May, Wed.–Mon. 9–noon and 2–6.*

❸❾ The **Musée d'Art Sacré** (Museum of Religious Art) has a collection of altarpieces and religious sculptures in the appropriate setting of a former church. ✉ *17 rue Ste-Anne,* ☎ *03–80–30–65–91.* 🎫 *8 frs.* ⊘ *Wed.–Mon. 9–noon and 2–6.*

❹⓪ The **Musée d'Histoire Naturelle** (Natural History Museum) sits behind the train station in the impressive botanical garden, the **Jardin de l'Arquebuse.** The garden is a pleasant place to stroll amid the wide variety of trees and tropical flowers. ✉ *1 av. Albert-I,* ☎ *03–80–76–82–76 museum, 03–80–76–82–84 garden.* 🎫 *Museum 11 frs, garden free.* ⊘ *Museum Wed.–Mon. 9–noon and 2–6; garden daily 7:30–6 (until 8 PM in summer).*

More links with Dijon's medieval past can be found west of the town center, just off avenue Albert-I beyond the train station. Keep an eye **❹❶** out for the exuberant 15th-century gateway to the **Chartreuse de Champmol**—all that remains of a former charter house. Next to it is the **Puits de Moïse,** the so-called Well of Moses, with six large, compellingly realistic medieval statues on a hexagonal base (1395–1405).

Dining and Lodging

Restaurants abound in Dijon, but there are three very popular areas for casual dining. One is around place Darcy, a square that caters to all tastes and budgets: Choose from the bustling Concorde brasserie, the quiet bar of the Hôtel de la Cloche, the underground Caveau de la Porte Guillaume wine-and-snack bar, or—for your sweet tooth—the Pâtisserie Darcy. For a really inexpensive meal, try the cafeteria Le Fluncy on boulevard de la Trémouille (near place Darcy). Two other areas for casual dining in the evening are place Émile Zola and the old market (Les Halles), along rue Bannelier.

$$$ ✕ **Central Grill Rôtisserie.** This grill room, attached to the Central Ibis hotel (☞ *below*), is a good alternative to the gastronomic sophistication of Dijon. There's carpaccio and smoked salmon in addition to heavier *abats* (organ meats). ⊠ *3 pl. Grangier,* ☏ *03–80–30–44–00. AE, DC, MC, V. Closed Sun.*

$$–$$$ ✕ **Dame Aquitaine.** In a happy marriage between two of France's greatest gastronomic regions, chef Monique Saléra and her husband create a wonderful blend of regional cuisines. The foie gras and duck, in confit or with cèpes, come from Saléra's native Pau; the coq au vin, snails, and *lapin à la moutarde* (rabbit with mustard) from her husband's Burgundy. The moderate prix-fixe menus are good value; the dining room, in a medieval crypt, is atmospheric. ⊠ *23 pl. Boussuet,* ☏ *03–80–30–45–65. Reservations essential. AE, DC, MC, V. Closed Sun. No lunch Mon.*

$$–$$$ ✕ **Thibert.** The refined menu at this Art Deco restaurant changes regularly, but cabbage stuffed with snails, prawns with peas, truffles, and sorbets in black-and-white chocolate figure among the tours de force. It's also a remarkable value for the money. ⊠ *10 pl. Wilson,* ☏ *03–80–67–74–64. Reservations essential. Jacket and tie. AE, MC, V. Closed Sun., early Jan., and Aug. No lunch Mon.*

$$ ✕ **Toison d'Or.** A collection of superbly restored 16th-century build-
★   ings, belonging to the Burgundian Company of Wine Tasters, forms the backdrop to this fine restaurant. It is lavishly furnished and quaint (candlelight is de rigueur in the evening). The food is sophisticated: Try the langoustines with ginger, and the nougat and honey dessert. After dinner visit the small wine museum in the cellar. ⊠ *18 rue Ste-Anne,* ☏ *03–80–30–73–52. Reservations essential. Jacket required. AE, DC, MC, V. No dinner Sun.*

$ ✕ **Bistrot des Halles.** Of the many restaurants in the area, this one offers the best value. Well-prepared dishes range from escargots to sautéed fresh fish in a beurre blanc. Dine either at the sidewalk tables or inside, where traditional French decor of mirrors and polished wood dominates. ⊠ *10 rue Bannelier,* ☏ *03–80–49–94–15. MC, V. No dinner Sun.*

$ ✕ **Les Moules Zola.** For mussel lovers, this is the place. Mussels and only mussels—prepared a half dozen ways, from traditional *moules marinières* (mussels cooked with white wine) to mussels with Dijon mustard—are served. Large picture windows look over the square and the ambience is jovial—conversation hums to the music of empty shells clattering into bowls as diners plough through mounds of mussels. ⊠ *3 pl. Émile Zola,* ☏ *03–80–58–93–26. Reservations essential. MC, V.*

$ ✕ **Restaurant du Sauvage.** Full of atmosphere, the restaurant in the Hostellerie du Sauvage (☞ *below*) serves a range of grilled meats and fish at under 100 francs for a three-course, prix-fixe menu. A huge chimney wall with fireplaces on either side separates the bar from the dining room. ⊠ *64 rue Monge,* ☏ *03–80–41–31–21. MC, V.*

$$$$ ▥ **Phillipe le Bon Hôtel.** This hotel, affiliated with the Toison d'Or restaurant (☞ *above*), has moderately priced, smallish, modern, L-shape rooms. The ones overlooking the courtyard garden are so wonderfully quiet that you'd never know you were sleeping in a provincial capital. ⊠ *18 rue Ste-Anne, 21000,* ☏ *03–80–30–73–52,* ℻ *03–80–30–95–51. 27 rooms. Restaurant. AE, DC, MC, V.*

$$$ ▥ **Chapeau Rouge.** Off the maze of corridors within the venerable, thick stone walls of this hotel near the cathedral are rooms with old-fashioned furniture. Try to avoid the twin beds—they are narrow and short. The restaurant, renowned as a haven of classic regional cuisine, serves snails cooked in basil and stuffed pigeon. The staff and the owner, Patrick Lagrange, are attentive. ⊠ *5 rue Michelet, 21000,* ☏ *03–80–30–28–10,* ℻ *03–80–30–33–89. 29 rooms. Restaurant, bar. AE, DC, MC, V.*

$$ 🏨 **Central Ibis.** This central, old, established hotel, now part of a national chain, offers comfort in excess of price. Rooms are ordinary yet clean. ✉ *3 pl. Grangier, 21000,* ☎ *03–80–30–44–00,* FAX *03–80–30–77–12. 90 rooms. Restaurant, air-conditioning. AE, DC, MC, V.*

$$ 🏨 **Hôtel Wilson.** This hotel in a 17th-century post house is connected by a walkway to the Thibert restaurant (☞ *above*). Rooms are modern and comfortable. ✉ *1 rue Longvic, 21000,* ☎ *03–80–66–82–50,* FAX *03–80–36–41–54. 27 rooms. AE, MC, V.*

$ 🏨 **Hostellerie du Sauvage.** In a courtyard off a busy street in the old quarter, this small, quiet hotel is a real find. Its old-fashioned rooms facing the courtyard, though far from stylish, are very quiet. ✉ *64 rue Monge, 21000,* ☎ *03–80–41–31–21,* FAX *03–80–42–06–07. 23 rooms. Restaurant, bar, parking (fee). MC, V.*

Nightlife and the Arts

Dijon stages **L'Été Musical** (Musical Summer), a music festival in June and July with a little bit of everything; the tourist office (☞ Burgundy A to Z, *below*) can supply the details. For three days in June you'll encounter **Arts in the Streets** (☎ 03–80–65–91–00 for information), an event where several hundred painters exhibit their work. During the **Bell-Ringing Festival** in mid-August, all the churches' bells chime to their own tune. In September, Dijon puts on the **Festival International de Folklore.** November in Dijon is the time for the **International Gastronomy Fair.**

L'An Fer (✉ 8 rue Pierre-Marceau, ☎ 03–80–70–03–69) caters to a slightly youngish clientele. **Bahia Brazil** (✉ 39 rue des Godrans, ☎ 03–80–30–90–19), a piano bar, is pleasant for a romantic drink. **L'Endroit** (✉ Centre Dauphine, ☎ 03–80–30–60–63) is a popular Dijon disco. **Le Messire** (✉ 3 rue Jules-Mercier, ☎ 03–80–30–16–40) is a bar attracting an older crowd.

Shopping

The auction houses in Dijon are good places to prospect for antiques and works of art. Tempting food items—mustard, snails, and candy (including snail-shaped chocolates—escargots de Bourgogne) can easily be found in the heart of Dijon's pedestrian streets.

En Route A31 connects Dijon to Beaune, 40 km (25 mi) south. But if you prefer a leisurely route through the vineyards, chug along D122, past venerable properties such as Gevrey-Chambertin, Chambolle-Musigny, and Morey-St-Denis, to Clos de Vougeot.

Clos de Vougeot

④² *17 km (11 mi) south of Dijon.*

The reason to come to Vougeot is to see its medieval castle with its famous vineyard. The **Château du Clos de Vougeot** was constructed by Cistercian monks in the 12th century and completed during the Renaissance; it's best known as the seat of Burgundy's elite company of wine lovers, the Confrérie des Chevaliers du Tastevin, who gather here in November at the start of an annual three-day festival, Les Trois Glorieuses. You can admire the château's cellars, where ceremonies are held, and ogle the huge grape presses. ☎ *03–80–62–86–09. ◷ 17 frs. ☉ Apr.–Sept., weekdays and Sun. 9–7, Sat. 9–6:30; Oct.–Mar., weekdays and Sun. 9–11:30 and 2–5:30, Sat. 9–5.*

Dining and Lodging

$$$$ ✕🏨 **Château de Gilly.** Formerly an abbey and a government-run cultural center, the château is now part of the Relais & Châteaux group.

Vestiges of the abbey remain: painted ceilings and a vaulted wine cellar adorned with tapestries. Rooms are filled with good-quality reproductions; size varies with price. The best, No. 46, has a sitting room and a view of the circular pool. The menu includes classical Bourgogne dishes—coq au vin and Charolais—and contemporary French cooking—*coquilles St-Jacques* (scallops) on a bed of tomato puree. "An elegant form of dress" at dinner is requested. ✉ *Gilly-les-Cîteaux, 21640,* ☎ *03–80–62–89–98,* 🖷 *03–80–62–82–34. 47 rooms. Restaurant, pool, 2 tennis courts, meeting rooms. AE, DC, MC, V.*

Nuits-St-Georges

㊸ *22 km (14 mi) south of Dijon, 22 km (14 mi) north of Beaune.*

Wine has been made in Nuits-St-Georges, south of Clos de Vougeot and north of Beaune, since Roman times; its "dry, tonic, and generous qualities" were recommended to Louis XIV for medicinal use. There isn't much to see or do here—it mostly serves as a good stop while visiting the surrounding area.

Dining

$ ✕ **Au Bois de Charmois.** Three kilometers (2 miles) out of Nuits-St-Georges, on the way toward Meuilley, is this marvelous little inn serving local fare at great prices—a three-course lunch (sample the huge plate of garlicky frogs' legs) is only 72 francs. An even less expensive menu is available at weekday lunch. It's especially pleasant to sit in the courtyard under the ancient trees, though even on chilly, gray days the small dining room is full of good cheer. ✉ *rte. de la Serrée,* ☎ *03–80–61–04–79. MC, V. Closed Mon.*

Beaune

㊹ *26 km (16 mi) south of Vougeot, 40 km (25 mi) south of Dijon, 315 km (197 mi) southeast of Paris.*

Despite the hordes of tourists, Beaune remains one of France's most attractive provincial towns. Some of the region's finest vineyards are ★ owned by the **Hospices de Beaune** (also known as the Hôtel-Dieu), founded in 1443 as a hospital. A visit to the Hospices (across from the city's tourist office) is one of the highlights of a stay in Beaune; its gorgeous tiled roofs have become an icon of Burgundy, and in fact the same glowing colors and intricate patterns are seen throughout the region. The Hospices carried on its medical activities until 1971, its nurses still wearing their strange medieval uniforms. The hospital's history is retraced in the museum, whose wide-ranging collections contain some weird and wonderful medical instruments of the 15th century. You can also see a collection of tapestries, including Rogier Van der Weyden's stirringly composed medieval Flemish masterpiece, *The Last Judgment.* A son-et-lumière show is presented every evening from April to mid-November. ✉ *rue de l'Hôtel-Dieu,* ☎ *03–80–25–45–00.* 🖃 *32 frs.* ☉ *Late Mar.–mid-Nov., daily 9–6:30; mid-Nov.–Mar., daily 9–11:30 and 2–5:30.*

A good series of tapestries, relating the life of the Virgin, can be admired in Beaune's main church, the 12th-century **Collégiale Notre-Dame.** ✉ *Just off av. de la République.*

There are few more delightful experiences than a visit to the candle-lit cellars of the **Marché aux Vins** (Wine Market). Here—for the price of admission—you can taste several of the regional wines, beginning with whites and fruity Beaujolais and ending with such big reds as Gevrey-Chambertin. The new collection of Grands Vins des Hospices de Beaune is also on the list. (You can also visit most of the Burgundian vineyards themselves and get free tastings of their wines, which may be more interesting than those available at the Marché aux Vins. Of course, they hope that you'll buy a case or two.) Perhaps the best reason to visit the Marché aux Vins is for the building's Burgundian Romanesque architecture mixed with Gothic additions. Even Viollet-le-Duc left his mark by adding the galleries to the right of the portal. ⊠ *7 rue Nicolas Rolin,* ☎ *03–80–25–08–20.* ⊠ *Entry and tasting 50 frs.* ☉ *Easter–3rd weekend in Nov., daily 9:30–noon and 2:30–6:30; late Nov.–Easter, daily 9:30–noon and 2:30–6.*

Dining and Lodging

$$ ✕ **Auberge St-Vincent.** The best thing about this restaurant is that it's opposite the Hospices. Not surprisingly, it pulls in as many tourists as locals. Though the cuisine and ambience are undistinguished, the grilled lobster tails flambéed with whiskey are quite a show. Service is attentive and the wine list lengthy, but order carefully, or the meal becomes expensive. Good choices are the *daurade* (sea bream) in a mille-feuille shell and the roast lamb. ⊠ *pl. de la Halle,* ☎ *03–80–22–42–34. Reservations essential. AE, DC, MC, V.*

$$ ✕ **L'Écusson.** Don't be put off by its unprepossessing exterior. This is a comfortable, friendly, thick-carpeted restaurant with good value, prix-fixe menus. Showcased is chef Jean-Pierre Senelet's sure-footed culinary mastery in dishes like duck liver with ham and spinach, and rabbit terrine with tarragon. ⊠ *pl. Malmédy,* ☎ *03–80–24–03–82. Reservations essential. AE, DC, MC, V. Closed Sun. and Feb.*

$–$$ ✕ **Le Gourmandin.** In the center of Beaune, this no-nonsense restaurant serves regional fare—beef Bourguignon and *tourte de canard* (duck pie)—and a good range of wines from small vineyards. The decor is simple, in the style of a 1930s café, with black and white tabletops and art posters on the walls. Seating in front is tight. ⊠ *8 pl. Carnot,* ☎ *03–80–24–07–88. AE, MC, V. Closed Wed. and late Dec.–early Jan. No dinner Tues.*

$–$$ ✕ **La Grilladine.** Chef Pierre Lenko's cuisine, though not elaborate, is
★ good, hearty Burgundy fare: beef Bourguignon and oeufs en meurette. The prix-fixe menus are extremely reasonable. The ambience is warm and cheerful: rose-pink tablecloths, exposed stone walls, and an ancient beam supporting the ceiling. One room is for nonsmokers. ⊠ *17 rue Maufoux,* ☎ *03–80–22–22–36. Reservations essential. MC, V. Closed Mon. and end Nov.–mid-Dec.*

$$$$ ✕⊡ **Hostellerie de Levernois.** The Crotet's marvelous hotel-restau-
★ rant gleams with light from its large picture windows. Rooms are traditionally furnished and have a comfortably elegant bourgeois feel; those in the modern building in the landscaped garden are done in natural wood and warm pastels. In the kitchen, Jean works with his son, Christophe, who has a more "nouvelle" approach. The combination makes for one of the most exciting dining rooms in Burgundy. Meals are occasions to be savored, but they are also expensive; menus begin at 390 francs (200 francs at lunch). ⊠ *rte. de Verdun-sur-le-Doubs, Levernois 21200 (10 km/6 mi east of Beaune),* ☎ *03–80–24–73–58,* 𝖥𝖠𝖷 *03–80–22–78–00. 14 rooms. Restaurant. AE, DC, MC, V. Closed last 2 wks of Dec.*

$$$–$$$$ ✕⊡ **Lameloise.** This small hotel on the outskirts of Chagny, south of Beaune, may be the only Relais & Châteaux property to stock crayons for kids. But don't be misled: The clientele is well heeled. Rooms are fresh and deluxe, with token rustic touches. Confident and consistent, chef-owner Jacques Lameloise cooks luxurious but not stuffy dishes—scallops in black olive juice or veal kidney in shallot puree. ⊠ *36 pl. d'Armes, 71150 Chagny (14 km/9 mi south of Beaune),* ☎ *03–85–*

87–08–85, FAX *03–85–87–03–57. 8 rooms. Restaurant. AE, MC, V. Closed late Dec.–late Jan.*

$$ ✕🏨 **Central.** A well-run establishment with several modernized rooms, the Central lives up to its name. The stone-walled restaurant is cozy—some might say cramped—and the consistently good cuisine is popular with locals, who come to enjoy *oeufs en meurette* (eggs cooked in a red wine sauce), and coq au vin. Service is efficient, if a little hurried. The evening meal is obligatory in July and August. ✉ *2 rue Victor-Millot, 21200,* ☎ *03–80–24–77–24,* FAX *03–80–22–30–40. 20 rooms. Restaurant. MC, V. Closed Dec.–Jan.*

$$$ 🏨 **Le Cep.** A five-minute walk from the main square, Beaune's top hotel
★ has large rooms tastefully furnished with antiques. It is a combination of several ancient town houses—the oldest circa 1547—whose courtyards have been made into a small garden. The ground-floor rooms have exposed wood beams. Choose one facing the courtyard, such as No. 303. Service is efficient, if a little curt, and can be harried when tour groups check in and out. ✉ *27 rue Maufoux, 21200,* ☎ *03–80–22–35–48,* FAX *03–80–22–76–80. 53 rooms. Restaurant. AE, DC, MC, V.*

$$$ 🏨 **La Poste.** The front rooms of this French provincial hotel look over ramparts and the rear ones look over vineyards. Inspect the room before accepting it—some (Room 205, for example) are not as good as others. The long, narrow restaurant breathes tradition. The setting compensates somewhat for the uninventive cuisine, as does the fabulous wine list. Service is briskly professional. ✉ *1 bd. Clemenceau, 21200,* ☎ *03–80–22–08–11,* FAX *03–80–24–19–71. 21 rooms, 9 suites. Restaurant. AE, DC, MC, V. Closed winter.*

$$–$$$ 🏨 **Château de Chorey-les-Beaune.** To really soak up the flavor of the vineyards, stay at the Germain family's winery and B&B, north of Beaune. Guest rooms are up a circular, stone staircase; furnishings are from the attic. Though it's a bit rustic and casual, it's the kind of place where you can open the windows and let the country air, perfumed by grapes, waft in. A good breakfast is served, but no dinner; you may have a chance to try their wine before going out to eat in Beaune. ✉ *21200 Chorey-les-Beaune (1½ km/1 mi north of Beaune),* ☎ *03–80–22–06–05,* FAX *03–80–24–03–93. 7 rooms. Breakfast room. MC, V. Closed Dec.–Apr.*

$$ 🏨 **Hôtel de la Cloche.** In the heart of town, this hotel is in a 15th-century residence. Rooms are neatly furnished with care and attention by the owners, M. and Mme. Lamy, both of whom are always on hand to assist. The best rooms, those with a full bath, are more expensive; the smaller, delightful attic rooms with a shower and separate toilet are less. Breakfast is served on the garden terrace in summer. ✉ *40–42 rue du Faubourg-Madeleine, 21200,* ☎ *03–80–24–66–33,* FAX *03–80–24–04–24. 22 rooms. Restaurant. MC, V.*

The Arts

In July, Beaune celebrates its annual **International Festival of Baroque Music,** which draws big stars of the music world. Beaune's famous wine festival, **Les Trois Glorieuses,** is held on the third Sunday in November at the Hospices.

Chalon-sur-Saône

45 *29 km (18 mi) south of Beaune, 127 km (79 mi) north of Lyon.*

Chalon-sur-Saône has its medieval heart near the **Église St-Vincent**—a former cathedral displaying a jumble of styles—close to the banks of the River Saône. This area was reconstructed to have an Old World charm, but the rest of Chalon is a modern, commercial, cosmopolitan city—the cultural and shopping center of southern Burgundy. Chalon is the birthplace of Nicéphore Niepce (1765–1833), whose early experiments, developed further by Jacques Daguerre, qualify him as the father of photography.

The **Musée Nicéphore Niepce,** occupying an 18th-century house overlooking the Saône, retraces the early history of photography and motion pictures with the help of some pioneering equipment. It also includes a selection of contemporary photographic work and a lunar camera used during the U.S. *Apollo* program. But the star of the museum is the primitive camera used to take the first photographs in 1816. ⊠ *20 quai des Messageries,* ☎ *03–85–48–41–98.* ◪ *10 frs, free Wed.* ◷ *Sept.–June, Wed.–Mon. 9:30–11:30 and 2:30–5:30; July–Aug., Wed.–Mon. 10–6.*

Dining and Lodging

$$–$$$ ✕◫ **Moulin d'Hautrive.** Once a mill built by Cistercian monks in the
★ 12th century, it is now a comfortable hotel in the country north of Chalon-sur-Saône and south of Beaune. Every room has blackened ancient beams, antiques, and bric-a-brac. The restaurant's four-course, 240-franc menu may include sautéed foie gras, adequate *maigret de canard* (duck breast), and a delicious salad with *bleu de Bresse* (blue cheese). The restaurant is closed Monday and Tuesday. ⊠ *Hameau de Chaublanc, 71350 St-Gervais-en-Vallière (28 km/17 mi from Chalon, 14 km/9 mi from Beaune),* ☎ *03–85–91–55–56,* ℻ *03–85–91–89– 65. 22 rooms. Restaurant, pool, tennis court. AE, MC, V. Closed Jan.*

$$ ✕◫ **St-Georges.** Close to the train station and town center, the friendly, white-walled St-Georges hotel is tastefully modernized and has many spacious rooms. Its cozy restaurant is known locally for its efficient service and menus of outstanding value. You can't go wrong with the duck in white pepper, foie gras with truffles, or roast pigeon. ⊠ *32 av. Jean-Jaurès, 71100,* ☎ *03–85–48–27–05,* ℻ *03–85–93–23–88. 48 rooms. Restaurant. AE, DC, MC, V.*

Tournus

㊻ *24 km (15 mi) south of Chalon-sur-Saône, 35 km (22 mi) north of Mâcon.*

Tournus, which retains much of the charm of the Middle Ages and the Renaissance and has one of Burgundy's most spectacular and best-preserved Romanesque buildings, has long been overshadowed as a tourist attraction by other Burgundian medieval towns. But an effort is under way to give Tournus its due. The **Musée de Greuze,** dedicated to religious art, is supposed to open in late 1999. And the **tourist office** (⊠ *2 pl. Carnot,* ☎ *03–85–51–13–10*) has produced a map of the town's many *traboules*—its hidden, covered walkways. It's also a great spot for a picnic, especially along the left bank (*rive gauche*) of the Saône River.

The abbey church of **St-Philibert,** despite its massiveness—unadorned cylindrical pillars more than 4 ft thick support the nave—is spacious and light. No effort was made to decorate or embellish the interior, whose sole hint of frivolity is the alternating red and white stones in the nave arches. The crypt and former abbey buildings, including the cloister and magnificent 12th-century refectory, can also be visited. ⊠ *pl. de l'Abbaye.*

Dining and Lodging

$$ ✕◫ **Aux Terrasses.** For a most enjoyable meal that takes advantage
★ of the region's products at reasonable prices, try chef Pariaut's light version of classic Burgundian cuisine: coq au vin, escargots in garlic butter, and *poulet de Bresse* (chicken roasted with wine sauce). Desserts are simple but good. Many French, German, and Dutch travelers stop

here for dinner and a night's rest. Rooms are reasonably large, comfortable, and each decorated differently in muted tones. ⊠ *18 av. du 23-Janvier, 71700,* ☎ *03–85–51–01–74,* FAX *03–85–51–09–99. 30 rooms. Restaurant. MC, V. Closed early Jan.–early Feb.*

$$ ✕🏨 **Le Rempart.** This hotel has adequate rooms that are modern, functional, and fresh in appearance. Double-glazed windows keep out traffic noise. At the "gastronomic" restaurant, prix-fixe dinners begin at 155 francs, and the cooking, though competently prepared by chef Daniel Rogie, doesn't live up to its reputation; you may wish to dine elsewhere. ⊠ *2 av. Gambetta, 71700,* ☎ *03–85–51–10–56,* FAX *03–85–40–77–22. 32 rooms, 6 suites. Restaurant, bar, air-conditioning. AE, DC, MC, V.*

$ ✕🏨 **Le Coq d'Or.** For inexpensive prix-fixe menus, this cheerful hotel-restaurant is just the spot. Many dishes are cooked on an open-hearth grill, and the exposed beams, peach tablecloths, and friendly service contribute to its cozy gaiety. The traditional fare is reliable, from onion soup and steak to poulet de Bresse and fruit tarts. Rooms are barebones but clean. The best, No. 8, is at the quiet back of the building. ⊠ *1 rue Pasteur, 71700,* ☎ *03–85–51–35–91. 6 rooms. Restaurant. MC, V.*

En Route   The best way to reach Cluny from Tournus is to use picturesque D14. Along the way, you pass the fortified hilltop town of **Brancion,** with its old castle and soaring keep, before turning left at Cormatin.

Cluny

㊼   *33 km (20 mi) southwest of Tournus, 50 km (31 mi) south of Chalon-sur-Saône, 26 km (16 mi) northwest of Mâcon.*

The village of Cluny is famous for its medieval abbey, which was once the center of a vast Christian empire and is now a tourist mecca. Founded in the 10th century, the **Ancienne Abbaye** was the biggest church in Europe until the 16th century, when Michelangelo built St. Peter's in Rome. Cluny's medieval abbots were as powerful as popes; in 1098, Pope Urban II (himself a Cluniac) assured the head of his old abbey that Cluny was the "light of the world." That assertion, of dubious religious validity, has not stood the test of time, and today Cluny stands in ruins—a reminder of the limits of human grandeur.

The ruins nonetheless suggest the size and glory of the abbey at its zenith. Only the **Clocher de l'Eau-Bénite** (a majestic bell tower) and the right arms of the two transepts, climbing 100 ft above the ground, remain. The 13th-century **farinier** (flour mill), with its fine chestnut roof and collection of statues, can also be seen. The gardens contain an ancient lime tree, reputedly several hundred years old, named Abélard, after the controversial philosopher, who sought shelter at the abbey in 1142. A small **museum** displays religious paintings, sculptures rescued from demolished portions of the abbey, and the remains of the *bibliothèque des moines* (monks' library). ☎ *03–85–59–12–79.* 🎟 *Abbey and museum 33 frs , museum only 15 frs.* ☉ *Abbey and museum Nov.–Mar., daily 10:30–11:30 and 2–4; Apr.–June, daily 9:30–noon and 2–6; July–Sept., daily 9–7; Oct., daily 10–noon and 2–5. Museum closed Tues.*

Dining and Lodging

$$–$$$ ✕🏨 **Bourgogne.** There's no better place to get into Cluny's medieval mood than the Bourgogne. The old-fashioned hotel building, dating from 1817, stands where other parts of the abbey used to be. There is a small garden and an atmospheric restaurant with sober pink decor and comfortable, if slightly stodgy, cuisine: foie gras, snails, and the more exotic fish with ginger. The evening meal is mandatory in July

and August. ⊠ *pl. de l'Abbaye, 71250,* ☎ *03–85–59–00–58,* FAX *03–85–59–03–73. 14 rooms. Restaurant. AE, DC, V. Closed mid-Nov.– early Mar.*

$–$$ ✕🏠 **Hôtel de l'Abbaye.** This modest hotel is five minutes' walk from the center of the village. The three rooms to the right of the dining room are the most recently decorated and the best value. The restaurant serves rich, hearty local fare that's less elaborate than at the Bourgogne (☞ *above*) but better (according to the chef, who did his training there): Try the chicken fricassee in a white Mâcon sauce or the confit of rabbit. The prix-fixe menus are very reasonable. ⊠ *av. Charles-de-Gaulle, 71250,* ☎ *03–85–59–11–14,* FAX *03–85–59–09–76. 14 rooms, 9 with bath. Restaurant. MC, V. Closed mid-Jan.–mid-Feb.*

The Arts
The ruined abbey of Cluny forms the backdrop of the **Grandes Heures de Cluny** (☎ 03–85–59–05–34 for details), a classical music festival held in August.

En Route   On the road (D980/N79) between Cluny and Mâcon, stop just as you leave town to admire the giant rocky outcrop of **Solutré** on your right, towering above the vineyard of Pouilly-Fuissé, renowned for its white wine. Excavations around the Rock of Solutré have revealed the presence of prehistoric man—and prehistoric horse (so many horses, in fact, that one school of thought asserts that the poor beasts were driven over the top of the cliff to crash to their death below).

Mâcon

48   *25 km (16 mi) southeast of Cluny, 58 km (36 mi) south of Chalon-sur-Saône, 69 km (43 mi) north of Lyon.*

Mâcon is a bustling town, best known for its wine fair in May and for its pesky stone bridge across the Saône, whose low arches are a headache for the pilots of large river barges. The Romantic poet Alphonse de Lamartine (1790–1869) was born in Mâcon. The two octagonal towers of the ruined **Cathédrale de St-Vincent** loom over the wide quays along the river in the old part of town. The upper story of the **Maison du Bois,** an ancient timbered house near the cathedral, leans out over the street.

BURGUNDY A TO Z

Arriving and Departing

By Car
The A6 expressway heads southeast from Paris through Burgundy, passing Sens, Auxerre, Chablis, Avallon, Beaune, and Mâcon before continuing on to Lyon and the south. A38 leads from A6 to Dijon, 290 km (180 mi) southeast of Paris; the trip takes 2½ hours. If you have more time, take N6 to Sens, just 120 km (75 mi) southeast of Paris; then continue southeast.

By Plane
Dijon has Burgundy's only commercial passenger **airport** (☎ 03–80–67–67–67), which serves domestic flights on Air Inter between Paris and Lyon.

By Train
The TGV (*Train à Grande Vitesse*) zips out of Paris (Gare de Lyon) to Dijon (75 minutes), Mâcon (100 minutes), and on to Lyon (2 hours). Trains run frequently, though the fastest Paris–Lyon trains do not stop at Dijon or go anywhere near it. A cross-country service links Dijon

to Reims (320 km/200 mi) in 3½ hours. Sens is on a mainline route from Paris (45 minutes).

Getting Around

By Car

Burgundy is best visited by car because its meandering country roads invite leisurely exploration. A6 is the main route through the region; N6 is a slower, prettier option. A38 provides a quick link between A6 and Dijon; A31 heads down from Dijon to Beaune (45 km/27 mi). Other smaller roads lead off the main routes to the little villages.

By Train

Train travel is unrewarding, especially since the infrequent cross-country trains chug along at the legendary speed of a Burgundian snail. You'll invariably have to change trains at La Roche-Migenne for Avallon, Auxerre, Clamecy, and Autun; and at Dijon for Beaune.

Contacts and Resources

Car Rental

Avis (⊠ 5 av. Foch, Dijon, ☎ 03–80–43–60–76). **Hertz** (⊠ 18 bis av. Foch, Dijon, ☎ 03–80–43–55–22). **Europcar** (⊠ 47 rue Guillaume-Tell, Dijon, ☎ 03–80–43–28–44).

Guided Tours

For general information on tours in Burgundy, write to the regional tourist office, the **Comité Régional du Tourisme** (⊠ 12 bd. Brosses, 21000 Dijon).

From April to November, **Air Escargot** (⊠ 71150 Remigny, ☎ 03–85–87–12–30) arranges hot-air balloon rides over the countryside. Tours of the old part of Beaune with a guide and a wine tasting at the city's oldest wine company can be arranged in advance through the **Beaune Tourist Office** (⊠ rue de l'Hôtel-Dieu, ☎ 03–80–26–21–30). Gastronomic weekends, including wine tastings, are organized by **Bourgogne Tour** (⊠ 11 rue de la Liberté, 21000 Dijon, ☎ 03–80–30–49–49).

Details about recommended bike routes and where to rent bicycles (train stations are a good bet) can be found at most **tourist offices. La Peurtantaine** (⊠ Accueil Morvan Environment, École du Bourg, 71550 Anost, ☎ 03–85–82–77–74) arranges bicycle tours of Burgundy.

Travel Agencies

Air France (⊠ 29 pl. Darcy, Dijon, ☎ 03–80–42–89–90). **Wagons-Lits** (⊠ 8 av. du Maréchal-Foch, Dijon, ☎ 03–80–45–26–26).

Visitor Information

Following are principal regional tourist offices: **Dijon** (⊠ 29 pl. Darcy, close to the cathedral, ☎ 03–80–45–15–84). **Auxerre** (⊠ 1 quai de la République, ☎ 03–86–52–06–19). **Mâcon** (⊠ 187 rue Carnot, ☎ 03–85–39–71–37). Addresses of other tourist offices in towns mentioned in this chapter: **Autun** (⊠ 3 av. Charles-de-Gaulle, ☎ 03–85–52–20–34). **Avallon** (⊠ 4 rue Bocquillot, ☎ 03–80–26–21–30). **Beaune** (⊠ rue de l'Hôtel-Dieu, ☎ 03–80–26–21–30). **Clamecy** (⊠ rue du Grand-Marché, ☎ 03–86–27–02–51). **Cluny** (⊠ 6 rue Mercière, ☎ 03–85–59–05–34). **Sens** (⊠ pl. Jean-Jaurès, ☎ 03–86–65–19–49). **Tournus** (⊠ 2 pl. Carnot, ☎ 03–85–51–13–10). **Troyes** (⊠ 16 bd. Carnot, ☎ 03–25–82–62–70; ⊠ rue Mignard, ☎ 03–25–73–36–88). **Vézelay** (⊠ rue St-Pierre, ☎ 03–86–33–23–69).

10 Lyon and the Alps

Beaujolais and the Rhône Valley

In this diverse region, earthly pleasures have been perfected and chefs rival their Parisian counterparts. You can ski in the shadow of Mont Blanc, hike along trails over Alpine slopes, sail across Lake Annecy, and enjoy the urban sophistication and cultural treasures of Lyon. A visit to the Roman sites and medieval towns will remind you of other eras, and a trip along the Beaujolais Wine Road will show you what the region has to offer today.

Revised and
updated by
Nigel Fisher

T'S HARD TO PIN A NAME ON THIS PART of east-central France. The government solution, "Lyon-Rhône-Alpes," although hardly poetic, at least covers the features: grand Lyon, the broad Rhône Valley, and the towering Alps on the Swiss-Italian frontiers. Despite the region's expressways and high-speed train lines, the pace is far from frenzied. The only city apart from Lyon is Grenoble, majestic in the foothills of the Alps.

Lyon has some of France's best cooking, best museums, and best theater. Small, timeless villages dot the area—medieval hilltop retreats and tranquil valley communities. Roman ruins are found along the Rhône and remains of prehistoric man in the Alps, which themselves provide some of the world's best skiing, not to mention Western Europe's highest mountain, Mont Blanc.

Pleasures and Pastimes

Dining

Food lovers around the world celebrate Lyon's cuisine. Robust specialties like *saveloy* (sausage) and *quenelles* (poached fish dumplings) appear on tables in restaurants from elegant on down. Traditional *bouchons* (taverns) with homey wooden benches, zinc counters, and paper tablecloths serve salads, pork products like garlicky *rosette* sausage, and sturdy main courses such as tripe, veal stew, and andouillette (chitterling sausage). The Dombes is rich in game and fowl; the chicken is famous, especially *poulet de Bresse,* usually cooked with cream. Thrush, partridge, and hare star along the Rhône. Local cheeses include St-Marcellin, Roquefort, Beaufort, Tomme, and goat's-milk Cabecou. Privas has its *marrons glacés* (candied chestnuts), Montélimar its nougats. Alpine rivers and lakes teem with pike and trout. In the Alps, try a raclette, melted cheese over potatoes. Mountain herbs yield liqueurs and aperitifs such as tangy, dark Suédois; sweet green Chartreuse; and bittersweet Suze (made from gentian).

CATEGORY	COST*
$$$$	over 400 frs
$$$	250 frs–400 frs
$$	125 frs–250 frs
$	under 125 frs

*per person for a three-course meal, including tax (20.6%) and tip but not wine

Lodging

Hotels and inns abound. At many you are expected to have your evening meal there, especially in summer. In winter, Alpine travelers must take *demi-pension*, with two meals, or *pension complète,* with three.

CATEGORY	COST*
$$$$	over 800 frs
$$$	550 frs–800 frs
$$	300 frs–550 frs
$	under 300 frs

*All prices are for a standard double room for two, including tax (20.6%) and service charge.

Skiing

The famous ski venue is Chamonix. Chic, expensive Megève, Courcheval, and fashionable Méribel are also world-class. Val d'Isère is one of Europe's poshest. Nearby Tignes and novice-friendly Morzine are also good bets. L'Alpe d'Huez is near Grenoble, and Serre-Chevalier is linked by cable car to Briançon. The ski season lasts from December through April.

Exploring Lyon and the Alps

East-central France can be divided into two areas: the Alps and "not the Alps." The second group includes Lyon, the country's "second city," a magnet for the surrounding region, including the vineyards of Beaujolais; and the area south of Lyon, dominated by the mighty Rhône as it flows toward the Mediterranean.

Great Itineraries

As you plan your trip, remember that you can whip along the highways. But on smaller roads and in the Alps, don't make your daily itineraries too ambitious.

Numbers in the text correspond to numbers in the margin and on Lyon and the Alps and Lyon maps.

IF YOU HAVE 3 DAYS

Concentrate on ⊞ **Lyon** ①–㉓, but take a day to head down the Rhône to see the Roman ruins in **Vienne** ㉚.

IF YOU HAVE 6 DAYS

Stay in ⊞ **Lyon** ①–㉓ for two days. If you love wine, leave a day early to travel up the Saône Valley, through the villages along the **Beaujolais Wine Road,** and then head to ⊞ **Bourg-en-Bresse** ㉗ or medieval ⊞ **Pérouges** ㉙ for the night. On day three, make ⊞ **Annecy** ㊸, with its medieval old town, your destination; be sure to drive around the lake to lovely ⊞ **Talloires**; stay in either one. The next day, travel along the narrow roads that connect small villages via mountain passes in the Alps. Stop in the fashionable mountain resort town of **Megève** ㊼ before you relish the drive to elegant ⊞ **Chambéry** ㊶. On day five, visit the abbey of **Grande Chartreuse** ㊵; then either go to **Grenoble** ㊴ to see the Grenoble Museum's fabulous collection or zip, via autoroute, to ⊞ **Valence** ㉟ to view the old town's cathedral and art museum. The next day drive through the spectacular Gorges Ardèche, if you are heading for Provence, and stop in **Privas** ㊲. Or return to Lyon via **Montélimar** ㊳, with a stop along the way at **Vienne** ㉚ to see the Roman sites.

IF YOU HAVE 8 DAYS

Spend three days in ⊞ **Lyon** ①–㉓ and another in ⊞ **Bourg-en-Bresse** ㉗ or ⊞ **Pérouges** ㉙. On day five, head south to **Vienne** ㉚; then continue on for an early lunch in **Serrières** ㉛ on the riverbank or in old **Annonay** ㉝. Go as far as ⊞ **Valence** ㉟ after seeing the château in **Tournon** ㉞ and the panoramic views near **St-Romain-de-Lerp.** Rise early on day six and speed to **Grenoble** ㊴; visit the **Grande Chartreuse** ㊵ abbey before lunch. In the afternoon explore **Aix-les-Bains** ㊷ and Lac du Bourget or ⊞ **Annecy** ㊸ and its lake; spend the night or, if you are short on time, stay near ⊞ **Chambéry** ㊶. On day seven, wake early to drive to **Thonon-les-Bains** ㊹ on Lac Léman, and then take D902 to ⊞ **Chamonix** ㊻ for the day's high point—a cable-car trip with staggering Mont Blanc views. The next day head deep into the Alps via **Albertville** ㊽, site of the 1992 Winter Olympics, stopping briefly in the resort town of **Bourg-St-Maurice** ㊾ on your way to tackle D902, the high Route de l'Iséran pass (closed November to June). Continue south on D902, past Valloire and more scenery to historic ⊞ **Briançon** ㊿. From here, over the Alps to Gap, you can pick up the Route Napoléon and drop down to the Riviera.

Lyon and the Alps

SWITZERLAND

ITALY

Lausanne

Montreux

Lac Léman

Évian-les-Bains **45**

Thonon-les-Bains **44**

Avoriaz

Morzine

Cluses

Bonneville

Annemasse

Geneva

Mijoux

Nantua

Frangy

Seyssel

Ambérieu-en-Bugey

Lagnieu

Belley

Morestel

La Tour-du-Pin

Bourgoin-Jallieu

Chamonix **46**

Mont-Blanc

Bourg-St-Maurice **49**

Les Arcs

Megève **47**

Flumet

Albertville **48**

La Clusaz

Menthon-St-Bernard

Tallojres

Duingt

Lac d'Annecy

Annecy **43**

Aix-les-Bains **42**

41

Lac du Bourget

Rhône

St-Laurent-en-Grandvaux

St-Claude

Lons-le-Saunier

Cuiseaux

Louhans

St-Trivier-de-Courtes

Tournus

Cormatin

Cluny

Fuissé

Juliénas

St-Amour

Chénas

Fleurie

Chiroubles

Odenas

Beaujolais Route du Vin

Mâcon

Pont de Veyle

Vonnas

Villié-Morgon

Villefranche-sur-Saône **26**

Bagnols

Bourg-en-Bresse **27**

Châtillon-sur-Chalaronne

Villars-les-Dombes **28**

LA DOMBES

Pérouges **29**

St-André de Covey

Ars-sur-Formans **25**

Saône

L'Arbresle **24**

Lyon **1 — 23**

TO BEAUNE

When to Tour Lyon and the Alps

Summer is the time to hike, explore isolated villages, and ogle vistas in the Alps; in winter, the focus is snow and skiing. Avoid early spring and late autumn, when many hotels close. At lower altitudes, autumn is best—the lakes warm, the grape harvest under way. Winter is dreariest, despite the beauty in the crystal mist over the Rhône. Midsummer can be hot and sticky. Lyon, not at its best in August, has festivals in fall.

LYON

Lyon and Marseille both claim to be France's "second city." In terms of size and industrial importance, Marseille probably grabs that title. But for tourist appeal, Lyon, 462 km (287 mi) southeast of Paris, is the clear winner. It's easily accessible by car or by train. Its scale is human. It has historic buildings and quaint *traboules,* passageways under buildings dating from the Renaissance (in Vieux Lyon) and the 19th century (in Croix Rousse). (During World War II, these traboules were used by the French Resistance to elude German street patrols.) The city's setting at the confluence of the Saône and Rhône is spectacular. And it has more good restaurants per square mile than any other European city except Paris.

Lyon's development owes much to its riverside site halfway between Paris and the Mediterranean and within striking distance of Switzerland, Italy, and the Alps. Lyonnais are proud that their city has been important for more than 2,000 years: Romans made it the capital of Gaul around 43 BC. Its name derives from the Roman Lugdunum, or "Hill of the Crow."

In the middle of Lyon is Presqu'île, a fingerlike peninsula between the rivers, only half a dozen blocks wide and about 10 km (6 mi) long, where modern Lyon throbs with shops, restaurants, museums, theaters, and an opera house. Across the Saône is Vieux Lyon (Old Lyon); above it is the old Roman district of Fourvière. To the north is the hilly Croix Rousse district, where you'll find more museums. Across the Rhône to the east is a mix of older residential areas and the ultramodern Part-Dieu business and office district. Consider taking advantage of the "Clés de Lyon," a three-day museum pass for 90 francs.

Vieux Lyon and Fourvière

Vieux Lyon has narrow cobblestone streets, 17th- and 18th-century mansions, small museums, and the city's cathedral. When the city developed as an important silk weaving town, Italian merchants and bankers built town houses in the area; the influence of Italian Renaissance architecture still dominates. Above Vieux Lyon, in the hilly Fourvière district, are the remains of Roman theaters and the Basilique de Notre-Dame, visible from all over the city.

A Good Walk

Start your walk armed with free maps from the Lyon tourist office on Presqu'île's **place Bellecour** ①. Cross the square and head north along lively rue du Président-Herriot; turn left onto place des Jacobins and explore rue Mercière and the small streets off it. Cross the Saône on the passerelle du Palais du Justice (foot bridge); now you are in Vieux Lyon. Facing you is the old Palais de Justice. Turn right, and then walk 200 yards along quai Romain Rolland to No. 36, where there is a traboule that leads to rue des Trois Maries. Take a right to get to small **place de la Baleine** ②. Exit the square on the left (north) side and go right on historic **rue St-Jean.** Head up to cobblestoned place du Change;

on your left is the **Loge du Change** ③ church. Take rue Soufflot and turn left onto rue de Gadagne. The Hôtel de Gadagne is home to two museums: the **Musée Historique de Lyon** ④, with medieval sculpture and local artifacts, and the **Musée de la Marionnette,** a puppet museum.

Walk south along **rue du Boeuf,** which runs parallel to rue St-Jean. Just off tiny place du Petit-Collège, at No. 16 is the **Maison du Crible** ⑤, with its pink tower. Use the traboule at No. 1 rue du Boeuf to lead you to 24 rue St-Jean. Turn right and then left onto rue de la Bombarde to get to the **Jardin Archéologique** ⑥, a small garden with two excavated churches. Alongside the gardens is the solid **Cathédrale St-Jean** ⑦, itself an architectural history lesson. The *ficelle* (funicular railway) runs from the cathedral to the top of Colline de Fourvière (Fourvière Hill). Take the montée de Fourvière to the **Théâtres Romains** ⑧, two ruined, Roman theaters. Overlooking the theaters is the semisubterranean **Musée de la Civilisation Gallo-Romaine** ⑨, a repository for Roman finds. Continue up the hill and take the first right to the mock-Byzantine **Basilique de Notre-Dame-de-Fourvière** ⑩.

Return to Vieux Lyon via the montée Nicolas-de-Lange, the stone staircase at the foot of the metal tower, the **Tour Métallique** ⑪. You will emerge alongside the St-Paul train station. Venture onto rue Juiverie, off place St-Paul, to see two splendid Renaissance mansions, the **Hôtel Paterin** ⑫ at No. 4 and the **Hôtel Bullioud** ⑬ at No. 8. On the northeast side of place St-Paul is the church of **St-Paul** ⑭. Behind the church, cross the river on the passerelle St-Vincent and take a left on quai St-Vincent; 200 yards along on the right is the **Jardin des Chartreux** ⑮, a small park. Cut through the park up to cours du Général Giraud, and then turn right to place Rouville. Rue de l'Annonciade leads from the square to the **Jardin des Plantes** ⑯, botanical gardens.

TIMING

Spend the morning ambling around Vieux Lyon and Fourvière, and then eat lunch in one of Vieux Lyon's many restaurants or have a picnic in the Jardin des Plantes. In the afternoon explore the Croix Rousse District (☞ *below*) and its many museums. Note that most museums are closed Monday.

Sights to See

⑩ **Basilique de Notre-Dame-de-Fourvière.** The pompous late-19th-century basilica, at the top of the ficelle, is, unfortunately, the symbol of Lyon. Its mock-Byzantine architecture and hilltop site make it a close cousin of Paris's Sacré-Coeur. Both were built to underline the might of the Roman Catholic Church after the Prussian defeat of France in 1870 gave rise to the birth of the anticlerical Third Republic. The excessive gilt, marble, and mosaics inside underscore that the church had wealth if not political clout. One of the few places in Lyon where you can't see the basilica is the adjacent terrace, whose panorama reveals the city, with the St-Jean cathedral in the foreground and the glass towers of the reconstructed Part-Dieu business complex glistening behind. For a yet more sweeping view, climb the 287 steps to the basilica observatory. ⊠ *pl. de Fourvière.* 🎫 *Observatory 10 frs.* ☉ *Observatory Easter–Oct., daily 10–noon and 2–6; Nov.–Easter, weekends 10–noon and 2–5. Basilica daily 8–noon and 2–6.*

⑦ **Cathédrale St-Jean.** No soaring roof or lofty spires can be found here. Solid and determined—it withstood the sieges of time, revolution, and war—the cathedral's stumpy facade is stuck almost bashfully onto the nave. Although the mishmash inside has its moments—the fabulous 13th-century stained-glass windows in the choir and the varied window tracery and vaulting in the side chapels—the interior lacks drama and harmony. But it is an architectural history lesson. The cathedral dates from the 12th century and the chancel is Romanesque, but construction continued over three centuries. The 14th-century astronomical clock, in the north transept, is a marvel of technology. It chimes a hymn to St. John on the hour at noon, 2, 3, and 4 PM as a screeching rooster and other automatons enact the Annunciation. To the right of the Cathédrale St-Jean stands the 12th-century **Manécanterie** (choir school). ⊠ *70 rue St-Jean,* ☎ *04–78–92–82–29.*

⑬ Hôtel Bullioud. This Renaissance mansion, close to the Hôtel Paterin, is noted for its courtyard, with an ingenious gallery (1536) built by Philibert Delorme, one of France's earliest and most accomplished exponents of classical architecture. He worked on the Loire Valley châteaux of Fontainebleau and Chenonceau. ⊠ *8 rue Juiverie, off pl. St-Paul.*

⑫ **Hôtel Paterin.** This splendid Renaissance mansion is one of many notable buildings in the area. ⊠ *4 rue Juiverie, off pl. St-Paul.*

⑥ **Jardin Archéologique** (Archaeological Garden). This garden contains the excavated ruins of two churches that succeeded one another on this spot. They were discovered after apartment buildings, constructed on the spot after the churches were destroyed in the Revolution, were undergoing repairs. When the apartment buildings were demolished, the foundations of the churches were unearthed. One arch still remains and forms part of the ornamentation in the garden. ⊠ *Entrance on rue de la Bombarde.*

⑮ **Jardin des Chartreux.** This garden is just one of several small, leafy parks in Lyon. It's a peaceful place to rest and eat a sandwich while admiring the splendid view of the river and Fourvière Hill. ⊠ *Entrance on quai St-Vincent.*

⑯ **Jardin des Plantes** (Botanical Garden). In this peaceful, luxurious Botanical Garden are remnants of the once-huge **Amphithéâtre des Trois Gauls** (Three Gauls Ampitheater) built in AD 19. ⊠ *Entrance on rue de la Tourette.* ☉ *Dawn to dusk.*

③ **Loge du Change** (Money Exchange). Germain Soufflot (architect of Paris's Panthéon; ☞ Chapter 2) constructed this building in 1747. ⊠ *pl. du Change.*

⑤ **Maison du Crible.** This 17th-century mansion is one of Lyon's oldest. In the courtyard you can glimpse a charming garden and the original Tour Rose—an elegant, pink tower. The higher the tower in those days, the greater the prestige; this one was owned by the tax collector. ⊠ *16 rue du Boeuf (off tiny pl. du Petit-Collège).* 🎟 *25 frs.* ☉ *Daily 10– noon and 2–6.*

⑨ **Musée de la Civilisation Gallo-Romaine** (Gallo-Roman Civilization Museum). Since 1933, systematic excavations have unearthed vestiges of Lyon's opulent Roman precursor. The statues, mosaics, vases, coins, and tombstones are excellently displayed at this semisubterranean museum next to the Roman Theaters (☞ *below*). The large, bronze Table Claudienne is inscribed with part of Emperor Claudius's speech to the Roman Senate in AD 48, conferring senatorial rights on the Roman citizens of Gaul. ⊠ *17 rue Clébert,* ☎ *04–72–38–81–90.* 🎟 *20 frs.* ☉ *Wed.–Sun. 9:30–noon and 2–6.*

👆 ④ **Musée Historique de Lyon** (Lyon Historical Museum). This museum is housed in the city's largest ensemble of Renaissance buildings, the Hôtel de Gadagne, built between the 14th and 16th centuries. Medieval sculpture, local furniture, pottery, paintings, and engravings are on display. Also housed here is the **Musée de la Marionnette** (Puppet Museum), tracing the history of marionettes beginning with Guignol and Madelon (Lyon's Punch and Judy, created by Laurent Mourguet in 1795). ⊠ *1 pl. du Petit-Collège,* ☎ *04–78–42–03–61.* 🎟 *25 frs.* ☉ *Wed.– Mon. 10:45–6 (until 8:30 Fri.).*

② **Place de la Baleine.** This small square is lined with 17th-century houses once owned by those who became rich from the silk trade.

① **Place Bellecour.** Shady, imposing place Bellecour is one of the largest squares in France and Lyon's fashionable center, midway between the Saône and the Rhône. Classical facades erected along its narrower sides in 1800 lend architectural interest. The large, bronze equestrian Louis XIV, installed in 1828, is by local sculptor Jean Lemot. On the south side of the square is the **tourist office.**

Rue du Boeuf. At the corner of place Neuve St-Jean and rue du Boeuf is one of Vieux Lyon's most famous signs, portraying the bull for which rue du Boeuf is named; it's by renowned French sculptor Jean de Bologne (1529–1608), trained in Renaissance Italy.

Rue St-Jean. Once Vieux Lyon's major thoroughfare, this street leads north from place de la Baleine to place du Change, where money changers operated during medieval trade fairs. Its elegant houses were largely built for illustrious Lyonnais bankers and silk merchants during the French Renaissance. No. 27 has an especially lovely courtyard. The houses once had just four stories; upper floors were added in the last century. Many area streets were named for their shops, still heralded by intricate iron signs.

⓮ St-Paul. The 12th-century church of St-Paul is noted for its octagonal lantern, its frieze of animal heads on the chancel, and its Flamboyant Gothic chapel. ⊠ *pl. St-Paul.*

❽ Théâtres Romains (Roman Theaters). Two ruined, semicircular Roman-built theaters are tucked into the hillside, just down from the summit of Fourvière. The **Grand Théâtre,** the oldest Roman theater in France, was built in 15 BC to seat 10,000. The smaller **Odéon,** with its geometric flooring, was designed for music and poetry performances. Come in September for the Lyon International Arts Festival. ⊠ *Colline Fourvière.* 🎫 *Free.* ☉ *Daily 9–dusk.*

⓫ Tour Métallique. Beyond the Fourvière Basilica is this skeletal metal tower built in 1893 and now a television transmitter. The stone staircase, the **Montée Nicolas-de-Lange,** at the foot of the tower, is a direct but steep route from the basilica to the St-Paul train station. ⊠ *Colline Fourvière.*

Presqu'île and the Croix Rousse District

Presqu'île, the peninsula flanked by the Saône and the Rhône, is the modern center of Lyon with fashionable shops, an array of restaurants and museums, and squares with fountains and 19th-century buildings. This is the core of Lyon, where you'll probably want to wander the streets from one river bank to the other and explore the area from place Bellecour to place des Terreaux.

The hilly district north of place des Terreaux, the Croix Rousse district, is flanked by the Jardins des Plantes on the west and the Rhône on the east. It once resounded to the clanking of looms churning out the silk and cloth that made Lyon famous. By the 19th century, more than 30,000 *canuts* (weavers) worked on looms on the upper floors of the houses. So tightly packed were the houses that the only way to transport fabrics was through the traboules, which had the additional advantage of protecting the cloth in bad weather.

A Good Walk

Armed with a detailed map available from the Lyon Tourist Office (☞ Guided Tours *in* Lyon and the Alps A to Z, *below*), you could spend hours "trabouling" in the area, which is still busy with textile merchants despite the demise of the old-style cottage industry of silk weaving. In the very northern part of the Croix Rousse District you can see old-time looms at the **Maison des Canuts** ⑱. For an impromptu tour of the area, walk along rue Imbert-Colomès. At No. 20, turn right through the traboule that leads to rue des Tables Claudiennes and right again across place Chardonnet. Take the passage Mermet alongside St-Poly-carpe church; then turn left onto rue Leynaud. A traboule at No. 32 leads to the Montée St-Sébastien. Here is a transfixing trompe l'oeil

In case you want to see the world.

At American Express, we're here to make your journey a smooth one. So we have over 1,700 travel service locations in over 120 countries ready to help. What else would you expect from the world's largest travel agency?

do more.

Travel

http://www.americanexpress.com/travel

In case you want to be welcomed there.

We're here to see that you're always welcomed at establishments everywhere. That's why millions of people carry the American Express® Card – for peace of mind, confidence, and security, around the world or just around the corner.

do more®

Cards

In case you're running low.

We're here to help with more than 118,000 Express Cash locations around the world. In order to enroll, just call American Express before you start your vacation.

do more

Express Cash

And just in case.

We're here with American Express® Travelers Cheques and Cheques *for Two.*® They're the safest way to carry money on your vacation and the surest way to get a refund, practically anywhere, anytime.
Another way we help you...

do more ®

Travelers Cheques

on the Mur des Canuts, a large wall painted with depictions of local citizens sitting and walking up a passageway of steps. Exit the Croix Rousse District by taking rue Romarin down to **place des Terreaux** ⑰.

The sizable place des Terreaux has two notable buildings: On the north side is the **Hôtel de Ville** ⑲, the Town Hall; on the south side is the elegant **Musée des Beaux-Arts** ⑳, the art museum. To reach the barrel-vaulted **Opéra de Lyon** ㉑, walk west across place des Terreaux and through the ground floor of the Hôtel de Ville (go around if it's closed). For a look at Lyon's fashionable shops, walk down the pedestrian-only rue de la République and cross place Bellecour. Continue 300 yards farther (now rue de la Charité) to the **Musée des Arts Décoratifs** ㉒, the Decorative Arts Museum. Next door is the **Musée Historique des Tissus** ㉓, the Fabric History Museum.

If you've seen all of Lyon's main cultural sights and want to indulge your children, take the métro from Perrache train station to Masséna, to the **Parc de la Tête d'Or.** If you're an architecture buff, take the métro from place Bellecour to Monplaisir-Lumière (it's a little bit of a long trip) and walk 10 minutes south along rue Antoine to the **Musée Urbain Tony Garnier,** usually referred to as the Cité de la Création.

TIMING

It will probably take you an hour to explore Presqu'île and the Croix Rousse District. The Musée des Beaux-Arts deserves at least two hours; the Musée des Arts Décoratifs and the Musée Historique des Tissus another couple of hours. You may want to leave these until the following day. Note that most museums are closed Monday and the Musée des Beaux-Arts is also closed Tuesday.

⑲ **Hôtel de Ville** (Town Hall). Architects Jules Hardouin-Mansart and Robert de Cotte redesigned the very impressive facade of the Town Hall after a 1674 fire. The rest of the building dates from the early 17th century. ⊠ *pl. des Terreaux.*

⑱ **Maison des Canuts** (Silkweavers Museum). Despite the industrialization of silk and textile production, old-time "Jacquard" looms are still in action at this historical house in the Croix Rousse. The weavers are happy to show children how to operate a miniature loom. ⊠ *12 rue d'Ivry,* ☎ *04–78–28–62–04.* ☜ *15 frs.* ⊙ *Weekdays 8:30–noon and 2–6:30, Sat. 9–noon and 2–6.*

★ ㉒ **Musée des Arts Décoratifs** (Decorative Arts Museum). Housed in an 18th-century mansion, this museum has fine collections of silverware, furniture, objets d'art, porcelain, and tapestries. ⊠ *34 rue de la Charité,* ☎ *04–78–37–15–05.* ☜ *26 frs (joint ticket with the nearby Musée Historique des Tissus;* ☞ *below).* ⊙ *Tues.–Sun. 10–noon and 2–5:30.*

⑳ **Musée des Beaux-Arts** (Fine Arts Museum). In the elegant 17th-century Palais St-Pierre, once a Benedictine abbey, this museum has one of France's largest collections of art after the Louvre, including Rodin's *Walker,* Byzantine ivories, Etruscan statues, and Egyptian artifacts. Amid old master, Impressionist, and modern paintings are works by the tight-knit Lyon School, characterized by exquisitely rendered flowers and overbearing religious sentimentality. Note Louis Janmot's *Poem of the Soul,* immaculately painted visions that are by turns heavenly, hellish, and downright spooky. ⊠ *Palais St-Pierre, 20 pl. des Terreaux,* ☎ *04–72–10–17–40.* ☜ *25 frs.* ⊙ *Wed.–Sun. 10:30–6.*

㉓ **Musée Historique des Tissus** (Fabric History Museum). On display is a fascinating exhibit of intricate carpets, tapestries, and silks, including Asian tapestries from as early as the 4th century, Turkish and Persian carpets from the 16th to the 18th centuries, and 18th-century Lyon silks. ⊠ *34 rue de la Charité,* ☎ *04–78–37–15–05.* 🎫 *28 frs (joint ticket with Musée des Arts Décoratifs;* ☞ *above).* 🕐 *Tues.–Sun. 10–noon and 2–5:30.*

Musée Urbain Tony Garnier (Tony Garnier Urban Museum). Also know as the Cité de la Création (City of Creation), this project was France's first attempt at low-income housing. In recent years the tenants have tried to bring some art and cheerfulness to their environment. Twenty-two giant murals depicting the work of Tony Garnier, the turn-of-the-century Lyon architect, are painted on the walls of huge housing projects built in 1920 and 1933. Artists from around the world, with the support of UNESCO, have added their vision to the creation of the ideal housing project. To get there, take the métro from place Bellecour to Monplaisir-Lumière and walk 10 minutes south along rue Antoine. ⊠ *bd. des États-Unis, Presqu'île.*

㉑ Opéra de Lyon. The barrel-vaulted Lyon Opera, a reincarnation of a moribund 1831 building, was built in the early '90s to a tune of 478 million francs. It incorporates a columned exterior, soaring glass vaulting, neoclassical public spaces, and the latest backstage magic. High above, looking out between the heroic statues lined up along the parapet, is a small restaurant, Les Muses (☞ Dining and Lodging, *below*). ⊠ *pl. de la Comédie,* ☎ *04–72–00–45–00 or 04–72–00–45–45 (tickets).*

☺ Parc de la Tête d'Or (Golden Head Park). On the banks of the Rhône, this 300-acre park has a lake, pony rides, and a small zoo. It's ideal for an afternoon's outing with children. Take the métro from Perrache train station to Masséna. ⊠ *pl. du Général-Leclerc, quai Charles-de-Gaulle.* 🎫 *Free.* 🕐 *Dawn–dusk.*

㉗ Place des Terreaux. The four majestic horses rearing up from a monumental 19th-century fountain in the middle of this large square are by Frédéric-Auguste Bartholdi, who also sculpted New York's Statue of Liberty. The two notable buildings sitting on either side are the Hôtel de Ville and the Musée des Beaux-Arts (☞ *above*).

Dining and Lodging

$$$$ ✕ **Léon de Lyon.** Chef Jean-Paul Lacombe's innovative uses of the region's butter, cream, and foie gras put this restaurant, in an old house, at the forefront of the city's gastronomic scene. Dishes such as fillet of veal with celery and leg of lamb with fava beans are memorable; suckling pig comes with foie gras, onions, and a truffle salad. Alcoves and wood paneling add to the atmosphere. ⊠ *1 rue Pléney,* ☎ *04–78–28–11–33. Reservations essential. Jacket required. MC, V. Closed mid-Aug. No dinner Sun., no lunch Mon.*

$$$$ ✕ **Paul Bocuse.** In this culinary shrine north of Lyon in Collonges-au-Mont-d'Or, the grand dining room makes a fitting backdrop for the creations of star chef Paul Bocuse. Elegantly dressed food lovers throng here to feast on his truffle soup and sea bass, although he is often away. Call ahead if you want to find out whether Bocuse or one of his chefs will be cooking, and book far in advance. ⊠ *50 quai de la Plage, Collonges-au-Mont-d'Or,* ☎ *04–72–27–85–85. Reservations essential. Jacket and tie. AE, DC, MC, V.*

$$$–$$$$ ✕ **Orsi.** Pierre Orsi's lavish restaurant, a pink stucco wonder, is by a tiny tree-lined square. Marble floors, brocade draperies, bronze nudes, and gilt-frame paintings make it glamorously festive. The foie gras ravioli with truffles and the mesclun with goat cheese are hard acts to follow, though the dessert of sliced figs with pistachio ice cream holds its own. ⊠ *3 pl. Kléber,* ☎ *04–79–89–57–68. Reservations essential. Jacket and tie. AE, V.*

$$ ✕ **Brasserie Georges.** This inexpensive brasserie at the end of rue de la Charité is one of the city's largest and oldest, founded in 1836 but now in a palatial Art Deco building. Meals range from hearty veal stew or sauerkraut and sausage to more refined fare. ⊠ *30 cours de Verdun,* ☎ *04–72–56–54–54. MC, V.*

$$ ✕ **Café des Fédérations.** For 80 years this sawdust-strewn café with homey red-checked tablecloths has reigned as one of the city's friendliest spots. Raymond Fulchiron not only serves deftly prepared local classics like *boudin blanc* (white-meat sausage) but also chats with you to make you feel at home. ⊠ *8 rue du Major-Martin,* ☎ *04–78–28–26–00. AE, DC, MC, V. Closed weekends and Aug.*

$$ ✕ **Les Muses.** High up under the glass vault of the Opéra de Lyon is
★ this small restaurant run by Philippe Chavent. Look out the glass front between statues of the Muses to the Hôtel de Ville. The nouvelle cuisine makes it hard to choose between the dishes, but don't pass up the salmon in butter sauce with watercress mousse. For price, the best value for dinner is the 159-franc menu. ⊠ *Opéra de Lyon,* ☎ *04–72–00–45–58. Reservations essential. AE, V.*

$$ ✕ **Le Nord.** Should you want to keep some change in your pocket and still sample cooking by Paul Bocuse–trained chefs (☞ Paul Bocuse, *above*), lunch at his bistro in downtown Lyon. Be sure to order the *frites* (fries)—they are some of the country's best. ⊠ *18 rue Neuve,* ☎ *04–72–10–69–69. AE, MC, V.*

$$ ✕ **Le Vivarais.** Roger Duffaud's simple, tidy restaurant is an outstanding culinary value. Don't expect napkins folded into flower shapes—the excitement is on your plate, with dishes like *lièvre royale* (hare rolled and stuffed with truffles and pâté). ⊠ *1 pl. du Dr-Gailleton,* ☎ *04–78–37–85–15. Reservations essential. MC, V. Closed Sun. and 1st 2 wks in Aug.*

$–$$ ✕ **Anticipation.** A new restaurant on the Lyon scene, Anticipation is the venue for light, creative dishes using the region's famed specialities such as poulet de Bresse. All this modern cuisine is the work of a former cook at Georges Blanc (☞ Dining and Lodging *in* Bourg-en-Bresse, *below*). The homey feel makes it a place where you can settle in for an evening of good fare and fun. ⊠ *rue Chavanne,* ☎ *04–78–30–91–92. MC, V. Closed Mon. No dinner Sun.*

$–$$ ✕ **Maison Villemanzy.** A former cook from Léon de Lyon (☞ *above*) has opened this delightful restaurant on the Croix Rousse hills. There are outstanding views from the balcony. The cuisine is a modern, lighter version of Lyonnais fare, though you should still expect veal and chicken cooked in butter and cream to be on the menu. ⊠ *5 montée St-Sébastien,* ☎ *04–78–39–37–00. MC, V. Closed Sun. and early Jan.–mid-Jan.*

$ ✕ **Brunet.** Tables are crammed together in this tiny *bouchon* (tavern) where the decor is limited to past menus inscribed on mirrors and a few photographs. The food is good, traditional Lyonnais fare; besides the mandatory andouillette sausage and tripe, there is usually excellent roast pork on the 98-franc menu. On a busy night expect it to be crowded—but it's all part of the fun. ⊠ *23 rue Claudia,* ☎ *04–78–37–44–31. MC, V. Closed Sun. in summer, Sun.–Mon. in winter, and Aug.*

$ ✕ **Hugon.** This typical, tiny bouchon with red-checked tablecloths is behind the Musée des Beaux-Arts. The owner drinks with patrons while Madame chops away in back. Go for a hunk of homemade pâté and stewed chicken in wine vinegar sauce or a plate of *ris de veau* (sweetbreads)—good, inexpensive food and plenty of it. ⊠ *12 rue Pizay,* ☎ *04–78–28–10–94. MC, V. Closed weekends and Aug.*

$ ✕ **Le Jura.** The rows of tables, the mosaic tile floor, and the absence of anything pretty gives this place the feel of a men's club. The mustached owner, looking as if he stepped out of the turn-of-the-century prints on the walls, acts gruffly with a smile as his wife rushes around. The game and steak dishes are robust, as is the *cassoulet des escargots* (stew of beans, mutton, and snails). Desserts are mediocre, so order the cheese. ⊠ *25 rue Tupin,* ☎ *04–78–42–20–57. MC, V. Closed Sun. and Aug.*

$ ✕ **Les Lyonnais.** This popular brasserie, decorated with local celebrities' photos, is particularly animated. The simple food—chicken simmered for hours in wine, meat stews, and grilled fish—is served on bare wood tables. A blackboard announces plats du jour, which are less expensive than items on the printed menu. ⊠ *1 rue Tramassac,* ☎ *04–78–37–64–82. MC, V. Closed Sun. and July 25–Aug. 20.*

$$$$ ✕ **La Tour Rose.** Philippe Chavent's silk-swathed Vieux Lyon hotel occupies several houses around a courtyard under a rose-washed tower; the glass-roof restaurant occupies a former chapel. Each room is named for an old silk factory and decorated in its goods; taffetas, plissés, and velvet cover walls, windows, and beds in daring, even startling styles. Dinner is an occasion and can be expensive, but if you limit yourself to the prix-fixe 295-franc menu of rabbit braised with olives and port wine, or some similar dish, you'll have a memorable (and affordable) dinner. ⊠ *22 rue du Boeuf, 69005,* ☎ *04–78–37–25–90, FAX 04–78–42–26–02. 12 rooms. Restaurant, bar. AE, DC, MC, V.*

$$$$ **La Cour des Loges.** Young Lyonnais architects teamed with Italian
★ designers to transform four Renaissance mansions into one of Lyon's most stylish hotels. It has an immense courtyard, spiral stone staircases, and exposed beams. Rooms range from fairly small to comfortably large and are either classic or contemporary in design. There is a cellar wine bar and a tapas bar. Concierge Gérard Ravet is not only a character, but he also knows Lyon inside out. ⊠ *6 rue du Boeuf, 69005,* ☎ *04–78–42–75–75, FAX 04–72–40–93–61. 63 rooms. Bar, tapas bar, breakfast room, indoor pool, hot tub, sauna, health club, library, meeting room. AE, DC, MC, V.*

$$$$ **Hôtel Saxe Lafayette.** There are times when a good chain hotel is needed: This one, owned by the Accord group, has super king-size beds, large bathrooms and towels, uniformity without problems, and an English-speaking staff. It's in Part-Dieu, the business section of town, not far from the train station (a shuttle is available), though this means it's a little less convenient for shopping or hanging out in Vieux Lyon. ⊠ *29 rue de Bonnel, 69003,* ☎ *04–72–61–90–90, FAX 04–72–61–17–54. 156 rooms. 2 restaurants, bar, in-room modem lines, health club. AE, DC, MC, V.*

$$$$ **Villa Florentine.** High above the old town, near the Roman theater and basilica, this pristine hotel was once a convent. It has beamed and vaulted ceilings, terraces everywhere, marvelous views, and a restaurant with refined cuisine. ⊠ *25–27 montée St-Barthélémy, 69005,* ☎ *04–72–56–56–56, FAX 04–72–40–90–56. 16 rooms, 3 suites. Restaurant, bar, breakfast room, pool, meeting rooms. AE, DC, MC, V.*

$$$ **Grande Hôtel Concorde.** Off place de la République is this Belle Époque hotel. Rooms have high ceilings and generally nondescript furniture except for one unique item. The staff is courteous and efficient. The restaurant has a very reasonable 78-franc lunch menu. ⊠ *11 rue Grôlée, 69002,* ☎ *04–72–40–45–45, FAX 04–78–37–52–55. 140 rooms. Restaurant, air-conditioning, meeting rooms. AE, DC, MC, V.*

$$$ **Hôtel des Artistes.** This intimate hotel on an elegant square opposite the Théâtre des Célestins has long been popular among artists; black-and-white photographs of them adorn lobby walls. Rooms are smallish but modern and comfortable, and the friendly reception and great location appeal to all comers. ⊠ *8 rue Gaspard-André, 69002,* ☎ *04–78–42–04–88, FAX 04–78–42–93–76. 45 rooms. AE, MC, V.*

$$–$$$ 🛏 **Grand Hôtel des Beaux-Arts.** Half of the rooms at this hotel are "inspired worlds" where an artist has developed a theme through his paintings. In Room 309, for instance, the paintings of Carmelo Zagari are used to lead you into the world of the theater. Should you want a more conventional sleeping environment, other rooms are traditionally furnished. A buffet breakfast is served. ⊠ *rue du Président Édouard-Herriot, pl. des Jacobins, 69002,* ☎ *04–78–38–09–50,* FAX *04–78–42–19–19. 80 rooms. AE, DC, MC, V.*

$ 🛏 **Bed et Breakfast à Lyon.** This nonprofit agency can house you for one night or several: singles are 120–290 francs; doubles are 170–390 francs. The agency is open weekdays 2 PM–6 PM. ⊠ *4 rue Joliot-Curie, 69005,* ☎ *04–72–57–99–22,* FAX *04–72–57–92–51. No credit cards.*

$ 🛏 **Hôtel du Théâtre.** The friendly and enthusiastic owner is sufficient enough reason to recommend this small hotel. But its location and reasonable prices make it even more commendable. Rooms are simple but clean; those overlooking place des Célestins not only have a theatrical view but also a bathroom with a tub (330 francs). Those facing the side have a shower only. Breakfast is included. ⊠ *10 rue de Savoie, 69002,* ☎ *04–78–42–33–32,* FAX *04–72–40–00–61. 24 rooms. MC, V.*

Nightlife and the Arts

Lyon is the region's liveliest arts center; check the weekly *Lyon-Poche,* published on Wednesday and sold at newsstands, for cultural events and goings-on at the dozens of discos, bars, and clubs.

For darts and pints and jazz on weekends, head to the **Albion Public House** (⊠ 12 rue Ste-Catherine, 1ᵉʳ, ☎ 04–78–28–33–00), where they even accept British pounds. The low-key, chic **L'Alibi** (⊠ 13 quai Romain-Roland, 5ᵉ, ☎ 04–78–42–04–66) has a laser show along with the music. **Bar Live** (⊠ 13 pl. Jules Terry, ☎ 04–72–74–04–41) is in the old Brotteaux train station and is the current drinking haunt. Romantics rendezvous at the **Bar de la Tour Rose** (⊠ 22 rue du Boeuf, 5ᵉ, ☎ 04–78–37–25–90).

Bouchon aux Vin (⊠ 64 rue Mercière, 2ᵉ, ☎ 04–78–42–88–90) is a wine bar with 30-plus vintages. Computer jocks head into cyberspace at **Le Chantier** (⊠ 18–20 rue Ste-Catherine, 1ᵉʳ, ☎ 04–78–39–05–56) while their friends listen to jazz and nibble on tapas. Caribbean and African music pulses at **Le Club des Iles** (⊠ 1 Grande Rue des Feuillants, 1ᵉʳ, ☎ 04–78–39–16–35). Live jazz is played in the stone-vaulted basement of **Hot Club** (⊠ 26 rue Lanterne, 1ᵉʳ, ☎ 04–78–39–54–74). A gay crowd is found among the 1930s decor at **La Ruche** (⊠ 22 rue Gentil, 2ᵉ, ☎ 04–78–39–03–82). **Villa Florentine** (⊠ 25 montée St-Barthélémy, 5ᵉ, ☎ 04–72–56–56–56) is a quiet spot for a drink accompanied by a harpist on Friday and Saturday.

Café-Théâtre de L'Accessoire (⊠ 26 rue de l'Annonciade, ☎ 04–78–27–84–84) and **Espace Gerson** (⊠ 1 pl. Gerson, ☎ 04–78–27–96–99) are two café-theaters where you can eat and drink while watching a revue. The **Opéra de Lyon** (⊠ 1 pl. de la Comédie, ☎ 04–72–00–45–45) presents plays, concerts, ballets, and opera from October to June. Lyon's Société de Musique de Chambre performs at **Salle Molière** (⊠ 18 quai Bondy, ☎ 04–78–28–03–11).

Early fall sees the renowned **Biennale de la Danse** (Dance Biennial; even years). September is the time for the **Foire aux Tupiniers** (☎ 04–78–37–00–68), a pottery fair. October brings the **Festival Bach** (☎ 04–78–72–75–31). The **Biennale d'Art Contemporain** (Contemporary Art Biennial; ☎ 04–78–30–50–66) is held odd years in October. The **Festival du Vieux Lyon** (☎ 04–78–42–39–04) is a musical festival in

November and December. On December 8 (Feast of the Immaculate Conception) lights go on city-wide for the marvelous **Fête de Lumière** (Festival of Lights).

Shopping

Lyon has the region's best shopping; it is still the nation's silk-and-textiles capital, and all big-name designers have shops here. For chic clothing try the stores on rue du Président Édouard-Herriot and rue de la République in the center of town. Lyon's biggest shopping mall is the **Part-Dieu Shopping Center** (⊠ rue du Dr-Bouchut, ☎ 04–72–60–60–62), where there are 14 cinemas and 250 shops.

France's major department stores are well represented in Lyon, including **Galeries Lafayette** (⊠ In the Part-Dieu Shopping Center, ☎ 04–72–61–44–44; ⊠ 6 pl. des Cordeliers, ☎ 04–72–40–48–00; ⊠ 200 bd. Pinel, ☎ 04–78–77–82–12). There's also a **Printemps** (⊠ 42 rue de la République, ☎ 04–72–41–29–29).

Captiva (⊠ 10 rue de la Charité, ☎ 04–78–37–96–15) is the boutique of a young designer who works mainly in silk. **Les Gones** (⊠ 33 rue Leynaud, ☎ 04–78–28–40–78), in the Croix Rousse quarter, is a boutique carrying the silk creations of several young designers. The workshop of **Monsieur Georges Mattelon** (⊠ rue d'Ivry, ☎ 04–78–28–62–04) is one of the oldest silk weavers in Lyon.

Lyonnais designer **Clémentine** (⊠ 18 rue Émile-Zola) is good for well-cut, tailored clothing. **Étincelle** (⊠ 34 rue St-Jean) has trendy outfits for youngsters.

For antiques, wander down **rue Auguste-Comte** (from place Bellecour to Perrache). **Image en Cours** (⊠ 26 rue du Boeuf) sells superb engravings. **La Maison des Canuts** (⊠ 10–12 rue d'Ivry, Croix Rousse) carries local textiles. Fabrics can be also found at the **Boutique des Soyeux Lyonnais** (⊠ 3 rue du Boeuf).

For arts and crafts there are several places where you can find irresistible objects. Look for Lyonnais puppets on **place du Change.** Or try the **Marché des Artistes** (Artists' Market; ⊠ quai Romain Rolland, 5ᵉ), every Sunday morning from 7 to 1. Also held on Sunday morning is the **Marché des Artisans** (Crafts Market; ⊠ quai Fulchiron, 5ᵉ). A **Marché des Puces** (Flea Market; ⊠ 1 rue du Canal in Villeurbanne; take Bus No. 37) takes place on Thursday and Saturday mornings 8–noon and on Sunday 6–1. For **secondhand books,** try the market along quai de la Pêcherie (2ᵉ) near place Bellecour, held every Saturday and Sunday 10–6.

Food markets are held Tuesday through Sunday on boulevard de la Croix-Rousse (⊠ 4ᵉ), at Les Halles on cours Lafayette (⊠ 3ᵉ), on quai Victor Augagneur (⊠ 3ᵉ), and on quai St-Antoine (⊠ 2ᵉ). A wine shop with an excellent selection is **À Ma Vigne** (⊠ 18 rue Vaubecour, ☎ 04–78–37–05–29). **Cave de la Côte** (⊠ 5 rue Pleney, ☎ 04–78–39–93–20) also has good wines. For chocolates, head to **Bernachon** (⊠ 42 cours Franklin-Roosevelt); some say it is the best *chocolaterie* in France. **La Boîte à Dessert** (⊠ 1 rue de l'Ancienne-Préfecture) makes luscious peach turnovers. For culinary variety, shop **Les Halles** (⊠ 102 cours Lafayette). **Pignol** (⊠ 17 rue Émile-Zola) is good for meats and sandwich makings. **Reynon** (⊠ 13 rue des Archers) is the place for charcuterie.

BEAUJOLAIS AND LA DOMBES

North of Lyon along the Saône are the vineyards of Beaujolais, a thrill if you're an oenophile. East of the Saône is the fertile land of La Dombes, where ornithologists flock to see the migratory bird life. North of La Dombes and east of the Beaujolais wine villages is Bourg-en-Bresse, home to a marvelous church and poultry that delights gourmets; it makes a good base after Lyon. South toward the Rhône, the great river of southern France, is the well-preserved medieval village of Pérouges.

L'Arbresle

㉔ *16 km (10 mi) northwest of Lyon.*

If you love modern architecture, don't miss Eveux, outside L'Arbresle. Here the stark, blocky Dominican convent of **Ste-Marie de la Tourette** protrudes over the hillside, resting on slender pillars that look like stilts and revealing the minimalist sensibilities of architect Le Corbusier, who designed it in 1957–59. ☎ 04–74–01–01–03. ☜ *20 frs.* ☽ *July–Aug., daily 9–noon and 2–6; Sept.–June, weekends 2–6.*

Ars-sur-Formans

㉕ *30 km (19 mi) northeast of L'Arbresle; 36 km (22 mi) north of Lyon via A6, Villefranche exit.*

Each year 400,000 pilgrims invade this village (population 719) to honor the Curé d'Ars, Jean-Baptiste Vianney (1786–1859), patron saint of parish priests. Arriving in Ars in 1818, he was soon known as a charismatic confessor of unparalleled godliness and was famed as a "saint" well before his death in 1859 and canonization in 1925. The village church, enlarged to accommodate pilgrims, retains Vianney's confessional and embalmed body; his Saint's Day is August 4. Seventeen tableaux chart Vianney's life at the **Historial du St-Curé-d'Ars.** ☒ *Le Tonneau,* ☎ *04–74–00–70–22.* ☜ *28 frs.* ☽ *Apr.–Oct., daily 10–12:30 and 1:30–7; Nov.–Mar., weekends 2–6.*

Villefranche-sur-Saône

㉖ *6 km (4 mi) east of Ars-sur-Formans, 31 km (19 mi) north of Lyon.*

The lively industrial town of Villefranche-sur-Saône is the capital of the Beaujolais region and is known for its *vin nouveau* (new wine). This youthful, fruity, red wine, thanks to marketing hype, is eagerly gulped down every year around the world on the third Thursday of November (when it's officially released).

Dining and Lodging

$$$$
★ ✕🏠 **Château de Bagnols.** This exquisite, small medieval castle, southwest of Villefranche, began life in the 13th century. Period glassware, fabrics, and porcelain were copied to complement the antique furniture. Adorning the walls are 17th- and 18th-century murals inspired by Lyon's textile industry. Rooms are huge, as are the regal bathrooms. Those in the main château evoke the 18th century; the ones in the converted stables and carriage houses are designed and furnished in a more contemporary mode. Periodically, wine tastings are held in the beautiful stone *cuvage* (wine-pressing room). ☒ *69620 Bagnols (15 km/9 mi southwest of Villefranche on D38 to Tarare),* ☎ *04–74–71–40–00,* 𝖥𝖠𝖷 *04–74–71–40–49. 12 rooms, 8 suites. Restaurant, library, meeting rooms. AE, DC, MC, V.*

Beaujolais Route du Vin

16 km (10 mi) north of Villefranche-sur-Saône, 49 km (30 mi) north of Lyon.

Not all Beaujolais wine is promoted as vin nouveau—that's just a marketing gimmick every November 19. Wine classed as "Beaujolais Villages" is higher in alcohol and produced from a clearly defined region northwest of Villefranche. Beaujolais is made from one single variety of grape, the Gamay. However, there are 12 different appellations: Beaujolais, Beaujolais Villages, Brouilly, Chénas, Chiroubles, Côte de Brouilly, Fleurie, Juliénas, Morgon, Moulin à Vent, Régnié, and St-Amour. The Beaujolais Route du Vin (Wine Road), a narrow strip just 23 km (14 mi) long, is home to nine of these deluxe Beaujolais wines, also known as *crus*. Most villages have a *cave* (communal cellar) or *coopérative*, where you can taste and buy. The **École Beaujolaise des Vins** (Beaujolais School of Wine; ⊠ Villefranche, ☎ 04–74–02–22–81) organizes lessons in wine tasting and on setting up your own cellar.

In the southernmost and largest vineyard of the Beaujolais crus is **Odenas,** producing Brouilly, a soft, fruity wine best drunk young. In the vineyard's center is towering Mont Brouilly, a hill whose vines produce a tougher, firmer wine classified as Côte de Brouilly. From Odenas, take D68, via St-Lager to **Villié-Morgon,** in the heart of the Morgon vineyard; robust wines that age well are produced here. At Monternot, east of Villié-Morgon, you will find the 15th-century **Château de Corcelles,** noted for its Renaissance galleries, canopied courtyard well, and medieval carvings in its chapel. The guardroom is now an atmospheric tasting cellar. ⊠ *Off D9 from Villié-Morgon,* ☎ *04–74–66–72–42.* ⊙ *Mon.–Sat. 10–noon and 2:30–6:30.*

From Villié-Morgon, D68 wiggles north through several more wine villages, including **Chiroubles,** where a rare, light wine that is best drunk young is produced. The wines from **Fleurie** are elegant and flowery. Well-known **Chénas** is home to two crus: the robust, velvety, and expensive Moulin à Vent, and the fruity and underestimated Chénas. The wines of **Juliénas** are sturdy and a deep color; sample them in the cellar of the town church (closed Tuesday and lunchtime), amid bacchanalian decor. **St-Amour,** west of Juliénas, produces light but firm reds and a limited quantity of whites. The famous white Pouilly-Fuissé comes from the area around **Fuissé.**

Bourg-en-Bresse

🕗 *43 km (27 mi) east of St-Amour on N79, 65 km (40 mi) northeast of Lyon.*

Cheerful Bourg-en-Bresse is esteemed among gastronomes for its fowl, striking-looking chickens with plump white bodies and bright blue feet—the *poulet de Bresse*. The town's southeasternmost district, Brou, is its most interesting and the site of a striking church. This is a good place to stay before or after a trip along the Beaujolais Wine Road (☞ *above*).

The **Église de Brou,** a marvel of Flamboyant Gothic, is no longer in religious use. The church was built between 1506 and 1532 by Margaret of Austria in memory of her husband Philibert le Beau, duke of Savoy, and their finely sculpted tombs highlight the rich interior. **Son-et-lumière** shows—on Easter and Pentecost Sunday and Monday, and on Thursday, Saturday, and Sunday from May through September—are magical. At press time a massive restoration of the roof was under way, bringing it back to its 16th-century state. When it's done, it will have the same gorgeous, multicolor, intricate patterns found throughout Burgundy. The museum in the nearby **cloister** stands out for its paintings: 16th- and 17th-century Flemish and Dutch artists keep company with 17th- and 18th-century French and Italian masters, 19th-century artists of the Lyon School, Gustave Doré, and contemporary local painters. ⊠ *63 bd. de Brou,* ☎ *04–74–45–39–00.* ⊡ *Church and museum 32 frs.* ☉ *Apr.–Sept., daily 9–noon and 2–6:30; Oct.–Mar., daily 9–noon and 2–5.*

Dining and Lodging

$$$
★
✕ **L'Auberge Bressane.** The location, looking out on the Brou church, makes this modern, polished spot a good bet. Chef Jean-Pierre Vullin's preparations are becoming more and more consistent and always interesting. Frogs' legs, and Bresse chicken with morel mushroom cream sauce are specialties; also try the *quenelles de brochet* (poached fish dumplings). Jean-Pierre wanders through the dining room ready for a chat while his staff provides excellent service. Don't miss the house aperitif, a champagne cocktail with fresh strawberry puree. The wine list has 300 vintages. ⊠ *166 bd. de Brou,* ☎ *04–74–22–22–68. Reservations essential. Jacket and tie. AE, DC, MC, V.*

$$–$$$
✕ **La Petite Auberge.** This cozy flower-decked inn is in the countryside on the outskirts of town. Motherly Mme. Bertrand provides games for children. Chef Philippe Garnier has a subtle way with mullet (he grills it in saffron butter) and Bresse chicken (browned in tangy cider vinegar). ⊠ *St-Just, rte. de Ceyzeriat,* ☎ *04–74–22–30–04. MC, V. Closed Jan. and Tues. No dinner Mon.*

$$$$
✕🏠 **Georges Blanc.** This simple 19th-century inn, full of beautiful rugs, grandfather clocks, and antique country furniture, makes a fine setting for Blanc's innovative preparations. Indulge in frogs' legs, wine from the extensive list, and the superb desserts. The restaurant is closed Wednesday and Thursday (except for dinner June–mid-September). The 30 guest rooms range from (relatively) simple to downright luxurious. It's worth the trip from Bourg-en-Bresse, though only if you have money to burn and want to eat in every luxury restaurant in France. ⊠ *pl. du Marché, 01540 Vonnas (19 km/12 mi from Bourg-en-Bresse),* ☎ *04–74–50–90–90,* 🆑 *04–74–50–08–80. 30 rooms. Restaurant, pool, tennis court, helipad. AE, DC, MC, V. Reservations essential. Closed Jan.–mid-Feb.*

$$
✕🏠 **La France.** La France is not memorable, but it is centrally located. Rooms are old-fashioned and on the dreary side, though spacious. In contrast, the staff is cheerful and helpful. The separately run restaurant, under chef Jacques Guy, serves regional cooking, using fresh produce from the surrounding rich farmlands, including the famed Bresse chicken and succulent river prawns. ⊠ *19 pl. Bernard, 01000,* ☎ *04–74–23–30–24,* 🆑 *04–74–23–69–90. 45 rooms. Restaurant. AE, DC, MC, V.*

Villars-les-Dombes

㉘ *29 km (18 mi) south of Bourg-en-Bresse, 37 km (23 mi) north of Lyon.*

Villars-les-Dombes is the unofficial capital of La Dombes, an area once covered by a glacier. When the ice retreated, it left a network of lakes and ponds that draws anglers and bird-watchers today. The 56-acre **Parc des Oiseaux,** one of Europe's finest bird sanctuaries, is home to 400 species of birds (some 2,000 from five continents); 435 aviaries house species from waders to birds of prey; and tropical birds in vivid hues fill the indoor birdhouse. Allow two hours. ⊠ *Off N83,* ☎ *04–74–98–05–54.* ⊡ *35 frs.* ☉ *Easter–Sept., daily 9–7:30; Oct.–Easter, daily 9–dusk.*

En Route N83 skirts the Dombes region's largest lake, the **Grand Étang de Birieux,** en route from Villars-les-Dombes to St-André de Covey.

Pérouges

★ ㉙ *21 km (13 mi) southeast of Villars-les-Dombes, 36 km (22 mi) north-east of Lyon.*

Wonderfully preserved (though a little too precious), hilltop Pérouges, with its medieval houses and narrow cobbled streets surrounded by ramparts, is just 200 yards across. Hand weavers brought it prosperity; the Industrial Revolution meant their downfall, and by the late 19th century, the population had dwindled from 1,500 to 12. Now the government has restored the most interesting houses; a potter, bookbinder, cabinetmaker, and weaver have given the town a new lease on life. A number of restaurants make Pérouges a good lunch stop.

Encircling the town is **rue des Rondes**; from it there are fine views of the countryside and, on clear days, the Alps. Park your car by the main gateway, **Porte d'En-Haut,** alongside the 15th-century fortress-church. Rue du Prince, the town's main street, leads to the **Maison des Princes de Savoie** (Palace of the Princes of Savoie), formerly the home of the influential Savoie family that once controlled the eastern part of France. Note the fine watchtower. **Place de la Halle,** a pretty square with great charm, around the corner from the Maison des Princes de Savoie, is the site of a lime tree planted in 1792. The **Musée de Vieux Pérouges** (Old Pérouges Museum), to one side of the place de la Halle, contains local artifacts and a reconstructed weaver's workshop. The medieval garden alongside has an array of rare medicinal plants. ✉ *pl. du Tilleul,* ☎ *04–74–61–00–88.* 🎟 *18 frs.* ☉ *Daily 10–noon and 2–6; closed Wed. and Thurs. morning Oct.–Apr.*

Lodging

$$$–$$$$ 🏨 **Hostellerie du Vieux Pérouges.** Extraordinary even by French stan-
★   dards, this historic inn has antiques, glossy wood floors and tables, and gigantic stone hearths. Rooms in the geranium-decked 15th-century manor are more spacious (but also nearly twice the cost) than those in the annex and have marble bathrooms and period furniture. In the restaurant, dishes are served on pewter plates by waitresses in folk costumes; the crayfish is particularly good. Prices are high: The simple three-course menu, for instance, is 190 francs. Fortunately, there are other places to eat, on or close to the square, so if the Hostellerie's menu isn't tempting, skip it and eat elsewhere. ✉ *pl. du Tilleul, 01800 Pérouges,* ☎ *04–74–61–00–88,* 🖷 *04–74–34–77–90. 28 rooms. Restaurant, meeting rooms. MC, V.*

THE RHÔNE VALLEY

At Lyon, the Rhône, joined by the Saône, truly comes into its own, plummeting south in search of the Mediterranean. The river's progress is often spectacular, as steep vineyards conjure up vistas that are more readily associated with the river's Germanic cousin, the Rhine. All along the way, small-town vintners invite you to sample their wines. Roman towns like Vienne and Valence reflect the Rhône's importance as a trading route. To the west is the rugged, rustic Ardèche *département* (province), where time seems to have stood still.

Vienne

㉚ *27 km (17 mi) south of Lyon via A7.*

One of Roman Gaul's most important towns, Vienne became a religious and cultural center under its count-archbishops in the Middle Ages and retains historic charm, despite being a major road and train junction. The tourist office anchors cours Brillier in the leafy shadow of the Jardin Public (Public Gardens). A 27-franc "passport" available here admits you to most local monuments and museums.

On quai Jean-Jaurès, beside the Rhône, is the church of **St-Pierre.** Note the rectangular 12th-century Romanesque bell tower with its arcaded tiers. The lower church walls date from the 6th century. Although religious wars deprived the cathedral of **St-Maurice** of many statues, much original decoration is intact; the portals on the 15th-century facade are carved with Old Testament scenes. The cathedral was built between the 12th and 16th centuries, with later additions, such as the splendid 18th-century mausoleum, right of the altar. A frieze of the zodiac adorns the entrance to the vaulted passage that once led to the cloisters but now opens onto place St-Paul.

Place du Palais is the site of the remains of the **Temple d'Auguste et de Livie** (Temple of Augustus and Livia), accessible via place St-Paul and rue Clémentine; they probably date, in part, from Vienne's earliest Roman settlements (1st century BC). The Corinthian columns were walled in during the 11th century, when the temple was used as a church; in 1833 Prosper Mérimée intervened to have the temple restored. The last vestige of the city's sizable Roman baths is a **Roman gateway** (⊠ rue Chantelouve) decorated with delicate friezes.

The **Théâtre Romain** (Roman Theater), on rue de la Charité, is one of the largest in Gaul (143 yards across). It held 13,000 spectators and is only slightly smaller than Rome's Theater of Marcellus. Rubble buried Vienne's theater until 1922; 46 rows of seats, some marble flooring, and the frieze on the stage have been excavated. Concerts take place here in summer. ⊠ 7 rue du Cirque, ☎ 04–74–85–39–23. 🎫 11 frs. ⊙ Apr.–mid-Oct., Wed.–Mon. 9:30–1 and 2–6; mid-Oct.–Mar., Wed.–Sat. 10–noon and 2–5, Sun. 1:30–5:30.

Rue des Orfèvres (off rue de la Charité) is lined with Renaissance facades and distinguished by the church of **St-André-le-Bas,** once part of a powerful abbey. If possible, venture past the restoration now in progress to see the finely sculpted 12th-century capitals (made of Roman stone) and the 17th-century wooden statue of St. Andrew. The cloisters are best during the music festival held here and at the cathedral from June to August. ⊠ cour St-André, ☎ 04–74–85–18–49. 🎫 9 frs. ⊙ Apr.–mid-Oct., Wed.–Mon. 9:30–1 and 2–6; mid-Oct.–Mar., Wed.–Sat. 10–noon and 2–5, Sun. 2–6.

Across the Rhône from the town center is the excavated **Cité Gallo-Romaine** (Gallo-Roman City), where the Romans built spectacular villas. 🎫 Free. ⊙ Daily 9–6.

Dining

$$ ✕ **Le Bec Fin.** An inexpensive weekday menu makes this unpretentious eatery opposite the cathedral good for lunch and dinner. The steak and freshwater fish seldom disappoint and occasionally display a deft touch (turbot cooked with saffron). The dining room has an understated elegance. ⊠ 7 pl. St-Maurice, ☎ 04–74–85–76–72. Reservations essential at dinner. Jacket required at dinner. MC, V. Closed Mon. No dinner Sun.

Serrières

③ 32 km (20 mi) south of Vienne, 59 km (37 mi) south of Lyon.

River boats traditionally stop at little Serrières, on the Rhône's west bank. Life on the water is depicted at the **Musée des Mariniers du Rhône** (Boatmen's Museum), in the wooden-roofed Gothic chapel of St-Sornin. ☎ 04–75–34–01–26. 🎫 12 frs. ⊙ Apr.–Oct., weekends 3–6.

Dining and Lodging

$$–$$$ ✕🏨 **Schaeffer.** In a sophisticated setting, chef Bernard Mathé dishes up inventive variants of traditional French dishes: smoked duck cutlet in lentil stew or lamb with eggplant in anchovy butter. The number of desserts is overwhelming, but pistachio cake with bitter chocolate is the clear winner. Reservations are essential and a jacket is required at the restaurant, which is closed Sunday night and Monday. Guest rooms are decorated in contemporary style. ⊠ *quai Jules Roche, 07340,* ☎ *04–75–34–00–07,* ℻ *04–75–34–08–79. 12 rooms. Restaurant. AE, DC, V. Closed 1st 3 wks Jan.*

Hauterives

㉜ *28 km (17 mi) east of Serrières, 40 km (25 mi) south of Vienne.*

Hauterives would be just another quaint village if not for the **Palais Idéal,** one of Western Europe's weirdest constructions. A fantasy constructed entirely of stones, it was the life work of a local postman, Ferdinand Cheval (1836–1924), haunted by visions of faraway mosques and temples. One of many wall inscriptions reads "1879–1912: 10,000 days, 93,000 hours, 33 years of toil." ☎ *04–75–68–81–19.* ⊠ *24 frs.* ⊙ *Daily 9–7 (9:30–5 in winter).*

Dining and Lodging

$$ ✕🏨 **Le Relais.** This comfortable, rustic inn is a stone's throw from the Palais Idéal. The good-size guest rooms have a country look, with chunky wooden desks and wicker chairs. The same warm, golden colors dominate the cozy restaurant, where you can enjoy roast partridge and delicately seasoned frogs' legs (no dinner Sunday). Half board is mandatory in summer. ⊠ *pl. de l'Église, 26390,* ☎ *04–75–68–81–12,* ℻ *04–75–68–92–42. 13 rooms. Restaurant. AE, DC, V. Closed Mon. and Jan.–Feb.*

Annonay

㉝ *44 km (27 mi) south of Vienne, 43 km (27 mi) southeast of St-Étienne.*

The narrow streets and passageways of central Annonay are full of character. The town, which grew up around the leather industry, is best known as the home of Joseph and Étienne Montgolfier, who, in 1783, invented the hot-air balloon (known in French as *une montgolfière*). The first flight was on June 4, 1783, from place des Cordeliers (although a commemorating obelisk is on avenue Marc-Seguin); the flight lasted a half hour and went to 6,500 ft.

Local history and folklore are evoked at the **Musée Vivarais César Filhol,** between the Mairie (Town Hall) and Notre-Dame church. ⊠ *15 rue Béchetoille,* ☎ *04–75–67–67–93.* ⊠ *12 frs.* ⊙ *June–Aug., Tues.–Sun. 2–6; Sept.–May, Wed. and weekends 2–6.*

Tournon

㉞ *37 km (23 mi) southeast of Annonay, 59 km (37) mi) south of Vienne.*

Tournon is on the Rhône at the foot of granite hills. A hefty 15th- to 16th-century **Château** is its chief attraction. The castle's twin terraces have wonderful views of the old town, the river, and—towering above Tain-l'Hermitage across the Rhône—the steep vineyards that produce Hermitage wine, one of the region's most refined, and costly, reds. The museum of local history, in the château—the **Musée Rhodanien**—explores the life of Annonay-born engineer Marc Seguin (1786–1875), who built the first suspension bridge over the Rhône at Tournon in 1825 (demolished in 1965). ⊠ *pl. Auguste-Faure,* ☎ *04–75–07–15–96.*

⊟ *15 frs.* ⊙ *June–Aug., Wed.–Mon. 10–noon and 2–6; Apr.–May and Sept.–Oct., Wed.–Mon. 2–6.*

⟳ A ride on one of France's last steam trains, the **Chemin de Fer du Vivarais,** makes an adventurous two-hour trip, 33 km (21 mi) along the narrow, rocky Doux Valley to Lamastre and back to Tournon. Departures are from Tournon station. ☎ *04–78–28–83–34.* ⊟ *Round-trip 150 frs.* ⊙ *June–Aug., daily 10 AM; May and Sept., weekends 10 AM.*

Dining and Lodging

$$ ✕ **Jean-Marc Reynaud.** Tain-l'Hermitage, across the Rhône from Tournon, is home to this fine restaurant with a comfortable, traditional dining room and a magnificent river view. The classic cuisine is excellent; specialties include poached egg with foie gras, and pigeon fillet in black-currant sauce. ⊠ *82 av. du Président-Roosevelt, Tain-l'Hermitage,* ☎ *04–75–08–07–96. AE, DC, MC, V. Closed Mon., Jan., and 1 wk in Aug. No dinner Sun.*

$$$ ✕⊡ **Michel Chabran.** This sophisticated hotel-restaurant is decidedly modern with its Danish-style furniture, floral displays, and airy picture windows overlooking the garden. The cuisine, such as mille-feuille de foie gras with artichokes, grilled fillet of *rouget* (red mullet) and lobster, and lamb from Rémuzat, is imaginative and light. The restaurant is closed Sunday dinner and Monday in winter. ⊠ *29 av. du 45ᵉ Parallèle, 26600 Pont de l'Isère (on the east bank of the Rhône at Pont de l'Isère, 10 km/6 mi south of Tournon via N7 and 7 km/4 mi north of Valence),* ☎ *04–75–84–60–09,* 🖷 *04–75–84–59–65. 12 rooms. Restaurant. MC, V.*

En Route From Tournon's place Jean-Jaurès, slightly inland from the château, follow signs to narrow, twisting **Route Panoramique;** the views en route to the old village of **St-Romain-de-Lerps** are breathtaking. In good weather, the panorama at St-Romain includes 13 *départements,* Mont Blanc to the east, and arid Mont Ventoux to the south. D287 winds down to St-Péray and Valence; topping the **Montagne de Crussol,** 650 ft above the plain, is the ruined 12th-century **Château de Crussol.**

Valence

③⑤ *17 km (11 mi) south of Tournon, 92 km (57 mi) west of Grenoble, 127 km (79 mi) north of Avignon.*

Largish Valence, the Drôme *département* capital, is the region's market center. Steep-curbed alleyways called *côtes* extend into the old town from the Rhône. At the center of the old town is the cathedral of **St-Apollinaire.** Although begun in the 12th century in the Romanesque style, it is not as old as it looks: Parts of it were rebuilt in the 17th century and the belfry in the 19th. The **Musée des Beaux-Arts** (Fine Arts Museum), next to the cathedral of St-Apollinaire, in the former 18th-century Bishops' Palace, displays archaeological finds as well as sculpture and furniture along with drawings by landscapist Hubert Robert (1733–1808). ⊠ *pl. des Ormeaux,* ☎ *04–75–79–20–80.* ⊟ *14 frs.* ⊙ *Mon.–Tues. and Thurs.–Fri. 2–6, Wed. and weekends 9–noon and 2–6.*

Dining and Lodging

$$$$ ✕⊡ **Pic.** The Pic family are the undisputed kings among Drôme restaurateurs. Their food is subtle and original, such as the truffle-flavored *galettes* (pancakes) and the asparagus with caviar. A special lunch-only menu is available for 290 francs. Comfortable, embroidered armchairs lend warmth to the carpeted peach dining room. In summer you can eat on the terrace. Reservations are essential and a jacket required at the restaurant, which is closed Sunday night and Wednesday. Elegant

guest rooms and two opulent suites are also available; book in advance. ⊠ 285 av. Victor-Hugo, 26000, ☎ 04–75–44–15–32, FAX 04–75–40–96–03. 12 rooms, 2 suites. Restaurant. AE, DC, V. Closed Aug.

Shopping

In the small town of Romans, 15 minutes east of Valence via D532, are a score of retail outlets for designer shoes. Romans, with its tradition of leather making, has become the major factory center for the production of high-quality shoes. Many of the top European designers are represented and their products may be had at bargain prices from any number of stores, such as **Charles Jourdan** (⊠ Galerie Fan Halles, ☎ 04–75–02–32–36), **Chaussures Tchlin** (⊠ quai Chopin, ☎ 04–75–72–51–41), and **Stephane Kelian** (⊠ 11 pl. Charles-de-Gaulle, ☎ 04–75–05–23–26).

En Route   The best route between Valence and Privas is N8 on the right bank of the Rhône; after 16 km (10 mi) and just before La Voulte, turn onto attractive D120, which follows the Eyrieux Valley as far as Les Ollières-sur-Eyrieux; then turn south along D2, under the horse chestnut trees.

Cliousclat

❸ *21 km (13 mi) south of Valence, 27 km (17 mi) north of Montélimar.*

Less than 10 km (6 mi) off A7 and N7, the roads running south from Valence to Montélimar and on to Provence, is the delightful, tiny village of Cliousclat. It's built on a side of hill with just one narrow street running through it. There's not much to do or see, but its charming atmosphere and its gorgeous views make it very appealing. While you're here, however, drop in at the small **Histoires de Poteries** (Pottery History Museum) to see the work of local potters. You might buy some of the lovely wares, too. ☎ 04–75–63–15–60. ⊡ 10 frs. ☉ Apr.–June, Tues.–Sun. 2–7; July–Aug., daily 10–1 and 2–8; Sept., Tues.–Sun. 10–noon and 2–7; Oct., Tues.–Sun. 2–6.

Dining and Lodging

$$ ✕⚏ **La Treille Muscate.** Between Lyon and Avignon there is no better place
★ to spend a night than at this gem of a hotel. Each rooms is made unique by items collected from antiques shops. Clay-tile floors covered with throw rugs add to the provincial charm. No. 11, the most delightful, has a huge terrace looking over fields to the Rhône. Dinner is a pleasure: It's inexpensive (135 francs for four courses), and, though perhaps not of the highest gourmet caliber, is tasty and made from top-quality products, such as Sisteron lamb, Mediterranean fish, and homemade foie gras. The wine list is also extremely reasonable. The friendly owner, Mme. deLaître, speaks English fluently, but politely refrains from doing so until you have exhausted your French. ⊠ Cliousclat, 26270, ☎ 04–75–63–13–10, FAX 04–75–63–10–79. 12 rooms. Restaurant. MC, V. Closed Jan.

Privas

❸ *41 km (25 mi) southwest of Valence.*

The capital of the spectacular Ardèche *département*, renowned for its caves and rocky gorges, Privas makes a good base for exploring the region. The tourist office, just off place Charles-de-Gaulle, can provide details. A Protestant stronghold during the 16th-century Wars of Religion, Privas was razed by Louis XIII in 1629, after 16 days of siege. The Pont Louis XIII (Louis XIII Bridge), over the River Ouvèze, commemorates the town's return to royal good graces. It eventually became a peaceful administrative town, best known for the production of that French delicacy known as *marrons glacés* (candied chestnuts).

Dining

$–$$ ✕ **Lous Esclos.** This strikingly modern restaurant has more windows than walls—all overlooking the wild Ardèche landscape. The chef's masterpieces include goose and snail in flaky pastry—at prices that are too good to be true. ⊠ *Alissas (5 km/3 mi southeast of Privas on D2),* ☎ *04–75–65–12–73. AE, V. Closed late-Dec.–mid-Jan.*

The Ardèche Valley

Aubenas is 30 km (18 mi) south of Privas on N104, 74 km (46 mi) northeast of Alés; Pont-St-Esprit is 43 km (27 mi) south of Montélimar, 45 km (28 mi) north of Avignon.

For the 120 km (75 mi) that the Ardèche River flows from its source to the Rhône, there is a spectacular variety of nature—basins of orchards, vertical cliffs, and spectacular gorges—plus medieval villages guarded by castles perched high up on rocky promontories. A good base is in or near the small town of **Aubenas,** which has a thriving silk industry and a 12th-century castle (with later additions) that is now the town hall. The Ardèche River's source can be traced at the **Col de la Chavade** (4,154 ft); take N102 west from Aubenas toward **Mayres,** 38 km (24 mi) upstream.

East of Aubenas via D104 and D579 is a 40-km (25-mi) stretch known as **La Valée Moyenne** (Middle Valley), where you'll find a number of small villages and a dramatic gorge. Pass through Rochecolombe and Balazuc to get to the small medieval village of **Voqümé.** Just before Ruoms, make a detour right on D245 for 3½ km (2 mi) en route to the tiny village of **Labesume.** The houses here are all built out of natural stone and, as if camouflaged, seem unnoticeable except for their balconies. Labesume is at the southern end of the **Gorges de la Beaume,** a 40-km (25-mi) gorge cut through by the Beaume River as it tumbles down from the Tanarque Massif to join the Ardèche River at Ruoms.

The last 58 km (35 mi) of the valley, from Vallon-Pont-d'Arc to Pont-St-Esprit, is particularly magnificent. Here you'll find another dramatic gorge, the 41-km-long (26-mi-long) **Gorges de l'Ardèche.** Route D290 runs from Vallon-Pont-d'Arc along the edge of the gorge on the side of the Gras Plâteau; stop periodically to look down. Your first stop should be at the **Pont d'Arc.** Here the river flows under a natural arch 112 ft high and 194 ft wide. From here on the river makes some spectacular bends and varies from tumbling through rapids to gently meandering. The most dramatic view of the gorge is from **Serre de Toure Belvedere,** about 11 km (7 mi) from Vallon, where you can peer down 750 ft to the river. Another 11 km (7 mi) along, the **Gournier Belevedere** gives you a view of the river tumbling its way through the Gournier Toupine Rocks. All along the gorge are caverns and grottoes. The best is **Marzal Aven,** with its large variety of calcite formations. To reach it turn left onto D590 just after the Gournier Belevedere and drive about 5 km (3 mi); the entrance to the main cave is down 743 steps to the **Salle du Tombeau** (Tomb Cave), where translucent sheets of stalactites seem like shielding drapes to bear and deer bones. Spend a fascinating hour underground being guided through the fantastic caves; take a sweater, as it can be chilly. ☒ *33 frs.* ۩ *Mid-Apr.–Sept., daily 9–6; mid-Mar.–mid-Apr. and Oct.–Nov., weekends 11, 3, and 5.*

Take one last look at the gorge at the **Ranc-Pointu Belvedere,** where the Le Louby River joins the Ardèche. This viewpoint overlooks the river's last enclosed bend, so don't pass up a stop here. The gorge then ends and the countryside opens up to a fertile valley. Cross over the suspension bridge at **Pont-St-Esprit** and turn left on D941 to reach the Rhône and the north–south route A7 heading toward Montélimar.

Lodging

$$ 🏨 **Les Cedres.** A friendly husband-and-wife team (she speaks English) efficiently manages this moderate hotel. Rooms are functional and small but clean; ask for one overlooking the garden (though they are smaller and more expensive) instead of the parking lot. Half have small terraces; only those without are air-conditioned. Dinner is moderately priced and enjoyable though nothing fancy—just simple, good fare of sautéed fish, regional stews, and meats with Provençal sauces. Breakfasts are a little disappointing. ✉ *07260, Joyeuse (20 km/12 mi southwest of Aubenas),* ☎ *04–75–39–40–60,* ℻ *04–75–39–90–16. 45 rooms. Restaurant, pool, fishing. MC, V.*

$$ 🏨 **Le Panoramic.** The name of this place just outside Aubenas is no idle boast: Rooms have sweeping views of the Ardèche Valley and the Cévennes hills. It's worth paying extra for one with a balcony as rooms are pretty small. One drawback is that N104 goes by the hotel, and, though it quiets down at night, it can be annoying. But the friendly family who runs the hotel is a real plus. The restaurant's fare—such as lamb chops with artichoke—is good if not exceptional, but the view more than makes up for it. Desserts are praiseworthy, especially those made with *marrons* (chestnuts). ✉ *Col de l'Escrinet, 07200, Aubenas,* ☎ *04–75–87–10–11,* ℻ *04–75–87–10–34. 26 rooms. Restaurant, pool. MC, V.*

Outdoor Activities and Sports

If you're interested in kayaking or canoeing through the Gorges de l'Ardèche, contact **Alpha Bateaux** (✉ 07150, Vallon Pont d'Arc, ☎ 04–75–88–08–29).

Montélimar

🔢 *43 km (27 mi) north of Pont-St-Esprit, 35 km (22 mi) southeast of Privas, 83 km (52 mi) north of Avignon.*

The town got its name from the 12th- to 14th-century fortress of **Château des Mont Adhémar,** in a park surveying town and valley. ✉ *24 rue du Château,* ☎ *04–75–01–07–85.* 🎫 *12 frs.* ☉ *Daily 9:30–11:30 and 2–5:30; closed Tues. Nov.–Mar.*

At the **Musée de la Miniature** (Miniatures Museum), a collection of very small pieces (a little *Mona Lisa,* a tiny chess game, a minimicroscope, etc.) from all over the world are displayed. ✉ *28 pl. de l'Hôtel de Ville,* ☎ *04–75–53–79–24.* 🎫 *30 frs.* ☉ *June–mid-Sept., daily 10–6; mid-Sept.–Dec. and Feb.–May, Wed.–Sun. 2–6.*

Montélimar's nougat has been famous since the end of the 17th century, soon after the first almond trees were introduced to the area. Almonds mixed with honey replaced the then traditional walnut cake known as *nux gatum* or "nougo." The nougat is made with melted honey and sugar, and whipped egg whites. The addition of more sugar at high temperatures creates a paste that characterizes Montélimar's nougat. Vanilla, almonds, and pistachios are then added, and the paste is poured in moulds lined with unleavened bread. The nougat must have a minimum of 30% almonds (or 28% almonds and 2% pistachios) and 25% honey; ordinary nougat needs to have only a minimum of 15% almonds or hazelnuts. At least a dozen shops specialize in the candy, among them **Nougat Chabert & Guillot** (✉ 9 rue Ch. Chalbert, ☎ 04–75–00–82–00) and **Nougat Diane de Poyters** (✉ 99 av. Jean-Jaurès, ☎ 04–75–01–04–95).

Dining and Lodging

$$$ ✕🍽 **Les Hospitaliers.** This tasteful, modern hotel with sweeping views is in tiny hilltop Le Poët-Laval, east of Montélimar. With its stone walls and red-tile roof, the hotel is perfect in its medieval setting. In cold weather, escape from the large but tacky rooms to the immense stone hearth in the sitting room. The airy restaurant serves local specialties; the thrush pâté with truffles is especially good. ⊠ *Le Vieux Village, 26160 Le Poët-Laval (22 km/14 mi east of Montélimar),* ☎ *04–75–46–22–32,* FAX *04–75–46–49–99. 20 rooms. Restaurant, pool. AE, DC, MC, V. Closed mid-Nov.–Feb.*

Outdoor Activities and Sports

Horses can be rented from the **equestrian center** (⊠ Ile Montmélian). A pleasant par-72 **golf course** is found at Château Le Monard (⊠ Montboucher-sur-Labron, Montélimar).

GRENOBLE AND THE ALPS

In winter, some of the world's best skiing is found in the Alps; in summer, chic spas, shimmering lakes, and hilltop trails come into their own. The Savoie and Haute-Savoie *départements* occupy the most impressive territory; Grenoble, in the Dauphiné, is the Alps' gateway and the area's only city. It's all at the nexus of highways from Marseille, Valence, Lyon, Geneva, and Turin.

Grenoble

㊴ *104 km (65 mi) southeast of Lyon, 138 km (86 mi) northeast of Montélimar.*

Cosmopolitan Grenoble's skyscrapers seem intimidating by homey French standards. But along with the city's nuclear research plant, they bear witness to the fierce local desire to move with the times. Grenoble is also home to a large university and is the birthplace of the great French novelist Stendhal. All around are proud mountains, dramatic gorges, and hidden valleys.

☺ A **cable car,** starting at quai St-Stéphane-Jay, on the north side of the River Isère, whisks you up to the hilltop and its **Fort de la Bastille,** where there are splendid views. 🎟 *35 frs round-trip.* ☉ *Apr.–Oct., daily 9 AM–midnight; Nov.–Dec. and Feb.–Mar., daily 10–6.*

Rue Maurice-Gignoux is home to gardens, cafés, mansions, and a 17th-century convent that contains the **Musée Dauphinois,** a lively museum with local folk art. The "Premiers Alpins" exhibit explores the evolution of the Alps and its inhabitants. ⊠ *30 rue Maurice-Gignoux,* ☎ *04–76–85–19–01.* 🎟 *15 frs, free Wed.* ☉ *Wed.–Mon. 9–noon and 2–6.*

The church of **St-Laurent,** near the Musée Dauphinois (☞ *above*), has an atmospheric 6th-century crypt—one of the country's oldest Christian monuments—supported by a row of formidable marble pillars. ⊠ *2 pl. St-Laurent,* ☎ *04–76–44–78–68.* 🎟 *15 frs.* ☉ *Wed.–Mon. 10–noon and 2–6.*

Place de Lavalette, on the south side of the river where most of Grenoble is concentrated, is the home to the **Musée de Grenoble,** formerly the Musée de Peinture et de Sculpture (Painting and Sculpture Museum). Founded in 1796 and since enlarged, it is one of France's oldest museums and the first to concentrate on modern art (Picasso donated his *Femme Lisant* in 1921); a modern addition incorporates the medieval Tour de l'Isle (Island Tower), a Grenoble landmark. The collection includes 4,000 paintings and 5,500 drawings, among them works from the Italian Renaissance, Rubens, Flemish still lifes, Zurbarán, and Canaletto; Impressionists such as Renoir and Monet; and 20th-century works by Matisse (*Intérieur aux Aubergines*), Signac, Derain, Vlaminck, Magritte, Ernst, Miró, and Dubuffet. Modern sculpture adorns the gardens. ⊠ *5 pl. de Lavalette,* ☎ *04–76–63–44–44.* 🖃 *25 frs.* ☉ *Wed. 11–10, Thurs.–Mon. 11–7.*

Dining and Lodging

\$\$–\$\$\$ ✕🏠 **Alpotel.** This reasonably priced chain hotel is modern and functional; comfortable rather than plush; and handily situated on a main boulevard a few minutes from the old town. The bustling restaurant's inventive menu has such delicacies as crab saveloy with cress and poached salmon with pink butter. ⊠ *12 bd. du Mal-Joffre, 38000,* ☎ *04–76–87–88–41,* 🖷 *04–76–47–58–42. 88 rooms. Restaurant, bar. AE, DC, MC, V.*

\$\$ ✕🏠 **Château de la Commanderie.** The 13th-century building, in a southern suburb, has been owned by the same family for 200 years; ancestral portraits peer down on grandfather clocks juxtaposed against Baroque blackamoors. The 20th-century addition, housing guest rooms, is a modern disappointment with furnishings that have seen better days. Still, rates are moderate and dining is a pleasure. Try the hot oysters coated with chopped watercress or venison fillet. The restaurant is closed weekends, except July and August. ⊠ *17 av. D'Echirolles, 38320 Eybens (5 km/3 mi from Grenoble),* ☎ *04–76–25–34–58,* 🖷 *04–76–24–07–31. 25 rooms. Restaurant, meeting rooms. AE, DC, MC, V.*

Nightlife and the Arts

Look for the monthly *Grenoble-Spectacles* for a list of events around town. **Le Joker** (⊠ 1 Grande-Rue) is a lively, youthful disco. **La Soupe aux Choux** (⊠ 7 rte. de Lyon) is the spot for jazz.

Cinq Jours de Jazz is just that—five days of jazz—in February or March. In summer, classical fare characterizes the **Session Internationale de Grenoble-Isère.**

Outdoor Activities and Sports

The **Maison de la Randonée** (⊠ 7 rue Voltaire, ☎ 04–76–51–76–00) has information on hiking around Grenoble.

En Route   If you have time only for a brief glimpse of the Alps, take N91 out of Grenoble to Briançon, past the spectacular mountain scenery of L'Alpe d'Huez, Les Deux Alpes, and the Col du Galibier. Or take D512 north from Grenoble for 17 km (11 mi), fork left, and follow small D57-D as far as you can (only a few miles) before leaving your car for the 30-minute climb to the top of the 6,000-ft Charmant Som peak. Your reward: a stunning view of the Grande Chartreuse monastery (☞ *below*) to the north.

Grande Chartreuse

④⓪   *23 km (14 mi) north of Grenoble; head north on D512 and fork left 8 km (5 mi) on D520-B just before St-Pierre-de-Chartreuse.*

St. Bruno founded this 12-acre monastery in 1084; it later spawned 24 other charterhouses in Europe. Burned and rebuilt several times, it was stripped of possessions during the French Revolution, when the monks were expelled. On their return, they resumed making their sweet liqueur, Chartreuse, whose herb-based formulas are known today to only three monks. Today it is sold worldwide and is a main source of income for the monastery. Enclosed by wooded heights and limestone crags, the monastery is austere and serene. Although it is not open to visitors, you can see the road to it.

The **Musée de la Correrie,** near the road to the monastery, has exhibits on monastic life and sells the monks' distillation. ☎ 04–76–88–60–45. ⬚ 20 frs. ⊙ Easter–Oct., daily 9:30–noon and 2–6.

Chartreuse is also sold in **Voiron,** 26 km (16 mi) west of St-Pierre-de-Chartreuse and 27 km (17 mi) northwest of Grenoble; free tastings are provided. ⊠ 10 bd. Edgar-Kofler, ☎ 04–76–05–81–77. ⊙ Daily except winter weekends, 8:30–11:30 and 2–5:30.

Chambéry

④ 44 km (27 mi) northeast of Voiron, 40 km (25 mi) north of St-Pierre-de-Chartreuse, 55 km (34 mi) north of Grenoble.

Elegant old Chambéry is the region's shopping hub. Townspeople congregate for coffee and people-watching on pedestrian-only **place St-Léger.**

The town's highlight is the 14th-century **Château des Ducs de Savoie.** Its Gothic **Ste-Chapelle** has good stained glass and houses a replica of the Turin Shroud, thought by many to have been Christ's burial wrappings, and by others to have been a hoax. ⊠ rue Basse du Château, ☎ no phone. ⬚ 27 frs. ⊙ Guided tours May–June and Sept., daily at 10:30 and 2:30; July–Aug., daily at 10:30, 2:30, 3:30, 4:30, and 5:30; Mar.–Apr. and Oct.–Nov., Sat. at 2:15, Sun. at 3:30.

Dining and Lodging

$$$$ ×⊡ **Château de Candie.** This rambling manor on a hill east of Cham-
★   béry makes a delightful base. Owner Didier Lhostis, an avid antiques collector, spent four years renovating. Linger over a lavish breakfast in your large room—No. 106, a corner room with a view, has honey-gold beams, a grandfather clock, and a carved armoire. For dinner, the chef's dishes include rabbit terrine with shallot compote and escalope de fruits de mer (seafood arranged in the shape of a lobster). ⊠ rue du Bois de Candie, 73000 Chambéry-le-Vieux (6 km/4 mi east of Chambéry), ☎ 04–79–96–63–00, FAX 04–79–96–63–10. 20 rooms, 4 suites. Restaurant. AE, MC, V.

Outdoor Activities and Sports

Go horseback riding in the foothills of the Alps with a horse from the **Centre Équestre** (⊠ Chenin des Bigornes, Voglans, ☎ 04–79–54–47–52).

Aix-les-Bains

④ 14 km (9 mi) north of Chambéry, 106 km (65 mi) east of Lyon.

The family resort and spa town of Aix-les-Bains takes advantage of its position on the eastern side of **Lac du Bourget,** the largest natural fresh-water lake in France, with a fashionable lakeshore esplanade. Although the lake is icy cold, you can sail, fish, play golf and tennis, or picnic on the 25 acres of parkland at the water's edge. (Try to avoid it on weekends, when it gets really crowded.) The main town of Aix is 3 km (2 mi) inland from the lake itself. Its sole reason for being is its thermal waters. Many small hotels line the streets, and streams of visitors take to the baths each day. In the evening, they play the slot machines at the casino and attend tea dances.

The Roman Temple of Diana (2nd to 3rd centuries AD) now houses the **Musée Archéologique** (Archaeology Museum); enter via the tourist office on place Mollard. The ruins of the original Roman baths are underneath the present **Thermes Nationaux** (National Thermal Baths),

built in 1934. ☉ *Guided tours only Apr.–Oct., Mon.–Sat. at 3 PM;
Nov.–Mar., Wed. at 3 PM.*

OFF THE
BEATEN PATH

ABBAYE DE HAUTECOMBE – Mass is celebrated with Gregorian chants at
this picturesque spot, a half-hour boat ride from Aix-les-Bains. ☎ 04–79–
54–26–12. ☞ *60 frs. Departures from the Grand Pont, Mar.–June and
Sept.–Oct., daily at 2:30; July–Aug., daily at 9:30, 2, 2:30, 3, 3:30,
and 4:30.*

Outdoor Activities and Sports

Some brave souls pursue water sports on the lake, but most swim in
the local *piscine* (pool; ⊠ av. Daniel-Rops). There's also an attractive
18-hole **golf course** (⊠ av. du Golf).

En Route   Fast A41 links Aix-les-Bains and Annecy. Prettier, if longer: Go 24 km
(15 mi) on D911; turn left onto D912 at La Charniaz to snake the 24
km (15 mi) north to Annecy along the Montagne du Semnoz.

Annecy

🔹 *33 km (20 mi) north of Aix-les-Bains, 137 km (85 mi) east of Lyon,
43 km (27 mi) southwest of Geneva.*

Jewel-like Annecy is on crystal-clear **Lac d'Annecy,** surrounded by
snow-tipped peaks. Though the canals, flower-decked bridges, and cobbled pedestrian streets are filled on market days—Tuesday and Friday—
with shoppers and tourists, the town is still tranquil. Does the River
Thiou seem to flow the "wrong way" (out of the lake)? You're right:
It drains the lake, feeding the town's canals. Most of the old town is
now a pedestrian zone lined with half-timber houses. Here is where
the best restaurants are, so you'll probably be back in the evening.

Meander through the old town, starting on the small island in the River
Thiou, at the 12th-century **Palais de l'Isle** (Island Palace), once home
to courts of law and a prison, now a landmark and one of France's
most photographed sites. It houses the **Musée d'Histoire d'Annecy** (Museum of Annecy) and is where tours of the old prisons and cultural exhibitions begin. ☎ 04–50–33–87–30. ☞ *20 frs.* ☉ *June–Sept.,
Wed.–Mon. 10–6; Oct.–May, Wed.–Mon. 10–noon and 2–6.*

From the towers of the medieval **Château d'Annecy,** high on a hill opposite the Palais, there are good views of the lake. This mighty castle
of four towers (the oldest is from the 12th century) has a stout defensive outer wall and an inner courtyard whose several dwellings reflect
different eras of Annecy history (covered in a small permanent exhibit
on-site). ☎ 04–50–33–87–31. ☞ *30 frs.* ☉ *June–Sept., Wed.–Mon.
10–6; Oct.–May, Wed.–Mon. 10–noon and 2–6.*

A drive around Lake Annecy—or at least along its eastern shore, which
is the most attractive—is a must; set aside a half day for the 40-km
(25-mi) trip. Picturesque **Talloires,** on the eastern side, has hotels and
restaurants. Just after Veyrier-du-Lac, keep your eyes open for the privately owned medieval **Château de Duingt.**

On the western shore is the intimate-feeling **Château de Menthon-St-
Bernard,** which you can tour, though it's not really worth going out
of the way to see. ☎ 04–50–60–12–05. ☞ *28 frs.* ☉ *Tours July–Aug.,
daily at 2–4:30; open Thurs. May, June, and Sept, Thurs. and weekends 2–4:30*

Dining and Lodging

$ ✕ **L'Étage.** This small, second-floor restaurant serves inexpensive local
fare—from cheese and beef fondue to grilled freshwater fish from

Lake Annecy, and raclette (a round of cheese baked over potatoes) made from the local Reblochon cheese. Minimal furnishings and plain wood tables give it rather an austere look, but the often lively crowd makes up for it by creating an atmosphere of bonhomie. ⊠ *13 rue Paquier,* ☎ *04–50–51–03–28. MC, V. Closed Mon.*

$ ✕ **Le Petit Zinc.** Near the Pont-Moren bridge in the old quarter, this cozy, beamed bistro serves reasonably priced meals. Locals especially throng here for lunch for the cheese croquettes and salad, roast pork, and good carafes of wine—so show up early. ⊠ *11 rue du Pont-Moren,* ☎ *04–50–51–12–93. No credit cards.*

$$$$ ✕🏨 **Impérial Palace.** Though the Palace, across the lake from the town center, is Annecy's leading hotel, it lacks character. In contrast to its Belle Époque exterior, the spacious, high-ceilinged guest rooms are done in the subdued colors so loved by contemporary designers. The better rooms face the public gardens on the lake; waking up to breakfast on the terrace is a great way to start the day. Service is professional, but you pay for it, including a 50-franc charge for making international credit card calls. Fine cuisine is served in the stylish La Voile (jacket and tie required); Le Jackpot Café in the casino is acceptable and less costly. ⊠ *32 av. Albigny, 74000,* ☎ *04–50–09–30–00,* 🇫🇦🇽 *04–50–09–33–33. 98 rooms. 2 restaurants, casino. AE, DC, MC, V.*

$$$$ ✕🏨 **Père Bise.** This deluxe inn on the lake has a leafy veranda, fine views, and a classy restaurant (with less-than-perfect service). Chef Sophie Bise's grilled lobster with spicy tomato and her puff pastry with potatoes, foie gras, and truffles are memorable. You'll also find a superb wine list and the famous *marjolaine*, a multilayer chocolate-and-nut cake. Alas, some of the non-air-conditioned rooms are stuffy and the better ones are very expensive. ⊠ *rte. du Port, 74290 Talloires,* ☎ *04–50–60–72–01,* 🇫🇦🇽 *04–50–60–73–05. 25 rooms, 9 suites. Restaurant. AE, DC, MC, V. Closed Dec.–Mar.*

$$ 🏨 **Hôtel du Palais de l'Isle.** Steps away from the lake, in the heart of
★ old Annecy, is this delightful small hotel. Without destroying the building's ancient feel, rooms have a cheery, contemporary look and Starck furnishings; some have a view of the Palais de l'Isle. Rates reflect size of the room. Breakfast is served. Though the area is pedestrian-only, you can drive up to unload luggage. ⊠ *13 rue Perrière, 74000,* ☎ *04–50–45–86–87,* 🇫🇦🇽 *04–50–51–87–15. 26 rooms. MC, V.*

Outdoor Activities and Sports

Bikes can be rented at the **train station** (⊠ pl. de la Gare). Mountain bikes are available from **Loca Sports** (⊠ 37 av. de Loverchy, ☎ 04–50–45–44–33) and **Sports Passion** (⊠ 3 av. du Parmelan, ☎ 04–50–51–46–28).

Thonon-les-Bains

㊹ *74 km (46 mi) east of Annecy, 37 km (23 mi) northeast of Geneva.*

Most of the south side of **Lake Geneva** (Lac Léman in French) is French, not Swiss, and is popular for its thermal waters. However, Thonon-les-Bains, a fashionable summer resort on the lake, primarily draws Geneva residents.

Évian-les-Bains

㊺ *9 km (6 mi) east of Thonon-les-Bains, 83 km (52 mi) east of Annecy.*

People stay in chic Évian-les-Bains as much to be seen as to enjoy the creature comforts and spa facilities of its deluxe hotels. In late afternoon, they promenade along the lake—a constitutional that precedes formal dinner parties. Its mineral waters, which are bottled for export throughout the world, began to achieve fame in the early 18th century.

En Route   Many small and lesser known Alpine **ski resorts** lie south of Lake Geneva, accessible via riverside D902: **Morzine**; **Avoriaz**, accessible via Thonon-les-Bains and by cable car (or D338) from Morzine; and **Cluses**. From Cluses, take N205 left along the Arve Valley to get to Chamonix.

Chamonix

46   *96 km (60 mi) south of Thonon-les-Bains, 94 km (58 mi) east of Annecy, 83 km (51 mi) southeast of Geneva.*

Chamonix is the oldest and biggest of the French winter-sports resort towns. It was the site of the first Winter Olympics, held in 1924. As a ski resort it has its limitations, however: The ski areas are spread out, none of them are very large, and the lower slopes often suffer from poor snow conditions. On the other hand, some runs are extremely memorable, such as the 20-km (12-mi) run through the **Vallée Blanche** or the off-trail area of **Les Grands Montets**. As a summer resort, it's great for hiking, climbing, and enjoying outstanding views.

The world's highest **cable car** soars 12,000 ft up the Aiguille du Midi, for positively staggering views of 15,700-ft **Mont Blanc**, Europe's loftiest peak. Be prepared for a lengthy wait, both going up and coming down—and wear warm clothing. ⊠ *185 frs round-trip.* ☉ *May–Sept., daily 8–4:45; Oct.–Apr., daily 8–3:45.*

Dining and Lodging

$$$ ✕🏨 **Albert I & Milan.** At Chamonix's most desirable hotel, rooms are furnished with elegant reproductions; most have balconies. Many, such as No. 33, have unsurpassed views of Mont Blanc. Choose between rooms in the original building and Alpine lodge–style accommodations—with contemporary rustic elegance in the complex known as Le Hameau. The dining room also has stupendous Mont Blanc views. Pierre Carrier's cuisine is best characterized as perfectly prepared and presented, though sometimes not so interesting or original. ⊠ *119 impasse du Montenvers, 74400,* ☎ *04–50–53–05–09,* FAX *04–50–55–95–48. 17 rooms, 12 suites. Restaurant, pool, hot tub, sauna. AE, DC, MC, V. Closed 2 wks mid-May.*

Nightlife

Chamonix is a lively place at night with its discos and late-night bars. A popular place to start or end the evening is at the **Casino** (⊠ pl. de Saussure, ☎ 04–50–53–07–65), which has a bar, a restaurant, roulette, blackjack, and punto banco. Entrance to the casino is 75 francs, though it's free for the slot machine rooms.

Outdoor Activities and Sports

Contact the **Chamonix Tourist Office** (☞ Lyon and the Alps A to Z, *below*) for information on skiing in the area. Want to try bob sledding? Two approximately 3,000-ft-long runs are open winter and summer at **Parc de Loisirs des Planards** (☎ 04–50–53–08–07). Chamonix's indoor **skating rink** (☎ 04–50–53–12–36) is open all year round, Thursday–Tuesday 3–6 and Wednesday 3–11. Admission costs 23 francs and skates are 16 francs.

The **Sports Centre Olympide** (☎ 04–50–53–09–07) has an indoor and outdoor, Olympic-size pool. Hang gliding and paragliding can be arranged through **Chamonix Parapente** (☎ 04–50–55–99–22). **Espace Sensations** (☎ 04–50–55–99–49) also organizes hang gliding and paragliding for a cost of 500 francs. Mont Blanc provides the backdrop to golf at the course in **Les Praz de Chamonix** (⊠ rte. de Tignes,

☎ 04–50–53–06–28); it's open daily May–November; greens fees are 300 francs. Horseback rides are organized by the **Club Hippique La Guérinière** (☎ 04–50–53–42–84); an hour's trek costs 95 francs.

Megève

47 *35 km (22 mi) west of Chamonix, 69 km (43 mi) southeast of Geneva.*

Idyllic Alpine Megève is not only a major ski resort but also a chic winter watering hole that draws royalty, celebrities, and big wallets from all over the world. In summer it's popular with golfers. From Megève, the drive along N212 to Albertville goes along one of the prettiest little gorges in the Alps.

Dining and Lodging

$$$$ ✕▥ **Chalet-Hôtel du Mont d'Arbois.** This rustic but sophisticated
★   mountain resort overlooking Megève is run by Nadine de Rothschild. The hotel is part of a vast, upscale development next to the ski lifts, 3 km (2 mi) up from Megève on Mont d'Arbois. Most come here for a few days or more to ski or hike. Rooms have fine views, antiques, and down comforters. The restaurant is the most prestigious in the area; delicious spit-roasted meats and fish (try salmon in red-wine sauce) are served. On the superb wine list are many bottles from the Rothschilds' Bordeaux vineyards. ⊠ *447 chemin Rocaille, 74120,* ☎ *04–50–21–25–03,* FAX *04–50–21–24–79. 20 rooms, 1 suite. Restaurant, pool, sauna, 18-hole golf course, tennis courts. AE, DC, MC, V. Closed Apr.–mid-June, Oct.–mid-Dec.*

$$ ✕▥ **Les Cîmes.** Friendly owners M. and Mme. Bourdin put their hearts into running this tiny, reasonably priced hotel with small, neat rooms and a pleasant little restaurant. Simple food is served, such as roast lamb or grilled fish. Breakfast is included in room rates. The only drawback is that the hotel is on the main street entering Megève from Chamonix and can be a little noisy. ⊠ *341 av. Charles Feige, 74120,* ☎ *04–50–21–01–71,* FAX *04–50–58–70–95. 8 rooms. Restaurant. MC, V.*

Outdoor Activities and Sports

For information about skiing in the area, contact the **Megève Tourist Office** (☞ Lyon and the Alps A to Z, *below*). In summer, you can play at the 18-hole **Megève Golf Course** (⊠ Mont d'Arbois).

Albertville

48 *32 km (20 mi) southwest of Megève, 80 km (50 mi) northeast of Grenoble.*

Albertville, in the Arly Valley, was the site of the 1992 Winter Olympics. To the south are other serious ski resorts, where many of the Olympic competitions were held. As a result, you'll find some of France's most up-to-date ski facilities in the area, though Albertville itself is more of a transit town to the slopes around it than a resort.

Courchevel, at the base of a vast north-facing Alpine amphitheater whose snows last long into spring, started out as a rustic Savoyard village; it's now oh-so-chic, composed of a quartet of planned ski villages named for their metric elevation. **Méribel,** with Courchevel, is part of the Les Trois Vallées (Three Valleys) area, with **Val Thorens** and **Les Menuires.**

Bourg-St-Maurice

49 *53 km (33 mi) east of Albertville on the spectacular D925 (becomes D902), 76 km (47 mi) south of Chamonix.*

In winter, Bourg-St-Maurice, in the Isère Valley, is a bustling ski station. In summer, it's a popular base for hiking, mountain biking, and kayaking along the Isère. **Les Arcs** ski resort is 11 km (7 mi) up the mountain peaks that rise up more than 9,900 ft from Bourg-St-Maurice. **Tignes,** another major ski resort, is 20 km (12 mi) beyond Les Arcs via D902. **Val d'Isère,** a favorite ski resort among the rich and famous, is 31 km (19 mi) from Bourg-St-Maurice. An extensive network of chairlifts and cable cars connects Tignes and Val d'Isère with other, smaller resorts—La Daille, Les Boisses, and Les Brévières.

Outdoor Activities and Sports

A map of hiking trails and information about skiing in Les Arcs is available at the **Bourg-St-Maurice Tourist Office** (⌖ pl. de la Gare, ☎ 04–79–07–04–92), across from the train station. **Le Lac Tourist Office** (☎ 04–79–06–50–09) in Tignes can help you organize all kinds of sporting activities in the area. Mountain bikes can be rented from **Cyclo Minoret** (⌖ 66 av. Général-Leclerc, ☎ 04–79–07–70–16). **L'Espace Killy** (☎ 04–79–06–00–35) encompasses Val d'Isère and Tignes, with more than 100 lifts and endless skiing possibilities.

En Route　From Val d'Isère to Bonneval-sur-Arc (at 9,084 ft the country's highest mountain pass, accessible only between July and late October), take the **Route de l'Iséran,** D902, for some magnificent views. From Bonneval-sur-Arc, continue on D902 to **Lanslevillard,** which is tucked in beneath an old church on a rocky outcrop; soon after the town, D902 broadens into N6. Farther along N6 is Modane, and just beyond, the 13-km (9-mi) **Tunnel du Fréjus,** which leads to Italy. At St-Michel de Maurienne, pick up D902 south, now called the **Route du Galibier.** Usually closed November to May, it twists between France and Italy in rugged grandeur, passing through the busy ski village of **Valloire.** Enjoy the spectacular views along the Route du Galibier as you wind up the barren **Col du Galibier,** one of the French Alps' highest passes. A short walk to the 8,900-ft summit (follow signs) yields a panorama of the southern Alps. Just afterward, stop to admire a monument to Henri Desgranges, founder of the Tour de France bike race, and spare a thought for the hapless cyclists who pedal up here each July. Eight kilometers (5 miles) past the Col du Galibier, before N91, is 6,750-ft **Col du Lautaret,** alive with wildflowers in summer.

Briançon

★ ⑳　*117 km (73 mi) southeast of Grenoble, 52 km (32 mi) south of Valloire.*

Altitudinous Briançon combines historic appeal with direct access to the Serre-Chevalier ski complex, accessible via cable car from the lower town. The old town, referred to as the (Upper Town) or Briançon-Vauban, was remodeled by Vauban from 1692 onward. His three-tiered defensive outworks proved their worth in 1815 by keeping marauding Austro-Sardinian troops at bay in the aftermath of Waterloo. The **Porte Pignerol** is one of the town's four gateways.

Since the area is famed for its sunny microclimate (300 days of rays a year), it's not surprising that both towers of the early 18th-century **Collégiale Notre-Dame** have a sundial; it's accessible via avenue Vauban, to the right after you enter the old town through Porte Pignerol. There are two more sundials on bustling place d'Armes, which leads to the 's main street, **Grande Gargouille,** also called Grande Rue. Admire the fine doorway at No. 64, built in 1714, and the **Fontaine François I,** whose spouts whimsically take the shape of elephants' heads. Rue du Pont-Asfeld, off Grande Rue, leads past the Chapelle des Pénitents and the **Église des Cordeliers** (down stone stairs), renowned for its 15th-century frescoes. The daring **Pont d'Asfeld** (Asfeld Bridge), at the end of rue du Pont-Asfeld, straddles the River Durance. Admire the view, and then head along chemin de Rond, beneath the citadel, back to Porte Pignerol.

Dining and Lodging

$$ ✕🏨 **Auberge du Choucas.** Just over the Col du Lautaret and up the road from Briançon is this cozy hotel in the village of Monetier-les-Bains, which is popular with hikers and skiers. Mountains rise on either side. Owner Mme. Sánchez-Ventura and her daughter are very welcoming. The chalet-type, wood-paneled rooms make the most of limited space (bathrooms, too, are small); many have little balconies. The three duplexes are good if you're traveling with children. Dinner in the vaulted restaurant—before an open fire in winter—is pleasant. The kitchen is striving to establish a reputation for gourmet food at affordable prices. The house wine, a Côte du Rhone, is unusually good for the price. ✉ *05220 Monetier-les-Bains (15 km/9 mi from Briançon)*, ☎ *04–92–24–42–73*, 📠 *04–92–24–51–60. 22 rooms. Restaurant. MC, V.*

$$ 🏨 **Vauban.** Despite its name, this in-town hotel is in a modern, unpretentious, comfortable, and convenient building—300 yards from the train station and a 10-minute walk down from the . Many rooms have balconies. The best face south on the fourth floor. Service tends to be a little abrupt for one-nighters; the management prefers that you arrange for a demi-pension and stay several days. ✉ *13 av. du Général-de-Gaulle, 05100*, ☎ *04–92–21–12–11*, 📠 *04–92–50–58–20. 44 rooms. Restaurant, bar. MC, V. Closed early Nov.–Dec.*

Outdoor Activities and Sports

The **Comité Départemental du Tourisme des Hautes-Alpes** (✉ B.P. 46 05002 Gap Cedex, ☎ 04–92–53–62–00) has a list of a number of *gîtes* (rustic B&Bs, or refuges) with horse stables throughout the region; this is an ideal way to fully appreciate the magnificence of the Hautes-Alpes. For fishing vacations, contact the **Association des gîtes de France** (☎ 04–92–51–31–45), which has a list of accommodations where you can get fishing permits.

Château-Queyras

51 *29 km (18 mi) south of Briançon.*

Château-Queyras is perched on a hilltop above the Guil Valley. A **fort** has stood here since the 14th century. Cross the drawbridge to visit the casemates, courtyard, and 14th-century keep. 🎫 *18 frs.* ☉ *Mid-June–early Sept., Wed.–Mon. 10–7.*

En Route From Château-Queyras, drive south on D902 along the crystal-clear River Guil, beneath pine-covered slopes and the jagged Combe du Queyras.

Montdauphin

52 *15 km (9 mi) southwest of Château-Queyras, 36 km (22 mi) south of Briançon.*

Montdauphin sits on a barren promontory at 3,400 ft. Vauban chose this strategic site for a new citadel and used local pink stone to build a fortified town from scratch. He intended to attract a community, but only soldiers lived here until 1980, when artisans and craftsmen moved in. The 18th-century **arsenal** outlines Montdauphin's construction—it took nearly a century. Other highlights include the **poudrière** (powder mill), with its vaulted upper chamber and larch-beam ground floor;

the airy **church**; and the huge beamed roof of the **Caserne Rocham-beau** (the barracks). Overall, though the scenery is spectacular, the town is disappointing. ☎ *04–92–45–17–80 for guided tours.* 🎫 *32 frs for tour of buildings.* 🕐 *Buildings Tues.–Sun. 9–5*

LYON AND THE ALPS A TO Z

Arriving and Departing

By Car

A6 speeds south from Paris to Lyon (463 km/287 mi). The Tunnel de Fourvière, which cuts through Lyon, is a classic hazard, and at peak times you may sit for hours. From Marseille, Lyon is 313 km (194 mi) north on A7. To get to Grenoble (568 km/352 mi from Paris) from Lyon, take A43. Coming from the south, take A7 to Valence and then swing east on A49 to Grenoble.

By Plane

The international airport is in **Satolas** (☎ 04–72–22–72–21 for flight information), 26 km (16 mi) east of Lyon. **Air Inter, British Airways,** and many other major carriers have connecting services from Paris into Lyon-Satolas. Air Inter also flies between Paris and Grenoble. Frequent shuttle buses run from the airport to the center of Lyon between 5 AM and 9 PM, and for the train station 6 AM and 11 PM; journey time is 35–45 minutes; the fare is 45 francs. A taxi into Lyon costs about 200 francs. There's also a bus from Satolas to Grenoble; journey time is just over an hour, and the fare is 120 francs.

By Train

The high-speed TGV (*Trains à Grande Vitesse*) to Lyon leaves from Paris (Gare de Lyon) hourly and arrives in just two hours. There are also six TGVs daily between Charles de Gaulle airport near Paris and Lyon. The TGV also has less frequent service to Grenoble and villages in the Alps, especially in winter.

Getting Around

By Bus

Buses cover the entire region, but Lyon and Grenoble are the two main bus stations for long distance (national and international) routes. From these towns, buses go to the smaller towns.

By Car

Regional roads are fast and well maintained, though smaller mountainous routes can be difficult to navigate and high passes may be closed in winter.

By Métro

Lyon's good subway system serves both of the city's train stations. A single ticket costs 8 francs, and a 10-ticket book 68 francs. A day pass for bus and métro is 24 francs (available from bus drivers and the automated machines in the métro).

By Plane

There are domestic airports at Grenoble, Valence, Annecy, Chambéry, and Aix-les-Bains.

By Taxi

Lyon Espace Affairés (☎ 04–78–39–26–11) runs a fleet of well-kept taxi-vans in the city.

By Train

Major rail junctions include Grenoble, Annecy, Valence, Chambéry, and Lyon, with frequent train service to other points. Albertville is the rail station for continuing by bus up into the Alps to the ski resorts of Val d'Isère, Courchevel, and Megève.

Contacts and Resources

Car Rental

Avis (⊠ 1 av. du Dr-Desfrançois, Chambéry, ☎ 04–79–33–58–54; ⊠ Aéroport de Lyon-Satolas, ☎ 04–72–22–75–25). **Hertz** (⊠ 16 rue Émile-Gueymard, Grenoble, ☎ 04–76–43–12–92; ⊠ 11 rue Pasteur, Valence, ☎ 04–75–44–39–45).

Emergencies

In Lyon there are several all-night pharmacies. One of the largest, with an equivalence chart of foreign medicines, is **Pharmacie Blanchet** (⊠ 5 pl. des Cordeliers, ☎ 04–78–37–81–31).

Guided Tours

The **Lyon Tourist Office** (⊠ pl. Bellecour, ☎ 04–72–77–69–69) organizes walking tours of the city in English, as well as minibus tours. To survey Lyon by air, contact the **Aéro-Club du Rhône et du Sud-Est** (⊠ Aéroport de Lyon-Bron, 69500 Bron, ☎ 04–78–26–83–97). **Navig-Inter** (⊠ 13 bis quai Rambaud, 69002 Lyon, ☎ 04–78–42–96–81) arranges daily boat trips from Lyon along the Saône and Rhône rivers. **Philibert** (⊠ 24 av. Barthélémy-Thimonier, B.P. 16, 69300 Caluire, ☎ 04–72–23–10–56, FAX 04–72–27–00–97) runs bus tours of the region from April to October starting in Lyon.

Travel Agencies

American Express (⊠ 6 rue Childebert, 69002 Lyon, ☎ 04–78–37–40–69). **Wagons-Lits** (⊠ 76 rue des Alliés, 38100 Grenoble, ☎ 04–76–40–47–78; ⊠ 48 bd. Vauban, 26000 Valence, ☎ 04–75–42–02–04).

Visitor Information

Contact the **Comité Régional du Tourisme Rhône-Alpes** (⊠ 78 rte. de Paris, 69260 Charbonnières-les-Bains, ☎ 04–72–59–21–59) for Lyon and the Alps. The **Maison du Tourisme** (⊠ 14 rue de la République, B.P. 227, 38019 Grenoble, ☎ 04–76–42–41–41) deals with the Isère *département* and the area around Grenoble.

Local tourist offices for towns mentioned in this chapter include the following: **Annecy** (⊠ Centre Bonlieu, 1 rue Jean-Jaurès, ☎ 04–50–45–00–33). **Briançon** (⊠ 1 pl. du Temple, ☎ 04–92–21–08–50). **Bourg-en-Bresse** (⊠ 6 av. d'Alsace-Lorraine, ☎ 04–74–22–49–40). **Chambéry** (⊠ 24 bd. de la Colonne, ☎ 04–79–33–42–47). **Chamonix** (⊠ 85 pl. du Triangle de l'Amitié, ☎ 04–50–53–00–24). **Courchevel** (⊠ La Croisette, ☎ 04–79–08–00–29). **Évian-les-Bains** (⊠ pl. d'Allinges, ☎ 04–50–75–04–26). **Grenoble** (⊠ 14 rue de la République, ☎ 04–76–42–41–41; ⊠ Train station, ☎ 04–76–54–34–36). **Lyon** (⊠ pl. Bellecour, ☎ 04–78–42–25–75; ⊠ av. Adolphe Max, near cathedral, ☎ 04–78–42–25–75; ⊠ Perrache train station). **Megève** (⊠ rue Monseigneur Conseil, ☎ 04–50–21–27–28). **Montélimar** (⊠ av. Rochemaure, ☎ 04–75–01–00–20). **Privas** (⊠ 3 rue Elie-Reynier, ☎ 04–75–64–33–35). **Valence** (⊠ parvis de la gare, ☎ 04–75–44–90–40). **Vienne** (⊠ cours Brillier, ☎ 04–74–85–12–62).

11 The Massif Central and Auvergne

The Parc National des Volcans, the Gorges du Tarn, and Rocamadour

Metropolitan pleasures are scarce in the Massif Central and Auvergne, but wide-open spaces, volcanic peaks, and gorges abound. This is a land of early to bed and early to rise, of hearty meals, and of delight in nature. The thrill of unblemished countryside and the awe of spectacular panoramas are reminders of our basic relationship to the earth.

WINDSWEPT PLAINS, SNOWCAPPED mountains, volcanic plateaus, deep ravines, and thick forests are at the heart of the Massif Central and Auvergne, France's geographic center. To outsiders this isolated and insular land is forbidding; even for inhabitants, it has made life hard. In the old days, it is said, people trained their dogs to lie on top of them for warmth; dangers, real and imagined, lurked everywhere.

Revised and updated by Nigel Fisher

The region has been a battleground since the dawn of history: Romans versus Arvernes (the original Celtic settlers); Gauls versus Visigoths; Charlemagne versus Saracens; the Duke of Dakotan versus Frankish kings Pépin I and II; English Plantagenets versus French kings in the Hundred Years' War; the dukes of Bourbon versus Francis I; and Huguenots versus Catholics in the Wars of Religion. By the Revolution, the Auvergnois had had enough; they kept to themselves and managed to escape most of of the Revolution's excesses. In World War II, Nazi puppet Pétain set up a figurehead French government at Vichy, and thus the region was spared from bombing. Though embroiled in tumultuous history, the people of the Massif Central and Auvergne have never been part of courtly France. Their heritage is the rugged geography.

Pleasures and Pastimes

Dining

Food in the Massif Central and Auvergne is fuel for the body; fine dining it is not. But there are a few regional specialties: *aligot* (puree of potatoes with Tomme de Cantal cheese and garlic), *cousinat* (chestnut soup), *sanflorin* (fried pork and herbs in pastry), and *salmis de colvert Cévenole* (wild duck sautéed in red wine and onions). Several well-known cheeses are also made here: Roquefort, creamy Bleu d'Auvergne, Gaperon with garlic, and the delightfully nutty St-Nectaire. In summer, bakers turn *myrtilles* (blueberries) into pies and tarts.

CATEGORY	COST*
$$$$	over 400 frs
$$$	250 frs–400 frs
$$	125 frs–250 frs
$	under 125 frs

*per person for a three-course meal, including tax (20.6%) and tip but not drinks

Lodging

Because the region was difficult to get to for so long, you won't find a large selection of accommodations. The larger towns generally have modest hotels; the villages have small inns; a few châteaux dot the countryside. In July and August rates are higher and rooms are at a premium, so be sure to make reservations in advance. Many hotels are closed from November to March.

CATEGORY	COST*
$$$$	over 800 frs
$$$	550 frs–800 frs
$$	300 frs–550 frs
$	under 300 frs

*All prices are for a standard double room for two, including tax (20.6%) and service charge.

Outdoor Activities and Sports

Few tourists venture up to the region's volcanic peaks or along its gorges, making the Massif Central a great alternative to the Alps for outdoor adventures. Bicycling and mountain biking (mountain bikes are known as *vélo touts terrains,* or VTT, in France) over the hills and along country roads is a good way to see the region; bikes can be rented at train stations in most towns. For serious hiking or ardent ambling strike out along the extensive network of trails that crisscross the large Parc National des Volcans and follow the Gorges du Tarn. Kayaking down the Gorges du Tarn is also popular. For gentler walking from village to village and valley to valley follow the Monts du Cantal. During winter there is limited skiing around Le Mont-Dore and Mt. Aigoual in the Causses.

Exploring the Massif Central and Auvergne

France's heartland offers dramatic untouched terrain, quiet medieval villages, imposing castles, and few large towns: Clermont-Ferrand (population 150,000), in the center of the region, is the major metropolis; elegant, infamous Vichy and industrial St-Étienne are two other cities. The expansive Parc National des Volcans, the grand Gorges du Tarn, and the magnificent Cévennes mountains, crisscrossed with canyons, are favorite destinations of nature lovers.

Great Itineraries

Because the Massif Central is so big, it's almost impossible to see everything in one short trip. But with 3–10 days, you can get a good sense of the region.

Numbers in the text correspond to numbers in the margin and on The Massif Central and Auvergne map.

IF YOU HAVE 3 DAYS

Begin your first day in ⓣ **Bourges** ①, the former, short-lived capital of France. Spend the night nearby at the Château de la Commanderie. On day two, explore Bourbonnais country, with stops in **Bourbon-l'Archambault** ③ and **Souvigny** ④. Head to medieval ⓣ **Moulins** ⑤ for the night. On day three, drive through the **Parc National des Volcans** to see the natural wonder the **Puy-de-Dôme** ⑭; then visit the Romanesque church in **Orcival** ⑮.

IF YOU HAVE 10 DAYS

You can cover much of the region by car, if you don't mind a lot of driving. Begin with lunch in ⓣ **Bourges** ①, and then head to the Château de la Commanderie in nearby St-Amand-Montrand for the night. The second day explore **Bourbon-l'Archambault** ③, **Souvigny** ④, and ⓣ **Moulins** ⑤, home of the Bourbons and a good place to stay the night. On day three, pass through **Vichy** ⑦ on your way to **Thiers** ⑧; stop in ⓣ **Roanne** ⑨ for the night and try to dine at the superb Troisgros restaurant. The following day drive south to **Le Puy-en-Velay** ⑪ and on to ⓣ **Millau** ㉝; stay overnight there or in one of the towns closer to the ⓣ **Gorges du Tarn** ㉞. The next day explore the gorge, and then drive through the Corniches des Cévennes to ⓣ **Anduze** ㊱. On day six retrace your steps by winding through the **Gorges de la Jonte** ㊳ back to Millau; then head south to the impressive **Cirque de Navacelles** ㊶. Stop in the cheese-producing caves at **Roquefort-sur-Soulzon** ㉜ on your way to beautiful ⓣ **Plaisance** ㉛; have a fantastic dinner at Les Magnolias. The following day head to **Rodez** ㉚ to see its pink sandstone cathedral, en route to the basilica in **Conques** ㉙. By nightfall get to ⓣ **Cahors** ㉖ on the Lot River. Explore Cahors and **St-Cirq-Lapopie** ㉗ on the morning of day eight; in the afternoon drive to ⓣ **Rocamadour** ㉕, the wondrous pilgrim village carved into a rock face. On day nine work your way northeast to medieval ⓣ **Salers** ㉑. Spend the last day traveling through the **Parc National des Volcans** around the **Puy-de-Dôme** ⑭ on your way to ⓣ **Clermont-Ferrand** ⑬.

When to Tour the Massif Central and Auvergne

Autumn, when the sun is still warm on the shimmering, golden trees, and early spring, especially May, when the wildflowers are in bloom, are the best times to visit central France. In summer it's hot and the sky is cloudy; in winter it's cold.

THE MASSIF CENTRAL AND AUVERGNE

The Massif Central is roughly demarcated by Burgundy, the Rhône River, Languedoc-Roussillon, and the Dordogne River valley. From Bourges to Montluçon the area is known as the Bourbonnais, for the dynasty of kings that it spawned. Auvergne—the core of central France—stretches from Montluçon to Aurillac and is characterized by *puys* (craggy lava peaks). To the west, along the Dordogne and Lot rivers, is the region known as the Dordogne.

Bourges

❶ *243 km (151 mi) south of Paris, 70 km (42 mi) west of Nevers, 153 km (92 mi) east of Tours.*

Find your way to Bourges, and you'll find yourself at the center of France. Modern times have largely passed it by, and the result is a preserved market town with medieval cathedral and streets. Pedestrian-only rue Mirabeau and rue Coursarlon are lined with timber-frame houses and are particularly appealing places to stroll and shop.

★ Approaching the town, you'll see the towers of the 13th-century **Cathédrale St-Étienne.** The central portal is a masterpiece of sculpture: Cherubim, angels, saints, and prophets cluster in the archway. The interior is unlike that of any other Gothic cathedral. The height of the side aisles that flank the nave is an astonishing 65 ft—high enough to allow windows to be placed above the level of the second side aisles. ⊠ *Off rue Porte Jaune.*

The **Palais Jacques-Coeur** is one of the most luxurious Gothic dwellings in France. Notice its vaulted chapel, the wooden ceilings covered with original paintings, and the dining room with its tapestries and massive fireplace. ⊠ *rue Jacques-Coeur,* ☎ *02–48–24–06–87.* 🎫 *31 frs.* ☉ *Daily 9–noon and 2–6. 45-min guided tours only, begin 15 mins after the hr.*

Dining and Lodging

$$$ ✕☷ **Château de la Commanderie.** You won't regret going out of your
★ way to reach this impressive 11th-century château. Rooms are large and elegantly furnished. Join the hosts, the Comte and Comtesse de Jouffrey-Gonsans, for an aperitif before meals in the paneled dining room. The food is well-prepared family fare—often with perfectly aged Charolais beef. ⊠ *Farges-Allichamps, 18200 St-Amand-Montrond (44 km/27 mi south of Bourges on N144),* ☎ *02–48–61–04–19,* ℻ *02–48–61–01–84. 7 rooms, 1 suite. Restaurant. MC, V.*

$$ ✕☷ **Arcantis et Angleterre.** This efficient hotel in the center of town, close to the palace, is popular with business travelers. Rooms have modern conveniences but little character. The restaurant, decorated in Louis XVI style, has prix-fixe menus starting at 120 francs. ⊠ *1 pl. des Quatre-Piliers, 18000 Bourges,* ☎ *02–48–24–68–51,* ℻ *02–48–65–21–41. 31 rooms. Restaurant, bar, minibars. AE, DC, MC, V.*

$$ ✕☷ **Auberge du Moulin de Chaméron.** Out in the country with only the owls to keep you awake at night, this hotel is a peaceful place to stay. Though rooms are in a modern, almost motel-like building and are small and have standard hotel furnishings that make them seem even smaller, most of them open out onto the lovely garden. At the other

end of the garden is the restaurant in a former mill. Dining outside on the terrace in the twilight or in either of the cozy, beamed dining rooms is a fine way to end the day. The cooking is not fancy, but the produce is fresh and the beef is prime Charolais; menus run 130 to 190 francs. ✉ *18210 Bannegon (40 km/25 mi from Bourges)*, ☎ *02–48–61–83–80 hotel, 02–48–61–84–48 restaurant*, ℻ *02–48–61–84–92. 25 rooms. Restaurant. MC, V. Closed mid-Nov.–Mar.*

Montluçon

② *94 km (58 mi) south of Bourges.*

Montluçon is best known for its Bourbon castle and its old quarter, where small 16th- and 17th-century houses line the streets. Built during the Hundred Years' War, the **Château de Montluçon** is remarkably well preserved. The **Musée du Vieux Château** (Old Castle Museum) has a collection of local artifacts from the 18th and 19th centuries including a historical account of the hurdy-gurdy, a traditional stringed instrument. ☎ *04–70–05–00–06.* ⌑ *15 frs.* ☉ *Tues.–Sun. 10–noon and 2:30–6.*

En Route On the way to Bourbon-l'Archambault, make a stop in the delightful rural town of **Cosne-d'Allier** (Exit 10 off A71 to D94 east), where locals come to market.

Bourbon-l'Archambault

③ *48 km (58 mi) northeast of Montluçon.*

During the 17th, 18th, and 19th centuries, Bourbon-l'Archambault was a ritzy thermal spa; illustrious figures such as Talleyrand, France's powerful foreign minister, took the waters here. But the fleeting fancy for fashionable spas left the town a little less noble. However, the weathered buildings and the ruined 14th-century **Château**—once the quarters of the noble tourists—still have an appealing faded glory. ✉ *rue du Château*, ☎ *No phone.* ☉ *Mid-Apr.–mid-Oct., daily 2–6.*

Souvigny

④ *14 km (9 mi) southeast of Bourbon-l'Archambault.*

Small, picturesque Souvigny is dominated by its surprisingly large church. Built in the 11th, 12th, and 15th centuries of pale golden stone, the **Prieuré St-Pierre** appears light compared to most other Auvergne buildings, which are made out of volcanic stone. This village was the financial base of the Bourbon fortunes, solid enough to enable them to establish a royal dynasty.

Dining

$ ✕ **Auberge des Tilleuls.** In an old town house on a small square near
★ the priory, this little restaurant serves innovative cuisine at exceptional prices. Especially good is the hearty beef casserole with a rich, zesty sauce. ✉ *pl. St-Eloi*, ☎ *04–70–43–60–70. MC, V. Closed Mon.*

Moulins

⑤ *12 km (7 mi) east of Souvigny, 291 km (182 mi) south of Paris, 98 km (61 mi) southeast of Bourges, 54 km (32 mi) southeast of Nevers.*

Once the capital of the dukes of Bourbon, Moulins has a compact, medieval center, dominated by its cathedral. The oldest part (1474–1507) of the **Cathédrale Notre-Dame** (✉ *rue de Paris*), in Flamboyant Gothic style, is known for its stained-glass windows. In the 15th century such windows served as picturebooks for illiterate peasants, enabling them to follow the story of the crusades of Louis IX. The cathedral's other medieval treasure is the triptych of the *Maître de Moulins*, painted toward the end of the 15th century. Notice that the Virgin is not as richly clothed as the Duke and Duchess of Bourbon, who commissioned the painting!

The town's belfry, known as the **Jacquemart** (⊠ pl. de l'Hôtel), was built in 1232 and rebuilt in 1946 after having ignited during a fireworks display. **The Musée du Folklore** (Folklore Museum), in a 15th-century mansion next door to the Jacquemart, is filled with costumes, farming implements, and other reminders of Moulins's past. ⊠ *pl. de l'Hôtel*, ☎ *04–70–44–39–03.* ⌑ *10 frs.* ⊙ *Tues.–Sun. 9:30–noon and 2–5:30.*

Dining and Lodging

$$$ ✕⊞ **Hôtel de Paris-Jacquemart.** This family-owned hotel, just a block
★   from the town's medieval quarter, is a genuine delight—traditional France at its best. Service is efficient and welcoming. Rooms are suitably large, with high ceilings and 19th-century antiques. The menus—between 170 and 230 francs—might include *paillette d'homard* (lobster in thin pastry wafers and rich sauce) and a chariot of pastries. ⊠ *21 rue de Paris, 03000 Moulins,* ☎ *04–70–44–00–58,* ☒ *04–70–34–05–39. 28 rooms. Restaurant. AE, DC, MC, V.*

St-Pourçain-sur-Sioule

❻ *31 km (19 mi) south of Moulins, 27 km (18 mi) northwest of Vichy.*

Most of the region's wine comes from the attractive little village of St-Pourçain-sur-Sioule—one of the oldest viticulture centers in France. The wine, which varies considerably in quality and price, is generally not found in other parts of France and is often a good value.

Lodging

$$$ ⊞ **Château de Boussac.** Although the turrets and moat suggest its defensive past, this château is fully modernized. The property is a working Charolais cattle farm and is quiet. Guest rooms are furnished with antiques. In the evening, have an aperitif with the Marquis and Marquise de Longueil before the table d'hôte dinner (advance arrangements required). Lovely breakfasts are served in your room. ⊠ *Target, 03140 Chantelle (10 km/6 mi from St-Pourçain on D987),* ☎ *04–70–40–63–20,* ☒ *04–70–40–60–03. 4 rooms. MC, V. Closed Dec.–Mar.*

Vichy

❼ *30 km (19 mi) south of St-Pourçain-sur-Sioule, 54 km (33 mi) north of Clermont-Ferrand, 349 km (216 mi) south of Paris.*

Vichy is the most elegant city in Auvergne. Yet it does not have the depth of character you'd expect from a town whose mineral waters attracted the Romans and, later, Paris haute society. Nobles such as the Marquise de Sévigné and the Duchess of Angoulême started the trend in the 17th century; then the arrival of Napoléon III in the mid-19th century and the railroad in the early 20th century attracted the middle classes.

When France fell to the Germans in 1940 and the country was divided under direct and indirect German control, the Pétain government moved to Vichy. Hotels served as embassies and ministries. After the war, the puppet government left a stain of infamy on the city. Today Vichy is trying to overcome its past, as well as the perception that it's only a place for retirement. A stretch of the River Allier is being transformed into a lake, and large conference facilities and thermal baths have been built. Although there are no old, famous buildings to admire, the city has a **Thermal Spa** (⊠ rue Callou, ☎ 04–70–97–39–59) that looks like a mosque and a **Grand Casino** with an opera house in the Parc des Sources. Around the park is a shopping area; the **tourist office** (⊠ 19 rue du Parc, ☎ 04–70–98–71–94) is on the western side.

Dining and Lodging

$$ ✕ **L'Alambic.** Chef-owner Jean-Jacques Barbot is a master with local produce. He grills fish from nearby streams with endives and an anise-based sauce, bakes his *sandre* (whitefish) with a mustard coating, and makes lentil salad with the famous, tiny *lentilles de Puy*. ⊠ *8 rue Nicolas-Larbaud,* ☎ *04–70–59–12–71. MC, V. Closed early Mar., early Sept., and Mon. No lunch Tues.*

$$ 🏠 **Hôtel Averna.** This hotel in an 18th-century building in the center of town provides excellent value for the money. Rooms are modest but functional; bathrooms are clean. ⊠ *12 rue Debrest, 03200 Vichy,* ☎ *04–70–31–31–19,* 𝖥𝖠𝖷 *04–70–97–86–43. 26 rooms. AE, DC, MC, V. Closed mid-Dec.–Jan.*

Thiers

🔘   *34 km (21 mi) south of Vichy, 47 km (29 mi) northeast of Clermont-Ferrand.*

Built on a steep hill, Thiers is a slightly grimy but nonetheless fascinating 18th- and 19th-century town that is famous for its cutlery. It supplies 70% of France's cutting needs, producing everything from table knives to daggers. In the old days, while the River Durolle turned the massive grindstones, craftsmen would lie on planks over the icy water to hone their blades on the stone. Today's factories use less exotic methods, but the tourist office gives demonstrations of the old way (as well as maps and information). Be prepared for stiff walking—the streets run only up and down!

Follow rue Conchette, then rue Bourg to appealing place du Pirou, where there is a wonderful example of ancient, half-timber architecture, the 15th-century **Maison du Pirou** (Pirou House). At No. 11 rue de Pirou is the **Maison des Sept Péchés Capitaux** (House of the Seven Deadly Sins)—look at the carvings on the ends of the beams and you'll know why. On rue de la Coutellerie are old knife-making workshops and the 15th-century **Maison des Coutelliers** (Cutlery House), a small museum and workshop with demonstrations of five centuries of knife-making. ⊠ *58 rue de la Coutellerie,* ☎ *04–73–80–58–86.* 🎫 *15 frs.* ⏲ *May–Oct., daily 9–noon and 2–5; Nov.–Apr., weekdays 2–6.*

Roanne

🔘   *59 km (37 mi) east of Thiers, 87 km (54 mi) west of Lyon, 98 km (61 mi) southeast of Moulins, 389 km (243 mi) south of Paris.*

The industrial city of Roanne is on everyone's itinerary for only one reason—the world-famous Troisgros restaurant.

Dining and Lodging

$$$$ ✕🏠 **Troisgros.** One of the most revered restaurants in France serves a
★   seven-course feast, the Menu dans la Tradition (540 francs), which might include lightly sautéed foie gras with grilled groundnuts, frogs'-leg lasagna, regional cheeses, and fantastic desserts. The surprisingly ordinary dining room has comfortable chairs and big windows. Service is at your table before you know you need it. There are also several high-design guest rooms, which are luxurious and comfortable. ⊠ *pl. Jean Troisgros (across from train station), 42300,* ☎ *04–77–71–66–97,* 𝖥𝖠𝖷 *04–77–70–39–77. 13 rooms. Restaurant. AE, DC, MC, V.*

St-Étienne

10 *84 km (52 mi) south of Roanne, 147 km (91 mi) southeast of Cler-mont-Ferrand, 56 km (35 mi) southwest of Lyon.*

The former mining city of St-Étienne (population 200,000) is better known for its soccer team than for its attractions, though it does have a good museum. And in June of 1998, the city hosted some matches of the World Cup in soccer.

The fine **Musée d'Art et d'Industrie** (Art and Industry Museum) has paintings (Rubens, Whistler, Monet) as well as exhibits on local industry. ⊠ *2 pl. Louis-Comte,* ☎ *04–77–33–04–85.* ⌨ *Free.* ⊙ *Wed. 2–5, Thurs.–Mon. 10–noon and 2–5.*

OFF THE BEATEN PATH **LA CHAISE-DIEU** – "The Chair of God" abbey, about 40 km (25 mi) north of Le Puy-en-Velay via N102 and D906, has splendid red-and-black frescoes of the *Danse Macabre* (Death dancing with the nobility, bourgeoisie, and peasants).

Le Puy-en-Velay

11 *76 km (47 mi) southwest of St-Étienne.*

Le Puy-en-Velay is a stunning sight, built up on the *puys* that rise from the fertile valley like pyramids. These solidified-lava peaks are crowned with man-made monuments: on the lowest, a statue of St. Joseph and the Infant Jesus; on the highest, the 11th-century chapel of St-Michel; on another, a huge statue of the Virgin. Most spectacular of the monuments is the Romanesque cathedral **Notre-Dame-du-Puy,** built of polychrome lava and balanced atop the fourth narrow pinnacle, reachable only by a long flight of steps.

St-Flour

12 *110 km (69 mi) east of Le Puy-en-Velay, 74 km (46 mi) west of Aurilac.*

St-Flour is a medieval enclave perched on the edge of an escarpment with cliffs dropping down on three sides. The age of the town becomes even more apparent as you drive from the newer *ville basse* (lower town) up to ancient *ville haute* (upper town). Narrow cobblestone streets meander between 16th- and 17th-century buildings. The town has a couple of museums that may appeal to you if you're interested in French history and culture.

The **Musée de la Haute-Auvergne** (Auvergne Museum), in the former bishop's palace, presents some local archaeological finds but is mostly filled with artifacts and furnishings used by residents over the last 300 years. ⊠ *1 pl. d'Armes,* ☎ *04–71–60–61–20.* ⌨ *25 frs.* ⊙ *Apr. 15–Oct. 15, daily 10–noon and 2–6; Oct. 16–Apr. 14, Mon.–Sat. 10–noon and 2–6.*

Across the square from the Musée de la Haute-Auvergne is the **Musée Alfred Douët.** The 13th-century building, renovated in the 16th century, has on display tapestries and furnishings from the 16th, 17th, and 18th centuries. The items are laid out just as they might have been when the building was occupied by the consul-general, enabling you to get a sense of that era. ⊠ *pl. d'Armes,* ☎ *04–71–60–44–99.* ⌨ *25 frs.* ⊙ *Mid-Apr.–mid-Oct., daily 10–noon and 2–6; mid-Oct.–mid-Apr., Mon.–Sat. 10–noon and 2–6.*

Dining and Lodging

$$ ✕🏨 **Grand Hôtel de l'Europe.** The choice of hotels in St-Flour's haute ville is limited; the family-run Europe is the best. A long, horizontal building on the edge of town, it overlooks the valley below and the hills beyond—a large part of the hotel's appeal. Ask for a room, and a table in the restaurant, with a view of the valley. Rooms, though not large, are old-fashioned, homey, and comfortable. ✉ *12–13 cours Spy des Ternes, 15100,* ☎ *04–71–60–03–64,* 🅵🅰🆇 *04–71–60–03–45. 43 rooms. Bar, breakfast room, restaurant. MC, V.*

Clermont-Ferrand

⓭ *130 km (80 mi) northwest of Le Puy-en-Velay, 40 km (24 mi) west of Thiers, 400 km (248 mi) south of Paris, 178 km (110 mi) west of Lyon.*

Known to historians as the hometown of Vercingétorix, who rallied the Arvernes to defeat Julius Caesar in 52 BC and who is immortalized in Astérix comic books, Clermont-Ferrand is the only large city in Auvergne. A bustling, modern commercial center that is the Michelin tire company's headquarters, Clermont-Ferrand probably won't draw you for more than a few hours. But the city is an ideal transfer point to the rest of Auvergne. It has some good museums and a small old quarter dominated by its cathedral.

The monolithic **Cathédrale Notre-Dame-de-l'Assomption** (✉ pl. de la Victoire) was built of a special black volcanic stone that enabled the pillars to be thinner and the interior to soar to greater heights than ever before. Built 200 years earlier out of yellow sandstone, the Romanesque **Notre-Dame-du-Port** (✉ rue du Port) has an entirely different feel from the cathedral. Note the raised choir with carved capitals that illustrate such tales as the struggle of Virtue and Vice and the fall of Adam and Eve.

Housed in a former Ursuline convent, the **Musée des Beaux-Arts** (Fine Arts Museum) has a beautifully designed exhibit on the history of painting and sculpture. ✉ *pl. Louis-Deteix,* ☎ *04–73–23–08–49.* 🎫 *23 frs.* ⊙ *Tues.–Sun. 11–7.*

The **Musée du Ranquet** houses an assortment of artifacts, from ancient musical instruments to the world's first calculating machine, invented in the 17th century by native son Blaise Pascal. ✉ *34 rue des Gras,* ☎ *04–73–37–38–63.* 🎫 *12 frs.* ⊙ *Tues.–Sat. 10–noon and 2–6 (until 5 in winter), Sun. 2–5.*

Dining and Lodging

$$$ ✕ **Bernard Audrieux.** Chef Bernard Audrieux cooks deceptively sim-
★   ple dishes such as salmon with truffle sauce and *escalope de foie chaud de canard* (sliced hot duck liver). The restaurant's elegance—cream-color walls, white linens, and well-spaced tables—matches the prices (the least expensive prix-fixe menu is 165 francs), but not the suburban location. ✉ *rte. de la Baroque (3 km/2 mi northwest of Clermont-Ferrand on D641A),* ☎ *04–73–37–00–26. AE, DC, MC, V. Closed Sun. and mid-July–mid-Aug. No lunch Sat.*

$$ 🏨 **Hôtel de Lyon.** Convenience is the chief attribute of this down-to-earth hotel in the center of town. Rooms are clean and service is perfunctory but efficient. ✉ *16 pl. de Jaude, 63000,* ☎ *04–73–93–32–55,* 🅵🅰🆇 *04–73–93–54–33. 32 rooms. Restaurant. MC, V.*

Parc National des Volcans and Puy-de-Dôme

★ **⓮** *18 km (11 mi) west of Royat on D68, 24 km (15 mi) west of Clermont-Ferrand.*

Stretching 150 km (90 mi) from north to south, the Parc National des Volcans (National Park of Volcanoes) contains 80 or so dormant volcanoes, with all kinds of craters, dikes, domes, prismatic lava flows, caldera cones, and basaltic plateaus. The volanoes are (relatively) young; the most recent is only 6,000 to 8,000 years old, which explains why their shapes are so well preserved.

At 4,806 ft, the Puy-de-Dôme is the highest volcano in the Mont-Dôme range. The Romans built a temple to Mercury here; the ruins of the temple were uncovered in 1872. The number of tourists, especially in July and August, is tremendous—Puy-de-Dôme is one of the three most-visited sights in France. Give yourself the best part of the day here, and bring your walking shoes so that you can follow the trails up to magnificent panoramas. For those set on a bird's-eye view, parasailing, hot-air ballooning, and hang-gliding can be arranged. ☞ *25 frs per car.* ☉ *Mar. and Nov., daily 8–6; Apr. and Oct., daily 8–8; May–Sept., daily 7–10 PM; Dec., weekends 7–5:30.*

Orcival

⑮ *13 km (8 mi) southwest of Puy-de-Dôme, 22 km (14 mi) southwest of Clermont-Ferrand.*

Mont-Dôme was a major hurdle for pilgrims making the long walk to Santiago de Compostela in Spain. To house them, five major sanctuaries—St-Austremoine d'Issoire, Notre-Dame-du-Port, Notre-Dame d'Orcival, St-Nectaire, and St-Saturnin—were erected in the 12th century. **Notre-Dame d'Orcival** (1146–78) was the most famous of these vaulted Romanesque hospices. Step inside to inspect a most unusual statue of the Virgin carrying an adult-looking child.

En Route From Orcival take D27, which joins D983, for a beautiful ride over the **Col de Guery** pass, at 4,160 ft.

Le Mont-Dore

⑯ *19 km (12 mi) south of Orcival.*

Le Mont-Dore, on the Dordogne River at the head of the sheltered Chaudefour Valley, was once a Roman spa town. Today there are still hot springs, though the town now derives much of its income as a convenient, although not particularly attractive, summer and winter resort town. There are ski trails radiating from the town center, a *téléphérique* (cable car) to the peaks, and mostly intermediate slopes leading down.

Dining and Lodging

$ ✕ **Le Boeuf dans l'Assiette.** This restaurant provides simple fare for ravenous skiers and hikers. With a three-course menu and a bottle of St-Pourçain wine, two people can replenish their energy for less than 175 francs. ⊠ *9 av. Michel-Bertrand,* ☎ *04–73–65–01–23. MC, V.*

$$ ▣ **Château de Bassignac.** This fortified 16th-century manor has just
★ four rooms, decorated with an assortment of family antiques. Bassignac is still a working farm, but the Bessons leave that aspect of business to their children. M. Besson is an artist who often gives painting classes; Mme. Besson acts like everyone's mother. In the evening, you can sit before the fire mellowing with a glass of Armagnac. In winter, the château is only open by advance arrangement. ⊠ *Brousse, 15240 Bassignac (on edge of village, 14 km/9 mi southwest of Bort-les-Orgues on D922; 55 km/34 mi from Le Mont Dore),* ☎ ℻ *04–71–40–82–82. 4 rooms. Fishing. No credit cards.*

St-Nectaire

⑰ *16 km (10 mi) east of Le Mont-Dore, 44 km (27 mi) southwest of Cler-mont-Ferrand.*

In the upper part of the village of St-Nectaire is a Romanesque hos-pice—you may want to give thanks after the drive over the passes. But your true reward is St-Nectaire's superb, soft, nutty-tasting cheese, made since the 3rd century.

Lodging

$$ ☒ **Relais Mercure.** On the site of the former Roman baths, in a digni-fied 19th-century building, is this attractive, modern hotel. Soaring ceil-ings in the palatial public areas and picture windows in the restaurant and bar give it a light, airy feel. Part of the reliable Mercure chain, the hotel has all the amenities, from cable TV to direct-dial phones and in-room modem lines. The grounds in back, rising protectively from the hotel, are a tranquil arboretum, with specimen trees and quiet walks. ⊠ *63710 St-Nectaire,* ☎ *04–73–88–57–00,* FAX *04–73–88–57–02. 71 rooms. Bar, restaurant, in-room modem lines, 1 indoor and 1 out-door pool, sauna, health club, meeting rooms. AE, MC, V.*

Montpeyroux

⑱ *20 km (12 mi) east of St-Nectaire, 23 km (13 mi) south of Clermont-Ferrand.*

This medieval village, perched on a knoll just 8 km (5 mi) off A75 Exit 7, has made a comeback. By the early 19th century, 445 inhabitants lived behind its granite walls, going out each day to the vineyards. Then came phylloxera, in the later part of the century, which destroyed the vines. The village's population dwindled to 125 people, and once proud homes fell into disrepair. In the 1970s, however, came recogni-tion in France that its many medieval relics needed to be preserved and Montpeyroux's rebirth began. Now the village has 360 residents, re-stored houses, and a festival of flowers every third week in May. There isn't actually that much to see here, except for the 13th-century round *donjon* (keep), which is open to the public and can be climbed, and a restaurant or two. Nonetheless, it is the views from the village of the sprawling landscape and the distant volcanic mountains, and the seren-ity of the place, that makes it so appealing.

Lodging

$–$$ ☒ **Chez Astruc.** Sometime during your stay at this charming four-story house, owner Marcel Astruc will inevitably show you photographs of the building's emergence from a ruin to its present state. The building has two entrances: one from the village's lower street into the break-fast room–lounge–bar area; another from its highest, rue Donjon. Mar-cel and his wife live on the upper floor; guest rooms are on the lower three. Ask for a room on the second floor; two have balconies and views of the surrounding countryside. Though they are not large, rooms are pleasant, if a little fussily decorated. But best of all is Astruc's enthu-siasm for the village—he is its mayor—and his knowledge of the area. ⊠ *63720 Montpeyroux,* ☎ *04–74–36–66–22. 4 rooms. Bar, break-fast room. No credit cards.*

Besse

⑲ *6 km (4 mi) east of St-Nectaire.*

Besse, like many of the other small, old farming villages in the moun-tainous Mont-Dôme region, has become a popular winter-sports and summer hiking center. If you are here on Monday, go to the cheese market—Auvergne's wheel of life. A favorite excursion from Besse is to nearby **Lac Pavin,** a perfectly symmetrical caldera lake. Anglers come here to fish for mammoth-size trout called *omble chevalier*—delicious in the hands of a good chef.

En Route The route south from Besse is splendid if you take D978 through the Monts du Cantal and Condat and Riom-les-Montagnes. The route becomes even more dramatic when, at Riom, D62 leads to the Pas de Peyrol. West from Besse, D680 heads through the Cirque de Falgoux, whose twists and turns will require all your attention.

Pas de Peyrol

㉚ *38 km (23 mi) south of Besse.*

At nearly 5,249 ft, the Pas de Peyrol is Auvergne's highest pass. Leave your car in the parking lot and take the 30-minute walk to the summit of ★**Puy Mary.** The views from here are tremendous: 13 valleys radiate from the mountain, funneling their streams into some of France's major rivers.

Salers

★ **㉑** *11 km (7 mi) west of Pas de Peyrol, 20 km (12 mi) south of Mauriac, 43 km (25 mi) north of Aurillac.*

Medieval Salers, perched on a bluff above the Maronne Valley, is filled with tourists. But the town cannot fail to seduce you, too. In the 15th century, the people of Salers, feeling isolated in the country, began building protective ramparts and, subsequently, won the right to govern themselves. Many of the 15th- and 16th-century houses, built of black lava stone, remain and are now filled with boutiques and small restaurants. Although this was once an important cattle-market town, farming today plays a smaller role than tourism—though you still may be woken up by the sound of cowbells. On market days, **Grande Place,** in the heart of the village, is very busy.

Fifteen to 20 kilometers (9 to 12 miles) south of Salers, the valley ridges are so beautiful that you could spend a day or two exploring the tiny, winding roads. The *cols* (mountain passes) are high enough (plus or minus 3,000 ft) to have snow in the winter, but they are really quite gentle and they provide a good view of the comely valleys below. Find your way to the small *hameau* (hamlet) of **Fontanges,** with its tiny chapel hollowed out of a limestone bluff on which stands a white Madonna. The sweet hillside village of Tournemire and its **Château Anjony** are also worth a visit. *Château:* ☎ *04–71–40–23–22.* 💶 *25 frs.* ⊙ *Mar.– mid-Nov., Mon.–Sat. 2–5:30.*

Lodging

$$–$$$ 🏰 **Château de la Vigne.** Rebuilt in the 15th century, this château on ★ a hillcrest still retains elements of its past as an 8th-century Merovingian castle and then a medieval fortress. The Parc National des Volcans is visible in the distance. Family coats of arms and stained-glass windows decorate the best guest room, the large Chambre Troubadour; it is said that Jean-Jacques Rousseau stayed here in 1767. Otherwise, furnishings are sparse and bathrooms makeshift. Dinner (reservations required) with owners Mme. and M. du Fayet de la Tour is served in the splendid dining room. Regional foods are used and the aperitifs include local dandelion wine. ✉ *15700 Ally (16 km/10 mi from Salers),* ☎ *FAX 04–71–69–00–20. 4 rooms. Dining room. No credit cards. Closed mid-Oct.–late Mar.*

$$–$$$ 🏠 **Hostellerie de la Maronne.** In a tranquil valley, this converted 19th-century farmhouse has well-kept, modern rooms, some with balconies. Furnishings, however, are department-store variety. The lounge and bar are pleasant, but the most care has been put into the dining room and the glassed-in kitchen. Dinner provides an opportunity to savor the best Salers beef, though the cuisine itself is not worth a special trip. ⊠ *Le Treil, 15140 St-Martin-Valmeroux (6 km/4 mi from Salers),* ☎ *04–71–69–20–33,* FAX *04–71–69–28–22. 17 rooms. Restaurant, bar, lobby lounge. MC, V. Closed Nov. 1–Easter.*

$$ 🏠 **Hôtel des Ramparts.** From its position atop the ramparts, this hotel has spectacular panoramic views. Rooms are simple and functional. The management likes to quote half-pension rates, which you should resist if you are staying for more than one night. ⊠ *esplanade de Barrouze, 15410 Salers,* ☎ *04–71–40–70–33,* FAX *04–71–40–75–32. 18 rooms. Restaurant. MC, V. Closed late-Oct.–late Dec.*

Aurillac

㉒   *42 km (26 mi) south of Salers, 157 km (97 mi) southwest of Clermont-Ferrand.*

The prefecture and market town of Aurillac, at the edge of the Monts du Cantal, bustles by day and becomes a sleepy country village by night. The oldest part of town—a small area—has an old cheese market, ancient houses, and narrow streets that twist along the banks of the River Jordanne. Locals and tourists spend their days at the cafés on **place du Palais-de-Justice,** the main square. Stop by the **tourist office** here for a free walking-tour map—well worth following.

At the **Musée d'Art et d'Archéologie** (Art and Archaeology Museum), remains of a Gallo-Roman temple and various religious objects are on display. A unique collection of umbrellas from the past three centuries—about half of all French umbrellas are made in Aurillac—is also housed here. ⊠ *Centre Pierre Mendès-France, 37 rue des Carmes,* ☎ *04–71–45–46–10.* 💺 *15 frs.* ☉ *Apr.–Oct., Tues.–Sun. 10–noon and 2–6; July–Aug., daily 10–noon and 2–6.*

On the south side of Aurillac is the **National Stud Farm** of Aurillac. The stables accommodate 22 stallions from standardbreds to Arabians. ☎ *04–71–64–19–61.* 💺 *20 frs (guided tours only).* ☉ *Mid-July–mid-Sept. (tours daily at 10, 11, 2, 3, 4, and 5).*

Dining and Lodging

$$ ✕ **Poivre & Sel.** This intimate, friendly bistro serves a refined version of Auvergne fare. It is a good place to try Salers beef, as well as other regional dishes such as *salmis de colvert Cévenole* (ragout of game). ⊠ *4 rte. du 14-Juillet,* ☎ *04–71–64–20–20. MC, V. Closed Mon.*

$ ✕ **Le Bistro.** For genuine Auvergne grub come to this little bistro with Formica tables and a long bar. Two fine regional specialties served are *truffade* (sautéed potato slices covered with melted cheese) and *choux farcis* (stuffed cabbage). ⊠ *23 rue Gambetta,* ☎ *04–71–48–01–04. Reservations not accepted. MC, V.*

$$ 🏠 **Grand Hôtel de Bordeaux.** There are advantages to this Best Western hotel—its central location and its private garage. Rooms are compact but clean, functional, and adequate. ⊠ *2 av. de la République, 15000,* ☎ *04–71–48–01–84,* FAX *04–71–48–49–93. 33 rooms. Bar. AE, DC, MC, V.*

Laguiole

㉓ *85 km (53 mi) southeast of Aurillac, 56 km (35 mi) north of Rodez.*

On the high basalt plateau, Laguiole is more than 3,000 ft above sea level. Locals claim that their home is nature at its purest. In winter, the wind roars across the land, piling up snow on ski trails; in summer, the sun scorches the land; in spring and fall, the angled sunlight dances on the granite outcroppings. The town is known for its hardy breed of Aubrac cattle; for its distinctive cheese made from unpasteurized cows' milk, flavored by the varied local flora; and for its spring-hinged pocket knife. You can visit the factory, the **Societé Forge de Laguiole** (☎ 05–65–48–43–34), where the knives with a slightly curved handle and a long blade are made; buy one here or in town.

Dining and Lodging

$$$$ ✕▥ **Michel Bras.** Despite the flowery prose used by the Bras to describe their contemporary hotel-restaurant, it does not really "mold itself perfectly to the countryside," but stands on a promontory like a spaceship about to be launched. Others have described it as a glass barn with wooden sheds alongside. To be fair, the rooms are full of light, creature comforts are everywhere, and the views of the granite outcrops are haunting. But the main draw is Michel Bras's unique creations—foie gras with apricots and honey vinegar, and asparagus with truffle vinaigrette—as well as his more classic Aubrac beef and wild boar dishes. ✉ *rte. de l'Aubrac, 12210,* ☎ *05–65–44–32–24,* FAX *05–65–48–47–02. 15 rooms. Restaurant. AE, DC, MC, V. Closed Nov.–Mar.*

$$ ✕▥ **Grand Hôtel Auguy.** An excellent alternative to the high-priced Michel Bras (☞ *above*), the Auguy has basic rooms with just enough space for a bed, a desk, and a couple of armchairs. Ask for one of the quieter rooms, away from the street. Owner Isabelle Auguy is a creative cook who uses her grandparents' rustic recipes, giving them a lighter touch. The foie gras salad is a delight, as are the Aubrac beef and fresh trout. ✉ *2 allée de l'Amicale, 12210,* ☎ *04–65–44–31–11,* FAX *04–65–51–50–81. 30 rooms. Restaurant, bar, lobby lounge. MC, V.*

St-Céré

㉔ *65 km (40 mi) west of Aurillac, 28 km (17 mi) east of Rocamadour.*

A small, medieval village on the Bave River, a tributary of the Dordogne, St-Céré is an ideal base for exploring the area. During World War II, the town was a center for the Resistance. Overlooking its ancient houses are the ruins of the **Château de St-Laurent-les-Tours,** whose two partially restored keeps date from the 12th and 15th centuries. Two kilometers (1 mile) west is another castle worth checking out, the 16th-century **Château du Montal.**

Dining and Lodging

$ ✕▥ **Ferme de la Rivière.** Make yourself at home at this charming farm-
★ house on the edge of the beautiful village of Autoire, just outside St-Céré. Rooms have ancient, exposed beams and gabled ceilings. Rates are extremely reasonable at 200 francs for two, including breakfast, and an extra 85 francs per person for an excellent table d'hôte dinner. ✉ *Autoire, 46400 St-Céré,* ☎ *05–65–38–18–01. 3 rooms. No credit cards.*

En Route Between St-Céré and Rocamadour, along D673, is the **Causses de Gramat,** an extensive limestone plateau where stubbly trees claw the white-gray earth.

Rocamadour

★ ㉕ *28 km (17 mi) west of St-Céré.*

Rocamadour is a medieval village that seems to defy the laws of gravity; it surges out of a cliff 1,500 ft above the Alzou River gorge. The town got its name after the discovery in 1166 of the 1,000-year-old body of St. Amadour "quite whole." The body was moved to the cathedral, where it began to work miracles. Pilgrims flocked to the site, climbing the 216 steps to the church on their knees. Making the climb on foot is sufficient reminder of the medieval penchant for agonizing penance; today an elevator lifts weary souls. The village is especially mobbed with pilgrims and tourists in summer. Cars are not allowed; park in the lot below the town or in L'Hospitalet, 1½ km (1 mi) away.

The staircase and elevator up to the **Cité Religieuse** start from place de la Carreta; if you walk, pause at the landing 141 steps up to admire the fort. Once up, you'll see tiny place St-Amadour and its seven sanctuaries: the basilica of **St-Sauveur** opposite the staircase; the **St-Amadour crypt** under the basilica; the chapel of **Notre-Dame** to the left; the chapels of **John the Baptist, St-Blaise,** and **Ste-Anne** to the right; and the Romanesque chapel of **St-Michel,** built into an overhanging cliff. St-Michel's two 12th-century frescoes—depicting the Annunciation and the Visitation—have survived in superb condition. ⊠ *Centre d'Accueil Notre-Dame.* ⊙ *Guided tours Mon.–Sat. 9–5;* ⊠ *tips at visitors' discretion; English-speaking guide available.*

The village itself, though very touristy, is full of beautifully restored medieval houses. One of the finest is the 15th-century **Hôtel de Ville,** near the Porte Salmon, which houses the **tourist office** and an excellent collection of tapestries. ⊠ *Free.* ⊙ *Mon.–Sat. 10–noon and 3–8.*

Dining and Lodging

$$ ✕⊡ **Le Beau Site.** This is the best of the few old-town hotels. The charm of the ancient beams, exposed stone, and open hearth in the foyer ends as you climb the stairs; rooms are modern and functional. The dining room overlooks the canyon, and best of all, you can park inside Rocamadour if you stay here. ⊠ *Cité Médiévale, 46500,* ☎ *05–65–33–63–08,* FAX *05–65–33–65–23. 55 rooms. Restaurant. MC, V. Closed mid-Dec.–mid-Jan.*

Cahors

㉖ *56 km (35 mi) south of Rocamadour.*

Once an opulent Gallo-Roman town, Cahors, sitting snugly within a loop of the River Lot, is famous for its tannic red wine, known to the Romans as black wine. Many of the small estates in the area have tastings. The town's finest sight is the **Pont Valentré,** a bridge, with elegant towers, that is a spellbinding feat of medieval engineering. Also look for the fortresslike **Cathédrale St-Étienne** (⊠ Off rue du Mar. Joffre), with its cupolas. Its cloisters connect to the courtyard of the archdeaconry, which is awash with Renaissance decoration and thronged with visitors who come for the art exhibits.

Dining and Lodging

$$$-$$$$ ✕⊡ **Château de Mercuès.** Just outside Cahors, this hotel in the former home of the Counts of Cahors has older rooms in baronial splendor (ask for one of these), as well as boring, modern ones (which tend to attract mosquitoes). One of the best rooms is Tour, with a unique ceiling that slides back to expose the shaft of the turret. Duck, lamb, and truffles reign in the restaurant, but the high prices lead you to expect more creativity than is produced. Service also tends to be rather

slack until you make the staff aware that you expect your needs fulfilled immediately. ⊠ *46090 Mercuès (6 km/4 mi west of Cahors on the road to Villeneuve-sur-Lot),* ☎ *05–65–20–00–01,* 🆀 *05–65–20–05–72. 25 rooms, 9 suites. Restaurant, pool, 2 tennis courts, helipad. AE, DC, MC, V. Closed Nov.–mid-Mar.*

\$\$\$–\$\$\$\$ ✕🏨 **Terminus.** Only a two-minute walk from the train station, this small, ivy-covered hotel is deep in the heart of truffle country. The young owners go out of their way to assist. The restaurant, La Balandre, is the town's best. The decor is mostly Roaring '20s. Truffles as well as exceptional *brandade* (puree of cod and potatoes) are served. ⊠ *5 av. Charles-de-Freycinet, 46000,* ☎ *05–65–35–24–50,* 🆀 *05–65–22–06–40. 22 rooms. Restaurant. AE, MC, V. Closed 2 wks in Feb., 1 wk in June. No dinner Sun.*

St-Cirq-Lapopie

㉗ *25 km (16 mi) east of Cahors: Take D653 in the direction of Figeac; after 8 km (5 mi) turn right on D662 and continue along the Lot River until a sign directs you over a one-lane bridge.*

The beautiful, 13th-century village of St-Cirq-Lapopie (pronounced san-*sare*) is on a rocky spur 262 ft up, with nothing but a vertical drop to the Lot River below. Filled with artisans' workshops, and not yet renovated à la Disney, the town has so many dramatic views that you may end up spending several hours here. A mostly ruined château can be reached by a stiff walk along the path that starts near the Hôtel de Ville. Stop by the tourist office in the center of town for information.

Lodging

\$\$ 🏨 **La Pelerissa.** This jewel of a hotel is very small and simple, but the ancient building has all the atmosphere that you'd expect to find in this medieval village. Room 3 has a view of the village; No. 4 has a view of the valley and the Lot River. There are also a couple of rooms in the garden with less grand views. The lounge is a snug place to relax in the evening, especially in front of the open fire. ⊠ *46330 St-Cirq-Lapopie,* ☎ *05–65–31–25–14,* 🆀 *05–65–30–25–52. 8 rooms. Restaurant. MC, V. Closed Nov.–Mar.*

Figeac

㉘ *43 km (27 mi) northwest of St-Cirq-Lapopie.*

The old town of Figeac, which has a lively Saturday-morning market, was a stopping point for pilgrims heading toward Santiago de Compostela. Many of the 13th-, 14th-, and 15th-century houses in the old part of town have been carefully restored; note their octagonal chimneys and *soleilhos* (open attics used for drying flowers and wood). The elegant, 13th-century **Hôtel de la Monnaie,** a block from the River Célé, is a characteristic old Figeac house. It was probably used as a money-changing office in the Middle Ages. Today it houses the **tourist office** and a museum of relics. ⊠ *pl. Vival,* ☎ *05–65–34–06–25.* 🎫 *Free.* ☉ *July–Aug., daily 10–noon and 2:30–6:30; Sept.–June, Mon.–Sat. 3–5.*

Jean-François Champollion (1790–1830), one of the first men to decipher Egyptian hieroglyphics, was born in Figeac. The **Musée Champollion** (leave place Vival on rue 11-Novembre, take the first left, and follow it as it veers right) contains a casting of the Rosetta stone, discovered in the Nile River delta, which Champollion used to decode Pharaonic dialect. ⊠ *5 impasse Champollion,* ☎ *05–65–34–66–18.* 🎫 *22 frs.* ☉ *May–Sept., Tues.–Sat. 10–noon and 2:30–6:30.*

Dining and Lodging

$$$$ ✕🏯 **Château du Viguier du Roy.** Everything—the tower, the cloister, the gardens, the wooden beams, the tapestries, and the canopied beds—in this medieval palace, once the residence of the king's *viguier* (representative), has been painstakingly restored. Rooms throughout are regal. The restaurant, La Dinée du Viguier, is excellent. ✉ *rue Droite, 46100,* ☎ *05–65–50–05–05,* FAX *05–65–50–06–06. 17 rooms, 3 suites. Restaurant. AE, DC, MC, V. Closed early–mid-Dec. and early Jan.–Feb.*

$$–$$$ 🏯 **Ferme Auberge Domaine des Villedieu.** This lovely farmhouse, partly dating from the 16th century, is lovingly run by the Villedieus. Not only can you look forward to cozy rooms in outbuildings, but you can also hope for cassoulet in front of the fire in a bubbling earthenware casserole and homemade foie gras. ✉ *rte. D13, Vallée du Célé, Boussac 46100 (10 km/6 mi from Figeac),* ☎ *05–65–40–06–63,* FAX *05–65–40–09–22. 4 rooms. Dining Room. AE, DC, MC, V.*

En Route Leave Figeac on the road to Rodez and take D52, a small road on your left: It leads through the beautiful Lot Valley to D901, which goes to Conques.

Conques

㉙ *44 km (27 mi) east of Figeac.*

The pretty, red-ocher houses of Conques harmonize perfectly with the surrounding rocky gorge. The village was home to a Benedictine abbey whose outstanding Romanesque church was one of the principal stopping points on the pilgrimage route between Le Puy-de-Dôme and Santiago de Compostela.

Begun in the early 11th century, the abbey church of **Ste-Foy** had its heyday in the 12th and 13th centuries, after which the flood of pilgrims and their revenue dried up. The two centuries of success were due to the purloined relics of Ste-Foy (St. Faith), a 13-year-old Christian girl who was martyred in 303 in Agen, where her remains were jealousy guarded. A monk from Conques venerated them so highly that he traveled to Agen, joined the community of St. Faith, and won their trust. After 10 years they put him in charge of guarding the saint's relics, whereupon he stole them and brought them back to Conques. Devastated by Huguenot hordes, the church languished until the 19th century, when the writer Prosper Mérimée raised the money to salvage it. Ste-Foy clings to a hill so steep that even driving and walking—let alone building—are precarious. The church's interior is high and dignified; the ambulatory was given a lot of wear by medieval pilgrims, who admired the church's most precious relic, a 10th-century wooden statue of Ste-Foy encrusted with gold and precious stones. You can see it in the treasury, off the recently restored cloister.

The **Musée Docteur Joseph-Fau** (Trésor II), opposite the pilgrims' fountain near Ste-Foy, houses a collection of furniture, statues, tapestries, and sculpture. 🏛 *22 frs.* ☉ *Sept.–June, Mon.–Sat. 9–noon and 2–6, Sun. 2–6; July–Aug., Mon.–Sat. 9–noon and 2–7, Sun. 2–7.*

Rodez

㉚ *39 km (24 mi) south of Conques.*

Rodez, capital of the Aveyron, stands on a windswept hill. At its center is the pink sandstone **Cathédrale Notre-Dame** (13th–15th centuries). Its bulk is lightened by decorative upper stories, completed in the 17th century, and by the magnificent 285-ft bell tower. The renovated **Cité Quartier,** once ruled by medieval bishops, lies behind the cathedral. On tiny place de l'Olmet, just off place du Bourg, is the 16th-century **Maison d'Armagnac,** a fine Renaissance mansion with a courtyard and an ornate facade covered with medallion emblems of the Counts of Rodez. The extensively modernized **Musée Denys Puech,** an art museum, is just east of the wide boulevard that circles the old town. ⊠ *pl. Clemenceau,* ☎ *05–65–42–70–64.* ☑ *17 frs.* ⊘ *Mon. 2–8, Wed.–Sat. 10–noon and 3–7, Sun. 3–7.*

Dining and Lodging

$–$$ ✕☒ **La Diligence.** Talented chef Joel Delmas makes succulent mille-
★ feuilles of lamb kidneys and a superb banana coconut tart, among other fine dishes. Equally impressive are the prices: Prix-fixe lunches start at 89 francs. The restaurant is closed for dinner Sunday and Tuesday, for lunch Monday and for dinner Monday April–June, and for lunch and dinner on Wednesdays October–March. Rooms, furnished in modern style, are not luxurious, but they are adequate and modestly priced. ⊠ *12330 Vallady (10 km/6 mi northwest of Rodez on Rte. N140 near the village of Nuces),* ☎ *05–65–72–60–20,* ℻ *no fax. 7 rooms. Restaurant. MC, V. Closed Jan. and 1st 2 wks of Sept.*

En Route If you are traveling from Rodez to Millau and have time, skip N88 and take the shorter and prettier route D28, off N88.

Plaisance

③ *71 km (44 mi) south of Rodez, 70 km (43 mi) west of Millau.*

Plaisance is typical of many of the villages tucked into the Tarn Valley and the rolling, wooded hills that serve as watersheds for the Tarn River. In this relatively undiscovered part of France, take a day to hike along the many trails that traverse the verdant hills.

Dining and Lodging

$$ ✕☒ **Les Magnolias.** Rustic charm and sophisticated cooking at this 14th-
★ century inn are orchestrated by jocular owner Francis Roussel. Sample his foie gras—Roussel is only too happy to divulge his secret. He has a flair for finding tastes that complement one another: grilled cheese in duck bouillon, for example, and perch in red wine sauce. The ambience is wonderfully medieval, with oak beams and stone staircases. Rooms are simple and slightly eclectic. ⊠ *12550 Plaisance,* ☎ *05–65–99–77–34,* ℻ *05–65–99–70–57. 6 rooms. Restaurant. AE, MC, V. Closed mid-Nov.–mid-Mar.*

Roquefort-sur-Soulzon

③ *24 km (15 mi) south of Millau.*

So widely sought after is Roquefort cheese that the milk from local sheep is not enough—30% of it now comes from the Pyrénées and Corsica. Foul play, you may say, but what makes Roquefort is not the milk but the place it is stored—in the seven levels of the caves at Roquefort-sur-Soulzon, home to the *Penicillium glaucum roquefortii* bacteria. The caves are between 7°C (45°F) and 9°C (48°F), the temperature that the Penicillium likes, year-round. These happy bacteria float through the air inoculating the cheeses for three months. Take a sweater. ☎ *05–65–58–59–58.* ☑ *Guided tour 15 frs.* ⊘ *July–Aug., daily 9:30–6; Sept.–June, daily 9:30–11:30 and 2–5.*

Millau

③ *66 km (41 mi) southeast of Rodez, 70 km (43 mi) east of Plaisance, 248 km (154 mi) south of Clermont-Ferrand.*

Millau is primarily a good jumping-off point for exploring the magnificent gorges (☞ below) that cut through the limestone *causses* (plateaus). Give yourself time to wander through the old quarter, especially around place du Maréchal-Foch, with its 800-year-old arcades. Browse through the shops on place des Mandarous and place de la Tine for leather goods, by-products of all those sheep producing milk for Roquefort cheese.

In Roman times, Millau produced pottery and sent its vases as far afield as Scotland. Some of these artifacts, collected from the nearby archaeological site, are in the **Musée de Millau.** ⊠ *Hôtel de Pégayrolles, pl. Foch,* ☎ *05–65–59–01–08.* 🎫 *22 frs.* ☉ *Mon.–Sat. 10–noon and 2–6.*

Dining and Lodging

$$ ✕🏠 **Château de Creissels.** This hotel, in an ancient 12th-century fort, has rooms furnished in simple country style and more modern decor. Dinner is served in the vaulted cellar, which has a medieval atmosphere. ⊠ *rte. de Ste-Afrique, 12100 Millau (3 km/2 mi outside of town on D992),* ☎ *05–65–60–31–79,* 𝔽𝔸𝕏 *05–65–61–24–63. 31 rooms, 26 with bath or shower. Restaurant. MC, V. Closed mid-Dec.–mid-Feb.*

Outdoor Activities and Sports

Mountain bikes, a good way to explore the gorges, can be rented from **William Orts** (⊠ 21 bd. de l'Ayrolle, ☎ 05–65–61–14–29).

Gorges du Tarn

★ ❸ *Extends from Le Rozier (16 km/10 mi northeast of Millau) to Florac, 75 km (47 mi) to the northeast.*

Though not quite as awesome as the Grand Canyon, the Gorges du Tarn (Tarn Gorge) is very beautiful and dramatic. Route D907 leads into its mouth and runs along it, 1,968 ft below the cliff top. Beginning at **Le Rozier,** the Tarn River, flowing out of the gorge, is joined by the Jonte, coming from the Gorges de la Jonte (☞ below). Follow D907B to **Les Vignes,** where the gorge opens into a little valley. Take D995 to the top, along some challenging switchbacks, and follow signs for **Point Sublime,** where you'll find views that justify the name. After Les Vignes, the gorge becomes the most dramatic, with sheer cliffs and rock face dappled with grays, whites, and blues. In summer you can take a boat through this stretch; a bus takes you to the embarkation point.

At the **Cirque des Baumes,** just before the village of La Malène, the cliffs form a natural amphitheater. Continue on to **Les Détroits,** the gorge's narrowest section, where the tumbling waters squeeze through. After passing **La Malène,** note the 15th-century **Château de la Caze,** with its imposing array of turrets. Beyond the castle, just before the village of St-Chély-du-Tarn, is the **Cirque de Pournadoires** and, catercorner, another, larger natural amphitheater. On summer nights it is the site of a son-et-lumière show. But don't make a point of seeing it: The gorge looks far more beautiful under natural light.

Ste-Énimie, the gorge's major town, is mired in summer by a flood of tourists. In its little church, ceramic tiles tell the 7th-century legend of Ste-Énimie, the beautiful sister of the Frankish king. When she was about to marry, she fell ill with leprosy and was scorned by her suitor. On the advice of an angel she was cured at the fountain of Burle, where she then founded a convent. Its ruins can still be seen, as can the fountain. From Ste-Énimie, the road winds through the valley, opening out just before the small market town of **Florac.**

Dining and Lodging

$ ✕⊞ **Le Vallon.** Locals are drawn year-round by the simple yet good fare at this restaurant-inn in the touristy town of Ispagnac, along the gorge. For 85 francs you get four courses, which might include an omelet, a salad, a casserole, and some cheese. Rooms are simple, clean, and inexpensive. ⊠ *rte. D907B, 48320 Ispagnac,* ☎ 04–66–44–21–24, FAX 04–66–44–26–05. *24 rooms, most with bath. Restaurant, bar. MC, V.*

Outdoor Activities and Sports

For kayaking down through the Gorges du Tarn, try **Canyon Location** (⊠ rte. de Millau, Ste-Énimie, ☎ 04–66–48–50–52). Trips can be as short as 9 km (5½ mi) and as long as 72 km (50 mi). Another outfit for kayaking the Gorges du Tarn, which also organizes horseback riding, rents mountain bikes, and sends you riding the winds in a hang glider (*parapente*), is **FREMYC** (⊠ Meyrueis, ☎ 04–66–45–61–54).

En Route Between Florac and St-Jean-du-Gard, the **Corniches des Cévennes** road winds its way through spectacular scenery. Follow D907 from Florac; then take a left on D983 toward St-Laurent-de-Trèves. From here the road ascends the **Col du Rey,** high above the valley.

St-Jean-du-Gard

③⑤ *53 km (33 mi) southeast of Florac.*

In the old days, bolts of silk made their way from St-Jean-du-Gard, on the Gardon River, to Paris couture houses. But hard times came to the town when clothing makers began importing silk from elsewhere. Now most of what is left of the silk industry is represented by the **Musée des Vallées Cévenoles.** ⊠ *95 Grand Rue,* ☎ 04–66–85–10–48. ☞ *12 frs.* ☉ *June–Sept., Tues.–Sat. 9–noon and 2–5, Sun. 2–5.*

Anduze

③⑥ *7 km (4 mi) southeast of St-Jean-du-Gard, 14 km (9 mi) east of Alès, 46 km (29 mi) east of Nîmes.*

Once a Huguenot stronghold, this pretty village had such mighty bulwarks that Louis XIII left it alone and sacked nearby Alès instead. The peace treaty stipulated that Anduze's fortifications be torn down; now only the 14th-century **Tour d'Horloge** (Clock Tower) remains.

Dining and Lodging

$$–$$$ ✕⊞ **La Ranquet.** The hilly, wooded setting; the comfortable, spacious
★ rooms; and top-ranking chef Annie Majourel are all reasons to come here. Majourel's menus (two moderately priced) change monthly, but you can expect such delightful dishes as roast wild boar and orange praline mousse. Be sure to visit the herb garden: It's both a delightful education and explains why Majourel's cooking is so aromatic. The restaurant is closed Tuesday and Wednesday in winter. ⊠ *rte. de St-Hippolyte, 30140 Tornac (6 km/4 mi southwest of Anduze),* ☎ 04–66–77–51–63, FAX 04–66–77–55–62. *10 rooms. Restaurant, piano bar, air-conditioning, pool. Closed mid-Nov.–Dec. 25 and Feb.*

Meyrueis

③⑦ *35 km (22 mi) southwest of Florac, 43 km (27 mi) east of Millau.*

The Jonte and Betuzon rivers join at the village of Meyrueis, which is 2,300 ft high. Its warm days and cool nights make it a perfect base for exploring the gorgeous Gorges du Tarn (☞ *above*), Gorges de la Jonte (☞ *below*), and other nearby caves, causses, and cirques. Meyrueis itself has a medieval round tower, part of ancient fortifications, which houses the tourist office, and a ruined château high above. The narrow streets of the oldest part of town, once within the walls, conceal a minuscule Jewish quarter and a noble house you can stay in. A self-guided walking tour will introduce you to everyone worth knowing about in Meyrueis, as well as show you where they lived, prayed, and administered justice.

Dining and Lodging

$$$ ✕☉ **Château d'Ayres.** A Benedictine monastery before the Wars of Re-
★ ligion, this aristocratic manor house has been transformed into a marvelous country retreat, a mile out of Meyrueis. A serene pool reflects the Virginia creeper–covered building, and the spacious grounds contain a tennis court and swimming pool. Lunch is served on the gravel courtyard or on the lawn. Step inside to comfortable public spaces and two dining rooms where delightful Auvergne meals are served: Superb lamb, Aubrac beef, Mt. Aigoual mushrooms, and goat cheese are just a few of the regional riches. Up the broad stone staircase are spacious, high-ceilinged guest rooms with a mix of antiques and newer, comfortable furnishings. ✉ *rte. d'Ayres, 48150,* ☎ *04–66–45–60–10,* FAX *04–66–45–62–26. 24 rooms, 3 suites. Restaurant, pool, tennis court, horseback riding. AE, DC, MC, V. Closed mid-Nov.–late Mar.*

$ ☉ **La Renaissance.** Just off shady place d'Orléans is this small, 16th-century *hôtel particulier* (mansion) owned by the Bourguet family since it was built. Over the centuries, they have furnished it with antiques, beautiful linenfold paneling, and family portraits. Don't expect to find telephones in rooms (there are TVs) or an elevator. There's a nice breakfast room overlooking the garden, but other meals are served at the neighboring Hôtel du St-Sauveur (also owned by the Bourguets), whose restaurant and wine list are of gastronomic note. ✉ *rue de la Ville, 48150,* ☎ *04–66–45–60–19,* FAX *04–66–45–62–12. 20 rooms. Breakfast room. MC, V.*

Gorges de la Jonte

38 *Extends from Meyrueis (35 km/22 mi southwest of Florac) 21 km/13 mi west to Le Rozier (16 km/10 mi northeast of Millau).*

The splendid Gorges de la Jonte (Jonte Gorge) is narrower than the Gorges du Tarn (☞ above), thus easier to see across and into. At its depths is the Jonte River. Start from the village of **Meyrueis** (☞ *above*), where the gorge is at its broadest. Within a short distance, the gorge narrows, and the eroded limestone cliffs form strange pinnacle shapes. A good spot to stop for a snack is **Les Douzes,** where you can then proceed to the deepest part of the gorge. The road winds along the cliff side. Past **Truel,** a cluster of houses clinging to the cliff face, is a lookout where, for a moment, the view opens to reveal two levels of cliff—**Les Terrasses de Truel**—then closes again before Le Rozier.

Canyon de la Dourbie

39 *Extends from Millau 40 km (25 mi) southeast to Nant.*

The most peaceful of the gorges ending in Millau is the Canyon de la Dourbie. Though it has its share of limestone cliffs and eroded rocks, the gorge's verdant, meadow-covered downstream section is the most interesting. Follow the gorge to the hilltop village of **St-Véran** and the ruined castle once owned by the Marquis de Montcalm, defender of the Battle of Québec. Farther on, where the Trévezel joins the Dourbie, beautiful **Cantobre** clings as if by magic to the cliff. Its tiny houses are prized and even its name says it is extraordinary: *Cantobre,* from *quant obra,* means "what a masterpiece." Past Cantobre is a fertile valley and the pleasant town of **Nant,** which contains a marvelous, arcaded 14th-century covered market and the plain but beautiful church of **St-Pierre,** built in 1135.

Dining and Lodging

$ ✕🏨 **Hôtel des Voyageurs.** A very reasonable 78-franc menu, including, perhaps, a country terrine, confit of duck, fresh mountain trout, and cheese or dessert, is available. The winter dining room is austere; the cool, vaulted summer dining room looks out on a vine-covered terrace. Ask for a room overlooking the lively square and don't expect *House & Garden* decor—many rooms have linoleum floors. ✉ *pl. St-Jacques, 12230 Nant,* ☎ *05–65–62–26–88,* FAX *05–65–62–15–64. 11 rooms, 6 with shower. Restaurant. MC, V. Closed Jan.–Feb.*

La Couvertoirade

⑩ *18 km (11 mi) south of Nant, 25 km (16 mi) west of Le Vigan, 33 km (21 mi) southeast of Millau.*

This perfectly intact medieval village was home to the Knights Templar in the 12th century and later the Knights of St. John, who built the encircling ramparts about 1450. Now classified as one of France's most beautiful villages, it is home to a few craftsmen. Wander through town and look at the pretty stone houses; then visit the fortress, the church, and a small historical museum. ✆ *Fortress, church, and museum 20 frs.* ☉ *Daily 10–noon and 2–4.*

Cirque de Navacelles

⑪ *18 km (5 mi) east of La Couvertoirade, 19 km (12 mi) southwest of Le Vigan, 68 km (42 mi) southeast of Millau. Take D158 south from Alzon (halfway between La Couvertoirade and Le Vigan) to Blandas, then D713.*

The River Vis, cutting its way for aeons between the Causse de Blandas and the Causse du Larzac, produced a small wonder, the Cirque de Navacelles, in an abandoned meander. From a viewpoint along the road you can see where, long ago, the river looped around a little hill and later took a shortcut through the neck of the loop. Within the loop formed by the river is the village of **Navacelles.** Follow the road down through a series of hairpins to the valley floor (a third of the way down there is a place to park and take a 3-km/2-mi hike to the river along a marked, sometimes steep, trail). Or take route D130 up the far side of the canyon to the village of **La Baume-Auriol** for more remarkable views. Route N9 leads back to Millau or south to Montpellier.

THE MASSIF CENTRAL AND AUVERGNE A TO Z

Arriving and Departing

By Car

Take A10 from Paris to Orléans, then A71 into the center of France. From Paris, Bourges is 229 km (137 mi) and Clermont-Ferrand is 378 km (243 mi). Coming from Lyon, it takes less than 90 minutes to drive the 179 km (111 mi) on A72 to Clermont-Ferrand. Entry into Auvergne from the south (☞ Chapter 15) is mostly on small, curving, national roads, though the new A75 will eventually link Montpellier with Clermont-Ferrand through Millau; portions of the autoroute are already completed and open to vehicles.

By Plane

The major airport for the region, at **Clermont-Ferrand** (☎ 04–73–62–71–00), has regularly scheduled flights to Paris (Orly), Bordeaux, Dijon, Lyon, Marseille, Nantes, Nice, and Toulouse on Air France and Air Inter and direct international flights to Geneva, Milan, and London on Air France, British Airways, and Swissair. **TAT** (Transport Aérien Transrégional) flies from Paris's Orly airport to Rodez (☎ 01–42–79–05–05 for reservations in Paris, ☎ 05–65–42–20–30 in Rodez).

By Train

The fastest way from Paris (Gare de Lyon) to Clermont-Ferrand, the capital of Auvergne, is on the high-speed TGV (*Trains à Grande Vitesse*) via Lyon, where you change for the regular train to Clermont-Ferrand (☎ 04–73–92–50–50). Regular SNCF trains also go from Paris to Bourges and Clermont-Ferrand and from Nîmes to Clermont-Ferrand.

Getting Around

By Car

There is really only one way to really explore the region, and that is by car. Although national highways will get you from one place to another fairly expediently, the region's beauty is best discovered on the regional roads that twist through the mountains and along the gorges.

Contacts and Resources

Car Rental

Avis (✉ 57 rue Bonnabaud, Clermont-Ferrand, ☎ 04–73–93–39–90; ✉ Clermont-Ferrand airport, ☎ 04–73–91–18–08). **Europcar** (✉ rue Émile-Loubet, ☎ 04–73–92–70–26; ✉ Clermont-Ferrand airport, ☎ 04–73–92–70–26 at the airport). **Hertz** (✉ 71 av. de l'Union Soviétique, Clermont-Ferrand, ☎ 04–73–92–36–10; ✉ Clermont-Ferrand airport, ☎ 04–73–62–71–93).

Guided Tours

Rafting trips of the Gorges du Tarn can be arranged through the following: **Service Loisirs** (✉ Haute-Loire, ☎ 05–61–09–20–80); **Association Le Merlet** (✉ rte. de Nîmes, St-Jean du Gard, ☎ 04–66–85–18–19). From April to November float through the skies above the volcanoes in a balloon; contact **Objectif** (✉ 43 av. Julien, 63011 Clermont-Ferrand, ☎ 04–73–35–32–01).

Travel Agencies

Centre Auvergne Tourisme (✉ 9 rue Ballainvilliers, 63000 Clermont-Ferrand, ☎ 04–73–90–10–20). **Voyagers Maisonneuve** (✉ 24 rue Georges-Clemenceau, 63000 Clermont-Ferrand, ☎ 04–73–93–16–72).

Visitor Information

Main regional tourist office: **Comité Régional du Tourisme** (✉ 43 av. Julien, 63011 Clermont-Ferrand, ☎ 04–73–93–04–03).

Local tourist offices: **Allier** (✉ 11 rue François-Péron, 03000 Moulins, ☎ 04–70–44–14–14). **Aveyron** (✉ pl. Maréchal-Foch, 12000 Rodez, ☎ 05–65–68–02–27). **Cantal** (✉ 28 av. Gambetta, 15018 Aurillac, ☎ 04–71–09–91–43). **Haute-Loire** (✉ 12 bd. Phillippe-Jourde, 43012 Le Puy-en-Velay, ☎ 04–71–09–66–66). **Lot** (✉ pl. François-Mitterrand, 46000 Cahors, ☎ 05–65–53–20–65). **Lozère** (✉ 14 bd. Henri-Bourrillon, 48000 Mende, ☎ 04–66–48–48–48). **Puy-de-Dôme** (✉ 26 rue St-Esprit, 63000 Clermont-Ferrand, ☎ 04–73–42–21–21).

12 Provence

Nîmes, Arles, Avignon, Marseille, and Aix-en-Provence

Provence means dazzling light and rugged, rocky countryside interspersed with vineyards, fields of lavender, and olive groves. The Romans staked their first claim here and left riches behind; van Gogh and Cézanne taught us to see it through their eyes; then Peter Mayle bought a house and the world was not far behind. From Montpellier to Toulon, from Orange to the sea, this alluring land still seduces.

Updated by
Nigel Fisher
and Nancy
Coons

AS YOU APPROACH PROVENCE, there is a magical moment when the north is finally left behind: Cypresses and red-tile roofs appear; you hear the screech of the cicadas and catch the scent of wild thyme and lavender. Even along the highway, oleanders flower on the central strip against a backdrop of harsh, brightly lit landscapes that inspired the paintings of Paul Cézanne and Vincent van Gogh.

Provence lies in the south of France, bordered by Italy to the east and the blue waters of the Mediterranean. The Romans called it Provincia—the Province—for it was the first part of Gaul they occupied. Roman remains litter the ground in well-preserved profusion. The theater and triumphal arch at Orange, the amphitheater at Nîmes, and the aqueduct at Pont-du-Gard are considered the best of their kind.

Provençal life continues at an old-fashioned pace. Hot afternoons tend to mean siestas, with signs of life discernible only as the shadows under the *platanes* (plane trees) start to lengthen and lethargic locals saunter out to play *boules* (the French version of bocce) and drink long, cooling *pastis,* an anise-based aperitif. The famous mistral—a fierce, cold wind that races through the Rhône Valley—is another feature of Provence. Thankfully, clear blue skies usually follow in its wake.

The Rhône, the great river of southern France, splits in two at Arles, 24 km (15 mi) before reaching the Mediterranean: the Petit Rhône crosses the marshy region known as the Camargue on its way to Stes-Maries-de-la-Mer, while the Grand Rhône heads off to Fos, an industrial port just along the coast from Marseille. North of Marseille lies Aix-en-Provence, whose old-time elegance reflects its former role as regional capital. We've extended Provence's traditional boundaries westward slightly into Languedoc, to include historic Nîmes and the dynamic university town of Montpellier.

Pleasures and Pastimes

Bullfighting

Provence's most popular summer spectator sport is bullfighting, both Spanish-style or the kinder *courses libres,* where the bulls have star billing and are often regarded as local heroes (they always live to fight another day). Spectacles are held in the Roman arenas in Arles and Nîmes and in surrounding villages.

Dining

In the old days, Provençal cooking was based on olive oil, fruit, and vegetables; garlic and wild herbs improved the scant meat dishes. The current gastronomic scene is a far cry from this frugality: Parisian chefs have created internationally renowned restaurants to satisfy demanding palates. Still, there's a lot to be said for simple Provençal food—pastis, that pale yellow, anise-based aperitif; *tapenade,* a delicious paste of olives, capers, and anchovies,; aioli, a garlicky mayonnaise; and grilled lamb and beef with a chilled bottle of rosé. Locals like to end their meal with a round of goat cheese and fruit.

Throughout Provence, specialties include *saucisson d'Arles,* salami; *soupe au pistou,* a traditional summer dish strong on basil; *anchoïade,* anchovies served with vegetables; *soupe de poissons,* a fish soup perfumed with olives, laurel, fennel, and saffron; *daube provençale,* stewed beef cooked in wine with carrots, onions, olives, and aromatic herbs; *aïou,* a mayonnaise with olive oil and garlic served with dried codfish; and *brouffado,* stuffed beef mixed with garlic and onions and served with capers and anchovies.

In Marseille, bouillabaisse is a specialty. But beware: The high-priced versions use fresh fish and can be delicious, but cheaper ones are often of dubious origins. Steer clear of the cheap fish restaurants, many with brisk ladies out front who deliver throaty sales pitches.

CATEGORY	COST*
$$$$	over 400 frs
$$$	250 frs–400 frs
$$	125 frs–250 frs
$	under 125 frs

per person for a three-course meal, including tax (20.6%) and tip but not wine

Lodging

Accommodations in this oft-visited part of France range from luxurious villas to elegantly converted *mas* (farmhouses) to modest city-center hotels. Service is often less than prompt, a casualty of the sweltering summer heat. Reservations are essential for much of the year and many hotels are closed in winter.

CATEGORY	COST*
$$$$	over 800 frs
$$$	550 frs–800 frs
$$	300 frs–550 frs
$	under 300 frs

All prices are for a standard double room for two, including tax (20.6%) and service charge.

Outdoor Activities and Sports

Provence provides a plethora of outdoor activities. You can sail and windsurf at La Grande Motte, Stes-Maries-de-la-Mer, Martigues (near Marseille), Cassis, Hyères-Plage, and the Iles de Porquerolles, in the south; ride through the Camargue on a horse rented from a local stable; tool around the Bouches-du-Rhône on a bike rented from the train station; or hike along blazed trails in the Luberon Mountains or Les Calanques.

Exploring Provence

Provence falls easily into three areas. The Camargue is at the heart of the first, though you might venture briefly into Languedoc to see the fine old towns of Nîmes, famed for its Roman arena, and Montpellier, known for its university, before wheeling back to visit the Roman remains at Arles and St-Rémy. In the second area, which falls within the boundaries of the Vaucluse, begin at Avignon and head north to Orange and Vaison-la-Romaine; the main natural feature here is Mont Ventoux, towering above the surrounding plains. The third area encompasses Aix-en-Provence, then stretches south to Marseille and east along the coast to Toulon.

Great Itineraries

The popular book entitled *A Year in Provence* dictates just that, but even a year might not be long enough to soak up all the charm of this captivating region. In 3 days you can see most of the major Roman towns: Nîmes, Arles, and Avignon; with 7 days you can easily add Montpellier, Orange, and Aix-en-Provence; with 10 days you can cover all the important towns, add Marseille and the hill towns in the Luberon mountains, and relax on a Mediterranean *plage* (beach). The following are suggested itineraries for seeing the area; another option is to base yourself in one place and take day trips from there.

Numbers in the text correspond to numbers in the margin and on the Provence, Nîmes, Avignon, and Marseille maps.

IF YOU HAVE 3 DAYS

Begin your trip at the **Pont du Gard** ①, the 2,000-year-old Roman aqueduct; then head for **Nîmes** ②–⑪ to see the Arènes and the Maison Carrée. Try to make the 30-minute drive to the former Roman city of ☒ **Arles** ⑰ before the 5 PM rush hour. Hopefully, you'll have an hour or two to explore the city. Spend the next morning in Arles; then drive, after lunch, through the countryside, stopping in medieval **Les Baux-de-Provence** ⑲ and the castle in **Tarascon** ㉑; stay overnight in ☒ **St-Rémy-de-Provence** ⑳. On your last day go to the walled city of **Avignon** ㉓–㉚ to see the famous Palais des Papes.

IF YOU HAVE 7 DAYS

Visit **Orange** ㉜ on your first day before stopping to see the **Pont du Gard** ①. Spend the night and the next morning in ☒ **Nîmes** ②–⑪. In the afternoon, drive to the fortified town of **Aigues-Mortes** ⑮ and make a slight detour through the Camargue to ☒ **Arles** ⑰. The next morning, explore Arles's Roman remains. Try to get to **Les Baux-de-Provence** ⑲ by lunchtime, and then continue to ☒ **St-Rémy-de-Provence** ⑳ to explore Roman ruins and see where van Gogh painted. On day four, wend your way via **Tarascon** ㉑ to ☒ **Avignon** ㉓–㉚. The following day, head through **L'Isle-sur-la-Sorgue** ㊳ and **Gordes** ㊵, in the Luberon Mountains, on your way south to ☒ **Aix-en-Provence** ㊸–㊿; spend two nights and a day there visiting the marvelous 18th-century mansions and museums.

IF YOU HAVE 10 DAYS

Stay in ☒ **Avignon** ㉓–㉚ your first two nights, making trips to **Orange** ㉜, **Vaison-la-Romaine** ㉝, and **Mont Ventoux** ㉟. On your third day stop at the **Pont du Gard** ① on your way to ☒ **Nîmes** ②–⑪ for the afternoon and night. The fourth day head to the university town of **Montpellier** ⑫, then east past the resort town of **La Grande Motte** ⑭ to medieval **Aigues-Mortes** ⑮. Plan on several hours to explore the Camargue and visit the fortresslike church at **Stes-Maries-de-la-Mer** ⑯. By nightfall, be in the Roman city of ☒ **Arles** ⑰. Spend the morning of day five sightseeing in Arles; then make the short drive to ☒ **St-Rémy-de-Provence** ⑳ for the night by way of **Les Baux-de-Provence** ⑲ and **Tarascon** ㉑. On the sixth day, head to the Luberon Mountains; visit **L'Isle-sur-la-Sorgue** ㊳ and stay overnight in ☒ **Gordes** ㊵ or ☒ **Venasque** ㊲. Make ☒ **Aix-en-Provence** ㊸–㊿ your destination on days seven and eight. Aim for ☒ **Marseille** ㊿–㊸ on your 9th and 10th days—despite its raunchy reputation, it has a classical vitality all its own.

When to Tour Provence

Spring and fall are the best months to experience the dazzling light, rugged rocky countryside, fields of lavender, and fruitful vineyards of Provence. In summer, it gets very hot and very crowded on the beaches. Still, if you are interested in seeing the bullfights, this is the time to come. Winter has some nice days, but it often rains, and the razor-sharp mistral cuts to the bone.

NÎMES AND THE CAMARGUE

Though Roman remains are found throughout Provence, their presence is strongest where the rivers meander their way to the sea on the region's western flank: the beautiful aqueduct at Pont du Gard, the are-

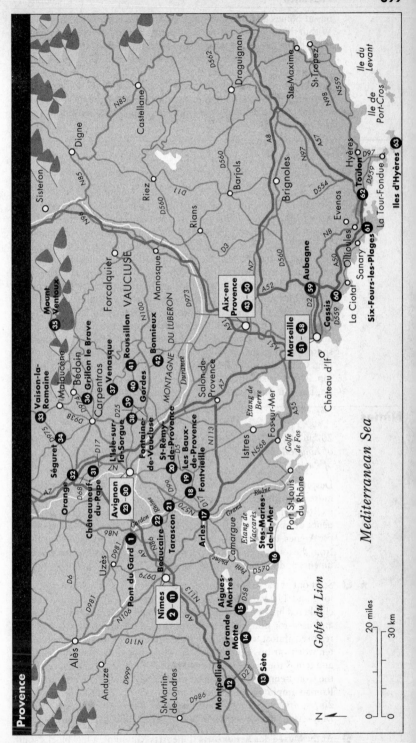

Mediterranean Sea

Golfe du Lion

Ile du Levant

Ile de Port-Cros

Iles d'Hyères 63

N

0   20 miles
0   30 km

nas at Nîmes and Arles, and the excavations at St-Rémy de Provence. Within this area are strange landscapes: the arid outcrops around Les Baux-de-Provence and the marshy wilderness of the Camargue. Formed by the sprawling Rhône delta and extending over 800 square km (300 square mi), the Camargue is an area of endless horizons, vast pools, low flat plains, innumerable species of migrating birds, and sturdy, free-roaming gray horses. The entire terrain is flat and not many feet above sea level, so occasionally the river bursts its banks and floods the entire region.

Pont du Gard

★ ❶ *22 km (13 mi) southwest of Avignon, 37 km (23 mi) southwest of Orange, 48 km (30 mi) north of Arles.*

No other sight in Provence can rival the Pont du Gard, this huge, three-tier aqueduct midway between Avignon and Nîmes (off the N86 highway) that symbolically links the 20th century to the area's Roman past. Erected 2,000 years ago as part of a 48-km (30-mi) canal supplying water to Roman Nîmes, the Pont du Gard is astonishingly well preserved. Its setting, spanning a rocky gorge 150 ft above the River Gardon, is nothing less than spectacular. There is no entry fee, though it costs 22 francs to park on the Rive Gauche (north side), which is less commercial and a shorter walk to the aqueduct, and 18 francs to park on the Rive Droite (south side), which has the most tour buses and is a longer walk to the aqueduct and the tourist office. Early morning spares you the crowds and lets you appreciate the magical natural setting. Gauge the full majesty of the Pont du Gard by walking along the top. The tourist office does lead guided tours, often at 10 AM and 1 PM, but you should check for the most current schedule.

Nîmes

20 km (13 mi) southwest of the Pont du Gard, 43 km (26 mi) south of Avignon, 121 km (74 mi) west of Marseille, 711 km (427 mi) south of Paris.

Despite its relatively charmless urban ambiance, Nimes surpasses its more atmospheric neighbors with superbly preserved treasures from its Roman past. Nemausus, as Nîmes was then known, grew to prominence during the reign of Caesar Augustus (27 BC–AD 14) and still has the Arènes, temple, and watchtower. A 60-franc "passport," available from the tourist office, admits you to all the town's museums and monuments and is valid for three days.

★ ❷ Start out at the **Arènes** (Roman Arena), which is more than 140 yards long and 110 yards wide, with a seating capacity of 21,000. After a checkered history—it was transformed into a fortress by the Visigoths and used for housing in medieval times—the amphitheater has been restored almost to its original look. An inflatable roof covers it in winter, when various exhibits and shows occupy the space, and bullfights and tennis tournaments are held here in summer. A smaller version of the Colosseum in Rome, this is considered the world's best-preserved Roman amphitheater. ⊠ *bd. Victor-Hugo,* ☎ *04–66–67–29–11.* 🖾 *26 frs; joint ticket to Arènes and Tour Magne (☞ below) 32 frs.* ☉ May–Mar., daily 9–noon and 2–6; Apr., guided visits only.

❸ At the **Musée des Beaux-Arts** (Fine Arts Museum), a few blocks south of the Arènes, you can admire a vast Roman mosaic; the marriage ceremony depicted provides intriguing insights into the Roman aristocratic lifestyle. Old master paintings (by Nicolas Poussin, Pieter Brueghel, Peter

Paul Rubens) and sculpture (by Auguste Rodin) form the mainstay of the collection. ⊠ *rue de la Cité-Foulc,* ☎ *04–66–67–38–21.* 🖅 *26 frs.* 🕑 *Tues.–Sat. 11–6.*

❹ The **Musée Archéologique et d'Histoire Naturelle** (Museum of Archaeology and Natural History), a few blocks northeast of the Arènes, is rich in local archaeological finds, mainly statues, busts, friezes, tools, glass, coins, and pottery. ⊠ *bd. de l'Amiral-Courbet,* ☎ *04–66–67–25–57.* 🖅 *26 frs.* 🕑 *Tues.–Sun. 11–6.*

❺ Destroyed and rebuilt in several stages, with particular damage by Protestants who slaughtered eight priests from the neighboring *eveché* (bishop's house), the **Cathédrale Notre-Dame et St-Castor** still shows traces of its Romanesque origins in the classically symmetrical facade and a miraculously preserved frieze, with lively Biblical portraiture reminiscent in style of the Bayeux Tapestry. Inside, look for the 4th-century sarcophagus (third chapel on the right) and a magnificent 17th-century chapel (in the apse), recently restored. ⊠ *pl. aux Herbes.*

❻ The **Musée du Vieux Nîmes** (Museum of Old Nîmes), opposite the cathedral in the 17th-century Bishop's Palace, has embroidered garments in exotic and vibrant displays. Nîmes used to be a cloth-manufacturing center and lent its name to what has become one of the world's most popular fabrics—denim (*de Nîmes*—from Nîmes). ⊠ *pl. aux Herbes,* ☎ *04–66–36–00–64.* 🖅 *26 frs.* 🕑 *Tues.–Sun. 11–6.*

★ ❼ Despite its name, which means "square house," the **Maison Carrée** is an oblong Roman temple that sits lonely and forlorn in the middle of a busy downtown square; the building now holds exhibitions. The exquisite carvings along the cornice and on the Corinthian capitals rank as some of the finest in Roman architecture. Thomas Jefferson admired the Maison Carrée's chaste lines of columns so much that he had them copied for the Virginia state capitol in Richmond. ⊠ *bd. Victor-Hugo*, ☎ *04–66–67–29–11*. ⊠ *Free*. ☉ *May–Oct., daily 9–7; Nov.–Apr., daily 9–6.*

❽ The glass-fronted **Musée d'Art Contemporain** (Contemporary Art Museum), often called the Carrée d'Art (it's directly opposite the Maison Carrée), showcases international painting and sculpture from 1960 onward. ⊠ *pl. de la Maison Carrée*, ☎ *04–66–76–35–35*. ⊠ *26 frs.* ☉ *Tues.–Sun. 11–6.*

❾ The **Jardin de la Fontaine** (Fountain Garden), an elaborate, formal garden, was landscaped on the site of the Roman baths in the 18th century, when the Source de Nemausus, a once-sacred spring, was channeled into pools and a canal.

❿ Just northwest of the Jardin de la Fontaine is the shattered Roman ruin known as the **Temple de Diane** (Diana's Temple), which dates from the 2nd century BC. The temple's function is unknown, though it is thought to be part of a larger Roman complex that is still unexcavated. In the Middle Ages, Benedictine nuns occupied the building before it was converted into a church. Destruction came in the Wars of Religion.

⓫ At the far end of the Jardin de la Fontaine is the **Tour Magne** (Magne Tower)—a stumpy pre-Roman tower that was probably used as a lookout post. Despite having lost 30 ft during the course of time, it still provides fine views of Nîmes for anyone energetic enough to climb the 140 steps up. ⊠ *quai de la Fontaine*, ☎ *04–66–67–29–11*. ⊠ *Tour Magne 12 frs, joint ticket with Arènes (☞ above) 32 frs.* ☉ *May–Oct., daily 9–7; Nov.–Apr., daily 9–12:30 and 1:30–6.*

Dining and Lodging

$$–$$$ ✕ **L'Enclos de la Fontaine.** Nîmes's most fashionable restaurant is in the Impérator hotel (☞ *below*), with warm-weather dining in an idyllic garden court. Chef Jean-Michel Nigon provides such inventive dishes as iced, dill-perfumed langoustine soup. ⊠ *15 rue Gaston-Boissier*, ☎ *04–66–21–90–30*. *AE, DC, MC, V.*

$ ✕ **Michel's Wine Bar.** Owned by a former sommelier, this restaurant offers good food and wine at very reasonable prices. You may opt to dine on the sidewalk terrace, adjacent to the square, or inside. Menus run 98 francs and up, or you can choose just one or two dishes from the à la carte menu, such as a marvelous salad with foie gras followed by fried calamari or an entrecôte. ⊠ *11 square de la Couronne*, ☎ *04–66–76–19–59*. *MC, V. Closed Mon.*

$ ✕ **Chez Jacotte.** Candlelight on rich tones of oxblood, cobalt, and ochre
★ enhance the warm bohemian welcome of red-haired Jacotte, who coddles her guests and artist friends with blackboard specials. Watch for scrambled eggs with truffles and asparagus, rich ravioli with basil, bulgar wheat with chicken fricassee—updated with a Far-East tang of coriander or red peppercorn. ⊠ *15 rue Fresque (Impasse)*, ☎ *04–66–21–64–59*. *MC, V . Closed Sun, Mon. No lunch Sat.*

$ ✕ **Nicolas.** You'll hear the noise of this homey place before you open the door. A friendly, frazzled staff serves up delicious *bourride* (fish soup) and other local specialties. ⊠ *1 rue Poise*, ☎ *04–66–67–50–47*. *AE, MC, V. Closed Mon., 1st 2 wks in July, and mid-Dec.–1st wk in Jan. No lunch Sat.*

$$–$$$ ▥ **Impérator.** This little palace-hotel, part of the Concorde hotel group,
★ is Nîmes's best. It has been tastefully modernized with sensibly arranged furnishings. Ask for a room overlooking the attractive garden and if you are lucky, you may get No. 104, which is a good size and has a whirlpool bath. ⊠ *15 rue Gaston-Boissier, 30900*, ☎ *04–66–21–90–30*, ℻ *04–66–67–70–25. 62 rooms. Restaurant. AE, DC, MC, V.*

$–$$ ⊡ **Royal Hôtel.** Jazz, Art Deco ironwork, and caged birds set the Latin tone at this bohemian, shabby-chic urban hotel, where whitewash and scrubbed concrete set off 1930s details and trendy flea-market finds. Bathrooms are newly tiled, and creature comforts up to date. Its Spanish restaurant serves tapas on pedestrain place d'Assas, but the lobby bar is where you'd expect to run across Picasso or Hemingway, slumming over absinthe. ⊠ *3 bd. Alphonse Daudet, 30000,* ☎ *04–66–67–28–36,* FAX *04–66–21–68–97. 27 rooms. Restaurant. AE, DC, MC, V.*

$ ✕ **Amphithéâtre.** Just behind the arena, this big, solid old private home has fallen into the hands of a loving landlord, who has stripped 18th-century double doors and fitted rooms with restored-wood details and antiques. A generous breakfast buffet is served in the dining room. ⊠ *4 rue des Arènes, 30420 ,* ☎ *04–66–67–28–51,* FAX *04–66–67–07–79. 17 rooms. Breakfast room . AE, MC, V.*

Outdoor Activities and Sports

Aquatropic (⊠ 39 rue de la Hostellerie, ☎ 04–66–38–31–00) is an indoor swimming pool with a difference: Wave machines, slides, water cannons, and bubble baths add to the fun for kids and adults alike. It's open weekdays 10–8 and weekends 10–7, for a cost of 35 francs.

Shopping

The **flower market** (⊠ bd. Jean-Jaurès) takes place Monday mornings, and also features food, clothing, linens, and pottery.

Montpellier

⑫ *50 km (30 mi) southwest of Nîmes, 94 km (58 mi) southwest of Avignon, 152 km (91 mi) north of Perpignan.*

Montpellier is a comparatively young town, a mere 1,000 years old; no Romans settled here. Ever since medieval times, its reputation has been linked to its university, which was founded in the 14th century. Its medical school in particular was so highly esteemed in the 16th century that the great writer François Rabelais left his native Loire Valley to take his doctorate here. Nowadays, the student population of 20,000 helps keep Montpellier young.

The 17th-century town center has been improved by an imaginative urban planning program, and several streets and squares are banned to cars. The heart of Montpellier is **place de la Comédie,** a wide square with cafés and terraces laid out before the handsome 19th-century facade of the civic theater.

Boulevard Sarrail leads north from place de la Comédie, past the leafy esplanade with its rows of plane trees, to the **Musée Fabre.** The museum's collection of art highlights important works by Gustave Courbet (notably *Bonjour Monsieur Courbet*) and Eugène Delacroix (*Femmes d'Alger*), as well as paintings by Frédéric Bazille—whose death during the Franco-Prussian War deprived Impressionism of one of its earliest exponents. ⊠ 37 bd. Sarrail, ☎ 04–67–14–83–00. ⊡ 20 frs. ☉ Tues.–Fri. 9–5:30, weekends 9:30–5.

In the heart of old Montpellier—a maze of crooked, bustling streets ideal for shopping and strolling—rue Foch strikes a more disciplined note, slicing straight east to west, to the pride of Montpellier, the **promenade du Peyrou.** An equestrian statue of Louis XIV rides triumphant, and carved friezes and columns mask a water tower at the far end of this long, broad, tree-shaded terrace with majestic steps. Water used to arrive along the St-Clément aqueduct, an imposing two-tier structure; locals still cluster beneath its arches to play boules.

Boulevard Henri IV runs north from the promenade du Peyrou to France's oldest botanical garden, the **Jardin des Plantes,** planted by order of Henri IV in 1593. An exceptional range of plants, flowers, and trees grows here. ⌨ *Free.* ☺ *Gardens Mon.–Sat. 9–noon and 2–5. Greenhouses weekdays 9–noon and 2–5, Sat. 9–noon.*

Within walking distance of Old Montpellier is the **Antigone** district, a fine example of innovative urban planning. Not so long ago Montpellier was in the doldrums, but with the effort of city planners and local industries, the city transformed itself into a hub of economic activity. This ideal neighborhood, designed by the Catalan architect Ricard Borfill, covers 100-plus acres with plazas, esplanades, shops, restaurants, and low-income housing, all constructed out of stone-color, pre-stressed concrete. Be sure to visit **place du Nombre d'Or**—symmetrically composed of curves—and the 1-km-long (½-mi-long) vista that stretches down a mall of cypress trees to the glass-fronted **Hotel du District.**

Dining and Lodging

$$–$$$ ✕ **Le Chandelier.** On the sixth floor of a building in the Antigone dis-
★   trict, this restaurant has dramatic views, impeccable service, and more than acceptable trendy pink decor. And Gilbert Furlan's inventive cuisine is delicious: Sample his chilled artichoke and rabbit soup or sea bass with crushed olives. Cinnamon-honey ice cream makes a fine dessert. The only complaint is the high-priced à la carte menu; you're better off opting for the prix-fixe ones. ⌂ *267 av. Léon Blum,* ☎ *04–67–15–34–38. Reservations essential. AE, DC, MC, V. Closed part of Feb., 1st 2 wks in Aug., and Sun. No lunch Mon.*

$$ ✕ **L'Olivier.** Though locals praise this small, 10-table restaurant, Chef Breton doesn't quite deserve it. Nonetheless, this place is recommendable because prices are within reason (160 and 190 francs for the two four-course menus; more for à la carte) and dishes are good if not perfect. His fish dishes, for instance, are light and perfectly cooked, though lacking in just the right sauce to fully bring out the fish's flavor. In winter, the scallops with cèpes are worth trying, as is the *poulet de Bresse* (Bresse chicken). ⌂ *12 rue Aristide Olivier,* ☎ *04–67–92–86–28. Reservations essential. AE, DC, MC, V. Closed Aug. and Mon. No dinner Sun.*

$$ ✕ **Petit Jardin.** As the name implies, there is a leafy garden, as well as a flower-bedecked dining room. Owner Roland Heilmann has made a rapid name for himself with such regional dishes as bourride and the *piperade* omelet with king-size prawns. ⌂ *20 rue Jean-Jacques-Rousseau,* ☎ *04–67–60–78–78. Reservations essential. AE, DC, MC, V. Closed Mon. and Jan.–Mar. No dinner Sun.*

$–$$ ✕ **Le César.** In the heart of the Antigone district, this lunch spot is ideal on a sunny day when you can sit outside, though the brasserie-style ambience is also pleasant. Choose from typical regional cuisine— *bouillinade* (a local version of bouillabaisse) or tuna with red wine and shallot-based sauce—on the à la carte menu. Or order the 70-franc *menu rapide* (two-course menu) or the 100-franc, four-course meal. ⌂ *pl. du Nombre d'Or,* ☎ *04–67–64–87–87. MC, V.*

$–$$ ✕ **Le Restaurant de Terroir.** This restaurant is in the headquarters of the Syndicat des Vignerons Côteaux du Languedoc—the folks who ensure that the region's wines are up to standard—so you can bet that wine is an important part of the menu. The lunch menu du jour—not the best in the area, but certainly good—may comprise mussels in butter sauce, grilled *dorade* (sea bream), and pasta simmered in octopus ink. Meals are served in the pleasant, stone-vaulted cellar or on the terrace. After, visit the Maison du Vin, where the syndicat's best wines are sold at good prices. ⌂ *Mas de Saporta, Lattes (from downtown Montpellier follow signs to des Prés D'Arènes; the restaurant is near*

the Montpellier Sud interchange of autoroute A9), ☎ 04–67–06–04–
40. *MC, V. Closed Sun. No dinner Sat.*

$$$ 🏨 **Sofitel Antigone.** At the edge of the Antigone district and within walking distance of old Montpellier is this modern hotel. Up-to-date conveniences and a professional staff make up for any lack of warmth. Rooms are reasonably large by French standards and have king-size beds. (Note that the difference between "standard" and "privilege" rooms is 100 francs, a larger television, and a trouser press.) On the top (eighth) floor is a breakfast room and cocktail bar overlooking the outdoor pool. Ask about special packages, including golfing. ⊠ *1 rue des Pertuisanes, 34000,* ☎ *04–67–99–72–72,* 𝖥𝖠𝖷 *04–67–65–17–50. 90 rooms. Bar, breakfast room, pool. AE, DC, MC, V.*

$$ 🏨 **Le Guilhem.** In the heart of the historic district, this 16th-century
★ *maison-particulier*-turned-hotel has charmingly furnished little rooms in shades of yellow and powder blue; many look onto the garden. All is quiet, except for the ringing bell at the nearby cathedral. Owners M. and Mme. Charpentier are superb hosts. ⊠ *18 rue Jean-Jacques Rousseau, 34000,* ☎ *04–67–52–90–90,* 𝖥𝖠𝖷 *04–67–60–67–67. 33 rooms. Parking (fee). MC, V.*

Nightlife and the Arts
La Croisière (⊠ Espace Latipolia, rte. de Palavas, ☎ 04–67–64–19–52), a lively disco, is in Lattes, on the south side of Montpellier. **Gyssertin** (⊠ rte. de Palavas, ☎ 04–67–22–45–82), also a dance club, is in Lattes. In the center of town, **Le Petit Negresco** (⊠ 6 pl. Jean Jaurès, ☎ 04–67–66–02–10) has tapas and live music. Concerts are performed at the 19th-century **Théâtre des Treize Vents** (⊠ allée Jules-Milhau, ☎ 04–67–58–08–13).

Sète

⑬ *29 km (18 mi) south of Montpellier.*

In Sète you can get a breath of salt air, have a delightful seafood lunch, and swim in the Mediterranean along the 15 km (9 mi) of sandy beaches that stretch to the Cap d'Agde. The old town is built on a limestone outcrop, Mont St-Clair, which was once an island but is now linked to the mainland by two narrow sand spits. Head first for the town center and the **Vieux Port** (Old Port) where colorful fishing boats auction off their catches. Running north from the harbor is the **Canal de Sète,** full of moored fishing and tourist boats ready to take you on a tour of the harbor or even on a day trip to Aigues-Mortes. **La Marine,** the quayside street, is lined with seafood restaurants. And be sure to take a trip up **Mont St-Clair** (574 ft) for panoramic views of Sète, the lagoons, and, on a clear day, the distant Pyrénées to the southwest and the Alps to the east.

OFF THE
BEATEN PATH
ABBAYE DE VALMAGNE – Just outside the village of Villeveyrac, 20 km (12 mi) from Sète, is the Valmagne Abbey. Not many individuals own an abbey, but the Baron de Gaudert d'Allaines does—as well as its vineyard. The abbey was established in 1138 under the Benedictine Order but transferred its allegiance to the Cistercians two decades later. It prospered until the Wars of Religion when one of the abbots joined the Protestant camp and came back in the dead of night to hack to death all the other brothers. After the Revolution, the abbey was sold off and became the property of the Gaudert d'Allaines's family. Eight generations later, they decided to restore the abbey, whose church, some 274 ft in length and 76 ft in height, had been used to store mammoth wine casks (one holds about 10,400 gallons). The wine is now stored in a nearby building, but the casks remain. The most delightful part of the

abbey is its cloisters, with its golden stonework, Tuscany Gardens, and beautiful fountain enclosed by filigreed stone (this abbey is one of the few to have an intact fountain). The guided tour of the abbey ends in the wine-tasting room and wine shop, where the purchase of a bottle or two could benefit your next picnic. ⊠ *rte. D5.* ☜ *25 frs.* ☉ *Apr.–Nov., Mon.–Sat. 10–noon and 2–4.*

Dining

$$ ✕ **La Palangrotte.** Don't miss out on Alain Gémignani's subtly prepared seafood creations. His specialty, the *rémoulade* (a mixture with spicy sauce) of marinated fresh salmon with shrimp, fillet of grouper, and a confit of vegetables, is particularly good. Lunch menus begin at 110 francs, but the 150-franc menu has the best choices. Decor is contemporary. ⊠ *39 quai de la Marine,* ☎ *04–67–74–80–25. AE, DC, MC, V. Closed Mon. No dinner Sun.*

$ ✕ **La Rascasse.** This place has one of the best-value prix-fixe menus along this restaurant-filled street. Sea scallops, oysters, and turbot in white wine sauce are some of the local favorites. ⊠ *27 quai de la Marine,* ☎ *04–67–74–38–46. MC, V.*

La Grande Motte

⓮ *20 km (12 mi) south of Montpellier, 87 km (54 mi) east of Béziers, 45 km (28 mi) west of Nîmes.*

The arid, rocky landscape of the Midi region of Languedoc begins to change as you head southeast from Montpellier along the coast on D21, en route to the Camargue, past pools and lagoons, to La Grande Motte. The town is the most lavish—and, some would say, ugliest— of a string of modern resort towns built along the coast. The mosquitoes that once infested this watery area have finally been vanquished, and tourists have taken their place. La Grande Motte was only a glint in an architect's eye back in the late 1960s; since then, its arresting pyramidal apartment blocks have influenced several French resorts.

Dining

$$ ✕ **Alexandre-Amirauté.** Tons of oysters are cultivated in the nearby *étangs* (lagoons); you can sample them in the elegant surrounds of Louis XV furnishings while gazing out over the Mediterranean. Other choices include a splendid array of seafood dishes. ⊠ *345 esplanade Maurice-Justin,* ☎ *04–67–56–63–63. AE, MC, V. Closed Mon. No dinner Sun.*

Aigues-Mortes

⓯ *13 km (8 mi) east of La Grande Motte, 41 km (25 mi) south of Nîmes, 48 km (30 mi) southwest of Arles.*

Created at the behest of Louis IX (St. Louis) in the 13th century, Aigues-Mortes is an astonishing relic of early town planning. Medieval streets are usually crooked; at Aigues-Mortes, however, a grid plan was adopted, hemmed in by sturdy walls sprouting towers at regular intervals. The town was originally a port, and Louis used it as a base for his Crusades to the Holy Land. The sea has long since receded, though, and Aigues-Mortes's size and importance have gone away with it. In the center of the old city is the elegant place St-Louis, with restaurants galore. Here, it seems, every tourist gathers around midday to plunk down at a sidewalk table and relish the atmosphere during the mandatory two-hour lunch break.

Unlike most of the medieval buildings, the **remparts** (fortifications) remain intact. Walk along the top of the city ramparts and admire some remarkable views across the town and salt marshes. You can also explore the powerful **Tour de Constance** (Constance Tower), originally designed as a fortress-keep and used in the 18th century as a prison for Protestants who refused to convert to official state Catholicism. One such unfortunate, Marie Durand, languished here for 38 years. Abraham Mazel was luckier. He spent 10 months chiseling a hole in the wall, while his companions sang psalms to distract the jailers. The ruse worked: Mazel and 16 others escaped. ☎ 04–66–53–61–55. ☑ 32 frs. ☉ Tower and ramparts Apr.–Oct., daily 9–7; Nov.–Mar., 9:30–noon and 2–5:30.

Lodging

$$$ ⊞ **Les Templiers.** In a 17th-century residence within the ramparts is this delightful hotel. Bare walls and terra-cotta tiled floors set the stage. Furnishings are classically simple and include many antiques. The owners know they have taste and charge accordingly—560 francs for a double bed in a small room with a view of the garden, 760 francs for a king-size bed and a view. On the ground floor are two, small cozy sitting areas; breakfast, weather permitting, is served in the small courtyard. ⊠ 23 rue de la République, 30220, ☎ 04–66–53–66–56, ℻ 04–66–53–69–61. 10 rooms. Free parking. MC, V. Closed Nov.–Mar.

$$ ⊞ **St-Louis.** Within the rampart walls, close to the Tour de Constance and just off lively place St-Louis, is this homey little hotel. Its medieval construction of cool stone is overlaid by Provençal charm and comfort. Rooms, which are pleasantly decorated if not stylish, look out on the garden below the ramparts or on to the sunny street. In winter, dinner is served in the beamed restaurant, and, in summer, in the shady garden. ⊠ 10 rue Amiral Courbet, 30220, ☎ 04–66–53–72–68, ℻ 04–66–53–75–92. 22 rooms. Restaurant, parking. AE, DC, MC, V.

Stes-Maries-de-la-Mer

⓰ 32 km (20 mi) southeast of Aigues-Mortes, 129 km (80 mi) west of Marseille, 39 km (24 mi) south of Arles.

Stes-Maries-de-la-Mer is a commercialized resort town, frequented mainly by British tourists in search of the Camargue's principal sandy beach, 4 km (2½ mi) of dunes and flat sand. Even if you just have a day, the beach makes a great picnic spot. Park in the lots on the east side of town or along the road to the west.

The town's tiny, dark fortress-church, the **Église de Stes-Maries,** houses caskets containing relics of the "Holy Maries" after whom the town is named. Legend has it that Mary Jacobi (the sister of the Virgin), Mary Magdalene, Mary Salome (mother of the apostles James and John), and their black servant Sarah were washed up here around AD 40 after being abandoned at sea. Their adopted town rapidly became a site of pilgrimage, the most important site for Gypsies. Sarah was adopted as their patron saint, and to this day, Gypsies from all over the world make pilgrimages to Stes-Maries in late May and late October, while guitar-strumming pseudo-gypsies serenade tourists throughout the summer.

To the north of Stes-Maries-de-la-Mer, in the center of the Camargue, is the 30-acre **Parc Ornithologique** (Ornithologic Park), independent of the vast Réserve Nationale, in the marshlands west of the reserve's Étang de Vaccarès. It is a private protected environment for vegetation and wildlife: Birds from northern Europe and Siberia spend the winter here, while flamingos flock here in summer. ☎ 04–90–97–82–62. ☑ 33 frs. ☉ Mar.–Oct., daily 8–dusk; Nov.–Feb., daily 10–dusk.

Arles

⑰ *38 km (24 mi) north of Stes-Maries-de-la-Mer, 92 km (57 mi) northwest of Marseille, 36 km (22 mi) south of Avignon, 31 km (19 mi) east
of Nîmes.*

The first inhabitants of Arles were probably the Greeks, who arrived
from Marseille in the 6th century BC. The Romans, however, left a
stronger mark, constructing the theater and amphitheater that remain
the biggest tourist attractions. Arles used to be a thriving port before
the Mediterranean receded over what is now the Camargue. It was also
the site of the southernmost bridge over the Rhône and became a commercial crossroads; merchants from as far afield as Arabia, Assyria,
and Africa would linger here to do business on their way from Rome
to Spain or northern Europe.

The Dutch painter Vincent van Gogh produced much of his best
work—and chopped off his ear—in Arles during a frenzied 15-month
spell (1888–89) just before his suicide at 37. Unfortunately, the houses
he lived in are no longer standing—they were destroyed during World
War II—but part of one of his most famous subjects remains: the **Pont
de Trinquetaille,** across the Rhône. Van Gogh's rendering of the bridge,
painted in 1888, was auctioned a century later for $20 million. Local
art museums can't compete with that type of bidding—which is one
reason none of van Gogh's works are displayed there. Another is that
Arles failed to appreciate him; he was jeered at and eventually packed
off to the nearest lunatic asylum in St-Rémy (☞ *below*). The city has
since softened, and now you'll find signs with reproductions of famous
van Gogh paintings at the spots where he set up his easel; the tourist
office has produced a free booklet mapping 10 places where he painted.

Before van Gogh was embraced by Arles, the city chose to name the
local museum, the **Musée Réattu,** after Jacques Réattu, a local painter
of dazzling mediocrity. His works fill three rooms, van Gogh's none.
But there are modern drawings and paintings by Pablo Picasso, Fernand Léger, and Maurice de Vlaminck, as well as a notable photography section. ✉ *rue du Grand-Prieuré,* ☎ *04–90–49–37–58.* 🎫 *15
frs; joint ticket to all monuments and museums in Arles 55 frs.* ⊙ *June–
Sept., daily 9:30–7; Nov.–Mar., daily 10–12:30 and 2–5; Apr.–May
and Oct., daily 9:30–12:30 and 2–6.*

★ Reminders of Roman society are found at the ruins of the **Palais Constantin,** on the site of the **Thermes de la Trouille** (Trouille Baths),
Provence's largest Roman baths. ✉ *rue Dominique-Maisto.* 🎫 *12 frs;
joint ticket to all Arles museums and monuments 55 frs.* ⊙ *June–Sept.,
daily 9:30–7; Nov.–Mar., daily 10–12:30 and 2–5; Apr.–May and Oct.,
daily 9:30–12:30 and 2–6.*

The most notable Roman sight is the 26,000-capacity **Arènes** (Arena),
built in the 1st century AD for circuses and gladiator combats. The arena
is 150 yards long and as wide as a football field, with each of its two
stories composed of 60 arches; the original top tier has long since crum-
bled, and the three square towers were added in the Middle Ages. Climb
to the upper story for some satisfying views. Despite its age, the amphitheater still sees a lot of action, mainly Sunday afternoon bullfights. ✉ *Rond-Point des Arènes,* ☎ *04–90–96–03–70.* 🎫 *15 frs;
joint ticket to all Arles museums and monuments 55 frs.* ⊙ *June–Sept.,
daily 8:30–7; Nov.–Mar., daily 9–noon and 2–4:30; Apr.–May and
Oct., daily 9–12:30 and 2–6:30.*

★ The bits of marble column scattered around the grassy enclosure of
the diminished remains of the **Théâtre Antique** (Roman Theater), just

100 yards from the Arènes, hint poignantly at the theater's onetime grandeur. The capacity may have shrunk from 7,000 to a few hundred, but the orchestra pit and a few tiers of seats are still used for the city's Music and Drama Festival each July. ⊠ *rue du Cloître,* ☎ *04–90–96–93–30 for ticket information.* 🏛 *15 frs; joint ticket to all Arles museums and monuments 55 frs.* ۩ *June–Sept., daily 8:30–7; Nov.–Mar., daily 9–noon and 2–4:30; Apr.–May and Oct., daily 9–12:30 and 2–6:30.*

The church of **St-Trophime,** on place de la République in the center of Arles, dates mainly from the 11th and 12th centuries; subsequent additions have not spoiled its architectural harmony. Take time to admire the accomplished 12th-century sculptures flanking the main portal, featuring the *Last Judgment,* the apostles, the Nativity, and various saints. There are other well-crafted sculptures in the cloisters. ⊠ *rue de l'Hôtel-de-Ville,* ☎ *04–90–49–36–36.* 🏛 *Cloisters 15 frs; joint ticket to all Arles museums and monuments 55 frs.* ۩ *June–Sept., daily 8:30–7; Nov.–Mar., daily 9–noon and 2–4:30; Apr.–May and Oct., daily 9–12:30 and 2–6:30.*

Below a former 17th-century Jesuit chapel is the double, horseshoe-shape cavern known as the **Cryptoporticus.** It's surprisingly vast—295 ft long and 197 ft wide—with galleries on three sides of the rectangle. At the beginning of the 1st century BC, it served as the foundations for the Roman forum. Aside from giving the grand monuments support, the gallery was probably used as a granary. ⊠ *rue Balze.* 🏛 *15 frs; joint ticket to all Arles museums and monuments 55 frs.* ۩ *June–Sept., daily 8:30–7; Nov.–Mar., daily 9–noon and 2–4:30; Apr.–May and Oct., daily 9–12:30 and 2–6:30.*

The **Muséon Arlaten,** a folklore museum, is housed in a 16th-century mansion just off boulevard Georges Clemenceau. The displays of costumes and headdresses, puppets, and waxworks were lovingly assembled by that great 19th-century Provençal poet Frédéric Mistral. ⊠ *29 rue de la République,* ☎ *04–90–96–08–23.* 🏛 *15 frs; joint ticket to all Arles museums and monuments 55 frs.* ۩ *June–Sept., daily 8:30–7; Nov.–Mar., Tues.–Sun. 9–noon and 2–4:30; Apr.–May and Oct., Tues.–Sun. 9–12:30 and 2–6:30.*

The fountains in the **Jardin d'Hiver** (Winter Garden), the public garden at the east end of the boulevard des Lices, figure in several of van Gogh's paintings.

The **Alyscamps** starts at the allée des Sarcophages, on the southeast side of town. This was a prestigious burial site from Roman times through the Middle Ages. A host of important finds have been excavated here, many of which are exhibited in the town's museums. Empty tombs and sarcophagi line the allée des Sarcophages, creating a gloomy atmosphere in gray weather. ☎ *04–90–49–36–87.* 🏛 *12 frs.* ۩ *Daily 9–5.*

In a high-concept, triangular, blue building on the southwest side of town (across highway N113), by the Rhone, is the modern **Musée de l'Arles Antique** (Museum of Ancient Arles), where many of Arles's vast collections of Roman artifacts and prehistory findings are gathered. If you haven't understood why Arles is referred to as the "Petite Rome des Gaules," you will after a visit here. There are 18 rooms: Two contain artifacts from 7,000 BC until 46 BC, when Julius Caesar's VI legion was stationed in Arles and the Roman era began. The next four rooms house great monuments of Roman art and architecture (you can climb a platform for ariel views); four others cover the economy of Roman Arles. The last six display domestic and religious art and sculpture and portray the culture of Roman Arles and the later arrival of Christian-

ity. ⊠ *Presqu'Ile du Cirque Romain*, ☎ 04–90–18–88–89. 🎟 *35 frs.*
🕐 *Apr.–Sept., daily 9–7; Oct.–Mar., daily 9:30–12 and 2–5:45.*

Dining and Lodging

$$$ ✕ **Lou Marquès.** Chef Pascal Renaud pleases with nouvelle cuisine and traditional Provençal dishes in his fashionable restaurant in the Jules César hotel (☞ *below*). ⊠ *bd. des Lices*, ☎ 04–90–93–43–20. *AE, DC, MC, V.*

$$ ✕ **Le Vaccarès.** In the footsteps of his father and grandfather, chef Bernard Dumas serves classic Provençal dishes. Try his mussels dressed in herbs and garlic. The dining room is as elegant as the cuisine. ⊠ *11 rue Favorin*, ☎ 04–90–96–06–17. *Reservations essential. MC, V. Closed mid-Jan.–mid-Feb. and Mon. No dinner Sun.*

$–$$ ✕ **Lou Caleu.** Behind the Roman Theater is a street lined with numerous restaurants; Lou Caleu is the best. It's also a good value: Dinner for two costs under 300 francs (lunch is even less). The dozen or so tables are clustered together, so you can expect to rub shoulders with other diners. Every dish is well prepared, but you may want to steer clear of the *entrecôte de toro* (fighting bull)—it's the nature of the beast, not the cooking. ⊠ *27 rue Porte de Laure*, ☎ 04–90–49–71–77. *AE, DC, MC, V.*

$$ ✕ **L'Affenage.** A vast smorgasbord of Provençal hors d'oeuvres draws
★ loyal locals to this former fire-horse shed. Come here for heaping crockery platters of tapenade, chickpeas in cumin, and ham carved off the bone—then dig into roasted potatoes and lamb chops grilled in the great stone fireplace. In summer you can opt for just the buffet and go back for seconds and thirds. ⊠ *4 rue Molière*, ☎ 04–90–96–07–67. *Reservations essential. Closed Sun. No dinner Wed.*

$$ ✕ **La Gueule du Loup.** The couple who owns this place serves as hosts, waiters, and chefs of serious cuisine—such as monkfish and squid in saffron, lamb in pastry lined with tapenade, and creme brulée perfumed with orange blossoms. And they manage to maintain a super-cool ambience with jazz and vintage posters that bring the stone-and-beam setting up to date. ⊠ *39 rue des Arènes*, ☎ 04–90–96–96–69. *MC, V. Closed Sun. No dinner Mon.*

$$$$ 🏨 **Jules César.** This elegant landmark was originally a Carmelite convent. Rooms, on the small side, have Provençal antiques and rich Soleiado fabrics; many overlook the 17th-century cloisters where breakfast is served, or the peaceful garden. ⊠ *bd. des Lices, 13200*, ☎ 04–90–93–43–20, FAX 04–90–93–33–47. *55 rooms. Restaurant, pool. AE, DC, MC, V. Closed Nov.–late Dec.*

$$$ 🏨 **Arlatan.** Follow the signposts from place du Forum to the pic-
★ turesque street where you'll find this 15th-century house, the former home of the counts of Arlatan, built on the site of a 4th-century basilica (tiled flooring dating from this period is visible below glass casing). Antiques, quarry tiles, pretty fabrics, and tapestries lend it the aristocratic atmosphere. There is a fountain in the garden court, a private bar, and a lovely dining room where breakfast is served ⊠ *26 rue du Sauvage, 13200*, ☎ 04–90–93–56–66, FAX 04–90–49–68–45. *51 rooms. Bar, dining room. AE, DC, MC, V.*

$$$ 🏨 **Nord-Pinus.** J. Peterman would feel right at home in this quintessentially Mediterranean hotel on the place du Forum; Hemingway did. Travel relics, kilims, angular wrought iron, and colorful ceramics make it ideal for literary types, fashion models, and decor magazines (keep your eyes peeled—off-season, of course—for Kate Moss, Christian Lacroix, Juliette Binoche, and others). The brasserie, all checked damask, beveled glass and terrazzo tile, is the *dernier cri* (last word) in insider chic. ⊠ *pl. du Forum, 13200*, ☎ 04–90–47–17–16, FAX 04–90–93–34–00. *26 rooms. Bar, brasserie . AE, DC, MC, V.*

$ 🏨 **Hôtel Calendal.** The cheery Provençal colors of this small hotel next to the Arènes reflect the spirit of the hotel and its staff, most of whom speak English. Rooms overlook the amphitheater or the courtyard garden; some sleep four. Light meals are served in the tearoom. ⊠ *22 pl. du Docteur Pomme, 13200,* ☎ *04–90–96–11–89,* FAX *04–90–96–05–84. 27 rooms. Restaurant, air-conditioning. AE, MC, V.*

$ 🏨 **Muette.** With 12th-century exposed stone walls, a 15th-century spi-
★ ral staircase, weathered wood, and an old-town setting, a hotelier wouldn't have to try very hard to please. But the couple who owns this place does: Antiques, sparkling white-and-blue-tile baths, hairdryers, good mattresses, Provençal prints, and fresh sunflowers show that Alain and Brigitte care. ⊠ *15 rue des Suisses, 13200,* ☎ *04–90–96–15–39,* FAX *04–90–49–73–16. 18 rooms. AE, MC, V.*

The Arts

The **International Photography Festival** takes place in July at the Théâtre Antique (⊠ rue de la Calade/rue du Cloître).

Shopping

Delicately patterned Provençal print fabrics can be found at **Souleiado** (⊠ 18 bd. des Lices). Fruit, vegetables, and household goods are sold at the **market** on Wednesday at boulevard des Lices and boulevard Clemenceau and on Saturday morning at boulevard Émile Combes.

Fontvieille

⑱ *10 km (6 mi) east of Arles: Take N570 toward Avignon, and almost immediately turn right on D17.*

The striking village of Fontvieille, among the limestone hills, is best known as the home of writer Alphonse Daudet. In the well-preserved, charming **Moulin de Daudet** (Daudet's Windmill), just up D33 on a hill in the outskirts of the village, 19th-century writer Alphonse Daudet dreamed up his short stories, *Lettres de Mon Moulin.* Inside there's a small museum devoted to Daudet, and you can walk upstairs to see the original milling system. ☎ *04–90–54–60–78.* 🎟 *10 frs.* ☉ *Apr.–Oct., daily 9–noon and 2–7; Nov.–Dec. and Feb.–Mar., daily 10–noon.*

Dining and Lodging

$$$–$$$$ ✕🏨 **La Regalido.** Though it's very popular, some feel that this member of the Relais & Châteaux group is overdone and a bit too commercialized. Rooms, some of which are quite small, feel cluttered with French floral furnishings. The enchanting, stone-terraced garden full of flowering plants, however, may be good enough reason for staying here. From late spring to early fall, meals are served in the garden instead of in the barrel-ceilinged dining room. Unfortunately, the chef-owner's fare, as pleasant as it is, doesn't always live up to its reputation. ⊠ *rue F. Mistral, 13990,* ☎ *04–90–54–60–22,* FAX *04–90–54–64–29. 15 rooms. Restaurant. AE, DC, MC, V. Closed Jan.*

Les Baux-de-Provence

★ **⑲** *18 km (11 mi) northeast of Arles, 29 km (18 mi) south of Avignon, 8 km (5 mi) east of Fontvieille.*

Perched on a mighty spur of rock high above the surrounding country-side with its vines, olive trees, and quarries, Les Baux-de-Provence is an amazing place. The mineral bauxite was discovered here in 1821. Half of Les Baux is composed of tiny climbing streets and ancient stone houses inhabited, for the most part, by local craftsmen. The other half, the **Château des Baux,** is a mass of medieval ruins, vestiges of Les Baux's glorious past, when the town had 6,000 inhabitants and the defensive impregnability of its rocky site far outweighed its isolation and poor access. Cars must be left in the parking lot (20 francs) at the entrance to the village.

The 16th-century **Hôtel des Porcelets,** close to the 12th-century church of St-Vincent (where local shepherds continue an age-old tradition of herding their lambs to midnight mass at Christmas), now contains the **Musée Yves Brayer,** devoted exclusively to its namesake's works. This 20th-century artist's paintings, which are figurative and accessible to the point of naïveté, feature Italy, Spain, and even Asia, but demonstrate most of all his love of Provence. Brayer's grave lies in the château cemetery. ⊠ *pl. Hervain,* ☎ *04–90–54–36–99.* 🖾 *20 frs.* ☉ *Apr.– Sept., daily 10–12:30 and 2–6:30; Oct.–Dec. and mid-Feb.–Mar. 10–12:30 and 2–5.*

Climb up the rue Neuve and enter the **Château** via the **Musée d'Histoire des Baux,** in the 15th-century home of the family de la Tour du Brau. On display are relics of Les Baux's prehistory, architectural details, regional pottery, and a fascinating model of the 13th-century fortifications and castle. Then step out into the windswept aerie once known as the *"ville morte"* or *"dead city,"* where ruins and foundations sketch a skeletal map of this once impenetrable fortress. Reconstructions of medieval war weapons, including a catapult, draw crowds. A 13th-century castle stands at one end of the cliff top and, at the other, the **Tour Paravelle** (Paravelle Tower) and the **Monument Charloun Rieu.** From here, there's a magnificent view of Arles and the Camargue as far as Stes-Maries-de-la-Mer. In the tiny **Chapelle St-Blaise** is a sound-and-slide show of artworks by Van Gogh, Cezanne, and Gauguin, all depicting the surrounding landscape. ⊠ *La Citadelle,* ☎ *04–90–54–37–37.* 🖾 *35 frs.* ☉ *Mar.–June and Sept–Nov., daily 9– 7:30; July–Aug., daily 9–8:30; Nov. and Feb., daily 9–6 Feb.; Dec.– Jan., daily 9–5.*

One kilometer (½ mile) north of Les Baux, off D27, is the **Cathédrale d'Images,** where the majestic setting of the old limestone quarries, with their towering rock faces and stone pillars, is used as a colossal screen for nature-themed films (Jacques Cousteau gets frequent billing). ⊠ *rte. de Maillane,* ☎ *04–90–54–38–65.* 🖾 *43 frs.* ☉ *Mid-Mar.–mid-Nov., daily 10–7; mid-Nov–mid-Dec. and mid-Jan.–mid-Mar, daily 10–6. Some special exhibitions mid-Dec.–mid-Jan.*

Dining and Lodging

$$$$ ✕🖾 **L'Oustau de la Baumanière.** Sheltered by rocky cliffs below the village of Les Baux, this hotel, with its formal terrace and large swimming pool, has the air of a Roman palazzo. Chef Jean-André Charial's hallowed reputation continues to attract culinary pilgrims, despite ups and downs. Ups include ravioli *de truffes aux poireaux* (stuffed with truffles and leeks), and his famous *gigot de sept heures* (seven-hour lamb). (Be sure to make reservations and note that the restaurant is closed Wednesday and Thursday lunch, November–Christmas and January–February.) The breezy, private, bungalow-like rooms are beautifully furnished with antiques. Those in the main house convey grandeur—enormous chimneys, sumptuous fabrics, and solid armoires. A few hundred feet away are 15 less-formal rooms and, in a third, small, vine-covered building, three more simple but charming ones. ⊠ *Val d'Enfer, 13520,* ☎ *04–90–54–33–07,* 🅵🅰🆇 *04–90–54–40–46. 25 rooms. Restaurant, pool, 2 tennis courts, horseback riding. AE, DC, MC, V. Closed mid Jan.–early Mar.*

$ 🖾 **La Reine Jeanne.** Jacques Brel and Winston Churchill were loyal to this modest but majestically placed inn right at the entrance to the village. Here they could stand on balconies and look over rugged views worthy of the châteaux up the street. Rooms are small, simple and—despite the vinyl-padded furniture—lovingly decorated with terra cotta and stencil prints. Reserve in advance for one of the two rooms with a balcony. But even in one of the tiny interior rooms you'll get to spend a quiet evening in lovely Les Baux after the tourists have left. The good home-cooking restaurant has views from inside and seating on a pretty terrace.✉ 13520, ☎ 04–90–54–32–06, ℻ 04–90–54–32–33. 10 rooms. Restaurant. MC, V.

St-Rémy-de-Provence

★ ⑳ *8 km (5 mi) north of Les Baux, 24 km (15 mi) east of Arles, 19 km (12 mi) south of Avignon.*

The small market town of St-Rémy-de-Provence was an important trading post in the 6th century BC. The Phocaeans enlarged the town with Greek-style houses. But disaster struck when the invading Teutons ravaged the country in the latter part of the 1st century BC. Peace was not secured until the Roman general Marius drove the invaders out, defeating them at the battle of St-Victoire in 102 BC—a famous date in the history of the taming of southern Gaul. St-Rémy, known as Glanum to the Romans, was rebuilt, and it is the architectural remains from these Roman days that has placed the town on the cultural map. Temples, baths, forum, and houses have been excavated, while the Mausoleum and Arc Municipal welcome you as you enter the town. After the Romans left, the town was rebuilt under the auspices of the Abbaye de St-Remi of Rheims. Today it is a quintessential Provençal town with fountains in its squares and tree-lined streets. No wonder Vincent van Gogh chose to spend a year (1889) here at the asylum to ease his mental anguish. Consider making it your base for exploring the area, and try to be in town for the Wednesday market.

The Roman **Mausolée** (Mausoleum) was erected around AD 100; the four bas-reliefs around its base, depicting ancient battle scenes, are stunningly preserved. The mausoleum is composed of four archways topped by a circular colonnade. The nearby **Arc Municipal** (Municipal Arch) is a few decades older and has suffered heavily; the upper half has crumbled away, although you can still make out some of the stone carvings.

Excavations of **Glanum** began in 1921, and one-tenth of the original Roman town has now been unearthed. The remains, spread over 300 yards along what was once the Aurelian Way between Arles and Milan, are less spectacular than the arch and mausoleum, but you can still see that they were once temples, fountains, gateways, baths, houses, and a forum. ☎ 04–90–92–23–79. ✑ 36 frs. ☉ Apr.–Sept., daily 9–noon and 2–5; Oct.–Mar., daily 9:30–noon and 2–5.

Many of the finds—statues, pottery, and jewelry—are at the town museum, the **Musée Archéologique** (Archaeology Museum). ✉ Hôtel de Sade, rue Parage, ☎ 04–90–92–64–04. ✑ 15 frs. ☉ June–Sept., daily 9–noon and 2–6; Apr.–May and Oct., weekends 10–noon, weekdays 3–6.

The 12th-century **Monastère de St-Paul-de-Mausolée** (St. Paul of the Mausoleum Monastery), the asylum where van Gogh spent a year resting and painting, is a short walk from Glanum. Still a psychiatric hospital, only the 12th-century church with an 18th-century facade, the Romanesque cloisters, and the small gift shop (with works of art by patients for sale) are open to the public. Along the paths between the monastery and Glanum, there are signs with reproductions of van Gogh's paintings at the spots where he is believed to have worked on

several masterpieces, including *Starry Night*. ☎ 04–90–92–77–00.
🎫 10 frs. ☉ *May–Sept., daily 8–7; Oct.–Apr., daily 8–5.*

Dining and Lodging

$$$$ ☒ **Château des Alpilles.** At the end of an alley of grand old platanes,
this early 19th-century manor house lords over a vast park off D31.
If public spaces and atmosphere are cool and spare, room decor is warm
and fussy, with lush Provençal prints and polished antiques. Outer buildings offer more modern apartments with kitchenettes, and the pool-
side grill gives you a perspective on the noble park that its first owners
probably never saw. ☒ *Ancienne rte. du Grès, 13210,* ☎ *04–90–92–
03–33,* 🗚 *04–90–92–45–17. 15 rooms, 4 suites. Pool, sauna, 2 tennis courts. AE, DC, MC, V. Closed mid-Nov.–mid-Dec. and
Jan.–mid-Feb.*

$$$$ ✕☒ **Domaine de Valmouraine.** Hospitable owner Judith McHugo,
★ who speaks English and excellent French, has turned this genteel
Provençal manor into a home-away-from-home for both French and
foreign guests. Furnishings are tasteful and comfortable. Rooms are
reasonably large and bathrooms modern. In the restaurant, the young
chef expresses his creativity, whether in a recipe using freshly caught
hare or seafood from the Mediterranean. ☒ *Petite rte. des Baux (D27),
13210,* ☎ *04–90–92–44–62,* 🗚 *04–90–92–37–32. 14 rooms.
Restaurant, outdoor pool, tennis court. AE, DC, MC, V.*

$$$ ☒ **Mas de Cornud.** An American mans the wine cellar and an Egyp-
tian runs the professional kitchen, but the attitude is pure Provence:
David and Nito Carpitras have turned their farmhouse, just outside
St-Rémy, into a private inn (make reservations in advance). Through-
out the house and guest rooms are French country furniture and ob-
jects from around the world. Guests and hosts unwind with a nightly
pastis-and-boules match. Table d'hôte dinners, cooking classes, and tours
can be arranged. Breakfast is included. ☒ *rte. de Mas-Blanc, 13210,*
☎ *04–90–92–39–32,* 🗚 *04–90–92–55–99. 6 rooms. Dining room,
pool. No credit cards. Closed Jan.–Feb.*

Tarascon

㉑ *16 km (10 mi) west of St-Rémy, 17 km (11 mi) north of Arles, 25 km
(15 mi) east of Nîmes.*

The mythical Tarasque, a monster that would emerge from the Rhône
to gobble up children and cattle, came from Tarascon. Luckily, St.
Martha, who washed up at Stes-Maries-de-la-Mer, allegedly tamed the
beast with a sprinkle of holy water, after which the inhabitants slashed
it to pieces. This dramatic event is celebrated on the last weekend in June
with a parade and immortalized by Alphonse Daudet in his tales of a
folk hero known to all French schoolchildren as Tartarin de Tarascon.

One highlight of a visit to Tarascon is its formidable 12th-century
Château, intended to protect the town from any beast or man that might
be tempted to emulate the Tarasque's fiendish deeds. The castle's mas-
sive stone walls, towering 150 ft above the rocky banks of the Rhône,
are among the most daunting in France, so it's not surprising that the
castle was used as a prison for centuries. Since 1926, however, the chapels,
vaulted royal apartments, and stone carvings of the interior have been
restored to less-intimidating glory. ☎ *04–90–91–01–93.* 🎫 *28 frs.*
☉ *July–Aug., daily 9–7; Sept. and Apr.–June, daily 9–noon and 2–
6; Oct.–Mar., daily 2–5.*

Dining and Lodging

$$ ☒ **Hôtel de Provence.** Rooms vary a great deal at this pleasant, traditional, enthusiastically run hotel. Especially nice are the ones that open

onto the large balcony, where breakfast is served in summer. Note, however, that the balcony is communal and that you must close the shutters at night for privacy. Rooms on the other side of the building look out on other houses. ⊠ *7 bd. Victor-Hugo, 13150 ,* ☎ *04–90–91–06–43,* FAX *04–90–43–58–13. 11 rooms. MC, V.*

Beaucaire

㉒ *2 km (1 mi) west of Tarascon, 26 km (16 mi) south of Avignon.*

☝ Eye to eye with Tarascon's château on the opposite bank of the Rhône is Beaucaire's equally impressive **Château.** It was built on the site of a Roman camp in the 11th century but was remodeled 200 years later and then dismantled in the 17th century on the orders of Cardinal Richelieu. What is left are the ramparts, two towers, the restored Romanesque chapel, and the barbican that defended the castle's entrance. Inside the ramparts a spectacle takes place—Les Aigles de Beaucaire—when birds of prey are handled by falconers in medieval costume. ☎ *04–66–59–26–72.* ▱ *Château free; bird show 45 frs.* ☉ *Late Mar.–early Nov., Thurs.–Tues., with bird shows at 2, 3, 4, and 5.*

THE VAUCLUSE

Though the Roman presence is still evident in this region, especially in Orange and at Vaison-la-Romaine, Avignon's more recent history revolves around its being the seat of the papacy in the 14th century. The outstanding geographic feature of this hilly landscape with stubbly trees is Mont Ventoux, but it's the small villages in the Luberon mountains—Venasque, Gordes, Roussillon—that will win your heart.

Avignon

24 km (15 mi) northeast of Tarascon, 82 km (51 mi) northwest of Aix-en-Provence, 95 km (59 mi) northwest of Marseille, 224 km (140 mi) south of Lyon.

A warren of medieval alleys nestling behind a protective ring of stocky towers, Avignon is possibly best known for its Pont d'Avignon, the St-Bénezet bridge, which many will remember singing about during their nursery-rhyme days. No one dances across the bridge these days, however; it was amputated in midstream in the 17th century, when a storm washed half of it away. Still, Avignon has lots to offer, starting with the Palais des Papes (Papal Palace), where seven exiled popes camped between 1309 and 1377 after fleeing from the corruption and civil strife of Rome. Avignon remained papal property until 1791, and elegant mansions bear witness to the town's 18th-century prosperity. From the **tourist office** (⊠ *41 cours Jean-Jaurès*), rue de la République, Avignon's main street, leads past shops and cafés to place de l'Horloge and place du Palais.

★ ㉓ The colossal **Palais des Papes** (Papal Palace) creates a disconcertingly fortresslike impression, underlined by the austerity of its interior decor. Most of the furnishings were returned to Rome with the papacy, and others were dispersed during the French Revolution. Some imagination is required to picture it in medieval splendor, awash with color and with worldly clerics enjoying what the 14th-century Italian poet Petrarch called "licentious banquets." On close inspection, two different styles of building emerge at the palace: the severe **Palais Vieux** (Old Palace), built between 1334 and 1342 by Pope Benedict XII, a member of the Cistercian order, which frowned on frivolity, and the more decorative **Palais Nouveau** (New Palace), built in the following decade by the artsy, lavish-living Pope Clement VI. The Great Court, where visitors arrive, links the two.

The main rooms of the Palais Vieux are the **Consistory** (Council Hall), decorated with some excellent 14th-century frescoes by Simone Martini; the **Chapelle St-Jean** (original frescoes by Matteo Giovanetti); the **Grand Tinel,** or Salle des Festins, with a majestic vaulted roof and a series of 18th-century Gobelin tapestries; the **Chapelle St-Martial** (more Matteo frescoes); the **Chambre du Cerf,** with a richly decorated ceiling, murals featuring a stag hunt, and a delightful view of Avignon; the **Chambre de Parement** (Papal Antechamber); and the **Chambre à Coucher** (Papal Bedchamber). The principal attractions of the Palais Nouveau are the **Grande Audience,** a magnificent two-nave hall on the ground floor, and, upstairs, the **Chapelle Clémentine,** where the college of cardinals gathered to elect the new pope. ⊠ *pl. du Palais,* ☎ *04–90–27–50–73.* 🎟 *35 frs.* ☉ *Apr.–Oct., daily 9–7; Nov.–Mar., daily 9–12:45 and 2–6.*

㉔ Avignon's 12th-century **Cathédrale,** not far from the Palais des Papes, contains the Gothic tomb of Pope John XII.

㉕ From the **Rocher des Doms** (Bluff of the Doms), a large, attractive park just east of the cathedral, you can get a look at Avignon and the Rhône.

㉖ The first bridge to span the Rhône at Avignon is the celebrated **Pont St-Bénezet**—built, according to legend, by a local shepherd named Bénezet in the 12th century. Though only half of the original 900 yards remains, it's worth strolling along, to enjoy the views and to visit the tiny **Chapelle St-Nicolas,** which juts out over the river. ☎ *04–90–85–60–16 for tourist office next to bridge for information.* 🎟 *Bridge 15 frs.* ☉ *Apr.–Sept., daily 9–6:30; Oct.–Mar., Tues.–Sun. 9–1 and 2–5.*

㉗ The medieval **Petit Palais** (Little Palace), between Pont St-Bénezet and the Rocher des Doms garden, was once home to cardinals and archbishops. Nowadays it contains an outstanding collection of old masters, led by the Italian schools of Venice, Siena, and Florence (note Sandro Botticelli's *Virgin and Child*). ⊠ *21 pl. du Palais,* ☎ *04–90–86–44–58.* 🎟 *20 frs.* ☉ *Wed.–Mon. 9:30–noon and 2–6.*

㉘ Venture into the narrow, winding, shop-lined streets of old Avignon, south of the Papal Palace, to get to a sturdy 17th-century Baroque chapel fronted by an imposing facade and housing the **Musée Lapidaire.** On display are a variety of archaeological finds—including the remains of Avignon's Arc de Triomphe. ⊠ *27 rue de la République,* ☎ *04–90–85–75–38.* 🎟 *10 frs.* ☉ *Wed.–Mon. 10–noon and 2–6.*

㉙ An 18th-century town house is home to the **Musée Calvet.** It features an extensive collection of mainly French paintings from the 16th century on, including works by Théodore Géricault, Camille Corot, Édouard Manet, Raoul Dufy, Maurice de Vlaminck, and the Italian artist Amedeo Modigliani. Greek, Roman, and Etruscan statuettes are also displayed. ⊠ *65 rue Joseph-Vernet,* ☎ *04–90–86–33–84.* 🎟 *30 frs.* ☉ *Wed.–Mon. 10–6.*

㉚ **Le Cloître des Arts** (Art Cloister), in an 18th-century building two doors down from the Musée Calvet, opened in 1996 as a venue for concerts and expositions. Another salon was opened in 1998 to exhibit paintings and art from the 20th century. Enhancing the tranquil setting is the cloister, where there is a restaurant and a tearoom—ideal for quiet relaxation and a quick read on what to visit next. ⊠ *83 rue Joseph-Vernet,* ☎ *04–90–82–70–60.* ☉ *Mon. 10–7:30, Tues.–Sat. 10 AM–midnight.*

Avignon

Dining and Lodging

$$$$ ✕ **La Mirande.** Tapestries warm the walls of the large airy dining room in the Hôtel de la Mirande (☞ *below*), where chef Alain Davi presents his deceptively simple dishes. Try the terrine *de gibier au foie gras* (of game and goose liver) or the *crepinette de faisan* (pheasant sausage). In winter, Coisel teams up with other Avignon chefs to give cooking lessons. ⊠ *pl. de la Mirande,* ☎ *04–90–85–93–93. AE, DC, MC, V.*

$$$ ✕ **Hiély-Lucullus.** According to most authorities, this restaurant num-
★ bers among the top 50 in France, although André Chaussy has now taken over as chef for the legendary Pierre Hiély. The upstairs dining room has a quiet, dignified charm. Classic delicacies include crayfish tails in scrambled eggs inside a puff pastry, and roast cod with juniper berries. ⊠ *5 rue de la République,* ☎ *04–90–86–17–07. Reservations essential. AE, V. Closed most of Jan., last 2 wks in June, and Mon. No lunch Tues. Oct.–June.*

$$$ ✕ **Jardin des Frênes.** The specialty at this excellent restaurant in the Hostellerie les Frênes (☞ *below*) is stylish country cuisine. The pigeon with black truffles in a puff-pastry case is always a good bet. ⊠ *645 av. des Vertes-Rives, Montfavet (5 km/3 mi outside Avignon),* ☎ *04–90–31–17–93. AE, DC, MC, V. Closed Nov.–early Mar.*

$$$ ✕ **La Vieille Fontaine.** This restaurant in the Europe hotel (☞ *below*) serves respectable regional cuisine. In summer, enjoy chicken with wild mushrooms or duck liver outside in the stone courtyard. ⊠ *12 pl. Crillon,* ☎ *04–90–82–66–92. AE, DC, MC, V. Closed Sun. No lunch Sat.*

$$ ✕ **La Cuisine de Reine.** In the trendy new Cloître des Arts (☞ *above*)
★   is this chic bistro sporting *theatrical dell'arte* decor. The young, laid-back wait staff serves up eclectic dishes from the blackboard: Simple but serious in execution, these include duck in rosemary honey, herbed lamb chops, and salmon tartare with eggplant caviar. Or join the cashmere and loafer set for the 120F Saturday brunch buffet. ⊠ *83 rue Joseph Vernet,* ☎ *04–90–85–99–04. AE, DC, MC, V. Closed Sun. No dinner Mon..*

$ ✕ **Le Grand Café.** In a massive former factory behind the Pope's Palace, a hip entertainment complex has sprung up, including a serious international cinema, a bar, and this popular bistro. Gigantic mirrors hang against crumbling plaster and brick, and votive candles half-light the raw metal framework—an inspiring setting for intense film-talk and a late supper foie gras, goat cheese, or marinated artichokes. ⊠ *La Manutention, 4 rue des Escaliers Ste-Anne,* ☎ *04–90–86–86–77. MC, V. Closed Mon. (except July).*

$ ✕ **NaniType.** By 12:30 all the inside and outside tables are occupied at this popular, central spot (it's just off rue de la République). There are two good reasons: The price is right—about 55 francs for one large lunch course and 30 francs for a carafe of wine; and the food is creative and served in generous portions, including salads, kebabs, and quiche. ⊠ *29 rue Théodore Aubanel,* ☎ *04–90–82–60–90. No credit cards. Closed Nov.–May. No dinner Sun.–Wed.*

★ ⊞ **Hôtel de la Mirande.** Superbly restored and richly decorated with exquisite reproduction fabrics and beeswaxed antiques, this designer's dream hotel is just below the Papal Palace in a car-free zone. Its enclosed garden is a breakfast and dinner oasis, and its central lounge a skylit and jazz-warmed haven. Rooms are both gorgeous and comfy; bathrooms are luxurious, with Victorian touches. Half the rooms face the garden, the other half the palace facade; a few even have tiny ultra-private balconies with rooftop views.⊠ *pl. de la Mirande, 84000,* ☎ *04–90–85–93–93,* ℻ *04–90–86–26–85. 19 rooms, 1 suite. Restaurant, bar. AE, DC, MC, V.*

$$$ ⊞ **Cloître St-Louis.** Although close to Avignon's train station, this serene hotel stands calm within its sturdy 17th-century walls, its windows surrounding a courtyard lined with grand old trees. The early Baroque building, erected by the Jesuits in 1611, was a theological school and later a hospital before it became a hotel at the beginning of the decade. The interior is more modern, but plays on the cool, old stone. ⊠ *20 rue du Portail-Boquier, 84000,* ☎ *04–90–27–55–55,* ℻ *04–90–82–24–01. 80 rooms. Restaurant, bar, pool. AE, DC, MC, V.*

$$$ ⊞ **Hôtel d'Europe.** This 16th-century town house became a hotel in Napoleonic times. The great man himself was one of the very first customers; since then, everyone from crowned heads of state to Robert and Elizabeth Browning has stayed here. The spacious guest rooms are filled with period furniture and have lavish bathrooms. ⊠ *12 pl. Crillon, 84000,* ☎ *04–90–14–76–76,* ℻ *04–90–85–43–66. 47 rooms. Restaurant. AE, DC, MC, V.*

$$$ ⊞ **Hostellerie les Frênes.** This luxurious hotel in a country house has gardens to ramble in, splashing fountains, and individually decorated

rooms in styles ranging from subtle modern to art deco. ⊠ *645 av. des Vertes-Rives, 84140 Montfavet (5 km/3 mi outside Avignon),* ☎ *04–90–31–17–93,* 🅵🅰🆇 *04–90–23–95–03. 15 rooms. Restaurant, pool, sauna. AE, DC, MC, V. Closed Nov.–early Mar.*

$$ 🏨 **Hôtel du Blauvac.** Just off rue de la République and place de l'Horloge, this 17th-century nobleman's home has been divided into guest rooms, many with exposed stonework, aged-oak detailing, and lovely tall windows that look, alas, onto backstreet walls. But prretty fabrics and a warm welcome more than compensate. ⊠ *11 rue de la Bancasse 84000,* ☎ *04–90–86–34–11.* 🅵🅰🆇 *04–90–86–27–41. 16 rooms. Bar. AE, DC, MC, V.*

$ 🏨 **Hôtel de la Bourse.** Down a quiet street, away from the traffic noise of Avignon's main avenues, and only 250 yards from the train station, is this small budget hotel. Rooms, on narrow corridors, are clean and reasonably large for the price; bathrooms are small. The staff is cheery. ⊠ *6 rue du Portail Boquier, 84000,* ☎ *04–90–82–34–43. 11 rooms. Restaurant. No credit cards.*

$ 🏨 **Hôtel Colbert.** This very reasonably priced hotel is 50 yards from the tourist office. Rooms are small and basic but air-conditioned. ⊠ *7 rue Agricol Perdiquier, 84000,* ☎ *04–90–86–20–20. 15 rooms, most with shower. Air-conditioning. No credit cards.*

$ 🏨 **Hôtel de Mons.** Off place de l'Horloge, this little hotel was once a 12th-century chapel that was turned into a house in 1821 when Napoléon's chaplain, Étienne Morel de Mons, lived here for nine years. Certain modernizations have been carried out since then, but it remains a very simple place. Rooms are compact but comfortable; some have exposed brick walls and beamed ceilings. ⊠ *5 rue de Mons, 84000,* ☎ *04–90–82–57–16,* 🅵🅰🆇 *04–90–85–19–15. 11 rooms. MC, V.*

Nightlife and the Arts

If you want to see a cabaret, head for **Les Ambassadeurs** (⊠ 27 rue Bancasse, ☎ 04–90–86–31–55). The prestigious **Festival de Théâtre Avignon** (⊠ pl. du Palais, ☎ 04–90–82–67–08), held the last three weeks of July, is centered in the Grand Courtyard of the Palais des Papes and throughout the streets of Avignon.

Outdoor Activities and Sports

Barthelasse (⊠ chemin du Mont Blanc, ☎ 04–90–85–83–48) rents horses to experienced equestrians and gives riding lessons to children.

Châteauneuf-du-Pape

③ *18 km (11 mi) north of Avignon, 23 km (14 mi) west of Carpentras.*

The hillside village of Châteauneuf-du-Pape was founded in the 14th century. The popes who lived here knew their wine: The vineyard here is still regarded as the best of the southern Rhône. The reds of Châteauneuf need three to five years to mature; the whites may be enjoyed in their first two years. The production of Châteauneuf is quite unusual in that the wine is produced from 13 different authorized vine varieties. The best time to visit the town is the first weekend in August for the **Fête de la Véraison,** when wine-tasting stands are set up, arts and crafts are exhibited, and a historical show is performed. If you're not into wine, the town isn't that interesting. A walk up to the château provides exercise and a sweeping view of the surrounding patchwork of vineyards, but the castle itself is in ruins.

Several producers stage tastings in the village and sell distinctive wine bottles emblazoned with the crossed-key papal crest. Like many vintners, **Père Ansèlme** (⊠ rte. d'Avignon, ☎ 04–90–83–70–07) gives a free guided tour of his winery (with a tasting afterward) with the hope that you'll buy a bottle or two.

Dining

$–$$ ✕ **Le Pistou.** On the street leading up to the ruined château is this restaurant serving regional cuisine, including, of course, soupe au pistou, the traditional summer dish strong on basil, and *anchoïade,* anchovies served with vegetables. Either dine inside or out on the terrace; prix-fixe menus start at 83 francs. In winter, "Provençal Evenings" are held, when a musician and storyteller entertains. ⊠ *15 rue Joseph Ducos,* ☎ *04–90–83–71–75. MC, V. Closed Mon. No dinner Sun.*

Orange

③② *10 km (6 mi) north of Châteauneuf-du-Pape, 31 km (19 mi) north of Avignon, 193 km (121 mi) south of Lyon.*

Orange is a small, pleasant town that sinks into total siesta somnolence during hot afternoons but at other times buzzes with visitors keen on admiring its Roman remains.

★ The magnificent, semicircular **Théâtre Antique,** in the center of town, is the best-preserved remains of a theater from the ancient world. It was built just before the birth of Christ, to the same dimensions as that of Arles. Orange's theater, however, has a mighty screen wall and steeply climbing terraces carved into the hillside. Seven thousand spectators can crowd in; the acoustics are superb. This is the only Roman theater that still possesses its original Imperial statue, of Caesar Augustus—one of the tallest in existence—which stands, 12 ft tall, in the middle of the screen. ⊠ *pl. des Frères-Mounet,* ☎ *04–90–34–70–88.* 🎫 *30 frs; joint ticket with Musée Municipal.* ☉ *Apr.–Oct., daily 9–6:30; Nov.–Mar., daily 9–noon and 1:30–5.*

The **Parc de la Colline St-Eutrope** (St. Eutrope Hill Park), the banked garden behind the Théâtre Antique, yields a fine view of the theater and of the 6,000-ft Mont Ventoux to the east.

The venerable **Arc de Triomphe** (Triumphal Arch)—a 70-ft central arch flanked by two smaller ones, the whole topped by a massive entablature—towered over the old Via Agrippa between Arles and Lyon and was probably built around AD 25 in honor of the Gallic Wars. The carvings on the north side depict the legionnaires' battles with the Gauls and Caesar's naval showdown with the ships of Marseille. Today the arch presides over a busy traffic circle.

Dining and Lodging

$$–$$$ ✕ **Le Pigraillet.** One of Orange's best lunch spots is Le Pigraillet, on
★ the chemin Colline St-Eutrope at the far end of the gardens. You may want to eat in the garden, or seek shelter from the mistral in the glassed-in terrace. The modern cuisine includes crab ravioli and duck breast in the muscat wine of nearby Beaumes-de-Venise. ⊠ *chemin de la Colline St-Eutrope,* ☎ *04–90–34–44–25. Reservations essential. MC, V. Closed Jan.–Feb. and Mon.*

$$ 🏨 **Arène.** In the town center, on a quiet square shaded by tall plane trees, is this comfortable old hotel. Look forward to a warm welcome and a labryinth of densely decorated rooms, the nicest of which look out over the square. ⊠ *pl. de Langes, 84100,* ☎ *04–90–11–40–40,* FAX *04–90–11–40–45. 30 rooms. Air-conditioning. AE, DC, MC, V. Closed three weeks in Nov.*

The Arts

An **International Opera Festival** takes place the last two weeks of July in the Théâtre Antique (☞ *above*).

Shopping

Fruit, herbs, honey, and truffles can be purchased at the **market** (⊠ cours Aristide-Briand) on Thursday morning. Provençal print fabrics can be found at **Souleiado** (⊠ 5 rue Joseph-Vernet).

Vaison-la-Romaine

③③   *27 km (17 mi) northeast of Orange, 30 km (19 mi) northeast of Avignon.*

Vaison-la-Romaine, as its name suggests, was once a Roman town. The ruins are more extensive, though less spectacular than Orange's; they can be found on either side of avenue du Général-de-Gaulle.

Parts of houses, villas, a basilica, and a theater have been unearthed; interesting finds are housed in the small **Musée Archéologique Théo Desplans** (Théo Desplans Archaeology Museum). With its lush lawns and colorful flower beds, the entire site suggests a historical garden. ☎ 04–90–36–02–11. ⊠ *Ruins and museum 40 frs. ☉ June–Sept., daily 10–1 and 2:30–5:45 (until 6:45 June–Aug.); Oct.–May, daily 10–noon and 2–4:30.*

Before leaving Vaison, pause to admire the 2,000-year-old **Pont Romain** (Roman Bridge) over the River Ouvèze and venture briefly into the medieval town across the river.

Dining and Lodging

$$ ✕⊞ **Le Beffroi.** On a hill in the old town is this hotel in a 16th-century mansion, with a 17th-century annex. Rooms are spacious, comfortable, and filled with old furniture; the best have views of the gardens. In the restaurant, enjoy wonderful lamb terrine with apples, saddle of hare, and baked dorade; it's closed from late December to early March and for lunch during the week. ⊠ *rue de l'Évêché, 84110,* ☎ *04–90–36–04–71,* ℻ *04–90–36–24–78. 22 rooms. Restaurant. AE, DC, MC, V. Closed mid-Feb.–mid-Mar. and mid-Nov.–mid-Dec.*

$$ ⊞ **Évêché.** Stay in one of the Verdiers' four rooms in this turreted, 17th-century former bishop's palace in the medieval part of town. The warm welcome and the rustic charm—exposed beams and wooden bedsteads—have garnered a loyal following among travelers who prefer character to modern luxury. Breakfast is served on a terrace overlooking the Ouvèze Valley; this is the time to try out your French as the Verdiers' English is rudimentary. Advance reservations are essential. ⊠ *rue de l'Évêché, 84110,* ☎ *04–90–36–13–46,* ℻ *04–90–36–32–43. 4 rooms. No credit cards.*

Seguret

③④   *10 km (6 mi) west of Vaison-la-Romaine, 40 km (25 mi) northeast of Avignon.*

The tower of a medieval castle dominates this hillside village where few cars are narrow enough to negotiate its cobbled streets and certainly could not manage the stairways that link the hillside streets. There are a few boutiques, but as of yet, Seguret is not as commercialized as some of Provence's other appealing hill towns. **Rue des Posternes,** lined with ancient houses, is a particularly appealing street. Pass by the 15th-century Mascarons fountain on your way up to the 12th-century church of **St-Denis.** From the nearby lookout, gaze over the valley to the **Dentelles de Montmirail,** an outline of craggy peaks, eroded in needle-like pinnacles that have formed a ridge reminiscent of a cock's comb.

Dining and Lodging

$$$ ✕🏨 **La Table du Comtat.** Wind your way up to the top of the village and this small hotel-restaurant with a breathtaking view over the plains of Comtat-Venaissin. Chef Gomez's fare is sophisticated; the 135-franc lunch menu may include lamb from Les Alpilles and dorade in citron butter sauce. (The restaurant is closed Tuesday night and Wednesday.) Rooms are comfortable but on the small side for the price. Ask for one with a view, though others face the garden and have a balcony. ⊠ *Just after pl. de l'Église, 84110,* ☎ *04–90–46–91–49,* 🖷 *04–90–46–94–27. 8 rooms. Restaurant. AE, DC, MC, V. Closed Feb.*

Mont Ventoux

㉟ *16 km (10 mi) southeast of Vaison-la-Romaine.*

A huge mountain that looms above the surrounding plains, Mont Ventoux is known reverentially as Le Ventoux. Weather conditions on this whalelike bulk can vary dramatically: In summer, few places in France experience such scorching heat; in winter, the Ventoux's snow-topped peak recalls the Alps. Its arid heights sometimes provide a grueling setting for the Tour de France cycling race; British bicyclist Tommy Simpson collapsed and died under the Ventoux's pitiless sun in 1967. D974 winds its way from Malaucène up to the summit, 6,250 ft above sea level. Stay on D974 as it doubles back around the southern slopes, then runs from Bédoin toward Carpentras.

Crillon le Brave

㊱ *12 km (7 mi) south of Malaucène (via Caromb), 21 km (13 mi) southeast of Vaison-la-Romaine.*

The main reason to come to this tiny village is to stay or dine at its hotel, the Hostellerie de Crillon le Brave (☞ *Dining and Lodging, below*). But it's also pleasant—perched on a knoll in a valley shielded by Mont Ventoux, with the craggy hills of the Dentelles in one direction and the hills of the Luberon in another. At one time, some 500 inhabitants huddled behind its fortified walls, but after World War II, families left (it had no running water or electricity) and houses fell into ruin. Even the church was in dire straits and had to sell tiles off its buildings to sustain itself. Then in the 1960s, a Parisian purchased the rectory and started to make it into a country home. This building, along with eight others, was later bought by a Canadian firm and made into the elegant Hostellerie de Crillon. Pride in the village was further enhanced when, in 1967, the statue of Crillon Le Brave, France's most notable soldier hero of the 16th century, was moved from place du Palais des Papes in Avignon to the village square. Today, though the village still doesn't have even a *boulangerie* (bakery), the wrecker's ball has been held at bay. The village makes a good base camp for exploring the region, if you can afford to stay at the hotel; with no other commercial establishments in the village, you are a captive of the hotel.

Dining and Lodging

$$$$ ✕🏨 **Hostellerie de Crillon le Brave.** The views from the hotel's nine interconnected hilltop houses are as elevated as its prices. But for this you get a rarefied atmosphere of medieval luxury. Faultless decor informs cozy salons and guest rooms, some with terraces looking out onto infinity. Fountains splash in the garden overlooking the pool. In the stone-vaulted dining room, refined French cuisine is served—pan-roasted foie gras on peppered toast and *côte d'agneau* (lamb chop), slightly flavored with anise. Most of the staff speak English, and most guests are from the United States or Canada. ⊠ *pl. de l'Église, 84410,*

☎ 04–90–65–61–61, 800/461–6247 in the U.S., FAX 04–90–65–62–86. 21 rooms. Restaurant, pool. AE, DC, MC, V.

Venasque

③⑦ 36 km (23 mi) southeast of Mont Ventoux, 16 km (12 mi) north of Gordes, 12 km (7 mi) southeast of Carpentras, 35 km (22 mi) northeast of Avignon.

Once the capital of Comtat Venaissin, the large agricultural region east of Avignon, Venasque now only has a population of fewer than 675 inhabitants. The village, tucked inside fortified walls, stands proudly on a hill overlooking the Carpentras Plain. The ambience is wonderfully medieval and tranquil—enough to enjoy in itself—but be sure to pop into **Notre-Dame** church, one of France's oldest buildings, to see the baptistery dating from the 6th century and remodeled in the 11th.

Dining and Lodging

$$$ ✕🔢 **Auberge La Fontaine.** This ancient, renovated house makes an ideal base for exploring the region. Its eight small apartments have eclectic furnishings; one is ultramodern, whereas the others are more traditional. The hotel abuts other village buildings, so there are no views. On the first floor is a small lounge and restaurant serving four-course dinners; on the ground floor is a bistro for lighter meals. ✉ 84210, ☎ 04–90–66–02–96, FAX 04–90–66–13–14. 8 apartments. 2 restaurants, kitchenettes. MC, V.

L'Isle-sur-la-Sorgue

③⑧ 18 km (11 mi) south of Malaucène, 41 km (25 mi) southeast of Orange, 26 km (16 mi) east of Avignon.

At L'Isle-sur-la-Sorgue the River Sorgue splits into a number of channels. The river once turned the waterwheels of the town's silk factories. Silkworms were cultivated locally, one reason for the profusion of mulberry trees in the region. Some of the waterwheels are still in place; you can see these as you stroll along the banks of the river. The richly decorated 17th-century church, the **Collégiale Notre-Dame-des-Anges**, is also of interest. Follow the signs to Le Partage des Eaux, where the rivers meet—the small park here is perfect for picnicking.

Dining and Lodging

$ ✕ **Lou Nego Chin.** Locals love this riverside institution, where in winter you dine in the cramped but atmosperic dining room (chinoiserie linens, bright-hued tiles); in summer, tables are strewn across the (quiet) street, on a wooden deck on the river. Ask for a spot at the edge, so you can watch the ducks cavorting, and order the inexpensive house wine and the 60-franc menu du jour, which consists of a salad and a main dish—usually lamb chops or grilled fish. Depending on what is available, you may or may not forgo dessert (an additional 30 francs). ✉ 12 quai Jean-Jaurès, ☎ 04–90–20–88–03. MC, V. Closed Mon. No dinner Sun.

$ ✕🔢 **La Gueulardière.** After a Sunday of antiquing along the canals, you can dine and sleep in a setting full of collectible finds, from the school posters in the restaurant to the oak armoires and brass beds that furnish the simple lodgings, just up the street. Each room has French windows that open onto the enclosed garden courtyard, where you can enjoy a private breakfast in the shade. ✉ 1 rue d'Apt 84800, ☎ 04–90–38–10–52, FAX 04–90–20–83–70. 5 rooms. Restaurant. AE, DC, MC, V.

Fontaine-de-Vaucluse

39 *8 km (5 mi) east of L'Isle-sur-la-Sorgue, 33 km (20 mi) east of Avignon.*

The "fountain" in Fontaine-de-Vaucluse is the site of the Sorgue River's emergence from underground imprisonment: Water wells up from a cavern at the floot of steep cliffs and cascades dramatically over boulders towern town. This is the picture in springtime or after heavy rains; with summer's drought and crowds, the scene may be less spectacular. Vaucluse stems from the Latin *vallis clausa* (enclosed valley), which is how the village is laid out—it's surrounded on three sides by towering cliffs.

The great poet Petrarch sought solace for 16 years in Fontaine-de-Vaucluse, treasuring his romantic ideal, the lovely Laura. He had fallen passionately in love with her while in Avignon, but she was married and virtuous. Petrarch could only consummate his love for her in his poetry. During his exile she died in Avignon of the plague. Today, if you ignore the summer crowds, you can still sense the serenity that Petrarch saw.

Dining and Lodging

$$ ✕🔟 **Le Parc.** This old-fashioned hotel on the banks of the roaring river has a waterfront terrace and several rooms overlooking the river or the château, which is illuminated at night. Rooms are plain, solid and comfortable; those facing the garden are wonderfully quiet. The restaurant (closed Wednesday) serves a number of prix-fixe menus; specialties range from pasta with foie gras to duckling with berries. ⊠ *rue de Bourgades, 84800,* ☎ *04–90–20–31–57,* 🄵🄰🄇 *04–90–20–27–03. 12 rooms. Restaurant. AE, DC, MC, V. Jan.–mid-Feb.*

$–$$ 🔟 **La Maison aux Fruits.** Before you enter you know an artist lives here and that this small bed-and-breakfast run by Roseline Giorgis is a special place. The carved front door and the painted woodwork prepare you for the faux marble, murals, painted ceilings, and other works of art inside. A lovely oval staircase takes you up to a sitting and dining room and a terrace. There's also a little apartment rented by the week. ⊠ *rue de l'Isle de Sorgue, 84800,* ☎ *04–90–20–39–15,* 🄵🄰🄇 *04–90–20–27–08. 2 rooms, 1 apartment. No credit cards.*

$ 🔟 **Le Grand Jas.** In a renovated farmhouse just out of the nearby village of Lagnes is this little B&B. It has three comfortable, rustic rooms with exposed beams, as well as a pleasant, high-ceilinged common area. With arrangements, you can enjoy a table d'hôte dinner in the large kitchen–dining room. Lagnes makes a good base: It's a sweet hilltop village with a couple of small restaurants and a café-bar. ⊠ *rue du Bariot, 84800, Lagnes (8 km/5 mi from Fontaine-de-Vaucluse via D1004),* ☎ *04–90–20–25–12,* 🄵🄰🄇 *04–90–20–29–17. 3 rooms. Dining room. No credit cards.*

Gordes

40 *16 km (10 mi) southeast of Fontaine-de-Vaucluse, 35 km (22 mi) east of Avignon.*

Gordes is only a short distance from Fontaine-de-Vaucluse, but you need to wind your way south, east, and then north on D100-A, D100, D2, and D15 to skirt the impassable hillside. The golden-stone village is perched dramatically on its own hill. On the summit is the Renaissance **Château,** with its collection of mind-stretching photo paintings by pop artist Pol Mara, who lived in Gordes until his death. ☎ *04–90–72–02–89.* 🎫 *25 frs.* ☺ *Wed.–Mon. 10–noon and 2–6.*

Just outside Gordes, on a lane heading north from D2, follow signs to the **Village des Bories.** Found throughout this region of Provence, the bizarre and fascinating little stone hovels called *bories* are concentrated 20-some strong in an ancient community. Their origins are provocatively vague: Built as shepherds' shelters with tight-fitting, morterless stone in a hivelike form, they may date back to the Celts, the Ligurians, even the Iron Age—and were inhabited or used for sheep through the 18th century. ☎ 04–90–72–03–48. ☜ 30 frs. ☽ daily 9 to sunset or 8 PM, whichever comes first.

In a wild valley some 4 km (2 mi) north of Gordes (via D177) is the beautiful 12th-century **Abbaye de Sénanque.** In 1969 its Cistercian monks moved to the island of St-Honorat, off the shore of Cannes, and the admirably preserved buildings here, under the stewardship of a few remaining monks, are now a cultural center that presents concerts and exhibitions. The dormitory, refectory, church, and chapter house can be visited, along with an odd museum devoted to the Sahara's Tuareg nomads. ☎ 04–90–72–05–72. ☜ 20 frs. ☽ Mar.–Oct., Mon.–Sat. 10–noon and 2–6, Sun. 2–6; Nov.–Feb., weekdays 2–5, weekends 2–6.

Dining and Lodging

$$$ ✕ **Comptoir du Victuailler.** You'll find only 10 tables at this tiny restaurant where elegantly simple meals—using only the freshest local capon, guinea fowl, asparagus, artichokes, and truffles—are served. The fruit sorbets are a revelation. ⌗ pl. du Château, ☎ 04–90–72–01–31. Reservations essential. MC, V. Closed mid-Nov.–mid-Dec., mid-Jan.–mid-Mar., and Wed. Sept.–May. No dinner Tues.

$$$ ⌖ **Domaine de l'Enclos.** Small, private stone cottages with panoramic views make up this charming hotel just outside Gordes. The simple exteriors suggest a rustic interior, but furnishings are modern, functional, and utilitarian. Opt for the demi-pension for a one-night stay, a better value than paying for rooms and meals separately, which makes the hotel overpriced. The restaurant's menu of good nouvelle dishes varies with the season; if it's available, try the excellent aromatic duck. ⌗ rte. de Sénanque, 84220, ☎ 04–90–72–08–22, ℻ 04–90–72–03–03. 14 rooms. Restaurant, pool, tennis court. AE, DC, MC, V.

$$–$$$ ⌖ **Les Romarins.** At this small inn you can gaze across the valley at Gordes while you breakfast on a sheltered terrace in the morning sun. Rooms are clean, well lighted, and feel spacious—ask for either No. 1, in the main building, from whose white-curtained windows you can see forever, or the room with a terrace in the atelier. Warm Oriental rugs, antique furniture around the fireplace in the sitting room, and a pool add to your contentment. ⌗ rte. de Sénanque, 84220, ☎ 04–90–72–12–13, ℻ 04–90–72–13–13. 10 rooms. Pool. AE, MC, V.

Roussillon

❹① 10 km (6 mi) east of Gordes, 45 km (28 mi) east of Avignon.

Roussillon is a picturesque hilltop village with houses built from a distinctive orange and pink stone. This is ocher country, and local quarrying has slashed the cliffs into bizarre shapes. If you are short of time, the view of the village is better than the sights in it.

Bonnieux

❹② 11 km (7 mi) south of Roussillon, 45 km (28 mi) north of Aix-en-Provence.

Bonnieux is one of several wondrous villages perched high on an arrid hilltop in the Vaucluse. Wander around, and then climb to the terrace of the old church (not to be confused with the big 19th-century Église Neuve, in the lower part of the village) for a sweeping view of Gordes, Roussillon, and the ruined château of Lacoste, once home to the notorious marquis de Sade.

Dining and Lodging

$$–$$$ ✕ **Le Fournil.** In a natural grotto lit by candles and torches, this restaurant would be memorable even without its trendy decor (jade and gold cement tiles, mix-and-match jacquard linens) and stylishly presented cuisine. But add adventurous fare (tomato-crisped pigs-feet galette), subtle seafood dishes, an informed wine list, and the option of sitting on the terrace by the fountain, and you have an experience to note in your travel diary. ⊠ *5 pl. Carnot, 84480,* ☎ *04–90–75–83–62. MC, V. Closed Mon. and mid-Nov.–mid-Dec., and mid-Jan.–mid-Feb. No lunch Sat. July–Aug.*

$$–$$$ 🏨 **Hostellerie du Prieuré.** In its tranformation to a hotel, this former 17th-century priory has kept its architectural authenticity. Mme. Caroline Coutaz runs it efficiently and enthusiastically, and she happily gives advice on traveling around the Luberon. Rooms have a mix of antiques and collectables. A few, such as No. 9, have a private balcony; others have a view of the garden, a green oasis where you can dine in summer. The large lounge with leather chairs and sofas is a good place to linger. ⊠ *In the center of the village, 84480,* ☎ *04–90–75–80– 78,* FAX *04–90–75–96–00. 10 rooms. Restaurant. MC, V.*

$$ 🏨 **Le Clos du Buis.** This Gîtes de France bed & breakfast opened in 1997 after a complete restoration. Whitewashed and quarry tiles, lovely new bathrooms, and carefully juxtaposed antiques create a regional look in rooms. Public spaces have scrubbed floorboards, quarry tiles, exposed stone, and a fireplace, and are open to guests around the clock. There's even a pool and a pretty garden, all overlooking the valley from the village center. ⊠ *rue Victor Hugo, 84480,* ☎ *04–90–75– 88–48,* FAX *04–90–75–88–57. 6 rooms. Pool. MC, V.*

AIX-EN-PROVENCE AND THE MEDITERRANEAN COAST

The southeastern part of this area of Provence, on the edge of the Côte d'Azur, is dominated by two major towns: Aix-en-Provence, considered the capital of Provence and the most cultural town in the region; and Marseille, a vibrant port town that combines seediness and fashion, and metropolitain feistiness with classical grace. For a breathtaking experience of the dramatic contrast between the azure Mediterranean sea and the rocky, olive tree–filled hills, take a trip along the coast from Marseille to Toulon and make an excursion to the Iles d'Hyères.

Aix-en-Provence

★ *48 km (29 mi) southeast of Bonnieux, 82 km (51 mi) southeast of Avignon, 176 km (109 mi) west of Nice, 759 km (474 mi) south of Paris.*

Many villages, but few towns, are as well preserved as the traditional capital of Provence: elegant Aix-en-Provence. The Romans were drawn here by the presence of thermal springs; the name Aix originates from Aquae Sextiae (Waters of Sextius) in honor of the consul who reputedly founded the town in 122 BC. Twenty years later, a vast army of Germanic invaders was defeated by General Marius at a neighboring mountain, known ever since as Mont Ste-Victoire. Marius remains a popular local first name to this day.

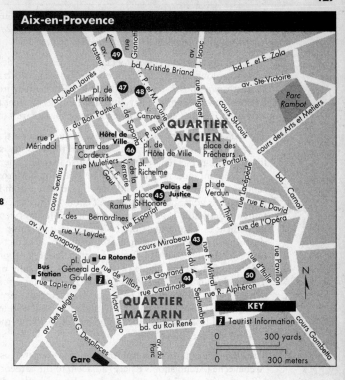

Aix-en-Provence numbers two of France's most creative geniuses among its sons: the post-Impressionist Paul Cézanne (1839–1906), many of whose paintings feature the nearby countryside, especially Mont Ste-Victoire (though Cézanne would not recognize it now, after the forest fire that ravaged its slopes in 1990); and the novelist Émile Zola (1840–1902), who, in several of his works, described Aix ("Plassans") and his boyhood friendship with Cézanne.

43 The celebrated **cours Mirabeau,** flanked with intertwining plane trees, is the town's nerve center, a graceful, lively avenue with the feel of a toned-down, intimate Champs-Élysées. It divides Old Aix into two, with narrow medieval streets to the north and sophisticated, haughty 18th-century mansions to the south. Begin your visit at the west end of cours Mirabeau; the **tourist office** is close by (⊠ 2 pl. du Général-de-Gaulle). Halfway down is the **Fontaine des Neuf Canons** (Fountain of the Nine Cannons), dating from 1691, and farther along is the **Fontaine d'Eau Thermale** (Thermal Water Fountain), built in 1734.

South of cours Mirabeau the streets are straight and rationally planned, flanked with symmetrical mansions imbued with classical elegance. Rue du Quatre-Septembre, three-quarters of the way down cours Mirabeau, **44** leads to the splendid **Fontaine des Quatre Dauphins** (Four Princes Fountain; ⊠ pl. des Quatre Dauphins), where sculpted dolphins play in a fountain erected in 1667.

45 The **Musée d'Histoire Naturelle** (Natural History Museum) is in the sumptuous **Hôtel Boyer d'Éguilles,** erected in 1675 and worth a visit itself for its fine woodwork, sculpture, and murals. The highlight of the museum is its rare collection of dinosaur eggs, accompanied by life-size models of the dinosaurs that roamed locally 65 million years ago. To get here from cours Mirabeau, turn left down rue Clemenceau to place St-Honoré, and then make a left again onto rue Espariat. Also notice on rue Espariat the sculpted facade of the **Hôtel d'Albertas** (built in 1707) at No. 10. ⊠ *6 rue Espariat,* ☎ *04–42–26–23–67.* ⊡ *15 frs.* ⊘ *Mon.–Sat. 10–noon and 2–6, Sun. 2–6.*

46 To get to the **Hôtel de Ville** (City Hall; ⊠ pl. de l'Hôtel de Ville), wend your way down rue Aude, north off rue Esperiat, which is lined with ancient town houses. Pause to admire its 17th-century iron gates and balcony and the 16th-century Tour de l'Horloge (former town belfry) alongside. Then stop for a coffee in one of the square's many cafés.

47 The **Cathédrale St-Sauveur** (⊠ rue de la Roque), just north of the Hôtel de Ville, juxtaposes so many eras of architectural history, so clearly delineated and preserved, it's a survey course in itself. There's a double nave, Romanesque and Gothic side by side, and a Merovingian (5th century) baptistery, its colonnade mostly recovered from Roman temples to other gods. But if that weren't enough, the cathedral also contains a remarkable 15th-century triptych, painted by Nicolas Froment in the heat of inspiration from his travels in Italy. Entitled *Triptyque du Buisson Ardent* (*Burning Bush Triptych*), it depicts King René (duke of Anjou, count of Provence, and titular king of Sicily) and Queen Joan kneeling beside the Virgin. Alas, it's only open now on Tuesdays from 3 to 4 PM, when a sacristan or porter discusses its hidden meanings. Shutters also hide the ornate 16th-century carvings on the cathedral portals, opened by a guide who will also lead you into the tranquil Romanesque cloisters next door to admire the carved pillars and slender colonnades.

48 The highlight of the **Musée des Tapisseries** (Tapestry Museum), in the **Archevêché** (Archbishop's Palace) adjacent to the cathedral, is a magnificent suite of 17 tapestries made in Beauvais that date, like the palace itself, from the 17th and 18th centuries. Nine woven panels illustrate the adventures of Don Quixote. ⊠ *28 pl. des Martyrs-de-la-Résistance,* ☎ *04–42–23–09–91.* ⊡ *14 frs.* ⊘ *Wed.–Mon. 10–noon and 2–5:45.*

49 No major paintings are on display at the **Atelier Paul Cézanne** (Paul Cézanne's Studio), but the great man's studio remains as he left it at the time of his death in 1906, scattered with his pipe, clothing, and other personal possessions, many of which he painted in his still lifes. Cézanne's pioneering work, with its interest in angular forms, paved the way for the Cubist style of the early 20th century. To get to his studio from the town center, take rue de la Roque north to the broad, leafy boulevard that encircles Old Aix. Head up avenue Pasteur, opposite, and then turn right onto avenue Paul-Cézanne. Fans of Cézanne can pick up a map of his "footsteps" at the tourist office: Gold studs in the pavement chronicle where the painter worked, went to school, and got married. ⊠ *9 av. Paul-Cézanne,* ☎ *04–42–21–06–53.* ⊡ *15 frs.* ⊘ *Wed.–Mon. 10–noon and 2–5.*

50 The **Musée Granet,** south of the cours Mirabeau, is named after another of Aix's artistic sons: François Granet (1775–1849), whose works are good examples of the formal, at times sentimental, style of art popular during the first half of the 19th century. Cézanne is also represented here with several oils and watercolors, as are European painters from the 16th to the 19th century and archaeological finds from Egypt, Greece, and the Roman Empire. ⊠ *13 rue Cardinale, pl. St-Jean de Malte,* ☎ *04–42–38–14–70.* ⊡ *18 frs.* ⊘ *Wed.–Mon. 10–noon and 2–6.*

Dining and Lodging

$$$ ✕ **Le Clos de la Violette.** Aix's best restaurant is in a residential dis-
★ trict north of the old town. Chef Jean-Marc Banzo uses local ingredients in his nouvelle and traditional recipes, such as *saumon vapeur*

(aromatic steamed salmon) and oyster and calamari salad. Enjoy his fine dishes under the chestnut trees or in the airy pink-and-blue dining room. The moderately priced weekday lunch menu is well worth the trek. ⊠ *10 av. de la Violette,* ☎ *04–42–23–30–71. Jacket required. AE, MC, V. Closed Sun., early Nov., and most of Mar. No lunch Mon.*

$$ ✕ **Les Bacchanales.** This small, intimate establishment in the old quarter of Aix is worth tracking down. From the 130-franc menu, sample the *marbré de lapereau* (stuffed baby rabbit) or the salmon with a light tomato sauce. For dessert, the *tarte aux pommes soufflées* (apple tart soufflé) is particularly good. ⊠ *10 rue de la Couronne,* ☎ *04–42–27–21–06. MC, V. Closed Wed. No lunch Thurs.*

$ ✕ **Le Bistro Latin.** Whether you sit up or downstairs, the tables are tight, but the feel is friendly. The 98-franc *menu du marché* (based on what the chef bought from the market that day) might include excellent *magret de canard* (duck) in a light cream sauce or flavorful lamb casserole. For an appetizer, hope that the tiny morsels of lamb in puff pastry showered in beurre blanc are available. ⊠ *18 rue de la Couronne,* ☎ *04–42–38–22–88. MC, V. Closed Sun. No lunch Mon.*

$$$ ✕⌂ **Relais Ste-Victoire.** The main reason to stay at this country inn is to dine on chef Jugy-Berges's modern Provençal cooking—eggs poached with truffles, delicately flavored roast partridge, and *tarte au châtaigne* (chestnut tart). (The restaurant is closed Sunday dinner and Monday.) Rooms are more than adequate: Tile floors shine, fabrics cover the walls, and glass doors lead onto private balconies. But the single beds joined by one bedspread can slip apart and romantics end up on the floor. ⊠ *From Aix, take N7 toward Nice; then follow signs for Bearecueil (15 km/9 mi east of Aix), 13100 Beaurecueil ,* ☎ *04–42–66–94–98,* FAX *04–42–66–85–96. 10 rooms. Restaurant, pool. AE, DC, MC, V. Closed 1st wk Jan., 1 wk Feb., and 1 wk Nov. (call in advance for exact dates).*

$$$$ ⌂ **Le Pigonnet.** A 10-minute walk from the cours Mirabeau takes you to this refined, family-run hotel. Here in the wonderful gardens, Cézanne caught distant Mont Ste-Victoire on canvas. The high-ceilinged rooms are furnished with family heirlooms and Provençal armoires; the slightly higher-priced ones look out over the garden. La Riviera restaurant is happily more traditional than nouvelle; local meats and game are served, as well as fish from the Mediterranean. ⊠ *5 av. du Pigonnet, 13090,* ☎ *04–42–59–02–90,* FAX *04–42–59–47–77. 53 rooms. Restaurant, pool, meeting rooms. AE, DC, MC, V.*

$$$$ ⌂ **Villa Gallici.** On a slight rise just outside town, this Relais & Châteaux
★ hotel breathes country fragrance. The terrace and the garden with swimming pool are shaded by hundred-year-old cypress trees. Rooms have separate sitting areas; fabric with green and rust chinoiserie covers the walls and the floor-to-ceiling windows. In the restaurant (open dinner only; closed Monday, November–April), light, unpretentious offerings from Le Clos de la Violette next door are served. More elaborate meals are served at the restaurant itself (closed Sunday). ⊠ *av. de la Violette, 13100,* ☎ *04–42–23–29–23,* FAX *04–42–96–30–45. 22 rooms, 4 suites. Restaurant, pool. AE, DC, MC, V.*

$$–$$$ ⌂ **Nègre-Coste.** A cours Mirabeau location makes this hotel both a convenient and atmospheric choice. The elegant 18th-century town house features luxurious Old World decor in public areas, but rooms—with all-weather carpet, scarred beds, and linoleum bathrooms—need updating. The view of cours Mirabeau and the sunlight make the front rooms worth the extra bit of noise (kept to a minimum by double-glazed windows). This place is very popular, so make reservations far in advance. ⊠ *33 cours Mirabeau, 13100,* ☎ *04–42–27–74–22,* FAX *04–42–26–80–93. 37 rooms. AE, DC, MC, V.*

$–$$ 🖼 **Quatre Dauphins.** In the quiet old neighborhood below the cours
★   Mirabeau, this modest but impeccable hotel offers pretty, comfortable
little rooms spruced up with *boutis* (Provençal quilts), quarry tiles, jute,
and painted furniture. The top floor rooms are charming, but can be
hot in summer (they don't have air-conditioning). But the house-proud
yet unassuming owner-host does his best to please. ⊠ *55 rue Roux
Alphéran, 13100,* ☎ *04–42–38–16–39,* ꜰᴀx *04–42–38–60–19. 12
rooms. MC, V.*

Nightlife and the Arts

If you love roulette and blackjack, head to the **Casino Municipal d'Aix
Thermal** (⊠ 2 bis av. Napoléon-Bonaparte, ☎ 04–42–26–30–33), open
from 3 PM to 2 AM. **Le Scat Club** (⊠ 11 rue de la Verrerie, ☎ 04–42–
23–00–23) is a good spot for jazz.

Opera and classical concerts are performed throughout the year at the
18th-century **Théâtre Municipal** (⊠ 17 rue de l'Opéra, ☎ 04–42–38–
44–71). The **Festival International des Arts et Musique,** with first-class
opera, symphonic concerts, and chamber music, flourishes from mid-
July to mid-August; its principal venue is the Théâtre de l'Archevêché
(⊠ pl. des Martyrs-de-la-Résistance). The **Festival International de
Danse** (International Dance Festival; ⊠ Espace Gambetta, cours Gambetta, ☎ 04–42–96–05–01), known as Danse à Aix, features modern and jazz dance in July. Tickets go on sale two weeks before the show
and can be purchased at the tourist office. In August, there's a **Summer Jazz Festival.**

Outdoor Activities and Sports

The tourist office has information on hiking or bicycling up **Mont Ste-
Victoire. Golf International du Château de l'Arc** (⊠ Off D6, in Fuveau,
20 km/32 mi from Aix, ☎ 04–42–53–28–38) is an 18-hole course
open to the public. **Sellerie Lou Mazet** (⊠ off N113, in Lançon-de-
Provence, 27 km/17 mi from Aix , ☎ 04–90–42–89–38) arranges
horseback excursions in the Camargue for 250 to 400 francs a day.

Shopping

Deliciously fragrant soaps and *calissons d'Aix,* ingeniously sculpted
marzipan figures, are two specialties of Aix. **Makaire** (⊠ 2 rue Thiers,
near pl. du Palais, ☎ 04–42–38–19–63) has very nice stationery, fountain pens, and books. One thousand different models of *santons,* the
colorful, painted clay figures traditionally placed around a Christmas
crib, can be found at **Santons Fouque** (⊠ 65 cours Gambetta). **Riederer**
(⊠ 6 rue Thiers, ☎ 04–42–38–19–69) makes irresistible chocolates
and pastries. An **antiques market** is held on Tuesday, Thursday, and
Saturday mornings on place de Verdun. Lovely blooms of all sorts are
found at the **flower market** (⊠ pl. de l'Hôtel-de-Ville) on Tuesday, Thursday, and Saturday mornings. A **produce market** takes place on place
Richel every morning and place des Prêcheurs on Tuesday, Thursday,
and Saturday mornings.

Marseille

*31 km (19 mi) south of Aix-en-Provence, 188 km (117 mi) west of Nice,
772 km (483 mi) south of Paris.*

Marseille, the Mediterranean's largest port, is not crowded with tourist
goodies, nor is its reputation as a big, dirty city entirely unjustified,
but it still has more going for it than many realize: a craggy mountain
hinterland that provides a spectacular backdrop, superb coastal views
of nearby islands, and the sights and smells of a Mediterranean melt-
ing pot where different peoples have mingled for centuries—ever since
the Phocaean Greeks invaded in around 600 BC. The most recent im-

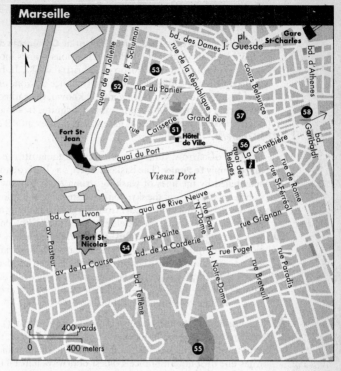

Marseille

migrants come from North Africa. The large city is divided into 16 *arrondissements* (districts). An efficient bus and métro system can get you around. To get into town from the airport, 25 km (16 mi) away, take the 44-franc shuttle bus, or a taxi for about 230 francs.

At the heart of Marseille is the **Vieux Port** (Old Harbor), an intimate, picturesque harbor packed with fishing boats and pleasure craft, and the sizable, ugly industrial docks next to it. For 5 francs round-trip or 3 francs one-way you can cross the harbor on a ferry that runs every few minutes. Restaurants line the quays, where the owners serve gleaming fresh sardines. The Marseillais can be an irascible lot: Louis XIV built the Fort St-Nicolas, at the entry of the Vieux Port, with the guns facing inland to keep the citizens in order. The famous, chaotic Marseille **fish market** is held here every day.

A short way down the quay (as you look out to sea) is the elegant 17th-century **Hôtel de Ville** (Town Hall).

Running east from the Vieux Port is the legendary **La Canebière**—known as the "Can O' Beer" to sailors from around the world—where stately mansions recall faded glory. Many an operetta has been inspired by the avenue, and it was still talked about by Legionnaires in the late 1950s, though by then what was left of the action could only be found in the Quartier de Panier. The avenue has been on the decline in recent years, but cafés and restaurants continue to provide an upbeat pulse. The **tourist office** is at No. 4.

51 Costumes, engravings, and paintings depicting 18th-century Marseille are on display at the **Musée du Vieux Marseille** (Museum of Old Marseille), housed in the Maison Diamantée, a 16th-century mansion with an elaborate interior staircase just behind the town hall. After renovations, the museum is scheduled to be reopened by early 1999. ⊠ *rue* *de la Prison,* ☎ *04–91–55–10–19.* 🎟 *12 frs.* ◷ *Tues.–Sun. 11–6 in summer, 10–5 in winter.*

52 Marseille's pompous, striped neo-Byzantine **Cathédrale de la Major** is a few blocks from the Vieux Port. Its various domes look utterly incongruous against the backdrop of industrial docks. If, however, you climb up rue du Panier behind the city police station, or *archevêché* (archbishop's seat), as it is irreverently known, the cathedral's silhouette, facing out over the Mediterranean, acquires fresh significance as a symbol of Marseille's role as gateway to the Levant. ✉ *esplanade de la Tourette.*

The grid of narrow, tumbledown streets leading off rue du Panier is called simply **Le Panier** (The Basket). There's a claustrophobic feel here, heightened by the lines of washing strung from window to window, sometimes blotting out the sky; you can taste some of the dowdy, Naples-like essence of Marseille. Apart from the colorful, sleazy ambience, Le Panier is worth visiting for the elegantly restored 17th-century hospice

53 now housing a museum, the **Musée de la Vieille-Charité** (Ancient Hospice Museum). Excellent art exhibitions are held here, and the architecture—a shallow-domed chapel in the middle of an arcaded, three-story courtyard—displays subtlety lacking in the cathedral. ✉ *2 rue de la Charité,* ☎ *04–91–14–58–80.* 🎟 *10 frs (20 frs for exhibitions).* ◷ *Tues.–Sun. 11–6 in summer, 10–5 in winter.*

54 The **Basilique St-Victor,** on the south side of the Vieux Port, stands in the shadow of the Fort St-Nicolas (which can't be visited). With its powerful tower and thick-set walls, the basilica itself resembles a fortress; it has one of southern France's oldest doorways (circa 1140), a 13th-century nave, and a 14th-century chancel and transept. Downstairs, you'll find the murky 5th-century underground crypt, with its collection of ancient sarcophagi. ✉ *rue Sainte.* 🎟 *Crypt 10 frs.* ◷ *Daily 8–6.*

A brisk 1-km (½-mi) walk up boulevard Tellène from the Vieux Port, followed by a trudge up a steep flight of steps, takes you to the foot

55 of **Notre-Dame de la Garde.** This church, a flashy 19th-century cousin of the Sacré-Coeur in Paris and Fourvière in Lyon, features a similar hilltop location. The expansive view stretches from the hinterland mountains to the sea via the Cité Radieuse, a controversial 1950s housing project by architect Le Corbusier. The church's interior is generously endowed with bombastic murals, mosaics, and marble. At the top of the tower, the great gilded statue of the Virgin stands sentinel over the Vieux Port, 500 ft below. If you are not up to the hike, Bus 60 from the port is an easy way up. ✉ *pl. du Colonel-Edon,* ☎ *04–91–13–40–80.* ◷ *Daily 7 AM–8 PM in summer, 7–7 in winter.*

56 The **Musée de la Marine** (Nautical Museum) is housed in the big, white **Palais de la Bourse** (Stock Exchange). It gives a history of the port and has an interesting display of model ships. ✉ *Palais de la Bourse, La Canebière,* ☎ *04–91–39–33–33.* 🎟 *10 frs.* ◷ *Daily 10–6.*

57 The **Jardin des Vestiges** (Garden of the Remains), a public park behind the Palais de Bourse, contains the excavated ruins of Greek and Roman fortifications and foundations. Here you will find the little **Musée d'Histoire de Marseille** (Marseille History Museum), featuring exhibits related to the town's history. One of the highlights is a 60-ft Roman boat. ✉ *Centre Bourse,* ☎ *04–91–90–42–22.* 🎟 *15 frs.* ◷ *Mon.–Sat. noon–7.*

58 The **Musée des Beaux-Arts** (Fine Arts Museum), in the imposing **Palais Longchamp**, was built in 1860 by Henri Espérandieu (1829–74), the architect of Notre-Dame de la Garde (☞ *above*). The museum's collection of paintings and sculptures includes works by 18th-century Italian artist Giovanni Battista Tiepolo, Rubens, and French caricaturist and painter Honoré Daumier. ⊠ *bd. Longchamp,* ☎ *04–91–14–59–30.* ▨ *10 frs.* ♡ *Tues.–Sun. 11–6 in summer, 10–5 in winter.*

Marseille is no seaside resort, but a scenic 5-km (3-mi) coast road—**corniche du Président-J.-F.-Kennedy**—links the Vieux Port to the newly created Prado beaches in the swanky parts of southern Marseille. There are breathtaking views across the sea toward the rocky Iles de Frioul (Frioul Islands), which can be visited by boat.

Ferries leave the Vieux Port hourly in summer and frequently in winter to visit the Château d'If and the Frioul Islands; the trip takes 90 minutes and the cost is 45 francs to Château d'If or Frioul and 70 francs to both. The very name of **Château d'If,** the castle where political prisoners were held captive down the ages, speaks of romance and derring-do. Alexandre Dumas condemned his fictional hero the Count of Monte Cristo to be shut up in a cell here, before the wily count made his celebrated escape through a hole in the wall. Contrary to legend, the man in the iron mask, whose cell is still being shown, was not actually imprisoned here. ☎ *04–91–59–02–30.* ▨ *25 frs.* ♡ *Apr.–Sept., daily 9–7; Oct.–Mar., Tues.–Sun. 9–5:30.*

Dining and Lodging

$$$ ✕ **Chez Fonfon.** Tucked into a story-book, film-set of a tiny fishing port, this landmark still draws the Marseillais for the best bouillabaisse in the world. Past diners lured by the top-quality seafood have included John Wayne and Nikita Khrushchev. You'll also find rock fish soup, lobster grilled over a wood fire, and dorade in a rock-salt crust. Although the owner's son, Alexandre Pinna, has taken over for the late, great chef Fonfon, the cachet remains. ⊠ *140 rue du Vallon des Auffes,* ☎ *04–91–52–14–38. Reservations essential. AE, DC, MC, V. Closed 2 wks in Jan. No dinner Sun.*

$$ ✕ **Dar Djerba.** This is one of the best North African restaurants scattered throughout Marseille, specializing in couscous of all kinds (with lamb, chicken, or even quail) as well as Arab coffees and pastries. ⊠ *15 cours Julien,* ☎ *04–91–48–55–36. Reservations essential in summer. DC, MC, V.*

$$ ✕ **Les Galinettes/Chez Madie.** Of the dozens of seafood restaurants that
★ actively court you as you stroll the horseshoe of the Vieux Port, this is one of the best: Seated under the shaded arcade before a white and blue panorama of boats, loyals choose from a fish-of-the-day menu selected from the stands just steps away. Bouillabaisse is a ceremony that requires advance ordering. ⊠ *138 quai du Port,* ☎ *04–91–90–40–87. AE, DC, MC, V. Closed Mon. and most of Aug. No dinner Sun.*

$ ✕ **Côté Grill.** On this delightful square one block south of the Vieux Port, in Le Quartier de l'Arsenal, are several reasonably priced restaurants (more expensive and more touristy ones are on the side streets off the square); Côté Grill is the best. At lunch, for 59 francs you can select from a marvelous buffet of appetizers—enough to constitute a meal in itself—and a choice of three main courses, such as fish, entrecôte, or pasta. Or opt for the 69-franc buffet menu. ⊠ *pl. Thiars,* ☎ *04–91–55–02–63. MC, V.*

$$$ ✕▥ **Le Petit Nice.** Only the smallest of signs marks the turnoff from
★ the corniche to the rocky promontory 1½ km (1 mi) from the Vieux Port, where you'll find this extraordinarily glamourous hideway, which out-Riviera's any hotel in Nice. The chef-owner is renowned for his regional recipes, with a lighter, creative touch, served in the many-windowed dining room. The menu focuses on seafood like grilled *coquilles St-Jacques* (scallops) with baby artichokes, though game is

available in late fall. (The restaurant is closed Saturday lunch and Sunday, off-season.) Rooms have smooth stone floors; rich, rare woods; and almost no doors or walls. Most have sea views. ⊠ *Anse de Maldormé, corniche J.-F.-Kennedy, 13007,* ☎ *04–91–59–25–92,* 𝖥𝖠𝖷 *04–91–59–28–08. 15 rooms. Restaurant, pool. AE, DC, MC, V.*

$$$ ✕🏨 **Sofitel.** Mainly because of its idyllic views, the Sofitel has more appeal than most other modern chain hotels. Rooms with a balcony are more expensive, but the pleasure of breakfast in the morning sunshine is worth the splurge. The top-floor restaurant, Les Trois Forts, has stunning panoramic views and delicious Provençal fare; the red mullet with pepper is superb. ⊠ *36 bd. Charles-Livon, 13007,* ☎ *04–91–15–59–00,* 𝖥𝖠𝖷 *04–91–15–59–50. 130 rooms, 3 suites. Restaurant, pool. AE, DC, MC, V.*

$$$ 🏨 **Mercure Beauvau Vieux Port.** Charming Old World opulence char-
★   acterizes this hotel in a totally modernized 200-year-old coaching inn on the Vieux Port. Wood paneling, fine paintings, genuine antique furniture, and exceptional service enhance a stay here. The best rooms look out onto the port. ⊠ *4 rue Beauvau, 13001,* ☎ *04–91–54–91–00, 800/MERCURE in the U.S., 0171/621–1962 in the U.K.;* 𝖥𝖠𝖷 *04–91–54–15–76. 71 rooms. Bar, breakfast room. AE, DC, MC, V.*

$–$$ 🏨 **Alize.** On the Vieux Port, with its front rooms taking in postcard views, this straightforward lodging was recently modernized to include tight double-glazed windows, slick modular baths, and a laminate-and-all-weather-carpet look. But public spaces have exposed stone and preserved details, and a glass elevator whisks you to your floor. Overall, it's an excellent value and location for the price range. ⊠ *35 quai des Belges, 13001,* ☎ *04–91–33–66–97,* 𝖥𝖠𝖷 *04–91–54–80–06. 37 rooms. Air-conditioning. AE, DC, MC, V.*

Nightlife and the Arts

Marseille's nightlife lasts into the wee hours of the morning. The under-40 set be-bops at the temple of jazz, **L'Orleans** (⊠ 1 quai de Rive Neuve, ☎ 04–91–33–87–27). **Le Pelle Mele** (⊠ 45 pl. aux Huiles, ☎ 04–91–54–85–26) has a piano bar and, on special nights, jazz combos. **Le Trolleybus** (⊠ 24 quai de Rive Neuve, ☎ 04–91–54–30–45) has concerts, three dance "grottoes," and the most alternative feel of all the clubs. In July, the large **Festival de Marseille** celebrates the city's rich Mediterranean heritage with concerts and exhibits.

Outdoor Activities and Sports

Though Marseille is not known for its seashore, the city does have numerous beaches—most are shingle, whereas some are made of sand and grass. The best, however, are found in *Les Calanques,* the picturesque coves along the coastline between Marseille and Cassis (☞ *below*). Bus 83 or Bus 19 takes you to the sandy **Plages de Prado. Plage des Catalans,** on Anse des Catalans in the city area, is the most popular beach, but there is an admission charge. To get there, take Bus 83 or Line 1 on the métro from the Vieux Port. You can also find your own little beach on the **Iles de Frioul,** reached from the Château d'If. Sailboats can be rented from **Midi Nautisme** (⊠ 13 pl. aux Huiles, ☎ 04–91–54–86–09).

Shopping

Leading south from La Canebière, busy rue Paradis, rue St-Ferréol, and rue de Rome are good shopping streets. **Four des Navettes** (⊠ 136 rue Sainte, ☎ 04–91–33–32–12), up the street from the basilica, is a bakery where orange-spice, shuttle-shape *navette* loaves have been made for more than 200 years.

Aubagne

 16 km (10 mi) east of Marseille, 36 km (22 mi) south of Aix-en-Provence.

Aubagne is proud of its native son, the dramatist, filmmaker, and chronicler of all things Provençal, Marcel Pagnol, best known as author of *Jean de Florette* and *Manon des Sources*. In this easy-going, plane-tree shaded market town, you can spend the morning comparing asparagus at the farmers' stands (produce with Aubagne labels are pesticide-free), digging through used Pagnol books and collectibles in the old town, or studying the miniature dioramas of scenes from Pagnol stories at Le Monde de Marcel Pagnol. The characters are all *santons* (miniature clay figures), which Aubagne also claims as a local product; the craft, originally from Marseille, focused here when artisans moved inland to benefit from local clay.

Aubagne is also the headquarters of the French Foreign Legion (to get there, take a left off D2 onto D44A just before Aubagne). The legion was created in 1831 and accepts recruits from all nations, no questions asked. The discipline and camaraderie instilled among its motley team of adventurers, criminals, and mercenaries has helped the legion forge a reputation for exceptional valor—a reputation romanticized by songs and films in which sweaty deeds of heroism are performed under the desert sun. The **Musée du Képi Blanc,** named after the distinctive white caps of the *légionnaires,* does its best to polish the image by way of medals, uniforms, weapons, and photographs. ✉ *Caserne Viénot,* ☎ *04–42–03–03–20.* 🎟 *Free.* ☉ *June–Sept., Tues.–Sun. 9–noon and 2–5; Oct.–May, Wed. and weekends 9–noon.*

Cassis

 11 km (7 mi) south of Aubagne, 30 km (19 mi) east of Marseille, 42 km (26 mi) west of Toulon.

Cafés, restaurants, and seafood shops cluster around the harbor and three beaches in the beautifully situated fishing village of Cassis, at the foot of Europe's highest cliff, the 1,300-ft Cap Canaille. Boats leave the harbor from quai St-Pierre to the neighboring **calanques,** the lovely coves in long creeks that weave their way between towering white-stone cliffs. The most spectacular and the farthest of the three calanques visited by boat is **En-Vau.** Take the boat there and walk back along the scenic footpath.

Dining and Lodging

\$\$\$ ✕🏠 **Jardin d'Emile.** Tucked back from the waterfront under quarried
★ cliffs and massive parasol pines, this chic yet homey inn takes in views of the cape from the restaurant and half the rooms. But view or not, rooms are intimate and welcoming, with rubbed-chalk walls, quilts, scrubbed pine, weathered stone, Salerne tiles, and dimmers to enhance the honeymoon atmosphere. The restaurant is as atmopheric, on a permanant sheltered garden terrace surrounded by greenery and, by night, the illuminated cliffs. Regional specialties with a cosmopolitan twist—such as harbor-fresh tuna grilled with soy—are served on local pottery. ✉ *Plage du Bestouan, 13260,* ☎ *04–42–01–80–55,* 🖷 *04–42–01–80–70. 7 rooms. Restaurant. AE, DC, MC, V.*

En Route   From Cassis, a daring clifftop road runs along the top of Cap Canaille to the shipbuilding base of **La Ciotat,** 13 km (8 mi) away. From La Ciotat, follow D559 for 19 km (12 mi), through the popular beach resort and wine center Bandol, to **Sanary,** whose old streets and picturesque seafront invite exploration.

Six-Fours-les-Plages

⑥₁   *28 km (17 mi) east of Cassis, 58 km (36 mi) east of Marseille.*

Six-Fours-les-Plages, on the dramatic Cap Sicié peninsula, is a sprawling town of limited interest, though three nearby sites deserve a visit. The **Fort of Six-Fours,** at the top of a steep hill, is a military base closed to the public, but the views from here across the Bay of Toulon are stupendous; follow the signs from town. The former parish church of **St-Pierre,** near the fort, features a Romanesque nave and a rich medieval altarpiece by Louis Bréa. Archaeological digs to the right of the entrance have revealed Roman walls on the site.

Just north of Six-Fours (take D63 and turn left following signs marked MONUMENT HISTORIQUE) is the small stone chapel of **Notre-Dame de Pépiole,** hemmed in by pines and cypresses. It is one of the oldest Christian buildings in France, dating from the 5th century. The simple interior has survived the years in remarkably good shape, although the colorful stained glass that fills the tiny windows is modern—composed mainly of broken bottles! ☺ *Most afternoons.*

En Route   A right on D616, around the **Cap Sicié** (Cape Sicié), will take you to more fine panoramas and a colossal view across the Bay of Toulon. For another scenic route, take D11 to Ollioules, 5 km (3 mi); then follow N8 (direction Le Beausset) through a 5-km (3-mi) route that twists its scenic way beneath the awesome chalky rock faces of the spectacular **Gorge d'Ollioules.** A right on D462 will take you to the village of **Evenos,** a patchwork of inhabited and ruined houses dominated by an abandoned cliff-top castle.

Toulon

⑥₂   *16 km (10 mi) east of Six-Fours, 42 km (26 mi) east of Cassis, 64 km (40 mi) east of Marseille.*

Toulon is France's leading Mediterranean naval base. Leave your car in the underground parking lot at place de la Liberté, head along boulevard de Strasbourg, and turn right after the theater into rue Berthelot. It leads into the pedestrian-only streets that constitutes the heart of old Toulon. Shops and colorful stalls make it an attractive area by day, but it's best avoided at night.

Avenue de la République, an ugly array of concrete apartment blocks, runs parallel to the waterfront, where yachts and pleasure boats—some available for trips to the Iles d'Hyères or around the bay—add bright splashes of color. At the western edge of the quay is the **Musée Naval** (Naval Museum), with large models of ships, figureheads, paintings, and other items related to Toulon's maritime history. ⊠ *pl. Monsenergue,* ☎ *04–94–02–02–01.* ☐ *22 frs.* ☺ *Wed.–Mon. 9–noon and 2–5.*

Mighty hills surround Toulon. **Mont Faron,** at 1,600 ft, is the highest of all. Either drive to the top, taking the circular route du Faron in either direction, or make the six-minute ascent by cable car from boulevard de l'Amiral Jean-Vence. ☎ *04–94–92–68–25.* ☐ *37 frs.* ☺ *Daily 9:15–noon and 2:15–6; closed Mon. and Sept.–May.*

Dining

$ ✕ **La Ferme.** Good-value menus and a cozy setting make this little home-style eatery a sensible choice for lunch. The 85-franc three-course menu usually has a fish terrine or mussels appetizer, followed by pork, steak, or a fillet of sole, and ends with a dessert. ⊠ *6 pl. Louis-Blanc,* ☎ *04–94–42–69–77. MC, V. Closed Sun. and Aug.*

Outdoor Activities and Sports

On a sunny day, set out for a game at **Golf de Valcros** (⊠ La Londe–Les Maures, 37 km/23 mi east of Toulouse off of N98, ☎ 04–94–66–81–02). Sailboats and sail boards can be rented from **Wanako Centre du Nautisme** (⊠ av. du Dr-Robin, Hyères, 19 km/12 mi east of Toulouse, ☎ 04–94–57–77–20), starting at 300 francs a day.

Shopping

The celebrated **fish, fruit, and household-goods market** (⊠ cours Lafayette) takes place near the harbor Monday through Saturday mornings.

Iles d'Hyères

63 *Boats leave frequently from La Tour-Fondue, at the tip of the narrow Giens peninsula (every ½ hour in July and Aug., every 60 or 90 mins at other times) for the 20-minute trip to Ile de Porquerolles. Boats for Ile de Port-Cros and Ile du Levant leave from Hyères-Plages and, farther along, from Port-de-Miramar and Le Lavandou.*

Iles d'Hyères is an archipelago that spans some 32 km (20 mi) and consists of three main islands—**Porquerolles, Port-Cros,** and **Le Levant.** The boat trip from La Tour-Fondue to Ile de Porquerolles, the largest island, takes 20 minutes and costs 80 francs round-trip. Should you leave from Le Lavandou, the 30-minute round-trip to Levant or to Port-Cros is 103 francs and the 50-minute round-trip to Porquerolles is 137 francs. The island's village has several small hotels and restaurants, but the main reason to come here is to escape the modern world. Filmmakers love the island and use it as a handy base for shooting tropical or South Sea Island–type scenery. You can stroll across it, from the harbor to *le phare* (the lighthouse), in about 90 minutes, or head east among luxuriant flowers and thick woods. Ile de Port-Cros, a national park, has delightful, well-marked hiking trails. Ile du Levant is long and rocky and much less interesting; the French Navy owns part of it, and most of the rest is a nudist camp.

Dining and Lodging

$$$ ✕⌂ **Mas du Langoustier.** Amid stunningly lush terrain at the westernmost
★ point of Ile de Porquerolles, 3 km (2 mi) from the harbor, this luxurious hideout is a popular getaway for the yacht and helicopter set, and a standard day-trip from high-season St-Tropez. Owner Mme. Richard will pick you up at the port; she's the granddaughter of the lucky woman who was given this island as a wedding gift. Choose between big new California-style modern rooms and cosseted old-style rooms in the original building. Chef Joël Guillet creates inspired southern cuisine, to be accompanied by the rare island rosé. ⊠ *Pointe du Langoustier, 83400 Ile de Porquerolles,* ☎ *04–94–58–30–09,* ℻ *04–94–58–36–02. 51 rooms. Restaurant, tennis court, beach, billiards. AE, DC, MC, V. Closed Nov.–Apr.*

PROVENCE A TO Z

Arriving and Departing

By Car

A6/A7 (a toll road) from Paris, known as the Autoroute du Soleil—the Highway of the Sun—takes you straight to Provence, whereupon it divides at Orange, 659 km (412 mi) from Paris; the trip can be done in a fast five hours or so.

By Plane

Marseille and Montpellier are served by frequent flights from Paris and London, and daily flights from Paris arrive at the smaller airport at Nîmes, which serves Arles and the Camargue (the trip takes about an hour). There are direct flights in the summer from the United States to Nice, 160 km (100 mi) from Aix-en-Provence.

By Train

The high-speed TGV (*Trains à Grande Vitesse*) goes from Paris (Gare de Lyon) to Avignon in less than four hours. Add another hour for Marseille, Nîmes, and Montpellier. For other destinations you must change to local trains.

Getting Around

By Bicycle

Bikes can be rented from the train stations in Aix-en-Provence, Arles, Avignon, Marseille, Montpellier, Nîmes, and Orange for a cost of about 40 francs per day. Contact the **Comité Départemental de Cyclotourisme** (⊠ les Passadoires, 84420 Piolenc) for a list of scenic bike routes in Provence.

By Bus

A moderately good network of bus services links places not served, or badly served, by train. If you plan to explore Provence by bus, Avignon, Marseille, Aix-en-Provence, and Arles are good bases. Avignon is also where excursion bus tours and boat trips down the Rhône start.

By Car

After route A7 divides at Orange, A9 heads west to Nîmes and Montpellier (765 km/475 mi from Paris), and continues into the Pyrénées and across the Spanish border. Route A7 continues southeast from Orange to Marseille on the coast (1,100 km/680 mi from Paris), while A8 goes to Aix-en-Provence (with a spur to Toulon) and then to the Riviera and Italy.

By Train

After the main line of the TGV divides at Avignon, the westbound link of the TGV heads to Nîmes, Montpellier (less than five hours from Paris by TGV), and points west. The southeast-bound link of the TGV takes in Marseille (also under five hours from Paris by TGV), Toulon, and the Riviera. There are also frequent, daily, local trains to other towns in the region from these main TGV stops.

Contacts and Resources

Car Rental

Avis (⊠ Gare SNCF, av. Paulin Talbot, Arles, ☎ 04–90–96–82–42; ⊠ 1800 av. Maréchal Juin, Nîmes, ☎ 04–66–29–05–33; ⊠ 11 cours Gambetta, Aix-en-Provence, ☎ 04–42–21–64–16; ⊠ 267 bd. National, Marseille, ☎ 04–91–50–70–11). **Budget** (⊠ 40 bd. de Plombières, Marseille, ☎ 04–91–64–40–03; ⊠ Marignane Airport, Marseille, ☎ 04–42–14–24–55). **Europcar** (⊠ 2 bis av. Victor-Hugo, Arles, ☎ 04–90–93–23–24; ⊠ 27 av. St-Ruf, Avignon, ☎ 04–90–82–49–85; ⊠ 68 cours Aristide Briand, Orange, ☎ 04–90–51–67–53; ⊠ Airport, Montpellier, ☎ 04–67–99–82–00). **Hertz** (⊠ Parking des Gares, 18 rue Jules-Ferry, Montpellier, ☎ 04–67–58–65–18; ⊠ 5 bd. de Prague, Nîmes, ☎ 04–66–76–25–91; ⊠ Marignane Airport, Marseille, ☎ 04–42–14–32–70).

Guided Tours

The regional tourist offices' "52 Week" program pools 52 tours organized by various agencies, allowing you to choose from myriad tours throughout the year, including wine tasting, sailing, hang gliding, golfing, gastronomy, and cultural exploration (☞ Visitor Information, *below*). In addition, local tourist offices arrange many tours, ranging from one-hour guided walks to excursions that take a week or longer by bus, bicycle, horseback, or foot. The **Aix-en-Provence Office du Tourisme** (⊠ 2 pl. du Général-de-Gaulle, ☎ 04–42–16–11–61) gives city tours in English, July–September. The **Arles Office du Tourisme** (⊠ 35 pl. de la République, ☎ 04–90–18–41–22) employs 15 guide-lecturers who run tours of the town and region. The **Comité Départemental du Tourisme** (⊠ 13 roux de Brignoles, 13006 Marseille, ☎ 04–91–13–84–13) arranges bus tours in the area. **Loisirs-Acceuil** (⊠ Domaine de Vergon, 13370 Mallemort, ☎ 04–90–59–49–39) runs bus tours of the region. **S.A.A.F.** (⊠ 110 bd. des Dames, 13002 Marseille, ☎ 04–91–91–10–91) organizes a two-day tour of Marseille and Avignon.

The **Association de Tourisme Équestre** (⊠ chemin St-Julien, 30133 Les Angles, ☎ 04–90–25–38–91) can give you information about horseback riding tours. **Cheval Nomade** (⊠ col du Pointu, Bonnieux, ☎ 04–90–74–40–48) specializes in tours by horseback. The **Marseille Office Municipal du Tourisme** features a six-day guided tour on horseback.

Outdoor Activities and Sports

For a list of hiking trails and outfitters, contact the **Comité Départemental de la Randonnée Pédestre** (⊠ 307 av. Foch, Orange, ☎ 04–90–51–14–86). The **Comité Régional du Tourisme du Languedoc-Roussillon** (☞ *below*) publishes a brochure on golf courses in the area and sells a pass good for 14 different courses.

For information about kayaking down the Sorgue River contact **Kayak Vert** (⊠ 84800, Fontaine de Vaucluse, ☎ 04–90–20–35–44). For information about kayaking through the Camargue and down the Petit Rhône, contact **Kayak Vert Camargue** (⊠ Mas de Baumelle, 13460, Stes-Maries-de-la-Mer, ☎ 04–09–56–06–47).

Travel Agencies

Midi-Libre Voyages (⊠ 40 bd. Victor-Hugo, Nîmes, ☎ 04–66–67–45–34). **Wagons-Lits** (⊠ 2 rue Olivier, Avignon, ☎ 04–90–82–20–56; ⊠ 225 av. du Prado, Marseille, ☎ 04–91–79–30–80; ⊠ 3 rue des Cordeliers, Aix-en-Provence, ☎ 04–42–96–31–88).

Visitor Information

Provence's regional tourist offices accept written inquiries only. The **Comité Régional du Tourisme du Languedoc-Roussillon** (⊠ 20 rue de la République, 34000 Montpellier, ☎ 04–67–22–81–00) provides information on all towns west of the Rhône River. The remainder of towns covered in this chapter are handled by the **Comité Régional du Tourisme de Provence-Alpes-Côte d'Azur** (⊠ 13 roux de Brignoles, 13006 Marseille, ☎ 04–91–13–84–13) and the **Chambre Départementale de Tourisme de Vaucluse** (⊠ la Balance, pl. Campana, B.P. 147, 84008 Avignon, ☎ 04–90–86–43–42).

Local tourist offices for major towns covered in this chapter are as follows: **Aix-en-Provence** (⊠ 2 pl. du Général-de-Gaulle, ☎ 04–42–16–11–61). **Arles** (⊠ esplanade Charles-de-Gaulle, ☎ 04–90–18–41–20). **Avignon** (⊠ 41 cours Jean-Jaurès, ☎ 04–90–82–65–11). **Marseille** (⊠ 4 La Canebière, ☎ 04–91–13–89–00). **Montpellier** (⊠ pl. René-Devic, ☎ 04–67–58–67–58). **Nîmes** (⊠ 6 rue Auguste, ☎ 04–66–67–29–11). **Toulon** (⊠ pl. des Riaux, ☎ 04–94–18–53–00).

13 The Riviera

St-Tropez to Monaco

The fabled Riviera is France's open door to the color and emotion of southern Europe and the Mediterranean. Without the Pyrénées or the Alps blocking the way, it's an easy slide into Monaco and Italy, across the border. The distinct light and feeling here have not only attracted movie stars but have also inspired artists, from Renoir to Matisse to Picasso, who came to live in the medieval hill town of Vence, enjoy the beaches and tiny streets of St-Tropez, and revel in the ochre and pastel hues of old Nice.

THE RIVIERA CONJURES UP IMAGES of fabulous yachts and villas, movie stars and palaces, and budding starlets sunning themselves on ribbons of golden sand. But the truth is that most beaches, at least east of Cannes, are small and pebbly, and that, in summer, vacationing crowds fill up the concrete high-rises and roadside campsites—on weekends it can take two hours to drive the last 10 km (6 mi) into St-Tropez. Yes, the film stars are here—but in their private villas. When the merely wealthy come, they come off-season, in the spring and fall.

Revised and updated by Nancy Coons

That said, the Riviera is still worth visiting, even in summer, as long as you're selective about the places you go. Inland are fortified medieval towns perched on mountaintops, high above the sea. The light that Renoir and Matisse came to capture is as magical here as ever (it pays to get up early to see it) and fields of roses and lavender still send their heady perfume up to these fortified towns, where craftspeople make and sell their wares, as did their predecessors in the Middle Ages.

It's impossible to be bored along the Riviera. You can try a different beach or restaurant every day. When you've had enough sun, you can visit pottery towns like Vallauris, where Picasso worked, or the perfumeries at Grasse. You can drive along dizzying gorges, almost as deep as the Grand Canyon. You can disco or gamble the night away in Monte Carlo and shop in Cannes or Nice. And only minutes from the beaches are some of the world's most famous modern art museums.

Pleasures and Pastimes

Beaches

If you like your beaches sandy, stick to those between St-Tropez and Antibes; most of the others are pebbly, though Menton and Monaco have imported vast tons of sand to spread around their shores. Private beaches are everywhere. You'll have to pay to use them (between 80 and 140 francs a day), but they usually have a café or restaurant, cabanas and showers, mattresses and umbrellas, and a parade of people in stylish swimwear.

Dining

Although prices often scale Parisian heights, the Riviera shares its cuisine with Provence—vegetable and fish dishes prepared with vivid seasonings. The most famous is bouillabaisse, a fish stew. Local fish is scarce, however, so dishes like *loup flambé* (sea bass with fennel and anise liqueur), braised tuna, and even fresh sardines are priced accordingly. *Estocaficada* (fish stew with garlic and olives) is a Nice specialty as are *pan bagna* (tuna, egg, and anchovies in a salad-stuffed bun) and *poulpe à la niçoise* (octopus in tomato sauce). With Italy so close, it's no surprise that many menus feature such specialties as ravioli, potato gnocchi, vegetable *soupe au pistou* (a seasoned, aromatic soup), and *pissaladière* (a version of pizza with olives, anchovies, and caramelized onions). Anise-flavored pastis is the Riviera's number one drink.

CATEGORY	COST*
$$$$	over 500 frs
$$$	250 frs–500 frs
$$	150 frs–250 frs
$	under 150 frs

per person for a three-course meal, including tax (20.6%) and tip but not wine

Lodging

Hotels on the Riviera can push opulence to the sublime—or the ridiculous. Pastel colors, gilt, plush, and a weakness for Art Deco are the decorators' staples in the hotels catering to the beau monde. The glamour comes hand in hand with hefty price tags, however. Inexpensive hotels do exist, but they're found mainly on dull outskirts of big centers and in less fashionable "family" resort towns, with the notable exceptions of less expensive inns in the hilltop villages above the coast.

CATEGORY	COST*
$$$$	over 1,000 frs
$$$	600 frs–1,000 frs
$$	300 frs–600 frs
$	under 300 frs

All prices are for a standard double room for two, including tax (20.6%) and service charge.

Exploring the Riviera

Also known as the Côte d'Azur, the French Riviera stretches for 120 km (75 mi) along the Mediterranean coastline, from St-Tropez to the Italian border. It's best to begin exploring the region on the western end at St-Tropez. Make Cannes and Antibes your next targets; then head inland to the medieval *villages perchés* (hilltop villages) of Grasse, Vence, and St-Paul-de-Vence. Lastly, visit the area to the east that includes Cagnes, Nice, and Monaco.

Great Itineraries

The towns along the Mediterranean are quite close together—Antibes is practically a suburb of Cannes, and St-Paul-de-Vence is just a 10-minute drive inland from Nice—so you can see many places in a short amount of time (the only problem is that you may want to stay forever). If you have limited time, it is possible, even advisable, to rush along the coast and see it all.

Numbers in the text and in the margins correspond to numbers on The Riviera: St-Tropez to Cannes; The Riviera: Cannes to Menton; Nice; and Monaco maps.

IF YOU HAVE 3 DAYS

Start in **St-Tropez** ①. In the afternoon, loop through the ancient villages of **Ramatuelle** ② and **Gassin** ③. Then drive from **Fréjus** ⑥, an old Roman town, along the Corniche de l'Esterel to **La Napoule** ⑨, with a stop, if you have time, at the Château de La Napoule Art Foundation. Get to world-famous ⚑ **Cannes** ⑩ by evening. On day two explore Cannes and then drive either to ancient **Antibes** ⑬ or up to the perfume-producing town of **Grasse** ⑰, just 20 minutes inland; from either, it's an easy jaunt to the medieval hilltop villages of ⚑ **Vence** ⑳ and ⚑ **St-Paul-de-Vence** ㉑, both good stopovers. The next day head to **Cagnes-sur-Mer** ㉒ to see the Renoir museum, and then go to the faded but graceful city of ⚑ **Nice** ㉔–㊿.

IF YOU HAVE 5 DAYS

Follow the three-day tour at a more relaxed pace, spending a night in both ⚑ **St-Tropez** ① and ⚑ **Antibes** ⑬ and stopping in the medieval town of **Èze** ㊻ on your way to Monte Carlo.

IF YOU HAVE 7 DAYS

Follow the five-day itinerary, with lunch in **Cagnes-sur-Mer** ㉒ on your way to ⚑ **Nice** ㉔–㊿ for a night and day. On the sixth day, drive along the Moyenne Corniche, stopping in **Èze** ㊺, then heading on to ⚑ **Monaco** ㊻–㊾ for the night. On day seven visit **Roquebrune** ㊴ and ⚑

Menton ㊴. Extra days would give you time to drive inland up the Route Napoleon to the Grand Canyon du Verdon, with its hair-raising drive along the Corniche Sublime (D71).

When to Tour the Riviera

October, May, and June are optimal times to be on the Riviera. Summer is too hot and too crowded, unless you want to be part of the banks of sunbathers watching each other on the beach. From early November through Easter, many of the most famous places are closed—but the locals go on living, enjoying having the markets and restaurants to themselves and room to stroll the waterfront in peace.

ST-TROPEZ, CANNES, AND ANTIBES

The *caps* (capes) of St-Tropez and Antibes look across the Corniche de l'Estérel at each other with little but the Iles de Lérins between them. The 60 km (37 mi) of towns, beaches, and the small but vibrant city of Cannes comprise an intense combination of riches that have made this coast into one of France's most sought-after destinations.

St-Tropez

❶ *73 km (45 mi) east of Toulon and southwest of Cannes, 878 km (549 mi) southeast of Paris.*

Old money never came to St-Tropez, but Brigitte Bardot did—with her director Roger Vadim in 1956 to film *And God Created Woman*. The town has never been the same since. Actually, the village was first "discovered" by the writer Guy de Maupassant (1850–93) and again, later, by the French painter Paul Signac (1863–1935), who came in 1892 and brought his friends—Matisse, Pierre Bonnard, and others. The writer Colette moved into a villa here between the two world wars and contributed to its notoriety. What attracted them was the pure, radiant light and the colors of the landscape.

Anything associated with the distant past almost seems absurd in St-Tropez. Still, the place has a history that predates the invention of the bikini, and people have been finding reasons to come here for centuries. First, in AD 68 there was a Roman soldier from Pisa named Torpes who was beheaded for professing his Christian faith in the presence of the emperor Nero. The headless body was put in a boat between a dog and a cock and sent drifting out to sea. The body eventually floated ashore, perfectly preserved, still watched over by the two animals. The buried remains became a place of pilgrimage, which by the 4th century was called St-Tropez. In the late 15th century, under the Genovese, St-Tropez became a small independent republic. Since then, people—and celebrities—have come for the sun and the sea. In summer, the population swells from 7,000 to 64,000.

Off-season is the time to come, but even in summer there are reasons to stay. The soft, sandy beaches are the best on the coast. Take an early morning stroll along the harbor or down the narrow medieval streets—the rest of the town will still be sleeping—and you'll see just how pretty St-Tropez is, with its tiny squares and rich, pastel-color houses. There are trendy boutiques and many cafés with colored awnings. Five minutes from town, you'll be in a green world of vineyards, fields, and mountains crowned with medieval villages. Perhaps it's the soft light, perhaps the rich fields and faded pastels, but nowhere else along the coast will you experience so completely the magic of the Riviera. Be forewarned, however: The name alone prompts an inflation in restaurant and hotel prices that belies the town's small scale.

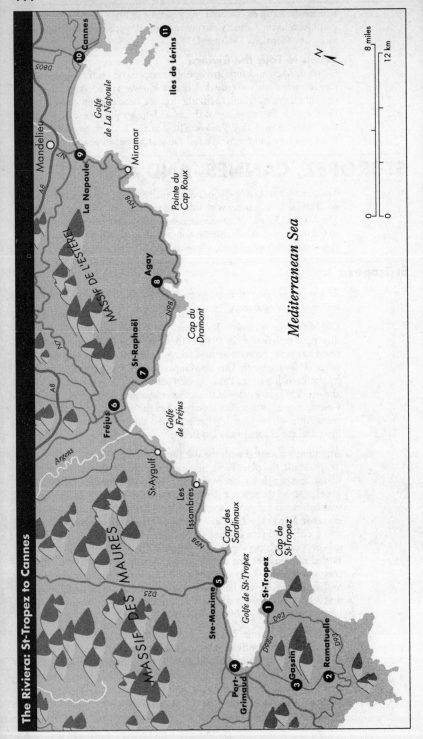

The Riviera: St-Tropez to Cannes

① St-Tropez
② Ramatuelle
③ Gassin
④ Port-Grimaud
⑤ Ste-Maxime
⑥ Fréjus
⑦ St-Raphaël
⑧ Agay
⑨ La Napoule
⑩ Cannes
⑪ Iles de Lérins

Cannes
Mandelieu
La Napoule
Miramar
Pointe du Cap Roux
Agay
St-Raphaël
Cap du Dramont
Fréjus
Golfe de Fréjus
St-Aygulf
Les Issambres
Cap des Sardinaux
Ste-Maxime
Golfe de St-Tropez
Port-Grimaud
St-Tropez
Cap de St-Tropez
Gassin
Ramatuelle

MASSIF DE L'ESTÉREL
MASSIF DES MAURES

Golfe de La Napoule
Iles de Lérins

Mediterranean Sea

Argens

A8
N7
D25
N98
D93
D98a
D805
N7

8 miles
12 km

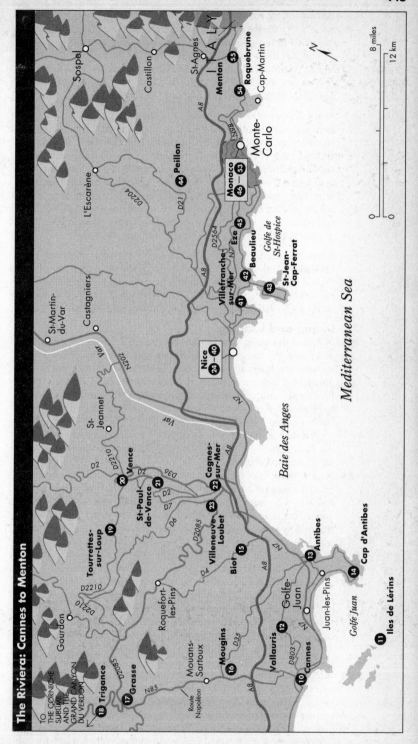

The Riviera: Cannes to Menton

Walk along the harbor, filled with pleasure boats, and along the break-
★ water, to the **Musée de l'Annonciade** (Annunciation Museum), a church
converted into a major art museum. The collection of Impressionist
paintings is filled with views of St-Tropez by Matisse, Bonnard, Paul
Signac, Maurice de Vlaminck, and others. ⊠ *quai de l'Épi/pl. Georges
Grammont,* ☎ *04–94–97–04–01.* ⊡ *30 frs.* ☉ *June–Sept., Wed.–
Mon. 10–noon and 3–7; Oct.–May, Wed.–Mon. 10–noon and 2–6.*

At the center of the half-moon quay surrounding the **Vieux Port** (Old
Port) is the **tourist office** (⊠ On the corner of rue de la Citadelle). Cafés
on the harbor provide dress-circle seats for admiring the St-Tropez scene,
and most everybody at some time hangs out at places like **Le Gorille**
(⊠ quai Suffren), **Café de Paris** (⊠ quai Suffren), and **Sénéquier's** (⊠
quai Jaurès), where women whose dogs match their coats drink 23-
franc espressos. Less than 20 yards from the tourist office up rue de
la Citadelle on the left is a covered **fish market**—it's small but has a
marvelous array of *fruits de mer* (seafood). Pass through the market
to a delightful tiny square with produce stalls and shops.

Commanding views across the bay to Ste-Maxime are found at the
Citadelle, a 16th-century fortress. Its keep is home to the **Musée Naval**
(Naval Museum), stocked with marine paintings and ship models. ⊠
rue de la Citadelle, ☎ *04–94–97–59–43.* ⊡ *25 frs.* ☉ *Nov.–Easter,
Wed.–Mon. 10–5; Easter–Oct., 10–noon and 2–4:30.*

Dining and Lodging

$$$ ✕ **Bistrot des Lices.** Overlooking a symmetrical forest of plane trees
and rocked by the gentle tonk of *pétanque* (a version of lawn bowl-
ing), terrace diners at this St-Tropez landmark relish the earthy yet so-
phisticated cuisine of Breton-born chef Laurent Tarridec. Try his
Provençal menu, of, perhaps, cold roast rabbit or truffle-potato soup;
lamb shoulder confit; an embarrassment of cheeses; and tender date
bonbons. If you find it too crowded, ask for a table in the intimate back
garden. Inside, formality is softened by a warm ochre glow. ⊠ *3 pl.
des Lices,* ☎ *04–94–97–29–00. AE, DC, MC, V. Closed mid-Jan.–
Mar. and mid-Nov.–Dec. 25.*

$$ ✕ **Le Girelier.** Like his father before him, chef Yves Rouet makes an
effort to prepare Mediterranean-only fish for his buffed and bronze
clientele, who enjoy the casual sea-shanty decor and the highly visible
Vieux Port terrace tables. Grilling is the order of the day, with most
fish sold by weight, but this is a stronghold for bouillabaisse. If you're
watching your pennies, try one of the reasonable daily specials, for 90
to 140 francs. ⊠ *quai Jean-Jaurès,* ☎ *04–94–97–03–87. AE, DC,
MC, V. Closed Oct.–Mar. (with the occasional exception).*

$$ ✕ **Lou Revelen.** Strike a pose on the throw-pillowed couch by the fire-
place, or people-watch from the terrace: This smart, stagey restaurant
caters to the glamorous or wannabes. There's also, not incidentally,
good Provençal cooking, with menus beginning at 160 francs. Try duck
carpaccio, garlicky-sweet eggplant terrine, and basil-perfumed lamb.
The fennel-grilled fish-of-the-day is a mainstay. ⊠ *bd. d'Aumale,* ☎
04–94–97–06–34. MC, V.

$$$$ ✕▦ **Byblos.** The Byblos resembles a Provençal village, with cottage-
like suites grouped around courtyards. Inside, the atmosphere is dis-
tinctly Casbah, with lots of heavy damask, a leopard-skin bar, and Persian
carpets on the dining-room ceiling. If you can't afford to stay here, at
least go to use the pool (for a steep fee). The restaurant, Les Arcades,
is lucky to have the talented Philippe Audibert as chef; watch for sub-
tle roast St-Pierre in lemon verbena, or stellar grilled sardines. ⊠ *av.
Paul Signac, 83990,* ☎ *04–94–56–68–00,* 𝐅𝐀𝐗 *04–94–56–68–01. 47*

rooms, 55 suites. Restaurant, pool, exercise room, nightclub. AE, DC, MC, V. Closed mid-Oct.–mid-Mar.

$$$$ 🏨 **Le Mas de Chastelas.** Just off the commercial access loop before you get to the center of St-Tropez is this inn in a former silkworm farm. The owner keeps the 18th-century main house stripped of art and color but lavishes the lovely garden "villas" with luxurious peach and terra-cotta decor. But its true heart is its garden—a gorgeous landscape of mimosas and palms surrounding no fewer than two idyllic swimming pools. ✉ *quartier Bertaud, Grande Bastide, 83580 Gassin,* ☎ *04–94–56–71–71,* ℻ *04–94–56–71–56. 16 rooms, 13 duplexes. Restaurant, 2 pools. AE, DC, MC, V.*

$$$ 🏨 **Ermitage.** This hotel near the heart of St-Tropez has old-fashioned
★ charm. The rooms' white walls are offset by strong primary colors on the beds and windows; ask for one overlooking the garden and the town, or the sea. The friendly bar always seems open, and owner Annie Bolloreis is more than willing to chat (in English) on the virtues and vices of her hometown. ✉ *av. Paul-Signac, 83990,* ☎ *04–94–97–52–33,* ℻ *04–94–97–10–43. 26 rooms. Bar. AE, DC, MC, V.*

$$ 🏨 **Le Baron.** This bargain lodging has small, simple, brocante-furnished rooms, with full bathrooms. All overlook the Citadelle's green park, some from tiny balconies. If you're more than two, ask for the pretty loft-suite, with its private spiral-stair entrance. Breakfast is served in the cozy "library" bar. ✉ *23 rue de l'Aïoli, 83990,* ☎ *04–94–97–06–57,* ℻ *04–94–97–09–44. 11 rooms. AE, DC, MC, V.*

Nightlife and the Arts

St-Tropez's major concert hall, which doubles as a cinema, is the **Salle de la Renaissance** (✉ pl. des Lices, ☎ 04–94–97–48–16). The hottest night spot in St-Tropez is **Les Caves du Roy** in the Byblos Hotel (✉ av. Paul-Signac, ☎ 04–94–56–68–00); the decor is stunningly vulgar, but the *très chic* clientele doesn't seem to mind. Look your best if you want to get in.

Outdoor Activities and Sports

The best **beaches** (*plages*) are scattered along a 5-km (3-mi) stretch reached by the route des Plages (beach road); the most fashionable are **Moorea, Tahiti Plage,** and **Club 55.** You'll see lots of topless bathers; some beaches allow total nudity. Those beaches close to town—**Plage des Greniers** and the **Bouillabaisse**—are great for families, but French vacationers snub them, preferring the 10-km (6-mi) sandy crescent at **Les Salins** and **Pampelonne,** 3 km (2 mi) from town. Bicycles are an ideal way to get to the beach; try **M. Mas** (✉ rue Quaranta, ☎ 04–94–97–00–60) or **Holiday Bikes** (✉ rte des Tamaris, ☎ 04–94–79–87–75).

Shopping

Rue Sibilli is a street with all kinds of trendy boutiques. **Souleiado** (✉ av. du 8-mai-1945) sells very French printed fabrics and clothes. Vegetables, fruit, and daily games of *boules* (also known as pétanque—a kind of lawn bowling) are found at the **produce market** (✉ pl. Carnot) on Tuesday and Saturday. The **clothing and antiques market** (✉ pl. des Lices) takes place on Tuesday and Saturday.

Ramatuelle

❷ *12 km (7 mi) southwest of St-Tropez.*

The old market town of Ramatuelle is a 20-minute drive south of St-Tropez through fields and vineyards. The ancient houses are huddled together on the slope of a rocky spur 440 ft above the sea, and the central square has a 17th-century church and a huge 300-year-old elm.

Surrounding the square are narrow, twisting streets with medieval archways and vaulted passages.

En Route   From Ramatuelle, the ride through vineyards and woods full of twisted cork-oaks to the hilltop village of Gassin is lovely and takes you over the highest point of the peninsula (1,070 ft).

Gassin

❸ *7 km (4 mi) north of Ramatuelle, 7 km (4 mi) south of St-Tropez.*

The hilltop village of Gassin, with its venerable old houses and 12th-century Romanesque church, has managed to maintain its medieval appearance. When it gets really hot at the beaches, people come up here to have a drink and contemplate the view and the vineyards.

Port-Grimaud

❹ *6 km (3 mi) north of Gassin, 6 km (4 mi) west of St-Tropez.*

On your way along the coast, stop at Port-Grimaud, a modern architect's idea of a Provençal fishing village–cum–Venice, built into the gulf for the yachting crowd—each house with its own mooring. Particularly appealing are the harmonious pastel colors, which have weathered nicely, and the graceful bridges over the canals.

Ste-Maxime

❺ *8 km (5 mi) east of Port-Grimaud, 33 km (20 mi) east of St-Tropez.*

Lively Ste-Maxime, across the gulf from St-Tropez, is a family resort with fine sandy beaches. Surrounded by the red mountains of the Massif des Maures, the heavily built-up waterfront, bristling with parking-garage-style apartments and hotels, offers a concentration of comforts and necessities within spitting distance of the beach.

En Route   The coastline between Ste-Maxime and Cannes consists of a succession of bays and beaches. Minor resorts—curious mixtures of lush villas, campsites, and fast-food stands—have sprung up wherever nature permits.

Fréjus

❻ *19 km (12 mi) northeast of St-Maxime, 52 km (32 mi) northeast of St-Tropez.*

Fréjus was founded by Julius Caesar as Forum Julii in 49 BC, and it is thought that the Roman city grew to 40,000 people—10,000 more than the population today. The Roman remains are modest but impressive and consist of part of the theater, an arena, a long series of chunks of aqueduct, and city walls. In the heart of the atmospheric hilltop old
★ town is the **Cathédrale.** Though it dates from the 10th century, its richly worked choir stalls belong to the 15th century. The austere baptistery alongside it, square on the outside and octagonal inside, is thought to date from AD 400, making it one of France's oldest buildings. The cloisters have an unusual combination of round and pointed arches. ⊠ *pl. Formigé.* ⊙ *Oct.–Mar., Tues.–Sun. 9–noon and 2–5; Apr.–Sept., daily 9–noon and 2–5.* ⌨ *Cathedral free; cloisters, baptistery, and museum 25 frs.*

St-Raphaël

❼ *4 km (2 mi) east of Fréjus, 36 km (22 mi) north of St-Tropez.*

St-Raphaël, next door to Fréjus, is a sprawling family resort city, best known as the railway stop for St-Tropez. It is also a major sailing center, has five golf courses, and draws the weary and indulgent to its sea-water-based thalassotherapy. It was here that the Allied forces landed in their offensive against the Germans in August 1944. The busy downtown is anchored by a **casino** (⊠ Square de Gand☎ 04–94–95–10–59). Stop in at the **tourist office** (⊠ rue Waledack-Rousseau, ☎ 04–94–19–52–52).

Lodging

$ 🏨 **Le Thimotée.** The new owners of this bargain lodging are throwing
★   themselves wholeheartedly into improving this already attractive 19th-century villa (with doubleglazing, bright-painted woodwork, and new carpet). They've also restored the tropical garden, with its grand palms and pines shading the walk to the pretty little swimming pool. They're helpful, too: They will rent you a bike, book an excursion, and pick you up at the train station. Though it's tucked away in a neighborhood far from the urban waterfront, top-floor rooms have poster-perfect sea views. ⊠ *375 bd. Christian-Lafon, 83700,* ☎ *04–94–40–49–49. 12 rooms. Pool. AE, MC, V.*

En Route   The rugged **Massif de l'Estérel,** between St-Raphaël and Cannes, is a hiker's dream, made up of volcanic rocks (porphyry) carved by the sea into dreamlike shapes. The harshness of the landscape is softened by patches of lavender, cane apple, and gorse. Take N7, the mountain route to the north, or stay on N98, the coastal road, past tiny rust-color beaches and sheer rock faces plunging into the sea. Some 15 trails strike out from designated parking sites along the way; ask about them at the St-Raphaël tourist office across from the train station (☞ *above*).

Agay

❽   *10 km (6 mi) east of St-Raphaël.*

Surrounded by the red rock of the Estérel and the growing clutter of its own development, Agay has the best-protected anchorage along the Estérel coast and was once used as a deep-water anchorage by traders from ancient Greece. It was near here that writer Antoine de St-Exupéry (*The Little Prince*) was shot down in July 1944, having just flown over his family castle on his last mission.

Mandelieu–La Napoule

❾   *24 km (15 mi) northeast of Agay, 10 km (6 mi) southwest of Cannes.*

Joining the waterfront sailing resort of Mandelieu with the picturesque old town of La Napoule, this varied double village makes a good place to stay. If you're an art buff, stop at the **Château de La Napoule/Fondation Henry Clews** to see the eccentric work of the American sculptor Henry Clews. A cynic and reputed sadist, Clews had, as one critic remarked, a knowledge of anatomy worthy of Michelangelo and the bizarre imagination of Edgar Allan Poe. ⊠ *av. Henry-Clews,* ☎ *04–93–49–95–05.* 🎫 *25 frs.* ☉ *Guided visits Mar.–Nov., Wed.–Mon. at 3 and 4; July–Aug., Wed.–Mon. at 3, 4, and 5.*

Dining and Lodging

$$ ✕ **Le Boucanier.** The drab, low-slung dining room is upstaged by
★   wraparound plate-glass views of the marina and château at this waterfront favorite. Locals gather here for mountains of oysters and whole fish, simply grilled and impeccably filleted tableside. The seafood, market fresh, speaks for itself: No one interferes beyond a drizzle of fruity olive oil, a pinch of rock salt, or a brief flambée in pastis. ⊠ *Port La Napoule,* ☎ *04–93–49–80–51. AE, DC, MC, V.*

$$$ ⌷ **Le Domaine d'Olival.** Set back from the coast, on its own vast land-scaped grounds along the Siagne River, is this charming inn. The sleek rooms, efficiently designed by the architect-owner, have built-in fur-niture and small kitchenettes. Balconies overlook the semitropical gar-den. ⌂ *778 av. de la Mer, 06210,* ☎ *04–93–49–31–00,* FAX *04–92–97–69–28. 18 apartments. Air-conditioning, kitchenettes, tennis court. AE, DC, MC, V. Closed Nov.–mid-Jan.*

$$$ ✕⌷ **Royal Hôtel Casino.** A glossy, modern pocket edition of the Loews in Monte Carlo (☞ *below*), this hotel offers deluxe comforts on a grand scale. Streamlined rooms in soft pastels have balconies and sea views from all sides. At the informal yet glamorous restaurant-grill you can dine on such dishes as artichokes with scampi and lightly grilled *rouget* (red mul-let) with kasha while you gaze out over the floodlit swimming pool. ⌂ *605 av. Général-de-Gaulle, 06210,* ☎ *04–92–97–70–00,* FAX *04–93–49–51–50. 211 rooms. 2 restaurants, bar, pool, sauna, 2 tennis courts, exercise room, cabaret, casino, travel services. AE, DC, MC, V.*

Outdoor Activities and Sports

Ask for the *"Star du Siècle"* brochure at the tourist office for details about canoeing, bicycling, riding, climbing, rambling, hang gliding, and rafting. There are also facilities for boating, golfing, horseback riding, and tennis, and eight beaches with waterskiing, jet-skiing, deep-sea div-ing, and windsurfing. **Club de Plongée de la Rague** (⌂ port de la Rague, ☎ 04–93–49–74–33) gives deep-sea diving lessons to any-one over age eight. The **Plongée International Center** (⌂ port Cannes Marina, ☎ 04–93–49–01–01) rents diving gear. Small sailboats and windsurfing equipment can be rented from **Maison de la Mer** (⌂ RN 98, ☎ 04–93–49–88–77). **Poney Club San Estello** (⌂ Domaine de Barbossi, 3 mi/2 km inland from Mandelieu–La Napoule on N7, ☎ 04–93–49–36–26) rents horses and gives lessons to children and adults. The 18 hole **Riviera Golf Club** (⌂ av. des Amazones, ☎ 04–92–97–67–67) is open to the public.

Cannes

⑩ *73 km (45 mi) northeast of St-Tropez, 33 km (21 mi) southwest of Nice, 908 km (567 mi) southeast of Paris.*

Cosmopolitan, sophisticated, smart—these are words that describe the most lively and flourishing town on the Riviera. Cannes is a resort town—unlike Nice, which is a city—that exists only for the pleasure of its guests. It's a tasteful and expensive breeding ground for the up-scale, a sybaritic heaven for those who believe that life is short and sin has something to do with the absence of a tan.

★   Alongside the narrow beach runs a broad, elegant promenade bordered by palm trees and flowers, known as **La Croisette.** All along the prom-enade are cafés, boutiques, and luxury hotels. Speedboats and water-skiers glide by; little waves lick the beach, lined with prostrate bodies. Behind the promenade lies the town, and beyond, the hills with the villas of the very rich. At one end of La Croisette is the **Palm Beach Casino** and a modern harbor for some of the most luxurious yachts in the world. As you walk in this direction you'll pass the **Parc de la Roserie,** where some 14,000 roses nod their heads in the wind.At the other end of La Croisette is the modern **Palais des Festivals** (Festival Hall), the site of the famous Cannes Film Festival; you can join the tourists tak-ing snapshots of each other on the famous red-carpeted steps or fit-ting their hands into the sidewalk palm-prints of Dépardieu, Streep, and Stallone. Just past the Festival Hall is **place du Général-de-Gaulle** and the **Vieux Port** (Old Port), where pleasure boats are moored.

Behind the Vieux Port, on **allées de la Liberté,** is a tree-shaded area where flowers are sold in the morning, boules is played in the afternoon, and a flea market is held on Saturday. Stop for restoration at one of the outdoor kiosks; the **Kiosque des Sports** is the best. The **Hôtel de Ville** (Town Hall), an ornate structure with an elegant stairway, is on rue Félix-Faure. Parallel to this street is **rue Meynadier,** Cannes's old main street, now a busy pedestrian area lined with 18th-century houses converted to youth-oriented boutiques. **Rue Louis-Blanc,** off rue Meynadier, is home to the colorful Forville vegetable and general produce market. Continue along the street to get to the **Église Miséricorde,** with its tiny bell tower.

Le Suquet is the town's oldest quarter, known as *le berceau* (the cradle) of Cannes. To reach it, take a right turn off rue Félix Faure onto rue St-Antoine and continue spiraling up through rue du Suquet to the top of a 197-ft hill. In the 12th-century tower overlooking the rooftops of Cannes is the **Musée de la Castre** (Castle Museum), filled with Provençal paintings, ethnological artifacts, and medieval archaeological finds. ⊠ *pl. de la Castre,* ☎ *04–93–38–55–26.* ☎ *10 frs.* ☉ *Oct.–Mar., Wed.–Mon. 10–noon and 2–5; Apr.–Jun., Wed.–Mon. 10–noon and 2–6; July–Sept., Wed.–Mon. 10–noon and 2–7.*

Dining and Lodging

$$ ✕ **Chez Astoux.** For seafood, this stands out among the other restaurants overlooking the leisurely scene at the far west end of La Croisette. Linen-covered tables on the terrace sport showy, tiered platters of fresh seafood, and bowls of bouillabaisse. You can also order seafood platters from here to go—don't confuse it with Brun around the corner, which trades on the Astoux name but is not as good. ⊠ *43 rue Félix-Faure,* ☎ *04–93–39–06–22. AE, DC, MC, V.*

$ ✕ **Au Bec Fin.** Despite its '60s-era luncheonette decor, devoted regulars attest to the quality of this anti-chic, family-run bistro near the train station. It's distinguished by its crowds of spirited local clientele and homey food. The prix-fixe menus are an excellent value; grilled sardines, the day's catch with fennel, *choucroute* (sauerkraut and sausage), and lentils are often the main dishes. ⊠ *12 rue du 24-août,* ☎ *04–93–38–35–86. AE, DC, MC, V. Closed Sun. and mid-Dec.–mid-Jan. No dinner Sat.*

$ ✕ **Bouchon d'Objectif.** Popular and unpretentious, this tiny bistro serves
★ inexpensive Provençal menus prepared with a sophisticated twist. Watch for terrine of hare with sultanas and Armagnac, stuffed sardines, or a trio of fresh fish with aïoli. An ever-changing gallery display of photography adds a hip touch to the simple yellow-and-aqua decor. ⊠ *6 rue Maréchal-Joffre,* ☎ *04–93–39–98–38. AE, MC, V. Closed Mon.*

$ ✕ **Montagard.** This extraordinary newcomer serves elegant, imagina-
★ tive vegetarian cuisine—rare in France—in a chic, low-key setting and at startlingly low prices (such as the copious three-course quick-lunch menu for 95 francs). A complex orchestration of crudités may include avocado, spinach, and lentils, as well as walnuts, sultanas, and currants; the *tourte* (tart) stuffed with pumpkin and chestnuts may be trimmed with deep-fried pumpkin rings and ruby beet chips. Strains of Keith Jarrett waft through the artful ocher setting. ⊠ *6 rue Maréchal-Joffre,* ☎ *04–93–39–98–38. MC, V. Closed Sun. No lunch Mon.*

$$$$ ✕⊡ **Carlton.** As one of the turn-of-the-century pioneers of this resort
★ town, this neoclassical landmark staked out the best position: La Croisette seems to radiate from its central spot on the waterfront. The Carlton sits right on the sidewalk—the better for you to be seen on the popular brasserie's terrace. The main film festival banquets take place in its gilt-and-marble Grand Salon, as do, alas, year-round conferences. Seafront rooms have a retro Laura Ashley look; those on the back compensate with cheery Provençal prints. The restaurant, Bel Otero,

next to the exclusive seventh-floor casino, is one of Cannes's finest. ⊠ *58 bd. de la Croisette, 06414,* ☎ *04–93–06–40–06,* FAX *04–93–06–40–25. 310 rooms, 28 suites. 4 restaurants, bar, air-conditioning, health club, beach, casino. AE, DC, MC, V.*

$$$$ ✕🔟 **Martinez.** A Hollywood-style face-lift has restored the Art Deco
  ★   Martinez to a theatrical version of its original '30s glamour. Renovated rooms now have a splashy neo-Deco look—be sure to ask for one of these or for one on the seaside with gorgeous views. Avoid those on the interior overlooking the grim parking lot and the shabby, still-unrenovated ones on the second floor. The Palme d'Or restaurant is has plush, extravagant decor, but despite all that, chef Christian Willer draws lavish praise for his modern Mediterranean cuisine. ⊠ *73 bd. de la Croisette, 06400,* ☎ *04–92–98–73–00,* FAX *04–93–39–67–82. 397 rooms, 12 apartments. 3 restaurants, bar, air-conditioning, pool, beach. AE, DC, MC, V. Closed mid-Nov.–mid-Jan.*

$$$$ ✕🔟 **Noga Hilton.** On the site of the old Palais des Festivals, the in-your-face modern facade of the Noga gives way to interiors that are just as bold and glossy. Inside are lipstick-red leather lobby chairs, a dizzying atrium design, and high-gloss wood, chrome, and mirrors, the better to reflect the geometric-print carpets. But the hotel maintains a posh integrity, with a seamlessly professional staff and a sense of hushed luxury that denies the volume of decor. The good Mediterranean restaurant, La Scala, has tables high above La Croisette and the waterfront. But don't miss the rooftop sunbathing terrace, with grill and bar around the plunge pool. ⊠ *50 bd. de la Croisette, 06400,* ☎ *04–92–99–70–00,* FAX *04–92–99–70–11. 184 rooms, 45 suites. 3 restaurants, 3 bars, air-conditioning, pool, exercise room, beach. AE, DC, MC, V.*

$$$$ 🔟 **Majestic.** Classical statuary and tapestries set the aristocratic tone at this other "palace" hotel lining La Croisette. Grand but gracious, it has a quieter feel than most of its neighbors. The (smallish) pool is behind a landscaped hillock so that you can't be seen. The Egyptian–Art Deco bar gives a nod to cinematic glamour. Though some rooms are fussy, most are now done in subdued golds and burgundies. Ask for one of the newly redone rooms, carefully renovated in retro style. ⊠ *14 bd. de la Croisette, 06400,* ☎ *04–92–98–77–00,* FAX *04–93–38–97–90. 298 rooms, 24 apartments. Restaurant, bar, air-conditioning, pool, hairdresser, sauna, parking (fee). AE, DC, MC, V. Closed mid-Nov.–Dec.*

$$$ 🔟 **Le Fouquet's.** If you're looking for a comfortable base from which to explore in a quiet residential neighborhood, this is the place. The ambience is welcoming—from the brightly lit archway, plants, and mirrors to the large rooms, decorated in warm shades and decked out with lots of French flounce. ⊠ *2 Rond-Point Duboys-d'Angers, 06400,* ☎ *04–93–38–75–81,* FAX *04–92–98–03–39. 10 rooms. AE, DC, MC, V. Closed Nov.–Dec.*

$$ 🔟 **Molière.** Plush, intimate, and low-key, this inexpensive hotel has pretty
  ★   tiled baths and small rooms in cool shades of peach, indigo, and white-waxed oak. Nearly all overlook the vast enclosed front garden, where palms and cypress shade terrace tables, and breakfast is served alfresco most of the year. ⊠ *5 rue Molière, 06400,* ☎ *04–93–68–16–16,* FAX *04–93–68–29–57. AE, MC, V. Closed mid-Nov.–end Dec.*

$ 🔟 **Albert I**er**.** In a quiet residential area above the Forville market—a 10-minute walk downhill to La Croisette and beach—this neo-Deco mansion has pretty rooms in pastels, tidy tile baths, and an enclosed garden setting. You can have breakfast on the flowered, shady terrace or in the family-style salon. The hotel has had one owner for 17 years, and it shows in the details. ⊠ *68 av. de Grasse, 06400,* ☎ *04–93–39–24–04,* FAX *04–93–38–83–75. 11 rooms. MC, V.*

Nightlife and the Arts

The Riviera's cultural calendar is splashy and star-studded and never more so than during the **International Film Festival** in May. The film screenings are not open to the public, so unless you have a pass, your star-studded glimpses will be on the streets or in restaurants—though if you hang around in a tux, a stray ticket might come your way.

The hottest disco of the moment is **Le Cat Corner** (⊠ 22 rue Macé, ☎ 04–93–39–31–31). **Jimmy'z** (⊠ Palais des Festivals, ☎ 04–93–68–00–07) admits celebrities, stars, and starlets, but not necessarily everyone else; the cabaret shows are legendary. After many metamorphoses, **Studio-Circus** is back and once again one of the main disco draws (⊠ 48 bd. de la République, ☎ 04–93–68–13–13).

Cannes has two casinos. The famous **Casino Croisette** (⊠ Palais des Festivals, ☎ 04–93–38–12–11), which traces its pedigree back to 1907, draws more crowds to its slot machines than any other casino in France. The **Carlton Casino Club** (⊠ 58 bd. de la Croisette, ☎ 04–93–68–00–33), a relative newcomer to the Cannes nightlife scene, encourages an exclusive atmosphere in its seventh-floor hideaway.

Outdoor Activities and Sports

Most **beaches** along La Croisette are owned by hotels and/or restaurants, though this doesn't necessarily mean the hotels or restaurants front the beach. It does mean that they own a patch of beachfront bearing their name, from which they rent chaise longues, mats, and umbrellas to the public and hotel guests (who also pay). One of the most fashionable beaches belongs to the **Carlton** hotel (☞ Dining and Lodging, *above*). Other fee beaches include the one at the **Martinez**, which has the largest strip in Cannes; **Long Beach**; and **Rado Plage**. Public beaches are easily recognizable by the crowds.

Camper & Nicholson's (⊠ Port Canto, ☎ 04–93–43–16–75) rents motorboats and sailboats. Sailboats can also be rented from the **Yacht Club de Cannes** (⊠ Palm Beach Port, ☎ 04–93–43–05–90). Get windsurfing equipment from the **Centre Nautique Municipal** (⊠ 9 rue Esprit-Violet, ☎ 04–92–18–88–88). Bicycles can be rented from the **train station** (⊠ pl. de la Gare); tool around town or take a scenic ride to Cap Ferrat along the coast road. Golf courses in town include **Golf de Biot** (⊠ La Bastide du Roy, ☎ 04–93–65–08–48). Or try **Golf Cannes-Mandelieu** (⊠ rte. du Golf, ☎ 04–93–49–55–39).

Shopping

The same chic designer labels that you find in Paris (Chanel, Yves Saint Laurent, Christian Dior, etc.) can be found for similar prices in Cannes on La Croisette, Rond-Point Duboys-d'Angers, rue des Belges, rue des Serbes, and rue d'Antibes. To satisfy a sweet tooth, head to **Schwartz** (⊠ 75 bd. de la République), which is renowned for its candy and macaroons. Almost anything, from strings of garlic to secondhand gravy boats, can be found at the **market** (⊠ allées de la Liberté) held every Saturday. On the first and third Saturday of each month, an array of old books, posters, and postcards is on sale at the **Marché du Livre Ancien et des Vieux Papiers** (⊠ pl. de la Justice).

Iles de Lérins

⓫ *15- to 30-min boat ride from Cannes Harbor.*

You may want to take a day trip to the peaceful Iles de Lérins (Lerin Islands) off the coast of Cannes to escape the crowds. Competitive ferries leave from the Vieux Port (near the Palais des Festivals) approximately every hour (look for the Horizon/Caribbes company—better boats than those of Estérel Chanticlair). Buy tickets for each island or one for both for 60 francs. It's a 15-minute, 50-franc trip to **Ste-Marguerite,** an island of wooded hills and a tiny main street lined with restaurants and vacation houses. An evocative old fort houses the **Musée de la Mer** (Sea Museum), a small bird preserve with cormorants, and lots of quiet tidal pools. A 30-minute, 55-franc trip takes you to the wilder and even quieter **St-Honorat,** named for the monk who started the monastery on the island.

Vallauris

⑫ *5 km (3 mi) north of Cannes on D803, 6 km (4 mi) west of Antibes.*

Ceramics are on sale throughout the pottery-making center of Vallauris, and several workshops can be visited. Picasso spurred a resurgence of activity when he settled here in 1947 and created some whimsically beautiful pieces. The fresco in the tunnel-like medieval chapel of the former priory—now the **Musée National Picasso**—was done by the great man himself. The showstopper: his monumental *La Guerre et la Paix* (*War and Peace*). ✉ *pl. de la Libération,* ☎ 04–93–64–16–05. ≦ *15 frs.* ☉ *July–Aug., Wed.–Mon. 10–7; Sept.–June, 10–noon and 2–6.*

Antibes

⑬ *11 km (7 mi) northeast of Cannes.*

Founded as a Greek trading port in the 4th century BC, Antibes is now a resort town, fishing port, and, until recently, an important rose-growing center. Antibes officially forms one town (dubbed "Juan-tibes") with the newer Juan-les-Pins to the south, where beach and nightlife attract a younger and less affluent crowd. In summer, the mood is especially frenetic. Avenue de l'Amiral-Grasse runs along the seafront from the harbor to the marketplace, a colorful sight most mornings.

The **Église de l'Immaculée Conception** (Church of the Immaculate Conception; ✉ av. de l'Amiral Grasse) has intricately carved portals (dating from 1710) and a 1515 altarpiece by Nice artist Louis Bréa (circa 1455–1523).

★ The **Château Grimaldi,** built in the 12th century by the ruling family of Monaco and extensively rebuilt in the 16th century, is reached by steps near the Church of the Immaculate Conception. Tear yourself away from the sunbaked terrace overlooking the sea to go inside the **Musée Picasso.** Roman remains are on exhibit, but the more than 300 works of Picasso—who occupied the château during his most cheerful and energetic period, filling it with nymphs, fauns, and centaurs—hold center stage. ✉ *pl. du Château,* ☎ 04–93–90–54–20. ≦ *30 frs.* ☉ *June–Sept., Wed.–Mon. 10–6; Oct.–May, Wed.–Mon. 10–noon and 2–6.*

St-André Bastion, constructed by the military engineer Sébastien de Vauban in the late 17th century, is home to the **Musée Archéologique** (Archaeology Museum). Here 4,000 years of local history are illustrated. ✉ *promenade de l'Amiral-Grasse,* ☎ 04–92–90–54–35. ≦ *15 frs.* ☉ *Dec.–Oct., Tues.–Sun. 9–noon and 2–6.*

If you want a change of venue, ferries leave from Juan-les-Pins to the **Iles de Lérins** (☞ *above*) hourly in summer.

Dining and Lodging

$$–$$$ ✕ **La Bonne Auberge.** In a graceful inn set back from the overbuilt sprawl along N7, chef Philippe Rostang cooks up classic, conservative specialties such as lamb in thyme with kidneys, lobster ravioli, and airy soufflés

on his seasonal menus. The dining room is a flower-filled haven of exposed beams, dim lantern lighting, and rose-color walls; huge glass windows allow you to view the inspired work in the kitchen. ⊠ *Quartier de la Brague,* ☎ 04–93–33–36–65. *Jacket required. AE, MC, V. Closed Mon. and mid-Nov.–mid-Dec. No dinner Sun., no lunch Tues.*

$$ ✕ **Le Brûlot.** One street back from the thriving market, this bistro is
★ one of the busiest in Antibes. Burly chef Christian Blancheri horses anything from suckling pigs to apple pies in and out of his roaring wood oven, and it's all delicious. The decor is rustic and chaotic and the seating so close it's almost unavoidable to become part of one large unruly mob at this popular spot. ⊠ *3 rue Frédéric-Isnard,* ☎ *04–93–34–17–76. MC, V. Closed Sun., last 2 wks of Aug., and last wk of Dec.–1st wk of Jan. No lunch Mon.*

$$$$ ✕🏠 **Juana.** This luxuriously renovated '30s hotel, near the casino
★ and a couple of blocks from the beach, is run by the second generation of the Barrache family. Service is attentive and rooms are large and individually decorated with creature comforts in mind. Pine trees tower over the grounds and the white marble pool. Chef Christian Morisset wins praise for his fine seafood at La Terrasse, one of the best restaurants on the Côte d'Azur. ⊠ *av. Georges-Gallice, 06160 Juan-les-Pins,* ☎ 04–93–61–08–70, FAX 04–93–61–76–60. *45 rooms. Restaurant, bar, pool. AE, MC, V. Closed late Oct.–mid-Apr.*

$$ ✕🏠 **Auberge Provençale.** The six rooms in this onetime abbey, complete with exposed beams, canopied beds, and lovely antique furniture, have just had a thorough face-lift but have kept their charm. The dining room and the covered garden are decorated with the same impeccable taste; the menu features fresh seafood, duck grilled over wood coals, and excellent bouillabaisse. The restaurant is closed Monday and Tuesday lunch. ⊠ *61 pl. Nationale, 06600Antibes,* ☎ *04–93–34–13–24,* FAX *04–93–34–89–88. 6 rooms. Restaurant. AE, DC, MC, V. Closed Jan.*

$$ 🏠 **Le Mas Djoliba.** There are only 14 rooms in this converted Provençal farmhouse, surrounded by greenery. The salon features an airy bamboo-shoot motif, and the rooms, painted in a range of pastel shades, have antique furnishings. Choose between views of the park or the sea. ⊠ *29 av. de Provence, 06600 Antibes,* ☎ 04–93–34–02–48, FAX 04–93–34–05–81. *14 rooms. Restaurant, pool. AE, DC, MC, V. Closed Jan.*

Nightlife and the Arts

The **Eden Casino** (⊠ bd. Baudoin, Juan-les-Pins, ☎ 04–92–93–71–71) draws a young crowd. If you're ready to party till dawn, head to **La Siesta** (⊠ rte. du Bord de Mer, Antibes, ☎ 04–93–33–01–18), an enormous setup with dance floors, bars, and roulette; it's only open in summer.

Outdoor Activities and Sports

Bicycles and motorcycles can be rented from **Holiday Bikes** (⊠ 93 bd. Wilson, Juan, ☎ 04–93–61–51–51). **Juan Midi Location** (⊠ 93 bd. Wilson, Juan, ☎ 04–92–93–05–06) also rents bikes and motorcycles.

Cap d'Antibes

★ ⑭ *2 km (1 mi) from Antibes.*

The Cap d'Antibes peninsula is rich and residential, with beaches, views, and large villas hidden in luxurious vegetation. You gain some appreciation of the wealth in this area when you pass by the Hôtel du Cap Eden Roc on boulevard Kennedy as you cross from Juan-les-Pins onto the peninsula. Barely 3 km long by 1½ km wide (2 mi long by 1 mi wide), it's perfect for a day's outing from Antibes.

Take a walk along the path known as the **Sentier des Douaniers,** the Customs Officers' Trail. At **Pointe Bacon** there is a striking view of the Baie des Anges (Bay of Angels) toward Nice.

Climb up to the **Plateau de la Garoupe** for a sweeping view inland over the Estérel massif and the Alps. The **Sanctuaire de la Garoupe** (Sailors' Chapel) has a 14th-century icon, a statue of Our Lady of Safe Home-coming, and numerous frescoes and votive offerings. The *phare* (light-house) on the Plateau de la Garoupe has a powerful beam that carries more than 64 km (40 mi) out to sea. ⊠ *Plateau de la Garoupe.* 🏛 *Light-house free.* ☼ *Nov.–Mar., weekdays 3–5:30; Apr.–Oct., daily 8:30–noon and 2–5:30.*

The lovely **Jardin Thuret** (Thuret Garden) was established by botanist Gustave Thuret (1817–75) in 1856 as France's first garden for sub-tropical plants and trees; it is now run by the Ministry of Agriculture. ⊠ *bd. du Cap.* 🏛 *Free.* ☼ *Weekdays 8:30–noon and 2:30–5:30.*

At the southwest tip of the peninsula, opposite the luxurious Grand Hôtel du Cap d'Antibes, is the **Musée Naval et Napoléonien** (Naval and Napoleonic Museum), a former battery, where you can spend an interesting hour scanning Napoleonic proclamations and viewing scale models of oceangoing ships. ⊠ *Batterie du Grillon, av. Kennedy,* ☎ *04–93–61–45–32.* 🏛 *20 frs.* ☼ *Weekdays 9:30–noon and 2:15–6, Sat. 9:30–noon.*

Dining and Lodging

$$$–$$$$ ✕ **Restaurant de Bacon.** At the Riviera's top spot for bouillabaisse and
★ Mediterranean fish, the prices generally match the quality, except for the bargain 250-franc lunch and dinner menus. The Sordellos have owned Bacon since 1948 and don't regard a fish as fresh unless it's still twitch-ing. Ask for a table outside on the terrace overlooking the old port and the bay. ⊠ *bd. de Bacon,* ☎ *04–93–61–50–02. Reservations essen-tial. Jacket required. AE, DC, MC, V. Closed Mon. (except July–Aug.) and Nov.–Jan.*

$$ 🏨 **Manoir Castel Garoupe Axa.** This old inn is known locally as Motel Axa, after owner Mme. Axa. She speaks little English but smiles and a minimal grasp of French will do. Not deluxe by any means, it's a friendly place and only two minutes from the beach. Rooms have bal-conies with countryside views. Breakfast is served. ⊠ *959 bd. de la Garoupe, 06600,* ☎ *04–93–61–36–51,* 🖷 *04–93–67–74–88. 27 rooms. Kitchenettes, pool, tennis court. MC, V. Closed early Nov.–mid-Mar.*

Biot

⓯ *4 km (3 mi) northeast of Antibes on N7 and D4, 11 km (7 mi) north-east of Cannes, 22 km (14 mi) southwest of Nice.*

Once a center of terra-cotta jar making, the picturesque old village of Biot has made a name for itself now as an artsy ceramics and glass cen-ter and as a focal point for the art of Fernand Léger (1881–1955), its most famous citizen.

Léger lived in Biot until his death, and hundreds of his paintings, ce-ramics, and tapestries are on display at the strikingly designed **Musée National Fernand Léger.** Léger's stylistic evolution is traced from his early flirtation with Cubism to his ultimate preference for flat ex-panses of primary color and shades of gray, separated by thick black lines. ⊠ *chemin du Val de Pomme,* ☎ *04–92–91–50–30.* 🏛 *38 frs.* ☼ *Apr.–Sept., Wed.–Mon. 10–12:30 and 2–6; Oct.–Mar., Wed.–Mon. 10–12:30 and 2–5:30.*

At the famous **Verrerie de Biot** (Biot Glassworks) you can observe the glassblowers at work, visit the extensive galleries of art glass, and start a collection of unique bubbled-glass goblets, cruets, and pitchers. There's only one Biot Glassworks (follow the pink signs); the others are imitations. ⊠ *5 chemin des Combes,* ☎ *04–93–65–03–00.* ⊙ *Mon.–Sat. 9–6:30, Sun. 10:30–1 and 2:30–6:30.*

Dining and Lodging

$ ✕⌂ **Galerie des Arcades.** Tucked away behind a quiet palm-lined
★ square in the old town, this combination hotel–restaurant–art gallery draws a chic and loyal clientele. They come to browse in the gallery, enjoy a weekend in one of the extraordinary guest rooms, or dine on the serious, unpretentious, authentic Provençal food (in the $$ category). Eat at the checked-cloth covered tables either under the arcades or the cozy beams indoors. Then ask for one of the *grandes chambres* (large roooms) and revel in antiquity: four-poster beds, stone sinks and fireplaces, beams, and a tapestry-rich color scheme. (The smaller rooms are nothing to write home about.) ⊠ *14 pl. des Arcades, 06410,* ☎ *04–93–65–01–04,* ℻ *04–93–65–01–05. 12 rooms. Restaurant. AE, DC, MC, V.*

CANNES TO MENTON

Begin in the medieval hill towns of Provence, and then dip down through Nice and Monaco to balmy Menton (close to the Italian border). The eastern part of the Riviera has an extraordinary range of sights, from the Grand Canyon du Verdon to the casinos at Monte Carlo.

Mougins

⑯ *8 km (5 mi) north of Cannes, 12 km (7 mi) northwest of Antibes, 32 km (20 mi) southwest of Nice.*

From quaint, fortified, hilltop Mougins, with its cluster of ancient houses dating from the 15th century, you can see Cannes and the Golfe de Napoule. Unfortunately, Mougins' popularity means that you have to park at the bottom of the hill and hike into the old village, which is a little hard to find behind the new houses and shopping centers that form Cannes's suburban sprawl. Don't be misled by signs for Mougins-le-Haut, a huge real-estate development that has become a village in its own right. Be sure to stop in at the **Notre-Dame-de-Vie** hermitage, one of the village's most interesting sights. Also look out for the **Chapelle St-Barthelmy,** with its 17th-century bell tower roofed in colored tiles.

Dining and Lodging

$$$$ ✕⌂ **Moulin de Mougins.** Housed in a 16th-century olive mill is a small
★ inn and one of the country's most famous restaurants. Since celebrity chef Roger Vergé gave over most responsibility to Serge Chollet, the loyal clientele has begun to sigh with nostalgia for the good old days. It's still one of the best in the region, however, with its specialties redolent of southern markets: white asparagus, sweet garlic, the freshest fish. The intimate beamed dining rooms, with oil paintings, plants, and porcelain tableware, are perfect for world-class fare. In summer, dine outside under the awnings. Reservations are essential for the restaurant, which is closed Monday. Rooms are elegantly rustic; the apartments are small but deluxe. ⊠ *Notre-Dame-de-Vie, 06250,* ☎ *04–93–75–78–24,* ℻ *04–93–90–18–55. 3 rooms, 2 apartments. Restaurant. AE, DC, MC, V. Closed Feb.–Mar.*

Grasse

⑰ *10 km (6 mi) northwest of Mougins, 17 km (10½ mi) northwest of Cannes, 22 km (14 mi) northwest of Antibes, 42 km (25 mi) southwest of Nice.*

If touring a perfume factory in a tacky modern town is your idea of pleasure, by all means visit Grasse. If you had visited four centuries ago, when the town specialized in leather, you would have come for gloves. In the 16th century, when scented gloves became the rage, the town began cultivating flowers and distilling essences. That was the beginning of the perfume industry. Today some three-fourths of the world's essences are made here from wild lavender, jasmine, violets, daffodils, and other sweet-smelling flowers. Five thousand producers supply some 20 factories and six cooperatives. If you've ever wondered why perfume is so expensive, consider that it takes 10,000 flowers to produce 2.2 pounds of jasmine petals and that nearly 1 ton of petals is needed to distill 1½ quarts of essence. Sophisticated Parisian perfumers mix Grasse essences into their own secret formulas; perfumes made and sold in Grasse are considerably less subtle. You can, of course, buy Parisian perfumes in Grasse at Parisian prices.

Several **perfume houses** welcome visitors—daily 9–noon and 2–6, free— for a whiff of their products and an explanation of how the perfumes are made: **Galimard** (⊠ 73 rte. de Cannes, ☎ 04–93–09–20–00); **Molinard** (⊠ 60 bd. Victor-Hugo, ☎ 04–93–36–01–62); and **Fragonard** (⊠ 20 bd. Fragonard, ☎ 04–93–36–44–65), which is conveniently central and has its own museum.

At the **Musée International de la Parfumerie** (International Museum of Perfume), the history and manufacturing process of perfume are explained. Old machinery, pots, and flasks can be admired; toiletry, cosmetics, and makeup accessories are on display. ⊠ 8 pl. du Cours, ☎ 04–93–36–80–20. ☞ 14 frs. ⓢ Oct.–May, Wed.–Sun. 10–noon and 2–5; June–Sept., daily 10–7.

The artist Jean-Honoré Fragonard (1732–1806) was born in Grasse, and many of his pictures, etchings, drawings, and sketches—plus others by his son Alexandre-Evariste and his grandson Théophile—are hung in the 17th-century **Musée Fragonard.** ⊠ 23 bd. Fragonard, ☎ 04–93–36–02–71. ☞ 20 frs. ⓢ Oct.–May, Wed.–Sun. 10–noon and 2–5; June–Sept., daily 10–noon and 2–7. First Sun. of the month is free.

The **Musée d'Art et d'Histoire de Provence** (Provence Museum of Art and History), just down the street from the Musée Fragonard, in an 18th-century mansion, houses a collection of china and Provençal furniture, folk art, and tools. ⊠ 2 rue Mirabeau, ☎ 04–93–36–01–61. ☞ 10 frs. ⓢ Apr.–Oct., Mon.–Sat. 10–noon and 2–6; Nov.–Mar., Mon.–Sat. 10–noon and 2–5.

Route Napoléon

176 km (110 mi) from Grasse to Sisteron.

One of the most famous and panoramic roads in France is the Route Napoléon, taken by Napoléon Bonaparte in 1815 after his escape from imprisonment on the Mediterranean island of Elba. Napoléon landed at Golfe-Juan, near Cannes, on March 1, and forged northwest to Grasse and through dramatic, hilly countryside to Castellane, Digne, and Sisteron. In Napoléon's day, most of this road (now N85) was little more than a winding dirt track. Commemorative plaques bearing the imperial eagle stud the route, inspired by Napoléon's remark, "The eagle will fly from steeple to steeple until it reaches the towers of Notre-Dame." That prediction came true. Napoléon covered the 176 km (110 mi) from the coast to Sisteron in just four days, romped north through Grenoble and Burgundy, and entered Paris in triumph on May 20.

Except for the occasional inn with the name Napoléon, there are no historical buildings or monuments, bar the plaques. It is the panoramic views as the road winds its way up into the Alps that make this route so worth traveling. Unless you are heading north to Grenoble, you can easily make a circular day trip along the Route Napoléon, starting from the coast at Grasse. Without stopping, you could reach Sisteron in 90 minutes, so take your time and stop for a picnic along the way. Sisteron, which is guarded by a medieval citadel perched 1,650 ft above the river, is the gateway between Provence and Dauphine. It is also famous for its lamb, the best according to Provençal chefs. At Sisteron, pick up autoroute A51 down to Aix-en-Provence (☞ Chapter 12), and then join A6 to return to the Riviera.

The Corniche Sublime and the Grand Canyon du Verdon

From Grasse, take the Route Napoléon (N85), and turn left after 43 km (27 mi) on D21, which becomes D71 at Comps-sur-Artuby.

The Route Napoléon leads to another spectacular road—the Corniche Sublime (D71), which runs along the south side of the Grand Canyon du Verdon, France's answer to the Grand Canyon. The Corniche Sublime is not a road for you if you're afraid of heights. The narrow lane—just wide enough for two cars to scrape by—snakes its way for 40 km (25 mi), along the cliffside, 3,000 ft above the gorge and the tiny River Verdon. At times the river disappears from view beneath the sheer rock face. At the far end of the gorge you'll arrive at the sparkling blue Lac de Ste-Croix, where you may want to stop for a picnic and a walk.

Trigance

⓲ *72 km (45 mi) north of Grasse.*

Trigance, a tiny village of stone houses and some 60 souls, is arranged in rampartlike rings around the château. The **Chapelle St-Roch** stands sentinel to the labyrinth of narrow alleys winding to the ancient bell tower and the church of **St-Michel.**

Dining and Lodging

$$–$$$ ✕🏠 **Château de Trigance.** Not much remains of the 9th-century original, except for the barrel vaulting in the lounge and dining room. Hospitable owner Monsieur Thomas has spent the last decade reconstructing the castle. The setting, on top of a bluff above a small village, gives commanding views of the surrounding hills. Rooms are comfortable, some romantic, with four-posters and stone walls. The dining atmosphere is wonderful; the culinary art, average. ✉ 83840 Trigance, ☎ 04–94–76–91–18, 🖷 04–94–85–68–99. 8 rooms, 2 apartments. Restaurant, helipad. AE, DC, MC, V. Closed early Nov.–mid-Mar.

Tourrettes-sur-Loup

⓳ *20 km (12 mi) east of Grasse via D2085 and D2210, 20 km (12 mi) west of Nice.*

The outer houses of Tourrettes form a rampart on a rocky plateau, 1,300 ft above a valley full of violets. The town is much less commercialized than many others in the area; its shops are filled not with postcards and scented soaps but with the work of dedicated artisans. A rough stone path takes you on a circular route around the rim of the town, past their workshops: Ask the local tourist office for a map that locates each of the shops. Also worth visiting is the single-nave 14th-century church with its notable wooden altar.

Vence

20   *5 km (3 mi) east of Tourrettes-sur-Loup, 22 km (13 mi) north of Nice.*

When you arrive in Vence, leave your car on avenue Foch and climb up to the **Vieille Ville** (Old Town), the medieval town. It is a maze of narrow streets with a central square, the place du Peyra. The beauty of this area is that there are real shops—great wine stores, *fromageries* (cheese shops), and *charcuteries* (butcher shops)—aside from touristy restaurants.

The Romans were the first to settle on the 1,000-ft hill. Rising above the medieval ramparts and traffic-free streets of the Old Town is the **Cathédrale.** It was built on the site of a temple to Mars between the 11th and 18th centuries, using Roman stones with inscribed dates of AD 239. Of special note is a Marc Chagall mosaic of Moses in the bulrushes and the ornate 15th-century wooden choir stalls. ⊠ *pl. Clemenceau.*

★   On the outskirts of Vence, toward St-Jeannet, is the **Chapelle du Rosaire,** a small chapel decorated with beguiling simplicity and clarity by Matisse between 1947 and 1951. The walls, floor, and ceiling are gleaming white, and there are small stained-glass windows in cool greens and blues. "Despite its imperfections I think it is my masterpiece . . . the result of a lifetime devoted to the search for truth," wrote Matisse, who designed and dedicated the chapel when he was in his eighties and nearly blind. ⊠ *av. Henri-Matisse,* ☎ *04–93–58–03–26.* ⊠ *Free.* ☉ *Tues. and Thurs. 10–11:30 and 2–5:30.*

Dining and Lodging

$ ✕ **Le Passe Muraille.** Food at Patrick and Michele Louasse's little restaurant is well prepared and occasionally innovative. Excellent Sisteron lamb and fresh seafood from Nice are often on the menu. In both the ground-floor and stone-arched cellar dining rooms, tables are tight. Patrick's true love is music (he graduated from the Paris conservatory) and Michele has a marvelous voice, so as the evening winds down, he plays and she sings. ⊠ *2 rue du Peyra,* ☎ *04–93–58–10–21. MC, V. Closed Tues.*

$$$$ ✕▥ **Château St-Martin.** The secluded, elite St-Martin stands on the site of a Templar castle, surrounded by tall, shady trees. Rooms are exquisitely decorated with antiques and brocade; those in the tower are smaller and less expensive. The excellent restaurant serves Provençal-inspired dishes. ⊠ *av. des Templiers, 06140,* ☎ *04–93–58–02–02,* ℻ *04–93–24–08–91. 24 rooms, 10 apartments. Restaurant, pool, 2 tennis courts. AE, DC, MC, V. Closed Nov.–May.*

$$ ▥ **Villa Roseraie.** Although there's no rose garden, a giant magnolia
★   spreads its venerable branches over the terrace. The delightful owners, M. and Mme. Ganier, speak excellent English and are quick to help. Mme. Ganier has marvelously decorated the rooms with antiques and warm fabrics; No 2, with its ochre walls and wrought-iron bed, is particularly special; all have sunny southern exposure. Super breakfasts are served on the terrace. ⊠ *51 av. Henri-Giraud, 06140,* ☎ *04–93–58–02–20,* ℻ *04–93–58–99–31. 14 rooms. Pool. AE, MC, V.*

St-Paul-de-Vence

㉑ *4 km (2½ mi) south of Vence on D2, 18 km (11 mi) north of Nice.*

St-Paul-de-Vence is a perfectly preserved medieval town, every weathered crack and cranny brimming with heavy-scented tropical flora. Not even the hordes of tourists—to which the village now caters—can destroy its ancient charm. You can walk the narrow, cobbled streets in perhaps 15 minutes, but you'll probably need another hour to visit the shops. Your best bet is to come in the late afternoon, when the tour buses are gone, and enjoy a drink among the Klees and Picassos in the Colombe d'Or (☞ *Dining and Lodging, below*). Be sure to stop into the remarkable 12th-century Gothic church. The treasury is rich in 12th- to 15th-century pieces, including processional crosses, reliquaries, and an enamel Virgin and Child.

★ Many people come here just to see the **Fondation Maeght** (founded in 1964 by art dealer Aimé Maeght). It's not just a small modern art museum but an extraordinary marriage of the arc-and-plane architecture of José Sert; the looming sculptures of Miró, Moore, and Giacometti; and a humbling hilltop setting of pines, vines, and flowing planes of water. The rooms inside mount an intriguing and ever-varying combination of modern masters, including the wise and funny late-life masterwork *La Vie* by Chagall. ☎ *04–93–32–81–63.* 🖅 *45 frs.* ☉ *July–Sept., daily 10–7; Oct.–June, daily 10–12:30 and 2:30–6.*

Dining and Lodging

\$\$\$ ✕🏠 **Colombe d'Or.** Although you'll have to pay for your room or meal
★ with cash or a credit card, Picasso, Klee, Dufy, Utrillo—all friends of the former owner—paid to stay and eat at this country-feeling inn with the paintings decorating the walls. You may well run into French film stars here, who bask in the fig-shaded garden like their forerunners Montand and Signoret . . . and don't complain about the restaurant's relatively ordinary food. ⊠ *pl. Général-de-Gaulle, 06570,* ☎ *04–93–32–80–02,* 🕿 *04–93–32–77–78. 24 rooms. Restaurant, pool. AE, DC, MC, V. Closed mid-Nov.–late Dec.*

\$\$ ✕🏠 **Les Remparts.** This simple, rustic inn built into the town ramparts is a handy alternative if you don't mind tiny rooms. Excellent Provençal cuisine is served in the restaurant, where the corner table is one of the finest perches in Provence. If you're staying at the hotel, you have the privilege of being able to drive into the village, following the ramparts (otherwise, the town is car free). ⊠ *72 rue Grande, 06570,* ☎ 🕿 *04– 93–32–09–88. 8 rooms, 5 with bath. Restaurant. AE, MC, V. Closed mid-Nov.–late Dec.*

Cagnes-sur-Mer

㉒ *6 km (4 mi) south of St-Paul-de-Vence via D2.*

An attractive castle and a Renoir museum make Cagnes-sur-Mer worth a visit. The **Château,** once a medieval fortress, is perched on a hilltop within the walls of Haut-de-Cagnes. Much of its Renaissance decoration—frescoes, plasterwork, and fireplaces—remains intact, and the third floor hosts an art gallery devoted to Mediterranean artists, including Chagall and Raoul Dufy. ⊠ *pl. Grimaldi,* ☎ *04–93–20–87–29.* 🖅 *20 frs.* ☉ *Easter–mid-Oct., Wed.–Mon. 10–noon and 2:30–6:30; mid-Oct.–Easter, Wed.–Mon. 10–noon and 2–5.*

Painter Auguste Renoir (1841–1919) spent the last 12 years of his life at Cagnes, and his home has been preserved as the **Musée Renoir.** See his studio, as well as some of his work and a bronze statue of Venus nestled amid the fruit trees in the colorful garden. ⊠ *av. des Collettes,*

☏ *04–93–20–61–07.* ⌑ *20 frs.* ☉ *June–Oct., daily 10–noon and 2–6; Nov.–May, Wed.–Mon. 10–noon and 2–5.*

Villeneuve-Loubet

㉓ *1½ km (1 mi) west of Cagnes-sur-Mer.*

The tiny village of Villeneuve-Loubet is best known for its gourmet shrine, the **Fondation Escoffier,** a museum dedicated to Auguste Escoffier (1846–1935), one of Europe's top chefs. As kitchen overlord at the London Carlton and the Paris Ritz, he invented, among other dishes, peach melba. The museum, in the house where he was born, displays some elaborate creations in sugar and marzipan and a collection of 15,000 lip-smacking menus. ✉ *3 rue Escoffier,* ☏ *04–93–20–80–51.* ⌑ *10 frs.* ☉ *Dec.–Oct., Tues.–Sun. 2–6; July–Aug., Tues.–Sun 2–7.*

Nice

12 km (7 mi) northeast of Cagnes-sur-Mer via N7, 960 km (600 mi) southeast of Paris.

The congested road from Cagnes to Nice at the wrong time of day or year can be enough to put you off the Riviera for life. Tedious concrete constructions assault the eye; the railroad on one side and the stony shore on the other offer scant respite. Soon, however, you'll arrive at the Queen of the Riviera—Nice. Less glamorous, less sophisticated, and less expensive than Cannes, Nice is also older and more weathered. A big, sprawling city of 350,000 people—five times as many as Cannes—it has a life and vitality that survive when tourists pack their bags and go home.

Nice is worth a visit, but should you stay here? On the negative side, its beaches are cramped and pebbly, though that's true for much of the Riviera. It's congested with traffic and many of its hotels are run-down. On the positive side, Nice is likely to have hotel space, at prices you can afford. If you are using public transportation, it's a convenient base from which to explore the coast, Monte Carlo, and the medieval towns in the interior. It has its share of first-class restaurants, nightclubs, and shops, and an evening stroll through the Latin-flavored old town or along the promenade des Anglais is something to savor.

㉔ We suggest that you divide your visit to Nice into three short walks, using the arcaded **place Masséna,** the city's main square, as your starting point. You may wish to buy a museum pass (available at any of the museums) if you plan on seeing more than five municipally owned museums. Individual admission to municipal museums is 25 francs; the pass is 120 francs.

㉕ From place Masséna, head west through the fountains and gardens of the **Jardin Albert I** to the promenade des Anglais, built, as the name indicates, by the English community in 1824. Traffic on this multilane highway can be heavy, but once you have crossed to the seafront, there are fine views, across private beaches, of the Baie des Anges.

㉖ The **Palais Masséna,** just off the promenade des Anglais, houses the **Musée d'Art et d'Histoire** (Art and History Museum), concerned principally with the Napoleonic era and, in particular, with the life of local-born general André Masséna (1756–1817). Bonaparte rewarded the general for his heroic exploits during the Italian campaign with the sonorous sobriquet *L'Enfant Chéri de la Victoire* (The Cherished Child of Victory). Sections of the museum evoke the history of Nice and its carnival; there are also some fine Renaissance paintings. ✉ *65 rue de*

Nice

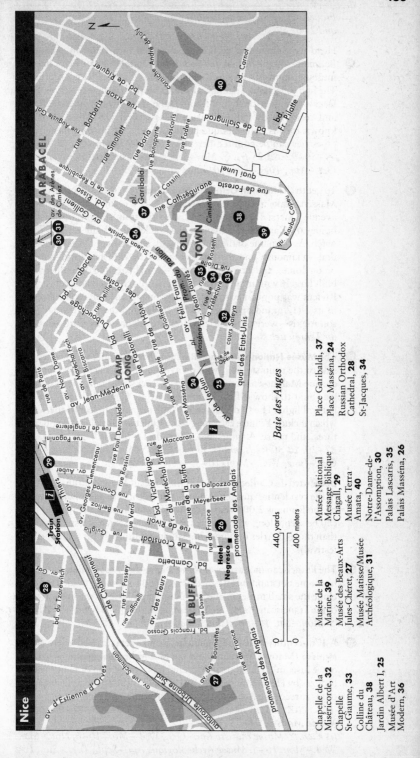

Chapelle de la
Miséricorde, **32**

Chapelle
St-Giaume, **33**

Colline du
Château, **38**

Jardin Albert I, **25**

Musée d'Art
Modern, **36**

Musée de la
Marine, **39**

Musée des Beaux-Arts
Jules-Chéret, **27**

Musée Matisse/Musée
Archéologique, **31**

Musée National
Message Biblique
Chagall, **29**

Musée Terra
Amata, **40**

Notre-Dame-de-
l'Assomption, **30**

Palais Lascaris, **35**

Palais Masséna, **26**

Place Garibaldi, **37**

Place Masséna, **24**

Russian Orthodox
Cathedral, **28**

St-Jacques, **34**

440 yards

400 meters

Baie des Anges

France, ☎ *04–93–88–11–34.* 🖾 *25 frs.* ⊙ *Tues.–Sun. 10–noon and 2–6.*

㉗ Head west along rue de France, and then turn right up avenue des Baumettes to the **Musée des Beaux-Arts Jules-Chéret,** Nice's fine-arts museum, built in 1878 as a palatial mansion for a Russian princess. The rich collection of paintings includes works by Auguste Renoir, Edgar Degas, Claude Monet, and Raoul Dufy; sculptures by Auguste Rodin; and ceramics by Pablo Picasso. Jules Chéret (1836–1932) is best known for his Belle Époque posters; several of his oils, pastels, and tapestries can be admired here. ✉ *33 av. des Baumettes,* ☎ *04–93–44–50–72.* 🖾 *25 frs.* ⊙ *May–Sept., Tues.–Sun. 10–noon and 2–6; Oct.–Apr., Tues.–Sun. 10–noon and 2–5.*

㉘ To get to the **Russian Orthodox Cathedral** from the north side of place Masséna, take avenue Jean-Médecin, Nice's main shopping street, to avenue Thiers: Take a left (west), pass the train station, turn right on boulevard Gambetta, then make the first left onto boulevard du Tzarewitch. As the name of the street suggests, the Russian Orthodox Cathedral—a famously unorthodox Nice landmark, with its colorful ceramics, onion domes, and icon-filled interior—is right around the corner. It was built largely with money from Czar Nicholas II (early this century, the Riviera was popular with Russian top brass, too). But within six years of its 1912 grand opening, Czar Nicholas and the "Czarevitch"—his son Alexis—were dead and the Romanov dynasty overthrown. ✉ *bd. du Tzarewitch.*

㉙ The **Musée National Message Biblique Marc Chagall,** on the northeast side of the train station (head up avenue Thiers, then take a left onto avenue Malausséna, cross the railway tracks, and take the first right), was built to show off the paintings of Marc Chagall (1887–1985) in natural light. The Old Testament is the primary subject of the works, which include 17 huge canvases, 195 preliminary sketches, several sculptures, and nearly 40 gouaches. ✉ *av. du Dr-Ménard,* ☎ *04–93–53–87–20.* 🖾 *30 frs (summer 38 frs).* ⊙ *July–Sept., Wed.–Mon. 10–6; Oct.–June, Wed.–Mon. 10–5.*

Boulevard de Cimiez, just east of the Chagall Museum, runs northeast to the residential quarter of Nice—the hilltop site of **Cimiez,** occupied by the Romans 2,000 years ago. The foundations of the Roman town can be seen, along with vestiges of the arena, which is less spectacular than those at Arles or Nîmes but still in use (notably for a summer jazz festival).

㉚ The Franciscan monastery of **Notre-Dame-de-l'Assomption,** in Cimiez, has some outstanding late-medieval religious pictures; guided tours include the small museum and an audiovisual show on the life and work of the Franciscans. ✉ *pl. du Monastère,* ☎ *04–93–81–00–04.* 🖾 *Free.* ⊙ *Mon.–Sat. 10–noon and 3–6.*

㉛ A 17th-century Italian villa amid the Roman remains houses the **Musée Matisse** (Matisse Museum) and the **Musée Archéologique** (Archaeology Museum). The Matisse Museum has a collection of paintings and bronzes by Henri Matisse (1869–1954), illustrating the different stages of his career. The Archaeology Museum contains a plethora of ancient objects. ✉ *164 av. des Arènes-de-Cimiez,* ☎ *04–93–81–08–08 for Musée Matisse, 04–93–81–59–57 for Musée Archéologique.* 🖾 *25 frs each.* ⊙ *Musée Matisse Apr.–Oct., Wed.–Mon. 10–6; Nov.–Mar., Wed.–Mon. 10–5. Musée Archéologique Apr.–Sept., Tues.–Sun. 10–noon and 2–6; Oct.–Mar., Tues.–Sun. 10–1 and 2–5.*

★ **Vieux Nice** (Old Nice), on the eastern side of the city, is one of the delights of the Riviera. Cars are forbidden on streets that are so narrow that their buildings crowd out the sky. The winding alleyways are lined with faded 17th- and 18th-century buildings. Flowers cascade from window boxes on soft-pastel-color walls. **Cours Saleya** is one of the main thoroughfares and the sight of a colorful morning market.

Stroll along the cours Saleya to reach the central 18th-century church, 32 the **Chapelle de la Miséricorde** (☒ cours Saleya), renowned for its ornate Baroque interior and sculpted decoration.

33 The **Chapelle St-Giaume** (☒ rue de la Poissonnerie), one block north of the cours Saleya, is also known as the Chapelle de l'Annonciation and, to make it more confusing, referred to by locals as the Chapelle de Ste-Rita. Stop in to admire its gleaming Baroque interior and grand altarpieces.

34 **St-Jacques** (☒ rue de Jésus), around the corner from St-Giaume, features on the ceiling an explosion of painted angels and scenes from the life of St. James. Built in the 17th century along the lines of the Gesù Church in Rome, it became a popular place for notable families to sponsor small chapels on either side of the barrel-vaulted nave.

35 The elegant **Palais Lascaris**, just north of St-Jacques, was built in the mid-17th century in the Genovese style for the Count of Vintimiglia, whose family had supported the emperors of Nicaea in Asia Minor during the 13th century. It is decorated with paintings and tapestries and has a particularly grand staircase and a reconstructed 18th-century pharmacy. ☒ *15 rue Droite,* ☎ *04–93–62–05–54.* ☒ *25 frs.* ☉ *Dec.– Oct., Tues.–Sun. 10–noon and 2–6.*

36 The state-of-the-art **Musée d'Art Modern** (Modern Art Museum) has four marble-fronted towers overlooking a sculpture-laden concourse. Its collection of French and international abstract and figurative art from the late 1950s onward is outstanding. ☒ *promenade des Arts,* ☎ *04–93–62–61–62.* ☒ *25 frs.* ☉ *Wed.–Mon. 11–6 (Fri. till 10).*

37 **Place Garibaldi,** east of the Modern Art Museum, was built in the 18th century in Piedmont style with yellow ochre stone. It used to be the northern edge of the city; now it is a symbol separating Vieux Nice and the new city sprawling inland. The statue in the center of the square is of Giuseppe Garibaldi, one of the principal authors of the Italian revolution of 1860 and a friend of France. On the south side is the **Chapelle du St-Sépulcre**, a Baroque 18th-century building under the auspices of the religious order Les Penitents Bleus.

38 Dominating Vieux Nice is the **Colline du Château** (Castle Hill), a romantic cliff fortified many centuries before Christ. It's fun to explore the ruins of the 6th-century castle and the surrounding garden. The 39 small **Musée de la Marine** (Naval Museum) is in the 16th-century **Tour Bellanda** (Bellanda Tower). It contains models, instruments, and documents charting the history of the port of Nice. The elevator between the tower and the quay operates daily 9 to 7 in summer and 2 to 6 in winter. ☒ *rue du Château,* ☎ *04–93–80–47–61.* ☒ *15 frs.* ☉ *June–Sept., Wed.–Sun. 10–noon and 2–7; Oct.–May, Wed.–Sun. 10–noon and 2–5.*

Relics of a local settlement that was active 400,000 years ago are in 40 the **Musée Terra Amata** (Terra Amata was the name of this ancient community). Recorded commentaries in English and films explain the lifestyle of prehistoric dwellers. At press time it was temporarily closed until spring 1999. ☒ *25 bd. Carnot,* ☎ *04–93–55–59–93.* ☒ *25 frs.* ☉ *Oct.–mid-Sept., Tues.–Sun. 9–noon and 2–6.*

CORSICA – If you have a day or two to spare, a high-speed ferry will whisk you to Corsica (☞ Chapter 14) for less than 300 francs: 2½ hours to Calvi or 3½ hours to Bastia. These ferries, operated by SNCM Ferry-terranée (☎ 04–93–13–66–66), depart from Nice twice a day.

Dining and Lodging

$$$ ✕ L'Ane Rouge. In the Vieux Port, this restaurant has been famous for generations as *the* place to go to for fish and seafood. The reputation of chef Michel Devillers is beyond question. But despite the new, sunny look and the fine cuisine, the feeling here is too serious and too expensive. ⊠ *7 quai des Deux-Emmanuel,* ☎ *04–93–89–49–63. Reservations essential. AE, DC, MC, V. Closed Wed. in winter.*

$$ ✕ Grand Café de Turin. Whether you crowd onto a banquette in the dark, low-ceilinged bar or win a table under the arcaded porticoes on place Garibaldi, this is the place to go for shellfish in Nice. Order a bottle of something cold, spread butter on the sliced brown bread, and devour the sea snails, clams, *fines de claires* oysters, and urchins by the dozen set out before you. It's packed afternoon and night. ⊠ *5 pl. Garibaldi,* ☎ *04–93–62–29–52. AE, DC, MC, V. Closed June.*

$$ ✕ La Mérenda. The back-to-bistro boom climaxed here when Dominique
★ Le Stanc retired his crown at the Negresco (☞ *below*)to take over this tiny, unpretentious landmark of Provençal cuisine. Now he and his wife work in the miniature open kitchen creating the ultimate versions of stuffed sardines, pistou, slow-simmered *daubes* (beef stews), and the quintessential stockfish (the local lutefisk). It's one man's private mission; stop by in person to reserve entry to the inner sanctum. ⊠ *4 rue de la Terrasse,* ☎ *no phone. No credit cards. Closed weekends*

$$ ✕ L'Olivier. Franck Musso bakes his own bread and serves up sturdy Provençal dishes (fish soup, snail ravioli, beignets, and tripe), while his brother Christian provides guests with a cheerful welcome to the small, cozy dining room that locals love. Watch for bargain lunch specials. ⊠ *2 pl. Garibaldi,* ☎ *04–93–26–89–09. Reservations essential. AE, MC, V. Closed Sun. and Aug. No lunch Wed.*

$–$$ ✕ La Cambuse. A marketplace greasy spoon, this *bouchon* (tavern) on
★ the cours Saleya packs the sunny outside tables as well as the somber, spare barroom. The cooking is straightforward and portions generous, from sardine beignets to classic "stuffed" vegetables (eggplant, peppers, mushrooms, zucchini with spicy crumb stuffing, marinated in garlicky olive oil); watch for the fish du jour. ⊠ *5 cours Saleya,* ☎ *04–93–80–12–31. MC, V. Closed Sun.*

$$$$ ✕⊡ Château des Ollières. The genteel owner of this fantastic neo-Mo-
★ roccan palace, once the dream house of Prince Lobnov-Rostowsky, has restored it. Its eight rooms are furnished as in a private home, with period details—herringbone parquet, crown moldings, chandeliers—in mint condition. Deluxe rooms have vast marble baths and fine old furniture; standard rooms are filled with toile de Jouy. The candlelit restaurant functions as a table d'hôte—one prix-fixe menu each day—and in summer expands into the extraordinary tropical garden-estate. Only the noise of the highway reminds you of the current epoch. ⊠ *39 av. des Baumettes, 06000,* ☎ *04–92–15–77–99,* FAX *04–92–15–77–98. 8 rooms. Restaurant. AE, MC, V.*

$$$$ ✕⊡ Negresco. Its pink cupola the symbol of Riviera glamour, this faded Belle Époque landmark retains much of its architectural excess, rescued by the eccentric vision of its owner of 40 years. Each floor is devoted to eras of French history, but the one that dominates is the 1960s, from the plastic-glitter bathtubs to the Vasarely-op-art carpet to the photos of Liz and Dick in the bar. Its restaurant, however, is still Nice's finest: Le Chantecler features the artistry of chef Alain Llorca, trained by Le Stanc (☞ La Mérenda, *above*) and Alain Ducasse. ⊠ *37* *promenade des Anglais, 06000,* ☎ *04–93–88–39–51,* FAX *04–93–88–35–68. 122 rooms. 2 restaurants, bar, beach. AE, DC, MC, V.*

$$$$ ✕🏨 **La Pérouse.** Just past the old town, at the foot of the château, this
★ antipalace is a secret treasure cut into the cliff (an elevator takes you up to reception). Most rooms have breathtaking views of the Baie des Anges. Some of the best not only overlook the azure sea but also look down into an intimate garden with lemon trees and a cliff-side pool. A sundeck and sauna by the pool, as well as valet parking, add to the sense of private luxury. Rooms are fair-sized; some sport somber plaids; others have painted provençal furniture. The restaurant serves meals in the candelit garden, May–September. ✉ *11 quai Rauba-Capéu, 06300,* ☎ *04–93–62–34–63,* FAX *04–93–62–59–41. 64 rooms. Restaurant, air-conditioning, pool, sauna. AE, DC, MC, V.*

$$$–$$$$ ✕🏨 **Beau Rivage.** Occupying an imposing late-19th-century town house near the cours Saleya, this hotel is just a few steps from the best parts of old Nice and the beach. Artists at the nearby opera are pampered by its pretty rooms, decorated in soothing pastels. ✉ *24 rue St-François-de-Paule, 06000,* ☎ *04–93–80–80–70,* FAX *04–93–80–55–77. 108 rooms. Restaurant, beach. AE, DC, MC, V.*

$$ 🏨 **Florence.** This old yet modernized hotel, just off rue Jean-Médecin (Nice's major shopping street), is recommended for friendly service, comfort (air-conditioning), and style (marble bathrooms). ✉ *3 rue Paul-Déroulède, 06000,* ☎ *04–93–88–46–87,* FAX *04–93–88–43–65. 56 rooms. Air-conditioning. AE, DC, MC, V.*

$$ 🏨 **La Fontaine.** Downtown and a block from the waterfront is this small, comfortable, immaculate, and simply designed hotel in cheery blues and yellows. It even has a pretty little courtyard where breakfast is served. ✉ *49 rue de France, 06000,* ☎ *04–93–88–30–38,* FAX *04–93–88–98–11. 29 rooms. Breakfast room, air-conditioning. AE, DC, MC, V.*

$$ 🏨 **Mirabeau.** Two hundred yards from the train station on busy avenue Malausséna, and a good 15-minute walk from the beach, is this stylishly renovated hotel. Plants, flowers, and leather armchairs brighten up the lobby-breakfast area; rooms, with floral-pattern quilts and functional modern furniture, vary in size. Nos. 206 and 406 are especially pleasant. The owners are extremely friendly and always ready to assist. ✉ *15 av. Malausséna, 06000,* ☎ *04–93–88–33–67,* FAX *04–93–16–14–08. 42 rooms. Bar, air-conditioning. AE, MC, V.*

$$ 🏨 **Windsor.** This is a memorably eccentric hotel with a vision: Most of its white-on-white rooms either have frescoes of mythic themes or are works of artists' whimsy. (Make sure to request one with air-conditioning, if you want it.) It also has a "relaxation room" on the top floor where you can exercise, meditate, or have a steam bath and massage. But the real draw of this otherwordly place is its astonishing garden—a paradise of lemon, magnolia, and palm trees, and even a tiny pool—in the middle of a city block. You can breakfast or dine here by candlelight (guests only). If all this sounds like your cup of tea, then overlook the slightly tatty public spaces and immerse yourself in an exotism that is particularly Niçoise. ✉ *11 rue Dalpozzo, 06000,* ☎ *04–93–88–59–35,* FAX *04–93–88–94–57. 57 rooms. Restaurant, bar, pool. AE, DC, MC, V.*

$ 🏨 **Felix.** On popular, pedestrian rue Masséna and a block from the beach,
★ this tiny hotel is owned by a hard-working couple (both fluent in English) who make you feel welcome. It's also Nice's best bargain. Rooms are compact but neat and bright, so they don't feel as small, and four have tiny balconies with ringside seats over the pedestrian thoroughfare. There's also TV with CNN. ✉ *41 rue Masséna, 06000,* ☎ *04–93–88–67–73,* FAX *04–93–16–15–78. 14 rooms. Air-conditioning. AE, DC, MC, V.*

$ 🏨 **La Mer.** This small hotel is close to Vieux Nice and the seafront. Though rooms are spartan (and carpets sometimes frayed), the location and prices are good, and the staff is generally pleasant. Ask for a room away from the square to be sure of a quiet night. ✉ *4 pl. Masséna, 06000,* ☎ *04–93–92–09–10,* FAX *04–93–85–00–64. 12 rooms. AE, MC, V.*

Nightlife and the Arts

Of course, another amusing way to spend your money is to gamble it away. At the **casino** (✉ promenade des Anglais), you can try your luck or simply stroll through for a glimpse of the sophisticated clientele and surroundings.

The **jazz festival,** in July, draws international performers from around the world. The **Théâtre de Verdure** (✉ Jardin Albert I) is another spot for jazz and pop; concerts relocate to the **Arènes de Cimiez** in summer. Check local papers for specific venues and information. Classical music and ballet performances take place at the **Acropolis** (✉ Palais des Congrès, Esplanade John-F.-Kennedy, ☎ 04–93–92–80–00). The season at the **Opéra de Nice** (✉ 4 rue St-François-de-Paul, ☎ 04–92–17–40–40) runs from September to June. The **Théâtre Municipal Francis-Gag** (✉ 4 rue St-Joseph, ☎ 04–93–62–00–03) is the place for drama. Plays are also performed at the **Théâtre de Nice** (✉ promenade des Arts, ☎ 04–93–80–52–60).

Outdoor Activities and Sports

Nice's **beaches** extend along the Baie des Anges. **Ruhl Plage** is one of the most popular, with a good restaurant and facilities for waterskiing, windsurfing, and children's swimming lessons. **Neptune Plage** has all that plus a sauna.

Rent bicycles at the **train station** (✉ 17 av. Thiers), and then take the coast road to Cap d'Antibes or ride through the hills to Villefranche-sur-Mer. In winter, **skiing** is the sport of choice: Nice is just 97 km (60 mi) from **Valberg** (4,600 ft), **Auron** (5,250 ft), and **Isola** (6,500 ft) in the Alps.

Shopping

The main shopping street, **avenue Jean-Médecin,** runs inland from place Masséna; all needs and most tastes are catered to in its big department stores (Galeries Lafayette, Prisunic, and the split-level Étoile mall). Olive oil by the gallon, in cans sporting colorful, old-fashioned labels, is sold at tiny **Alziari** (✉ 14 rue St-François-de-Paule); from November to April you can visit Alziari's "oil mill" (✉ 318 bd. de la Madeleine). **Henri Auer** (✉ 7 rue St-François-de-Paule) has a good selection of crystallized fruit, a Nice specialty. Seafood of all kinds is sold at the **fish market** (✉ pl. St-François). The **flea market** (✉ pl. Robilante) by the Old Port is held Tuesday through Saturday and every first Sunday of the month. The daily **flower market** (✉ cours Saleya) features all kinds of plants and mounds of fruits and vegetables. Mondays, check out the **brocante** (collectibles) market (✉ cours Saleya).

En Route   There are three scenic roads at various heights above the coast between Nice and Monte Carlo, a distance of about 19 km (12 mi). All are called "corniches"—literally, a projecting molding along the top of a building or wall. The **Basse Corniche** (lower road) is the busiest and slowest route because it passes through all the coastal towns. The **Moyenne Corniche** (middle road) is high enough for views and close enough for details. It passes the perched village of Èze. The **Grande Corniche** (upper road) winds some 1,300 to 1,600 ft above the sea, with sweeping views of the coast—though it's dangerous to stop and look (there's not really enough space along the side of the road). It follows the Via

Aurelia, the great Roman military road that brought Roman legions from Italy to Gaul (France). In 1806 Napoléon rebuilt the road and sent Gallic troops into Italy. The best advice is to take the Moyenne Corniche one way and the Grande Corniche the other. The view from the upper route is best in the early morning or evening.

Villefranche-sur-Mer

④ *4 km (2½ mi) east of Nice via the Basse Corniche (N98).*

Be sure to include Villefranche on a tour of Cap Ferrat; it is the least commercialized of the Riviera's old fishing ports. With its steep, narrow streets—one, rue Obscure, is actually a tunnel winding down to the sea—the town is a miniature version of old Marseille. It is also a stage set of brightly colored houses, and thus has been a location for a number of films. The 17th-century church of **St-Michel** (⊠ pl. Poullan), in the center of the old town, has a strikingly realistic Christ carved of boxwood by an unknown convict.

The **Cocteau Chapel,** also known as **St-Pierre-des-Pêcheurs,** near the port, is a small Romanesque chapel that was once used for storing fishing nets and was decorated by French writer and painter Jean Cocteau in 1957. Walk through the flames of the Apocalypse (represented by staring eyes on either side of the door) and enter a room filled with frescoes of St. Peter, Gypsies, and the women of Villefranche. ⊠ *pl. Pollanais.* 🎫 *12 frs.* ☉ *Mid-June–mid-Sept., Tues.–Sun. 10–noon and 4–8:30; mid-Sept.–mid-Nov. 9:30–noon and 2–6; end Dec.–Mar., Tues.–Sun. 9–noon and 2–6:30; Apr.–mid-June, Tues.–Sun. 9:30–noon and 3–5.*

Guarding Villefranche is the **Citadelle,** built in 1557 on the site of a smaller fort. On the orders of the Sun King, Louis XIV, the citadel was partially demolished along with the other defenses of the county of Nice. Much of the fort and its imposing walls still remains, however. Housed here is the **Hôtel de Ville** and the **Fondation Musée Volti,** a museum with a collection of contemporary sculpture. ☎ *04–93–76–33–33.* 🎫 *Free.* ☉ *Citadel: always open; Museum: July, Aug., Mon., Wed–Sat. 10–noon and 3–7, Sun 10–noon; June, Sept. 9–noon and 3–6; Oct.–May, 10–noon and 2–5.*

Lodging

$$$ 🏨 **Hôtel Welcome.** When Villefranche was fashionably exclusive, writer Somerset Maugham stayed in one of the low-ceilinged *chambres bâteaux* (boat rooms) on the top floor. These romantic little rooms (especially No. 56) with private balconies feel as if they are cabins in a ship. You may, however, prefer the lighter, more traditionally furnished rooms with bay views. Prices reflect the hotel's superb location on the quai in the old village (two rooms have views of both the bay and the harbor) rather than luxury. But this is the only place in the old village you would want to stay. ⊠ *quai Courbet, 06230,* ☎ *04–93–76–76–93,* 📠 *04–93–01–88–81. Restaurant. MC, V. Closed mid-Nov.–mid-Dec.*

Beaulieu

④ *6 km (4 mi) east of Villefranche-sur-Mer, 10 km (6 mi) east of Nice.*

Beaulieu was a turn-of-the-century high-society haunt, and you can still get a flavor for how things used to be if you walk along the promenade, sometimes called Petite Afrique (Little Africa) because of its magnificent palm trees.

In the early part of the century, a rich amateur archaeologist named
Théodore Reinach asked an Italian architect to build an authentic
Greek house for him here. The **Villa Kérylos** is a faithful reproduction,
made from cool Carrara marble, alabaster, and rare fruitwoods. The
furniture, of wood inlaid with ivory, bronze, and leather, was copied
from drawings of Greek interiors found on ancient vases and mosaics.
⊠ *rue Gustave-Eiffel,* ☎ *04–93–01–01–44.* ⊠ *40 frs.* ☉ *July–Aug.,
weekdays 3–7, weekends 10:30–12:30 and 3–7; Sept.–June, Tues.–
Fri. 2–6, weekends 10:30–12:30 and 2–6.*

St-Jean-Cap-Ferrat

㊸ *1 km (½ mi) south of Beaulieu on D25.*

The lush peninsula of St-Jean-Cap-Ferrat has 17 acres of gardens, as
well as a richly varied art museum. The **Musée Ephrussi de Rothschild**
reflects the sensibilities of its former owner, Mme. Ephrussi de Rothschild, sister of Baron Édouard de Rothschild. An insatiable collector,
she surrounded herself with an eclectic but tasteful collection of French
paintings, Louis XIII furniture, rare Sèvres porcelain, and objets d'art
from the Far East. The remarkable gardens provide a mini–world
tour: Provençal-, Japanese-, Spanish-, and Florentine-style gardens
surround the centerpiece, a garden shaped in the form of a boat. ⊠
Villa Ile-de-France, ☎ *04–93–01–33–09.* ⊠ *28 frs; guided tours 15
frs extra.* ☉ *June–Sept., daily 10–6; Nov.–Feb., weekdays 2–6, weekends 10–6.*

Peillon

㊹ *19 km (12 mi) northeast of Nice via D2204 and D21, then right up
the mountain.*

Of all the perched villages along the Riviera, the fortified medieval town
of Peillon, on a craggy mountaintop more than 1,000 ft above the sea,
is the most spectacular and the least spoiled. Unchanged since the
Middle Ages (thanks to a ban on souvenir shops), the village has only
a few narrow streets and many steps and covered alleys. There's really
nothing to do here but look—which is why the tour buses stay away,
leaving Peillon uncommercialized for the 50 families who live here—
including professionals summering away from Paris and artists who
want to escape the craziness of the world below. You can, however,
visit the **Chapelle des Pénitents Blancs** (Chapel of the White Penitents)—the key is available at the Auberge de la Madone (☞ *below*).

Dining and Lodging

$$ ✕▥ **Auberge de la Madone.** Above a tiny square at the edge of town,
this charming inn serves a lunch of regional cuisine on its idyllic shaded
veranda. The modern little rooms have exposed beams; some have ter-
races and fabulous views. ⊠ *06440 Peillon Village,* ☎ *03–93–79–
91–17,* ⊠ *03–93–79–99–36. 17 rooms. Restaurant. MC, V. Closed
mid-Oct.–mid-Dec. and early Jan.–late Jan.*

Èze

㊺ *2 km (1 mi) east of Beaulieu, 12 km (7 mi) east of Nice, 8 km (5 mi)
west of Monte Carlo.*

Almost every tour from Nice to Monaco includes a visit to the medieval
hill town of Èze, perched on a rocky spur near the Moyenne Corniche,
some 1,300 ft above the sea. (Don't confuse Èze with the beach town
of Èze-sur-Mer, which is down by the water on the Basse Corniche. If
you arrive by train from Nice, there is a shuttle bus, in summer, be-

tween Èze-sur-Mer and Èze Village.) Although Èze has its share of serious craftspeople, most of its vendors cater to the crowds of tourists.

Enter the town through the fortified 14th-century gate and wander down the narrow, cobbled streets with vaulted passageways and stairs. The church is from the 18th century, but the small **Chapelle des Pénitents Blancs** (Chapel of the White Penitents) dates from 1306 and contains a 13th-century gilded wooden Spanish Christ and some notable 16th-century paintings. Crafts shops and those oriented toward tourists line the streets leading to the ruins of the **Château,** which has a scenic belvedere.

Near the top of the village is the **Jardin Exotique,** a garden with exotic flowers and cacti. It's worth the admission price, but it's not as nice as the one in Monte Carlo. ⊠ *rue du Château,* ☎ *04–93–41–10–30.* ☞ *8 frs.* ☉ *June–Sept., 9–7:30; Oct.–May, 9–noon and 2–7.*

If you're not going to Grasse (☞ *above*), consider visiting a branch of a Grasse perfumery, **La Parfumerie Fragonard,** in front of the public gardens. ⊠ *Moyenne Corniche,* ☎ *04–93–41–05–05.* ☞ *Free.* ☉ *Daily 8:30–6:30.*

Dining and Lodging

$$$$ ✕☐ **Château de la Chèvre d'Or.** A member of the Relais & Châteaux
★ group, this hotel is made up of a number of ancient houses whose mellow stone walls are set off by terra-cotta pots brimming with geraniums. Rooms, in creamy shades, are small but airy and embellished with antiques; some command fairy-tale views of rock and sea. The bar is in a medieval room with stone walls and Louis XIII furniture. The restaurant is dignified but pricey. Swallow the price and you can enjoy beautifully presented cuisine, scented, as chef Mazot likes to say, with the perfumes of Provence. ⊠ *rue du Barri, 06360,* ☎ *04–92–10–66–66,* FAX *04–93–41–06–72. 22 rooms, 8 apartments. Restaurant, bar, café, pool. AE, DC, MC, V. Closed Dec.–Feb.*

Monaco

8 km (5 mi) east of Èze on the Moyenne Corniche, 20 km (12 mi) east of Nice.

The Principality of Monaco covers just 473 acres and would fit comfortably inside New York's Central Park or a family farm in Iowa. Its 5,000 citizens would fill only a small fraction of the seats in Yankee Stadium. Note that when calling Monaco from France or elsewhere, you must first dial the country code, 377.

The present ruler, Prince Rainier III, traces his ancestry to Otto Canella, who was born in 1070. The Grimaldi dynasty began with Otto's great-great-great-grandson, Francesco Grimaldi, also known as Frank the Rogue. Expelled from Genoa, Frank and his cronies disguised themselves as monks and seized, in 1297, the fortified medieval town known today as Le Rocher (The Rock). Except for a short break under Napoléon, the Grimaldis have been here ever since, which makes them the oldest reigning family in Europe. On the Grimaldi coat of arms are two monks holding swords (look up and you'll see them above the main door as you enter the palace).

Back in the 1850s, a Grimaldi named Charles III made a decision that turned the Rock into a giant blue chip. Needing revenues but not wanting to impose additional taxes on his subjects, he contracted with a company to open a gambling facility. The first spin of the roulette wheel was on December 14, 1856. There was no easy way to reach Monaco then—no carriage roads or railroads—so no one came. Be-

Monaco

tween March 15 and March 20, 1857, one person entered the casino—and won two francs. In 1868, however, the railroad reached Monaco, filled with wheezing Englishmen who came to escape the London fog. The effects were immediate. Profits were so great that Charles eventually abolished all direct taxes.

Almost overnight, a threadbare principality became an elegant watering hole for European society. Dukes (and their mistresses) and duchesses (and their gigolos) danced and dined their way through a world of spinning roulette wheels and bubbling champagne—preening themselves for nights at the opera, where such artists as Vaslav Nijinsky, Sarah Bernhardt, and Enrico Caruso came to perform.

Monte Carlo—the modern gambling town with elegant shops, manmade beaches, high-rise hotels, and a few Belle Époque hotels—is actually only one of four parts of Monaco. The second part is **Old Monaco**, the medieval town on the Rock, 200 ft above the sea. It's here that Prince Rainier lives. The third area is **La Condamine**, the commercial harbor area with apartments and businesses. **Fontvieille**, the fourth area of Monaco, is an industrial district on 20 acres of reclaimed land.

Start at the **tourist office** (⊠ av. de la Costa, ☎ 92–16–61–16), just north of the casino gardens. Ask for the useful English booklet *Getting Around in the Principality* to give you an idea about which buses you can use. For what to see and where to find it, request the booklet *Monaco's Tourist Attractions.*

★ ㊻ Place du Casino is the center of Monte Carlo, and the **casino** is a must-see, even if you don't bet a sou. You may find it fun to count the Jaguars and Rolls-Royces parked outside and breathe on the windows of shops selling Yves Saint Laurent dresses and fabulous jewels. Into the gold-leaf splendor of the casino, where fortunes have been won and shirts have been lost, the hopeful traipse from tour buses to tempt fate at slot machines beneath the gilt-edged rococo ceiling. The main gambling hall, once called the European Room, has been renamed the **Salle Americaine** and fitted with 150 one-armed bandits from Chicago. Adjoining it is the **Salon Rose,** now a bar where unclad nymphs float about on the ceiling smoking cigarillos. The **Salles Privées** (Private Rooms) are for high rollers. Jacket and tie are required in the back rooms, which open at 4 PM. Bring your passport (under-21s not admitted). ⊠ *pl. du Casino.* ☉ *Noon–the last die is thrown.*

In the true spirit of the town, it seems that the **Opéra,** with its 18-ton gilt-bronze chandelier, is part of the casino complex. The designer, Charles Garnier, also built the Paris Opéra (☞ Chapter 2). ⊠ *pl. du Casino.*

㊼ The serious gamblers, some say, play at **Loews Casino.** It opens weekdays at 4 PM and weekends at 1 PM. You may want to try parking here, since parking near the old casino is almost impossible.

㊽ From place des Moulins there is an escalator down to the Larvotto beach complex, artfully created with imported sand, and the **Musée National** (National Musem), housed in a Garnier villa within a rose garden. This museum has a beguiling collection of 18th- and 19th-century dolls and mechanical automatons. ⊠ *17 av. Princesse-Grace,* ☎ *93–30–91–26.* ☐ *26 frs.* ☉ *Easter–Aug., daily 10–6:30; Sept.–Easter, daily 10–12:15 and 2:30–6:30.*

㊾ Prince Rainier spends much of the year in his grand Italianate **Palais du Prince** (Prince's Palace) on the Rock. The changing of the guard takes place here each morning at 11:55, and the State Apartments can be visited in summer. ☎ *93–25–18–31.* ☐ *35 frs; joint ticket with Musée Napoléon (☞ below) 40 frs.* ☉ *June–Oct., daily 9:30–6:30.*

One wing of the palace, open throughout the year, is taken up by the **Musée Napoléon,** filled with Napoleonic souvenirs and documents related to Monaco's history. ☎ *93–25–18–31.* ☐ *20 frs; joint ticket with palace apartments (☞ above).* ☉ *June–Oct., daily 9:30–6:30.*

㊿ The **Cathédrale,** a short stroll though the medieval alleyways near the Napoléon Museum, is a neo-Romanesque monstrosity (1875–84), with several important paintings of the Nice school. ⊠ *rue Col de Castro.*

�945 One of Monaco's most outstanding showpieces, the **Musée Océanographique** (Oceanography Museum), is an important research institute once headed by the late, great underwater explorer and film-maker Jacques Cousteau (1910–1997); his films are shown in the museum cinema. Prince Rainier's great-grandfather Albert I (1848–1922), an accomplished marine biologist, founded the institute in 1910. It now has two exploration ships, laboratories, and a staff of 60 scientists. Non-scientific visitors may wish to go straight to the well-arranged and generously stocked aquarium in the basement. Other floors are devoted to Prince Albert's collection of seashells and whale skeletons and to Cousteau's diving equipment. For a fine view and a restorative drink, take the elevator to the roof terrace. ⊠ *av. St-Martin,* ☎ *93–15–36–00.* ☜ *60 frs.* ☼ *July–Aug., daily 9–8; Sept. and Apr.–June, daily 9:30–7; Oct.–Mar, daily 9:30–6.*

52 Six hundred varieties of cacti and succulents cling to a sheer rock face at the **Jardin Exotique** (Tropical Garden), a brisk half-hour walk west from the palace. ⊠ *bd. du Jardin Exotique,* ☎ *93–30–33–65.*

53 The **Musée d'Anthropologie Préhistorique** (Museum of Prehistoric Anthropology), on the grounds of the Tropical Garden (☞ *above*), contains bones, tools, and other artifacts. Shapes of the stalactites and stalagmites in the cavernous grotto (entered from the gardens) resemble the cacti outside. ⊠ *56 bis bd. du Jardin Exotique,* ☎ *93–15–80–06.* ☜ *38 frs.* ☼ *May–Sept., daily 9–7; Oct.–April , daily 9–6 or until dusk.*

Dining and Lodging

$$$$ ✕ **Louis XV.** This restaurant, in the Hôtel de Paris (☞ *below*), stuns
★ with royal decor and superb food made by chef Alain Ducasse, one of Europe's most celebrated chefs. Ducasse often refers to his deceptively simple style as "country cooking." Using the sensual flavors of Provence and northern Italy and nothing but the finest produce, he creates dishes such as braised baby pigeon with duck foie gras and milk-fed lamb stuffed with a mixture fragrant with black olives. ⊠ *Hôtel de Paris, pl. du Casino,* ☎ *92–16–30–01. AE, MC, V. Closed Tues. and mid-June–Aug. (except Wed. dinner)*

$$–$$$ ✕ **Port.** Harbor views from the terrace and top-notch Italian food make the Port a good choice. The large, varied menu includes homemade pasta, seafood, and fish risotto. ⊠ *quai Albert-I,* ☎ *93–50–77–21. AE, DC, MC, V. Closed Mon. and Nov.*

$–$$ ✕ **Polpetta.** This popular little trattoria is close enough to the Italian
★ border to pass for the real McCoy. If it's on the menu, go for the vegetable soupe au pistou and the *risotto al porcini* (risotto with wild mushrooms). ⊠ *2 rue Paradis,* ☎ *93–50–67–84. Reservations essential in summer. MC, V. Closed Tues. and Feb. No lunch Sat.*

$ ✕ **Le Bistrot.** At this restaurant, popular with locals and tourists at lunch, you can sit outside and watch the activities of the port, sit inside at banquettes, or just have a drink at the bar. The 60-franc menu du jour might include grilled sardines or a small entrecôte steak. ⊠ *21 bd. Albert-I,* ☎ *93–30–26–88. MC, V. Closed Sun. No dinner Sat.*

$$$$ ✕▥ **Hermitage.** Even if you're not staying, come to see the glass-dome Art Nouveau vestibule and the white-stucco rococo corridor leading to the lavish dining room, where pink marble columns hold up a gilded, frescoed ceiling. The adjacent terrace has a tinkling pianist in summer and a view of the harbor. Rooms are comfortable but far less stylish; not all face the sea—and these are priced accordingly. The hotel is one block west of the casino. ⊠ *square Beaumarchais, B.P. 277, 98005,* ☎ *92–16–40–00,* ℻ *92–16–38–52. 197 rooms, 34 apartments. Restaurant, bar, pool. AE, DC, MC, V.*

$$$$ ✕▥ **Hôtel de Paris.** This hotel has one of the most prestigious addresses, and you pay for it at every turn. The hotel exudes the ambience of an era in which kings and grand dukes were regulars, though the hallways and public areas are not as striking as you might expect. The spacious, yellow-painted rooms have high ceilings, floral-patterned curtains, and white, wood furniture; from some you can view the sea or the casino. Dinner is served in the superb Louis XV (☞ *above*); breakfast (Continental runs 150 francs) is served on the terrace in Le Côte Jardin; and Mediterranean-style cuisine is served in Le Grill. ⊠ *pl. du Casino, 98000,* ☎ *92–16–30–00,* FAX *92–16–38–50. 143 rooms, 41 suites, and 19 junior suites. 4 restaurants, 1 indoor and 1 outdoor pool, spa. AE, DC, MC, V.*

$$$$ ✕▥ **Loews.** Big, brash, and more than a touch vulgar, Loews has a plush extravagance on a scale Donald Trump would envy. Contemporary rooms are decorated in ice cream shades. Celebrities mix with sheikhs in the bars, casino, and restaurants. Diehard football fans can watch the Super Bowl by satellite; those in search of live entertainment can head for the Folie Russe cabaret. ⊠ *12 av. des Spélugues, 98000,* ☎ *93–50–65–00,* FAX *93–30–01–57. 650 rooms, 69 apartments. 3 restaurants, 3 bars, pool, hot tub, health club, cabaret, casino. AE, DC, MC, V.*

$$ ▥ **Alexandra.** The friendly proprietress, Mme. Larouquie, makes foreign visitors feel right at home at this central, comfortable spot. Though the color schemes clash and the decor is spare, bathrooms are big and newly redone. ⊠ *35 bd. Princesse-Charlotte, 98000,* ☎ *93–50–63– 13,* FAX *92–16–06–48. 55 rooms. Air-conditioning. AE, DC, MC, V.*

Nightlife and the Arts

There's no need to go to bed before dawn in Monte Carlo when you can go to the **casino** (⊠ pl. du Casino). **Sparco Café** (⊠ 19 av. Charles-III) is a piano bar that often attracts good jazz singers. **Jimmy's** (⊠ On rue Sporting, Sept.–June; on av. Princesse-Grace, July–Oct.) is a fun spot. If you can't get in to Jimmy's, try the neighboring **Parady's** (⊠ av. Princesse-Grace), with a chic and slightly younger crowd. The **Living Room** (⊠ 7 av. des Spélugues) is a popular, crowded bar open year-round. **Tiffany's** (⊠ 3 av. des Spélugues) is another year-round hot spot.

Monte Carlo's spring arts festival, **Printemps des Arts,** takes place from early April to mid-May and includes the world's top ballet, operatic, symphonic, and chamber performers. Year-round, ballet and classical music can be enjoyed at the **Salle Garnier** (⊠ pl. du Casino, ☎ 92–16–22–99). The **Théâtre Princesse Grace** (⊠ 12 av. d'Ostende, ☎ 93–25–32–27) stages a number of plays during the spring festival; off-season, there's usually a new show each week.

Outdoor Activities and Sports

The best **beaches** in Monte Carlo are **Plage Monte Carlo** and **Plage du Larvotto,** the public beach. Both are off avenue Princesse-Grace and have a variety of water-sports facilities.

The 18-hole **Golf de Monte Carlo** (⊠ rte. du Mont-Agel, La Turbie, ☎ 04–93–41–09–11) is open to the public. Diving equipment can be rented from the **Under Water Diving Club** (⊠ quai des Sanbarbani, ☎ 92–05–91–78).

The **Monte Carlo Tennis Tournament** is held during the spring arts festival. When the tennis stops, the auto racing begins: The **Grand Prix de Monaco** (☎ 93–15–26–00 for information) takes place in mid-May.

Roquebrune

🚳 *5 km (3 mi) east of Monaco.*

The hilltop village of Roquebrune has a Carolingian castle, medieval houses, covered steps, and narrow streets. The adjacent Cap Martin peninsula is colonized by wealthy villa dwellers. Near the tip, on avenue Winston-Churchill, is the start of a coastal walking path—the promenade Le Corbusier—that leads to Monte Carlo in 1½ hours.

Menton

⑤⑤ *9 km (5½ mi) east of Monaco.*

Next door to Roquebrune is Menton, a comparatively quiet resort town with the warmest climate on the Riviera. Lemon trees flourish here, as do senior citizens, enticed by a long strand of beaches. Menton likes to call itself the Pearl of the Riviera—beautiful, respectable, and not grossly expensive.

Walk eastward from the casino along promenade du Soleil to the harbor where there is a small 17th-century fort housing the **Musée Cocteau.** Writer, artist, and filmmaker Jean Cocteau (1889–1963) once worked here. The museum has a fantastic array of his paintings, drawings, stage sets, and a large mosaic. ⊠ *Bastion du Port, 111 quai Napoléon-III,* ☎ *04–93–57–72–30.* ☒ *Free.* ☉ *Wed.–Sun. 10–noon and 2–6.*

The quaint **Vieille Ville** (Old Town) above the jetty has an Italian feel to it, with its pretty squares and lively market. The church of **St-Michel** (⊠ rue St-Michel) has an ornate Baroque interior and altarpiece of St. Michael slaying a dragon. Chamber music concerts take place in the square on summer nights. Walk up through the old town to get to the **Vieux Cimetière** (Old Cemetery) and a magnificent view of the Old Town and coast. Here lie Victorian foreigners who hoped (in vain, as the dates on the tombstones reveal) that Menton's balmy climate would reverse the ravages of tuberculosis.

In the center of town is the **Hôtel de Ville** (Town Hall). The **Salle des Mariages,** the room in which marriage ceremonies are conducted, has vibrant allegorical frescoes by Cocteau; a tape in English helps to interpret them. ⊠ *17 av. de la République.* ☒ *5 frs.* ☉ *Weekdays 8:30–12:30 and 1:30–5.*

On the west side of town is the **Palais Carnolès,** an 18th-century villa once used as a summer retreat by the princes of Monaco. The gardens are beautiful, and the collection of European paintings (13th to 18th century) is extensive. ⊠ *3 av. de la Madone,* ☎ *04–93–35–49–71.* ☒ *Free.* ☉ *Wed.–Sun. 10–noon and 2–6.*

Dining and Lodging

$$–$$$ ✕▥ **Aiglon.** Sweep down the curving stone stair to the terrazzo mo-
★ saic lobby of this lovely 1880 garden-villa and wander out for a drink or a meal by the pool. Or settle onto your little balcony overlooking the grounds and a tiny wedge of sea. There's a room for every whim, all soft-edged, comfortable, and romantic. The poolside restaurant, Le Riaumont, serves classic seafood by candlelight; breakfast is served in a shady garden shelter. It's a three-minute walk to the beach. ⊠ *7 av. de la Madone, 06502,* ☎ *04–93–57–55–55,* ﬁﬄ *04–93–35–92–39. 28 rooms, 2 apartments. Restaurant, bar. AE, MC, V.*

$$ ✕▥ **Londres.** This small, family-owned central hotel is close to the beach and the casino. Rooms are plain but clean; those in the back are cooler. The restaurant serves solid, traditional French cuisine; in summer, meals are served in the small garden. The restaurant is closed Wednesday. ⊠ *15 av. Carnot, B.P. 73, 06502,* ☎ *04–93–35–74–62,* ﬁﬄ *04–93–41–77–78. 27 rooms. Restaurant, bar. AE, MC, V.*

Nightlife and the Arts

The **casino** (⊠ promenade de Soleil) has the usual slot machines and roulette tables, as well as top-class cabaret in its Club 06. In August, the **Festival de Musique de Chambre** (Chamber Music Festival) takes place in the St-Michel church. The **Fête du Citron** (Lemon Festival) at the end of February celebrates the lemon with Rose Bowl–parade-like floats and sculptures, all made of real fruit.

THE RIVIERA A TO Z

Arriving and Departing

By Car

If you're traveling from Paris by car, you can avoid a lengthy drive by taking the overnight motor-rail (*train-auto-couchette*) service to St-Raphaël or Nice, which departs from Paris (Gare de Bercy). Otherwise, leave Paris by A6 (becoming A7 after Lyon), which continues down to Avignon. Here A8 branches off east toward Italy, with convenient exit-entry points for all major towns (except St-Tropez, which is some 30 km/19 mi south on a minor road branching off A8). Driving non-stop from Paris to Nice takes about eight hours; if you are driving from Provence (such as Aix-en-Provence) to Nice, allow 90 minutes.

By Plane

The area's only international airport is the **Aéroport Nice–Côte d'Azur** in Nice (☎ 04–93–21–30–12). **Air France** has many flights to Paris daily. **Corse Méditerranée** has flights to Corsica.

By Train

The high-speed TGV (*Trains à Grande Vitesse*) from Paris (Gare de Lyon) to Nice takes about six hours and 30 minutes. Regular SNCF trains from Paris to Nice take more than 10 hours, so reserve a *couchette* (an overnight sleeping car). Frequent daily local trains run along the coast from Nice to Menton. For Monaco, take a connecting train out of Nice; the trip takes 30 to 40 minutes.

Getting Around

By Bus

Local buses cover a network of routes along the Riviera and stop at many out-of-the-way places that can't be reached by train. Timetables are available from tourist offices, train stations, and local bus depots (*gares routières*).

By Car

If you prefer to avoid the slower, albeit spectacularly scenic, coastal roads (especially in summer), opt for the Italy-bound A8. While trains are convenient along the coast, it is really only with a car that you can appreciate the beauty of the inland hills and villages.

By Train

The train is a practical and inexpensive way of getting around the Riviera and stops at dozens of stations. Pick up a schedule at any of the local train stations to plan your times, but don't worry too much about missing a trai, as they run frequently during the day. Nice's **train station** (⊠ av. Thiers, ☎ 04–93–87–50–50) serves all lines along the Riviera. Note that the pretty Nice–Digne line is not run by the SNCF but by the **Chemin de Fer de Provence** (⊠ Gare du Sud, 33 av. Malausséna, Nice, ☎ 04–93–88–28–56).

Contacts and Resources

Car Rental

Avis (⊠ 9 av. d'Ostende, Monaco, ☎ 04–93–30–17–53; ⊠ av. du 8-mai-1945, St-Tropez, ☎ 04–94–97–03–10). **Europcar** (⊠ 9 av. Thiers, Menton, ☎ 04–93–28–21–80). **Hertz** (⊠ 147 rue d'Antibes,

Cannes, ☎ 04–93–99–04–20; ⊠ 12 av. de Suède, Nice, ☎ 04–93–87–11–87).

Guided Tours

Local tourist offices have loads of suggestions about gourmandizing, golfing, and walking tours, among others. You can also try one of the following tour companies. **Gallus Excursions 80** (⊠ 24 quai Lunel, 06000 Nice, ☎ 04–92–04–28–30) runs enjoyable daylong jaunts by boat to the Iles de Lérins; the cost is about 80 francs. **Santa Azur** (⊠ 11 av. Jean-Médecin, 06000 Nice, ☎ 04–93–85–46–81, ℻ 04–93–87–90–08) organizes a variety of bus tours (most starting from the bus station, or gare routière, on promenade du Paillon in Nice, but sometimes with pickups in Menton, Cannes, or Antibes).

Travel Agencies

American Express (⊠ 8 rue des Belges, Cannes, ☎ 04–93–38–15–87; ⊠ 11 promenade des Anglais, Nice, ☎ 04–93–16–53–53). **Carlson Wagons-Lits** (⊠ 2 av. Monte Carlo, Monaco, ☎ 04–97–97–35–15).

Visitor Information

The Riviera's regional tourist office is the **Comité Régional du Tourisme de Riviera-Côte d'Azur** (⊠ 55 promenade des Anglais, 06000 Nice); it accepts written inquiries only.

Local tourist offices in major towns covered in this chapter are as follows: **Antibes** (⊠ 11 pl. du Général-de-Gaulle, ☎ 04–92–90–53–00). **Cannes** (⊠ Palais des Festivals, 1 La Croisette, ☎ 04–93–39–01–01). **Fréjus** (⊠ 325 rue Jean-Jaurès, ☎ 04–93–39–24–53). **Grasse** (⊠ 22 cours Honoré-Cresp, ☎ 04–93–36–03–56). **Juan-les-Pins** (⊠ 51 bd. Charles-Guillaumont, ☎ 04–92–90–53–05). **Mandelieu–La Napoule** (⊠ 272 av. Henry-Clews, ☎ 04–92–97–86–46). **Menton** (⊠ Palais de l'Europe, av. Boyer, ☎ 04–93–57–57–00). **Monte Carlo** (⊠ 2a bd. des Moulins, ☎ 92–16–61–66). **Nice** (⊠ av. Thiers, ☎ 04–93–87–07–07). **St-Tropez** (⊠ quai Jean-Jaurès, ☎ 04–94–97–45–21). **Vence** (⊠ pl. du Grand-Jardin, ☎ 04–93–58–06–38).

14 Corsica

This Mediterranean "mountain in the sea," off the coast of Monaco, is known for its striking, unspoiled scenery and its rich, cultural treasures. Come here to visit the port city of Bastia, explore a chestnut forest, climb to Corte's citadel, and laze on a beach in Calvi. Or come to admire the cliffs of Bonifacio, see Napoléon's birthplace in Ajaccio, listen to traditional folk music, and delight in fine yet simple Corsican cuisine.

Revised and
updated by
George Semler

ANCIENT MEDITERRANEAN PORTS, artistic and archaeological treasures, crystalline waters, granite peaks, and pine forests make Corsica one of France's most beautiful regions. For thousands of years, its natural resources and strategic location, 168 km (105 mi) south of Monaco and just 81 km (50 mi) west of Italy, have made Corsica a prize hotly contested by many Mediterranean civilizations. You can still see vestiges of those invaders—the city-state of Genoa ruled Corsica for more than 200 years, leaving behind impressive citadels and bridges and a network of nearly 100 medieval watchtowers that still encircle the island. The Italian influence is also apparent in village architecture and in the Corsican language, a combination of Italian, Tuscan dialect, and Latin.

Although it's only 215 km (133 mi) long and 81 km (50 mi) wide, Corsica seems much larger—partly because rugged, mountainous terrain makes for slow traveling and partly because the landscape and the culture vary so much from one "micro-region" to another. Much of Corsica that is not wooded or cultivated is covered with a dense thicket of undergrowth called the *maquis*. The maquis is made up of a variety of sweet-smelling plants including lavender, myrtle, and heather that gave Corsica one of its nicknames, "the perfumed isle." The maquis is also famous for harboring a motley crew of fugitives. In Corsica, you didn't head for the hills, you headed for the maquis.

There has always been a rough legend associated with the island, stemming mainly from a tradition of apparent lawlessness and deeply entrenched clannishness. As justice from "the Continent," whether France or Italy, was usually slow and often unsatisfying, Corsican clans frequently fought each other in blood feuds of revenge. The term "vendetta" is, in fact, Corsica's prime contribution to world lexicography.

Corsica is especially famous as the birthplace of Napoléon Bonaparte. Although he never returned to the island after beginning his military career, you can visit his family's home in Ajaccio. Perhaps better suited to the island's individualist character is Corsica's real national hero, Pasquale Paoli, who framed the world's first constitution for the independent Corsican republic in 1755 and whose ideas significantly influenced the French Revolution as well as the founding fathers of the United States.

Pleasures and Pastimes

Architecture and Archaeology

Corsica is superbly endowed with cultural riches ranging from megalithic monuments to Roman ruins to Baroque churches to Genoan bridges. Forts, mills, bell towers, tombs, *bergeries* (shepherds' huts), mountain refuges, lookout towers, and traditional farmhouses are all characteristic parts of the uniquely Corsican patrimony.

Dining

Authentic Corsican fare based on free-range livestock, game (especially wild boar), herbs, and wild mushrooms is best found in the tiny villages of the mountainous interior between October and April. *Civets* (delicious meaty stews) feature prominently on menus, as do many versions of the prototypical, hearty Corsican soup (alternately known as *soupe paysanne, soupe corse,* and *soupe de montagne*), made from herbs and vegetables simmered for hours with a ham bone. Seafood dishes are available on the coast: particularly good is *aziminu,* a rich bouillabaisse. Everywhere you'll find all kinds of *charcuterie* (pork products): *Lonzu* (shoulder), *coppa* (fillet), and *figatelli* (liver sausage) are standard cuts, along with *prisuttu* (cured ham).

Corsican cheeses include *brocciu* (pronounced *bro*-cho), similar to ricotta and used in omelettes, *fiadone* (cheesecake), *fritelli* (chestnut-flour doughnuts), and as stuffing for trout or rabbit; *bastelicaccia*, a soft, creamy sheep cheese; and *sartenais*, a harder and sharper cheese. Many of the most powerful cheeses are simply designated as *brebis* (sheep) or *chèvre* (goat). Chestnuts and chestnut flour also play an important part in Corsican gastronomy: in *castagna* (chestnut in Corsican), a cake; *panetta*, a kind of bread; *canistrelli*, dry cookies; *beignets* (fried dough), often made of chestnut flour; *pulenta*, a doughy chestnut-flour bread; and *pietra*, chestnut beer. Be sure to try some of Corsica's fine wines: Orenga de Gaffory or Gentile, from the Patrimonio vineyards; Domaine Peraldi Clos du Cardinal from Ajaccio; and Fiumicicoli from Sartène.

CATEGORY	COST*
$$$$	over 350 frs
$$$	250 frs–350 frs
$$	125 frs–250 frs
$	under 125 frs

per person for a three-course meal, including tax (20.6%) and tip but not wine

Lodging

The amount of building around Porto-Vecchio in the 1950s was so horrifying to Corsicans that they resolved to avoid excessive tourist-driven development. Instead, *fermes-auberges* (farmhouse-inns) are being restored at a rapid clip and tastefully designed new hotels are being built. During the peak season (July to mid-September) prices are higher and some hotels insist that you have breakfast and dinner there. The best seaside hotels are priced only marginally lower than in the Riviera, but lodging in the interior villages remains substantially cheaper. Off-season, good prices can be found all over.

CATEGORY	COST*
$$$$	over 750 frs
$$$	400 frs–750 frs
$$	250 frs–400 frs
$	under 250 frs

All prices are for a standard double room for two, including tax (20.6%) and service charge.

Outdoor Activities

From the wild, undeveloped strands of Cap Corse (Cape Corsica) to the Riviera-like tourist beaches near Calvi and Propriano, the island's coastline offers astonishing variety. In summer, during the *canicule* (literally, "dog days") Corsicans take to the rivers, always cooler than the Mediterranean. Others take on the rugged GR 20 (Grande Randonnée 20): Considered one of Europe's greatest hiking trails, it requires 70 to 100 hours to complete. Planned in stages from one mountain refuge to another, the well-marked GR 20 is the ultimate way to see Corsica. If you are traveling by car, short probes along the GR 20 are easily feasible. Check with tourist offices and/or bookstores for guides.

Exploring Corsica

Both leaving Marseille (on the excellent SNCM *Ferryterranée*, which also departs from Toulon and Nice) in the sunset and arriving in Ajaccio as the sun rises are among the finest moments of any trip to Corsica. Napoléon claimed he could identify the fragrance of the Corsican maquis from many miles away at sea; approaching the island by airplane seems like heresy. The northern half of the island (Haute Corse) is generally wilder than the southern half (Corse du Sud), which is hotter and more barren. On the other hand, southern Corsica's archaeological sites at Filitosa and Pianu de Levie, the Col de Bavella and its majestic laricio pine forest, and the towns of Sartène and Bonifacio all rank indisputably among the island's finest treasures. The least interesting part of the island is the coast between Porto-Vecchio and Bastia; the prettiest route is the one around Cap Corse. If you spend too much time at sea level, you'll miss the dramatic heights for which the island is famous. Also be sure to brush up on your French before you go outside the main towns—the port city of Bastia and the French capital, Ajaccio (pronounced ah-*jack*-sio)—it's difficult to find people who speak English.

Great Itineraries

Three days is barely sufficient time to visit Corsica's three main cities and some of the island's prettiest scenery. In 5 days you can cover most of Haute Corse and in 10 days it is possible, though not necessarily advisable, to see the whole island: The danger is of spending too much time car-bound. One approach is to settle in Corte, near the island's center, sallying forth each day to different attractions.

Numbers in the text correspond to numbers in the margin and on the Corsica and Ajaccio maps.

IF YOU HAVE 3 DAYS

Ajaccio ①–⑦ is a good place to start. A two-hour drive over the Vizzavona pass to ☒ **Corte** ⑮ will place you at the island's historical heart for the night. Explore the **Restonica gorges** and Corte the next day. On day three, drive through the chestnut-covered **La Castagniccia** region, visiting the small villages along the way. Find your way out of La Castagniccia via Folelli, stopping for lunch in **Murato** ㉝. Save the afternoon and evening for exploring **Bastia** ㊾, before shipping out for the mainland.

IF YOU HAVE 5 DAYS

Follow the three-day itinerary, and then spend the fourth and fifth nights in or near ☒ **Bastia** ㊾. Tour Cap Corse on day four, starting out on the eastern side, stopping for lunch in the fishing port of **Centuri** ㊲, and visiting **Nonza** ㊱, **St-Florent** ㉞, and the **Patrimonio** ㉟ vineyards before driving up over the Col de Teghime (if possible at sunset). Spend day five exploring Bastia, and then head back to the mainland.

IF YOU HAVE 10 DAYS

Start in **Ajaccio** ①–⑦ and reach the megalithic site at **Filitosa** ⑨ by noon. Have a late lunch in **Sartène** ⑩ and drive into ☒ **Bonifacio** ⑪ as the sun sets into the sea. The next day, get to the laricio pine forest near the **Col de Bavella** ⑬ to see or even walk to the famous granite peaks. Tiny D268 comes out on the east coast at N198, which will take you up to **Aléria** ⑭ and into ☒ **Corte** ⑮ on N200. Make Corte your base: Devote day three to Corte and the Restonica gorges; day four to the **Asco Valley**; day five to the small villages in **La Castagniccia.** On day six, take **La Scala di Santa Regina** road through the Aitone Forest. Spend the night in ☒ **Ota** ㉒. Pass through the Scandola Natural Reserve on day seven, reaching the Riviera-like ☒ **Calvi** ㉕ by evening. Go to the beach in Calvi on day eight. In the evening drive through La Balagne to **L'Ile Rousse** ㉛ and medieval ☒ **Lama** ㉜. On the ninth day drive around Cap Corse and spend the night in ☒ **Erbalunga** ㊳, in ☒ **Bastia** ㊾, or in ☒ **San Martino di Lota** ㊵. On the morning of day 10, hike up to the Bocca di Santo Lunardo or go to the beach at Erbalunga; in the afternoon explore Bastia, and then head back to the mainland.

When to Tour Corsica

The best time to visit Corsica is fall or spring, when the weather is cool.

Corsica

TO NICE

TO NICE

TO MARSEILLE

TO MARSEILLE, TOULON

TO MARSEILLE, TOULON

TO MARSEILLE, TOULON

TO GENOA, LIVORNO

TO NICE, TOULON, MARSEILLE

TO MARSEILLE

TO SARDINIA

TO SARDINIA

TO SARDINIA

Centuri 37
D80
Macinaggio
Ragliano
Cap Corse Peninsula Pino
D180
Canari
Canelle
Monte Stello
Sisco
Nonza 36
D80
Erbalunga
40 38
San Martino di Lota
Patrimonio 35
39 **Bastia**
St-Florent 34
D81 Oletta
Lama
HAUTE-CORSE (UPPER CORSICA)
L'Ile Rousse
Algajola 30
31 **Pigna**
N1192 32 **Murato** 33
Ostricone Valley
D82
N193
Casamozza Mariana
Golo
Calvi 25 N197 28
Sant'Antonino 27
LA BALAGNE
Cateri 26
D151 Cassano
N197
Calenzana
Asco 20
D47
Ponte Leccia 16
D515
La Porta 18 D506 Folelli
Réserve Naturel de Scandola
Haut-Asco 21
Asco Valley
Morosaglia 17
19 **LA CASTAGNICCIA**
Monte Cinto
Calacuccia
D84
Piedicroce
D81
Partinello
Gorges de la Spelunca 22
Col de Verghio
Scala di Santa Regina
15 **Corte**
D71 Prunete
Golfe de Porto
Porto 23
Ota
Evisa
Gorges de la Restonica
N200
N198
Piana 24 D81 D84
LES CALANCHES
Cargèse
D70 Vico
Sagone
Tiuccia
Golfe de Sagone
N193
Gravona
Prunelli
Vivario
Ghisoni
D69
Tavignano
14 **Aléria**
D343
Ghisonaccia
N198
Ajaccio
1 — 7
N196
Cauro
Iles Sanguinaires
Golfe d'Ajaccio
8 **Porticcio**
Petreto-Bicchisano
Taravo
D69
Parc Naturel Régional
Solenzara
D268
13 **Col de Bavella**
9 **Filitosa**
Olmeto
Zonza
CORSE-DU-SUD (SOUTHERN CORSICA)
D368
Capo di Muro
Propriano
Cauria
10 **Sartène**
N196
12
Golfe di Porto-Vecchio
Porto-Vecchio
Mediterranean Sea
N
Figari
D859
N198
Tyrrhenian Sea
0 40 miles
0 60 km
11 **Bonifacio**
Iles Lavezzi
TO SARDINIA

Most Corsican culinary specialties are at their best between October and April. Try to avoid July and August, when French and Italian vacationers fill hotels and push up prices. In winter, the island has the best weather in France, but a majority of the hotels and restaurants are closed.

CORSE DU SUD

Corse du Sud includes the French administrative capital of Ajaccio, the mountainous zones of the Cinarca and Alta Rocca, megalithic treasures at Filitosa and Levie, and the fortresslike towns of Sartène, Bonifacio, and Porto-Vecchio. Perhaps because Southern Corsica is on the French side of the island, it seems more Continentalized. Forest fires in 1994, and the resulting flooding, scarred much of the southern part of the island, though the irrepressible maquis quickly repaired much of the damage.

Ajaccio

40 mins by plane, 5–10 hrs by ferry from Marseilles, Nice, or Toulon.

Ajaccio, Napoléon's birthplace and Corsica's modern capital, is a busy town with a bustling port, beautiful beaches, ancient streets, and one of the best collections of paintings south of the Louvre. Set out for the **city market,** a lovely square where every morning except Monday you can admire the enticing array of produce and seafood. Be sure to try the traditional, chestnut-flour beignets.

Rows of stately palm trees lead up to a marble statue of Napoléon on **place Maréchal-Foch,** the city's main square. The **Hôtel de Ville** (Town Hall) has an Empire-style Grand Salon hung with portraits of a long line of Bonapartes. You'll find a fine bust of Letizia, Napoléon's formidable mother; a bronze death mask of the emperor himself; and a frescoed ceiling that portrays Napoléon's meteoric rise. ⊠ *pl. Maréchal-Foch.* ☎ *7 frs.* ☉ *Apr.–Oct., weekdays 9–noon and 2:30–5:30; Nov.–Mar., weekdays 9–noon and 2–5.*

Napoléon was born on August 15, 1769, in the large, middle-class, 18th-century **Maison Bonaparte** (Bonaparte House). Today the building houses a museum with portraits and cameos of the entire Bonaparte clan. Search out the two family trees woven out of human hair. ⊠ *rue St-Charles.* ☎ *22 frs.* ☉ *Mon. 2–5, Tues.–Sat. 10–noon and 2–5, Sun. 10–noon.*

At the corner of rue St-Charles and rue Roi de Rome, are the city's oldest houses, opposite the tiny church of **St-Jean Baptiste** (St. John the Baptist). They were built shortly after the town was founded in 1492. The 16th-century Baroque **Cathédrale** where Napoléon was baptized is at the end of rue St-Charles. The interior is covered with trompe l'oeil frescoes, and the high altar, from an old church in Lucca, Italy, was donated by Napoléon's sister Eliza after he made her princess of Tuscany. Above the altar, look for Eugène Delacroix's famous painting *Virgin of Sacré Coeur.* ⊠ *rue F.-Conti.*

Before leaving Ajaccio, go to the Renaissance-style **Chapelle Impérial** (Imperial Chapel), built in 1857 by Napoléon's nephew, Napoléon III, to accommodate the tombs of the Bonaparte family. (The great man himself is buried, however, in the Hôtel des Invalides in Paris; ☞ Chapter 2.) A Coptic crucifix taken from Egypt during the general's 1798 campaign hangs over the main altar. ⊠ *50 rue Fesch.* ☎ *12 frs.* ☉ *Tues.–Sat. 10–12:30 and 3–7.*

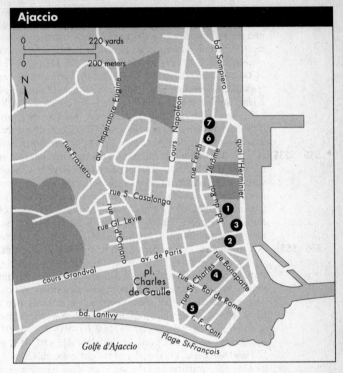

Ajaccio

★ **7** The **Musée Fesch** houses what is considered the best collection of Italian masters Botticelli, Canaletto, and De Tura outside Florence and Paris—part of a collection of 30,000 paintings bought at bargain prices following the French Revolution by Napoléon's uncle, Cardinal Fesch, the archbishop of Lyon. ⊠ *50 rue Fesch,* ☎ *04–95–21–48–17.* 🖃 *27 frs.* ☉ *Apr.–Oct., Wed.–Mon. 9:30–noon and 3–6:30 (July and Aug., also Tues.–Sat. 9–midnight); Nov.–Mar., Wed.–Mon. 9:30–noon and 2:30–6.*

NEED A BREAK?	After visiting the old quarter, make your way down to the plage St-François and stop at the **Café Fesch** for coffee while you contemplate the Golfe d'Ajaccio.

Dining and Lodging

$$–$$$ ✕ **A La Funtana.** A fountain greets diners at the door of this gourmet restaurant, named for a popular Corsican folk song. Fresh flowers and Oriental carpets are the only touch of decoration in the simple white dining room. The house specialty is homemade foie gras; other dishes worth sampling include *morilles* (morels) in foie gras and homemade sorbets. ⊠ *7 rue Notre-Dame,* ☎ *04–95–21–78–04. AE, DC, MC, V. Closed June and Sun.–Mon.*

$$ ✕ **Auberge de Prunelli.** This cheerful riverside inn overlooking the
★ Prunelli River has an excellent 175-franc five-course menu. Dine on brocciu omelets, trout, roast lamb, and figatelli sausage. ⊠ *Pisciatellu (about 11 km/7 mi south of Ajaccio just off N196; look for the turn-off onto D55B just before crossing the river),* ☎ *04–95–20–02–75. Reservations essential. MC, V. Closed Tues. and possibly (not sure due to new management) Oct.–Nov.*

$$ ✕ **Le Maximilien.** Across from the cathedral, this stylish spot is one of the hottest places for dinner. Chef-owner Serge Alain Gros serves Continental cuisine to a smart crowd interested in something more than local cooking. The cassoulet *périgord* (with duck, sausage, and white beans) and the *lotte au foie gras de canard* (monkfish with goose liver) are interesting combinations of maritime and upland products. ⊠ *rue Eugène-Macchini,* ☎ *04–95–51–36–39. AE, DC, MC, V. Closed Mon.*

$ ✕ **Da Mamma.** Just after 13 rue Fesch, turn into passage de la Guinghetta, where there is a small, shady square of the same name. Under a leafy rubber tree you might, in season, try a *civet de sanglier* (wild boar stew) with *trompettes de la mort* (wild mushrooms) served in a bubbling earthenware casserole. ⊠ *2 passage Guinghetta,* ☎ *04–95–21–39–44. AE, MC, V. Closed Feb.–Oct. No lunch Sun.–Mon.*

$$$–$$$$ ✕🔝 **La Dolce Vita.** Spread out on flower-filled terraces at the edge of the Gulf of Ajaccio, La Dolce Vita has a lavish Italianate decor and a spectacular swimming pool overlooking the sea. Its restaurant ranks as one of the island's best for gourmet interpretations of traditional Corsican dishes. ⊠ *rte. des Iles Sanguinaires, 20000 (8 km/5 mi from the center of town),* ☎ *04–95–52–00–93,* 🄵🄰🄷 *04–95–52–07–15. 32 rooms. Restaurant, bar, pool. AE, DC, MC, V. Closed Nov.–Easter.*

$$$–$$$$ ✕🔝 **Eden Roc.** The modern Eden Roc overlooks the gulf in Ajaccio's most exclusive suburb. Gardens surround the swimming pool, and a tiny beach lies across the road. Rooms are large and luxurious, each with a terrace and sea view. The restaurant, no longer considered the gourmet haven it once was, nevertheless remains one of Ajaccio's finest. ⊠ *rte. des Iles Sanguinaires, 20000 (8 km/5 mi from the center of town),* ☎ *04–95–52–01–47,* 🄵🄰🄷 *04–95–52–05–03. 45 rooms. Restaurant, piano bar, pool, health club. AE, DC, MC, V.*

$$ 🔝 **Hôtel San Carlu.** On the edge of the old town, this friendly hotel over-
★ looking the ramparts and the sea is an ideal base for exploring Ajaccio. Rooms are clean and comfortable; those on the gulf side on the third floor get an abundance of morning sunshine streaming across the bed and even into the bathtub. ⊠ *8 bd. Danielle-Casanova, 20000,* ☎ *04–95–21–13–84,* 🄵🄰🄷 *04–95–21–09–99. 40 rooms. AE, DC, MC, V.*

Nightlife and the Arts

Ajaccio's hottest night spots are 4 km (2 mi) north of town in the new Santalino district. **La Cinquième Avenue** (⊠ rte. des Iles Sanguinaires) is the reigning dance-until-dawn venue for all ages, the younger the better. **Le Satélite** (⊠ rte. des Iles Sanguinaires) is another nearby hotspot. **Le Sun Club** (⊠ rte. des Iles Sanguinaires) is also trendy at the moment.

Have a drink to the tinkling of a piano at **Le Brazil Café** (⊠ 28 cours Grandval). **Le Cohiba** (⊠ blvd. Lantivy, 1 Résidence Diamant) is a new and very popular bar. **La Place** (⊠ blvd. Lantivy) is another popular piano bar.

The **Fête de la Miséricorde** (Feast of Our Lady of Mercy) on March 18 features the Procession de la Madunnuccia (Procession of the Madonna), Ajaccio's patron saint. In May Ajaccio celebrates during its festive **Carnival.** In July you can attend the **Rencontres Internationales de Musique,** a gathering of classical and operatic musicians. A major festival, the **Fêtes Napoléoniennes,** takes place on August 15, Napoléon's birthday.

Outdoor Activities and Sports

BMS (⊠ quai de la Citadelle, ☎ 04–95–21–33–75) rents bicycles year-round. **Locacorse** (⊠ 10 av. Bévérini-Vico, ☎ 04–95–20–71–20) has bike rentals from April through September. Horseback riding is ideal along the former mule paths; the **Centre de Randonnées Équestres de St-Georges** (⊠ Domaine de Campiccioli, rte. de Vigna Piana, ☎ 04–95–25–34–83) rents horses and organizes outings. The **Poney-Club d'Ajaccio** (⊠ Campo dell' Oro, ☎ 04–95–23–03–10) also rents horses. For fishing, swimming, underwater diving, kayaking, or wind-surfing, head to **Club des Calanques** (⊠ Hôtel des Calanques, rte. des Sanguinaires, ☎ 04–95–21–39–65). **Les Dauphins** (⊠ rte. des Sanguinaires, plage de Barbicaja, ☎ 04–95–52–07–78) also has water-sports gear. For information about sailing, contact the **Ligue Corse de Voile** (⊠ Port de la Citadelle, ☎ 04–95–21–07–79). Another place where you can get a sailboat is the **Tahiti Nautic Club d'Ajaccio** (⊠ Plage du Ricanto, ☎ 04–95–20–05–95).

Shopping

Much more than just a bookstore specializing in books about Corsica, **Librairie la Marge** (⊠ 7 rue Emmanuelle-Arène) is a hub of Corsican culture, where you can buy music and attend poetry readings. **Paese Nostru** (⊠ passage Guinguetta) sells Corsican crafts of all kinds. **U Tilaghju** (⊠ rue Forcioli Conti), one of several artisan shops near the cathedral, has an impressive collection of ceramics.

Porticcio

8 *17 km (10½ mi) south of Ajaccio on N196.*

Across the Prunelli River south of Ajaccio, Porticcio is the capital's fancy suburb and luxurious beach resort town. It's primarily notable for its seawater cures at the **Institut de Thalassothérapie** (Institute of Thalassotherapy) on the Punta di Porticcio and the *grand luxe* Le Maquis hotel (☞ *below*).

Dining and Lodging

$$$–$$$$ X🄣 **Le Maquis.** The evocatively named Maquis ranks as one of the island's (and Europe's) finest *hôtels de charme*. The quaint, ivy-covered building reaches down to a private beach. Rooms have views of the sea or the hills. At the candlelit restaurant, with ancient beams and wicker chairs, a blend of traditional and nouvelle cuisine is served: fish tartare, scrambled eggs with truffles, and fresh tagliatelles. ⊠ *D55, 20166 Porticcio,* ☎ *04–95–25–05–55,* 🄵🄰🄾 *04–95–25–11–70. 27 rooms. Restaurant, 1 indoor and 1 outdoor pool, tennis court, beach. AE, DC, MC, V.*

Outdoor Activities and Sports

Bikes are a great way to explore the beach; **Avis** (⊠ in the Hôtel Marina Viva) rents them. Kids love **Aqua Cyrné Gliss** (⊠ follow the signs in Porticcio, ☎ 04–95–25–17–48), a water park with water slides and swimming pools. Admission is 70 francs and it's open mid-June–mid-September, daily 10:30–7, plus two nights a week (usually Tuesday and Friday).

Filitosa

9 *71 km (43 mi) southeast of Ajaccio off N196.*

Filitosa is the site of Corsica's largest grouping of megalithic menhir statues. Bizarre, life-size stone figures of ancient warriors rise up mysteriously from the undulating terrain, many with human faces that have been eroded and flattened with time. A small museum on the site houses archaeological finds, including the menhir known as Scalsa Murta, whose delicately carved spine and rib cage make it difficult to believe the statue dates from some 3,000 years BC. Be sure to buy the excellent guidebook in English (30 francs) by experts Cesari and Acquaviva. You can study it over a snack at the pleasant museum café. ⊠ *Contact the Centre Préhistorique Filitosa,* ☎ *04–95–74–00–91 for information.* 🄰 *Guided tours in English 25 frs.* ☉ *June–Aug., daily 8–7.*

Sartène

⑩ *27 km (16 mi) southeast of Filitosa on N196.*

The hillside town of Sartène was called the "most Corsican of all Corsican towns" by French novelist Prosper Mérimée. Dorothy Carrington, author of *Granite Island*, the definitive work on Corsica, described it as one of the least-changed places on Corsica. Founded in the 16th century, Sartène has survived pirate raids and bloody feuding among the town's families. The word "vendetta" is believed to have originated here as the result of a 19th-century family feud so serious that French troops were brought in as a peace-keeping buffer force. Centuries of fighting have left the town with a somewhat eerie and menacing atmosphere. Perhaps adding to this is the annual Good Friday *catenacciu* (enchaining) procession in which an anonymous penitent, dragging ankle chains, lugs a heavy cross through the village streets.

The most interesting part of town is **Vieux Sartène** (Old Sartène), surrounded by ancient ramparts. Start at place de la Libération, the main square. To one side is the **Hôtel de Ville**, the former Genoese governor's palace. For a taste of the Middle Ages, slip through the tunnel in the town hall to place du Maggiu and the old quarter of **Santa Anna**, a somber warren of narrow, cobbled streets lined with granite houses. Scarcely 100 yards from the Hôtel de Ville (Town Hall), down a steep and winding street, a 12th-century *tour de guet* (watchtower) stands out in sharp contrast to the modern apartment buildings behind.

Sartène is the center for research into Corsica's prehistory, due to its proximity to Pianu de Levie and numerous dolmens and megalithic statues. For a look at some of the island's best prehistoric relics, stop by the **Musée Départemental de Préhistoire et de Protohistoire de la Corse** (Regional Museum of Corsican Prehistory) in the town's former prison. ⊠ *rue Croce,* ☎ *04–95–77–01–09.* 🎟 *17 frs.* ☉ *Apr.–Oct., Mon.–Sat. 10–noon and 2–6; Nov.–Mar., weekdays 10–noon and 2–5.*

Dining

$$ ✕ **Auberge de Santa Barbara.** This excellent restaurant is just 1 km (½ mi) north of Sartène. Known as one of the best half dozen or so practitioners of authentic Corsican cuisine on the island, chef Giselle Lovighi also serves innovative seafood specialties such as shrimp soufflée and crayfish salad. ⊠ *Alzone, Sartène,* ☎ *04–95–77–09–06. MC, V. Closed Mon. and Nov.–Easter.*

Outdoor Activities and Sports

In Propriano, just north of Sartène, horses can be rented from the **Ferme Équestre de Baracci** (⊠ Propriano, ☎ 04–95–76–08–02). Five- to 15-day seaside and mountain outings can also be arranged here. Another way to see the area is to hike along the **Tra Mare a Mare** (Sea-to-Sea Trail) from Propriano to Porto-Vecchio. Roadside information points suggest itineraries.

Bonifacio

★ **⑪** *54 km (33 mi) southeast of Sartène via N196.*

The ancient fortress town of Bonifacio occupies a spectacular clifftop setting above a harbor carved from limestone cliffs. It is just 13 km (8 mi) from Sardinia, and local speech is heavily influenced by the accent and idiom of the neighboring Italian island. Established in the 12th century as Genoa's first Corsican stronghold, Bonifacio remained Genoese through centuries of battles and sieges. As you wander the narrow streets of the **Haute Ville** (Upper Village), inside the walls of the citadel, think of Homer's *Odyssey*. It was here, in the harbor, that classics scholars have placed the catastrophic encounter between Ulysses's fleet and the vicious Laestrygonians who hurled boulders down from the cliffs.

From place d'Armes at the city gate, enter the **Bastion de l'Étendard** (Bastion of the Standard); you can still see the system of weights and pulleys used to pull up the drawbridge. The former garrison now houses life-size dioramas of Bonifacio's history. ⌨ *20 frs.* ☉ *Mid-June– mid-Sept., daily 9–7.*

In the center of the maze of cobbled streets that makes up the citadel is the 12th-century church of **Ste-Marie-Majeure,** with buttresses attaching it to surrounding houses. Inside the church, note the Renaissance baptismal font, carved in bas-relief, and the 3rd-century white marble Roman sarcophagus. Walk around the back to see the loggia, which is built above a huge cistern that contained water for use in times of siege, as were the circular silos throughout the town.

From Bonifacio, you can take a **boat trip** to the **Dragon Grottoes** and **Venus's Bath** (the trip takes one hour on boats that set out every 15 minutes during July and August) or the **Lavezzi Islands.** Call 04–95– 75–05–93 for information; boats leave from outside Hôtel La Caravelle.

Dining and Lodging

$$ ★ ✕ **U Ceppu.** Just outside of Bonifacio, this rustic, barn-size restaurant features grilled meats and seafood prepared in the dining room on a big open hearth—for instance, smoked salmon and wild boar stew. Picture windows look out on lobster pots bobbing in the bay and scattered on the beach. ⌧ *L'Auberge de Santa Manza (about 5 km/3 mi east of Bonifacio on the road to Santa Manza beach),* ☎ *04–95–73– 02–34. AE, MC, V. No lunch Mon.–Sat.*

$–$$ ✕ **Les 4 Vents.** This friendly restaurant is popular with the yachting crowd and with families. In winter, the kitchen serves up Alsace specialties like sauerkraut and sausages. In summer the focus is on barbecued fish and meats, as well as typical Corsican dishes. ⌧ *29 quai Bando di Ferro,* ☎ *04–95–73–07–50. No credit cards. Closed Tues.*

$ ✕ **Restaurant du Pêcheur.** People often line the sidewalk waiting to dine at this tiny, authentic seafood spot. True to its name, the restaurant is run by fishermen who serve the catch of the day straight from the sea. There's no written menu, so ask what's available. ⌧ *14 rue Doria,* ☎ *04–95–73–12–56. Reservations not accepted. MC, V. Closed Nov.– Easter.*

$$$–$$$$ ⌂ **Hôtel le Genovese.** This small, personal hotel is built into the ramparts of the upper town's citadel. Rooms glow with peach fabric wall coverings; those upstairs have superb views, which is the best part about the hotel. ⌧ *quartier de Citadelle, Haute Ville, 20169,* ☎ *04–95–73– 12–34,* FAX *04–95–73–09–03. 14 rooms. Bar. AE, DC, MC, V.*

Nightlife and the Arts

Party until dawn at **Le Langoustier** (⌧ quai Comparetti, ☎ 04–95– 73–01–44) in the port. Or drive out to **Amnesia** (⌧ 10 km/6 mi from town on the Porto-Vecchio road, ☎ 04–95–72–12–27), the dance club of choice.

The **Fête Millénaire de Bonifacio,** Bonifacio's celebration of the 1,000th anniversary of its founding, has been held in late August for the last two years and is threatening to become an annual event, with concerts, processions, and street dances.

Outdoor Activities and Sports

The area around Bonifacio is ideal for water sports; contact **Club Atoll** (⌧ rte. de Porto-Vecchio, ☎ 04–95–73–02–83). The best golf course on Corsica (and one of the best in the Mediterranean), a 20,106-ft par-

72 gem designed by Robert Trent Jones, is at **Sperone** (⊠ Domaine de Sperone, ☎ 04–95–73–17–13) just east of Bonifacio.

Shopping
Pierres de Cade (⊠ Haute Ville) has a good selection of beautiful objects carved from Corsica's rich chestnut and juniper trees.

Porto-Vecchio

⑫ *27 km (16 mi) north of Bonifacio via N198.*

The old walled town of Porto-Vecchio has become synonymous with mass tourism dominated by tour operators from Italy, so you might want to consider skipping it. The town's network of medieval streets has now been largely given over to bistros, boutiques, and cafés. Nonetheless, the Gulf of Porto-Vecchio is lined with beautiful beaches.

Dining and Lodging

$$–$$$$ ✕☷ **Grand Hôtel de Cala Rossa.** This mansion-hotel, close to the beach, showcases modern design—nothing jars, from the curves of the heavy white walls to the contemporary paintings. The luxurious rooms vary greatly in price. Corsican-style nouvelle dishes are featured in the restaurant; you can't go wrong with the roast kid or the fresh-mint omelet. ⊠ *Cala Rossa, 20137 (8 km/5 mi north of Porto-Vecchio),* ☎ *04–95–71–61–51,* 𝖥𝖠𝖷 *04–95–71–60–11. 50 rooms. Restaurant, tennis court. AE, DC, MC, V. Closed Nov.–Apr.*

$$–$$$ ✕☷ **Moby Dick.** This sophisticated modern hotel is nearly surrounded by water and sandy beaches. Rooms, done in blue and white, look out on this scene. The restaurant serves a good-value buffet lunch and both a "normal" and *gastronomique* (gargantuan) menu at dinner. The crayfish is delicious. ⊠ *baie de Santa Giulia, 20137 (8 km/5 mi south of town),* ☎ *04–95–70–43–23,* 𝖥𝖠𝖷 *04–95–70–01–54. 44 rooms. Restaurant, beach. AE, DC, MC, V. Closed Nov.–Apr.*

En Route Porto-Vecchio backs onto Corsica's largest cork oak forest, **L'Ospédale.** An excursion across the forest on D368, climbing 49 km (30 mi) to the mountain pass of **Col de Bavella,** might be one of your most memorable and should under no circumstances be missed in favor of the flat, straight road up the east coast.

Col de Bavella

⑬ *50 km (31 mi) northeast of Porto-Vecchio on D368 and D268.*

The granite peaks known as the **Aiguilles de Bavella** (Needles of Bavella) tower some 6,562 ft overhead as you reach the Col de Bavella (Bavella Pass). Hiking trails are well marked. The narrow but mostly well-paved roadway over the pass will take you back to the coast along the Solenzara River. If you stop and look carefully, you may be able to see wild Corsican trout dining on aquatic insects.

Dining

$ ✕ **Le Refuge.** Near the top of the spectacular drive from Porto-Vecchio to the Col de Bavella, follow signs for Le Refuge, an inexpensive little hikers' inn. Here you can enjoy a welcoming lunch of Corsican mountain fare by a roaring fire. ⊠ *Cartalavonu (2 km/1½ mi off D368 to the left),* ☎ *04–95–70–00–39. No credit cards.*

Aléria

⑭ *32 km (20 mi) north of Solenzara on N198, 70 km (63 mi) north of Porto-Vecchio.*

Just before the village of Aléria are the ruins of the Roman city of the same name. On a pine-studded plateau is the carefully restored 16th-century **Fort de Matra,** which houses the Musée Jérôme Carcopino. On display are pottery and tools found on the site, as well as Etruscan, Greek, and Roman artifacts dating from as far back as 500 BC. ▱ *15 frs. ⊙ Apr.–Oct., daily 8–noon and 2–7; Nov.–Mar., Mon.–Sat. 8–noon and 2–5.*

Dining and Lodging

$$ ✕ **Chez Mathieu.** This beach-side restaurant, open year-round, specializes in very fresh *loup* (sea bass) and *dorade* (sea bream). In summer, dinner on the beach at sunset before driving back up into the mountains at Corte can give you—aside from the fresh fish—a sense of Corsica's unique geographical diversity. ✉ *plage Padulone,* ☎ *04–95–57–12–03. AE, MC, V.*

Outdoor Activities and Sports

Aléria's **beach** stretches north from the mouth of the Tavignano River and gets increasingly wild the farther you go. It's a fine place for surf casting, swimming, or sailing. **Camping-Bungalows Marina d'Aléria** (✉ At the intersection of N200 and the beach, ☎ 04–95–57–01–42) rents all kinds of nautical equipment.

Shopping

For antique ceramic reproductions, try the shops near the entrance to the Roman ruins.

HAUTE CORSE

Haute Corse (Upper Corsica) encompasses the northeastern end of the island and is, indeed, higher in mean altitude than Corse-du-Sud, topped by the 8,876-ft Monte Cinto. Most Corsica enthusiasts agree that Haute Corse is richer in what is most Corsican about this "mountain in the sea": highland forests, remote villages, hidden cultural gems, and alpine lakes and streams. In the center of Haute Corse is the city of Corte, Corsica's heart and soul. To the east is the forested region of La Castagniccia, named for the abundance of *châtaigniers* (castagna, or chestnut trees). It is one of the most colorful parts of Corsica, especially in the fall, when leaves and chestnuts cover the ground. Driving through the forest's tiny roadways, you'll find villages with stunning Baroque churches and houses still roofed in traditional blue-gray slate. To the north is Cap Corse: The 105-km (65-mi) drive along the coastal route D80, from the town of Patrimonio to the city of Bastia, takes about three hours (four with lunch in Centuri and five with a run up the Col de Ste-Lucie). The road is better on the east coast, and there are fewer reasons to stop.

Corte

⑮ *48 km (30 mi) northwest of Aléria on N200, 83 km (51 mi) northeast of Ajaccio, 70 km (43 mi) southwest of Bastia.*

Among spectacular cliffs and gorges at the confluence of the Tavignano, Restonica, and Orta rivers, Corte is the spiritual heart and soul of Corsica. Capital of Pasquale Paoli's government from 1755 to 1769, it was also where Paoli established the Corsican University in 1765. Closed by the victorious French in 1769, the university, always a symbol of Corsican identity, was reopened in 1981.

To reach the upper town and the 15th-century château looking over the rivers, walk up the cobblestone ramp from place Pasquale-Paoli. Stop in lovely **place Gaffori** at one of the cafés or restaurants. Note the bullet-pocked house where the Corsican hero Gian Pietro Gaffori and his wife, Faustina, held off the Genoans in 1750.

★ The **Citadelle,** a Vauban-style fortress (1769–78), is built around the original, 15th-century fortification at the highest point of the cliff, with the river below. It contains the **Musée de la Corse** (Corsica Museum), a museum dedicated to the island's history and ethnography. ☎ 04–95–45–25–45. ⌦ 35 frs. ☉ Nov.–Apr., Tues.–Sat. 10–5; May–Oct., daily 10–8.

The **Palais National** (National Palace), just outside the citadel and above place Gaffori, is the ancient residence of Genoa's representatives in Corsica and was the seat of the Corsican parliament from 1755 to 1769. The building is now part of the Corsican University at Corte. ⌧ pl. du Poilu. ☉ Weekdays 2–6.

For an unforgettable view of the river junction and the Genoan bridge below, the citadel's tiny watchtower above and the mountains behind, walk left along the citadel wall to the **Belvedere.**

Leave the Haute Ville and go through the **Quartier de Chiostra** (Alleyway Quarter). Follow the cobblestone path (as you look down) to the right from the Belvedere, bearing right and across at the **Chapelle St-Théophile.** Coming into the tiny square on your left, don't miss the flying stone staircase on the opposite wall, or the prehistoric fertility goddess carved into the wall to the left next to the pottery artisans shop. After leaving this little space, continue downhill and you will rejoin the ramp leading into place Pasquale-Paoli.

A nice excursion from Corte is a day at the **Gorges de la Restonica** (Restonica Gorge). Drive up the Restonica Valley and leave your car at the end of the road. A two-hour climb will take you to **Lac de Mélo,** a trout-filled mountain lake, 6,528 ft above sea level, surrounded by a circle of craggy granite peaks. Another, more strenuous hour up takes you to the usually snow-bordered lake, the **Lac de Capitello.** Information on trails is available from the tourist office (☞ Corsica A to Z, below) or the Parc Naturel Régional (☞ below). At the top of the drivable part of the Restonica Gorge, in the stone shepherds' huts at the **Bergeries de Grotelle,** light meals are served.

Dining and Lodging

$$ ✕☷ **Auberge de la Restonica–Hôtel Dominique Colonna.** Over the
★ crystalline Restonica River, this cozy inn—known for its hearty Corsican fare—has rooms in the hunting lodge, the original building, and the modern new annex across the parking lot. Owner Dominique "Dumé" Colonna, one of France's great soccer stars, drops by from time to time. ⌧ Vallée de la Restonica, 20250, ☎ 04–95–46–09–58, ℻ 04–95–61–03–91. 35 rooms. Restaurant. AE, DC, MC, V.

Outdoor Activities and Sports

In summer, you can get information on hiking and trail maps from the local office of the **Parc Naturel Régional de la Corse** (☞ Corsica A to Z, below), on the road about halfway between Corte and the Auberge de la Restonica.

Ponte Leccia

⑯ 24 km (15 mi) north of Corte on N193, 14 km (9 mi) northeast of Morosaglia, 24 km (15 mi) north of Corte.

Ponte Leccia is the entry point to La Castagniccia: take D71 southeast into the forest. A rail and road crossing with gas stations and a supermarket, the town has little else to recommend it.

Morosaglia

⑰ *14 km (9 mi) southeast of Ponte Leccia, 9 km (5 mi) east of La Porta.*

The town of Morosaglia is the birthplace of Pasquale Paoli. Letters, portraits, and memorabilia from Paoli's life are on display at the **Maison de Pasquale Paoli** (Pasquale Paoli House). ☎ 04−95−61−04−97. ⊙ *Daily 9−noon and 2:30−7:30; in winter, 1−5 only.*

La Porta

⑱ *9 km (5 mi) west of Morosaglia, 14½ km (9 mi) north of Piedicroce on D515.*

As the name of the village suggests, La Porta is the doorway to La Castagniccia. The **St-Jean-Baptiste** church here is widely accepted as the crowning glory of Corsican Baroque art. The bright ochre facade and the five-story bell tower are feasts for the eyes, as are the paintings inside.

Dining

$$ ✕ **L'Ampugnani−Chez Elisabeth.** This excellent restaurant is known throughout Corsica as one of the top gourmet experiences in La Castagniccia. Specializing in *cuisine du terroir* (local country cooking), the chef reinvents the leg of lamb with herbs from the surrounding hills and brings new meaning to the notion of *figatellu* (liver sausage). ⊠ *La Porta,* ☎ 04−95−39−22−00. *Reservations essential. MC, V. Closed Mon. Oct.−Easter.*

Piedicroce

⑲ *14 km (9 mi) south of La Porta on D515, 66 km (40 mi) south of Bastia.*

Piedicroce's panoramic view of La Castagniccia is superb. Be sure to stop in the vividly painted Baroque church of **St-Pierre-et-St-Paul,** one of the finest of its type in the area. The nearby mineral springs of **Orezza** are reputed to have miraculous powers. The **Fium Alto stream,** running along the road that goes northeast to Folelli, is one of Corsica's best trout streams. To exit La Castagniccia, follow signs for **Folelli** (37 km/22 mi north) or Bastia (66 km/40 mi north).

Dining and Lodging

$$ ✕ **U Fragnu.** After you've exited La Castagniccia at Folelli, head north to this place for some exquisite cuisine du terroir. The Garelli family has cooked for the French premier as representatives of Corsican gastronomy, and Mme. Garelli is a specialist in *soupe de berger* (shepherd's soup)—a recipe restored after much research. ⊠ *rte. de Vescovato, Venzolasca (7 km/4 mi north of Folelli on N198, then 2 km/1 mi up D37),* ☎ 04−95−36−62−33. *Reservations essential. No credit cards. No lunch Thurs.−Sat. Nov.−Mar.*

$$ ✕▥ **Le Refuge.** A handy midway point in the labyrinthine La Castagniccia, this hotel-restaurant is a good place to stop for a Corsican beer,
★ a superb meal based on the Rafalli family's home-processed charcuterie, and a night's sleep in the small but cozy quarters. Rooms are suspended over the valley of the Fium Alto stream. ⊠ *20229 Piedicroce,* ☎ 04−95−35−82−65, ℻ 04−95−35−84−42. *20 rooms. Restaurant. MC, V. Closed Nov.*

Asco

⑳ *22 km (13 mi) west of Ponte Leccia: 2 km (1 mi) north of Ponte Leccia, D147 turns off N197 toward the village of Asco, 16 km (10 mi) away.*

The Asco Valley is studded with beehives, and honey and cheese abound in Asco's shops. Don't miss the Genoan bridge below Asco or, even better, a swim in the river. Above Asco the granite gorge becomes a cool pine forest, perfect for hiking. Follow the road for another 12 km (7 mi) past the village, ending at the top against a wall of mountains. The valley runs west to an awe-inspiring barrier of mountains crowned by **Monte Cinto,** rising to 8,795 ft, the highest point in Corsica. As you travel up the valley, the maquis-covered valley gives way to a sheer granite gorge hung with sweet-smelling juniper. This is certainly a drive well worth making in daylight, although if your time is short you can see it on the way down the next day.

Haut-Asco

㉑ *13 km (8 mi) west of Asco.*

Haut-Asco is the starting point for the eight- to nine-hour walk up **Monte Cinto** and back down again. From the top, on a clear day, you can see the entire island and even the Appennines on the Italian mainland. Clouds and mist gather after about 10 AM, however, particularly in summer. For this reason a 4 AM start is recommended. Questions can be answered at Le Chalet (☞ *below*).

Dining and Lodging

$ ✕🏨 **Le Chalet.** This tidy hideaway at the very top of the island has an impeccable restaurant serving Corsican cuisine. Walls are covered with photographs of famous mountaineers. Along with the 22 private rooms there is also a hiker's dormitory, a bar, and a store selling supplies to trekkers, who use the chalet as a way station from the GR 20. ✉ *20276 Haut-Asco,* ☎ *04–95–47–85–84,* 🖷 *04–95–30–25–59. 22 rooms, plus dormitory with shared bath. Restaurant, bar, shop. MC, V. Closed early Nov.–early May.*

Outdoor Activities and Sports

From at least December to April, Corsica's upper reaches are snowed in and there is both alpine and cross-country skiing; consult the **Club Alpin Français** (☎ 04–95–22–73–81) in Ajaccio. For information about hiking up Monte Cinto, contact the **Parc Naturel Régional de la Corse** (☞ Corsica A to Z, *below*).

La Scala di Santa Regina

★ *9 km (5 mi) south of Ponte Leccia, D84 leaves N193, starts up the Golo River, and turns into La Scala di Santa Regina.*

This road, known as La Scala di Santa Regina (Stairway of the Holy Queen), is one of the most spectacular on the island. It's also one of the most difficult to navigate, especially in winter. The route follows the twisty path of the Golo River, which has carved its way through layers of red granite, forming dramatic gorges and waterfalls. Be prepared for herds of animals to cross the road. Follow the road to the **Col de Verghio** (Verghio Pass), where there are superb views of Tafunatu, the legendary perforated mountain, and Monte Cinto. On the way up, you'll pass through the **Valdo Niello Forest,** Corsica's most important woodlands, filled with pines and beeches. The col is considered the border between Haute-Corse and Corse-du-Sud. As you descend from the Verghio Pass through the **Forêt d'Aitone** (Aitone Forest), note how well manicured it is—the pigs, goats, and sheep running rampant through the tall laricio pines keep it this way. As you pass the village of Evisa, with its orange roofs, look across the impressive **Gorges de Spelunca** (Spelunca Gorge) to see the hill village of Ota. A small road on the right will take you across the gorge, where there's an ancient Genoese-built bridge.

Ota

㉒ *16 km (10 mi) northwest of Evisa on La Scala di Santa Regina.*

The tiny village of Ota, overlooking the **Gorges de Spelunca** (Spelunca Gorge), has traditional stone houses that seem to be suspended on the mountainside, an amazing view of the surrounding mountains, and a number of trailheads. It's an excellent base for hiking in the area.

Dining and Lodging

$ ✕⊞ **Chez Félix.** This homey place serves as dining room, taxi stand, and town hall. Cheerful owner Marinette Ceccaldi cooks up heaping portions of Corsican specialties ranging from wild boar to chestnut-flour beignets. Suites are decorated with curios and antiques, each with a balcony overlooking the gorge; rooms are comfortable and rustic. Some have private bathrooms, others share. The hotel has a van that will transport you out to hiking routes. ✉ *pl. de la Fontaine, 20150,* ☎ FAX *04–95–26–12–92. 4 2-bedroom apartments, 36 beds in 4 and 6-bed rooms with shared bath. Restaurant. No credit cards.*

Porto and Les Calanches

㉓ *5 km (3 mi) west of Ota, 30 km (19 mi) south of Calvi.*

The flashy resort town of Porto doesn't have much character, but its setting on the crystalline **Golfe de Porto** (Gulf of Porto), surrounded by massive pink granite mountains, is superb. Activity focuses on the small port, where there is a boardwalk with restaurants and hotels. A short hike from the boardwalk will bring you to a 16th-century Genoese tower that overlooks the bay. Boat excursions leave daily for the **Réserve Naturel de Scandola** (☞ *below*).

Detour south of Porto on D81 to get to **Les Calanches,** jagged outcroppings of red rock considered among the most extraordinary natural sites in France. There are arches and stelae, standing rock formations shaped like animals and phantasmagorical human faces.

Piana

★ **㉔** *11 km (7 mi) south of Porto, 71 km (44 mi) north of Ajaccio.*

Piana overlooks Les Calanches and the Golfe de Porto. Explore the crooked streets of the old town and climb up to the old fortress at the top of **Capo Rosso** to admire the craggy rocks that jut out from the water.

Dining and Lodging

$$ ✕⊞ **Les Roches Rouges.** On the hillside just below the Capo Rosso, this rambling old mansion has a distinctive British flavor. Don't be misled by the crumbling facade; the hotel is still being renovated. Most rooms are monastic, but the irrepressible owner, Mady, and the hotel's stunning location make the hotel a winner. The vast Imperial-style restaurant is classified as a historic monument; go for the fish soup or grilled lobster. ✉ *rte. de Porto, 20115,* ☎ *04–95–27–81–81,* FAX *04–95–27–81–76. 20 rooms. Restaurant. AE, DC, MC, V. Closed Nov.–Mar.*

$$–$$$ ⊞ **Capo Rosso.** The Capo Rosso sits high in the hills overlooking the gulf, just yards from Les Calanches. The views—whether seen from your room, the outdoor pool, or the restaurant's terrace—are dramatic. Unfortunately, the modern rooms are functional rather than charming. ✉ *20115 Piana,* ☎ *04–95–27–82–40,* FAX *04–95–27–80–00. 70 rooms. Restaurant, pool. AE, DC, MC, V. Closed mid-Oct.–Easter.*

Calvi

㉕ *92 km (58 mi) north of Piana, 159 km (100 mi) north of Ajaccio.*

Calvi, Corsica's slice of the Riviera, has been described by Dorothy Carrington as "an oasis of pleasure on an otherwise austere island." Calvi grew rich by supplying products to Genoa; its citizens remained loyal supporters of Genoa long after the rest of the island declared independence. Calvi also claims to be the birthplace of Christopher Columbus. During the 18th century the town endured assaults from Corsican nationalists, including celebrated patriot Pasquale Paoli. Today, Calvi sees a summertime invasion of tourists, drawn to the 6 km (4 mi) stretch of sandy white beach, the citadel, and the booming night life.

The Genoese **Citadelle,** perched on a rocky promontory at the tip of the bay, competes with the beach as a major attraction. An inscription above the drawbridge, *Civitas Calvi semper fidelis,* "The citizens of Calvi always faithful," reflects the town's unswerving allegiance to Genoa. At the welcome center, just inside the gates, you can see a video on the city's history and take a guided tour in English (three times a day) or a self-guided walking tour. ⊠ *Up the hill off av. de l'Uruguay,* ☎ *04–95–65–36–74.* 🎫 *Guided tour and video show 50 frs.* ☉ *Tour Easter–early Oct., daily at 10, 4:30, and 6:30*

Stop in at the 13th-century church of **St-Jean-Baptiste**; it contains an interesting Renaissance baptismal font. Look up to see the rows of pews screened by grillwork: the chaste young women of Calvi's upper classes sat here. ⊠ *pl. d'Armes.*

OFF THE BEATEN PATH **GOLFE DE GIROLATA AND RÉSERVE NATUREL DE SCANDOLA –** North of Porto are the Gulf of Girolata and the Scandola Natural Reserve, a dazzling sanctuary of maquis and underwater park where all hunting, fishing, and camping are prohibited. Founded in 1975, Scandola is managed by the Parc Naturel Régional and is inhabited by dolphins, falcons, ospreys, and many other strains of flora and fauna that have thrived here protected for the last 20 years. Excursions leave Calvi and Porto, accessible only by boat, daily at 9 AM from April through October.

Dining and Lodging

$$$ **★** ✕ **Chez Tao.** At Chez Tao, a mandatory stop on almost everyone's itinerary, you can rub elbows with the town's glitterati in the ocher-color 16th-century vaults that look out over the bay. Seafood is what everyone eats, but food plays second fiddle to the atmosphere, which includes Corsican folk singing and piano until the wee hours. ⊠ *pl. de la Citadelle,* ☎ *04–95–65–00–73. AE, DC, MC, V. Closed mid-Sept.–Easter.*

$$$ ✕ **L'Île de Beauté.** One of Calvi's most celebrated restaurants, it has been pulling in crowds since 1929. Metal suns adorn the walls of the dining room, where the menu features a variety of seafood and upland dishes ranging from lobster fricassee to wild boar stew. ⊠ *quai Landry,* ☎ *04–95–65–00–46. AE, DC, MC, V. Closed Oct.–Apr. No lunch Wed.*

$–$$ ✕ **U San Carlu.** Good, classic Corsican and French cooking at reasonable prices makes U San Carlu a favorite. The brick-vaulted dining room is in a 16th-century building that was once a hospital. In summer, you can eat outdoors on the palm-shaded patio. Specialties include steak in Roquefort and prawns flamed in brandy; there's also an excellent daily menu. ⊠ *10 pl. St-Charles,* ☎ *04–95–65–92–20. AE, DC, MC, V. Closed Wed. mid-Oct.–mid-May. No dinner Tues.*

$ ✕ **Le Poème.** Drop in at Martine Abitbol's friendly restaurant in the citadel for Corsican cuisine or tea. (She also has a café of the same name in New York City's SoHo neigborhood.) ⊠ *9 rue Ste-Antoine,* ☎ *04–95–65–23–85. No credit cards. Closed mid-Oct.–June.*

$$$ ✕▦ **Le Signoria.** This 17th-century country manor and annex have
★ homey bedrooms and large bathrooms. From the pool and patio there are panoramic views of the mountains and the bay. The renowned restaurant serves imaginative, regional cuisine. It is closed for lunch, except for weekends from July through August. ⊠ *rte. de la Forêt de Bonifato, 20260 (about 5 km/3 mi from Calvi),* ☎ *04–95–65–23–73,* ℻ *04–95–65–33–20. 10 rooms. Restaurant, bar, pool, Turkish bath. AE, MC, V. Closed Nov.–Easter.*

$$$$ ▦ **La Villa.** On a hill with marvelous views of the town and the citadel, this Relais & Châteaux hotel feels like a modern Italian villa. The architecture leans heavily toward arched loggias and wrought iron; fountains, paintings, and sculpture abound. Rooms are large and have terra-cotta floors and balconies. The canopied dining area overlooks the pool, surrounded by a fragrant garden. ⊠ *chemin de Notre Dame de la Serra, 20260,* ☎ *04–95–65–10–10,* ℻ *04–95–65–10–50. 25 rooms. Restaurant, bar, pool, beauty salon, Turkish bath. AE, DC, MC, V. Closed Jan.–Mar.*

$$ ▦ **Le Magnolia.** Rooms in this cozy 19th-century former mansion between the church and the marketplace are named after French literary figures: "Verlaine" overlooks rooftops to the port. Cupids and cherubs perch over beds. The restaurant is in the garden under a giant magnolia tree—thus the name of the hotel. ⊠ *pl. du Marché,* ☎ *04–95–65–19–16,* ℻ *04–95–65–34–52. 12 rooms. Restaurant, air-conditioning, minibars. DC, MC, V. Closed Jan.–Feb.*

Nightlife and the Arts

On the outskirts of town, **La Camargue** (⊠ on N167) is the biggest dance club; a free *navette* (shuttle bus) cruises downtown Calvi until dawn collecting and returning club goers. The cabaret-restaurant **Chez Tao** (⊠ pl. de la Citadelle, ☎ 04–95–65–00–73) is the "in" spot in town.

The **Calvi Jazz Festival** takes place in mid-June. **Rencontres Polyphoniques,** an international choral festival, is held in mid-September. **Festiventu,** a celebration of wind-powered sports, musical instruments, and scientific artifacts, happens in late October.

Outdoor Activities and Sports

The **GR 20** begins near Calvi and follows the watershed line on the crests of the mountains, northwest–southeast to Ste-Lucie de Porto-Vecchio. Contact the tourist office (☞ Corsica A to Z, *below*) for information. For water-sports, diving, and boating information and equipment rental, contact **Calvi Nautique Club** (⊠ Port de Plaisance, ☎ 04–95–65–10–65). The **Centre Équestre de Calvi** (⊠ rte. de Pietramaggiore, ☎ 04–95–65–22–22) arranges tours on horseback.

Shopping

The major shopping streets are rue Clemenceau and boulevard Wilson. Look for pottery, for which the region is known. Corsican knives are another specialty item, as are regional charcuterie, cheeses, and jams.

Calenzana

㉖ *13 km (8 mi) from Calvi: Head east on N197 for 5 km (3 mi), then south on D151.*

Leave the Calvi region via the rose-color hill towns of La Balagne, known as the garden of Corsica. This remained a feudal society right up until the French Revolution. Calenzana, once a hideout for Corsica's notorious bandits, lies among the olive groves. The 11th-century church of **Ste-Restitute,** about 1 km (½ mi) beyond town, has an altar backed by medieval frescoes depicting the life of St. Restitute. Legend has it that the saint was martyred here in the 3rd century, and when the people of the town began building a church on another site, the stone blocks were moved here each night by two huge white bulls. Apparently, this happened several times before the townsfolk finally got the divine message and changed building sites.

En Route   From Calenzana, serpentine D151 winds around hillsides dotted with picturesque villages. Most are surrounded by walls and have the same layout: a central area surrounded by short streets leading out like the spokes of a wheel, ending with a final house built into the village walls.

Cateri

㉗   *18 km (11 mi) north of Calenzana on D151.*

The cheese-making center of Cateri (or Catteri, as it is often spelled), in La Balagne, is known for its unique bell-tower facade, a scrolled and pilastered pediment that is a miniature replica of Notre-Dame-des-Anges, of which it is part.

Dining

\$ ✕ **Restaurant A Lataria.** This little spot just beyond the crossroads of Cateri has a flower-filled terrace with views of the village and the sea. The Corsican and Mediterranean fare, such as paella and brocciu lasagna, is a good value. ⊠ *Just outside Cateri,* ☎ *04–95–61–71–44. Closed Oct.–May.*

Sant'Antonino

㉘   *7 km (4 mi) north of Cateri on D13, and across the gorge.*

The medieval stone village of Sant'Antonino, believed to date from the 9th century, is one of the oldest still-inhabited places on the island.

Pigna

㉙   *7 km (4 mi) northeast of Sant'Antonino on D151.*

The unusual village of Pigna is dedicated to bringing back traditional Corsican music and crafts. Here you can listen to folk songs in cafés, visit workshops, and buy handmade musical instruments. The **Casa Musicale** (☞ *below*), a concert hall, auberge, and restaurant, is at the center of it all. During the first half of July, the Casa Musicale hosts a Festivoce (singing festival) of vocalists and a capella groups.

Dining and Lodging

\$ ✕▥ **Casa Musicale.** This unique spot has traditional local cuisine, music of all kinds—often authentic Corsican polyphonic singing—and a lovely view over La Balagne down to Calvi. Rooms are simple but elegant, with whitewashed walls and rustic furniture; they sleep two, three, or four. ⊠ *20220 Pigna,* ☎ *04–95–61–77–31,* ☏ *04–95–61–77–81. 7 rooms. MC, V. Closed Mon. and Jan.–Feb.*

Shopping

Casa di l'Artigiani sells a wide range of local crafts, from jam and honey to musical instruments and handknitted sweaters.

Algajola

㉚   *8 km (5 mi) east of Pigna, 10 km (6 mi) southwest of L'Ile Rousse on N197.*

Built in the 16th century, the village of Algajola is another ancient fortress, the last and smallest of the seven citadel towns built by the Genoese on Corsica's shores. A low-key and friendly resort, it has a perfect crescent beach that attracts crowds.

Dining and Lodging

$$ ✗⊞ **L'Ondine.** Nestled into the rocks at the edge of a sandy cove, L'Ondine is part of a pleasantly landscaped village of single-story, beige stucco buildings. The dining room, serving typical Corsican maritime cuisine, commands a million-dollar view of the beach and Algajola. ✉ *7 rue à Marina, 20220,* ☎ *04–95–60–70–02,* FAX *04–95–60–60–36. 55 rooms. Restaurant, bar, pool. MC, V. Closed late Oct.–late Mar.*

L'Ile Rousse

③ *10 km (6 mi) northeast of Algajola, 37 km (22 mi) southwest of St-Florent.*

L'Ile Rousse, named for the mass of reddish rock now connected to the town by a causeway, is a favorite spot of French vacationers who come to bask in its Riviera-like atmosphere. A small two-car train runs from here along the coast to Calvi, delivering sun worshipers to beaches not accessible by road.

Dining and Lodging

$$ ✗⊞ **A Pasturella.** This picturesque hotel has simple rooms with modern furnishings and geranium-filled window boxes; most overlook the mountains. The well-known restaurant specializes in seafood and Corsican dishes. Though it's unusual, rates are not higher in July and August. ✉ *20220 Monticello (5 km/3 mi outside of L'Ile Rousse),* ☎ *04–95–60–05–65,* FAX *04–95–60–21–78. 14 rooms. Restaurant, bar. AE, MC, V. Closed mid-Nov.–mid-Dec.*

Outdoor Activities and Sports

Two of the best **beaches** in the area are the **Plage d'Ostriconi,** at the mouth of the Ostriconi River (20 km/13 mi north of town), and the wilder and much-frequented-by-nudists **Plage Saleccia,** used in the 1960s filming of *The Longest Day.*

Shopping

Baked goods, local wines, and herbs from the maquis can be bought at the **market** (✉ pl. Paoli) every morning except Monday.

Lama

③ *15 km (9 mi) southeast of L'Ile Rousse, 57 km (24 mi) north of Corte.*

The charmingly restored medieval village of Lama is only 10 minutes up the Ostriconi Valley and is a handy place to spend a night on your way to Cap Corse. Everyone from the mayor to the local children works to accommodate visitors; people say hello in the streets and seem to know where you are staying. Once a prosperous olive-growing town, the village was nearly deserted after a 1971 fire destroyed 35,000 olive trees in one afternoon. Carefully cultivated tourism has put Lama back on the map.

Dining and Lodging

$$ ✗ **U Campu Latinu.** Skillfully built into an ancient bergerie using old stone and drywall construction, this flower-festooned restaurant overlooks Lama, the sea, and the mountains. Try an omelet or lasagna prepared with mint and brocciu or lamb grilled over coals with maquis herbs. ✉ *At the top of the village of Lama; walk or drive up from the main square,* ☎ *04–95–48–23–83. DC, MC, V. Closed Sept.–June.*

$$–$$$ ✕⊡ **Ferme Équestre de L'Ostriconi.** Pierre-Jean and Christine Costa make you part of their life, whether on horseback, on a wild boar hunt, or by showing you Lama's hidden corners and secret spots. Lodgings are in small stone cottages that sleep two to eight. The lively restaurant, open year-round, is the town's informal nerve center. Excellent Corsican specialties are served, such as a mint and brocciu omelet, and roast kid. ✉ 20218 Lama, ☎ 04–95–48–22–99, FAX 04–95–48–21–49. 50 cottages. Restaurant, kitchenettes. DC, MC, V.

Outdoor Activities and Sports

Riding along the old mule trails on horseback is an excellent way to see the countryside; contact **Ferme Équestre de L'Ostriconi** (☞ above).

Murato

㉝ 15 km (9 mi) west of Lama, 12 km (7 mi) south of Bastia: Take N193 to D82 to D305 at Rutalli.

The village of Murato has two excellent restaurants and an extraordinary 12th-century Pisan church. The polychrome, green-and-white marble **Église Mosaïque de San Michele** overlooks the Golfe de St-Florent and sometimes even the mainland.

Dining

$$ ✕ **Le Ferme Campo di Monte.** The Julliards prepare some of Corsica's
★ best, most authentic fare at this lovely 350-year-old farmhouse. Be sure to try the *storzapreti* (brocciu croquettes). ✉ D305 Rutali-Murato, ☎ 04–95–37–64–60. Reservations essential. AE, DC, MC, V. Closed weekdays Sept.–June.

St-Florent

㉞ 28 km (17 mi) northeast of the exit for Lama on D81, 46 km (28½ mi) northeast of L'Ile Rousse.

St-Florent is a postcard-perfect village nestled into the crook of the Golfe de St-Florent between the rich Nebbio Valley and the desert of Agriates. The town has a crumbling citadel and a yacht basin ringed by shops and restaurants. Be sure to seek out the interesting Romanesque **Santa Maria Assunta,** just outside the village. Standing in isolated splendor among the vineyards, this 12th-century limestone church is one of only two Pisan churches remaining on the island. The facade and interior columns support a menagerie of sculpted human faces, snakes, snails, and mythical animals. ✉ rue Agostino Giustiniani.

Dining

$$$ ✕ **La Rascasse.** This fine restaurant overlooking the port is known for its excellent fish stews and fresh seafood dishes. Try to get an upstairs table for a better view of the gulf. The *civet de lotte* (stewed sea bass) and the warm scallop salad are especially good. ✉ esplanade du Port, ☎ 04–95–37–06–99. AE, DC, MC, V. Closed Mon. Apr.–June, Sept.

Patrimonio

㉟ 5 km (3 mi) northeast of St-Florent, 18 km (11 mi) west of Bastia.

Patrimonio lies at the base of the Cap Corse peninsula, among acres of vineyards that produce some of Corsica's best red wine. The Antoine Arena vineyards are gaining ground steadily, but the **Orenga de Gaffory** label is the most famous. Tours of the vineyard and art gallery can be arranged. ☎ 04–95–37–11–38. ☺ Weekdays 9–noon and 3–6.

Nightlife and the Arts

The **Nuits de la Guitare** music festival during the third week of July is one of Corsica's top musical events, featuring blues, jazz, and flamenco guitarists from all over the world.

Outdoor Activities and Sports

One of the most spectacular mountain **hiking** routes in Corsica follows the crest of Cap Corse over the 4,287-ft Monte Stello, from which you can see hills of Tuscany and Provence. Contact the Parc Naturel Régional de la Corse (☞ Corsica A to Z, *below*) for details.

Nonza

36 *14 km (9 mi) north of Patrimonio, 8 km (5 mi) south of Canelle.*

On your way along Cap Corse, be sure to stop in Nonza. This vertiginous crag seems impossibly high over its famous black beach, the legacy of a former asbestos mine down the coast at Canari. The beach is accessible only by 600 steps leading down from Nonza, and no doubt this is the reason it's usually deserted. The chapel is dedicated to the martyred St. Julie, whose severed breasts became the double fountain, known as the *Fontaine aux Mamelles* (Fountain of Mammaries) on the way down to the beach. The spectacular gravity-defying tower was constructed by Pasquale Paoli in 1760. Its squared corners made it easier to defend, as famed Captain Casella proved in 1768 when he stood off 1,200 French troops.

Dining and Lodging

$$ ╳▨ **Auberge Patrizi.** On a shady terrace in the center of town, this place serves excellent Corsican cuisine in a lively setting. There are also rooms—small and a little close to the road—with spectacular views. ⊠ *pl. du Village, 20217,* ☎ *04–95–37–82–16,* ℻ *04–95–37–86–40. 13 rooms. AE, MC, V. Closed Nov.–Mar.*

Centuri

37 *55 km (34 mi) north of Patrimonio, 41 km (25 mi) north of Nonza.*

Centuri is a good place to stop for lunch on your way around Cap Corse. Watch for the arrival of the fishing boats at the end of the afternoon; the town is known as Cap Corse's top fishing port.

Dining and Lodging

$$$ ╳▨ **Le Vieux Moulin.** If you're after Old World charm and authentic Corsican flavor, this is the place. The main house was built in 1870 as a private residence; the eight-room annex is more recent but no less inviting, with bougainvillea cascading from its balconies. Boat rides and fishing trips can be arranged, and there are tennis courts and golf nearby. The restaurant specializes in seafood: Try the bouillabaisse. ⊠ *rte. de Cap Corse, 20238 Centuri Port,* , ☎ *04–95–35–60–15,* ℻ *04–95–35–60–24. 14 rooms. Restaurant. AE, DC, MC, V. Closed Nov.–Mar.*

En Route From Centuri, continue along the D80 coastal road to the **belvedere** near the Moulin Mattei windmill at Col de Serra, on the tip of the peninsula. As you round the tip, you can see some of Corsica's 90 **Genoan watchtowers,** as well as the Giraglia island with its lighthouse. Take D253 north to reach the fishing village of **Barcaggio.** A long, sandy beach extends east from the village, ending in a path leading to the 16th-century Tour D'Agnello. The **Finocchiarola Islands,** a protected aviary reserve visitable by boat from Macinaggio, are visible off the northeast corner of the peninsula. As you head down the east coast of Cap Corse on D80, you might want to make a detour on D180 through the **Col de Ste-Lucie** to the **Tour de Sénèque,** home of the Roman philosopher and writer Seneca after he was exiled for seducing the niece of Emperor Claudius. Farther south on D80, a drive up D32 to the town of **Sisco** will take you to within a 2-km (1-mi) walk of the Romanesque church of San Michele, built in 1030.

Erbalunga

38 *40 km (25 mi) southeast of Centuri, 10 km (6 mi) north of Bastia.*

Erbalunga is one of the most charming villages on Cap Corse's east coast, with stone houses sloping gently down to a Genoan tower built into a rock ledge. Probably as a result of Erbalunga's aesthetic grace, though possibly because it was French poet Paul Valéry's ancestral home, a colony of artists settled here in the '20s.

Lodging

$$–$$$ ⊠ **Castel Brando.** This 19th-century mansion has dark green shutters
★ and terra-cotta tiles. The large rooms are furnished with country-style antiques and dried flowers. The large pool and the terrace, where breakfast is served, are in the garden. ⊠ *Off of D80 (mailing address: B.P. 20), 20222 Erbalunga,* ☎ *04–95–30–10–30,* ℻ *04–95–33–98– 18. 16 rooms. Air-conditioning, kitchenettes, pool. AE, MC, V. Closed late Oct.–Apr.*

Bastia

39 *10 km (6 mi) south of Erbalunga, 23 km (14 mi) east of St-Florent, 93 km (58 mi) northeast of Calvi, 170 km (105 mi) north of Bonifacio, 153 km (95 mi) northeast of Ajaccio.*

Bastia's name comes from the *bastaglia,* or fortress, that the Genoese built here in the 14th century as a stronghold against rebellious islanders and potential invaders. Today, the city is Corsica's business center and largest town. Despite sprawling suburbs, the center of Bastia retains the timeless, salty flavor of an ancient Mediterranean port.

The **Terra Vecchia** (Old Town) is small enough to be explored on foot. Start at the wide, palm-filled **place St-Nicolas,** bordered on one side by the sea and on the other by two blocks of cafés that stretch out along **boulevard Général-de-Gaulle.** These cafés with their tables spilling into the square are the hub of Bastia's social life. Head south on boulevard Général-de-Gaulle, which becomes rue Napoléon, for two blocks to the **Église de la Conception** (Church of the Conception), occupying a pebble-studded square. Step inside to admire the church's ornate 18th-century interior, although the lighting is poor and you'll need a bright day to see much. The walls are covered with a riot of wood carvings, gold, and marble, and the ceiling is painted with vibrant frescoes. ⊠ *rue Napoléon.*

The **place du Marché,** the market square, brimming with activity every morning except Monday, is behind the church. The warren of tiny streets that make up the old fishermen's quarter begins at the far side of the square. To the south is the picturesque **Vieux Port** (Old Port), along quai des Martyrs de la Libération, dominated by the hilltop citadel. The harbor, lined with excellent seafood restaurants, is home to million-dollar yachts, but you can still find many bright red-and-blue fishing boats and tangles of old nets and lines. A walk around the port takes you to **Terra Nova** (New Town), a maze of not-so-new streets and houses at the base of the 15th-century fortress. Climb the stairs to the top for a sweeping view of the Italian islands of Capraia, Elba, and Montecristo.

Stop in at the **Palais des Nobles Douzes** (also known as the Palais des Gouverneurs Genois, or Genoese Governors' Palace), whose vaulted, colonnaded galleries now house the **Musée d'Ethnographie Corse** (Corsican Ethnographic Museum), with collections detailing the island's history. Look for the 18th-century rebel flag with the black head and white headband. Behind the ancient defense tower, a tiny stairway leads past the *Casablanca,* a French submarine used by the Resistance. The swastikas on the turret are from downed Nazi aircraft. ⊠ *pl. du Donjon,* ☎ *04–95–31–09–12.* 🎫 *20 frs.* ☉ *Weekdays 9–noon and 2–6, weekends 10–noon and 2–5.*

A network of cobbled alleyways rambles across the citadel to the 15th-century **Cathédrale Ste-Marie** (⊠ rue Notre-Dame). Inside, classic Baroque abounds in an explosion of gilt decoration. The 18th-century silver statue of the Assumption is paraded at the head of a religious procession every August 15. The sumptuous Baroque style of the **Chapelle Ste-Croix** (Chapel of the Holy Cross), behind the cathedral, makes it look more like a theater than a church. The chapel owes its name to a blackened oak crucifix, "Christ of the Miracles," discovered by fishermen at sea in 1428 and venerated to this day by Bastia's fishing community.

Dining and Lodging

$$–$$$ ✕ **La Citadella.** This rustic and intimate spot is near the Governor's Palace on the heights of the Terra Nova. In the middle of the restaurant is an ancient oil press, and the ambience is romantic day and night. The cuisine, too, is always excellent: Try the rock fish soup, a lovely dark and thick potage. ⊠ *5 rue du Dragon,* ☎ *04–95–31–44–70. AE, MC, V. Closed Sun.*

$$ ✕ **A Scaletta.** Enjoy the view of the Old Port as you choose from a host ★ of fish and seafood specials from this popular spot. (Lavezzi next door has the same view and considerably higher prices.) The cuisine in this rollicking little bistro is traditional Corsican with maritime leanings. ⊠ *4 rue St-Jean,* ☎ *04–95–32–28–70. AE, DC, MC, V. Closed Sun.*

$$$ 🏨 **Pietracap.** Perched on a hillside five minutes north of Bastia, Pietracap is a strikingly modern hotel nestled into a fragrant garden. The large rooms have stark, white modern furnishings and balconies. The lobby and hallways are decorated with bold canvases painted by the amiable owner's brother. ⊠ *20 rte. de San Martino di Lota, 20200 Pietranera-Bastia,* ☎ *04–95–31–64–63,* 🖷 *04–95–31–39–00. 42 rooms. Bar, restaurant, pool, bicycles. AE, DC, MC, V. Closed mid-Dec.–early Mar.*

$$ 🏨 **Posta Vecchia.** The greatest feature of this hotel in an old building not far from place St-Nicolas is its quai-side location. The unpretentious rooms have floral wallpaper and wood-beam ceilings; some are small. Ask for one in the main house facing the port. ⊠ *quai des Martyrs-de-la-Libération, 20200,* ☎ *04–95–32–32–38,* 🖷 *04–95–32–14–05. 49 rooms. AE, DC, MC, V.*

Nightlife and the Arts

L'Alba (⊠ 22 quai des Martyrs-de-la-Libération, ☎ 04–95–31–13–25) is a piano bar with occasional cabaret and floor shows. **Apocalypse** (⊠ in La Marana, 10 km/6 mi south of Bastia, ☎ 04–95–33–36–83) is *the* place to go dancing. A younger set gathers at **Mayflower** (⊠ port de Plaisance, ☎ 04–95–32–33–14) to hear loud rock and roll. Musicians fill the lively patio of the **Pub Chez Assunta** (⊠ pl. Fontaine Nueve 4, ☎ 04–95–34–11–40) on most summer nights. For a night of traditional Corsican music, head to **U-Fanale** (⊠ Vieux Port, ☎ 04–95–32–68–38).

One of Corsica's major carnivals, the **Fête du Christ Noir** (Feast of the Black Christ), dedicated to Bastia's most important religious icon, takes place on the May 3. The **Fête de St-Jean,** on Midsummer's Eve (June 23), means concerts in all of Bastia's Baroque spaces. A **Film Festival of Mediterranean Cultures** is held every November. An **International Music Festival** takes place in early December.

Outdoor Activities and Sports

Golf at the nine-hole **Bastia Golf Club** (⊠ Castellarèse, rte. de l'aéroport, Borgo, 12 km/7 mi south of Bastia, ☎ 04–95–38–33–99). **Corsica Loisirs** (⊠ 31 av. Émile-Sari, ☎ 04–95–32–54–34) organizes fishing outings and rents equipment. Bikes can be rented from **Objectif Nature** (⊠ 3 rue Notre-Dame-de-Lourdes, ☎ 04–95–32–54–34). Get a horse from the **Société Hippique Urbaine de Bastia La Marana** (☎ 04–95–33–53–08 or 04–95–30–37–62) and go galloping along the coast.

Shopping

Casa di l'Artigiani (⊠ 5 rue des Terrasses) has a wide selection of local crafts. The **Mattei Cap Corse** store (⊠ pl. St-Nicolas) sells the Mattei family's special Cap Corse liqueur (made from grapes). At the **market** (⊠ pl. du Marché, behind St-Jean-Baptiste), everything from local cheeses to charcuterie to myrtle liqueur is sold on weekday mornings.

San Martino di Lota

40 *12 km (7 mi) north of Bastia.*

Just 20 minutes from downtown Bastia, the turnoff to the perched village of San Martino di Lota winds through thick vegetation as the flat blue expanse of the Tyrrhenian Sea spreads out below. A hike up the **Bocca di Santo Lunardo** (a mountain pass) above the village is a great way to develop a ravenous appetite: It's a six- to eight-hour round-trip trek with fantastic views of Cap Corse, the Tyrrhenian, and the Tuscan hills.

Dining and Lodging

\$\$ ✕▥ **La Corniche.** The Anziani family runs this excellent hotel-restaurant serving Corsican fare—*cabri aux herbes du maquis* (roast kid in herbs from the maquis) and wild boar terrine. The restaurant is closed Sunday dinner and Monday from October to April. Rooms have panoramic views of the Tyrrhenian. ⊠ *20200 San Martino di Lota,* ☎ *04–95–31–40–98,* FAX *04–95–32–37–69. 18 rooms. Restaurant. AE, DC, MC, V. Closed late Dec.–late Jan.*

CORSICA A TO Z

Arriving and Departing

By Ferry

Regular car ferries run from Marseille, Nice, and Toulon to Ajaccio, Bastia, Calvi, L'Ile Rousse, and Propriano. These crossings take from 5 to 10 hours, with sleeping cabins available. The high-speed ferry from Nice to either Calvi or Bastia takes about three hours. Packages including the crossing with a car, onboard cabin, and hotel in Corsica are available from SNCM.

CMN (⊠ Compagnie Méridionale de Navigation, Ajaccio, ☎ 04–95–21–20–34; ⊠ Bastia, ☎ 04–95–31–63–38). **SNCM** (Société Nationale Maritime Corse-Méditérranée; ⊠ Paris, ☎ 01–49–24–24–24; ⊠ Marseille, ☎ 04–91–56–30–30; ⊠ Nice, ☎ 04–93–13–66–99; ⊠ Toulon, ☎ 04–94–16–66–66; ⊠ Ajaccio, ☎ 04–95–29–66–99;

⊠ Bastia, ☎ 04–95–54–66–88; ⊠ Calvi, ☎ 04–95–65–01–38; ⊠ L'Ile Rousse, ☎ 04–95–60–09–56).

Connections from the Italian mainland are run by **Corsica Ferries** (⊠ Bastia, ☎ 04–95–32–95–95; ⊠ Genoa, Italy, ☎ 010–59–33–01). **Moby Lines** (⊠ Bastia, ☎ 04–95–31–46–29; ⊠ Bonifacio, ☎ 04–95–73–00–29; ⊠ Genoa, ☎ 010–20–56–51) also runs Italian mainland connections.

Sardinia can be reached by ferry from Bastia or Bonifacio on **Navarma Lines** (⊠ 4 rue Luce-de-Casablanca, 20200 Bastia, ☎ 04–95–31–46–29; ⊠ At the port in Bonifacio, ☎ 04–95–73–00–29). **Saremar** (⊠ Gare Maritime, 20169 Bonifacio, ☎ 04–95–73–06–75) also runs ferries to Sardinia.

By Plane

Corsica has four major airports: Ajaccio, Bastia, Calvi, and Figari. **Air Inter** (☎ 04–95–29–45–45 Ajaccio; 01–45–46–90–00 Paris) has daily service connecting Paris and Lyon with Ajaccio, Bastia, and Calvi. **Compagnie Corse Méditérranée** (☎ 04–95–29–05–00 Ajaccio) connects Ajaccio and Bastia to Nice and Marseille, with several flights a day. **Delta Airlines** (☎ 800/241–4141) connects with Air Inter for flights from the United States to Corsica from May to October. **TAT** (Transport Aérien Transrégional; ☎ 05–05–50–05 toll free in France; 04–95–71–01–20 Figari) flies to Figari from Paris.

The airports at Ajaccio and Bastia run regular **shuttle-bus** services to and from town. At Figari, a bus meets all incoming flights and will take passengers as far as Bonifacio and Porto-Vecchio for about 100 francs. If you arrive at Calvi, take a **taxi** into the town center for about 100 francs.

Getting Around

By Bus

The local bus network is geared to residents who take it to school and work. At least two buses a day connect all the southern towns with Ajaccio, while northern towns are connected by bus to Bastia.

By Car

Though driving is undoubtedly the best way to explore the island's scenic stretches, note that winding, mountainous roads and uneven surfaces can actually double or triple your expected travel time. The Michelin 1/200,000 map No. 90 is essential. Be prepared for spelling anomalies, many of which are simply Corsican instead of French. Drive defensively: Drivers tend to circulate at terrifying speeds.

By Plane

Following are airlines with interisland flights: **Air Balagne** (☎ 04–95–65–02–97). **ATM** (Air Transport Méditérranée; ☎ 04–95–76–04–99). **Kyrnair** (☎ 04–95–20–52–29).

By Train

The main line of Corsica's simple rail network runs from Ajaccio, in the west, to Corte, in the central valley, then divides at Ponte Leccia. From here, one line continues to L'Ile Rousse and Calvi in the north and the other to Bastia in the northeast. Another daily service runs four times daily between Ajaccio and Bastia. In summer, a small train connects Calvi and L'Ile Rousse, stopping at numerous beaches and resorts. Following are numbers for local train stations: **Ajaccio** (☎ 04–95–23–11–03); **Bastia** (☎ 04–95–32–60–06); **Calvi** (☎ 04–95–65–00–61); and **Corte** (☎ 04–15–46–00–87).

Contacts and Resources

Car Rental

Avis Ollandini (⊠ Ajaccio airport, ☎ 04–95–23–25–14). **Europcar** (⊠ 1 rue du Nouveau Port, Bastia, ☎ 04–95–31–59–29). **Hertz** (⊠ Ajaccio airport, ☎ 04–95–22–14–84; ⊠ 8 cours Grandval, Ajaccio, ☎ 04–95–21–70–94; ⊠ square St-Victor, Bastia, ☎ 04–95–31–14–24; ⊠ quai du Commerce, Bonifacio, ☎ 04–95–73–02–47; ⊠ 2 rue Maréchal-Joffre, Calvi, ☎ 04–95–65–06–64) serves the entire island with 18 offices at all the airports, harbors, and major towns. Be sure to reserve at least two weeks in advance in July and August.

Guided Tours

Much of Corsica's most spectacular scenery is best viewed from the water. **Colombo Line** (⊠ quai Landry, ☎ 04–95–65–32–10) and **Promenades en Mer** (⊠ Porto Marine, ☎ 04–95–26–15–16) in Calvi organize whole-day tours in glass-bottom boats of Girolata, the Scandola nature reserve, and the Golfe de Porto. **Promenades en Mer** (⊠ Port de l'Amirauté, 20000 Ajaccio, ☎ 04–95–23–23–38) organizes daily trips (at 9 AM and 2 PM) to the Iles Sanguinaires. **Vedettes Christina** (☎ 04–95–73–14–69) and **Vedettes Méditérranée** (☎ 04–95–73–07–71) arrange outings from Bonifacio to the Iles Lavezzi, Les Calanches, and Les Grottes.

Canoeing, kayaking, and rafting are popular pastimes on the inland mountain rivers in the area; for details, write the **Association Municipale de Ponte-Leccia** (⊠ 20218 Ponte Leccia). Two- and three-day guided hikes through the mountains and lake region are organized by the **Associu di Muntagnoli Corsi** (⊠ quartier Pentaniedda, 20122 Quenza, ☎ 04–95–78–64–05).

Ollandini (⊠ 1 rte. d'Alata, Ajaccio, ☎ 04–95–21–10–12) arranges whole- and half-day bus tours of the island, leaving from Ajaccio. **ATM** (☎ 04–95–76–04–99) and **Kyrnair** (☎ 04–95–20–52–29) arrange sightseeing tours by plane.

Travel Agencies

Corse Itineraries (⊠ 32 cours Napoléon, Ajaccio, ☎ 04–95–51–01–10, FAX 04–45–21–52–30). **Corse Voyages** (⊠ Immeuble Les Remparts, bd. Wilson, Calvi, ☎ 04–95–65–26–71). **Cyrnea Tourisme** (⊠ 9 av. Xavier-Luciani, Corte, ☎ 04–95–46–24–62, FAX 04–95–46–11–22). **Kallistour** (⊠ 6 av. Maréchal-Sebastiani, Bastia, ☎ 04–95–31–71–49, FAX 04–95–32–35–73).

Visitor Information

The **Agence du Tourisme de la Corse** (⊠ 17 bd. Roi-Jérôme, 20000 Ajaccio, ☎ 04–95–51–77–77, FAX 04–95–51–14–40) can provide information about the whole island. The **Parc Naturel Régional de la Corse** (⊠ rue du Général-Fiorella; mailing address: B.P. 417, 20100 Ajaccio; ☎ 04–95–21–56–54), Corsica's wildlife and natural-resource management authority, controlling well over a third of the island, can provide trail maps, booklets, and a wide range of information.

Local tourist offices are as follows: **Ajaccio** (⊠ Hôtel de Ville, pl. Foch, ☎ 04–95–51–53–03). **Bastia** (⊠ pl. St-Nicolas, ☎ 04–95–31–00–89). **Bonifacio** (⊠ rue des Deux Moulins, ☎ 04–95–73–11–88). **Calvi** (⊠ port de Plaisance, ☎ 04–95–65–16–67). **Corte** (⊠ La Citadelle, ☎ 04–95–46–24–20). **Porticcio** (⊠ 428 bd. Rive Sud, ☎ 04–95–25–01–00). **Sartène** (⊠ rue Borgo, ☎ 04–95–77–15–40).

15 Toulouse, the Midi-Pyrénées, and Roussillon

The Midi-Pyrénées and Roussillon form the main body of France's traditional southwestern Languedoc region. Languedoc, named for the local medieval language, Langue d'Oc (literally, "language of yes"), possesses some of France's finest and most varied treasures: the wild peaks of the Pyrénées, colorful Mediterranean fishing villages, and cosmopolitan Toulouse. A cultural capital at the end of the last millennium, Toulouse is still one of France's liveliest and loveliest cities.

Revised and
updated by
George Semler

THE MIDI-PYRÉNÉES IS FRANCE'S largest region, spreading over 75,000 square km (28,500 square mi) from the Dordogne in the north to the Spanish border along the Pyrénées in the south. This chapter covers Roussillon and all of the Midi-Pyrénées except the southwest, or Hautes-Pyrénées (☞ Chapter 16). With its mountains, lakes, rivers, and arid limestone plateaus, this is the perfect region for nature lovers, sports enthusiasts, and gastronomes.

The Pyrénées, Western Europe's highest mountain range after the Alps, give birth to the Garonne, the great Atlantic-bound river of Toulouse and Bordeaux. The Garonne is joined by the Rivers Aveyron and Tarn (as well as by the Lot and the Célée to the north), flowing east to west, all of which carve out steep gorges and wide green valleys.

Toulouse is an upbeat university center with a rhythm more redolent of Spain (two hours' drive away) than of the drowsy French provinces. The city is known as the Ville Rose (Pink City) because of the ruddy glow of its redbrick buildings. The Canal du Midi, built in the 17th century, passes through Toulouse and continues east, near the medieval walls of Carcassonne, on its way from the Atlantic to the Mediterranean.

Other highlights include the picturesque hilltop village of Cordes north of Toulouse; the Ariège Valley, with its Merens horses and medieval villages; and the fishing village of Collioure, where Matisse and Derain committed chromatic mayhem in the early years of this century. There are three outstanding art museums: the Musée Ingres in Montauban, devoted to one of France's most accomplished pre-Impressionist painters; the Musée Toulouse-Lautrec in Albi, with its unique collection of works by the leading observer of Belle Époque cabaret; and the Musée d'Art Modern in Céret, with its Picassos, Braques, and Chagalls.

Roussillon—between Narbonne and the Spanish border—is easy to reach from Toulouse. Perpignan, its capital, has a bustling, Iberian feel. There are strong linguistic and historic ties with Catalonia: The area was ceded to France as recently as 1659. The streets of even the smallest towns display the Catalan colors of *sang et or* (blood and gold).

Pleasures and Pastimes

Dining

The region is known for rich and strongly seasoned cooking: Garlic and goose fat are generously used. Be sure to try some of the renowned foie gras and confit *de canard* (of duck). The most famous regional dish is cassoulet, a succulent white-bean stew with confit *d'oie* (of goose) or confit de canard, spicy sausage, pork, and sometimes lamb. Cheaper specialties include *garbure,* mixed vegetables served as a broth or puree; *farci du lauragais,* a kind of pork pancake; and *gigot de sept heures,* a leg of lamb cooked for seven hours. Finish your meal with a glass of Armagnac, distilled throughout the Gers *département* (province). You'll see signs for *dégustation* (tasting) just about everywhere.

CATEGORY	COST*
$$$$	over 400 frs
$$$	250 frs–400 frs
$$	125 frs–250 frs
$	under 125 frs

*per person for a three-course meal, including tax (20.6%) and tip but not wine

Lodging

Hotels range from Mediterranean modern to medieval baronial; most are small and cozy rather than luxurious. Toulouse has the usual range of big-city hotels; make reservations well in advance if you plan to visit in spring or fall.

CATEGORY	COST*
$$$$	over 800 frs
$$$	550 frs–800 frs
$$	300 frs–550 frs
$	under 300 frs

*All prices are for a standard double room, including tax (20.6%) and service charge.

Outdoor Activities and Sports

The Pyrénées Orientales (eastern Pyrénées) between Prades and Foix offer great walking, though sturdy legs come in handy. The rough waters of the Tarn and Aveyron gorges are perfect for canoeing and kayaking; the peaceful River Quercy is better for a gentler trip. Skiing—downhill or cross-country—is excellent in the Pyrénées, with more than two dozen ski resorts along the central and eastern part of the range. There are also equestrian tours, fishing opportunities, and several superb golf courses.

Exploring the Midi-Pyrénées

This region can be divided into three areas. The first covers Toulouse, a lively city imbued with culture and history. The second encompasses the area to the north and west of Toulouse, including Albi, the Lot Valley, Montauban, and verdant Gascony—the Gers *département*. The third extends east into Roussillon at Carcassonne, up through the Ariège and through the Pyrénées Orientales to the Mediterranean before swinging north through Perpignan and Narbonne.

Great Itineraries

Getting to know the large Midi-Pyrénées and Roussillon regions would take several weeks or even years. But it is possible to sample their finest offerings in 3 to 10 days, if that's all you have.

Numbers in the text correspond to numbers in the margin and on The Midi-Pyrénées and Roussillon and Toulouse maps.

IF YOU HAVE 3 DAYS

Bask in the rich rose color of ⛫ **Toulouse** ①–㉓ for a day, and then head to **Cordes** ㉕, a fortified medieval village. Make Toulouse-Lautrec's hometown, ⛫ **Albi** ㉔, your home for the night: Locals argue that it's a deeper rose hue than Toulouse—you can decide. On day three, explore the medieval citadel at ⛫ **Carcassonne** ㉜.

IF YOU HAVE 7 DAYS

Spend the first day and a half in ⛫ **Toulouse** ①–㉓; then drive west to ⛫ **Auch** ㉛, the capital of the Gers *département*. Next head north to **Condom** ㉙, in the Armagnac region, for a taste of the famous brandy. On your way to the cloisters at ⛫ **Moissac** ㉗, roam around the old Roman town of **Lectoure** ㉘. On day three, study up on the university town of **Montauban** ㉖ before stepping back in time in medieval **Cordes** ㉕. Spend the night at ⛫ **Albi** ㉔ or at the delightful inn in nearby Plaisance (☞ Plaisance *in* Chapter 11). Go south to **Carcassonne** ㉜ for more medieval history, on the fourth day, before going to **Mirepoix** ㉝, near the castle town of ⛫ **Foix** ㉞, for the night. The next day drive into the Pyrénées, passing through **Tarascon-sur-Ariège** ㉟ to see the Grotte de Niaux, the mountain resorts of **Ax-les-Thermes** ㊱ and

Font-Romeu ㊲, and the Vauban fortress town of **Mont-Louis** ㊴. Spend the night in nearby 🚉 **Eyne** ㊳ before continuing east out of the Pyrénées toward the Mediterranean. Stop in the fortified town of **Villefranche-de-Conflent** ㊵ and the Abbaye de St-Martin-de-Canigou. Pass through the spa town of **Vernet-les-Bains** ㊶ on your way to **Prades** ㊷ and the Abbaye de St-Michel-de-Cuxa, and **Céret** ㊸. Spend the sixth night in Roussillon's historic capital, 🚉 **Perpignan** ㊺, or the fishing village of 🚉 **Collioure** ㊹. On the final day, drive north to **Salses** ㊻, where Hannibal once passed through, before leaving this region at **Narbonne** ㊼.

Old Toulouse

The area between the boulevards and the Garonne forms the historic nucleus of Toulouse. Originally part of Roman Gaul, later capital for Visigoths and Carolingians, by the year AD 1000 Toulouse was one of the artistic and literary centers of medieval Europe. Despite the 13th-century defeat by the lords of northern France, Toulouse quickly reemerged as a cultural and commercial power and has remained so ever since. The religious and civil structures throughout this part of town bear witness to this illustrious past, even as the city's booming student life provides a dynamic present. This is the heart of Toulouse, with the place du Capitole at its center.

A Good Walk

Start on the **place du Capitole** ①, stopping at the *donjon* (keep) next to the **Capitole/Hôtel de Ville** ②, where there is a tourist office with maps. Rue du Taur, off the square, leads to **Notre-Dame du Taur** ③. Continue along rue du Taur to the **Ancien Collège de Périgord** ④, to see the oldest part of the medieval university. The emblematic church of **St-Sernin** ⑤ is at the end of rue du Taur on place St-Sernin. Next door is the **Musée St-Raymond** ⑥, the city's archaeological museum.

Leave place St-Sernin and cut out along rue Bellegarde to the boulevard de Strasbourg, where the open-air vegetable and produce market is held. Take the boulevard to rue Victor-Hugo and the **Marché Victor Hugo** ⑦, the large market halls. Find your way back to place du Capitole, cross the square, and take rue Gambetta to rue Lakanal; a right will take you to the **Église des Jacobins** ⑧, one of Toulouse's greatest structures.

Back on rue Gambetta, to your right, is the opulent **Hôtel de Bernuy** ⑨. Cut through rue J.-Suau to **place de la Daurade** ⑩. **Notre-Dame de la Daurade** ⑪ is the church on your left. After a pause here, continue up the quai de Tounis past the sculpted façade of the École des Beaux-Arts toward the **Pont Neuf** ⑫. Turn left on rue de Metz, continuing down to the **Hôtel d'Assézat** ⑬, home to the **Fondation Bemberg** and its excellent collection of paintings. If you are interested in religious art, pop over to the **Musée des Augustins** ⑭.

Take a left on rue des Changes, once part of the Roman road that sliced through Toulouse from north to south; today it's a chic pedestrian-only shopping area. Stop to admire the **Hôtel d'Astorg** ⑮ at No. 16, the **Hôtel d'Arnault Brucelles** ⑯ at No. 19, and the **Hôtel Delpech** ⑰ at No. 20. Continue along rue des Changes to the intersection with rue de Temponières. Note the handsome wood and brick building on the far right corner, and the faux-granite at the near left, complete with painted lines between the "stones" and trompe l'oeil windows bricked in and painted, a reminder of the legendary window tax all good citizens struggled to avoid. The next street to the left, rue Tripière, loops through place du May onto rue du May, which leads to the **Musée du Vieux Toulouse** ⑱ housed in the Hôtel Dumay (sic) at No. 7. Continue past

Le Bol Bu tearoom and the small Renaissance doorway at No. 16 to rejoin what was rue des Changes, now rue St-Rome. Turn left and have a look at (and a whiff of) the delicious Berdoncle dry goods store at No. 38. Then continue back to place du Capitole.

TIMING

This walk covers some 3 km (2 mi) and should take from three to four hours depending on how long you spend at each sight. Places close punctually at noon, so it is essential that you get an early start. Or, better yet, take a long lunch, too, continuing on again after 2 PM when places reopen.

Sights to See

❹ Ancien Collège de Périgord (Old Périgord College). This wooden structure, on the street side of the courtyard, is the oldest remnant of the 14th-century residential college. ⊠ *56–58 rue du Taur.*

❷ Capitole/Hôtel de Ville (Capital/Town Hall). The 18th-century Capitole is home to the Hôtel de Ville and the city's highly regarded opera company. The reception rooms are open when not in use for official functions or weddings. Halfway up the **Grand Escalier** (Grand Staircase) hangs a large painting of the *Jeux Floraux* (Floral Games), organized by a literary society created in 1324 to promote the local language, Langue d'Oc. The festival continues to this day: Poets give public readings here each May, and the best are awarded silver- and gold-plated violets, one of the emblems of Toulouse.

At the top of the stairs is the **Salle Gervaise**, a hall used for weddings, beneath a series of paintings inspired by the theme of love and marriage. The mural at the far end of the room portrays the Isle of Cythères, where Venus received her lovers, alluding to the French euphemism for getting married: *embarquer pour Cythères* (to embark or shove off for Cythères). Four more giant paintings in the **Salle Henri-Martin**, named for the artist (1860–1943), show the passing seasons set against the eternal Garonne. Look for Jean Jaurès, one of France's greatest socialists (1859–1914), in *Les Rêveurs* (*The Dreamers*); he's wearing a boater and a beige coat. At the far left end of the elegant **Salle des Illustres** (Hall of the Illustrious) is a large painting of a fortress under siege, portraying the women of Toulouse killing Simon de Montfort, leader of the Albigensian crusade against the Cathars, during the siege of Toulouse in 1218. ⊠ *pl. du Capitole,* ☎ *05–61–11–34–12.* ☑ *Free.* ⏱ *Weekdays 8:30–5, weekends 10–6.*

❽ Église des Jacobins. An extraordinary structure built in the 1230s for the Dominicans (dubbed Jacobins in 1217 for their Parisian base in rue St-Jacques), this church has two rows of columns running the length of the nave—a standard feature of Dominican churches. The column farthest from the entrance is one of the world's two or three finest examples of palm-tree vaulting. The original refectory is used for temporary art exhibitions. In summer, the cloister hosts piano concerts ("Piano Jacobins"). ⊠ *rue Lakanal.*

❶❻ Hôtel d'Arnault Brucelles. One of Toulouse's tallest and best towers can be found at this 16th-century mansion. ⊠ *19 rue des Changes.*

❶❸ Hôtel d'Assézat/Fondation Bemberg. Built in 1555 by Toulouse's top Renaissance architect, Nicolas Bachelier, this mansion, considered the city's most elegant, has arcades and ornately carved doorways. It is now home to the Fondation Bemberg, an exceptional collection of paintings ranging from Tiepolo to Toulouse-Lautrec. Climb to the top of the tower for splendid views over the city's rooftops. ⊠ *rue de Metz.* ☑ *25 frs.* ⏱ *Daily 10–noon and 2–6.*

Toulouse

⑮ Hôtel d'Astorg. This 16th-century mansion is notable for its lovely wooden stairways and galleries and for its top-floor *mirande,* a wood-ceilinged observation deck. This isn't an official site; you can just explore it on your own. ⊠ *16 rue des Changes.*

⑨ Hôtel de Bernuy. Now part of a school, this mansion, around the corner from the Église des Jacobins, was built for Jean de Bernuy in the 16th century when Toulouse was at its most prosperous. De Bernuy, a merchant, made his fortune exporting dye, and his wealth is reflected in the use of stone, a costly material in this region of brick, and by the octagonal stair tower, the highest in the city. You may wander freely around the courtyard. ⊠ *rue Gambetta.*

⑰ Hôtel Delpech. Distinguishing this mansion are the biblical inscriptions in Latin carved in stone under the windows. ⊠ *20 rue des Changes.*

⑦ Marché Victor Hugo (Victor Hugo Market). This hangarlike indoor market is always a refreshing stop. Consider eating lunch at one of the seven upstairs restaurants. **Chez Attila,** just to the left at the top of the stairs, is the best of them. ⊠ *pl. Victor-Hugo.*

⑭ Musée des Augustins (Augustinian Museum). Housed in a medieval Augustinian convent, the museum uses the sacristy, chapter house, and cloisters for displaying an outstanding array of Romanesque sculpture and religious paintings. ⊠ *rue de Metz,* ☎ *05–61–23–55–07.* ⌁ *10 frs (free Sun.).* ⊘ *Wed. 10–9, Thurs.–Mon. 10–5.*

❻ Musée St-Raymond. The city's archaeological museum, next to the basilica of St-Sernin (☞ *below*), has an extensive collection of imperial Roman busts, as well as ancient coins, vases, and jewelry. ⊠ *pl. St-Sernin,* ☎ *05–61–22–21–85.* ⌁ *10 frs.* ⊘ *Mon. and Wed.–Sat. 8–noon and 2–6, Sun. noon–6.*

⑱ Musée du Vieux Toulouse (Museum of Old Toulouse). This museum is worthwhile for the building itself as much as for its collection of Toulouse memorabilia, paintings, sculptures, and documents. Be sure to note the ground floor fireplace and wooden ceiling. ⊠ *7 rue du May,* ☎ *05–61–13–97–24.* ⌁ *10 frs.* ⊘ *June–Sept., Mon.–Sat. 3–6.*

⑪ Notre-Dame de la Daurade. Overlooking the River Garonne is this 18th-century church. The name Daurade comes from *doré* (gilt), referring to the golden reflection given off by the mosaics decorating the 5th-century temple to the Virgin Mary that once stood on this site. ⊠ *pl. de la Daurade.*

❸ Notre-Dame du Taur. Built on the spot where St. Saturnin (or Sernin), the martyred bishop of Toulouse, was dragged to his death in AD 257 by a rampaging bull, this church is famous for its *cloche-mur,* or wall tower. The wall looks like an extension of the facade and has inspired many similar versions throughout the region. ⊠ *rue du Taur.*

❶ Place du Capitole. A vast, open square lined with shops and cafés in the city center, it is a good spot for getting your bearings. There is a parking lot underneath.

❿ Place de la Daurade. This is one of Toulouse's nicest squares. Check out the quay-side walks suggested at the top of the ramp down to the Garonne and note the Restaurant-Péniche (barge) moored along the quay. A stop at Café des Artistes is almost obligatory. Just past the church you'll find a romantic view of the Pont Neuf.

⑫ Pont Neuf (New Bridge). The graceful span of the Pont Neuf opened to traffic in 1632. It leads your eye to the **Château d'Eau,** a 19th-century water tower at the far end, now used for photography exhibits. The remains of the old bridge—one arch and the lighter-color outline on the brick wall of the **Hôtel Dieu** (hospital)—are visible across the river. The 16th-century hospital was used for pilgrims on their way to Santiago de Compostela. Just over the bridge, on a clear day in winter, the snowcapped peaks of the Pyrénées are visible in the distance, which is said to be a sign of imminent rain.

★ ❺ St-Sernin. Toulouse's most famous landmark and the world's largest Romanesque church once belonged to a Benedictine abbey, built in the 11th century to house pilgrims on their way to Santiago de Compostela in Spain. When illuminated at night, St-Sernin's five-tier octagonal tower glows red against the sky. Not all the tiers are the same: The first three, with their rounded windows, are Romanesque; the upper two, with their pointed Gothic windows, were added around 1300. ⊠ *rue du Taur,* ☎ *05–61–21–70–18.* ⌁ *Crypt 10 frs.* ⊘ *Daily 10–11:30 and 2:30–5:30.*

South of rue de Metz

South of rue de Metz are St-Étienne Cathedral and the antiques district, along rue Perchepinte. All around are streets lined with some of the city's finest town houses.

A Good Walk

From the **Cathédrale St-Étienne** ⑲ walk down rue Fermat to rue Perchepinte. The street, lined with 18th-century houses, makes up the antiques district. At place Perchepinte cut across to rue de la Pleau. At No. 13 is the **Musée Paul Dupuy** ⑳, a museum of medieval arts. Take a right on rue Ozenne and note No. 9, the 15th-century Hôtel de Dahus. To get to the **Muséum d'Histoire Naturelle** ㉑, go the other direction on rue Ozenne. If you choose, instead, to continue on from No. 9, you'll come to rue du Languedoc: Look at No. 36, the 15th- and 16th-century mansion Hôtel du Vieux Raisin, with its unusual octagonal tower. Across the street is the Marché des Carmes, a market worth a stop. Continue back down rue du Languedoc to place du Salin, where farmers sell homemade foie gras on market mornings. Rue de la Dalbade, parallel to the Garonne, leads past one stately facade after another. The finest is No. 25, the **Hôtel de Clary** ㉒. Continue up the street to the church of **Notre-Dame de la Dalbade** ㉓.

TIMING

This walk will take you two or three hours. Note that the market is only open in the morning.

Sights to See

⑲ **Cathédrale St-Étienne.** The cathedral was erected in stages between the 13th and 17th centuries, though the nave and choir languished unfinished because of a lack of funds. A fine collection of 16th- and 17th-century tapestries traces the life of St. Stephen. Fronting the cathedral is the city's oldest fountain, dating from the 16th century. ⌂ *pl. St-Étienne.*

㉒ **Hôtel de Clary.** This mansion, known as the Hôtel de Pierre because of its unusual solid *pierre* (stone) construction—at the time considered a sign of great wealth—is one of the finest 17th- and 18th-century mansions on the street. The ornately sculpted stone facade was built in 1608 by parliamentary president François de Clary. ⌂ *25 rue de la Daurade.*

⑳ **Musée Paul Dupuy.** This museum, dedicated to medieval applied arts, is housed in the Hôtel Pierre Besson, a 16th-century mansion. ⌂ *13 rue de la Pleau,* ☎ *06–61–22–21–82.* ▨ *15 frs.* ☉ *Wed. 10–9, Thurs.–Mon. 10–5.*

㉑ **Muséum d'Histoire Naturelle.** Surrounded by gardens, the Natural History Museum has a varied collection of stuffed birds and prehistoric exhibits. ⌂ *35 allée Jules-Guesde,* ☎ *05–61–52–00–14.* ▨ *8 frs.* ☉ *Wed.–Mon. 10–5.*

㉓ **Notre-Dame de la Dalbade.** Originally Sancta Maria de Ecclesia Alba in Langue d'Oc (Ste-Marie de l'Église Blanche in French, or Holy Mary of the White Church), the name of the church evolved into "de albata" and later Dalbade. One of its outstanding features today is the colorful 19th-century ceramic tympanum over the Renaissance door. ⌂ *pl. de la Dalbade.*

Dining and Lodging

$$$$ ✕ **Jardins de l'Opéra.** One of the most fashionable restaurants in town is in the Grand Hôtel de l'Opéra (☞ *below*). Intimate dining rooms and a covered terrace around a little pond make for undeniable, if slightly

over-formal, charm. The food is a successful mix of innovation and traditional Gascon fare: for example, ravioli stuffed with foie gras. ✉ *1 pl. du Capitole,* ☎ *05–61–21–82–66. Reservations essential. AE, DC, MC, V.*

$$$ ✕ **Brasserie des Beaux-Arts.** This spot overlooking the Pont Neuf is the place to be at sunset. Watch the colors change over the Garonne from a window or sidewalk table while enjoying the delicious seafood, including all kinds of oysters. The house white wine goes along quite nicely, as does the impeccable service. ✉ *1 quai de la Daurade,* ☎ *05–61–21–21–12. AE, DC, MC, V.*

$$–$$$ ✕ **Au Pois Gourmand.** A 30-minute walk or 10-minute cab ride down the Garonne from the Pont Neuf will bring you to one of the best restaurants in Toulouse. In Jean-Claude Plazzotta's lovely wooden house, sample foie gras, lamb, magret de canard, squab, and kid. A specialist in wild mushrooms and spices, Plazzotta takes you on a memorable gastronomical tour. In summer, dine in the garden or on the balcony overlooking the Garonne. (If you're walking, go down the right bank to the Pont des Catalanes, cross to the left bank, and continue along the gravel walkway to the fourth bridge downstream.) ✉ *3 rue Heybrard,* ☎ *05–61–31–95–95. AE, DC, MC, V. Closed Sun. No lunch Sat.*

$$–$$$ ✕ **La Corde.** This little hideaway is worth taking the time to find. Built
★ into a lovely 15th-century corner tower hidden in the courtyard of the 16th-century Hôtel Bolé, La Corde claims the distinction of being the oldest restaurant in Toulouse. Try the *effiloché de canard aux pêches* (shredded duck with caramelized peach). ✉ *4 rue Jules-Chalande,* ☎ *05–61–29–09–43. AE, DC, MC, V. Closed Sun. No lunch Mon.*

$$ ✕ **Chez Emile.** There are two dining rooms at this restaurant: The ground floor has a seafood menu that changes daily; if it's available, have the turbot in ginger. Upstairs is a cozy hideaway for when you want a more traditional taste of Toulouse: cassoulet, *magret de canard* (duck breast), and other sturdy choices. ✉ *13 pl. St-Georges,* ☎ *05–61–21–05–56. Reservations essential. AE, DC, MC, V. Closed last wk in Aug. and Sun.–Mon.*

$$$$ 🏨 **Grand Hôtel de l'Opéra.** This downtown doyen has an Old World
★ feeling. The comfortably plush rooms are decorated in traditional style and soothing pastels yet lack none of the usual modern conveniences. The three restaurants have a range of cuisine, from provincial bistro to international gourmet to Indian curry. ✉ *1 pl. du Capitole, 31000,* ☎ *05–61–21–82–66,* 🖷 *05–61–23–41–04. 49 rooms. 3 restaurants, café, pool, health club. AE, DC, MC, V.*

$$$ 🏨 **Château de Garrevaques.** Equidistant (50 km/31 mi) from Toulouse, Carcassonne, and Albi, this castle makes a great base. Built in 1470 and rebuilt in the early 19th century, the château is on 8 acres of parkland. Mme. Combes is a helpful hostess, the château's 15th generation, and will guide you through the family heirlooms and antiques. Continental breakfast is included in the room rates. The table d'hôte dinner costs extra and is plain family fare. Advance reservations are required. ✉ *81700 Garrevaques (5 km/3 mi northwest of Revel),* ☎ *05–63–75–04–54,* 🖷 *05–63–70–26–44. 7 rooms, 2 suites. Pool, tennis court, billiards. AE, MC, V.*

$$$ 🏨 **Hôtel des Beaux-Arts.** In the thick of the most Toulousain part of
★ town, over the Pont Neuf and next to the Hôtel d'Assézat, this cozy place has small but tastefully decorated rooms; the best have a tiny breakfast terrace overlooking the Garonne. The management is attentive. ✉ *1 pl. du Pont-Neuf, 31000,* ☎ *05–61–23–40–50,* 🖷 *05–61–22–02–27. 20 rooms. Breakfast room. AE, DC, MC, V.*

$–$$ 🏨 **Hôtel Albert I.** The building is rather ordinary and the reception area is just functional, but rooms are cheerful and as spacious as you can expect from a hotel in the heart of Toulouse. The extremely personable owner, Mme. Hilaire, is on hand to chat and to give suggestions on where to dine and shop. A Continental breakfast is served. ⊠ *8 rue Rivals, 31000,* ☎ *05–61–21–17–91,* FAX *05–61–21–09–64. 46 rooms. Breakfast room. MC, V.*

$ 🖬 **Hôtel du Grand Balcon.** This charmingly down-at-the-heels spot has views of place du Capitole from some of its corner rooms. Antoine de St-Exupéry, author of *The Little Prince,* stayed here with his fellow aviators early this century. ⊠ *8 rue Romiguières, 31000,* ☎ *05–61–21– 48–08,* FAX *05–61–21–59–98. 50 rooms. Breakfast room. MC, V. Closed mid-Dec.–early Jan. and 1st 3 wks Aug.*

Nightlife and the Arts

Toulouse's classical, lyrical, and chamber music orchestras; dramatic arts center; and ballet are all listed as national companies—no mean feat in this arts-oriented country. For a schedule of current programs, contact the city tourist office. If you want to stay up late—and they do in Toulouse—a complete list of clubs and discos can be found in the weekly *Toulouse Pratique,* available at any newsstand.

Bagamoyo (⊠ 27 rue des Couteliers, ☎ 05–62–26–11–36) is a lively place for nocturnal snacks of simple but delicious African fare. **Bar Basque** (⊠ 7 pl. St-Pierre, ☎ 05–61–21–55–64) is one of the many good watering holes around place St-Pierre. Brazilian guitarists perform at **La Bonita** (⊠ 112 Grand-Rue St-Michel, ☎ 05–62–26–36– 45). For jazz, try **Le Café des Allées** (⊠ 64 allée Charles-de-Fitte, ☎ 05–62–27–14–46), a hothouse for local musicians. **Café Le Griot** (⊠ 34 rue des Blanchers, ☎ 05–62–36–41–56) features a number of American duos and trios.

At **El Mexicano** (⊠ 37 rue de l'Industrie, ☎ 05–61–63–17–36) a crush of people inhales tequila and 3-inch steaks. **La Péniche** (⊠ Canal de Brienne, 90 allée de Barcelone, ☎ 05–61–21–13–40) is a local gay bar. Begin your night on the town at **Père Louis** (⊠ 45 rue des Tourneurs, ☎ 05–61–21–33–45), an old-fashioned winery (and restaurant) with barrels for tables and vintage photographs. **Puerto Habana** (⊠ 12 port St-Étienne, ☎ 05–61–54–45–61) is the place for salsa music. If you're looking for onion soup and other treats in the wee hours, head for **St-André** (⊠ 39 rue St-Rome, ☎ 05–61–22–56–37), open 7 PM to dawn (closed Sunday). Local glitterati and theater stars go to **L'Ubu** (⊠ 16 rue St-Rome, ☎ 05–61–23–97–80), the city's top night spot for 20 years.

The main theaters in Toulouse are the **Halle Aux Grains** (⊠ pl. Dupuy, ☎ 05–61–63–18–65); **Théâtre du Capitole** (⊠ pl. du Capitole, ☎ 05– 61–23–21–35); **Théâtre Daniel Sorano** (⊠ 35 allée Jules-Guesde, ☎ 05–61–25–66–87). **Théâtre de la Digue** (⊠ 3 rue de la Digue, ☎ 05– 61–42–97–79); and **Théâtre du Taur** (⊠ 69 rue du Taur, ☎ 05–61– 21–77–13). So many opera singers perform at the **Théâtre du Capitole** and the **Halle aux Grains** that the city is known as the *capitale du bel canto* (capital of the bel canto). The opera season lasts from October until late May, with occasional summer presentations. A wide variety of dance companies perform in Toulouse: The **Ballet du Capitole** stages classical ballets. **Ballet-Théâtre Joseph Russilo** and **Compagnie Jean-Marc Matos** put on modern dance concerts. The **Centre National Chorégraphique de Toulouse** welcomes international companies each year in the St-Cyprien quarter.

Outdoor Activities and Sports

Toulouse is just 100 km (60 mi) from the nearest peaks. For information about hiking, skiing, mountain refuges, and just about anything having to do with the Pyrénées, check with the **Pyrénées Club** (✉ 29 rue du Taur, ☎ 05–61–21–11–44). There are two good 18-hole golf courses near Toulouse: **Golf Club de Toulouse** (✉ Vieille Toulouse, ☎ 05–61–73–45–48) and **Golf Club de Toulouse Palmola** (✉ rte. d'Albi, ☎ 05–61–84–20–50). If you want to go horseback riding, try **Poney City** (✉ St-Paul, 40 km/25 mi east of Toulouse, ☎ 05–63–42–06–45).

Shopping

Toulouse is a chic design outlet for clothing and artifacts of all kinds. **Rue St-Rome, rue des Changes,** and **rue d'Alsace-Lorraine** are all good shopping streets. And don't skip **Bourdoncle** (✉ 38 rue St-Rome), a dry goods shop.

ALBI AND THE GERS

Along the banks of the Tarn to the northeast of Toulouse is Albi, Toulouse's rival in rose colors. West from Albi, along the river, the land opens up to the rural Gers *département,* home of the heady brandy Armagnac and heart of the former dukedom of Gascony. It's studded with châteaux—from simple medieval fortresses to ambitious classical residences—and tiny, isolated villages.

Albi

★ ㉔ *75 km (47 mi) northeast of Toulouse.*

Toulouse-Lautrec's native Albi is a well-preserved and busy provincial market town. In its heyday, Albi was a major center for Cathars, members of a dualistic and ascetic religious movement critical of the hierarchical and worldly ways of the Catholic Church. Pick up a copy of the excellent visitor's booklet (in English) from the tourist office (✉ pl. Ste-Cécile, ☎ 05–63–49–48–80), and follow the walking tours—of the old city, the old ramparts, and the banks of the River Tarn.

The huge **Cathédrale Ste-Cécile,** with its intimidating clifflike walls, resembles a cross between a castle and an ocean liner. It was constructed as a symbol of the church's return to power after the 13th-century crusade that wiped out the Cathars. The interior is an astonishingly ornate reply to the massive austerity of the outer walls. Maestro Donnelli and a team of 16th-century Italian artists covered every possible surface with religious scenes and brightly colored patterns. The most striking fresco is a 15th-century depiction of the Last Judgment on the west wall. ✉ *pl. Ste-Cécile.*

★ The **Palais de la Berbie** (Berbie Palace), between the cathedral and the Pont Vieux (Old Bridge), was built in 1265 as a defensive fortress. The gardens were created by André Le Nôtre, known for the Versailles gardens. In 1905, the fortress became a museum, the **Musée Toulouse-Lautrec,** honoring Albi's most famous son: Belle Époque painter Henri de Toulouse-Lautrec (1864–1901). Toulouse-Lautrec left Albi for Paris in 1882 and soon became famous for his colorful and tumultuous evocations of the bohemian glamour in and around Montmartre. Despite his aristocratic origins (Lautrec is a town not far from Toulouse), Henri cut a far-from-noble figure. He was less than 5 ft tall (due to a genetic bone deficiency) and pursued a decadent life that led to an early grave. With more than 1,000 of the artist's works, the Albi exhibit is the country's largest Toulouse-Lautrec collection. ✉ *Just off pl. Ste-*

Cécile, ☎ 05–63–49–48–70. ⊠ 25 frs, gardens free. ☉ May–Sept., daily 10–noon and 2–6; Oct.–Apr., Wed.–Mon. 10–noon and 2–5.

After visiting the Palais de la Berbie, stroll around the old town. Leaving the palace behind you, walk to the 11th- to 15th-century college and **Cloître de St-Salvy** (cloister; ⊠ rue St-Cécile). Next, visit Albi's finest restored traditional house, the **Maison du Vieil Albi** (Old Albi House; ⊠ On the corner of rue de la Croix-Blanche and Puech-Bérenguer). If you're a real fan of Toulouse-Lautrec, stop by his birthplace, the **Maison Natale de Toulouse-Lautrec** (⊠ 14 rue Henri de Toulouse-Lautrec). Rue de l'Hôtel de Ville, two streets west of the Maison Natale, leads past the *Mairie* (Town Hall), with its hanging globes of flowers, to Albi's main square, **place du Vigan.** Take a break in one of the two main cafés, Le Pontie or Le Vigan.

Dining and Lodging

$$$ ✕ **Le Moulin de la Mothe.** This onetime mill on the banks of the Tarn is neatly tucked in to the river, surrounded by lush vegetation. Chef-owner Michel Pellaprat specializes in inventive cooking based on high-quality local products. ⊠ *rue de Lamothe,* ☎ 05–63–60–38–15. AE, MC, V. Closed Wed. Sept.–June. No dinner Sun. Sept.–June.

$$ ✕ **Le Jardin des Quatre Saisons.** There are two reasons for this restaurant's excellent reputation: its good-value menu and its fish dishes. Owner-chef Georges Bermond's house specialties include mussels baked with leeks and *suprême de sandre* (a freshwater fish similar to a pickerel cooked in wine). ⊠ *19 bd. de Strasbourg,* ☎ 05–63–60–77–76. AE, MC, V. Closed Mon.

$$$–$$$$ ✕🛏 **La Réserve.** A 5-acre park surrounds this modern, hacienda-style building with arched windows, terraces, and a garden that stretches to the river. Guest rooms are spacious, but those in the main building have the most charm, with elegant reproduction furniture and lots of pretty knickknacks. The restaurant (closed from November to April) serves tempting local specialties; the salmon with grapefruit is a good bet. ⊠ *rte. de Cordes, 81000 Fonvialane (5 km/3 mi outside town),* ☎ 05–63–60–80–80, FAX 05–63–47–63–60. 24 rooms. Restaurant, pool, tennis court. AE, DC, MC, V.

$$–$$$ ✕🛏 **Hostellerie St-Antoine.** Founded in 1734, this is one of the oldest hostelries in France. It's in the center of town, but it's quiet. Modern renovations have made it eminently comfortable. Room 30 has a pleasing view of the garden; its pristine white furnishings create a spacious atmosphere. The superb restaurant serves classical cuisine—rich and delicious foie gras de canard, and saddle of hare with a foie gras–based sauce. ⊠ *15 rue St-Antoine, 81000,* ☎ 05–63–54–04–60, FAX 05–63–47–10–47. 50 rooms. Restaurant, parking (fee). AE, DC, MC, V.

$$ ✕🛏 **Hôtel Chiffre.** This hotel in a centrally located town house has impeccably decorated rooms that overlook a cozy garden retreat. The restaurant, the Bateau Ivre, run by chef Michel Gouty, is one of Albi's finest. ⊠ *50 rue Séré-de-Rivières, 81000,* ☎ 05–63–54–04–60, FAX 05–63–47–20–61. 40 rooms. Restaurant. AE, DC, MC, V.

$$ ✕🛏 **Mercure Albi Bastides.** This converted 18th-century *vermicellerie* (noodle mill), across the river from the old center of Albi, has rooms that are functional and modern, if somewhat cramped. The views of the Tarn and the Pont Vieux are spectacular, however. In the stylish restaurant, try chef Gérard Belbèze's regional specialties or his "Toulouse-Lautrec menu." ⊠ *41 rue Porta, 81000,* ☎ 05–63–47–66–66, FAX 05–63–46–18–40; 800/637–2873 U.S. reservations; 0181/741–3100 U.K. reservations. 56 rooms. Restaurant, free parking. AE, DC, MC, V.

$$–$$$ 🛏 **La Pérouse.** This tastefully decorated enclave is centrally located and supremely quiet and intimate. Rooms are comfortable and the garden is a lush and shady spot to rest between sorties in and around Albi.

There's also a secluded swimming pool. ⊠ *21 pl. Lapérouse, 81000,* ☎ *05–63–54–69–22,* ℻ *05–63–38–03–69. 22 rooms. Pool, tennis court. AE, DC, MC, V.*

$$ ⊡ **Le George V.** This little in-town bed-and-breakfast is near the cathedral and the train station. Each room is unique, and the garden makes a nice retreat in summer. ⊠ *29 av. Maréchal-Joffre,* ☎ *05–63–54–24–16,* ℻ *05–63–49–90–78. 9 rooms. Pool, tennis court. AE, DC, MC, V.*

Outdoor Activities and Sports

Eighteen-hole golf courses can be found at **Golf d'Albi** (⊠ Château de Lasbordes, ☎ 05–63–54–98–07) and **Golf de Florentin** (⊠ Le Bosc, Florentin, 28 km/17 mi from Albi, ☎ 05–63–55–20–50).

Shopping

Around **place Ste-Cécile** there are numerous clothing, book, music, and antiques shops. The finest foie gras in town is found at **Albi Foie Gras** (⊠ 29 rue Mariès, ☎ 05–63–38–21–23). You won't want to miss **L'Artisan Chocolatier** (⊠ 4 rue Dr- Camboulives, on pl. du Vigan, ☎ 05–63–38–95–33), Michael Belin's famous chocolate emporium. There are many **produce markets** in Albi: One takes place Tuesday through Sunday in the market halls near the cathedral; another is held on Sunday morning at place Ste-Cécile. A Saturday morning **flea and antiques market** is held in the Halle du Castelviel (⊠ pl. du Castelviel).

Cordes

★ ㉕ *25 km (15 mi) northwest of Albi, 80 km (50 mi) northeast of Toulouse.*

The picture-book hilltop village of Cordes, built in 1222 by Count Raymond VII of Toulouse, is one of the most impressively preserved *bastides* (fortified medieval towns built along a strict grid plan) in all of France. When mists steal up from the Cérou Valley and enshroud the hillside, Cordes appears to hover in midair, hence its tacky nickname, Cordes-sur-Ciel (Cordes-on-Sky/Heaven). Many of the restored medieval houses are occupied by artisans and craftspeople; the best crafts shops are found along the main street, **Grande-Rue.** The village's venerable covered market, supported by 24 octagonal stone pillars, is also noteworthy, as is the nearby well, which is more than 300 ft deep.

Dining and Lodging

$$$ ✕⊡ **Le Grand Écuyer.** The dramatic hilltop setting of this hotel suits ★ it well—it is a perfectly preserved medieval mansion. Rooms have period furnishings; the best, Planol, Horizon, and Ciel, have grand views of the rolling countryside. Yves Thuriès is one of the region's best chefs and chocolatiers; sample his salmon and sole twist in vanilla, or the guinea fowl supreme in pastry. Menus begin around 200 francs and culminate in an over-500-franc, seven-course gourmet extravaganza. ⊠ *rue Voltaire, 81170,* ☎ *05–63–56–01–03,* ℻ *05–63–56–16–99. 13 rooms. Restaurant. AE, DC, MC, V. Closed mid-Oct.–early Apr.*

$$ ✕⊡ **L'Hostellerie du Vieux Cordes.** This magnificent 13th-century ★ house has a lovely courtyard, shaded by a 200-year-old wisteria and dotted with tiny white tables. Guest rooms are richly decorated but not nearly as opulent as the vast crimson dining rooms. Bernard Lafuente, Yves Thuriès's (☞ *above*) brother-in-law, is an accomplished chef. There are no fixed menus; each dish costs 50 francs. It's closed Monday from November to Easter and in January. ⊠ *rue St-Michel, 81170,* ☎ *05–63–56–00–12,* ℻ *05–63–56–02–47. 21 rooms. Restaurant. AE, DC, MC, V. Closed Jan.*

Montauban

26 *59 km (37 mi) west of Cordes, 52 km (32 mi) north of Toulouse.*

Montauban, built in 1844, was one of the first *bastides* (fortified towns) in France. It is best known as the birthplace of the great painter Jean-Auguste-Dominique Ingres (1780–1867) and is home to a superb collection of his works.

Ingres was the last of the great French classicists, who favored line over color and used classical antiquity as a source for subject matter. However, Ingres fell out of favor with the strict neoclassicists of his day as a result of his unusual combination of superb draftsmanship and sensuality. Later, artists such as Degas, Renoir, and Picasso ackowledged their debt to Ingres and today he is undergoing a strong revival; looking at his works, with their quasiphotographic realism, it's easy to see

★ why. The **Musée Ingres,** overlooking the Tarn River, is housed in what was originally the château of Edward the Black Prince (1330–76), who was briefly ruler of the English principality of Aquitaine. The château was later converted to a Bishop's Palace in the 17th century. Ingres has the second floor to himself; note the contrast between his love of myth (*Ossian's Dream*) and his deadpan, uncompromising portraiture (*Madame Gonse*). Most of the paintings are from Ingres's excellent private collection, ranging from his followers (Théodore Chassériau) and precursors (Jacques-Louis David) to old masters. ⊠ *19 rue de l'Hôtel de Ville,* ☎ *05–63–22–12–92.* ⌨ *20 frs.* ⏲ *July–Aug., Mon.–Sat. 9:30–noon and 1:30–6, Sun. 1:30–6; Sept.–June, Tues.–Sat. 10–noon and 2–6.*

Other attractions in Montauban include the 14th-century **Pont Vieux** (Old Bridge), with its seven pointed arches. The mid-13th-century **Église St-Jacques,** with its Toulouse-style steeple, is also noteworthy. The town's 17th- to 18th-century **Notre-Dame Cathedral** features Ingres's masterpiece: *Vow of Louis XIII.*

Moissac

27 *29 km (18 mi) west of Montauban, 72 km (45 mi) north of Toulouse.*

Moissac has the largest and arguably the most beautiful Romanesque cloisters standing today as well as one of the region's most remarkable abbey churches. The "port"— built at the confluence of the Tarn, Aveyron, and Garonne, and the lateral canal—is also a peculiar attraction. Little is left of the original 7th-century ★**Abbaye St-Pierre,** and religious wars laid waste its 11th-century replacement. Today's abbey, dating mostly from the 15th century, narrowly escaped demolition in this century when the Bordeaux-Sète railroad was rerouted within feet of the cloisters, sparing the precious columns around the arcades. Each of the 76 capitals has a unique pattern of animals, geometric motifs, and religious or historical scenes. The highlight of the abbey church is the 12th-century south portal, topped with carvings illustrating the Apocalypse. The **Musée des Arts et Traditions Populaires** (Folk Art Museum), in the abbey, contains regional treasures and a room of local costumes. ⊠ *6 bis rue de l'Abbaye,* ☎ *05–63–04–05–73.* ⌨ *Cloisters and museum 25 frs.* ⏲ *Tues.–Sun. 9–noon and 2–5 (until 6 Apr.–June and Sept.; until 7 July–Aug.).*

Lodging

$$–$$$ 🏨 **Château St-Roch.** This neo-Renaissance château, with turrets and spirals, is an eye-stopper. Guest rooms are huge, with coffered ceilings and French doors leading onto terraces. Other rooms are on display for 25 francs. Two drawbacks: the barracklike bar and the dining room, in a separate modern building. The food is just acceptable, so consider eating elsewhere. On the plus side, breakfasts—brought to your room—include good coffee and fresh bread. English is not spoken, but a few words of French will get you by. ⊠ *82340 Le Pin (19 km/12 mi west of Moissac; 5 km/3 mi east of Auvillar)*, ☎ *05–63–95–95–22*, F⨯A⨯X *05–63–94–85–54. 15 rooms. Restaurant, bar. MC, V. Closed Jan.–Apr.*

Lectoure

28 *57 km (35 mi) southwest of Moissac, 94 km (58 mi) northwest of Toulouse.*

Once a Roman city and a fortified Gallic town, Lectoure stands on a promontory above the Gers Valley in the heart of the former dukedom of Gascony. Lectoure was ravaged in 1473 when Louis XI attacked its fortress and established direct royal rule by killing the last count of Armagnac. But there's still plenty to see in its old arched streets. The 13th-century **Fontaine Diane** (Diana's Fountain) on rue Fontélie is the town's most interesting monument, as well as a visual feast. The 15th- to 16th-century **Cathédrale St-Gervais et St-Protais** is an enormous structure for a town of this size and is an immense trove of art and architectural treats.

The **Musée Municipal** (Town Museum), near the cathedral, is installed in the vaulted cellars of the former **Palais Épiscopal** (Bishop's Palace), now the town hall. Its collection contains a dramatic group of 20 pagan altars, engraved with Latin inscriptions and heads of sacrificial bulls discovered under the choir of the cathedral in 1640. ⊠ *Hôtel de Ville*, ☎ *05–62–68–70–22.* ☜ *25 frs.* ☾ *Daily 9–noon and 2–6.*

Dining and Lodging

$$–$$$ ✕☶ **Hôtel de Bastard.** There's nothing illegitimate about this excellent hotel and restaurant run by Jean-Luc Arnaud. The 18th-century estate is charming and the rooms comfortable and renovated. The cuisine is innovative and carefully prepared with fresh local produce. The duck with asparagus and raspberry vinegar is especially good. ⊠ *rue Lagrange, 32700*, ☎ *05–62–68–82–44*, F⨯A⨯X *05–62–68–76–81. 28 rooms. Restaurant. AE, DC, MC, V. Closed Jan.–mid-Feb.*

Condom

29 *24 km (15 mi) west of Lectoure via D7, 123 km (76 mi) northwest of Toulouse.*

A town of seven churches, Condom is in the heart of Ténarèze, one of the three regions that produces Armagnac. Condom's location on the River Baïse made it an excellent base for exporting the local brandy to Bordeaux and Bayonne on the Atlantic coast. The musty **Musée de l'Armagnac** (Armagnac Museum), in an 18th-century annex of the former Bishop's Palace in the town center, details the production process. Armagnac is distilled only once (unlike cognac, which is distilled twice); you can inspect the copper alembics. ⊠ *2 rue Jules-Ferry*, ☎ *05–62–28–31–41.* ☜ *15 frs.* ☾ *June–Sept., Tues.–Sun. 10–noon and 2–6; Oct.–May, Tues.–Sat. 10–noon and 2–4.*

Worth an excursion is **Larressingle**, just 10 km (6 mi) west of Condom. A fortified village known as the little Carcassonne of the Gers, it has high walls with crenellated battlements concealing stately town houses and a Romanesque church.

Six kilometers (4 miles) southwest of Condom via D931/D208 is the **Château de Cassaigne**, once the country residence of the bishops of Condom. The vineyards surrounding this 13th-century manor were originally cultivated for wine, with only the unconsumed leftovers distilled to make brandy. By the 17th century, the English were importing Armagnac in large quantities; ever since, brandy production has been the château's main raison d'être. You can visit the château's 17th-century cellars, where the Armagnac is stored in oak barrels that give it an amber color, and the 16th-century vaulted kitchen, where you can taste and buy brandy. There's also a small museum. ☎ 05–62–28–04–02. ☞ *Free.* ☉ *Mar.–mid-Oct., daily 9–noon and 2–7; mid-Oct.–Feb., Mon.–Sat. 9–noon and 2–6:30.*

OFF THE BEATEN PATH	**ABBAYE DE FLARAN –** Find your way from Condom to the 12th-century Flaran Abbey, just over 4 km (2½ mi) away from the Château de Cassaigne, via D142. In 1971 regional authorities took over the abbey, renovated it, and converted the guests' quarters into a cultural center for temporary exhibits. The abbey was built by Cistercian monks under St. Bernard; the monks' rooms on the second floor, overlooking the cloisters, remain largely unchanged. Have a look at the impressive sacristy, with its ribbed arches resting on one central column. ✉ *Valence-sur-Baïse,* ☎ *05–62–28–50–19.* ☞ *25 frs.* ☉ *July–Aug., daily 9:30–7; Sept.– June, Wed.–Mon. 9:30–noon and 2–6.*

Dining and Lodging

$$$ ✕🏨 **La Bastide Gasconne.** In Barbotan-les-Thermes, west of Condom, this sumptuously decorated 18th-century bastide near an immense lake houses a fine hotel-restaurant. Cognac or Armagnac and coffee by the open hearth make a suitably grand finale to the modern interpretations of traditional local specialties. (Reservations are essential in the restaurant.) Rooms feature quaint-chic touches such as antiques and colorful tiling in bathrooms. ✉ *av. des Thermes, 32150 Barbotan-les-Thermes (36 km/21 mi west of Condom),* ☎ *05–62–08–31–00,* ℻ *05–62–08–31–99. 30 rooms. Restaurant, pool, tennis court. AE, DC, MC, V. Closed Nov.–Mar.*

$$ 🏨 **Hôtel des Trois Lys.** You can recognize this hotel in the heart of Condom by its 18th-century facade. Most of the furnishings are Empire reproductions. The high-ceiling guest rooms vary in size; the smaller ones are a little cramped. The bar is open for evening aperitifs, and in summer, breakfast is served on the terrace overlooking the pool. ✉ *38 rue Gambetta, 32100,* ☎ *05–62–28–33–33,* ℻ *05–62–28–41– 85. 10 rooms. Restaurant, bar, pool. AE, DC, MC, V. Closed Feb.*

Fleurance

㉚   *30 km (19 mi) east of Condom, 83 km (51 mi) northwest of Toulouse.*

Fleurance is one of several bastide towns in the Armagnac region with a grid square street plan. Particularly notable is the Gothic **St-Laurent** church, with three stained-glass windows by Arnaud de Moles, whose most famous windows are in Auch (☞ *below*).

Auch

㉛   *24 km (15 mi) south of Fleurance, 79 km (40 mi) west of Toulouse.*

Auch, the capital of the Gers *département,* is best known for its stunning Gothic cathedral. The **Cathédrale Ste-Marie,** in the center of town, dates from the 15th and 16th centuries. Most of the stained-glass windows in the choir were done by Arnaud de Moles; they portray biblical figures and handsome pre-Christian sibyls, or prophetesses. The oak choir stalls are carved with more than 1,500 figures, both biblical and mythological; they took 50 years to complete. In June, classical music concerts are held here. ✉ *pl. Salinis.* ☞ *15 frs.* ☉ *Daily 8–noon and 2–6.*

Cross place Salinis to the terrace overlooking the River Gers. A monumental flight of 232 steps leads down to the riverbank. Halfway down is the **statue of D'Artagnan,** the musketeer immortalized by Alexandre Dumas. Although Dumas set the action of his historical drama *The Three Musketeers* in the 1620s, the true D'Artagnan—Charles de Batz—was born in 1620, probably at Castlemore near Lupiac, and did not become a musketeer until 1645.

On the other side of the cathedral, behind the former Archbishop's Palace (now the Préfecture), is the **Musée des Jacobins,** with a fine collection of Latin-American art and pre-Columbian pottery. The museum also contains Gallo-Roman relics; look for the white-marble epitaph dedicated by a grief-stricken mistress to her dog Myia. ⊠ *rue Daumesnil,* ☎ *05−62−05−74−79.* 🎫 *15 frs.* ⊙ *May−Oct., Tues.−Sun. 10−noon and 2−6; Nov.−Apr., Tues.−Sat. 10−noon and 2−4.*

Dining and Lodging

$$$
★

✕⊡ **Hôtel de France.** The ambience at this celebrated restaurant is as warm as at any corner bistro, with a bit of extra plush thrown in for good measure. Renowned chef André Daguin creates traditional Gascon cuisine with a masterly touch; his best dishes include cod in flaky pastry with a whipped liver sauce, and magret de canard. Save room for dessert—such as chocolates in Banyuls (sweet wine from Banyuls-sur-Mer in the Roussillon). (The restaurant is closed Sunday dinner and Monday all day.) The charming guest rooms have exposed wood beams. Ask about two-day, off-season packages. ⊠ *pl. de la Libération, 32000,* ☎ *05−62−61−71−71,* 📠 *05−62−61−71−81. 29 rooms. Restaurant. AE, DC, MC, V. Closed Jan.*

$−$$

✕⊡ **Ténarèze.** This stately hotel-restaurant is in the spa town of Castéra-Verduzan, northwest of Auch. Rooms are traditionally decorated, with heavy velvet draperies and lace trim. The restaurant, Le Florida, is now independently run and the hotel is associated with the nearby thermal baths center. ⊠ *Castéra-Verduzan (25 km/15 mi northwest of Auch on D390),* ☎ *05−62−68−10−22,* 📠 *05−62−68−14−69. 24 rooms, 13 with bath. Restaurant. AE, DC, MC, V. Closed late Oct.−early Apr.*

Shopping

Caves de l'Hôtel de France (⊠ rue d'Étigny) sells a wide selection of Armagnac.

ROUSSILLON

Draw a line between Toulouse and Narbonne, on the Mediterranean: The area to the south down to the Pyrénées, long part of the Catalonia-dominated House of Aragón, is known as the Roussillon. Rolling plains sweep along the northern border; the Pyrénées line the southern end; and craggy hills, divided by gorges, lie in between. On the eastern side is the Mediterranean and the Côte Vermeille (Yellow Coast); on the western side is the Ariège Valley.

Carcassonne

㉜ *88 km (55 mi) southeast of Toulouse, 105 km (65 mi) south of Albi.*

On a hill overlooking lush green countryside and the River Aude, Carcassonne is a storybook medieval town with the longest walls in Europe. The circle of towers and battlements is said to be the setting for Charles Perrault's *Puss in Boots.* The town is divided by the river into two parts—La Cité, the fortified upper town, and the rest, the lower, newer city (the *ville basse*), known simply as Carcassonne. Unless you are staying at a hotel in the upper town, private vehicles are not permitted; you must park in the lot (15 francs) across the road from the drawbridge. Be aware that the train station is in the lower town, and that means a cab ride or a 45-minute walk up to the old city. Plan on spending at least a couple of hours exploring the walls and peering over the battlements across sun-drenched plains toward the distant Pyrénées.

The earliest sections of the wall, built by the Romans in the 1st century AD, were later enlarged by the Visigoths in the 5th century. During the 13th century, Louis IX (St. Louis) and his son Philip the Bold strengthened the fortifications and gave Carcassonne much of its present-day appearance. Still, in 1835, the Historic Monument Inspector (and poet) Prosper Mérimée was appalled by the dilapidated state of the walls, and by 1844 Viollet-le-Duc was at work restoring them. Once inside the walls of the upper town, 20th-century tourism takes over. The streets are lined with souvenir shops, crafts boutiques, and restaurants. Staying overnight within the ancient walls lets you savor the timeless atmosphere after the hordes of visitors are gone.

The 12th-century **Château Comtal** is the last inner bastion of Carcassonne. It has a drawbridge and a museum, the **Musée Lapidaire,** where stone sculptures found in the area are on display. ☎ 04–68–25–01–66. ☒ 32 frs. ☉ June–Sept., daily 9–6; Oct–May, daily 9–noon and 2–5.

The best part about the *ville basse* (lower city), built between the River Aude and the Canal du Midi, is the **Musée des Beaux-Arts** (Fine Arts Museum), which houses a nice collection of porcelain, 17th- and 18th-century Flemish paintings, and works by local artists—including some stirring battle scenes by Jacques Gamelin (1738–1803). ☒ *rue Verdun,* ☎ 04–68–72–47–22. ☒ Free. ☉ Mon.–Sat. 10–noon and 2–5.

Dining and Lodging

$$ ✕ **Le Languedoc.** This restaurant in the *ville basse* serves up a light version of the region's specialties, from confit to game. The flowery patio in this country house is a perfect spot for a long evening dinner in June. Be sure to try the quail with foie gras, if available. ☒ *32 allée d'Iéna,* ☎ 04–68–25–22–17. Closed mid-Dec.–mid-Jan. and Mon. No dinner Sun. July–Oct.

$$$$ ✕🏠 **Domaine d'Auriac.** Former rugby player Bernard Rigaudis and family maintain a countrified atmosphere in this 19th-century manor house southwest of Carcassonne. Room prices vary according to the size and view; the largest look out over the magnificent park and vineyards. In the dining room, festooned with copper pots, traditional Languedoc cuisine is served. A Relais & Châteaux property, it tends to charge even more than top dollar—a superior room runs more than 1,500 francs and a good after-dinner brandy can cost 400 francs—but the quality is undeniable. ☒ *rte. de St-Hilaire, 11330 Auriac (4 km/2½ mi southwest of Carcassonne),* ☎ 04–68–25–72–22, ℻ 04–68–47–35–54. 28 rooms. Restaurant, air-conditioning, pool, 18-hole golf course, tennis court. AE, MC, V. Closed last 2 wks of Feb., last 2 wks of Nov., 1st wk of Dec.

$$$$ 🏠 **La Cité.** This is *the* spot for royalty and celebrities in Carcassonne. Enter the ivy-covered building and you'll be surrounded by the kind of luxurious creature comforts the ascetic Cathars would have decried. Have afternoon tea in the library or in the garden. Change for dinner in your spacious, high-ceilinged room. No. 21 is a good choice for views of the sun hitting the snow-covered Pyrenean peaks, or dropping down behind them. ☒ *pl. de l'Église, 11000 La Cité de Carcassonne,* ☎ 04–68–25–03–34, ℻ 04–68–71–50–15. 60 rooms, 3 suites. Restaurant, pool. AE, DC, MC, V. Closed early Jan.–mid-Feb.

$$ 🏨 **Hôtel Montségur.** With its *ville basse* location, this hotel is especially
convenient. Rooms on the first two floors feature Louis XV and Louis
XVI furniture, some of it genuine, while those above are more romantic,
with gilt-iron bedsteads set under the sloping oak beams. ⊠ *27 allée
d'Iéna, 11000,* ☎ *04–68–25–31–41,* 𝖥𝖠𝖷 *04–68–47–13–22. 21
rooms. Restaurant. DC, MC, V. Closed mid-Dec.–mid-Jan.*

The Arts

Carcassonne hosts a major arts festival in July, featuring dance, the-
ater, classical music, and jazz; for details, contact the **Théâtre Munici-
pal** (⊠ B.P. 236 rue Courtejaire, 11005, ☎ 04–68–25–33–13;
04–68–77–71–26 reservations).

Mirepoix

㉝ *48 km (29 mi) southwest of Carcassonne, 88 km (53 mi) southeast of
Toulouse.*

The 13th-century walled town of Mirepoix is in the heart of Cathar
country. It's built around a lovely, medieval main square, **place Général-
Leclerc,** which is surrounded by 13th- to 15th-century houses with in-
tricately carved timbers that form arcades or porticoes called *couverts.*
A good time to come is during Mirepoix's medieval festival in July, when
a historical procession is held on the third Sunday of the month.

Dining and Lodging

$$–$$$ ✕ **La Porte d'Aval.** Next to one of Mirepoix's key monuments, a for-
tified entryway, this elegant spot serves quail, wild pigeon, fresh fish,
and a sampling of *cuisine du terroir* (down-home French country cook-
ing). The terrace is the place to be in summer. ⊠ *cours Maréchal de
Mirepoix,* ☎ *05–61–68–19–19. AE, DC, MC, V. Closed Mon. and
early–mid-Jan.*

$$$ 🏨 **La Maison des Consuls.** This extraordinary hotel on Mirepoix's
★ medieval central square is a classified historic site. The 500-year-old
carved timber gargoyles concentrated around the hotel facade make
the exquisitely restored interior even more surprising. Each room is decorated in a different color, most with exposed beams. The Chambre
de Dame Louise and the Chambre du Maréchal, both overlooking the
square, are the best. ⊠ *pl. des Couverts, 09500 Mirepoix,* ☎ *05–61–
68–81–81,* 𝖥𝖠𝖷 *05–61–68–81–15. 7 rooms. MC, V.*

Foix

㉞ *35 km (22 mi) southwest of Mirepoix, 84 km (52 mi) south of Toulouse,
16 km (10 mi) north of Tarascon-sur-Ariège, 138 km (86 mi) west of
Perpignan.*

Nestled in the Ariège Valley is Foix, capital of the Ariège *département.*
Notice the fancy 19th-century administrative buildings to the south of
avenue Fauré, the town's major thoroughfare. The **Château de Foix,**
sitting impregnably on a promontory above the town and river, has
three enormous towers that reach skyward like sentinels. The castle
museum details regional history and archaeological finds. ⊠ *rue Mer-
cadal,* ☎ *05–61–65–56–05.* 🎟 *25 frs.* ☉ *Daily 10–noon and 2–5:30.*

A 5-km (3-mi) drive northwest from Foix along D1 leads to the **Rivière Souterraine de Labouiche** (Labouiche Subterranean River), a mysterious underground river whose waters have tunneled a 5-km (3-mi)
gallery through the limestone. The 75-minute boat trip covers a 1½-
km (1-mi) stretch, past weirdly shaped, subtly lit stalactites and stalagmites, ending with a subterranean waterfall. Dry land is 230 ft

overhead. ☎ *05–61–65–04–11.* 🎟 *40 frs.* ⊙ *Apr.–mid-June and mid-Sept.–mid-Nov. 2–5, mid-June–mid-Sept. 10–noon and 2–5.*

Dining and Lodging

$$–$$$ ✕ **Le Phoebus.** Come here for the views across the Ariège and over the Château de Foix, which once belonged to the illustrious Gaston Phoebus himself, the most famous of the counts of Foix. Come here, too, for the excellent specialties of game in season, and cuisine du terroir, such as *foie de canard mi-cuit* (half-cooked duck liver) and *râble de lièvre au poivrade* (hare in pepper sauce). ⊠ *3 cours Irénée Cros,* ☎ *05–61–65–10–42. MC, V. Closed Mon. and mid-July–mid-Aug. No lunch Sat.*

$$ ✕🏨 **Audoye-Lons.** This former post house in the town center has comfortable, modernized rooms that vary in size. The restaurant is reasonably priced and overlooks the Ariège River; it is closed Saturday in winter. ⊠ *4 pl. Georges-Duthil, 09000,* ☎ *05–61–65–52–44,* 🖷 *05–61–02–68–18. 35 rooms, 24 with bath or shower. Restaurant. AE, DC, MC, V. Closed mid-Dec.–mid-Jan.*

Outdoor Activities and Sports

The rivers and mountain lakes here are excellent trout habitat. Beginner and advanced fishing courses are run by **Loisirs Accueil** (⊠ Service Pêche, 14 rue Lazéma, 09000, ☎ 05–61–65–01–15).

Tarascon-sur-Ariège

③⑤ *16 km (10 mi) south of Foix.*

Tarascon is best known for its superb, extensive grotto, with its collection of prehistoric art second only to Lascaux (☞ Chapter 17). As you enter Tarascon, veer left along D8 to the **Grotte de Niaux,** which contains scores of red-and-black Magdalenian rock paintings done in charcoal and iron oxide. Stylized horses, goats, deer, and bison, dating from about 20,000 BC, gallop around a naturally circular underground gallery (known as the Salon Noir, or Black Room) 1 km (½ mi) inside the entrance. Now that the famous caves at Lascaux in the Dordogne can be seen only in reproduction, this is the finest assembly of prehistoric art open to the public anywhere in France. ☎ *05–61–05–88–37 (guided tours only; call ahead for reservations and to check schedule).* 🎟 *40 frs.* ⊙ *July–Sept., tours daily every 45 mins 8:30–11:30 and 1:30–5:15; Oct.–June, tours daily at 11, 3, and 4:30.*

Ax-les-Thermes

③⑥ *26 km (15 mi) southeast of Tarascon-sur-Ariège.*

A summer and winter resort town, Ax-les-Thermes has more than 80 mineral springs. Alpine ski stations at Ax-Bonascre and Ascou-Pailhères and nordic areas at Plateau de Beille and Domaine de Chioula along with Ax's thermal hot springs are an unbeatable winter combination. Crisscrossing the surrounding heights are 400 km (248 mi) of trails.

Font-Romeu

③⑦ *75 km (45 mi) southeast of Ax-les-Thermes, 87 km (54 mi) southeast of Tarascon-sur-Ariège.*

Font-Romeu first became a high-altitude vacation spot in 1920. French Olympians trained here for the Mexico City games of 1968. Excellent indoor and outdoor sports facilities include ski lifts, an ice rink, a riding school, a swimming pool, tennis courts, and a golf course.

Dining and Lodging

$–$$ ✕🏨 **Carlit.** This modern resort hotel is the traditional Font-Romeu haven and is popular with French families vacationing in the mountains. The staff can arrange a ski instructor or mountain guide for you or organize a minibus excursion to nearby Spain and Andorra. Prices are highest in ski season and midsummer. The restaurant serves hearty mountain fare (demi-pension is mandatory during peak periods). ⊠ *av. du Dr-Capelle, 66120,* ☎ *04–68–30–80–30,* FAX *04–68–30–80–68. 58 rooms. Restaurant, bar, brasserie, pool. MC, V. Closed Nov.–mid-Dec.*

Eyne

38 *12 km (7 mi) southeast of Font-Romeu.*

Eyne, with a grand total of no (zero) in-town commercial establishments—not a café, not a bakery—is one of the purest villages remaining in the broad Pyrenean valley of the Cerdagne. The village has a nationally classified botanical park, the **Vall d'Eyne,** where Atlantic and Mediterranean weather systems and vegetation converge. In the park are archaeological walks to menhirs and Neolithic dolmens, and a ski station uphill.

Dining and Lodging

$$ ✕🏨 **Cal Pai.** This 17th-century country farmhouse is a *gîte d'étape* (way station for hikers and skiers) with table d'hôte (dinners with the host) of uncommon design and quality (reservations are essential). The impeccable taste of owner-builder-manager-chefs Françoise and Jean-Pierre—in both decoration and cuisine—makes this an unforgettable place. ⊠ *Eyne Village,* ☎ *04–68–04–06–96. 12 rooms with shared bath. Dining room. MC, V.*

Mont-Louis

39 *5 km (3 mi) east of Eyne, 30 km (18 mi) west of Villefranche-de-Conflent.*

This fortified village, at 5,200 ft—France's highest—was set up as a border stronghold by Vauban in 1679 and commands views over the Cerdagne Valley to the west, the Capcir to the north, and the Conflent to the east. The ramparts and the citadel, never attacked, are perfectly preserved. A solar oven—over the bridge and inside the portal in the town—is the only one in France in commercial use and is a key attraction.

Dining and Lodging

$$ ✕🏨 **Lou Roubaillou.** Widely recommended as the best value and top cuisine in Mont-Louis, Pierre and Christiane Duval's tiny flower-covered hideaway is the place to go. Rooms are simple, small, and cozy. The cuisine is rich in sauces based on Pyrenean herbs, wild mushrooms, and game. Try the *civet d'isard* (mountain-goat stew). Reservations are essential. ⊠ *rue des Écoles Laïques, 66210,* ☎ *04–68–04–23–26,* FAX *04–68–04–14–09. 14 rooms, 7 with bath. MC, V. Closed May and Oct.–Dec.*

Villefranche-de-Conflent

40 *30 km (18 mi) east of Mont-Louis, 6 km (4 mi) west of Prades.*

Named for its location at the confluence of the Têt and Cady rivers, this village combines elements of an 11th-century fortress with Vauban improvements from the 17th century. Cross the tiny St-Pierre bridge over the Têt and use the pink marble "stairway of a thousand steps" to climb up to Fort-Liberia for views of the village, the Canigou, and the valleys east to Prade.

Dining and Lodging

$$$ ✕ **Auberge St-Paul.** One of the best-known tables in the area, this warm stone-surrounded refuge is known for its fine Catalan cuisine. Sample the *truite à la llosa* (trout on slate slabs) or the civet d'isard. ⊠ *7 pl. de l'Église,* ☎ *04–68–96–30–95. Reservations essential. MC, V. Closed Mon.*

$$ ✕ 🏨 **Auberge du Cèdre.** This comfortable little inn over the river commands fine views of the fortress. Rooms are small but cozy. Pyrenean and Catalan specialties are served on a little glassed-in porch suspended over the Têt. Reservations are essential at the restaurant; call before you go to make sure it's open. ⊠ *Domaine Ste-Eulalie, 66500,* ☎ *04–68–96–37–37,* FAX *04–68–05–35–32. 10 rooms. Restaurant. AE, DC, MC, V. Closed Nov. and early Jan.*

Vernet-les-Bains

㊶ *12 km (7 mi) west of Prades, 55 km (34 mi) west of Perpignan.*

English writer Rudyard Kipling came to take the waters in Vernet-les-Bains, a long-established spa town. The hilltop village church is dwarfed by the imposing Mont Canigou behind. Even higher up is the medieval abbey. Leave your car in Casteil, 2 km (1¼ mi) farther, and complete the journey to the **Abbaye St-Martin du Canigou** on foot. Brace yourself for the steep half-hour climb; the abbey is perched on a triangular promontory at an altitude of nearly 3,600 ft. Although the abbey was diligently restored by the bishop of Perpignan early this century, part of the cloisters, along with the higher (and larger) of the two churches, date from the 11th century. The lower church, dedicated to Notre-Dame-sous-Terre, is even older. Rising above is a stocky, battlemented bell tower. ☎ *04–68–05–50–03.* 🎫 *15 frs.* ☉ *Daily 10– 12:30 and 2:30–5.*

Prades

㊷ *6 km (4 mi) east of Villefranche-de-Conflent, 43 km (27 mi) west of Perpignan.*

Once home to Catalan cellist Pablo Casals, the market town of Prades is famous for its annual summer music festival, the **Festival Pablo Casals,** which takes place from late July to mid-August. Founded by ★ Casals in 1950, the festival is primarily held at the medieval **Abbaye de St-Michel de Cuxa,** 3 km (2 mi) south of town on D27. One of the gems of the Pyrénées, the abbey's sturdy, crenellated, four-story bell tower is visible from afar. If the remains of the cloisters here seem familiar, it may be because you have seen the missing pieces at New York City's Cloisters museum; they were purchased by American sculptor George Grey Barnard in 1907 and subsequently by the Metropolitan Museum in 1925. The 10th-century pre-Romanesque church is a superb aesthetic and acoustical venue for the summer cello concerts.

Céret

㊸ *68 km (41 mi) southeast of Prades, 35 km (21 mi) west of Collioure.*

Picasso, Braque, Juan Gris, and many other artists found this small Pyrenean town surrounded by cherry orchards irresistible at the beginning of this century. Others, such as Chagall in the late '20s, followed. The ★ result is a museum, the **Musée d'Art Moderne** (Modern Art Museum), housing an extraordinary collection of paintings by these 20th-century masters. ⊠ *8 bis Maréchal-Joffre,* ☎ *04–68–87–27–76.* ☉ *May–Sept., Wed.–Mon. 10–6.*

After visiting the Modern Art Museum, stroll through pretty **Vieux Céret** (Old Céret): Find your way through the **place des Neufs Jets** (Nine Fountains Square), around the church, and out to the lovely fortified **Porte de France** gateway. Then walk over the single-arched **Vieux Pont** (Old Bridge).

Dining

$$$
★ ╳ **Les Feuillants.** Widely known as one of the top restaurants in the area, this elegant place combines cuisine, wine, and traditional design in another manifestation of Céret's superb and surprising artistic endowment. Marie Louise and Didier Banyols, sommelier and chef respectively, produce spectacular fare, such as *rouelles de homard Bretagne au Banyuls et châtaignes* (sliced Brittany lobster in sweet wine and chestnuts). ⊠ *1 bd. La Fayette,* ☎ *04–68–87–37–88. AE, DC, MC, V. No lunch Sat.*

Collioure

44 *35 km (21 mi) east of Céret, 27 km (17 mi) southeast of Perpignan.*

This pretty seaside fishing village with a sheltered natural harbor has become a summer magnet for tourists and should be strenuously avoided in July and August. Painters such as Henri Matisse, André Derain, Henri Martin, and Georges Braque—who were dubbed "Fauves" for their "savage" (*fauve* means wild animal) approach to color and form— were among the early discoverers of Collioure. The view they admired remains largely unchanged today: To the north, the rocky Ilot St-Vincent juts out into the sea, a modern lighthouse at its tip, while inland, the Albères range rises to connect the Pyrénées with the Mediterranean.

Near the old Quartier du Mouré is the 17th-century church of **Notre-Dame-des-Anges** (⊠ pl. de l'Église). It has exuberantly carved altarpieces and a pink-domed bell tower that doubled as the original lighthouse.

A slender jetty divides the Boramar beach, beneath the church, from the small landing area at the foot of the **Château Royal,** a 15th-century castle remodeled by Vauban 200 years later. ☎ *04–68–82–06–43.* 🕮 *20 frs.* ☉ *Mar.–Oct., daily 10–noon and 2–5.*

Dining and Lodging

$$–$$$
╳🏠 **Relais des Trois Mas.** Overlooking Collioure from the cliffs south of town, this hotel has small but interestingly furnished rooms—headboards, for example, are made from antique Spanish doors. Rooms are named for painters whose work appears on the bathroom tiles. The views are spectacular. Below is a pebbled beach, though you may prefer the small pool (hewn from rock) or the huge Jacuzzi. Dine at the restaurant, La Balette, on the terrace or in one of the two small dining rooms looking over the harbor. ⊠ *rte. de Port-Vendres, 66190,* ☎ *04–68–82–05–07,* FAX *04–68–82–38–08. 19 rooms, 4 suites. Restaurant, 2 dining rooms, pool, hot tub, exercise room, beach. AE, DC, MC, V. Closed mid-Nov.–mid-Dec.*

$$
★ ╳🏠 **Les Templiers.** Universally considered the "soul" of Collioure, no visit is complete without a stop here. Owner Jojo Pous, son of the force behind Collioure's art colony, has more than 2,500 original works hanging from every nook and cranny. The bar itself is a work of art, curved like the hull of a skiff and ending with a wood sculpture of a mermaid suckling an infant sailor. The mostly Catalan cuisine is excellent, and the rooms overlooking the château are cozy. ⊠ *quai de l'Amirauté, 66190,* ☎ *04–68–98–31–10,* FAX *04–68–98–01–24. 43 rooms. Restaurant, bar, café. AE, DC, MC, V. Closed early Jan.–early Feb.*

Perpignan

⑤ *16 km (10 mi) south of Salses, 64 km (40 mi) south of Narbonne.*

During medieval times, Perpignan was the second city of Catalonia (after Barcelona), before falling to Louis XIII's French army in 1642. The Spanish influence is evident in Perpignan's leading monument, the fortified **Palais des Rois de Majorque** (King of Majorca Palace) begun in the 14th century by James II of Majorca. Highlights here are the majestic **Cour d'Honneur** (Courtyard of Honor), the two-tier Flamboyant Gothic chapel of **Ste-Croix**, and the **Grande Salle** (Great Hall) with its monumental fireplaces. ⊠ *rue des Archers,* ☎ *04–68–34–48–29.* ▨ *10 frs.* ☉ *Daily 9–5.*

The center of town is marked by the medieval monument, the 14th-century **Le Castillet,** with its tall, crenellated twin towers. Originally this hulking brick building was the main gate to the city; later it was used as a prison. Now the **Casa Pairal,** a museum devoted to Catalan art and traditions, is housed here. ⊠ *pl. de Verdun,* ☎ *04–68–35–42–05.* ▨ *Free.* ☉ *Wed.–Mon. 9–noon and 2–6.*

The **promenade des Plantanes,** across boulevard Wilson from Le Castillet, is a cheerful place to stroll among flowers, plane trees, and fountains. To see more interesting medieval buildings, walk along the streets—the **Petite Rue des Fabriques d'En Nabot** is the best—near Le Castillet and the adjacent place de la Loge, the town's nerve center. Note the frilly wrought-iron campanile and dramatic medieval crucifix on the **Cathédrale St-Jean** (⊠ pl.Gambetta). The **Loge de Mer** (Maritime Exchange; ⊠ rue de la Loge), a graceful 14th-century building, was once the chamber of commerce for maritime trade. The 15th-century **Palais de la Députation** (⊠ rue de la Loge) was once the seat of the permanent deputy or representative of the Catalan Corts (Parliament). The massive arched entryway is typical of the Catalonian or House of Aragon civil design of that period.

Dining and Lodging

$$$–$$$$ ✕ **Chapon Fin.** An upscale crowd pours into this excellent restaurant in the Park hotel (☞ *below*) to sample the subtle, understated cuisine. Three prix-fixe menus showcase authentic Mediterranean food. ⊠ *18 bd. Jean-Bourrat,* ☎ *04–68–35–14–14. AE, DC, MC, V. Closed Sun. No lunch Mon.*

$$ ✕ **La Casa Sansa.** This very Catalan, very popular restaurant serves
★ fine regional specialties in an atmosphere thick with tastefully designed local color. Paintings crowd the walls with Roussillon themes. ⊠ *2 rue Fabrique d'en Nadal,* ☎ *04–68–34–21–84. Reservations essential. AE, DC, MC, V. Closed Sun. No lunch Mon.*

$$$ ☷ **Park.** Don't be deceived by the undistinguished facade: This fam-
★ ily-run hotel enjoys ironclad prestige in Perpignan. Athough some rooms are small, most are luxurious, soundproof, and air-conditioned. ⊠ *18 bd. Jean-Bourrat, 66000,* ☎ *04–68–35–14–14,* ☎ *04–68–35–48–18. 67 rooms. Restaurant. AE, DC, MC, V.*

$–$$ ☷ **Hôtel de la Poste et de la Perdrix.** If you're looking for an inexpensive place with old French charm in the center of town next to Le Castillet, don't miss this little spot. Rooms, like the hotel, are simple and poetic, as opposed to overcomfortable and prosaic. The cuisine is Catalan. ⊠ *6 rue Fabriques Nabot, 66000,* ☎ *04–68–34–42–53,* ☎ *04–68–34–58–20. 38 rooms. Restaurant. AE, DC, MC, V.*

Shopping

Rue des Marchands, near Le Castillet, is thick with chic shops. **Maison Quinta** (⊠ rue Louis Blanc) is a top design and architectural artifacts store. Excellent local ceramics can be found at the picturesque

Sant Vicens crafts center (⊠ rue Sant Vicens, off D22 east of the town center).

Salses

🚇 *16 km (10 mi) north of Perpignan, 48 km (30 mi) south of Narbonne.*

Salses has a history of sieges. Hannibal stormed through the town with his elephants on his way to the Alps in 218 BC, though no trace of his passage remains. The colossal and well-preserved **Fort de Salses,** built by Ferdinand of Aragon in 1497 and equipped for 300 horses and 1,000 soldiers, fell to the French under Cardinal Richelieu in 1642 after a three-year siege. Bulky round towers ring the rectangular inner fort, and the five-story keep, with its narrow corridors and small-scale drawbridges, was designed to keep the fort's governor safe to the last. ☎ 04–68–38–60–13. 🎫 25 frs. ☉ July–Aug., daily 9–6; Sept.–June, daily 9:30–11:30 and 2–5:30 (until 4 Nov.–Easter).

Narbonne

🚇 *64 km (40 mi) north of Perpignan, 60 km (37 mi) east of Carcassonne, 94 km (58 mi) south of Montpellier.*

In Roman times, bustling, industrial Narbonne was the second-largest town in Gaul (after Lyon) and an important port, though today little remains of its Roman past. Until the sea receded during the Middle Ages, Narbonne prospered. The town's former wealth is evinced in the 14th-century **Cathédral St-Just;** its vaults rise 133 ft from the floor, making it the tallest cathedral in southern France. Only Beauvais and Amiens, in Picardy, are taller, and as at Beauvais, the nave at Narbonne was never built. ⊠ *rue Armand-Gauthier.*

Richly sculpted cloisters link the cathedral to the former **Palais des Archevêques** (Archbishops' Palace), now home to the museums of archaeology, art, and history. Note the enormous palace kitchen and the late-13th-century keep, the **Donjon Gilles-Aycelin;** climb the 180 steps to the top for a view of the region and the town. ⊠ *Palais des Archevêques,* ☎ *04–68–90–30–30.* 🎫 *28 frs (includes all town museums).* ☉ *May–Sept., daily 9–noon and 2–6; Oct.–Apr., Tues.–Sun. 10–noon and 2–5:30.*

On the south side of the Canal de la Robine is the **Musée Lapidaire** (Sculpture Museum), housed in the handsome, 13th-century former church of **Notre-Dame de la Mourguié.** Classical busts, ancient sarcophagi, lintels, and Gallo-Roman inscriptions await you. ⊠ *pl. Lamourguier,* ☎ *04–68–65–53–58.* 🎫 *28 frs (includes all town museums).* ☉ *May–Sept., daily 9–noon and 2–6; Oct.–Apr., Tues.–Sun. 10–noon and 2–5:30.*

For the nearest decent beach, follow pretty D168 as it winds its way over the Montagne de la Clape to **Narbonne-Plage,** 15 km (9 mi) away. Just up the coast at St-Pierre-sur-Mer is the curious **Gouffre de l'Oeil-Doux,** an inland lake fed by seawater.

🦁 Some 3,000 wild animals roam freely in the 500-acre, pond-studded **Réserve Africaine de Sigean,** 15 km (9 mi) south of Narbonne. The reserve was designed by France's leading game expert, the vicomte de La Panouse, who is best known for cross-breeding lions and tigers. ☎ 04–68–48–20–20. 🎫 100 frs. ☉ Daily 9–6:30 (until 5 in winter).

OFF THE BEATEN PATH **ABBAYE DE FONTFROIDE** – Roughly 11 km (7 mi) southwest of Narbonne is the Fontfroide Abbey, one of the largest and best preserved in France. Founded in 1093, it is surrounded by cypress trees—the type of setting beloved of Cistercian monks. Pope Benedict XII was abbot here from

1311 to 1317, and the finest monastic buildings—including the church, flower-bedecked cloisters, chapter house, and dormitory—date from his time. Especially noteworthy is the rose garden, with 2,000 bushes. ✉ *Head west from Narbonne on N113 and turn left 5 km (3 mi) from town center onto D613; 7 km (4½ mi) farther is a sign for the abbey down a small road to the left.* ☎ *04-68-45-11-08.* 🎫 *Guided tours only 34 frs.* ☉ *Daily 10–noon and 2–5:30; tours every 45 mins in summer, hourly in winter; closed weekday mornings in winter.*

Dining and Lodging

$$$ ✕🏨 **Le Relais du Val d'Orbieu.** Good hotels are scarce in Narbonne. The most commodious, though a bit overpriced, is this hostelry west of town. Owner Jean-Pierre Gonsalvez speaks English and is extremely helpful. Designed around a courtyard, most rooms are reached through covered arcades. The better ones are pleasantly simple, with bare tile floors and large French windows leading onto terraces; the standard ones (100 francs less) are slightly smaller and do not have terraces or views. The dining room lacks intimacy, but the wine list has good local wines at reasonable prices. ✉ *D24, 11200 Ornaisons (14 km/8 mi west of Narbonne),* ☎ *04–68–27–10–27,* 🖷 *04–68–27–52–44. 20 rooms. Restaurant, pool, tennis court. AE, DC, MC, V.*

$$ ✕🏨 **Languedoc.** In this old-fashioned, turn-of-the-century hotel downtown, the smallish rooms vary in style and comfort; a full bath is an extra 100 francs. La Coupole restaurant serves inexpensive regional dishes with menus starting at 90 francs; it is closed Sunday dinner and Monday. ✉ *22 bd. Gambetta, 11100,* ☎ *04–68–65–14–74,* 🖷 *04–68–65–81–48. 38 rooms, 34 with bath or shower; 2 suites. Restaurant, piano bar. AE, DC, MC, V.*

TOULOUSE, THE MIDI-PYRÉNÉES, AND ROUSSILLON A TO Z

Arriving and Departing

By Car

The fastest route from Paris to Toulouse (700 km/435 mi southwest) is via Bordeaux on A10, then A62; journey time is about nine hours. If you choose to head south over the Pyrénées to Barcelona, the Tunnel du Puymorens saves a half hour of switchbacks between Hospitalet and Porta, but in good weather and with time to spare, the drive over the Puymorens pass is spectacular. Plan on taking three hours between Toulouse and Font-Romeu and another three to Barcelona. The fastest route from Toulouse to Barcelona is the three- to four-hour, 421-km (253-mi) drive via Carcassonne and Perpignan on A61 and A9, which becomes A7 at Le Perthus.

By Plane

All international flights arrive at Toulouse's **Blagnac Airport** (☎ 05–61–42–44–65), a 20-minute drive from the center of the city. **Air France** (☎ 08–02–80–28–02) has regular flights between Toulouse and most European capitals. **TAT** (Transport Aérien Transrégional) has direct flights from Paris's Orly Airport to Rodez (reservations: ☎ 01–42–79–05–05 Paris, ☎ 05–65–42–20–30 Rodez).

Airport shuttles run regularly (every half hour between 8:15 AM and 8:45 PM) from the airport to the bus station in Toulouse (at the train station; fare 25 francs) and also at 9:20, 10, and 10:45 PM. From Toulouse bus station to the airport, buses leave at 5:30 AM, 6, 7, 7:30, and then every half hour until 8:30 PM.

By Train

Trains for the southwest leave from Paris (Gare d'Austerlitz). There are direct trains to Toulouse (six to seven hours), Carcassonne (seven to eight hours), and Montauban (six hours). For Rodez (seven to eight hours), change in Brive, and for Auch (more than eight hours), in Toulouse. Seven trains leave Paris (Gare de Lyon) daily for Narbonne (six hours) and Perpignan (seven hours); a change at Montpellier is often necessary. Note that at least one high-speed TGV (*Train à Grande Vitesse*) per day leaves Paris (Gare Montparnasse) for Toulouse; journey time is five hours.

Getting Around

By Car

A62 slices through the region on its way to the coast at Narbonne, where A9 heads south to Perpignan. At Toulouse, where A62 becomes A61, various highways fan out in all directions: N117 to Pau, N20 to Montauban and Cahors, and N88 to Albi and Rodez.

By Train

The French rail network in the southwest provides regular services to all towns.

Contacts and Resources

Car Rental

Avis (⊠ 13 bd. Conflent, Perpignan, ☎ 04–68–34–26–71; ⊠ Blagnac Airport, Toulouse, ☎ 05–61–30–04–94). **Hertz** (⊠ pl. Lagarrasic, Auch, ☎ 05–62–05–26–26; ⊠ 5 av. Chamier, Montauban, ☎ 05–63–20–29–00).

Guided Tours

Contact the **Toulouse Tourist Office** (⊠ Donjon du Capitole, ☎ 05–61–11–02–22) for information about walking tours and bus tours in and around Toulouse. The **Comité Régional du Tourisme** (⊠ CRT, 54 bd. de l'Endouchure, 31200 Toulouse, ☎ 05–61–13–55–55) has a brochure, "1,001 Escapes in the Midi-Pyrénées," with descriptions of weekends and short organized package vacations.

Music Festivals

There are 50 music festivals a year in smaller towns throughout the region; the Comité Régional du Tourisme (CRT) and larger tourist offices can provide a list of dates and addresses, or contact the **Délégation Musicale Régionale** (⊠ 56 rue du Taur, 31080 Toulouse, ☎ 05–61–29–21–00).

Outdoor Activities and Sports

For information on canoeing or kayaking, contact the **Ligue de Canoë-Kayak** (⊠ 16 rue Guillemin-Tarayre, 31000 Toulouse, ☎ 05–61–62–65–05). For information on hiking or horseback riding, contact the **Comité de Randonnées Midi-Pyrénées** (⊠ CORAMIP, 14 rue Bayard, 31000 Toulouse, ☎ 05–61–99–44–00). Local tourist offices also have detailed maps of more than 3,220 km (2,000 mi) of marked trails. The **Comité Régional du Tourisme du Languedoc-Roussillon** (⊠ 20 rue de la République, 24000 Montpellier, ☎ 04–67–22–81–00) publishes a brochure on golf courses in the area and sells a pass good for 14 different courses.

Travel Agencies

Havas (⊠ 73 rue d'Alsace-Lorraine, Toulouse, ☎ 05–61–23–16–35). **Wagons-Lits** (⊠ Voyages Dépêche, 42 bis rue d'Alsace-Lorraine, Toulouse, ☎ 05–62–15–42–70).

Visitor Information

The regional tourist office for the Midi-Pyrénées is the **Comité Régional du Tourisme** (⊠ CRT, 54 bd. de l'Endouchure, 31200 Toulouse, ☎ 05–61–13–55–55). For Pyrénées-Roussillon, contact the **Comité Départemental de Tourisme** (⊠ quai de Lattre de Tassigny, B.P. 540, 66005 Perpignan, ☎ 04–68–34–29–94).

Local tourist offices are as follows: **Albi** (⊠ pl. Ste-Cécile, ☎ 05–63–49–48–80). **Auch** (⊠ 1 rue Dessoles, ☎ 05–62–05–22–89). **Carcassonne** (⊠ 15 bd. Camille-Pelletan, ☎ 04–68–25–07–04). **Ceret** (⊠ 1 bd. Clemenceau, ☎ 04–68–87–00–53). **Collioure** (⊠ pl. 18-juin, ☎ 04–68–82–15–47). **Mont-Louis** (⊠ rue Vauban, ☎ 04–68–04–21–97). **Narbonne** (⊠ pl. Roger-Salengro, ☎ 04–68–65–15–60). **Perpignan** (⊠ quai de Lattre de Tassigny, ☎ 04–68–66–30–30). **Prades** (⊠ 4 rue Victor-Hugo, ☎ 04–68–05–41–02). **Toulouse** (⊠ Donjon du Capitole, ☎ 05–61–11–02–22).

16 Pays Basque, Béarn, and the Hautes-Pyrénées

Some of France's most varied treasures are concentrated in this southwest corner of the country, from sandy beaches to the Pyrénées' highest peaks. You can begin at Bayonne and Biarritz on the Atlantic coast, then travel east through the cultural landscape of the Basque Pyrénées. After, continue on to Pau, capital of Bérn and the center of the Hautes-Pyrénées, then on to Tarbes, Lourdes, and Gavarnie.

Revised and
updated by
George Semler

FRENCH BASQUE COUNTRY, the Atlantic Pyrénées, and the Hautes-Pyrénées, stretching along the border with Spain, have a rich variety of cultures and landscapes to explore. The three French Basque provinces—Labourd, Soule, and Basse Navarre—have a distinct culture with a mysterious and ancient non–Indo-European language of its own. East of the ski town of Pierre-St-Martin, on the eastern edge of Basque Country, is Béarn, with its splendid capital city of Pau and its valleys descending from the Pyrénées—Aspe, Ossau, and Barétous. East through the Aubisque pass, at the far end of Bérn, is the region known as La Bigorre, the heart of the Hautes-Pyrénées. Here peaks such as Vignemale (10,820 ft) and Balaïtous (10,321 ft) compete with some of France's most legendary natural treasures: the Cirque de Gavarnie, Cirque de Troumouse, and the Brèche de Roland.

Pleasures and Pastimes

Dining

Dining in the Basque Country is invariably a feast, whether it's seafood or upland dishes ranging from beef to lamb to game birds such as the famous migratory *palombes* (wood pigeons). Dishes to keep in mind include *ttoro* (hake stew), *pipérade* (tomatoes and green peppers cooked in olive oil, and often scrambled eggs), *bakalao "al pil-pil"* (cod cooked in oil "*al pil-pil*"—so slowly that the oil makes this bubbling noise as the fish creates its own sauce), *marmitako* (tuna and potato stew), and *zikiro* (roast lamb). Béarn is famous for its *garbure,* thick vegetable soup with *confit de canard* (preserved duck) and *fèves* (broad beans). *Civets* (stews) made with *isard* (wild goat) or wild boar are another Béarn specialty. La Bigorre and the Hautes-Pyrénées are equally dedicated to garbure, though they may call it *soupe paysanne bigourdane* (Bigorran peasant soup) to distinguish their cuisine from that of the neighboring Béarn.

CATEGORY	COST*
$$$$	over 400 frs
$$$	250 frs–400 frs
$$	125 frs–250 frs
$	under 125 frs

*per person for a three-course meal, including tax (20.6%) and tip but not wine

Hiking

The Pyrénées are best explored on foot. And you'll really appreciate the hearty mountain cuisine if you get out of the car and hike along the gorges and into the mountains. The lengthy GR (*Grande Randonnée*) 10, a trail marked by discreet red and white paint spots, runs all the way from the Atlantic at Hendaye to Banyuls-sur-Mer on the Mediterranean, through villages and up and down the mountains. Along the way are mountain refuges. The HRP (*Haute Randonnée Pyrénéenne,* High Pyrenean Trail) stays closer to the border crest, following the terrain through both France and Spain, irrespective of national borders. Local trails are also well indicated, usually with blue or yellow markings. Some of the classic walks in the Basque Pyrénées include the Iparla Ridge walk between Bidarrai and St-Étienne-de-Baïgorry, and the Holçarté gorge walk between Larrau and Ste-Engrâce. Trail maps are available from tourist offices.

Lodging

From palatial beachside splendor in Biarritz to simple mountain auberges in the Basque and Béarn country to Pyrenean refuges in the Hautes-Pyrénées, the gamut of lodging in southwest France is ample. For top value and camaraderie, look for *gîtes* (rustic bed-and-breakfasts and way stations for hikers and skiers), where all guests dine together. Be sure to book summer lodging on the Basque coast well in advance, particularly for August. In the Hautes-Pyrénées, only Gavarnie during its third-week-of-July music festival presents a potential booking problem. Even better: Make it up as you go along; the surprises are usually very pleasant.

CATEGORY	COST*
$$$$	over 800 frs
$$$	550 frs–800 frs
$$	300 frs–550 frs
$	under 300 frs

All prices are for a standard double room, including tax (20.6%) and service charge.

Basque Sports

Perhaps the best known and most spectacular of Basque sports is the ancestral ball game of pelota, from the medieval *jeux de paume* (literally "palm" games). Pelota is a fundamental part of rural Basque culture. A Basque village without a *fronton* (backboard and pelota court) is as unimaginable as an American town without a baseball diamond. There are many versions and variations on this graceful and rapid sport, played with the bare hand, with wooden bats, or with curved basket-like gloves. Other rural Basque sports include scything, wood chopping and sawing, sack hauling, stone lifting, long distance racing, oxen hauling, tug-of-war, and whaleboat regatta competitions.

Exploring Pays Basque, Béarn, and the Hautes-Pyrénées

Bayonne and Pau are the urban book ends for this southwest corner of France. But whether you approach from the Atlantic or the Mediterranean end, you won't want to miss Gavarnie, Ste-Engrâce, St-Jean-Pied-de-Port, Sauveterre-de-Béarn, Ainhoa, or St-Jean-de-Luz. Trans-Pyrenean hikers generally prefer moving west to east for a variety of reasons, but one of the best is the superior illumination provided by the late afternoon and evening sunlight during the prime months of May to October.

Great Itineraries

Consider Dax and Eugénie-les-Bains as excellent side trips to the basic itinerary outlined here. Begin in Bayonne, exploring the Basque coast, and then head east into the Basque Pyrénées. Explore the Béarn as carefully as time permits—Sauveterre-de-Béarn, Oloron-Ste-Marie, and Pau—before continuing on to La Bigorre, the Hautes-Pyrénées, and Gavarnie.

Numbers in the text correspond to numbers in the margin and on the Pays Basque, Béarn, and the Hautes-Pyrénées and Toulouse maps.

IF YOU HAVE 3 DAYS

There is nothing leisurely about this three-day tour, nor is there time to do much walking, for which reason it is recommended only if you have limited time and unlimited curiosity. Begin in **Bayonne** ①, spending a morning exploring the town. See the cathedral and the Bonnat Museum before hitting **Biarritz** ④ for afternoon tea. Spend the night in ☒ **St-Jean-de-Luz** ⑤. On day two drive through **Sare** ⑥ and **Ainhoa** ⑦ and past **Pas de Roland** ⑧ on the way up the Nive River to **St-Jean-**

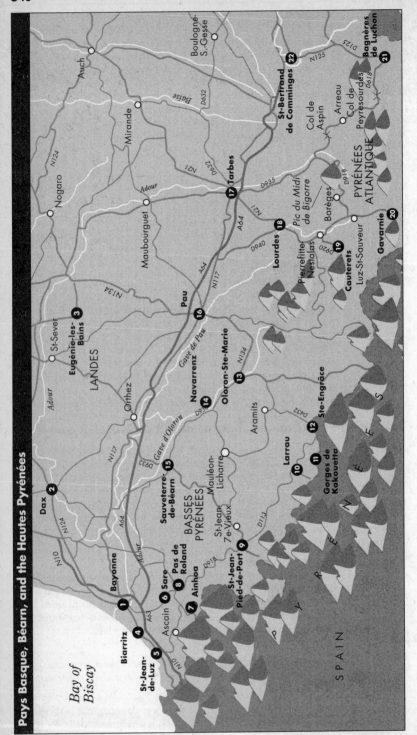

Pays Basque, Béarn, and the Hautes Pyrénées

Pied-de-Port ⑨ for lunch. Explore the Haute Soule during the afternoon: Drive through the Irati Forest, to **Larrau** ⑩, and **Ste-Engrâce** ⑫ on the way through **Oloron-Ste-Marie** ⑬ to 🏨 **Pau** ⑯ for the night. On day three have a look around Pau, see **Lourdes** ⑱ at midday, and get up to 🏨 **Gavarnie** ⑳ in time to see the sunset from the legendary Hôtel du Cirque.

IF YOU HAVE 7 DAYS

Begin in **Bayonne** ①, spending a morning exploring the town. See the cathedral and the Bonnat Museum before going to **Dax** ② for a bullfight and 🏨 **Eugénie-les-Bains** ③ for dinner and the night. The next day, head back to the coast at **Biarritz** ④ for some time at the beach. Spend the night in 🏨 **St-Jean-de-Luz** ⑤. On day three climb La Rhune (or take the little train to the top) for a stunning view over the entire Basque coast. Drive through **Sare** ⑥ and **Ainhoa** ⑦ and past **Pas de Roland** ⑧ on the way up the Nive River to 🏨 **St-Jean-Pied-de-Port** ⑨ for the night. Explore the town and the Haute Soule the next morning: Drive through the Irati Forest to 🏨 **Larrau** ⑩ and do the Holçarté Gorges walk to 🏨 **Ste-Engrâce** ⑫ if there is time. Return to Larrau if not. On day five explore the lower Soule, **Oloron-Ste-Marie** ⑬, and 🏨 **Pau** ⑯. On day six walk around Pau, see **Lourdes** ⑱ at lunchtime, and get up to 🏨 **Gavarnie** ⑳ in time to see the sunset from the Hôtel du Cirque. On day seven explore around Gavarnie.

When to Tour Pays Basque, Béarn, and the Hautes-Pyrénées

Easter to All Saints' Day—early May through late October—is the best time to explore this region. Beach life ends and much of the Pyrénées is snowed in during the winter; many hotels and restaurants close. Only for skiing and the pleasure of the nearly total absence of tourism is winter recommendable. The best months of all are June and September; July is the only month you can be nearly 100% sure of, say, walking safely over the glacier to the Brèche de Roland.

BAYONNE AND THE BASQUE COAST

Bayonne, a port town, is the capital of French Basque Country and seat of the annual pelota championships, that most emblematic of Basque sports. Its aegis extends along the Basque coast from the swanky resort town of Biarritz to the charming fishing town of St-Jean-de-Luz and on to Hendaye, on the border with Spain.

Bayonne

❶ *48 km (30 mi) southwest of Dax, 184 km (114 mi) south of Bordeaux, 295 km (183 mi) west of Toulouse.*

Originally a 4th-century Roman fort or *castrum,* and from 1151 to 1451 a British colony, Bayonne, the most Basque city in France, stands at the confluence of the Adour and the Nive. The town's two rivers and five bridges lend a definite nautical feel to this small gem of a city, even though the port is spread out along the Adour estuary leading out to the sea 5 km (3 mi) away. Bayonne's quai-front houses, place Pasteur's leafy intimacy, the Château-Vieux, the 18th-century houses along rue Prébendé, and the 17th-century ramparts are some of the town's best features. Bayonne's 13th-century **Cathédrale** (alternately called Ste-Marie or Notre-Dame) is one of France's southernmost examples of Gothic architecture. The 13th- to 14th-century cloisters are especially lovely. The airy, modernized **Musée Bonnat** houses a notable collection of 19th-century paintings. ⊠ *5 rue Jacques-Lafitte,* ☎ *05–59–59–08–52.* 🎟 *18 frs.* ⊙ *Wed.–Mon. 10–noon and 2:30–6:30.*

Dining and Lodging

$$ ✕ **Euskalduna.** This profoundly Basque establishment serves the best
★ *cuisine du terroir* (homestyle regional cooking) in Bayonne. The sur-
roundings are exactly as rustic and maritime as they should be. The fare
is authentic and hearty, featuring fresh fish dishes as well as upland spe-
cialties from the Basque hills. ⊠ *61 rue Pannecau,* ☎ *05–59–59–28–
02. MC, V. Closed Sun.–Mon., and early–mid-June, mid–late Oct.*

$$$ ✕🖫 **Le Grand Hôtel.** Just down the street from the Château-Vieux, this
central spot has pleasant, comfortable rooms with an Old World feel.
Its restaurant, Les Carmes, is excellent. ⊠ *21 rue Thiers, 64100,* ☎
05–59–59–14–61, 🖹 *05–59–25–61–70. 58 rooms. Restaurant.
AE, DC, MC, V.*

Dax

❷ *143 km (89 mi) south of Arcachon, 145 km (90 mi) south of Bordeaux.*

Known in Roman times as Aquae Tarbellicae, Dax has been famous
for 2,000 years for its thermal springs. The daughter of Caesar Augustus
came here to soothe her aches and pains and was the first in a long line
of seasonal guests. Steaming water gushes out of the lion-headed Néhé
fountain in the center of town. Take a walk through the parks and gardens and along the banks of the River Adour. Of note are the sculptures and 11th-century bas-reliefs on the church of **St-Paul-les-Dax** and
the cathedral of **Notre-Dame.** But people generally come to Dax for the
waters; unless you plan to do so, you may not want to make the stop.

Eugénie-les-Bains

❸ *68 km (42 mi) east of Dax, 140 km (87 mi) south of Bordeaux.*

Eugénie-les-Bains's heyday was a century ago when Empress Eugénie
popularized it with her visits. In gratitude for her patronage, the villagers changed the name of the town. The village was forgotten until
Michel and Christine Guérard brought it back to life in 1973 by re-
creating one of the most fashionable thermal retreats in France. The
spa has 13 therapeutic treatments for everything from weight loss to
rheumatism. Two springs are certified by the French Ministry of Health,
"l'Impératrice" and the "Christine-Marie," whose 39°C (102°F) waters come from nearly 1,300 ft below the earth's surface.

Dining and Lodging

$$ ✕ **La Ferme aux Grives.** In addition to the spa, the Guérards own this
delightfully re-created old coaching inn, where the bounty of nature
is the theme. A banquet table is laid out with vegetables and breads,
darkened beams give a rich hue, and hunting paintings cover the walls.
The three-course 170-franc menu may include a vinaigrette of grilled
pears over locally cured ham, milk-fed lamb roasted in a pastry shell,
and a huge meringue with Chantilly sauce. ⊠ *Eugénie-les-Bains,* ☎
05–58–51–19–08. MC, V. Closed Jan.–mid-Feb.

$$$$ ✕🖫 **Les Prés d'Eugénie.** People come from all over to enjoy chef
★ Michel Guérard's superb *tourte sauvagine de Garenne et du canard
au foie gras* (marinated wild rabbit and duck baked with foie gras in
pastry) and taste-bud-tingling *coquilles St-Jacques* (scallops). Grandeur
prevails. Rooms are formal, though not outstandingly designed. Those
in the former 18th-century convent have an understated luxury. ⊠ *40320
Eugénie-les-Bains,* ☎ *05–58–05–06–07, 05–58–05–05–05 for
restaurant reservations,* 🖹 *05–58–51–13–59. 44 rooms. Restau-
rant, pool, 9-hole golf course, 2 tennis courts, exercise room. AE, DC,
MC, V.*

Biarritz

④ *8 km (5 mi) south of Bayonne, 190 km (118 mi) southwest of Bordeaux, 50 km (31 mi) north of San Sebastián, 115 km (69 mi) west of Pau.*

Biarritz rose to prominence in the 19th century when upstart emperor Napoléon III took to spending his holidays here on the prompting of his Spanish wife, Eugénie. Although not as stylish as it once was, the town is making a comeback with a new casino and a new convention center. The narrow streets around the cozy 16th-century church of **St-Martin** are delightful to stroll. The harbor of **Port des Pêcheurs** (Fishers' Port), too, provides a tantalizing glimpse of the Biarritz of old. The **beaches** still attract crowds—particularly the fine, sandy beaches of **Grande Plage** and the neighboring **Plage Miramar,** both amid craggy natural beauty.

Dining and Lodging

$$ ✕ **Les Platanes.** Chef-owner Arnaud Daguin specializes in adapting country recipes and giving them a lighter touch. Be sure to try his foie gras, which he gets from his hometown in Gers. The decor of the restaurant, in an old Basque town house, is comfortably formal. ⊠ *32 av. Beau-Soleil,* ☎ *05–59–23–13–68. Jacket and tie. MC, V. Closed Mon. No lunch Tues.*

$$$$ ✕☒ **Palais.** This majestic redbrick hotel, with immense driveway,
★ lawns, and semicircular dining room, exudes a stylish, opulent, aristocratic air that stops short of decadence. Empress Eugénie, wife of Napoléon III, left her mark here a century ago. Rooms are spacious; the 2,000-franc ones facing the ocean are especially grand. In the restaurant, La Rotonde, chef Jean-Marie Gautier creates deft, innovative fare reflecting Basque Country's Atlantic and Pyrenean resources. Specialties range from lobster gazpacho to roast suckling lamb. Informal lunch is served on the terrace facing the curved pool above the Atlantic. ⊠ *1 av. de l'Impératrice, 64200,* ☎ *05–59–24–09–40,* ℻ *05–59–41–67–99. 134 rooms, 20 suites. 3 restaurants, 2 bars, pool, sauna. AE, DC, MC, V. Annual winter closing varies.*

$$$ ✕☒ **Café de Paris.** This well-known hotel is also a popular Biarritz
★ restaurant—in fact, two. One is an elegant (and expensive) gourmet restaurant featuring such items as *ris de veau* (calf's sweetbreads) and fish served with an imaginative nouvelle touch. The other is a less formal brasserie (with the same chefs). The haute cuisine restaurant is closed for lunch, as well as for dinner on Sunday; the brasserie is always open. Rooms are luxurious and have ocean views. ⊠ *5 pl. Bellevue, 64200,* ☎ *05–59–24–19–53,* ℻ *05–59–24–18–20. 19 rooms. Restaurant. AE, DC, V.*

$$–$$$ ✕☒ **Windsor.** This hotel, built in the 1920s, is close to the casino and beach. The restaurant serves a variety of dishes, including terrine de foie gras with Armagnac and ravioli stuffed with crab. Rooms are modern and cozy; those with sea views cost about twice as much as those facing the inner courtyard. ⊠ *19 bd. du Général-de-Gaulle, 64200,* ☎ *05–59–24–08–52,* ℻ *05–59–24–98–90. 49 rooms. Restaurant. AE, MC, V. Closed Jan.–mid-Mar.*

Nightlife and the Arts

At the **Casino de Biarritz** (⊠ 1 av. Édouard-VII, ☎ 05–59–22–77–77) you can wrestle with the one-armed bandit, play blackjack, or, alternatively, lose some pounds at the Flamingo disco. To keep your connections in cyberspace, **Internet & Café** (⊠ 5 rue Jauerry, ☎ 05–59–24–03–31) behind the post office provides the link. A comfortable hangout both day and night is the small **Le Queen's Bar** (⊠ 25 pl. Clemenceau, ☎ 05–59–24–70–65), where the young at heart gather in the evening and the not-so-shy take the mike to do karaoke.

Outdoor Activities and Sports

Côte Basque Surf Training (⌧ 10 rue Larrepunte, ☎ 05–59–23–15–31) gives body-boarding and surfing lessons. The **Freedom Surf Shop** (⌧ 2 av. de la Reine Victoria, ☎ 05–59–38–40–25) gives surfing lessons and rents equipment. **Désertours Aventure** (⌧ 65 av. Maréchal-Juin, ☎ 05–59–41–22–02) arranges rafting trips on the Nive River and four-wheel-drive vehicle trips through the Atlantic Pyrénées. **Golf de Biarritz** (⌧ 2 av. Edith-Cavell, ☎ 05–59–03–71–80) has an 18-hole, par-69 course. You can watch pelota, that Basque specialty, being played on Wednesday and Saturday at 9 PM in July, August, and September, at the **Parc des Sports d'Aguilera** (☎ 05–59–23–91–09).

St-Jean-de-Luz

★ ❺   *23 km (16 mi) southwest of Bayonne, 24 km (18 mi) northeast of San Sebastián, 54 km (32 mi) west of St-Jean-Pied-de-Port, 128 km (77 mi) west of Pau.*

Along the coast between Biarritz and the Spanish border, St-Jean-de-Luz has old streets, a curious church, a colorful harbor, and an elegant beach. The tree-lined **place Louis-XIV,** alongside the **Hôtel de Ville** (Town Hall), with its narrow courtyard and dainty statue of Louis XIV on horseback, is the hub of the town. The church of **St-Jean-Baptiste** has unusual wooden galleries lining the walls creating a theaterlike effect. ⌧ *pl. des Corsaires.*

Of particular note is the **Maison de l'Infante** (Princess's House), between the harbor and the bay, where Maria Teresa of Spain stayed prior to her wedding to the Sun King. The foursquare mansion now houses the **Musée Grévin,** which contains worthy 17th-century furnishings and period costumes. ⌧ *quai de l'Infante,* ☎ 05–59–51–24–88. ⌧ *33 frs.* ☉ *Apr.–Oct., daily 10:30–noon and 2–6:30; Nov.–Mar., by appointment.*

Dining and Lodging

$$$ ✕ **La Coupole.** In this semicircular gourmet restaurant in the Grand Hôtel (☞ *below*), look out at the bay while feasting on chef Patrice Demangel's excellent regional specialties: confit of lobster, baby lamb from the Pyrénées, and a luscious dessert of three chocolate flowers in a vanilla sauce. ⌧ *43 bd. Thiers,* ☎ 05–59–26–35–36. *AE, DC, MC, V. Closed late Oct.–early Apr.*

$$$ ✕ **Txalupa.** The name means "skiff or small boat" in Basque, and you feel like you're in one this close to the bay—yachts and fishing vessels go about their business just a few yards away. This well-known haunt with a terrace over the port serves the famous *jambon de Bayonne* (Bayonne ham) in vinegar and garlic sauce, as well as fresh fish and natural products such as wild mushrooms. ⌧ *pl. Louis-XIV,* ☎ 05–59–51–85–52. *AE, DC, MC, V.*

$ ✕ **Chez Pablo.** This place is a local institution. The simple, home-style menu is based on what the fishing fleet caught that morning. Long tables covered with red and white tablecloths, benches, and plastered walls make for a casual meal. There is also a room laid out with cutlery and glasses, but this is for regulars. ⌧ *rue M. Etcheto,* ☎ 05–56–26–37–81. *No credit cards. Closed Sun.*

$$$ ⌂ **Le Grand Hôtel.** Although it is the town's leading hotel, it is not as grand as you might expect—rooms have seen better days. But a major plus is that it is on the waterfront, and Suites 301 and 302 have terraces over the bay. ⌧ *43 bd. Thiers, 64500,* ☎ 05–59–26–35–36, FAX 05–59–51–19–91. *43 rooms, 3 suites. Restaurant. AE, DC, MC, V. Closed late Oct.–early Apr.*

THE ATLANTIC PYRÉNÉES

Watching the Pyrénées grow from rolling green foothills in the Basque Country to jagged limestone peaks in the Béarn to glacier-studded granite massifs in the Hautes-Pyrénées is an exciting process. The Atlantic Pyrénées' first major peak is at La Rhune (2,969 ft), known as the Balcon du Côte Basque (Balcony of the Basque Coast). The highest Basque peak is at Orhi (6,617 ft), and the Béarn's highest is Pic d'Anie (8,510 ft). Not until Vignemale (10,820 ft) in the Haute Pyrénées does the altitude surpass the 10,000-ft mark. Starting east from St-Jean-de-Luz up the Nivelle river, a series of picturesque villages serve as stepping stones into the Pyrénées.

Sare

❻ *14 km (8 mi) southeast of St-Jean-de-Luz; 9 km (5½ mi) southwest of Ainhoa on D118: Take the first left.*

The tiny village of Sare is one of the most beautiful in France. Shady streets, a large fronton (for pelota), and a lovely three-tier church are among its chief assets.

Up the Sare Valley is the panoramic Col de Lizarrieta and the **Grottes de Sare,** where you can take a guided tour (in five languages) for 1 km (½ mi) underground and see a son-et-lumière show. ☎ *05–59–54–21–88.* 🎟 *30 frs.* ☉ *Mid-Feb.–Dec.*

☝ West of Sare on D4, at the Col de St-Ignace, take the **Petit Train de la Rhune,** a tiny wood-paneled cogwheel train that reaches the dizzying speed of 5 mph while climbing up La Rhune peak. The views of the Bay of Biscay, the Pyrénées, and the grassy hills of the Basque farmland are wonderful. 🎟 *45 frs.* ☉ *Round-trip (1 hr): Easter vacation and May–June, daily 10 and 3; July–Sept., daily every 35 mins.*

Ainhoa

❼ *9 km (5½ mi) east of Sare, 23 km (14 mi) southeast of St-Jean-de-Luz, 31 km (19 mi) northwest of St-Jean-Pied-de-Port.*

The classical Basque village of Ainhoa is one of the prettiest towns in France. The streets are lined with one lovely house after another, complete with whitewashed walls, flower-filled balconies, brightly painted shutters, and carved master beams. The church of **Notre-Dame de l'Assomption** is a three-tier delight, with carved railings and woodwork.

Lodging

$$ 🏨 **Hôtel Ohantzea.** Across from the church, this classical Basque house, with a beautiful facade and garden, was a farm in the 17th century. The original antiques and the many paintings by artists who traded them for lodging all make this comfortable space as much of a museum as a hotel. Ask for a room with a balcony overlooking the garden. ⊠ *rue Principale, 64250,* ☎ *05–59–29–90–50,* 📠 *no fax. 9 rooms. MC, V. Closed Dec.–Jan.*

Pas de Roland

❽ *15 km (9 mi) east of Ainhoa; 30 km (18 mi) northwest of St-Jean-Pied-de-Port; follow signs for Itxassou and proceed past the town up to the pass.*

Legend has it that it was at the Pas de Roland (Roland's Footprint) where the legendary medieval hero Roland, to allow Charlemagne's troops to pass, cut a breach through a boulder with his mystical sword

Durandal, in the process leaving his footprint in the rock. The evidence remains.

Dining and Lodging

$$ ✕▦ **Hôtel du Mont Roland.** Just upstream of the Pas de Roland, this rustic little inn is a good place for a meal or a night. Home-grown native trout are available from the hotel's private pool, or have the *pipérade basquaise au jambon* (an egg dish with tomatoes, green peppers, onions, and ham). Rooms are simple but clean and cozy. ⊠ *Laxîa, 64250 Itxassou,* ☎ *05–59–29–75–23,* ▣ *no fax. 9 rooms with showers and sinks, WC in the hall. Restaurant. MC, V. Closed Jan.*

St-Jean-Pied-de-Port

❾ *54 km (33 mi) east of Biarritz, 46 km (28 mi) west of Larrau.*

St-Jean-Pied-de-Port, a fortified town on the Nive River, got its name from its position at the foot (*pied*) of the *port* (mountain pass) of Roncevaux (Roncesvalles). The pass was the setting for *La Chanson de Roland* (*The Song of Roland*), the 11th-century epic poem considered the real beginning of French literature. The bustling town center, a major stop for pilgrims en route to Santiago de Compostela, seems, after a tour through the Soule, like a frenzied metropolitan center—even in winter. In summer, especially around the time of Pamplona's San Fermin blowout (the running of the bulls, July 7–14), the place is filled to the gills and is somewhere between exciting and unbearable.

Walk into the old section through the Porte de France just behind and to the left of the tourist office, climb the steps on the left up to the walkway circling the ramparts, and walk around to the stone stairway down to the rue de l'Église. The street leads down to the magnificent doorway of **Notre-Dame-du-Bout-du-Pont** (Our Lady of the End of the Bridge), a characteristic Basque three-tier structure: men above, women below, and the choir loft above that. Walk out on the bridge, the **Pont Notre-Dame,** near the church of Notre-Dame-du-Bout-du-Pont, and watch the wild trout in the Nive, which is also a scheduled Atlantic salmon stream. Fishing is *défendu* (forbidden) in town. Follow the left bank upstream to get to another wooden bridge. Cross there and then walk around and back through town, crossing back to the left bank on the main road. At the **Relais de la Nive** bar and café (hanging over the river at the north end of the bridge in the center of town), admire the reflection of the Notre-Dame bridge upstream and watch the trout working in the current as you sip your coffee.

Take **rue de la Citadelle,** running from the square in front of the church, to see the **La Maison Arcanzola** (Arcanzola House) at No. 32 (1510), the **Maison des Évêques** (Bishops' House) at No. 39, and the famous **Prison des Évêques** (Bishops' Prison) next door. Continue along rue de la Citadelle to get to the **Citadelle** up above, a classic Vauban fortress, now occupied by a school.

Dining and Lodging

$$–$$$ ✕ **Chez Arbillaga.** Tucked inside the citadel ramparts, this lively bistro is a sound choice for lunch or dinner. The food represents what the Basques do best: simple cooking of excellent quality, such as *agneau de lait à la broche* (roast lamb) in winter or *coquilles St-Jacques au lard fumé* (scallops with bacon) in summer. ⊠ *8 rue de l'Église,* ☎ *05–59–37–06–44. MC, V. Closed 1st 2 wks of June and Oct. and Wed. Jan.–May.*

$$$ ✕▦ **Les Pyrénées.** In this inn is the best restaurant in town, specializ-
★ ing in nouvelle Basque cuisine, such as ravioli and prawns with caviar sauce or the hot wild-mushroom terrine. Rooms are modern and vary in size; four have balconies. ⊠ *19 pl. du Général-de-Gaulle, 64220,*

☎ 05–59–37–01–01, ℻ 05–59–37–18–97. *18 rooms, 2 apart-ments. Restaurant, pool. AE, DC, MC, V. Closed last 3 wks of Jan., late Nov.–late Dec.*

$$ ✕🏠 **Central Hôtel.** This family-run hotel and restaurant over the Nive has the best quality for price in town. The owners speak Basque, Span-ish, French, English, and some German as well, so communicating is no problem. Trout for breakfast can be literally (though illegally) caught from the rooms over the river. There is a wonderful, 200-year-old, handmade oak staircase. The cuisine is superb: Try the *magret de canard* (duck breast). ✉ *1 pl. Charles-de-Gaulle, 64220,* ☎ *05–59–37–00–22,* ℻ *05–59–37–27–79. 14 rooms. Restaurant. AE, DC, MC, V. Closed mid-Dec.–early Mar.*

En Route The road between St-Jean-Pied-de-Port and Larrau twists through mountain passes (Col de Burdinkurutzeta and Col de Organbideska), offering views north over the Arbailles Forest and the sweeping Basque hills as it enters the vast Iraty forest to the south. The Iraty forest, one of Europe's largest stands of beech, provided masts for the Spanish and French fleets up through the 18th century.

Larrau

⓾ *46 km (28 mi) east of St-Jean-Pied-de-Port, 20 km (12 mi) west of Ste-Engrâce, 42 km (26 mi) southwest of Oloron-Ste-Marie.*

Larrau is a cozy way station on the road over the Larrau pass into Spain. There are several hotels of distinction in the town and several ex-traordinarily ancient and rustic mountain houses. Once known for its 19th-century forges, Larrau is now a winter base camp for hunters and a summer center for hikers. It's a good departure point for the **Holçarté Gorges walk.** This classic trek is a 90-minute round-trip hike includ-ing a spectacular bridge that hangs 561 ft above the rocky stream bed. The well-marked trail begins at the Logibar inn (☞ Dining and Lodg-ing, *below*), 3 km (2 mi) east of Larrau.

Dining and Lodging

$$–$$$ ✕🏠 **Hôtel Etxemaïté.** This country inn has spectacular views and is one
★ of the area's top dining spots. The dining room seems suspended over the garden and is often full in summer. The hotel has several examples of the *susulia*, a Basque chair and table combination designed to allow two people to sit and dine comfortably by the fire. The Basque cook-ing is excellent: Terrine *de poule au foie gras* (hen with duck liver) is one good choice. The restaurant is closed for Sunday dinner and Mon-day from mid-November to mid-May. ✉ *rte. D26, 64560 Larrau,* ☎ *05–59–28–61–45,* ℻ *05–59–28–72–71. 16 rooms. DC, MC, V. Closed mid–late Jan.*

$ ✕🏠 **Logibar.** This simple inn with a *gîte d'étape* (way station) for hik-ers attached serves nonpareil garbure and an even better *omelette aux cèpes* (wild mushroom omelet). Rooms are tiny but cozy, and the Qui-hilliry family, in its fourth generation of commanding this well-known spot, has a knack for making you feel at home. ✉ *rte. D26, 64560 Larrau,* ☎ *05–59–28–61–14,* ℻ *05–59–28–61–14. 12 rooms. MC, V. Closed early Dec.–early Mar.*

Gorges de Kakuetta

⓫ *13 km (8 mi) east of Larrau, 3 km (2 mi) west of Ste-Engrâe.*

A right turn onto D113 at the junction of the Uhaitxa and Larrau rivers will take you toward Ste-Engrâce past one of the area's great natural phenomena, the Gorges de Kakuetta (the Basque spelling). Just west of Ste-Engrâce is the gorge, a famous canyon cut through the limestone cliffs by the Uhaitxa River. At times as narrow as 12 ft across, the gorge reaches depths of over 350 m (1,155 ft). Stairways are cut into the rock, and hanging bridges span the watercourse. A waterfall and a grotto mark the end of the climb, a two-hour walk round-trip. This hike is recommended only during low-water conditions, normally between June and October. Good hiking shoes are indispensable. ☎ 05–59–28–73–44. 🎫 15 frs. ⊙ Mid-Mar.–mid-Nov., daily 8 AM–dark

Ste-Engrâce

⑫ 66 km (40 mi) east of St-Jean-Pied-de-Port, 37 km (23 mi) southwest of Oloron-Ste-Marie, 100 km (62 mi) southwest of Pau.

Ste-Engrâce was once an important medieval pilgrimage site. Pilgrims on the way to Santiago de Compostela, in northwest Spain, flocked to Ste-Engrâce's lovely 11th-century church, **Ste-Engrâce,** to venerate the arm of Sancta Gracia. A young Portuguese noblewoman, Sancta Gracia was martyred around the year 300. In 1569, pillaging Calvinists removed the cherished relic. A ring finger was sent from Zaragoza, the scene of her martyrdom, to replace the stolen arm. The church has an asymmetrical, slanting roof, redolent of *maison Basque* (Basque house) design. Its gray stone contrasts eerily with the green hills and fields behind. The ornate interior is a surprising contrast to the church's stark exterior. The town remains a key crossroads for pilgrims traveling to Santiago and trans-Pyrenean trekkers going east across the "dragon's back."

Dining and Lodging

$ ✕🏠 **Auberge Elichalt.** This cozy hikers' inn has 50 beds in varying conditions, all good. There are double rooms, dormitory beds, and an apartment for rent, all in the shadow of the church. M. and Mme. Burguburu ("town's end" in Basque) can recommend hikes into the mountains. ✉ 64560 Ste-Engrâce, ☎ 05–59–28–61–63, FAX 05–59–28–75–54. *5 double rooms, 1 apartment for 5, 40 dormitory beds with shared bath. No credit cards.*

Outdoor Activities and Sports

The nearby ski station, 10 km (6 mi) away in **Pierre-St-Martin,** has alpine and Nordic skiing. If you're interested in fly-fishing, the **Gave d'Oloron,** the river (in Bérn dialect) flowing through Sauveterre-de-Béarn, is both a trout and an Atlantic salmon fishery. On the D919 between Aramits and Oloron-Ste-Marie, look for the Vert River and the nearby town of **Féas.** The gentle Vert Valley, with a meadow brook running through it, is well populated with trout and is a great place for fishing.

En Route   Ste-Engrâce is at the eastern edge of the Basque Country in the **Haute Soule** (Upper Soule), part of the Soule, the smallest of the Basque provinces. Nearly all the inhabitants speak Euskera (Basque), a non–Indo-European language of uncertain (though probably native Iberian) origins. The **Basse Soule** (Lower Soule), also known as the Barétous region, is an undulating and moist transitional zone between Basque Country and Béarn, characterized by rolling green hills and corn fields. To explore the Basse Soule, take D132 from Pierre-St-Martin down to Arette. Drive the loop beginning west toward **Aramits, Lanne, Trois-Villes,** and **Gotein,** with its characteristic *clocher-calvaire,* a three-peaked bell tower designed as an evocation of Calvary. Just short of Mauléon-Licharre on D918 is the rustic 11th-century **Chapelle St-Jean-de-Berraute,** built by the Order of Malta for pilgrims on the way to Santiago de Compostela. **Mauléon-Licharre,** capital of the Soule, is on the banks of the Saison. Stop to see the 16th-century **Hôtel de Maytie** (also known as the Château d'Andurain), the 17th-century **Hôtel de**

Montréal, and the remains of a 12th-century fortress. The next village, L'Hôpital-St-Blaise, has a 12th-century church with Moorish characteristics very probably imported from south of the Pyrénées by the same architect who designed the Sainte-Croix church in Oloron-Ste-Marie. From L'Hôpital-St-Blaise, a right on D936 will take you into Oloron-Ste-Marie. A left on D936 will take you to Navarrenx and Sauveterre-de-Béarn, two of the most spectacular towns in the Soule region.

Oloron-Ste-Marie

⑬ *33 km (20½ mi) southwest of Pau on N134.*

Oloron-Ste-Marie straddles the confluence of two rivers, the Gave d'Aspe and the Gave d'Ossau. Trout and even the occasional Atlantic salmon can be spotted when the sun is out. Originally an Iberian and later a Roman military outpost, the town was made a stronghold by the viscounts of Béarn in the 11th century.

The **quartier Ste-Croix** occupies the once fortified point between the two rivers and is the most interesting part of town. The fortresslike church of **Ste-Croix**, with its Moorish-influenced cupola; the two Renaissance buildings nearby; and the 14th-century **Tour Grède** (Grède Tower) are the main attractions. A walk around the **promenade Bellevue** along the ramparts below the west side of the church will give you a view down the Aspe Valley and into the mountains behind.

Dining and Lodging

$–$$ ✕ **Le Biscondau.** Come here to sample one of the finest garbures, the hearty peasant vegetable soup, in Oloron. The view over the Gave d'Ossau is at its best from the terrace in summer. ⊠ *7 rue de la Filature,* ☎ *05–59–39–06–15. DC, MC, V. Closed Mon.*

$$–$$$ ✕▥ **Hôtel Darroze.** This traditional hotel is on a quiet corner next to the town hall. Rooms overlook the rooftops of Oloron and on to the Pyrénées. The restaurant, one of the town's best, is decorated with old murals depicting Oloron's confluence of gaves, or rivers. Be sure to try the *tourtière Gasconne flambé à l'Armagnac* (Gascon pigeon in flaming Armagnac). The restaurant is closed Sunday dinner and Monday all day. ⊠ *4 pl. de la Mairie,* ☎ *05–59–39–00–99,* 🖷 *05–59–39–17–88. 30 rooms. Restaurant. AE, DC, MC, V.*

$ ▥ **Chambre d'Hôtes Paris.** This bed-and-breakfast in Féas, run by Christian and Marie-France Paris, is a bargain, especially if you like fly-fishing. Christian, a registered guide, knows every trout in the Barétous—by name. ⊠ *64570 Féas (7½ km/5 mi past Oloron-Ste-Marie),* ☎ *05–59–39–01–10. 3 rooms. No credit cards. Closed late Dec.– early Jan.*

Navarrenx

⑭ *19 km (11 mi) northwest of Oloron-Ste-Marie.* Perched over the Gave d'Oloron, Navarrenx was built in 1316 as a *bastide* (fortified town) at an important crossroads on the Santiago de Compostela pilgrimage route. Henri d'Albret, King of Navarre, constructed the present ramparts in 1540. The bastion of Porte St-Antoine, with its miniaturesque turret, is one of the Soule's most emblematic sights. "Si You Ti Baou," the town motto ("If I should see you," in Béarnais) refers to the cannon guarding the approach to the town across the bridge. The Gave d'Oloron is an excellent river for trout and salmon fishing (an important part of Navarrenx tradition). Every year there is a salmon fishing championship, and the townsfolk line the banks of the best pool upstream from the bridge.

Dining and Lodging

$$ ╳⛨ **Le Commerce.** As the best restaurant and most traditional lodging in Navarrenx, the Commerce is an easy choice. Rooms are old-fashioned and cozy and have renovated, spacious bathrooms. The exquisite menu features such items as *pigeonnaux au style bécasse* (squab, woodcock style), fragrant dark meat in a Madeira sauce, or *foie gras frais au myrtille* (fresh duck liver in a berry sauce). ⊠ *pl. des Casernes, 64190.* ☎ *05–59–66–50–16,* FAX *05–59–66–52–67. 38 rooms. Restaurant. AE, DC, MC, V.*

Sauveterre-de-Béarn

⑮   *19 km (11 mi) northwest of Navarrenx, 39 km (23 mi) northwest of Oloron-Ste-Marie, 39 km (23 mi) northeasat of St-Jean-Pied-de-Port.*Make your first stop the terrace next to the church: The view of the Gave d'Oloron, the fortified 12th-century drawbridge, the lovely Montréal tower, and the Pyrénées rising in the distance is among the finest in the region. The bridge, known both as the **Vieux Pont** (Old Bridge) and the Pont de la Légende (Bridge of the Legend), was named after the legend of Sancie, widow of Gaston V de Béarn. Subjected to the Judgment of God in 1170 after being accused of murdering a child after her husband's death, she was thrown, bound hand and foot, from the bridge by order of the King of Navarre, her brother. When the river carried her safely to the bank, she was cleared of all charges.

Dining and Lodging

$$–$$$ ╳⛨ **Hôtel du Vieux Pont.** Former British journalists Paul and Sandie Williams have beautifully restored this medieval manor house built into the town's fortified 12th-century drawbridge. The views over the river and up to the ramparts of Sauveterre are superb. Rooms range from cozy and comfortable to grand and baronial (ask for the one on the corner with two views of the river and an immense bathroom). Excellent cuisine is served in the restaurant (especially if you bring home fresh trout or salmon), including such dishes as magret de canard and poulet basquaise and a good choice of local wines. ⊠ *rue du Pont de la Légende, 64390 Sauveterre-de-Béarn,* ☎ *05–59–38–95–11,* FAX *05–59–38–99–10. 7 rooms. Restaurant. AE, DC, MC, V.*

Pau

⑯   *106 km (63 mi) east of Bayonne and Biarritz.*

The busy and elegant town of Pau is the historic capital of Béarn, a state annexed to France in 1620. Pau was "discovered" in 1815 by British officers returning from the Peninsular War in Spain, and it soon became a prominent winter resort town. Fifty years later, English-speaking inhabitants made up one-third of Pau's population. They started the Pont-Long steeplechase, still one of the most challenging in Europe, in 1841; created France's first golf course here, in 1856; and introduced fox hunting to the region.

Pau's regal past is commemorated at the **Château,** begun in the 14th century by Gaston Phoebus, the flamboyant count of Béarn. The building was transformed into a Renaissance palace in the 16th century by Marguerite d'Angoulême, sister of François I. Marguerite's grandson, the future King Henri IV, was born in the château in 1553. Temporary exhibits connected to Henri's life and times are staged regularly. His cradle, a giant turtle shell, is on exhibit in his bedroom, one of the sumptuous, tapestry-lined royal apartments. ⊠ *rue du Château,* ☎ *05–59–82–38–00.* ▦ *26 frs, Sun. 14 frs.* ☉ *Apr.–Oct., daily 9:30–11:30 and 2–5:45; Nov.–Mar., daily 9:30–11:30 and 2–4:30.*

The **Musée Béarnais,** on the fourth floor of the château, gives an overview of the region, encompassing everything from fauna to furniture to festival costumes. There is a reconstructed Béarn house and displays of local crafts. ☎ 05–59–27–07–36. 🎫 8 frs. ⊙ Apr.–Oct., daily 9:30–12:30 and 2:30–6:30; Nov.–Mar., daily 9:30–12:30 and 2:30–5:30.

Dining and Lodging

$$–$$$ ✕ **Gousse d'Ail.** In the Hédas district, the deep mid-city canyon in the oldest part of Pau, this lovely hideaway is tucked under the stairway at the end of the street. Traditional Béarn and international cuisine are served. Try the magret de canard cooked over coals. ⊠ 12 rue du Hédas, ☎ 05–59–27–31–55, FAX 05–59–06–10–53. MC, V. Closed Sun. No lunch Sat.

$$ 🏨 **Hôtel de Gramont.** Within sight of the château gardens, the Gramont is a convenient base for exploring Pau. Ask for one of the *chambres mansardées* (dormered bedrooms) under the eaves. ⊠ 3 pl. de Gramont, 64000, ☎ 05–59–27–84–04, FAX 05–59–27–62–23. 36 rooms. Breakfast room. AE, DC, MC, V.

Nightlife and the Arts

During the music and arts **Festival de Pau** there are events almost every evening, nearly all of them gratis, mid-July–late-August.

THE HAUTES-PYRÉNÉES

The *département* (province) of the Hautes-Pyrénées, traditionally known as La Bigorre, includes the highest and most spectacular natural resources in the cordillera. La Bigorre's border with the Ossau Valley and Béarn country is the Col d'Aubisque southeast of Oloron-Ste-Marie; its eastern border with the Haute Garonne is at the Col de Peyresourde just west of Bagnères-de-Luchon. The legendary Cirque de Gavarnie, the Vignemale peak (10,817 ft) and glacier, the Balaïtous peak (10,312 ft), and the Cirque de Troumouse are among the major attractions in the Haute Pyrénées.

Tarbes

⑰ 40 km (24 mi) east of Pau, 152 km (94 mi) southwest of Toulouse, 214 km (133 mi) southeast of Bordeaux.

If your point of entry into the Hautes-Pyrénées is Tarbes, stop in the **tourist office** (⊠ 3 cours Gambetta, ☎ 05–62–51–30–31) for information, brochures, and maps of the region. The city is the commercial and administrative center of the Pyrénées region and of no burning interest as a tourist destination. But you might enjoy a stroll around the pretty **Jardin Massey** amid the abundance of summer flowers.

Lourdes

⑱ 41 km (27 mi) southeast of Pau, 19 km (12 mi) southwest of Tarbes.

Each year some 5 million pilgrims flock to Lourdes, many in quest of a miraculous cure for sickness or disability. Whether it's worth seeing is another question. The area surrounding the famous churches and grotto is woefully lacking in beauty. Out of season, the acres of nearly empty parking lots echo. Shops are shuttered and restaurants are closed. In season, a milling throng jostles to get a glimpse of the grotto lurking behind a forest of votive candles.

The history of this Catholic mecca is relatively recent. In February 1858, Bernadette Soubirous, a 14-year-old miller's daughter, claimed the Virgin Mary had appeared to her in the **Grotte de Massabielle** near the River Gave de Pau. During the night, Bernadette dug at the ground in the grotto, releasing a gush of water from a spot where no spring existed. From then on, pilgrims thronged the Massabielle rock in response to the water's supposed healing powers. But church authorities reacted skeptically. It took four years of inquiry for the miracle to be authenticated by Rome and a sanctuary erected over the grotto. In 1864 the first organized procession was held. Today there are six official annual pilgrimages, the most important on August 15.

In 1958 Lourdes celebrated the centenary of Bernadette Soubirous's visions by constructing the world's largest underground church, the **Basilique St-Pie X.** The basilica looks more like a parking lot than a church, but it can accommodate 20,000 people—more than the permanent population of the entire town.

Two other **basilicas** stand above St-Pie X: the neo-Byzantine **Basilique Rosaire** (1889) and the tall, white basilica of **Basilique Supérieure** (1871). Both are open throughout the day, but their spiritual function far outweighs their aesthetic appeal.

The **Pavillon Notre-Dame,** across from St-Pie X, houses the **Musée Bernadette,** with mementos of Bernadette's life and an illustrated history of the pilgrimages. In the basement is the **Musée d'Art Sacré du Gemmail** (Museum of Stained-Glass Mosaic Religious Art). *Gemmail* is a modern approach to the stained-glass technique, involving the assembly of broken glass. ⊠ *72 rue de la Grotte,* ☎ *05–62–94–13–15.* 🎫 *Free.* ☉ *July–Nov., daily 9:30–11:45 and 2:30–6:15; Dec.–June, Wed.–Mon. 9:30–11:45 and 2:30–5:45.*

Just across the river is the **Moulin de Boly** (Boly Mill), where Bernadette was born on January 7, 1844. ⊠ *12 rue Bernadette-Soubirous.* 🎫 *Free.* ☉ *Easter–mid-Oct., daily 9:30–11:45 and 2:30–5:45.*

You can also visit the **cachot,** a shabby little room where Bernadette and her family lived. ⊠ *15 rue des Petits-Fossés,* ☎ *05–62–94–51–30.* 🎫 *Free.* ☉ *Easter–mid-Oct., daily 9:30–11:45 and 2:30–5:30; mid-Oct.–Easter, daily 2:30–5:30.*

The **Château** on the hill above town can be reached on foot or by escalator. In the 17th and 18th centuries, the castle was used as a prison; now it contains the **Musée Pyrénéen,** one of France's best provincial museums, devoted to the region's popular customs and arts. ⊠ *25 rue du Fort,* ☎ *05–62–94–02–04.* 🎫 *32 frs.* ☉ *Easter–mid-Oct., daily 9–noon and 2–7 (last admission at 6); mid-Oct.–Easter, Wed.–Mon. 9–noon and 2–7.*

Dining and Lodging

$$ ✕🏨 **Hôtel Albert/La Taverne de Bigorre.** The Moreau family's popular establishment serves traditional French mountain cooking such as the hearty garbure. Rooms are clean and comfortable, with a personal touch that is very welcome in Lourdes. ⊠ *21 pl. du Champ Commun, 65100,* ☎ *05–62–94–75–00,* 📠 *05–62–94–78–45. 27 rooms. Restaurant. AE, DC, MC, V. Closed mid-Nov.–mid-Dec. and Jan.*

Cauterets

⑲ *30 km (19 mi) south of Lourdes, 49 km (30 mi) south of Tarbes.*

Cauterets is a spa-resort town deep in the mountains, where you can sometimes ski until May. Ever since Roman times, Cauterets's thermal springs have been revered as a miracle cure for female sterility. Virile novelist Victor Hugo (1802–85) womanized here, and Lady Aurore

Dudevant—better known as the writer George Sand (1804–76)—discovered her feminism.

En Route South from Cauterets is the Pont d'Espagne, where steep-twisting D920 peters out. Continue on foot or by chairlift to the plateau and a view over the bright blue **Lac de Gaube,** fed by the river of the same name. Return via Cauterets to Pierrefitte-Nestalas and turn right on D921 and the Gorge de Luz to Gavarnie.

Gavarnie

❷ *30 km (19 mi) south of Cauterets on D921, 50 km (31 mi) south of Lourdes.*

The village of Gavarnie is a good base for exploring the mountains in the region. For starters, it is at the foot of the **Cirque de Gavarnie,** one of the world's most remarkable examples of glacial erosion and a daunting challenge to mountaineers. Horses and donkeys, rented in the village, can take you to the head of the valley where the Hôtel du Cirque (☞ Dining and Lodging, *below*) has hosted six generations of visitors. When the upper snows melt, numerous streams tumble down from the cliffs to form spectacular waterfalls; the greatest of them—the **Grande Cascade**—drops nearly 1,400 ft.

Another dramatic sight is 2 km (7 mi) west of the village of Gavarnie. Take D921 up to the Col de Boucharo, where you can park and walk five hours up to the **Brèche de Roland** glacier (you cross it during the last two hours). For a taste of mountain life, have lunch high up in the Club Alpin Français Refuge de Sarradets ou de la Brèche dormitory. This is a serious climb, only feasible from mid-June to mid-September, for which you need hiking equipment and need to be in very good shape. Crampons and ice axes are available for rent in Gavarnie; check with the Gavarnie tourist office for weather reports and for information about guided tours.

Dining and Lodging

$$ ✕ **Hôtel du Cirque.** With its legendary views of the Cirque de Gavarnie, this spot is magic at sunset. Despite its name, it's just a restaurant, but not just any one: The garbure here is as delicious as the sunset. Seventh-generation owner Pierre Vergez claims his recipe using water from the Cirque and *cocos de Tarbes* (Tarbes broad beans) is unique. ⊠ *1-hr walk above the village of Gavarnie, 65120,* ☎ *05–62–92–48–02. Restaurant, bar, café. MC, V. Closed mid-Sept.–mid-June.*

$$ ✕▣ **Hôtel Marboré.** This multigabled house built over a rushing mountain brook offers all the history and tradition of Gavarnie along with delightful creature comforts. Rooms are bright and pleasant and look out onto lush hillside meadows. Owner-manager Roselyne Fillastre is a kind and lively hostess who attends to her guests with great warmth and vivacity. The restaurant, too, is excellent: Look forward to fine cuisine prepared with the freshest ingredients. ⊠ *Village de Gavarnie, 65120,* ☎ *05–62–92–40–40,* ℻ *05–62–92–40–30. 13 rooms. Restaurant. MC, V.*

Nightlife and the Arts

Every July, Gavarnie holds an outdoor ballet and music performance, **La Fête des Pyrénées,** using the Cirque de Gavarnie as a backdrop. Showtime is at sunset. Contact the tourist office (☎ 05–62–92–49–10) for information.

En Route The dramatic mountain scenery is impressive all along D921 between Luz-St-Sauveur and Gavarnie. If you continue east, along D918 toward **Arreau,** the road passes through the lively little spa town of **Barèges** and under the brow of the mighty **Pic du Midi de Bigorre,** a mountain peak towering nearly 10,000 feet above the **Col du Tourmalet** pass. **Luz-St-Sauveur** is 61 km (38 mi) from Arreau along the tortuous twists of the D918. The finest views—and the sharpest curves—are found toward the **Col d'Aspin** pass. Another spectacular road is D618 from Arreau over the **Col de Peyresourde** to Bagnères de Luchon.

Bagnères de Luchon

㉑ *150 km (93 mi) east of Gavarnie.*

The largest and most fashionable Pyrenean spa is Bagnères de Luchon (simply known as Luchon), at the head of a lush valley. The Romans considered Luchon to rank second as a spa only to Naples. Thermal waters here cater to the vocal cords: Opera singers, lawyers, and politicians hoarse from electoral promises all pile in to breathe in the healing vapors.

OFF THE
BEATEN PATH

SUPERBAGNÈRES – Above Luchon is the ski resort of Superbagnères, reached by a serpentine road (D46). On the way up, admire the breathtaking views of the Maladeta Massif and the Pyrénées' highest peak, Aneto (11,165 ft), across the border in Spain.

St-Bertrand de Comminges

㉒ *32 km (20 mi) north of Bagnères de Luchon, 57 km (35 mi) southeast of Tarbes, 107 km (66 mi) southwest of Toulouse.*

A Roman road led directly from Luchon to St-Bertrand de Comminges (then a huge town of 60,000). This delightful village, whose inhabitants number just 500 today, is dwarfed beneath the imposing, (mostly) 12th-century **Cathédrale Ste-Marie.** Old houses, sloping alleyways, and crafts shops add to the charm.

PAYS BASQUE, BÉARN, AND THE HAUTES-PYRÉNÉES A TO Z

Arriving and Departing

By Car

A64 connects Pau and Bayonne in under an hour, and A63 runs up and down the Atlantic coast. National Route 117 connects Hendaye with Toulouse via Pau and Tarbes. National Route 134 connects Bordeaux, Pau, Oloron-Ste-Marie, and Spain via the Col de Somport and Jaca.

By Plane

Biarritz–Parme Airport (☎ 05–59–43–83–83) serves Bayonne and Biarritz and has several daily flights to and from Paris, and several weekly to London, Marseille, Geneva, Lyon, Nice, and Pau. **Pau-Pyrénées International Airport** (☎ 05–59–33–33–00) has 10 flights daily to and from Paris as well as flights to Nantes, Lyon, Marseille, Nice, Biarritz, Madrid, Rome, Venice, Milan, and Geneva. **Air France** (☎ 05–59–27–27–28) flies from Paris and other major European destinations to Biarritz and Pau.

By Train

High-speed trains (TGV, *Trains à Grande Vitesse*) cover the 800 km (500 mi) from Paris to Bayonne in 4½ hours. To get to Pau, take the TGV to Bordeaux (3 hours) and connect to Pau (2 hours). Bayonne and Toulouse are connected by local SNCF trains via Pau, Tarbes,

Lourdes, Lannemezan, and St-Gaudens. A local express runs along the Nive from Bayonne to St-Jean-Pied-de-Port stopping at 12 stations along the way.

Getting Around

By Car
Roads are occasionally slow and tortuous in the mountains, but valley and riverside roads are generally smoother. D132, which goes between Arette and Pierre-St-Martin, can get snowed in between mid-November and Mid-May, as can N134 through the Valley d'Aspe and the Col de Somport into Spain.

By Plane
Air Inter (☎ 05−59−33−34−35) flies to Pau, Bayonne, Biarritz. **Air Littoral** (☎ 05−59−33−26−64) flies between Biarritz, Pau, Toulouse, Nice, and Marseille.

By Train
Bayonne is the central train hub; the TGV arrives here from Paris. Local trains go between Bayonne and Biarritz and from Bayonne into the Atlantic Pyrénées; the trip is slower but very picturesque. Hendaye is connected to Bayonne and to San Sebastián via the famous "*topo*" (mole) train, so called for the number of tunnels it passes through.

Contacts and Resources

Car Rental
Car rental agencies at **Biarritz-Parme airport** include the following: Alfa Citer (☎ 05−59−23−67−95); ALS Eurorent (☎ 05−59−23−05−96); Avis (☎ 05−59−23−67−92); Budget (☎ 05−59−23−58−62); Eurodollar (☎ 05−59−41−21−12); Europcar (☎ 05−59−23−90−68); and Hertz (☎ 05−59−43−92−92). Car rentals at **Bayonne SNCF station** are as follows: Alfa Citer (☎ 05−59−55−10−50), Ada Location (☎ 05−59−55−71−96); Aquitaine Location (☎ 05−59−55−30−55); and Europcar (☎ 05−59−55−38−20). At **Hendaye:** Avis (☎ 05−59−20−79−04). **St-Jean-de-Luz:** Avis (☎ 05−59−26−76−66). Rental agencies at **Pau−Pyrénées International airport** include the following: Alfa Citer (☎ 05−59−33−25−00); Avis (☎ 05−59−33−27−13); Budget (☎ 05−59−33−77−45); Europcar (☎ 05−59−33−24−31); and Hertz (☎ 05−59−33−16−38).

Guided Tours
In Biarritz, **Aitzin** (☎ 05−59−24−36−05) organizes tours of Bayonne, Biarritz, the Basque coast, and the Basque Pyrénées. The **Association des Guides** (☎ 05−59−30−44−01) in Pau arranges tours with guides of the city, the Pyrénées, and Béarn and Basque Country. The **Bayonne Tourist Office** (☎ 05−59−46−01−46) gives guided tours of the city. **Guides Culturels Pyrénéens** (☎ 05−62−44−15−44) in Tarbes arranges a variety of tours, including such themes as cave painting, art and architecture, Basque sports, hiking, and horseback riding.

Travel Agencies
Bayonne: Agence Garrouste (✉ 10 rue Thiers, ☎ 05−59−59−02−35); Havas Voyages (✉ 5 rue Lormand, ☎ 05−59−46−29−26). **Biarritz**: Adour Voyages (✉ 3 rue Gardères, ☎ 05−59−24−14−25); Saga Tours (✉ 4 av. du Maréchal-Foch, ☎ 05−59−24−39−39). **Lourdes**: L'Accueil Pyrénéen (✉ 26 av. Maransin, ☎ 05−62−94−15−62); American Express (✉ 14 Chausée du Bourg, ☎ 05−62−94−40−84; note that they receive mail but don't do any banking transactions); Maison du Pélerin (✉ 12 av. Maransin, ☎ 05−62−94−70−05). **Pau**: Havas Voy-

ages (⊠ pl. Clemenceau, ☎ 05–59–27–86–86); **Sud Ouest Agence des Voyages** (⊠ 11 rue Maréchal-Foch, ☎ 05–59–27–16–88).

Visitor Information

The addresses of tourist offices in towns mentioned in this chapter are as follows: **Bayonne** (⊠ pl. des Basques, ☎ 05–59–46–01–46). **Biarritz** (⊠ 1 square Ixelles, ☎ 05–59–23–37–00). **Gavarnie** (⊠ In center of village, ☎ 05–62–92–49–10). **Lourdes** (⊠ pl. Beyramalu, ☎ 05–62–42–77–40). **Pau** (⊠ pl. Royale, ☎ 05–59–27–27–08). **St-Jean-de-Luz** (⊠ pl. Foch, ☎ 05–59–26–03–16). **St-Jean-Pied-de-Port** (⊠ 14 pl. Charles-de-Gaulle, ☎ 05–59–37–03–57).

17 Poitou-Charentes, Périgord, and Northern Aquitaine

Bordeaux, La Rochelle, and St-Émilion

Let the vast beaches near Royan, the waterways of "Green Venice," and the famed vineyards of Médoc draw you to this region along the Atlantic coast. Inland, see castles and châteaux recalling medieval battles, and Romanesque abbeys and cathedrals echoing with history. Sip splendid wine with oysters in Bordeaux and savor Périgord truffles and foie gras.

Revised and
updated by
Simon Hewitt

IF THERE'S A FORMULA FOR ENJOYING this region, it should include exploring cultural spots, relaxing by the sea, tasting wine, and eating oysters, truffles, and foie gras. Swaths of sandy beaches line the Atlantic coast: Well-heeled resorts, like Royan and Arcachon, are thronged with glistening bodies baking in the sun. The world-famous vineyards of Médoc, Sauternes, Graves, Entre-Deux-Mers, and St-Émilion surround the elegant 18th-century city of Bordeaux.

But if you prefer solitude, you won't have any trouble discovering vast, underpopulated stretches inland in Poitou-Charentes and Périgord. Between La Rochelle and Poitiers lies the Marais Poitevin, a marshy area known as Green Venice for its crisscrossing small canals. The rolling countryside of Périgord and Limousin—often referred to as the Dordogne for the river that flows through it—is chockful of riverside châteaux, medieval villages, and prehistoric sites.

For three centuries during the Middle Ages, this region was a battlefield in the wars between the French and the English. Of the castles and châteaux dotting the area, those at Biron, Hautefort, and Beynac are among the best. Robust Romanesque architecture is more characteristic of this area than the airy Gothic style found elsewhere in France: Poitiers showcases the best examples, notably Notre-Dame-la-Grande, with its richly worked facade, though the Romanesque can also be admired at the nearby abbey of St-Savin, and at Angoulême and Périgueux.

Pleasures and Pastimes

Beaches

French families concentrate on the resort towns of Royan and Arcachon, but there are plenty of other huge beaches where you can escape the crowds: along the forest-girdled Côte Sauvage (Wild Coast) north of Royan; along the coast of the islands of Ré, Aix, and Oléron; and beneath the huge dunes south of Arcachon.

Boat Trips

Although the region's two main islands, the Ile de Ré and the Ile d'Oléron, are now linked to the mainland by bridges, boats still ply the Atlantic waters south of La Rochelle, visiting Fort Boyard and docking at the Ile d'Aix. Explore the oyster beds of the Baie de Seudre or make an excursion across the Gironde to the Coubre lighthouse, stranded on a sandbank in mid-estuary. Ferries ply the Gironde from Royan and Blaye; punts, steered with long poles, float peacefully along the canals of the Marais Poitevin; and the Dordogne River is a favorite with canoers.

Dining

Truffles, foie gras, walnuts, plums, trout, eel, oysters, and myriad succulent species of mushrooms jostle for attention on restaurant menus. The hearty food of Périgord, the rich dairy produce of Poitou, and shoals of succulent seafood from the Atlantic make for diversified tables. The versatile wines of Bordeaux make fine accompaniments to most regional dishes. Cognac is de rigueur at the end of a meal, sweet tangy pineau—made from cognac and unfermented grape juice—at the start.

CATEGORY	COST*
$$$$	over 400 frs
$$$	250 frs–400 frs
$$	125 frs–250 frs
$	under 125 frs

*per person for a three-course meal, including tax (20.6%) and tip but not wine

Lodging

Vacationers flock to the coast and islands, and for miles around, hotels are booked solid months in advance. Farther inland—except for the Dordogne Valley—the situation is easier, but there aren't as many places to stay. Advance booking is particularly desirable in Bordeaux and Périgord, where hotels fill up quickly in midsummer. Many country or small-town hotels expect you to have at least one dinner there, and, if you can have two meals a day with lodging and stay several nights, it will save you money. Prices off-season (October–May) often drop as much as 20%.

CATEGORY	COST*
$$$$	over 800 frs
$$$	600 frs–800 frs
$$	300 frs–600 frs
$	under 300 frs

All prices are for a standard double room for two, including tax (20.6%) and service charge.

Wine

No other part of France has such a concentrated wealth of top-class vineyards. The versatile Bordeaux region yields sweet and dry whites and fruity or full-bodied reds from a huge domain extending either side of the Gironde (Blaye and Bourg to the north, Médoc to the south), and inland along the Garonne (Sauternes) and Dordogne (St-Émilion, Fronsac, Pomerol) or in between these two rivers (Entre-Deux-Mers). Farther north, the rolling hills of Cognac produce the world's finest brandy. Less familiar appellations are also worth seeking out, including Bergerac, Pécharmant, and Monbazillac along the Dordogne, and the lighter whites and reds of the Fiefs Vendéens, northeast of La Rochelle.

Exploring Poitou-Charentes, Périgord, and Northern Aquitaine

The rural region of Poitou-Charentes, to the north, stretches from Poitiers through the canals around Niort to the seacoast town of La Rochelle and back through Cognac country to Angoulême. To the southeast are the medieval villages, cliff-top châteaux, and prehistoric sites of Périgord and Limousin. To the west, in northern Aquitaine (the Roman name for Land of Water), lies the city of Bordeaux and the surrounding vineyards.

Great Itineraries

To see all of the region in one trip would be over-ambitious, so you need to be selective about where you go. If you love the beach and the outdoors, head to the Royan peninsula or the islands of Ré and Oléron. If you're a gourmet, go straight to the Dordogne; if wine is your passion, use Bordeaux as your base. For nature, seek out the Marais-Poitevin. Following are some suggested itineraries.

Numbers in the text correspond to numbers in the margin and on the Poitou-Charentes, Périgord, and Northern Aquitaine map.

IF YOU HAVE 4 DAYS

Begin in **Poitiers** ①, known for its Romanesque cathedral and an easy hour's drive from the Loire Valley—add another hour if you are coming from Paris. Try to get to ⊞ **Cognac** ⑩ or ⊞ **Jarnac** ⑪ by afternoon, so that you have time to visit a *chais*, or brandy warehouse. The following day enter Périgord via hilltop **Angoulême** ⑫ and quaint **Brantôme** ⑭. Rest up in ⊞ **Hautefort** ⑯ or the medieval market town of ⊞ **Sarlat-la-Canéda** ⑲. The next day follow the Dordogne River to ⊞ **La**

Roque-Gageac ㉑, huddled beneath a towering gray cliff—make it your base for exploring the castle at **Beynac** ㉒, the fortified medieval village of **Monpazier** ㉓, the hilltop château in **Biron** ㉔, the cave paintings at the **Grotte de Lascaux** ⑰, or the Musée Nationale de Préhistoire in **Les Eyzies-de-Tayac** ⑱. On the fourth day, lunch in medieval **St-Émilion** ㉞ and end the day in ▦ **Bordeaux** ㉖–㉜.

IF YOU HAVE 6 DAYS

Follow the four-day itinerary to ▦ **Bordeaux** ㉖–㉜. On the fifth day, visit the Médoc vineyards near Bordeaux or the beaches around **Arcachon** ㊱; then return to Bordeaux for another night. The next morning, head north through the Médoc vineyards and cross the Gironde estuary to **Royan** ㉝; then drive up to ▦ **La Rochelle** ④, stopping for lunch in **Brouage** ⑦. On day six, explore the **Marais Poitevin** ③ and the archaeology and fine arts museums in **Niort** ②.

When to Tour Poitou-Charentes, Périgord, and Northern Aquitaine

Spring and autumn are the best times to visit—there aren't as many tourists around and the weather is still pleasant. The *vendanges* (grape harvests) usually begin about mid-September in the Bordeaux region (though you can't visit the wineries at this time), and a fortnight later in the Cognac region to the north. A number of hotels close from the end of October through March.

POITOU-CHARENTES

Occupying the northern part of the region, this area known as Poitou-Charentes extends from Poitiers to the coastal towns of La Rochelle and Brouage and south to the Gironde Estuary. Between Niort and La Rochelle lies the marshy region of the Marais Poitevin.

Poitiers

★ ❶ *340 km (212 mi) southwest of Paris, 100 km (62 mi) south of Tours, 120 km (75 mi) northwest of Limoges.*

Thanks to its majestic hilltop setting above the River Clain and its position halfway along the Bordeaux–Paris trade route, Poitiers became an important commercial, religious, and university town in the Middle Ages. Life quieted down after the 17th century, but tranquillity has resulted in excellent architectural preservation.

The church of **Notre-Dame-la-Grande,** in the town center, is an impressive example of the Romanesque architecture so common in western France. Its 12th-century facade is framed by rounded arches and decorated with a multitude of bas-reliefs and sculptures while its dark interior is enlivened with reproduction murals painted in the mid-19th century to brighten the church. ⊠ *rue des Cordeliers.*

The **Cathédrale de St-Pierre,** a few hundred yards beyond Notre-Dame-la-Grande, was built from the 12th to the 14th century. The largest church in Poitiers, it has a distinctive facade marked by two asymmetrical towers. The imposing interior is noted for its 13th-century stained glass and 13th-century wooden choir stalls, thought to be the oldest in France. ⊠ *pl. de la Cathédrale.*

The **Musée Ste-Croix,** in a modern building off rue Jean-Jaurès, houses archaeological discoveries, traditional regional crafts, and European paintings from the 15th to the 19th century of good, though not outstanding, quality. The museum is part of a triad of museums. The **Musée de Chièvres** (⊠ 9 rue Victor-Hugo, ☎ 05–49–41–42–21) displays

Poitou-Charentes, Périgord, and Northern Aquitaine

Renaissance furniture, ceramics, and old master paintings. The **Hypogée Martyrium** (⊠ 44 rue du Père-de-la-Croix, ☎ 05–49–01–68–85) is a subterranean chapel with ancient sarcophagi and sculptures. ⊠ *61 rue St-Simplicien,* ☎ *05–49–41–07–53.* 🖼 *15 frs (includes the museums of Chièvres and Hypogée); free Tues.* ☉ *All museums Tues.– Fri. 10–noon and 1–5, weekends 10–noon and 2–6.*

Next to the Musée Ste-Croix is the 4th-century **Baptistère St-Jean,** the oldest Christian building in France. Its heavy stone bulk, some 12 ft beneath ground level, includes a rectangular baptismal chamber; go inside to see the octagonal basin for baptism by total immersion. ⊠ *rue Jean-Jaurès.* 🖼 *5 frs.* ☉ *Easter–Oct., daily 10–12:30 and 2–4:30; Nov.–Easter, Thurs.–Tues. 2–4:30.*

The oldest of Poitiers's churches is **St-Hilaire-le-Grand,** part of which dates from the early 11th century. Inside, a semicircular, mosaic-floor choir rises high above the level of the nave, and striking frescoes ornament the chapels around the east end. ⊠ *rue St-Hilaire.*

At **Futuroscope,** just north of Poitiers, you can experience futuristic thrills in "simulated seating" (which moves, tilts, and jolts) and interactive cinema. ⊠ *Poitiers (Exit 18 off A10),* ☎ *05–49–49–30–80.* 🖼 *140– 185 frs according to season.* ☉ *Mid-June–Aug., weekdays 9–6, weekends 9 AM–11 PM; Apr.–mid-June and Sept.–Oct., weekends 9 AM– 11 PM.*

Dining and Lodging

$$ ✕ **Maxime.** Reasonable prix-fixe menus and chef Christian Rougier's cooking have made Maxime a crowd-pleaser. Enjoy foie gras and duck salad in the pastel dining room lined with '30s-style frescoes. ⊠ *4 rue St-Nicolas,* ☎ *05–49–41–09–55. Reservations essential. AE, MC, V. Closed weekends and most of July–Aug.*

$$ 🏨 **Europe.** An early 19th-century building with a modern extension houses this unpretentious hotel in the middle of town. Because it is off the main street and has a forecourt, rooms are quiet. There is also a pleasant garden in the back for an afternoon tea or an evening aperitif. ⊠ *39 rue Carnot, 86000,* ☎ *05–49–88–12–00,* FAX *05–49–88–97–30. 88 rooms. MC, V.*

Nightlife and the Arts

For a night of dancing, head to **Black House** (⊠ 195 av. du 8-mai-1945, ☎ 05–49–57–08–21). **La Grand'Goule** (⊠ 46 rue du Pigeon-Blanc, ☎ 05–49–50–41–36) is a split-level disco with good ambience. At **Le Théâtre Scène Nationale de Poitiers** (⊠ 1 pl. du Maréchal-Leclerc, ☎ 05–49–41–28–33), mainly French works are performed.

OFF THE BEATEN PATH
ST-SAVIN – The tiny village of St-Savin (40 km/25 mi east of Poitiers via N151) is famous for its impressively large medieval abbey. Inside the 11th-century **Abbaye de St-Savin,** carved monsters run riot on the column capitals, and well-preserved paintings, dating from the building's construction, decorate the walls. Swaying folds of cloth and enormous hands lend life to the biblical figures.

Niort

❷ *74 km (46 mi) southwest of Poitiers via A10, 125 km (83 mi) southeast of Nantes.*

Niort is a complacent, middle-class town best known as the capital of the French insurance industry. But the remains of its medieval fortress and its two museums—archaeology and fine arts—make it worth a stop. All that is left of the Plantagenet Castle built at the end of the 12th century by English kings Henry II and Richard the Lionhearted is the massive *donjon* (keep), with its two square towers dominating the River Sèvre. Inside is a museum with an extensive collection of arms and local costumes. ⊠ *rue Duguesclin,* ☎ *05–49–28–14–28.* 🎫 *20 frs.* ☉ *Apr.–Oct., Wed.–Mon. 9–noon and 2–6; Nov.–Mar., Wed.–Mon. 9–noon and 2–5.*

Just off rue Victor-Hugo is the old town hall, a triangular building completed in 1535. It now houses the **Musée du Pilori,** with a collection of local archaeological finds and Renaissance artifacts. The highlight is an ebony chest encrusted with gold and silver. ⊠ *pl. du Pilori,* ☎ *05–49–28–51–73.* 🎫 *15 frs.* ☉ *Apr.–Oct., Wed.–Mon. 9–noon and 2–6; Nov.–Mar., Wed.–Mon. 9–noon and 2–5.*

On rue St-Jean, the oldest street in Niort, is the **Musée des Beaux-Arts** (Fine Arts Museum), where tapestries, gold and enamelware, and 17th- to 18th-century paintings are on display. ⊠ *rue St-Jean,* ☎ *05–49–24–97–84.* 🎫 *21 frs.* ☉ *Wed.–Mon. 9–noon and 2–6.*

In Échiré, north of Niort, the **Laiterie Co-opérative** (Cooperative Dairy) makes some of the best butter in the world.

The Marais Poitevin

★ ❸ *Coulon is 11 km (7 mi) west of Niort; Maillezais is 29 km (18 mi) west of Niort.*

Coulon is the best base for exploring the Marais Poitevin—France's "Green Venice"—an extraordinary region of canals and lush fields. Willow, ash, and alder trees line the rivers and canals of the Marais; artichokes, onions, melons, and garlic are grown in the fields alongside. The only way to explore the Marais proper is by rowboat—or, more typically, on a *pigouille* (a flat, narrow boat maneuvered with a long pole), which you can find in Coulon. They cost about 90 francs per hour per boat, maximum six persons, or you can hire a boat with a guide (for 45 minutes at 120 francs). If your French is decent, you'll get an earful of local lore as well as a ride. The town also has a lovely medieval church and a delightful, privately run folk museum, the **Musée Maraichin** (⊠ rue de l'Église). There are no regular hours: Just show up and see if it's open; donations are accepted.

In the countryside northwest of Coulon, there is little but the occasional pretty village—**Maillezais** (18 km/11 mi northwest) is one of these. The main reason to come here is to see the ruins of its abbey. Maillezais used to be a bishop's seat and a powerful Benedictine monastery, but all that remains of the **Abbaye de Maillezais** are the 14th-century cloister and refectory, the 11th-century porch, and the 15th-century transept. ☎ *05–51–00–70–11.* 🎟 *16 frs.* ☉ *Nov.–Mar., Fri.–Wed. 9–12:30 and 2–6; Apr.–Oct., daily 9–8.*

Dining and Lodging

$–$$ ✕🏠 **Au Marais.** The Merrières' small, waterside inn and restaurant is delightful. Light, regional fare, with prix-fixe menus of 95 francs and 150 francs, is served in the restaurant (closed Sunday dinner and Monday). Sample the succulent mussels in dill sauce or the veal chops in Madeira sauce, and, for dessert, the crunchy crème brûlée. Rooms are plain yet clean and reasonably priced. ⊠ *48 quai Louis-Tardy, 79510 Coulon,* ☎ *05–49–35–90–43,* 🆒 *05–49–35–81–98. 11 rooms. Restaurant. MC, V. Closed mid-Nov.–mid-Mar.*

Outdoor Activities and Sports

One of the best ways to explore the area is by bicycle (a detailed map is advisable), rented from **La Libellule** (⊠ 94 quai Louis-Tardy, Coulon, ☎ 05–49–35–83–42).

En Route Between Maillezais and the Atlantic Coast, the **Marais Mouillé** (Wet Marsh) gradually dries up and a flat, barren, eerie landscape appears: the **Marais Desséché** (Dry Marsh). To get to the coast from Maillezais, head south along D15, then turn right after La Ronde onto narrow D262, which hugs the straight banks of the Canal de la Branche as far as Marans, once a thriving seaport but now linked to the sea only by canal. D105 sneaks seaward from Marans. At the first major crossroad, 8 km (5 mi) past Marans, turn left along D9 toward La Rochelle, 16 km (10 mi) away.

La Rochelle

❹ *48 km (30 mi) southwest of Maillezais, 64 km (40 mi) southwest of Niort.*

La Rochelle is an appealing town, a vibrant collection of the old and the new. Its ancient streets are off its harbor, the picturesque Vieux Port. Standing sentinel on either side of the port are two fortresslike 14th-century *tours* (towers) known as **Tour de la Chaîne** (to the right) and **Tour St-Nicolas** (to the left)—climb to the top for a view of the bay toward the Ile d'Aix. ☒ *Each tower 18 frs.* ☉ *Mid-Feb.–mid-Nov., daily 10–noon and 2–6; mid-Nov.–mid-Feb., daily 2–6.*

From the towers, follow the western wall of the Vieux Port to cours des Dames, a spacious avenue lined with sturdy trees and 18th-century houses. It leads to the **Porte de la Grosse Horloge** (Gate of the Big Clock), a massive stone gate marking the entrance to the narrow, bustling streets of the old town. From the gate, head down rue du Palais and onto rue Gargoulleau: Halfway down on the left is the 18th-century Bishop's Palace, now the **Musée des Beaux-Arts** (Museum of Fine Arts). ☒ *28 rue Gargoulleau,* ☎ *05–46–41–64–65.* ☒ *18 frs.* ☉ *Mon. and Wed.–Sat.10:30–12:30 and 1:30–6, Sun. 3–6.*

The **Muséum d'Histoire Naturelle** (Museum of Natural History), housed in an elegant mansion, contains extensive collections of rocks, coral, and shell work. Other items range from a tribal idol from Easter Island to a giraffe (now stuffed) given as a gift to King Charles X (reigned 1824–30). ☒ *28 rue Albert-I,* ☎ *05–46–41–18–25.* ☒ *18 frs.* ☉ *Apr.– Oct., Tues.–Sun. 10–noon and 2–6; Nov.–Mar., Tues.–Sat. 10–noon and 2–5, Sun. 2–5.*

Not far from the Bishop's Palace is an 18th-century building containing the **Musée du Nouveau-Monde** (New World Museum). Old maps, engravings, watercolors, and even wallpaper evoke the commercial links between La Rochelle and the New World. ☒ *10 rue Fleuriau,* ☎ *05– 46–41–46–50.* ☒ *18 frs.* ☉ *Wed.–Mon. 10:30–12:30 and 1:30–6, Sun. 3–6.*

In summer, boats operated by Ré Croisières leave La Rochelle harbor daily for cruises to the nearby **îles** (islands): **Ile de Ré, Ile d'Aix,** and **Fort Boyard.** ☒ *Buy tickets from Agence de La Rochelle, Bassin d'É-chouage, Vieux Port,* ☎ *05–07–65–43–42 or 05–46–09–39–00.* ☒ *Round-trip: Ile de Ré, 75 frs; Ile d'Aix and Fort Boyard, 96 frs.*

Dining and Lodging

$–$$ ✕ **André.** The salty decor is somewhat excessive—fishing nets and posters of ocean liners—but the food and service have so much gusto that you'll be caught up in the mood, especially if you order the monumental seafood platter and wash it down with white Charentes wine. ☒ *5 rue St-Jean,* ☎ *05–46–41–28–24. AE, DC, MC, V.*

$–$$ ✕ **Les Quatre Sergents.** On a street in the north side of the Vieux Port, where good restaurants abound, this place serves delightful, traditional seafood with distinctive sauces. Plants grow in every nook and cranny, shielding one table from another—it's like dining in a winter garden. ☒ *49 rue St-Jean du Pérot,* ☎ *05–46–41–35–80. AE, DC, MC, V. Closed Mon. No dinner Sun.*

$ ✕ **Pub Lutèce.** More of a brasserie than a pub, this cheerful spot with brass rails and comfortable banquettes serves good, inexpensive food from mussels to confit *de canard* (of duck). Conversation and bustle are as much the reason for coming as the wholesome fare. ☒ *6 bis rue St-Sauveur,* ☎ *05–46–41–40–80. MC, V.*

$$ 🏨 **Hôtel de la Monnaie.** This 17th-century house by the Vieux Port has a wonderful lobby and cobblestone courtyard. Rooms are less inspiring; the quietest overlook the courtyard. Bathrooms have a tub and hand-held shower. Free parking is available adjacent to the hotel, a definite plus as it's only a few minutes' walk from the harbor and town. ☒ *3 rue de la Monnaie, 17000,* ☎ *05–46–50–65–65,* FAX *05–46–50–63–19. 32 rooms, 4 suites. Free parking. AE, DC, MC, V.*

$$ 🏠 **33 rue Thiers.** Amiable Maybelle Iribe, an expatriate American who
★ has a wealth of local knowledge, owns this inn in a private town house.
With advance notice, she will prepare a splendid dinner from fresh market products. You're likely to eat in the kitchen and, if you want, pick
up some cooking tips (Maybelle teaches cooking classes). Rooms are
large and wonderfully furnished, expressing the owner's idiosyncrasies:
The Mexican Room is gaily decorated with cheerful colors; the Blue
Room is also a delight. ⊠ *33 rue Thiers, 17000,* ☎ *05–46–41–62–
23,* FAX *05–46–41–10–76. 8 rooms. Dining room. MC, V.*

$$ 🏠 **Tour de Nesle.** This 19th-century hotel is around the corner from
quai Valin. Rooms are a bit cramped but up-to-date; some have a view
across the canal. Breakfast is served. ⊠ *2 quai Louis-Durand, 17000,*
☎ *05–46–41–30–72,* FAX *05–46–41–95–17. 28 rooms. Breakfast
room. MC, V.*

Outdoor Activities and Sports

A good way to get around town is on a bicycle; rent one from the
Boobaloo (⊠ promenade de la Concurrence, ☎ 05–46–41–02–24).
Held over Pentecost, La Rochelle's major festival, the **Fêtes de la Mer,**
is a celebration inspired by the sea, with regattas and sailboats on display in the harbor.

Shopping

La Rochelle will impress you as more than a port town if you are here
on a Wednesday or Saturday for the **market** in the old town.

Ile de Ré

❺ *11 km (7 mi) west of La Rochelle.*

A bridge (round-trip toll is 112 francs) curves across from La Rochelle
to the cheerful Ile de Ré, just 26 km (16 mi) long and never more than
6 km (4 mi) wide. Vineyards sweep over the eastern part of the island
while oyster beds straddle the shallow waters to the west. The first village on the north coast reached from the mainland is **La Flotte.** The
rectangular harbor hiding tiny fishing boats is surrounded by sturdy
houses ready to stand against Atlantic gales. Ten kilometers (6 miles)
farther on is the largest village on the island, **St-Martin de Ré** (population 3,000). It has a lively harbor and a citadel built by ace military
architect Sébastien de Vauban in 1681. Many of its streets also date
from the 17th century, and the villagers' low, white houses are typical
of that period. **Ars,** a smaller village 10 km (6 mi) farther west, has a
black-and-white church spire and a cute harbor. If you go all the way
to the northwestern end of Ile de Ré, be sure to climb up the **Phare de
la Baleine** (Whale Lighthouse) for sweeping views of the Atlantic. At
its foot is the Café de la Phare, which has a surprising Art Deco setting
full of artsy '30s lamps and serves a good *poutargue,* a local specialty made from smoked cod roe and accompanied by shallots and
sour cream.

Dining and Lodging

$$$ ✕🏠 **Le Richelieu.** Eat chef Dominique Bourgeois's seafood as you gaze
at the ocean. Let lobster and smoked oysters spark your taste buds for
the excellent grilled turbot in beurre blanc and superb wine. Guest rooms
are innocuously furnished but have all the amenities, from bathrobes
to balconies. A separate building houses masseurs, beauticians, and thalassotherapy equipment. A beach fronts the hotel, but it's better for
strolling than lounging. ⊠ *44 av. de la Plage, 17630 La Flotte-en-Ré,*
☎ *05–46–09–60–70,* FAX *05–46–09–50–59. 45 rooms. Restaurant,
pool, beauty salon, massage, spa, 2 tennis courts, beach. AE, DC, MC,
V. Closed early Jan.–mid-Feb.*

Rochefort

❻ *32 km (20 mi) south of La Rochelle via N137.*

Rochefort was built from scratch in the 1660s as a naval base for Louis XIV's fleet to defend France's Atlantic coast from English attack. The extraordinary **Corderie Royale** facing the Charente River—a 400-yard-long building used for making ship ropes—dates from that time. The stately 17th-century **Église St-Louis** (Church of St-Louis) has a classical interior and a majestic Corinthian portico. The town acquired more recent fame as scene of the French movie industry's best-loved musical, Jacques Demy's *Les Demoiselles de Rochefort,* starring Gene Kelly and Catherine Deneuve. Much of the action takes place on the main square, **place Colbert**; the opening titles were shot at the **pont Transbordeur,** a magnificent turn-of-the-century iron transporter bridge just south of the town, the last of its kind in France to remain operational before being replaced by a modern road bridge in the late 1960s.

Although his books are little known to English speakers, don't miss the former home of Pierre Loti (1850–1923). As befits a son of Rochefort, Loti was an avid sailor and explorer, and his exotic tales are reflected in the **Maison Pierre-Loti.** From the outside, this looks just like any other house in an unremarkable street. Inside, however, not only is it full of Persian silks and Turkish silverware, but, using Arabic arches and carved ceilings, entire rooms have been transformed into chambers from a mosque or an Ottoman palace. ⊠ *141 rue Pierre-Loti,* ☎ *05–46–99–16–88.* 🎫 *30 frs.* ☼ *Apr.–Sept., Mon. and Wed.–Sat. 10–noon and 2–5, Sun. 2–5; Oct.–Mar., Wed.–Mon. 2–4.*

Brouage

❼ *12 km (7 mi) southwest of Rochefort via D3.*

The ancient town of Brouage's 17th-century walls loom sullenly above deserted marshland. Samuel de Champlain, who founded Québec in 1608, was born in Brouage—then a major port. Stroll around the walls for a view across the marsh toward the sea—now more than 3 km (2 mi) away—and then visit the village church to learn more of Champlain's tale. You can muse on the fate of Louis XIV's sweetheart Marie Mancini, who retired here in 1659 after learning that her regal suitor had wed the Infanta of Spain for reasons of state.

Ile d'Oléron

❽ *16 km (10 mi) southwest of Brouage via D3/D26.*

Sand dunes ring the Ile d'Oléron (Oléron Island) to the north and west. Oyster beds line the eastern shores, notably along the **Route des Huîtres** (Oyster Road). South of this road is the **Château d'Oléron,** a ruined 17th-century castle.

En Route Back on the mainland, stop briefly in **Marennes,** facing Ile d'Oléron, to climb its elegant 250-ft church spire for a fine view of Oléron and the Atlantic on one side, and the **Baie de Seudre** (Bay of the Seudre) on the other. Then take the toll bridge across the bay and head left to **La Tremblade,** where boats leave daily in summer for tours of the bay and islands. Oyster beds line the bay and, armed with a good map (best is the blue IGN map no. 1332 ET), you can explore the shantylike arrays of brightly colored huts and fishing boats used by oyster farmers at **Arvert** and **Chaillevette.** Don't miss the picturesque village of **Mornac,** with its foursquare tower and tumbling main street. **Saujon,** at the foot of the bay, is home to a steam train that chugs up a disused branch line to La Tremblade on summer Sundays. From Saujon, take N150 24 km (15 mi) northeast to Saintes.

Saintes

9 *24 km (15 mi) northeast of Saujon via N150, 40 km (25 mi) southeast of Rochefort, 138 km (86 mi) southwest of Poitiers.*

On the banks of the River Charente, Saintes is a city of stately serenity, littered with religious edifices and Roman ruins dating from the 1st century. Saintes owes its development to the salt marshes that first attracted the Romans to the area some 2,000 years ago. The Romans left their mark with the impressive **Arènes** (Amphitheater). There are several better-preserved examples in France, but few as old. You'll find it to the west of the town center, close to the church of St-Eutrope with its mighty spire. The **Arc de Germanicus,** built in AD 19 on the banks of the Charente, is another grand Roman vestige.

Climbing above the red roofs of the old town is the **Cathédrale St-Pierre,** which seems to stagger beneath the weight of its stocky tower. Engineering caution foiled plans for the traditional pointed spire, so the tower was given a shallow dome—incongruous, perhaps, but distinctive. The austere 16th-century interior is lined with circular pillars of formidable circumference. The narrow pedestrian-only streets clustered around the cathedral contrast with the broad boulevards that slice through the town and over the river. ✉ *pl. du Synode.*

Saintes's ecclesiastical pride and joy is the **Abbaye aux Dames** (Women's Abbey), consecrated in 1047. The abbey church is fronted by an exquisite, intricately carved, arcaded facade. Although the Romanesque choir remains largely in its original form, the rest of the interior is less harmonious, as the abbey fell on hard times after the death of the last abbess—the 30th—in 1792. It became a prison, then a barracks, and now it is a cultural center for expositions. The brasserie opposite the abbey portals has inexpensive lunch menus (65–100 francs). ✉ *7 pl. de l'Abbaye,* ☎ *05–46–97–48–48.* ⏱ *June–Sept., daily 10–12:30 and 2–7; Oct.–May, Wed. and Sat. 10–12:30 and 2–7, Thurs.–Fri. and Sun.–Tues. 2–7; closed Dec.*

Dining and Lodging

$$$ ✗▥ **Relais du Bois St-Georges.** Rooms in this hotel vary; some have contemporary furnishings, others traditional; some are miniduplexes with loft beds, others small with fold-down beds (one is named "Count de Monte Cristo's Prison Cell"); many have separate sitting areas. Service is enthusiastic because the staff has input in running the hotel. The restaurant looks out over the gardens and a lake. Specialties from the Charente region and seafood become eye-catching creations in the hands of chef Jérôme Emery. ✉ *Le Pinier, rte. de Royan, 17100,* ☎ *05–46–93–50–99,* ℻ *05–46–93–34–93. 27 rooms, 3 suites. Restaurant, bar, indoor pool, croquet, meeting rooms. MC, V.*

$$–$$$ ✗▥ **Moulin de Marcouze.** You, too, can feast like a brandy baron—if
★ you make the 30-minute drive from Saintes to Mosnac, where an old watermill has been transformed into a sophisticated restaurant. The style is understated: spacious layout, artwork, and food that is innovative but not flashy (sautéed sole fillet or duck pie with truffles). At midday, local executives come for power lunches; dinner is more peaceful. ✉ *rte. de St-Georges, 17240 Mosnac (33 km/20 mi south of Saintes, 34 km/21 mi southwest of Cognac),* ☎ *05–46–70–46–16,* ℻ *05–46–70–48–14. 10 rooms. Restaurant, pool, helipad. AE, DC, MC, V. Closed Feb. and 1 wk in Nov.*

Cognac

⑩ *27 km (17 mi) southeast of Saintes via D24, 120 km (75 mi) north-east of Bordeaux.*

The black-walled town of Cognac seems an unlikely home for one of the world's most successful drink trades. You may be disappointed initially by the town's unpretentious appearance, but like the drink, it tends to grow on you. Cognac owed its early development to the transport of salt and wine along the River Charente. When 16th-century Dutch merchants discovered that the local wine was both tastier and easier to transport if distilled, the town became the heart of the brandy industry. Most cognac houses organize visits of their premises and chais. Wherever you decide to go, you will literally soak up the atmosphere of cognac; 3% of the precious cask-bound liquid evaporates every year! This has two consequences: Each chais smells delicious, and a small, black fungus, which feeds on cognac's alcoholic fumes, forms on walls throughout the town.

The leading monument in Cognac is the former **Château de Cognac,** now on the premises of Otard Cognac. Volatile Renaissance monarch François I was born here in 1494. The remaining buildings are something of a hodgepodge, though the stocky towers recall the site's fortified origins. The tour of Otard Cognac combines its own propaganda with historical comment on the drink itself. At the end you get to sample free cognac, and you can buy some at vastly reduced prices. ⊠ *127 bd. Denfert-Rochereau,* ☎ *05–45–36–88–88.* 🎫 *Free.* ☉ *Guided tours daily on the hr 10–noon and 2–5 (except Sun. Oct.–May).*

Hennessy, along the banks of the Charente and easily recognized by the company's mercenary emblem—an ax-wielding arm carved in stone—includes in its tour a cheerful jaunt across the Charente in old-fashioned boats. ⊠ *rue Richonne,* ☎ *05–45–35–72–72.* ☉ *June–Sept., Mon.–Sat. 9–5:30; Oct.–May, weekdays 9–11 and 1:30–5:30.*

Martell gives the most polished guided tour of the Cognac houses, and its chais are perhaps more picturesque than Hennessy's. ⊠ *pl. Édouard-Martell,* ☎ *05–45–36–33–33.* ☉ *July–Aug., weekdays 9–5, weekends 10–4:30; June and Sept., weekdays 9–11 and 1:30–5; Oct.–May, weekdays 9–11 and 2–5.*

Rue Saulnier, alongside the Hennessy premises, is the most atmospheric of the somber, sloping, cobbled streets that compose the core of Cognac, dominated by the tower of **St-Léger,** a church with a notably large Flamboyant Gothic rose window.

Busy boulevard Denfert-Rochereau twines around the old town, passing the town hall and the neighboring **Musée Municipal** (Town Museum). ⊠ *48 bd. Denfert-Rochereau,* ☎ *05–45–32–07–25.* 🎫 *15 frs.* ☉ *June–Sept., Wed.–Mon. 10–noon and 2–5:30; Oct.–May, Wed.–Mon. 2–5:30.*

Dining and Lodging

$$ ✕🎫 **Pigeons Blancs.** "White Pigeons," a modernized coaching inn on
★ spacious grounds 1½ km (1 mi) from the center of Cognac, has been owned by the same family since the 17th century. Each room is different: No. 32 has a gabled ceiling supported by an ancient beam and a skylight. The major draw, though, is chef Jacques Tachet's cuisine: Try his milk-fed lamb with *jus d'ail doux* (sweet garlic) or grilled escargots. The three-course, prix-fixe menu is a find at 138 francs. You can arrange to have two meals per day with your room rate. ⊠ *110*

rue Jules-Brisson, 16100, ☎ *05–45–82–16–36,* FAX *05–45–82–29–29. 6 rooms. Restaurant. AE, DC, MC, V. Closed 1st ½ of Jan.*

Nightlife and the Arts

La Maison Blanche (⊠ 2 impasse de Moulins) is the place to party every night. Each September Cognac hosts a **crime film festival.**

Outdoor Activities and Sports

Hit the greens at the local 18-hole **golf course** (⊠ In the village of St-Brice, 5 km/3 mi from Cognac, ☎ 05–45–32–18–17); fees range from 300 francs in peak season to 200 francs off-season.

Shopping

A bottle of old cognac makes a fine souvenir; try **La Cognathèque** (⊠ 10 pl. Jean-Monnet) in Cognac itself, though you can sometimes find the same item infinitely cheaper at a local producer.

Jarnac

⓫ *14 km (9 mi) east of Cognac via N141.*

The village of Jarnac is primarily known as the birthplace of the late president François Mitterrand, who is buried in the local cemetery. Several excellent cognac firms are found here as well. **Hine** (⊠ quai de l'Orangerie, ☎ 05–45–81–11–38), one of Jarnac's cognac firms, organizes visits of its riverbank premises. **Courvoisier** (⊠ pl. du Château, ☎ 05–45–35–55–55), in a bombastic redbrick factory, gives tours of its premises and its chais.

Dining and Lodging

$ ✕🏠 **Maison Karina.** Co-owner Niki Legon is an English woman who
★ describes herself as a cupboard cook: She starts with a recipe, then looks into her cupboard to see what to add. The result is that no dish is ever the same, be it canard *à la pineau* (with pineau, a sweet, cognac-based aperitif of the region) or *côtes de porc* (pork chops). Rooms have exposed beams and walls. You'll not find cognac from Cognac in the cozy bar but from Jarnac and from some excellent lesser-known houses such as Louis Royet. ⊠ *Bois-Faucon, 16200 Sigogne (off D736, 8 km/5 mi north of Jarnac),* ☎ *05–45–36–26–26,* FAX *05–45–81–10–93. 7 rooms, 2 suites. Restaurant, bar, pool, 18-hole golf course, tennis court, horseback riding. MC, V.*

Angoulême

⓬ *28 km (17 mi) east of Jarnac via N141, 116 km (72 mi) south of Poitiers, 86 km (54 mi) northwest of Périgueux.*

Angoulême is divided, like many other French towns, between an old, picturesque section perched around a hilltop cathedral and a modern, industrial part sprawling along the valley and railroad below. The 19th-century novelist Honoré de Balzac is one of the town's adopted sons; Balzac described Angoulême in his meaty novel *Lost Illusions.* In the **Ville Haute** (Upper Town), known as "le plateau," there are stunning views from the ramparts and a warren of quaint old streets around the Hôtel de Ville (Town Hall).

The 12th-century **Cathédrale d'Angoulême** bears little resemblance to the majority of its French counterparts because of the cupolas topping each of its three bays, a style popular in the southwest. The cathedral was partly destroyed by Calvinists in 1562, then restored in a heavy-handed manner in 1634 and 1866. Its main attraction is the magnificent Romanesque facade, whose layers of rounded arches bear 70 stone statues and bas-reliefs illustrating the Last Judgment. ⊠ *pl. St-Pierre.*

Dining and Lodging

$ ✕ **La Tour des Valois.** This restaurant diagonally across from the market has a good choice of regional food. Sample one of the veal dishes—the one using the local mustard from Jarnac is particularly good—and the locally made foie gras. ⊠ *7 rue Massillon,* ☎ *05–45–95–23–64. Reservations not accepted. MC, V. Closed Sun. No lunch Sat.*

$$$ ✕🏨 **Château de Nieuil.** An avenue of trees opening onto a circular lawn leads to this former hunting lodge—a huge château with towers. Rooms vary: Some have traditional furnishings and pastel blue fabric; others have a *petit salon* (small sitting area) or a garden view. Unfortunately, the reception area is small. The formidable dining room has a large stone fireplace with sculpted family crests and a multifaceted chandelier. Enjoy superb lamb (a regional specialty) or scallop of milk-fed veal with grapes. The wine list is impressive, but you need to search for an affordable bottle. ⊠ *16270 Nieuil (off N141 between Angoulême and Limoges),* ☎ *05–45–71–36–38,* 𝔽𝔸𝕏 *05–45–71–46–45. 14 rooms, 3 suites. Restaurant, pool, tennis court, fishing, helipad. AE, DC, MC, V. Closed Nov.–Mar.*

$$ 🏨 **Mercure Hôtel de France.** On the edge of the Ville Haute, across from the covered market, this hotel has a traditional air. From the garden there are fine views of the city. Rooms are decorated in light blues with striped curtains and bedspreads. Solid, unpretentious regional cuisine is served in the restaurant (closed lunch Sunday, and all day Sunday September to May). The staff is professional and accustomed to speaking English. ⊠ *1 pl. des Halles, 16000,* ☎ *05–45–95–47–95, 0181/ 741–3100 in U.K., 800/637–2873 in U.S.;* 𝔽𝔸𝕏 *05–45–92–02–70. 90 rooms. Restaurant, bar. AE, DC, V.*

PÉRIGORD AND LIMOUSIN

Stretching along the Dordogne, Isle, Dronne, and Auvezère rivers, this wooded region's rolling hills and valleys are full of romantic riverside châteaux, small medieval villages, and prehistoric sites. You may want to spend a week exploring the small country roads and picnicking on the riverbanks.

Limoges

⑬ *104 km (65 mi) northeast of Angoulême, 120 km (75 mi) southeast of Poitiers, 102 km (64 mi) northeast of Périgueux.*

Limoges, capital of Limousin, is famous for its porcelain. Every other shop, especially on rue Jean-Jaurès, rue du Clocher, rue du Consulat, and rue St-Michel, seems to sell it. You can get a good overview of what is produced by the factories at the **Limoges-Castel Centre de Démonstration** (demonstration center). ⊠ *Pavillon de la Porcelaine, 40 av. du Président-Kennedy,* ☎ *05–55–30–21–86.* ☉ *Mid-Apr.–mid-Oct., daily 8:30–6; mid-Oct.–mid-Apr., Mon.–Sat. 8:30–6.*

The best porcelain made over the last two centuries is on display at the **Musée National Adrien-Dubouché.** It also has a good technical section introducing the process that gave rise to the four principal ceramic groups: terra-cotta, glazed earthenware, stoneware, and porcelain. ⊠ *8 pl. Winston-Churchill,* ☎ *05–55–33–08–50.* 💴 *20 frs.* ☉ *Wed.– Mon. 10–noon and 1:30–5:15.*

At the **Musée Municipal de l'Évêché** (Town Museum in the 18th-century Bishop's Palace), there's an extensive array of ceramics—from the 12th to the 20th century—and an archaeological section on Limoges Roman history. Look, too, for the few works of Renoir. Limoges was his birthplace. ⊠ *pl. de l'Évêché,* ☎ *05–55–34–44–09.* ⚌ *Free.* ☉ *Wed.–Mon. 10–11:45 and 2–6 (until 5 Oct.–June).*

The **Cathédrale St-Étienne,** across from the Bishop's Palace, was begun in 1273 and closely resembles the cathedrals of Narbonne and Clermont-Ferrand, with their extremely high vaults—the trademark of architect Jean Deschamps. ⊠ *pl. de la Cathédrale.*

OFF THE
BEATEN PATH

ORADOUR-SUR-GLANE – This village 22 km (14 mi) northwest of Limoges stands as a chilling reminder of Nazi barbarism. On the night of June 10, 1944, the Germans stormed the village, herded the men into a barn, the women and children into the church, and slew them. Some believe they mistook it for another town, reputed to harbor the Resistance. Some 642 people, including 205 children, were murdered. Ten villagers survived by hiding under the corpses. A new town was established with the same name 1 km (½ mi) away, leaving this village just as it was that evening. ⚌ *Donation of 30 frs to visit village.* ☉ *Daily 9–sunset.*

Brantôme

⑭ *88 km (55 mi) southwest of Limoges via N21 and D78, 59 km (37 mi) southeast of Angoulême via D939.*

The beautiful old town of Brantôme, with its abbey, village square, small streets, and bridges across the sparkling waters of the River Dronne, will either be your entry to or exit from the Dordogne. It deserves a stop, even if you just take a walk along the river. At night, the abbey is floodlit and the reflecting light on the river adds to the romance of the stars.

Some 21 km (13 mi) northwest of Brantôme, on the Angoulême road, is the **Château de Mareuil.** The magnificent, 14th to 15th-century fortified castle has been in the Montebello family for generations (the Duke of Montebello, Marshal Lannes, took part in the coup d'état that brought Napoléon to power and then became one of the Corsican's ablest generals). Be sure to see the Gothic chapel with ribbed vaulting inside the left tower, the prisons, and the living quarters. Restoration, with the help of government grants, is an ongoing process. ⊠ *rue du Château, Mareuil,* ☎ *05–53–60–74–13.* ⚌ *15 frs.* ☉ *Wed.–Mon. 2–4:30.*

Dining and Lodging

$$$ ✕⌂ **Château de Vieux Mareuil.** This modern, courtyard-style manor is built on the foundations of an ancient farmhouse. Most rooms are contemporary and tasteful, with spacious bathrooms and small terraces. High ceilings, thick stone walls, and exposed beams make Tour 1, in the old part of the building, particularly special. Nouvelle cuisine is served in two small dining rooms; the *cabecou* (local goat cheese) salad and the *navarin* (ragout) of lamb are delicious. ⊠ *Chanet, rte. d'Angoulême-Périgueux, 24340 Vieux Mareuil (15 km/9 mi north of Brantôme),* ☎ *05–53–60–77–15,* 𝔽𝔸𝕏 *05–53–56–49–33. 14 rooms, 2 suites. Restaurant, pool. MC, V. Closed Sept.–Apr.*

$$ ⌂ **Château Laborie.** In the countryside 6 km (4 mi) north of Brantôme is this château, a step above your usual B&B. A long avenue of *tilleuls*

(linden trees) leads to the moat and impressive facade. Owner Mme. Duseau is an amiable hostess who chats with guests and offers advice on where to dine (one of these suggestions, the Terrace des Jardins, is well below par). Rooms, furnished with hand-me-down antiques, are comfortable, if a little stilted, though two rooms on the first floor are warmer and have less bourgeois pretense. ⊠ *24530 Champagnac-de Belair (3 km/2 mi from Brantôme in the direction of Angoulême),* ☎ *05–53–54–22–99,* FAX *05–53–08–53–78. 5 rooms. Breakfast room, pool. No credit cards. Closed early Nov.–Easter.*

Périgueux

🚲 *27 km (19 mi) south of Brantome via D939.*

Périgueux, the ancient capital of Périgord, is best known for its weird-looking cathedral. Finished in 1173 and restored in the 19th century, the **Cathédrale St-Front** might be on loan from Istanbul, given its shallow, scale-pattern domes and elongated, conical cupolas sprouting from the roof like baby minarets. You may be struck by similarities with the Byzantine-style Sacré-Coeur in Paris (☞ Chapter 2); that's no coincidence—architect Paul Abadie (1812–84) worked on both. ⊠ *pl. de la Clautre.*

Hautefort

🚲 *45 km (28 mi) northeast of Périgueux via D5.*

The only reason to come to Hautefort is to see its castle, which presents a disarmingly arrogant face to the world. The skyline of the ★ **Château de Hautefort** bristles with high roofs, domes, chimneys, and cupolas. The square-lined Renaissance left wing clashes with the muscular, round towers of the right wing as the only surviving section of the original medieval castle—the gateway and drawbridge—referees in the middle. Adorning the inside are 17th-century furniture and tapestries. ⊠ *Off of N89 and D704,* ☎ *05–53–50–51–23.* 🎫 *28 frs.* ☉ *Easter–Nov., daily 2–6; Dec.–Easter, Sun. 2–6.*

Dining and Lodging

$$ ✕🏨 **Manoir d'Hautegente.** This old, ivy-covered manor is in a pastoral ★ setting with a lily pond, sheep in a paddock, and a 13th-century windmill. Inside, the simple rooms have beige, patterned-fabric wallpaper and colorful curtains that match the bedspreads. Regional fare, such as homemade foie gras, is given a balanced lightness in the hands of the chef. ⊠ *Haute Gente, 24120 Coly (6 km/4 mi south of Hautefort, 26 km/16 mi north of Sarlat),* ☎ *05–53–51–68–03,* FAX *05–53–50–38–52. 10 rooms. Restaurant, pool. MC, V. Closed Nov.*

Grotte de Lascaux

🚲 *32 km (20 mi) south of Hautefort via D704 and D65.*

The famous Grotte de Lascaux, or Lascaux Cave, in Montignac in the Vézère Valley, contains hundreds of mesmerizing prehistoric wall paintings—thought to be at least 20,000 years old. They were discovered by chance in 1940. Although the caves have been sealed off to prevent irreparable damage, two of the galleries and many of the paintings have been reproduced in vivid detail in the Lascaux 2 exhibition center nearby. Be sure to purchase tickets for the caves at the tourist office in the town of Montignac before going. ⊠ *Off of rte. Montignac-Les-Eyzies,* ☎ *05–53–51–95–03.* 🎫 *50 frs.* ☉ *Tues.–Sun. 10–noon and 2–5:30.*

Les Eyzies-de-Tayac

⑱ *27 km (19 mi) southwest of Lascaux via D704.*

Many signs of prehistoric man have been discovered in the vicinity of Les Eyzies; a number of excavated caves and grottoes, some with wall paintings, are open for public viewing. The **Grotte du Grand-Roc** has weird-shape crystalline stalactites and stalagmites in its rocky cavern. ⊠ *Look for signs in town,* ☎ *05–53–06–92–70.* ☞ *30 frs.* ☼ *Feb.– May and Sept.–Dec., daily 10–5; June–Aug., daily 9–7.*

At the **Musée Nationale de Préhistoire** (National Museum of Prehistory), in a Renaissance château, you can examine many artifacts, including primitive sculpture, furniture, and tools. You can also get ideas at the museum about excavation sites to visit in the region. ⊠ *Look for signs for the Grotte du Grand-Roc in town,* ☎ *05–53–06–45– 45.* ☞ *24 frs.* ☼ *Apr.–Oct., Wed.–Mon. 9:30–noon and 2–6; Nov.– Mar., Wed.–Mon. 9:30–noon and 2–5.*

Dining and Lodging

$$$–$$$$ **✗⌂ Le Vieux Logis.** A member of the Relais & Châteaux group, this
★ rambling old stone house at the edge of Tremolat is one of the best hotels in Dordogne. The warmly decorated rooms vary in size; most face the well-tended garden and a rushing brook. One favorite, No. 22, has a terra-cotta tile floor, exposed beams, stone walls, and a suitelike bathroom. For dinner, the five-course Menu Vieux Logis (250 francs) might include the chef's forte, pigeon terrine. The restaurant is closed Tuesday from mid-January through May. ⊠ *24510 Tremolat (8 km/5 mi west of Les Eyzies-de-Tayac),* ☎ *05–53–22–80–06,* 𝖥𝖠𝖷 *05–53–22– 84–89. 19 rooms, 3 suites. Restaurant, pool. AE, DC, MC, V.*

$$$ **✗⌂ Le Centenaire.** Although it is a stylish, modern, comfortable hotel, Le Centenaire is known first as a restaurant. Chef Roland Mazère adds flair to the preparation of local specialties: risotto with truffles, or snails with ravioli and gazpacho. The dining room, with its gold-color stone and wooden beams, retains local character. The restaurant is closed Tuesday lunch; a jacket is required. Rooms, especially at the lower end of the price scale, are pretty small. ⊠ *24620 Les Eyzies-de-Tayac,* ☎ *05–53–06–97–18,* 𝖥𝖠𝖷 *05–53–06–92–41. 21 rooms. Restaurant, pool, sauna, health club. MC, V. Closed Nov.–Mar.*

En Route From Les Eyzies to Sarlat, on twisty D47, you'll pass the elegant **Château de Puymartin** (☎ *05–53–59–29–97*); it's open April–October, daily 10–noon; admission is 32 francs.

Sarlat-la-Canéda

★ ⑲ *21 km (12 mi) southeast of Les Eyzies via D47.*

Another Périgord gem is the small town of Sarlat-la-Canéda, which is hectic during the Saturday market—all the geese on sale are proof of the local addiction to foie gras. To do justice to the town's golden-stone splendor, wander through its medieval streets, aided by the tourist office's walking map.

Of particular note is rue de la Liberté, which leads to **place du Peyrou,** occupied on one corner by the pointed-gable Renaissance house where writer-orator Étienne de la Boétie (1530–63) was born. The elaborate turret-topped tower of the **Cathédrale St-Sacerdos** (⊠ pl. du Peyrou), begun in the 12th century, is the oldest part of the building and, along with the choir, all that remains of the original Romanesque cathedral. The sloping garden behind the cathedral, the **Cour de l'Évêché** (Bishop's Courtyard), contains a strange, conical tower known as the **Lanterne des Morts** (Lantern of the Dead), which was occasionally used as a funeral chapel.

Rue d'Albusse, adjoining the garden behind the cathedral, and rue de la Salamandre are narrow, twisty streets that head to place de la Liberté and the 17th-century **Hôtel de Ville.** Opposite the town hall is the rickety former church of **Ste-Marie,** overlooking place des Oies. Ste-Marie points the way to Sarlat's most interesting street, **rue des Consuls.** Among its medieval buildings are the **Hôtel Plamon,** with broad windows that resemble those of a Gothic church, and, opposite, the 15th-century Hôtel de Vassal.

☾ The **Musée-Aquarium** shows the fish found in the local rivers: salmon, eel, pike, perch, trout, and even sturgeon, rarely seen outside the Caspian Sea. ⊠ *3 rue du Commandant-Maratuel,* ☎ *05–53–59–44–58.* ⊡ *32 frs.* ☯ *June–mid-Sept., daily 10–7; mid-Sept.–Oct. and Apr.–May, daily 10–noon and 2–6.*

Dining and Lodging

$$$–$$$$ ✕⊞ **Château de la Treyne.** Part of the Relais & Châteaux chain, this small hotel east of Sarlat serenely guards the Dordogne River, as it has since the 14th century. Dinner is served in a delightful paneled room with old portraits and a roaring fire. Spacious rooms are traditionally furnished with 19th-century paintings and country antiques. During high season, you are expected to dine at the hotel. ⊠ *La Treyne, 46200 Lacave (40 km/25 mi east of Sarlat),* ☎ *05–65–32–66–66,* FAX *05–65–37–06–70. 14 rooms. Restaurant, pool, sauna, tennis court. MC, V. Closed mid-Nov.–Easter.*

$–$$ ✕⊞ **Hôtels St-Albert et Montaigne.** The Garrigou family has two ho-★ tels on this delightful square in the center of town. The Montaigne is in a manor; ask for lovely Room 33, with exposed beams. The St-Albert has varying-size, simply furnished rooms. Hearty regional fare is served in the restaurant. Over dinner, discuss your next day's itinerary with M. Garrigou: He not only knows the region well, he is also the town's backroom politician. The restaurant is closed Sunday dinner and Monday from November to mid-April. ⊠ *10 pl. Pasteur, 24200,* ☎ *05–53–31–55–55,* FAX *05–53–59–19–99. 56 rooms, 6 suites. Restaurant. AE, MC, V. Closed Nov.–mid-Apr.*

Domme

㉑ *11 km (7 mi) south of Sarlat via D46.*

The historic cliff-top village of Domme lies across the Dordogne River from La Roque-Gageac. It is famous for its **grottes** (caves), where prehistoric bison and rhinoceros bones have been discovered. You can visit the 500-yard-long illuminated **galleries,** lined with stalagmites and stalactites. ⊠ *Entrance on pl. de la Halle.* ⊡ *28 frs.* ☯ *Apr.–Sept., daily 9:30–noon and 2–6; Mar. and Oct., daily 2–6.*

Dining and Lodging

$$ ✕⊞ **L'Esplanade.** Make sure your room looks over the Dordogne—it's the expansive view that makes this hotel special. Rooms are small but modern, and the staff speaks English. Salmon and trout top the menu; dining à la carte can be pricey. The restaurant is closed Sunday dinner and Monday off-season. ⊠ *rue du Pont-Carrat, 24250 Domme,* ☎ *05–53–28–31–41,* FAX *05–53–28–49–92. 19 rooms. Restaurant. AE, MC, V. Closed mid-Nov.–mid-Feb.*

La Roque-Gageac

㉑ *5 km (3 mi) northwest of Domme via D703.*

A short distance up the Dordogne River from Beynac, huddled beneath a towering gray cliff, is La Roque-Gageac, one of the best-restored villages in the Dordogne Valley. Crafts shops line its narrow streets, dominated by the outlines of the 19th-century mock-medieval Château de Malartrie and the Manoir de Tarde, with its cylindrical turret.

Dining and Lodging

$$ ✕🏠 **La Plume d'Oie.** This small inn overlooks the river and the limestone cliffs. Rooms, decorated in light fabrics and wicker furniture, vary in size and price. La Plume d'Oie's major raison d'être, however, is the stone-walled restaurant, at which you are expected to have at least one meal. Chef-owner Marc-Pierre Walker prepares classical regional cuisine: fillet of beef cooked in red wine and ragout of foie gras. The restaurant is closed Monday. ✉ *24250 La Roque-Gageac,* ☎ *05–53–29–57–05,* FAX *05–53–31–04–81. 4 rooms. Restaurant, minibars. MC, V. Closed late Nov.–mid-Dec. and Feb.*

Beynac

㉒ *5 km (3 mi) northwest of La Roque-Gageac via D703.*

The main reason to visit Beynac is to see its medieval castle. Daringly perched atop a sheer cliff face beside an abrupt bend in the Dordogne, the 13th-century **Château de Beynac** has unforgettable, muscular architecture and staggering views from its battlements. ☎ *05–53–29–50–40.* 🖾 *32 frs.* ☉ *Mar.–mid-Nov., daily 10–noon and 2–5; July–Aug., daily 10–7.*

Dining and Lodging

$$ ✕🏠 **Auberge du Noyer.** This inn, in a small, 18th-century building 5 km (3 mi) outside La Bugue (west of Beynac), is owned by two expats from England. The comfortable rooms, decorated in provincial style, are in the main building or in the former barn (avoid the ground-floor barn rooms: you can hear the upstairs plumbing). The good four-course prix-fixe dinner menu is made up of soup, a starter, a main dish, such as magret de canard or fresh trout, and cheese or dessert. ✉ *Le Reclaud-de-Bouny-Bas, 24260 Le Bugue (5 km/3 mi outside the village; 22 km/14 mi or 20 min from Beynac),* ☎ *05–53–07–11–73,* FAX *05–53–54–57–44. 10 rooms. Restaurant, pool. MC, V. Closed Nov.–Mar.*

En Route   Cross the Dordogne just upstream from Beynac; then turn right on D53 to pass the ruined castle of **Castlenaud,** open May–November, daily 10–7. Just 5 km (3 mi) farther on is the **Château des Milandes,** once owned by the American-born cabaret star of Roaring '20s Paris, Josephine Baker. It is open May–October, daily 9:30–11:30 and 2–6. Then turn inland along D53 (via Belvès) southwest to Monpazier.

Monpazier

㉓ *39 km (24 mi) southwest of Beynac via D703, D710, and D53.*

On the south bank of the Dordogne River is the tiny town of Monpazier, one of France's best-preserved *bastides* (fortified medieval towns with regimented street plans). It was built in ocher-color stone by English king Edward I in 1284 to protect the southern flank of his French possessions. The bastide has three stone gateways (of an original six), a large central square, and the church of **St-Dominique,** housing 35 carved wooden choir stalls and a would-be relic of the True Cross. Opposite the church is the finest medieval building in town, the **Maison du Chapître** (Chapter House), once used as a barn for storing grain. Its wood-beam roof is constructed of chestnut to repel web-spinning spiders.

Biron

㉔ *8 km (5 mi) south of Monpazier via D53.*

Stop in Biron to see its hilltop castle, the **Château de Biron.** Highlights of a visit to the castle which, along with the keep, square tower, and chapel, dates from the Middle Ages, include monumental staircases and the kitchen with its huge stone slabs. The classical buildings were completed in 1730. English Romantic poet Lord Byron (1788–1824) is claimed as a distant descendant of the Gontaut-Biron family, who lived here for 14 generations. ☎ 05–53–63–13–39. ⊡ 24 frs. ☉ Feb.– June and Sept.–Nov., Wed.–Mon. 9–11:30 and 2–6; July–Aug., daily 9–11:30 and 2–6.

En Route   Head west from Monpazier along D2 to another bastide town, **Villeréal.** Then take D207 to **Issigeac,** a well-preserved old town with numerous medieval houses.

Continue northwest via D14 to the hilltop village of **Monbazillac,** where there are spectacular views of the sweet-wine-producing vineyards that tumble north toward the Dordogne. The squat corner towers of the beautifully proportioned 16th-century gray-stone **Château** pay tribute to the fortress tradition of the Middle Ages, but the large windows and sloping roofs reveal the Renaissance influence. Regional furniture and an ornate, early 17th-century bedchamber enliven the interior. A wine tasting is provided at the end of your tour to tempt you into buying a case or two. ⊡ 32 frs. ☉ Mid-Feb.–Dec., daily 10– noon and 2–4:15.

Bergerac

㉕ *6 km (4 mi) north of Monbazillac via D13, 57 km (35 mi) east of St-Émilion, 48 km (30 mi) southwest of Périgueux.*

Bergerac is a lively town with ancient half-timber houses, narrow alleys, and a colorful Saturday market. Guided walking tours of its old town, lasting 90 minutes and costing 22 francs, leave from the **tourist office** (☎ 05–53–57–03–11). You can also take an hour-long cruise on the Dordogne for 40 francs: Check with the tourist office or the cruise company (☎ 05–53–24–58–80).

The **Couvent des Récollets,** a former convent, is also in the wine business. The convent's stone-and-brick buildings range in date from the 12th to the 17th century and include galleries, a large vaulted cellar, and a cloister, where the **Maison du Vin** (Wine Center) dishes out information on—and samples of—local wines. ⊠ *pl. de la Myrpe,* ☎ 05– 53–63–57–57. ⊡ 25 frs. ☉ July–Aug., daily tours every hr 10:30–11:30 and 1:30–5:30; mid-May–June and Sept.–mid-Oct., Tues.–Sat. at 3:30 and 4:30.

Not only are there vineyards in the region, but there are also tobacco plantations. Learn about this local industry from its American origins to its spread worldwide at the **Musée du Tabac** (Tobacco Museum), a museum housed in the haughty 17th-century Maison Peyrarède near the quayside. ⊠ 10 rue de l'Ancien-Pont, ☎ 05–53–63–04–13. ⊡ 15 frs. ☉ Tues.–Fri. 10–noon and 2–6, Sat. 10–noon and 2–5, Sun. 2:30–6:30.

Dining and Lodging

$$ ✕☷ **Hôtel Bordeaux.** One of the better hotels in town, the Bordeaux has contemporary furnishings and neat rooms. Request one on the garden-courtyard or No. 22, which is slightly more spacious. Though you're not obliged to eat at the restaurant, it's difficult to refuse the marinated salmon in anisette and lime or the panfried escallop de foie gras. Owner M. Maury speaks fluent English. ✉ *38 pl. Gambetta, 24100,* ☎ *05–53–57–12–83,* FAX *05–53–57–72–14. 40 rooms. Restaurant, bar, pool. AE, DC, MC, V. Closed mid-Dec.–Jan.*

$$ ✕☷ **La Petite Auberge.** Head south to Razac d'Eymet to find this
★ modernized old country house. Rooms are tidy and cozy; for an extra 100 francs you might be tempted to stay in No. 7, the spacious ground-floor suite with a fireplace and kitchenette. Locals come to dine on the light version of Périgord cooking, particularly confit de canard, foie gras, and walnut tart, as well as vegetarian dishes. The restaurant is closed Sunday and Monday from September to June. ✉ *Le Royère, 24500 Razac d'Eymet (4 km/2 mi east of D933, before the town of Eymet),* ☎ *05–53–24–69–27,* FAX *05–53–61–02–63. 7 rooms, 2 suites. Restaurant, pool. MC, V.*

THE BORDEAUX REGION

Bordeaux, the commercial and cultural center of southwest France, is ringed by renowned vineyards: Graves and pretty Sauternes to the south; Pomerol and St-Émilion to the east; and, to the northwest, the dusty Médoc peninsula, looking across the Gironde Estuary at the vineyards of Bourg and Blaye. Head southwest and you'll find great swaths of pine forest, huge sand dunes, and the fancy resort of Arcachon with its lagoon.

Bordeaux

88 km (55 mi) west of Bergerac, 580 km (360 mi) southwest of Paris, 240 km (150 mi) northwest of Toulouse, 190 km (118 mi) northeast of Biarritz.

Bordeaux, the capital of southwest France and the region's largest city, has tried to diversify its tourist appeal—its May music festival is a major crowd puller—but the city remains synonymous with the wine trade: Wine shippers have long based their headquarters along the banks of the Garonne.

An aura of 18th-century elegance permeates downtown Bordeaux, where fine shops invite exploration. To the south of the city center are the old docklands, targeted for renewal but still a bit shady. As a whole, Bordeaux is a less exuberant city than most others in France. To get a feel for the historic port of Bordeaux, take the 90-minute boat tour, weekdays from the Embarcadères des Quinconces at around 3; the cost is 56 francs.

For a view of the picturesque quayside, stroll across the Garonne on
㉖ Pont de Pierre (Peter's Bridge); built by Napoléon at the start of the 19th century, the bridge makes spectacular viewing itself.

Two blocks from the riverbank, along cours Chapeau-Rouge, is the
㉗ city's leading 18th-century monument: the **Grand Théâtre**, designed by architect Victor Louis and built between 1773 and 1780. Its elegant exterior is ringed by graceful Corinthian columns, and the majestic foyer, with its two-winged staircase and cupola, inspired Charles Garnier's design for the Paris Opéra. The theater-hall has a frescoed ceiling, a shimmering chandelier composed of 14,000 Bohemian crystals, and,

it is said, perfect acoustics. ⊠ *pl. de la Comédie,* ☎ *05–57–81–90–81.* 🎫 *32 frs. Contact tourist office for guided tours.*

㉘ The tree-lined allées de Tourny and cours du XXX-Juillet reel off from the Grand Théâtre. At the start of the cours du XXX-Juillet is the **CIVB,** headquarters of the Bordeaux wine trade, where information can be had and samples tasted; you can make purchases at the **Vinothèque,** opposite. At the far end of the cours is the **esplanade des Quinconces,** a vast square overlooking the Garonne. One kilometer (½ mile) north

㉙ of the esplanade is the ambitious **Cité Mondiale du Vin** (World of Wine Center), part office block, part shopping mall, and part cultural center, all focusing on the world of wine. ⊠ *Entry at 25 quai des Chartrons.*

㉚ Just a block in from the river is **place de la Bourse,** an important 18th-century landmark. A provincial reply to Paris's celebrated place Vendôme, the square (built 1730–55) is surrounded by airy, large-windowed buildings designed by the era's most esteemed architect, Jacques-Ange Gabriel.

㉛ Narrow streets wind from the river to the **Cathédrale St-André.** This hefty edifice isn't one of France's better Gothic cathedrals, but the soaring 14th-century chancel makes an interesting contrast with the earlier, more severe nave. Excellent—albeit grimy—stone carvings adorn the facade. ⊠ *pl. Pey-Berland.*

㉜ The **Musée des Beaux-Arts,** across the tidy gardens behind the luxurious Hôtel de Ville, has a notable collection of works spanning the 15th–20th centuries, with important paintings by Paolo Veronese (*Apostle's Head*), Camille Corot (*Bath of Diana*), and Odilon Redon (*Chariot of Apollo*) and sculptures by Auguste Rodin. ⊠ *20 cours d'Albret,* ☎ *05–56–10–16–93.* 🎫 *18 frs.* ☉ *Wed.–Mon. 10–6.*

One of the region's most famous wine-producing châteaux is actually within the city limits: Follow N250 southwest from central Bordeaux (direction Arcachon) for 3 km (2 mi) to the district of Pessac, home to **Haut-Brion,** producer of the only non-Médoc wine to be ranked a *premier cru* (the most elite wine classification). The white, classical château surveys the celebrated pebbly soil. The wines produced at **La Mission-Haut Brion,** across the road, are almost as sought after.

Dining and Lodging

Old Bordeaux has many small restaurants, particularly around the 18th-century place du Parlement, like bustling L'Ombrière (No. 14), with fairly priced steaks, and pricey Chez Philippe (No. 1), one of the city's top fish restaurants. What is lacking are charming hotels. You may want to consider staying outside Bordeaux, at the Château Lamothe in St-Sulpice et Cameyrac, 20 km (12 mi) east of the city (☞ St-Émilion Lodging, *below*), for instance.

$$ ✕ **Vieux Bordeaux.** This lively, much-acclaimed nouvelle-cuisine haunt
★ lies on the fringe of the old town. Chef Michel Bordage's menu is short but of high quality, complemented by three 160-franc prix-fixe menus. His fish dishes are particularly tasty, such as the grilled *bar* (bass) on a peppery galette of crab. ⊠ *27 rue Buhan,* ☎ *05–56–52–94–36. AE, MC, V. Closed Sun., Aug., and 1 wk in Feb. No lunch Sat.*

$–$$ ✕ **Gravelier.** Anne-Marie, daughter of Pierre Troisgros of Roanne (☞ Chapter 11), married Yves Gravelier, and they combined their culinary talents. In sparse decor, full of light and openness, imaginative cuisine is served: fillets of *rouget* (red mullet) with foie gras and pigeon pot pie with Chinese cabbage. The 95-franc lunch menu is a good deal. ⊠ *114 cours de Verdun,* ☎ *05–56–48–17–15. AE, DC, MC, V. Closed Sun. and 1st 2 wks in Aug. No lunch Sat.*

$ ✕ **La Cafetière.** On a small street a block and a half from place du Parlement, La Cafetière has only half a dozen tables in an intimate, cozy atmosphere. The salads are enormous, the confit de canard tasty. ⊠ *14 rue des Faussets,* ☎ *05–56–51–66–55. MC, V. Closed Sun.*

$$$ ✕🖫 **Burdigala.** Of the three luxury hotels in Bordeaux, Burdigala (Latin for Bordeaux) is the only one within walking distance of the center of town. The modern exterior is extremely unappealing, but the inside is comfortable. The soundproof rooms are smart and neat; No. 416 is especially quiet and sunny. Deluxe rooms have marble bathrooms with whirlpool baths. The Jardin du Burdigala restaurant serves nouvelle haute cuisine. ⊠ *115 rue Georges-Bonnac, 33000,* ☎ *05–56–90–16–16,* 🖷 *05–56–93–15–06. 76 rooms, 7 suites. Restaurant, meeting rooms. AE, DC, MC, V.*

$$$ ✕🖫 **Hôtel Ste-Catherine.** This fashionable hotel is in a 19th-century building in the old part of town. Service is limited, but the reception staff is helpful. The compact rooms are decorated with light floral fabrics. Beautifully presented, light nouvelle cuisine is served in the dining room with 12th-century vaulted ceilings. ⊠ *27 rue du Parlement-Ste-Catherine, 33000,* ☎ *05–56–81–95–12,* 🖷 *05–56–44–50–51. 83 rooms, 3 suites. Restaurant, piano bar. AE, DC, MC, V.*

$$–$$$ 🖫 **Bayonne.** Rooms in this hotel in an 18th-century building in the heart of town have standard furnishings. Where the Bayonne stands out is in its relative newness, its excellent location, and the freshness of its rooms. A simple breakfast is served. ⊠ *15 cours de l'Intendance (enter from the small rue Martignace, off the street), 33000,* ☎ *05–56–48–00–88,* 🖷 *05–56–52–03–79. 36 rooms. Breakfast room. AE, DC, MC, V.*

$–$$ 🖫 **Hôtel des Quatre Soeurs.** This inexpensive gem, more of a rooming house than a hotel, near the Grand Théâtre has well-kept rooms of varying sizes and prices. In the adjoining café you may be treated to classical music on many afternoons. The owner, Mme. Defalque, is pleasant and helpful. ⊠ *6 cours du XXX-juillet, 33000,* ☎ *05–56–48–16–00,* 𝖥𝖠𝖷 *05–54–01–04–28. 35 rooms. Bar, café. MC, V.*

Nightlife and the Arts

Les Argentiers (⊠ 33 rue des Argentiers), a respected and long-established Bordeaux hangout, is the place for jazz. **L'Aztécal** (⊠ 61 rue du Pas-St-Georges) is a comfortable bar. **Cabaret Andalucia** (⊠ 7 quai Bacalan) is a happening spot. Dance the night away at **Sénéchal** (⊠ 57 bis quai de Paludate).

The **Grand Théâtre** (⊠ pl. de la Comédie, ☎ 05–56–90–91–60) puts on performances of French plays and occasionally operas. Bordeaux's **International Musical May** is a leading event on France's cultural calendar for classical concerts.

Shopping

Between the cathedral and the Grand Théâtre are numerous pedestrian streets where stylish shops abound. For an exceptional selection of cheeses, go to **Jean d'Alos** (⊠ 4 rue Montesquieu). The **Maison de Tourisme et du Vin** (⊠ On the Route du Médoc in Pauillac, north of Bordeaux) has a vast selection of claret. **Vinothèque** (⊠ 8 cours du XXX-Juillet) sells top-ranking Bordeaux wines.

The Médoc

North of Bordeaux, the Route du Médoc wine road (D2) twines through the Médoc Peninsula, a strange, dusty region. Even the vines in Médoc look dusty, and so does the ugly town of **Margaux,** the area's unofficial capital, 27 km (17 mi) northwest of Bordeaux. Yet the small, arid communes and châteaux of Haut-Médoc have such venerable names as Margaux, St-Julien, Pauillac, and St-Estèphe. **Château Margaux,** an elegant, coolly restrained classical building of 1802, and three wineries at Pauillac—Lafite-Rothschild, Latour, and Mouton-Rothschild—are recognized as producers of premiers crus, their wines qualifying with Graves's Haut-Brion as Bordeaux's top five reds. Of all the towns and villages in the Médoc region, **Pauillac** is the nicest; you may want to stroll along the riverfront and stop for refreshments at one of the restaurants.

Stop off at **Soulac-sur-Mer,** a small resort overlooking the Atlantic Ocean. Soulac's 12th-century basilica of **Notre-Dame de la Fin-des-Terres** deserves to have an outlandish history, given its name—Our Lady of the Ends of the Earth—and it does. By 1800 it had been almost completely embedded in drifting sands and was dug out and restored only 100 years ago. At the tip of the peninsula, near a memorial commemorating the landing of U.S. troops in 1917, is the **Pointe de Grave,** where you can take the *bac* (ferry) across the Gironde to Royan; it runs four times daily and costs 135 francs per car and 36 francs per passenger. During the half-hour crossing, keep an eye out for the **Phare de Cordouan** on your left, a lighthouse that looks as if it's emerging from the sea (it's actually built on a sandbank).

Royan

㉝ *104 km (65 mi) north of Bordeaux, 40 km (25 mi) south of Rochefort.*

Royan is a commercialized resort town whose vast seafront is packed to the gills in summer, although there are prettier beaches just north (Pontaillac and St-Palais). Boats leave Royan in summer for trips along the Gironde Estuary and across to the Phare de Cordouan (☞ *above*).

Royan was tastefully rebuilt after being destroyed by Nazi bombing in 1945. The imaginative, domed, octagonal, concrete **Marché Central** (Central Market) merits a visit. In the **Église Notre-Dame,** an enormous concrete church with a breathtaking oval interior, the huge, unsupported sweep of the curved ceiling is a technical tour de force. The elegant church tower dominates the town skyline.

En Route Down the coast from Royan along D25 is the pleasant resort town of **St-Georges-de-Didonne.** Continue south through pine forest and past chalky cliffs to **Meschers** and Les Grottes de Matata, where you can sip tea or eat ice cream on a flower-bedecked terrace overlooking the estuary, from June through September. From Meschers, head south to **Talmont,** an unspoiled village renowned for its gently proportioned 12th-century church jutting out over the waters on a rocky promontory. Stay on D145, pause at the cheerful little harbor at **Mortagne-sur-Gironde**; then continue through rolling hills, with beguiling views over the Gironde Estuary and vineyards used first for cognac then, as you progress south, Bordeaux wines. **Blaye** is home to a vast Vauban citadel and a ferry across the estuary to Lamarque in the Médoc (four times a day for 90 francs per car and 25 francs per passenger). A scenic riverside road continues to **Bourg,** famed for its lightish red wines. From Bourg, head southwest toward Libourne, skirting the town to the north to explore the vineyards of **Fronsac, Pomerol,** and **Lalande-de-Pomerol,** close to St-Émilion.

St-Émilion

★ ③④ *56 km (35 mi) west of Bergerac, 35 km (23 mi) east of Bordeaux.*

Suddenly, the sun-fired flatlands of Pomerol break into hills and send you tumbling into St-Émilion. This jewel of a town has old buildings of golden stone, ruined town walls, well-kept ramparts offering pleasing views, and a church hewn into a cliff. Sloping vineyards invade from all sides, and thousands of tourists invade down the middle.

The medieval streets are filled with wine stores (St-Émilions reach maturity earlier than other Bordeaux reds and offer better value for the money than either Medocs or Graves), crafts shops, and bakeries selling macaroons, a local specialty. Tours of the pretty local vineyards—Château Pétrus and Cheval Blanc, among others—including wine tastings, are organized by the tourist office, the **Syndicat d'Initiative** (✉ pl. des Créneaux, ☎ 05–57–55–28–28), as are train rides through the vineyards.

A stroll along the 13th-century ramparts takes you to the **Château du Roi** (King's Castle), built by occupying sovereign Henry III of England (1216–72). From the castle ramparts, steps lead down to **place du Marché,** a wooded square where cafés remain open late into the balmy summer night. Beware of the inflated prices at the café tables.

The **Église Monolithe,** lining one side of the place du Marché, is one of France's largest underground churches, hewn out of the rock face between the 9th and 12th centuries. ✉ *pl. du Marché.* ⌚ *34 frs.* ☉ *Tours leave every 45 mins from tourist office, 10 AM–5 PM, and cover church, citadel, Catacombes, and Grotte de l'Ermitage.* Just south of the town walls is the **Château Ausone,** an estate that is ranked with Cheval Blanc as producing the finest wine of St-Émilion.

Dining and Lodging

$$ ✕ **Chez Germaine.** Family cooking and regional dishes are the focus at this central St-Émilion eatery. The candlelit upstairs dining room and

the terrace are both pleasant places to enjoy the reasonably priced set menus. Grilled meats and fish are house specialties; for dessert, go for the almond macaroons. ⊠ *13 rue du Clocher,* ☎ *05–57–74–49–34. DC, V. Closed Sun.–Mon. and mid-Dec.–mid-Jan.*

$$$$ ✕🏨 **Grand Barrail.** This turn-of-the-century estate just outside of St-Émilion has been converted into a luxury hotel, albeit a little stiff and Germanic. Rooms are unusually large for a French hotel and are smartly furnished; about half are in the former stables. The talented young chef serves traditional regional fare in the small dining room. St-Émilions constitute at least 60% of the impressive wine list. ⊠ *9 rue Marzelle, 33330 (4 km/2½ mi northwest of St-Émilion),* ☎ *05–57–55–37–00,* 🖷 *05–57–55–37–49. 28 rooms. Restaurant, pool. AE, DC, MC, V.*

$$$ ✕🏨 **Hostellerie de Plaisance.** Across from the tourist office in the
★ upper part of town is this sought-after hotel. Rooms are furnished in warm, appealing style; the Descault Room has an excellent view of the vineyards. Dinner matches the St-Émilion wines; if you are not staying here, make this your number one choice for a leisurely lunch or dinner. The restaurant tends to be overbooked, so be ready to be turned away or fight for your rights. ⊠ *5 pl. du Clocher, 33330,* ☎ *05–57–24–72–35,* 🖷 *05–57–55–07–55. 12 rooms. Restaurant. AE, DC, MC, V. Closed Dec.–Jan.*

$$ ✕🏨 **Auberge de la Commanderie.** Close to the ramparts is this two-story, 19th-century hotel with a garden and a view of the vineyards. Rooms are small but clean and individually decorated. The attractive restaurant, often frequented by nonguests, serves hearty regional fare, such as confit de canard, steaks, and gizzard salad, and a good selection of local wines; it's closed Tuesday, except in July and August. ⊠ *2 rue de la Porte-Brunet, 33300,* ☎ *05–57–24–70–19,* 🖷 *05–57– 74–44–53. 15 rooms. Restaurant. MC, V. Closed late Dec.–Feb.*

$$$ 🏨 **Château Lamothe.** St-Émilion's hotels are mostly in-and-out tourist stops and Bordeaux's lack charm; a delightful alternative is this private manor house (advance reservations required) halfway between the two. The large guest rooms have big four-poster beds with soft cotton sheets; you may find them a little too frilly, but they are very comfortable. Invariably the friendly hosts, M. and Mme. Bastide, will join you for an aperitif or breakfast. Jacques Bastide speaks English and is extremely helpful. ⊠ *6 rte. du Stade, 33450 St-Sulpice et Cameyrac (25 km/16 mi northeast of St-Émilion, 20 km/12 mi west of Bordeaux),* ☎ *05– 56–30–82–16,* 🖷 *05–56–30–88–33. 3 rooms. MC, V.*

En Route   Cross the Dordogne at Brannes, 8 km (5 mi) south of St-Émilion, and head southwest along D11, via Targon, through the region known as **Entre-Deux-Mers** (Between Two Seas, i.e., the Dordogne and Garonne rivers), whose dry white wine is particularly flavorsome if made from the vineyards near the ruins of the **Château de Haut-Bénauge.** Soon after the ruined castle, D11 collides with the Garonne at **Cadillac.** Turn left along D10 to the picturesque villages of **Loupiac** and **Ste-Croix-du-Mont,** sandwiched between the river and hillside vineyards producing sweet white wine.

Cross the Garonne at Langon and head west on D8 into the **Sauternes** vineyards, home to what is generally acclaimed as the finest sweet wine in the world. Nothing in the grubby village of Sauternes would tell you that mind-boggling wealth lurks amid the picturesque vine-laden slopes and hollows. The village has a wine shop where bottles gather dust on rickety shelves, next to handwritten price tags demanding 1,000 francs (about $160) and more. Making Sauternes is a tricky business. Autumn mists steal up the valleys to promote *Botrytis cinerea*, a form of "noble rot" called *pourriture noble,* which sucks moisture out of the grapes, leaving a high proportion of sugar. Not all grapes achieve the required degree of over-ripeness simultaneously; up to seven successive harvests are undertaken at **Château d'Yquem**, a little more than 1½ km (1 mi) north of Sauternes, to assure the optimum selection. This painstaking attention to detail, added to a centuries-old reputation and soil ideally suited to making sweet white wine, enables bottles of Yquem to obtain prices more appropriate to liquid gold. If you do splurge on a recent vintage, you may as well lock it away; Yquem needs to wait a good 10 years before coming into its own and will reward decades of patience.

Heading northwest toward Bordeaux, you encounter the vineyards of the **Graves** region, so called because of its gravelly soil. This is the region's most historic appellation: A lightish-red wine known as clairet was esteemed by English occupiers during the Middle Ages. White wine—both dry and sweet—is also produced, some of the best at the Domaine de Chevalier in **Léognan**, 10 km (6 mi) southwest of Bordeaux. From near here, pick up arrow-straight N250, which shoots though the swaths of evergreen forest known as Les Landes toward Arcachon.

Arcachon

③⑤ *64 km (40 mi) southwest of Bordeaux via N250.*

In the midst of the sandy pine forest of Les Landes is the resort town of Arcachon. It became a resort in the 1850s when the new railroad connected it with Bordeaux. These days, Arcachon is a lively, busy boating center, with three jetties protruding over its sandy beaches. From boulevard de la Mer, there are good views toward Cap Ferret, across the narrow straits that mark the divide between lagoon and ocean.

Arcachon is at the southernmost tip of a chain of lakes connected by streams and canals. The largest is the 19-km-long (12-mi-long) **Lac d'Hourtin-Carcans.** The small town of **Hourtin**, with a marina and 460-yard jetty, stands on its northernmost shore. In the center of this chain is the smaller **Lac de Lacanau,** which teems with pike, perch, and eel and is linked by the **Canal de Lège** to the **Bassin d'Arcachon.** The lagoon is renowned both for its variety of migratory birds and for its excellent oysters, clustered around the **Ile aux Oiseaux** (Island of Birds), a small island in the middle. In addition, there are three more lakes south of Arachon: the **Étang de Cazaux**, the **Étang de Biscarosse**, and the small **Étang d'Aureilhan.** Of note is the town of **Mimizan,** which was swamped in roving sand during the 18th century; sand still surrounds its ruined Benedictine abbey. But the highlight of a visit to Archachon (actually 6 km/4 mi south) is probably the mighty **Dune du Pyla,** a wall of sand that, at more than 370 ft high, counts as Europe's highest sand dune.

Nightlife and the Arts

Activities are ongoing at Arcachon's **casino** (✉ 163 bd. de la Plage). Arcachon's major festival, celebrating the sea, is the **Fêtes de la Mer,** held in mid-August.

Outdoor Activities and Sports

Both Arcachon and Lacanau, to the north, have 18-hole **golf courses** (✉ Archachon, ☎ 05–56–54–44–00; ✉ Lacanau, ☎ 05–56–26–35–50).

POITOU-CHARENTES, PÉRIGORD, AND NORTHERN AQUITAINE A TO Z

Arriving and Departing

By Car

As the capital of southwest France, Bordeaux has superb transport links with Paris, Spain, and even the Mediterranean (A62 expressway via Toulouse). The A10 Paris–Bordeaux expressway passes close to Poitiers, Niort (exit 23 for La Rochelle), and Saintes before continuing toward Spain as A63.

By Plane

Frequent daily flights link Bordeaux and the domestic airport at Limoges with Paris on **Air Inter-Europe** (☎ 08–02–80–28–02), a subsidiary of Air France.

By Train

Superfast TGV (*Trains à Grande Vitesse*) Atlantique service links Paris (Gare Montparnasse) to Bordeaux—584 km (365 mi) in three hours—with stops at Poitiers and Angoulême (change for Jarnac, Cognac, and Saintes); and to La Rochelle—467 km (292 mi) in three hours—with a stop in Niort. Trains link Bordeaux to Lyon (8–9 hours) and Nice (8 hours) via Toulouse. Six trains daily make the 3½-hour, 400-km (250-mi) trip from Paris to Limoges.

Getting Around

By Car

Fast N137 connects La Rochelle with Saintes via Rochefort; Angoulême is linked to Bordeaux and Poitiers by N10 and to Limoges by N141; and D936 runs along the Dordogne Valley to Bergerac. N89 links Bordeaux to Périgueux, continuing to Limoges as N21.

By Train

Bordeaux is the region's major train hub (☞ Arriving and Departing By Train, *above*). Trains run regularly from Bordeaux to Bergerac (80 minutes), with occasional stops at St-Émilion, and, three times daily, to Sarlat (nearly 3 hours). At least six trains daily make the 90-minute journey from Bordeaux to Périgueux, and four continue to Limoges (2 hours, 20 minutes). Poitiers is the connecting point for Niort, La Rochelle, and Rochefort; Angoulême is the connecting point for Jarnac, Cognac, and Saintes.

Contacts and Resources

Car Rental

Avis (✉ 59 rue Peyronnet, Bordeaux, ☎ 05–56–92–69–38; ✉ 133 bd. du Grand-Cerf, Poitiers, ☎ 05–49–58–13–00; ✉ 166 bd. Joffre, La Rochelle, ☎ 05–46–41–13–55). **Hertz** (✉ pl. de la Gare, Bergerac, ☎ 05–53–57–19–27; ✉ 105 bd. du Grand-Cerf, Poitiers, ☎ 05–49–58–24–24).

Guided Tours

Horizons Européens (✉ Française de Tourisme, 3 rue d'Alger, 75001 Paris, ☎ 01–42–60–31–25) organizes a seven-day bus tour of Dordogne and Périgord, leaving from Paris.

Travel Agencies

American Express (✉ 14 cours de l'Intendance, Bordeaux, ☎ 05–56–00–63–33). **Wagons-Lits** (✉ 43 rue de la Porte-Dijeaux, Bordeaux, ☎ 05–56–52–92–70).

Visitor Information

Suggestions about wine tours and tastings, as well as information on local and regional sights, are available at the **Bordeaux Office de Tourisme** (⊠ 12 cours du XXX-Juillet, ☎ 05–56–00–66–00), which also provides a round-the-clock answering service in English.

The addresses of other tourist offices in towns mentioned in this chapter are as follows: **Angoulême** (⊠ 7 bis rue du Chat, ☎ 05–45–95–16–84). **Bergerac** (⊠ 97 rue Neuve d'Argenson, ☎ 05–53–57–03–11). **Cognac** (⊠ 16 rue du XIV-Juillet, ☎ 05–45–82–10–71). **Limoges** (⊠ bd. Fleurus, ☎ 05–55–34–46–87). **La Rochelle** (⊠ pl. de la Petite-Sirène, ☎ 05–46–41–14–68). **Niort** (⊠ rue Ernest-Pérochon, ☎ 05–49–24–18–79). **Poitiers** (⊠ 8 rue des Grandes-Écoles, ☎ 05–49–41–21–24). **Rochefort** (⊠ av. Sadi-Carnot, ☎ 05–46–99–08–60). **Royan** (⊠ Palais des Congrès, ☎ 05–46–23–00–00). **St-Émilion** (⊠ 15 rue du Clocher, ☎ 05–57–55–28–28). **Saintes** (⊠ 62 cours National, ☎ 05–46–74–23–82). **Sarlat** (⊠ pl. de la Liberté, ☎ 05–53–31–45–45).

18 Portraits of France

FRANCE AT A GLANCE: A CHRONOLOGY

ca. 3500 BC   Megalithic stone complexes erected at Carnac, Brittany.

ca. 1500 BC   Lascaux cave paintings executed (Dordogne, southwest France).

ca. 600 BC   Greek colonists found Marseille.

after 500 BC   Celts appear in France.

58–51 BC   Julius Caesar conquers Gaul; writes up the war in *De Bello Gallico*.

52 BC   Lutetia, later to become Paris, is built by the Gallo-Romans.

46 BC   Roman amphitheater built at Arles.

14 BC   The Pont du Gard aqueduct at Nîmes is erected.

AD 406   Invasion by the Vandals (Germanic tribes).

451   Attila invades and is defeated at Châlons.

The Merovingian Dynasty

486–511   Clovis, king of the Franks (481–511), defeats the Roman governor of Gaul and founds the Merovingian Dynasty. Great monasteries, such as those at Tours, Limoges, and Chartres, become centers of culture.

497   Franks convert to Christianity.

567   The Frankish kingdom is divided into three parts—the eastern countries (Austrasia), later to become Belgium and Germany; the western countries (Neustria), later to become France; and Burgundy.

The Carolingian Dynasty

768–78   Charlemagne (768–814) becomes king of the Franks (768); conquers northern Italy (774); and is defeated by the Moors at Roncesvalles, Spain, after which he consolidates the Pyrénées border (778).

800   The pope crowns Charlemagne Holy Roman Emperor in Rome. Charlemagne expands the French kingdom far beyond its present borders and establishes a center for learning at his capital, Aix-la-Chapelle (Aachen, in present-day Germany).

814–987   Death of Charlemagne. The Carolingian line continues through a dozen or so monarchs, with a batch called Charles (the Bald, the Fat, the Simple) and a sprinkling of Louis. Under the Treaty of Verdun (843), the empire is divided in two—the eastern half becoming Germany, the western half France.

The Capetian Dynasty

987   Hugh Capet (987–996) is made king of France and establishes the principle of hereditary rule for his descendants. Settled conditions and the increased power of the church see the flowering of Romanesque architecture in the cathedrals of Autun and Angoulême.

1066   Norman conquest of England by William the Conqueror (1028–87).

1067   Work begins on the Romanesque Bayeux Tapestry, celebrating the Norman Conquest.

ca. 1100   First universities in Europe include one in Paris. Development of European vernacular verse: *Chanson de Roland*.

1140   The Gothic style of architecture first appears at St-Denis and later becomes fully developed at the cathedrals of Chartres, Reims, Amiens, and Paris's Notre-Dame.

ca. 1150 Struggle between the Anglo-Norman kings (Angevin Empire) and the French; when Eleanor of Aquitaine switches husbands (from Louis VII of France to Henry II of England), her extensive lands pass to English rule.

1257 The Sorbonne University is founded in Paris.

1270 Louis IX (1226–70), the only French king to achieve sainthood, dies in Tunis on the seventh and last Crusade.

1302–07 Philippe IV the Fair (1285–1314) calls together the first States-General, predecessor to the French Parliament. He disbands the Knights Templars to gain their wealth (1307).

1309 Pope, under pressure, leaves a corrupt and disorderly Rome for Avignon in southern France, seat of the papacy for nearly 70 years.

The Valois Dynasty

1337–1453 Hundred Years' War between France and England: fighting for control of those areas of France gained by the English crown following the marriage of Eleanor of Aquitaine and Henry II.

1348–50 The Black Death rages in France.

1428–31 Joan of Arc (1412–31), the Maid of Orléans, sparks the revival of French fortunes in the Hundred Years' War but is captured by the English and burned at the stake at Rouen.

1434 Johannes Gutenberg invents the printing press in Strasbourg, Alsace.

1453 France finally defeats England, terminating the Hundred Years' War and English claims to the French throne.

1475 Burgundy at the height of its power under Charles the Bald.

1494 Italian wars: beginning of Franco-Hapsburg struggle for hegemony in Europe.

1515–47 Reign of François I, who imports Italian artists, including Leonardo da Vinci (1452–1519), and brings the Renaissance to France. The château of Fontainebleau is begun (1528).

1558 France captures Calais, England's last territory on French soil.

1562–98 Wars of Religion: Catholics versus Huguenots (French Protestants).

The Bourbon Dynasty

1589 The first Bourbon king, Henri IV (1589–1610), is a Protestant who converts to Catholicism and achieves peace in France. He signs the Edict of Nantes, giving limited freedom of worship to Protestants. The development of Renaissance Paris begins.

ca. 1610 Scientific revolution in Europe begins, marked by the discoveries of mathematician and philosopher René Descartes (1596–1650).

1643–1715 Reign of Louis XIV, the Sun King, a monarch who builds the Baroque power base of Versailles and presents Europe with a glorious view of France. With his first minister, Colbert, Louis makes France, by force of arms, the most powerful nation-state in Europe. He persecutes the Huguenots, who emigrate in great numbers, nearly ruining the French economy.

1660 Classical period of French culture: dramatists Pierre Corneille (1606–84), Jean-Baptiste Molière (1622–73), and Jean Racine (1639–99), and painter Nicolas Poussin (1594–1665).

ca. 1715 Rococo art and decoration develop in Parisian boudoirs and salons, typified by the painter Antoine Watteau (1684–1721) and, later, François Boucher (1703–70) and Jean-Honoré Fragonard (1732–1806).

1700– onward Writer and pedagogue François-Marien Voltaire (1694–1778) is a central figure in the French Enlightenment, along with Jean-Jacques Rousseau (1712–78) and Denis Diderot (1713–84), who, in 1751, compiles the first modern encyclopedia. The ideals of the Enlightenment—for reason and scientific method and against social and political injustices—pave the way for the French Revolution. In the arts, painter Jacques-Louis David (1748–1825) reinforces revolutionary creeds in his neoclassical works.

1756–63 The Seven Years' War results in France's losing most of its overseas possessions and in England's becoming a world power.

1776 The French assist the Americans in the Revolutionary War. Ideals of liberty cross the Atlantic with the returning troops to reinforce new social concepts.

The French Revolution

1789–1804 The Bastille is stormed on July 14, 1789. Following upon early Republican ideals comes the Reign of Terror and the administration of the Directory under Robespierre. There are widespread political executions—Louis XVI and Marie Antoinette are guillotined in 1793. Reaction sets in, and the instigators of the Terror are themselves executed (1794). Napoléon Bonaparte enters the champion of the Directory (1795–99) and is installed as First Consul during the Consulate (1799–1804).

The First Empire

1804 Napoléon crowns himself emperor of France at Notre-Dame in the presence of the pope.

1805–12 Napoléon conquers most of Europe. The Napoleonic Age is marked by a neoclassical artistic style called Empire as well as by the rise of Romanticism—characterized by such writers as François-Auguste-René de Chateaubriand (1768–1848) and Marie-Henri Stendhal (1783–1842), and the painters Eugène Delacroix (1798–1863) and Théodore Géricault (1791–1824)—which is to dominate the arts of the 19th century.

1812–14 Winter cold and Russian determination defeat Napoléon outside Moscow. The emperor abdicates and is transported to Elba.

Restoration of the Bourbons

1814–15 Louis XVIII, brother of the executed Louis XVI, regains the throne after the Congress of Vienna settles peace terms.

1815 The Hundred Days: Napoléon returns from Elba and musters an army on his march to the capital but lacks national support. He is defeated at Waterloo (June 18) and exiled to the island of St-Helena in the south Atlantic.

1821 Napoléon dies in exile.

1830 Bourbon king Charles X, locked into a pre-Revolutionary state of mind, abdicates. A brief upheaval (Three Glorious Days) brings Louis-Philippe, the Citizen King, to the throne.

1840 Napoléon's remains are brought back to Paris.

1846–48 Severe industrial and farming depression contributes to Louis-Philippe's abdication (1848).

Second Republic and Second Empire

1848–52 Louis-Napoléon (nephew and step-grandson of Napoléon I) is elected president of the short-lived Second Republic. He makes a successful attempt to assume supreme power and is declared emperor of France, taking the title Napoléon III.

ca. 1850 The ensuing period is characterized in the arts by the emergence of realist painters, such as Jean-François Millet (1814–75), Honoré Daumier (1808–79), and Gustave Courbet (1819–77), and late-Romantic writers, among them Victor Hugo (1802–85), Honoré de Balzac (1799–1850), and Charles Baudelaire (1821–87).

1863 Napoléon III inaugurates the Salon des Refusés in response to critical opinion. It includes work by Édouard Manet (1832–83), Claude Monet (1840–1926), and Paul Cézanne (1839–1906) and is commonly regarded as the birthplace of Impressionism and of modern art in general.

The Third Republic

1870–71 The Franco-Prussian War sees Paris besieged by and fall to the Germans. Napoléon III takes refuge in England. France loses Alsace and Lorraine to Prussia before the peace treaty is signed.

1871–1914 Before World War I, France expands its industries and builds vast colonial empires in North Africa and Southeast Asia. Sculptor Auguste Rodin (1840–1917), composers Maurice Ravel (1875–1937) and Claude Debussy (1862–1918), and poets such as Stéphane Mallarmé (1842–98) and Paul Verlaine (1844–96) set the stage for Modernism.

1870s Emergence of the Impressionist school of painting: Claude Monet, Auguste Renoir (1841–1919), Camille Pissarro (1830–1903), and Edgar Degas (1834–1917).

1889 The Eiffel Tower is built for the Paris World Exhibition. Centennial of the French Revolution.

1894–1906 Franco-Russian Alliance (1894). Dreyfus affair: The spy trial and its anti-Semitic backlash shock France.

1900 Paris holds World Exposition.

1904 The Entente Cordiale: England and France become firm allies.

1914–18 During World War I, France fights with the Allies, opposing Germany, Austria-Hungary, and Turkey. Germany invades France; most of the big battles (Vimy Ridge, Verdun, Somme, Marne) are fought in trenches in northern France. French casualties exceed 5 million. With the Treaty of Versailles (1919), France regains Alsace and Lorraine and attempts to exact financial and economic reparations from Germany.

1918–39 Between wars, Paris attracts artists and writers, including Americans Ernest Hemingway (1899–1961) and Gertrude Stein (1874–1946). France nourishes major artistic and philosophical movements: Constructivism, Dadaism, Surrealism, and Existentialism.

1939–45 At the beginning of World War II, France sides with the Allies until invaded and defeated by Germany in 1940. The French government, under Marshal Philippe Pétain (1856–1951), moves to Vichy and cooperates with the Nazis. French overseas colonies split between allegiance to the legal government of Vichy and declaration for the Free French Resistance, led (from London) by General Charles de Gaulle (1890–1970).

1944 D day, June 6: The Allies land on the beaches of Normandy and successfully invade France. Additional Allied forces land in Provence. Paris is liberated in August 1944, and France declares full allegiance to the Allies.

1944–46 A provisional government takes power under General de Gaulle; American aid assists French recovery.

The Fourth Republic

1946 France adopts a new constitution; French women gain the right to vote.

1946–54 In the French-Indochina War, France is unable to regain control of its colonies in Southeast Asia. The 1954 Geneva Agreement establishes two governments in Vietnam: one in the north, under the Communist leader Ho Chi Minh, and one in the south, under the emperor Bao Dai. U.S. involvement eventually leads to French withdrawal.

1954–62 The Algerian War leads to Algeria's independence from France. Other French African colonies gain independence.

1957 The Treaty of Rome establishes the European Economic Community (now known as the European Union—EU) with France as one of its members.

The Fifth Republic

1958–69 De Gaulle is the first president under a new constitution; he resigns in 1969, a year after widespread disturbances begun by student riots in Paris.

1976 The first supersonic transatlantic passenger service begins with the Anglo-French Concorde.

1981 François Mitterrand (1916–1996) is elected the first Socialist president of France since World War II.

1988 Mitterrand is elected for a second term.

1990 TGV (*Train à Grande Vitesse*) clocks a world record—515 kph (322 mph)—on a practice run. Channel Tunnel link-up between France and England begins.

1993 After nine years of painstaking renovations by I. M. Pei, American-Chinese architect, the Richelieu Wing of the Louvre is opened to the public, doubling the museum's exhibition space.

1994 The Channel Tunnel (or Chunnel) opens; trains link London to Paris in three hours.

1995 Jacques Chirac, mayor of Paris, is elected president. Paris becomes the focus of extremist terrorist bomb attacks and is crippled by one of the country's worst strikes of public employees in its history.

1997 The world's largest library, the Bibliothèque Nationale François-Mitterrand, is inaugurated in Paris. President Jacques Chirac calls early elections, a Socialist coalition wins a majority, and Lionel Jospin is appointed prime minister.

1998 France hosts Soccer World Cup, with final on July 12 at giant new stadium, the Stade de France, in St-Denis near Paris.

THE ART OF FRENCH COOKING

BORN BRITISH, naturalized American, I am an unabashed chauvinist about French food. To wander through a French open market, the vegetables overflowing from their crates, the fruits cascading in casual heaps on the counter, is a sensual pleasure. To linger outside a bakery in the early morning, watching the fresh breads and croissants being lined up in regimental rows, must awaken the most fickle appetite. Just to read the menu posted outside a modest café alerts the imagination to pleasures to come.

Best of all, the French are happy to share their enthusiasm for good food with others. There are more good restaurants and eating places in France than in any other European country; the streets are lined with delicatessens, butchers, cheese shops, bakeries, and pastry shops. And I have yet to find a Frenchman, cantankerous though he may be, who does not warm to anyone who shows an interest in his national passion for wines and fine cuisine.

Fine cuisine does not necessarily mean fancy cuisine. Masters though French chefs are of the soufflé and the butter sauce, the salmon in aspic, and the strawberry *feuilleté* (puff pastry), such delicacies are reserved for celebration. Everyday fare is much more likely to be roast chicken, steak and *frites* (fries), omelet, or pork chop. Bread, eaten without butter, is mandatory at main meals, while the bottle of mineral water is almost as common as wine.

Where the French do score is in the variety and quality of their ingredients. Part of the credit must go to climate and geography—just look at the length of the French coastline and the part seafood plays in the cooking of Normandy, Brittany, and Provence. Count the number of rivers with fertile valleys for cattle and crops. Olives and fruit flourish in the Mediterranean sun, while the region from southwest of Paris running up north to the Belgian border is one of the great breadbaskets of Europe.

No one but the French identifies three basic styles of cuisine—classical, nouvelle, and regional. No other European nation pays so much attention to menus and recipes.

Most sophisticated are the sauces and soufflés, the *mousselines* and *macédoines* of classical cuisine. Starting in the 17th century, successive generations of chefs have lovingly documented their dishes, developing an intellectual discipline from what is an essentially practical art. As a style, classical cuisine is now outmoded, but its techniques form the basis of rigorous professional training in French cooking. In some measure, all other styles of cooking are based on its principles.

Nouvelle cuisine, for instance, is directly descended from the classics. Launched with great fanfare more than 20 years ago, it takes a fresh, lighter approach, with simpler sauces and a colorful view of presentation. First-course salads, often with hot additions of shellfish, chicken liver, or bacon, have become routine. For a while, cooks experimented with such way-out combinations as vanilla with lobster and chicken with raspberries, but now new-style cooking has settled down, establishing its own classics. Typical are *magrets de canard* (boned duck breast) sautéed like steak and served with a brown sauce of wine or green peppercorns, and pot-au-feu made of fish rather than the usual beef.

COOKS HAVE RECENTLY made a refreshing return toward country-style cooking. Indeed, many cooks never left it, for classical and nouvelle cuisines are almost exclusively the concern of professionals. However, regional dishes are cooked by everyone—chefs, housewives, grandma, and the café on the corner.

The city of Lyon exemplifies the best of regional cuisine. It features such local specialties as poached eggs in *meurette* (red-wine sauce), *quenelles* (fish dumplings) in crayfish sauce, sausage with pistachios, and chocolate *gâteau* (cake). The Lyonnais hotly dispute Paris's title of gastronomic capital of France, pointing to the number of prestigious restaurants in their city. What is more, some of the world's finest wines are produced only 90 miles north, in Burgundy.

LYON MAY REPRESENT the best of French regional cooking, but there's plenty to look for elsewhere. Compare the sole of Normandy, cooked with mussels in cream sauce, with the sea bass of Provence, flamed with dried fennel or baked with tomatoes and thyme. Contrast the butter cakes of Brittany with the yeast breads of Alsace, the braised endive of Picardy with the gratin of cardoons (a type of artichoke) found in the south.

Authentic regional specialties are based on local products. They have a character that may depend on climate (cream cakes survive in Normandy but not in Provence) or geography (each mountain area has its own dried sausages and hams). History brought spice bread to Dijon, legacy of the days when the dukes of Burgundy controlled Flanders and the spice trade. Ethnic heritage explains ravioli around Nice on the Italian border, waffles in the north near Belgium, and dumplings close to Germany. Modern ethnic influences show up in cities, with many an Arab pastry shop started by Algerian immigrants and many a restaurant run by Vietnamese.

Fundamental to French existence is the baker, the *boulanger*. From medieval times, legislation has governed the weight and content of loaves of bread, with stringent penalties for such crimes as adulteration with sand or sawdust. Today the government pegs the price of white bread, and you'll find the famous long loaves a bargain compared with the price of brioche, croissants, or loaves of whole wheat (*pain complet*), rye (*pain de seigle*), and bran (*pain de son*). White bread can be bought as thin *flûtes* to slice for soup; as baguettes; or as the common, thicker loaves known simply as *pains*.

Since French bread stays fresh for only a few hours, it is baked in the morning for midday and baked again in the afternoon. A baker's day starts at 4 AM to give the dough time to rise. Sadly, there is a lack of recruits, so more and more French bread is being produced industrially, without the right nutty flavor and chew to the crisp crust. The clue to bread baked on the spot is the heady smell of fermenting yeast, so sniff out a neighborhood bakery before you buy.

IF BREAD IS THE STAFF of French life, pastry is the sugar icing. The window of a city pastry shop (in the country, bakery and pastry shop are often combined) is a wonderland of éclairs and meringues, madeleines, and puff pastry, spun sugar, and caramel. You'll find pies laden with seasonal fruit, nut cakes, and chocolate cakes, plus the baker's specialty, for he is certain to have one. Survey them with a sharp eye; they should be small (good ingredients are expensive) and impeccably alike in color and size (the sign of an expert craftsman). Last, the window should not be overflowing; because of the high cost, the temptation to cram the shelves with leftovers from the day before is strong.

THE CHARCUTERIE is almost as French an institution as the bakery. *Chair cuite* means "cooked meat," and a charcuterie is a kind of delicatessen, specializing in pâtés, terrines, ham, and sausages. A charcuterie also sells long-lasting salads, such as cucumber, tomato, or grated carrot vinaigrette and root celery (celeriac) *rémoulade* (with mustard mayonnaise). Cooked "dishes of the day" may include coq au vin and *choucroute alsacienne* (sauerkraut with smoked pork hock). Often you'll also find such condiments as pickles, plus a modest selection of wines, cheeses, and desserts—rice pudding or baked apple, for example. Only bread is needed to complete the meal, and you're set for the world's best picnic!

French cheese deserves, and gets, close attention. Choosing a cheese is as delicate a matter as deciding on the right wine. In a good cheese shop you will be welcome to sample any of the cut cheeses, and assistants will gladly offer advice. One cardinal rule is to look for *fromage fermier* (farmhouse cheese), a rough equivalent of château-bottled wine. If the label says *lait cru* (raw milk)—even better; only when milk is unpasteurized does the flavor of some cheeses, Camembert, for example, develop properly. Try to keep a cheese cool without refrigeration and eat it as soon as you can. Delicate soft cheeses like Brie can become overripe within a matter of hours, one reason it is rare to find a wide-ranging selection of cheeses in a restaurant.

MANY OTHER KINDS of specialty stores exist, often for local products. In Dijon, for instance, you'll find shops selling mustards in ornamental pots; in Gascony (near Bordeaux), it's foie gras and canned confit (preserved duck or goose). But the most famous concentration of food shops in the world must be clustered around place de la Madeleine in Paris. On one corner stands Fauchon, dean of luxury food emporiums. Just across the square stands Hédiard, specializing in spices, rare fruits, and preserves.

The Madeleine crossroads may be unique, but with a bit of persistence, a more modest version can be found in most French towns in the weekly market, often held in a picturesque open hall that may be centuries old. Markets start early, typically around 8 AM, and often disband at noon. In Paris, street markets continue to thrive in almost every quarter, and although the main wholesale market of Les Halles has moved to the suburbs, the area around rue Coquillière is still worth exploring for its maze of truffle vendors, game purveyors, and professional kitchen-equipment outlets.

French markets are still dominated by the season—there is little or no sign of frozen produce and meats. The first baby lamb heralds Christmas; little chickens arrive around Easter, together with kid and asparagus. Autumn excitement comes with game—venison, pheasant, and wild boar. Even cheeses look and taste different according to the time of year.

If you're an early riser, there's a long wait until lunch, for snacks are not a French habit. The structure of a meal, its timing, and its content are taken seriously. The "grazing" phenomenon of minimeals snatched here and there throughout the day is almost unheard of, and snacks are regarded as spoiling the appetite, not to mention being nutritionally unsound.

Still, the French light breakfast can come as no surprise; its unbeatable wake-up combination of croissant, brioche, or crusty roll with coffee has swept much of the world. Traditionally, the coffee comes as café au lait, milky and steaming in a wide two-handled bowl for dipping the bread.

At noon you'll be rewarded by what, for most Frenchmen, remains the main meal of the day. In much of the country, everything stops for two hours; children return from school, and museums and businesses lock their doors. The pattern is much the same in large provincial cities. Restaurants, bistros, and cafés are crammed with diners, most of whom eat at least two and often three or more courses.

LUNCH KEEPS FRENCH adults going until evening, but you may want to follow the example of schoolchildren, who are allowed a treat on the way home. Often it is a *pain au chocolat* (chocolate croissant). By 8 PM, you'll be ready for dinner and one of the greatest pleasures France has to offer.

The choice of restaurants in France is a feast in itself. At least once during your trip you may want to indulge in an outstanding occasion. But restaurants are just the beginning. You can also eat out in cafés, bistros, brasseries, fast-food outlets (they, too, have reached France), or auberges, which range from staid country inns to sybaritic hideaways.

Simplest is the café (where the espresso machine is king), offering drinks and such snacks as *croque monsieur* (toasted ham and cheese sandwich), *oeufs sur le plat* (fried eggs), *le hot dog,* and foot-long sandwiches of French bread. Larger-city cafés serve hot meals, such dishes as onion soup and braised beef with vegetables, consumed on marble-topped tables to a background of cheerful banter. Like English pubs, French cafés are a way of life, a focal point for gossip and dominoes in practically every village.

The bistro, once interchangeable with the café, has recently taken a fashionable turn. In cities, instead of sawdust on the floor and a zinc-topped counter, you may find that a bistro is designer-decorated, serving new-style cuisine to a trendy, chattering crowd. If you're lucky the food will be as witty and colorful as the clientele.

With few exceptions, brasseries remain unchanged—great bustling places with white-aproned waiters and hearty food. Go to them for oysters on the half shell and fine seafood, garlic snails, *boudin* (black pudding), sauerkraut, and vast ice cream desserts. Originally a brasserie brewed beer, and since many brewers came from

Alsace on the borders of Germany, the cooking reflects their origins.

Training is an important factor in maintaining the standards of French cooking. Professional chefs begin their three-year apprenticeship at age 16, starting in baking, pastry, or cuisine and later branching out into such specialties as aspic work and sugar sculpture. To be a *chocolatier* is a career in itself. Much more than a manual trade, cooking in France aspires to being an art, and its exponents achieve celebrity status. Each decade has its stars, their rise and fall a constant source of eager speculation in the press and at the table.

The importance placed on food in France is echoed by the number of gastronomic societies, from the Chevaliers du Tastevin to the Chaîne des Rôtisseurs and the Confrérie des Cordons Bleus, to mention only three. The French believe that good eating, at whatever level, is an art that merits considerable time and attention. They have done the hard work, and, as a traveler, you can reap the benefits.

— Anne Willan

Anne Willan is president and founder of the École de Cuisine La Varenne in Paris. Her food column in the *Washington Post* is widely syndicated and her books include *French Regional Cooking* and *La Varenne's Cooking Course*.

AN INTRODUCTION TO FRENCH WINE

ALTHOUGH FRANCE marginally trails Italy as the largest wine-producing country in the world, the reputation of French wines is second to none. That's partly because of luck—the exceptional variety of France's soils and climate—and partly because of 2,000 years of know-how. Few understand better than the French which grapes produce the best wines and where.

The credentials of French wines have been internationally established since at least 1787, when Thomas Jefferson went down to Bordeaux and splurged on bottles of 1784 Château d'Yquem and Château Margaux, for prices that were, he reported, "indeed dear." Jefferson knew his wines: In 1855, both Yquem and Margaux were officially classified among Bordeaux's top five. In 1986, Jefferson's unopened bottle of Yquem rated $56,000 at auction. The Margaux—of which Jefferson boasted "there cannot be a better bottle of Bordeaux" (in fact, it was a half bottle)—was sold for $30,000 in 1987.

With such eminent roots, it is no surprise that the United States is the richest export market for French wines, along with Great Britain. France, like Italy, produces about 20% of the world's wine—more than double that of Spain and Russia and four times as much as the United States. Nearly a quarter of a million people in France make and sell wine. Many more produce it for their own consumption.

Bordeaux's reputation dates from the Middle Ages. From 1152 to 1453, along with much of what is now western France, Bordeaux belonged to England. The light red wine then produced was known as *clairet,* the origin of our word "claret." Champagne, on the other hand, has existed as we know it only since 1700, when—thanks to the introduction of strong bottles, cork stoppers, and the blending of wines from different vineyards—its sparkle was first captured by a blind monk, Dom Pérignon. The abbey at Hautvillers, where he lived, is a pilgrimage site for champagne aficionados. So is the monster oak barrel languishing in the Épernay cellars of the Mercier firm: It has a mind-boggling capacity of 200,000 bottles, and 24 thirsty oxen spent three weeks carting it to the Paris Exhibition in 1889.

Such publicity coups have brought champagne fame, fortune—and problems. Like cognac (a brandy produced in a strictly defined area north of Bordeaux), its name is illegally exploited worldwide by would-be imitators. Producers of the real McCoy fight such fraud in international law courts, but it is a hapless struggle. It has proved easier for French authorities to attack fraud in their own backyard. Thomas Jefferson, who cagily noted that his expensive wines were "bought on the spot and therefore genuine," would have enjoyed perusing today's legal texts. Their bureaucratic aridity may be of no succor to the thirsty tourist, but their role is essential in ensuring that the wine in your glass is precisely what the bottle says it is.

Prominently printed on any self-respecting French wine label is the term Appellation d'Origine Contrôlée (often abbreviated AC). Such wines have to meet stringent requirements. Yield, production methods, and geographic limits are meticulously controlled, as are the varieties of grapes that are permitted (sometimes one, sometimes several—no fewer than 13 types of grapes can be used at Châteauneuf-du-Pape), and the requisite degree of alcohol (all wines must respect a minimum, ranging from 8.5% for the sunless, sharp, white Gros Plant Nantais to 13% for sweet whites like Sauternes). AC wines now account for nearly a third of production, a figure that has doubled in 20 years.

THE NEXT CATEGORY, Vin Délimité de Qualité Supérieure (VDQS), accounts for about 10% of French wines. It is a sort of second division for wines that may be promoted to the AC category if they prove their mettle and show signs of steady improvement. Then come the Vins de Pays, regional titles with fewer restrictions, that account for about 15% of production.

The simplest classification is Vin de Table, a poor relation in terms of price, if not necessarily quality.

Each bottle tells a tale. Usually the fancier it is, the more it has to hide. Beware of garish labels. Also, note where the wine was bottled: If it was not bottled on the spot (*mise en bouteille à la propriété/au domaine/au château*) or at least by a local merchant (often the case with burgundies), it should be treated with suspicion.

Napoléon, incidentally, was partial to unblended burgundy and, in a fit of alcoholic lucidity, once revealed the secret of his military genius: "No wine—no soldiers!" The English took the rival view of battle before wine: General Palmer celebrated victory over Napoléon at Waterloo by galloping down to Margaux and founding Château Palmer.

The vineyards of Margaux are among the ugliest in France, lost amid the flat, dusty plains of Médoc. Bordeaux is better represented at historic St-Émilion, with its cascading cobbled streets, or at Sauternes, where the noble rot (a fungus that sucks water from the grapes, leaving them sweeter) steals up the riverbanks as autumn mists vanish in the summer skies. From the chilly hills of Champagne in the north to the sun-pelted slopes of the southern Midi, vines cover France. Steep-banked terraces tower above the River Rhône. The vineyards of Alsace sway and ripple into the foothills of the Vosges. Chalky cliffs, cellars, and caves line the softly lit Loire Valley.

Names of wines can be as charming as the scenery. The Loire Valley yields Vin de Pays du Jardin de la France—Country Wine from the Garden of France. Entre-Deux-Mers quaintly translates as Between Two Seas (actually the Garonne and Dordogne rivers). It's difficult to resist flowery Fleurie, lovable St-Amour, sober Bouzy, or—if you overindulge—an early Graves.

More than a hundred different types of grapes exist in France. Some sound delicious. Try wrapping your tongue around Mourvèdre, Bourboulenc, Gewürtztraminer, or Sciacarello. Visualize a bunch of Barbarossa ("red beard"), Folle Blanche ("crazy white"), or Fer ("iron"). Some names are confusing: The Auxerrois grape is used at Cahors, not near Auxerre; the Beaunois is used near Auxerre, not near Beaune; the St-Émilion is used for making cognac, not St-Émilion; while the Melon de Bourgogne has nothing to do with melons or burgundy (it's a white grape grown near the Atlantic coast).

YOU CAN BUY local wines from a cooperative (which handles wines from a number of local growers) or from an individual producer. Although the big champagne houses in Reims and Épernay organize slick, informative visits, the leading Bordeaux châteaux are only just beginning to—partly because the Bordelais are notoriously reserved, mainly because they have had no need to seduce passersby: Bulk orders account for 99% of their sales. You can obtain parsimonious gulps of second-string clarets at the Maison du Vin on the cours du XXX-juillet in central Bordeaux, but, unfortunately, there is nothing to match the Marché aux Vins in the Burgundian town of Beaune, where a string of fine burgundies can be sampled for a modest sum.

Different occasions warrant different wines. If you're buying wine for a picnic, go for something simple, such as a rosé or fruity red (Beaujolais or Gamay de Touraine). Full-bodied reds from the hottest regions of France are likely to knock you out if you drink them at lunchtime. Beware of restaurant wine lists designed to beef up the price of your meal, and always go for the house wine rather than a vague description such as "Bordeaux" or "Côtes du Rhône"; if there's no year or precise origin, don't expect quality. If wine is made locally, try it; you may not come across it elsewhere, and regional cuisine is invariably tailored to regional wines.

The harvests, or *vendanges,* begin in September and can last into December. In Sauternes, the grapes have to rot before being picked, and at Château d'Yquem, up to seven successive manual harvests may be required, with each grape inspected individually and picked only after achieving the right degree of maturity (by which time it looks a foul, shriveled mess). The year's biggest celebration, however, is the appearance of Beaujolais Nouveau on the third Thursday of November. Wine villages pay tribute to their patron saint on January 22, St. Vincent's Day.

Other wines to look out for include two from the Jura region of eastern France. Vin

Jaune, also made from grapes picked late, is kept in oak barrels for six years or longer while yeasts form on the surface; the result is a wine (with a unique, nutty flavor sometimes likened to sherry) that can last for more than a hundred years. The grapes that produce the strong, amber-color Vin de Paille are left for two months on straw mats while the juice is drawn out and the sugar concentration intensifies.

CHAMPAGNE OFFERS tiny quantities of wine without a fizz. Still reds and whites made near Reims are known as Côteaux Champenois while, far to the south, there is even a still pink, Rosé des Riceys: rare, delicious, and expensive. Neither the truly black wine of Cahors nor the sweet white Jurançon of the Pyrénées is easy to find, unlike the sand wines (Vins de Sable) of Provence, which are made from vines that creep right down to the beach. There are even vines in and around Paris, at Suresnes and Montmartre, where the harvest is celebrated behind the basilica of Sacré-Coeur on the first weekend of October; unfortunately, the resultant wine is often undrinkable.

Don't be a prisoner of fashion. Marketing men have convinced the British that Muscadet is *the* dry white, while Americans jostle for Pouilly-Fumé and Sancerre—fine wines, certainly, but in overhyped demand and therefore of poor value. Try instead to ferret out unfamiliar, peasanty wines, concocted by authentic local characters. If you hunt around, you may meet someone like Marcel.

Marcel makes illegal wines out of illegal vines in a lost corner of Burgundy that is off both the beaten track and the straight and narrow. People say—maps and guidebooks, anyway—there aren't any vines in Marcel's bit of Burgundy. We ambled over the Canal du Nivernais and scrambled up a hill. The hill became a street and the street

a village square. There was a large sign on the square saying LOCAL WINE. It was 12:15. The wine merchant was closed for lunch. Till 3. We sidled hopefully into a bar. "Local wine? Not here. Try Gaston by the church."

Gaston sold it, all right, and sloshed some into cracked glass beakers. We stared solemnly at the wine, and all the flat-hatted old men playing cards in the corner stared solemnly at us. We shared impressions. Unexpected. Perky but pale. Seemed friendly, but you never know.

Gaston leaned confidentially forward, stroked his mustache, and asked, "Want some more?" Yes. "Try that fellow there who's just gone out." Which fellow? "Marcel," said Gaston, adding helpfully, "The one in the flat hat."

Eventually—many country roads and twisty bends later—we tracked Marcel down. Who were we? We'd come about the wine. What wine? His wine. Marcel looked suspicious. His *excellent* wine. Marcel mellowed and got out the key to his cellar. We clattered down the slimy steps, taste buds tingling. Marcel grabbed a bottle. The wine's freshness came soaring through the dinge. Its sunniness pierced the murk. Marcel tossed back a glass and belched.

We murmured a few clichés of admiration. Marcel downed another glass, receded into the darkest, dirtiest depths of his cellar and rummaged under a heap of jerricans. Out popped a bottle as black as ink. Marcel squirted some into a glass, dashed it back and said, "Let's finish the bottle!"

Drinking this thick, cloying illegality was like being half-strangled in a velvet curtain. We fought our way free and staggered to the car with a crate. Marcel turned his back on us, brandished his francs triumphantly, and watered his garden in celebration.

—Simon Hewitt

A SURVEY OF FRENCH ARCHITECTURE

DESPITE THE RAVAGES OF wars throughout the centuries, France retains examples of nearly every historic and regional style.

Each region has its own characteristics. The dark red brick of the north stands in contrast to the pink brick of Toulouse, as does the white, chalky stone of the Cognac and Champagne regions when compared with the pink sandstone of the Vosges. Roofs vary as well, from the steep slopes of Alsace to the flat, orange-tiled expanses of the Midi and the colorful slate patterns of Burgundy.

Medieval black-and-white timber-frame houses survive in towns north of the Loire, such as Troyes, Dinan, Rennes, and the Petite France sector of Strasbourg. Castles perch grandly on cliffs throughout the southwest; hilltop villages survey the vineyards and olive groves of Provence in the southeast. Grim gateways repel strangers in the Charente region, whereas flower-strewn balconies welcome them to Alsace. Flemish belfries and Spanish gables flourish in the north, while the Germans, armed with their heavy Gothic-Renaissance style, transformed parts of Strasbourg into a Gallic Berlin.

Although the cave paintings at Lascaux in the Dordogne and the freestanding *menhirs* of Brittany prove that Frenchmen (or their ancestors) have created and constructed since prehistoric times, the first great builders were the Romans. Their efforts—mostly in ruins—are found throughout France, especially in the south. The amphitheaters of Nîmes and Arles, the theater of Orange, and the Pont du Gard aqueduct are masterpieces equal to anything in Italy. Autun, Saintes, and Reims have proud Roman arches, and even the sprawling cities of Lyon and Paris house Roman remains.

With occasional exceptions, such as the 5th-century chapel at La Pépiole, near Toulon, the next architectural style of note was the Carolingian, in the 9th and 10th centuries. Surviving examples include the Basse-Oeuvre at Beauvais and the octagonal abbey church of Ottmarsheim in Alsace. The massive Romanesque style that succeeded Carolingian differed in various ways—with its stone (as opposed to wood) ceilings or vaults, its introduction of windows high up the walls, and its preference for stone sculpture over such superficial ornament as mosaic and painting. Many 10th- and 11th-century Romanesque buildings survive in Burgundy, Alsace, the Auvergne, and western France, notably Poitiers, with the intricately carved west front of the church of Notre-Dame-la-Grande.

The airier Gothic of the great French cathedrals built between the 12th and 16th centuries represented a fundamental departure from Romanesque. The most obvious visual change: Pointed arches replaced round ones. Just as important, though, was a new vaulting structure based on intersecting ribbed vaults, which sprang across the roof from column to column. Outward thrust was borne by flying buttresses, slender arches linking the outer walls to freestanding columns, often topped by spiky pinnacles. Whereas Romanesque architecture had thick, blocky walls with little room for window space, Gothic architecture, technically more sophisticated, replaced stone with stained glass.

Most medieval churches were built in the form of a cross, often topped by a tower in Romanesque churches. The nave, divided into bays (the spaces between columns) and flanked on either side by aisles, formed the main body of the church, with the east end, known as the chancel, containing the choir and altar. Many Gothic churches also have a number of small chapels behind the high altar, forming an outline known as the *chevet*, or apse.

ROMANESQUE AND GOTHIC churches are divided into three or four distinct vertical sections, like strata. Forestlike rows of pillars, topped by carved capitals, spring from the ground either to a gallery or triforium (an arcade of small columns and arches, originally of stone, later filled with glass), then to a clerestory (row of windows) above. The Romanesque facade was intended as an ornate screen and was sometimes fronted by a large porch (or narthex). The tympanum, a large sculpted panel above the central doorway (usually representing Christ in Judgment or Glory), was retained in the Gothic facade, which also featured huge portals, a circular rose window, a statue gallery, and lofty towers. Other towers, over the crossing or alongside the transepts, gradually lost favor: The stone bulls on top of the many-towered cathedral of Laon mourn a dying breed.

POINTED ARCHES and ribbed vaults were first used during the 1130s at Sens and St-Denis—home of Abbot Suger, the leading political figure of the day. Within a decade, local bishops had followed Suger's lead, and huge Gothic cathedrals were under way at Noyon, Senlis, and Laon. As France expanded during the early Middle Ages from its Parisian epicenter, Gothic went with it. But the Gothic style did not displace the Romanesque overnight. Many Romanesque churches survive as crypts beneath later buildings (as at Dijon Cathedral, for example). Similarly, Romanesque naves were conserved at Mont-St-Michel, Vézelay, and Le Mans despite the addition of new Gothic chancels. At Strasbourg Cathedral, the reverse is true and a Romanesque chancel survives.

As the Gothic style evolved, less and less stone was used, and churches became delicate, almost skeletal. Paris's Ste-Chapelle is the most famous example, though as a stained-glass showcase, its scale doesn't match that of Metz Cathedral or St-Urbain in Troyes. The circular rose window spans through the Middle Ages like a leitmotif, evolving from 13th-century geometric splendor at St-Denis and Notre-Dame in Paris to a petal-like fluidity during the first half of the 16th century.

Height was another Gothic quest. Roofs soared higher and higher—until that at Beauvais Cathedral came crashing down in 1284. Notre-Dame of Paris is 106 feet high, but later cathedrals are even taller: Chartres climbs 114 ft; Bourges 120; Reims 124; Amiens 137; and Beauvais an ill-fated 153.

THE CHAMBIGES family, last in a long line of medieval master masons and star glaziers, played a major role in the development of the Flamboyant style. When the bishop of Beauvais was planning a grandiose transept he sent for Martin Chambiges, tempting him away from Sens and keeping him jealously at Beauvais for 30 years. Some see in the flamelike Flamboyant style the last shrieks of Gothic decadence. But while its decorative profusion smacks of sculptural self-indulgence (St-Pierre in Caen is a good example), there are some admirable Flamboyant churches—take St-Séverin (Paris) and St-Nicolas de Port near Nancy.

In the 16th century, Gothic architecture was subject to the influx of Renaissance ideas, given official encouragement when François I (1515–47) invited Italian painters and architects Il Rosso, Primaticcio, and Leonardo da Vinci to his court. Renaissance architecture, marked by a stylistic return to ancient Rome, existed side by side with Gothic throughout the 16th century. In a number of Paris churches you will see classical columns and ornaments superimposed on Gothic structures (St-Étienne-du-Mont, St-Gervais, and St-Eustache are the best examples). While Gothic was essentially an ecclesiastical style, the chief creations of Renaissance architecture were the châteaux of noblemen, princes, and kings. In the Loire Valley, medieval castles (like Chinon) gradually yielded to ideals of comfort and luxury (like Cheverny). Along the way, Renaissance proportion and daintiness were mingled with medieval massiveness, as at Azay-le-Rideau and Amboise.

TO CONTRAST the Renaissance style with the Baroque, its successor, compare the pink-brick arcades of the place des Vosges in Paris (1612) with the grand, solemn stonework of the place Vendôme, built in 1685 across town. A similar difference can be observed between the intimate château of Fontainebleau (mid-16th century) and the immense palace of Versailles (late 17th century).

Baroque imbued the classical style with drama and a sense of movement: Take a look at Mansart's dome surging above Paris's Hôtel des Invalides, or the powerful rhythms of Charles Perrault's Louvre facade. Yet only in northern France, under the temporary influence of Spanish occupiers, did Latin exuberance find an outlet, typified in the soaring curls on the colossal belfry of St-Amand-les-Eaux near Lille. The overblown fantasies of Baroque in Italy, Spain, southern Germany, and Austria—wild curves, broken outlines, and sculptural overkill—were held firmly in check by the French love of discipline. Whole towns survive to remind us: The rigid plan and identical houses of Richelieu, south of Chinon, are restrained and austere.

The 18th century saw several major provincial building programs in the neoclassical style—a more literal, toned-down interpretation of antique precedent. The state rooms of Strasbourg's Château des Rohan, the charming place Stanislas in Nancy, and the Grand Théâtre and place de la Bourse in Bordeaux are top examples. Baroque, however, continued to dominate church building until the early 19th century (witness the cathedrals of Nancy and Arras). Many clerics commissioned architects to dress up Gothic buildings in classical apparel, sticking pilasters on columns or transforming pointed arches into rounded ones. Louis XIV set the tone by remodeling the choir of Notre-Dame in Paris in 1708, but Autun Cathedral—revamped throughout—is the most extreme example of such architectural rethink.

NAPOLÉON USHERED in the 19th century with the Arc de Triomphe, which remained unfinished for 20 years—typifying the hesitations of a century bereft of original ideas. Iron made its appearance—most obviously at the Eiffel Tower, most frequently accompanied by glass in train stations and covered markets.

The 19th century bequeathed us Paris as we know it, with Baron Haussmann carving boulevards through the city. Luckily, Haussmann's seven-story buildings have proved sufficiently large and imposing to withstand the rapacious onslaughts of modern developers, and central Paris has remained unchanged for 100 years. But it's not surprising that the showpiece of Haussmann's Paris, the Opéra, is a pompous jumble of styles.

THINGS PERKED UP in the 20th century. While such Paris landmarks as the Grand and Petit Palais and opulent town halls throughout the country were faithful to conservative taste, Émile Gallé and Hector Guimard led an artistic revolution known as Art Nouveau, with sinuous, nature-based forms. The Paris métro, ornamented by iron railings and canopies, is the most familiar example. A reaction occurred in the straighter lines of Art Deco, which first turned up at the Théâtre des Champs-Élysées in 1913. At the same time, the French developed a taste for reinforced concrete that they have never lost. Its most imaginative exponent was Swiss-born Le Corbusier, an architectural Picasso whose best work (like the chapel at Ronchamp in eastern France) obeys few established rules.

In the first half of the 20th century, much energy was spent repairing the damage of two world wars: Many towns had to be rebuilt almost from scratch. The result at its worst was bland and hurried (Amiens, Reims), at its best spacious, rational, and monumentally austere (Le Havre). Official buildings—like town halls and train stations—number among the most significant buildings of the period.

The most-visited postwar building in France is Paris's futuristic Pompidou Center. Its pipes and workings are on the outside, ensuring that the interior is uncluttered to a fault. Paris's latter-day skyscrapers have—with the exception of the Tour Montparnasse—been banished to the city outskirts, notably at La Défense. There, the giant glass-and-concrete arch known as La Tête Défense has cemented a vista that stretches along avenue de la Grande Armée, past the Arc de Triomphe, down the Champs-Élysées, across place de la Concorde, and over the Tuileries to the gleaming glass pyramid of the Louvre.

—Simon Hewitt

BOOKS AND VIDEOS

THE BEST INTRODUCTION to modern France, surveying social, political, and economic developments, is John Ardagh's *France Today*. A witty, but less complete, survey of the country and its people is Theodore Zeldin's *The French*. Another entry on the list is Richard Bernstein's *Fragile Glory*. An immensely popular, if slightly satiric, introduction to French country life is provided by Peter Mayle's two autobiographical books on Provence, *A Year in Provence* and *Toujours Provence*, as well as by his novel *Chasing Cézanne*.

Nancy Mitford's readable *The Sun King* covers the regal grandeur of the 17th century, while Alfred Cobban's workmanlike *History of Modern France* describes trends and events from the death of Louis XIV up to 1962. Another readable and fascinating book about French history is Barbara Tuchman's *A Distant Mirror*. Dorothy Carrington's classic work on Corsica, *Granite Island: A Portrait of Corsica*, is available at the library. For a history of Paris from the Revolution to the Belle Époque, look for Johannes Willms's *Paris: Capital of Europe*. For modern French history, particularly the Vichy Era, a good bet is Robert Paxton's *Vichy France and the Jews*. Alice Kaplan's *French Lessons* is an engaging memoir about her passion for the French language and her connection to France. For a scholarly study of Romanesque and Gothic architecture, read Henri Focillon's thoughtfully illustrated *The Art of the West*, available at the library.

As for books about French wine and cuisine, Patricia Wells's *The Food Lover's Guide to Paris* and *The Food Lover's Guide to France* provide a good beginning. Waverly Root's *The Food of France* is a great accompaniment to any trip. Alexis Lichine's *Guide to Wines and Vineyards of France* is still the classic wine guide, though it's now only available from the library. For more books about French wine, try Robert M. Parker's *Bordeaux: A Comprehensive Guide to the Wines Produced from 1961–1990* and *Wines of the Rhône Valley*. A. J. Liebling's *Between Meals* provides a more literary and entertaining look at the fine art of eating in France.

Charles Dickens in *A Tale of Two Cities,* George Orwell in *Down and Out in Paris and London,* Ernest Hemingway, notably in *A Moveable Feast,* F. Scott Fitzgerald in *Tender is the Night,* and Gertrude Stein in *Paris, France* are just some of the authors who have written about Paris in English. The novels of Émile Zola—*La Curée, L'Assommoir, Nana,* and *La Débâcle*—are mostly set in Provence or in Paris, emerging from mid-19th-century reconstruction amid backstreet squalor and brash glamour. A good thriller set in France is *Assignment in Brittany* by Helen MacInnes.

If you want to see France on film before you go, consider renting one of the following films: Louis Malle's *Au Revoir Les Enfants* (1987), which takes place during World War II in Provins in Ile-de-France; Krzysztof Kieslowski's *The Double Life of Véronique* (1991), a mysterious drama set in Paris and Poland; *Everyone Says I Love You* (1996), a Woody Allen comedy with Paris as a backdrop; *Jean de Florette* (1986) or *My Father's Glory* (1990), Claude Berri's and Yves Robert's views of rural Provençal life; *My Favorite Season* (1993), André Techiné's family drama set in southwest France; *Mr. Hulot's Holiday* (1953), Jacques Tati's classic comedy on the beach in Brittany; *Ready to Wear* (1994), Robert Altman's send-up of the fashion industry in Paris; *The Return of Martin Guerre* (1982), Daniel Vigne's vision of 16th-century village life; *A Sunday in the Country* (1984), Bertrand Tavernier's story of a day in the life of an elderly painter on his country estate; *To Catch a Thief* (1955), Alfred Hitchcock's mystery set on the French Riviera, with Grace Kelly and Cary Grant; and *When the Cat's Away* (1996), Cédric Klapisch's story of a young woman searching for her lost cat in the Bastille neighborhood of Paris.

FRENCH VOCABULARY

One of the trickiest French sounds to pronounce is the nasal final *n* sound (whether or not the *n* is actually the last letter of the word). You should try to pronounce it as a sort of nasal grunt—as in "huh." The vowel that precedes the *n* will govern the vowel sound of the word, and in this list we precede the final *n* with an *h* to remind you to be nasal.

Another problem sound is the ubiquitous but untransliterable *eu,* as in *bleu* (blue) or *deux* (two), and the very similar sound in *je* (I), *ce* (this), and *de* (of). The closest equivalent might be the vowel sound in "put," but rounded.

Words and Phrases

	English	French	Pronunciation
Basics			
	Yes/no	Oui/non	wee/nohn
	Please	S'il vous plaît	seel voo **play**
	Thank you	Merci	mair-**see**
	You're welcome	De rien	deh ree-**ehn**
	That's all right	Il n'y a pas de quoi	eel nee ah pah de **kwah**
	Excuse me, sorry	Pardon	pahr-**dohn**
	Sorry!	Désolé(e)	day-zoh-**lay**
	Good morning/afternoon	Bonjour	bohn-**zhoor**
	Good evening	Bonsoir	bohn-**swahr**
	Goodbye	Au revoir	o ruh-**vwahr**
	Mr. (Sir)	Monsieur	muh-**syuh**
	Mrs. (Ma'am)	Madame	ma-**dam**
	Miss	Mademoiselle	mad-mwa-**zel**
	Pleased to meet you	Enchanté(e)	ohn-shahn-**tay**
	How are you?	Comment ça va?	kuh-mahn-sa-**va**
	Very well, thanks	Très bien, merci	tray bee-ehn, mair-**see**
	And you?	Et vous?	ay **voo**?
Numbers			
	one	un	uhn
	two	deux	deuh
	three	trois	twah
	four	quatre	**kaht**-ruh
	five	cinq	sank
	six	six	seess
	seven	sept	set
	eight	huit	wheat
	nine	neuf	nuff
	ten	dix	deess
	eleven	onze	ohnz
	twelve	douze	dooz

thirteen	treize	trehz
fourteen	quatorze	kah-**torz**
fifteen	quinze	kanz
sixteen	seize	sez
seventeen	dix-sept	deez-**set**
eighteen	dix-huit	deez-**wheat**
nineteen	dix-neuf	deez-**nuff**
twenty	vingt	vehn
twenty-one	vingt-et-un	vehnt-ay-**uhn**
thirty	trente	trahnt
forty	quarante	ka-**rahnt**
fifty	cinquante	sang-**kahnt**
sixty	soixante	swa-**sahnt**
seventy	soixante-dix	swa-sahnt-**deess**
eighty	quatre-vingts	kaht-ruh-**vehn**
ninety	quatre-vingt-dix	kaht-ruh-vehn-**deess**
one-hundred	cent	sahn
one-thousand	mille	meel

Colors

black	noir	nwahr
blue	bleu	bleuh
brown	brun/marron	bruhn/mar-**rohn**
green	vert	vair
orange	orange	o-**rahnj**
pink	rose	rose
red	rouge	rooje
violet	violette	vee-o-**let**
white	blanc	blahnk
yellow	jaune	zhone

Days of the Week

Sunday	dimanche	**dee**-mahnsh
Monday	lundi	**luhn**-dee
Tuesday	mardi	**mahr**-dee
Wednesday	mercredi	**mair**-kruh-dee
Thursday	jeudi	**zhuh**-dee
Friday	vendredi	**vawn**-druh-dee
Saturday	samedi	**sahm**-dee

Months

January	janvier	**zhahn**-vee-ay
February	février	**feh**-vree-ay
March	mars	marce
April	avril	a-**vreel**
May	mai	meh
June	juin	zhwehn
July	juillet	**zhwee**-ay
August	août	oot
September	septembre	sep-**tahm**-bruh
October	octobre	awk-**to**-bruh
November	novembre	no-**vahm**-bruh
December	décembre	day-**sahm**-bruh

Useful Phrases

Do you speak . . . English?	Parlez-vous . . . anglais?	par-lay **voo** **ahn**-glay
I don't speak . . . French	Je ne parle pas . . . français	zhuh nuh parl **pah** frahn-**say**
I don't understand	Je ne comprends pas	zhuh nuh kohm-prahn **pah**
I understand	Je comprends	zhuh kohm-**prahn**
I don't know	Je ne sais pas	zhuh nuh say **pah**
I'm American/ British	Je suis américain/ anglais	zhuh sweez a-may-ree-**kehn**/ahn-**glay**
What's your name?	Comment vous appelez-vous?	ko-mahn voo za-pell-ay-**voo**
My name is . . .	Je m'appelle . . .	zhuh ma-**pell** . . .
What time is it?	Quelle heure est-il?	kel air eh-**teel**
How?	Comment?	ko-**mahn**
When?	Quand?	kahn
Yesterday	Hier	yair
Today	Aujourd'hui	o-zhoor-**dwee**
Tomorrow	Demain	duh-**mehn**
This morning/ afternoon	Ce matin/cet après-midi	suh ma-**tehn**/set ah-pray-mee-**dee**
Tonight	Ce soir	suh **swahr**
What?	Quoi?	kwah
What is it?	Qu'est-ce que c'est?	kess-kuh-**say**
Why?	Pourquoi?	**poor**-kwa
Who?	Qui?	kee
Where is . . .	Où se trouve . . .	oo suh **troov**
the train station?	la gare?	la gar
the subway?	la station de?	la sta-**syon** duh
station?	métro?	may-**tro**
the bus stop?	l'arrêt de bus?	la-**ray** duh **booss**
the airport?	l'aérogare?	lay-ro-**gar**
the post office?	la poste?	la post
the bank?	la banque?	la bahnk
the hotel?	l'hôtel?	lo-**tel**
the store?	le magasin?	luh ma-ga-**zehn**
the cashier?	la caisse?	la **kess**
the museum?	le musée?	luh mew-**zay**
the hospital?	l'hôpital?	lo-pee-**tahl**
the elevator?	l'ascenseur?	la-sahn-**seuhr**
the telephone?	le téléphone?	luh tay-lay-**phone**
Where are the rest rooms?	Où sont les toilettes?	oo sohn lay twah-**let**
Here/there	Ici/là	ee-**see**/la
Left/right	A gauche/à droite	a goash/a drwaht
Straight ahead	Tout droit	too drwah

Is it near/far?	C'est près/loin?	say pray/lwehn
I'd like . . .	Je voudrais . . .	zhuh voo-**dray**
a room	une chambre	ewn **shahm**-bruh
the key	la clé	la clay
a newspaper	un journal	uhn zhoor-**nahl**
a stamp	un timbre	uhn **tam**-bruh
I'd like to buy . . .	Je voudrais acheter . . .	zhuh voo-**dray** **ahsh**-tay
a cigar	un cigare	uhn see-**gar**
cigarettes	des cigarettes	day see-ga-**ret**
matches	des allumettes	days a-loo-**met**
dictionary	un dictionnaire	uhn deek-see-oh-**nare**
soap	du savon	dew sah-**vohn**
city map	un plan de ville	uhn plahn de **veel**
road map	une carte routière	ewn cart roo-tee-**air**
magazine	une revue	ewn reh-**vu**
envelopes	des enveloppes	dayz ahn-veh-**lope**
writing paper	du papier à lettres	dew pa-pee-**ay** a **let**-ruh
airmail writing paper	du papier avion	dew pa-pee-**ay** a-vee-**ohn**
postcard	une carte postale	ewn cart pos-**tal**
How much is it?	C'est combien?	say comb-bee-**ehn**
It's expensive/cheap	C'est cher/pas cher	say share/pa share
A little/a lot	Un peu/beaucoup	uhn peuh/bo-**koo**
More/less	Plus/moins	plu/mwehn
Enough/too (much)	Assez/trop	a-say/tro
I am ill/sick	Je suis malade	zhuh swee ma-**lahd**
Call a . . . doctor	Appelez un . . . médecin	a-play uhn mayd-**sehn**
Help!	Au secours!	o suh-**koor**
Stop!	Arrêtez!	a-reh-**tay**
Fire!	Au feu!	o fuh
Caution!/Look out!	Attention!	a-tahn-see-**ohn**

Dining Out

A bottle of . . .	une bouteille de . . .	ewn boo-**tay** duh
A cup of . . .	une tasse de . . .	ewn **tass** duh
A glass of . . .	un verre de . . .	uhn **vair** duh
Ashtray	un cendrier	uhn sahn-dree-**ay**
Bill/check	l'addition	la-dee-see-**ohn**
Bread	du pain	dew pan
Breakfast	le petit-déjeuner	luh puh-**tee** day-zhuh-**nay**
Butter	du beurre	dew burr
Cheers!	A votre santé!	ah vo-truh sahn-**tay**
Cocktail/aperitif	un apéritif	uhn ah-pay-ree-**teef**

Dinner	le dîner	luh dee-**nay**
Special of the day	le plat du jour	luh plah dew **zhoor**
Enjoy!	Bon appétit!	bohn a-pay-**tee**
Fixed-price menu	le menu	luh may-**new**
Fork	une fourchette	ewn four-**shet**
I am diabetic	Je suis diabétique	zhuh swee dee-ah-bay-**teek**
I am on a diet	Je suis au régime	zhuh sweez oray-**jeem**
I am vegetarian	Je suis végé-tarien(ne)	zhuh swee vay-zhay-ta-ree-**en**
I cannot eat . . .	Je ne peux pas manger de . . .	zhuh nuh **puh** pah mahn-**jay** deh
I'd like to order	Je voudrais commander	zhuh voo-**dray** ko-mahn-**day**
I'm hungry/thirsty	J'ai faim/soif	zhay fahm/swahf
Is service/the tip included?	Le service est-il compris?	luh sair-**veess** ay-teel com-**pree**
It's good/bad	C'est bon/mauvais	say bohn/mo-**vay**
It's hot/cold	C'est chaud/froid	say sho/frwah
Knife	un couteau	uhn koo-**toe**
Lunch	le déjeuner	luh day-zhuh-**nay**
Menu	la carte	la cart
Napkin	une serviette	ewn sair-vee-**et**
Pepper	du poivre	dew **pwah**-vruh
Plate	une assiette	ewn a-see-**et**
Please give me . . .	Merci de me donner . . .	Mair-**see** deh meh doe-**nay**
Salt	du sel	dew sell
Spoon	une cuillère	ewn kwee-**air**
Sugar	du sucre	dew **sook**-ruh
Waiter!/Waitress!	Monsieur!/Mademoiselle!	muh-**syuh**/mad-mwa-**zel**
Wine list	la carte des vins	la **cart** day van

MENU GUIDE

French	English

General Dining

Entrée	Appetizer/Starter
Garniture au choix	Choice of vegetable side
Selon arrivage	When available
Supplément/En sus	Extra charge
Sur commande	Made to order

Breakfast

Confiture	Jam
Miel	Honey
Oeuf à la coque	Boiled egg
Oeufs au bacon	Bacon and eggs
Oeufs sur le plat	Fried eggs
Oeufs brouillés	Scrambled eggs
Tartine	Bread with butter or jam

Appetizers/Starters

Anchois	Anchovies
Andouille(tte)	Chitterling sausage
Assiette de charcuterie	Assorted pork products
Crudités	Mixed raw vegetable salad
Escargots	Snails
Jambon	Ham
Jambonneau	Cured pig's knuckle
Pâté	Liver puree blended with meat
Quenelles	Light dumplings
Saucisson	Dried sausage
Terrine	Pâté in an earthenware pot

Soups

Bisque	Shellfish soup
Bouillabaisse	Fish and seafood stew
Julienne	Vegetable soup
Potage/Soupe	Soup
Potage parmentier	Thick potato soup
Pot-au-feu	Stew of meat and vegetables
Soupe du jour	Soup of the day
Soupe à l'oignon gratinée	French onion soup
Soupe au pistou	Provençal vegetable soup
Velouté de . . .	Cream of . . .
Vichyssoise	Cold leek and potato cream soup

Fish and Seafood

Bar	Bass
Bourride	Fish stew from Marseilles
Brandade de morue	Creamed salt cod
Brochet	Pike
Cabillaud/Morue	Fresh cod
Calmar	Squid
Coquilles St-Jacques	Scallops
Crabe	Crab
Crevettes	Shrimp
Daurade	Sea bream

Écrevisses	Prawns/crayfish
Harengs	Herring
Homard	Lobster
Huîtres	Oysters
Langouste	Spiny lobster
Langoustine	Prawn/lobster
Lotte	Monkfish
Lotte de mer	Angler
Loup	Catfish
Maquereau	Mackerel
Matelote	Fish stew in wine
Moules	Mussels
Palourdes	Clams
Perche	Perch
Poulpe	Octopus
Raie	Skate
Rascasse	Scorpion-fish
Rouget	Red mullet
Saumon	Salmon
Thon	Tuna
Truite	Trout

Meat

Agneau	Lamb
Ballotine	Boned, stuffed, and rolled
Blanquette de veau	Veal stew with a white-sauce base
Boeuf	Beef
Boeuf à la Bourguignonne	Beef stew
Boudin blanc	Sausage made with white meat
Boudin noir	Sausage made with pig's blood
Boulettes de viande	Meatballs
Brochette	Kabob
Cassoulet	Casserole of white beans, meat
Cervelle	Brains
Châteaubriand	Double fillet steak
Côtelettes	Chops
Choucroute garnie	Sausages and cured pork served with sauerkraut
Côte de boeuf	T-bone steak
Côte	Rib
Cuisses de grenouilles	Frogs' legs
Entrecôte	Rib or rib-eye steak
Épaule	Shoulder
Escalope	Cutlet
Foie	Liver
Gigot	Leg
Langue	Tongue
Médaillon	Tenderloin steak
Pavé	Thick slice of boned beef
Pieds de cochon	Pig's feet
Porc	Pork
Ragoût	Stew
Ris de veau	Veal sweetbreads
Rognons	Kidneys
Saucisses	Sausages
Selle	Saddle

Tournedos	Tenderloin of T-bone steak
Veau	Veal
Viande	Meat

Methods of Preparation

À point	Medium
À l'étouffée	Stewed
Au four	Baked
Bien cuit	Well-done
Bleu	Very rare
Bouilli	Boiled
Braisé	Braised
Frit	Fried
Grillé	Grilled
Rôti	Roast
Saignant	Rare
Sauté/poêlée	Sautéed

Game and Poultry

Blanc de volaille	Chicken breast
Caille	Quail
Canard/Caneton	Duck/duckling
Cerf/Chevreuil	Venison
Coq au vin	Chicken stewed in red wine
Dinde/Dindonneau	Turkey/Young turkey
Faisan	Pheasant
Lapin	Rabbit
Lièvre	Wild hare
Oie	Goose
Pigeon/Pigeonneau	Pigeon/Squab
Pintade/Pintadeau	Guinea fowl/Young guinea fowl
Poularde	Fattened pullet
Poulet/Poussin	Chicken/Spring chicken
Sanglier/Marcassin	Wild boar/Young wild boar
Volaille	Fowl

Vegetables

Artichaut	Artichoke
Asperge	Asparagus
Aubergine	Eggplant
Carottes	Carrots
Champignons	Mushrooms
Chou-fleur	Cauliflower
Chou (rouge)	Cabbage (red)
Choux de Bruxelles	Brussels sprouts
Courgette	Zucchini
Cresson	Watercress
Épinard	Spinach
Haricots blancs/verts	White kidney/green beans
Laitue	Lettuce
Lentilles	Lentils
Maïs	Corn
Oignons	Onions
Petits pois	Peas
Poireaux	Leeks
Poivrons	Peppers

Pomme de terre	Potato
Pommes frites	French fries
Tomates	Tomatoes

Sauces and Preparations

Béarnaise	Vinegar, egg yolks, white wine, shallots, tarragon
Béchamel	White sauce
Bordelaise	Mushrooms, red wine, shallots, beef marrow
Bourguignon	Red wine, herbs
Chasseur	Wine, mushrooms, shallots
Diable	Hot pepper
Forestière	Mushrooms
Hollandaise	Egg yolks, butter, vinegar
Indienne	Curry
Madère	With Madeira wine
Marinière	White wine, mussel broth, egg yolks
Meunière	Brown butter, parsley, lemon juice
Périgueux	With goose or duck liver puree and truffles
Poivrade	Pepper sauce
Provençale	Onions, tomatoes, garlic

Fruits and Nuts

Abricot	Apricot
Amandes	Almonds
Ananas	Pineapple
Cacahouètes	Peanuts
Cassis	Black currants
Cerises	Cherries
Citron/Citron vert	Lemon/Lime
Figues	Figs
Fraises	Strawberries
Framboises	Raspberries
Fruits secs	Dried fruit
Groseilles	Red currants
Marrons	Chestnuts
Melon	Melon
Mûres	Blackberries
Noisettes	Hazelnuts
Noix de coco	Coconut
Noix	Walnuts
Pamplemousse	Grapefruit
Pêche	Peach
Poire	Pear
Pomme	Apple
Pruneaux	Prunes
Prunes	Plums
Raisins blancs/noirs	Grapes green/purple
Raisins secs	Raisins

Desserts

Coupe (glacée)	Sundae
Crêpe	Thin pancake
Crème brûlée	Custard with caramelized topping

Crème caramel	Caramel-coated custard
Crème Chantilly	Whipped cream
Gâteau au chocolat	Chocolate cake
Glace	Ice cream
Mousse au chocolat	Chocolate mousse
Sabayon	Egg-and-wine-based custard
Tarte aux pommes	Apple pie
Tarte tatin	Caramelized apple tart
Tourte	Layer cake

Alcoholic Drinks

À l'eau	With water
Avec des glaçons	On the rocks
Kir	Chilled white wine mixed with black-currant syrup
Bière	Beer
blonde/brune	*light/dark*
Calvados	Apple brandy from Normandy
Eau-de-vie	Brandy
Liqueur	Cordial
Poire William	Pear brandy
Porto	Port
Vin	Wine
sec	*dry/neat*
brut	*very dry*
léger	*light*
doux	*sweet*
rouge	*red*
rosé	*rosé*
mousseux	*sparkling*
blanc	*white*

Nonalcoholic Drinks

Café	Coffee
noir	*black*
crème	*with steamed milk/cream*
au lait	*with steamed milk*
décaféiné	*caffeine-free*
Express	Espresso
Chocolat chaud	Hot chocolate
Eau minérale	Mineral water
gazeuse/non gazeuse	*carbonated/still*
Jus de . . .	. . . juice
Lait	Milk
Limonade	Lemonade
Thé	Tea
au lait/au citron	*with milk/lemon*
glacé	*Iced tea*
Tisane	Herb tea

INDEX

Music

N

Nightlife and the Arts

NOTES

Looking for a different kind of vacation?

Fodor's makes it easy with a full line of international guidebooks to suit a variety of interests—from adventure to romance to language help.

At bookstores everywhere.
www.fodors.com

WHEREVER YOU TRAVEL, *H*ELP IS NEVER FAR AWAY.

From planning your trip to

providing travel assistance along

the way, American Express®

Travel Service Offices are

always there to help

you do more.

American Express Travel Service
Offices are found in central locations
throughout France.

Travel

http://www.americanexpress.com/travel